W9-BXZ-111

DICTIONARY
OF
WARS

DICTIONARY OF WARS

Revised Edition

George Childs Kohn

Checkmark Books™
An imprint of Facts On File, Inc.

Dictionary of Wars, Revised Edition

Copyright © 1999 by George Childs Kohn

All rights reserved. No part of this book may be reproduced or utilized in any form or by any means, electronic or mechanical, including photocopying, recording, or by any information storage or retrieval systems, without permission in writing from the publisher. For information contact:

Checkmark Books
An imprint of Facts On File, Inc.
11 Penn Plaza
New York NY 10001

Library of Congress Cataloging-in-Publication Data

Kohn, George C.
    Dictionary of wars / George Childs Kohn. — Rev. ed.
        p.   cm.
    Includes indexes.
    ISBN 0-8160-3928-3 (hc)—ISBN 0-8160-4157-1 (pbk.) (alk. paper)
    1. Military history—Dictionaries. I. Title
D25.A2K63   1999
355'.009—dc21   98-49684

Checkmark Books are available at special discounts when purchased in bulk quantities for businesses, associations, institutions or sales promotions. Please call our Special Sales Department in New York at (212) 967-8800 or (800) 322-8755.

You can find Facts On File on the World Wide Web at http://www.factsonfile.com

Text design by Grace M. Ferrara
Cover design by Cathy Rincon

Printed in the United States of America

MP FOF 10 9 8 7 6 5 4 3 2
    pbk 10 9 8 7 6 5 4 3 2 1

This book is printed on acid-free paper.

CONTENTS

PREFACE

More than a dozen years have passed since the *Dictionary of Wars'* first publication—years full of violence, terrorism, rebellion, insurrection, revolution, and war in many parts of the world. Thus, in this fast-moving, eventful era, it seems desirable to bring this well-received reference source historically up to date, to cover recent bloody insurgencies and military operations in the last decades of the 20th century.

Dangerous continuing conflicts have developed particularly in Africa, the Asian subcontinent, and the Balkan and Transcaucasian regions. Religious or sectarian, ethnic, and racial conflict has become a major factor in today's political, economic, and social world, as it often was in the past but was at times overlooked. In addition, distortions and imbalances in the world economy, affecting entire nations and the lives of millions of people, have hindered efforts to find peaceful solutions to numerous conflicts. Violent rebels or secessionist groups are able to keep countries in a state of turmoil and terror for long periods of time. Few countries today have actually declared war formally upon one another, and humanity thankfully has been spared another high-intensity world war. And yet local and regional hostility and spite remain widespread, with adamant dissidents and rebellious factions creating as much belligerence and bloodshed as ever. Our inhumanity to one another seems to remain a constant.

This enlarged revised edition will, we hope, again gain the approval of all those seeking a convenient and comprehensive source for past and present armed conflicts. The original text has been carefully checked and, when needed, amended. There are more than 70 new articles, thus expanding the book to more than 1,800 main entries. I have aimed to stimulate rather than jade the reader's appetite for knowledge and understanding. Selection of information and its concision have been done with considerable care; I hope my judgments have been satisfactory and wise.

Finally, many thanks are extended to the following for their help and contributions: Elizabeth Cluggish, Ashwinee Sadanand, and Suzanne Solensky. Thanks also go to Facts On File's editorial director, Laurie Likoff, and editors Chris Hollander and Mary Kay Linge, all of whom have given encouragement and support during the various stages of the revision.

PREFACE TO THE FIRST EDITION

The compilation of the *Dictionary of Wars* was an endeavor to fill a large gap on the reference-book shelf. The real need for a single-volume reference work that deals exclusively and concisely with the world's military conflicts, from classical antiquity to the present, became more obvious as the task of researching and writing progressed. I hope the final product meets the needs of both the general reader and student, providing a quick, convenient, authoritative, and comprehensive source of information on the major wars, revolutions, revolts, and rebellions that have for so long been a part of history.

No one-volume reference work like this can possibly include every war. Space limitations preclude total comprehensiveness. Furthermore, dealing with a subject of so wide a range of time and territory—wars in all parts of the world from 2000 B.C. to the present—compels a certain subjectivity in choosing what to include and what to exclude. But I have still covered the entire sweep of the globe in selecting entries, and I feel that the presentation gives the reader a clear idea of the amazingly diverse conflicts that have plagued humankind.

War has a long and intriguing history and has been a prominent feature of human existence ever since the day when rival men—or women—decided to settle their differences by use of force. In many instances, the history of a people is the history of its wars. I have defined war fairly broadly, to mean an overt, armed conflict carried on between nations or states (international war) or between parties, factions, or people in the same state (civil war). There are multifarious reasons for war. International war usually arises from territorial disputes, injustice against people of one country by those of another, problems of race and prejudice, commercial and economic competition and coercion, envy of military might, or sheer cupidity for conquest. Civil war generally results from rival claims for sovereign power in a state or from struggles to win political, civil, or religious liberties of some sort. An organized effort to seize power, to overthrow a government, or to escape oppression is frequently termed a rebellion, insurrection, uprising, or revolt, which, if successful, becomes known as a revolution. These kinds of conflicts, as well as conquests, invasions, sieges, massacres, raids, and key mutinies, are included in *Dictionary of Wars*. In addition, there are separate entries for a number of exceptionally complex and significant battles.

It is not the intention of this book to interpret conflicts; that is left to works of limited geographical and historical breadth. Of prime concern is the military information, although political, social, and cultural influences are often specified in order to gain a fuller, more understandable picture of a conflict. Emphasis is placed on gathering essential and pertinent facts into a reasonably smooth narrative. Each entry gives the name(s) of the conflict, the dates it spanned, how it began, the opposing sides involved, a concise description or summary of events, and the outcome or significance. In addition, kings, emperors, generals, rebels, and so forth, when mentioned, are followed by their birth and death dates (or active dates).

Throughout, conflicts are listed in alphabetical order under their most accessible or commonly familiar names, some of which are widely recognized (for example, Napoleonic Wars, Crimean War, the Crusades), others of which are less familiar (Barons' War, Taiping Rebellion, Chaco War), and still others quite unfamiliar (Holy Roman Empire-Papacy War of 1081–84, Burmese-Laotian War of 1558, Hukbalahap Rebellion). Numerous conflicts are known by two or more names, and the dictionary alleviates the problem of looking up these conflicts by cross-referring to the main entry in a *see reference*. Thus, when looking up Dutch War of Independence, the reader is directed to EIGHTY YEARS' WAR. Conflicts having the same name but different dates are listed in chronological order, despite the fact that the dates may not follow alphabetically (for instance, Janissaries' Revolt of 1730 precedes Janissaries' Revolt of 1807–8, which precedes Janissaries' Revolt of 1826); this time frame helps the reader pursue the general military history in some lands.

The reader may want to check the cross-references set in small capital letters within many entries to attain a wider perspective on a particular conflict. Finally, the names of the wars, revolts, and conflicts are listed in the Geographical Index, in which wars are arranged chronologically under the country or polity (state, empire, and so on) connected with them. Such larger land areas as Africa, Arabia, Asia Minor, Central America, and the Caribbean are also listed in the index to make it easier to look up their conflicts. We have also included an Index of Names in order to aid readers who need information about particular military and political leaders.

I wish to express particular thanks for assistance in the writing of this book to Mary L. Allison, Judith W. Augusta, Cynthia S. Pomerleau, Mary Ann Ryer, and Howard G. Zettler. Their help facilitated the work, and their acceptance of the completed book itself indicates to me success in filling that void on the reference shelf. I would also like to thank Ed Knappman, Publisher of Facts On File, and James Warren, the editor of the book, for their support.

——*George Childs Kohn*

DICTIONARY
OF
WARS

A

Abbasid Revolution of A.D. 747–50 (Abu Muslim's Revolt) The Abbasids, Muslim Arabs who claimed descent from Abbas (d. 653), uncle of the prophet Muhammad (570–632), opposed the ruling Ummayyad family. Led by Abu Muslim (728?–55), the Abbasids openly revolted in 747, seizing Merv in the province of Khorasan in northeastern Persia. Marwan II (d. 750), the last Ummayyad caliph, attempted to crush the Abbasids, but his forces lost battles at Nishapur, Jurjan, Nehawand, and Kerbela. The revolt spread to other provinces in the Muslim Empire. When the Abbasids decisively defeated the Ummayyads at the Great Zab River in 750, Marwan fled to Egypt, where he was soon murdered. Abu al-Abbas as-Saffan (722–54), a close friend of Abu Muslim, proclaimed himself the first Abbasid caliph at Kufa, a Mesopotamian city near the Euphrates River. See also MUSLIM CIVIL WAR OF A.D. 743–47.

Abd el-Kader, First War of (1832–34) Abd el-Kader (1808–83), Muslim leader and emir of Mascara, led Algerians in a war of harassment against invading French troops in Oran and Mostaganem. He was successful, forcing the French to sign the Desmichels Treaty of 1834, which recognized Abd el-Kader as the dey (governor) of Mascara and gave him control of the interior of Oran. France signed the treaty with the hope that Abd el-Kader could be used as a French agent in Algeria. **Second War of Abd el-Kader** (1835–37). French troops continued to oppose Abd el-Kader's united Algerian tribes but lost many battles. In 1837, the Treaty of Tafna was signed, giving Abd el-Kader control of most of the interior of Algeria; France retained only a few ports. With his territorial acquisitions, Abd el-Kader organized a true Muslim state, using religious sentiment to unify the Algerians. **Third War of Abd el-Kader** (1840–47). In December 1840, France sent Marshal Thomas R. Bugeaud (1784–1849) to Algeria to begin a concerted military campaign to conquer Abd el-Kader's Algerians. The French drove Abd el-Kader into Morocco in 1841, where he enlisted the Moroccans as allies in his war against the French. Abd el-Kader used his rifle-armed cavalry effectively, conducting incessant raids against French troops and then retreating. Finally, however, the French army under Bugeaud attacked Abd el-Kader's 45,000-man army at the Isly River on August 14, 1844, and decisively defeated it. After the Battle of Isly, Abd el-Kader took refuge in Morocco again in 1846 and, with a small band, fought small skirmishes against the French. Having lost the support of the sultan of Morocco and with few men left, Abd el-Kader surrendered to French general Christophe Lamoricière (1806–65) in 1847.

Abd el-Krim's Revolt See RIF WAR OF 1919–26.

1

Abnaki War, First (1675–78) The Abnaki (Abenaki) Indians lived in what is now Maine, New Hampshire, and Vermont, and, as allies of the French, they carried on a campaign against the English settlers in the area for 50 years. When the Wampanoag under King Philip (Metacomet) (d. 1676) rose up against the English colonists in New England in 1675 (see KING PHILIP'S WAR), they were joined by many of the eastern Indian tribes, including the Abnaki. For about three years the Abnaki fought the English along the Maine frontier, pushing back the white settlers. Indian raids on scattered farmhouses and small settlements were continuous and devastating, eventually resulting in a peace treaty in 1678. The English colonists promised to pay an annual tribute to the Abnaki. **Second Abnaki War** (1702–12). Shortly after the outbreak of QUEEN ANNE'S WAR in 1702, the Abnaki Indians and French forces attacked English settlements on Maine's frontier. About 300 settlers were killed in towns from Wells to Casco. The Indians continued to make raids for 10 years and ceased only when the English and French made peace with the Treaty of Utrecht. Without the support of the French, the Abnaki were unable to defeat the English and were forced to sue for peace in 1712. **Third Abnaki War** (1722–25). Further encroachment by English settlers in Maine angered the Abnaki, who were incited to hold their ground by the French Jesuit missionary Sebastien Rasles (1657?–1724). When the English tried to seize Rasles, the Abnaki raided the settlements at Brunswick, Arrowsick, and Merry-Meeting Bay. The Massachusetts government then declared war on the "eastern Indians," meaning primarily the Abnaki and their allies. Bloody battles took place at Norridgewock (1724), where Rasles was slain, and at Fryeburg on the upper Sacco River (1725). Peace conferences at Boston and Casco Bay brought an end to the war. See also LOVEWELL'S "WAR."

Abu Muslim's Revolt   See ABBASID REVOLUTION OF A.D. 747–50.

Abyssinian-Italian Wars   See ITALO-ETHIO-PIAN WARS.

Achaean-Spartan Wars   See SPARTAN-ACHAEAN WARS.

Achaean War (146 B.C.) The Achaeans, a people of ancient south-central Greece, formed a confederation of Peloponnesian city-states, the Achaean League, for mutual protection against enemies. The Achaeans attempted to force Sparta, which was under Roman protection, to join. In 146, a Roman army under Lucius Mummius Achaicus (fl. mid-100s) invaded Greece and defeated the Achaean army, which consisted mainly of poorly trained slaves, near Corinth. Afterward the Romans sacked Corinth and burned it to the ground. They then dissolved the Achaean League and subjugated all of Greece.

Achinese Rebellion of 1953–59   Muslim Achinese (Achenese) rebels in northern Sumatra protested against the annexation of the state of Achin or Acheh (now Atjeh) to the republic of Indonesia, formed in 1950. On September 20, 1953, Tengku Daud Beureuh, military governor of Achin before its annexation, led an open armed rebellion against the Indonesian government of President Sukarno (1901–70). Achinese attacked police and army posts, attempting to obtain more arms for a full-scale rebellion. Scattered guerrilla fighting continued until a cease-fire was arranged in March 1957, with Achin declared a separate province. Native revolts broke out on other Indonesian islands that sought more autonomy. The Achinese rebels renewed fighting, which resulted in Sukarno declaring Achin a special district with autonomy in matters of religion and local law.

Achinese War (1873–1907) After the British recognized Dutch influence in Achin or Acheh (now Atjeh), a Muslim state in northern Sumatra, the Dutch sent two expeditions to conquer the rebellious Achinese people in 1873. The Achinese palace in the capital, Kutaradja, was seized. In 1903 the sultan of Achin, Muhammad Daud, concluded a treaty with the Dutch, recognizing Dutch sovereignty over the area and relinquishing his throne. However, many Achinese refused to accept Dutch rule and continued to wage war. Slowly, using a "castle strategy" (establishing fortresses for Dutch troops throughout the area), the Dutch were able to pacify the Achinese by the end of 1907.

Actian War   See ROMAN CIVIL WAR OF 43–31 B.C.

Aegospotami, Battle of   (405 B.C.)   Hoping to cut the Athenian grain supply route through the Hellespont (Dardanelles) during the Second or Great PELOPONNESIAN WAR, Lysander (d. 395), the Spartan commander, led a naval force that besieged and captured Lampsacus, a city on the Hellespont allied with Athens at the time (405). With every ship they could gather, the Athenians under Admiral Conon (d. c. 390) sailed to confront the aggressors but were unable to lure them into battle. After a five-day standoff, the Athenians, ignoring a warning by Alcibiades (c. 450–404), moored their vessels in a bad position off the Gallipoli peninsula (western Turkey) near the mouth of the Aegospotami River and went ashore in large numbers. Lysander's fleet surprised the Athenian fleet, attacking and seizing about 180 enemy ships (Conon with 20 vessels managed to escape); about 4,000 captured Athenians were murdered. Its fleet gone, its grain route closed, its allies (save Samos) in revolt, and its port besieged by Lysander's forces, Athens was in a perilous state after Aegospotami.

Aethelbald's Wars   (A.D. 733–50)   The supremacy of the kingdom of Mercia in Anglo-Saxon England was assured in the eighth century by two great kings, Aethelbald (fl. 716–57) and Offa (fl. 757–96). Aethelbald enlarged Mercia by conquering and occupying (733) the Somerset district of British Dumnonia, reducing British holdings in the south to Devon and Cornwall. In 749 he broke a 60-year peace with Northumbria by devastating large areas. Several vassal kings received his help in border conflicts with the Welsh (743). For the most part, Aethelbald was a powerful ruler, seeking peace and earning the title "king of Britain." Only once in war was he defeated—a police action in the Wessex area of Boergfeord (Burford) failed—but the loss did not affect Mercia's hegemony over Wessex. Though his reign was glorious, his end was not: Aethelbald was murdered by his bodyguard in 757. His cousin Offa succeeded him. See also OFFA'S WARS; OSWALD'S WARS.

Aethelfrith's Wars   (A.D. 593–616)   Major internecine strife among the Anglo-Saxon Heptarchy began with Aethelfrith (fl. 593–616), ruler of the Anglian kingdom of Bernicia. He had united his kingdom with another Anglian state, Deira, by marrying its princess and exiling its male heir, Edwin (585–632). To protect his borders, he fought (603) and defeated the Scot (Irish) king of Dal Riata and the Britons of Strathclyde at Degasaston (Dawson Rig, Liddesdale?), making Anglians dominant from east to west below the Firth of Forth. Now king of Northumbria (a union of Bernicia and Deira), Aethelfrith, in 616, battled at Chester against 1,250 monks from Bangor, Wales, slaughtering 1,200 and gaining control over an area separating the Scottish Welsh from Wales proper. Edwin, meanwhile, had secured aid from the king of East Anglia; he attacked and killed Aethelfrith near modern Nottingham in 616; he then dominated Northumbria until he lost his life in a battle with the Welsh of Gwynedd (632). See also OSWALD'S WARS; SAXON RAIDS OF A.D. c. 550–77.

Afghan Civil War of 1928–29   Amanullah Khan (1892–1960), emir (sovereign) of Afghanistan, had been attempting to modernize his country when opponents to his internal reforms caused a large-scale revolt in November 1928. In mid-January 1929, Amanullah abdicated in favor of his weak older brother, but an outlaw leader led a strong band to capture the Afghan capital of Kabul and proclaimed himself emir as Habibullah Ghazi (d. 1929). At Kandahar, Amanullah assembled an army and began a march on Kabul to retake the throne in the spring of 1929; he was defeated en route and fled from the country. Other claimants to the throne were also unsuccessful. General Muhammad Nadir Khan (1880–1933), an Afghan officer and Amanullah's cousin, organized an army after returning from Europe and marched against Habibullah, defeating him and taking Kabul in October 1929. Habibullah was captured and executed, and his victorious foe took the throne, renaming himself Nadir Shah. With British assistance, he instituted reforms, restored order and placated the loyal followers of Amanullah. In 1932, he established a constitutional government.

Afghan Civil War of 1979–   The Soviet invasion of Afghanistan in late December 1979 dramatized a momentous failure in Soviet foreign policy. When Afghanistan became a republic in 1973, the Soviet Union increased its efforts to make the country an economically dependent buffer state against Pakistan, which had Chinese connections, by supporting radical political parties like the Khalq (People's Democratic) Party. The Soviets, however, forgot that the introduction of modern ideas, whether western or marxist, had always met the resistance of conservative Afghan Muslim tribes; successive Afghan governments had attempted reforms without much success. In 1978, Khalq militants overthrew and assassinated Afghanistan's first president; a Khalq leader became president but was ousted by his prime minister (September 1979), who himself was overthrown (December 27, 1979) by another leftist, Babrak Karmal (1929–), who was backed by the Soviets. When Karmal's attempt to impose Russianization met with armed resistance, he asked for and received Soviet aid to crush the opposition. Despite having modern equipment, more than 100,000 Soviet troops found it difficult to defeat the Afghan rebels, whose guerrilla tactics and sabotage confused the invaders. Ancient tribal antagonisms and linguistic differences prevented the development of a unified strategy by the rebels to defeat the Soviets and the official Afghanistan army, the latter so riddled by defections that in 1984 the Kabul government was forcibly drafting 14-year-olds. The civil war, labeled by some as the Soviets' "Vietnam," embarrassed the Soviet Union internationally. In 1986 Karmal resigned, supposedly in ill health, and was replaced as president by former police leader Muhammad Najibullah (1947–96). After the Soviet Union withdrew its troops from Afghanistan, as required under a United Nations–mediated peace accord (April 1988), competing moderate and fundamentalist Muslim factions began fighting the government and each other for control. Among numerous ethnic war rivals were Hezb-i-Islami and Hezb-i-Wahadat (two strong fundamentalist groups), both of which allied themselves at times with other groups to gain military superiority. In 1992 Najibullah was forced from office by rebels, who established a moderate Islamic regime at Kabul, the capital. But rival Muslim militias soon opposed the government, whose military forces were led by Ahmad Shah Masoud. Another powerful faction, the Taliban, which advocated a harsh form of Islamic rule, condemned the other factions as corrupt, gained much military success (1994), and rejected a UN peace proposal (1995). Taliban forces seized Kabul from Masoud's forces in early October 1996, executed Najibullah, and had squashed allied opposition groups by 1997. In control of two-thirds of Afghanistan, Taliban troops failed to capture the city of Mazari-i-Sharif, a stronghold of northern allied factions, including Masoud's forces. By 1998 the war had reached a stalemate, with ethnic hostilities still rampant; more than 2 million Afghans had died since the war began. In mid-March 1999, the warring groups (along with the ruling Taliban) agreed to a power-sharing deal that could lead to an armistice.

Afghan-Maratha War of 1758–61   The death of Nadir Shah (1688–1747) caused his Persian empire to break up (see PERSIAN CIVIL WAR OF 1747–60). Afghanistan became independent under Ahmad Shah Durrani (1722?–73), who wanted control of western Hindustan (the Punjab and upper Ganges area); two invasions (1748 and 1751) enabled him to annex the Punjab; during a 1756–57 invasion, he sacked Delhi, retained the Maratha puppet Alamgir II (fl. 1754–59), and returned to Kabul to quiet opposition there. Ordered by the Delhi vizier to eject the Afghans from the Punjab, the Marathas, then at the zenith of their power under Balaji Rao (fl. 1740–61) and believing they had a call to take over the area, went to war. At first, they were stunningly victorious: 1758 saw the occupation of Lahore and the defeat of Sirhind. But Ahmad returned in a fourth invasion (1759), retook Lahore, occupied Delhi, witnessed the murder of Alamgir II (killed lest he support the Afghans), and refused the Mogul throne. Instead, he made Shah Alam II (1728–1806) the Mogul emperor. In Poona, Balaji Rao sent toward Delhi the largest Maratha army ever assembled, estimated at 300,000 men. Ahmad preached a jihad (Islamic holy war) and assembled a smaller but better equipped army. In 1761, the armies met at Panipat; in a one-day battle (January 14), about 75,000 Marathas were killed, along with their leaders; 30,000 were captured and ransomed. Ahmad's victorious army, however, forced him to return to Kabul. Although Shah Alam retained his throne, British and Maratha forces, with noble Muslim and Hindu families, divided the Mogul Empire among themselves; the British gradually destroyed the Marathas during the three MARATHA WARS.

Afghan-Persian Wars   See PERSIAN-AFGHAN WARS.

Afghan Rebellions of 1709–26 Much of present-day Afghanistan was ruled by the Safavid Persians in the 17th century. Taking advantage of Safavid weakness in 1709, Ghilzai Afghans rose in rebellion at Kandahar, ousted their Persian governor, and set up an independent Afghan state. In 1711, a large Persian army besieged Kandahar but was driven back because of Afghan sorties. Other attempts by the Persians failed. The Abdali Afghans rebelled at Herat in 1717 and seized the city, joining with the Uzbeks to ravage the surrounding area. In an effort to retake Herat in 1719, a 30,000-man Persian army became confused in battle and was defeated. In 1721–22 a large army of Ghilzai Afghans invaded Persia, captured Kerman and Shiraz, and continued on to the Persian capital, Isfahan. Persian forces failed to halt the Afghans, who afterward besieged Isfahan for six months and forced its surrender in October 1722, when the inhabitants were starving. Safavid weakness also attracted the Russians (see RUSSO-PERSIAN WAR OF 1722–23) and the Ottoman Turks, who occupied parts of western Persia. The PERSIAN CIVIL WAR OF 1725–30 created further chaos. The Afghans, after capturing Tehran in 1725 and defeating both the Russians and Ottomans in separate battles in 1726, seemed supreme, but the sudden rise of Nadir Khan (1688–1747) as Persia's military leader postponed Afghan liberation until Nadir's assassination (see PERSIAN-AFGHAN WAR OF 1726–38).

Afghan Revolt of A.D. 699–701 See MUSLIM REVOLT OF A.D. 699–701.

Afghan War, First (1839–42)   Fearing the growth of Russian influence over Dost Muhammad (1793–1863), emir of Afghanistan, the British attempted to replace him with a former emir more sympathetic to their desire to protect the northern approaches to India. In 1839, Dost Muhammad was deposed by the British army and imprisoned. Escaping, he made a futile attempt to reestablish his regime and was deported to India. But the combination of harsh winters and intractable Afghan opposition forced the British to evacuate in January 1842. Retreating troops were set upon by Afghan tribesmen and almost completely annihilated. The following year Dost Muhammad was restored to leadership. **Second Afghan War** (1878–80). Sher Ali (1825–79), who succeeded his father, Dost Muhammad, as emir, alarmed the British by negotiating with the Russians and declining to receive a British mission. In November 1878, British forces invaded Afghanistan. Sher Ali sought aid from the Russians, who advised him to make peace. Upon his death in 1879, his son, Yakub Khan (1849–1923), concluded a treaty ceding the Khyber Pass and other strategic areas to the British. But when the British envoy was murdered, British troops once again occupied Kabul, forcing Yakub to flee. The conflict ended with the accession of Abd Ar-Rahman Khan (1844?–1901), Dost Muhammad's grandson, who supported British interests and established a strong central government in Afghanistan. **Third Afghan War** (1919). When Amanullah Khan (1892–1960) became emir in 1919, he resolved to transform Afghanistan into a modern state free of foreign domination. His proclamation of independence threatened India, provoking renewed hostilities with Great Britain. This brief struggle was terminated by the Treaty of Rawalpindi, which recognized the independence of Afghanistan in both internal and foreign affairs. See also PERSIAN-AFGHAN WAR OF 1836–38.

Afghan War between Ghur and Ghazna (1148–52)   After the death of Mahmud of Ghazna (971–1030), his kingdom of Ghazna (Ghazni) in present-day Afghanistan and Iran declined in power, and Ghur (Ghowr), a subordinate Afghan hill state, rose up against its master. Under the Shansabanis dynasty, the Ghurids attacked the capital city of Ghazna in 1151, laid siege, and ultimately sacked it in 1152. All Ghaznavids were driven into India. The city of Ghazna was not entirely destroyed, for in 1175, before the Indian conquests of Muhammad of Ghur (d. 1206) began, it was made a subsidiary Ghurid capital after its seizure permitted the expulsion of its then-ruling Oguz Turkmen nomads. See also MAHMUD OF GHAZNA, CONQUESTS OF; MUHAMMAD OF GHUR, CONQUESTS OF.

Agathocles' Massacre (317 B.C.)   Agathocles (360?–289), a Sicilian, was twice exiled from Syracuse because of his constant grasping for power. In 317, he returned with an army drawn from cities unhappily controlled by Syracuse and established himself forcibly as *strategos autocrator*, becoming tyrant in all but name. He also appropriated the title "general plenipotentiary," one accorded in the past only to Dionysius the Elder (c. 430–367). To ensure his control, he eliminated his political opposition and members of the Council of Six Hundred, who governed Syracusans, an estimated 10,000 persons in all. Secure, he was then free to continue the struggle against Carthage. See also AGATHOCLES' WAR AGAINST CARTHAGE.

Agathocles' War against Carthage   (311–306 B.C.)   Tyrant of Syracuse, Agathocles (360?–289) had shown early military ability under Timoleon (d. 337). Emulating the demagoguery of Dionysius the Elder (c. 430–367), he decided to attack Carthage on its home territory and invaded the shores of Africa in 311. The Carthaginians, aided by Syracusan oligarchs opposed to Agathocles, swiftly defeated the Syracusans at Licata and separately laid siege to Syracuse. Agathocles fled, returning to Africa in 310 with an army that defeated the Carthaginians so thoroughly that he could return to Sicily in 308 to achieve the collapse of the Carthaginian blockade. In his absence, however, his remaining African force was defeated in 307 by the Carthaginians. Forced by a variety of reasons, he made peace with Carthage, reestablishing the western Sicilian boundary set after the third of the DIONYSIUS WARS. Carthage remained at peace for almost 30 years until its war against Pyrrhus of Epirus. See also CARTHAGINIAN WAR AGAINST PYRRHUS OF EPIRUS; TIMOLEON'S WAR.

Agincourt, Battle of (1415)   The 1412 Normandy-Bordeaux raid by the English and the 1413 crowning of King Henry V (1387–1422) renewed England's interest in France, now weakened by the ARMAGNAC-BURGUNDIAN CIVIL WAR and the CABOCHIEN REVOLT, and reopened the HUNDRED YEARS' WAR. Henry took Harfleur in 1415 and marched toward Calais with about 9,000 men, only to be stopped by more than 30,000 French soldiers at Agincourt on October 25, 1415. The French faced rain-wet ploughed fields. Henry waited for them to charge and bog down in the mud. English archers cut down two French advances; Henry's men then attacked from the rear. The French broke and fled. This bloody but remarkable battle, where perhaps 5,000 Frenchmen died, preceded Normandy's recapture by the English and forced the humiliating 1420 Treaty of Troyes.

Albanian Rebellion of 1997   Europe's poorest country, Albania disintegrated into anarchy and armed revolt soon after pyramid investment schemes failed in January 1997. The schemes (actually fronts for laundering money and dealing in weapons) could no longer make payments once the number of investors grew to include the vast majority of Albanians, who had been lured by get-rich-quick promises. Beginning in February thousands of citizens gathered daily, demanding reimbursement by the government, which they suspected of profiting from the schemes. By March 1997, the protests had turned violent in the south, especially around the port city Vlore (Vlora), where numerous residents armed themselves with weapons looted from army barracks. On March 2 President Sali Berisha (1944–   ) declared a state of emergency, but rioting and destruction spread throughout the country, gripping the capital, Tirana, for two weeks. Although the government quelled revolts in the north, in mid-March rebels still controlled towns in the south. Fearing the spread of unrest outside Albania's borders—and alarmed at the third wave of refugees from the country in a decade—the United Nations on March 28 authorized a force of 7,000 to direct relief efforts and to restore order. In elections in June and July 1997, Berisha and his party were voted out of power, and all UN forces left Albania by August 11.

Albanian-Turkish Wars of 1443–78   George Castriota, better known as Skanderbeg (1405–68), son of an Albanian prince, was taken at a young age as a hostage to the court of Ottoman sultan Murad II (1403?–51), where he became a favorite, received the name Iskander ("Alexander") and the honorific *bey* ("lord"), converted to Islam, and was put in charge of an army. He could have become lost in the luxury of the Ottoman court had he not remembered his heritage. When Albania was in danger of attack by Turkish armies, Skanderbeg escaped (1443) to his homeland, formed a league of otherwise quarrelsome Albanian nobles, reconverted to Christianity, seized the supposedly impregnable fortress of Krujë to begin a struggle against Turkish domination (1443), and successfully repulsed 13 Turkish invasions between 1444 and 1466. In 1450, his defeat of a siege of Krujë by Murad's forces made him a hero in the western world and the recipient of aid from Venice, Naples, Hungary, and the papacy. His troops, who often used guerrilla tactics, were almost always successful. A major victory in 1461 enabled him to force a 10-year truce on the Porte (Ottoman government), only to break it himself in response to a papal request for a new crusade (1463). His men raided Macedonia (1463) and defeated the Turks in 1464 and 1465; the last, a heavy siege of Krujë by Sultan Muhammad II "the Conqueror" (1429–81), devastated the country and cost Skanderbeg his allies, who deserted him. After his death, the Albanian nobles resumed their quarrels but continued a desultory warfare against the Ottomans, who regained control of Albania by 1478.

Albanian Uprising of 1910   The Albanians had assisted the Young Turks of the Ottoman Empire because of a promise that Albania would have autonomy and relief from repressive Turkish taxation. However, once in power, the Young Turks reneged and, instead, levied new taxes on the Albanians. About 8,000 Albanians in the northern part of the country rebelled in March 1910. The uprising soon spread to Korçë in southeastern Albania and into western Macedonia. The Albanian leaders met in Montenegro, adopted a memorandum demanding self-government for Albania, and sent it to the Turkish government, which rejected it. A large Turkish army brutally crushed the uprising in June 1910.

Albanian Uprisings of 1932, 1935, and 1937
Albania's King Zog I (1895–1961) faced insurrections in 1932, 1935, and 1937 from groups of liberal reformers and marxist-oriented Muslim radicals (the majority of the country's population were and are Muslims). A dictator who ruled autocratically to preserve Albania's feudal society, Zog put down these relatively small and poorly planned uprisings easily. Surprisingly, his punishment was lenient: only a few ringleaders were executed; minor social and administrative reforms were undertaken. Zog's rule ended on April 7, 1939, when Italy, Albania's sole foreign support, simultaneously declared the kingdom a protectorate and invaded (Italian Fascist forces shelled towns and occupied Albania, which was annexed by Italy), forcing Zog to flee into exile. See also WORLD WAR II IN THE BALKANS.

Albigensian Crusade (1208–29)   The Albigenses, a sect of religious reformers in southern France, were called heretics by the Roman Catholic Church, and in 1208 Pope Innocent III (1161–1216) proclaimed a crusade against them. Northern French forces under Simon IV de Montfort (1160?–1218) turned the crusade into a political war, ending the independence of the southern French nobles. Montfort's troops crushed the nobles and the Albigenses at the Battle of Muret on September 12, 1213. However, the heresies persisted, and the war continued. Albigensian leader Raymond VI (1156–1222), who had been defeated at Muret, withstood a siege at Toulouse by Montfort in 1218 and regained territory lost to the crusaders. In 1226, French forces of King Louis VIII (1187–1226) captured most of Languedoc, a region in southern France, and suppressed the Albigenses. Under the Treaty of Meaux in 1229, the county of Toulouse was put under French Capetian rule. See also ARAGONESE-FRENCH WAR OF 1209–13.

Alexander's Asiatic Campaign (329–327   B.C.)
Departing from Ecbatana in Media (ancient country in present-day northwestern Iran), Alexander the Great (356–323) and his troops began a difficult easterly march (see ALEXANDER THE GREAT, CON-

QUESTS OF). Supplies were so low that he actually paid some of his men to return home. Finding his respected foe Darius III (d. 330) stabbed to death had given Alexander an additional motive for the campaign: to capture Bessus (d. 329), Darius's murderer. Alexander subdued northern Parthia and Sogdiana (two ancient Persian countries), caught Bessus, and then threatened to punish the Dailamites severely for kidnapping his beloved war horse Bucephalus, which was returned to him. Turning south, then northeast toward modern Kabul, Afghanistan, he subdued Bactria (an ancient Persian satrapy that became a Greek kingdom), marrying Roxana (d. 311), a Bactrian princess, in 327. His troops reconquered Sogdiana and took Gandhara in present-day northwestern Pakistan. Bactria and Sogdiana then rebelled, requiring long campaigns to keep order. Overcoming a plot to kill him, Alexander marched his men into India in late 327 (see ALEXANDER'S INVASION OF INDIA).

Alexander's Invasion of India (327–325   B.C.)
About 90,000 troops led by Alexander the Great (356–323) wintered in the Hindu Kush (high mountain range on the present-day Afghanistan-Pakistan border) and then advanced southeast toward the Indus River, reaching its tributaries by the summer of 327 (see ALEXANDER THE GREAT, CONQUESTS OF). Once the troops left Bactria, they had to adapt to strange conditions: unknown climates, alternately hostile and friendly natives, and elephants—all of which Alexander somehow had to overcome. The Khyber Pass near the Indus saw a difficult siege at AORNOS; the plains of the Punjab presented a hostile raja (Hindu chief), who, however, became Alexander's friend after the Battle of the HYDASPES RIVER in 326. Alexander continued toward the Beas tributary of the Indus and would have continued, despite the monsoon season, but his men longed for home. In 326, they began backtracking along the old Indus riverbed, stopping near what is modern Karachi in 325 and pausing along the way west to conquer the Malli, despite the wounding of Alexander.

Alexander the Great, Conquests of (334–323 B.C.) After the murder of his father Philip II (382–336), Alexander (356–323) found himself king of Macedonia, at age 20, and controller of Greece. Military actions, including a savage destruction of Thebes in 336, secured that control; Alexander was ready to fulfill his father's plan to punish Persia for the GRECO-PERSIAN WARS and its later dominance (see CORINTHIAN WAR; SOCIAL WAR OF 357–355 B.C.). His minor motive was to replenish Macedonia's bare coffers. Alexander's army of some 30,000 infantry and 5,000 cavalry crossed the Dardanelles in 334, briefly detoured for Alexander to pray in Troy at Achilles' tomb, and that year defeated the Persians under Darius III (d. 330) at the Granicus River. Taking Phrygian cities to injure the Persian fleet, Alexander entered northern Syria and defeated Darius at the Battle of ISSUS in 333. To disable the Persian fleet completely, he next entered Phoenicia, easily taking some cities and besieging TYRE, then conquering Syria. In 332, he liberated Egypt and in 330 was declared a son of Amon (Egypt's supreme deity). Alexander returned to Syria in 331, defeated Darius at the Battle of GAUGAMELA, seized Babylon and Susa, sacked Persepolis, and pursued Darius to Ecbatana in 330. Since 331 Alexander had begun to show signs of orientalization; he called himself "King of Kings" (a Persian title) and wore Persian dress. Some troops objected to his change and rebelled, but he quelled them by executing their leaders. Discovering his foe Darius dead, murdered by a cousin, Bessus (who was captured and crucified in 329), Alexander covered Darius's corpse with his own robe before a royal funeral. Wintering in 330 near the Hindu Kush, Alexander launched in 329 his Asiatic campaign (see ALEXANDER'S ASIATIC CAMPAIGN). Capturing by 327 the area around Bactria (Afghanistan) and establishing the easternmost of his many Alexandrias (cities), he traveled southeast to start his invasion of India (see ALEXANDER'S INVASION OF INDIA), where he staged his remarkable siege of AORNOS in 327 and fought his most problem-ridden battle at the HYDASPES RIVER in 326. Continuous reinforcement made his army now number 120,000 men, who, upon reaching the Beas River in India—11,000 miles from Macedonia—refused to go on. Alexander conceded, had a fleet built in 325 at another Alexandria, and divided his army. Some men went with him through the Makran desert, suffering many disasters and deaths. In 324 his armies were reunited at Susa, where, to realize his dream of Asians and Greeks living in harmony, he ordered intermarriages, himself marrying Darius's daughter Barsine (one of Alexander's several wives), who was later murdered in 309. In addition, Alexander eliminated inept and corrupt officials, Greek and Persian, sent his soldiers home, issued a proclamation calling Greek exiles home, and ordered that he be considered a god. He crushed a final army mutiny, traveled to Babylon in 323, and, while preparing an Arabian campaign, caught a fever and soon died. See also DIADOCHI, WARS OF THE.

Alexandrian Massacre (A.D. 215) After a punitive expedition against invading Goths in the lower Danube area, Roman Emperor Caracalla (Marcus Aurelius Antoninus) (A.D. 188–217) planned a military campaign against the Parthians, stopping in A.D. 215 at Alexandria, Egypt, to visit before proceeding to Parthia (northeast Iran). Some Alexandrians made reference to his past heinous crimes (he had killed his wife and his brother Geta and many of Geta's loyal followers) and the villainy of his Syrian mother, Julia Domna. In response, Caracalla ordered the execution of thousands of inhabitants, notably military-age young men; many, especially Christians, managed to escape the bloodshed. Two years later, the cruel Caracalla was assassinated by some of his officers at Carrhae in Mesopotamia—at the start of another foray against Parthia.

Alexandrian Succession, War of the See DIADOCHI, WARS OF THE.

Algerian-French Wars of 1832–47   See ABD EL-KADER, WARS OF.

Algerian-Moroccan War of 1963–64   The separation of Algeria from France (see ALGERIAN WAR OF 1954–62) pleased neither Algeria nor Morocco (to which France relinquished its rights in 1956), for their shared boundary had been established by the French without consulting either former possession. Demands for adjustment from Algeria's President Ahmed Ben Bella (1918–   ) were ignored, and, in October 1963, Algerian and Moroccan forces began a border war in which many lives were lost. The fledgling Organization of African Unity (OAU), led by Ethiopian emperor Haile Selassie (1891–1975) and Mali's President Modibo Keita (1915–77), intervened and was able to arrange a cease-fire (February 20, 1964). But relations between Algeria and Morocco remained strained. The border clashes resumed in 1967; later, in 1976, when the former Spanish Sahara became independent and was renamed Western Sahara, Algeria and Morocco began a low-keyed military dispute over ownership of that region (see SPANISH-SAHARAN WAR).

Algerian Civil War of 1992–   Divisions between Islamic fundamentalists and secular and moderately religious Algerians erupted into an unprecedented reign of terror when Algeria's military-backed government cancelled parliamentary elections in 1992, which the Islamic Salvation Front (ISF), an organization intent on governing by Koranic law, was set to win. The Front, which had gathered support not only for its conservative religious views but also for its promise to end economic hardship and repressive military rule, then split into a moderate wing and a number of armed extremist factions. The most notorious of these, the Armed Islamic Group, was believed largely responsible for the series of village massacres that characterized the war. About 70,000 civilians were butchered (1993–98) in surprise raids throughout the country, especially in places where members of civil defense groups were believed by the militants to be located.

Western governments remained mostly silent in the first few years of the conflict, including France, Algeria's colonial master until 1962 (after the bloody ALGERIAN WAR OF 1954–62 had resulted in the country's independence). Acute French fears of Algerian terrorism spreading to France were confirmed by bombings in Paris in 1995 and 1996. In November 1996, Algeria's President Liamine Zeroual (1941–   ) adopted a repressive constitution, partly in an effort to destroy the ISF, but in the face of more and more killings, multiparty elections were held in June 1997. The government won with a huge majority, reflecting most Algerians' disillusionment with the religious opposition. In September 1997 the ISF unilaterally declared a truce, but continued bloodshed made it clear the ISF had little control over the terrorists. In early 1998 the government, criticized internationally for its failure to protect its citizens, announced plans to reinforce civilian self-defense units. Some observers suspected Algeria's government of allowing terror to flourish in order to consolidate its political power.

Algerian War of 1954–62   Algerian Muslims of the Front de Libération National (FLN), or the National Liberation Front, began open warfare against French rule in Algeria in 1954. They raided French army installations and European holdings. In 1957, the Paris government refused to grant Algeria independence, and thousands of French troops were sent to crush the Algerian rebels. After taking office as French president in 1958, Charles de Gaulle (1890–1970) offered a plan of self-determination for Algeria and later sought an honorable cease-fire with Algerian rebel leaders in 1960. Raoul Salan (1899–1984), a French military officer, helped stage an unsuccessful French army insurrection in Algiers in April 1961, trying to thwart Algerian independence from France. French and Algerian rebel leaders signed a cease-fire agreement in March 1962, but Salan led the illegal Algerian Secret Army Organization (OAS) in revolt against it. French forces seized Salan, but the French-OAS war continued. On July 1, 1962, Algerians, voting in a national referendum, approved independence, and two days later France recognized Algeria's sovereignty.

Algerine War (1815) Early in 1815, an outbreak of piracy off the Barbary Coast of North Africa renewed a centuries-old threat to American trade in the Mediterranean. The United States, its attention no longer diverted by the WAR OF 1812, sent Commodore Stephen Decatur (1779–1820) to the area in command of a large naval force. Quickly capturing the Algerian flagship *Machuda* off Cape de Gat, Spain, Decatur sailed into the harbor of Algiers and secured a treaty that provided for an end to tributes, release of all American captives, and a large indemnity, thus ensuring the safety of American commerce. See also TRIPOLITAN WAR.

Algonquian-Dutch War (1641–45) The Algonquian Indians were angered by Dutch settlers taking over Indian lands on what are now Staten Island and in Hackensack, N.J. When Dutch colonial administrator William Kieft (1597–1647) demanded a tribute from the Algonquian, the Indians attacked the settlers on Staten Island and Manhattan in the summer of 1641. Bloody fighting continued until a truce was arranged the next year. In February 1643, Mohawk Indian warriors, armed by the settlers, attacked the Algonquian, who retaliated with new raids against the Dutch. After much bloodshed and many reprisals, the Dutch, aided by the Mohawks, forced the Algonquian to retreat and imposed peace in August 1645. See also DUTCH-INDIAN WARS OF 1655–64.

Allies, Wars of the   See SOCIAL WARS.

Almohad Conquest of Muslim Spain (1146–72) The Almohads, a puritanical Berber Muslim sect, became rivals of the Almoravids, another Berber Muslim sect, in northwest Africa, where they had established a militant religious confederation about 1125. Many inhabitants of Muslim Spain desired to overthrow their Almoravid overlords, increasingly corrupted by the luxury of their Spanish courts (see ALMORAVID CONQUEST OF MUSLIM SPAIN). In May 1146, the Almohads invaded southernmost Spain, lured by a call for help to oust the Almoravids; Tarifa and Algeciras fell to the Almohads, who immediately moved northward under the leadership of Abd al-Mumin (d. 1163), who was proclaimed ruler of Muslim Spain in 1146. The Almoravids were evicted from Seville (January 1147), and later they surrendered Córdoba and Jaén to the Almohads, who had received reinforcements from Africa. Forging ahead beyond former Almoravid holdings, the Almohads captured Málaga (1153), Granada (1154), and then successfully invested Almería, a Moorish fortress-city captured earlier in 1147 by King Alfonso VII (d. 1157) of Castile and León in a spectacular siege. During the 1150s, opposition to the Almohads was mainly led by ibn-Mardanish (d. 1172), ruler of the Moorish kingdom of Murcia in southeastern Spain. Abd al-Mumin, preoccupied with problems at home, left Spain's subjugation to his sons and returned to North Africa. In 1162, ibn-Mardanish's forces were routed in battle near Granada and were defeated again near Murcia three years later. Afterward ibn-Mardanish's followers sought peace with the Almohads, and at his death ibn-Mardanish advised his son to accept the Almohad caliph's suzerainty, thereby making complete the Almohad conquest of al-Andalus (southern Spain).

Almoravid Conquest of Muslim Spain (1086–94) Threatened with possible conquest by King Alfonso VI (1030–1109) of Castile and León, the emirs (rulers) of Seville, Granada, and Badajoz requested help from an ascetic Berber Muslim North African sect, the Almoravids, despite the risk of subjugation by them. In June 1086, an Almoravid army landed at Algeciras, Spain, and was soon joined by the Seville, Granada, and Málaga emirs and their forces; they then advanced to the north toward Badajoz. Responding to this incursion, Alfonso's troops, with Aragonese support, encountered a combined Almoravid and Moorish (Spanish

Muslim) army, led by Yusuf ibn Tashfin (d. 1106), at the Battle of Zallaqa, near Badajoz, on October 23, 1088; the Castilian-Aragonese forces were crushed as French nobles arrived too late with reinforcements to save the day. Soon afterward the Almoravid sovereign, Yusuf ibn Tashfin, returned to North Africa, but battle victories by the Christians under Rodrigo Díaz de Vivar, familiarly known as the Cid (1040?–99) and successful Christian forays into Moorish territory brought Yusuf ibn Tashfin back to Spain in June 1089. Some petty rulers joined him in battling Alfonso without success, causing him to retreat to Morocco (North Africa). Again returning to Spain, he led the Almoravids to victory in Málaga and Granada and evicted the emirs. When Seville was menaced by the Almoravids, its emir, Muhammad al-Mutamid (1040–95), sought help from Alfonso, whose aid, however, failed to prevent the fall of Seville in November 1091. Badajoz fell to the Almoravid invaders in 1094. Except for the region and city of Valencia (see CID'S CONQUEST OF VALENCIA, THE), the entire southern Iberian peninsula was now in the hands of the Almoravids. See also ALMOHAD CONQUEST OF MUSLIM SPAIN.

Alnwick, First Battle of (1093) An early king of Scotland, Malcolm III Canmore (d. 1093) lived in England until 1066, when he took up residence in Scotland after the Normans won at Hastings (see NORMAN CONQUEST). He sheltered the Saxon pretender Edgar the Atheling (1060?–1125) and married his sister, who aided Malcolm in civilizing Scotland. Raids into Northumbria and Cumberland in 1072, designed to gain territory and protect Scotland's independence, brought Norman retaliation. In 1093, to forestall a Norman invasion, Malcolm attacked Alnwick in Northumbria but was killed during an ambush. His death put Scotland in a state of turmoil for 30 years. **Second Battle of Alnwick** (1174). William the Lion (1143–1214) became king of Scotland in 1165 and made the first of many French-Scottish treaties (he resented the loss of Northumbria by his predecessor to the English). When King Henry II (1133–89) of England faced

insurrection from his sons and barons (see ANGLO-NORMAN REBELLION OF 1173–74) and Prince Henry, his son, promised Northumbria and Cumberland in exchange for a diversion, William the Lion laid siege to Alnwick, now a great fortress. The Scots were rash and careless on a foggy day, posting no guards. The English, assembling unseen, inflicted a costly defeat. William the Lion, unhorsed, was captured and taken to Falaise, in France, where, before his release, he agreed to humiliating terms as Henry's vassal.

Amboina Massacre (1623) English traders followed the Dutch to the East Indies (the Malay Archipelago, Indochina, and India) and settled on the Molucca island of Amboina (Ambon) in present-day east Indonesia. There the Dutch East India Company was already established to deal with the spice growers. When the island's Dutch governor suspected the English traders, together with some Japanese mercenaries, of plotting to kill him and seize the Dutch garrison on Amboina, he secured the arrest of the supposed plotters, who were then tortured in order to win confessions of guilt. In February 1623, 10 Englishmen, 10 Japanese, and one Portuguese were executed. The English, whose factory on Amboina was taken by the Dutch, abandoned the spice trade in most parts of the East Indies and concentrated their efforts in India. See also PORTUGUESE-DUTCH WARS IN THE EAST INDIES.

American Civil War See CIVIL WAR, U.S.

American-French Quasi-War (1798–1800) French interference with American shipping during the FRENCH REVOLUTIONARY WARS resulted in an undeclared war between the United States and France that was fought mainly in the West Indies. (France, allied with the Americans since 1778 and outraged by the 1794 Jay Treaty settling some territorial differences between the British and Americans, had seized U.S. merchant ships bound for England; the XYZ Affair in Paris [French demand for money in order to begin U.S.-sought trade and amity negotiations] had angered U.S. president John Adams [1735–1826], whose report led to congressional repudiation of the 1778 U.S.-French treaty, suspension of trade with France, and authorization of the capture of French warships.) More than 85 French ships were seized by U.S. naval vessels (the U.S. Navy Department had been formed in May 1798). The 36-gun U.S.S. *Constellation* commanded by Thomas Truxtun (1755–1822) captured the 40-gun French frigate *Insurgente* off Nevis on February 9, 1799, and defeated the 52-gun French warship *La Vengeance* off Guadeloupe on February 1–2, 1800 (the latter French ship managed to escape at night). The convention of 1800 ended the fighting, with the United States and France agreeing to the mutual abrogation of the 1778 treaty and the assumption by the United States of claims by its citizens against France for the recent seizures of American merchant vessels. See also FRIES REBELLION.

American Revolution (1775–83) General Thomas Gage (1721–87), governor of Massachusetts, attempting to enforce British parliamentary acts deeply resented by the American colonists as "taxation without representation" and hoping to stave off armed rebellion, dispatched British redcoats (soldiers) to seize guns and ammunition stored by the colonists at Concord, Mass. Minutemen (Americans "ready to fight at a minute's notice") resisted at Lexington and Concord, forcing a British retreat in April 1775. Colonial troops soon captured Fort Ticonderoga and Crown Point on Lake Champlain. Although the British under General William Howe (1729–1814) established a foothold at the Battle of Bunker Hill on June 17, 1775, the British victory was costly (they lost almost half their strength), and American troops under General George Washington (1732–99) gradually consolidated their position around Boston, Mass. On July 4, 1776, the Continental Congress issued its Declaration of Independence, announcing separation of the American colonies from Great Britain and formation of the United States. However, Howe's troops soon forced Washington's Continental Army

to retreat in New York and seized Philadelphia, the colonial capital, the following year (1777). The British attempted to split the American colonies in half by moving an army south from Canada; British general John Burgoyne (1722–92) recaptured Ticonderoga and Crown Point but suffered a crushing defeat at the Battle of Saratoga in October 1777, surrendering to American general Horatio Gates (1727–1806). The French allied themselves with the Americans, bolstering the Americans' position despite a discouraging winter (1777–78) at Valley Forge, Pa., and a confounded defeat at the Battle of Monmouth, N.J., on June 28, 1778. American privateers scored some impressive naval victories, most notable of which was the capture of the British warship *Serapis* by John Paul Jones (1747–92), American commander of the *Bonhomme Richard*, a rebuilt French ship, after a great naval battle off England's coast on September 23, 1779. After 1778, the action shifted to the South, with British successes in Savannah, Ga., and Charleston, S.C. But American forces under Nathanael Greene (1742–86), Francis Marion (1732?–95), and Daniel Morgan (1736–1802) harassed the British and won battles in Virginia, South Carolina, and Georgia. American raids continued, with crucial French contributions. At Yorktown, Va., in October 1781, colonial forces under Washington, Comte de Rochambeau (1725–1807), Marquis de Lafayette (1757–1834), and Baron Friedrich von Steuben (1730–94) surrounded the British under General Charles Cornwallis (1738–1805), who was waiting for reinforcements. A French naval force blocked any escape by sea. After several unsuccessful attempts to break through the American-French lines, Cornwallis surrendered on October 19. Most of the fighting ceased (see BRITISH-INDIAN RAIDS OF 1782), but not until the 1783 Treaty of Paris, by which Britain formally recognized American independence, was it certain that the revolution was over. See also BOSTON MASSACRE; WAR OF 1812.

Amistad Mutiny (1839) The Spanish schooner *La Amistad*, with 53 black African slaves aboard, left Havana to go to another Cuban port in July 1839.

Led by Cinque (1813?–80), so named by slave traders but whose real name was Sengbe Pieh, the slaves mutinied and killed the captain and the ship's cook. Ignorant of navigation, the slaves kept two crew members to sail the ship to Africa and put the others over the side in boats. The two navigators, however, stealthily steered the ship northward. After about 50 days it wound up off Long Island, was seized by a U.S. warship, and was taken to New London, Conn., where Cinque and the other mutineers were charged with piracy and murder. Abolitionists defended them and appealed their case to the U.S. Supreme Court, where former president John Quincy Adams (1767–1848) eloquently argued their case, despite efforts of the administration of U.S. president Martin Van Buren (1782–1862) to return the Africans to their masters. On March 9, 1841, the Court ruled that Cinque and his men be set free on grounds that the slave trade was illegal; they were returned to Sierra Leone in West Africa. See also CREOLE MUTINY.

Amphissean War   See SACRED WAR, FOURTH.

Amritsar Massacre (1919) On April 12, 1919, in the city of Amritsar in the Punjab, India, five British citizens were killed during a riot by Indian nationalists, who were protesting the British Rowlatt bills, two strong antisedition measures. The next day, April 13, about 10,000 unarmed Indians assembled in Amritsar, again protesting the bills. Refusing to disperse, the Indians were fired upon by Gurkha troops under the command of British brigadier general Reginald Dyer (1864–1927); 379 Indians were killed and about 1,200 wounded. After the shooting, Dyer imposed martial law and ordered floggings and public humiliations. Dyer's actions were denounced in the British House of Commons but upheld in the House of Lords. An army council later called the massacre "an error in judgment."

Anastasius II, Revolt of (A.D. 720–21) As the result of an army mutiny in 715, Byzantine emperor Anastasius II (d. 721) was deposed and replaced by Theodosius III (d. after 717). Leo the Isaurian (680?–741), the chief Byzantine general, refused to recognize Theodosius and supported a plot to reinstall Anastasius, who had fled and become a monk in Thessalonica. Muslims, meanwhile, had invaded the Byzantine Empire (see BYZANTINE-MUSLIM WAR OF A.D. 698–718). Seeing a chance to seize the throne himself, Leo led his forces to Constantinople, forced Theodosius to abdicate, and became emperor in 717. In 720, army officers and others, led by Anastasius, began a revolt in Sicily to dethrone Leo, who immediately dispatched troops to the area. The rebels gave up; Anastasius was seized and executed in 721. See also CONSTANTINOPLE, SIEGE OF.

Anderson's Raid (1864) Under the leadership of William Anderson (d. 1864), a band of Confederate irregulars, among them Jesse James (1846–82) and his brother Frank (1843–1915), descended upon Centralia, Mo., on September 27, 1864. After attacking a stagecoach, they captured a train and killed 24 unarmed Union soldiers; they then robbed the passengers and burned the train. When three companies of Union troops arrived on the scene, "Bloody Bill" Anderson and his gang virtually wiped out the Union forces. See also CIVIL WAR, U.S.; QUANTRILL'S RAIDS.

Andrews's Raid (Great Locomotive Chase) (1862) During the U.S. CIVIL WAR (1861–65), on the night of April 22, 1862, 22 volunteer Union soldiers led by James J. Andrews (d. 1862) went deep into Confederate territory to cut the rail line between Marietta, Ga., and Chattanooga, Tenn. The soldiers hijacked a Western & Atlantic Railway train pulled by a locomotive called the "General" and headed toward Chattanooga, intending to destroy bridges and communication lines. Confederate soldiers quickly chased them in another locomotive, the "Texas," and caught them after about 90 miles when the "General" ran out of fuel. Andrews and seven other Unionists were executed as spies. Those who survived Confederate prison camps became the first recipients of the Congressional Medal of Honor.

Anglian-Pictish War of A.D. 685 From 593 to 641 rivalry between the independent Anglian kingdoms of Bernicia and Deira for political dominance in their territory, known as Northumbria (see AETHELFRITH'S WARS; OSWALD'S WARS), led to the emergence of Mercia as the dominant kingdom of the Anglo-Saxon Heptarchy (see SAXON RAIDS OF A.D. c. 550–77). The rivalry also prevented the Anglo-Saxon conquest of what is now modern Scotland, where north Welsh in Strathclyde, Scots (Irish) in Dal Riada (Argyllshire), and indigenous Picts fought for supremacy. Under a king named Brude or Bruidhe (fl. c. 670–95), the Picts had warred against Strathclyde Britons since 672 and attracted the hostile attention of the Northumbrian ruler Ecgfrith (fl. 671–85), who assembled a huge army, marched through Lothian, and reached a site called Nectan's Mere (now Dunnichen in Angus) to meet an equally large army led by Brude. There, Ecgfrith was defeated and killed in battle (685); his death weakened Northumbria, costing it all its territory beyond the Firth of Forth, and eventually allowed Scotland to gain independence from Anglo-Saxon England for a time.

Anglo-Afghan Wars See AFGHAN WARS.

Anglo-Boer Wars See BOER WARS.

Anglo-Burmese War, First (1824–26) Burmese occupation of Assam and Manipur in northeastern India led to war with the British. In 1824, British naval forces under Sir Archibald Campbell (1769–1843) seized Rangoon, which Burmese forces were unable to recapture in 1825. British-led Indian troops moved up the Irrawaddy River and, at the same time, took control of coastal regions. The Burmese suffered a defeat near Ava on the Irrawaddy. By the Treaty of Yandabo in February 1826, the Burmese ceded Assam, Manipur, Arakan, and the Tenasserim coast to the British. **Second Anglo-Burmese War** (1852). British seizure of a ship belonging to the Burmese king helped provoke another war (the British hoped to secure an all-land route between their colonies in India and Singapore). Rangoon and Pegu in southern Burma were taken by British-Indian forces. A revolt in Rangoon led to the ouster of Burmese king Pagan Min (d. 1880) by his brother Mindon Min (1814–78), who accepted British annexation of southern Burma. **Third Anglo-Burmese War** (1885). Burmese king Thibaw (1858–1916), who favored the French and negotiated with them to build a railroad from Mandalay to the Indian border, openly defied the British by not accepting a British envoy. Thus provoked, the British seized Mandalay and northern Burma, which was annexed to India. Thibaw, deposed, was sent to India, but Burmese guerrilla forces fought British troops for four more years before they were pacified.

Anglo-Chinese Wars See OPIUM WARS.

Anglo-Dutch War in Java (1810–11) The governor-general of the Dutch East Indies, Herman Willem Daendels (1762–1818), fortified the island of Java (part of Indonesia) against possible British attack (see NAPOLEONIC WARS). In 1810 a strong British East India Company expedition under Gilbert Elliot, first earl of Minto (1751–1814), governor-general of India, conquered the French islands of Bourbon (Réunion) and Mauritius in the Indian Ocean and the Dutch East Indian possessions of Amboina (Ambon) and the Molucca Islands. Afterward it moved against Java, captured the port city of Batavia (Djakarta) in August 1811, and forced the Dutch to surrender at Semarang on September 17, 1811. Java, Palembang (in Sumatra), Macassar (Makasar, Celebes), and Timor were ceded to the British. Appointed lieutenant governor of Java, Sir Thomas Stamford Raffles (1781–1826) ended oppressive Dutch administrative methods, liberalized the system of land tenure, and extended trade. In 1816, the British returned Java and other East Indian possessions to the Dutch as part of the accord ending the Napoleonic Wars. See also JAVA WAR, GREAT; NANING WAR.

Anglo-Dutch War in West Africa (1664–65) After the English founded colonies in the New World, they needed slaves to farm the land and do the heavy work. They entered into the slave trade along West Africa's Gold Coast (Ghana) by establishing numerous posts and forts and later (1664) by taking Cape Coast fortress from the Dutch, who were infuriated because they considered the territory their own. In 1664, a Dutch naval squadron under Admiral Michiel de Ruyter (1607–76) attacked and destroyed some English posts and forts; Cape Coast remained in English hands. The Dutch, who had lost the island of St. Helena in the South Atlantic, captured the Gold Coast fort of Kormantine from the English in 1665. The Treaty of Breda in 1667 recognized the Dutch claim to the area. In 1672, the Royal African Company, chartered by England's King Charles II (1630–85), constructed new trading posts on the coast at Dixcove, Sekondi, Accra, and elsewhere to export gold and slaves. See also DUTCH WAR, SECOND.

Anglo-Dutch Wars See DUTCH WARS.

Anglo-French War of 1109–13 Robert Curthose (1054?–1134), duke of Normandy, a thorn in his father's side (see WILLIAM I'S INVASION OF NORMANDY), attempted to bedevil his younger brother King Henry I (1068–1135) of England by vainly invading England (1101) and then causing Henry to invade Normandy, defeat him (see TINCHEBRAI, BATTLE OF), and take control of Normandy himself (1107). Robert's mentor was King Louis VI (1081–1137) of France, who, following in the footsteps of his father King Philip I (1052–1108), opposed the English in Normandy constantly and urged rebellion. In 1109, Henry and his forces went to France because the Vexin, a valuable French region in Normandy, had been politically divided by Louis, the Angevin leaders, and Robert's son. Louis's

side did badly in a sporadic series of raids against and truces with the English (see ANGLO-FRENCH WAR OF 1116–19).

Anglo-French War of 1116–19 The combination of sporadic raids and truces, alternating with varieties of intrigues, that characterized the ANGLO-FRENCH WAR OF 1109–13 apparently was a comfortable pastime for King Louis VI (1081–1137) of France. The objective of his military attempts to keep England off balance during this new war was to secure control of the regions of Maine and Brittany in northwestern France. At first, though holding their own, the French fought poorly. In 1119, a major battle occurred at Brémule, where the French were decisively defeated. Louis found himself forced to agree that suzerainty over Maine and Brittany belonged to England.

Anglo-French War of 1123–35 English troops led by King Henry I (1068–1135) invaded northwestern France to secure England's control over the region of Maine (see ANGLO-FRENCH WAR OF 1116–19). Among Henry's opponents was Fulk V (1092–1143) of Anjou, to whose daughter he had planned to marry his son. But the son died (1120), and Henry instead married his daughter Matilda (1102–67) to Fulk's son Geoffrey Plantagenet (1113–51), despite the war. Militarily sporadic before 1128, the war became one of attrition, ending with Henry's death in 1135. The marriage of Matilda and Geoffrey in 1128, designed to bring peace, engendered its own conflict (see ENGLISH DYNASTIC WAR OF 1138–54).

Anglo-French War of 1159–89 When Henry of Anjou became England's King Henry II (1133–89), he ruled so large an empire in England and Europe that he angered and frightened his feudal overlord, King Louis VII (1120–80) of France. Too weak militarily to fight openly, Louis used intrigue and his wits to keep Henry off balance. Anxious to press a claim to Toulouse, Henry and his forces invaded from Normandy in 1159 but found Louis already there. Because he would not attack his feudal superior, Henry ordered his troops to retreat; he made peace but vowed revenge. Louis continued to undermine Henry, encouraging revolt in the English-held territories in France. In 1173, he persuaded Henry's sons to rebel (see ANGLO-NORMAN REBELLION OF 1173–74); he manipulated Henry's queen, Eleanor of Aquitaine (1122?–1204), jealous of her husband's amours; and her sons conspired against their father to gain more authority. Louis's death in 1180 ended hostilities briefly. In 1183, Duke Richard (1157–99) of Aquitaine, later King Richard I the Lion-Heart of England, put down a rebellion against him and, in 1189, aided by his brother John (1167–1216), later King John of England, and by France's King Philip II (1165–1223), warred with his father, Henry, whose death (1189) brought Richard to the English throne. See also HENRY II'S CAMPAIGNS IN WALES.

Anglo-French War of 1202–04   When King John I (1167–1216) of England carried off the fiancee of a French nobleman and rejected a summons to answer for this crime, King Philip II (1165–1223) of France, technically his suzerain, declared him a felon and used this pretext to claim John's French holdings. In the ensuing war, John lost Anjou, Brittany, Maine, Normandy, and Touraine, the most notable actions occurring at Château Gaillard, an English outpost on the Seine River, which Philip's forces besieged from 1203 to 1204, and at the city of Rouen in Normandy. John retained control of his territory south of the Loire River, however. Philip, anticipating retaliation, established a semipermanent royal army during this period.

Anglo-French War of 1213–14   King John I (1167–1216) of England forged an alliance with his nephew, Holy Roman Emperor Otto IV (1174?–1218), and Count Ferdinand (1186–1233) of Flanders, in an effort to regain the northwestern French territory lost to King Philip II (1165–1223) of France in the ANGLO-FRENCH WAR OF 1202–04. John's invasion of Poitou failed as a diversionary tactic, for his allies, Otto and Ferdinand, were soundly defeated by Philip at the Battle of Bouvines in Flanders on July 27, 1214, a victory that consolidated Capetian power and brought widespread acclaim to Philip in France. See also ALBIGENSIAN CRUSADE.

Anglo-French War of 1242–43   Hostilities between the French and English crowns resumed with an invasion of France by King Henry III (1207–72) of England in alliance with his vassals in southern France. Victories by French king Louis IX (1214–70) at Taillebourg and Saintes demoralized the southerners, forcing Henry to make a truce at Bordeaux. But Louis, troubled by scruples of conscience and eager to embark upon the Seventh Crusade, failed to follow up with a decisive peace arrangement, and the continued English presence in France sowed the seeds of future conflicts.

Anglo-French War of 1294–98   Bickering over administrative rights in Aquitaine came to a head when the French occupied English strongholds in Gascony, leading King Edward I (1239–1307) of England to renounce his vassalship to King Philip IV (1268–1314) of France. In the ensuing war, Philip, forging a coalition with Scotland, pushed deep into Gascony. Edward attempted a counteroffensive in league with a series of allies, but, upon crossing the English Channel in 1297 to join troops from Flanders, he was foiled at Furnes by the French. A truce concluded at Vyve-Saint-Bavon was followed by arrangements for two royal intermarriages designed to secure a lasting peace.

Anglo-French War of 1300–03   Despite a truce between France and England in 1298 (see ANGLO-FRENCH WAR OF 1294–98), England's Flemish allies pursued their own grudge against France. The decisive defeat of the French heavy cavalry (knights on horseback) by the Flemish infantry (pikemen) in 1302 near Courtrai in western Flanders (see SPURS, FIRST BATTLE OF THE) greatly improved England's negotiating stance, and in the Peace of Paris of 1303, the English recovered their holdings in Gascony, essentially restoring the status quo ante bellum.

Anglo-French War of 1475   King Edward IV (1442–83) of England, seeking revenge for French interference in the struggle between the houses of York and Lancaster for the throne of England (see ROSES, WARS OF THE), declared war against France in alliance with Charles the Bold (1433–77) of Burgundy. Edward's army crossed the English Channel and landed successfully at Calais, but, lacking supplies and support from its allies, engaged in no military action. At Picquigny, Edward and King Louis XI (1423–83) of France negotiated an agreement whereby Edward withdrew his troops in return for a substantial cash settlement.

Anglo-French War of 1542–46   Anglo-French relationships after 1453 (see HUNDRED YEARS' WAR) were uneasy and usually negative. King Henry VIII (1491–1547) of England had held the balance of power between the Holy Roman Empire and France in 1511, when he allied himself with the emperor; he invaded France in 1513, winning at Guinegate (see SPURS, BATTLE OF THE). In 1522, Henry's forces invaded France again, as French influence in Scotland prompted fighting to break out there (see AN-GLO-SCOTTISH WAR OF 1542–49). In 1542, Henry again allied with the emperor against French king Francis I (1494–1547). Landing with a force in 1543, Henry captured Boulogne in 1544, the same year that the emperor made peace. Henry followed suit in 1546, forcing the French to recognize English control of Boulogne in a treaty. The war had cost Henry two million pounds.

Anglo-French War of 1549–50   Despite the peace made at the end of the ANGLO-FRENCH WAR OF 1542–46, the French were anxious to regain Boulogne and thus apply pressure on England. Diplomatic maneuvering, aid to the Scots involved in the ANGLO-SCOTTISH WAR OF 1542–49, and naval and military diversions in the Boulogne area—actions just short of all-out war—alternately alarmed and

harassed the English. In 1549, French king Henry II (1519–59) declared war and, in a combination of sea and land actions (including the bribery of England's German mercenaries), encircled the city. The French, however, could not capture Boulogne, and so they bought it—in a backdoor victory—in 1550 from the war-weary English, who were heavily in debt from the last two wars with France.

Anglo-French War of 1557–60   In 1557, King Philip II (1527–98) of Spain, husband of England's Queen Mary I (1516–58), gained England's support in a war with France. It was a very unpopular war in England, for it was not a national conflict; instead it had begun at the behest of the aged Pope Paul IV (1417–71), who hated Spain and vowed to defeat it (see HAPSBURG-VALOIS WAR OF 1547–59). Also the war was costly for England, because Calais, England's last link with Crécy (see HUNDRED YEARS' WAR), was captured by the French army under the second duc de Guise, François de Lorraine (1519–63), in 1558. Otherwise militarily insignificant, the war ended in the 1560 Treaty of Edinburgh, which made peace, gained French recognition of Elizabeth I (1553–1603) as English queen, and provided for the withdrawal of foreign troops.

Anglo-French War of 1627–28   England's King Charles I (1600–1649) was sympathetic to the rebellious Huguenots (French Protestants) besieged at La Rochelle by French government troops during the start of the Third BEARNESE REVOLT. The Huguenots had rebelled against expected repressive measures by Cardinal Richelieu (1585–1642), who considered the group an obstacle to his plans for increased governmental centralization. Charles ultimately resorted to forced loans to finance the sending of three naval fleets to relieve La Rochelle. After a 14-month siege, during which the English forces were repelled, French troops personally led by Richelieu captured the city in October 1628. See also THIRTY YEARS' WAR.

Anglo-French Wars in India.   See CARNATIC WARS; SEVEN YEARS' WAR.

Anglo-Irish Civil War of 1916–21   Irish nationalistic feeling developed strongly after the Anglo-Irish Union of 1800. This caused increased Irish resentment and insurrection and later led to legislative attempts to gain home rule, which was granted by the British Parliament in 1914 but postponed until 1920 because of WORLD WAR I. Frustrated by the delay, the Irish began the final phase of their struggle against the British government in the unsuccessful 1916 EASTER UPRISING. After executing the uprising's leaders, the British tried (1917) to achieve an all-Ireland consensus through an Irish National Convention, but then (1918) destroyed their achievement by announcing a never-fulfilled plan to draft Irishmen for the European war. The Irish reacted both politically and with terrorism. The Sinn Féin, an Irish political society seeking independence from Britain, won 73 of the parliamentary seats assigned to the Irish, refused to go to London, and set up the Dáil Éireann (Irish Assembly). The British promptly arrested 36 members of the society, but the remaining 37 ratified the Irish republic proclaimed during the Easter Uprising. A collision course now seemed inevitable; a provisional Irish government and court system were established. The Irish Republican Army and the Irish Volunteers engaged in two and a half years of guerrilla warfare, called "the Troubles" by the Irish, which was a counterterrorist struggle against the Royal Irish Constabulary (Black and Tans), supported by British troops, and included isolated heroic acts like the successful 1920 hunger strike of the Lord Mayor of Cork. The British government was slowly conciliated; granting a separate Irish parliament, it saw the Sinn Féin take almost all seats (1920). A truce begun in 1921 led to an Anglo-Irish treaty, which was opposed by both Ulster (Northern Ireland) and Dublin (Eire) because it split the country. Nevertheless, granted both free state and dominion status (1921), Dublin accepted the partition and became the capital of the Irish Free State in 1922.

Anglo-Norman Rebellion of 1173–74   Only the tactical genius of Henry II (1133–89) enabled him to avoid being overcome by his four rebellious sons and his no longer loving wife. He had assigned each son lands overseas in an empire stretching from Scotland to the Pyrenees, but had allowed them no real power. Ever contentious, all but the youngest, John (1167–1216), fled to France, claiming independence. Counseled and aided by their mother, Eleanor of Aquitaine (1122–1204), and the king of France, they began a revolt in Normandy and Brittany. Simultaneously, disgruntled barons and the Scottish king William the Lion (1143–1214) rebelled in England. Henry's forces were victorious in every skirmish on both sides of the English Channel during this straggling war, and by late 1174 all powers were imploring Henry's pardon. His sons gained subsidies but no additional powers. The barons were reduced in rank, and William, an English prisoner, was forced to make Scotland an English fief. See also ANGLO-FRENCH WAR OF 1159–89.

Anglo-Persian War of 1856–57   The British supported the Afghans against the Persians, who had invaded Afghanistan in an attempt to capture Herat (see PERSIAN-AFGHAN WAR OF 1855–57). On November 1, 1856, Britain declared war on Persia and in January 1857 seized the port of Bushire (or Bushehr) on the Persian Gulf. A British-Indian expedition, led by Sir James Outram (1803–63), was successful against the Persians, who sued for peace in March 1857. A treaty was signed, asking no Persian concessions except recognition of Afghan boundaries and Persian evacuation from Afghan soil.

Anglo-Portuguese "War" of 1612–30   The English (later British) East India Company, chartered by Queen Elizabeth I (1533–1603) in 1600, hoped to deprive the Dutch of their spice trade monopoly in the East Indies. When English merchants arrived in India, however, they discovered that their chief competitors there were the Portuguese, who controlled the Indian Ocean from trading centers in western India, such as Goa. In 1611, an English settlement was established at Masulpatam on India's east coast. Ships of the English East India Company, armed for battle, fought and defeated (1612, 1614)

Portuguese warships on India's western seas off Surat, where the English acquired trading rights in 1612 and set up a factory (post). The English adopted a policy of harassment and subversion, which took several forms: interference with Portuguese shipping, support of rebellious groups in their enemy's colonies, and assistance to countries anxious to escape Portuguese control. The English and Dutch East India companies secured trading stations along the Indian coast, at the expense of the Portuguese. An agreement (1630) between the governor-generals of Goa and Surat stopped the hostilities and gave trading rights in Portuguese centers in India to other nations. Portuguese activity in the region declined afterward. See also AMBOINA MASSACRE; PORTUGUESE-DUTCH WARS IN THE EAST INDIES.

Anglo-Scottish War of 1079–80 Despite gaining Scottish homage in 1072 (see WILLIAM I'S INVASION OF SCOTLAND), William I "the Conqueror" (1027?–87) failed to effect a royal peace north of the Yorkshire river Tees. King Malcolm III Canmore (d. 1093) of Scotland, anxious for an excuse to invade England and control disputed areas, found one in the rebellion of William's eldest son, Robert Curthose (1054?–1134), duke of Normandy (see WILLIAM I'S INVASION OF NORMANDY). In 1079, Malcolm's troops overran Northumbria as far south as the Tyne River. With Anglo-Norman forces, William came to Scotland in 1080 and, as in 1072, imposed new conditions on his vassal without the necessity of battle; minor skirmishes occurred constantly. To secure England's northern boundary, William erected a defensive castle at Newcastle-on-Tyne. But Malcolm, truly incorrigible, continued his resistance (see WILLIAM II'S INVASION OF SCOTLAND).

Anglo-Scottish War of 1214–16 Before Runnymede and the Magna Carta (1215), the English barons had requested that King Alexander II (1198–1249) of Scotland invade England against King John (1167–1216). After John had manipulated the pope to declare the Magna Carta void (the document gave less power to the English kings and certain rights to the barons) and the English barons began to revolt, Alexander acted, harrying John's supporters in the north of England and, as a matter of course, defeating the last Gaelic pretenders to his throne. He did not engage in any major battles, nor did he involve himself in the barons' and French attacks (see ANGLO-FRENCH WAR OF 1213–14), even after John's death in 1216. Indeed, he actually became son-in-law to John's successor, Henry III (1207–72).

Anglo-Scottish War of 1295–96 See SCOTTISH WAR OF 1295–96.

Anglo-Scottish War of 1314–28 See SCOTTISH WAR OF 1314–28.

Anglo-Scottish War of 1482 Alexander Stuart (1454?–85), duke of Albany and brother of King James III (1452–88) of Scotland, had pretensions to the throne and intrigued with King Edward IV (1442–83) of England to seize it. Soon the chief menace to the Crown, Archibald "Red" Douglas (1449–1514), joined Albany, who was arrested and imprisoned by James in 1479. Albany escaped and fled first to France and then to England. In 1482, Douglas, accompanied by other nobles and joining an invading English army led by Albany, captured James at Lauder. There, Douglas humiliated James by hanging his favorites from a bridge, ordering him home to Edinburgh, and, with Albany, ruling the country. The English went on to recapture Berwick (see SCOTTISH WAR OF 1314–28) before they left Scotland. Truces were negotiated in 1484, 1487, and 1491. See also BARONS' REVOLT OF 1488, SCOTTISH.

Anglo-Scottish War of 1513 King James IV (1473–1513) of Scotland, nicknamed "Rex Pacificator," tried zealously to achieve a balance of power in Europe and avoid war. But papal anger at France created a Holy League in 1511 and endangered Scotland's 1491 peace with England. James renewed the "Auld Alliance" with France in 1512 and, when war in France began, sent King Henry VIII (1491–1547) of England a last call for peace. Henry replied belligerently, claiming overlordship of Scotland, and James invaded England in 1513. The Scots met English forces at Flodden, outnumbering them two to one. English weaponry proved superior, however, and the Scots were massacred. James was slain, along with nine earls and 14 lords; Henry denied James burial, and his body was permanently lost. Heavy English losses and Henry's French war prevented further action. James's infant son was crowned James V (1512–42). He would endure troublesome border warfare for almost 30 years thereafter.

Anglo-Scottish War of 1542–49   King Henry VIII (1491–1547) of England wanted to control Scotland. When plans for royal intermarriage failed, and because Ireland offered its crown to Scotland, Henry provoked war by illegally declaring himself overlord. A 1542 invasion of Cumberland followed. At Solway Moss, the mutinous and feebly led Scottish army of King James V (1512–42) met a much smaller English force and was utterly smashed. James died soon after, and his only child, Mary (1542–87), was crowned queen in 1543. Henry's English forces attacked Edinburgh in 1544, and, in what the Scots called the "Rough Wooing," pillaged and destroyed, but without gaining surrender. A 1545 plot with Scottish dissidents failed, but a 1547 battle at Pinkie Cleugh routed the Scots. Henry VIII died, and Somerset the Protector, to betroth the young Queen Mary to King Edward VI (1537–53), sent ships and troops with little success. Edinburgh was occupied, but, following a 1549 treaty between England and France, hostilities in Scotland ceased.

Anglo-Scottish War of 1559–60   The Protestant-Catholic struggle in Scotland became so intense in 1559 that Mary of Guise (1515–60), widow of King James V (1512–42) of Scotland, shut herself up in Leith Castle and asked for and received French help. The Scottish Protestants asked Queen Elizabeth I

(1533–1603) for relief, and she sent both an English fleet and an army, which laid siege to Leith for many months. Two treaties ended this "peaceful war" in 1560: the Treaty of Berwick, a Scottish-English mutual defense pact, and the Treaty of Edinburgh, which withdrew foreign troops and pledged peace between France and England. The Scottish Kirk (Presbyterian Church) was now free to grow. See also ANGLO-FRENCH WAR OF 1557–60.

Anglo-Siamese War   (1687)   In 1684, a British East India Company factory was forced to close as the foreign policy of Siam (now Thailand), directed by a Greek adventurer named Phaulkon (d. 1688), swung to the favor of the French. England was slow to act. In 1686, a royal proclamation withdrew the right of Englishmen to serve on foreign ships, and, to implement it and press for payment of damages for the factory, two English ships were sent to Siam. They arrived shortly after a French fleet had been sent scurrying. Overnight shelling sank one English ship, killed sailors ashore, and forced the second to flee. Although war was declared soon after, it was not pursued; an antiforeign coup in 1688 toppled Phaulkon, and Siam closed its ports to all foreigners for 150 years.

Anglo-Sikh Wars   See SIKH WARS.

Anglo-Spanish War of 1587–1604   During their later reigns, England's Queen Elizabeth I (1533–1603) and Spain's King Philip II (1527–98) began a long, confused war at sea, in the Netherlands, in France, and in Spain. The war, whose most spectacular incident was the defeat of the SPANISH ARMADA in 1588, had become inevitable by 1585, when England sent troops to aid Protestant, Spanish-resisting Holland. Raids by the English under Sir Francis Drake (1540?–96) in 1587 on Cádiz, Spain, slowed the development of the Armada, impressed the then-Spanish Lisbonites, and captured a valuable Spanish treasure vessel. Following the great victory over the Armada, English forces under the earl of Leicester were defeated in the Spanish Netherlands, an English-Portuguese fleet larger than the Armada failed to win Lisbon from the Spanish, and two English expeditions won success in France. The war gradually dwindled into raids by England's "sea dogs" (buccaneers), especially upon Spanish ships at Cádiz in 1596 and 1598. As the raids continued, Philip died in 1598 and Elizabeth in 1603; a treaty in 1604 brought peace. See also DRAKE'S RAIDS IN THE CARIBBEAN.

Anglo-Spanish War of 1655–59   Oliver Cromwell (1599–1658), Lord Protector of England, desired an alliance with Spain, but his demands for Spanish trade concessions ended all negotiations. To punish Spain, he sent an expedition under Admiral Sir William Penn (1621–70) to attack the West Indian Spanish colonies of Santo Domingo and Jamaica, which were captured in 1655. Allied with France, England challenged Spain in the West Indies and on the high seas. Off Cádiz, Spain, in 1656, a large, valuable Spanish treasure fleet was seized. English ships under Admiral Robert Blake (1599–1657) destroyed Spanish vessels at the Canary Islands and at Veracruz, Mexico, in 1657. The Spanish suffered a resounding defeat by an Anglo-French army under Henri, vicomte de Turenne (1611–75), at the Battle of the Dunes at Dunkirk in northern France on June 14, 1658. Spain lost many Flemish towns to England, and the 1659 Peace of the Pyrenees reduced Spain to near impotence. See also DEVOLUTION, WAR OF; DUTCH WARS.

Anglo-Spanish War of 1727–29   (Franco-Spanish War of 1727–29) By the 1725 Treaty of Vienna, Spain's diplomatic representative Jan Willem, duke of Ripperdá (1680–1737), concluded an alliance between King Philip V (1683–1746) of Spain and Holy Roman Emperor Charles VI (1685–1740), who agreed to use Austrian "persuasion" to secure Britain's cession of Gibraltar and Minorca to Spain. To counter this new alliance, Britain's State Secretary Charles Townshend (1674–1738) arranged the Treaty of Hanover (September 3, 1725), which formed an alliance among Britain, France, and Hol-

land (and, later, Sweden, Denmark, and small German states) for mutual protection and the destruction of the commercially threatening Ostend Company, a trading company operating from the Austrian Netherlands and rivaling the British and Dutch East India companies. Britain and France refused to allow Philip's son, Charles (1716–88), to go to Italy to rule the duchies to which he had succession rights (see QUADRUPLE ALLIANCE, WAR OF THE). In February 1727, Spain declared war on Britain and besieged Gibraltar, but Austria, fearful of the power of the Hanover alliance, remained neutral. The British attempted to seize Spanish treasure fleets in the West Indies to prevent riches from being used to induce Austria's entry into the war; Porto Bello in Panama was blockaded by British warships, which also patrolled the Spanish Main's coast and engaged in minor naval battles. Through the efforts of France's Cardinal André Hercule de Fleury (1653–1743), an armistice was arranged that ended the overt warring in May 1727, but peace negotiations dragged on until Spain's Queen Elizabeth Farnese (1692–1766), hearing of Austria's breach of its Spanish martial provisions, furiously rejected the Spanish-Austrian alliance. By the Treaty of Seville on November 9, 1729, Spain accepted the terms of the 1713 Peace of Utrecht (see SPANISH SUCCESSION, WAR OF THE), recognized British control of Gibraltar, and granted trade privileges to Britain and France, both of which agreed to Charles's succession to the Farnese Italian duchies of Parma, Piacenza, and Tuscany. These terms were agreed to by Emperor Charles in the second Treaty of Vienna (July 22, 1731), and Charles then inherited the Farnese duchies.

Angolan Civil War of 1975–91   When the Popular Movement for the Liberation of Angola (MPLA) gained control of Angola's central government in 1976 (see ANGOLAN WAR OF INDEPENDENCE), the National Union for the Total Independence of Angola (UNITA) and the National Front for the Liberation of Angola (FNLA), two separate factions fighting for ascendancy, refused to recognize the new marxist-oriented government. In 1977, the MPLA captured the last major stronghold of the UNITA, whose leaders then fled to neighboring Zaire and Zambia, where they regrouped and revived their guerrilla warfare against the MPLA. White mercenaries, South Africans, and Portuguese frequently aided UNITA militarily, and covert American arms and assistance were reportedly received as well. In 1977, UNITA initiated a series of guerrilla raids on urban areas in Angola; a rebellion that UNITA supported was crushed. The following year a government offensive against the guerrillas failed to dislodge them from the large areas they controlled in southern Angola. Being sympathetic to South Africa, UNITA let South African forces maintain bases in its territory for raids into Namibia, or South West Africa (see NAMIBIAN WAR OF INDEPENDENCE). In the early 1980s, UNITA guerrillas had extended their control to central and southeast Angola. They won the support of Great Britain, France, the United States, Saudi Arabia, and a number of African nations, while the MPLA was backed by the Soviet Union and Cuba. The continual warfare disrupted Angola's economy and displaced one-sixth of its people, many of whom were forced to become refugees in Zaire, Zambia, and the Congo. The United States refused to recognize Angola's government as long as Cuban troops were in the country. In late 1988 U.S.-mediated talks led to a signed peace accord, after which South Africa removed its troops, but the fighting continued between the marxist MPLA government and the UNITA rebels. Another truce in June 1989, signed by Angola's President José Eduardo dos Santos (1942–) and UNITA leader Jonas Savimbi (1934–), also failed to end hostilities. Cuba removed its troops in May 1991. After a year of negotiations, led by the Soviet Union and the U.S., Santos and Savimbi signed a peace treaty in Lisbon, Portugal, on May 31, 1991, officially ending the 16-year civil war. It lasted only 18 months before fighting flared up between UNITA rebels and the government, which the U.S. now recognized after years of backing the UNITA. A month before, UNITA had lost parliamentary elections that the United Nations deemed free and fair; Savimbi de-

clared them fraudulent. UNITA resumed fighting and gained control of much of the countryside. On November 20, 1994, both sides signed a truce that gave limited power, through government concessions, to the rebels. Because UNITA later balked, the UN Security Council voted (1997) to impose sanctions on it. The government and UNITA accused each other of responsibility for the massacre of more than 200 persons in Lunda Norte province in July 1998. To put pressure on UNITA to implement the 1994 truce (Lusaka Protocol), government forces launched offensives against the rebel strongholds of Andulo and Bailundo in December 1998; UNITA responded by taking the northern town of Mbanza Congo in late January 1999.

Angolan War of Independence (1961–76) Antonio de Oliveira Salazar (1889–1970), virtual dictator of Portugal, had no intention of relinquishing control of his country's colonies in Africa, but events proved otherwise. In Portuguese West Africa (Angola), in February 1961, the marxist-oriented Popular Movement for the Liberation of Angola (MPLA) began a revolt against the repressive colonial government in the capital of Luanda; about a month later antigovernment guerrilla warfare led by the moderate Union of the Peoples of Angola (UPA) broke out in the northern provinces. The rebels were ruthlessly suppressed, and an estimated 20,000 black Africans were killed in the fighting. The revolt, however, smoldered on as the MPLA shifted its activities to the country's eastern section, where it waged guerrilla campaigns from bases in neighboring Zambia. In 1966, the UPA split into the pro-Western, socialist National Front for the Liberation of Angola (FNLA) and the pro-Western National Union for the Total Independence of Angola (UNITA), which moved its guerrilla operations into the south-central region. The antigovernment guerrillas confined their actions to ambushes and hit-and-run attacks, but they were persistent and tied down a sizable Portuguese force. By the late 1960s, half of Portugal's national budget was being spent on its armed forces in Africa (see GUINEA-BISSAUAN WAR OF INDE-

PENDENCE; MOZAMBICAN WAR OF INDEPENDENCE). Young Portuguese army officers came to resent the unrelieved bush fighting and the inefficiency of the bureaucracy running the war in Lisbon, Portugal's capital; and in April 1974, they toppled the national government and installed a leftist regime that was willing to relinquish Portuguese West Africa, once an orderly succession in rule could be ensured. Twice the three main liberation movements—MPLA, FNLA, and UNITA—formed a coalition, and twice the coalitions collapsed. When the Portuguese finally withdrew in November 1975, they left a country divided by civil war, with the UNITA and FNLA pitted against the MPLA. The MPLA held the capital and its port, through which Cuban soldiers, Soviet technicians, and Soviet arms entered the country in support of the MPLA. This aid turned the tide. Although South African forces and American supplies came to the aid of UNITA and FNLA, the MPLA and its Cuban-Soviet allies overcame the opposition parties by February 1976. UNITA tried to maintain its guerrilla war despite the withdrawal of South African troops and the cessation of U.S. aid. Winning an apparent victory, the MPLA seized control of the government and was recognized by the Organization of African Unity (OAU) as the legitimate authority in the newly independent Angola. Portuguese colonialism in Africa had ended. See also ANGOLAN CIVIL WAR OF 1975–91.

Angora, Battle of (1402) After his conquest of Baghdad, Aleppo, and Damascus, Tamerlane (Timur) (1336–1405), by now called the "Prince of Destruction," led his forces into the Ottoman Empire in 1402 (see TAMERLANE, CONQUESTS OF). Already 66 years old, he felt able to challenge the great Ottoman general and sultan Bayazid I (1347–1403), victor over the crusaders at Nicopolis (see NICOPOLIS, CRUSADE OF). Bayazid, whose forces were besieging Constantinople (Istanbul), interrupted the siege to march toward Tamerlane, who, always ready for subterfuge, led his 160,000-man army into the mountains. Thinking Tamerlane

was withdrawing, Bayazid made camp on the plain near Angora (Ankara), left supplies there, and chased Tamerlane, who doubled back, captured the camp, and stood ready to face the superior, but now undersupplied and, more important, waterless Ottoman Turks. Bayazid's surprising ingenuousness cost him many Ottoman princes and Tatar (Tartar) forces, who went over to Tamerlane. Amid desperate fighting, Bayazid, who was outgeneraled, was captured; he died in captivity, deranged. Apparently uninterested in controlling the Ottoman territory (which required a decade to recover), Tamerlane and his army returned to Samarkand, his capital.

An Lu-shan, Revolt of (A.D. 755–63) An Lu-shan (703–57), who was of Persian and Turkish descent, grew up in Mongolia and, when a young man, moved to China, where he joined the army. He rose rapidly through the ranks and eventually became the military governor of three northern Chinese provinces and a court favorite of Emperor Hsüan Tsung (Xuan Zong) (685–762) of the T'ang dynasty. When the emperor's powerful chief minister died, An Lu-shan applied for the post but was denied it. In anger, he returned to his provinces, rounded up his army, and marched on Loyang, China's eastern capital. After seizing Loyang, An Lu-shan proclaimed himself emperor of the Great Yen dynasty. His rebel followers advanced on the imperial capital, Ch'ang-an (Sian, Xi'an), but were checked for six months by the T'ang forces. Ch'ang-an was finally taken, forcing the emperor to flee. An Lu-shan, who had stayed behind in Loyang and was in bad health, was murdered by either a eunuch slave or his treacherous eldest son in early 757. Nevertheless, his revolt continued for six more years with much fierce fighting and loss of life. Though unsuccessful, it damaged the prestige of the government and established the precedent that strong military leaders, rather than scholars, had the most influence at court.

Annamese-Chinese Wars   See   CHINESE-AN-NAMESE WARS; VIETNAMESE-CHINESE WARS.

Aornos, Siege of (327 B.C.) The reputation of Alexander the Great (356–323) as a besieger reached its zenith in the Khyber Pass near Aornos (Pir Sarai), where rebel highland tribesmen pursued by Alexander's troops had found refuge on the 7,000-foot-high rocky plateau. Aornos could not be starved out, nor could it be surrounded by the usual siege machines. Alexander had an 800-foot-deep ravine filled in to hold his catapults and to reach the north face of the plateau. One night he took 30 men with him to scale the cliff and, near the last ledge, gave them the right to be first. The natives bombarded the ledge with boulders, killing all 30 men. On the third night, to the sound of native victory drums, Alexander tried again; his Shield Bearers killed all the Indians. Alexander had altars built to the goddess Athena—her easternmost shrines—and then continued down the Indus Valley (see ALEXANDER'S INVASION OF INDIA). See also ALEXANDER THE GREAT, CONQUESTS OF.

Apache and Navaho War of 1860–65 Both the Apache and Navaho (Navajo) were warlike tribes who inhabited mainly what is now New Mexico and Arizona. Their warriors resisted the encroachment of white civilization upon their territory. In the 1850s, U.S. troops built a series of forts in the Southwest to protect and encourage while settlements there. In 1860, both tribes took to the warpath on their sturdy, fast-footed ponies and spread destruction throughout the area, while stealing guns, ammunition, cattle, horses, and other booty. In 1861, Cochise (1815?–74), a Chiricahua Apache, and five other Indian chiefs were seized and accused, wrongly, of cattle rustling and kidnapping a boy from a ranch. One chief was slain, Cochise escaped, and the four others were soon hanged, With many warriors, Cochise waged a bloody war of revenge against the whites during the U.S. CIVIL WAR, which drew many federal troops away from the Southwest and thus allowed Cochise to wreak havoc there with little opposition for a period. In 1862, the First California Infantry was ambushed at Apache Pass, but the two mountain howitzers the soldiers had brought along saved the day and put the Indians to flight. Union troops had to be transferred from the East, where they were fighting the Confederates. In 1863–64, Colonel Christopher "Kit" Carson (1809–69), an experienced Indian fighter, led the First New Mexico Volunteers in a campaign against the Indians, who were to be killed outright and their women and children taken prisoner; Carson's force killed more than 650 Apache and captured over 9,000. In 1865, the Navaho surrendered and agreed to settle on a reservation on the Pecos River in New Mexico. Cochise and the Apache retreated to the mountains and continued to make raids.

Apache War of 1871–73 The Apache Indians of the Southwest resisted the advance of the white American settlers and U.S. troops. They constantly made swift raids and then retreated to their mountain hideouts. After the slaughter of more than 100 Apache, mostly women and children, at the CAMP GRANT MASSACRE, the Indians went on the warpath in great numbers. In 1871, U.S. general George Crook (1829–90), who stated that the Indians would have to be defeated before peace could be arranged, took charge of American troops stationed in the New Mexico and Arizona territories, split them into small squads, and sent them out to capture or kill the Apache. He led forces against the Chiricahua Apache chief Cochise (1815?–74), who finally signed a treaty of peace in 1872 and agreed that his people would live on an Indian reservation. Other Apache under Chiefs Victorio (d. 1880) and Geronimo (1829–1909) fought on, but they were continually harried by army troops and suffered shortages of food and ammunition. Worn out by the fighting, the Indians capitulated in April 1873, and were sent to live on the San Carlos reservation in Arizona. Peace was only temporary, for the Apache loathed the restrictions of reservation life and were angry because the whites did not adhere to agreements. After a few years the Indians began to break out of the reservations and resume marauding.

Apache War of 1876–86   The restrictive life on the reservation did not agree with the Apache, especially when game was scarce and their families were hungry. After several drunken Apache killed a white station master, and U.S. troops tried to remove hundreds of innocent Indians to a more remote reservation, war erupted again (see APACHE WAR OF 1871–73). Roving Apache bands led by Victorio (d. 1880) and Geronimo (1829–1909) terrorized most of the Arizona and New Mexico territories, killing prospectors and herders and stealing horses and guns. When army troops came too close, they fled over the border into Mexico, where the Americans could not follow. The Apache continued their raids from across the border, where they were joined by Comanche Indians and other renegades. Victorio also terrorized Mexico with his band until he was killed in 1880. Geronimo's people took refuge in the Sierra Madre mountains, from which they ventured forth to steal cattle and ammunition. Troops led by U.S. Generals George Crook (1829–90) and Nelson A. Miles (1839–1925) battled the Indians under Geronimo for a number of years until an Apache turncoat led Crook's men to Geronimo's stronghold in the mountains in 1883. The Indians were taken by surprise, and Crook induced them to surrender. They agreed to start anew on the White Mountain reservation, but in 1885 Geronimo and his followers broke away again and returned to plundering. But constant harassment by U.S. forces led to their surrender a year later. Geronimo and other Apache were sent to a federal prison in Florida. Later, Geronimo was allowed to return to the West, where he lived out his life near Fort Sill, Okla.

Appenzell War (1403–11)   The painful struggles involved in the collapse of the European feudal social structure are illustrated in the Appenzell War. In the early 1400s, Appenzell was a Swiss district feudatory to the Abbey of St. Gall. The town of St. Gall, an Imperial (free) town with an extensive textile trade, applied for help to Appenzell when its former suzerain, the abbey, illegally demanded a return to earlier status and assessments. Appenzell allied itself with Schwyz, another Imperial town, and the group defied the abbey. A monastic army then attacked Appenzell and was defeated in 1403. With assistance from the oppressive Hapsburg duke, Frederick of Austria (fl. 1380–1410), the abbey attacked both the village and Appenzell in 1405, but lost again. King Rupert (1352–1410) of Germany groundlessly ordered the rebels to return to the control of the abbey, but Appenzell (and, by association, the town of St. Gall) earned the protection of the Swiss Confederacy in 1411, against which Rupert was powerless. (Today Appenzell is a Swiss canton; St. Gall has over 400,000 people; the abbey is a museum.)

Arab-Byzantine Wars   See BYZANTINE-MUSLIM WARS.

Arab Conquests   See BYZANTINE-MUSLIM WARS; MUSLIM CONQUESTS.

Arab-Israeli War of 1948–49   The creation of the Jewish state of Israel in 1948 was opposed by the Arab states, which considered Israel Arab territory. Arab armed forces from Egypt, Syria, Transjordan (Jordan), Lebanon, and Iraq invaded Israel on May 14, 1948 (the day the state of Israel was proclaimed) and took control of territory in southern and eastern Palestine. Jordanian troops seized Jerusalem's Old City but were unable to take the New City. The Israelis managed to halt the Arab advance, and the United Nations succeeded in securing a four-week truce in June. After fighting resumed in July, the Israeli forces gained territory until another truce went into effect for about three months. Israeli forces then pushed back the Arab armies on all fronts and gained possession of the Negev desert region (except for the coastal Gaza Strip). Between February and July of 1949, Israel signed armistice agreements with Egypt, Syria, and Transjordan (Iraq refused to sign but withdrew its forces). At the end of the war, Israel occupied most of the disputed areas in Palestine, had increased its territory by about one-half, and had developed a formidable standing army. About 400,000 Palestinian Arabs, who fled from Israel during the war, settled in refugee camps in neighboring Arab countries. See also ARAB-IS-RAELI WAR OF 1956.

Arab-Israeli War of 1956 (Suez or Sinai War) Nationalization of the Suez Canal by Egypt's President Gamal Abdel Nasser (1918–70) in July 1956 precipitated a crisis in Britain, France, and the United States. Egypt rejected international operation of the canal. The British and French governments, concerned about the protection of their interests in the Middle East, held secret meetings with Israel in Paris at which it was arranged that Israel would attack the Suez Canal. Ostensibly functioning as a neutral force, British and French military intervention would then separate the belligerents and protect the canal. The purpose of this collusion between the British, French and Israelis was to topple Nasser. On October 29, 1956, the prearranged Israeli attack took place. The Israelis captured the Gaza Strip, Sharm el-Sheikh and several other important places before the British and French governments ordered Israel and Egypt to cease fire and withdraw from the area. Israel, as planned, complied, but the Egyptians, as expected, refused. On November 5, 1956, Anglo-French paratroopers landed near Port Said and attacked and killed Egyptian troops. The following day, Egypt and Israel accepted a cease-fire arranged by the United Nations, which sent an emergency force (UNEF) to supervise it. Under strong U.S. pressure, the Anglo-French force was eventually withdrawn, and Britain's prime minister, Anthony Eden, was persuaded to resign. (In 1957, Israel turned the Gaza Strip and Sharm el-Sheikh over to the UNEF.) See also SIX-DAY WAR.

Arab-Israeli War of 1967 See SIX-DAY WAR.

Arab-Israeli War of 1973 (Yom Kippur War, "October War," or War of the Ramadan) Fighting continued off and on between the Arabs and Israelis after the SIX-DAY WAR of 1967. Arab states, frustrated over Israeli refusal to negotiate the return of occupied territories, launched a surprise two-pronged attack on Israel on October 6, 1973, the Jewish holy day of Yom Kippur. Egyptian forces of President Anwar Sadat (1918–81) attacked from the east across the Suez Canal, while Syrian troops moved from the north into Israel. The Egyptian and Syrian armies, joined by Iraqi, Jordanian, and Libyan military units, inflicted heavy losses on the Israelis, who were caught off guard. The Israeli armies eventually retaliated and drove into Syria to within 20 miles of Damascus and encircled the Egyptian army by crossing the Suez and establishing troops on the canal's west bank. A cease-fire, called for by the United States and the Soviet Union, was agreed to by Israel and Egypt, but fighting continued until a United Nations peacekeeping force was moved into the war zone and a cease-fire agreement was signed on November 11, 1973. By a peace agreement in 1974, Israel agreed to withdraw into the Sinai, west of the Mitla and Gidi passes, and Egypt reduced its forces on the Suez's east bank. A UN buffer zone was established between Syria and Israel.

Arab Uprising in German East Africa (1888–90) The German East Africa Company, founded in 1885 by Carl Peters (1856–1918), governed the territory known as German East Africa (Tanzania). In 1888, Arabs in the coastal region rose up against the German administrators, whose aggressive conduct was resented (the Germans had obtained a lease from the sultan of Zanzibar for his territory along the coast). Joined by black Africans, the Arabs fought the Germans, who were aided by the British, for over two years. In January 1891, the German government, which had helped the German East Africa Company suppress the uprising, took over the territory, declared it a protectorate, and sent Peters to govern it as imperial high commissioner. See also WAHEHE WAR.

Aragonese-Castilian War of 1109–12   After King Alfonso I "the Battler" (1073?–1134) of Aragon married Queen Urraca (1081–1126) of Castile in 1109, the two immediately quarreled and the hoped-for union of Aragon and Castile seemed to vanish. Their personal clashes became the basis of war between the nobles of the two Spanish kingdoms, with battles fought between Alfonso's troops and those gathered by Urraca, her family, and Castilian partisans. Though Alfonso won the Battle of Sepúlveda in 1111, the war continued with minor engagements until the dissolution of the marriage and the political union of Aragon and Castile in 1112. Alfonso, who afterward returned to his kingdom, later captured Saragossa from the Moors in 1118, thus expanding Aragon below the Ebro River.

Aragonese Civil War of 1347–48 When King Pedro IV (1319–87) of Aragon proclaimed one of his daughters heir to the throne, the nobles disputed the claim under the rights and privileges granted to them in charters by former Aragonese kings Pedro III (1239–85) and his son Alfonso III (1265–91). In December 1347, open warfare broke out, and the nobles' forces won a victory and forced Pedro IV to bequeath the throne to a male acceptable to the nobles. The king was held captive at Valencia in May 1348 while attempting to negotiate peace with the nobles, but was released because of the Black Death. His loyalists finally defeated the nobles at the Battle of Eppila on July 21, 1348; Pedro IV then withdrew the charters of the nobles.

Aragonese Conquest of Sardinia (1323–26) In the 1295 Treaty of Anagni, King James II (1260?–1327) of Aragon gave up rights to Sicily in exchange for control of Sardinia and Corsica (see SICILIAN VESPERS, WAR OF THE). The Italian cities of Pisa and Genoa had interests on Corsica and Sardinia, which were dominated by the Pisans in the cities of Cagliari and Iglesias. James, who intended to expand Aragon's Mediterranean holdings, did not pursue control of Sardinia until 1323, when he sent a fleet, commanded by his son Alfonso (1299–1336), later King Alfonso IV, to pacify the Pisans and Genoese. By 1326, Iglesias and Cagliari were in Aragonese hands and the Pisans were defeated. However, the expulsion of the Pisans and Genoese from Sardinia was not completed until 1421. The Aragonese were unable to drive the

Genoese rulers from Corsica, which fell under Genoa's full control in 1434. See also ARAGONESE-GENOESE WAR OF 1352–54.

Aragonese-French War of 1209–13 After the Christian crusaders helped King Pedro II (1174–1213) of Aragon destroy the Muslim kingdom at Valencia in 1209, they marched into Provence, an Aragonese holding in France, where heretic Albigensians were gaining a following, to continue the ALBIGENSIAN CRUSADE proclaimed by the pope. When the crusade became a war between northern and southern French nobles, Pedro supported his brother-in-law, Raymond VI (1156–1222), count of Toulouse, in his fight against Simon IV de Montfort (1160?–1218), leader of the northern nobles. In 1213, Pedro died fighting Simon's troops at the Battle of Muret in southern France; Spanish influence north of the Pyrenees ended with his death.

Aragonese-French War of 1284–85 Pope Martin IV (1210?–85) backed the Angevin French claim to Sicily (see SICILIAN VESPERS, WAR OF THE). Declaring that King Pedro III (1239–85) of Aragon had forfeited his right to rule Aragon because of his supposed conspiratorial intrusion into Sicilian affairs, Martin excommunicated Pedro and made Charles of Valois (1270–1325), third son of King Philip III (1245–85) of France, king of Aragon and Sicily. French forces, led by Philip and Charles, invaded Aragon in 1284, won a victory at Gerona, but were subsequently forced by the Aragonese under Pedro to retreat. Disease, which had devastated the ranks of the French army in Aragon, also claimed the life of Philip on the march home.

Aragonese-Genoese War of 1352–54 When the Sardinians rose up against their Aragonese rulers, the Genoese, former rulers of the island (Sardinia), took the opportunity to recapture it (see ARAGONESE CONQUEST OF SARDINIA). King Pedro IV (1319–87) of Aragon secured help from the Venetians and Catalans, and these allies pursued the

Genoese on the high seas and defeated them in a naval battle in 1352. However, a storm disrupted the allied fleet, allowing the Genoese to regroup and attack Sardinia and Corsica. The Genoese proclaimed Mariano de Arborea (d. 1368) king of Sardinia. In 1353, the allies defeated the Genoese near Alghero off the Sardinian coast. King Pedro went to Sardinia the next year and managed to suppress most of the rebels, but opposition to Aragonese rule persisted until well into the next century.

Aragonese-Neapolitan War of 1435–42   René I (1409–80), duke of Anjou, inherited a claim to the throne of Naples through Queen Joanna II (1371–1435) of Naples. King Alfonso V (1396–1458) of Aragon, who had been made heir to the Neapolitan throne by Joanna in 1421 and then disinherited in 1423 (Joanna opposed his attempt to seize the crown), prepared an attack on Naples in 1435 but was defeated at the port of Gaeta. Alfonso was captured by the Genoese and later released with the help of the duke of Milan, with whom he made an alliance to join in the fight against Naples. In 1442, Alfonso defeated René in battle, took possession of Naples, and proclaimed himself king (recognized by the pope in 1443).

Arapaho War of 1864–68   See CHEYENNE AND ARAPAHO WAR OF 1864–68.

Araucanian Wars   See SPANISH CONQUEST OF CHILE.

Arbela, Battle of   See GAUGAMELA, BATTLE OF.

Arcadian War   (c. 471–469 B.C.)   Sparta, a militaristic oligarchic Greek city-state in the Peloponnesus that wanted to dominate the area, came into conflict with some cities of Arcadia, a mountainous region in central Peloponnesus (Sparta hoped to match the growing power and prosperity of Athens to the north). In a long war (c. 580–550) against Arcadia's chief city-state, Tegea, Sparta failed to win and instead made an alliance with its former foe. Later, when Sparta's authority in the Peloponnesus had declined, Tegea forsook Sparta to ally itself with Argos, a Peloponnesian city to the east. After the Spartans fought an inconclusive battle at Tegea, all the Arcadian cities, except Mantinea, allied against Sparta, which then mobilized in strength and decisively defeated the Arcadians at the Battle of Dipaea (c. 470); at the time Argos was preoccupied fighting and subduing the neighboring cities of Mycenae and Tiryns, thus unable to aid Tegea, which shortly afterward yielded to Sparta. Spartan hegemony was recovered in the Peloponnesus. About 100 years later the strong-walled Arcadian city of Megalopolis was founded by General Epaminondas (418?–362) of Thebes as headquarters of an Arcadian League formed (370) to contain Sparta (see THEBAN-SPARTAN WAR OF 379–371 B.C.). See also ARGIVE WAR; MESSENIAN WAR, THIRD.

Archidamian War   (431–421 B.C.)   King Archidamus II (fl. 476–427) of Sparta led an invasion of Attica, near Athens, triggering the first phase of the GREAT PELOPONNESIAN WAR between the two great Greek powers, Athens and Sparta. Pericles (495?–429) restrained his battle-hungry troops behind the walls of Athens, opting instead to launch naval raids from the harbor at Piraeus. A series of victories safeguarded Athens by blockading its enemies. Then an outbreak of the plague weakened Athens and killed Pericles; Sparta seized the initiative, capturing Plataea in 427. Athens responded by seizing Sphacteria in 425, spurning Spartan peace overtures. Sparta now waged a brilliant offensive in northeastern Greece and took several Athenian cities, including Olynthus. Finally, Sparta scored a decisive victory at Amphipolis, where both Brasidas (d. 422), leader of Sparta, and Cleon (d. 422), Pericles's successor, were killed. Nicias (d. 413), the new Athenian leader, arranged an uneasy peace that left the major issues unresolved, thus setting the stage for renewed hostilities and Athens's ultimate ruination.

"Archive War" (1842) In 1836, Texas broke away from Mexico and declared itself an independent republic (see TEXAN WAR OF INDEPENDENCE). The Gulf Coast city of Houston, founded in 1836 and named in honor of Samuel Houston (1793–1863), served as the republic's capital from 1837 to 1839, when it was moved to Austin. When an invasion by Mexicans and Indians seemed imminent in 1842, Texas's President Houston moved his administration to the city of Houston and ordered that the government archives be transferred there from Austin. Citizens of Austin, fearing that if the archives were moved the capital itself would soon be relocated, hid the official records. Houston sent an armed force to do his bidding, while confusion and secret dealings prevailed. At the end of the year, soldiers dug up the hidden archives and loaded them on wagons for the trip to Houston, but irate citizens pursued the wagons and forcibly brought them back to Austin. Rather than risk the destruction of the republic's records, Houston agreed that the capital would remain in Austin, where it remains today.

Ardashir's War with Rome See ROMAN-PERSIAN WAR OF A.D. 230–33.

Ardennes, Battle of the See BULGE, BATTLE OF THE.

Ardoin's Revolt (1002) Ardoin (Arduin) (d. 1015), marquis of Ivrea, led the Lombards in northern Italy in a successful revolt against the rule of Holy Roman Emperor Otto III (980–1002), who earlier had declared himself king of Lombardy and now planned to create an "ecclesiastical empire" centered in Rome. Though opposed by Italian bishops, Ardoin won the support of the lay nobles and was proclaimed king of the Lombards at Pavia in February 1002, shortly after the death of Otto. See also ARDOIN'S WARS.

Ardoin's Wars (1004–1014) German king Henry II (973–1024) had sought to regain control of Lombardy ruled by King Ardoin (Arduin) (d. 1015) since 1002 (see ARDOIN'S REVOLT). Henry's forces marched into northern Italy, overwhelmed Ardoin's troops, and occupied Pavia. There, while Henry was being crowned king of Lombardy, the townspeople fought Henry's forces, and the city was nearly destroyed. Uncertain of ascendancy, Henry fled and returned to Germany. Ardoin, supported by some Italian nobles, attacked the bishops who had backed Henry. In 1013, Henry went to Rome, where he crushed an Italian rebellion (encouraged by Ardoin) and was proclaimed Holy Roman Emperor by the pope on February 14, 1014. Ardoin, who considered himself the Italian king, seized Verceilli (west of Milan) and besieged Novara and Como, but Henry's forces again overwhelmed Ardoin's men. Ardoin retired to the Fruttuaria monastery near Turin, where he died the next year.

Argentine-Brazilian War of 1825–28 Uruguayan revolutionary Juan Antonio Lavalleja (1784–1853) and his small group, called the "Thirty-three Immortals," declared Banda Oriental (Uruguay) independent from Brazil in 1825. Argentina, which hoped to acquire the province, supported the Uruguayans, causing Brazil to declare war on Argentina and to blockade the port of Buenos Aires. On February 20, 1827, an Argentine-Uruguayan army defeated the Brazilians on the pampas of Cisplatina at the Battle of Ituzaingó. Protests from Britain, France, and the United States forced Brazil to discontinue its blockade. Through British mediation, a peace treaty was signed, creating an independent Uruguay as a buffer state between Brazil and Argentina. See also ARGENTINE WAR OF INDEPENDENCE; URUGUAYAN REVOLT OF 1811–16.

Argentine Civil War of 1851–52 See MONTEVIDEO, SIEGE OF.

Argentine Civil War of 1859 Buenos Aires remained an independent province, refusing to join the Argentine Confederation, which had been formed in 1852–53 and led, since 1854, by President

Justo José de Urquiza (1800–1870). Urquiza's government, with its capital at Paraná in the province of Entre Ríos, was hindered in its efforts to improve foreign trade and domestic business by dissident Buenos Aires, which retained for itself monies from tariffs on imported goods. Deciding to use force to reduce Buenos Aires, Urquiza led confederation troops against a provincial army under Bartolomé Mitre (1821–1906), leader of the dissidents, and was victorious at the Battle of Cepeda on October 23, 1859. As a result, Buenos Aires was incorporated into the confederation. See also MONTEVIDEO, SIEGE OF.

Argentine Civil War of 1861 Governmental differences between the province of Buenos Aires and the Argentine union resulted in the former's secession (1861) under the leadership of Bartolomé Mitre (1821–1906), governor of Buenos Aires since 1860. Civil war erupted, and at the Battle of Pavón in the province of Santa Fe, on September 17, 1861, a Buenos Aires army commanded by Mitre won a surprising victory when federal forces under General Justo José de Urquiza (1800–1870), who had become governor of Entre Ríos province after giving up the Argentine presidency in 1860, withdrew from the battlefield; Urquiza also withdrew from politics and left Mitre to form a new national government, whose capital was moved from Paraná to Buenos Aires. In 1862, Mitre was elected president of a united Argentina; he instituted liberal reforms and increased the authority of the federal government in the provinces. Provincial insurrections were easily put down several times during his six-year presidential term. See also MITRE'S REBELLION.

Argentine "Dirty War" (1976–83) On March 24, 1976, in a well-planned coup, the Argentine armed forces overthrew the government of President Isabel Martínez de Perón (1931–), who was held in "protective custody." A three-man military junta, headed by General Jorge Rafael Videla (1925–), took charge and began a ruthless campaign against liberals, leftists, and political terrorists. Anyone suspected of favoring these groups was subject to arbitrary arrest, and those who had illegally profited from the former corrupt Peronist government were prosecuted. People were kidnapped on the streets and never seen again; the prisons overflowed with so-called political prisoners, and torture was common; there were no trials or pretense of legal process. An estimated 11,000 Argentines disappeared between 1976 and 1982, and the flagrant violations of human rights caused the U.S. government under President James E. Carter, Jr. (1924–), to stop sending military aid to Argentina. Several prominent prisoners were freed and allowed to leave the country, and gradually the security forces decreased their "dirty war" activities in response to adverse worldwide public opinion. With the return to civilian government on December 10, 1983, Argentina's newly elected president Raul Alfonsín (1926–) announced plans to prosecute the nine military leaders who ruled during the "dirty war," or reign of terror, from 1976 until the restoration of democracy in 1983. After an eight-month-long trial in Buenos Aires in 1985, Videla and his navy commander, Admiral Emilo Massera (1925–), were found guilty of homicide, illegal detention, and other human rights violations and were sentenced to life imprisonment. Three codefendants, including General Roberto Eduardo Viola (1924–), who succeeded Videla as president, were found guilty of lesser charges and received sentences ranging from four and a half to 17 years. The remaining four officers were acquitted. In January 1991, Argentina's President Carlos Saúl Menem (1930–), seeking to quell discontent in the military (four army uprisings had occurred since 1983), issued pardons to imprisoned military personnel, including Videla, which resulted in much public protest and outrage. See also FALKLAND ISLANDS/ISLAS MALVINAS WAR.

Argentine Revolt of 1951 Argentina became a virtual dictatorship under President Juan Domingo Perón (1895–1974), who was assisted in the government by his wife Eva, or Evita (1919–52). In 1951, the country's economy was in bad shape, with decreasing export trade, climbing inflation, and striking railway workers, firemen, and engineers. Declaring martial law, Perón broke the strikers with force and claimed they were instigated by "foreign agitators." He suspended publication of *La Prensa*, Argentina's largest independent newspaper, which had criticized the government; riots erupted over the paper's suspension. The government confiscated the paper after its publisher fled the country. Perón attempted to have his wife nominated for vice president, but the prospect of a woman succeeding to the presidency and as commander of armed forces outraged some army generals, who led an unsuccessful revolt in September 1951. Eva withdrew her bid for the vice presidency; and in the national election on November 11, 1951, Perón was reelected president by a two to one popular majority.

Argentine Revolt of 1955   Juan Domingo Perón (1895–1974), president and dictator of Argentina, began to lose power after the death of his wife Eva or Evita (1919–52), who had a strong political following among women, labor, and the poor. Many Argentines were also upset by the deteriorating economy and increasing totalitarianism. Fearing a growing Christian socialist movement, Perón turned against the Roman Catholic Church, a former ally; priests were arrested for supposedly meddling in labor unions, politics, and student organizations; clerical teachers were fired from state-controlled schools and universities; the government stopped all financial support of church educational institutions; and outdoor religious celebrations were prohibited. Opposition to these severe measures increased, and many government officials resigned in protest. Perón introduced bills to end religious instruction in the schools and to tax church property. Catholics held religious processions that turned into antigovernment demonstrations, which the police ruthlessly suppressed. After a Corpus Christi celebration in June 1955, two high-ranking bishops were deported. The Vatican retaliated by excommunicating Perón (June 16, 1955), and that same day part of the navy and air force staged an unsuccessful revolt in Buenos Aires, the capital. Dissatisfaction spread as Perón's grip on the country weakened. Perón offered to resign (August 31, 1955), but the working classes indicated continued support for him by calling a general strike until he promised to remain in office. On September 16, 1955, army revolts against Perón broke out in Córdoba, Rosario, Santa Fe, and Paraná; the navy and air force soon joined and threatened to bomb Buenos Aires unless Perón resigned. With the army, navy, and air force converging on the capital, Perón took refuge on a Paraguayan gunboat anchored in the harbor and later flew to Paraguay and on to exile in Spain. On September 23, 1955, five days after Perón had been ousted, General Eduardo Lonardi (1896–1956) became provisional president, but his predecessor's influence on Argentine politics remained strong (see PERÓNIST REVOLTS OF 1956–57), and the Peronistas are still a force to be reckoned with in Argentina.

Argentine Revolts of 1962–63   In Argentina's local and congressional elections of 1962, Perónist candidates were permitted on the ballot for the first time since the ouster of their leader, Juan Domingo Perón (1895–1974), as president in 1955 (see ARGENTINE REVOLT OF 1955). The Peronistas won 45 out of 86 seats in the Chamber of Deputies and 9 of 14 governorships. This outcome so enraged the strongly anti-Perónist top military leaders, ultraconservatives known as the "Gorillas," that they refused to permit the elected Peronistas to take their seats in the government. A general strike ensued that threw the country into chaos. When Argentina's President Arturo Frondizi (1908–95) refused to resign (his political moderation was blamed for the Peronistas' success), the Gorillas deposed and exiled him and seized control of the government. Soon the president of the Senate became a puppet dictator and ruled until free elections were held in 1963. Meanwhile, much internal fighting took place within the armed forces over whether to allow elections or establish a dictatorship. In late 1962, General Juan Carlos Ongania (1914–), commander in chief of the army, took the position that the armed forces should remove themselves from politics, but other military leaders attempted to assert the political power of the military on the civilian government. The Peronistas were forbidden to run candidates in the 1963 elections, so, in protest, they cast blank ballots as they had in 1957 (see PERÓNIST REVOLTS OF 1956–57). In the midst of this explosive political situation full of intrigues, secret alliances, street fighting, intimidating methods of the military, and popular unrest, Arturo Umberto Illia (1900–1983), a semileftist, was elected president. The Argentine economy was in shambles, the hatreds of opposing parties were hardened, and the fervor of the Peronistas was still strong after the so-called "Black Year."

Argentine War of Independence (1806–16) In 1806, Britain, cut off from former trading partners during the NAPOLEONIC WARS, sent an expedition to the Río de la Plata (estuary between Argentina and Uruguay) in an attempt to take possession of part of the surrounding area. Colonial militia under Santiago de Liniers (1756–1810) defeated the British invaders and forced them to withdraw from Buenos Aires. In 1807, a larger, 8,000-man British expedition seized Montevideo and then Buenos Aires before Liniers was able to force the British to leave the area of the Río de la Plata. News of Napoleon's advance into Spain (see PENINSULAR WAR) and the deposing of Spanish King Ferdinand VII (1784–1833) reached Buenos Aires, where the Spanish viceroy was removed and replaced by a provisional junta, including Cornelio Saavedra (1760–1828), Mariano Moreno (1778–1811), Manuel Belgrano (1770–1820), and Bernardino Rivadavia (1780–1845), who set up the United Provinces of the Río de la Plata. While feigning loyalty to the Spanish Crown, the junta exiled royal officials, eased trade regulations, and unsuccessfully invited allegiance from the provinces of the former Spanish viceroyalty (present-day Argentina, Uruguay, Paraguay, and Bolivia). Violent internal disagreements and clashes led to the replacement of the junta by a triumvirate in September 1811. An Argentine congress met at Tucumán, declaring Argentine independence and adopting a constitution in 1816. Juan Martín de Pueyr-

rdón (1776–1850) was installed as supreme dictator on July 9, 1816, directing an Argentine congress consisting of delegates from Buenos Aires and a few nearby provinces. See also CHILEAN WAR OF INDEPENDENCE; PARAGUAYAN WAR OF INDEPENDENCE; URUGUAYAN REVOLT OF 1811–16.

Argive War (494 B.C.) The Greek city-states of Argos and Sparta were rivals for supremacy in the Peloponnesus in the sixth century B.C. (for a long time much of the region had been dominated by the Argives, who had notably defeated the Spartans at Hysiae in 669). In 510, Sparta's King Cleomenes I (d. 490) led an army to Athens, a city-state in Attica that challenged Sparta's ascendancy, and drove out the Athenian tyrant Hippias (fl. 527–510). He tried to set up a pro-Spartan oligarchy but was expelled by Cleisthenes (570?–after 510), the founder of Athenian democracy, in 507. Still trying to increase Spartan power, Cleomenes marched toward Argos; his troops surprised the Argive soldiers (who were dining) and defeated them at the Battle of Sepeia (494) near Tiryns. Argos lost its paramountcy in the Peloponnesus after Cleomenes seized the city in 494. See also ARCADIAN WAR.

Arikara "War" (1823) The Arikara (Rees) Indians went on the warpath when white fur hunters began encroaching on their lands along the upper Missouri River in the Dakotas. A bloody Arikara attack (1823) on trappers led to the first U.S. Army punitive expedition against an American Plains Indian tribe. Troops under Colonel Henry H. Leavenworth (1783–1834) inflicted damages on Arikara villages, opening up areas for the whites; moving northward, the Arikara eventually settled on Fort Berthold reservation, N.Dak., in the 1860s.

Armada, Spanish See SPANISH ARMADA, DEFEAT OF THE.

Armagnac-Burgundian Civil War (1411–13) John "the Fearless" (1371–1419), duke of Burgundy, ordered the assassination of Louis (1372–1407), duke of Orléans, brother of the recurrently insane King Charles VI (1368–1422) of France, triggering minor conflicts that eventually culminated in open warfare for control of France. Loosely allied with the English and backed by the Cabochiens, an association of tradespeople seeking governmental reform (see CABOCHIEN REVOLT), the Burgundians temporarily overpowered the Orleanists, led by Bernard VII (d. 1418), count of Armagnac, father-in-law of Louis's son Charles (1391–1465), duke of Orléans. But the Cabochiens' continued reign of terror antagonized the bourgeoisie, who in a decisive move threw their support to the Orléanists. After his ouster in 1413, John once again sought English aid (see HUNDRED YEARS' WAR).

Armenian-Azerbaijani War of 1988–94   In late February and March 1988 Armenia (predominantly Christian) and neighboring Azerbaijan (mostly Shiite Muslim) began violently pressing their longtime territorial claims to Nagorno-Karabakh, a mostly mountainous agricultural region located within Azerbaijan's boundaries but home mainly to Armenians. Bloody ethnic clashes also occurred over control of Nakhichevan, a smaller area bordering Iran and separated from Azerbaijan by a strip of Armenian territory. Situated in the southwestern part of the Soviet Union, between the Black and Caspian Seas, the two republics of Armenia and Azerbaijan soon turned their ethnic conflict into a popular revolt against Soviet rule. When Azerbaijani militants called for the republic's reunification with part of northern Iran, Moscow declared a state of emergency and, in late January 1990, sent 11,000 troops to help the 6,000 Soviet soldiers already in Azerbaijan; they invaded the republic's capital city of Baku. Thus the conflict, which had begun with skirmishes with hunting rifles, escalated to battles with missiles, tanks, and heavy artillery. In the late summer of 1991 Azerbaijan and then Armenia declared independence, but they did not become real independent states until the Soviet Union dissolved on December 26, 1991. Efforts to resolve the war by the United Nations, Iran, and others failed in 1991

and 1992. Fighting resumed, with both sides blaming the other for truce violations. In May 1994 Russia mediated a ceasefire, with Armenian soldiers in control of Nagorno-Karabakh. Sporadic fighting has occurred since, and no progress has been made toward a political settlement to end the conflict.

Armenian Massacres of 1894–97   Armenians attempted a revolutionary movement to secure independence from oppressive Turkish rule, provoking disturbances in various cities throughout the Ottoman Empire. In retaliation and on orders from Turkish Sultan Abdul-Hamid II (1842–1918), Kurdish cavalry and Turkish soldiers conducted systematic massacres of Armenians at Sassun, Constantinople, Trabzon, Erzurum, Bitlis, Kurun, Maras, and other places. The suffering of the Armenians aroused the humane nations of the world and led to investigations, but nothing significant was done. After the collapse of the Armenian revolutionary movement in 1897, the massacres were temporarily halted. An estimated 250,000 Armenians were killed during the period. Armenians continued to suffer persecution, and the sultan's plan of extermination or deportation was carried out more stealthily.

Armenian Massacres of 1909   Thousands of Armenians were killed by the Turks during several massacres in the province of Cilicia in present-day southern Turkey in April 1909. Turkish sultan Abdul-Hamid II (1842–1918) had ordered the killings after the Armenian revolutionaries, seeking freedom from Turkish oppression, had provoked the Muslim officials and inhabitants of Armenia by their attacks and demonstrations. The United States and other major world powers intervened to stop the cruel slaughter. See also YOUNG TURKS' REBELLION.

Armenian Massacres of 1915   Armenian revolutionaries, hoping to achieve independence for Armenia, captured the Turkish fortress at Van in the eastern Ottoman Empire on April 20, 1915. The Russians aided the Armenians in holding the fortress from May to August 1915, when the Turks regained control of it. The Young Turks' government, considering the Armenians a dangerous people and accusing them of helping the Russian invaders in WORLD WAR I, ordered all Armenians to be either massacred or deported. About 1 million Armenians fled or were killed; nearly 600,000 died of starvation, disease, and exhaustion during a forced march through swampy regions and deserts of Syria and Mesopotamia (now part of Iraq). When Armenians were unable to march any farther, they were often massacred by their Turkish captors.

Armenian-Roman Wars   See ROMAN-ARMENIAN WARS.

Aroostook War (1838–39)   The 1783 Treaty of Paris, which ended the AMERICAN REVOLUTION, had failed to establish the U.S.-Canadian border between Maine and New Brunswick. Maine farmers wanted to cultivate the farmlands of the Aroostook River valley, which Canadian lumbermen considered their land for logging. When a squad of Maine land agents was arrested by the Canadians for trying to remove the lumberjacks from the area, Maine officials called out the militia, and New Brunswick did the same. U.S. president Martin Van Buren (1782–1862) sent a small federal force under General Winfield Scott (1786–1866) to the Aroostook area. In March 1839, Scott successfully negotiated an agreement with the British authorities of New Brunswick and a boundary commission was set up to settle the dispute. It was not until the Webster-Ashburton Treaty was signed in 1842 that the boundary through about 12,000 contested square miles was settled after a "battle of maps." The war in the Aroostook was undeclared and bloodless, except for bloody noses and much hard feeling on both sides.

Arrabel, Revolt of the   See SUBURB, REVOLT OF THE.

Arrow War   See OPIUM WAR, SECOND.

Arundel's Rebellion (1549)   The religious and economic policies of King Henry VIII (1491–1547) negatively affected both the rich and the poor in England. Humphrey Arundel (1513–50), an important landholder in Cornwall, reacted to a 1549 peasants' insurrection in Devon and Cornwall against enclosures and Catholic suppression by assuming its leadership. At first triumphant, the Cornish rebels attacked Exeter. After a two-day losing battle with royal forces, they fled, only to be defeated again at Samford Courtenay. Arundel fled to Launceston, where he was seized, sent to London, and executed at Tyburn.

Asens' Uprising (1185–89)   The Asen (Assen) brothers, John (d. 1196) and Peter (d. 1197), led a large uprising of Bulgars and Vlachs against Byzantine rule in 1185. They proclaimed independence for Bulgaria, and John was crowned ruler as John Asen I at Tirnovo. A Byzantine army under Emperor Isaac II Angelus (d. 1204) crushed the Bulgarians in 1186. The Asen brothers regrouped their forces, obtained support from the Cumans (Kumans), a nomadic Turkic people, and led many devastating raids against the Byzantines in Thrace and Macedonia. After the Byzantines were defeated at the Battle of Berrhoe in 1189, Isaac II Angelus accepted a truce with the Asens, acknowledging the formation of a new Bulgarian state between the Balkan Mountains and the Danube River.

Ashanti War, First (1824–31)   The Ashanti tribal confederation in West Africa began expanding its territory in the early 1800s, moving toward the adjoining British-held Gold Coast (in present-day Ghana). Sir Charles M'Carthy (1770–1824), governor of the British posts along the Gold Coast, tried to protect the settlers and coastal tribes from the Ashanti warriors, but was defeated and killed. Britain sent reinforcements, and the Ashantis were defeated in 1827. The Ashantis gave up sovereignty over parts of the coastal region in 1831. **Second**

Ashanti War (1873–74). The Ashantis, who had been raiding British posts on the Gold Coast from 1863 to 1872, finally invaded the area in 1873. Some 20,000 Ashanti warriors overwhelmed the British and took control until General Sir Garnet Wolsely (1833–1913) was made the new governor and was given British reinforcements. The British soldiers then penetrated the Ashanti line to Kumasi, the Ashanti capital, and leveled the city in February 1874. By the Treaty of Fomena, the Ashanti were forced to pay a heavy indemnity of 50,000 ounces of gold and were compelled to end their practice of human sacrifices. **Third Ashanti War** (1893–94). The new Ashanti ruler, Prempeh (1871–1931), sent raiding parties into the British territory. Bloody skirmishes occurred, and the British attempted to force Prempeh to accept a treaty. In 1894, the Ashantis reluctantly accepted a British protectorate in the region. **Fourth Ashanti War** (1895–96). Prempeh refused to pay an indemnity imposed by the British after the third war and to honor the British residents of the area. War broke out. British troops again took Kumasi, the Ashanti capital, and captured Prempeh and other Ashanti leaders, and deported them. The Ashanti confederation was dissolved, and the protectorate secured.

Assyrian-Hurrian Wars (c. 1350–1245 B.C.) The Assyrians and Hurrians were contemporary empire builders in Anatolia (Turkey) during the second millennium (see HURRIAN CONQUESTS). The Hurrians gained power in northeastern Anatolia about 1700; the earliest Assyrian dynasty began to rule from its capital at Ashur (Qal'at Sharqat, Iraq) on the Tigris River about 1670. At that time, Assyria was an autonomous vassal state of the Hurrian kingdom of Mitanni. About 1350, a conflict arose between the Assyrian ruler Ashur-uballit (fl. c. 1365–c. 1330) and the Mitanni king Tushratta (fl. 14th cent.), for Assyria attacked Mitanni, perhaps with help from the Hittite ruler Suppiluliumas (c. 1375–c. 1335) (see HITTITE-HURRIAN WARS). The Mitanni kingdom, already weakened by a Hittite victory in 1380, lost parts of northeastern Mesopotamia and thereby contributed to the founding of the Assyrian Empire. In 1325, Mitanni and Assyria became allied for a brief time, cooperating in freeing the Mitanni subkingdom of Hanigabat from Hittite control. However, according to Assyrian chronicles, undatable wars occurred under Adadnirari I (fl. c. 1307–1275), who defeated two consecutive Mitanni kings; all of Mesopotamia became a province of Assyria. Hanigabat remained an enemy of Assyria, and King Shalmaneser I (fl. c. 1274–1245) of Assyria succeeded in reducing the last Hurrian kingdom to an Assyrian province, despite Hittite-Babylonian efforts to preserve it for its strategic importance to the control of southern Syria.

Assyrian Wars of c. 1244–c. 1200 B.C. Its wars with the Hurrian kingdom of Mitanni ended (see ASSYRIAN-HURRIAN WARS), Assyria's Old Kingdom freely opposed its remaining rivals, the Hittites and Babylonians. The kingdom's fourth aggressive leader was King Tukulti-Ninurta I (fl.c. 1244–c. 1208). Known in Greek legends as Ninos, he was honored in the naming of Assyria's fourth capital city, Ninua (the Hebrew form is Nineveh), for his guidance enabled the Assyrians to be victorious over the Hittites, who had been weakened by wars with the Egyptians (see KADESH, BATTLE OF). The Assyrians defeated and deported thousands of people to control their newly won territories in Mesopotamia and eastern Anatolia (Turkey), effectively ending the Hittites' New Kingdom (see HITTITE CONQUEST OF ANATOLIA). Tukulti-Ninurta also began the Assyrian fight with expansive Babylonia; his forces plundered the city of Babylon and, for the first time in Assyrian history, looted and destroyed its temples. Tukulti-Ninurta, however, was a tyrant; a rebellion by his sons took his life in 1208, allowing Babylonia, especially later under King Nebuchadnezzar I (fl. 1146–1123), to become briefly dominant because of the collapse of Assyria's Old Kingdom about 1200.

Assyrian Wars of c. 1200–c. 1032 B.C. The military fortunes of Assyria's Middle Kingdom were inconsequential until the reign of King Tiglath-pileser I (fl. c. 1115–c. 1077). Until then, Assyria had been too weak to take advantage of a colossal defeat of the Babylonians (c. 1180) by the Elamites. During his rule, Tiglath-pileser rejuvenated the Assyrians to overpower the small Hurrian kingdom of Muski in southern Armenia and to restrain the Aramaeans. After 1100, Assyria conquered northern Babylonia, plundering the city of Babylon a second time, but failed to secure its southern territories. Tiglath-pileser's death brought on another period of Assyrian decline; the Aramaeans rose up to plague both Assyria and Babylonia in northern Syria and central Mesopotamia.

Assyrian Wars of c. 1032–c. 746 B.C. Gaining control of the rapidly multiplying Aramaean city-states was the primary objective of the Assyrian New Kingdom's activities until about 891 B.C. Six minor wars had established Assyrian-Aramaean boundaries. A second Assyrian enemy was northern Babylonia, which had been reduced to vassal status by two wars between 930 and 904. Under Assyria's King Ashurnasirpal II (fl. 884–859), Assyria introduced major deployment of cavalry and developed heavy siege machinery. Both aided in effecting control of northern Mesopotamia. The Assyrians under King Shalmaneser III (fl. 859–825) went on to take control of northern Syria, but they failed to conquer the city of Damascus and fought indecisive wars in Cilicia and Armenia. Shalmaneser dominated, without conquest, Babylonia's south (southern Mesopotamia). King Shamshi-Adad V (fl. 824–811) of Assyria added Chaldea to the empire, and later King Shalmaneser IV (fl. 782–772) successfully incorporated parts of Armenia into Assyria. However, military actions against Damascus brought on Shalmaneser's defeat and death and caused Assyria to lose most of Syria, and, in the classic Assyrian pattern, to begin a succession rivalry that resulted in a three-decade-long decline in the empire's power.

Assyrian Wars of c. 746–609 B.C. The Assyrian Empire achieved its greatest size under King Tiglath-pileser III (fl. 745–727), a general elevated by a coup to the throne. He and his autonomous vassals defeated the rebellious Babylonians even as other Assyrian troops conquered the Syrian Urartu in 743, took Arpad in 740, and defeated a northern Syrian coalition in 738, a victory that forced all Syrian princes and eastern Anatolia (Turkey) to pay tribute. In a 735–733 war in Palestine, with the kingdom of Judah as his ally, Tiglath-pileser defeated Israel and took much territory. A 732 victory over Damascus caused its destruction and forced Arabia to pay tribute. Of his successors, three continued to increase Assyrian power. The Assyrians under King Sargon II (fl. 722–705) defeated the Elamites in 721, the same year in which they conquered Samaria and made Israel a vassal state, deporting some 27,000 Israelites to eastern Syria to become the legendary 10 lost tribes. Sargon II defeated an Egyptian army at Gaza in 720, put down a rebellion in Cilicia in 716 that had been fostered by Phrygia's historical King Midas (fl. 8th cent.), and established another Assyrian capital named after himself, Dur Sharrukin (Khorsabad, Iraq). King Sennacherib (fl. 705–681) of Assyria had a stormier reign, defeating a resurgent Babylonia under an Aramaean usurper. His campaign in 702 into western Persia, Syria, and Palestine endangered Jerusalem, and a drive against constantly rebellious Babylonia (c. 700–681) ended in the razing and flooding of the city of Babylon. His assassination in 681 brought to power his son Esarhaddon (d. 669), who made peace with the Babylonians and the Elamites. He waged war on Egypt, seizing the city of Memphis in 671. His son Ashurbanipal (fl. 669–626) reigned while Assyria began its final decline. Egypt regained its independence in 656; southern Babylonia, attacked by Elamites, fell under repeated attacks from 652 to 648; a victorious Ashurbanipal intervened from 647 through 646, punishing the Elamites, entering Persia, and seizing the Elamites' major city of Susa. There was Assyrian civil war after 635, when Ashurbanipal's sons fought for the throne while he was still alive, enabling the Chaldeans to occupy Babylon in 629 and, under King Nabopolasar (fl. 625–605), to establish the Neo-Babylonian Empire. The Scythians laid waste to Syria and Palestine in 626; the Babylonians drove out the Assyrians in

623; and the Medes made their first attack on the Assyrian capital of Nineveh in 616. Despite the fall and destruction of NINEVEH in 612, the Assyrian Empire did not collapse for three more years. A remnant of the Assyrian army crowned its commander king in a new capital at Harran (Haran), which suffered partial destruction from attacking Medes and Babylonians in 610. The army surrendered in 609, and the Assyrians thereafter disappeared completely from written history. See also CARCHEMISH, BATTLE OF; MEGIDDO, SECOND BATTLE OF.

Asturian Uprising of 1934 In Spain in the early 1930s, political parties were polarized, chiefly over the powers to be granted the Roman Catholic Church. In 1934, the united Socialist Party developed a scheme to keep the right-wing, pro-church Confederación Española de Derechas Autónomos (CEDA) from joining the increasingly confused and despotic Spanish government; it planned a nationwide general strike, an uprising in Madrid, and a declaration of an independent republic in Catalonia (see CATALAN REVOLT OF 1934). On October 5, 1934, over 70,000 highly unionized, communist-oriented miners in Asturias (region in northwestern Spain) rose in revolt, occupying the city of Oviedo and taking control of much of the area within a few hours. However, Francisco Franco (1892–1975) and another general led Spanish Foreign Legion and government forces to Asturias, where they brutally put down the uprising in two weeks. The miners had burned churches and killed about 40 persons, including 29 priests. The government troops killed an estimated 3,000 and took about 35,000 prisoners, who were tortured and tried well into 1935. The ferocity of the government divided the Spanish people and helped to precipitate the SPANISH CIVIL WAR OF 1936-39.

Atlantic, Battle of the (1940–43) After the start of WORLD WAR II, Great Britain blockaded the German-controlled areas of Europe, but the blockade was ineffective, largely because of the feared German U-boats (submarines) that constantly preyed on British

vessels. Many Allied merchant ships carrying food and war materiel to Britain were torpedoed and sunk by U-boats in the North Atlantic, thus forcing the need for food rationing in the British Isles in 1940. U-boats also destroyed aircraft carriers, battleships, destroyers, and other warships. When the United States began Lend-Lease shipments of goods to European nations, whose defense was vital to that of America, U.S. naval vessels began patrolling the western North Atlantic, while British Royal Air Force planes watched the sea lanes in the east. Large convoys of American and Canadian merchant ships assembled west of Iceland to be escorted across the Atlantic by British warships. After the U.S. destroyer *Reuben James* was sunk by a U-boat off Iceland on October 31, 1941 (about 100 of its crew were lost), the U.S. Congress repealed the Neutrality Act, and U.S. ships armed themselves and entered war zones. In 1942 and early 1943, sinkings by U-boats increased when the Germans began hunting their targets in so-called "wolf packs," groups of as many as 15 to 20 submarines making coordinated attacks. The British, however, had invented two devices that eventually turned the tables—high-frequency direction finding and centrimetric radar, both of which enabled the Allies to pinpoint the location of U-boats and sink them. So many submarines were sunk that the Germans could not disrupt shipping much after mid-1943, and the Allies soon controlled the sea lanes of the Atlantic and elsewhere.

Augsburg, War of the League of See GRAND ALLIANCE, WAR OF THE.

Aurangzeb, Wars of (1636–57) Before he became Mogul emperor in India, Aurangzeb (1618–1707) acted as military leader under his father's orders. In 1636, he was made nawab (viceroy) of the Deccan region and was charged with ensuring the peacefulness of newly subjugated Bijapur and Golconda (two sultanates) and preventing the expansion of the Maratha kingdom in the west Deccan. His forces seized forts from the Marathas and annexed new territories until 1644, when his elder brother's intrigues, a factor negatively affecting Aurangzeb's military success, forced him to withdraw. Made governor of troublesome Gujarat in 1645, Aurangzeb was soon transferred to the even more difficult governorship of Balkh in Transoxania (1647), where his forces gained a clear-cut victory over militant Uzbek Turks. Persian aid, however, enabled the Turks to force out the imperial Mogul army; Aurangzeb became governor of Multan province. Summoned to protect Kandahar from the Persians, he and his troops arrived too late to do more than establish an unsuccessful siege (see MOGUL-PERSIAN WAR OF 1649–53). This failure was redeemed by his victory over the Persians at Shah Mir a few months later (1650). In 1652, Aurangzeb returned to Kandahar to establish a second but equally ineffective siege. Sent again to the Deccan in disgrace (1653), he warred with success upon Golconda and Bijapur (1656–57), only to be undercut in imposing peace terms by his brother and father. His further campaigns in the Deccan were stopped by the MOGUL CIVIL WAR OF 1657–59.

Aurelian's War against Tetricus (A.D. 273–74) In 270, Gaius Pius Esuvius Tetricus (d. c. 276), a Gallic noble, was proclaimed emperor of Gaul (France), Britain, and northern Spain. His provincial empire was disrupted by mutinies in his army and by Germanic invaders (see ROMAN-GOTHIC WARS). Seeking to reunite Tetricus's territory with the empire, Roman emperor Aurelian (212?–75) led an army across the Alps and marched north through Gaul. In late 273, he met and battled Tetricus at Châlons-sur-Marne, where the latter deserted to the enemy as his Gauls went down to defeat. Within several months, Aurelian had gained control of his rival's empire and united it with Rome. Tetricus was displayed during the emperor's triumphal march in Rome (274); he was later pardoned and made governor of southern Italy.

Aurelian's War against Zenobia (A.D. 271–73) While Rome was preoccupied fighting the Goths in eastern Europe (see ROMAN-GOTHIC WARS), Queen Zenobia (d. after 274) of Palmyra, a city in central Syria, took the opportunity to extend her territory in Syria, Asia Minor, and Egypt. In 271, she proclaimed her independence of Rome by setting up her son, Vaballathus (d. 273?), as emperor and herself as empress. When the new Roman emperor Aurelian (212?–75) heard this, he led an army east to Asia Minor. Near Antioch, in 271, he successfully fought the famous armored and mounted lancers and archers of Palmyra, who withdrew in good order pursued by the Romans. Aurelian again defeated them at the Battle of Emesa (Homs, Syria) in 272 and afterward besieged Palmyra, where Zenobia surrendered, was forgiven by Aurelian, and remained in control with her son. Aurelian left, but he soon returned when Zenobia again declared her independence. The Romans recaptured Palmyra; Zenobia was taken prisoner as she was trying to escape and was brought to Rome, where she was displayed in chains in Aurelian's triumphal procession in 274; Vaballathus was thought to have been slain near the war's end. Palmyra was demolished by the Romans.

Australian Irish Convict Revolt (1804)   A group of Irish criminals and political prisoners who had been transported to Australia, many without trial, attempted armed rebellion at Castle Hill, outside Sydney, in March 1804. The conspiracy was betrayed, martial law imposed, and the uprising easily put down. Eight men were hanged, and others were flogged. The remaining ringleaders were removed to the newly founded penal colony of Newcastle on the Hunter River.

Australian Rum Rebellion (1808)   William Bligh (1754–1817), governor of New South Wales, Australia, prohibited offering spirits in payment for commodities. Though many colonists supported his attempts to normalize trade, others resented his interference. A series of charges and countercharges culminated in a military rebellion in January 1808, and in Bligh's arrest by the acting commandant of the New South Wales Corps. For over a year Bligh remained confined. Finally he agreed to set sail for England, but once aboard he turned back and attempted to resume control of Sydney. In 1809, the British government, recognizing the impasse between governor and military, recalled Bligh. The commandant was later found guilty of mutiny.

Austrian Netherlands Civil War of 1477–92   The marriage of Austrian archduke Maximilian (1459–1519), later Holy Roman Emperor, to Mary of Burgundy (1457–82) in 1477 gained him the Netherlands as part of her inheritance; with it, he acquired two closely related problems: sporadic war with France over Burgundy (see FRANCO-AUSTRIAN WAR OF 1477–93) and resistance from the Netherlands, causing intermittent civil war marked by French meddling. Like the Swiss (see AUSTRO-SWISS WARS), the Netherlanders were used to a large measure of freedom and wanted more. Mary and Maximilian, however, restricted autonomy as they tried to establish a strong central government despite the French war's necessitating a restoration of local privileges to pay military expenses. The Netherlanders' resistance reached its zenith in 1482 with Mary's death. Then Maximilian claimed to be the Netherlands' regent for his son Philip (1478–1506). Flanders, chiefly the cities of Bruges and Ghent, disallowed Maximilian's claim, held the child prisoner, and, through cunning advice from the French, supported the 1482 Austro-Dutch Treaty of Arras, which cost Maximilian Burgundy. Maximilian's forces battled in Flanders until 1485 to regain his son. Then, resuming his centralization efforts and pursuing the war, Maximilian offended the Netherlanders and botched two invasions of France (1486, 1487). He summoned his legislature to Bruges in 1487, but when he attempted to bring German mercenaries with him, Bruges closed its gates and held him prisoner for four months. Troops under his father, Holy Roman Emperor Frederick III (1415–93), marched to relieve him in 1488 and witnessed Maximilian's humiliation in the so-called "Peace of Bruges," when his legislature forced him to promise a constitution granting federative autonomy. Both Hapsburg rulers—Maximilian and Frederick—went to Germany in 1488, but Maximilian, repudiating his promise at Bruges while making momentary peace with France in 1489, returned to the Netherlands, where civil war broke out again from 1490 to 1492, with most Flemish cities partici-

pating. On the sidelines, France promised to ensure the projected 1488 constitution, but did not intervene. Maximilian put down a rebellion in Ghent in 1491 and a Netherlanders' revolt over high taxes in 1492. His forces besieged Sluys, helping bring about pleas for peace from the Netherlanders, whose leader, Philip of Cleves (fl. 1480s–90s), had been captured in 1492. Peace came on Maximilian's terms that year. With his territories acquired through inheritance now secured for his son, Maximilian carried on the war with France, winning at Dournon in 1493 and benefiting from that year's Peace of Senlis. See also "MAD WAR."

Austrian Revolution of 1848–49   The revolt in Paris in February 1848 (see FRENCH REVOLUTION OF 1848) prompted the outbreak of other demonstrations for political and economic reform, especially in the Austrian Empire (see "FIVE DAYS" REVOLT; HUNGARIAN REVOLUTION OF 1848–49; ITALIAN REVOLUTION OF 1848–49). As in France and Germany (see GERMAN REVOLUTION OF 1848), the Austrian revolt had initial success but ended ultimately in failure. In Vienna, a peaceful demonstration on March 13, 1848, turned violent; suburban uprisings occurred, and the Austrian government became so frightened that the archconservative foreign minister Metternich (1773–1859) was dismissed by the emperor and then fled to England. On March 15, 1848, to quiet agitation, Emperor Ferdinand (1793–1875) promised a liberal constitution, allowed freedom of the press, and set up a council of ministers. But promises and accomplishments were far apart. Three constitutions were prepared; the first, the Pillersdorf Constitution, was ready by April 8, 1848; a representative Diet was accorded Bohemia, and a separate constitution was promised to Prague. The Pillersdorf document envisioned a constitutional monarchy and extended suffrage to all citizens. But the emperor's prime minister attempted to foil it by dissolving the Reichstag (legislature) and arresting reformers. Public outcry, but no violence, compelled the legislature to reassemble, and the document was published on April 25, 1848. Then the reforming process stalled because the government was busy in other Austrian territories. On October 6, 1848, a new uprising occurred in Vienna; three days were needed to repress it brutally. The Reichstag began work on another representative but less liberal constitution, and soon after the emperor abdicated (December 2, 1848) in favor of his reactionary son Francis Joseph (1830–1916). The Reichstag was moved to Moravia and then dismissed. Almost a year after the Vienna uprising, the final constitution appeared (March 4, 1849), allowing national equality, a limited form of representation, the abolition of feudalism and serfdom, and a reformed judiciary. Neither so liberal nor so democratic as the Pillersdorf document, it was received with docility, a meekness reinforced by the invitation (May 1849) of Russian troops to "protect" the Austrian Empire.

Austrian Succession, War of the   (1740–48) When Holy Roman Emperor Charles VI (1685–1740) died, several claimants challenged the Pragmatic Sanction (1713) whereby his daughter Maria Theresa (1717–80) succeeded her father as ruler of the Austrian (Hapsburg) lands. Some European countries were ready to divide up part of the Austrian Empire. King Frederick II "the Great" (1712–86) of Prussia posed the most serious threat, pressing his dubious claim to Silesia by invading that region in 1740 (see SILESIAN WAR, FIRST). For a variety of motives, France, Spain, Bavaria, and Saxony then united with Frederick, and a general power struggle ensued among the states of Europe. Only Britain, an enemy of Spain in the War of JENKINS' EAR, at first aided Maria Theresa, whose forces moved about Europe in a war containing some 20 important battles, five of them large-scale. Her troops first lost to Frederick's (1741), and she hoped to ensure his neutrality by letting Prussia have Silesia (1742), for Prague had fallen to the Bavarians and French in 1741. In 1742, her soldiers laid siege to Prague, seized it, and overran Bavaria. The Austrian queen gained Saxony as an ally in 1743 and induced Sardinia to help contain Spain and Naples in Italy. French forces, pushed westward toward the Rhine by the rejuvenated armies of Maria Theresa, confronted a marching British army at Dettingen, Bavaria. There, on June 27, 1743, the French cavalry attacked prematurely, and the British

infantry, led personally by King George II (1683–1760) and supported by Hessians and Hanoverians, destroyed it before assistance arrived. The French then retreated across the Rhine and remained on the west side, precluding any further action in Germany or Austria. Instead, they began to move toward Austria's territories in the Netherlands. In 1744, alarmed at Austrian successes, Frederick reentered the fray (see SILESIAN WAR, SECOND). The French moved into the Austrian Netherlands, transferred from Spain after the War of the SPANISH SUCCESSION, and besieged Tournai. The Austrian allies, an Anglo-Dutch-Hanoverian army under Duke William of Cumberland (1721–65), attacked the French under Marshal Saxe (1696–1750) at Fontenoy on May 11, 1745, but were routed by a great French counterattack. Tournai surrendered, and the French went on to seize Brussels. Meanwhile, after Bavaria's claimant to the Austrian throne died (1745), Austria and Bavaria made peace, with Bavaria receiving back all lands taken by Austria in return for its support of Maria Theresa's husband as Holy Roman Emperor Francis I (1700–1765). This peace isolated Prussia, and the empire's troops advanced into Silesia to oppose 65,000 Prussians concentrated there. But Frederick, always alacritous, attacked the empire's vanguard on June 4, 1745, at Hohenfriedeberg, routing it before the main force could arrive. Then the Prussians charged the main body, causing the enemy to take flight under heavy pursuit. Two armies of the Holy Roman Empire advanced toward Berlin, Prussia's capital. At Hennersdorf, on the Silesian-Saxon border, one of the armies was crushed by Frederick's men on November 24, 1745. A second Prussian force moved to stop the other Imperial army, mainly Saxon, attacking and defeating it at Kesselsdorf near Dresden on December 14, 1745. Eleven days later, Maria Theresa, whose armies had suffered four defeats in seven months and were demoralized, agreed to the Treaty of Dresden, which recognized Frederick's control of Silesia and Maria Theresa's husband's election as emperor, but military operations continued in Flanders and in Italy, with phases of the war also going on in North America and India (see CARNATIC WARS; KING GEORGE'S WAR). The participants finally grew weary and concluded the Treaty of Aix-la-Chapelle on October 18, 1748, which recognized the Pragmatic Sanction, ensured Frederick's annexation of Silesia, and awarded some Italian lands to Spain, but it failed to resolve the colonial conflicts involving France and Britain. See also FRENCH AND INDIAN WAR; SEVEN YEARS' WAR.

Austro-Hungarian War of 1439–57   See HAPS-BURG DYNASTIC WAR OF 1439–57.

Austro-Prussian War of 1756–63   See SEVEN YEARS' WAR.

Austro-Prussian War of 1866   See SEVEN WEEKS' WAR.

Austro-Russian-Turkish War   See RUSSO-TURK-ISH WAR OF 1736–39.

Austro-Swiss War of 1385–88   The communities and cantons of Switzerland were the prey of aggrandizing dynastic houses during the 13th and 14th centuries, chiefly the Leopoldine (eastern) branch of the House of Hapsburg. These pressures had led the political units to cooperate informally for mutual defense; in 1291, in what is sometimes called the "Swiss Revolt" of that year, three (Uri, Schwyz, and Unterwalden) formed the Everlasting League, the nucleus of the long-enduring Swiss Confederation. The confederation had withstood the Hapsburgs at Morgarten (1315), resisted Bavaria and gained Imperial attention (1355), and lost Zurich briefly to the Hapsburgs (1368), only to face another Hapsburg aggression in 1385 by Leopold III (1351–86), duke of Austria, whose attempts to gain territory in Swabia in southern Germany had spilled over into confederation territory. By year's end, Lucerne's forces occupied Hapsburg-controlled Rothenburg and Sempach. Leopold led a strong invasion of Switzerland to offset the occupation of his territories, and near the village of Sempach, a column of heavy Austrian cavalry dismounted and easily drove through the Swiss vanguard from Lucerne only to face

the main forces of the Swiss Confederation and to lose to their halberds and pikes. A second column of dismounted cavalrymen was slaughtered before it could organize and advance. A third Austrian column fled, and Leopold, with all his dismounted knights, perished in battle. The momentous defeat of Leopold boosted the morale of the Swiss Confederation, which was victorious in all subsequent actions of the war, including the Battle of Nafels in 1388. There, the troops of Glarus lay in ambush, disorganized the Austrian forces by an avalanche of boulders, and then routed both cavalry and infantry. A truce followed, during which the Swiss improved their military organization. The Austrians lost ground, signing a 20-year peace with Zurich (1394), abandoning rights in Lucerne, Zug, and Glarus (which became a confederation member after the victory at Näfels). Now eight members strong—Uri, Schwyz, Unterwalden, Lucerne, Zürich, Bern, Zug, and Glarus—the confederation became a dependent of the Holy Roman Emperor (who, although a Hapsburg, was not friendly toward the Austrian branch), and Switzerland, for all practical purposes, was autonomous.

Austro-Swiss War of 1460   Despite the expulsion of the Austrians from the Aargau in 1450 (see OLD ZURICH WAR), Switzerland was still not free of the expansionist Austrian House of Hapsburg. Sigismund (d. 1496), duke of Austria, inherited Tyrol; in addition, Holy Roman Emperor Frederick III (1415–93), himself a Hapsburg but of a rival branch, had to balance his assertions of Imperial rights in Switzerland against pressing for the Hapsburg family's rights. He chose, mistakenly, to back the family and attempted to split the Swiss Confederation. But he mistook the loyalty and the power of the confederation, which had grown to include the abbeys of St. Gall, Rapperswil, and Stein am Rhein as allies and Appenzell and Steinhausen as members. As emperor, Frederick menaced the confederation but did not attack it. The Swiss acted in 1460, when Duke Sigismund was excommunicated over the usual investiture issue (see HOLY ROMAN EMPIRE-PAPACY WARS), by sending their soldiers north as far as the Rhine River, meeting almost no opposition. Swiss troops occupied Frauenfeld, vainly besieged Winterthur, and wrested the Thurgau canton from Sigismund's men. The Peace of Constance in 1461 left the Hapsburgs with only a few strongholds south of the Rhine and permitted the Swiss to be free of aggrandizement until the Hapsburg defeat in the AUSTRO-SWISS WAR OF 1499.

Austro-Swiss War of 1499 (Swiss-Swabian War) Driven out of the Aargau and thus out of Switzerland, the Hapsburgs of Austria sought revenge. Hapsburg Holy Roman Emperor Maximilian I (1459–1519) attempted to force imperial control and taxation upon territories in eastern Switzerland (the Austro-Swiss border was in contention). Aided by the French, the Swiss resisted and forced the empire into war. Most of the empire's soldiers were Swabians (southern Germans), who fared badly, losing minor battles at Vaduz, Walgan, Bruderholz, and Schwaderloo and major battles at Frastenz, Calven, and Dornach (the decisive Swiss victory came on July 22, 1499). The Treaty of Basel on September 22, 1499, forced Maximilian to give independence to the Swiss.

Austro-Turkish War of 1529–33 By the end of the HUNGARIAN-TURKISH WAR OF 1521–26, the Ottoman Turks had control of two-thirds of Hungary, but Austria had not been humbled, which forced John Zápolya (1487–1540), newly crowned king of Ottoman Hungary, into Poland in 1527. He turned to Constantinople (Istanbul) and the Turks for aid against the Austrians, and Sultan Süleyman I "the Magnificent" (1496–1566), vowing to capture Vienna, mobilized and marched in 1529. From the beginning, his campaign was doomed: he had left too late, the trek to Belgrade took three months, the weather was bad, and Vienna had used the delay to build its defenses. The Ottoman siege of Vienna (September 27–October 14, 1529) failed, and Süleyman withdrew, with the Austrians in pursuit. Zápolya was safe in Buda, and Archduke Ferdinand (1503–64) of Austria was still frightened enough to offer tribute in

exchange for all of Hungary. The war should have stopped, but Süleyman was so humiliated and angry that he tried again to crush the Austrians in 1532. He left Constantinople early but got bogged down by the Austrians at the fortress at Güns (Koszeg), where the Turks' monthlong siege (August 1532) was repulsed. His army then made destructive raids marching toward Belgrade but finally turned back. In 1533, a truce was conceded to Ferdinand, and Süleyman returned home to pursue the TURKO-PERSIAN WAR OF 1529–33. Ottoman soldiers, however, intoxicated by the joys of raids, plundered, killed, and raped merrily on until their depredations helped lead to the renewal of hostilities (see AUSTRO-TURKISH WAR OF 1537–47).

Austro-Turkish War of 1537–47 Two incidents helped provoke Ottoman Sultan Süleyman I "the Magnificent" (1496–1566) to renew his war against Vienna (see AUSTRO-TURKISH WAR OF 1529–33): 24,000 Austrians and Bohemians had vainly attacked the Ottoman fortress at Essek in 1537; in Moldavia, the current governor was suspected of intrigue with Vienna. In 1538, Süleyman occupied Moldavia and installed a new governor. John Zápolya (1487–1540), king of Hungary, and Archduke Ferdinand (1503–64) of Austria concluded a solemn but foolish pact to forestall war between them: each would keep what he had control of until Zápolya's death; if he died childless (John was still a bachelor), Ferdinand would inherit his lands. John neither consulted nor informed Süleyman. He married (1539) and died the next year, leaving an infant son, John II Sigismund (1540–71). Ferdinand claimed to be heir and marched his forces toward Buda, Hungary's capital; Süleyman found himself in a major crisis. The Ottomans hastily occupied Buda in 1541, conquered nearby Pest, and then ordered the return of all territories acquired by the Austrians since Zápolya's death while agreeing to Ferdinand's offer to pay tribute for Austrian Hungary. The Austrians demurred. In 1543, a carefully planned Turkish expedition departed from Belgrade and captured all fortresses on the way to Buda, taking Grau and Stuhlweissenberg, the largest in the area. Süleyman, the leader, then returned to Constantinople

(Istanbul) to take part in the ongoing TURKO-PERSIAN WAR OF 1526–55, but his beys (governors) continued his campaign, seizing Styria, Carinthia, and Croatia in 1544. Hard pressed and lacking outside help, Ferdinand sued for a truce in 1545, an unhappy development for the Turks, who, winning, did not want to stop fighting. Hostilities, however, did cease, but a peace was not signed until 1547 at Adrianople and then only for a five-year period. Ferdinand retained Austrian Hungary for an annual tribute of 30,000 ducats (gold coins) to the Ottoman Empire. But he was restless and treacherous (see AUSTRO-TURKISH WAR OF 1551–53).

Austro-Turkish War of 1551–53   The Peace of Adrianople ending the AUSTRO-TURKISH WAR OF 1537–47 did not last its intended five years. Austria's Archduke Ferdinand (1503–64) was unhappy that the Ottoman pashalik (province of a pasha) of Buda separated Austrian Hungary from Transylvania. Previously, the queen mother of Hungary's John II Sigismund (1540–71) had protested to the Porte (Ottoman government) that her assigned adviser and regent for John, George Martinuzzi (1482–1551), had assumed too much power and had tried to have her give up Transylvania for equivalent Austrian areas, especially Silesia, in 1551. In order to ensure this exchange, Ferdinand had besieged Lippa, Transylvania's capital. Martinuzzi served as the go-between. An Ottoman army was sent to capture Lippa and establish a garrison there. Ferdinand suspected Martinuzzi of being a traitor and had him murdered. In three separate military actions, the Ottomans captured three fortresses and conquered Temesvar and made it a new Turkish province, but failed to capture the fortress at Erlau (Eger) in 1552. An armistice of sorts ended the fighting the next year, with the main Ottoman army being recalled to pursue a new campaign in the TURKO-PERSIAN WAR OF 1526–55. The Austrians vainly took advantage of the unofficial truce to attempt diplomatic annexation of Austrian Hungary. Formal peace came 10 years later, and it merely renewed the terms of the 1547 accord. Thus, three Hungaries existed: Austrian, Ottoman (Buda), and Transylvanian; each was kept fully prepared for new hostilities.

Austro-Turkish War of 1566   After the Ottoman siege of Malta (1565) was checked by the Knights Hospitalers (Order of St. John), led by Jean de La Valette (1494–1568), Ottoman Sultan Süleyman I "the Magnificent" (1496–1566) wished for a final triumph to vindicate both himself and his belief in Ottoman invincibility. He also wanted to avenge his defeat at Erlau (Eger) in the AUSTRO-TURKISH WAR OF 1551–53 and used as his pretext for war the failure of Holy Roman Emperor Ferdinand I's (1503–64) successor, Maximilian II (1527–76), to pay the tribute due for Austro-Hungarian and Austrian attacks made against Transylvania. In 1566, a very large Ottoman force led by Süleyman besieged the fortress town of Szigetvár; it destroyed the town but failed to take the fortress, whose Croatian commander, Miklos Zrinyi (1508–66), vowed to fight to the last man. When the fortress's walls were nearly crumbled, Zrinyi set time fuses to his powder magazine and led a sortie, during which he and his men were killed. Süleyman had died two days earlier, but the fact was kept secret so that his army could complete the overthrow of the fortress with zeal. Charging into the fortress, some 3,000 Turks were blown apart when the powder magazine exploded. After their Pyrrhic victory, the remaining Ottomans, informed of Süleyman's death, carried his embalmed body to Constantinople (Istanbul) for burial. See also VENETIAN-TURKISH WAR OF 1570–73.

Austro-Turkish War of 1591–1606   (Fifteen Years' War or "Long War") Border strife between Austrian and Ottoman Hungary, intermittent since the earliest Austro-Turkish war, became more violent during 1591; and the defeat of Bosnian Ottomans by Croatian troops at Sissek (Sisak) in 1593 enlarged the hostilities into a full-scale war. The longest continuous conflict in the many pitting Austria against the Ottoman Empire, its original focus was a small part of Austrian Hungary north of the fortress of Esztergom (Gran), but the Porte (Ottoman government) lost control of so much of central Hungary and Rumania from 1593 through 1595 that the next 11 years were devoted to recovering these territories. Only one victory (Raab, 1594) brightened these years of war for the Ottomans, who were harassed by the defection of Moldavia, Wallachia, and Transylvania to Vienna (1594) and attacks from Dnieper Cossacks by land and sea. The Turks lost Esztergom in 1595 and almost immediately thereafter were sorely routed at Giurgiu. Ottoman sultan Muhammad III (1567–1603) came to Hungary to lead his troops personally and was victorious at Erlau (Eger) in 1596 just before an almost miraculous Ottoman win at Mezokeresztes, where the Ottoman infantry had deserted en masse and Muhammad urged retreat. However, Muhammad's war council had demurred, and, angered, he had taken the Prophet's standard, positioned himself with his remaining troops, and turned the tide; 30,000 Germans and Hungarians died. Muhammad returned to Constantinople (Istanbul), bewildered at his audacity. The war, with Austria occupying Transylvania, generally became a battle of fortresses. Austria recovered Raab but failed at Buda (1598), as did the Turks at Varazdin in the same year. In 1599, the Austrians asked for peace, but the Ottomans refused, seized Kanizsa (1600), but lost Stuhlweissenberg (1601). During 1602–04, the Austrians again failed to capture Buda, and the Turks failed to take Pest. But, in 1605, the Ottomans seized Esztergom, Visigrad, Veszperm, and Palota, regaining territories lost through 1595. Transylvania returned to the Ottoman fold under Stephen Bocskay (1557–1606), who led a rebellion (1604) with Turkish support against the Hapsburg (Austrian) Holy Roman Emperor's efforts to impose Roman Catholicism on Hungary; Bocskay's reward was to be made prince of Transylvania, a title recognized by the Turks. He made a separate peace with the emperor—the Treaty of Vienna (1606), which granted both Hungaries religious freedom. The war's main peace between Austria and the Ottoman Empire, now hard pressed by the TURKO-PERSIAN WAR OF 1603–12, was made by the Treaty of Zsitva-Torok (1606), the first peace signed by the Turks outside Constantinople. The Porte renounced its claim to Esztergom territory, cancelled Austria's annual tribute in exchange for a single payment of 200,000 gulden, and promised to address the emperor by his formal titles in future diplomacy. In 15 years of war, the Porte had gained only the fortresses of Erlau and Kanizsa and had indicated its inability to expand farther into Europe.

Austro-Turkish War of 1663–64   Having restored order in Transylvania (see TRANSYLVANIAN-TURKISH WAR OF 1657–62), the Turkish force, led by Grand Vizier Fazil Ahmed Koprulu Pasha (1635–76) and enlarged by Wallachian and Rumanian Christians offended by the Hapsburg (Austrian) counter-reformation (see THIRTY YEARS' WAR), was regarded as an army of liberation from Hapsburg tyranny. It overran the Hungarian-Transylvanian areas in 1663, capturing Buda and, in a surprise attack, overwhelming the fortress of Neuhäusel in a victory second only to Mezökeresztes in the AUSTRO-TURKISH WAR OF 1591–1606. After wintering in Belgrade, the Turkish army renewed its advance on Austrian Hungary, taking as many fortresses as possible on the road to Vienna and causing the Austrians under Holy Roman Emperor Leopold I (1640–1705) to begin peace negotiations. Before ratifying the peace terms, the Turks planned to hold the area north of the Raab River, but fortune and bad weather ruled otherwise. Half of the Turkish army had crossed the river in the area of the Convent of St. Gotthard, but rain and flooding prevented the second half from crossing. The advance force was defeated by Austrian cavalry under Raimund Montecuccoli (1609–80) in the Battle of St. Gotthard (or Raab River) on August 1, 1664. This first great Turkish defeat forced the Treaty of Vasvar, a 20-year truce, which confirmed Turkish suzerainty over Transylvania but removed Austrian and Ottoman troops from the area to reduce confrontation. The Turks kept the fortresses they had seized. See also VIENNA, SIEGE OF.

Austro-Turkish War of 1683–99   The Turkish invasion of Austria in 1683 (see VIENNA, SIEGE OF) plunged Austria, allied with Poland, into war with the Ottoman Empire. Austrian-Polish forces under King John III Sobieski (1624–96) of Poland pursued the Turks, forcing them out of northwestern Hungary by late 1683. Pope Innocent XI (1611–89) instigated a crusading Holy League, made up of the Holy Roman Empire, Venice, Poland, and, after 1686, Moscow, to battle the Ottomans, who were driven out of Buda, their capital of Hungary, in early September 1686. Southern Hungary and much of Transylvania came under Hapsburg (Austrian) control in 1687, and Belgrade and Serbia were taken by the Austrians the next year. Ottoman sultan Süleyman II (1642–91) sent invading forces into Transylvania, which were at first successful before being defeated decisively in 1691, and into Serbia, recapturing it and Belgrade in 1690. Austria, which had become deeply involved in the War of the GRAND ALLIANCE with France, did not press against the Turks, and thus an unfixed border ensued for more than five years. When a large Ottoman army marched from Belgrade to invade Hungary, an Imperial army under Prince Eugene of Savoy (1663–1736) advanced and attacked it at the Battle of Senta (Zenta) on September 11, 1697. The Ottomans suffered a crushing defeat and were never again a serious threat to Hungary. The war was ended by the Treaty of Karlowitz on January 26, 1699; Austria gained control of Hungary (except the Banat of Temesvar), Transylvania, Croatia, and Slavonia; Venice got the Morea (Peloponnesus) and much of Dalmatia; Poland received Podolia; and the Turks kept Belgrade and Serbia. See also RUSSO-TURKISH WAR OF 1695–1700; VENETIAN-TURKISH WAR OF 1685–99.

Austro-Turkish War of 1716–18   Officially neutral during 1714, when the Ottoman Empire was fighting the VENETIAN-TURKISH WAR OF 1714–18, Austria, influenced by the brilliant Savoyard strategist, Prince Eugene (1663–1736), made a defensive alliance with Venice in 1716. Arguing that the Porte (Ottoman government) had broken the 1669 Treaty of Karlowitz and endangered Dalmatia (and therefore Austria's Croatian and Styrian territories), Austria mounted an offensive, and some 60,000 troops under Eugene routed the Turks at the Battle of Peterwardein on the Danube River on August 5, 1716. Losing 6,000 men and over 100 artillery pieces, the Turks were afterward slow to recover their discipline, for their grand vizier had

been mortally wounded. Eugene took advantage of their confusion to capture Temesvar, the last Ottoman fortress in Hungary, and to besiege Belgrade, the strongest Ottoman fortification in the Balkans. A large Ottoman army moved rapidly to confront Eugene's Austrian troops, who, at first, fared badly in battle, but a surprise charge by Eugene's cavalry scattered the Turks and won victory. Belgrade surrendered on August 21, 1717. Austrian forces then occupied much of Serbia, Wallachia, and other Balkan areas and began to advance on Constantinople (Istanbul) when the Ottomans sued for peace. In 1718, the Treaty of Passarowitz awarded Temesvar, Belgrade, and part of Wallachia to Austria. See also RUSSO-TURKISH WAR OF 1710–11.

Austro-Turkish War of 1737–39   See RUSSO-TURKISH WAR OF 1736–39.

Ava-Pegu Forty Years' War   See BURMESE CIVIL WAR OF 1368–1408.

Axe, War of the (1846–47)   Drought and a plague of locusts set the stage for yet another outbreak of fighting between Xhosa tribespeople and Europeans competing for pasture and farmland along the Great Fish River in southern Africa (see KAFFIR WARS). Cattle raiding escalated, and in 1846, British troops entered Kaffirland to force the Xhosa to surrender some wanted men (including a man caught allegedly stealing an axe from a store in Fort Beaufort but who escaped, thanks to a group of Xhosa—hence that war's name). The Xhosa triumphed, in turn invading colonial territory, but after some initial successes they were again driven out and their lands annexed. The British governor, Sir Harry Smith (1787–1860), attempted unsuccessfully to intimidate the defeated Xhosa chiefs into a permanent peace by blowing up a wagonload of gunpowder in their presence.

Ayutthayan-Chiengmai Wars See THAI WARS

B

Babi Yar Massacre (1941) In September 1941, large numbers of Ukrainian Jews and communists in Nazi-occupied Kiev (Kyyiv) were summoned to report to designated places of registration. Many were then transported to a deep gully called Babi Yar ("Old Woman's Gully") outside the city, where they were machine-gunned in front of pre-dug graves by Nazi SS (Schutzstaffel) troops under the command of General Otto Rasch (1891–1948). The mass graves were covered with dirt by bulldozers. Thousands of inhabitants of Kiev (perhaps 100,000), including at least 34,000 Jews, were massacred by the Nazis in two days.

Babri Mosque, Destruction of the (1992) On December 6, 1992, the historic Babri Masjid (mosque) in the holy town of Ayodhya, in northern India, was demolished by Hindu militants during a political rally organized by the Bharatiya Janata Party (BJP), India's opposition right-wing Hindu nationalist party. This aroused Muslim and anti-Muslim sentiments and unleashed violent clashes across the region as the Congress Party-led government promised to rebuild the mosque. Built in 1528 by Mogul (Muslim) emperor Babur (1483–1530) on the site of a Hindu temple honoring the warrior-god Rama, the mosque had been the focus of sectarian conflict over the years and was ordered closed in 1949. However, in 1984, Hindu fundamentalists campaigned on a promise to destroy the mosque

and, in September 1990, a BJP-led protest march on the mosque ended in communal rioting (1,000 casualties nationwide), forcing the resignation of the current prime minister, V. P. Singh (1931–), who headed a coalition of centrist parties. The BJP government in the state of Uttar Pradesh was directed by the Supreme Court not to tamper with the disputed property. On December 6, thousands of Hindus voluntarily pulled down the mosque, reducing it to rubble. Rioting by angry Muslims afterward resulted in the death of 1,150 persons throughout India. Before being arrested on December 8, 1992, thousands of BJP activists erected a makeshift Hindu temple amid the ruins. Ten other mosques and several Muslim homes in the area were also attacked. Meanwhile, the violence spread across the country from Mumbai (formerly Bombay) to Assam, and hundreds of fatalities were reported in the first two days alone. The arrest of six Hindu-fundamentalist leaders sparked calls for a nationwide strike. On December 15, the Congress government at the center outlawed all BJP state governments. More than 3,000 militants who had threatened to storm the site again were arrested on December 25. As the situation eased elsewhere, it flared up again in Mumbai on January 6, 1993, when Hindu mobs (responding to calls from the right-wing Hindu Shiv Sena party) attacked and burned Muslim homes and businesses, reportedly with the connivance of the police. By the end of that week, some 100,000 people fled the city and over 600 were killed. On January 16, 1993, the

Indian cabinet resigned to allow the prime minister, P. V. Narasimha Rao (1921–), to reshuffle his cabinet. Then, in March 1993, Mumbai was terrorized by a series of explosions, which destroyed buildings and killed over 250 people. The Srikrishna Commission was appointed to investigate the January riots, and its report was not officially released until 1998 because the government in the state of Maharashtra (of which Mumbai is the capital) was led by the right-wing Shiv Sena, which was implicated in instigating the riots of 1993.

Babur, Conquests of (1524–29) On his father's side, the fifth descendant of Tamerlane (1336–1405) and the 14th of Genghis Khan (1167?–1227) on his mother's, Babur ("lion") (1483–1530) was an opportunist who developed this trait through experience. King of Transoxanian Fergana at the age of 14, he lost the kingdom to his own relatives and acquired his military skills through battles with them. In 1503, learning of Tamerlane's past Indian victory in 1398 (see TAMERLANE'S INVASION OF INDIA), Babur vowed to duplicate his ancestor's feat rather than continue vainly in attempting to recover his ancestral home. His help as ruler of Kabul in what is now Afghanistan was asked in 1524 by the governor of the Punjab against his brother, the Delhi sultan Ibrahim Lodi (fl. 1517–26). Babur welcomed the invitation, gathered Afghan allies, and defeated an imperial Indian army near Lahore. His appointment of his own tribe (the Chagatai Turks) as administrators angered his allies, who went home to establish the Sur dynasty. Babur, nonetheless, went on with 25,000 troops to meet Ibrahim Lodi's force of 40,000 at Panipat. Both armies sat for eight days, daring each other to attack; Ibrahim did (April 21, 1526), but his charge was stalled by Babur's defense: a line of 700 carts tied together, rather like the ring of Conestoga wagons of American pioneer days. Babur's forces, the first outside the Ottoman Empire to be armed with guns, then charged; the Delhi line broke and fled; Ibrahim was killed. Sending his son Humayun (1508–56) ahead to seize Agra's treasury, Babur reached Delhi, India, on April 25, 1526, had the *khutba* (sacred address) read in the mosque in his name, and became the Mogul emperor of Hindustan

(the Ganges plain of north India). Retaining his throne proved relatively easy. Babur fought Mewar forces at Khanua or Fatehpur Sikri (March 16, 1527); using his Panipat strategy again, he won. Hindu Gwalior fell to him in 1528, and the last of the Lodi dynasty and his Afghan allies were defeated in 1529 at the confluence of the Ganges and Gogra rivers. Conquering the rest of India was left to Babur's descendants, for he died in 1530 and was buried in his favorite garden in Kabul. See also DELHI SULTANATE WARS WITH JAUNPUR; MOGUL WAR AGAINST GUJARAT, FIRST; MOGUL WARS AGAINST THE SUR DYNASTY, EARLY.

Babylon, Destruction of (689 B.C.) The Assyrian Empire ruled by King Sennacherib (d. 681) became disturbed by internal rebellion in Babylonia, where Chaldean and Aramaean tribes, aided by the Elamites across the Persian Gulf, sought to oust the Assyrian subkings and take control themselves. Sennacherib launched a military campaign to suppress the rebels and stabilize the situation. His forces won the Battle of Halule on the Diyala River against the Chaldeans and Elamites in 691. However, because of severe battle losses, Sennacherib temporarily ceased his campaign until 689, when he besieged the city of Babylon. After a nine-month siege, Babylon fell to the Assyrians, who then destroyed the city entirely and diverted the waters of the Arakhatu Canal to flow over the ruins. Babylon's inner city was virtually uninhabited for the next eight years, when the rebuilding of Babylon began.

Babylonian Captivity of Jerusalem (586–538 B.C.) In 601 B.C., the king of Judah (southern Palestine) renounced his Babylonian vassal status acquired after the Battle of CARCHEMISH, allied himself with Egypt, but suffered in 598 a Babylonian occupation of Jerusalem, Judah's major city. Zedekiah (fl. early 6th cent.) was crowned the new vassal king in 597, and Judah allied again with Egypt, leading to a Babylonian military expedition into the area in 589. Zedekiah and the citizens of Jerusalem rose in revolt against the Babylonians, who began in 588 an 18-

month siege of Jerusalem. The Jewish prophet Jeremiah (650?–585?) urged the surrender of the city to prevent its destruction, but its citizens held out, hoping vainly for Egyptian aid; many starved. When Jerusalem's walls were breached in 587, Zedekiah and others fled toward Jericho, hoping to regroup. They were captured, and Babylonian revenge began. Zedekiah was blinded, a customary punishment for traitors, and many of the other leaders were executed. The city was burned, and its walls leveled. Following a standard Near Eastern practice, its citizens were deported; only the poor were left. Judah itself was reduced to an estimated 20,000 people. Most citizens exiled in Babylonia remained faithful Jews, and when Babylonia fell to Persian control under King Cyrus "the Great" (600? 529) in 538, the Jews were granted permission to return home. Numerous Jews, prosperous and fearful, remained, but those who trekked the 800 miles to Jerusalem began to rebuild the temple, completing the construction in 516 and fulfilling the prophecy that the captivity would last 70 years.

Bacon's Rebellion (1676) When Sir William Berkeley (1606–77), governor of Virginia, failed to fend off Indian attacks, Nathaniel Bacon (1647–76) mounted two unauthorized attacks against the local Indians, including some friendly tribes. Bacon then won election to the new House of Burgesses but was arrested when he tried to take his seat. Soon released, he and his yeoman supporters marched on Jamestown, forcing the assembly at gunpoint to commission further action against the Indians. Berkeley fled but returned to reclaim Jamestown. After a bloody clash, Bacon regained control and set the town afire. When Bacon died suddenly, the rebellion fizzled, and Berkeley retaliated harshly before returning to England to defend his Indian policy.

Bactrian-Parthian War (c. 170–c. 160 B.C.) Taken from Persia by Alexander the Great (356–323) in 328, Bactria (now part of Afghanistan and Russia) developed into a powerful state, becoming independent in 256. Both the Seleucid Empire

(the Hellenistic government in Persia) and the Parthian nation wanted to control it, chiefly because of Bactrian trade with China. The Seleucids sent Eucratides (d. 159) to Bactria in 167 to battle against Demetrius (c. 200–167), its enterprising ruler. Meanwhile, Mithridates I (171–138) of Parthia took advantage of the fighting by attacking Bactria's frontiers. Eucratides slew Demetrius in 167 and became ruler of Bactria and its military leader, restricting Parthian gains to small areas before the war ended.

Bactrian-Syrian War (208–206 B.C.) The prosperous, independent kingdom of Bactria in north-central Asia had once been part of the ancient Persian Empire. In 208, Antiochus III "the Great" (242–187), the Seleucid king of Syria, decided to unite the area with his empire, which extended into Persia, and led an army northeastward. The Syrian invasion was opposed by King Arsaces III (212–171) of Parthia, whose forces suffered defeat; Arsaces then appealed to Bactria's King Euthydemus (fl. late 3rd cent.) for help. Combined Bactrian-Parthian forces battled against the Syrians on the banks of the Arius (Harirud) River in 208 but were routed. Arsaces made peace with Antiochus and recognized Seleucid suzerainty; Euthydemus, however, withdrew with his troops to his capital, Bactra (Balkh, Afghanistan), where they successfully resisted a two-year Syrian siege. Finally Antiochus, realizing he could not permanently subdue the fierce mountain peoples of Bactria, although he had won the war, concluded a peace with Euthydemus, who kept his kingdom while accepting Seleucid suzerainty.

Bahmani Civil War of c. 1490–1512 Under the last sultan of Bahmani, Shihab-ud-Din Mahmud (fl. 1482–1518), the large Delhi sultanate in India began to split asunder. The cause was a rivalry between the old Turkish nobles and newcomers in his administration from Afghanistan and Persia (Iran)—a rivalry that was essentially sectarian because the newcomers were Shi'ites in a fundamentally Sunni sultanate. At first, the civil war was not open, involving acts of omission—the sultan's orders were ignored. Military missions were ineffective and finally ceased; about 1490, dissident nobles and provincial governors became semi-independent, ultimately establishing the kingdoms of Bijapur, Berar, and Ahmadnagar. The last provincial governor to secede from the Delhi sultanate was Qutub-ul-Mulik (fl. early 1500s), who founded the Qutub Shahi dynasty in Golconda and declared it an independent sultanate (1512). A Shi'ite rather than a Sunni, Qutub-ul-Mulik made Golconda the first openly Shi'ite kingdom in the Deccan. Little resistance took place, and in 1518 Golconda became one of the successor states of the former sultanate of Bahmani. It was eventually absorbed by the Mogul Empire in 1687 (see MARATHA-MOGUL WARS).

Bahmani-Delhi Sultanate War (1346–47) Moves toward centralization in India by the second Tughluk sultan of Delhi, Muhammad (fl. 1325–51), proved disastrous. In trying to consolidate control in south India, he lost command of the north and then ultimately lost authority in the south. In 1327, the sultan established a new Muslim province and created a provincial capital by renaming Deogir, the former Yadavan capital, Daulatabad and populating it with forced emigration from Delhi. The new residents found being a Muslim minority in a Hindu district unendurable and began to resist Delhi's rule. Their opposition became a revolt in 1346, when Hasan Gangu founded the Bahmani dynasty as Alaud-Din Bahman Shah and reigned until 1358. An army was sent from Delhi (1347), but (as was the case in the MADURA REVOLT OF 1334–35) it was recalled north before deposing Alaud-Din. Under his leadership, Muslim control of the western Deccan area was consolidated, and Warangal was made a feudatory. Much of the Bahmani sultanate's 175-year history involved wars with Hindu kingdoms, especially the powerful realm of Vijayanagar (see VIJAYANAGAR WARS WITH BAHMANI).

Baldwin of Flanders, Revolt of (1006–7) In 1002, when Henry II "the Saint" (973–1024) be-

came king of Germany, succeeding his third cousin Otto III (980–1002), and designee as Holy Roman Emperor, he was sorely oppressed by many German princes and vassal states. To consolidate and extend the Ottonian kingdom, he fought widely and aroused the potential hostility of the West Frankish-Capetian duchy of Burgundy and its many vassals. One Burgundian vassal state, Flanders, under Count Baldwin IV (988–1035), expanded its holdings by taking Ghent and then violating German territory east of the Scheldt River by capturing Valenciennes (1006). Henry and Baldwin's overlord Robert "the Pious" (970?–1031) of Burgundy united briefly in 1006 to mount an unsuccessful expedition, making Baldwin and Robert enemies. In 1007, Henry, acting alone, brought a large army to the Scheldt, laid waste the territory, and forced Baldwin to surrender Valenciennes. Henry forgave Baldwin, gained him as his own vassal, and granted him control of Ghent.

Balkan War, First (1912–13) Just days after peace was concluded in the ITALO-TURKISH WAR OF 1911–12, the Porte (Ottoman government) found itself at war with Greece, Serbia, and Bulgaria, united for the first time in an effort to take possession of the remaining Turkish possessions in the Balkan peninsula. Soon joined by Montenegro, this Balkan League, like the Italians, argued that their nationals, all Christians, were being maltreated by Muslim Turks, especially in badly administered Macedonia. The league was at first ready to accept reforms, including autonomy for Macedonia, but the Porte hesitated and thus found itself, unprepared and badly officered, involved in violent hostilities. Greek forces advanced from the south, trapping a large Turkish army, capturing all its artillery and transport, and then liberating Salonika. Serbs moved from the north, defeating Turkish armies in battles at Kumanovo and Monastir (Bitola) in the fall of 1912. Bulgarians arrived from the east to invade Thrace, won victories at Kirk Kilissa and Lule Burgas, where they engaged the main Turkish army and drove it into retreat toward Constantinople (Istanbul), the Ottoman capital. Only Bulgarian supply problems saved Adrianople (Edirne) and Constantinople from being captured. Greece and Montenegro ignored a Bulgarian-Turkish armistice (December 3, 1912), and the London Peace Conference failed to settle the warring parties' conflicting aims in the Balkans. The Young Turks then seized control of the government at Constantinople, denounced the armistice, and renewed fighting. On March 26, 1912, Adrianople fell to a besieging Bulgarian-Serb force three weeks after the Greeks had forced the surrender of the Turks at Yannina (Ioánnina). With the fall of Scutari (Üsküdar) to Montenegrin troops on April 22, 1913, the Ottomans reluctantly accepted the Treaty of London imposed by the great powers, losing Crete and its European possessions (save the Chatalja and Gallipoli peninsulas). **Second Balkan War** (1913). The Young Turks soon rejected the peace conditions, causing hostilities to resume. Turkish chances for victory were good at first, for Bulgaria was at odds with the rest of the Balkan League over plans for dismembering Macedonia; its forces attacked Serbia in June 1913 (the Serbians were distressed over their failure to secure an Adriatic seaport, and the Montenegrins were vexed from giving up Scutari to the newly formed state of Albania). In July 1913, Bulgarian armies were checked by Serbian and Greek forces in separate actions. Rumania then declared war against Bulgaria and advanced troops toward Sofia. Turkish troops recaptured Adrianople on July 20, 1913. Bulgaria, which had sued for peace, accepted the Treaty of Bucharest (August 10, 1913) and thus ceded all of its territory gained in the first war to the other members of the Balkan League. The Porte retained Adrianople, but the Ottoman Empire had lost more than 80 percent of its Balkan territories and more than 70 percent of its European population. See also WORLD WAR I.

Bamian, Mongol Destruction of   (1221) Pursuing Jalal-ad-Din (d. 1231), son of the recently vanquished shah of Khwarizm (see BUKHARA, MONGOL DESTRUCTION OF), Genghis (Jenghiz, Chingis) Khan (1167?–1227) led his Mongol army south from Samarkand to Afghanistan, where Jalal-ad-

Din had formed a new Muslim army. (At Parwan, a Mongol defeat in a minor rout caused the unharmed Persian cities of Herat and Merv to rebel; Genghis Khan had them destroyed.) The Mongols were blocked near the Afghan city of Bamian, in a pass between the Hindu Kush and the Koh-i-Baba mountains. Genghis Khan began to besiege the city, and, angered by the death of a grandson at the hands of its defenders, he captured it after suffering heavy losses, razed it, and slaughtered all its inhabitants. Even the Mongols referred to Bamian as "the city of sorrow." Genghis Khan then continued his pursuit of Jalal-ad-Din into India (see INDUS RIVER, BATTLE OF). See also MONGOL-PERSIAN WAR, FIRST.

Bangladeshi Civil War of 1973–97   The indigenous, mainly Buddhist tribes (called Jumma) of the Chittagong Hill Tracts (CHT) region bordering India and Myanmar (Burma), long marginalized by the discriminatory policies of successive governments, established the Shanti Bahini (Peace Force), a resistance movement aimed at securing autonomy, in 1973. Bangladesh's government countered with its own insurgency measures and a military occupation that perpetrated human rights abuses, including arbitrary arrests and murders, arson, rape, forced evictions, and occupation of tribal lands. In the 1960s thousands of Jumma people were displaced when the Kaptai hydroelectric dam flooded one-10th of the CHT and 40 percent of its arable land. Thousands fled to India's eastern states of Arunachal Pradesh, Mizoram, and Tripura, where they faced discrimination. More contentious was the state-sponsored settlement in the 1970s of hundreds of thousands of Bengali Muslims from the crowded delta region into the CHT—often, on Jumma-owned land. As intended, this radically altered its demography, further alienated the tribes, and led to attacks between the two groups. Bangladesh's government signed a peace accord with the Jana Samhati Samiti (JSS)—the People's United Party in the CHT—on December 2, 1997, but it was not constitutionally guaranteed and did not include the withdrawal of the military, reverse the illegal settlement of tribal lands, or investigate the human rights abuses. It did, however, allow for the return of 50,000 refugees from Tripura. It provided for CHT's three districts to be administered by a Hill Council under a Tribal Affairs Ministry and for a Land Commission to resolve land ownership disputes. JSS and Shanti Bahini members were granted amnesty, but the ban on the JSS remained. Although a major step toward peace, the accord did not address the core issues of the conflict and continued negotiations are necessary.

Bannockburn, Battle of (1313–14) Scottish forces, led by Robert the Bruce (1274–1329), began a siege of English-held Stirling Castle in 1313, and King Edward II (1284–1327) of England responded by assembling a large and lavishly equipped army, then marching north. Outnumbered three to one, Bruce placed 8,000 men on a hill at Bannockburn, near Stirling, put his left flank in a dense woods and his right on a bend in the brook—in all, a 2,000-foot front. The English not only had to move up a hill but also had to cross a bog in order to reach it. Edward gave the order, and his heavily armored knights, with Scottish arrows and spears raining down on them, marched forward and began to sink in the marsh. Scottish spearmen drove back Edward's archers, and soon the English were retreating with the Scots in pursuit. Edward panicked and ran, followed by his remaining troops. The Scots considered their victory a sign of their independence, but Edward stubbornly refused to agree (see SCOTTISH WAR OF 1314–28). See also BRUCE'S REVOLT.

Bannock War (1878) The Bannock Indians, suffering from severe famine and receiving no help from the U.S. government, fled from the Fort Hall Reservation in southeastern Idaho in 1878. The Indians, led by Chief Buffalo Horn and joined by the Northern Paiute Indians (to whom the Bannocks were closely related), raided white settlements in search of food. U.S. cavalry under General Oliver Otis Howard (1830–1909), sent to crush the Bannocks, won two battles against the Indians in southern Idaho. After the massacre of about 140

Bannock men, women, and children at Charles's Ford in present-day Wyoming, the remaining Indians gave up and returned to the reservation.

Barbary Wars   See ALGERINE WAR; TRIPOLITAN WAR.

Bar Cocheba's Revolt (A.D. 132–35) Roman emperor Hadrian (76–139) inflamed the Jews of Judea by attempting to erect a shrine to Jupiter, supreme Roman god, on the site of the Temple at Jerusalem and by issuing decrees against circumcision and public instruction of Jewish law. Simon Bar Cocheba (Kokba) (d. 135), claiming to be the long-awaited Messiah, led a major revolt. At first the rebels were successful, but the Roman legions under Julius Severus (fl. 130s) gradually gained the upper hand, vanquishing 985 Palestinian cities. Bar Cocheba was slain defending Bethar. Many were killed in battle, and others perished of starvation, fire, and disease. Hadrian retaliated harshly by suppressing the practice of Judaism.

Barons' Revolt of 1387, English   Only 10 years old when he was crowned king of England, Richard II (1367–1400) resented his regency, and thus, when he gained sole power, appointed his friends to high office. When he made the earl of Oxford duke of Ireland, several barons, led by the duke of Gloucester, packed the "Merciless" Parliament of 1386, and as Lords Appellant brought charges of treason against Oxford and others. Oxford mustered 4,000 men and met Gloucester and the earl of Derby at Radcote Bridge in 1387; when his line broke, Oxford escaped. Other royal officers were captured and executed, and the barons ruled England until 1389.

Barons' Revolt of 1488, Scottish   Despite his 1482 humiliation at Lauder (see ANGLO-SCOTTISH WAR OF 1482), King James III (1452–88) of Scotland continued to be unpopular. In 1488, he was once again the victim of Archibald "Red" Douglas

(1449–1514), whose conspirators captured James's son. The king tried vainly to come to terms with them, fled to Stirling (where the keeper of the castle treasonably refused to grant him admission), and faced the conspirators' army at Sauchie Burn. There, injured by a fall from his horse, James was stabbed to death by an unknown assailant. His sorrowing son was crowned James IV (1473–1513), and Douglas became his regent.

Barons' War (1263–65)   King Henry III (1207–72) of England tried, despite the Magna Carta, to rule imperiously. His barons, led by Simon de Montfort (1208?–65), earl of Leicester, opposed him and his costly and inept policies and set up a commission of reform in 1259, which in turn governed badly. Renouncing earlier legal restraints, Henry then opposed the reform party. In 1263, Montfort led the English barons in revolt. At the Battle of Lewes in 1264, Henry's forces were outwitted and defeated by Montfort, and Henry, with his son and brother, was captured. Montfort ruled thereafter, establishing many reforms, including the first Commons representation. However, by these reforms, he angered the barons. When Henry's son Edward (1239–1307) escaped in 1265, he gathered English and Welsh support, defeated Montfort's son at Kenilworth, and then fought the decisive Battle of Evesham on August 4, 1265. There, Edward used a Montfort military strategy, which forced the reformers to approach their enemy over a narrow bridge in a slow column. Montfort was killed in the battle. Absolute royal rule was reinstated after all baronial resistance was stamped out in the next two years.

Barrackpore Mutiny (1824)   During the First ANGLO-BURMESE WAR, an Indian (sepoy) regiment mutinied at Barrackpore (Barrackpur), India, because the British military authorities ignored its social and religious customs. Ordered to go by ship to Burma—an act that defiled high-caste Hindus—the Indians petitioned for a reversal of the order. Their request was ignored. They then refused to parade, causing their commander to order them

surrounded and bombarded on November 2, 1824; they were forced to flee under fire. Disciplinary actions were severe: the mutiny's ringleaders were hanged, others were imprisoned, and the regiment was "erased" from the army list as a lesson to natives foolish enough to give religion priority over authorized orders. Soon the obtuse military authorities found themselves criticized for blockheadedness, rigidity, and unreasonable harshness.

Basque War for Independence (c. 1968–   )   The Basques, a distinct people of obscure origin living in the western Pyrenees in Spain and France, have long sought to regain self-government, lost after the SECOND CARLIST WAR. The Basque independence movement, which Spanish dictator Francisco Franco (1892–1975) tried to crush, came to life in 1959, when the radical nationalist ETA (Euzkadi Ta Askatasuna, meaning Basque Homeland and Freedom) party was formed to secure Basque political and cultural autonomy. In late 1970 Basque nationalists went to trial for the 1968 murder of a police official. Widespread dissent occurred after their convictions, which were then reduced. Various Basque militants carried on campaigns of violence against Spanish authorities and wealthy industrialists opposed to their aims. Terrorists bombed Madrid's airport and railway station in 1979, kidnapped and killed the chief engineer of the Lemoniz nuclear power plant in 1981, bombed a crowded supermarket in Barcelona in 1987, and set off more bombs in Madrid, Valencia, and León in late 1995. Spanish and French authorities cooperated to capture ETA militants. The Basque leader José Antonio Urrutikoetxea (1950–   ), also known as Josu Ternera, was arrested in Bayonne, France, in early 1989, and other leading ETA members were caught there in 1992. But Basque radicals carried on their kidnapping, murders, and bombings, thus hardening the government's stance against them in 1995 and 1996. ETA's campaign for independence continued mainly in Spain's four Basque northern provinces of Álava, Guipúzcoa, Vizcaya (Biscay), and Navarra—all of which is a region called Vascongadas—while the neighboring Basses-Pyrénées department in southwest France remained a strong Basque haven. In September 1998, the ETA declared a cease-fire, renounced violence, and sought an independent state through politics; it gained seats in the new Basque government during elections on October 25, 1998. In March 1999, France arrested the head of the ETA's military wing and five others in Paris; then nine Basque militants were arrested in Spain, certainly testing the ETA cease-fire.

Basuto War (1865–68) For many years, the Basutos under King Moshweshwe (c. 1786–1870) successfully resisted encroachments of the Boers of the Orange Free State, with whom they competed for pasture and farmland. By the mid-1860s, however, Moshweshwe's powers were waning and Boer strength had grown; and, as fighting intensified, the Boers gained the upper hand. Moshweshwe appealed for British protection, but British negotiators were unsuccessful, and by the Treaty of Thaba Bosiu in 1866 the Orange Free State acquired most of Basutoland. Further fighting erupted in 1867, but just as the Basutos approached total collapse, Sir Philip Wodehouse, British high commissioner, cut off the Orange Free State's ammunition supply and annexed Basutoland.

Batetelan Uprisings (1895–1900) In 1885, King Leopold II (1835–1909) of Belgium gained international recognition as head of the newly formed Congo Free State (Zaire) in equatorial Africa. He treated the vast area as his private domain, and his administrators were noted for their cruelty and harshness toward the black native Africans. In 1895, the Batetelas, a warlike native tribe that lived in the Lomani River and Lulua River areas of the Congo, rose up against their stern Belgian masters, but were soon suppressed. Two years later they revolted again and gained control of a large area in the eastern part of the Congo. Belgian forces under Baron François Dhanis (1861–1909) advanced against the Batetelas, who put up a fierce resistance for three years. Eventually the Belgians were able to crush the rebels and their strong leaders (October

1900). By parliamentary act in 1908, Belgium annexed the Congo, thus forming the Belgian Congo.

Bavarian Succession, War of the (1778–79). Upon the death of Bavarian elector Maximilian III Joseph (1727–77), ending the Wittelsbach line, the duchy of Bavaria passed to Charles Theodore (1724–99), Palatinate elector. With no legitimate issue, Charles Theodore concluded a treaty with Holy Roman Emperor Joseph II (1741–90) ceding Lower Bavaria to Austria. King Frederick II "the Great" (1712–86) of Prussia resisted this augmentation of Austrian power, mobilized his forces, and invaded Bohemia in July 1778. The resulting conflict between Prussia and Austria was more remarkable for hungry soldiers foraging for food than for any serious military engagement—hence its sobriquet "the potato war." Under the Treaty of Teschen in 1779, Charles Theodore's sovereignty was recognized, and Austria relinquished its claims to all but a fertile triangle of land along the Inn River.

Bavarian War of 1503–4 The death of the Wittelsbach family's George "the Rich" (d. 1503), baron of Bavaria-Landshut, initiated a three-way struggle for control of Bavaria, a region then ruled competitively by a motley collection of dukes. By tradition, the Landshut holdings should have gone to another branch of the family controlled by Albert (1467–1508), duke of Bavaria-Munich; but the branches were at odds, and sonless George had bequeathed his territory to his daughter and son-in-law (the son of the elector of Palatine). The Munich branch sought a legal adjustment, which ended in its favor, but the elector was not satisfied and gathered an army. Holy Roman Emperor Maximilian I (1459–1519) sent Imperial troops to enforce the legal ruling; they were joined by supportive German nobles. Fighting was sporadic and ended in 1504, when the intended heirs suddenly died. Everyone else won: Maximilian gained some coveted territories, the elector was solaced by the receipt of two areas, and Albert, whose gain was greatest, accidentally found himself able to fulfill his dream of uniting Bavaria under his authority.

Bay of Islands War (First Maori War) (1844–47) Angry about the WAIRAU MASSACRE, land appropriations, the shift of the colonial government to Auckland, and the losses in local population and income, a Maori chief named Hone Heke (fl. 1840s) of the northern Bay of Islands section of North Island, New Zealand, mounted a raid and cut down a British flagstaff at Russell (Kororareka) in July 1844, and later sacked the town in March 1845. Despite attempts by British colonial forces to stop him, Hone Heke and another chief, Kawiti (fl. 1840s), led Maori attacks on British settlements farther north until mid-1845. Then Sir George Grey (1812–98) was put in charge of the British forces; he defeated Kawiti in January 1846 and resolutely forced Hone Heke to cease fighting in 1847. As the new governor-general, Grey brought peace to New Zealand until 1860; the discovery of gold in Australia aided his efforts, for it gave a market to Maori and British-settler foodstuffs. However, disputes over lands led inexorably to the three TARANAKI WARS, also referred to collectively as the SECOND MAORI WAR.

Bay of Pigs Invasion (1961) The 1959 takeover of Cuba by Fidel Castro (1926–   ) and his revolutionary followers (see CUBAN REVOLUTION OF 1956–59) prompted the exodus of many Cubans, especially to the United States. When Castro's communist-oriented regime confiscated private property and established close ties to the Soviet Union, the United States imposed an embargo on all exports to Cuba (except food and medicine) and broke diplomatic relations (1960–61). Anti-Castro Cuban exiles demanded that the United States back an invasion of their homeland to topple the government; as early as 1960, the American Central Intelligence Agency (CIA) began to train an exile army in Guatemala. On April 17, 1961, about 1,400 exiles invaded southern Cuba at the Bahía de los Cochinos (Bay of Pigs), but were totally defeated by the Cuban

army by April 20; most of the invaders were killed or taken prisoner. Critics of this failure blamed the last-minute withdrawal of naval air support by U.S. president John F. Kennedy (1917–63), but closer investigation disclosed that the CIA scheme, meant to be secret but long a matter of public knowledge, had been based on faulty intelligence information, was poorly planned, and ultimately was poorly executed. The failed invasion aggravated already hostile U.S.-Cuban relations and eventually required the expenditure of $53 million in food and medicine (raised by private donors to meet Castro's ransom) to secure the release of the 1,113 surviving captive invaders (1962–65).

Bear Flag Revolt (1846) After the outbreak of the MEXICAN WAR, American settlers in California, led by Captain John C. Frémont (1813–90), expelled Mexican authorities and established an independent nation called the Bear Flag Republic at Sonoma on June 14, 1846. In July, an American squadron under Commodore John D. Sloat (1781–1867) captured California's capital, Monterey, hoisted the U.S. flag, and proclaimed California American territory. When General Stephen W. Kearny (1794–1848) arrived there in early 1847, he found California already in U.S. control under Frémont and Commodore Robert Stockton (1795–1866), Sloat's replacement. Stockton and Kearny vied for command, and Frémont backed Stockton. But the U.S. government sustained Kearny, and Frémont was court-martialed for insubordination. California was formally ceded by Mexico in 1848.

Béarnese Revolt, First (1621–22) When King Louis XIII (1601–43) of France attempted to reestablish Roman Catholicism and reclaim lost church property, the Huguenots (French Protestants) of Béarn, a province in southwestern France, under Henri, duke of Rohan (1579–1638), offered armed resistance to the French government. Though Louis's troops managed to recapture most strongholds accorded to the Huguenots by the Edict of

Nantes (see RELIGION, NINTH WAR OF) and to enforce suppression of Protestant assemblies, the Huguenots retained control of Montauban and La Rochelle. These struggles saw the rise of the influence of Armand Jean du Plessis, duke of Richelieu (1585–1642), who in 1622 was named a cardinal. **Second Béarnese Revolt** (1625–26). Duke Henri and his brother, Benjamin of Rohan and Soubise (1583–1642), launched another Huguenot revolt against the French government from their base at La Rochelle. Though the Protestants scored some initial naval successes, royalist forces under Duke Henri of Montmorency (1595–1632) were eventually able to establish a partial naval blockade around the Huguenot stronghold. **Third Béarnese Revolt** (1627–29). Hostilities between the Huguenots and the French government were renewed with an extended siege of La Rochelle under the direct supervision of Cardinal Richelieu. Vigorous land action, in combination with a complete maritime blockade that handily repulsed British naval reinforcements, virtually choked the city. Montmorency's defeat of the duke of Rohan in Languedoc put a permanent end to Huguenot hopes of political autonomy within France. But Richelieu, wisely respecting the potential economic contribution of the Huguenots, guaranteed them religious toleration in the Peace of Alais (Alès). See also ANGLO-FRENCH WAR OF 1627–28.

"Beer Hall Putsch" (1923)   Adolf Hitler (1889–1945), chairman of the Nazi party, led an abortive attempt to overthrow the republican government of Germany. On November 8, 1923, his storm troopers invaded a large political meeting in a Munich beer hall and coerced Bavarian leaders into proclaiming loyalty to the Nazis. But the leaders escaped and quickly mobilized the German army against the coup. Upon realizing that he lacked the support of the army, Hitler fled but was soon arrested. During his nine months' imprisonment in the Landsberg fortress, he dictated *Mein Kampf*, which became the bible of National Socialism. The putsch, though a fiasco, brought Hitler to national prominence, making him a hero to many Germans.

Bengalese-British War of 1686   After learning that the British East India Company was preparing to fortify the town of Hooghly or Hugli in the region of Bengal in northeastern India, the Mogul emperor of India, Aurangzeb (1618–1707), dispatched troops that sacked Hooghly in October 1686. The British had been raiding imperial Bengalese forts, using Hooghly as a military base, in retaliation against local customs officials who were trying to exact tolls. The British then moved down the Hooghly River to construct Fort William (Calcutta). Peace was finally concluded in 1690, when the British agreed to pay fees to continue their trade in Bengal. See also AURANGZEB, WARS OF.

Bengalese-British War of 1756–57   Siraj-ud-Dawlah (1732–57), nawab of Bengal, seized Calcutta from the British on June 20, 1756, when the British East India Company refused to stop fortifying Calcutta in expectation of the SEVEN YEARS' WAR. Siraj-ud-Dawlah seized the city within four days and used the company's own lockup, the so-called "Black Hole," to hold the Europeans who were not able to escape the siege. No accurate count of the prisoners kept in the underground dungeon is known, but estimates are that between 40 and 123 persons died after the first night. Former East India Company clerk-turned-soldier Robert Clive (1725–74) and Admiral Charles Watson (1714–57) led British forces that retook Calcutta on January 2, 1757, when the nawab was captured and executed. Clive subsequently installed Mir Ja'far (1691–1765), friendly to the British, as the new nawab.

Bengalese-British War of 1763–65   The British East India Company quarreled with the new nawab of Bengal, Mir Qasim (d. 1777), over taxation. When Qasim's forces tried to seize Patna, where the company had a factory, war began in 1763. The British forced Qasim to withdraw to Avadh, which the British seized after winning an important victory against the Bengalese at Buxar on October 22, 1764. Qasim, who received help from natives in western India, could not hold off the

British and was defeated in 1765. Robert Clive (1725–74) established two nawabs in Bengal, both under the control of a British resident, so that no Bengal ruler could again garner the finances to repeat Qasim's military actions.

Bengalese-Mogul War of 1742 After the devastating Persian raid on the Mogul capital of Delhi in 1739 (see PERSIAN INVASION OF MOGUL INDIA), the Mogul Empire became a pawn in the hands of the Marathas, a dominant Hindu people opposing the Moguls, and various opportunists. One adventurer, Ali Vardi Khan (1676–1756), seized power in Bengal and made the region virtually independent of the empire. He also became rich by cultivating Portuguese endeavors along the Hooghly or Hugli River and British enterprises in the Calcutta area. His single fear was the Marathas, especially so because the Maratha peshwa (prime minister) Balaji Rao (fl. 1740–61) had begun to push eastward, seizing the Mogul-held region of Bundelkhand (central India) and threatening Orissa, then a Bengal subregion. Balaji Rao had trouble controlling his generals, among them one Raghunath Bhonsle (fl. 1740s), who independently launched a Maratha expedition in Orissa (1741) and, in campaigns near Calcutta (1742), forced the British to dig their famous "Maratha ditch." Balaji Rao ordered Raghunath to deliver a portion of the Orissa plunder to him; he was refused. Then, in response to a request from Delhi, Balaji Rao sided with Ali Vardi Khan, ordered a large army to confront Raghunath's, and drove it halfway across India to Nagpur (1742). Other independent Maratha groups irritated Bengal until Ali Vardi's death. Then the British, after winning the Battle of Plassey against the Bengalese (June 23, 1757), seized control of Calcutta, and Bengal was permanently lost to the Mogul Empire. See also BENGALESE-BRITISH WAR OF 1756–57; SEVEN YEARS' WAR.

Berenice, War of See SYRIAN-EGYPTIAN WARS, SECOND AND THIRD.

Bhutanese-British War of 1865 After the British occupied Assam and made the area part of British India (1826), a longtime frontier dispute began with the state of Bhutan to the north. In the early 1860s, the Bhutanese took strategic frontier mountain passes (duars) from the Assamese and paid no heed to the British demand to surrender the lands or give tribute. In January 1865, a small British force invaded Bhutan, but the Bhutanese successfully resisted and evicted the British garrison at Dewangiri. A punitive expedition led by Sir Henry Tombs (1824–74) gradually suppressed the Bhutanese, who agreed to peace on November 11, 1865. By the Treaty of Sinchula, Bhutan ceded the southern passes and set free all captured British, and the British in return agreed to pay an annual subsidy to Bhutan for the passes.

Biafran-Nigerian War See NIGERIAN-BIAFRAN WAR.

Bishops' War, First (1639) At the urging of King Charles I (1600–1649) of England and Archbishop William Laud (1573–1645), the bishops of Scotland attempted to impose a new Book of Common Prayer upon the Scottish church in 1637. The Presbyterians resisted and, in February 1638, drew up a National Covenant pledging to maintain their religion against Anglican incursions. In November 1638, a general assembly of the Scottish church abolished the episcopate altogether and defied Charles's orders to disband. Charles attempted to wage war in 1639, but his weak and inexperienced troops were quickly repulsed by the Covenanters, and he was forced to accept the Pacification of Berwick, permitting the formation of the new Scottish general assembly. **Second Bishops' War** (1640). Strong differences remained between Charles and the Scottish Presbyterians, who opposed his attempts to impose Anglican innovations. The Edinburgh Assembly continued to defy the king, and in 1640 the Scots carried their fight into England, abetted by many sympathizers among the English gentry and nobility. Lacking reliable troops and adequate financing, Charles suffered humiliating defeats at the hands of the disciplined Scots. The resulting Treaty of Ripon provided that Scottish troops occupy northern England and receive 850 pounds a day until a new English parliament could hammer out the final terms of peace. Charles was thus forced to summon the Long Parliament in November 1640, setting the stage for the Great ENGLISH CIVIL WAR.

"Black and Tans" War   See ANGLO-IRISH CIVIL WAR OF 1916–21.

Black Hawk War (1832) In early April 1832, Sauk and Fox Indian tribes, led by Chief Black Hawk (1767–1838), crossed the Mississippi River into Illinois to reclaim tribal lands that supposedly were ceded to the United States in an 1804 treaty. Black Hawk, who wished only to farm the lands in peace, was pursued by the Illinois militia sent out by the governor. After winning a victory at Stillman's Run, Black Hawk's band decided to retire into Wisconsin. Militiamen caught up with the Indians as they were attempting to cross the Mississippi, and at the Battle of Wisconsin Heights won a partial victory; Black Hawk and some of his band managed to escape across the river. On August 2, 1832, the Illinois militia and U.S. troops, all under the command of General Henry Atkinson (1782–1842), attacked and massacred Black Hawk's band at the mouth of the Bad Axe River south of LaCrosse, Wis. Fewer than 150 of the more than 1,000 Indians survived. Black Hawk escaped and sought refuge with the Winnebago Indians, who turned him over to the whites for imprisonment in Fort Monroe, Va. In 1833, he was allowed to join the remainder of his tribe near Fort Des Moines, Iowa.

"Black Hole" of Calcutta   See BENGALESE-BRITISH WAR OF 1756–57.

Black Hundreds, Raids of the (1906–11) During the RUSSIAN REVOLUTION OF 1905, a reactionary, anti-Semitic group called the League of the Russian People, commonly referred to as the Black Hundreds, was secretly formed and unofficially sanctioned by the government. Made up primarily of landowners, wealthy peasants, bureaucrats, and police, the Black Hundreds attacked and killed revolutionaries in the Russian provinces. While organized local massacres (pogroms), especially of Jews, had been a regular part of Russian life since the assassination of Czar Alexander II (1818–81), they became particularly violent and frequent under the "respectable" leadership of the Black Hundreds, who instigated pogroms in more than 100 cities. In Odessa, a four-day slaughter of Jews and others occurred before order was restored. These ghastly repressions encouraged Russia's autocratic leaders to delay the enactment of the new constitution achieved in the 1905 revolution.

Black Patch War (1904–9) Growers of dark tobacco in the extreme western and southwestern parts of Kentucky, known as the Black Patch, opposed the monopolistic practices of the tobacco-buying companies, which controlled the markets and prices. A tobacco growers association was formed and attempted to boycott the buyers; night riders began terrorizing both buyers and growers (those who didn't join the association). Lawlessness prevailed in the area until 1907, when Kentucky's Governor A. E. Willson (1846–1931) declared martial law in 23 counties and used the state militia to fight the rebels and to take control of whole towns. In 1908, an agreement was reached between growers and buyers, whose monopoly was partially broken. Disgruntled night riders continued their violence into the next year, finding themselves now contending with armed citizens angered by their tactics. Thereafter dissension among members of the growers association helped end the fighting.

Black War (1804–30) European soldiers and settlers on Van Diemen's Land (Tasmania) harassed the native aborigines and seized valuable hunting lands belonging to them. When whites attacked and killed some aborigines on a hunting party in 1804, a protracted "bush war" broke out that greatly reduced the aborigine population during the next generation. Bushrangers, rural outlaws, robbed and killed both the whites and the aborigines during the period, causing additional terror and bloodshed. In 1830, the island's governor, Sir George Arthur (1784–1854), managed to capture and hang many of the bushrangers but failed to corral the aborigines with his "Black Line," a cordon of thousands of settlers sent into the bush to drive the aborigines out (only a boy and a woman were flushed out). The fighting, however, ended, and by 1835 the remaining aborigines had been persuaded to resettle on Flinders Island nearby.

"Bleeding Kansas" See POTTAWATOMIE MASSACRE; WAKARUSA WAR.

Blenheim, Battle of (1704) Early decisive battles in the War of the SPANISH SUCCESSION occurred at the Bavarian villages of Donauwörth and Blenheim. The former crippled a French drive toward the Austrian capital, Vienna, and the latter, in a remarkable feat of strategy, permanently stopped the French advance, drove Bavaria out of the war, and forced the French back to the Rhine River. Donauworth had only disorganized the French, who regrouped north of the Danube River near Blenheim. South of the river to attack Augsburg, John Churchill, first duke of Marlborough (1650–1722), led British forces to recross to the north bank of the tributary Nebel, where he was joined by Eugene, prince of Savoy (1663–1736), heading an Austrian army. Their allied line, some 52,000 men strong, put Marlborough in the center, Savoy on the right with additional cavalry and infantry, and another allied force on the left (Danube) side. The French, with almost 60,000 men in two armies of French and Bavarians under Count Camille de Tallard (1652–1728) and Maximilian II Emmanuel (1662–1726), were attacked twice by the allied left; the French drove them back. Savoy was busy holding his position against the French, whose center, weakened by its support of the flanks, was attacked by Marlborough's cavalry and routed; Marlborough

then wheeled left, driving many French into the Danube to drown. Split by this maneuver, the French infantry was trapped. Savoy's troops scattered those on his front. About 13,000 French were taken prisoner, and some 15,000 were wounded, killed, or drowned. Allied losses amounted to about 12,000.

Blitzkrieg (German Invasion of Poland) (1939) After the German partitioning and occupation of Czechoslovakia in 1938–39, it became obvious that Poland was the next nation Adolf Hitler (1889–1945), Germany's Führer (leader), wished to absorb into his Third Reich (German Nazi state). Frantic negotiations by the French, British, and Russians during the summer of 1939 came to naught. At dawn, on September 1, 1939, a well-prepared, well-equipped, largely mechanized German army swept across the Polish frontier and advanced rapidly toward Warsaw, Poland's capital. The German Luftwaffe (air force) bombed and destroyed most of the small Polish air force, disrupted the major rail and road transportation systems, and blasted the heavy industrial centers in Poland. A second German army invaded from East Prussia, and afterward the Russians, German allies at the time, invaded along the eastern border. Many Polish military units valiantly resisted the invaders, but they were poorly armed and undermobilized. The British and French were powerless to help their ally, Poland, although they did declare war on Germany (see WORLD WAR II). The German armored panzer (tank) divisions rolled forward across the plains of Poland, while the Polish armies were cut off from each other or tried vainly to rally at Warsaw, which was besieged and fell on September 27, 1939. Eight days later the last Polish resistance collapsed at Lublin. In a brief 35 days Poland had been crushed; Hitler's Blitzkrieg ("lightning war") was over.

Blood River, Battle of (1838) Moving northward from southernmost Africa to escape British domination (see KAFFIR WAR, SIXTH), Boer (Dutch) trekkers under Piet Retief (1780–1838) and Gerhardus Martinus Maritz (1797–1838) sought an agreement with Dingaan (d. 1840), king of the Zulus, allowing settlement in what is now Natal. Early in 1838, unarmed Boer negotiators were ambushed by Zulu warriors, who then attacked the trekkers' encampment (some 500 Boers, including Retief and Maritz, were slain during the attacks). Later that year Boer reinforcements arrived under Andries Pretorius (1799–1853), and, forging an alliance with Dingaan's brother and rival, Umpanda (d. 1872), the trekkers thoroughly routed the Zulus under Dingaan at the Battle of Blood River on December 16, 1838. (The water of a branch of the Buffalo River was reddened with the blood of about 3,000 slain Zulus, giving it thereafter the name Blood River.) The Boers established the Republic of Natal, which was annexed by the British in 1843. See also BOER-ZULU WAR OF 1838–39; ZULU WAR.

"Bloody Week"   See FRENCH CIVIL WAR OF 1871.

Boer Uprising of 1914–15   The Union of South Africa, established by the British in 1910, entered WORLD WAR I on the side of the Allies in 1914, and South Africa's Prime Minister Louis Botha (1862–1919) made preparations to invade neighboring German South West Africa (Namibia). But many of his Boer (Dutch) supporters balked, for they disliked the British (see BOER WARS) and favored Germany. Three army commanders led a Boer uprising, and by the end of 1914, some 12,000 rebels were up in arms in the Orange Free State and the Transvaal. Although the Boer rebels were former comrades, Botha did not hesitate to oppose them and was assisted by Jan Smuts (1870–1950), a former Boer general like the prime minister. Taking command of two campaigns himself, Botha defeated the rebels in the Transvaal and in the Free State in October and December 1914, respectively. The third and last rebel force was overcome in February 1915. Botha showed unusual clemency toward the rebels and their leaders and, by 1917, had set free all prisoners.

Boer War, First (Transvaal Revolt) (1880–81) Boer (Dutch) resentment against British annexation of the Transvaal (an independent Boer state) in 1877 eventually erupted in war in late 1880. The Boers took up arms, proclaiming a new South African Republic in the area. Under the leadership of President S. J. Paul Kruger (1825–1904) and General Piet Joubert (1831–1900), the Boers twice, at Laing's Nek and Ingogo, repulsed the British before handing them a resounding defeat at Majuba Hill on February 27, 1881. The Convention of Pretoria granted the South African Republic independence in internal affairs, but the British maintained an ambiguous "suzerainty" over the region. **Second or Great Boer War** (South African War) (1899–1902). The discovery of large, rich deposits of gold in the southern Transvaal (what is now Witwatersrand) in 1886 brought a rush of foreigners (mainly British) to the area and exacerbated British-Boer tensions. JAMESON'S RAID, in 1895, which was to incite an uprising there against the Boers, had further strained relations. Finally, when troops protecting British mining interests failed to comply with a Boer ultimatum to withdraw, the South African Republic (Transvaal) and its ally, the Orange Free State, declared war on Great Britain in October 1899. Well-equipped Boer forces, led by Joubert, Piet Cronjé (1840?–1911), Louis Botha (1862–1919), Jacobus H. De La Rey (1847–1914), and others, scored initial successes, seizing Kimberly, Mafeking, and Ladysmith. (Cronjé's victory at the Battle of Magersfontein on December 10–11, 1899, prevented the British under Paul S. Methuen [1845–1932] from relieving Kimberly, and Botha's victory at the Battle of Colenso on December 15, 1899, forced the British under Redvers H. Buller [1857–1915] to fall back and surrender Ladysmith.) However, in 1900, the war turned with the arrival of heavy British reinforcements under Field Marshal Lord (Frederick) Roberts (1832–1914) and General Lord (Horatio) Kitchener (1850–1916). Roberts advanced into the Orange Free State, seized its capital, Bloemfontein, on March 13, 1900, and soon occupied the country. The British then invaded the Transvaal and, in May–June 1900, captured Johannesburg and Pretoria, effectively crushing all Boer resistance on the battlefield. With the British formally annexing the Boer states, Roberts, believing the war was over, left for home, but it took Lord Kitchener's forces two more years of bitter fighting to subdue guerrilla units led by such Boer generals as Jan Smuts (1870–1950), Christiaan De Wet (1854–1922), Botha, and De La Rey. Through a line of blockhouses to split up the country and the placement of Boer women and children in concentration camps, Kitchener wore down Boer morale and systematically was able to destroy guerrilla units. By the Treaty of Vereeniging on May 31, 1902, British sovereignty was finally recognized by the Boers in exchange for a large indemnity and other concessions.

Boer-Zulu War of 1838–39   The Great Trek, the migration of Boer (Dutch) cattlemen into the Transvaal and away from British rule in South Africa, brought conflict between the Europeans and the Zulu people. One group of trekkers led by Piet Retief (1780–1838) asked the Zulu king, Dingaan (d. 1840), for a grant of land. Dingaan replied in the affirmative if Retief would retrieve some cattle stolen by a rival. Retief brought back the cattle, but instead of giving land, Dingaan treacherously turned against the Boers and massacred the entire party (February 6, 1838). Zulu warriors then attacked a Boer settlement at Weenen ("the place of weeping") in Natal and slaughtered 282 men, women, and children. The Boers organized an army to retaliate and, in April 1838, attacked a Zulu force; unknowingly drawn into an ambush, the Boers used their firearms to clear a path and escape, although many perished. Meanwhile a British force approached from the east; it also was lured into an ambush and surrounded by some 7,000 Zulus. Three times the British repelled the enemy, whose fourth charge succeeded in cutting the British force in half. One half tried to escape along the Tugela River, but only a few soldiers were successful. The other part was completely encircled and attacked again and again by the Zulus, who didn't stop until all the British were slain. The Boers organized another army and offered to enter into peace negotiations

with Dingaan, who dispatched a 10,000-man army instead. At the Battle of BLOOD RIVER on December 16, 1838, Dingaan's Zulu warriors were cut down by the Boers' gunfire and withdrew. The next year Dingaan's brother, Umpanda (d. 1872), conspired to seize the Zulu throne, and his supporters requested help from the white men, who were glad to give it. Together they confronted Dingaan's army and defeated it; Dingaan fled north and was later murdered. Thereafter the white men controlled the Natal region.

Bogomils' Revolt of 1086–91   The Bogomils, members of a religious sect in Bulgaria, with ties to the Paulicians (see PAULICIAN WAR OF A.D. 867–72), allied themselves with two nomadic Turkish groups, the Pechenegs (Patzinakes) and the Cumans (Kumans), and made raids into the eastern Balkan region of the Byzantine Empire. Byzantine forces, sent by Emperor Alexius I Comnenus (1048–1118), were defeated at what is now Silistra, Bulgaria, in 1086. Intertribal arguing about plunder finally caused the alliance to collapse. Alexius bought off the Bogomils, whom he took into his army to fight the Pechenegs (the Cumans moved northward). After unsuccessfully besieging Constantinople, the Pechenegs were pursued by the Byzantines, who defeated them at the Battle of Leburnion, drove them north across the Danube River, and virtually annihilated them in 1091.

Bohemian Civil War of 1390–1419   After finally settling the German TOWN WAR, Wenceslaus (1361–1419), king of Bohemia and Germany and Holy Roman Emperor, left the German nobles and their affairs alone, spending most of his time in Prague, Bohemia. There he became involved in a civil war with jealous and ambitious nobles, especially his cousin Jobst (1351–1411), margrave of Moravia, who imprisoned him for a time in Austria (1393–94). Afterward Wenceslaus lost much of his authority because the Bohemian nobles set up a council that governed the realm. The religious Hussite movement, led by John Huss (1369–1415), was supported by Wenceslaus, who became embroiled with the clergy, notably the archbishop of Prague (see HUSSITE WARS). In Germany, the electors deposed Wenceslaus as king in 1400, and in Bohemia, the nobles again held him prisoner in 1402–3 with the help of his half-brother, Sigismund (1368–1437), later king of Bohemia and Germany and Holy Roman Emperor. Although regaining the Bohemian throne, Wenceslaus continued to battle the opposing nobles, who had released him (twice) when they had gained minor concessions. Arguments and fights over the king's choices of candidates for higher offices and church reform disrupted the realm until his death, at which time Sigismund, who had become German king in 1411, took the Bohemian crown.

Bohemian Civil War of 1448–51   George of Podebrad (1420–71), head of the moderate Utraquist faction of the Hussite Protestants, opposed the Hapsburg party's prospective candidate for the Bohemian throne, Ladislas V "Posthumous" (1440–57), a minor, who was under the guardianship of Germany's King Frederick III (1415–93), later Holy Roman Emperor from 1452 to 1493. George rose to power with the help of other nationalists and captured Prague, the Bohemian capital, in 1448. After being defeated, the Hapsburgs reluctantly permitted him to govern, and Frederick meekly concurred. In 1451, the Bohemian diet (parliament) appointed George regent governor. After Ladislas V assumed his rule over Bohemia in 1453, George kept control of the kingdom, strengthening the central government at Prague and regaining Crown lands. Ladislas died suddenly in 1457, and George was elected the new king in 1458. See also HUSSITE WARS.

Bohemian Civil War of 1465–71   Pope Pius II (1405–64) ordered King George of Podebrad (1420–71) of Bohemia to abolish the Compactata, which had legitimized the Utraquist faction of the Hussite Protestants (see HUSSITE WARS). George refused and lost the backing of Bohemia's Roman Catholic nobles, who formed an alliance against him at Zelena Hora in 1465. The next year Pope Paul II (1417–71) declared George a heretic and excommunicated him, along with other Hussites; he persuaded King Matthias Corvinus (1440–90) of Hungary to fight George (see BOHEMIAN-HUNGARIAN WAR OF 1468–78). Matthias invaded Bohemia but was unsuccessful at first against George's forces. In 1469, the Catholic nobles voted Matthias king of Bohemia, and George, to save his throne, undertook negotiations with Poland's King Casimir IV (1427–92), sacrificing his sons' succession rights to the Bohemian throne. Later, Casimir's son, Prince Uladislas II (1456–1516), was chosen king of Bohemia (1471) after the death of George.

Bohemian-Hungarian War of 1260–70   Both Bohemia's King Ottokar II "the Great" (1230?–78) and Hungary's King Bela IV (1206–70) sought control of Austria and Styria, a duchy that had been a possession of the powerful Austrian House of Babenberg from 1192 until the extinction of the Babenberg male line in 1246. The Treaty of Ofen (1254) was concluded after clashes between Hungarian and Bohemian forces; Bela was to rule Styria and Ottokar got Austria. Later, the nobility of Styria rebelled, asking Ottokar to become their lord. At the Battle of Kressenbrunn in 1260, the Bohemians defeated the Hungarians, thus allowing Ottokar to seize Styria. The expansionism of the energetic Bohemian king continued with success, by force and by diplomacy, during an anarchic period in the Holy Roman Empire; many Austrian nobles resented Ottokar's power and rule, and some were executed for insurgence. On the death of Bela, who had vainly fought to check the advancing Bohemian empire until the very end, Ottokar headed the most powerful state in central Europe, with his domains extending from Silesia to the Adriatic. See also HAPSBURG-BOHEMIAN WAR OF 1274–78.

Bohemian-Hungarian War of 1468–78   Bohemia's King George of Podebrad (1420–71), head of the nationalists, earned the enmity of the Romanists (pro-papal and pro-Hapsburg people), especially the Roman Catholic nobles, who allied against him (see BOHEMIAN CIVIL WAR OF 1465–71). Pope Paul II (1417–71) excommunicated George and supported the Bohemian Catholics, lifting their duty of allegiance to the king. The ambitious King Matthias Corvinus (1440–90) of Hungary was induced by the pope to invade Bohemia in 1468 but met defeat in battle against George at the onset. However, Matthias's troops were able to seize Brno, the capital of Moravia, and on May 3, 1469 Catholic nobles declared Matthias king of Bohemia. Supporters of George then rallied during the next year when his son advanced with troops into Hungary. After George's death, Prince Uladislas II (1456–1516), a strong supporter of Bohemia's nationalists, was chosen Bohemian king on May 27, 1471. The National party became dominant and reflected a latent Bohemian anticlericalism. Uladislas carried on the war against the Romanists and Matthias but was unsuccessful, losing the regions of Moravia, Silesia, and Lusatia. The Peace of Olomouc on December 7, 1478 awarded the rule of Bohemia to Uladislas and that of Moravia, Silesia, and Lusatia to Matthias (but these three areas would revert to Bohemia on his death).

Bohemian-Palatine War (1618–23)   Protestant Bohemian nobles, resisting the Hapsburg (Austrian) imposition of Catholicism, angrily tossed three Catholic envoys from Vienna, Austria, out the window of the Hradschin Castle at Prague on May 23, 1618 (the Defenestration of Prague) and established an independent government, helping precipitate the THIRTY YEARS' WAR. The next year Bohemians gave their throne to the Protestant elector Frederick V (1596–1632) of Palatine instead of to Catholic Holy Roman Emperor Ferdinand II (1578–1637), causing forces of the Catholic League under Johan, count of Tilly (1559–1632), to invade Bohemia to support the emperor. At the Battle of White Mountain (Weisser Berg) on November 8, 1620, troops of the Holy Roman Empire and the Catholic League, led by Tilly, routed a Bohemian army under Prince Christian of Anhalt-Bernberg

(1568–1630). Prague was seized by Imperial forces, Catholicism was reimposed, and the Bohemian monarchy became an inherited Hapsburg right. Ferdinand ordered Frederick stripped of his Palatine title and made Duke Maximilian (1573–1651) of Bavaria, head of the Catholic League, the Elector of the Palatinate, which he occupied with the aid of Spanish troops. Frederick attempted to regain his lands, but after Tilly's combined Spanish and Catholic League forces defeated a German Protestant army at the Battle of Wimpfen on May 6, 1622 and Tilly's seizure of Heidelberg in September 1622, Frederick was formally deposed and Maximilian took the Palatine title. Diplomatic efforts by England, France, Sweden, and Denmark to provide aid against the Hapsburgs failed, and Denmark alone sought to contain the northward Imperial thrust (see DANISH WAR OF 1625–29).

Bohemian-Polish Wars   See POLISH-BOHEMIAN WARS.

Bolivian Guerrilla War of 1966–67   In Bolivia, in 1964, a military faction overthrew the discredited nationalistic government of President Victor Paz Estenssoro (1907–   ) and established a ruling junta, which dealt harshly with striking tin miners while currying favor with the peasantry. To Ernesto "Che" Guevara (1928–67), an Argentine-born revolutionary and a major in the Cuban army of Fidel Castro (1926–   ), Bolivia seemed the one country in South America that was ripe for a Cuban-like revolution (see CUBAN REVOLUTION OF 1956–59). In the fall of 1966, he and some 15 seasoned followers clandestinely arrived in Bolivia and set up a headquarters at Nancahuazu in a wild, unsettled region of the country. Unexpected troubles arose; their controller double-crossed them and absconded with a quarter of a million dollars, their food and supplies ran low, and the several warring factions of the Bolivian Communist Party failed to give the expected support to Guevara's insurgency. The Bolivian army learned of the guerrillas' presence and, assuming there was a large force of Cubans, sent several thousand troops to patrol the region; small skirmishes ensued in which the guerrillas usually triumphed. In March 1967, Bolivian fighter planes strafed the guerrillas' area while American Green Beret-trained army units began an encircling operation; authorities were still not sure if Guevara, who had been reported dead earlier, was directing the actions of the guerrillas. On April 26, 1967, a French and an Argentine courier, who were trying to leave Bolivia to tell the world of Guevara's existence and intentions, were captured by the army, which used them to stir up the Bolivian people against the "foreign invaders." Three months later the army staged a surprise attack against Guevara's camp on the Morocos River and seized irreplaceable equipment. Nine guerrillas were killed in an ambush at a river ford. By the fall of 1967, Guevara was retreating through the jungles with only 16 men against 1,500 soldiers in pursuit. A special army detachment discovered Guevara and his small band on the banks of the Yuro River on October 8, 1967; some were killed outright. Guevara was wounded and captured; he was taken to nearby La Higuera, where he was shot the next morning.

Bolivian National Revolution (1952) Although outlawed in Bolivia in 1946, the Movimiento Nacionalista Revolucionario (MNR), or National Revolutionary Movement, continued to have many thousands of Bolivian adherents who demanded land reform, control of the rich tin-mining industry, and justice. In the Bolivian presidential elections of 1951, the MNR won a plurality victory with its candidate Victor Paz Estenssoro (1907–), founder and leader of the MNR and former professor of economics, who was in exile in Argentina. The government claimed Estenssoro did not have the required majority and the president must be chosen by the congress. In order to prevent the MNR from coming to power, Bolivia's outgoing president resigned and turned the government over to a 10-man military junta, whose rule was anathema to many. On April 8–11, 1952, a popular revolt occurred in La Paz, Bolivia's administrative capital, and elsewhere; the MNR, supported by armed workers, ci-

vilians, and peasants and the national police, overthrew the military junta and recalled Paz Estenssoro from exile to take the presidency. As president he did what he had said he would do: nationalized the tin-mining industry, raised miners' wages, liquidated the vast holdings of powerful landholders, and distributed acres to landless Indians. Universal suffrage was granted, but Paz Estenssoro was ruthless to his political foes, many of whom he imprisoned. In one of Latin America's major revolutions, Bolivia had "suddenly broken loose from the chains of serfdom," and its people, especially the Indians, had gained civil and political rights which subsequent governments would have to recognize.

Bolivian Revolt of 1946 Tin from Bolivia was vital to the Allied war effort during WORLD WAR II. After the Bolivian government of President Enrique Peñaranda (1892–1970) declared war on the Axis powers (April 1943), a group of dissident army officers led by Colonel Gualberto Villaroel (1907–46) and supported by the National Revolutionary Movement (MNR), the Argentine government, and German agents in Buenos Aires, staged a successful coup, deposing Peñaranda (December 21, 1943) and installing Villaroel as president. Initially, the United States refused recognition of Villaroel's regime, but later granted it when Villaroel promised to cooperate with the Allies. With the decline of mineral prices, inflation, and unemployment at the end of the war, Bolivia suffered severe economic hardship, which helped bring on a popular revolt against the government at La Paz on July 17–21, 1946. The army did nothing to check rebellious soldiers, workers, and students; Villaroel was seized and hanged from a lamppost in front of the presidential palace. A provisional liberal government was installed and recognized by the United States and Argentina.

Bolivian Revolt of 1971 The arrest of 30 leaders of a right-wing demonstration in Santa Cruz, Bolivia, triggered a brief general revolt (August 19–22, 1971) that pitted peasants, students, miners, the air force, and other supporters of leftist president Juan José Torres (1921–) against most of the army and the conservative middle and upper classes. The government declared the arrests were to prevent a "fascist conspiracy," while the rightist rebels said they were fighting "to keep the country from falling into the hands of communism." The rebels gained control of Santa Cruz and Cochabamba and, a day later, after the air force had defected to them, captured La Paz, Bolivia's administrative capital. Torres fled to Peru and then to Chile, where he was granted asylum. A military-civilian coalition government was formed with rebel Colonel Hugo Banzer Suárez (1924–) as the head.

Bolivian War of Independence   See PERUVIAN WAR OF INDEPENDENCE.

Bolshevik Revolution (1917) Military reverses and shortages of goods during WORLD WAR I, combined with widespread distrust of governmental officials, brought about the downfall of the Russian czars. The first phase occurred in March 1917 (the FEBRUARY REVOLUTION by the Old Style calendar), when Nicholas II (1868–1918) failed to subdue rioting workers in Moscow and Petrograd (St. Petersburg). The Duma, or parliament, refusing to dissolve, established a provisional government under Prince Lvov (1861–1925). Nicholas abdicated and was later executed. Soviets, or revolutionary committees, around the country pressured for withdrawal from the war, encouraged by Vladimir I. Lenin (1870–1924), leader of the Bolsheviks, left-wing faction of the Russian marxists. An attempt to seize power failed, Lenin fled, and socialist moderate Alexander F. Kerensky (1881–1970) became premier. But Kerensky lost support, and Lenin returned to Petrograd to lead a bloodless coup in November (the OCTOBER REVOLUTION, O.S.), masterminded by Leon Trotsky (1879–1940). The Bolsheviks withdrew from WORLD WAR I and moved quickly to consolidate their power. Private property, class privilege, and sex discrimination were abolished, banks and industries nationalized, and opposition

suppressed with the aid of secret police. A bloody civil war ensued (see RUSSIAN CIVIL WAR OF 1918–21). See also KORNILOV'S REVOLT.

Bordeaux, Fall of (1453) Because no peace treaty was signed after Orléans (see ORLÉANS, SIEGE AT), the French made use of a 1435 Burgundian alliance, rebellion in English-held territories in France, and the truce of 1444–49 to unify, reorganize, and reform the government and military. In 1449, the French aided rebellious Normandy, taking Rouen and defeating the English brutally at Formigny in 1450 and Castillon in 1453. They used an improved gunpowder and the culverin, a long cannon that killed six to the longbow's one. The English, dismayed, captured Bordeaux in 1452. In power all around the Bordelais, the French laid siege, and in a few months the city was again French. No peace was signed, but the HUNDRED YEARS' WAR was essentially over.

Bosnian Civil War of 1992–95 Beginning several months later than fighting in the republics of Slovenia and Croatia (see SLOVENIAN WAR OF INDEPENDENCE and CROATIAN WAR FOR INDEPENDENCE), the Bosnian civil war was the most brutal chapter in the breakup of Yugoslavia. On February 29, 1992, the multiethnic republic of Bosnia and Herzegovina, where Catholic Croats, Orthodox Serbs, and Muslim Slavs lived side by side, passed a referendum for independence—but not all Bosnian Serbs agreed. Under the guise of protecting the Serb minority in Bosnia, Serbian leaders like Slobodan Milosevic (1941–) channeled arms and military support to them. In spring 1992, for example, the federal army, dominated by Serbs, shelled Croats and Muslims in Sarajevo, the Bosnian capital. Foreign governments responded with sanctions (not always tightly enforced) to keep fuel and weapons from Serbia, which had (in April 1992) joined the republic of Montenegro in a newer, smaller Yugoslavia. Bosnian Serb guerrillas carried out deadly campaigns of "ethnic cleansing," massacring members of other ethnic groups or expelling them from their homes to create exclusively Serb areas. Attacks on civilians and international relief workers disrupted supplies of food and other necessities just when such aid was most crucial: in what became the worst refugee crisis in Europe since World War II, millions of Bosnians (and Croatians) had been driven from their homes by July 1992. Alarmed by ethnic cleansing and other human rights abuses (which Croats and Muslims also engaged in, though to a lesser extent than did the Serbs), the United Nations resolved to punish such war crimes. In early 1994 the fierce three-way fighting became a war between two sides. In February and March the Muslims and Croats in Bosnia called a truce and formed a confederation, which in August agreed to a plan (developed by the United States, Russia, Britain, France, and Germany) for a 51–49 split of Bosnia, with the Serbs getting the lesser percentage. Despite the Muslim-Croat alliance, the peace proposal, and an ongoing arms embargo against all combatants (an embargo criticized abroad for maintaining Bosnian Serb dominance in weaponry), the fighting did not stop. In 1994 and 1995 Bosnian Serbs massacred residents of Sarajevo, Srebenica, and other cities that the United Nations had in May 1993 deemed "safe havens" for Muslim civilians. Neither NATO air strikes (beginning in April 1994) nor the cutoff of supplies from Serbia (as of August 1994) deterred the Bosnian Serbs, who blocked convoys of humanitarian aid and detained some of the 24,000 UN troops intended to stop hostilities. Like their allies in Serbia, the Bosnian Serbs wanted to unite all Serb-held lands of the former Yugoslavia. By September 1995, however, the Muslim-Croat alliance's conquests had reduced Serb-held territory in Bosnia from over two-thirds to just under one-half—the percentage allocated in the peace plan for the Serb autonomous region. On December 14, 1995, the leaders of Bosnia, Croatia, and Serbia signed the Dayton peace accords, officially ending the wars in Bosnia and Croatia after about 250,000 people died and more than 3 million others became refugees. NATO troops numbering 60,000 entered Bosnia to enforce the accords. In early 1998 about 30,000 NATO peacekeepers were still in Bosnia, which remained scarred by war and divided between the Muslim-Croat confederation and the Bosnian Serb region. Dozens of suspected war criminals had been indicted by the UN tribunal, including Bosnian Serb leader Radovan Karadzic (1945–) (who had resigned in June 1996), although many had not been arrested or tried.

Bosnian-Turkish War of 1459–63 Ottoman Turks and Hungarians battled each other for Serbia in the mid-15th century. In 1459, Sultan Muhammad II "the Conqueror" (1429–81) annexed the region and then turned his eyes toward Bosnia to the west. Bloody battles ensued before this region too came under Turkish control in 1463, but the Bosnians rebelled at certain places and were not fully subjugated until the HUNGARIAN-TURKISH WAR OF 1463–83.

Boston Massacre (1770) Colonists in Boston, Mass., strongly opposed the Townshend Acts, by which the British parliament had levied new taxes on them, and the forced quartering of "redcoats" (British troops) in their homes. On the evening of March 5, 1770, a group of dockworkers and others began to harass a British soldier on guard duty at the Boston customhouse. Seven other British soldiers, led by Captain Thomas Preston, soon arrived on the scene and tried unsuccessfully to disperse the unruly crowd. In the confusion, a soldier was knocked down, and the order to fire was heard by the soldiers. Five colonists, including Crispus Attucks (d. 1770), a black sailor and former slave, were shot to death by the British soldiers, who afterward were tried for murder. Preston and six others were acquitted; two other soldiers were found guilty of manslaughter, punished, and later discharged from service. See AMERICAN REVOLUTION.

Bosworth Field, Battle of (1485) Usurper, villain, and alleged murderer of his brother's sons, King Richard III (1452–85) of England was despised by

Lancastrians and opposed by many fellow Yorkists (see ROSES, WARS OF THE). Premature revolts were put down, but the Lancastrian claimant to the throne, Henry Tudor (1457–1509), invaded England with aid from France in 1485 and met Richard at Bosworth Field on August 22, 1485. Richard's cavalry charged. Then Richard signaled for reserves, only to discover that their treasonous leader was attacking the royal army. Richard valiantly and courageously entered the battle, but was struck from behind. Falling, he was stabbed to death. The Plantagenet line had ended, and the war was over.

Boudicca's Rebellion (A.D. 60–61) Suetonius Paulinus (d. after 69), Roman governor of Britain since 59, began a campaign to capture the island of Mona (Anglesey, Wales), a druid stronghold of resistance, but he was forced to return to southeast Britain when Boudicca (Boadicea) (d. 61), queen of the Iceni tribe, raised a rebellion against the Romans (60). The Iceni kingdom (Norfolk) had just been annexed by the Romans on the death of Boudicca's husband, King Prasutagus (d. 60), who had left no male heir and given his wealth to his daughters and Roman emperor Nero (37–68). The rebellion spread throughout East Anglia; Camulodunum (Colchester), Verulamium (St. Albans), and Londinium (London) were sacked by rebels; some 70,000 Romans and pro-Roman Britons were slain, according to the Roman historian Cornelius Tacitus (56?–120?), before Paulinus and his legions crushed the rebels and regained control. Boudicca reportedly poisoned herself, died of shock, or was killed. See also ROMAN CONQUEST OF BRITAIN.

Bounty Mutiny (1789) The H.M.S. *Bounty*, a British armed transport ship, was sent to deliver breadfruit plants from Tahiti in the Pacific to the British West Indies, where the plants were to be used as a food supply for the black slaves. On April 28, 1789, during the return voyage from Tahiti, much of the crew of the *Bounty*, led by master's mate Fletcher Christian (d. 1790), successfully mutinied against their captain, William Bligh (1754–1817).

Bligh and 18 other men were set adrift in a small open boat with some food and, after sailing nearly 4,000 miles, reached Timor in the East Indies. Some mutineers under Christian landed at Pitcairn Island in the South Pacific, where they founded a colony; other mutineers were later caught and imprisoned or executed.

Boxer Uprising (Boxer Rebellion) (1899–1901) A secret organization in the Chinese government, called the Society of the Righteous Harmonious Fists (hence "Boxers"), led an uprising against foreign missionaries and their Chinese converts to Christianity. Great Britain, France, Italy, Germany, Russia, Japan, and the United States sent military forces to Tientsin (Tianjin) and Peking (Beijing) to protect their besieged legations. China's empress dowager, Tz'u Hsi (Cixi) (1835–1908), supported the Boxers and ordered all foreigners to be killed. After bloody fighting, an international expedition subdued the Boxers and captured Peking and the Imperial City. The empress dowager fled to the north with her court. The Russians occupied southern Manchuria (see RUSSO-JAPANESE WAR OF 1904–5). Hostilities ended when the so-called Boxer Protocol was signed by China's imperial princes, Japan, and western nations. China was compelled to pay reparations and to permit foreign interests in China, whose administrative and territorial "rights" were preserved by mutual agreement among the foreign powers. See also OPIUM WARS.

Boyars' Revolt of 1564 The boyars (members of the Russian aristocracy) became extremely powerful politically during the minority (1533–44) of Prince Ivan IV "the Terrible" (1530–84). Afterward, he, who had himself crowned czar (emperor) in 1547, sought to subjugate them with the aid of the pro-czar military landed gentry (dvoriane). With the death of his wife Anastasia Romanov (d. 1560), a demoniacal aspect of Ivan's character seemed to be unleashed against the boyars, who had supposedly humiliated him during his childhood and whom he suspected of conspiracy. Ivan indulged in wholesale murder, slaying many boyars and their friends in what historians judge as a calculated move to gain full control over them. In 1564, his trusted military commander and adviser, Prince Andrei Kurbsky (1528?–83), who was a boyar, defected to Lithuania, greatly upsetting Ivan. Boyars revolted against Ivan's assassinations and ruthlessness, and Ivan blamed them and the clergy for Russia's troubles (see LIVONIAN WAR). Eventually Moscow's metropolitan (archbishop), afraid of a large popular revolt in favor of Ivan, agreed not to interfere in Ivan's prosecution of "state enemies" and delimited an extensive domain (oprichnina) directly under the czar's control. Helped by a newly formed corps (*oprichniks*), Ivan attacked the boyars, killing, imprisoning, and banishing many of them and taking their lands. The influence of the boyars had been significantly diminished by the time Ivan decided to abolish the oprichnina in 1572. See also TIME OF TROUBLES, RUSSIAN.

Brabant Revolution (1789–90)   Joseph II (1741–90), Austrian Hapsburg Holy Roman Emperor, instituted sweeping administrative and clerical changes in the Austrian Netherlands, rousing resentment among conservative and Catholic leaders. Late in 1789, the duchy of Brabant (now part of Belgium and the Netherlands) declared independence. Invading Austrian troops were defeated at Turnhout, and in early 1790, a confederative constitution was ratified. But the Brabantian leaders, Henri van der Noot (1731–1827) and Jean-François Vonck (1743–92), could not sustain a united front (Noot's conservatives opposed the fully representative form of government sought by Vonck's progressives, desiring a return to an oligarchic rule), and by December 1790, the new Holy Roman Emperor, Leopold II (1747–92), had forcibly restored Austrian rule in Brabant, repealing his predecessor's reforms. The victory proved short-lived, for within four years forces of the FRENCH REVOLUTION took over the area.

Brasidas's Invasion (424–423 B.C.)   The expense of carrying on the Second or Great PELOPONNESIAN WAR caused Cleon (d. 422), the Athenian leader, to treble the taxes paid by Athen's allies (424). Olynthus in Chalcidice and other allied cities revolted and sought Spartan help. Sparta's king sent General Brasidas (d. 422) with less than 2,000 soldiers (helot hoplites and mercenaries) to invade Thrace. Advancing through Thessaly, defeating two Athenian forces en route, and enlisting the aid of rebellious cities, Brasidas and his small army seized Athens's most important colony on the Chalcidice peninsula, Amphipolis, in Thrace. An Athenian naval squadron under Thucydides (c. 460–c. 400), the historian, had arrived too late to help Amphipolis's soldiers, who had urgently requested reinforcements, but later Thucydides' men prevented the invaders from taking the nearby port of Eion. Shortly after, Cleon charged Thucydides with negligence and exiled him for 20 years, and the Athenian council under Nicias (d. 413) set up a one-year truce. But Brasidas endangered Athens's supply route to Hellespontine grain, and in 423 Cleon led an attack on Amphipolis; he was surprised by Brasidas's troops and was defeated and killed in battle (Brasidas was also killed).

Brazilian Revolt of 1893–95   General Manuel Deodoro da Fonseca (1827–92), who led a bloodless army revolt (1889) that ended the Brazilian empire and established a federal republic, later became Brazil's first elected president in 1891. But that same year strong opposition to his dictatorial policies led to an almost bloodless revolt by the army and navy (he wanted to curtail the power of the military) that forced him to resign in favor of Vice President Floriano Peixoto (1842–95). But Peixoto, a general also, announced that Brazil needed a military dictator to purge its corruption. The navy, led by Admiral Custodio José de Mello (1845?–1902), became frightened; in September 1893, the entire navy mutinied under Mello's direction against the Peixoto government and took control of the harbor of Rio de Janeiro, the capital. Another revolt in the state of Rio Grande do Sol was backed by Mello; its followers gained control of much of southern Brazil but failed to capture the capital, attacked by a third rebel group advocating restoration of the monarchy. Peixoto's forces, including warships ordered from abroad, had much difficulty defeating Mello, who capitulated (April 16, 1894), and suppressing the other rebels; guerrilla activity continued in Rio Grande do Sol until August 1895, when it stopped suddenly upon Peixoto's death. Brazil's "first civilian president," Prudente José de Morais Barros (1841–1902), generally welcomed when he took office (1894), had to deal with militarism in government throughout his four-year tenure.

Brazilian Revolt of 1964   President João Goulart (1918–76) of Brazil headed a leftist-oriented government that was endorsed by the Sailors and Marines Association and other labor organizations. On March 25, 1964, about 1,400 sailors and marines seized a trades union building to protest the arrest of their association's president; the protesters refused to surrender to the minister of the navy, but two days later yielded to army troops and were promptly pardoned. Top military leaders were shocked and accused Goulart of not supporting them and of undermining discipline. Although Goulart agreed to investigate the amnesty, the Fourth Military Region staged a revolt against him (March 31, 1964) and was soon joined by other military regions. The army garrison at Rio de Janeiro fought against a few troops loyal to Goulart and soon took control of the city. A general strike called by the General Confederation of Workers completely disrupted daily life but failed to prevent the military takeover of the government. Goulart was forced to flee to Uruguay. The new government immediately began arresting all leftists and suspected communists and later expanded its purge to members of congress and officials who had been in Goulart's Labor Party.

Brazilian Revolution of 1930   (Gaucho Revolution)   Suffering from the worldwide Great Depression and the collapse of the coffee markets, Brazilians were discontented as the presidential election of 1930 approached. Incumbent president Washington Luiz Pereira de Souza (1869–1957) designated fellow Paulista (native of São Paulo), Julio Prestes (1898–1946), as the official conservative candidate in the election to succeed him. This, however, represented a break in the usual arrangement, under which the chief politicians in the Brazilian states of São Paulo and Minas Gerais had alternated in selecting presidential candidates. In the election, the leaders of Minas Gerais supported Getúlio Dornelles Vargas (1883–1954), governor of the state of Rio Grande do Sol, whose residents were referred to as *gauchos* (hence the name of the revolution). When Prestes was declared the winner (March 1930), his opponents in the southern states made plans to upset the results; Orwaldo Aranha (1894–1960), legal aide to Vargas, made a tour of army commands and found support for Vargas in the military. In October 1930, Vargas called for a revolt, promised numerous economic and political reforms, assembled state and national troops loyal to him, and made a trip by train to Brazil's capital, Rio de Janeiro. All opposition vanished, and in a bloodless revolution, he seized the presidency, forcing Luiz to resign and Prestes to take refuge in the British legation. This marked the end of the old, or first, republic.

Brazilian War of Independence   (1822–25)   As a result of the Napoleonic invasion of Portugal during the PENINSULAR WAR, the Portuguese royal family fled to Rio de Janeiro in Brazil, which became the seat of the Portuguese government. In 1821, King John VI (1769–1826), who had initiated reforms, including raising Brazil to equal status with Portugal in the empire and removing restrictions on Brazilian trade, returned to Portugal and left behind his eldest son, Dom Pedro (1798–1834), as prince regent. Attempts by Portugal to reduce Brazil again to subordinate status led to Dom Pedro's statement, the *Grito de Ypiranga*, proclaiming Brazilian independence and his crowning as Brazil's emperor in 1822. The Brazilian navy, organized and commanded by Lord Thomas Cochrane (1775–1860), blockaded the Portuguese garrisons at Bahia in

1823. Attacks by land and sea drove the Portuguese to leave in a large convoy and, failing to land at Maranhão (São Luis) (Cochrane had captured the port), to proceed across the Atlantic to Portugal. In 1824, Pedro I granted Brazil its first constitution, and in 1825, Portugal recognized Brazilian independence. See also ARGENTINE-BRAZILIAN WAR OF 1825–28; CHILEAN WAR OF INDEPENDENCE; PERUVIAN WAR OF INDEPENDENCE; PORTUGUESE CIVIL WAR OF 1823–24.

Breton Succession, War of the (1341–65) When Duke John III (1312–41) of Brittany died without an heir, his half-brother John of Montfort (d. 1345) and his nephew-in-law Charles of Blois (c. 1319–1364) sought support from King Edward III (1312–77) of England and King Philip VI (1293–1350) of France, respectively, for their rival claims to succession, initiating an important phase of the HUNDRED YEARS' WAR. Both countries invaded Brittany, locking horns at Rennes, Nantes, and Vannes in late 1342. Through the intervention of envoys from the new pope, Clement VI (1291–1352), the Truce of Malestroit brought about a temporary and indecisive end to hostilities. In 1345, the English army once again laid siege to French posts along the border of Brittany, attacking France on two other fronts as well. In 1347, Charles of Blois was captured near La Roche-Derrien and sent to the Tower of London for nine years. But Charles's wife, Jeanne of Penthièvre, carried on the struggle, and the French tasted defeat once again at Mauron in 1352. Repeated truces failed to end the fighting, until Charles of Blois was killed in the Battle of Auray in 1364. The following year the Treaty of Guérande recognized Montfort claims to the Breton succession. Duke John paid homage to the French Crown, and stability was restored to the region.

Britain, Battle of (1940)   After the fall of France to the invading Germans in WORLD WAR II (see FRANCE, BATTLE OF), the German Nazi war machine concentrated its efforts on Great Britain and planned to bomb the country into submission before sending an invasion force across the English Channel. On August 15, 1940, the Luftwaffe (German air force) sent its first massive wave of bombers over southern England, where they encountered stiff resistance from British fighter planes. At first the Luftwaffe focused with some success on airfields, and then it began to make bombing raids on London and other cities. During the blitz (intensive air raid) in September 1940, London suffered great damage and loss of life, but the will of the British people was not broken. The Royal Air Force fought on tenaciously and shot down many German aircraft. On September 15, 1940, the Germans made a climactic attempt to establish superiority in the air, but they failed. Germany's Führer (leader), Adolf Hitler (1889–1945), called off the invasion plan and resorted to indiscriminate bombing of large cities, notably London, with main attacks coming at night and continuing until May 1941. Prime Minister Winston Churchill (1874–1965) of Great Britain acknowledged the country's debt to the pilots of the Royal Air Force when he said, "Never in the field of conflict was so much owed by so many to so few."

British Colonial Wars in Africa (1900–1915)   By the turn of the 19th century, Great Britain had firmly established a hold on the west coast of Africa in Nigeria, the Gold Coast (Ghana), and Sierra Leone, but the territory was vast and the interior needed to be brought under control. British army officers and native soldiers had to bring peace to warring tribes, use force on tribes that attacked other natives living peacefully under British protection, and punish those natives who made slave raids or blockaded trade routes. The Ashantis rebelled at Kumasi in the Gold Coast in 1900, and it took eight months for the British to restore order. The Aros in Nigeria were subdued in 1901; Bauchi, Bornu, and Nassarawa provinces in Nigeria were subjugated in 1902; and successful British campaigns were waged against the Hausa states (neighboring black African Muslim states) in northern Nigeria in 1903 (the Kano and Sokoto areas were conquered). The British practice was to depose rulers or chiefs of troublesome tribes and replace them with men who were loyal to the British Crown. In 1914, a regiment from the Gold Coast invaded neighboring German Togoland (Togo) and quickly took control of it from the Germans (see WORLD WAR I). British and French forces won victories the following year in the German-held Cameroons and in German East Africa (Tanzania). In British East Africa (Kenya) a native revolt was crushed in 1906. See also ASHANTI WARS; BOER WARS; MATABELE-BRITISH WAR; SUDANESE WARS.

British-Indian Raids of 1782 Although the British had surrendered at Yorktown, Va., in October 1781, the fighting in the AMERICAN REVOLUTION was not yet over. Combined British and Indian forces continued to attack frontier settlements in the Old Northwest. On August 15, 1782, about 250 British and Indians, led by the American turncoat Simon Girty (1741–1818), raided across the Ohio River to attack Bryan's Station in Kentucky but were driven back and pursued by some 200 armed American backwoodsmen. Near Blue Licks, Ky., the pursuing Americans were ambushed by a large band of Indians, who killed about 70 of them. The ensuing unrest caused General George Rogers Clark (1752–1818) to lead a force of more than 1,000 men northward, destroying several Indian villages and securing control of the territory.

Brittany Civil Wars See BRETON SUCCESSION, WAR OF THE.

Brown's Raid on Harpers Ferry (1859) American abolitionist John Brown (1800–1859) planned to liberate the slaves by arming them and by establishing a base in the southern mountains to which blacks could flee and from which they could incite uprisings. As a first step, Brown and his band of 21 followers, which included his three sons and five blacks, assaulted and took control of the federal arsenal at Harpers Ferry, Va. (now in West Virginia), on the night of October 16, 1859. The next day Brown's band took possession of the town and held some of the citizens as hostages. Instead of retreating to the mountains with a large stock of arms, Brown and his men fortified themselves in the arsenal's engine room and battled the local militia. A company of U.S. Marines under Colonel Robert E. Lee (1807–70) arrived from Washington, D.C., and, on the morning of October 18, 1859, regained possession of the arsenal after a short but stubborn fight, in which Brown was wounded. Seventeen of Brown's men died in the raid. Brown was tried, found guilty of treason and murder, and hanged on December 2, 1859. See also POTTAWATOMIE MASSACRE.

Bruce's Revolt (1306–14) Personal ambition caused Robert the Bruce (1274–1329) to woo both sides during Scotland's quarrels with King Edward I (1239–1307) of England. Bruce had joined William Wallace (1272?–1305) after Falkirk (see WALLACE'S REVOLT), but in 1302 was on Edward's side. In 1306, however, while still in Edward's service, Bruce murdered a rival baron, assumed Wallace's leadership, and had himself crowned Scottish king at Scone. Edward again invaded and won at Methven, driving Bruce into exile in Ireland. The Scots rallied to him on his return in 1307, when his pikemen slaughtered a host of English cavalry at Loudon Hill. Edward died in 1307 at the beginning of a new campaign, and, after a feeble invasion in 1310, Edward II (1284–1327) abandoned his father's objectives for several years. During this period, Bruce made peace with most of his enemies, consolidated his forces, gained recognition as king from France, and got the Scottish clergy to side with him. In 1311, he attacked Durham and Hartlepool, and by 1314 he had recovered all the castles controlled by English garrisons except Berwick and Stirling. The latter had already undergone siege (see BANNOCKBURN, BATTLE OF). See also SCOTTISH WAR OF 1314–28.

Buckingham's Revolt (1483) Though married to a Woodville, the second duke of Buckingham, Henry Stafford (1454?–83), opposed Elizabeth Woodville (1437?–92), widow of Edward IV (1442–83) of England, in her attempt to become regent to their son, Edward V (1470–83). Buckingham supported Richard of Gloucester (1452–85), Edward IV's brother and Protector of the Realm, and aided Gloucester's attempt to usurp the throne as Richard III. Amply rewarded, Buckingham, nonetheless, mysteriously rebelled against Richard and gave his support to Henry Tudor (1457–1509) (see ROSES, WARS OF THE). In 1483, because floods prevented his army from joining others in an abortive revolt, Buckingham went into hiding; he was betrayed, tried, and beheaded. His sequestered properties were released by Henry VII (Henry Tudor) in 1485.

Buckshot War (1838) The Anti-Masonic party, led by Thaddeus Stevens (1792–1868) and supported by some Whigs, attempted to organize the Pennsylvania House of Representatives in Harrisburg, Pa., without seating the Democratic members from Philadelphia. An angry mob from Philadelphia descended on Harrisburg and threatened violence. The Pennsylvania governor, after having been denied the use of federal troops, called out militiamen and ordered them to load their guns with buckshot for riot control. The Democrats were admitted to the house, and order was restored.

Bukhara, Mongol Destruction of (1220)   In pursuit of the Khwarizmian shah after the Battle of Khojend (see MONGOL-PERSIAN WAR, FIRST), Genghis (Jenghiz, Chingis) Khan (1167?–1227) and his Mongol army faced a Khwarizmian defensive line established near the city of Bukhara in central Uzbek (south-central Asia). Genghis Khan arranged 10 cavalry divisions into four columns; three of them converged to crumple the shah's right (southern) flank near the city of Samarkand, and Genghis Khan took the fourth column (40,000 men) and approached Bukhara from the west (rear flank). This four-pronged Mongol maneuver of so many troops (some 100,000) exemplified a precision never surpassed by other military strategists. The shah concentrated on the larger forces, abandoning Bukhara. After a brief siege, the city was sacked and accidentally burned; its inhabitants died to a man. Afterward Genghis Khan and the other columns converged at Samarkand. Admitted to the city by traitors after a five-day Mongol siege in 1220, Genghis Khan partially duplicated the destruction of Bukhara. The shah escaped and was pursued northwestward (see MONGOL INVASION OF RUSSIA); Genghis Khan chased the shah's son to Bamian (see BAMIAN, MONGOL DESTRUCTION OF).

Bulgarian-Byzantine War of A.D. **755–72** Warfare broke out when the Bulgars, a Turkish-speaking people, demanded a tribute from Byzantine fortresses built in Thrace, a Bulgarian holding. Forces of Constantine V (718–75), emperor of the Byzantine Empire, defeated the Bulgars in Thrace during a Bulgarian invasion of the empire in 755. Byzantine forces again won at Marcellae in 759 and at Anchialus in 763. The Bulgars concluded a peace agreement in 767 that lasted five years. However, after learning of Bulgarian preparations for a surprise attack in 772, the Byzantines took up arms and conquered them again. Telets (731–64), a Bulgarian military leader who had become khan (lord) in 761, fought the Byzantines for three more years until Constantine's death in 775, when the Bulgars sued for peace.

Bulgarian-Byzantine War of A.D. **780–83**   In 780, the Byzantine Empire continued its conquest of the Bulgars, begun about 30 years earlier, and pushed the Bulgarian frontier bordering the empire to the north. Despite losing territory, Khan Kardam, ruler of the Bulgars, compelled Byzantine empress Irene (752–803) to renew Byzantine payments on an annual basis to the Bulgars in 792.

Bulgarian-Byzantine War of A.D. **809–17**   Emperor Nicephorus I (d. 811) led the Byzantine army into Bulgaria in 809 and captured Pliska, the Bulgar capital. Krum (d. 814), king of the Bulgars, repeated offers of peace, but Nicephorus rejected them. After Nicephorus was defeated and killed in a Bulgarian night attack in 811, the Bulgars won victories againts the Byzantines, though struggling under a rapid succession of rulers and confronting Charlemagne (742?–814) in the Frank's war against the Byzantine Empire in 803–10. Michael I, who ruled the Byzantines from 811 to 813, lost to the Bulgars at Versinikia in 813, when Leo the Armenian (d. 820), a Byzantine general, pulled his support and his Asian soldiers from the battlefield. Leo revolted against Michael and seized the Byzantine throne as Leo V. At Mesembria, in 817, Leo defeated the Bulgars and forced them to accept a 30-year peace. See also FRANKISH-BYZANTINE WAR OF A.D. 803–10.

Bulgarian-Byzantine War of A.D. 889–97   The Bulgars under Czar Symeon (d. 927) defeated the Greek army in 894, and the Byzantines, in retaliation for the defeat of an army of their empire, induced the Magyars, a Hungarian people, to attack Bulgaria in 895. Symeon allied himself with the Patzinaks, a nomadic people of southern Russia, and defeated the Magyars in the BULGAR-MAGYAR WAR OF A.D. 895. Symeon returned to the southern front to win a decisive victory over the Byzantine forces in 896, which led to peace the following year. The Byzantines agreed to pay an annual tribute to Symeon. The war, which had begun in 889 as a dispute over trade rights, had escalated into a contest for supreme rule, a goal Symeon continued to fight for.

Bulgarian-Byzantine War of A.D. 913–27   Czar Symeon (d. 927) of Bulgaria sought to defeat the Byzantines and advanced to their capital, Constantinople, in 913. However, he withdrew without fighting after securing tributes from the Byzantine Empire. During a palace revolt in 913, Empress Zoe (906–920) took the Byzantine throne. Symeon, realizing force was necessary to take the Byzantine Empire, advanced his troops, seizing Macedonia, Adrianople, and Albania from the Byzantines in 914. He took most of the Balkan peninsula and then invaded northern Greece and Thessaly in 918. During the next five years, Symeon advanced to the walls of Constantinople four times. But, unable to take the city without a strong naval fleet, Symeon's forces withdrew each time. The war ended when Symeon died in 927.

Bulgarian-Byzantine War of A.D. 981–1018   The Byzantines under Basil II (c. 958–1025) invaded Bulgaria but were defeated by the Bulgars under Czar Samuel (d. 1014) near Sofia in 981. Samuel's forces invaded Thessaly in eastern Greece in 896 to take Larissa and Dyrrhachium. Samuel, who took advantage of internal discord in the Byzantine Empire at that time, began to extend his control over eastern Bulgaria and beyond. However, Basil's Byzantine troops stopped the Bulgarian march, winning a tough campaign at Ochrida, the Bulgarian capital, and at Spercheios in 996. Basil then reclaimed Greece and Macedonia in 1003. Basil's army overwhelmed Samuel's army at Balathista in 1014, and about 15,000 Bulgarian soldiers were captured. Blinding virtually the entire Bulgarian army, Basil sent it back to Samuel, who thereupon died from the shock of seeing his blinded soldiers. By 1018, Basil, the "Slayer of the Bulgars," had incorporated Bulgaria into the Byzantine Empire, but allowed the country practical autonomy.

Bulgarian-Byzantine War of 1261–65   Bulgaria remained under Byzantine control from about 1018 to 1185, when an uprising forced the Byzantines to recognize Bulgaria as an independent empire. In 1261, the Byzantines, who had begun waging war to take control of Bulgaria once again, seized the Bulgarian ports of Anchialus and Mesembria. Byzantine emperor Michael VIII (1224–82) pushed the Bulgarian boundary beyond Haemus (the Balkan Mountains) in 1265. Returning from battle, Michael was ambushed and caught by the Bulgarians, who forced him to promise to return the two seaports taken in 1261. Michael never returned the ports, and the Bulgars, hoping to seize them, invaded the Byzantine Empire in 1272 but were unsuccessful and finally gave up their claim to them.

Bulgarian Revolt of 1040–41   Bulgarian rebels, led by Peter Deljan, grandson of Bulgarian czar

Samuel (d. 1014), openly rebelled against Byzantine rule, hoping to reassert Bulgarian independence (see BULGARIAN-BYZANTINE WAR OF A.D. 981–1018). Deljan was proclaimed czar in Belgrade in 1040, and soon Prince Alusianus, a member of the ruling family, joined him as coruler. The Bulgars attacked the Byzantine city of Thessalonica but were repulsed and had to retreat. Dissension occurred among Bulgarian rebel leaders, causing Alusianus to ambush and blind Deljan. The revolt collapsed afterward. See also MANIACES, REVOLT OF.

Bulgar-Magyar War of A.D. 895 The Magyars, a Hungarian people, were prompted by the Byzantines to attack the Bulgars, a Turkish-speaking people, who had invaded the Byzantine Empire (see BULGARIAN-BYZANTINE WAR OF A.D. 889–97). Under their chief, Árpád (c. 840–907), the Magyars suffered defeat by the Bulgars under Czar Symeon (d. 927) and the Patzinaks or Pechenegs of southern Russia. Forced from their ancestral home near the Black Sea, the Magyars moved into the Danube Valley where they took territory from the Slavs and set up a monarchy in what is now Hungary.

Bulge, Battle of the (Battle of the Ardennes) (1944–45) As a last desperate gamble to reverse Allied advances toward the Rhine and win the war (see WORLD WAR II), Adolf Hitler (1889–1945), Germany's Führer (leader), ordered an offensive against the Allies in the Ardennes Forest in Luxembourg and southern Belgium. It was in this area that the German armies had broken through Allied lines in May 1940 and had overrun Belgium and France. On December 16, 1944, Hitler's attack began in the Ardennes; the Allied line was held by four relatively inexperienced U.S. divisions, which were no match for the three German armies that were hurled against them. By the end of the first week, the Germans had advanced 50 miles on a 50-mile-long front. Bad weather prevented the Allies from using their air forces, but when the skies cleared, their bombers and fighter planes attacked, and American

resistance stiffened. U.S. general George S. Patton (1885–1945) rushed his Third Army to the defense of Bastogne in the Ardennes, and its arrival spelled the end to any hope of German success. On December 26, 1944, the Germans began a slow retreat, and the "bulge" they had caused in the Allies' line disappeared as they withdrew in January 1945. The Allied counteroffensive succeeded in driving the enemy back to its starting line by January 28, 1945. In the battle, the Germans suffered some 120,000 casulties and the loss of about 600 tanks, 1,600 aircraft, and 6,000 vehicles; the Allies had more than 75,000 casualties and lost some 730 tanks and tank destroyers.

Burgundian-Frankish War of A.D. 500 An internecine war broke out between King Gundobad (d. 516) of Burgundy and his brother Godegesil (d. 500) over rule of the kingdom. Clovis (c. 466–511), king of the Franks, intervened in support of Godegesil, and his Frankish soldiers won victory against Gundobad's Burgundians at Ouche. At Avignon, Gundobad successfully resisted a siege by Clovis, who then made peace with Gundobad. Godegesil had been previously defeated and killed by Gundobad during a battle at the Burgundian capital of Vienne.

Burgundian-Frankish War of A.D. 523–34 The four sons of Clovis (c. 466–511)—Theodoric I (d. 534), Clodomer (d. 524), Childebert I (d. 558), and Clotaire I (d. 561)—sought to enlarge the Frankish kingdom over which they shared in rule, each with his own domain. In 523, their forces moved into Burgundy and captured and killed Burgundian king Sigismund (d. 524). When Clodomer died in 524, Clotaire and Childebert seized his lands and murdered his children. That same year, Burgundian forces under Gundimar (d. 532), brother of Sigismund, defeated the Franks at the Battle of Vérerance and forced them to retreat. Burgundy remained independent until 532, when the Franks again invaded it. Gundimar was killed, and by 534 the Burgundian kingdom was in the hands of Clotaire and Childebert, who shared equally in its rule

(Theodoric's death that year ended his share). The Burgundian royal dynasty had been extinguished.

Burgundian-French Wars See FRANCO-BURGUNDIAN WARS.

Burgundian-Swiss War of 1339 The Swiss of Bern, a free city of the Holy Roman Empire, steadily extended their power by taking control of surrounding territories in the early 1300s. To check Bern's expansionism, invading Burgundians (about 15,000 strong, including infantry and cavalry) besieged the town of Laupen, acquired and defended by Bern, which received help from the three Swiss Forest cantons (Uri, Schwyz, and Unterwalden—the Everlasting League). Although outnumbered three to one, the Swiss infantry (pikemen and archers) charged, routed the Burgundians on the battlefield, and withstood a strong counterattack by the enemy's cavalry (June 21, 1339). The siege of Laupen was lifted. Swiss military valor and steadfastness had been displayed for the first time, and Bern's position as a leader in what is now Switzerland became firmly established. See also AUSTRO-SWISS WAR OF 1385–88.

Burgundian-Swiss War of 1474–77 Territorial expansion by Charles the Bold of Burgundy (1433–77) led to war with the Swiss in 1474. The Swiss, allied with the Germans and Austrians and aided by funds from the French king Louis XI (1423–83), a longtime enemy of Charles, repelled the Burgundians at Héricourt and took control of some Burgundian territory along the Swiss border. After Charles's forces killed the entire Swiss garrison at Granson in February 1476, the highly disciplined Swiss infantrymen routed the Burgundians at Granson on March 2, 1476, and at Morat on June 2, 1476. The Swiss moved into both battles without deploying and used superior military tactics to win victories. On January 5, 1477, at Nancy, Charles, with a new, reorganized Burgundian army, confronted the Swiss, who had advanced into Burgundian territory. The Burgundians were encircled and thoroughly defeated; Charles was slain while he and his army were in retreat. See also FRANCO-BURGUNDIAN WARS.

Burkina Faso Rebellion of 1987 Captain Blaise Compaoré (1951–) helped organize the successful 1983 military coup that installed Captain Thomas Sankara (1949–87) as president of the landlocked West African country of Burkina Faso (a former French colony known as Upper Volta, which gained independence in 1960 and later [1984] changed its name to Burkina Faso, meaning "Land of Upright Men" in the local Mossi and Dioula languages). Sankara—a popular, charismatic, and upright leader—improved the country's agriculture and public health services, but apparently his inchoate concentration of power helped lead to a bloody rebellion led by Compaoré, longtime upright friend and minister of state and justice, on October 15, 1987. In Ouagadougou (Wagaduga), the capital, rival groups of soldiers exchanged heavy gunfire, killing about 100 people; Sankara and 12 of his aides were shot to death and hastily buried in a mass grave. Compaoré became president, continued many of Sankara's policies, and headed a largely civilian and multiparty government in the 1990s.

Burma Campaign (Chindit War) (1943–45) Early in 1942 the Japanese invaded and occupied the country of Burma (now known as Myanmar) (see WORLD WAR II). They closed the Burma Road, the vital and only supply route from northern Burma to China. A British general, Orde Charles Wingate (1903–44), trained a band of British, Gurkha, and Burmese soldiers in the techniques of jungle warfare, and these men, called "Wingate's Raiders" or "Chindits," began in 1943 to make forays against Japanese airfields and communications stations. The U.S. effort against the Japanese in Burma was under the direction of General Joseph "Vinegar Joe" Stilwell (1883–1946), American commander in the China-Burma-India area. He trained a Chinese army in India and another in southern China in western fighting methods. In December 1943, a combined American-Chinese army set off to retake Burma from the north; it had to traverse rugged mountains and thick jungles and cross swift rivers, as well as fight experienced Japanese troops. In February 1944, the army was joined by 3,000 volunteers recruited by Stilwell's aide, Frank Dow Merrill (1903–55), and trained in long-range penetration tactics; the force became known as Merrill's Marauders. After incredible hardships, the Americans and Chinese seized the airfield at Myitkyina in northern Burma (May 17–18, 1944), which meant that Allied supplies and fresh troops could be flown in, but it took until August 3, 1944, and much hard fighting before the Japanese surrendered the city of Myitkyina. Meanwhile, the Chinese Expeditionary Force had moved against the Japanese at Lun-ling on the Burma Road. The "Battle for the Road" continued through 1944 and into 1945 with much bloody fighting; eventually some 400 communities were liberated by the Allies and the road was opened. This was the only Chinese victory over the Japanese in eight years of war (see SINO-JAPANESE WAR OF 1937–45).

Burmese-British Wars   See   ANGLO-BURMESE WARS.

Burmese-Chinese War of 1438–46   The Ming dynasty of China was anxious to conquer the Shan states in Upper Burma (see MONGOL-BURMESE WAR OF 1299–1300). Chinese forces, led by Wang Chi (d. 1445), invaded and were partly successful against the Shans. Wang Chi suffered defeat and was killed at Tagaung during an advance on Ava, the capital and home of King Narapati (1443–69) of Burma. Renewing and strengthening their invasion in 1446, the Chinese reached Ava and ordered Narapati to surrender and to hand over the Shan chief, Thonganbwa (d. 1446), who had received refuge there. Thonganbwa, seeing eventual Shan defeat, surrendered but soon committed suicide; Narapati also capitulated and accepted Ming suzerainty. The Shan-held city of Pagan, farther down the Irrawaddy River from Ava, was taken by the Chinese, who helped Narapati restore order in Upper Burma.

Burmese-Chinese War of 1658–61   The last Ming claimant to China's peacock throne, Prince Yung Li (Zhu Youlong) (1623–62), fled from the southern Chinese province of Yunnan after his forces suffered defeat at the hands of the Manchus (Ch'ing dynasty) in 1658. Burma's King Pindalè (d. 1661) gave the prince asylum in Sagaing on the Irrawaddy River, opposite the capital, Ava, in Upper Burma. Both Ming and Manchu armies invaded and occupied Burmese territory, where they battled each other and Pindalè's forces. The Chinese soldiers attacked Ava to overthrow Pindalè, who was treacherously murdered and replaced by his younger brother, Pyè Min (d. 1672). The Manchu governor of Yunnan demanded that the Burmese hand over Yung Li or suffer destruction; confronted by a 20,000-man Chinese army, Pyè Min complied with the demand. See also SIAMESE-BURMESE WAR OF 1660–62; THAI WAR OF 1660–62.

Burmese-Chinese War of 1765–69   Alarmed over the policy of aggrandizement pursued by Burma's King Hsinbyushin (d. 1776), whose forces had made forays into Chinese territory, China's Emperor Ch'ien Lung (Qianlong) (1711–99) launched an enormous military invasion of Burma, seizing most of the country's eastern part. Undaunted by defeat, the Burmese waged an incessant and vigorous guerrilla war and avoided direct battles with the larger Chinese armies. From their strategically located jungle forts, Hsinbyushin's forces, led by able generals, attacked the Chinese lines of communication and split the enemy into isolated groups. Unable to pin down the elusive Burmese in the jungles and suffering from heavy casualties, disease, and starvation, the Chinese sued for peace (they had invaded Burma four times, without real success, by 1769). The Burmese, realizing the enemy could eventually, through sheer numbers, defeat them, accepted terms, and the Chinese withdrew, leaving behind about 20,000 dead, their melted-down cannons, and their burned riverboats. See also BURMESE-MANIPURI WAR OF 1770; SIAMESE-BURMESE WAR OF 1764–69.

Burmese Civil War of 1368–1408   (Ava–Pegu Forty Years' War) In the 14th century, Burma was divided into a number of rival kingdoms, chief of which were Ava in Upper Burma and Pegu in Lower Burma. These two states, while waging war against each other, fought Toungoo (a state on the Ava-Pegu frontier), the neighboring Shan people, and the Arakan kingdom on the west coast. In 1368, in Ava, government ministers opposed the seizure of power by the newly widowed queen of King Thadominbaya (1343–68) and her soldier-bride-groom and supported instead Minkiswasawki (1331–1401), who soon evicted the usurpers. As Ava's king, Minkiswasawki settled the border war with Pegu in 1371. Later, when Razadarit (d. 1423) became Pegu's king in 1385, his uncle offered Pegu as a vassal state to Ava in return for Razadarit's overthrow. War broke out in Lower Burma; Shans in the north made raids into Ava, and Burmese from Prome (Pye) made a guerrilla-style attack on the Mons (natives of Pegu). In 1391, Razadarit and his forces ousted the Burmese from the fort of Myaung-mya in the Irrawaddy delta area; he then unsuccessfully sought an armistice with Ava. After Minkiswasawki's death in 1401, a succession dispute broke out, during which Razadarit launched several attacks to the north and sailed up the Irrawaddy River in 1406. Despite suffering some defeats en route, his flotilla reached and settled outside the town walls of Sagaing, across from Upper Burma's capital of Ava. Razadarit withdrew after negotiations, but his daughter's seizure at Prome to the south caused him to besiege that town. Ava's new king, Minhkaung (d. 1422), came to Prome's aid, seizing three forts of Nawin and massacring its inhabitants. Afterward some 300 Mon war canoes sailed up the Irrawaddy and laid waste towns. With his soldiers facing starvation, Minhkaung succeeded in making peace; the Ava-Pegu border was established below Prome, and prisoners were exchanged.

Burmese Civil War of 1408–17   Peace was short-lived between the Burmese kingdom of Ava in Upper Burma and the Mon kingdom of Pegu in Lower Burma (see BURMESE CIVIL WAR OF 1368–1408). Pegu's King Razadarit (d. 1423), who had successfully invaded the Arakan kingdom on Burma's western coast and placed a puppet on the throne (1406), persuaded northern Shan chiefs to distract Ava's King Minhkaung (d. 1422), who threatened to invade Pegu and Arakan. While Minhkaung was involved fighting in a northern Shan state, the Mons moved against the Ava-held town of Prome (Pye), thus necessitating Minhkaung's return south. In 1410, Burmese forces under Minhkaung's son, Crown Prince Minrekyawswa (d. 1416), invaded Arakan, ousted Razadarit's puppet ruler, but suffered defeat in the Irrawaddy River delta area. The Mons again assaulted Prome in 1412; two of Ava's armies, one coming by river and one by land, were victorious against the Mons until invading Shan troops from the north reached present-day Maymyo and forced a redeployment of Burmese forces (under Minrekyawswa) to meet this threat; the Shans were defeated and withdrew. In 1414–15, Minrekyawswa again invaded Pegu, drove Razadarit far south to Martaban, and threatened to destroy the Mon kingdom; another Shan attack in the north forced Minhkaung to recall his son from Pegu. Minrekyawswa renewed his invasion of Pegu the next year; in pursuit of Razadarit, he was accidentally crippled by an elephant, was captured, and chose execution rather than surrender. With his death the war wound down. Ava's forces helped the kingdom of Toungoo (between Ava and Pegu) repulse a Mon attack in 1416. Razadarit received Arakanese aid in repulsing Minhkaung's final attempt to conquer Pegu in 1417. Ava's forces retreated to confront new Shan incursions.

Burmese Civil War of 1426–40   After the death of Minhkaung (d. 1422), his son Hsinbyushin Thihatu (d. 1426) succeeded him as king of Ava in Upper Burma and inherited the periodic belligerency of the neighboring Shan people. While on a punitive campaign against the Shans, Hsinbyushin was betrayed by his Shan wife and murdered. Unrest increased in Upper Burma; the Shans began to dominate as Ava's power under king Mohnyinthado (d. 1440) lessened. To the south, the Burmese kingdom of Toungoo under the Shan Soalu (d. 1437) became semiautonomous, along with Taungdwingyi, Yamethin, and Pinlaung; the Shans helped these areas defend themselves against Ava. Toungoo allied itself with the Mon kingdom of Pegu in Lower Burma to assault Prome (Pye), a vassal state of Ava. When Soalu died in 1437, Pegu's king installed his son as ruler of Toungoo. By 1440, the Shans wielded power in Upper Burma, alongside Ava. See also BURMESE-CHINESE WAR OF 1438–46.

Burmese Civil War of 1527   In the early 16th century, the Shan state of Mohnyin (northeastern Burma) threw off its Chinese tributary status and stepped up its raids into the Burmese kingdom of Ava. In 1507, Ava tried appeasement to make peace with the Shans, who continued their attacks. Ava failed to gain support from the Burmese kingdom of Toungoo to the south. By 1524, invading Shans had seized Ava's border garrisons and control of the upper Irrawaddy River, on the left bank of which, at the Myitinge confluence, lay the capital city of Ava. There, in 1527, the Shans of Mohnyin waged a great battle, killing Ava's king and capturing and sacking the city. Most of Ava's citizens fled to Toungoo. The Shans installed Prince Thohanbwa (d. 1543) as king, and a terrible period of devastation ensued in the Burmese kingdom, with Buddhist temples looted, monks immolated, and libraries destroyed. The Shans held the city until 1555.

Burmese Civil War of 1535–46   King Tabinshwehti (1512–50) of Toungoo (northeastern Lower Burma) began a series of military campaigns in an attempt to unite the various kingdoms in Burma. He moved north into the Kyaukse granary area near where Burmese fleeing from invading Mohnyin Shans joined his troops to hold the invaders at bay. After consolidating his power in the upper Sittang Valley, Tabinshwehti launched an invasion of the Mon kingdom of Pegu in Lower Burma (1535), easily capturing Bassein and Myaungmya in the Irrawaddy delta area. The capital city of Pegu fell to him in 1539, causing the Mon king to take refuge in Prome (Pye). Tabinshwehti advanced on Prome but retreated upon the arrival of Shan soldiers from

Ava. With the help of Portuguese mercenaries, he seized the towns of Martaban and Moulmein and the coastal area south to Tavoy (1541). When Prome fell after a five-month siege (1542), Tabinshwehti had control of Lower Burma, and most of the Mon princes became his vassals. He repulsed a Shan-led assault on Prome in 1544 and extended his power up the Irrawaddy Valley to Pagan, where he was crowned "king of all Burma" in 1546. Pegu was made his capital. With an army, in 1547, Tabinshwehti attempted to conquer the Arakan kingdom on Burma's western coast; but while his men besieged its capital of Myohaung, Siamese forces moved against Tavoy, thus causing him to end the siege and march eastward to Siam (see SIAMESE-BURMESE WAR OF 1548).

Burmese Civil War of 1551–59   After the assassination of Burma's King Tabinshwehti (1512–50), the country broke up into various Mon- and Burmese-controlled areas. Smim Htaw (d. 1551), a Mon rebel leader, seized control of Pegu, overthrowing the Mon prince who had declared himself king. Tabinshwehti's brother-in-law, Bayinnaung (1515–81), set about trying to reunite the country. With the help of Portuguese mercenaries, he defeated a pretender to the throne at Toungoo, where he proclaimed himself king (1551). Moving south, Bayinnaung triumphed over Smim Htaw in battle outside Pegu (the Mon leader was soon executed). To subdue the fractious Shans in Upper Burma, Bayinnaung launched a large-scale invasion to the north, capturing the Shan-held former Burmese capital of Ava (March 1555). His forces moved through the Shan states, taking Hsipaw and other towns (1556) while en route southward into the Thai kingdom of Chiengmai, which surrendered without a fight. After the Burmese departed, Laotian ruler Setthathirat (1534–71) returned to Chiengmai to regain the throne, which his father had secured and passed to him. Bayinnaung's return prevented him from gaining control. Allying with the Shans, Setthathirat achieved a victory but eventually was forced to pull back; his alliance fell apart in 1559. See also BURMESE-LAOTIAN WAR OF 1564–65; SIAMESE-BURMESE WAR OF 1548.

Burmese Civil War of 1599

Burma's ruling Toungoo dynasty, under King Nanda Bayin (d. 1599), became weakened by the ongoing SIAMESE-BURMESE WAR OF 1593–1600, as well as by attacks from the Arakan kingdom (on present-day Burma's western coast). In 1599, Nanda Bayin's brothers—the governors of Ava, Prome (Pye), and Toungoo—joined in revolt against the central government at Pegu, the Burmese capital. Toungoo's governor paid for Arakan's help, and the Arakanese king sent troops and a fleet that captured the port of Syriam, south of Pegu. Nanda Bayin was captured when Pegu fell to the besiegers and taken in chains to Toungoo, where he was killed. Pegu was burned to the ground, its riches taken, and its people dispersed. Arakan awarded control of Syriam to Portuguese mercenary Felipe de Brito y Nicote (d. 1614). Invading Siamese forces, after occupying Pegu, pushed north to attack Toungoo but suffered a grave defeat by the Burmese and withdrew; Burma now split into a number of petty states. See also SIAMESE-BURMESE WAR OF 1607–18.

Burmese Civil War of 1740–52

While the Burmese rulers of the Toungoo dynasty were occupied fighting Manipuri invaders in Upper Burma (see BURMESE-MANIPURI WAR OF 1714–49), the Mon or Talaing people of Lower Burma seized control of Syriam and Martaban in a bloody uprising against Toungoo rule. Proclaiming their freedom, the Mons established an independent kingdom, with a Mon ex-monk as king at Pegu (their former capital). They moved northward in 1743, seizing Prome (Pye) and Toungoo (original home of the ruling dynasty); the opposing Burmese retaliated by capturing Syriam (1743), but the Mons soon retook the town and sought French help to defend it and Pegu (in 1751 Sieur de Bruno [d. 1756] arrived in Pegu in hope of gaining control of Lower Burma for France). In a systematic conquest of Upper Burma, initiated by King Binnya Dala (d. 1774), the Mons besieged the walls of Ava, the Burmese capital under the Toungoos, captured the city (1752), and utterly destroyed the dynasty.

Burmese Civil War of 1753–57

With the fall of Ava in Upper Burma to the Mons or Talaings (see BURMESE CIVIL WAR OF 1740–52), an underground resistance to Mon rule began under the leadership of village chieftain Alaungpaya (1714–60), who refused to pledge fealty to Mon king Binnya Dala (d. 1774). From his capital at Moksobomyo (Shwebo), Alaungpaya openly threatened the Mons, who abandoned Ava (1753) and later failed to retake control of the city (March 1754). Pursuing the Mons southward into Lower Burma, Alaungpaya's forces liberated Prome (Pye), repulsed a Mon attempt to recapture it (1755), and then captured Rangoon (May 1755). In 1756, the Mon port of Syriam was razed by Alaungpaya's invading Burmese, who seized and executed French officers, including their leader Sieur de Bruno (d. 1756), whose warships had given support to the Mons. The Mon capital at Pegu was captured and destroyed (1757); Binnya Dala was taken prisoner and held until Alaungpaya's son, Hsinbyushin (d. 1776), put him to death in 1774. Burma became unified under King Alaungpaya and his Konbaung dynasty.

Burmese Guerrilla War of 1948–

After the Union of Burma (Myanmar), an independent republic, was set up in early 1948, the Karens, Kachins, Shans, and other ethnic, minority groups began antigovernment revolts in an effort to achieve autonomous states. In south-central Burma, communists rebelled and helped the Karen guerrillas, who captured Mandalay and besieged the government in Rangoon, now known as Yangon. An independent Karen state was proclaimed at Toungoo (1949), causing government forces to attack and seize the city (1950). Although the main communist center at Prome (Pye) was also seized, separatist and communist rebels continued fighting. Meanwhile, Chinese Nationalist troops fleeing from the communist takeover in China (see CHINESE CIVIL WAR OF 1945–49) moved into eastern

Burma, where they resisted the Burmese government's attempts to remove them until, at the urging of the United Nations, they evacuated to Formosa (Taiwan) in 1953–54. By then Burmese troops under the able General U Ne Win (1911–) had regained control of most parts of the country. When the communists threatened to topple the unstable government, U Ne Win seized power but soon returned control to the civilians. Continuing rebel activity compelled him again to depose the civilian government four years later (1962) and establish a military dictatorship. Guerrilla activity persisted, and anti-communist riots occurred. U Ne Win was elected president in 1974 and reelected in 1978. Bloody clashes between the pro-Chinese Burmese Communist party (BCP) and government forces disrupted the country, helping foment trouble with the separatist groups, especially the Karens. In 1981, General U San Yu (1919–96) became president after U Ne Win relinquished the post; he held Burma together despite strong opposition from rebel factions. Widespread pro-democracy demonstrations and anti-government riots erupted in mid-1988, forcing U Ne Win to resign as chairman of the ruling party in July and allowing a military junta under General Saw Maung (1929–) to seize power in September. In 1989 the military rulers changed the country's name to the Union of Myanmar to reflect the diverse ethnic groups throughout, not just the majority Burmese. That same year Saw Maung's troops crushed large demonstrations and arrested many rebel leaders, notably Karens and Rohingyas (Muslims). For the first time in 30 years free multiparty parliamentary elections were held in May 1990, and the main opposition party, the National League for Democracy (NLD), won a decisive victory, despite its leaders being in jail or under house arrest. The military government, however, refused to relinquish control or hold new elections (there had been 93 opposition parties). Criticized for many human rights abuses, Saw Maung resigned in April 1992 suffering from a nervous disorder; General Than Shwe (1933–), army commander, succeeded him, ordered the release of some political prisoners, and enacted some reforms. Later, in 1996,

Than Shwe's military junta, the State Law and Order Restoration Council (SLORC), severely cracked down on all opponents, especially the NLD, which sought to write a new constitution for a new civilian government. Over 250 NLD members were arrested. In 1995, SLORC laid waste to the Karen rebel base in Manerplaw, home to other ethnic opposition organizations as well. The Mong Tai army now remained the sole major rebel group in the country. NLD leader Daw Aung San Suu Kyi (1945–), who had been awarded the 1991 Nobel Peace Prize and been under house arrest from 1989 to 1995, carried on her pro-democracy activities against Myanmar's military rulers, who continued to persecute groups in 1997, 1998, and 1999.

Burmese-Laotian War of 1558   The Laotian-held Thai kingdom of Chiengmai (northwestern Thailand) had sent agents to stir up and assist rebellions among the Shan tribesmen in Upper Burma. Burma's King Bayinnaung (1515–81), of the Toungoo dynasty, retaliated by invading and seizing the Chiengmai kingdom in April 1556. The Laotians under their competent leader Setthathirat (1534–71) came to the aid of their neighbors, the Chiengmai, but were unable to defeat the invading Burmese forces, which took care not to sack Chiengmai's capital and installed a puppet ruler. Later the Burmese army of occupation left Chiengmai, which came under Laotian rule again.

Burmese-Laotian War of 1564–65   Setthathirat (1534–71), ruler of the Laotian kingdom of Lan Xang and formerly controller of the neighboring Thai state of Chiengmai, became involved in the war between King Mahachakrabarti (d. 1569) of Ayutthaya or Siam (Thailand) and King Bayinnaung (1515–81) of the Toungoo dynasty of Burma (see SIAMESE-BURMESE WAR OF 1563–69). Burmese forces, marching eastward, overran and occupied Chiengmai and invaded Laotian territory, where they besieged the capital, Vientiane—the Laotian royal court at Muong Swa (Luang Prabang or Louangphrabang) had recently been moved there.

Continual strong Laotian guerrilla resistance forced the Burmese invaders to withdraw from the area in 1565. See also BURMESE CIVIL WAR OF 1551–59.

Burmese-Laotian War of 1571–75   After the death of the Laotian ruler Setthathirat (d. 1571), who frequently tried to help the Ayutthayans or Siamese in their wars against the Burmese and drive the Burmese out of the Shan states in Upper Burma, the Burmese once again invaded the Laotian kingdom of Lan Xang and later seized the capital of Viantiane in 1574 (in earlier Burmese-Laotian conflicts, Setthathirat's able military leadership had thwarted the invaders, who were eventually driven out). By 1575, Burma's King Bayinnaung (1515–81), who had been trying to conquer Laos for about 20 years, had gained complete control and placed a Laotian prince whom he had held hostage for 10 years on the Laotian throne. The Burmese ravaged the country, which fell into a chaotic state. See also SIAMESE-BURMESE WAR OF 1563–69.

Burmese-Laotian War of 1581–92   Laotians began a concerted effort to throw off the Burmese yoke after the death of Burma's King Bayinnaung (1515–81), who had held Laos as a kind of vassal state since 1575. Guerrillas battled the Burmese sporadically while Burma became involved in another war with Siam (see SIAMESE-BURMESE WAR OF 1584–92). In 1592, Laos secured its independence, but it soon lapsed into an anarchic state until Souligna-Vongsa (d. 1694) was crowned king in 1637, restored order, and made treaties with neighboring Siam and Vietnam, establishing borders.

Burmese-Manipuri War of 1714–49   Raja or Prince Gharib Newaz (fl. 18th cent.) of Manipur (state in northeastern India) sent his warriors, mostly on horseback, southeastward to raid and pillage neighboring Upper Burma, which was in a period of weak rule. The Manipuri (Meithei), who claimed their intention was to convert the Burmese (Buddhists) to Hinduism, took captive several thousand Burmese, using trickery. Repeated attacks and

lootings devastated Upper Burma; by 1737, the Manipuri had slaughtered two-thirds of the enemy's royal army, advancing several times to the Burmese capital of Ava (most victoriously in 1738). Inept Burmese military leadership gave victory to the smaller Manipuri army for many years. By 1749, however, the Burmese had regained enough military strength to overcome the invaders, and the Manipuri raja ceased waging war and gave the Burmese his 12-year-old daughter as a tribute of peace. See also BURMESE CIVIL WAR OF 1740–52.

Burmese-Manipuri War of 1755–58   The able Burmese military leader Alaungpaya (1714–60) sought to avenge the devastation done by the Manipuri (Meithei) raids into Upper Burma, especially against the Burmese capital of Ava in 1738. His forces invaded Manipur (state in northeastern India, bordering Burma) and set up garrisons there (1755). Local Manipuri villagers and warriors subsequently revolted against the Burmese soldiers, causing Alaungpaya to send a punitive expedition to the area. Many Manipuri villages were destroyed, thousands of inhabitants were taken prisoner, and many were forcibly resettled in Burma. Alaungpaya recruited the superb Manipuri horsemen for his own cavalry. See also BURMESE CIVIL WAR OF 1753–57.

Burmese-Manipuri War of 1764   In 1763, Hsinbyushin (d. 1776) became the third king of the ruling Konbaung dynasty of Burma, following his elder brother and father, Alaungpaya (1714–60), the dynasty's founder. Pursuing a policy of territorial expansion, he launched an invasion westward into the Hindu state of Manipur, much of which his army seized by December 1764. Many Manipuri (Meithei) prisoners of war were carried off to be slaves in Hsinbyushin's Burmese capital, Ava, and elsewhere. Hsinbyushin plotted to gain suzerainty over all of Manipur, believing that with the country under the Burmese yoke he would be in a good strategic position to attack British India. See also BURMESE-CHINESE WAR OF 1765–69.

Burmese-Manipuri War of 1770   Burmese general Maha Thihathura (fl. 1770s) had accepted peace terms with the Chinese and allowed them to return home at the end of the BURMESE-CHINESE WAR OF 1765–69. However, he was afraid to face his headstrong king, Hsinbyushin (d. 1776), who might easily order his execution for leniency with the enemy. To distract the king from further campaigns against the Chinese and Siamese (see SIAMESE-BURMESE WAR OF 1764–69), Maha Thihathura decided to invade Manipur (northeastern India) and put down a minor revolt against Burmese rule. The Manipuri (Meithei), still recovering from the last war with the Burmese six years before, were defeated in a three-day battle ending when the raja (prince) of Manipur fled. The Burmese then put their own candidate on the throne. Despite this victory, Maha Thihathura was disgraced at home by Hsinbyushin because of his forbearance with the Chinese.

Burmese-Portuguese War of 1613   Felipe de Brito y Nicote (d. 1614), a leading Portuguese mercenary serving in Burma, began to transform the Portuguese fort at Syriam in Lower Burma into a base for a Portuguese colony (see BURMESE CIVIL WAR OF 1599). But his forced conversions to Christianity and looting of temples antagonized the Burmese under King Anaukpetlun (d. 1628). In 1610, de Brito seized and imprisoned Anaukpetlun's vassal Natshinnaung (d. 1614), ruler of Toungoo, to punish him for his duplicitous alliances with both de Brito and Anaukpetlun. In retaliation, Anaukpetlun's forces invaded Syriam, tunneled into the fort, and captured it, along with de Brito and Natshinnaung, both of whom were executed the following year (de Brito was impaled). Though Burmese-Portuguese relations were severely set back, Burma gained international recognition for its triumph. See also SIAMESE-BURMESE WAR OF 1607–18.

Burmese-Siamese Wars   See SIAMESE-BURMESE WARS.

Burundian Civil War of 1972   Hundreds of years ago the very tall Tutsi (Watusi or Tusi), a warlike cattle-raising people, conquered the medium-height Hutu (Bahutu), peasant farmers, in east-central Africa. The former became the traditional aristocratic ruling minority and held the latter in feudal subjugation. When the country of Burundi gained independence from Belgium in 1962, a Tutsi monarchy was established there. Later a struggle for power ensued among the elite Tutsi; in 1966, the mwami (king) was deposed by a military coup, and a republic was created with the Tutsi caste still in control. In 1970, the suppressed Hutu attempted unsuccessfully to seize power, massacring many Tutsi during an uprising; most Hutu leaders were executed in reprisal. After the government crushed an attempt by the ousted mwami to regain power in April 1972 (the mwami was killed), armed revolts erupted throughout Burundi, with the Hutu violently attacking the Tutsi. In retaliation, the government slaughtered more than 100,000 Hutu to suppress them; the victorious Tutsi, who suffered the loss of about 10,000 lives, had firm control of the country within several months. Renewed fighting occurred in 1973, and thousands of Hutu fled to neighboring Zaire (Congo), Rwanda, and Tanzania. See also RUANDAN CIVIL WAR OF 1959–61.

Burundian Civil War of 1993–   Against a historical background of decades-long ethnic hatred and major outbreaks of strife (see BURUNDIAN CIVIL WAR OF 1972), Burundi's Hutu and Tutsi tribal factions plunged into another bloody power struggle in October 1993. Four months earlier Burundi's Tutsi-led government, bowing to international pressure, had agreed to hold open presidential elections; predictably, Hutu citizens, who comprise 85 percent of Burundi's population, voted Hutu banker Melchior Ndadaye (1953–93) into office, making him the first democratically elected president since the country gained independence from Belgium in 1962. Fearful of Hutu domination, Tutsi members of the Tutsi-dominated army assassinated Ndadaye, setting off a cycle of revenge killings that resulted in 50,000 deaths over the next several months, mostly among both Hutu and Tutsi civilians. The fighting created large numbers of refugees; over the next two years 250,000 Burundians, mostly Hutu, escaped to safety in neighboring Zaire (Congo) and Tanzania, countries also burdened by 2 million Rwandan Hutus who fled Rwanda after the genocide of Tutsi civilians in the spring of 1994 (see RWANDAN CIVIL WAR OF 1990–94). International pressure was applied once again, and in early 1994 Burundi formed a coalition government. In April 1994 Burundian president Cyprien Ntaryamira, a Hutu, was killed along with Rwandan president Juvénal Habyarimana in a plane shot down by Hutu extremists. In the summer of 1995 intense fighting broke out in the northwest between Hutu rebels infiltrating the area from the refugee camps in Zaire (see CONGOLESE [ZAIRIAN] CIVIL WAR OF 1996–97) and the still Tutsi led army. Later, on July 25, 1996, angered by the government's solicitation of foreign military intervention to help impose security for planned political discussions, the Burundian army staged a coup, surrounding government buildings in the capital city of Bujumbura and forcing the moderate Hutu president, Sylvestre Ntibantunganya (1956–   ), to seek safety in the U.S. ambassador's residence. The military leaders installed Pierre Buyoya (1949–   ), a Tutsi, as president. Turmoil from clashes between rebel Hutu and government Tutsi continued to disrupt Burundi in 1996–97. After government forces repulsed some 2,000 attacking Hutu rebels near Bujumbura in early 1998, the Organization of African Unity sponsored peace talks (June, July, October 1998), which brought no substantial progress. Rebel attacks led to more Burundian civilians fleeing the country.

Bushiri's Uprising (1888–90) Bushiri bin Salim (d. 1889) incited an uprising of coastal Arab slave traders against harsh German colonizers in German East Africa (now part of Tanzania). Hermann von Wissmann (1853–1905), a noted African explorer, was appointed German commissioner of East Africa in 1888 and ordered to put down the uprising. In early 1889, he arrived on the German East African coast with 600 Sudanese troops and proceeded to engage the rebel Arabs in skirmishes throughout the year. In December 1889, Wissmann's forces stormed and took Bagamoyo, a rebel stronghold, and Bushiri was captured and hung. While Wissmann was reestablishing order on land, the Germans, joined by the British, carried out a blockade of the coast, preventing the export of slaves and the import of weapons by the Arabs. By 1890, Wissmann had completely suppressed the rebels.

Byzantine-Avarian War of A.D. 595–602 The Avars, a Mongolian people who settled near the Volga River, invaded the Balkan peninsula held by the Byzantine Empire, causing Byzantine emperor Maurice (c. 539–602) to launch a campaign against them. An army led by Byzantine general Priscus defeated the Avars at the Battle of Viminacium south of the Danube River in 601. The Byzantines then drove the Avars back across the river but were prevented from pursuing them farther by the onset of winter. See also PHOCAS'S MUTINY.

Byzantine-Avarian War of A.D. 603–626 With the Byzantine army out of the field (see PHOCAS'S MUTINY), the Avars poured into Byzantine-ruled Macedonia, Thrace, and the Balkan peninsula. Byzantine emperor Phocas briefly halted the Avar invasion, paying a large tribute in 604. However, by 617 the Avars had reached the walls of Constantinople (Istanbul), and for the next three years they made raids on the city. The Byzantines, who were also occupied fighting the Persians in the east, checked the Avars and forced their retreat. However, in 626, an enormous Avar army, which included Slavs, Bulgars, and Germans, assaulted Constantinople. Persian naval ships aided the assault, which continued incessantly for 10 days (July 1–10, 626) by land and sea. Finally, the Avars, suffering lack of food, and the Persians, unable to land forces at Constantinople because of Byzantine naval strength, retreated from the field, giving victory to the Byzantines in one of history's greatest defenses.

Byzantine-Bulgarian Wars See BULGARIAN-BYZANTINE WARS.

Byzantine Civil War of 1094   Scythians, Seljuk Turks, and Normans tested the strength of the Byzantine Empire under its vigorous emperor Alexius I Comnenus (1048–1118) by mounting invasions, which were checked (see BYZANTINE-SELJUK TURK WAR OF 1064–81; NORMAN-BYZANTINE WARS). Alexius had to make concessions to powerful landed noblemen to keep the empire intact. In 1094, Constantine Diogenes (d. 1094?), a pretender to the throne, began a revolt with the help of the Cumans (Kumans), a nomadic Turkish people from Russia. Crossing the Danube River with a Cuman army, he marched south and besieged Adrianople (Edirne) in Thrace, but he suffered defeat by Alexius's forces at the Battle of Taurocomon. The emperor then strengthened both his imperial power and military forces to meet possible threats to the empire's unity. See also BYZANTINE-SELJUK TURK WAR OF 1110–17.

Byzantine Civil War of 1222–42   Two rival independent Greek states, Nicaea and Epirus, warred against each other and the Latin Empire of Constantinople in an attempt to restore the Byzantine Empire (see LATIN EMPIRE–BYZANTINE EMPIRE WAR, SECOND). John III (d. 1254), after successfully battling the two brothers of Theodore I Lascaris (c. 1175–1222) for the emperorship of Nicaea in 1222, defeated the Latin forces and became master of most of Asia Minor by 1225. When Theodore Ducas Angelus (fl. 1220–30), despot of Epirus, proclaimed himself Byzantine emperor that same year, John opposed him and dispatched forces that were later defeated at Adrianople (Edirne) in Thrace. In 1230, John's forces won against Theodore's and, with support from Bulgarians of Ivan II (d. 1241), besieged Constantinople (Istanbul) in 1235, but failed to take the city. After Ivan II died, John annexed territory in Bulgaria and again launched an attack on the despotate of Epirus, which was forced to accept domination by Nicaea in 1212. See also BYZANTINE WAR OF 1207–11.

Byzantine Civil War of 1259   Michael VIII Palaeologus (1225–82), regent for the rightful heir to the Nicaean throne, John IV Lascaris (1250?–1300?), proclaimed himself emperor in 1259. He then sent troops to defend the city of Thessalonica, captured by the Nicaeans in 1246 and now besieged by forces from Epirus. An attempt to negotiate a settlement failed, and at the Battle of Pelagonia in 1259, the Nicaeans defeated the Epireans, backed by Sicilian and French forces. This victory enabled Michael to capture Constantinople (Istanbul) and to reestablish the Byzantine Empire (see LATIN EMPIRE–BYZANTINE EMPIRE WAR, THIRD).

Byzantine Civil War of 1321–28   Byzantine emperor Andronicus II Palaeologus (1260–1332) denied the throne to his grandson Andronicus III Palaeologus (1296–1341), a rebellious youth who accidentally caused the death of his brother. In 1321, the younger Andronicus, supported by powerful Byzantine nobles who were angered by high taxes, led an uprising, assembled an army, and successfully battled the emperor's forces. In 1325, the elder Andronicus recognized him as co-emperor and ruler of the provinces of Thrace and Macedonia. The younger continued to oppose his grandfather, weakening the power of the Byzantine Empire in its war against invading Ottoman Turks (see BYZANTINE–OTTOMAN TURK WAR OF 1329–38). In 1328, Andronicus III forced his grandfather to abdicate and became sole emperor.

Byzantine Civil War of 1341–47   Byzantine chief minister John Cantacuzene (1292–1383) was named regent for Emperor John V Palaeologus (1332–91), who was too young to rule when his father Andronicus III Palaeologus (1296–1341) died. Cantacuzene attempted to claim the throne by declaring himself Emperor John VI on October 26, 1341. He allied himself with some Turks, as well as Serbs, who had also secretly agreed to help defend the Byzantine court of John V in Constantinople (Istanbul). Many Byzantines opposed John VI's takeover; an independent state was established at Thessalonica. Forces of John VI, with Turkish aid, seized Constantinople in 1347, and John ruled as emperor until 1355 (see BYZANTINE CIVIL WAR OF 1352–55). See also BYZANTINE–OTTOMAN TURK WAR OF 1359–99.

Byzantine Civil War of 1352–55   Byzantine emperor John VI Cantacuzene (1292–1383), who had seized the throne in 1341 (see BYZANTINE CIVIL WAR OF 1341–47), attempted to establish a well-knit empire and gave Cantacuzene family members rule over Byzantine territories. While John VI began to battle Turkish invasions into Thrace and Macedonia (see BYZANTINE–OTTOMAN TURK WAR OF 1359–99), John V Palaeologus (1332–91), ousted as emperor at Constantinople (Istanbul), gathered forces to overthrow John VI, whose troops encountered John V's at Adrianople (Edirne) in Thrace in 1352. Helped by some Turks, John VI's troops checked John V, who waged guerrilla warfare until 1354. Supporters of John V then stormed Constantinople and successfully drove John VI from the throne. John V, now sole emperor, retook by force in 1355 the territories ruled by Cantacuzene kinsmen.

Byzantine-Muslim War of A.D. 633–42   Muslim Arabs, in the name of Allah, began a war of conquest against the Byzantine Empire in 633. Led by Khalid ibn al-Walid (d. 642), the Muslims won victories against the Byzantine armies of Emperor Heraclius (575–641) in what is now Israel and western Jordan in 634 and 635. Khalid then took Damascus in southern Syria in 635. His Muslim army defeated the Byzantines at the Battle of the Yarmuk in 636, thus forcing the Byzantines to give up all of Syria. Jerusalem fell to the Muslims that same year, and Mesopotamia in 639. Khalid died in 642, and a new Muslim commander, Amr ibn el-Ass (d. 664), forced the now-retreating Byzantines to give up Alexandria in Egypt, which came fully under Muslim domination. See also MUSLIM CONQUEST OF PERSIA.

Byzantine-Muslim War of A.D. 645–56   Byzantine emperor Constans II (630–68) attempted to recapture the city of Alexandria from the Muslims (see BYZANTINE-MUSLIM WAR OF A.D. 633–42). The Byzantines, taking advantage of the dismissal by Caliph Uthman ibn Affan (d. 656) of Amr ibn el-Ass (d. 664) as Muslim governor of Alexandria, began to besiege the city and were at first quite successful. However, Amr was reinstated and roused the Muslims to defeat the Byzantines after a 14-month siege. The Muslims now made incursions into the Byzantine Empire to take more territory, seizing Cyprus and Byzantine Armenia in 653. Their goal was the capture of Constantinople (Istanbul), capital of the Byzantine Empire. With that in mind, Mu'awiyah (602?–80), the governor of Syria, developed the Muslims' first naval fleet. In a great naval battle off the coast of Lycia in 655, the Muslims defeated a Byzantine fleet under the command of Constans. Mu'awiyah suspended his advance on Constantinople, securing a truce with the Byzantines in order to return home to dispute the ascension of Ali ibn Abi Talib (600?–661) to the caliphate (see MUSLIM CIVIL WAR OF A.D. 657–61).

Byzantine-Muslim War of A.D. 668–79   Caliph Mu'awiyah (602?–80) began a new invasion of the Byzantine Empire (see BYZANTINE-MUSLIM WAR OF A.D. 645–56). His Muslim army seized the city of Chalcedon on the Bosporus Strait, opposite Constantinople (Istanbul), in 668. The next year the Muslims crossed the strait to attack Constantinople but were repulsed by the Byzantines, who used "Greek fire"—a flammable combination of quicklime, naphtha, sulfur, and sea water—to stop the invaders during assaults on the city walls. Later, the Byzantines destroyed the Arab army at the Battle of Amorium. An Arab naval fleet was defeated at the Battle of Cyzicus in the Sea of Marmara in 672; again the Byzantines used Greek fire to win victory. The Muslims, temporarily demoralized, returned to set up a blockade of Constantinople, which they besieged recurrently from 673 to 677. Greek fire held them at bay. When the Byzantines destroyed the Muslim fleet off Syllaeum in southern Asia Minor in 679, Mu'awiyah ended the war by suing for peace and agreeing to pay annual tributes of money, men, and horses to the Byzantines.

Byzantine-Muslim War of A.D. **698–718**   After the Muslims halted their invasion of the Byzantine Empire (see BYZANTINE-MUSLIM WAR OF A.D. 668–79), both they and the Byzantines engaged in constant minor warfare, making raids on each other's cities and territories. Full-scale war broke out in 698, when the Arabs assaulted and entirely destroyed the Byzantine-held city of Carthage in North Africa. When the Byzantines were driven from Utica, northwest of Carthage, by the Arabs in 699 (Utica was totally destroyed), they were virtually eliminated from North Africa. Because of ineffective leadership, the Byzantines were unable to halt invading Muslims in parts of the empire. Cilicia, in southeastern Asia Minor, was overrun by Arabs, who then invaded Pontus to the north. A succession of Byzantine army mutinies resulted in the overthrow of three emperors between 713 and 717, when Leo the Isaurian (680?–741), the chief Byzantine general, seized the throne as Leo III. By then, a large Muslim army was approaching the Byzantine capital (see ANASTASIUS II, REVOLT OF; CONSTANTINOPLE, SIEGE OF).

Byzantine-Muslim War of A.D. **739**   The Muslims under Caliph Hisham ibn Abd al-Malik (691–743), seeking to expand the caliphate (caliph's dominion), invaded the Byzantine Empire in the late 730s. They confronted the Byzantines of Emperor Leo III (680?–741) at the Battle of Akroinon or Acroinum in ancient Phrygia in Asia Minor in 739. The Byzantines repulsed the Muslims, forcing them to fall back toward Damascus, Syria, and temporarily secured Asia Minor from threat of Arab conquest.

Byzantine-Muslim War of A.D. **741–52**   Almost immediately after becoming Byzantine emperor, Constantine V (718–75) began a military campaign to regain lands lost to Muslim invaders of the empire. Taking advantage of internal strife among the Muslims in 741, he led forces into Syria, where he reconquered some border areas before being forced to return home to crush an army and religious revolt

(see ICONOCLASTIC WAR, SECOND). Afterward he reinvaded Syria, taking more land. Constantine's fleet defeated an Arab fleet near Cyprus, from which the Muslims were driven out in 746. By 752, Constantine had reclaimed Armenia after defeating the Muslims in several engagements there. See also MUSLIM CIVIL WAR OF A.D. 743–47.

Byzantine-Muslim War of A.D. **778–83**   The Muslims, conducting yearly raids into the Byzantine Empire, invaded Anatolia (what is now most of Turkey) in force in 778 but were decisively repulsed at the Battle of Germanicopolis. The Byzantine army of Emperor Leo IV (749–80) killed thousands of Muslims during and after the battle. To retaliate, Muslim caliph Muhammad al-Mahdi (742–86) assembled a large army of Mesopotamians, Syrians, and Khorasanians and led it northward in 780. Leo IV died, and because his successor, Constantine VI (771–97?), was only nine years old, his mother, Irene (752–803), became regent and ordered Byzantine forces to stop and annihilate the Muslims. The caliph's son, Harun al-Rashid (766–809), leading many charges against the Byzantines, won notable victories, allowing the Arabs to advance westward. In 783, the Muslims reached the Bosporus, near which they defeated the Byzantines at Nicomedia (Izmit or Kocaeli). Irene then sued for peace and accepted a three-year truce, agreeing to pay tribute.

Byzantine-Muslim War of A.D. **797–98**   After Harun al-Rashid (766–809) became Muslim caliph in 786, he ordered the rebuilding and fortification of Tarsus, a Byzantine city destroyed by the Arabs about 600, and established a fort at Hadath in preparation for an invasion of the Byzantine Empire. In 797, al-Rashid's forces advanced to the Byzantine cities of Ephesus and Ancyra (Ankara). Byzantine empress Irene (752–803) was forced to reinstate the payment of tributes agreed to by the truce that ended the BYZANTINE-MUSLIM WAR OF A.D. 778–83. (Irene did so because she had deliberately kept the Byzantine imperial forces weak to forestall a possible army mutiny against her; thus her forces were no match for the caliph's larger, more powerful army.)

Byzantine-Muslim War of A.D. 803–9   Byzantine emperor Nicephorus I (d. 811) broke the truce with the Muslims bought by Empress Irene (752–803) in 798 (see BYZANTINE-MUSLIM WAR OF A.D. 797–98). Nicephorus, certain of victory against the Muslims, had written an extremely insulting letter to Muslim caliph Harun al-Rashid (766–809), who replied by leading an invading army across the Taurus Mountains of Anatolia in 803 and seizing the Byzantine city of Heraclea Cybistra (Eregli). Nicephorus sued for peace, but almost immediately after agreeing to terms broke the truce. Al-Rashid invaded again, plundering and burning many cities in Anatolia as he advanced northward. Again Nicephorus sued for peace, and again broke it. The Muslims won victories on land and at sea, capturing Tyana and Ancyra (Ankara) in 806 and ravaging Rhodes and Cyprus between 805 and 807. A counteroffensive by Nicephorus forced the Muslims to relinquish captured Byzantine territory. In 809, a truce was arranged, which the emperor kept; by then, al-Rashid had set out personally to put down the KHORASAN REBELLION OF A.D. 806–9.

Byzantine-Muslim War of A.D. 830–41   Muslims, led by Caliph al-Ma'mun (785–833), made annual raids against the Byzantines in 830, 831, and 832. Although Byzantine emperor Theophilus (d. 842) sued for peace, al-Ma'mun obstinately refused to come to terms and continued his raids. While leading a Muslim expedition to take Amorium, a main Byzantine fortress, and Constantinople (Istanbul), al-Ma'mun died after capturing the town of Tyana. An indeterminate truce was then made, but it was broken in 837, when Theophilus gave aid to the Khurramite rebel Babak al-Khorrami (d. 838), who was trying to stamp out the religion of Islam (see KHURRAMITES' REVOLT). Theophilus led Byzantines as far as the Euphrates River in northeastern Syria, where he sacked the towns of Samosata and Zibatra. Abu Ishak al-Mu'tasim, who succeeded al-Ma'mun

as caliph, sought revenge and led the largest Muslim army ever assembled under one caliph—composed of Turkish slaves and guards and Arab warriors—into Anatolia (most of present-day Turkey) and defeated Theophilus's army at the Battle of Dazimon on the Halys River in July 838. The Muslims then besieged and captured Ancyra (Ankara) and Amorium. Al-Mu'tasim's plan to take Constantinople fell apart when his Arab fleet was destroyed in a storm while on its way there in 839. Theophilus's forces managed to push the Muslim invaders back to the frontier, and in 841 the emperor and al-Mu'tasim agreed to a truce.

Byzantine-Muslim War of A.D. 851–63   Constant Muslim raids into the Byzantine Empire led to a new Byzantine offensive in 851. A Byzantine amphibious force landed in Egypt and sacked the city of Damietta (Dumyat) in 853. In Anatolia (what is now most of Turkey), Byzantines advanced eastward to crush Muslim forces and take 10,000 prisoners in Amida (Diyarbakir). Muslims, aided by the Paulicans, a persecuted Christian heretical sect, defeated the Byzantines under Emperor Michael III (836–67) on the Euphrates River in northern Syria in 860. The war then became a series of skirmishes, resulting in a treaty and the exchange of prisoners. In 863, a large Muslim army under Abbasid general Omar (d. 863) invaded Anatolia, sacked the Black Sea port of Amisus (Samsun), and plundered the regions of Paphlagonia and Galatia. The Byzantines marched against this army, which had fallen back toward the Anti-Taurus Mountains, and destroyed it; Omar was slain in battle. Muslim and Arab expansion was temporarily halted in 863.

Byzantine-Muslim War of A.D. 871–85   Taking advantage of turmoil within the caliphate (see MUSLIM CIVIL WAR OF A.D. 861–70), Byzantine emperor Basil I (813?–86) decided to extend his eastern frontier. Byzantine forces marched to the upper Euphrates River at Samosata (Samsat), where they soundly defeated the Muslims in 873. Basil then launched an expedition to drive Muslim invaders from Sicily and southern Italy, where Bari was besieged and captured in 875 (land forces of the Holy Roman Emperor Louis II [d. 875] aided sea forces of Basil to defeat the Muslims there). Basil failed to drive the Muslims out of Sicily but succeeded in Italy at Tarentum (Taranto) in 880 and in Calabria in 885. Tarentum was made a refuge for Christians driven out of Sicily by the Muslims.

Byzantine-Muslim War of A.D. 960–76   Byzantine emperor Nicephorus II (d. 969) began a counteroffensive to stop invading Hamdanids, a Muslim sect in northern Syria, in eastern Anatolia. Byzantine forces seized the province of Cilicia, captured Adana and Tarsus in 965, advanced into Syria and northern Mesopotamia, and occupied Antioch and Aleppo by 969. The caliphate sued for peace, but John Tzimisces (925–76), who assassinated Nicephorus in 969 to become co-emperor, continued the Byzantine drive deep into Syria, taking Damascus in 974. At Jerusalem, in 976, the Fatimids checked the Byzantines, who stopped fighting when Tzimisces died later that year. See also MUSLIM CIVIL WAR OF A.D. 976–77.

Byzantine-Muslim War of A.D. 995–99   When the Hamdanids in Byzantine Syria were attacked by invading Fatimids of Egypt, they appealed to Byzantine emperor Basil II (958?–1025) for help. After aiding the Hamdanids in winning in 995, the Byzantines sacked the Arab city of Hims (formerly Emesa) in Syria to reassert their power over the Hamdanids, who were thought to be planning an invasion of the Byzantine Empire. Basil led Byzantine troops in a sweep through northern Syria in 999, forcing the Fatimids to fall back. Basil then negotiated a 10-year truce with them.

Byzantine-Muslim Wars of 1030–35   Dalmatian Muslim pirates, whom Venetian naval forces had defeated and whose strongholds of Curzola (Korcula) and Lagosta (Lastovo) had been seized in the late 10th century, continued to make depredations on commerce in the Adriatic Sea, causing Ragusa

(Dubrovnik, Yugoslavia) to join the Byzantine Empire (at the time co-ruled by Empress Zoë [980–1050] and her husband Emperor Romanus III Argyrus [968?–1034]) to wage a series of naval wars against these predators. In 1032, a combined Byzantine-Ragusan fleet crushed the pirates in the Adriatic; afterward, Byzantine warships, largely manned by mercenary Vikings, roamed the Mediterranean, triumphing over many Muslim pirates and laying waste to parts of North Africa's Muslim coast.

Byzantine-Norman Wars   See NORMAN-BYZANTINE WARS.

Byzantine-Ottoman Turk War of 1302–26   The Ottoman Turks of western Asia were pushed southward by Mongol hordes and moved into the territory of the Byzantine Empire. Led by Osman I (1258–1326), the Ottomans defeated the Byzantines near the city of Nicomedia near the Bosporus Strait in 1302. The Byzantines employed Spanish mercenaries, the Catalans, to fight the invading Turks (see CATALAN COMPANY, RAIDS BY THE). After the Catalans turned against them, the Byzantines found themselves under constant siege by the Ottomans, who set up a chain of fortified posts and encircled several of the empire's cities, including Bursa and Nicomedia. Bursa, besieged by the Ottomans for nine years, fell to the Turks in 1326, when the inhabitants were starving to death. Bursa was then made the capital of the Ottoman Empire. (When Adrianople [Edirne] fell in 1413, it replaced Bursa as the Ottoman capital.)

Byzantine–Ottoman Turk War of 1329–38   The Ottoman Turks under Orkhan (1279–1359), son and successor of Osman I (1258–1326), wisely settled on the Gallipoli peninsula (between the Aegean Sea and the Dardanelles) in the 1320s and then launched invasions into the Byzantine territories of Thrace and Macedonia. After the BYZANTINE CIVIL WAR OF 1321–28, the empire under Andronicus III Palaeologus (1296–1341) fell into dire financial and military straits and was unable to defeat the

Turkish invaders, who seized Nicaea in 1331 and Nicomedia in 1337. By 1338, the Ottomans had conquered western Asia Minor, and the emperor had reluctantly accepted Orkhan's terms of truce, needing the Turks as an ally against the Serbs and their expansionist leader Stephen Dushan (1308?–55).

Byzantine–Ottoman Turk War of 1359–99   After John V Palaeologus (1332–91) took the Byzantine throne from John VI Cantacuzene (1292–1383) in 1354, he unsuccessfully sought military aid from neighboring principalities to defend the empire against the invading Ottoman Turks. By 1359, Constantinople (Istanbul) was surrounded by the Turks, who had taken most of the Byzantine territories. Byzantine forces held the Turks at bay, and John V personally went to Rome in 1369 to beg for help. Meanwhile, the Turks continued their offensive, defeating the Serbs (who had invaded the empire to seize part of it) and afterward taking control of Macedonia in 1371. A Christian army of Serbs, Bulgars, Bosnians, Albanians, and others was decisively defeated by the Ottomans at the Battle of Kosovo in 1389. The Byzantine Empire had nearly crumbled. Now the Turks besieged Constantinople until 1399, when they were compelled by mercenaries to withdraw.

Byzantine–Ottoman Turk War of 1422   Byzantine emperor John VIII Palaeologus (1391–1448), hoping to cause disruption within the ranks and leadership of the Ottoman Empire, encouraged a Turkish pretender to take the rule from the ascending sultan, Murad II (1403–51). Murad crushed the plot in 1421 and then revoked all the privileges the Turks had accorded the Byzantines after the BYZANTINE–OTTOMAN TURK WAR OF 1359–99. The Ottomans assaulted Constantinople (Istanbul) in 1422 but, because of the strength of the city's walls and its defenders, were forced to retire. The siege might also have been called off by Murad, who had to return to the Ottoman capital to prevent another pretender, possibly Byzantine-encouraged, from seizing power.

Byzantine–Ottoman Turk War of 1453–61   After losing Constantinople (Istanbul) (see CONSTANTINOPLE, FALL OF) to the Ottoman Turks, the Byzantines attempted to hold on to the last territorial vestiges of the empire. The Turks, however, had no trouble taking the remaining Greek, Latin, and Slavic holdings in the Balkans and Anatolia (most of present-day Turkey) into their Ottoman Empire (Belgrade successfully withstood Turkish capture in 1456). In Greece the Turks captured Athens and the principality of Morea (Peloponnesus) in 1456. The last Greek successor state of the Byzantine Empire, Trebizond on the Black Sea, fell to the Turks when its emperor, David Comnenus (d. 1462?), was forced to surrender to Ottoman sultan Muhammad II "the Conqueror" (1429–81) in 1461.

Byzantine-Persian War of A.D. 603–28   A perpetual enemy to the Byzantine (Eastern Roman) Empire, Persia attacked the empire's borders in 603 and in 605 took Caesarea, an ancient port in Palestine. Emperor Heraclius (c. 575–641) forced Persia out of Caesarea in 611 and by 613 had besieged Antioch. Constant defeats then cost the Byzantines dearly. In 613 alone, Syria, Tarsus, and Armenia were lost; Jerusalem was sacked and its treasures stolen. The Persians reached the Bosporus in 615; in 619, Egypt was lost. Heraclius finally drove the Persians out of Armenia in 622, freed Asia Minor of their influence, and invaded Persia itself. In 626, his forces routed a Slav fleet and a Slav-Persian army besieging Constantinople (Istanbul). An alliance with the Khazar Turks kept the Persians busy in the Caucasus later that year while Heraclius reentered Persia. By 628, the Byzantines had regained all territory taken by Persia and regained the True Cross taken earlier from Jerusalem. See also JUSTINIAN'S WARS; ROMAN-PERSIAN WAR OF A.D. 502–6; ROMAN-PERSIAN WAR OF A.D. 572–91.

Byzantine Revolts of A.D. 976–89   The authority of Byzantine emperor Basil II (958?–1025) was challenged by a powerful general, Bardas Sclerus, who was the brother-in-law of former emperor John

Tzimisces (925–76). Proclaimed emperor by his army and the Melitene Arabs, Sclerus seized much territory in Asia Minor and Byzantine Syria. Basil's troops, led by Bardas Phocus (d. 989), defeated Sclerus's forces in battle in March 979, and Sclerus fled to the caliph of Baghdad, a friend. Later Sclerus collaborated with Phocus, who had turned against Basil, in a plot to seize the emperorship at Constantinople (Istanbul) in 988. Basil won victory over Phocus at the Battle of Abydos in Phrygia the following year. When Phocus died soon afterward, the revolt collapsed. See also BYZANTINE-MUSLIM WAR OF A.D. 960–76.

Byzantine-Russian War of A.D. 970–72 Although allied to the Byzantines, the Kievan Russians twice made disruptive shows of force (against Byzantine-held Bithynia in 911 and in the Danube Valley in 943) and were to do so again in 969 (see RUSSIAN-BULGARIAN WAR OF A.D. 969–72). The Russians, who had been called upon by the Byzantines to subdue the rebellious Bulgars, won several battles and then remained in Bulgaria because their Kievan prince, Sviatoslav (d. 972), wanted a western frontier. Threatened by Russian advances, the Byzantines under Emperor John Tzimisces (925–76) moved against the Russians and Bulgarians in 971, capturing Sviatoslav's puppet czar at Preslav after winning a great battle there. Tzimisces's forces then laid siege to Silistria on the Danube and gained Sviatoslav's surrender. The Russians abandoned their conquest of Bulgaria, which then fell to the Byzantines, losing its semi-independent status.

Byzantine–Seljuk Turk War of 1048–49 A powerful band of Seljuk Turks from western Asia invaded the eastern provinces of the Byzantine Empire, where they defeated the Armenians at Kars, fortress-city in Armenia. Byzantine forces, sent by Emperor Constantine IX Monomachus (c. 1000–1055), fought several battles against the Seljuks, who had settled in the region west of Lake Van (in eastern Turkey). The Seljuks were finally repulsed and forced to withdraw from the area in 1049.

Byzantine–Seljuk Turk War of 1064–81 Independent, rival Turkish groups invaded the Byzantine Empire for many years but were unable to secure much territory. Finally, one dominant Turkish group, the Seljuks, led by Alp Arslan (1029–72), captured Ani in eastern Anatolia (most of present-day Turkey) and ravaged Armenia in 1064. When the Seljuks invaded deep into Anatolia during the next three years, Byzantine emperor Romanus IV Diogenes (d. 1072) launched a counteroffensive and forced the Seljuks to retreat from Heraclea to Aleppo. However, the Seljuks again invaded the Byzantine Empire in 1070 and defeated the Byzantines at Sebastia. At the Armenian village of Manzikert, in August 1071, the Seljuks under Alp Arslan completely crushed the 50,000-man Byzantine army; Romanus was captured. Afterward the Seljuks overran much of Anatolia and killed many people. To fight the Turks, the Byzantines now recruited European mercenaries in large numbers to fill army ranks and, despite constant internal dissension, checked the Seljuk advance. Alexius I Comnenus (1048–1118), crowned Byzantine emperor in 1080, made peace with the Seljuks in 1081, giving them the territory they had captured. See also CRUSADE, FIRST.

Byzantine–Seljuk Turk War of 1110–17 The powerful Seljuk Turks again invaded the Byzantine Empire, raiding into Anatolia (most of present-day Turkey) as far as the Bosporus. However, because of internal dissension among Turkish leaders following the death of Seljuk leader Kilij Arslan I (d. 1108), the Seljuks became disunited, suffered defeat, and were forced to retreat back across Anatolia. The Byzantine army of Emperor Alexius I Comnenus (1048–1118) continued to wage war and routed the Turks at the Battle of Philomelion (Akshehr) in 1116. By 1117, the Turks had accepted a truce, with the Byzantines reclaiming all the coastal areas of Anatolia. The Seljuks established a sultanate, called Rum, in eastern Anatolia.

Byzantine–Seljuk Turk War of 1158–76 Byzantine emperor Manuel I Comnenus (1120?–80), fearing the Seljuk Turks would incorporate Anatolia (most of present-day Turkey) into their domain, complied with a request from Seljuk Turk leader Kilij Arslan II (d. 1192) for military aid. Kilij needed the aid to fight rival Turkish groups, and Manuel thought that if the Turks continued internal warring, they would weaken each other and he would have to fight only one enervated Turkish force in Anatolia at the end. Kilij, however, used the aid to every advantage, slaying his enemies and expanding his territory. To expel the Seljuks from Anatolia, Manuel organized a large Byzantine army, which encountered the Turks at Myriocephalum in September 1176. The Byzantines were losing the battle when Manuel sued for peace. Anatolia was lost to the Seljuks, marking the beginning of the collapse of the Byzantine Empire.

Byzantine-Sicilian Wars   See SICILIAN-BYZANTINE WARS.

Byzantine War of 1207–11   After the crusaders sacked Constantinople (Istanbul) in 1204 (see CRUSADE, FOURTH) and established the Latin Empire of Constantinople, the remainder of the Byzantine Empire split into three rival independent states or empires: Trebizond on the Black Sea, Epirus in western Greece, and Nicaea in Asia Minor. The exiled Byzantine emperor Alexius III Angelus (d. 1211) accepted the Seljuk Turks' offer of asylum. Seljuk Turks, urged by Alexius, invaded Nicaea in 1208 to force its ruler, Theodore I Lascaris (c. 1175–1222), to abdicate (Theodore had assumed the title emperor). The Seljuks were repulsed by Theodore's forces, which also successfully defended Nicaea against invasions by the emperors of Trebizond and crusaders. The constant tensions of Nicaea, Trebizond, and Epirus, each claiming the emperorship and individually fighting the Seljuk Turks, came to a head in 1211, when the Seljuks, accompanied by Alexius, who now wanted the crown of Nicaea, invaded Theodore's empire. Again the Seljuks were defeated; Alexius was captured by Theodore and sent to a monastery in Nicaea, where he soon died. See also BYZANTINE CIVIL WAR OF 1222–42.

Cabochien Revolt (1413)   A Parisian skinner called Simon Caboche (fl. 1407–18), whose real name was Simon Le Coustellier, led about 500 discontented French tradespeople (including members of the butchers' and skinners' guilds) in revolt against government corruption and extravagance. In April 1413, the so-called Cabochiens (Cabochians), who backed John "the Fearless" (1371–1419), duke of Burgundy, in the ARMAGNAC-BURGUNDIAN CIVIL WAR, violently stormed and seized the Bastille, the royal fortress-prison in Paris. France's King Charles VI (1368–1422) was forced to issue the *ordonnance cabochienne* (1413), which stipulated radical reforms. But continued Cabochien rioting antagonized the Parisian middle class, allowing Charles (1391–1465), duke of Orléans, the duke of Burgundy's rival, to suppress the Cabochiens and force the repeal of their ordinance. Hope for reform ended with this feudal reaction, helping England's quest for power. See also AGINCOURT, BATTLE OF; HUNDRED YEARS' WAR.

Cade's Rebellion (1450)   This revolt occurred near the end of the HUNDRED YEARS' WAR, revealing the effect of the conflict on England's populace. John or Jack Cade (d. 1450), who assumed the name John Mortimer and proclaimed himself a cousin of Richard (1411–60), duke of York, led a well-organized rebellion of small property owners, demanding lower taxes and prices, the dismissal of some minis-

ters of King Henry VI (1421–71), the end of royal corruption, and the recall of Richard, Henry's rival, who was in exile. Cade's army, whose men came mainly from Kent and Sussex, defeated a royalist army at Sevenoaks on June 18, 1450, then briefly occupied London, and there executed the loathed lord treasurer, thought responsible for all war losses in France. The rebels pillaged and burned until Londoners forced them from the city on July 6, 1450. A government pardon dispersed most of the rebels, but Cade continued his fight and was captured after being mortally wounded. The rebellion did help to break down royal authority and allowed Richard to return to England from Ireland, his home in exile. See also ROSES, WARS OF THE.

Caesar's War in Pontus (47 B.C.)   After the death of his father, Mithridates VI "the Great" (c. 132–63) (see MITHRIDATIC WARS), Pharnaces II (fl. 63–47) was confirmed as ruler of the Bosporus Cimmerius (Crimean region) by Pompey the Great (106–48), the Roman commander in the east. When the Pompeian supporters were fighting against Julius Caesar (100–44) in the Great ROMAN CIVIL WAR, Pharnaces seized the chance to re-create his father's kingdom of Pontus and enlarged his domains in Asia Minor through conquests. Leaving Egypt securely in Cleopatra's (69–30) hands, Caesar marched with his army north through Syria into Asia Minor. At the Battle of Zela in Pontus in May 47, his superior army easily defeated Pharnaces and his army. Caesar promptly dispatched to Rome his famous message: "Veni, vidi, vici" ("I came, I saw, I conquered"). The Pontic territory was divided among minor kings, and its mountain strongholds were demolished.

Cambodian Civil War of 1970–75 Cambodia (Kampuchea) became involved in the VIETNAM WAR when its ruler, Prince Norodom Sihanouk (1922–), tolerated communist infiltration and agitation at home and permitted North Vietnam to supply its forces in South Vietnam via the Port of Sihanoukville and the Ho Chi Minh Trail through Cambodia and to establish base areas there. When Sihanouk closed the port in 1970, North Vietnamese troops began to aid the Cambodian Communist Party (Khmer Rouge) in the fight against Sihanouk. However, while Sihanouk was abroad in March 1970, his government was overthrown in a pro-Western coup led by General Lon Nol (1913–), who demanded the withdrawal of North Vietnamese and Viet Cong troops from Cambodia (which was renamed the Khmer Republic, ending the old monarchy); Sihanouk set up a government-in-exile based in Peking. South Vietnamese and American troops, in support of Lon Nol, made incursions into Cambodian territory against enemy sanctuaries; U.S. bombing raids were increased. Lon Nol, who assumed Cambodia's presidency in 1972, could not check the steady advance of North Vietnamese and Khmer Rouge forces, which gradually took control of rural areas. Phnom Penh, the Cambodian capital, was shelled and besieged frequently between 1972 and 1975 (notably in March–April 1973). Despite U.S. airlifts of material to Phnom Penh, the city fell to the Khmer Rouge on April 16, 1975; the government of Lon Nol (who had fled by air) capitulated. Under a new constitution, Cambodia was renamed Democratic Kampuchea. Most of Phnom Penh's inhabitants were evacuated by the ruling Khmer Rouge; and in a terror campaign that, in percentage terms, exceeded the Holocaust, about 1 million persons died because of long forced marches to work in rural areas, starvation, and executions by the communists. See also KAMPUCHEAN CIVIL WAR OF 1978–98.

Cambodian Civil War of 1978–98 See KAMPUCHEAN CIVIL WAR OF 1978–98.

Cambodian Rebellion of 1811–12 King Ang Chan II (1791–1835) acknowledged both Siamese (Thai) and Vietnamese suzerainty over his country, Cambodia, hoping to keep peace by paying tribute to Siam and Vietnam. Ang Chan's brother sought Siamese aid in an attempt to usurp the throne (1811); King Rama II (1768–1824) of Siam sent an army, which helped to oust Ang Chan, who fled to southern Vietnam to secure aid to regain the throne. Vietnam's Emperor Gia Long (1762–1820) sent a large force whose intimidating presence in Cambodia caused the Siamese to withdraw without fighting. Ang Chan was enthroned again. See also SIAMESE-CAMBODIAN WAR OF 1831–34.

Cambodian-Siamese Wars See SIAMESE-CAMBODIAN WARS.

Cambrai, War of the League of See LEAGUE OF CAMBRAI, WAR OF THE.

Cameroonian Revolt of 1984 On April 6, 1984, dissident members of the presidential palace guard violently sought to seize political power in Yaoundé, the capital of Cameroon, in western central Africa on the Gulf of Guinea. The revolt was apparently ignited by an order by Cameroon's President Paul Biya (1933–), a southern Christian, to transfer all palace guards who came from the predominantly Muslim north. Armed forces loyal to Biya won victory over the rebels after several days of heavy fighting, in which at least 500 were killed. Over 1,000 dissident "regionalists and separatists" were arrested; 35 of them were immediately sentenced to death and executed. Soon after, the government declared a six-month-long state of emergency in Yaoundé and the surrounding region. Biya consolidated his political power and continually won re-election into the late 1990s.

Camisards' Rebellion (1702–10) In addition to ambitions revealed in the War of the SPANISH SUCCESSION, France's King Louis XIV (1638–1715) is negatively remembered for cruelties benefiting the Counter-Reformation. To force the French to practice Roman Catholic traditions, he revoked (1685) the 1598 Edict of Nantes granting civil liberties and political powers to Protestants. Reaction was strong but nonviolent until persecutions caused peasants of the Cévennes and Languedoc regions in southern France to kill a hated persecutor in 1702. Thereafter, French Protestants, called Camisards because of the white shirts (*camisas*) they wore to promote recognition during night raids, sacked and burned churches, expelling and sometimes murdering inimical priests. Their leaders were Jean Cavalier (1681?–1740) and Roland Laporte (1675–1704). Reprisals were extremely harsh; exterminations and the burning of entire villages were common. Laporte was killed in 1704; Cavalier, duped by concessions and promises from the royalist general and marshal of France, Claude Villars (1653–1734), capitulated (1704). Leaderless, the Camisards fought on sporadically through 1710; outlasting Louis, the persecutions continued until 1750.

Camp Grant Massacre (1871) About 150 white men and Papago Indians, who hated the Apache, stealthily crept into Camp Grant in southern Arizona territory on the night of April 30, 1871. They mercilessly slaughtered 108 men, women, and children of the Arivaipa Apache tribe, who had been striving for peace with the white settlers. Of those slain, only eight were men; most of the warriors were away hunting. The killers took 29 children hostage and later sold them in Mexico as slaves. Authorities arrested the leaders of the massacre, but they were soon acquitted. The slayings influenced the policy, developed by U.S. president Ulysses S. Grant (1822–85), of confining the Apache to Indian reservations, where "civilization" could be instilled in them. The massacre caused the start of the APACHE WAR OF 1871–73.

Canadian Rebellions of 1837 See MACKENZIE'S REBELLION; PAPINEAU'S REBELLION.

Candian War (1645–69) Ottoman sultan Ibrahim I (1615–48) began a campaign to conquer the Venetian colony of Candia (the island of Crete and its main city, Iráklion, both of which were called Candia by the Venetians). The Turks quickly gained a foothold on the island and began attempts to take the city of Candia (Iráklion) in 1648. Venetian ships meanwhile blockaded the Dardanelles, causing famine and revolt in Constantinople (Istanbul), and continually kept Candia supplied, permitting the Venetians, who, in later years, were under the inspired leadership of Francesco Morosini (1618–94), to hold the city for 22 years against the Turkish besiegers. Finally, Candia fell to the Turks under Muhammad IV (1641–91) in 1669 (Morosini surrendered after French forces, which had been aiding the Venetians, withdrew). A peace treaty left most of Crete in Turkish hands, and the Venetians relinquished control of many islands and outposts in the Aegean Sea and Dalmatian regions and now had little effective power in the eastern Mediterranean after being a ruling force there for about 500 years.

Cape Frontier Wars See KAFFIR WARS.

Carchemish, Battle of (605 B.C.) After the Second Battle of MEGIDDO, Egyptians in Palestine attempted to prevent the Babylonians from crossing their newly acquired territory of Syria into Palestine. Egyptian king Necho II (fl. c. 609–593) first fought against Babylonian king Nabopolasar (fl. 625–605) and then his son and successor Nebuchadnezzar II (d. 562), who led armies to victory in Syria. The Babylonians, who had divided the Assyrian Empire with the Medes in 609 (see ASSYRIAN WARS OF c. 746–609 B.C.), soon advanced to take over Palestine; Necho's Egyptian forces met them at Carchemish on the Euphrates River. The fighting was fierce, and Egyptian losses were heavy. The Babylonians pursued the fleeing, beaten Egyptians and caught them at Hamath near the Sea of

Galilee, where they fought them as fiercely as at Carchemish. By 604, the remaining Egyptians had been driven out of Palestine, and, though Egypt and Babylonia warred briefly in 601, the Asian possessions of Egypt had been lost.

Carlist War, First (1834–39) On the death of King Ferdinand VII (1784–1833) of Spain, his brother Don Carlos (1788–1855) and his conservative followers (the Carlists) opposed the succession to the throne of Queen Isabella II (1830–1904), Ferdinand's young daughter and designated heiress, who had been declared queen with military and government support under the regency of her mother, Maria Cristina (1806–78). The Carlists believed that Don Carlos was rightful heir based on the Salic Law prohibiting women from succeeding to the throne. The clergy and much of northern Spain (the Basques, Catalonia, Aragon, and Navarre) approved the reactionary Apostolic Party's declaration of Don Carlos as King Charles V of Spain, the first Carlist pretender. The Spanish government under Maria Cristina, who was supported by the liberals, formed the Quadruple Alliance with Portugal, France, and Britain and thus secured foreign aid against the Carlists, who were now engaged in revolution to overthrow the constitutional government and Cristina's followers (the Cristinos). General Tomás Zumalacárregui (1788–1835) led the Carlist forces to several victories in the north until 1835, when he was wounded in the leg at the unsuccessful siege of Bilbao and died of incompetent medical treatment. Afterward, the Cristinos and government forces under General Baldomero Espartero (1792–1879) were victorious, assisted by the so-called "Spanish Legion" from Britain and the French Foreign Legion, which distinguished itself in winning the Battles of Terapegui (1836) and Huesca (1837). Don Carlos was forced to withdraw from Madrid in 1837. On August 31, 1839, the Carlist commander in chief, Maroto (1785–1847), without instructions from Don Carlos, signed the Convention of Vergara, by which he and his forces joined the Cristinos in return for amnesty and freedom for the Basque and Navarre provinces. Don Carlos and some loyal followers thereupon fled to Bourges, France, leaving Carlist forces under "Father" Ramón Cabrera (1806–77) still fighting in Catalonia until they were routed by Espartero in July 1840. **Second Carlist War** (1873–76). After Queen Isabella was deposed (see SPANISH REVOLUTION OF 1868), the Cortes (national assembly) finally elected Duke Amadeus (1845–90) of Aosta, of the house of Savoy, as Spanish king in 1870. However, strong opposition from defeated candidates for the throne and from the populace and attempts on his life forced Amadeus to abdicate in 1873, at the same time as the radical-controlled Cortes proclaimed Spain's first republic. Immediately, the Carlists, who believed in the traditional monarchy, rose in revolt in support of Don Carlos III (1848–1909), grandson of the first Don Carlos and the third Carlist pretender to the throne. In the north, the Basques helped them seize much territory. In the south, towns established communes; the army fractionized as generals joined the Carlists, who took Alcoy, Seville, Cádiz, and Valencia, while other cities capitulated without battle. The city of Cartagena endured a four-month siege before surrendering. In January 1874, the republic collapsed and was replaced by a military dictatorship under General Francisco Serrano y Domínguez (1810–85), who dispatched troops to lift the Carlist siege of Bilbao. Spain was in chaos, wracked by a civil war of extreme savagery on both sides. Despite Carlist victories at Estella and Cuenca, the Spanish Bourbon monarchy was restored when military leaders placed Isabella's son, Alfonso XII (1857–85), on the throne as a constitutional king in late 1874. The next year Alfonso's forces were able to suppress the Carlists in Catalonia and Aragon, and they entered the Basque stronghold of Pamplona in February 1876, after a long siege. Don Carlos gave up the struggle and fled to France; some 10,000 Carlists were banished. The Basque provinces were forced to relinquish their unique tax and military systems. In July 1876, the newly elected Cortes ratified a new constitution. See also SPANISH CIVIL WAR OF 1840–43.

Carnatic War, First (1744–48) The War of the AUSTRIAN SUCCESSION reached India, where the French East India Company battled against the British East India Company for control of the Carnatic region in the south. Allied French and Indian forces led by Joseph-François Dupleix (1696–1763), French colonial governor in India, captured the city of Madras in 1746 and checked British efforts to help Indian allies in the Carnatic. Fighting ceased with the Treaty of Aix-la-Chapelle in Europe in 1748; Madras was restored to Great Britain (in return, Louisbourg [Louisburg], Nova Scotia, seized by the British during KING GEORGE'S WAR, was given back to France). **Second Carnatic War** (1749–54). The French and British East India companies resumed warfare, supporting different Muslim leaders for nawab (viceroy) of the Carnatic region. By 1751, Dupleix had gained control of the region and nearly the entire Deccan (plateau area covering most of peninsular India). Allied British and Indian forces led by Robert Clive (1725–74) captured the fortified town of Arcot on September 12, 1751, then brilliantly withstood a 53-day French assault, and later broke a French-Indian siege at Trichinopoly (Tiruchirappali) in the southeastern Carnatic. When Dupleix was recalled to Paris in 1754, all hope for a French empire in India disappeared. See also SEVEN YEARS' WAR.

Carthaginian Civil War (241–237 B.C.)   The power of Carthage in the western Mediterranean continued to decline after the CARTHAGINIAN WAR AGAINST PYRRHUS OF EPIRUS, especially because of the First PUNIC WAR. In 241, after losing its fleet to the Romans near Aegates (Egadi) Islands, Carthage saw the Romans take all of Sicily. Although Carthage still had two Punic wars to endure, Rome added indignity to defeat by fining Carthage 3,200 talents (ancient monetary units of weight). Almost immediately, other Carthaginian dependencies suffered rebellions by mercenaries, especially in Sar-

dinia. Carthage tried to punish the rebels, but Rome intervened, defeated the Carthaginians, took control of Sardinia and Corsica, and added the punishment of leveling a fine of 1,200 talents. Carthage was severely wounded, but was to exist, ailing, until the end of the Third PUNIC WAR in 146.

Carthaginian-Syracusan War (481–480 B.C.)   By 500 B.C., Carthage, an ancient city-state in North Africa, had established control in southern Italy and in all western Mediterranean islands except Sicily. To fill this gap, Carthage mounted a massive invasion under an early Hamilcar Barca (d. 480), landing in Panormus (Palermo) in 481 and advancing to Himera, where a siege of the city was mounted. Syracuse, a Greek city-state on Sicily, responded by sending a large force under Gelon (d. 478), its tyrant, against Hamilcar and his father-in-law (allegedly an encourager of the invasion). The Syracusans crushed the Carthaginian force and caused Hamilcar's death. The defeat was avenged 70 years later during HANNIBAL'S DESTRUCTION OF HIMERA.

Carthaginian War against Pyrrhus of Epirus   (278–276 B.C.)   Carthage resumed hostilities in Sicily accidentally as the result of Greco-Roman economic rivalry. Tarentum (Taranto) in Apulia, a Spartan colony able to withstand the power of the Romans until 272, had invited Pyrrhus (319–272), king of Epirus, to aid it. The Romans had violated a treaty by sending ships into Tarentum's gulf, only to have them sunk by the city's fleet. Pyrrhus had earlier contributed to the Roman pain by defeating them at Heraclea in 280 and at Asculum (Ascoli) in 279—the latter victory achieved by using a novel cavalry of elephants. The Carthaginians, feeling endangered, offered naval and financial aid to Rome; and Pyrrhus, at the request of Greek colonists, came to Sicily and won all its territory from the Carthaginians except Lilybaeum (Marsala). The Carthaginians were once again the minority power in the western Mediterranean, a condition lasting only until the CARTHAGINIAN CIVIL WAR. See also ROMAN WAR AGAINST PYRRHUS OF EPIRUS.

Carthaginian Wars   See PUNIC WARS.

Castilian Civil War of 1065–72   After King Ferdinand I (d. 1065) of Castile and León died, his realm was divided among his offspring. His eldest son, Sancho II (c. 1038–72), became king of Castile and sought to unify Spain under his rule. After unsuccessfully waging the "War of the THREE SANCHOS" against his cousins, he turned against his own brothers, King Alfonso VI (1030–1109) of León and García (fl. 1065–73) of Galicia. In 1068, Alfonso suffered defeat at Llantada but managed to hold on to his kingdom. Sancho ousted García from Galicia in 1071 and defeated Alfonso at Golpejera in 1072. Captured, Alfonso was banished from León and lived for a brief time at the Moorish court in Toledo, Spain. Alfonso's sister soon incited a revolt in León, and Sancho invested her in the fortified city of Zamora. While assaulting the city's walls, Sancho was slain by a disloyal knight, causing his army to break up and depart. Alfonso then returned and took control of both Castile and León (1072). García hoped to regain Galicia, his rightful inheritance, but instead was imprisoned for life by Alfonso (1073), who, as ruler of Castile, León, and Galicia, was now probably the strongest Christian king in Spain. See also ALMORAVID CONQUEST OF MUSLIM SPAIN.

Castilian Civil War of 1214–18   When Castile's monarchs, King Alfonso VIII (1155–1214) and Queen Eleanor (d. 1214), both died in the same year, their son ascended the throne at the age of 11, becoming King Henry I (1203–17), with his sister Berengaria (Berenguela) (1171–1246) as his guardian. A faction of nobles schemed to take control of Henry and the throne, causing Berengaria to yield her brother to a Castilian count under specific terms. But the count ignored his agreement, and by his autocratic behavior, he brought Castile to the brink of revolt and ruination. However, when Henry was killed accidentally in 1217, Berengaria, as royal heiress, became queen for a few months. At the request of her subjects, she yielded her rights of succession to her son by King Alfonso IX (d. 1230) of León, who was unaware of these actions, and her son was declared King Ferdinand III (1199–1252) of Castile on August 31, 1217. Ferdinand then proceeded to subdue the towns supporting the monarchial Castilian count. When Alfonso learned what had happened, he invaded Castile with the intention of joining both kingdoms (León and Castile) under his rule. But, seeing he had little support when Castilian nobles flocked to Ferdinand's side, Alfonso withdrew and, in August 1218, reached an amicable agreement with his son, who retained the Castilian throne and later inherited León on his father's death.

Castilian Civil War of 1474–79   Princess Isabella (1451–1504) of Castile married (1469) Prince Ferdinand (1452–1516) of Aragon in violation of an agreement made with her half brother, King Henry IV (1425–74) of Castile and León, who was consequently provoked to name his alleged daughter Juana la Beltraneja (1462–1530) of Portugal as royal heiress. Upon Henry's death in 1474, and despite Juana's prior swearing-in as queen of Castile, an agreement between Isabella and Ferdinand and a noble-cleric group established the couple's joint sovereign rule of Castile and León. Many barons, however, supported Juana, and to strengthen her position, they obtained her marriage by proxy to her uncle, King Alfonso V (1432–81) of Portugal. In return, Alfonso dispatched Portuguese troops, which seized Zamora fortress in León in 1475. Castilian forces, however, proved to be superior, taking the defecting barons' lands and inducing rebellious towns to rejoin Castile. They recaptured Zamora, and Alfonso's Portuguese troops were decisively defeated by Ferdinand's army at the Battle of Toro in March 1476. The city of Madrid, which had backed Juana, now yielded to the rule of King Ferdinand V and Queen Isabella I. When Alfonso failed to gain French aid, the barons negotiated successfully the Peace of Trujillo on September 14,

1479, accepting the joint sovereigns. Alfonso gave up claim to the Castilian throne, annulled his marriage to Juana, and ceded Spanish holdings in Estremadura and the Canary Islands. Ferdinand and Isabella recognized Portuguese conquests in Africa. Juana chose retirement to a convent in Portugal over marriage to the sovereigns' one-year-old son.

Castro's Revolution   See CUBAN REVOLUTION OF 1956–59.

Catalan Company, Raids by the (1302–11) Byzantine emperor Andronicus II Palaeologus (1260–1332), who had reduced the empire's armed forces as an economy measure, hired the Catalan Company, about 6,500 Spanish mercenaries led by Roger de Flor (d. 1305), to fight invading Ottoman Turks under Osman I (1258–1326). The Catalans defeated the Turks at Philadelphia in western Asia Minor in 1304. However, claiming they were not paid properly by the emperor, the Catalans rebelled and attacked Constantinople, which they were unable to capture. After the murder of Flor by imperial order, they sought revenge by pillaging and murdering throughout Byzantine territories, especially in Thrace and Macedonia. A scourge for years, the mercenaries finally advanced into Greece, where they set up a duchy at Athens in 1311.

Catalan Revolt of 1461–72 Rioting broke out in Catalonia, a region in northeastern Spain, over a dynastic dispute. Upon the death of the favored claimant to rule, the Catalonians proclaimed a republic and laid siege to Gerona, home of King Ferdinand I (1423–94) of Naples, nominal ruler of Catalonia as well. In 1462, King Louis XI (1423–83) of France supported King John II (1397–1479) of Aragon, Navarre, and Sicily as ruler of Catalonia. In opposition to this, Catalonian revolutionaries called first Henry IV (1425–74) of Castile, then Portuguese Constable Pedro (d. 1466), and then Réné I (1409–80) of Anjou to their throne. Réné sent his son John (d. 1470) of Calabria to Barcelona, Catalonia's chief city, to govern. After John's death,

Catalonia was subdued and came under the rule of King John of Aragon. The region declined as a powerful, "independent" region after the union of Aragon and Castile in 1479.

Catalan Revolt of 1640–59 Constantly agitating for autonomy, the Catalans, inhabitants of Catalonia in northeast Spain, opposed the governmental policies of the Count of Olivares (1587–1645), chief minister of King Philip IV (1605–65), who sought to centralize and impose new taxes. During the THIRTY YEARS' WAR, Castilian troops and government officials were quartered in Catalonia and proved extremely onerous to the Catalans, who openly revolted in June 1640, in what became known as the "Corpus of Blood." Rebels poured into the city of Barcelona on a murderous rampage, killing many Castilian authorities and the Spanish viceroy. Meanwhile, France's chief minister, Cardinal Richelieu (1585–1642), dispatched soldiers to Roussillon and occupied this region bordering Catalonia in 1642. The Catalan rebels established an independent republic while awaiting the onslaught of government troops and requested French aid. Under pressure of being crushed by Spanish troops, the rebels dissolved their fledgling state and proclaimed France's King Louis XIII (1601–43) count of Barcelona. Then some 5,000 French soldiers crossed the Pyrenees and besieged the Spanish royal stronghold at Tarragona, Catalonia. Louis personally arrived with more forces, and the French gained an advantage for a time. But the fighting lasted without a decisive outcome until the Catalans, nominally under French rule for 16 years, decided to rejoin Spain. In 1659, a peace treaty was signed at St-Jean-de-Luz. Roussillon became a French possession.

Catalan Revolt of 1934 Catalans, inhabitants of Catalonia, were perturbed by the swing of Spain's central government to the right, by its overturning of an agrarian law passed by the Catalan Generalided (local assembly), and by the slow implementation of a statute of autonomy for Catalonia.

Leftists and communists led a general strike on October 5, 1934; the semi-fascist Catalan police, called *escamots*, brutally opposed the leftist strikers, creating turmoil in Catalonia. On October 6, 1934, Spain's President Niceto Alcalá Zamora y Torres (1877–1949) proclaimed martial law throughout Spain, and that night Luis Companys (1883–1940), president of the Generalidad, declared Catalonia a fully independent republic. Immediately government troops moved in, killed several rebels, and squashed the separatist movement; the Catalan government, including Companys, was jailed for revolting against Spain's legal authority; the proclamation for Catalan autonomy was voided; and Madrid (the central government) regained control of Catalonia. See ASTURIAN UPRISING OF 1934; SPANISH CIVIL WAR OF 1936–39.

Catherine the Great's First War with the Turks (1768–74) (Russo-Turkish War of 1768–74) Czarina Catherine II "the Great" (1729–96) of Russia intervened militarily in Poland's succession problems and failed to comply with the terms of the treaty ending the RUSSO-TURKISH WAR OF 1736–39. The ill-prepared Ottoman Empire declared war in 1768 when Russian forces, pursuing Poles into Turkish lands, sacked a Turkish town. Turkish forces, with Austrian support, lost battles against the invading Russians in Georgia, Kabardia, Crimea, and the Baltic; when the main Ottoman army was routed along the Dniester River, the Russians overran Moldavia and Wallachia in 1769. The Turks, aided by Albanians, were able to quell a Russian-incited and -supported revolt in Greece in 1770. Nonetheless, the entire Ottoman fleet was destroyed by the Russians at the Battle of Çeçme in the Aegean Sea on July 6, 1770, and a Turkish-Tatar army, attempting to recapture Moldavia, was devastated and forced to retreat in August 1770. Turkish fortresses along the Danube, Dniester, and Pruth rivers were captured. An invading Russian army conquered the Crimea (1771), while in Egypt and Syria revolts broke out against Turkish rule but were eventually put down in 1773. At the Conference of Bucharest (1773) Russia proposed peace terms,

which the Ottomans rejected, and the war continued with Russian forces under the victorious Count Petr Rumiantsev (1725–96) moving south along the Danube to engage the main Ottoman army. Other Russians assaulted Varna and Silistria, and the Turkish grand vizier entered into peace negotiations with Rumiantsev. In June 1774, the Turks lost much of their main army when Russians under Count Aleksandr Suvorov (1729–1800) won a battle near Shumla. On July 16, 1774, the Treaty of Kuchuk-Kainardji was signed by the Turks and Russians, who were now involved in PUGACHEV'S REVOLT. Moldavia and Wallachia were returned to Turkish suzerainty; Crimea became independent; and Russia received control of much of the northern Black Sea coast and the ambiguous right to intervene in Turkish affairs to protect Orthodox interests (this provision created the ongoing "Eastern Question," what happened to European lands under Turkish control). **Catherine the Great's Second War with the Turks** (1787–92) (Russo-Turkish War of 1787–92). Russia's annexation of the Crimea (1783) and desire to make Georgia a protectorate, plus the Turks' attempts to foment a Tatar revolt, led to a renewal of Catherine's war (it was rumored that she desired to absorb the Ottoman Empire). In 1788, Suvorov repelled a Turkish effort to seize the Crimea, and Rumiantsev invaded Moldavia. The Russian Black Sea fleet commanded by the American naval hero John Paul Jones (1747–92), in the Russian service as a rear admiral, won two naval battles near the mouth of the Dnieper River in June 1788. In Moldavia and along the Black Sea, the Russians massacred the captured Turkish inhabitants of Chocim (Khotin), Jassy (Iasi), and Ochakov (1788) and, supported by Austrians, defeated the Ottomans at the Battle of Focsani on the Moldavian-Wallachian border (1789). Austrians repulsed invading Turks in Serbia and took Belgrade. With the accession of Austria's anti-Russian emperor Leopold II (1747–92) came an Austrian-Turkish peace treaty at Sistova in 1791, and Belgrade was returned to the Ottomans. As Russia continued its successful push into Ottoman territory, the sultan made peace by the Treaty of Jassy on January 9, 1792. Russia returned Moldavia but retained Ochakov and all conquered lands east of the Dniester River, which became the Ottoman-Russian border.

Catiline, Revolt of (63–62 B.C.) Lucius Sergius Catiline (108?–62), a Roman politician, was eager to be elected consul in Rome, but he failed to be chosen the third time in 63. Bitter and resentful, he determined to seize the office by force. His agents secretly sent money to supporters in Etruria to raise an army, while in Rome he conspired with friends to burn the city and arm the slaves. Marcus Tullius Cicero (106–43), the consul, learned of the plot and publicly accused Catiline in famous orations before the Senate. Catiline fled. The conspirators who remained in Rome continued their agitations and were arrested. On December 3, 63, they were condemned to death and executed without a trial, although this was illegal. Catiline himself died in battle a month later. The episode reveals the unrest and discontent of many Romans against the oligarchic ruling class.

Cavite Mutiny (1872) On January 20, 1872, some 200 Filipino soldiers in the Spanish army in the Philippines mutinied in the fort of San Felipe in Cavite, a province south of Manila. The mutineers were quickly subdued and later severely punished. The reactionary Spanish governor of the Philippines, using the uprising as a pretext to crush the fledgling Filipino independence movement, had many intellectuals and others who had been urging governmental reforms arrested on false charges of involvement. Arrested, tried for and found guilty of treason, and publicly executed were three Catholic priests, whose unjust deaths made them martyrs for the cause of Philippine freedom from Spanish control.

Cayuse War (1848–55) After the Cayuse Indians killed 14 whites and held 53 others captive until ransomed (see WHITMAN MASSACRE), about 500 settlers took up arms and marched through Cayuse territory (southeast Washington and northeast Oregon),

demanding the surrender of the warriors responsible for the crimes. U.S. troops and militiamen from the Oregon Territory were called in to suppress the Cayuse, who refused to make peace and raided settlements. Five captured Cayuse were tried and convicted of murder by a military commission and hanged on June 3, 1850. Bloodshed in the area continued until 1855, when the Indians were defeated and placed on a reservation with the Umatilla Indians. The Cayuse were greatly reduced in number by the war, and much of their tribal land was taken.

Celtiberian Wars (154–133 B.C.) Invading Roman forces fought cruel, bloody, and prolonged wars against the Celtic tribes of the Iberian peninsula (Spain and Portugal). The tribes inhabiting the mountainous region of Celtiberia (north-central Spain) constructed and defended immense hill forts, foremost of which was Numantia (see NUMANTIAN WAR). The Lusitani, a federation of warlike Celtic peoples in what is now central Portugal and western Spain, successfully resisted Roman penetration until 151, when both the Lusitanians and Celtiberians were defeated. Taking advantage of Rome's preoccupation with the Third PUNIC WAR, the tribes revolted about 147 and inflicted serious damage on the Romans. Viriathus (d. 139) led the Lusitanians and held the field for eight years of war (see LUSITANIAN WAR). Many Celtiberians were defeated (144) by Quintus Caecilius Metellus (d. 115) and his Roman legions, but those at Numantia repulsed attacks until a Roman army captured and occupied the fort in 140. But not until seven years later did the Numantians completely capitulate.

Central American Federation Civil Wars (1826̄29, 1838–40) The Central American Federation, a loose political union formed (1823) by Guatemala, El Salvador, Nicaragua, Honduras, and Costa Rica, elected its first president, Manuel José Arce (1783?–1847), a liberal from El Salvador, in 1825. Dissension between Conservatives (advocates of centralism and the church) and Liberals (backers of federalism and reform) disrupted the federation's congress in Guatemala City, the capital; Arce, quarreling with his own party, assumed dictatorial powers when the congress refused to enact his laws. Salvadoran Liberals tried to topple Arce at Guatemala City, which came under Conservative control (Arce's forces defeated the Salvadorans to keep the federation intact, thus winning Conservative support for Arce). Later Arce's army besieged San Salvador, whose defenders were relieved when Francisco Morazán (1792–1842), a Liberal, led an army from his native Honduras and liberated the city (1829). Morazán's forces then routed a Conservative army at Guatemala City; he seized power (1829), became the federation's president (1830), and moved its capital to San Salvador. However, he failed to end the conflicts among political factions in the states, and the Conservatives increasingly opposed him. In 1838, the congress dissolved the federation, whose states had more and more feared the hegemony of one state over another. Morazán tried in vain to regain control of Guatemala, now held by the rebel army of Rafael Carrera (1814–65), a ruthless arch-Conservative; Morazán's army was totally crushed at Guatemala City in March 1840, and he went into exile. He later (1842) returned to lead forces from Costa Rica in an unsuccessful attempt to reestablish the Central American Federation. Carrera became dictator of Guatemala and helped set up Conservative governments in the other independent states.

Ceylonese Rebellion of 1971 In 1948, Ceylon (Sri Lanka) gained independence from Britain and dominion status in the British Commonwealth. Constant friction between the country's Buddhist Sinhalese majority and the Hindu Tamil minority, plus economic troubles and strife among political parties, led to the 1959 assassination of Ceylon's Sinhalese prime minister, S. W. R. D. Bandaranaike (1899–1959), of the Sri Lanka Freedom Party (SLFP). His widow, Sirimavo Bandaranaike (1916–), became the SLFP's leader and later (1960) prime minister, creating a strongly leftist, pro-Sinhalese government opposed by both ends of the political and nationalistic spectrums. Replaced in the 1965 Ceylonese elections by a moderate socialist and pro-Western ruler, she reassumed power in 1970 and formed a new coalition government of the SLFP and the marxist socialist parties. Opposition from the extreme left and the marxist People's Liberation Front (PLF), impatient with the government's slow social reform, resulted in an attempted takeover of Colombo, the capital, and other cities (April–May 1971). Ceylon's government received military aid from the Soviet Union, India, Pakistan, and Britain, helping it suppress the rebels first in the cities and by mid-June in the rural and jungle areas. In 1972, Mrs. Bandaranaike proclaimed a republic, a new constitution, and a new name for the country—Sri Lanka ("resplendent land" in the Sinhalese language). But the majority-minority problem remained unresolved. See also SRI LANKAN CIVIL WAR OF 1983– .

Chaco War (1932–35) Ownership of the Chaco Boreal or Gran Chaco, a wasteland of some 100,000 square miles west of the Paraguay River and north of the Río Pilcomayo, had been in dispute between Bolivia and Paraguay since about 1825. Bolivia, which had lost its seacoast to Chile (see PACIFIC, WAR OF THE), saw a shipping route for its oil through the Chaco to the Atlantic via the Paraguay and Paraná Rivers. As Bolivian soldiers and colonists pushed into the Chaco, which was thought to contain large oil deposits, armed clashes occurred between them and the Paraguayans already inhabiting the region. In 1928, forces of the two nations attacked one another; outright war was averted while a Pan-American conference attempted unsuccessfully to settle the dispute through arbitration. Skirmishes took place until Paraguay launched a major offensive in 1932 and later formally declared war on Bolivia on May 10, 1933. The larger and better-equipped Bolivian armies, trained and commanded at first by a German general, Hans von Kundt (1869–1939), seized Paraguayan fortifications in northern and central Chaco, including the strategic Fortín (Fort) Boquerón (June 15, 1932). Afterward Paraguay, which regarded the struggle as a defense of its homeland, began a national mobilization effort and prepared a major offensive under Colonel José Felix Estigarribia (1888–1940). The Paraguayans were victorious under Estigarribia, who recaptured Fortín Boquerón and other forts and conquered most of the Chaco in 1934. General Enrique Penaranda (1892–1970) replaced Kundt as head of the Bolivian forces. On November 17, 1934, Estigarribia captured the key Bolivian fort of Ballivián and advanced into eastern Bolivia in early 1935 before being pushed back by counterattacks. The United States and five South American nations succeeded in arranging a truce between the two war-weary countries (June 12, 1935), which later signed the peace Treaty of Buenos Aires (July 21, 1938). Paraguay received most of the Chaco region, and Bolivia was given access to the Atlantic via the Paraguay and Paraná Rivers and the use of Puerto Casado as a free port.

Chad, French Conquest of (1897–1914) During the partition of Africa by the European powers at the end of the 19th century, France, Britain, and Germany made a race for Lake Chad, which was thought to be of great economic importance. France arrived first (1897) and took control of the eastern shores of the large lake. French explorer Émile Gentil (1866–1914), who had led an expedition down the Chari River to the lake's southern part, made a treaty with the sultan of Baguirmi and set up a French protectorate in the area. In 1900, French forces marched south from Algeria and east from Senegal and Niger, and they joined with Gentil's men to fight against Rabah Zobeir (d. 1900), a Muslim chieftain and follower of the Mahdi (see SUDANESE WAR OF 1881–85), and his African warriors. On April 22, 1900, at the Battle of Lakhta (Kusseri), Rabah was defeated, killed, and beheaded. Much bloody fighting was to follow, however. It took years to conquer the fanatical Senussi, a Muslim sect. The area of Kanem near Lake Chad was brought under French control in 1906, the area of Wadai in 1912, and finally the northern Chadian territory of Borkou in 1914. Chad was then organized as a French colony in French Equatorial Africa.

Chadian Civil War of 1965–96 Arab Muslim nomads and cattle herders live in northern Chad, while Bantu Christian and pagan farmers inhabit the south. In 1965, the northerners felt discriminated against by the Chadian government, which was dominated by the southerners. A civil war soon erupted between the north and south. A military coup in 1975 brought General Félix Malloum (b. 1932) to power as the Bantu ruler. His regime was opposed by the Libyan-backed Chadian National Liberation Front (FROLINAT), a rebel guerrilla movement, which had gained control of about 80 percent of the country by the end of 1978. When the government's northern stronghold in Tibesti was overrun, the French Foreign Legion arrived to help halt the guerrillas' offensive; a cease-fire was arranged, but was soon broken, and the guerrillas were pushed back. In 1979, Malloum was deposed and fled to Nigeria; a provisional government was formed with Goukouni Oueddi (1944–), a former FROLINAT leader, as president and Hissen Habré (1942–) as defense minister. A power struggle quickly developed between these two Muslim leaders. In late 1980, Libyan forces supporting Oueddi occupied N'Djamena, Chad's capital. Libya's head of state, Colonel Muammar al-Qaddafi (1943–), proclaimed a union of Chad and Libya, but there was much opposition to it; Libyan troops were withdrawn from Chad later that year (1981). In mid-1982, Habré's troops seized N'Djamena and forced Oueddi to flee. Chad was virtually partitioned at the 15th parallel; Oueddi's Libyan-sponsored guerrillas in the north fought to overthrow the government in the south of pro-Western Habré, who was backed by France. In early 1987 the war drastically changed when Oueddi's guerrillas turned against Libyan forces in the country (Oueddi had been shot and wounded by Libyans in October 1986). Oueddi then united with Habré to push the Libyans out of northern Chad. Habré's adviser, Colonel Idriss Déby (1952–), led the successful military attacks against Qaddafi's forces in 1987. Habré became president (1989), but in late 1990, Déby's guerrilla army overthrew Habré's government in N'Djamena, and Déby became president, immediately setting free some

400 Libyan prisoners (giving ripe suspicion to reports his army was supplied by Qaddafi). By 1994, Déby's government was confronted by about 40 opposition groups and six rebel movements; Déby foiled two coups against him in 1993 (one on behalf of Habré). The prolonged armed struggle ended in 1996, when the Chadian government signed peace agreements with various political and rebel groups in the north and south.

Chalukya Dynasty, Wars of the (A.D. 543–655) The collapse of the Gupta dynasty (see GUPTA DYNASTY, CONQUESTS OF THE) reduced all of India to a state of chaos and fostered important contests for regional dominance, the earliest involving the small states in central India's Deccan plateau. The conqueror was an outsider, a former petty chieftain who claimed royal (Rajput) lineage, Pulakesin I (d. 566). He established the Chalukya dynasty by capturing the hill fort of Vatapi (Badami) and seizing territories between the western Deccan and the Western Ghats from their Vakataka rulers. His son seized territories farther north, including the Konkan coast (modern Bombay state), focusing family pressure on the northwest coast in 597. Pulakesin II (fl. c. 610–42) continued this focus and brought Chalukyan influence to its early height, gaining parts of Gujarat (Kathiawar peninsula) and Malwa and, by winning the CHALUKYAN WAR AGAINST HARSHA (620), establishing the southern boundary of his kingdom at the Narmada (Narbada) River. His territories in the east stretched as far south as the Kistna River, for he annexed lands formerly controlled by the Andhra dynasty. He then turned east, seizing in 624 the Visnukindin east coast kingdom of Vengi (near Kalinga, now Orissa state) and founding an eastern Chalukya dynasty at Pishtapura on the Bay of Bengal, which lasted until 1070. His actions won the Chalukyas territories on both coasts of India, control of east Asian trade, and a barrier behind which to keep back ambitious south Indian kingdoms. But his conquest offended the Pallava dynasty, Parthians who had left the Ganges area to rule southern Dravidian-speaking areas as the first emperors of the south, taking control of a narrow strip

of the east coast and a capital at Kanchipuram (in Tamil Nadu state) from an early Chola dynasty. The Pallavas, who had wanted Vengi, raided the Deccan area from 641 through 647, taking Vatapi in 642 and killing Pulakesin II. Undismayed, the Chalukyas focused on Gujarat, gained sufficient power to recapture Vatapi in 655, and prepared for further action against the Pallavas (see CHALUKYAN-PALLAVAN WARS). See also CHALUKYAN-CHOLAN WARS; CHALUKYAN CIVIL WARS; CHALUKYAN-RASHTRAKUTAN WARS.

Chalukyan-Cholan Wars (A.D. c. 990–c. 1070) About 850, the Pallavan and Chalukyan pressures on the southern tip of India caused to come into prominence a revivified Chola dynasty. Once feudatory to the rulers of a pre-Gupta central Indian kingdom called Andhra, the Cholas were in 850 one of three kingdoms governing the southern end of the subcontinent—Kerala (Chera) in the west, Pandya on the very tip, and Chola in the east. By 950, despite many skirmishes with the Pallavas and the eastern Chalukyas, the Cholas controlled the entire area and were free to oppose the second western Chalukya dynasty (see CHOLAN-PANDYAN WAR OF A.D. c. 910). Invasions of the southern and western Deccan region began during 990–93, and the Cholas kept invading until 1021, when they stopped, apparently because their actions were fruitless. Switching to the offensive, Chalukyan forces under the eastern dynasty's Somesvara I (fl. 1043–68) began intensive military campaigns against the Cholas, who wanted control of Vengi for its influence on east Asian trade (they had held it briefly before the RASHTRAKUTAN-CHOLAN WAR OF A.D. c. 940–72). A major Cholan defeat in 1052 was countered by an equally important defeat of the Chalukyas in 1062. Conferences for peace ensued, and plans for intermarriage between the contending dynasties followed, ending with the eastern Chalukya dynasty's absorption into the Chola. The western dynasty continued without further wars with the Cholas; instead, after suffering a usurpation from about 1156 through 1167, it was absorbed by an alliance of rulers dominating the Telugu-speaking parts of the Deccan (1189). See also CHALUK-YAN CIVIL WAR OF c. 1156–81.

Chalukyan Civil War of c. 1156–81 Competition for power within the kingdoms of India was constant, especially so in the Deccan region, for a ruling dynasty had influence rather than authority in a subordinate kingdom because of the looseness of Indian feudal arrangements. A feudatory kingdom was expected to supply troops as needed and pay annual taxes, but a subordinate dynasty still ruled its own territory without interference and could, and often did, gain sufficient power to reverse the feudatory relationship. As happened in the CHALUKYAN-RASHTRAKUTAN WARS, a feudatory family, the Kalacuri, led by Bijjala (fl. 1156–67), rose against the Chalukyas and briefly usurped the throne. In true Indian fashion, Bijjala's successors fought among themselves, allowing the last important western Chalukyan ruler, Somesvara IV (fl. 1181–89), to reverse the usurpation and to pursue a second civil war, begun in 1180. See also CHALUKYA DYNASTY, WARS OF THE.

Chalukyan Civil War of 1180–89 In India, the western Chalukya dynasty held extensive territories at the time of Mahmud of Ghazna's death (1030), ranging from Kathiawar to the Kistna or Krishna River in south India. The dynasty's eastern boundary abutted the holdings of the eastern Chalukyas and its southern boundary reached the growing kingdom of the revitalized Cholas. Mahmud's conquests in the north (see MAHMUD OF GHAZNA, CONQUESTS OF) had upset the feudal relationships in the south, and the Chalukyas fought two civil wars, that of about 1156 to 1181 (see CHALUKYAN CIVIL WAR OF c. 1156–81) and a second against Telugu-speaking feudatories, the Hoysala and Yadava families, allied with the Kakatiya family, who had become a Cholan feudatory when the eastern Chalukya dynasty was absorbed by the Cholas (1070). The Chalukyas lost the three-cornered conflict and became a minor kingdom. In 1189, the Hoysala took southern territories in modern Mysore

(Karnataka) state; the Yadavas ruled areas south of the Narmada (Narbada) River. The reduced Chalukyan kingdom was squeezed between the two, blocked on the east by the Kakatiyas. But the status of the three victors was unstable, for control of coastal trade depended on sole sovereignty over the entire Deccan region, a power achieved by the Delhi sultanate in the 14th century (see DELHI SULTANATE RAIDS IN SOUTH INDIA).

Chalukyan-Pallavan Wars (A.D. 670–975) The Pallavas, who had defeated the western Chalukyas in 642 (see CHALUKYA DYNASTY, WARS OF THE), became the third dynasty to vie for dominance in India after the collapse of the Gupta dynasty (see GUPTA DYNASTY, CONQUESTS OF THE). While the western Chalukyas kept the Pallavas out of the Deccan region, the eastern Chalukyas pushed south of Vengi into the Nellore district, pinning the Pallavas inside the narrow strip of formerly Andhra coast from which they had fought 30 years before. Under Vikramaditya I (fl. 655–80), the temple-fort of Vatapi (Badami) was reestablished in 655 and the Pallavan capital at Kanchipuram, sacred to Hindus as "the Benares of the south," was captured and partly destroyed in 670. This action did not destroy the Pallavas; however, even after reinhabiting Kanchipuram, they avoided further important hostilities—perhaps sensing, as modern historians do, that they were militarily ineffective. Vikramaditya II (fl. 733–46), reigning in the west, warred sporadically with the Pallavas from 730 to 742 in a long campaign that resulted in a second overthrow of Kanchipuram (742). The Pallava dynasty then slowly declined, losing again to the Chalukyas at the end of the ninth century before being overpowered by their vassal dynasty, the Chola. The Chalukya dynasty had been weakened, too, and lost out in 752 to its own feudatory, the Rashtrakuta (see CHALUKYAN-RASHTRAKUTAN WARS). A second western Chalukya dynasty defeated the Rashtrakutas in 975 and reduced them again to vassalage. See also CHALUKYAN-CHOLAN WARS.

Chalukyan-Rashtrakutan Wars (A.D. 752, 973–75) One effect of the wars between the Pallava and the western Chalukya dynasties in India (see CHALUKYAN-PALLAVAN WARS) was a gradual weakening of the Chalukyas and a growth in power of their feudatory, the Rashtrakuta dynasty. By the middle of the eighth century, the Rashtrakutas had become so influential that, in 752, under their ruler Dantidurga (fl. 752–60), they overthrew and killed the western Chalukyan king, Kirtivarman II (d. 752), when they seized Vatapi (Badami). In ending the first western Chalukya dynasty, the Rashtrakutas took over territories in the western and central Deccan region and inherited former Vakatakan territory north of the Godavari River on the east coast and former Satavahanan areas in the northern Deccan. Because they also attempted to capture territories governing trade routes in the Ganges Valley, they were the first Deccan power to work for domination in northern India. Their supremacy did not affect the eastern Chalukya dynasty, nor did their power from a capital at Ellora (near Hyderabad) last long. In 973, the western Chalukyas under Taila II (fl. 973–97) began a military campaign to overthrow the Rashtrakutas and were successful two years later, when they began to fight the aggressive Cholas for complete dominance of India's prosperous east coast. See also CHALUKYAN-CHOLAN WARS.

Chalukyan War against Harsha (A.D. 620) After the fall of the Gupta dynasty (see GUPTA DYNASTY, CONQUEST OF THE), the second unification attempt in India was made by Harsha Vardhana (c. 590–c. 647), a prince of the kingdom of Sthanvisvara, near Delhi. Formerly a Gupta vassal, he hoped to restore Gupta holdings. Enthroned in 606, he began to build a large Indian empire, gaining influence from Gujarat in the west to Assam in the east and establishing a political unit on a feudal rather than centralized basis. Unable to take control of areas west of the Indus River (containing the vulnerable passes in the northwest), he attempted to gain territory in the south-central Deccan plateau area and faced severe opposition from the western Chalukya dynasty, then ruled by Pulakesin II (fl. 610–42). Harsha's defeat by the Chalukyan leader in 620 led to a treaty naming the Narmada (Narbada) River as the southern boundary of his empire and establishing that river as the traditional geographic division between northern and southern India. Harsha's military action was made because of his realization that the controller of the Deccan could dominate the trading areas of the eastern and western coasts of southern India. His defeat gave the Chalukya dynasty opportunities in the Gujarat (see CHALUKYA DYNASTY, WARS OF THE) and allowed Chalukyan control of the entire Deccan; Harsha's death, about 647, caused the unity of northern India to be broken until the establishment of the Islamic Delhi sultanate in the 13th century. In both northern and southern India, ambitious dynasties, such as the short-lived Pallava and both the early and late Chola dynasties, now found themselves opposed by the western and eastern Chalukya dynasties.

Cham-Chinese Wars See CHINESE-CHAM WARS.

Cham Civil War of 1150–60 After his victory over the Khmers (see KHMER-CHAM WAR OF 1144–50), Jaya Harivarman I (d. 1166–67), ruler of the kingdom of Champa (central Vietnam), was faced with frequent challenges to his authority, most notably by his brother-in-law, Vamsaraja (d. 1150?), whose rebellion was supported by Cham hill tribes. Suffering a defeat in 1150, Vamsaraja sought help from the ruler of Dai Viet or Annam (northern Vietnam), who sent 5,000 troops to him. Jaya Harivarman led troops from the Cham capital of Vijaya (Binh Dinh) into battle on the plains of Dalva and Lavang and was victorious; he inflicted heavy losses on Dai Viet's soldiers. His troops went on to pacify the rebellious Cham regions of Amaravati (Quang Nam) in 1151 and, after a hard five-year struggle, Panduranga in 1160.

Cham-Khmer Wars See KHMER-CHAM WARS.

Chamorro's Revolt See NICARAGUAN CIVIL WAR OF 1925–33.

Cham-Vietnamese Wars   See VIETNAMESE-CHAM WARS.

Charlemagne, Conquests of (A.D. 771–814) Upon the death of Pepin the Short (714?–68), the first Carolingian king of the Franks, his territories were divided up according to Frankish custom, and his two sons, Charles (742–814) and Carloman II (751–71), who were uncooperative (as seemed to be the usual Frankish practice), ruled the western Franks (Neustria) and the eastern Franks (Austrasia), respectively. When Carloman died, Charles took over his brother's territories, became king of all the Franks, and launched an exciting and edifying career that resulted in the development of a Frankish empire, Charles's anointing as the Western or Holy Roman Emperor, and his famous designation as Charlemagne ("Charles the Great"). His lasting greatness is to be found in his ecclesiastical, judicial, administrative, and educational efforts and achievements, all made possible by his military victories. His wars began early, for his seizure of Carloman's kingdom made him the enemy of Desiderius (fl. 756–74), the duke of Tuscany, whose belligerence (772) led to Charlemagne's invasion of Lombardy (see CHARLEMAGNE'S DEFEAT OF DESIDERIUS). Even as he prepared for Lombardy, he began a 32-year war against the pagan, wily Saxons (see CHARLEMAGNE'S WAR AGAINST THE SAXONS). He put down a rebellion in Lombardy in 776, suffered a defeat in northern Spain in 778 (see CHARLEMAGNE'S INVASION OF NORTHERN SPAIN), reinvaded Lombardy in 780 to make his son its king and strengthen the papacy, and then suffered a minor defeat by the Saxons, avenged by a blameworthy massacre in 782. Charlemagne managed to develop and run his burgeoning empire despite frequent invasions of Saxony (between the Elbe and Em rivers), a punitive war against Brittany in 786, a successful conquest of Bavaria in 787–88, the five-year war against the Avars (see FRANKISH-AVARIAN WAR OF A.D. 791–96), and a battleless campaign in Italy in 800, which ended with his crowning in Rome as Holy Roman Emperor. This Roman designation as "Augustus" led to an invasion of the rebellious papal territory of Beneventum in 801 and a war with the Byzantine Empire (see FRANKISH-BYZANTINE WAR OF A.D. 803–10). Charlemagne's forces finally defeated the Saxons in 804, subdued the unruly Bohemians in 805 and Slavic Wends in 806, and fought wars in 808–10 with the Danes and other Saxon allies who had not quit in 804. After 804, when he was 62 and ailing, Charlemagne no longer fought actively. He drew up laws for his empire and made his will in 811; upon the deaths of some of his children before his own perhaps he reflected upon all he had accomplished militarily and peacefully in his years of leadership, for he had fathered 18 children and prepared the way for his son, later King Louis I "the Pious" (778–840) of France, to be his successor in an undivided French empire. See also FRANKISH CIVIL WARS.

Charlemagne's Defeat of Desiderius   (A.D. 773–74) The Franks under Pepin the Short (714?–68) had successfully defended Rome against the invading Lombards (754, 756), some of whose territory had then been ceded to the pope by the "donation of Pepin" (the basis of the Papal States). Later Desiderius (fl. 756–74), duke of Tuscany and the last native Lombard king in Italy, whose daughter had married Charlemagne (742–814), king of the Franks, sought to gain independence for Lombardy, in vassalage to both the Franks and the papacy. Angered by Desiderius's actions, Charlemagne divorced his Lombard queen and took over the territories of his recently deceased brother Carloman II (751–71), whose queen and children Desiderius sheltered. When Desiderius began attacking Rome (771) and other papal possessions, Pope Adrian I (d. 795) asked Charlemagne for help. The Franks crossed the Italian Alps, seized Verona and Carloman's family (773), successfully besieged the Lombard capital, Pavia, and captured Desiderius, who was sent as a prisoner to a monastery near Liège (774). Frankish nobles arrived in great numbers, and Charlemagne, now that the Lombard succession was Carolingian, spent Easter of 774 in Rome, confirmed his father Pepin the Short's gift to the papacy, and thereafter called himself "King of the Franks and Lombards and Patrician of the Romans."

Charlemagne's Invasion of Northern Spain (A.D. 777–801)   Apparently feeling secure in Saxony (see CHARLEMAGNE'S WAR AGAINST THE SAXONS) and seeing Spain torn by internal strife, Charlemagne (742–814) led a large Frankish army in 777–78 southward across the Pyrenees to the city of Saragossa, Spain, where the Ummayyads were resisting another Muslim dynasty, the Abbasids. (Charlemagne's ambition to advance his empire, civilization, and Christianity motivated him in the invasion.) His army was not admitted to Saragossa and proceeded to ravage several towns. Called home because of problems in Saxony, Charlemagne evidently mistook Pamplona for a Moorish city; his forces razed it, angering the Christian Basques (Gascons) of Navarre, who, together with Muslims, ambushed and massacred Charlemagne's army's rearguard, led by his nephew Roland (d. 778), at Roncesvalles on August 15, 778. This battle in the Pyrenees became the basis of *La Chanson de Roland* (The Song of Roland), the famous epic poem, which made a legendary hero out of Roland. Charlemagne never again entered Spain, but the people of Aquitaine continued to skirmish with the Moors. The Franks managed to subdue the Basques and force the Moors south of the Ebro River in Spain. The city of Barcelona fell to the Franks after a long siege (800–801) and was included in the Spanish March, a Frankish province in northeastern Spain, set up to contain the Moors.

Charlemagne's War against the Saxons (A.D. 722? – 804)   Of the many military objectives of Charlemagne (742–814), the most durable was his attempt to contain and control the Saxons, the last heathen and independent tribe in Germany. Unlike their cousins in Britain, the Saxons were not readily receptive to Christianity; like their Slavic and Nordic neighbors, they were not immediately amenable to civilization. Because they were attracted to Frankish gains in wealth, they often made raids into

Austrasia (land of the eastern Franks), and Charlemagne spent 32 years and made 14 invasions into Saxony (between the Elbe and Em Rivers) in his attempt to subdue them. His first campaign against the Saxons in 772 was a harsh reprisal, destroying the column of Irminsul, Saxon symbol of the mythic tree that supported the world, and seizing its treasure. Uncowed by this indication of their gods' indifference, the Saxons continued raiding, forcing Charlemagne to mount a large army for a full-scale invasion in 775. But the Saxons fiercely and successfully resisted. Then Charlemagne's strategy changed; he gradually annexed Saxon territory, established forts, and sent missionaries. But his Germanic adversaries acquired a Westphalian leader, Widukind (d. 807?), who, with Danish and Slavic assistance, harassed Charlemagne from 777 to 785, once defeating the Franks in a badly executed attack on a Saxon camp in 782. In revenge, Charlemagne executed 4,500 Saxons in a massacre at Verden (782). The war was altered little when Widukind surrendered himself in 785 and was baptized a Christian the next year; and Charlemagne's campaign against the Saxons became so ruthless that Alcuin (735–804), the foremost scholar at the court of the Franks, complained politely. After a major Saxon rebellion occurred in 792, annual invasions of Saxony by Charlemagne's soldiers became the rule, and after 795 deportation of Saxons and replacement by Franks began in the area. The last active campaign of Charlemagne ended in the Saxon surrender of Nordalbingia (Holstein) in 804. The war had been cruel, but the effects were permanent. The Saxons became Christians but retained a tribal identity and dialect, even to this day. See also CHARLEMAGNE, CONQUESTS OF.

Charles's Ford Massacre   See BANNOCK WAR.

Chechen Revolt of 1994–96 (Russo-Chechen Civil War of 1994–96)   Following weeks of military deployment along the border of the mostly Muslim, autonomous province of Chechnya, and despite concurrent negotiations, Russian troops bombarded its capital city of Grozny on December 11, 1994, thus initiating a 21-month guerrilla and civil war that ended in August 1996 with a ceasefire and a peace accord. Chechnya, a small republic nestled in the North Caucasus Mountains between the Black and Caspian Seas, had declared its independence from the Russian Federation in 1991. However, Chechnya was not internationally recognized as a sovereign state, and western countries, including the United States, announced their intention to keep clear of what Russian president Boris Yeltsin (1931–) proclaimed a strictly domestic affair. Chechnya itself was divided into two main factions: one dedicated to total freedom from Russia, led by Chechen president and former Soviet air force general Dzhokhar Dudayev (d. 1996?), and the other favoring remaining part of the federation. Before Yeltsin's attack, the Chechen moderates were covertly supported by the Russians and proved effective in diminishing Dudayev's influence. However, once Yeltsin began his full-fledged military offensive—motivated by a wish to bolster his flagging popularity and a desire to demonstrate Russia's strength, as well as a stated intention to crush Chechnya's notorious crime culture—bonds with these Chechens were broken and they united with Dudayev. Yeltsin's actions incurred widespread criticism, among not only troops and rival politicians but also prominent government and military figures, including Yeltsin's human rights adviser Sergei Kovalyov (1959?–), Deputy Defense Minister Georgi Kondratyev (1944–), Afghan war hero Boris Gromov (1943–), and celebrated army commander Alexander Lebed (1950–). Fierce battles occurred between Russian troops with tanks and defiant rebels in Grozny, Kizlyar, and other cities; mercenaries fought on both sides; Chechen snipers killed numerous Russians. Yeltsin remained firm and the war continued, resulting in tens of thousands of deaths, about 400,000 refugees, and the destruction of much of Chechnya. In May 1996 Dudayev was reportedly shot to death by Russian troops. In September 1996 the relatively moderate president Aslan Maskhadov, who had been Chechnya's chief commander during the war, presided over the ensu-

ing peace. Although Yeltsin withdrew his forces from Chechnya and granted the Chechens self-government, he did not confer complete independence. A stalemate situation prevailed, with Chechnya still refusing to consider itself part of the Russian Federation, and Russia refusing to let Chechnya go but later (March 1999) ordering all its officials out of the separatist republic, amid a Chechen campaign of kidnappings.

Cherokee War of 1760–62   The Cherokee Indians lived in North and South Carolina and were among the most advanced of all the American Indian tribes. At first they had been friendly with the white settlers, but their chief, Attakullakulla ("Little Carpenter") (fl. early 1760s), persuaded them to resist further encroachment by the colonists. War raged along the Carolinas' frontier for two years, but the Indians were no match for the whites with their superior firearms and military skill. The Cherokee were beaten badly and forced to sue for peace. As a result, they had to cede a sizable portion of their territory, which opened the back country of the Carolinas to further settlement.

Cherry Valley Massacre (1778)   During the AMERICAN REVOLUTION, two Iroquois Indian villages on the New York frontier were destroyed by American colonial troops, who were trying to put pressure on Britain's Iroquois allies. In retaliation, some 500 enraged Iroquois under Chief Joseph Brant (1742–1807), accompanied by 200 Loyalist troops under Captain Walter N. Butler (d. 1781), attacked the fortified town of Cherry Valley, N.Y., on November 11, 1778. Every building in the town was burned to the ground, and about 50 defenders were massacred, including 20 soldiers and Colonel Ichabod Alden (1739–78), who was stationed at Cherry Valley with 200 men of the Seventh Massachusetts Continentals. Another 70 townspeople were wounded or captured before the attackers left. See also MINISINK MASSACRE; WYOMING VALLEY MASSACRE.

Chevy Chase, English Defeat at (1388) Barons charged with protecting the Scottish-English border often clashed. The year 1388 held a major victory for the Scots at Chevy Chase or Otterburn (the Scots' name), in Northumberland. Although the English force led by Henry "Hotspur" Percy (1366–1403) outnumbered the Scots three to one, the Scots, commanded by the earls of Douglas and Moray, pressed so closely that, out of fear of killing their own in the growing dusk, the English fired few arrows. Douglas was killed, but his followers rallied and slew 2,000 Englishmen as they fled in retreat. Percy was captured and later ransomed.

Cheyenne and Arapaho War of 1864–68 For several years the Cheyenne and Arapaho Indians abided by the treaty some of their chiefs had signed in 1861, but they could not live on the poor land that had been assigned to them as a reservation in the Colorado Territory. In 1864, several settlers claimed Indians had stolen their cattle and a hot-headed army detachment clashed with friendly Indians, who defended themselves and killed several soldiers. These small incidents stirred up the whites, whose leaders declared war on the Plains Indians, several of whose chiefs tried to negotiate peace. When these efforts failed, war parties of young braves began attacking the wagon trains along the main trails, burning and looting farms and outposts, and seizing stagecoach stations. In the fall of 1864, a peace-seeking U.S. major gave the Cheyenne permission to pitch their camp close to Fort Lyon, but his replacement ordered them away. Shortly after fresh troops arrived. They discovered the Cheyennes' winter camp and utterly destroyed it (see SAND CREEK MASSACRE). This bloody deed infuriated all the Indian tribes, and they rose against all whites from Colorado to Texas. In 1865, three army columns were sent against them, but the army fared poorly and only one Arapaho camp was wiped out. Then the war pretty much fizzled out. The southern tribes of the Cheyenne and Arapaho agreed to move south of the Arkansas River, where they roamed, making only occasional raids.

Cheyenne War of 1878 After the defeat of their allies, the Sioux (see SIOUX WAR OF 1876–77) and the northern Cheyenne Indians were sent south to the reservation of the southern Cheyenne in what is now Oklahoma. They were miserable there, and in September their chiefs, Dull Knife and Little Wolf, respectively, escaped from the reservation with about 300 followers. They made their way north to their former homeland (around the Platte River's headwaters), fighting off army troops that tried four times to stop them. After crossing the Union Pacific rail line, they split into two groups. The one lead by Little Wolf spent the winter hiding near the Lost Chokecherry River. The other under Dull Knife headed northwest, but unexpectedly ran into a cavalry company during a snowstorm. They were captured and taken to Camp Robinson. When they adamantly refused to return south, they were locked up and given no food, water, or fire despite the bitter cold. In desperation, the Cheyenne broke out of the barracks on a cold January night and ran for their lives. For 12 days they were pursued. Many were killed or wounded or perished of starvation and cold. The remaining 30 were cornered in a canyon and annihilated. Dull Knife and his family had become separated from the others and finally made their way to an Indian agency where they were hidden. The ruthless treatment of the Cheyenne caused a rising protest in much of the United States, and when Little Wolf's followers were apprehended and taken to Fort Keogh, they were treated humanely. Later Montana's Tongue River Reservation was established for them, the remnants of Dull Knife's band, and other northern Cheyenne who had not gone south.

Chiapas Rebellion of 1994 On January 1, 1994, an Indian peasant rebellion erupted in Mexico's southernmost state of Chiapas, on the Guatemalan border. Armed rebels, calling themselves the Zapatista National Liberation Army (EZLN), after Emiliano Zapata (1880–1919), a peasant hero in the MEXICAN REVOLT OF 1914–15, had longtime social and economic grievances against wealthy cattle ranchers and coffee growers, who were supported by police and government officials. The rebellion also coincided with the enactment of the North American Free Trade Agreement (NAFTA) between Mexico, Canada, and the United States, which the poor Maya-descended Indians saw as a boon to the rich and ruination to them because it would sharply lower coffee and corn prices. Some 2,000 peasant guerrillas, supported by Roman Catholic leaders, occupied San Cristóbal de las Casas and six other towns in the highlands of Chiapas. They seized a dozen police, ranchers, and others, and waged furious gun battles with government soldiers for 12 days before being driven into the mountains. A tentative accord was reached between the rebels and the government, which promised to redistribute illegal large landholdings to poor peasants, to begin a public works program, and to prohibit discrimination against the Indians. But a yearlong truce ended when, in February 1995, soldiers moved into rebel territory in Chiapas, arrested Zapatistas, and chased others into the Lacandón jungle. Chiapas still simmered at the brink of more hostilities. See also MEXICAN REVOLT OF 1996.

Chief Joseph's Uprising   See NEZ PERCE WAR.

Chiengmai-Ayutthayan Wars   See THAI WARS.

Children's Crusade (1212)   The crusading fever sweeping Europe in the early 1200s (see CRUSADE, FOURTH) even infected children. A French peasant boy, Stephen of Vendôme (fl. 1212), recruited thousands of boys and girls, many under the age of 12, and led them to Marseilles. The group set sail for Palestine to free the Holy Land, hoping to succeed where their elders had failed so dismally; the children were either shipwrecked or sold into slavery by unscrupulous skippers. Another group of thousands of German children, led by a boy preacher named Nicholas (fl. 1212), went to Italy but was turned back; many died of hunger, disease, and exposure.

Chilean Civil War of 1829–30   After Chilean dictator Bernardo O'Higgins (1778–1842) was deposed in 1823, Chile suffered a period of extreme disorder. Conservative, wealthy landowners and clergy coalesced to oppose liberal elements, composed mainly of the lower classes, who favored local autonomy, agrarian reform, and curtailment of clerical power. The promulgation of a liberal constitution in 1828 brought on a crisis, and civil war erupted in 1829. The conservatives backed General Joaquín Prieto (1786–1854), commander of the largest army garrison located at Concepcion; liberal forces were led by General Ramón Freire (1787–1851). On April 17, 1830, the opposing armies met at Lircay, where the conservatives won a decisive victory. Prieto became Chilean president and appointed Diego Portales (1793–1837) a minister in his cabinet; the latter became virtual dictator of the conservative government. See also PERUVIAN-BOLIVIAN CONFEDERATION, WAR OF THE.

Chilean Civil War of 1891   After the liberal José Manuel Balmaceda (1840–91) was elected president of Chile in 1886, he fostered public works, improved health care, and public education. In 1890, his programs met opposition in the Chilean congress, which rejected his budget. Balmaceda announced in early 1891 that he would proceed without the congress, which soon deposed him and appointed naval officer Jorge Montt (1845–1922) as provisional president. The navy supported the congress, while Balmaceda retained control of the army and exercised dictatorial powers in the capital city of Santiago. In August 1891, the navy landed 9,000 congressional troops at a point near Valparaiso, where many of Balmaceda's 10,000 troops refused to fight and thus allowed the city to be taken. Santiago fell to the congressional forces shortly; driven from office, Balmaceda gained asylum in the Argentine legation in the capital and, at the conclusion of his term of office, committed suicide on September 19, 1891.

Chilean Revolution of 1973   In 1970, Salvador Allende Gossens (1908–73), an avowed marxist, was elected president of Chile; in his campaign he had asserted he wanted to establish socialism within a democratic framework. His immediate task was to reform the economy, and he started by freezing prices and raising wages. Later he nationalized U.S.-owned copper mines and several heavy industries and broke up large plantations and distributed the land to peasants. These actions antagonized many foreign countries as well as Chile's middle and upper classes and right-wing parties. The economy worsened as food shortages developed, strikes cut production, foreign loan requests were refused, and inflation rose; street fighting, sabotage, and quarreling in congress were daily events. A two-month strike by owners of the trucking industry who resisted nationalization crippled the nation, which seemed on the verge of civil war. On September 11, 1973, the armed forces staged a successful coup d'état, overthrowing the government and seizing the presidential palace in Santiago, Allende apparently committed suicide during the military assault on the palace. Reportedly the U.S. Central Intelligence Agency helped plan and finance the plot against Allende. Chile then came under the rule of a four-man military junta, with General Augusto Pinochet Ugarte (1915–   ) as head.

Chilean War of Independence (1810–18) When news that Napoleon (1769–1821) had deposed King Ferdinand VII (1784–1833) of Spain (see PENINSULAR WAR) reached Chile, the Spanish captain-general was deposed, and a junta, outwardly professing loyalty to Ferdinand, took control and engaged in ousting colonial administrators and opening Chilean ports to free trade. Chile's revolutionary movement was torn by violent strife between the radical followers of José Miguel Carrera (1785–1821) and the moderates under Bernardo O'Higgins (1778–1842) from 1811 to 1814. This enabled the Spanish royalist army to defeat the revolutionaries at the Battle of Rancagua in 1814 and to reestablish royal control of Santiago. O'Higgins and Carrera then joined forces with José de San Martín (1778–1850), who for three years had been organizing and training an army at Mendoza in western Argentina for the liberation of Peru by way of Chile (see PERUVIAN WAR OF INDEPENDENCE). San Martín

soon exiled Carrera because of seditious activities. In early 1817, some 5,000 soldiers, led by San Martín, crossed the Andes—a feat never done before—and defeated the Spanish at the Battle of Chacabuco on February 12, 1817. San Martín took Santiago and proclaimed Chilean independence a year later. A final defeat of royalist forces by San Martín's army on the banks of the Maipo River on April 5, 1818, secured independence. Spain's hold on the Chilean coast and sea lanes was broken by Chile's small navy under the command of Lord Thomas Cochrane (1775–1860), an able British officer, who successfully bombarded Spanish forts and seized numerous warships between 1818 and 1820. See also ARGENTINE WAR OF INDEPENDENCE.

Chilean War with the Peruvian-Bolivian Confederation See PERUVIAN-BOLIVIAN CONFEDERATION, WAR OF THE.

Chindit War See BURMA CAMPAIGN.

Chinese-Annamese War of A.D. 907–39 With the fall of China's T'ang dynasty (907) and the outbreak of anarchy, the Chinese-controlled region of Annam ("Pacified South," a Chinese name resented by the native people) began a struggle for independence. The Annamese, who had obtained the right to choose their own mandarin governor in 906 (and later all government officials), skirmished with the Cantonese Chinese to the north. By 931, the Chinese had been evicted from Annam. When the Annamese leader was later murdered by a rebel army officer, his son-in-law, Ngo Quyen (897–944), marshaled nobles and peasants against the officer, who sought help from China. Having killed the officer, Ngo and his forces met the invading Chinese on the Bach Dang River in Annam. A clever strategist, Ngo ordered iron spikes hammered into the river bottom so that they were hidden at high tide. Chinese ships sailed up the river and, when the tide turned, were impaled on the spikes and trapped. This decisive defeat of the Chinese ended their control over Annam, except for a brief period later

(1407–28). Ngo became ruler of independent Annam, which stretched from the foothills of China's Yunnan south to the 17th parallel (roughly northern Vietnam).

Chinese-Annamese War of 1057–61   Chinese troops invaded the independent state of Dai Viet (northern Vietnam), which the Chinese continued to call disparagingly Annam ("Pacified South"), with the hope of conquering it. They were met and checked by defending troops at the Red River delta. The ensuing war lasted four years, and ultimately the Chinese were driven back into their territory to the north. During this war the neighboring Chams and Khmers invaded Dai Viet to seize territory. In 1061, the Vietnamese or Annamese marched south into Champa and extended their border south of the 17th parallel. Vietnamese peasant-soldiers then settled the seacoast area, eventually evicting the remaining Cham residents. See also VIETNAMESE-CHAM WAR OF 1000–1044.

Chinese-Annamese War of 1075–79   The Sung (Song) dynasty of China sought to secure its southern border with Dai Viet or Annam (northern Vietnam) and, allied with the Chams and Khmers, attacked this independent state, which was flourishing under the Ly dynasty. The Vietnamese or Annamese were defeated, and the Ly rulers ceded five border provinces to China in exchange for China's pullout. Later, by the treaty of 1084, these provinces were returned to Dai Viet and the border fixed. See also VIETNAMESE-CHINESE WARS.

Chinese-Burmese Wars   See BURMESE-CHINESE WARS.

Chinese-Cham War of A.D. 431–46   King Fan Hu-ta (d. c. 414) of Champa (kingdom in what is now central Vietnam) took advantage of unstable conditions in the collapsing Tsin or Chin dynasty of China and conducted raids into the Chinese-ruled territory of Nam Viet to the north (405 and 407).

In 413, he led an invasion north of Jih-nan (Ceyhan), but never returned. Later, in 431, Cham king Yang Mah II (402–47?) directed more than 100 boats in a plundering expedition along Jin-nan's coast in Chinese-held Tonkin (northern Vietnam). However, while the king was away, the Chinese retaliated by besieging Ch'ü-su, until bad weather forced a halt to the siege. Yang Mah's soldiers tried unsuccessfully to obtain the aid of Funan soldiers while fighting in Tonkin. Sporadic skirmishing continued until 446, when the new governor of Tonkin denounced the ongoing peace negotiations and besieged Ch'ü-su. He gained much booty when the city fell; his forces went on to capture and sack the Cham capital near Hue, expropriating much gold and taking control of Champa.

Chinese-Cham War of A.D. 605   Anarchy and weakness in the ruling Sui dynasty of China caused Cham king Sambhuvarman (d. 629) to end Chinese subjugation of his kingdom of Champa (in what is now central Vietnam). Later, however, when confronted by a reinvigorated China and its soldiers, he renewed Champa's payment of tribute to the Chinese in 595. After crushing rebellions in the Chinese-controlled provinces of Tonkin and Annam (in present-day northern Vietnam), Chinese forces under General Liu Fang (fl. early 600s) marched south, overwhelmed Sambhuvarman's army, seized Ch'ü-su, and looted the Cham capital at Tra-kieu (605). After the Chinese withdrew, Sambhuvarman retook control and asked the Chinese emperor, Yang Kuang (d. 618), for forgiveness.

Chinese Civil War of 1398–1402   Chu Yüan-chang (Hung-wu) (1328–98), founder of the Ming dynasty, drove out the Mongol invaders (see MONGOL-CHINESE WAR OF 1356–68) and restored China's economy and agriculture. Although six sons survived him, the throne passed to his grandson, Chu Yun-wen (Chien-wen, Jianwen) (1377–1440?), a young man of 16 who promptly began to break the power of his six ambitious uncles. Within a year he had reduced three of them to private citizens, one had committed suicide, and one had retired to a monastery, but Chu Ti (1359–1424), the prince of Yen, resisted in 1398 and gained control of all the northern provinces. In 1402, he marched on the imperial capital at Nanking (Nanjing), which his strong army surrounded; the walled city soon surrendered without much of a struggle, thanks in part to the help of court defectors. Chu Ti ascended the imperial throne as Yung Lo, the third Ming emperor, and Chu Yun-wen vanished, presumably having either died in his burning palace or escaped disguised as a Buddhist monk. The latter fate is thought most likely by many Chinese historians.

Chinese Civil War of 1621–44   Burdensome taxation, destruction wrought by Manchu raids (see MANCHU CONQUEST OF CHINA), devastating floods and famines, and political intrigues brought great suffering to millions of Chinese toward the end of the Ming dynasty, and revolts broke out in many places in the empire. Warlords recruited homeless men into their private armies and controlled large areas. One of the most powerful of these chiefs was Li Tzu-ch'eng (Li Zicheng) (1605?–45), who, in 1637, tried unsuccessfully to seize the capital of Szechwan (Sichuan). Still defiant, he led his army into the province of Shensi (Shaanxi) and in 1640 into Honan (Henan). By 1642, he was master of the provinces of Shensi and Honan (Henan) and the next year took control of Shansi (Shanxi) and declared himself emperor. In 1644, he marched at the head of 300,000 men to Peking (Beijing), the imperial capital. Two armies under rival commanders went out of the city to meet them, but because they did not cooperate, they were badly beaten, and the rebels entered the city in triumph. The last Ming emperor hung himself in despair, and Li assumed the throne for a brief period.

Chinese Civil War of 1674–81   See THREE FEUDATORIES, REVOLT OF THE.

Chinese Civil War of 1930–34   Although the Kuomintang (Nationalist) armies had reunited China in 1928 (see NORTHERN EXPEDITION), the problems of turning China into a modern state were enormous and complex. It could not be done in a few years, and discontent smoldered all over the country as former warlords tried to regain power and the peasants suffered the ravages of floods and famines. Revolts were put down in one province, and a fresh one broke out in another. However, the Kuomintang's Generalissimo Chiang Kai-shek (Jiang Jieshi) (1887–1975) considered his chief enemies to be the Communists, who had been driven from the large cities and found refuge in the Jing Gang mountains in the south. Five times between 1930 and 1934 Chiang's troops tried to encircle their strongholds. The first two efforts and the fourth failed. In the third campaign of 1931 a furious battle was fought at Goaxing with heavy losses on both sides. Chiang claimed a victory, but the Red (Communist) Army was not annihilated and moved its bases farther south. By 1933, Chinese Communist communes had been set up in four other remote provinces. The fifth campaign started in October 1933, with a 700,000-man Nationalist army. This time, with the coaching of a German general and the aid of modern planes and artillery, the Nationalist troops adopted a scorched-earth policy to starve the enemy into submission. Pillboxes, forts, and checkpoints on all roads discouraged the Communists' usual aggressive guerrilla methods, and the peasants were exterminated. The ruthless campaign continued for a year until the Communists in the southern mountains of China were finally dislodged and began their long trek to a new base (see LONG MARCH).

Chinese Civil War of 1945–49   After Japan's defeat in WORLD WAR II (see also WORLD WAR II IN CHINA; WORLD WAR II IN THE PACIFIC) and the expulsion of its troops from mainland China, both the Communists in the north and the Kuomintang (Nationalist) armies in the south rushed to seize the Chinese areas formerly occupied by the Japanese. American planes airlifted thousands of Kuomintang troops to Shanghai, Nanking (Nanjing), and other major Chinese cities; U.S. general George Marshall

(1880–1959) was sent to negotiate a peace between the opposing Chinese sides. Mao Tse-tung (Mao Zedong) (1893–1976), the Communist leader, seemed willing to bargain, but Chiang Kai-shek (Jiang Jieshi) (1887–1975), the Nationalist leader, adamantly refused to talk with the Communists. Marshall warned Chiang that China's faltering economy would collapse if negotiations were not conducted, but Chiang would not listen. Marshall reported that his mission had failed, and he returned home in early 1947. American troops were also withdrawn, but American military and economic aid continued. Meanwhile, whole divisions defected to the Communists; Kuomintang commanders quarreled among themselves and refused to take the offensive; and rampant inflation and government corruption discredited the once popular Kuomintang. In October 1948, about 300,000 Nationalist troops surrendered to the Communists in Manchuria, and two months later 66 Nationalist divisions were surrounded and captured—or they deserted—in north-central China. The following April the Communists crossed the Yangtze (Chang) River and spread throughout the south. Shanghai fell to them in May, Canton (Guangzhou) in October, and the former capital of Chungking (Chongqing) in November. In December 1949, Chiang, his Nationalist government, and their followers fled to the island of Formosa (Taiwan), where Chiang set up the Republic of China (1950). Millions of Chinese died in this civil war, and millions more were impoverished by the runaway inflation. American aid to the Kuomintang created anti-American sentiments among much of China's population. The Communists had triumphed and proclaimed the People's Republic of China (1949), with their capital at Peking (Beijing) and Mao as chairman; soon they would chart a completely new social, economic, and political course for China. See also SINO-JAPANESE WAR OF 1937–45.

Chinese Conquest of Nam Viet (111 B.C.) About 500 B.C., Chinese traders began traveling south into what is now northern Vietnam; Chinese forts were built near Hanoi during the Ch'in dynasty (221–207). The region was conquered by a renegade Chinese general, Chao T'o or Trieu Da (d. after 208), and incorporated by him into a kingdom established in southern China, known as the kingdom of Nan Yüeh or Nam Viet (c. 208). With the rise of the powerful Han dynasty in China, armed clashes between the Hans and Viets began about 181; invading Han forces arrived at the Red River delta in 113 and conquered Nam Viet in 111. Wu Ti (157–87), the Han emperor, annexed the kingdom to his Chinese empire. Nan Viet become the Chinese province of Giao Chi (later Giao Chau), which was split into nine military administrative units. Small groups of Chinese peasant-soldiers were sent to set up villages and build forts in Nam Viet, which the Chinese called Annam ("Pacified South"); later the Chinese introduced more advanced farming and irrigation techniques and their culture. See also CHINESE-ANNAMESE WARS; LY-BON'S REBELLION; TRUNG SISTERS' REBELLION.

Chinese "Cultural Revolution" (1966–69) Directed at young people, a new political campaign known as the Great Proletarian Cultural Revolution was launched by Mao-Tse-tung (Mao Zedong; 1893–1976), China's communist leader. Mao, whose power base was in the Chinese army, wanted to reseize control from the bureaucracies that had grown up in education, industrial management and agricultural and economic development and to encourage the continuation of the revolution in Chinese cultural life. Free rail passes were issued and hundreds of thousands of militant young men and women flocked to Peking (Beijing), China's capital, to march in massive parades reviewed by Mao in Tiananmen Square. These communists or Red Guards vied with each other to express their patriotism and devotion to Mao. They covered walls with posters denouncing Mao's enemies and traveled around China spreading the doctrines contained in Mao's "little red book." This endeavor to re-create and experience the fervor of the Red armies' LONG MARCH of 1934–1935 soon got out of hand, however. Bands of Red Guards destroyed works of art and historical relics, denounced intellectuals, burned books, and attacked those they considered elitists or anti-Mao. Schools and universities were closed, and the economy almost came to a standstill. Red Guards fought each other over ideological differences, and Chinese factions clashed with arms in most of the provinces, especially in the south. Gradually the violence and chaos waned as new Revolutionary Committees, which were made up of representatives of the army, the more responsible Red Guards, and peasants and workers, were organized to restore order and stamp out factionalism. In the spring of 1969, schools were reopened, but the universities did not reopen until September 1970. According to some accounts, the Cultural Revolution did succeed in eliminating many of the age-old differences between rich and poor and city and country, but it did so at enormous cost and loss.

Chinese-French War of 1883–85   See SINO-FRENCH WAR OF 1883–85.

Chinese-Korean Wars   See SINO-KOREAN WARS.

Chinese Revolts of 1865–81   Although a major revolt that had encompassed much of south China had been suppressed by 1865 (see TAIPING REBELLION), smaller, scattered rebellions continued to plague the Manchu (Ch'ing) dynasty for the next 16 years. The most important occurred in the Chinese provinces of Shensi (Shaanxi) and Kansu (Gansu) and in western Sinkiang (Xinjiang). The motives of the rebels varied considerably. Some were anti-Manchu revolutionary movements organized by secret societies as in the past (see "RED EYEBROW" REBELLION; "YELLOW TURBAN" REBELLION; FIVE PECKS OF RICE). Some were directed by strong anti-Western or anti-Christian sentiments, and their adherents opposed the broad treaty rights that had been granted to foreigners. Still other revolts were instigated by bands of roving bandits who sought to take advantage of the turmoil of the times to attack trade routes and travelers or to force towns and cities to pay them tribute for "protec-

tion." Whatever the causes, the Manchu military put down the revolts and executed their leaders.

Chinese Revolution of 1911–12   Although the Manchu (Ch'ing [Qing]) dynasty (1644–1911) had ruled China for more than 260 years, many Chinese still considered the Manchus (who originated in Manchuria) foreigners and hated them as such even as they hated and feared the western foreigners who had gained control of the coastal ports and had been granted concessions to build railroads, roads, and mines. Throughout the first decade of the 20th century, China seethed with unrest and turmoil, revolutionary societies sprang up everywhere, new public and private schools graduated students who wanted a better life for themselves and their countrymen, and overseas Chinese sent money home to finance reform and resistance movements. The weak Manchu emperor made some attempts at reform, but these were abruptly canceled by the dowager empress, who was out of touch with the realities in the country. On October 8, 1911, an explosion in the city of Hankow (Hankou) revealed the presence of a revolutionary group, whose leaders were promptly arrested and executed. Soldiers in Wuchang (part of Wuhan) across the Yangtze (Chang) River from Hankow knew of the group's plot and, fearing to be implicated, mutinied on October 10, 1911, sacked the governor's residence, took control of the city, and declared a rebellion against the Manchus. This date, celebrated as the "Double Ten," sparked similar uprisings all over the country. Soon all the provinces in the Yangtze Valley and southern and northwestern China were in the rebels' hands. They proclaimed their territory a republic. There was comparatively little bloodshed because most Chinese officials and military leaders realized the days of the Manchus were numbered. In desperation, the prince regent recalled the Assembly, an advisory body of appointed and elected members, which elected Yüan Shih-k'ai (1859–1916) prime minister, a post he reluctantly accepted. Yüan was the organizer of China's modern army and a capable leader who felt no strong devotion to the Manchus and wanted mainly to develop China as a strong modern nation under his direction. His army did retake several cities from the revolutionists, and then Yüan ordered the revolution to halt. Meanwhile the leader Sun Yat-sen (Sun Wen, Sun Yixian) (1866–1925), often called the "Father of the Chinese Republic," hurried home from America where he had been lecturing and raising funds for the revolution. On his return to China, he was offered the position of provisional president and was inaugurated on January 1, 1912, at the provisional capital in Nanking (Nanjing). Sun knew he had no military support and no government experience; he was chiefly a theorist and democratic idealist. Thus, when the young emperor, Hsüan T'ung (P'u-i, Puyi) (1906–67), abdicated on February 12, bringing the Ch'ing dynasty to an end, Sun resigned. The newly formed National Assembly then elected Yüan provisional president, and the north and south of China were reunited as a republic.

Chinese-Tibetan Wars   See SINO-TIBETAN WARS.

Chinese War against the Eastern Turks   (A.D. 629–30) The Eastern or Northern Turks occupied what is now Inner Mongolia at the time the T'ang dynasty replaced the Sui in 618. The widow and grandson of the former emperor had been given asylum by the Turks, and for a decade they had caused unrest on the northern frontier. T'ai Tsung (Taizong) (600–649), the energetic and capable Chinese emperor, realized the danger of an invasion and sent emissaries to stir up discontent among the tribes that paid unwilling allegiance to Hie-li (fl. 600s), the Turkish kagan (king). In 628, a revolt erupted, and the following year T'ai Tsung sent an army northward to support the rebels. During a battle Hie-li was taken prisoner, but T'ai Tsung treated him kindly when he was brought to the capital. He also was merciful to the defeated Turkish troops, many of whom he incorporated into the Chinese army.

Chinese War against the Western Turks, First   (A.D. 641–48)   The Chinese emperor T'ai Tsung (Taizong) (600–649) employed the same tactics against the Western Turks as he had against the Eastern Turks (see CHINESE WAR AGAINST THE EASTERN TURKS), namely, stirring up dissension among rival tribes and winning the allegiance of powerful chiefs. T'ai Tsung's armies were noted for their fierce cavalry, which drove the Turks westward from their strongholds in the mountains in Central Asia. The emperor wanted to subdue the Turks to prevent them from harassing caravans on the northern caravan route to the west, and he succeeded before his death in 649. **Second Chinese War against the Western Turks**   (A.D. 657–59). This was also fought in the steppes of Central Asia, mainly by nomad militia and cavalry who were loyal to the Chinese. The Uighur tribes had once been allies of the Turks, but they rejected them in 657 and helped the Chinese drive the Turks beyond the Pamirs (mountainous region in Central Asia, mainly in Tajikistan) and from what is modern Afghanistan.

Chinese War with the Khitans   (A.D. 979–1004) The Khitans were Mongol tribes who had occupied most of northeastern China as far south as the Yellow River (Huang Ho) by 950. They were ruled by a dynasty known as the Liao, which means "iron." The Sung dynasty was founded in China in 960 by Chao K'uang-yin (927–76), and in 979 his successor tried to regain from the Khitans the provinces of Chihli (Hopeh, Hebei) and Shansi (Shanxi). His first attempt to seize their capital at Peking (Beijing) failed, but seven years later he succeeded in reconquering northern Shansi and part of southern Chihli. The war continued under the third Sung emperor with ups and downs on both sides, but the Chinese slowly retook much of their former territory. Finally, at the Peace of Shanyuan in 1004, the Khitans agreed to abandon southern Chihli in return for northern districts of Shansi and an annual tribute of 100,000 ounces of silver and 200,000 rolls of silk. See also JUCHEN MONGOL CONQUEST OF THE LIAO.

Chinese War with Koxinga (1646–62) Cheng Ch'eng-kung (Zheng Cheng-gong), better known as Koxinga (1623–62), was a Chinese patriot for supporting the Ming dynasty against the invading Manchus, but he was also a ruthless pirate because of his depredations along the South China coast and islands. He established several bases from which his large pirate fleet could prey on shipping and Chinese coastal cities. In desperation, the Manchus (Ch'ing dynasty) evacuated people living along the coast and placed them behind guarded barriers some 10 miles inland, destroying their homes and fields to deprive Koxinga and his men of food and supplies. With the help of the Dutch, the Manchu forces then devastated the pirates' coastal strongholds. In retaliation, Koxinga stormed the island of Formosa (Taiwan), which was ruled by the Dutch, in 1661 and captured the Dutch garrison there, Fort Zealandia, after a long siege, in which hundreds of pirate ships were used. After Koxinga's death, his son and grandsons ruled the island until 1683, when it again became part of China. See also MANCHU CONQUEST OF CHINA.

Chinese War with Nanchao (A.D. 751–74) The area of present-day Yunnan and southern Szechwan (Sichuan) in southern China was inhabited by a Thai racial group known as the Shan in the eighth century. The Shan acknowledged the suzerainty of China. About 733, a Shan prince gained control over neighboring territory and proclaimed himself king of Nanchao ("Southern Princedom"). The emperor confirmed his title, and the king continued to pay tribute. When his son ascended the throne, he refused to be subservient to China. Although imperial forces tried to overpower the rebellious king, they could not prevail, and in 774 China recognized Nanchao as an independent state. Two decades later the Nanchaoans allied themselves with the Chinese against the Tibetans (see SINO-TIBETAN WAR OF A.D. 763–821).

Chinese War with the Tanguts, First (A.D. 990–1003) While the Chinese were preoccupied with the Khitans (see CHINESE WAR WITH THE KHITANS) in the northeast, another group of partly nomadic peoples living north of the Great Wall, the Tanguts, renounced their loyalty to the Sung dynasty rulers and proclaimed themselves an independent kingdom, later named the Hsi Hsia or Western Hsia. The Khitans recognized the new state immediately, and the Chinese made only feeble efforts to reassert their suzerainty. At that time they preferred to live in peace with their more warlike northern neighbors. **Second Chinese War with the Tanguts** (1040–43). The Tanguts (Hsi Hsia) invaded Chinese territory on their southern borders, hoping to conquer all of China, but were driven back with difficulty. To ensure no more raids on the frontier, the Chinese emperor agreed to pay the Hsi Hsia ruler an annual tribute of silver, silk, and tea, similar to the one paid the Khitans. A long period of peace ensued during which both the Tanguts and the Khitans adopted a Chinese lifestyle and culture.

Chioggia, War of (1378–81) Venice and Genoa, trade rivals, renewed fighting (see VENETIAN-GENOESE WAR OF 1350–55) after securing aid from their allies, Milan and Hungary, respectively. In 1379, after winning a naval victory over the Venetians at Pola (Pula, Yugoslavia), the Genoese, despite the loss of their chief admiral, Luciano Doria (d. 1379), during the battle, launched an attack on Venice itself. They seized the city of Chioggia just south of Venice and initiated a blockade to starve the Venetians into submission (the Hungarians had surrounded Venice on land). In the winter of 1380, the Venetian fleet under Vettore Pisani (1324–80) succeeded in blockading the Genoese at Chioggia and won a series of minor naval engagements in the Adriatic. Suffering from hunger and hardship, the Genoese were forced to surrender and hand over their fleet (about 4,000 Genoese were taken prisoner). Genoa, compelled to accept the Peace of Turin in 1381, was never again a threat to Venice's maritime superiority. See also HUNGARIAN-VENETIAN WAR OF 1378–81.

Chitral Campaign (1895) Tribesmen in Chitral (district in northernmost Pakistan) remained hostile to the British, who had entered the area and established an agency (1889). In 1895, a coup d'état in Chitral cost the life of the ruling chief, and the victors attempted to drive out the British representative, which necessitated the dispatch of a 16,000-man British expedition to reduce the rebels. At the Malakand Pass, on April 3, 1895, the invading troops overwhelmed some 12,000 Chitralis, who lost more than 500 men before giving up control of the pass; on the other side about 70 were killed or wounded. A British garrison was later set up in Chitral, which was annexed to British India. Tribal rebellions occurred, but the British presence eventually brought peace in 1898.

Chivington Massacre   See SAND CREEK MASSACRE.

Chmielnicki's Revolt (1648–54) Cossacks and peasants chafed under oppressive Polish rule in the Ukraine. Poland's King Ladislas IV (1595–1648) had built fortresses to suppress the Cossacks, slain captives, and rescinded agreed-upon rights. When more Polish troops were stationed in the Ukraine and the Cossacks were reduced nearly to serfdom, Bogdan Chmielnicki (1593?–1657), a member of the Ukrainian gentry angered by the Polish governor's confiscation of his lands and the subsequent mistreatment of his family, led the Cossacks in revolt, which soon grew into a national uprising of Ukrainians. Chmielnicki's army of Cossacks, Tatars (Tartars), and peasants won victories at first and invaded Poland as far as Lvov in 1648–49. After Ladislas died, the new Polish king, John II Casimir (1609–72), attempted to negotiate peace, but Polish nobles took up arms in opposition to him. Invading Cossacks besieged the king at Zborow, where a treaty (temporary) was signed in 1649 that legitimized Chmielnicki as hetman (chieftain) of the Cossacks and restored Cossack freedoms and rights. When Chmielnicki sought to install his son as leader in Moldavia, the Poles objected and resumed hostilities against him. At the Battle of Beresteczko in 1651, John II Casimir and a 150,000-man army defeated Chmielnicki and 200,000 Cossacks and Tatars. The Cossacks made peace, but Chmielnicki and some loyal followers carried on their fight. A Russo-Cossack treaty in 1654, recognizing the czar's rule in the Ukraine, helped precipitate the RUSSO-POLISH WAR OF 1654–56. See also POLISH-TURKISH WAR OF 1671–77.

Cholan-Pandyan War of A.D. c. 910   In India, the Cholan king, Parantaka I (fl. 907–53), enlarged his kingdom northward by taking control of the remnants of Pallavan territory soon after his accession to power. The Pallavan lands, however, had been coveted by the southern Pandya dynasty, allied with a small central Indian dynasty called the Ganga. Cholan forces easily defeated their rivals, who were not accustomed to territorial conflict, and thus gained influence in (but not complete control of) the entire southern tip of India—a task accomplished between 926 and 942. The later Cholan action, however, pitted them against the Rashtrakutas, successors of the first Chalukya dynasty, and the RASHTRAKUTAN-CHOLAN WAR OF A.D. c. 940–972 ensued. See also CHALUKYAN-CHOLAN WARS.

Chremonidean War (266–261 B.C.) The death of Pyrrhus (318?–272), king of Epirus, strengthened the position of King Antigonus II (c. 319–239) of Macedonia to gain full control of Greece (see DIADOCHI, WARS OF THE). Antigonus had tried previously to protect Macedonia from Greek revolts by a combination of garrisons and alliances with friendly governments, but Athens and Sparta formed an alliance in 267 with support from Egypt and declared war under the guidance of the motion's sponsor, Chremonides (fl. 260s), after whom the war is named. Antigonus did not want war, but he invaded Attica in 266. His forces defeated the Spartans near Corinth in 265 and withstood an Epirote invasion of Macedonia the next year. In 263, after the Macedon-blockading Egyptian fleet had departed, Antigonus's troops attacked Athens and gained its surrender in 262. A peace in 261 lasted for 10 years.

Christians' Revolt in Japan   See SHIMABARA REVOLT.

Cid's Conquest of Valencia, The (1089–94)   During the ALMORAVID CONQUEST of Muslim Spain, Rodrigo Díaz de Vivar, better known as the Cid (el Cid Campeador) (1040?–99), an independent Spanish traveling soldier nominally under the suzerainty of King Alfonso VI (1030–1109) of Castile and León, sought to take control of the independent Moorish (Spanish Muslim) kingdom of Valencia and its emir (ruler), al-Kadir (d. 1092). The Muslim Almoravids also wanted control of Valencia. In October 1092, Valencians, with Almoravid backing, rebelled and killed al-Kadir, but immediately the Cid and his private army invested the city of Valencia to prevent its capitulation to the Almoravids, who decided not to attack. The Valencians held out against the Cid, but finally starvation forced them to surrender on June 17, 1094, after a 20-month siege. As the new ruler of the city, the Cid allowed freedom of worship and property ownership subject to payment of tribute. In October 1094, Almoravid invaders were repulsed by his forces at the Battle of Cuarte outside the city walls and put to flight. Valencia remained under the rule of the Cid until his death in 1099; he checked a major assault by the Almoravids at the Battle of Bairen in 1097.

Cimmerian Invasion of Phrygia (c. 696–695 B.C.)   During their advance from western Siberia after 1000 B.C., the Scythians, fierce Indo-Iranian nomads, reached the Caucasus area and drove (8th cent.) an ancient Caucasian people, the Cimmerians, into Anatolia (Asiatic Turkey). The Cimmerians searched first for a homeland in eastern Anatolia, tried to enter Assyrian territory, but were forced into central Anatolia, where they invaded the ancient kingdom of Phrygia. During the reign of

Assyria's King Sennacherib (fl. 705–681), they brought an end to Phrygia's status as a major political power by destroying its capital, Gordium, and, according to Greek historian Herodotus (484?–425?), caused its king, the historical Midas (d.c. 695), to commit suicide. Called the *Gimarrai* in Assyrian records and *Gomer* in the Old Testament, the Cimmerians went on to harry Lydia before being driven by the Scythians into Cappadocia, where the Armenian name *Gamir* suggests their presence. Although its name lasted as the label of a geographic area under successive Anatolian rulers, Phrygia was never again a political entity.

Ciompi, Revolt of the (1378)   Florentine resentment against the reimposition of repressive Guelph (Guelf) Party rule, supported by the papacy, after the successful administration of "the Eight Saints" (see EIGHT SAINTS, WAR OF THE) welled up with the return of the Medicis in 1378. The *ciompi*, poor wool carders, forbidden to form a guild and thus denied political power, aroused the lower classes, including shopkeepers in minor guilds, in an attempt to establish a democratic government in Florence. In July 1378, the lower classes took over the government, and the *ciompi* were raised to the status of a guild. However, deteriorating economic conditions caused by the political upheaval soon led the minor guilds to abandon the *ciompi* and join the major guilds in overturning the new government and returning to another conservative social order, dominated by a new oligarchic group. The *ciompi* guild was abolished. Rioting and unrest persisted in Florence until 1382, when the major guilds finally regained dominance in the city. *Ciompi* leaders were killed or exiled, and the Guelph Party in time attained its former power.

Civil War, U.S (War between the States, War of the Rebellion, War of Secession, War for Southern Independence) (1861–65)   The complex causes of this conflict between the northern states of the Union and the southern states of the Confederacy were rooted in economic, social, political, and geographic differences between the two sections of the United States. Tensions had been building for decades, and every time a new state in the West was added, there was furious debate over whether or not slavery would be permitted in it. The election of Abraham Lincoln (1809–65) to the U.S. presidency in 1860 prompted South Carolina to call a state convention at which it decided to secede from the Union. Within two months, Georgia, Florida, Alabama, Mississippi, and Louisiana followed suit, and on February 8, 1861, they adopted a constitution for the provisional government of the Confederate States of America. Jefferson Davis (1808–89) was elected the Confederate president. The new nation quickly began confiscating federal property, such as forts and customhouses, but when it attempted to seize Fort Sumter in the Charleston, S.C., harbor, the federal commander resisted. The fort was bombarded by Confederate forces and surrendered (April 11–12, 1861), precipitating the start of the Civil War. The four wavering southern states—Virginia, North Carolina, Tennessee, and Arkansas—soon joined the Confederacy. For the next four years the opposing sides fought each other over thousands of miles in mountains, forests, fields, and on rivers and the sea. More than 2,400 battles and skirmishes took place, many of them bloody and destructive. Both sides were forced to conscript recruits for their armies, and both suffered many casualties. The South had expected Britain and perhaps France to support the Confederacy, but this did not happen officially; instead, Confederate export trade declined drastically when the Union's blockade of the southern ports became effective. At first the Confederate army commanded by General Robert E. Lee (1807–70) was successful in the East; major Confederate victories in Virginia occurred at Bull Run or Manassas (July 21, 1861 and August 29–30, 1862), during the Peninsular Campaign and Seven Days battles (April–July 1862), at Fredericksburg (December 13, 1862), and at Chancellorsville (May 2–4, 1863); but when Lee's army pushed into northern Maryland, it was stopped by a Union army under General George B. McClellan (1826–85) at Antietam Creek (Sharpsburg) on Sep-

tember 17, 1862, and when his army later invaded southern Pennsylvania, via the Shenandoah Valley, it was defeated by Union forces under General George G. Meade (1815–72) at Gettysburg on July 1–3, 1863. In the West the Union forces were very successful; General Ulysses S. Grant (1822–85) scored the first Union victories by capturing two forts on the Tennessee and Cumberland rivers. On April 6–7, 1862, he was again triumphant at the bloody Battle of Shiloh, Tenn., and the following year captured Vicksburg, Miss., and Chattanooga, Tenn. A Union naval fleet under Admiral David G. Farragut (1801–70) captured the port of New Orleans in April 1862, giving the Union control of the lower Mississippi. By the end of 1863, it controlled the entire river as well as many rivers in the northern part of the Confederacy. In 1864, Lincoln made Grant the Union's commander in chief, and he slowly forced Lee's army south toward Richmond, fighting the inconclusive Wilderness Campaign (May–June 1864). Meanwhile, General William T. Sherman (1820–91) and his Union army were advancing eastward through Tennessee and Georgia toward Atlanta, which they captured, occupied, and burned (September–November 1864) before continuing a devastating "march to the sea," to Savannah, Ga., carrying out a scorched-earth policy and cutting the South in half. After taking Savannah, Sherman moved north to join Grant. The Union armies were encircling the last Confederate forces in Virginia; Union general Philip H. Sheridan (1831–88), whose army had devastated the Shenandoah Valley's farmland (the Confederacy's breadbasket) between September 26 and October 8, 1864, won an important victory over Confederate general George E. Pickett (1825–75) at the crossroads near Dinwiddie Courthouse, Va. (Five Forts), on April 1, 1865. Petersburg, Va., was finally captured by the Union two days later, and soon Richmond, Va., the Confederacy's capital, fell. Realizing that further resistance was futile, Lee surrendered at Appomattox Courthouse on April 9, 1865. The war was over, and the Union was preserved but at a terrible price. The reconstruction period that followed was often vindictive and cruel; there was intolerance and bitterness on both sides, and the problems of racism and sectionalism still persist. See also BROWN'S RAID ON HARPERS FERRY; WAKARUSA WAR.

Claiborne's Rebellion (1644–46) Disputes over Crown grants led to conflict between Maryland and Virginia. Colonist William Claiborne (c. 1587–c. 1677) directed the Virginia forces with support from the colony's council. Twice secretary of state for Virginia, Claiborne had established a trade post in 1631 on Kent Island, territorially part of the 1609 grant to the Virginia Colony, but also granted to George Calvert, First Lord Baltimore (c. 1580–1632), as part of Maryland in 1632. Intermittent sea hostilities caused both colonies to appeal unsuccessfully to the Crown for redress. Meanwhile, Maryland seized Kent Island in 1637; Claiborne's forces recaptured it in 1644. Claiborne also successfully incited an insurrection by anti-Catholic Marylanders; forced Governor Leonard Calvert (1606–47), George Calvert's second son, into Virginia; and held Maryland from 1644 through 1646, when a 1642 Crown reassignment of the disputed land was effected.

Coalition, War of the First (1792–98) Flushed with victory during the first phase of the FRENCH REVOLUTIONARY WARS, the French Constitutional Convention offered aid to seekers of liberty everywhere, which, combined with the execution of King Louis XVI (1754–93) and the opening of the Scheldt estuary to French commerce, provoked Britain, Holland, Spain, Austria, Prussia, and Russia into forming the First Coalition against France. Early allied victories occurred at Neerwinden, Mainz, and Kaiserslautern, and the French were evicted from the Austrian Netherlands. But the demoralized French regrouped, formed citizen armies by mass mobilization of the population, and went on the offensive, driving the Prussians back across the Rhine. Russia, distracted by unrest in Poland, withdrew from the coalition in 1794. French successes compelled Holland (renamed the Batavian Republic) to make peace in 1795, followed by Prussia and Spain in the First and Second Treaties of Basel in 1795. Two years later, after being besieged at Mantua by the French under Napoleon (1769–1821), Austria concluded the Treaty of Campo Formio, ceding the Austrian Netherlands to France.

Coalition, War of the Second (1798–1801) French aggressions driving the pope from Rome and causing the formation of French-sponsored Roman, Ligurian, Cisalpine, and Helvetic republics triggered another coalition war (see COALITION, WAR OF THE FIRST), arraying Russia, Austria, Britain, Portugal, Naples, and the Ottoman Empire against France. Naples, quickly falling to the French in early 1799, was declared the Parthenopean Republic. However, in northern Italy that year, Russian forces under Aleksandr V. Suvorov (1729–1800), who was in conjunction with the Austrians, won important victories against the French at Cassano, Trebbia River, and Novi. The French-created buffer republics in Italy disintegrated as the French lost ground. Suvorov's Russians crossed the Alps into Switzerland, but dissension between the Austrians and Russians caused Suvorov's withdrawal from the war. The French under Napoleon (1769–1821), now First Consul, demolished the Austrians at the Battle of Marengo on June 14, 1800. Austrian resistance was completely broken after the French under Jean Victor Moreau (1763–1813) won at Hohenlinden on December 3, 1800. The Second Coalition collapsed when Austria signed the Peace of Lunéville on February 9, 1801. See also FRENCH REVOLUTIONARY WARS; NAPOLEONIC WARS.

Coalition, War of the Third (1805–7) During the NAPOLEONIC WARS, Napoleon (1769–1821), emperor of the French, proclaimed himself king of Italy in 1805 (he had annexed Genoa), causing a third coalition to be formed against him by Britain, Austria, Russia, and Sweden. Abandoning plans to invade England, Napoleon sent his Grand Army against the Austrians at Ulm, winning an overwhelming victory in October 1805. He then occupied Vienna and routed the Russians and Austrians at the Battle of Austerlitz on December 2, 1805. Austria was eliminated from the coalition and evicted from Italy by the Treaty of Pressburg. Prussia, joining the coalition in 1806, was promptly defeated at Jena and Auerstädt in October 1806. French forces under Napoleon fought an inconclusive battle against the Russians at Eylau in February 1807; Napoleon's advance on the Russian frontier was briefly checked. Russian forces were crushed by Napoleon's army at Friedland on June 14, 1807, and three days later Russia asked for a truce. By the Treaties of Tilsit in July 1807, France made peace with Russia and forced Prussia to give up half of its territory. Napoleon was now virtually in control of western and central Europe. See NAPOLEON'S INVASION OF RUSSIA.

Coalition Wars against Louis XIV   See DUTCH WAR, THIRD; GRAND ALLIANCE, WAR OF THE; SPANISH SUCCESSION, WAR OF THE.

Colombian Civil War of 1861   The early national history of Colombia saw a political division develop between conservatives, who favored a strong central government and a strong ecclesiastical establishment, and liberals, who desired strong state governments and a reduction of church authority. Though the conservatives controlled the presidency until 1849, that date saw the election of the liberal José Hilario López (c. 1800–1869). During his term in office, the liberals proclaimed a new constitution (1853), ended slavery, separated church and state, gave all adult males the vote, made almost all offices elective, and established the principles of federalism, in which local governments were nearly autonomous. This federalist constitution led to a weakening of central authority, frequent revolts, and a discrediting of liberals, which brought on the election of a conservative president, Mariano Ospina (1805–75), in 1857. In an effort to placate his opponents, Ospina proclaimed a new constitution in 1858 that embodied many federalist

principles and established the republic as the Granadan Confederation. The republic's states grew more independent, and in 1860 an attempt by the national government to inspect the electoral procedures of the states and to bring the state militias under its control resulted in civil war. General Tomas Cipriano de Mosquera (1798–1878), a liberal and the governor of Cauca, declared his state independent and marched with his army into Bogotá, the country's capital; Ospina was ousted and imprisoned, and Mosquera declared himself provisional president on July 18, 1861. See also "EPOCH OF CIVIL WARS," COLOMBIAN.

Colombian Civil War of 1899–1903   See THOUSAND DAYS, WAR OF A.

Colombian "Epoch of Civil Wars"   See "EPOCH OF CIVIL WARS," COLOMBIAN.

Colombian Guerrilla War of 1976–   In 1976, the government of Colombia instituted a state of siege against left-wing guerrilla groups that had been trying to foment civil war in the country. Leftist political violence continued and led to a government-decreed tough "security statute" (1978) that curtailed individual liberties and was objected to by liberals and the press. On January 1, 1979, guerrillas of the Movement of April 19 (M-19), which got its name from the date in 1970 when its notorious hero Gustavo Rojas Pinilla (1900–1975) lost the presidential election, captured more than 5,000 weapons form the main military arsenal in Bogotá, the capital. Hundreds of suspected leftist rebels were arrested and imprisoned; some were reportedly tortured. Another left-wing guerrilla movement, the Colombian Revolutionary Armed Forces (FARC), increased its violence against the government, blowing up army tanks and carrying out armed actions. In 1980, M-19 guerrillas seized 15 diplomats and others in a raid on a diplomatic reception at the Dominican Republic embassy in Bogotá. They demanded the release of 311 political prisoners and a $50 million ransom payment for setting free their hostages. A settlement was negotiated after 61 days, and the guerrillas fled safely to Havana, Cuba, with 12 hostages, who were then freed. Although many M-19 leaders were killed or captured in a violent shoot-out with Colombian army troops (March 18, 1981), the M-19 and FARC continued their subversive activities, along with other rebel groups, while right-wing paramilitary groups (death squads) engaged in reprisals against the guerrillas. An amnesty offered to the guerrillas by the government met with limited success (1982–83). On November 6, 1985, M-19 guerrillas seized the Palace of Justice in Bogotá; government forces stormed the building the next day, and 106 persons died in the battle, including 11 Supreme Court judges and all the rebels. An agreement to extradite narcotics suspects to the U.S. for trial ignited "drug wars" during 1986–90. Extreme drug-related violence caused the deaths of three candidates for president in 1990; César Gaviria Trujillo (1947–) of the Liberal Party won and moved to form a coalition government of Liberals, Conservatives, and other groups. FARC joined forces with another leftist guerrilla group, the National Liberation Army (ELN), and attacked about 50 strategic installations (1991); M-19 had disbanded along with two other rebel organizations after a new constitution went into effect in 1991, ratifying the non-extradition of Colombians to face trial abroad. Federal soldiers fought battles with guerrillas in Antioquia province (1992) and killed Pablo Escobar (1949–93), leader of the Medellín cocaine cartel. Afterward the Cali cartel gained strength and, by 1995, reportedly controlled up to 70 percent of the world's trade in cocaine. The Liberal government under Ernesto Samper Pizano (1950–), elected president in 1994, continued to battle the FARC and ELN guerrillas, who supported uprisings (1996) by growers of cocaine in Putumayo and Caquetá provinces (peasant farmers wanted compensation for loss of their drug crops due to the government cocaine eradication program). The FARC and ELN continued to attack oil pipelines, power lines, and police and military installations, where they at times took soldiers hostage until their demands were met (1996–98). In 1999, Colombia seemed split into three volatile regions: the north, ruled by right-wing paramilitary, drug-trafficking groups; the middle, ruled by a dysfunctional federal government and ineffective military; and the south, dominated by the FARC and ELN guerrillas, who controlled the borders and thrived on kidnappings and cocaine production.

Colombian Revolt of 1948   Colombia, plagued by social and economic problems, was also embroiled in a political feud between the country's two traditional parties, the Liberals and Conservatives, when Jorge Eliécer Gaitán (1902–48), popular left-wing Liberal leader, was assassinated on April 9, 1948, while a Pan-American conference was being held in Bogotá, the Colombian capital. Immediately riots and vandalism occurred throughout the country (this sudden outbreak of violence seems to have been the result of longtime pent-up frustration by the public over numerous local and national issues). Colombia was thrown into a constant state of insurrection and criminality from 1948 to 1958 (called "La Violencia"), a period during which more than 200,000 persons lost their lives and more than a billion dollars of property damage was done. Laureano Eleuterio Gómez (1889–1965), an archconservative, served as Colombia's president from 1950 until his ouster in 1953 in a coup led by Army Chief of Staff General Gustavo Rojas Pinilla (1900–1975), who ruled as a dictatorial president until his corrupt, brutal regime was deposed (1957) by a military junta supported by both Liberals and Conservatives. In 1958, democracy returned to Colombia upon the formation of a Liberal-Conservative coalition government (the National Front) under newly elected president Alberto Lleras Camargo (1906–90), who slowly stabilized the country's faltering economy and instituted agrarian reform.

Colombian War of Independence   (1810–19)   With the fall of Spanish king Ferdinand VII (1784–1833) during the PENINSULAR WAR in Spain, the town council at Bogotá in New Granada (Colombia) declared loyalty to the king, but by 1810 it had expelled royal officials and established a provincial junta. Most of the other large towns in New Granada also ousted Spanish authorities and formed juntas, some of which drafted constitutions. Instead of uniting for common defense against the royalists, the various juntas fought among themselves, weakening the revolutionary movement. Rebel forces commanded by Simón Bolívar (1783–1830) won some successes but were decisively defeated by Spanish troops led by Pablo Morillo (1777–1838) at Santa Mara in 1815. The royalists regained control of New Granada, and Bolívar fled to Jamaica and then Haiti. In 1816, after establishing a base at Angostura (Ciudad Bolívar) (see VENEZUELAN WAR OF INDEPENDENCE), Bolívar put into motion a daring plan, leading a ragged but well-armed 3,500-man army across Venezuela, over seven rivers, and over the high Andes to attack Bogotá. During the arduous march in June–July 1819, Bolívar's army was joined by forces under Francisco de Paula Santander (1792–1840) and volunteer European soldiers. More than 1,000 died on the way. At the Battle of Boyacá on August 7, 1819, the revolutionary army defeated the Spaniards; Bogotá was taken soon afterward, ensuring the independence of New Granada. Bolívar became the new republic's president and then returned to Angostura and the unfinished war in Venezuela. Later, in 1822, he and Antonio José de Sucre (1785–1830) moved patriot troops into Quito province (Ecuador) and fought bitter battles until Sucre's decisive victory near Pichincha volcano on May 24, 1822. What is now Ecuador was freed from Spanish rule and was persuaded by Bolívar to unite with Greater Colombia (Colombia, Panama, and Venezuela). See also PERUVIAN WAR OF INDEPENDENCE.

Comoran Rebellion of 1997   In the Indian Ocean between northern Mozambique and Madagascar lie the Comoros, consisting mainly of Grande Comore (Ngazidja), Anjouan (Nzwani), and Mohéli (Mwali), three predominantly Muslim islands, which gained independence from France in 1975.

Southeast of Anjouan lies Mayotte (Mahore), a largely Christian island that remains under French administration. In July 1997, Anjouan and Mohéli declared their independence, calling the Comoran (Comorian) government corrupt and seeking to reestablish ties with France. On September 3, about 300 troops were dispatched from Moroni, the capital on Grande Comore, to regain control of Anjouan, where secessionists put up heavy resistance with the use of foreign mercenaries, artillery, and other materiel; the troops were withdrawn several days later. Calling the secession "an internal affair," France declined to intervene; the Organization of African Unity (OAU) sponsored peace talks between the two sides. In late 1997, the Comoros's president appointed a native of Anjouan as his prime minister.

Comuneros' Uprising in New Granada (1781) By attempting to increase royal revenues through forced collection of back taxes and higher taxes on tobacco and liquor, the Spanish government in New Granada (Colombia, Panama, Venezuela, and Ecuador) aroused much hostility, leading to the outbreak of rioting at Socorro in March 1781. Quickly, groups of *comuneros*, citizens seeking democratic reforms under the leadership of three creoles—Juan Francisco Berbeo, Jose Antonio Galán, and Ambrosio Pisco—rose up throughout the country, overwhelming royal authorities and rejecting taxes. When Berbeo's *comunero* "army" prepared to march on the capital, Bogotá, negotiations immediately began, resulting in the authorities' capitulation to the *comuneros'* demands to end taxes and monopolies. The rebels then dispersed. However, the Spanish viceroy received reinforcements and led an army into the interior, where he thoroughly routed the *comuneros* and their Indian allies. Berbeo, Galán, and Pisco were captured; the former two were promptly executed, and the latter was punished by long-term imprisonment, along with many followers.

Comuneros' Uprising in Paraguay   (1723–35) José de Antequera y Castro (1690–1731) led the comuneros, citizens for democratic rights, against the repressive authority of the Spanish royal governor at Asunción, Paraguay. The governor was imprisoned, and Antequera assumed his office and upheld the rights of the people over those of the Spanish king. The viceroy of Peru repeatedly sent forces to remove Antequera but failed. In 1726, royal troops under the governor of Buenos Aires invaded and occupied Asunción; Antequera was captured, imprisoned in Lima, Peru, and finally beheaded on July 5, 1731. While in prison, Antequera inspired a fellow prisoner, Fernando Mompox, to carry on the fight against arbitrary and unjust rule in Paraguay. Comuneros under Mompox's leadership declared Paraguay an independent republic and held out against military expeditions sent to topple the government until 1735, when a force under Bruno Mauricio de Zabala (1682–1736) defeated the rebels. Spanish royal authority was promptly reestablished in Paraguay.

Comuneros' Uprising in Spain (1520–21)   Popular discontent with the autocratic rule of King Charles I (1500–1558) of Spain erupted into an uprising of the comuneros, Spanish advocates of constitutional and democratic government. The disparate factions of the comunero movement (nobles, bourgeoisie, and radicals) soon fell into disunity, with the nobles withdrawing and backing Charles. On April 23, 1521, royal forces defeated the comuneros at Villalar, after which the movement's leaders were caught and executed. Government authority was reestablished, with Charles having more power.

Congolese Civil War of 1960–68   Belgium granted independence to the Congo (Zaire) on June 30, 1960, but the leaders of this large new African republic, President Joseph Kasavubu (1910?–69) and leftist premier Patrice Lumumba (1925–61), were ill-prepared to bring a sense of national unity to its 22 million citizens from more than 200 tribes. Almost immediately tribal conflicts erupted, and units of the Congo army mutinied. On July 11, 1960,

Moise Tshombe (1919–69), leader of Katanga (Shaba) province, announced that his mineral-rich province was seceding from the Congo, and South Kasai province soon followed suit. Kasavubu and Lumumba requested military aid and a peacekeeping force from the United Nations; a UN force was sent for a four-year stay. Lumumba also appealed for help from the Soviet Union; the charge that he was a communist caused him to be dismissed from his post on September 5, 1960. Chaos followed, and nine days later Colonel Joseph-Désiré Mobutu, later called Mobutu Sese Seko (1930–97), army chief of staff, seized virtual control of the government. Lumumba was arrested about two months later and was mysteriously murdered in a prison in Katanga in February 1961. Violence and bloodshed characterized the years that followed, for the undisciplined Congo army troops were unable to maintain peace and order. In 1963, the UN persuaded Katanga to rejoin the Congo, and in mid-1964 UN forces left the Congo. Returning from exile, Tshombe was named premier (July 9, 1964), attempted forcibly to make peace with the various rebel groups, and introduced white mercenary troops and officers into the army (this was denounced by communist-bloc African nations). Tshombe, however, was no more able than his predecessor to bring peace to the vast country. Rebels seized many white hostages and held them at Stanleyville (Kisangani) until Belgian paratroopers, flown in on U.S. airplanes, rescued them (November 25–27, 1964). In a power struggle, Tshombe was ousted by Kasavubu on October 13, 1965, and again went into exile. The next month Mobutu deposed Kasavubu in a bloodless coup and named himself president of a military government, which gradually strengthened the central authority of the state. Local insurrections continued to flare up, and the loyalty of Katanga remained a problem. In 1967, the white mercenaries were dismissed from the Congo army and, in protest, occupied Stanleyville and Bukavu, the capital of Kivu province, with the help of Katangan rebels. A state of emergency was declared; Stanleyville was retaken after heavy fighting; the mercenaries and Katangans abandoned Bukavu, only to seize it again in August 1967. Congolese government forces recaptured the city, driving the mercenaries and their allies into neighboring Rwanda (October 1967). In 1968, the most persistent and widespread internal rebellion was crushed, and its leader executed. Tshombe was sentenced in absentia to death for treason and found refuge in Algeria, where he died in 1969. By then Mobutu was definitely firmly in control.

Congolese Civil War of 1997 In June 1997, disgruntled soldiers loyal to General Denis Sassou-Nguesso (1943–), president of the Republic of the Congo from 1979 to 1992, rose up to overthrow President Pascal Lissouba (1931–), who had tried to loosen the control of large French oil company Elf Aquitaine on his country's petroleum market since his election in 1992. Over 2,000 persons died during fighting and looting in the capital, Brazzaville, which was largely destroyed during the next four months. France evacuated foreign nationals and troops from its former colony. Calls for a cease-fire were ignored by the warring sides until a Gabon-mediated truce (July 5) ended intense combat. But sporadic fighting continued while Gabon and seven other African nations tried in vain to find a permanent solution to the conflict. In October 1997, Angola deployed fighter jets, tanks, and 3,500 troops to support Sassou-Nguesso's forces, which then seized Brazzaville and Pointe-Noire, the main coastal city. Lissouba fled to Burkina Faso, and the victorious Sassou-Nguesso called for reconciliation after assuming the presidency.

Congolese Civil War of 1998–   On August 3, 1998, in the easternmost part of the Democratic Republic of the Congo (formerly Zaire), rebellious, Tutsi-led troops seized control of Goma and Bukavu, announcing their intention to topple the government of Congolese president Laurent Kabila (1940–), who was accused of tribalism, power-grabbing, mismanagement, and extravagant living. Kabila had evidently discriminated against the Congo's Tutsi minority, known collectively as the Banyamulenge and closely tied to neighboring Rwanda (see RWANDAN CIVIL WAR OF 1990–94). Mainly consisting of Tutsis, Rwandan soldiers, and disenchanted Congolese, the rebels opened up battlefronts in both the east and west, capturing Kisangani and the Congo River port of Matadi respectively by mid-August. Rwanda's Minister of Defense Paul Kagame (1957?–) appeared to back the rebellion in the eastern Congo, with a hope perhaps to redraw the borders there to protect his Tutsi brothers. Zimbabwe's President Robert Mugabe (1924–) deployed troops to help Kabila fight off rebels advancing on the Congo's capital, Kinshasa. Angolan troops soon crossed into the Congo in support of Kabila's loyalist forces. The war threatened to engulf other African states, and chances of a negotiated settlement grew dim. In early 1999, in retaliation against attacks by Kabila's allies, rebels terrorized and slaughtered many civilians in eastern villages. See ZAIRIAN CIVIL WAR OF 1996–97.

Constantinople, Fall of (1453) Ottoman Turks encircled the Byzantine Empire and reduced it to Constantinople (Istanbul) and the surrounding area. On April 6, 1453, an 80,000-man Turkish army, led by Sultan Muhammad II (1429–81), called "the Conqueror," began a siege of Constantinople, defended by Byzantine Emperor Constantine XI Palaeologus (1404–53) and his 10,000-man army. The city was blockaded by the Turkish navy, which drove off an assisting Venetian naval fleet. Bombardments by Turkish cannons breached the massive city walls, which could no longer be blocked off by the Byzantines, and the Turks finally entered Constantinople on May 29, 1453. Constantine gallantly fought the Turks at one of the gates of the city until he was overwhelmed and slain. Muhammad allowed his warriors to plunder Constantinople for three days; the Byzantine Empire had come to an end. See also BYZANTINE–OTTOMAN TURK WAR OF 1422.

Constantinople, Siege of (A.D. 717–18) An 80,000-man Muslim army from Pergamum (Bergama), a city taken by the Muslims in 716 during the BYZANTINE-MUSLIM WAR OF A.D. 698–718, crossed the Hellespont (strait now called the Dardanelles) and laid siege to Constantinople (Istanbul), the Byzantine capital, in July 717. Emperor Leo III (680?–741) kept the Muslims at bay, employing "Greek fire"—a flammable composition of sulfur, naphtha, quicklime, and sea water—to force the invaders from the city's walls. Muslim caliph Sulayman (674–717) joined the assault, leading about 2,000 Arab warships with another 80,000 men through the Hellespont; but, after landing his force, he was driven back by Leo's Byzantine army. The Muslims camped for the winter and, with 50,000 reinforcements, attacked in the spring of 718. Leo's land and sea forces won victories. Bulgars under King Terbelis (fl. 710–20), then allied with the Byzantines against the Arabs, marched into Thrace and crushed the Muslims near Adrianople. In August 718, the Muslim army began a retreat back through Asia Minor, pursued by Leo's troops, and the Muslim fleet, with many soldiers aboard, left and was later almost entirely destroyed in a storm.

Corinthian-Corcyrean War (435–433 B.C.) Corcyra (Corfu or Kérkira), a Greek island colony in the Ionian Sea, began a naval war against its mother city of Corinth over the latter's attempt to control their joint mainland colony Epidamnus. In 435, when Corcyreans moved on Epidamnus, a Corinthian fleet of 75 ships tried to relieve the colony and suffered serious defeat by 80 Corcyrean triremes at the Gulf of Ambracia (Árta). Humiliated by the loss, Corinth built a larger fleet, while fearful Corcyra appealed to Athens for aid. Ten Athenian ships were sent to Corcyra. In the Battle of Sybota (433), the attacking Corinthian fleet was overwhelming the Corcyreans when additional Athenian warships arrived to force the Corinthians to withdraw and return home. Corinth bitterly resented the Corcyrean-Athenian alliance, which helped to precipitate the Second or Great PELOPONNESIAN WAR two years later.

Corinthian War (395–387 B.C.) After the peace of 404 (see PELOPONNESIAN WAR, SECOND OR GREAT), Thebes was so angry at Sparta's tyrannical dominance that it allied with its recent enemy, Athens; together, they established a coalition in 395. Thebes repelled a Spartan invasion of Boeotia, and Sparta's warring with Persia enabled Athens to use Persian money to rebuild its fleet; with it, Athens defeated a Spartan fleet at Cnidus in 394 and recovered many Aegean port cities by 390. Athens's defenses were rebuilt. On land, the triumphs were chiefly Spartan. Victory at Nemea (394) and the regaining of Persian aid enabled Sparta to win again at Coronea (394) and blockade Corinth (393) and Athens (392). Athens captured Corinth in 390 and put Argives in charge, but, by 387, Athens's only power, its fleet in the Dardanelles, was cut off by the Persian navy. Almost bankrupt, Athens had to accept a Persian peace (the "King's Peace," 386), dissolving Athenian alliances in the Aegean. Thebes lost control of Boeotian cities, and Argos evacuated Corinth. Only Sparta retained power, and then only at Persia's pleasure. See also THEBAN-SPARTAN WAR OF 379–371 B.C.

Corsican Revolts of 1729–69 Genoa, Italy, controlled the island of Corsica, whose native inhabitants increasingly resented Genoese tyranny. Led by local notables, Corsicans spontaneously rose in revolt, taking control of the island's interior and carrying on their fight for independence. German adventurer Baron Theodor Neuhof (1694–1756) landed on Corsica with help for the rebels, was for a period successful against the Genoese, and was proclaimed (1736) "King" Theodore I of Corsica. But, in late 1736, he suffered defeat and escaped from the island while civil war raged; returning twice (1738, 1743) in vain attempts to reestablish his "kingdom," he lost to the Genoese, who received French aid, and fled to England. In 1755, the Corsican nationalist Pasquale Paoli, whose father had led Corsicans in revolt in 1734–35 and had been a supporter of Neuhof, returned from exile abroad to lead his countrymen in a triumphant revolt against Genoese rule and was elected Corsica's president under a republican constitution (1755); the Genoese continued to fight Paoli, who introduced enlightened self-government and reforms. After 1764, France, Genoa's ally, engaged in war to topple Paoli and, in 1768, bought Corsica from Genoa, which had abandoned hope of ever subjugating the island. Superior French forces invaded, encountering vigorous resistance from Paoli's outnumbered but brilliantly generaled soldiers, who were eventually defeated (1769). Paoli escaped to England, and France annexed Corsica.

Corupedion, Battle of (281 B.C.) At Corupedion in ancient Lydia in western Asia Minor, a curious battle ended the military conflicts of the Diadochi (see DIADOCHI, WARS OF THE). Fought to determine possession of Asia Minor, it involved Lysimachus (c. 355–281) with Macedonian troops and Seleucus I (358?–280) with a Syrian army. Before the assembled troops, these two aged leaders engaged in single combat. Seleucus killed Lysimachus, and afterward his army routed the Macedonians. Now master of Asia Minor, Seleucus invaded Macedonia in 280 and was assassinated there. His son Antiochus I (c. 324–c. 261), took control of Egypt; Antigonus II (c. 319–239) became king of Macedonia. With Seleucus's death, despite struggles in Thrace and Macedonia until 276 to establish Antigonus II, the contests of the Diadochi were over. All of the original successors were dead.

Cossack and Peasant Revolts See CHMIELNICKI'S REVOLT; PUGACHEV'S REVOLT; RAZIN'S REVOLT.

Costa Rican Civil War of 1948 Costa Rica's presidential election of 1948 was won by Otilio Ulate (1895–1973), but the results were declared invalid and annulled by the congress on March 1, 1948. Immediately civil war broke out between Ulate's followers, led by Colonel José "Pepe" Figueres Ferrer (1906–90), a Costa Rican planter, and the supporters of the defeated presidential candidate, Rafael Calderón Guardia (1900–1970). Figueres's force, called the "Caribbean Legion," battled successfully against Calderón's forces, which included government troops and communists and which received outside aid from President Anastasio Somoza (1896–1956) of Nicaragua and President Tiburcio Carías Andino (1876–1969) of Honduras. On April 28, 1948, after about six weeks of fighting, Figueres entered the capital city of San José and ousted the government. On May 8, 1948, he established a ruling military junta, over which he presided for 18 months. The junta made revolutionary changes by dissolving the Costa Rican army, outlawing the Communist Party, nationalizing banks, and beginning civil service reform. There was opposition to these changes; on December 10, 1948, armed Calderónista rebels exiled in Nicaragua invaded Costa Rica but were repulsed, while the Organization of American States sent a commission to investigate Somoza's involvement in the invasion. In early 1949, a Costa Rican constitutional assembly met, confirmed the earlier election of Ulate, and drafted a new constitution. On November 8, 1949, Figueres turned over the government to Ulate.

Costa Rican Rebellion of 1955 José "Pepe" Figueres Ferrer (1906–90), a moderate socialist, was elected president of Costa Rica in 1953. Dictatorial president Anastasio Somoza (1896–1956) of Nicaragua claimed that members of the Caribbean Legion, a group of political exiles from Caribbean nations, participated in a plot to assassinate him with Figueres's help (the legion had backed Figueres in his election); Somoza apparently made plans to retaliate and supported Rafael Calderón Guardia (1900–1970), a disgruntled former president of Costa Rica, who led a band of rebels south from Nicaragua and seized the northern Costa Rican border town of Villa Quesada on the Pan American Highway (January 11, 1955). Figueres immediately appealed to the Organization of American States to investigate; its commission discovered that the rebels' supplies and war matériel were coming from Nicaragua. As soon as this was publicly announced, Nicaragua ceased supporting the rebels, who were mostly Costa Ricans. Meanwhile, the United States had sold four fighter planes to Costa Rica. Some heavy fighting occurred in several towns, but the rebels were no match for the popularly backed government forces and were driven north over the border into Nicaragua. In early 1956, Costa Rica and Nicaragua agreed to cooperate in a surveillance of their border.

Costa Rican Revolution of 1917   The proposed reforms of Alfredo González Flores (1877–after 1967), the elected democratic president of Costa Rica since 1913, were opposed by General Federico Tinoco Granados (1870–1931), who led a military revolt that overthrew González and his government (January 27, 1917). Tinoco set up a military dictatorship; in time, insurrections broke out against his despotic regime, which the United States refused to recognize and had denounced. Threatened by U.S. intervention, Tinoco resigned in May 1919; about a month later, U.S. Marines landed in Costa Rica to safeguard American interests there. In 1920, an orderly, democratic government was restored under the newly elected Costa Rican president, Julio Acosta García (1872–1954), whom the U.S. government recognized. The next year Costa Rica nearly went to war with neighboring Panama over a longtime boundary dispute; when Panamanian troops moved into disputed territory on the Pacific coast, fighting occurred until U.S. officials persuaded the Panamanians to evacuate the area, which Costa Rica held. The boundary was not fully fixed until 1941.

Count's War (1533–36)   Strong religious dissension in Denmark between Lutheran burghers (townspeople) and peasants and Roman Catholic nobles was reflected in the decision of the noble-dominated Rigsraad (state council), following the death of King Frederick I (1471?–1533), to govern temporarily without a king rather than accept a Lutheran partisan. Danish rebels, allied with the northern German city of Lübeck (see LÜBECK'S WAR OF 1531–36), sought to restore the imprisoned former Danish king, Christian II (1481–1559)(see KALMAR CIVIL WAR OF 1520–23), and to bring the cities of Copenhagen and Malmö into the Hanseatic League (mercantile league of cities in the Baltic). Supported by leading Jutland nobles and bishops, Frederick's eldest son and successor, Christian (1503–59), the Lutheran-educated duke of Holstein, led a military campaign against Count Christopher (c. 1504–66) of Oldenburg, who commanded the Lübeck and Danish forces favoring the restoration of Christian II (the war derived its name from Count Christopher, whose forces invaded and plundered Holstein, blockaded and captured Copenhagen, and later took Zealand, Malmö, and Skåne). Opposed by half of Denmark, Christian, as King Christian III (he had been elected king by the Rigsraad in 1534), wrested lands from the count's control and pushed back the count's armies to Ålborg in northern Jutland, which Christian's forces took in a bloody massacre in 1535. Swedish forces (Sweden had allied itself with Christian III) besieged Malmö, Landskrona, and Zealand. Christian's blockade of Copenhagen finally forced Count Christopher to surrender in late July 1536, and Christian took control of the Danish kingdom. Though Lübeck and its allies kept their trading rights, their power (and that of the Hanseatic League) was broken in the Baltic (Lübeck held the Danish island of Bornholm for 50 years as reimbursement for the war's expenses). Count Christopher was forced to swear never to enter Denmark again and returned home to Oldenburg in northern Germany. Christian III established the Lutheran Church in Denmark and imposed it on Norway.

Covenanters' Rebellion of 1666   King Charles II (1630–85) of England, Scotland, and Ireland was not a man of his word (like his father). He had signed the Solemn League and Covenant Agreement (see ENGLISH CIVIL WAR, SECOND) only to safeguard his advancement to the throne. Having no plans to return to Scotland, he ruled this country through a reformed Covenanter (Scottish Presbyterian) named John Maitland

(1616–82), duke of Lauderdale, and the Scottish Church through an archbishop of St. Andrews named James Sharp (1613–79), both of whom approved his restoration of the Anglican episcopacy (see BISHOPS' WAR, FIRST). The Covenanters were provoked and then angered when a rescissory act abolished all agreements of the Commonwealth (i.e., Cromwellian) era. All clergy appointed after 1649 were asked to resign, unauthorized (i.e., Presbyterian) services were banned, fines were levied, and Highland troops were based in the Lowlands. The Covenanters attacked Edinburgh and were defeated at the Battle of Pentland Hills on November 28, 1666, but nonetheless continued to defy Charles II's new restrictions.

Covenanters' Rebellion of 1679   Repressive measures against the Presbyterian Church undertaken by John Maitland (1616–82), duke of Lauderdale, one of the chief ministers of England's King Charles II (1630–85), angered the Covenanters (Scottish Presbyterians), causing them to rebel and murder Archbishop James Sharp (1613–79), a suppressor of their church. At Drumclog the Covenanters crushed a royalist force on June 1, 1679. The government then dispatched a strong force under Charles's illegitimate son James Scot (1649–85), duke of Monmouth, that decisively defeated the rebels at Bothwell Bridge on June 22, 1679; 1,400 prisoners were taken to Edinburgh and executed. Charles continued his oppressions against the Presbyterians, and later Covenant preachers openly advocated armed rebellion. The 1680s were to be known as "the killing time."

Covenanters' Rebellion of 1685   Upon the death of King Charles II (1630–85) of England, Scotland, and Ireland, James II (1633–1701), called James VII in Scotland, succeeded him and, as a Roman Catholic rightly suspected of planning to force Catholicism on Scotland and England, was distrusted and feared. His Scottish policy was actually similar to that of his father, Charles I (1600–1649), except for toleration of Catholics, and it too was opposed. The

earl of Argyll unsuccessfully attempted a Covenanters' rebellion in Scotland and was captured and executed; the duke of Monmouth, James Scot (1649–85), failed, too (see MONMOUTH'S REBELLION). England's opposition to Roman Catholicism became international when William of Orange (1650–1702), later King William III of England, Scotland, and Ireland, began to support and finance it. When William became king in 1688 (see GLORIOUS REVOLUTION) with James II's Protestant daughter Mary II (1662–94) as his queen, most of Scotland was satisfied. Only the Jacobites grumbled (see JACOBITE REBELLION OF 1689).

Cracow Insurrection (1846)   Although under Austrian, Russian, and Prussian protection, the small, free Republic of Cracow (the Polish city of Cracow [Krakow] and the area around it), established by the Congress of Vienna at the end of the NAPOLEONIC WARS (1815), became an important symbolic remnant of a once independent Poland (divided among Russia, Austria, and Prussia). In 1833–46, secret Polish revolutionaries tried in vain to effect their country's independence. In February–March 1846, the revolutionary leader Jan Tyssowski (1811–57) and others in Cracow fomented an insurrection in nearby Galicia (Austrian-ruled Poland) and elsewhere; in the countryside the rebels, mainly Polish nationalist landlords, became pitted against peasants, who remained loyal to Austria (and were paid a 10-florin bounty for capturing or killing a seditious landlord). The insurrection was suppressed by the Russians and Austrians, who forcibly moved into and occupied Cracow, which then ceased to exist as an independent entity; Austria attached Cracow to Galicia. The failure of the rebels weakened Polish participation in the more general liberal revolutions of 1848. See also POLISH REVOLUTION OF 1794.

Crécy, Battle of (1346)   King Edward III (1312–77) of England, busy with Scottish problems, delayed returning to the front in the HUNDRED YEARS' WAR until 1346, when he, the Black Prince

(Edward's son), and 20,000 men raided across France from Cherbourg. Some 60,000 French met them at Crécy, on a battlefield chosen by Edward, on August 26, 1346. Placing his main force halfway up a hill, with reserves at the top, Edward had longbowmen flank his front line. Arrows slaughtered the first three French infantry regiments and then riddled cavalry horses. English men-at-arms completed the slaughter of the French. The one-day battle, capped by the seizure of Calais, made Edward the most feared monarch in Europe.

Creek War (1813–14) The Creek Indians, who had been allies of the British during the WAR OF 1812, were angered by white encroachment on their hunting grounds in Georgia and Alabama. In 1813, some Creeks under Chief Red Eagle (William Weatherford) (1780?–1824) attacked and burned Fort Mims on the lower Alabama River, killing about 500 whites (see FORT MIMS MASSACRE). Afterward, U.S. militiamen, led by General Andrew Jackson (1767–1845), invaded Creek territory in central Alabama and destroyed two Indian villages—Talladega and Tallasahatchee—in the fall of 1813. Jackson pursued the Creek, and on March 27, 1814, his 3,000-man army attacked and defeated them at the Battle of Horseshoe Bend on the Tallapoosa River in eastern Alabama. More than 800 Creek warriors were killed, and the power of the Creek nation was completely broken. At the Treaty of Fort Jackson on August 9, 1814, the Creek were compelled to cede 23 million acres (half of Alabama and part of southern Georgia) to the whites.

Creole Mutiny (1841) The U.S. brigantine *Creole*, carrying 134 black slaves from Hampton Roads, Va., to New Orleans, was seized by the slaves during the voyage in November 1841. One white crewman was killed in the mutiny, led by the African–American Madison Washington (fl. 1840s). The ship was then sailed to the British port of Nassau in the Bahamas, where the British refused to hand over the ship or slaves, despite angry protests by the owners and American southerners. Ignoring the precedent set by the AMISTAD MUTINY case, U.S. secretary of state Daniel Webster (1782–1852) demanded the return of the slaves because they were the property of U.S. citizens. By British law, all the slaves were freed, except those who actually participated in the mutiny, who were charged with murder and imprisoned. In 1855, after the case was finally settled by arbitration between the two countries, Britain awarded $110,330 to the U.S. in compensation for lost slave property.

Cresap's War (1774) In what is now Ohio and West Virginia, fighting between white settlers and Indians increased sharply after Ohio's Yellow Creek (or Baker's Cabin) Massacre (April 30, 1774), in which the Shawnee Indian family of friendly Tahgah-jute (1725?–80), better known as James Logan, and some Mingo Indians were slaughtered by whites under Daniel Greathouse (fl. 1770s). Logan and others, however, accused Captain Michael Cresap (1742–75), the whites' militia leader in the region, of the massacre; Cresap, who was waging war against hostile Indians there, was evidently not responsible, but his war soon merged with LORD DUNMORE'S WAR, in which he fought under Colonel Andrew Lewis (1720–81).

Cretan Rebellion of 1770 Acquired by the Ottoman Empire in 1669, the island of Crete and its mainly Christian population were restive under Muslim occupation, increasingly so after Russia adopted the policy of stirring up the empire's foreign populations. Influenced by Russian agents, the Cretan merchant and shipowner Daskaloyiannis (d. 1770) preached rebellion in Crete's mountainous Sfakian area and led rebels north into the plains near Canea (Khania) in 1770. He did not receive expected Russian help, and Turkish counter-attacks drove the Sfakians back into the White Mountains under fierce pursuit. The Turks ordered surrender; Daskaloyiannis refused, and many Sfakians were killed fighting. A second Turkish order led him to surrender with 70 followers. His comrades were maltreated, and Daskaloyiannis, taken to the Turks'

Cretan capital at Candia (Iráklion) for questioning, was flayed to death. Confirmed in power, the Ottomans continued making Crete the worst-governed province in their empire.

Cretan Rebellion of 1821–22

The GREEK WAR OF INDEPENDENCE caused a bloody reaction in Crete, where the Turkish Janissaries (elite corps), already ill-famed for their cruelties, yielded to panic and began to massacre the Christian population. Armed bands roamed the streets of Cretan towns, strangling, drowning, or burning Christians. The metropolitan (archbishop) of Candia (Iráklion) was slaughtered with his congregation in his cathedral. Turks marauded in Sfakia in revenge for the CRETAN REBELLION OF 1770. After five months the Sfakians reacted by penning up the Turks in Cretan towns, causing a momentary peace that was broken by the invasion of Egyptian troops to aid the Turks. The invaders rapidly subdued eastern Crete, destroyed villages, burned forests, and forced the remaining rebels to hide in the caves of Sfakia. For his services, Pasha Muhammad Ali (1769?–1849) of Egypt was awarded the pashalik (a pasha's province) of Crete.

Cretan Uprising of 1866–68

The Christians on the island of Crete regarded their Turkish rulers with hatred (see CRETAN REBELLION OF 1821–22; GREEK WAR OF INDEPENDENCE). Christian raids from the area of Sfakia in Crete's White Mountains led the Ottoman Empire to consider all Cretans as hated Sfakians. When promised reforms failed to be promulgated by the Porte (Ottoman government), the Sfakians and city dwellers rose up simultaneously in 1866. Crete's pasha (governor) gained aid from Constantinople (Istanbul), but the insurgents forced the surrender of an entire Turkish army on the plain of Apokoronas in 1866. The insurgents then dispersed, and other Turks attacked the fortified monastery in Arkadi for revenge. Its powder magazine exploded and killed hundreds of refugee women and children there. Next, the Turks systematically destroyed areas in the White Mountains and then returned home in 1867. Greece and some western nations sent support to the Cretans, angering the Ottomans, who threatened on December 11, 1868, to blockade Greece if it did not desist. To avoid war, Greece complied, but the western nations, meeting in Paris in 1869, awarded Crete a measure of self-government, but too limited to forestall the CRETAN UPRISING OF 1896.

Cretan Uprising of 1896

The Ottoman Empire under Sultan Abdul-Hamid II (1842–1918) continued to rule the island of Crete to the benefit of its 10 percent minority Muslim population. The sultan pretended to promote reforms by alternately installing a Christian governor and then subjugating the Cretan Christians by installing an abusive Muslim. Cretans complained internationally and pushed for Greek intervention. In 1896, the Christians finally rose up, massacring Muslims and touching off a brief civil war. Greece sent troops to offset Turkish forces already on Crete. The great powers intervened, but with differing policies. Germany and Russia wanted to blockade Greece but retain Turkish troops; Britain pushed for Cretan autonomy, withdrawal of all Greek forces, and retention of some of the Porte's (Ottoman government) forces. Hostilities accelerated to cause the GRECO-TURKISH WAR OF 1897. The Cretan struggle continued; Germany and Austria withdrew occupation forces; Britain and then France worked for Cretan autonomy. After Muslims caused the death of the British vice consul, Britain changed some of its policies, forced the withdrawal of all Turkish forces from Crete, and helped make Prince George (1863–1913) of Greece Crete's high commissioner. This enabled the island to be free for the first time since its conquest by Rome almost two millennia earlier.

Cretan Uprising of 1935

Cretan-born statesman and politician Eleuthérios Venizélos (1864–1936), who had held the Greek premiership six times between 1910 and 1933, was leader of the antiroyalist Liberal Party, which opposed the Populist (royalist) Party and its leader Panayoti Tsaldaris (1868–1936), premier of

Greece since 1933. In early March 1935, the Venizélists—followers of Venizélos —rose up in arms in Crete, Athens, and Macedonia to protest the imminent restoration of the monarchy. (Greece had been governed as a republic since 1924.) Government forces under General George Kondylis (1879–1936) fought and defeated the rebelling Venizélists, who held out the longest in Crete; Venizélos was forced to flee to France, where he died in exile in Paris about a year later. In the fall of 1935, Kondylis engineered a successful coup against Tsaldaris, assumed the premiership, and prompted the parliament to recall Greece's King George II (1890–1947), who was in exile; an almost unanimous vote in a plebiscite resulted in the enthronement of George on November 25, 1935.

Crimean War (1853–56) Involved in a jurisdictional dispute over the Holy Places of Turkish-controlled Jerusalem, Czar Nicholas I (1796–1855) claimed the sole right to protect Orthodox Christians within the Ottoman Empire's territories. When the Ottomans rejected this, he ordered his forces to occupy Moldavia and Wallachia (tributaries to the empire), precipitating the Ottoman declaration of war in 1853 after Russia refused to withdraw its troops. When a Russian naval squadron bombarded and destroyed a Turkish flotilla at Sinop on the Black Sea (November 30, 1853), a combined French and British fleet moved into the area, ordering the Russians to withdraw. Russia's noncompliance led to a declaration of war by Britain and France, both of which feared Russian expansionism in the Middle East. Austria made a defensive pact with Prussia against Russia and, with Ottoman permission, moved troops into Moldavia and Wallachia, compelling the Russians to abandon the principalities in 1854. In September 1854, an allied expeditionary army of British, French, Sardinian, and Turkish soldiers landed on the Crimean peninsula and advanced against the Russians at Sevastopol. During the yearlong allied siege of Sevastopol, which finally fell when the Russians blew up and evacuated the fortress-city, British-French forces won important battles at Balaklava

(immortalized in Tennyson's poem "The Charge of the Light Brigade") and at Inkerman against the Russians under Prince Aleksandr Menshikov (1787–1869) in 1854. After the bloody capture of Malakov and Redan, two main Russian strong points overlooking Sevastopol, by French and British soldiers, respectively, on September 8–9, 1855, the allies secured the fortress-city, soon causing Czar Alexander II (1818–81), Nicholas's son and successor, to begin peace negotiations. In the Caucasus area, savage fighting took place during the successful Russian siege of Kars (1855), a Turkish fortress that succumbed to starvation and sickness before the arrival of a relief force. British-French forces bombarded Russian fortresses in the Baltic (1854–55). The czar agreed to peace, the terms of which were ratified at the Congress of Paris in 1856. The integrity of the Ottoman Empire was maintained; Russia relinquished its role as Orthodox protector in the empire; the self-governing status of Moldavia, Wallachia, and Serbia was protected; and doctrines relating to the principle of freedom of the seas were recognized.

Croatian War of Independence (1991–95) Under its nationalist president Franjo Tudjman (1922–   ), Croatia declared its independence from Yugoslavia on June 25, 1991, provoking an immediate response from the federal military. Unlike the brief fighting in Slovenia, the other breakaway republic (see SLOVENIAN WAR OF INDEPENDENCE), the clashes between federal troops and republic defense forces in Croatia erupted into full-scale war. Federal ships off the coast fired on targets in Croatia, while Croatian forces blockaded federal barracks, cutting off utilities and food; besieged soldiers then shelled nearby civilian areas. In 1991 Serbs constituted one-eighth of the Croatian population; encouraged and armed by the federal military, Serb guerrillas took control of about one-third of the republic, driving out members of other ethnic groups. Some federal leaders in Belgrade (the Yugoslav capital) disagreed with the aggressive tactics of the army, which they saw as acting in the interests of its Serb officers and not of the country as a whole. In January

1992, after at least 10,000 people had died in Croatia and after 14 cease-fires had been broken, a United Nations-sponsored truce took hold. For nearly three years 14,000 UN peacekeepers maintained an uneasy standoff between the Croatian defense forces and the rebel Serbs, who eventually declared their own republic of Krajina, consisting of the territory captured in 1991. As the July 1992 shelling of Dubrovnik by rebel Serbs shows, however, fighting never entirely stopped during those three years. At the same time, neighboring Bosnia and Herzegovina was also engulfed in war (see BOSNIAN CIVIL WAR OF 1992–95), and the Croats feared that Bosnian Serb advances in late 1994 would further embolden the Krajina Serbs. In May 1995 the Croatian army swept through one of the Krajina Serb enclaves, expelling the residents; the Serbs then sent missiles into the Croatian capital, Zagreb, killing a handful of people and injuring more than 150. The Serb retaliation did not halt the Croat offensive; by August Croatian troops had retaken most of the Serb-held land and had sent more than 100,000 Serbs fleeing. The war in Croatia (along with the war in Bosnia) officially ended on December 14, 1995, when leaders of Croatia, Bosnia, and Serbia signed the Dayton peace accords.

Cromwell's Irish Campaign (1649–50) When England's parliamentary Council of State asked Oliver Cromwell (1599–1658) to pursue royalists in Ireland in 1649 (see ENGLISH CIVIL WAR, SECOND), Cromwell went reluctantly but soon felt fulfilled. The royalists under the marquess of Ormond were defeated by the forces of the Protestant governor of Dublin and then went north to Drogheda, where Cromwell, threatening to slay all rebels found with weapons, ordered the killing of 2,000 as "a righteous judgment of God," and then he actively judged in like manner at Wexford. Cromwellian sieges took much of Ireland by mid-1650. The Cromwellian settlement was equally loathsome: England seized two-thirds of the country, colonized it, and transported thousands of inhabitants to wilderness or colonial areas. About a third of the population died.

Cromwell's Scottish Campaign (1650–51) To the Scots, who surrendered King Charles I (1600–1649) to the English in 1646 (see ENGLISH CIVIL WAR, SECOND), his beheading at Whitehall in London in 1649 was extremely dismaying. The marquess of Argyll, ruler of Scotland, proclaimed Charles's son king as Charles II (1630–85), and an unsuccessful attempt was made to have him invade Scotland from France in 1649. Charles, after pledging to support Presbyterianism in Scotland and England, arrived in 1650. Oliver Cromwell (1599–1658) immediately launched an invasion, routed a Scottish army at Dunbar, and occupied Edinburgh. Despite Cromwell's victories and because he had broken agreements to support Presbyterianism, the stubborn Scots crowned Charles at Scone in 1651. Cromwell reacted; his forces defeated a Scottish army at Stirling, gained control of Perth, and followed an ill-fated Scottish army into England. On September 3, 1651, Cromwell's army won the Battle of Worcester, defeating the Scots and their English royalist allies. Charles II was forced to flee to France, and Cromwell became "Lord Protector" of Scotland.

Crusade, First (1095–99) Threatened by Seljuk Turks, converts to Islam, Byzantine Emperor Alexius I (1048–1118) looked westward for help. At the Council of Clermont, Pope Urban II (c. 1042–99) exhorted Christians to recover the Holy Lands, promising plenary indulgences. In numbers exceeding all expectations, commoners as well as knights, mostly French, cried "Deus vult" ("God wills it") and donned crosses (hence the name Crusades). Preliminary skirmishes involving disorderly peasant bands under Peter "the Hermit" (c. 1050–1115) and Walter "the Penniless" (d. 1096), the so-called People's Crusade, resulted in defeat. The main crusading force—under such feudal lords as Raymond IV (c. 1038–1105) of Toulouse, Robert II (c. 1054–1134) of Normandy, Hugh of Vermandois (fl. 1090s), Bohemond I (c. 1056–1111) and his nephew Tancred (1076–1112) of Normandy, and brothers Baldwin (1058?–1118) and Godfrey (c. 1058–1100) of Bouillon—reached Constantinople

(Istanbul) in 1096–97, where most pledged fealty to Alexius. Crusaders took Nicaea in 1097, routed the Turks at Dorylaeum, and captured Antioch in 1098. In 1099, they stormed Jerusalem, murdering thousands of Muslims and Jews. Godfrey, declining a crown, governed Jerusalem as Defender of the Holy Sepulcher. Three fiefdoms were created: Edessa under Baldwin, Tripoli under Raymond, and Antioch under Bohemond. **Second Crusade** (1147–49). When the precariously held Edessa was recaptured by the Turks in 1144, Pope Eugenius III (d. 1153) issued a bull proclaiming a new crusade, which was eloquently preached by St. Bernard of Clairvaux (1090?–1153). King Conrad III (c. 1093–1152) of Germany and King Louis VII (c. 1120–80) of France answered the call by leading separate armies through the Balkans, where Byzantine emperor Manuel I (c. 1120–80) provided transport to Asia Minor. After the Germans were forced to retreat from Dorylaeum, the two armies merged at Acre for an ill-advised assault on Damascus. Internal conflicts among the crusaders contributed to an easy Turkish triumph. **Third Crusade** (1189–92). The fall of Jerusalem to Turkish chief Saladin (1137?–93) prompted Pope Gregory VIII (d. 1187) to launch a third crusade (see SALADIN'S HOLY WAR). The Holy Roman Emperor Frederick I Barbarossa (c. 1125–90), Richard I Lion-Heart (1157–99) of England, and Philip II (1165–1223) of France responded, though lacking support from Byzantine emperor Isaac II (d. 1204), now allied with Saladin. Frederick drowned en route, but some German troops joined Philip and Richard at Acre. Philip left following a quarrel, but Richard, after wresting Cyprus from the Byzantines, defeated Saladin at Arsuf in 1191 and reoccupied Jaffa. Though he never reached Jerusalem, he concluded a five-year truce permitting Christians free access to holy places. The Latin kingdom, however, was reduced to a coastal strip based at Acre. **Fourth Crusade** (1202–04). Pope Innocent III (c. 1160–1216) inaugurated a crusade against Muslim power in Egypt. Venetians, enlisted to provide transport, convinced the mostly French and Flemish crusaders to buy passage by helping recover Zara from Hungary. At Zara, Al-

exius (d. 1224), son of a deposed Byzantine emperor, persuaded the crusaders with promises of money and military aid to help him oust his uncle Alexius III (d. after 1210). A Venetian fleet entered the Bosporus, and Alexius III fled. But Alexius IV himself was soon assassinated, provoking the crusaders to defy the pope and sack Constantinople. Thus the crusade, completely diverted from its original purpose, effected establishment of a Latin empire on Byzantine territory, precluding reconciliation between the two churches. **Fifth Crusade** (1217–21). Citing the shame of the abortive CHILDREN'S CRUSADE, Innocent III and then Honorius III (d. 1227) preached a new effort, promulgated at the Lateran Council of 1215. The goal was again Egypt, to be used as leverage to regain Jerusalem. Under the divided leadership of John of Brienne (c. 1170–1237) and papal legate Pelagius (fl. 1210s), crusaders besieged Damietta. John favored accepting peace terms proffered by the Muslims, but Pelagius held out, hoping vainly for reinforcements from Holy Roman Emperor Frederick II (1194–1250). In 1221, Pelagius's advance on Cairo was thwarted by Nile floods, forcing acceptance of a truce less advantageous than terms rejected earlier. A notable incident was St. Francis of Assisi's (1182?–1226) evangelistic visit to Sultan Kamil (1180–1238). **Sixth Crusade** (1228–29). Shouldering responsibility for the failure of the Fifth Crusade, Holy Roman Emperor Frederick II embarked on a mission unique in being a diplomatic rather than military effort. He proceeded under excommunication, the pope having rejected illness as justification for his delayed departure. In 1229, he succeeded in negotiating a 10-year treaty with Sultan Kamil ceding Jerusalem and other holy places, whereupon he crowned himself king of Jerusalem, a title he had acquired by marriage. But the treaty precipitated much disorder, and upon its expiration, hostilities were renewed under Thibaut IV (1201–53) of Navarre and Champagne and Richard of Cornwall (1209–72). **Seventh Crusade** (1248–54). Despite the efforts of Thibaut of Navarre and Richard of Cornwall, Jerusalem was captured by Turkish and Egyptian Muslims in 1244, prompting Louis IX (1226–1270) of France to launch a new crusade against Egypt, supported by Pope Innocent IV (d. 1254). Crusaders recovered Damietta in 1249, but a poorly planned advance up the Nile was foiled at Mansura, and Louis himself was taken captive. Following his ransom and the surrender of Damietta, Louis negotiated the release of as many prisoners as possible and spent four years fortifying the kingdom's defenses before departing. **Eighth Crusade** (1270). When the brilliant Sultan Baybars (1233–77) captured Antioch in 1268, Louis IX made preparations for a new crusade. Probably influenced by the political maneuverings of his brother, Charles of Anjou (1226–85), Louis headed not eastward but toward North Africa. In Tunisia he succumbed to disease, cutting short the crusaders' advance. Charles arrived to negotiate the evacuation of the tattered troops. **Ninth Crusade** (1271–72). Prince Edward of England (1239–1307) reached North Africa too late to rescue Louis's efforts. He concluded a truce at Acre, then returned to England upon succeeding to the throne in 1272. With the fall of Tripoli in 1289 and of Acre, the last Christian outpost in the Holy Land, in 1291, the crusading era came largely to a close, though Constantinople remained in Christian hands until 1453 and Cyprus until 1571. See also BYZANTINE–SELJUK TURK WARS; CRUSADER-TURKISH WARS; LATIN EMPIRE–BYZANTINE EMPIRE WARS.

Crusader-Turkish Wars of 1100–1146   In 1100, after the First CRUSADE, the Seljuk Turks ambushed and seized Bohemond I (c. 1056–1111), crusader prince of Antioch, near Aleppo and then held him captive at Sivas in central Anatolia (Turkey). Three separate expeditions under Raymond IV (c. 1038–1105) of Toulouse, Stephen of Blois (1097?–1154), and other nobles set out across Anatolia to punish the Turks and free Bohemond; all three met disastrous defeat in battle (1101, 1102), with many lives lost. Baldwin I (1058–1118), who had assumed the title king of Jerusalem, sought to consolidate his position by attacking hostile Muslim Egyptians, who were far superior in number. At Ramla or Ramleh, he was victorious at first (1101), but suffered disaster in a second battle there (1102).

With another army, he soon routed the Egyptians at Jaffa and drove them south. Danish crusaders arrived at Jaffa to lend assistance against the "infidels." Released from prison in 1103, Bohemond returned to Antioch, attempting again the next year to crush the Muslims and losing the Battle of Harran. In 1107, Norway's King Sigurd I "the Crusader" (1089?–1130) led a force to the Holy Land and aided Baldwin in capturing Sidon; they failed to take Tyre from the Muslims in 1109. The fortress of Krak de Montréal was built (1115) by Baldwin to safeguard his kingdom in the south. After an unsuccessful campaign into Egypt (1118), Baldwin died and was succeeded as king of Jerusalem by his cousin Baldwin II (d. 1131), who continually fought the Turks in northern Syria. Invading Egyptian forces besieged Jerusalem without success in 1124. When the crusader-occupied city of Edessa fell (1144) to the Muslims under Zangi (1084–1146), a new papal call for another crusade brought together European armies for a cause (see CRUSADE, SECOND). See also BYZANTINE–SELJUK TURK WARS; SALADIN'S HOLY WAR.

Crusader-Turkish Wars of 1272–91   Both Muslim Turks and pagan Mongols, while fighting one another, attacked the Christian crusader states in the Holy Land, Palestine, and Syria, taking control of much territory after the mid-13th century (see CRUSADE, NINTH). Baybars (1233–77), Muslim Mamluk (Mameluke) sultan of Egypt, systematically conquered crusader strongholds; Safed was surrendered by the Knights Templars in 1266; Jaffa and Antioch fell in 1268; and the Knights Hospitalers' great fortress near Tripoli was seized by Baybars in 1271. The crusaders' doom was sealed. Forces under Prince Edward (1239–1307) of England arrived to subdue Muslims and Mongols in the Holy Land, but failed (1271–72). Quarrels among the crusader states helped speed up their disintegration. A short respite occurred with the death of Baybars, whose successor, Sultan Qala'un (d. 1290), led forces to victory against invading Mongols at the Battle of Homs or Hims in Syria (1281); this virtually ended the Mongol threat to Egypt. In 1289,

Qala'un drove the crusaders from Tripoli, whose harbor he destroyed to prevent the enemy from landing there again. A heroic defense of Acre, the crusaders' last important stronghold in the Holy Land, came to a disastrous end on May 19, 1291, when the Muslims captured it and massacred or enslaved the inhabitants. Afterward every Christian fortress on the Mediterranean coast was destroyed by the victorious Turks. See also LATIN EMPIRE–BYZANTINE EMPIRE WARS.

Cuban Revolt of 1917 In 1916, Mario García Menocal (1866–1941), Cuba's incumbent conservative president, was reelected to office, defeating Alfredo Zayas (1861–1934), the liberal candidate, in an election torn by strife and marred by fraud. The liberals protested Menocal's reelection because more votes were cast than there were qualified voters and some provincial returns were lost or altered. After Cuba's supreme court upheld the protest, new elections were scheduled for February 1917 in several provinces, but before they were completed, the liberals rose in revolt. José Miguel Gómez (1858–1921) prepared to lead liberal forces from Santa Clara to Havana, the Cuban capital, to overthrow the government, but Menocal enlisted volunteers, purchased arms from the United States, assembled an army, and blocked Gómez's advance. Various skirmishes ensued; a small force of U.S. Marines landed at Santiago in Oriente province, a liberal center, and restored order; within a few weeks (March 1917) Menocal's forces had crushed the rebels. U.S. president Woodrow Wilson (1856–1924) sought to maintain order in Cuba now that the United States was involved in WORLD WAR I and believed Menocal was more sympathetic to the Allies. Cuba declared war on Germany on April 7, 1917. Menocal, inaugurated as president on May 20, 1917, asked for and received U.S. troops, which remained in Cuba until 1923.

Cuban Revolts of 1930–33 In 1924, the liberal Gerardo Machado y Morales (1871–1939) was elected president of Cuba; he later secured a constitutional amendment providing for a six-year presidency and was reelected in 1928. Machado's dictatorial policies and suppression of freedoms were strongly opposed by students at the University of Havana, which was closed in 1930 because of severe student agitation; numerous students and faculty members were imprisoned or killed. In August 1931, a band of about 40 revolutionaries landed at the Cuban port of Gibara, seized the police station and town hall, distributed arms to the populace, and then moved inland toward Holguín, only to be speedily defeated by the army. Despite the failure of this revolt against Machado, Cubans banded together in secret revolutionary societies, notably the ABC. With between 30,000 and 40,000 members, the ABC used terrorism and sabotage against the government, whose reprisals were murderous. In June 1933, the secret groups agreed to accept mediation by the U.S. ambassador to Cuba, Sumner Welles (1892–1961), to end the violence, but shortly a general strike and a clash between police and citizens occurred. The army rebelled against Machado, forcing him from office on August 12, 1933; Carlos Manuel de Céspedes y Quesada (1871–1939) was installed as provisional president, but was ousted on September 5, 1933, by an army coup, staged by Sergeant Fulgencio Batista y Zaldívar (1901–73) in support of Professor Ramón Grau San Martín (1887–1969), who became president. Batista became commander in chief of the army and virtual dictator of Cuba.

Cuban Revolution of 1956–59 (Castro's Revolution) A general amnesty for political prisoners in May 1955 freed rebel leader Fidel Castro (1926–   ) and his followers from prison in Cuba (see 26TH OF JULY MOVEMENT); they promptly left for Mexico to reorganize their plans to overthrow Cuban dictator Fulgencio Batista y Zaldívar (1901–73), whose regime was marked by blatant corruption, police oppression, and embezzlement. In 1956, Castro and 81 followers returned to eastern Cuba in a yacht loaded with arms and ammunition; many of these "invaders" were slain or captured by Batista's forces (Castro was erroneously presumed dead), but the rest found refuge in the rugged Sierra Maestra mountain range in Oriente province. For the next two years Castro's rebels carried out a successful guerrilla campaign from their mountain stronghold, from which neither the army nor the police could dislodge them. Castro's ranks grew to several hundred as sympathizers joined the guerrilla bands, which intermittently raided military installations and destroyed property. In 1957, the rebels kidnapped 10 American civilians and 28 sailors, but released them without harm when the U.S. government and press angrily protested. Opposition to Batista's tyranny increased throughout Cuba, and admiration for the bearded revolutionaries who defied him grew apace. After calling for "total war" against Batista's regime, Castro took the offensive and moved out of the mountains in the fall of 1958. The rebels captured Santa Clara, the capital of Las Villas province, on December 31, 1958. Two days before, Major Ernesto "Che" Guevara (1928–67), Castro's comrade-in-arms, had gained a coup by capturing an armored train loaded with weapons at Santa Clara. Realizing that all support for his government had eroded, Batista fled with his family to the Dominican Republic on January 1, 1959, taking the loot he had accumulated and leaving the Cuban government in the hands of a three-man military junta. Two days later Castro led the first of his motley columns into Havana, Cuba's capital, where they were hailed enthusiastically by the people. The army made no attempt to stop the rebel forces; indeed, most of the military was on their side and welcomed them. A provisional government was quickly formed with Castro as premier; gradually Cuba was transformed into a communist state supported by the Soviet Union. See also BAY OF PIGS INVASION.

Cuban War of Independence (1895–98) The failure of Spain to institute promised political and economic reforms in its colony of Cuba led to increasing unrest after the TEN YEARS' WAR. New cries for Cuban independence were voiced by the Cuban Revolutionary Party (Partido Revolucionario Cubano) headquartered in New York City, leading to the return to Cuba of exiled writer José Julián Martí

(1853–95) and other former rebel leaders, including Antonio Maceo (1848–96), Máximo Gómez y Baez (1836–1905), and Calixto Garcia Iñiguez (1836?–98), and many expatriate troops. In 1895, the rebels established a republic in eastern Cuba and began fighting a guerrilla war against the Spanish. While avoiding head-to-head battles, they pushed the war into the west and were approaching Havana, Cuba's capital, when, in 1896, Spanish forces were placed under the command of General Valeriano Weyler y Nicolau (1838–1930), who had earlier (1868–73) fought against the Cuban rebels. Based in Havana, Weyler launched an offensive into the eastern provinces and began the controversial policy of placing Cuban civilians in "concentration camps," where inadequate food, inhumane conditions, and disease caused the deaths of thousands. By the end of 1896, Weyler's troops had driven the rebels back to the eastern end of the island. By publicizing these events and other Spanish atrocities, real and imaginary, the press in the United States created a "war fever" to intervene on behalf of the Cubans; it made little mention of the end of the camps, the recall of Weyler, and the Spanish offer of home rule for Cuba (all in 1897). American sentiment in favor of the rebels grew until the destruction of the battleship U.S.S. *Maine* in Havana harbor in 1898 brought on the SPANISH-AMERICAN WAR.

Culpeper's Rebellion (1677–79) The colonists in northern Carolina opposed the proprietary government, which supported the English trade laws placing heavy duties on goods and restricting trade to England. In December 1677, led by John Culpeper, they overthrew the government, imprisoned the deputy governor, Thomas Miller (who was also the customs collector), and other officials, and formed a new popular government with Culpeper as governor. Later, Miller escaped to England to plead his case before the English authorities; Culpeper was sent for to do the same. Though tried and found not guilty on charges of treason and embezzlement, Culpeper was removed by the proprietaries, who appointed a new governor and collector.

"Cultural Revolution" See CHINESE "CULTURAL REVOLUTION."

Cunaxa, Battle of (401 B.C.) Ambitious to take the Persian throne from his brother Artaxerxes II (d. 359), Cyrus the Younger (424?–401) hired more than 11,000 Greek mercenary soldiers idled by the end of the Great PELOPONNESIAN WAR. Ostensibly involved in a punitive expedition against Pisidia, the Greeks demurred when Babylon was revealed as their true goal, but an offer of double wages won them over. At Cunaxa, near Babylon, in 401, the Greeks, commanded by Clearchus (d. 401), and Cyrus's Persian rebel army met and battled against Artaxerxes's larger Persian army (some 100,000 troops). Victory seemed imminent for Cyrus until he was killed; his army then fell apart. The Greeks fought boldly but eventually had to give up the field. Afterward Tissaphernes (d. 395), Persian satrap in coastal Asia Minor, lured Clearchus and other Greek leaders to a conference, at which they were treacherously slain. The Greek mercenaries, about 10,000 in number, began a long retreat, pursued by Persians under Tissaphernes (see TEN THOUSAND, MARCH OF THE).

"Custer's Last Stand" See SIOUX WAR OF 1876–77.

Cypriot War of 1963–64, Greek-Turkish The independent Republic of Cyprus was officially established on August 16, 1960, to avoid its possible annexation by either Greece or Turkey. Cyprus, with a population about three-fourths Greeks and one-fourth Turks and others, was torn by strife politically and socially. Its president, Greek archbishop Makarios III (1913–77), who had foresworn union with Greece (enosis), was continually assailed by Turkish Cypriots claiming to be oppressed. Inhabitants of both Greece and Turkey influenced Greek and Turkish Cypriots, respectively, to acts of violence. Britain attempted to get those two rival countries to guarantee Cypriot peace. In late 1963, Turkish Cypriots, thinking their rights threatened by Greek attempts to alter the constitution, began fighting, causing the United Nations (UN) to send a peacekeeping force to Cyprus in March 1964. A possible Turkish invasion of the island was thwarted when U.S. president Lyndon B. Johnson (1908–73) warned against it, and, despite continued UN military presence on Cyprus, unabated battling persisted between Turkish and Greek Cypriots. In August 1964, when Turkish warplanes attacked Greek Cypriots, Makarios sought help from Egypt and the Soviet Union, but the UN soon arranged a cease-fire. Later, when the Cypriot government passed laws abolishing de facto abuse of the Turks' rights, the violence was reduced to grumbling and the threat of war between Greece and Turkey was quieted.

Cypriot War of 1974, Greek-Turkish The shaky peace established in Cyprus in 1964 (see CYPRIOT WAR OF 1963–64, GREEK-TURKISH) was oppugned by rival factions with increasing ferocity. An Athens-based terrorist organization, the EOKA, may have been behind an attempt to kill Cypriot president Makarios III (1913–77) in 1973 and the kidnapping of a government officer. Dissident bishops called a council that stripped Makarios of his spiritual office as archbishop, but a synod voided their action and punished them. In mid-July 1974, the Greek Cypriot National Guard, led by Greek officers from Greece, overthrew Makarios, who fled to London, and set up a new government that was expected to seek union (enosis) with Greece. The United Nations (UN) failed to act, and a London conference of all involved parties was unsuccessful. Invading Turkish forces fought the Greeks and won a large territory in northeastern Cyprus, whose inhabitants voted overwhelmingly to form a separate state. A UN-sponsored cease-fire on July 22, 1974, caused the war to decline to sporadic fighting, but the fall of the military government of Greece led to renewed war, then a standstill cease-fire on July 30, 1974, and the UN's establishment of a buffer zone between Greek and Turkish territories on the island. On August 16, 1974, the guarantors of the Cypriot constitution (Britain, Greece, and Turkey) arranged another cease-fire with the Turks, who now held almost 40 percent of the island. Makarios returned in late 1974, allowing Turkish autonomy in their territory but opposing the partition.

Czechoslovakia, Soviet Invasion of (1968)   Early in 1968, the Slovak leader Alexander Dubček (1921–92) became first secretary of the Communist Party of Czechoslovakia. A brief period of liberalization, labeled the "Prague spring," began, during which Dubček attempted to democratize Czechoslovakia by lifting press censorship, establishing ties to the West, promising increases in consumer goods, seeking autonomy for Slovakia within the larger state, and planning a new constitution that allowed individual liberties. The Soviet Union, used to governing Czechoslovakia and its other satellites rigidly, was alarmed, and a Soviet-Czech conference was held in the Slovak town of Cierna (July 29–August 1, 1968), from which the Soviet officials departed amicably. But their views changed, for on the night of August 20–21, 1968, Soviet forces, aided by troops from Bulgaria, Hungary, Poland, and East Germany, invaded Czechoslovakia, overcame minor resistance, and occupied the country (the invaders numbered at least 600,000). Dubček and other Czech leaders were arrested, taken to Moscow, forced to make concessions, and then returned home; a pro-Soviet communist regime was established firmly in Czechoslovakia. By April 1969, all of Dubček's reforms (except Slovak autonomy) had been invalidated, and Dubček was out of office. Justifying their action under the so-called Brezhnev doctrine ("the Soviet Union reserves the right to intervene militarily in the affairs of its East European Communist neighbors whenever its interests or security are significantly threatened"), the Soviets ordered arrests, union purges, and religious persecutions in 1970 to rid Czechoslovakia of its liberal tendencies. Many years later, in late 1989, the leaders of the Soviet Union, Bulgaria, Hungary, Poland, and East Germany publicly admitted that the 1968 invasion was unjustified "interference in the internal affairs of a sovereign Czechoslovakia."

D

Dacian War, First (A.D. 101–2) In 101, Roman Emperor Trajan (53–117) personally led an invasion of Dacia (roughly Rumania) because he considered its arrogant king, Decebalus (d. c. 107), a threat to the security of Rome's provinces to the south across the Danube River. The Dacians vigorously opposed the Romans, but in the second year of the war Trajan penetrated the heart of the kingdom and captured the capital, Sarmizegethusa; Decebalus was forced to make peace. He agreed to recognize Rome as overlord and to render military service. Trajan returned home after ordering that a permanent stone bridge be built across the Danube. **Second Dacian War** (A.D. 105–7). Decebalus's forces wiped out a Roman garrison stationed in Dacia and attacked a neighboring people allied to Rome. The next year, 106, Trajan again invaded the kingdom, seized the capital, and hunted down Dacians who did not surrender or flee from the area. In defeat, Decebalus committed suicide, and Dacia was made a Roman province peopled with settlers from Asia Minor and Syria. Trajan commemorated his victory by building a stone column with spiral reliefs depicting his campaign in Dacia; it may still be seen in Trajan's Forum in Rome.

Dacke's War (Dacke's Rebellion) (1542–43) The anti-Catholicism and harsh tax collection policies of Sweden's King Gustavus I (1496–1560) were fervently opposed by the peasants in the province of Smaland in southern Sweden. In the spring of 1542, they took up arms under the leadership of Nils Dacke (d. 1543?), a fugitive, and killed a number of tax collectors. The powerful Swedish noble, Svante Sture (1517–67), to whom the peasants offered their support to gain the throne, refused involvement in the civil war. Dacke's forces were victorious over a royal army, and a truce was agreed to by both sides in November 1542. Promising to cooperate with the peasants and alter the taxes, Gustavus simultaneously reinforced his troops in Smaland, and, in early 1543, royal forces decisively defeated the peasants in battle. Dacke supposedly died fighting. Other peasant leaders were executed, and Smaland's citizens were compelled to pay severe financial retribution. Nonetheless, Gustavus moderated his autocratic rule during the rest of his reign.

Dahomeyan-French War, First (1889–90) In 1889, the British and French signed agreements whereby the former ceded to the latter the city of Cotonou on the coast of Dahomey (Benin) in West Africa. The native Dahomeyans, who had no say in the matter, attacked a French force that landed at Cotonou, and fierce fighting ensued. A distinctive feature of the Dahomeyan army was its female soldiers (Amazons), who fought as boldly and well as the men and played a significant role in the war against the French. In 1890, a treaty was signed that ceded Cotonou and Porto Novo, another coastal city, to the French in exchange for an annual payment to King Behanzin (fl. 1889–94) of Dahomey. **Second Dahomeyan-French War** (1892). Although slavery had been abolished in Dahomey, King Behanzin continued to make slave raids into neighboring areas; he also attacked a French gunboat. These actions provoked another war with France. A French-Senegalese army under General Alfred-Amédée Dodds (1842–1922) landed in Dahomey and confronted the rebel native forces in the fall of 1892. The Dahomeyans were overwhelmed by superior numbers and firepower. Behanzin set fire to his capital at Abomey before the French entered it on November 17, 1892; he then fled to the north. Finally surrendering in early 1894, Behanzin was exiled to Martinique in the West Indies. His kingdom in Dahomey became a French colony.

Damascene War (280–279 B.C.)   Ptolemy II Philadelphus (309–246) was the second Macedonian king of Egypt, and he did much to increase the power of his kingdom and to beautify it. He was envious of the Seleucid kings of Syria and attacked their capital city of Damascus. The Syrians under King Antiochus I Soter (324–261) were badly defeated in battle by the Egyptians and lost a sizable amount of territory to them. This war was the first of a series of struggles between the Syrians and the Macedonian kings of Egypt (see SYRIAN–EGYPTIAN WARS).

Danish Civil War of 1137–57   When Danish king Erik II Emune (d. 1137) died without heirs, Denmark fell into disunity, with three princes claiming the throne. Canute V (d. 1157) and Sweyn III (d. 1157) were each elected king in different areas, causing a civil war to break out; the third claimant, Waldemar (1131–82), allied himself with Sweyn. When Canute obtained support from German king Conrad III (1093–1152) to continue the war, Conrad's nephew Frederick Barbarossa (1123?–90), later Holy Roman Emperor, intervened to grant Sweyn the kingship, with Canute to rule Zealand (Sjaelland) under the Crown. The settlement pleased no one, but peace was maintained when Waldemar persuaded the aspirants to accept lands in Jutland and Skane (extreme southern Sweden) instead of Zealand. Sweyn's harsh rule induced Waldemar to further mediation, and the

Danish kingdom was divided among the three claimants. During the ensuing celebration, Sweyn ordered his corulers assassinated. Canute was killed, but Waldemar escaped and conducted a campaign against Sweyn, whom he defeated and killed near Viborg in 1157. Waldemar, now sole king as Waldemar I "the Great," later launched the DANISH WAR AGAINST THE WENDS.

Danish-Estonian War of 1219–27   Religious divisions arose in Livonia (Estonia and part of Latvia) with the Christianization of the south. Denmark's King Waldemar II (1170–1241), supported by the Christian Livonian Knights of the Sword and the bishop of Riga, launched a crusade against the Estonians under Russia's Greek Christian influence, sailing a large force across the Baltic to Revel (Tallinn). Vastly outnumbered, the Estonian-Russian troops sued for peace while secretly strengthening their numbers. After the Danes were driven back by a surprise five-pronged Estonian attack, Waldemar, now bolstered by German reinforcements, retaliated and defeated the Estonian-Russian forces in 1219. Revel was captured and destroyed, and Waldemar built a fortress on the site, leaving a garrison to enforce conversion to Christianity. Danish sovereignty in Estonia was lost in 1227, when Waldemar was defeated by fractious Germans at the Battle of Bornhoved, but was regained in 1238 by an agreement with the Brothers of the Sword (Livonian Knights).

Danish-Lübeck War of 1501–12   See DANISH-SWEDISH WAR OF 1501–12.

Danish-Prussian War of 1864 (Schleswig-Holstein War)   The duchies of Schleswig and Holstein, with predominantly German populations, revolted against Danish control in 1848 and were occupied by Prussian troops commissioned by the German Confederation, which had claims to the duchies. Swedish forces assisting Denmark, threatened naval action by Britain against Prussia, and diplomatic backing from Russia helped restore Denmark's rights to Schleswig-Holstein (1850), whose inseparability as duchies was guaranteed afterward. However, in early 1864, Prussian troops under Prince Frederick Charles (1828–85), assisted by some Austrians, invaded and overran Schleswig-Holstein with little difficulty. On August 1, 1864, Denmark sued for peace and gave up its rights to the disputed duchies, which came under joint Prussian and Austrian rule by the Treaty of Gastein in 1865. Prussia's premier, Otto von Bismarck (1815–98), desired to annex both duchies, seeking a means to usurp Austrian administration of Schleswig (Holstein was put under Prussian administration; the duchy of Lauenburg was also under Prussian rule after the war). See also SEVEN WEEKS' WAR.

Danish-Swedish War of 1497–1500   When John I (1455–1513) was elected king of Denmark, he also became king of Norway and Sweden according to the terms of the Kalmar Union, which combined the three countries' crowns. Norway accepted him as king before long, but Swedish administrator Sten Sture the Elder (1440?–1503) denied John Sweden's rule. Growing impatient with Sture's vacillations about accepting the Union of Kalmar, John and his forces seized the union's political center, Kalmar, in southeastern Sweden in 1497. Sture then laid siege to Uppsala, the coronation place of Swedish kings, and intercepted John as he moved on Stockholm, Sweden's principal commercial center. The Danes defeated Sture's Dalecarlian (Dalarnan) reinforcements before they could join him, and Sture accepted defeat on good terms, receiving control of Finland and the two Bothnias (lands in the north around the Gulf of Bothnia). John was crowned king and made Sture grand master of the kingdom. See also DANISH-SWEDISH WAR OF 1501–12.

Danish-Swedish War of 1501–12   Christian (1481–1559), son of King John I (1455–1513) of Denmark, and others fomented rumors of plans by Grand Master Sten Sture the Elder (1440?–1503) to seize the Kalmar throne (Denmark, Sweden, and Norway) held by John. When John called upon Sture to explain himself, the grand master arrived with a large

armed retinue, and John fled fearfully to his Swedish citadel and later left for Denmark, leaving his queen and 1,000 troops to hold the citadel. With support from Lübeck and other Hanseatic ports, Sture led Swedish troops to capture Örebro and besiege Stockholm. John's queen surrendered. The Swedes were generally successful, and the Danes soon held only Kalmar and Borgholm. In 1502, southern Norway allied itself with Sweden, but Christian's cruel treatment of captured Norwegian rebels soon frightened it into submission. Christian led the Danes into Sweden, where he seized two fortresses in Västergötland and slaughtered the defenders. Sture died in 1503; his successor, Svante Nilsson Sture (c. 1460–1512), unsuccessfully besieged Kalmar and Borgholm. John convened a tribunal that proclaimed the Swedish fighters traitors, and Holy Roman Emperor Maximilian I (1459–1519) decreed aid to the Swedes a treasonable offense (a ruling aimed especially at Lübeck). Aided by Hanseatic towns, Sweden continued sporadic fighting against Denmark. During 1509–11, open warfare erupted among Lübeck, various Hanseatic towns, and Denmark. The fortunes of the parties seesawed until finally, in 1512, Lübeck and the Hanseatic League (wracked by internal dissension) signed a peace agreement to end support for Sweden. Hostilities soon ceased.

Danish-Swedish War of 1563–70   (Scandinavian Seven Years' War)   Antagonism arose when Denmark's young king Frederick II (1534–88) insisted on his right to use Sweden's coat of arms on his shield, and in retaliation Swedish king Erik XIV (1533–77) incorporated Denmark's arms into his. Other incidents fanned Erik's anger: Frederick's arrest of three Swedish ambassadors and his interception of a Swedish fleet. War was declared when Frederick intercepted a letter sent by Erik to Queen Elizabeth I (1533–1603) of England (Erik wrote love letters to Elizabeth and unsuccessfully sought to marry her). Nobles of Holstein, Schleswig, and Lübeck joined Frederick at Halland in southwestern Sweden and together besieged Elfsborg Älvsborg) to the east; Erik's forces moved into Skåne (Danish province in extreme southern Sweden). The Swedes triumphed in Norway (under Danish rule) but later lost the captured territory. The Danes, too, were unable to hold on to their conquered lands. The peace signed at Stettin in 1570 left the borders unchanged for the most part; Sweden gave Denmark Gotland and Elfsborg and some monetary reparation for the war. Denmark was granted the use of the Swedish three crowns' insignia pending a future decision, but Sweden was barred from incorporating Danish or Norwegian arms. See also SWEDISH CIVIL WAR OF 1562–68.

Danish-Swedish War of 1643–45   Fearful and envious of Swedish success in 1642 during the THIRTY YEARS' WAR, King Christian IV (1577–1648) of Denmark came to an understanding with Holy Roman Emperor Ferdinand III (1608–57). In response, Swedish troops commanded by Lennart Torstensson (1603–51) advanced to the Baltic area after abandoning a march on Vienna and promptly seized Schleswig-Holstein and Jutland. After defeating Swedish and Dutch ships in a naval battle on July 1, 1644, the Danes blockaded the Swedish fleet in Kiel Bay, but subsequently Dutch and Swedish vessels attacked and destroyed 17 Danish ships near Lolland, Denmark. With large portions of Denmark occupied by the Swedes, Christian was forced to accept harsh terms by the Peace of Brömsebro in 1645. Denmark ceded Gotland and Oesel (two Baltic islands) and some Norwegian lands and exempted Swedish-bound goods from shipping tolls through the Öresund.

Danish-Swedish War of 1675–79   Sweden's King Charles XI (1655–97) was allied with France's King Louis XIV (1638–1715) during the Third DUTCH WAR. Denmark's King Christian V (1646–99), wishing to regain Skåne (former Danish province in extreme southern Sweden), lost by the Treaty of Roeskilde in 1658 (see NORTHERN WAR, FIRST), entered the war, launching an invasion of Skåne in 1675. Danish warships under Admiral Niels Juel (1629–97) defeated the Swedish navy at the Battle of Jasmund, off Rugen, on May 25, 1676

(Juel won another naval battle over the Swedes near Copenhagen in 1677). But on land, Swedish forces under Charles were victorious against the Danes and their allies, the Brandenburgers, from 1676 to 1678. Denmark and Sweden made peace at Lund in Skåne (the Swedes won victory there in 1676), with Skåne remaining in Swedish hands.

Danish War against the Wends   (1160–68) While Denmark was in the midst of civil strife (see DANISH CIVIL WAR OF 1137–57), the Wends, a pagan Slavic people on the island of Rügen in the Baltic Sea off the German coast, continually harassed Danish and German coastal areas as pirates. King Waldemar I "the Great" (1131–82) initiated a campaign to conquer the Wends, whom Henry the Lion (1129–95), duke of Saxony, and Albert the Bear (c. 1100–1170), margrave of Brandenburg, had been crusading against since 1147. Danish soldier-stateman Absalon (1128–1201) led forces that besieged the Wend fortress at Arkona on Rügen. In 1168, the fortress fell, and the Wend inhabitants there and on Rügen surrendered to the Danes, who destroyed the pagan idols and temples. The Wends were subjugated and forced to accept Christianity.

Danish War of 1625–29   When the Hapsburgs (Austrians) interfered with Denmark's toll collection from ships passing to and from the Baltic Sea during the THIRTY YEARS' WAR, the Danes under King Christian IV (1577–1648) advanced against the forces of the Holy Roman Empire, or Hapsburgs. Failing to obtain aid from the Dutch and English, Christian's army was trounced at the Battle of Lutter on August 24–27, 1626, by Imperial troops led by Johan, count of Tilly (1559–1632); Christian lost about half of his men. Earlier that year, on April 25, 1626, Danish-German forces under Count Peter Ernst II Mansfeld (1580–1626) had suffered defeat at the Battle of Dessau by an Imperial army under Count Albrecht von Wallenstein (1583–1634). This disastrous effort to crush the Hapsburgs and another Wallenstein victory at the Battle of Wolgast on September 8, 1628 (over Christian), despite a successful defense against Wallenstein's besieging troops at Stralsund on the Baltic coast (1628), compelled Denmark to withdraw from the war (Treaty of Lübeck on June 7, 1629). Christian agreed not to interfere in German affairs and was assured his Danish lands in return.

Danish War with Holstein (1348) King Waldemar IV (1320?–75) of Denmark, attempting to unite the Danish kingdom, sought to regain control of Fünen (Fyn) Island, held by the county of Holstein in northwestern Germany as collateral on a debt. By 1348, the Holstein courts had granted Waldemar in the Treaty of Nebbegaard half of Fünen and a favorable opportunity to obtain the other half. But the treaty's terms were disputed, and only after resorting to arms, most successfully near Gamborg Castle, did the Danish king gain possession of all Fünen. Denmark's Jutland peninsula also came under his control in 1348. See also DANISH WARS WITH THE HANSEATIC LEAGUE.

Danish War with the Hanseatic League, First (1361–63) Danish king Waldemar IV (1320?–75), seeing Sweden preoccupied with problems in Norway, recovered former Danish lands in southern Sweden (Skane or Scania) in 1360. His army defeated a Swedish peasant army in Gotland in 1361, allowing the Danes to take the wealthy city of Wisby (Visby), a Swedish trade center of the Hanseatic League (mercantile league of northern German cities). A coalition of the Hanseatic League, Sweden, Mecklenburg, and Holstein opposed the Danish conquests, and war erupted. Copenhagen was sacked, but Waldemar's forces, using cannon, repulsed the Hanseatic fleets at the Battle of Helsingborg in 1362. The league was forced to accept peace terms in 1363 that greatly curtailed its trade privileges. Waldemar's daughter married King Haakon VI (1339–80) of Norway in 1365 in an effort to unite Denmark and Norway. **Second Danish War with the Hanseatic League** (1367–70). In 1367, the Hanseatic League, supported by Sweden, Mecklenburg, Holstein, and even by some dissident Danish

nobles, attacked Waldemar, who was battling civil strife at home and who then suddenly fled to Germany and left his privy council in charge. Despite Waldemar's success in persuading Brunswick, Brandenburg, and Pomerania to attack the league from the rear, the war went badly for Denmark, which was forced to conclude the Peace of Stralsund in 1370. The Hanseatic League was granted commercial rights and privileges, and Waldemar, who was allowed to return to Denmark, reluctantly accepted the league's trade in the country.

D'Annunzio's War (1919–20) Italy and Yugoslavia both claimed the Dalmatian port city of Fiume (Rijeka) at the end of WORLD WAR I. While the dispute was being negotiated, the Italian poet and soldier Gabriele D'Annunzio (1863–1938) led a filibustering expedition against Fiume (September 12, 1919), which he believed was rightfully Italy's and which he seized and occupied (his troops wore the black shirts that were to be part of the Fascist uniform). The autocratic rule D'Annunzio established at Fiume was opposed by the Italian government and others in Europe. After Italy and Yugoslavia signed the Treaty of Rapallo (November 12, 1920), by which Fiume was to be a free state, D'Annunzio declared war on Italy, but he was forced to evacuate Fiume after Italian forces bombarded the city (December 27, 1920). Political turmoil plagued Fiume's local government until its overthrow in a Fascist coup in 1922; then Italian troops occupied the city, which eventually (1947) was awarded to Yugoslavia. See also "MARCH ON ROME."

Dardanelles Campaign (Gallipoli Campaign) (1915) If Great Britain and France could gain control of the straits of the Dardanelles and the city of Constantinople (Istanbul), they would have access to the Black Sea and be able to ship supplies to their ally, Russia, during WORLD WAR I. In February 1915, an Anglo-French naval fleet entered the straits and knocked out several small Turkish forts at the entrance, but when it proceeded north to the more strongly fortified Turkish area, it suffered severe losses (caused by minefields) and was forced to withdraw. The Allies then decided to launch a land attack on the Gallipoli peninsula that guarded the straits. Anglo-French expeditionary forces landed at both ends of the straits, planning to crush the enemy in the middle. The Turks, however, aided by German artillery and officers, were firmly entrenched in the heights of the rugged terrain, and Allied naval bombardments were unable to dislodge them. Three bloody battles were waged between April and June 1915, during which the Allies gained and lost several thousand yards. In August 1915, another assault was attempted by the Allies, but it lacked drive and proved ineffectual. Finally, in December of that year, the high command acknowledged the hopelessness of the situation and evacuated the troops, who were suffering intensely from disease and thirst. British and French casualties for the entire campaign were about 250,000; the Turks suffered about the same.

Decembrists' Uprising (1825) Russian soldiers influenced by Western democratic ideas during the NAPOLEONIC WARS formed secret societies with the intention of replacing the czarist monarchy with a republic. An opportunity arose when a succession dispute occurred following the death of Czar Alexander I (1777–1825). Alexander's brother Constantine (1779–1831) had yielded his succession rights to his brother Nicholas (1796–1855); but without Constantine's public acknowledgment, Nicholas hesitated to take the throne. When a conspiracy of the Northern Society became known, the plotters, unprepared and without a specific program, led their regiments into St. Petersburg (Leningrad) to support "Constantine and Constitution" on December 26, 1825 (December 14 by the Old Style calendar), but the rebels arrived too late in Senate Square (Decembrist Square) to prevent the Russian officials from taking the oath of allegiance to Czar Nicholas I. When rebel soldiers refused to capitulate and were joined by stone-throwing citizens, government artillery men fired "a whiff of grapeshot" for an hour, routing the rebels. Paul Pestel (1794–1826), leader of a Kievan rebel group, was soon captured in southern Russia, and a military uprising was quelled on January 15, 1826. Lack of citizen

support for the St. Petersburg revolutionaries (Decembrists) and the others doomed the uprisings. Nicholas ordered the hanging of five leaders and exiled 100 others to Siberia. Here began the tradition of self-sacrificing revolution that continued throughout the 19th century in Russia.

Deerfield Massacre (1704) On the night of February 29, 1704, a band of 50 French soldiers and about 200 Indian allies fell upon the sleeping inhabitants of Deerfield, a small town on the western Massachusetts frontier. They killed 50 people outright and forced the remaining 111 to march back to Canada with them. Many died along the way, but eventually, after many negotiations, 60 were permitted to return to Deerfield. This bloody raid was one of the most savage to take place in New England during QUEEN ANNE'S WAR.

Delhi Sultanate Raids in South India   (1307–13) Stories of the riches of south India whetted the appetites of both Ala-ud-Din, second Khalji dynasty sultan of Delhi from 1296 to 1316, and that of the Ghurid slave-general Malik Kafur (d. 1316), for the enlargement and protection of the Delhi sultanate were proving expensive. Raised in a tradition of lucrative looting, the sultan decided to combine the collection of overdue tribute from the Yadavas with plundering, and in 1307 both he and Malik Kafur entered the Deccan region, taking Deogir and making the ruler of the country (Devagiri) a vassal of Delhi. The raid proved rewarding, and a second raid in 1309 on the Kakatiyan capital of Warangal was so beneficial that the military campaign continued southward (1310–11). It engulfed the Hoysalas; overran the deserted former capital of the Pandya state, Madurai; and reached the coast opposite Ceylon (Sri Lanka). The marauders carried off vast quantities of loot, but did not upset local administrations or depose rulers; instead, they demanded an annual tribute. A Muslim governor was installed at Madurai to oversee tribute collections and other matters. The Devagiri ruler failed to pay in 1313, as did the Kakatiyan chief in 1323. The first brought another raiding party from Delhi, which deposed the ruler (1313); the second brought deposition from Madurai. See also BAHMANI-DELHI SULTANATE WAR; CHALUKYAN CIVIL WARS; MAHMUD OF GHAZNA, CONQUESTS OF; MUHAMMAD OF GHUR, CONQUESTS OF.

Delhi Sultanate Wars with Ghazna and Ghur

(1208–28) The Muslim invaders of India in the 12th century (see MUHAMMAD OF GHUR, CONQUESTS OF) did not sever their connection with their Afghan kingdom in the west. Under the second ruler of the "slave dynasty" (Mamluks), Iltutmish (fl. 1211–36), Delhi, India, was the kingdom's primary capital and Ghur (Ghowr, Afghanistan) was the secondary. But other slave-generals had contested the right of Qutb-ud-Din Aybak (d. 1210) to succeed Muhammad of Ghur (d. 1206) as ruler, and it was necessary for him to defeat one rival slave-general at Ghazna (Ghazni, Afghanistan) in 1208. Iltutmish inherited his rivalry for power, as well as the continuing conflict of the Ghurids with the Khwarizm-shah dynasty over authority in Khwarizm (central Asian state). Iltutmish, who was already faced with subjugating Hindu chiefs in India, was patient; he allowed the rivals to come to him. A second rival, Yldiz (d. 1215), was driven from Ghazna by Khwarizm forces into the Punjab; Iltutmish defeated and captured him at Tarain in 1215. He then waited for Khwarizm troops to follow and was saved by the outbreak of the 1218 MONGOL-PERSIAN WAR. Instead of war, Iltutmish gained Khwarizm refugees, including the dynasty's heir, Jalal-ad-Din (d. 1231) (see INDUS RIVER, BATTLE OF). Diplomacy enabled him to get Jalal-ad-Din to move on without obtaining Delhi's help; diplomacy also enabled him to make Genghis (Jenghiz, Chingis) Khan (1167?–1227) decide to withdraw from India. And the depredations of war helped him defeat his last rival: Jalal-ad-Din's forces had done great damage to the rebellious slave-general Nasir-ud-Din Qabacha (fl. 1220s), whose military weakness enabled Iltutmish to force him out of Lahore and Multan in 1228, thereby gaining control of the Punjab for Delhi.

Delhi Sultanate Wars with Gujarat and Malwa

(1299–1312) In India, the death of the Delhi sultanate's ruler Balban (d. 1287) brought on a fierce struggle for power between the Afghans and the newer Turkish nobility, during which the princes of many Hindu states, especially the large kingdoms of Gujarat and Malwa, stopped being Delhi's tributaries. Ultimately, the Turks won, establishing the Khalji dynasty as rulers from 1290 to 1320. The second Khalji ruler, Ala-ud-Din (fl. 1296–1316), who murdered to usurp the throne, was determined to restore Delhi's finances by subjugating the Hindu princes. He began a series of raids and sieges in 1299, attacking Gujarat and subduing it in that year. Malwa proved to be less swiftly conquered, for Ala-ud-Din was repelling Mongol invasions from 1299 to 1308 at the same time. By staging hard-fought sieges against strong fortresses, he captured Ranthambhor (1301), Chitor (1303), and Mandu (1305). These sieges were extremely bloody, especially at Chitor, where the hopeless defenders observed the rite of *jauhor*, casting their wives and children upon a funeral pyre before staging a suicidal charge against the besiegers. Ala-ud-Din then began the DELHI SULTANATE RAIDS IN SOUTH INDIA, while he completed making the Rajput princes bow to Delhi by seizing Malwa's fortresses of Siwana (1308) and Jalor (1312).

Delhi Sultanate Wars with Jaunpur (c. 1414–93)

In India, in 1394, while two rival sultans of the Tughluk dynasty fought for the Delhi throne, the Sharqi dynasty of Jaunpur established a Muslim sultanate independent of Delhi. Civil war through 1397 prevented the Tughluk dynasty from reversing this action, and TAMERLANE'S INVASION OF INDIA in 1398 created such chaos that Delhi's authority dwindled as Malwa and Gujarat also became separate Muslim kingdoms in 1401. When the last Tughluk ruler died in 1413, the Sayyid dynasty, founded by Tamerlane's viceroy Khizur Khan (fl. 1414–21), took control of a kingdom consisting only of the city of Delhi and a small area surrounding it. The Sayyids concentrated on preserving what little they had. So Jaunpur prospered, and to sustain itself and to make the Hindus, who controlled the trade economy, feel secure, it practiced tolerance and uniform justice as did no other Muslim kingdom in India before the great Mogul Akbar (1542–1605). However, a second Timurid (Afghan) dynasty named Lodi was building strength in the Punjab and pushing slowly eastward to supersede the Sayyids in 1451 and to elevate Bahlul Lodi (fl. 1451–89) to the sultanate of Delhi. In 1452, the kingdom of Jaunpur began to fight not only for its very existence but also for its Muslim way of life. The warring was sporadic and indecisive until 1479, when a defeat led to Jaunpur's partial annexation by Delhi. Fighting continued, but Jaunpur grew steadily weaker until, in 1493, Sikander Lodi (fl. 1489–1517) completed the annexation. Jaunpur became part of the Lodi sultanate stretching across north India from the Punjab through Bihar to the border of Bengal during the time of the last Lodi sultan, Ibrahim (fl. 1517–26). Ibrahim, however, was the first to confront militarily and lose to Babur (1483–1530), a Timurid by blood, who became the first of the great Moguls in India (see BABUR, CONQUESTS OF).

Demerara Uprising (1823)   British sugarcane-plantation owners and Christian missionaries argued over social reform and rights for slave laborers in Demerara, a fertile coastal region in what is now Guyana. In 1823, about 12,000 slaves (many of them kinsfolk) rose up to gain freedom, raiding and seizing plantations. Accused of helping foment the rebellion was a sympathetic missionary, John Smith (d. 1823?), who died in jail awaiting execution. The slaves failed; hundreds of them were wounded or killed, and 33 were summarily tried and executed (only three whites died in the uprising). In 1831 Demerara was united with neighboring Berbice and Essequibo to form the crown colony of British Guiana, and slavery was abolished in all British colonies in 1833.

Demetrius, War of (239–229 B.C.)   Demetrius II (278?–229), son of Antigonus II (c. 319–239), inherited both Macedon and his father's problems with Greece (see CHREMONIDEAN WAR). To keep Epirus, he married its princess, but the country of Aetolia, desiring the province of Epirote Acarnania, and Achaea, a region hoping to control the whole Peloponnesian peninsula, allied themselves to oppose his control. Achaea seized Cleone and Heraea, but failed at Argos in 238. Rebel cities joined the Achaean League. Demetrius then invaded Boeotia (237–236), effectively splitting the Achaean and Aetolian leagues and causing the war to dwindle to isolated skirmishes. The war ended in 229 with Demetrius's death, but his nine-year-old son and regent had to face the loss of Epirus and Athens (229), troubles with Illyria, and the preludes to the SOCIAL WAR OF 219–217 B.C. Macedon was beginning to fall apart. See also ILLYRIAN WARS.

Devolution, War of (1667–68)   After the death of his father-in-law, King Philip IV (1605–65) of Spain, France's King Louis XIV (1638–1715) carefully laid plans to make the Spanish Netherlands French. Publicly, he explained that his Spanish queen, Marie Thérèse (1638–83), Philip's daughter, had renounced her rights there in exchange for a large dowry, which Spain had never paid; in addition, an old law gave her, as first born, inheritance rights of devolution, or succession, over her younger brother. Diplomatically, Louis had paralyzed his enemies: by treaty, the United Provinces (independent Netherlands, especially its chief member, Holland) were to remain uncommitted; Portugal's war kept Spain off balance (see SPANISH-PORTUGUESE WAR OF 1657–68); and a secret treaty kept England neutral. In 1667, French troops led by Henri, vicomte de Turenne (1611–75), invaded the Netherlands and won easy victories, capturing Flanders's chief city, Lille, within three months. The region of Franche-Comté was invaded and occupied in 14 days by the French under Louis II de Condé (1621–86) in February 1668. When Spain gave Portugal its independence and England, Sweden, and Holland formed an alliance to check French expansion (1668), Louis elected to stop the war and enter negotiations. By the Treaty of Aix-la-Chapelle on May 2, 1668, France gained fortresses and towns in the Spanish Netherlands and restored Franche-Comté to Spain. The question of devolution remained unsettled. See also DUTCH WAR, THIRD; GRAND ALLIANCE, WAR OF THE.

Diadochi, Wars of the (323–281 B.C.) The sudden death of Alexander the Great (356–323) raised problems concerning the preservation of his empire (see ALEXANDER THE GREAT, CONQUESTS OF), and the seven highest men in Alexander's command—the Diadochi ("successors")—began almost immediately to plot how to better themselves. The result was more than 40 years of convoluted intrigues, murders, and battles—a war of the Alexandrian succession. It centered around four questions. The first: who was to rule? The Diadochi compromised by establishing a co-kingship pairing Philip III Arrhidaeus (d. 317), Alexander's feeble-minded half-brother, and the unborn son of Alexander's wife Roxana (d. 311), to be named Alexander IV Aegeus (d. 311). The second question: who was to be regent? Antipater (d. 310), regent of Macedon during Alexander's conquests, took the job, though not unopposed. The LAMIAN WAR intervened and postponed the wrangling, and Antipater died. Question three: who succeeds? By this time, one of the successors, Perdiccas (d. 321), regent in Babylon, was dead, and the chief rivals were three: Antigonus I (c. 382–301), originally governor of Phrygia and the successor most concerned with uniting the empire; Cassander (358–297), Antipater's son; and Polyperchon (fl. c. 317–16), Antipater's appointment. Cassander allied himself with Lysimachus (c. 355–281), governor of Thrace, and Ptolemy I (d. 283?), governor of Egypt, to oppose Antigonus. Cassander harried Polyperchon, driving him from Macedon in 317. Philip III's wife made Cassander regent, angering Olympias (d. 316), Alexander's mother, who subsequently had Philip, his wife, and 100 Cassandrian friends murdered in 317. Polyperchon then returned until Cassander arrived as self-appointed regent and ordered the execution of Olympias. But Antigonus made himself Alexander IV's guardian in 315, and fierce battles rocked the empire until Cassander murdered Alexander and his mother in 311. One final question aroused the Diadochi: who was to be king? Against a background of battles and rumors of battles, Macedonia had five kings between 311 and 281, one of them twice: Cassander from 311 to 306; Antigonus from 306 until his death in the 301 Battle of IPSUS; Cassander again from 301 to 297 (a regency for Cassander's sons intervened, 297–294); Demetrius I (337?–283), Antigonus's son and a failure in his 305 siege of RHODES from 294 to 283; Lysimachus, who was killed in battle at CORUPEDION in 281; and Antigonus II (c. 319–239), claimant for the title in 283, who had to take Thrace to gain the throne in 276. Corupedion was the end of the military phase of the Diadochian wars; the death of Seleucus I (358?–280), king of Macedonia after Lysimachus, wiped out the successors. Alexander's empire was destroyed; the Seleucid dynasty controlled Syria, Mesopotamia, and Persia; the Ptolemies had Egypt and Asia Minor; and the Antigonids held Macedonia.

Dionysius War, First (398–397 B.C.) Dionysius the Elder (c. 430–367), tyrant of Syracuse, deviously initiated war to keep the Syracusans obedient to him and to repel the Carthaginian masters of much of Sicily. Leading 80,000 troops, Dionysius sacked Motya (Modica), a major Carthaginian stronghold. Carthaginians under Himilco (d. 396) countered by destroying the Syracusan fleet and laying siege to Syracuse. Gaining the support of Sparta and aided by plague in Himilco's army, Dionysius routed the Carthaginians. Except for Himilco's saving of the Carthaginian citizen-soldiers, the Syracusan victory was complete. Chagrined, Himilco committed suicide in 396. **Second Dionysius War** (393–392 B.C.). Carthage attempted to resume hostilities, but the forces of Dionysius were overwhelming. In 392, Dionysius forced the signing of a treaty, giving Syracuse control of most of Sicily and of the "foot" of Italy (Apulia and Calabria, both former Carthaginian territories). **Third Dionysius War** (382–376 B.C.). After a 10-year lapse in major confrontations, Dionysius led a large Syracusan force against the Carthaginians in western Sicily. At first he was victorious, but then he suffered a serious defeat at Cronium near Palermo. Control of western Sicilian lands was ceded to Carthage, with the Syracusan boundary being established at the Halycus (Platani) River. **Fourth Dionysius War** (368–367 B.C.). Dionysius again began a thrust into western Sicily, succeeding until his death during the blockade of Lilybaeum (Marsala) gave victory to the Carthaginians. He was followed by his son, Dionysius II (d. 344), who suspended the conflict between the rival city-states until TI-MOLEON'S WAR some 20 years later.

Dipo Negoro's War See JAVA WAR, GREAT.

Djibouti Civil War of 1991–94 In November 1991, the mainly Afar-supported Front for the Restoration of Unity and Democracy (FRUD) began fighting the Issa-dominated government of Djibouti (formerly the French territory of Afars and Issas), a small republic in northeast Africa on the south entrance to the Red Sea. Vying for power as the main ethnic groups, the Afars were in the north and west, and the Issas, related to the Somalis, were in the south. French peacekeeping forces were sent to help stop the fighting in early 1992; the Afar rebels then declared a unilateral ceasefire. But warring resumed in late 1992 near the town of Tadjoura, with dozens of persons killed and hundreds wounded. Under pressure, Djibouti's president, Hassan Gouled Aptidon (1916–), reshaped his government to form a careful balance between Afars and Issas in February 1993. The FRUD split apart because of disagreement over discussions with the government, which reached an agreement of reconciliation and peace with the principal FRUD faction on December 26, 1994. The constitution was revised, and seven FRUD leaders joined the government (1995). Some dissident FRUD rebels attacked and fought government troops in the north in 1997.

Dominican-Haitian Discord of 1963 The Dominicans were angry that the Haitians permitted the heirs and followers of former Dominican dictator Rafael Leónidas Trujillo Molina (1891–1961) to use their country as a base for plotting subversive activities in the Dominican Republic. The Haitians accused the Dominicans of giving sanctuary to Haitian opponents of François "Papa Doc" Duvalier (1907–71), Haiti's repressive president. In April 1963, former Haitian army officers reportedly tried to kill Duvalier's children, and many of those accused took refuge in the embassies of Latin American countries in Port-au-Prince, the Haitian capital. When Haitian police raided the Dominican embassy and held captive 22 refugees, the Dominican Republic broke off diplomatic relations and threatened to invade Haiti. The Organization of American States (OAS) mediated the dispute and eased the tension; Dominican troops, ready to invade, pulled back from the border; and many of the refugees were granted safe conduct out of Haiti (about 500 others escaped to the Dominican Republic). In an attempt to overthrow Duvalier, a small force of Haitian exiles, based in the Dominican Republic, invaded northern Haiti by sea on August 5, 1963, but the rebels were driven back across the border after two days of fighting. Hostilities erupted again in September that year when both sides shelled each other across the border. The OAS again intervened to make peace. That fall two hurricanes caused much destruction in the two neighboring hostile countries; in addition, the leftist Dominican government of President Juan Bosch (1909–) was overthrown by military leaders in a coup. The Haitian and Dominican governments, now preoccupied with pressing domestic problems, ceased further belligerency.

Dominican Republic Civil War of 1965–66 On September 25, 1963, Juan Bosch (1909–), socialist president of the Dominican Republic, was deposed by military leaders, who soon installed a civilian triumvirate to rule the country. On April 24, 1965, pro-Bosch army dissidents, aided by leftists, overthrew the government in Santo Domingo, the capital, where riots broke out and buildings were torched. However, the navy, air force, and some army units did not want Bosch to return to power, and they managed to regain control of much of the capital; their officers formed a rightist junta to rule until free elections could be held. Meanwhile, fighting continued between leftist and rightist factions, causing U.S. president Lyndon B. Johnson (1908–73) to send U.S. paratroopers and Marines to protect American interests and to prevent a communist takeover (April 28, 1965). The Organization of American States (OAS) arranged a truce on May 5, 1965; by that time almost 20,000 U.S. troops were in the Dominican Republic, and more than 2,000 Dominicans had been killed. Though the OAS's Inter-American Armed Force arrived to restore order, sporadic fighting persisted between pro-Bosch "rebels" and the military, which U.S. forces supported, throughout the rest of the year. The leaders of the rival factions agreed to set up a provisional government, and Bosch returned from abroad and called for the removal of OAS forces. The country was disrupted by leftist-instigated riots and a general strike in February 1966. Bosch lost the June presidential election to Joaquin Balaguer (1907–   ), a centrist; by October, all OAS and U.S. forces had withdrawn.

Dorian Invasions (c. 1120–950 B.C.) Prehistoric Greece experienced three major invasions of Greek-speakers: Mycenaeans (c. 2000 B.C.), armed with hard bronze weapons, who displaced an immigrant Anatolian culture; Achaeans (c. 1500–1400 B.C.), who chiefly co-existed with Mycenaean rulers; and Dorians, iron-weaponed, who overthrew the Mycenaeans and destroyed the Bronze Age economy of all of Greece. Originating in Epirus and southwest Macedonia, the Dorians invaded in two periods, the first a minor influx after 1400, for, as Thucydides (471?–400?) noted, they were servants to the Achaeans and participants in Achaean military actions against the Mycenaeans. Greek tradition states that the major influx occurred about 80 years after the TROJAN WAR, and modern archeology supports this tradition. Mariners and warriors, the Dorians came by sea and land through central Greece into the Peloponnesus, destroying one by one Mycenaean strongholds; however, Thebes's Cadmeia and Athens's Acropolis escaped destruction. The Dorians came in wave after wave, gaining control of areas, acquiring land and slaves, forcing many surviving residents east to the Aegean islands and Asia Minor, and then moving on to a new stronghold. The Dorians themselves eventually founded colonies in Italy, Sicily, and Asia Minor. Greek legend calls the invasion "the return of the Heraclids," for the first of the three main Dorian tribes (the Hylleis, Dymanes, and Pamphyloi) was traditionally ruled by Heracles's son Hyllus. But no clear Dorian record exists, perhaps because the Dorians may have originally been illiterate. Culturally inferior to the Achaeans except in iron, the Dorians nonetheless contributed to Greek culture in drama, poetry, and sculpture and created the solid, cold perfection of Doric architecture.

Dorr's Rebellion (1842) Thomas Wilson Dorr (1805–54), a Providence lawyer, organized the People's Party to reform the Rhode Island constitution and gain universal manhood suffrage. His supporters, the Dorrites, at an unofficial "people's convention," established a separate state government with Dorr as governor, opposed to the legitimate state government. Dorr tried unsuccessfully to seize the state arsenal at Providence to secure his position. His government, however, collapsed amid armed clashes between the Dorrites and the state militia, and Dorr fled from Rhode Island. In late 1842, the state government extended the vote to all native-born male whites.

Douglas Rebellion of 1455 The Douglas family, notorious for its attempts to control the throne of Scotland, was severely weakened during the reign of King James II (1430–60). The fifth earl, James's regent, died in 1439; the sixth and seventh earls were murdered to safeguard the Scottish Crown. The eighth, William (1425?–52), intent on revenge as well as power, schemed to become lieutenant-general of the realm and then conspired with other nobles to manipulate James. Confronted by the king in 1452, William refused to capitulate; James murdered him at Stirling Castle. William's brother James (1426–88), the ninth and last earl of Douglas, seized Inverness, but he was forced into exile in England after the Scottish forces of King James defeated the Douglas forces at the Battle of Arkenholm on May 12, 1455.

Dozsa's Rebellion (Hungarian Peasants' Revolt) (1514) Hungary's ambitious cardinal primate preached a crusade against the Turks, gathering an army of 100,000 peasants and appointing Gyorgy Dozsa (1470–1514) to lead it. When the crusade was suddenly and mysteriously suspended, the peasants refused to disband, deciding to march against their landlords and nobles, who had cruelly oppressed and exploited them in the past. The rebels ravaged the country, burning castles and killing nobles and their families until the lords' forces, led by John Zapolya (1487–1540), governor of Transylvania and later king of Hungary, defeated them at Temesvar. Dozsa was captured and executed (roasted alive). The Hungarian Diet of 1514 severely punished the surviving peasants, increasing their taxes and obligations, forcing them to pay for the damages caused by the revolt, and sentencing them to perpetual servitude.

Drake's Raids in the Caribbean (1585–86) Having been knighted in 1580 for previous service to England (successful raids on Spanish colonies and treasure ships, exploration and claiming lands for the Crown, and circumnavigating the world), Sir Francis Drake (1540?–96) led an English fleet of 29 ships to attack Spanish possessions in the Caribbean region. After failing to capture the Spanish treasure fleet, Drake's forces attacked the Spanish colony of Santo Domingo on the island of Hispaniola, burning much of it before the inhabitants paid him a ransom. Drake next besieged and sacked the Spanish Main's treasure city of Cartagena in present-day Colombia; its citizens also paid a ransom. With many captured pieces of Spanish artillery and much money, Drake set sail for England, stopping en route to plunder the Florida coast, including St. Augustine (which he burned), before arriving home in 1586 to advocate an attack on the SPANISH ARMADA being assembled in Spain. See also ANGLO-SPANISH WAR OF 1587–1604.

Druse-Ottoman Wars   See   OTTOMAN-DRUSE WARS.

Druse Rebellion of 1600–1607   In what is now Lebanon, Fakhr al-Din II (1572–1635) prepared to

regain the power previously held by his family (see OTTOMAN-DRUSE WAR OF 1585); his chief enemy was the Yamani party, headed by the ruler of Tripoli. Unlike his foe, Fakhr cultivated friendships and support among both Sunnis and Shi'ites, and he was the first to unite the Druse (Druze) and Maronite Christian districts. By 1600, the military activity by his private army had gained him control of Sidon and Beirut on the coast and also the enmity of both the Porte (Ottoman government) and Tripoli's ruler; fighting began between Fakhr's Kaysis party and the Yamanis. The Porte wavered in its support, favoring first one party and then the other, until Fakhr's victories became consistent. Ottoman help then led Fakhr to final supremacy in 1607; to prevent Ottoman interference in his emirate, he regularly sent ambassadors and bribes to Constantinople (Istanbul). See OTTOMAN-DRUSE WAR OF 1611–13.

Druse Rebellion of 1925–27   The Druses (Druzes), a small Islamic sect, in the French mandate of Syria protested their governor's tyrannical treatment but received no satisfaction from the French high commissioner. Opposed also to foreign control, they rebelled under Sultan al-Atrash (fl. 1914–27) in July 1925, and soon controlled most of the countryside. Syrian nationalists joined the Druses, and together they forced the French to withdraw from Damascus and then bombarded the city, killing many civilians. The French unleashed fierce attacks with heavy artillery and aerial bombing of Damascus, but the rebellion, which had spread into southern Lebanon, continued until June 1927, when Druse leaders accepted peace (Lebanon had been declared a republic by the French on May 23, 1927). French military officers, impressed by Druse bravery, tried to ensure conditions of harmony.

Dubh's Rebellion (1501–3)   King James IV (1473–1513) of Scotland, alternately friendly and authoritarian, attempted to solve the problem of controlling the north and west Highlands by putting power, but not land, into the hands of his Campbell

"Lord Lieutenant of the Isles." Donald Dubh (fl. early 1500s), son of Angus Og (see OG'S REBELLION), objected and led uprisings beginning in 1501. In 1503, the loyal Macdonalds, with Maclean assistance, defeated Dubh's forces and burned his hiding place in Inverness Castle, forcing Dubh to flee. Caught in 1506, he was imprisoned. Now in control, James established fortified strongholds in the Highlands to ensure peace.

Dunes, Battle of the   See NIEUWPOORT, BATTLE OF.

Dunkirk, Evacuation of (1940)   After German armies invaded Belgium on May 10–13, 1940, during WORLD WAR II, they turned their attention to seizing the English Channel ports on the northern French coast. They proceeded to bombard the ports heavily by air and by land, and hundreds of thousands of British, French, Belgian, and other Allied troops became trapped between the sea and the German lines. The British and French navies and merchant fleets, plus private trawlers, yachts, and other vessels, came to rescue the troops off the beaches at Dunkirk. For more than a week, from May 26 to June 4, 1940, more than 1,200 ships and boats of every description participated in the troops' evacuation, sailing back and forth across the channel bringing the exhausted soldiers to safety in England. Simultaneously, the Luftwaffe (German air force) attempted to destroy the fleeing Allies, bombing and strafing relentlessly. Many Allied vessels were sunk, including six destroyers, but most survived and succeeded in saving about 340,000 troops.

Dunmore's War   See LORD DUNMORE' WAR.

Dunsinane, Battle of (1054)   As the West Saxon kingdom of England gradually regained control of the Danelaw after 1042 (see VIKING RAIDS IN ENGLAND, LATER), King Edward the Confessor (1002?–1066) demanded that Scotland acknowledge England as its feudal overlord. When the Scots refused, he sent Earl Siward of Northumberland (d. 1055) to compel acknowledgment. With his nephew Malcolm Canmore (d. 1093), a Scottish prince, Siward and his forces invaded lowland Scotland in 1054 and at Dunsinane near Perth fought a fierce and costly (especially in English lives) battle with the Scots under their king, Macbeth (d. 1057), who was wounded. Siward retreated to England afterward. Macbeth, an effective and popular ruler disparaged by the playwright William Shakespeare, was later hunted down and killed by Malcolm, who acquired lowland Scotland as King Malcolm III.

Dupplin Moor, Battle of (1332)   The rulers of Scotland did not restore lands to pro-English nobles, as ordered in the 1328 Treaty of Northampton (see SCOTTISH WAR OF 1314–28), and consequently King Edward III (1312–77) of England was angered. He plotted to recover the Scottish throne for Edward Balliol (d. 1363) (see SCOTTISH WAR OF 1295–96) and finally invaded Scotland, meeting the Scots at Dupplin Moor on August 12, 1332. Attacking at night and using the Welsh-invented tactic of longbows and dismounted men-at-arms, the English troops defeated the Scots and killed their leader, the earl of Mar. Edward then had Balliol crowned at Scone, thus giving Scotland two kings, but disgruntled Scots drove Balliol back over the border (see HALIDON HILL, BATTLE OF).

Dutch-Indian Wars of 1655–64   While Governor Peter Stuyvesant (1592–1672) was absent from the Dutch colony of New Netherlands (much of present-day New York and New Jersey), a dispute occurred between the Dutch and Indians in Manhattan on September 6, 1655. War broke out that extended to Esopus, Long Island. Stuyvesant soon returned to make peace, to ransom hostages, and to set down laws restricting the actions of the Indians, a number of whom were Algonquian (see ALGONQUIN-DUTCH WAR). Manhattan was never again subjected to Indian attack, but Indian raids at Esopus in May 1658 caused the settlers there to appeal to Stuyvesant for help. The governor again made peace with the Indians and supervised the building of a palisade (wooden fortification set in the ground); but again he had to come to the aid of the settlers at Esopus when Indian attacks resumed in August 1658. Stuyvesant's forces subdued the Indians. However, Indian resentment over the harsh peace terms laid down by the governor led to renewed fighting near Esopus in 1663. The Dutch forced the Indians to surrender and to sign a treaty in 1664 that gave the settlers the Esopus Valley.

Dutch-Indonesian War of 1962   See INDONE-SIAN WARS OF 1957–62.

Dutch-Portuguese Wars in West Africa (c. 1620–55)   As early as the mid-15th century, Portuguese mariners had established posts along the western coast of Africa on Arguin Island, Guinea, Costa de Mina (later the Gold Coast), São Tomé Island, and on the shores of Portuguese West Africa (Angola). Originally they came searching for gold and ivory, but soon expanded their trade to include black natives, who were shipped as slaves by the thousands to Brazil and the Caribbean islands. Early in the 17th century, the Dutch, who had broken the Portuguese trade monopoly in the Indian Ocean, turned their attention to West Africa and built forts at Mouri, Gorée Island, and Rifisque. Engaging in the profitable slave trade, the Dutch competed with the Portuguese, and the rivals attacked each other's bases and ships whenever they had a chance. Between 1637 and 1642, the Dutch stormed the Portuguese forts of Elmina and Axim on the Ghana coast, the port of Luanda (in Angola), São Tomé, and parts of Brazil. The Portuguese managed to regain control of most places and retain supremacy along the Kongo (Bakongo) coast and in Guinea, but they lost territory to the Dutch and other Europeans in Ghana and the Gold Coast.

Dutch War, First (1652–54)   Two important achievements of the Commonwealth, the English government set up after the execution of King Charles I (1600–1649), were the doubling of the size of the royal navy and the Navigation Act of 1651 (see ENGLISH

CIVIL WAR, SECOND). The latter, designed to increase English trade, ordered imports to be handled by English ships with mainly English crews; it was meant to hurt the Dutch, Europe's chief sea merchant at the time, and the Dutch-East Indies trade; it provoked war. When a Dutch fleet failed in 1652 to dip its flag to an English squadron under Admiral Robert Blake (1599–1657), whose request to search the Dutch fleet was refused by its commander, Maarten Tromp (1597–1653), shooting occurred between the fleets, and soon after there were declarations of war. Nine naval engagements were fought, principally between Blake, aided by George Monck (1608–70), and Tromp, who was killed fighting with 1,600 other Dutch at the Battle of Scheveningen (Texel) on July 31, 1653. Blake lost only once, after which a Dutch fleet convoyed 500 merchant vessels safely to port. The Dutch got the Danes to close the Baltic to the English and took control of the Mediterranean during most of the war. England blockaded Holland and, in 1653, the starving Dutch sued for peace after Scheveningen. The Treaty of Westminster in April 1654 forced the Dutch to indemnify English merchants who had been harmed and prescribed a Dutch salute in English waters. The Anglo-Dutch commercial rivalry continued, however. **Second Dutch War** (1665–67). English attacks in 1663 on West African ports that were a source of the Dutch slave trade and the English seizure of New Amsterdam (New York) in 1664 helped provoke this conflict. At the Battle of Lowestoft in 1665, English naval ships (150 of them) under Prince James (1633–1701), later King James II, defeated a Dutch fleet of 100 ships under Jacob Opdam (d. 1665), who was killed along with several other Dutch and English naval leaders. Warships commanded by Monck suffered defeat by the Dutch under Admiral Michiel de Ruyter (1607–76) but later broke de Ruyter's blockade of the Thames River in 1666. Regardless, England's Restoration navy had proven to be inferior to Cromwell's because of maladministration, corruption, Crown-Parliament disputes, and mutinies by unpaid sailors. In June 1667, de Ruyter led a Dutch raid into the Thames, destroying 16 English ships on the Medway River at Chatham. This and the Great Plague (1665–66) and the Great Fire of London (1666) led England to seek peace. The Treaty of Breda in 1667 modified the trade laws in favor of the Dutch, who gained possession of present-day Surinam and recognized English control of what is now New York, New Jersey, and Delaware. **Third Dutch War** (1672–78). This conflict resulted from the plottings of Louis XIV (1638–1715) of France and the desire of King Charles II (1630–85) of England to rule his country single-handedly. Louis wanted the Belgian Netherlands as a French "natural boundary," but the Triple Alliance of England, Sweden, and Holland (1668) prevented its acquisition (see DEVOLUTION, WAR OF). To isolate Holland, Louis secretly bribed Sweden to quit the alliance, and, to hard-pressed Charles, he gave a pension, thus receiving English support. Louis attacked Holland in 1672, and England declared war. De Ruyter's Dutch warships staved off English and French fleets. The Dutch opened dikes, causing extensive flooding that held off invasions. Charles had promulgated a Declaration of Indulgence, so unpopular that Parliament passed the Test Act of 1673 and cut off funds for the war, in which England had failed in an attempt to blockade and invade Holland. In 1674, Parliament forced England out of the war and again allied England against France, which continued the fighting. French forces under Prince Louis II de Condé (1621–86) defeated the Dutch under William of Orange (1650–1702) at the Battle of Seneff in 1674. The Germans in the Rhineland were unable to repulse French campaigns under Henri, vicomte de Turenne (1611–75), losing at Sinzheim in 1674 and at Turckheim in 1675. The coalition armies (Dutch, Spanish, and German) made attempts to invade France but were upset by French forces, especially those commanded by Marshal François Créqui (1629?–87), who won important battles in the Alsace and Lorraine regions. In 1676, at Messina, Sicily, French troops crushed a Spanish army, and French warships under Admiral Abraham Duquesne (1610–88) defeated Dutch-Spanish naval forces under de Ruyter, who was mortally wounded (see MESSINAN REBELLION OF 1674–79). Much of Holland was overrun by the French during the war. Finally, with his armies generally victorious but threatened by England's reentry into the war and

by financial ruin at home, Louis decided to make peace in 1678; the Treaties of Nijmegen resulted between France and its coalition enemies (Holland, Spain, and the Holy Roman Empire); the Treaty of St. Germain forced the Elector of Brandenburg, who had opposed France in the war, to relinquish his conquests in Pomerania to Sweden, whose King Charles XI (1655–97) had been Louis's ally. See also DANISH-SWEDISH WAR OF 1675–79; GRAND ALLIANCE, WAR OF THE.

Dutch War in Brazil (1624–29)   In 1621, the Dutch West India Company was chartered to trade in the New World (North and South America) and, specifically, to deprive Portugal of its holdings there, as a similar company had done to Portugal in the Far East. In 1624, a company fleet of 26 Dutch ships commanded by Piet Heyn (1577–1629) sailed into Bahia (Baia) on the Brazilian coast and seized the port. In response, Spain, which had annexed Portugal in 1580 (see SPANISH-PORTUGUESE WAR OF 1580–89), sent 52 ships and 12,000 men under Fadrique de Toledo to expel the Dutch invaders. Heyn's forces were driven out, but returned in 1627 to recapture and plunder Bahia. Made an admiral in the Dutch navy, Heyn captured a Spanish treasure ship off Cuba in 1628. The enriched Dutch West India Company now dispatched 67 ships and 7,000 men, who seized Recife (city) and Pernambuco (region) in northeastern Brazil. The Dutch withdrew from the area in 1654, when the Portuguese inhabitants successfully revolted.

Dutch War of Independence   See EIGHTY YEARS' WAR.

Dutch War of 1780–84   The AMERICAN REVOLUTION made Great Britain an enemy of most European nations because the British refused to recognize neutrality in the war and seized ships indiscriminately. A League of Armed Neutrality was formed and threatened war against Britain if it did not stop its practices, but only Holland (a league member) actually suffered. The British, angry because Holland supplied French and Spanish arms to the American rebels through its West Indian Dutch base, St. Eustatius, declared war in 1780, captured and sank a number of Dutch vessels, and inflicted serious damage on Dutch trade. No naval or land battles occurred. In 1784, Britain apologized for its actions, pleading wartime necessity, when it concluded the Treaty of Paris.

E

Easter Uprising (Easter Rebellion) (1916) The sentiments behind the Easter Uprising (see ANGLO-IRISH CIVIL WAR OF 1916–21) found expression first in the founding of the Sinn Fein ("we, ourselves") in 1905, devoted to the cause of Irish home rule and to passive resistance toward all things British. The more radical members of the Sinn Fein wanted independence; the older Irish Republican Brotherhood (Fenians; IRB, later IRA) called openly for rebellion. The radicals sought to embarrass the British by vainly sending Sir Roger Casement (1864–1916) to Germany for help. The IRB and the Irish Volunteers split over the impending uprising, issuing orders, countermanding orders, and counter-countermanding orders. Loosely planned and finally confined to Dublin City, it was undermanned by 2,000 Irish Volunteers and a 200-member citizen army. Seizing (Easter Monday, April 24, 1916) the general post office as a headquarters for their leaders, Padhraic Pearse (1879–1916) and James Connolly (1870–1916), the Irish rebels proclaimed a republic and set up a provisional government. The British were taken by surprise, losing more than 460 men, but they managed to put down the uprising in a week. Dubliners condemned the rebellion until the leaders, including Casement, were tried and executed; then they venerated them. The uprising ruined the Irish Parliamentary party, but the Sinn Fein went on under the leadership of Eamon de Valera (1882–1975), and the IRA became an underground guerrilla force.

Ecuadoran Civil War of 1830–34 Ecuador withdrew from Greater Colombia in September 1830 and became an independent republic under the presidency of General Juan José Flores (1800–1864), a Venezuelan who had come to Ecuador with the liberating army of Simon Bolivar (1783–1830) and who now maintained his power under the autocratic constitution of 1830 with an army composed mainly of foreign soldiers. Flores ruled from the mountain city of Quito, composed of a largely conservative populace, while discontent brewed in the seaport of Guayaquil, populated by numerous liberals. An uprising began in 1834 in the coastal region under Vicente Rocafuerte (1783–1847) and aimed at removing the foreigners, including Flores. The latter remained in control, briefly jailed Rocafuerte, and then agreed that they should take turns in the presidency. In 1835, Rocafuerte became president and Flores became commander of the army. See also COLOMBIAN WAR OF INDEPENDENCE.

Ecuadoran-Colombian War of 1863 For years Ecuador and New Granada (Colombia) hotly disputed their common border, each wanting more territory. In 1861, conservative Gabriel García Moreno (1821–75) became Ecuadoran president and soon attempted to unify his country, which was sharply divided by class, regional, and language differences, by handing over much power to the

Roman Catholic Church, which he considered the people's chief social tie to achieving a sense of nationalism. Many Ecuadorans opposed his autocratic regime, which gave control of education and welfare to clerics and suppressed leading liberals and other opponents. New Granada's liberal president, Tomás Cipriano de Mosquera (1798–1878), backed rebellious Ecuadorans in an effort to topple García Moreno, who responded by sending a 6,000-man army under his elderly father-in-law, General Juan José Flores (1800–1864), to invade New Granada. On December 6, 1863, at the Battle of Cuaspad, some 4,000 Colombians under Mosquera utterly defeated the invaders, about 1,500 of whom were slain or wounded and 2,000 taken captive. The war ceased, and differences were settled by a treaty.

Ecuadoran-Peruvian Border War of 1995   A longstanding territorial dispute between Ecuador and Peru erupted in fighting on January 26, 1995, in the remote, rugged jungle mountains of the Cordillera del Cóndor, where a stretch of border had never been clearly marked and where deposits of gold, uranium, and oil supposedly lay. Peru claimed that the approximately 1,000-mile border between the two countries had been set by the 1942 Rio de Janeiro Protocol, which had confirmed its victory over Ecuador in a 10-day war in 1941 over territory. But Ecuador declared the protocol null in 1960, before the last 48 miles of the border had been marked. Vowing to enforce Peru's claim to the 48-mile stretch, President Alberto Fujimori (1938–) sent troops and warplanes into the region (between the Santiago and Zamora rivers); then Ecuador's president Sixto Durán Ballén (1922–) attempted to negotiate a peace. Each side accused the other of being the aggressor and deployed naval ships along their coasts. Finally a cease-fire and truce took effect on March 1, 1995, after tense peace talks, calling for demilitarization of the disputed jungle border. Peru reported losing several warplanes and almost 50 soldiers; Ecuador's official toll was about 30 dead and 300 wounded, but casualties on both sides most likely were greater. On October 26, 1998, the two countries signed a peace treaty defining the 48-mile stretch of border, creating a committee to resolve boundary issues peacefully, and setting down terms for bilateral trade and navigation rights.

Ecuadoran War of Independence   See COLOMBIAN WAR OF INDEPENDENCE.

Edward the Black Prince, Raids of (1355–56) After the English victories at CRÉCY and Calais during the HUNDRED YEARS' WAR, the Black Death (plague) and the demise of King Philip VI (1293–1350) caused a truce between England and France. Anxious for a lasting settlement, English king Edward III (1312–77) suggested in 1355 ending the war through French concession of Aquitaine, but French king John II (1319–64) rejected the proposal. King Edward and the Black Prince Edward quickly invaded France with a new army to resume the conflict. Scottish problems recalled Edward, but the Black Prince, with a small but hardy force of 8,000 men, raided devastatingly in Languedoc and continued up the Loire in 1356, to be met at Poitiers by 80,000 French soldiers under John (see POITIERS, BATTLE OF).

Egyptian War against the Wahabis (1811–18) During the 1730s, the Arabian theologian Muhammad ibn Abd al-Wahab (1703–92) preached a reformed Islam, declaring that all doctrinal or ritual accretions made after the Prophet's death were spurious and unorthodox. This primitive Islam, sometimes labeled puritan, swept Arabia after its adoption (1744) by the Saudi family; Wahabism remains today the official orthodoxy of Saudi Arabia. In the early 1800s, the Wahabi Saudis interfered, through piracy, with the Indian Ocean trade of Ottoman Egypt's chief ally and benefactor, Great Britain; Muhammad Ali (1769?–1849), pasha of Egypt, determined, with the consent of the Ottomans, that the Wahabis be put down. By 1811, the Wahabis, operating from their capital, Riyadh, had gained control of Mecca, Medina, and Jidda and threatened Syria, prompting the start of Muhammad Ali's campaign against them in Arabia, nominally a vassal of the Ottoman Empire. The Egyptian invading forces under Muhammad Ali and his son Ibrahim (1789–1848) fought bloody battles against the Wahabis in the desert and elsewhere for seven years. By 1818, the Egyptians had recovered the Muslim holy cities, thanks mainly to successful naval actions, and had control of the eastern coast of the Red Sea.

Eight Saints, War of the (1375–78)   Pope Gregory XI (1330–78) hoped to remove the papacy from Avignon, France, to Rome (in the so-called "Babylonian Captivity of the Church," 1309–77, the popes were in exile on French soil). Florence led a coalition of Italian states in revolt against papal authority, causing the pope to excommunicate the Florentines in 1376. Florence thereupon allied itself with Milan, and a Florentine eight-member council, the Otto di Guerra ("the Eight Saints"), directed the war against the pope. In 1377, an army under Robert of Geneva (d. 1394), sent by the pope, ruthlessly ravaged the Italian states in revolt, and Pope Gregory XI returned to Italy to take his seat in Rome. Helped by the intercession of Saint Catherine of Siena (1347–80), the papacy secured a compromise peace with Florence and, in return for a payment of 200,000 florins, rescinded the papal interdict imposed on Florence during the war.

Eighty Years' War (Netherlands or Dutch War of Independence) (1568–1648)   Dutch desire for autonomy and Hapsburg intransigence clashed after 1555, when Holy Roman Emperor Charles V (1500–1558) gave the Netherlands to his son Philip II (1527–98) of Spain. Philip lived and ruled unhappily in the Netherlands until 1559, battling with the Estates General while administering the usual Hapsburg policies: war, high taxes, and government centralization at the expense of old privileges. Angry at having to withdraw some Spanish garrisons, he left and thus created another grievance: unenlightened rule from a distant capital. He had so angered both southern Catholics and northern Calvinists that as early as 1562 minor uprisings occurred in Flanders and Brabant. In 1567, Philip sent the duke of Alva (Alba) (1507–82) to take control at the Brussels capital through a reign of terror, during which some 12,000 people died. When, in 1568, Holland and Zeeland rebelled, a lengthy, sporadic war for independence began. Early military activity was sparse, but Calvinist Dutch guerrillas, the Geuzen, conducted pillaging raids on land and piracy at sea; the Dutch won the first battle of the war at Heiligerles (1568), then promptly lost the second at Jemmingen. The Geuzen blockaded the sea outlet for Brussels, and by 1572, with the election of William the Silent (1533–84) of Nassau, prince of Orange, as chief ruler (stadtholder) of the Netherlands, areas near Brussels were captured by the Dutch. The Spanish began to lose and failed in a siege of Leiden in 1574. The southern states of the Netherlands joined the northern in the Pacification of Ghent (1576) to force out plundering (because unpaid) Spanish garrisons. Troops under the new Spanish governor, Alessandro Farnese (1545–92), reconquered the southern states, which were placated enough to accept the Spanish by the Union of Arras (1579). The northern states of the Netherlands allied themselves as the United Provinces (Union of Utrecht, 1579), seeking greater autonomy; in 1581, they formally declared their independence. For help, William the Silent turned experimentally to foreigners, gaining that of the duke of Anjou, who, in 1583, in an abortive attempt to seize Antwerp, revealed that his real purpose was to control the Netherlands for France. After William the Silent's assassination in 1584, the Spanish regained control of Flanders and Brabant, thus forcing the removal of the United Provinces' capital to the Hague. In 1586, an English expedition under Robert Dudley (1532–88), earl of Leicester, invaded the Netherlands to help the Dutch but was ineffectual and withdrew. The United Provinces resolved to fight alone under the guidance of William the Silent's son, Maurice of Nassau (1567–1625), now stadtholder. The Spanish, busy in other wars (see SPANISH ARMADA, DEFEAT OF THE; SPANISH-PORTUGUESE WAR OF 1580–89), did not attempt to invade the northern Netherlands; instead, a kind of unwritten truce prevailed, seriously broken only by Maurice's victory at the Battle of NIEUWPOORT (THE DUNES) in 1600 and the Spanish siege and capture of Ostend in 1601–4. The coexistence was ratified by a war-weary Spain in a 12-year truce (1609), which gave the United Provinces partial recognition. The war was resumed in 1621 to take advantage of Spain's involvement in the THIRTY YEARS' WAR. Dutch victories at Breda and Maastricht (1625), capture of a Spanish silver fleet off Cuba (1628), a Dutch treaty with France (1635), and destruction of the Spanish fleet at Downs (1639) prompted the Spanish to enter into peace negotiations. In the Peace of Westphalia in 1648, ending the Eighty and Thirty Years' wars, the southern states remained the Spanish Netherlands and the United Provinces finally won their full independence. See also AUSTRIAN NETHERLANDS CIVIL WAR OF 1477–92.

Emboabas, War of the (1708–9)   The discovery of gold in Minas Gerais in eastern Brazil in the 17th century caused conflict between the region's original settlers from São Paulo (Paulistas), who claimed exclusive right to the mineral wealth there, and the new settlers, mostly European immigrants, called *emboabas* (the Paulistas, many of whom were of Portuguese-Amerindian blood, regarded the newcomers as trespassers and tenderfeet, applying the term *emboabas* to them, while the *emboabas* thought of the Paulistas as uncouth and barbaric). Tension mounted for a decade, with the European newcomers finally outnumbering the Paulistas and with civil war erupting in 1708 for possession of the gold mines. The *emboabas,* supported by the colonial government, succeeded in displacing the Paulistas, who then moved west to Mato Grosso, where they found gold deposits in 1718.

Emmet's Insurrection (1803)   Robert Emmet (1778–1803) is highly regarded by Irish nationalists as the martyred leader of an abortive insurrection against the British, an uprising whose objective was to establish a republic based on French principles in

accord with the aims of Wolfe Tone (1763–98), founder of the United Irishmen and Emmet's idol (see UNITED IRISHMEN'S REVOLT). With the leaders of that organization, Emmet had spent 1800–2 in France, developing plans for the uprising, to be aided by the French. An accidental explosion at one of Emmet's secret arms caches made early action necessary in late July 1803, but confusion ruined the insurrection: one contingent of rebels never arrived, a second went home thinking the uprising postponed, and a third waited vainly for a signal someone forgot to give. Emmet and about 100 followers rashly and unsuccessfully stormed Dublin Castle. He then fled and hid in the mountains of Wicklow. Returning to be near his fiancée, he was captured, tried for treason, and hanged on September 20, 1803.

English Civil War, First or Great (1642–46)   King Charles I (1600–1649) of England believed that he ruled by divine right and that Parliament merely advised, and any rights Parliament had were his gift. Parliament, however, felt decision making should be shared. Both sides were unyielding. Charles wanted money for wars and Crown projects; he repeatedly assembled recalcitrant parliaments to obtain it. He continued despotic tax levies and unregulated trial courts and attempted to rule without Parliament for 11 years. His manner unaltered, he sequestered lands, collected taxes, imprisoned opponents, appointed hated advisers, and tried to force a High Church liturgy on Scotland (see BISHOPS' WARS). Unable to wage war effectively, Charles called a parliament in 1640 (the "Short"), which refused money unless grievances were discussed. Dismissing it in just three weeks, Charles summoned another 1640 parliament (the "Long," for it lasted until 1653) and found it full of opposition, including a growing Puritan faction. The assembly attacked Charles, passing laws to sweep away encroachments of despotism; it impeached and executed some advisers and ruled that Parliament's dissolution required agreement on both sides. The GREAT IRISH REBELLION began in 1641 and required an army, but Parliament, distrusting the king, put it under its own control, adding a plan for church reform demanded by the Puritans. Charles arrested its leaders, rejected a compromise, and gathered forces made up of nobles, Anglicans, and Roman Catholics, all with limited finances. The Parliamentarians mobilized the moneyed artisans and the merchant class in the south and west, and controlled the navy. Hostilities began in 1642 with skirmishes all over England. The first major battle, at Edgehill, ended in a draw. Charles established himself at Oxford and tried vainly to take London in 1643. His royalists, failing to conquer fortified places, had no real strength until they allied with the Scots in the Solemn League and Covenant: Charles agreed to "Presbyterianize" England in exchange for 20,000 men. The Scots invaded Yorkshire in 1644 and helped capture Newark briefly, but the royalists lost badly at Marston Moor because of brilliant cavalry maneuvers by a parliamentary regiment, the Ironsides, under Oliver Cromwell (1599–1658). In 1645, Cromwell, now second in command of all parliamentary forces, agreed to form a New Model Army: well-trained, well-paid troops who trounced Charles's forces at Naseby (see ANGLO-SCOTTISH WAR OF 1542–49) because Charles had received no Irish or Continental aid. Oxford fell in 1646; Charles fled to Scotland and surrendered to the Scots, thus ending the first civil war. **Second English Civil War** (1648–51). After Oxford, the Long Parliament tried refashioning both government and the church. Presbyterians attempted to implement the Solemn League and Covenant of 1643 by designing a Presbyterian system for England. This action alienated the army, and Parliament sought its demobilization. Hoping for restoration through foreign aid, Charles delayed his response to parliament's Presbyterian legislation. This angered the Scots, who turned him over to Parliament in 1646 for 400,000 pounds. Parliament offered him a limited monarchy, but the army, ready to execute him because he stubbornly rejected all compromises, seized him and marched to London, with Cromwell in full command. Charles escaped, fled to the Isle of Wight, and continued to negotiate with Parliament, foreign governments, and Scotland, again promising Presbyterianism in exchange for aid. The fighting resumed in 1648; uprisings in Kent, Essex, and Wales were suppressed. An invading Scottish army was defeated by Cromwell's army at Preston in northern England in 1648. Parliament again tried to obtain a compromise, but the army, dominated by Cromwell, got rid of the Presbyterians in 1648 through Pride's Purge (Thomas Pride [d. 1658], on army orders, expelled Presbyterians from Parliament on grounds they were royalists). The legislative remnant, known as the Rump Parliament, constituting itself a special court, brought Charles to trial for treason in 1649. He was the first English king ever tried, convicted, and executed. Parliament then ruled England through a Council of State, ordering Cromwell to counteract proclamations of Charles II (1630–85) in Ireland and Scotland (see CROMWELL'S IRISH CAMPAIGN; CROMWELL'S SCOTTISH CAMPAIGN). Charles II initiated invasions of England, but, after defeat at Worcester in 1651, he fled overseas. The tragic struggle was over, but England had still to heal its many wounds.

English Civil War of 1215–17   Appalled by the liberties extorted from him by the Magna Carta in 1215, King John (1167–1216) of England immediately asked for and received a papal decree voiding the charter. He summoned French mercenaries and freebooters and swiftly began war against the English barons. France sent siege guns to the barons and, when John's forces at first did well, offered to send Prince Louis (1187–1226). Thousands of English supported the barons, who offered Louis the English throne. In 1216, John died and Louis invaded, rapidly becoming master of southeastern England. Henry III (1207–72) was crowned, and his regent, William Marshal (1146?–1219), directed English forces that defeated Louis's navy at Dover and his besieging army at Lincoln, almost simultaneously, in 1217. The barons, conciliated by Marshal's reforms, had deserted Louis by then; Louis withdrew after concluding a peace treaty with Marshal in September 1217. See also BARONS' WAR.

English Dynastic War of 1138–54 Having lost his only son (1120) and fearing the appointment of his weak and unreliable nephew Stephen of Blois (1097?–1154) as his successor, England's King Henry I (1068–1135) arranged, with his barons, to have his daughter Matilda (1102–67) take the throne. When Henry died, the English barons and clergy offered the throne instead to Stephen, whose inability to keep peace and order caused the barons to rebel in 1138 in favor of Matilda. In 1139, forces of Matilda, who was helped by her half brother Robert (d. 1147), earl of Gloucester, began battling Stephen's supporters; Stephen was taken prisoner at Lincoln, England, in 1141. Uncrowned and arrogant, Matilda engendered further rebellion; her forces were defeated at Winchester and Robert was taken captive but soon freed in a prisoner exchange for Gloucester. Matilda was driven out of England in 1142. Stephen ruled anarchically, and civil war continued—after 1148, in favor of Matilda's son Henry Plantagenet (1133–89). After an indecisive battle at Wallingford, a truce was concluded in 1154, enabling Stephen to finish his reign; Henry was named to succeed him (see ANGLO-FRENCH WAR OF 1159–89). See also STANDARD, BATTLE OF THE.

English Invasions of Ireland (1394–99) The troubled reign of King Richard II (1367–1400) of England contained Irish problems important enough to prompt him to invade Ireland twice. Interclan strife affecting English administration led to the first of them in 1394. Little fighting occurred, but much successful parleying enabled him to gain the submission of 50 Irish chiefs and to knight five Irish kings before leaving in 1395. Fighting broke out, at first involving only the Irish. When his lieutenant was defeated and slain in late 1398, Richard returned, but had hardly landed when news arrived of HENRY OF BOLINGBROKE'S REVOLT in England. Richard was forced to return home.

English Revolution of 1688 See GLORIOUS REVOLUTION.

English-Scottish Wars See ANGLO-SCOTTISH WARS.

English Succession, War of the See GLORIOUS REVOLUTION; IRISH WAR OF 1689–91; JACOBITE REBELLION OF 1689–90.

"Epoch of Civil Wars," Colombian (1863–80) In 1861, the liberal general Tomás Cipriano de Mosquera (1798–1878) declared himself provisional president of Colombia (see COLOMBIAN CIVIL WAR OF 1861), thus beginning almost two decades of uneasy liberal rule. In 1863, a constituent assembly met at Río Negro, adopted a new federal constitution, and proclaimed the union of seven sovereign states as the United States of Colombia; the central government was kept weak with a presidential term of two years, after which the incumbent could not be reelected. Nevertheless, Mosquera was reelected president in 1865 after his first term in the office, which had been restricted to one year because he was mistrusted by many. Assuming dictatorial powers, he quarreled with his liberal party and the congress and was deposed and imprisoned (1867) and exiled for two years. The liberals now named a succession of presidents, who headed the lame central government for their limited terms, and provisional presidents, who served even shorter terms. There was continual disorder during this period, later referred to as the "Epoch of Civil Wars," with more than 40 local armed conflicts occurring among factions seeking control of individual states. In 1876, strong conservative opposition to the liberal president flared into open armed revolt in Cauca and several other states. Supported by both liberals and conservatives, Rafael Núñez (1825–94) was elected president in 1880 and, once in office, became increasingly conservative, strengthened the central government, and ended the state revolts.

Eritrean War of Independence   See ETHIOPIAN-ERITREAN GUERRILLA WAR.

Esopus War   See DUTCH-INDIAN WARS OF 1655–64.

Estonian Revolt of 1343–45 (St. George's Day Revolt) Danish and German nobles, holding much land in Estonia as fiefs since the DANISH-ESTONIAN WAR OF 1219–27, abused the Estonian peasants in violation of peace treaties granting them certain rights and freedoms. Sporadic violence by the peasantry against the oppressive nobles occurred until a major revolt erupted on St. George's Day (April 23) in 1343. Starting in Estonia's Harjumaa county, the revolt rapidly spread to surrounding areas, including the island of Oesel. More than 1,800 nobles were killed by the rebellious peasants, who besieged Revel (Tallinn) and requested help from Swedish forts in Finland. Responding to the nobles' plea for aid, the Teutonic Knights of Prussia entered the conflict, arranged a peace conference, and murdered the peasant leaders at the meeting. Near Revel, the knights then routed the peasants in battle before their Swedish supporters could arrive. Realizing the great difficulty of controlling the region, Denmark's King Waldemar IV (1320?–75) sold northern Estonia for 19,000 silver marks to the Teutonic Knights (August 1346), who gave its administration to a fellow order, the Livonian Knights.

Estonian War of Independence (1917–20) During WORLD WAR I, Russian-controlled Estonia proclaimed its independence on November 28, 1917, and immediately Bolshevik (Soviet) troops advanced to retake the country. However, to check the Bolsheviks, the Germans occupied Estonia (December 1917), which, under German defense, again declared its independence on February 24, 1918. By the Treaty of Brest-Litovsk, Germany forced Soviet Russia to give up the Baltic states (Estonia, Latvia, and Lithuania), but after Germany's defeat (November 11, 1918) and renunciation of the treaty, Soviet forces again invaded Estonia. They encountered fierce resistance by the Estonians, who were helped by a British flotilla in the Baltic, and were expelled in January 1919. An anti-Bolshevik army, assembled and led by Nikolai N. Yudenich (1862–1933), marched across the Estonian-Russian border in a valorous attempt to seize Petrograd (Leningrad) in October 1919. The Bolshevik leader Leon Trotsky (1879–1940), unnerved by this development (see RUSSIAN CIVIL WAR OF 1918–21), hastily gathered a motley army of workers and soldiers, which was able to repulse Yudenich's troops and force their retreat to Estonia. Estonia's independence was officially recognized by the Soviet government by the Treaty of Dorpat (Tartu) on February 2, 1920 (the country was occupied by Soviet troops during WORLD WAR II in 1940 and was then constituted as a Soviet republic).

Ethiopia, British Expedition in (1867–68) Made powerful by conquests, a petty Ethiopian (Abyssinian) chieftain named Kasa had himself crowned emperor as Tewodros (Theodore) II (1818–68) in 1855. His rule of Ethiopia began well, and he reformed both legal and administrative policies against a background of competition for trade and influence among foreign powers. But he grew emotionally unstable and erratic in his later years. Angry because Britain's Queen Victoria (1819–1901) had not answered a letter concerning increased British aid, Tewodros imprisoned several British consular officials at Magdala, his capital, in 1867. An Anglo-Indian expeditionary force (about 32,000 strong) under Robert C. Napier (1810–90) landed at the Ethiopian port of Zula on the Red Sea and moved inland, crossing the mountains and gaining allies from dissident tribes. After defeating Tewodros's troops in battle, Napier stormed and captured Magdala on April 13, 1868; immediately Tewodros committed suicide. Napier recovered the British captives, destroyed Magdala, and then left the country. See also ETHIOPIAN CIVIL WAR OF 1868–72.

Ethiopian Civil War of 1868–72   After the suicide of Ethiopia's Emperor Tewodros (Theodore) II

(1818–68), a civil war erupted among district chieftains seeking to succeed him on the throne. One contender promptly had himself crowned and began to attempt to bribe the others for their support. The chieftain of Tigre refused the title *ras* (prince) for his support, but the leader of Shewa agreed not to object as long as his district remained independent. The newly crowned king then warred against Tigre, but a series of minor encounters brought him only defeat because the Tigre troops had more modern weapons. In 1872, the chieftain of Tigre, victorious over all rivals, was crowned emperor as Yohannes (John) IV (1831–89); his reign was marked by local chieftains' revolts against his efforts at centralization; he was under pressure until his death in battle against Sudanese Mahdists.

Ethiopian-Egyptian War of 1875–77   Ismail Pasha (1830–95), the khedive of Egypt and nominally a vassal of the Ottoman sultan, aggressively pursued Egyptian colonization along the Red Sea coastline of Ethiopia (Abyssinia). By 1875, Egyptian forces occupied several Ethiopian seacoast ports and the inland city of Harar, which remained in Egyptian hands until 1887, long after Egypt had given up all attempts to colonize. Emperor Yohannes (John) IV (1831–89) of Ethiopia, who had declared war on Egypt in 1875, advanced his forces, who won at Aussa (1875) and again near Gura southwest of Mitsiwa (1876). Gura itself, and the town of Gondar, became the focus of another Egyptian campaign in 1877, which proved unsuccessful; afterward the Egyptians desisted. In 1879, Ismail Pasha, attempting to throw off foreign control, was deposed by the sultan, who replaced him with his son Tewfik Pasha (1852–92). See also ITALO-ETHIOPIAN WAR OF 1887–89.

Ethiopian-Eritrean Border War of 1998–   Both landlocked Ethiopia and neighboring Eritrea (on the Red Sea), feuding over currency and trade issues, laid claim to a 150-square-mile border region known as Badame in northern Ethiopia. There, on May 6, 1998, fighting erupted between Eritrean and Ethiopian troops, and within a month both sides were exchanging heavy artillery and tank fire. Eritrean aircraft bombed the northern Ethiopian towns of Adigrat and Mekele, while ground troops clashed on three fronts (one close to the Red Sea). Ethiopia retaliated with air strikes on Eritrea's capital, Asmara. By late June 1998, the intense fighting had killed hundreds of people (many were civilians), and diplomatic peace efforts by the United States and Rwanda floundered; both sides finally accepted a proposal to halt air raids, but in October 1998, they were moving men and arms to the border. In February 1999, serious fighting resumed, involving artillery, tanks, ground troops, and warplanes, over the claims of both countries to Badame; both sides suffered heavy losses, with Ethiopia claiming "significant victories," which Eritrea disclaimed. See also ETHIOPIAN-ERITREAN GUERRILLA WAR.

Ethiopian-Eritrean Guerrilla War (1961–91) Under British control from 1941 until 1952, Eritrea gained the status of an autonomous province under federal union with Ethiopia so that the latter could have a maritime frontier on the Red Sea. The change pleased only the Ethiopians, who immediately began to undercut Eritrea's autonomy by requiring Amharic as the official language and making all administrators Ethiopian, thus offending Christians and Muslims alike. As early as 1961, an armed struggle began, at first caused by the Cairo-based Eritrean Liberation Front (ELF); then, as the partisans argued among themselves, a new guerrilla party, the Eritrean People's Liberation Front (EPLF), appeared (1970), fielding some 10,000 rebel fighters. It was followed by a third party, the ELF/PLF. The rival parties focused much of their hostility upon each other, weakening the fight against the Ethiopian government, which made a massive military effort in 1967, forcing thousands of Eritreans to flee to Sudan. The establishment of martial law in Eritrea in 1971, a famine in 1973, the fall of Ethiopia's imperial government in 1974, another famine in 1975, the reduction of Ethiopian control to Eritrean urban centers in 1977, and rebellions in Ethiopia itself greatly complicated the war. With

Soviet and Cuban support, Ethiopian forces drove invading Somalis from the Ogaden region in the southeast (1978) and then launched two major offensives against Eritrean guerrillas, but with limited success (1978–79). Ethiopia's head of state, Lieutenant Colonel Mengistu Haile Mariam (1937–), who took power in 1977, established in 1984 a dictatorial communist regime determined to crush separatist movements in Eritrea, Ogaden, and Tigre (a northern region adjoining Eritrea). By 1989, the principal guerrilla organizations—the EPLF and the Tigre People's Liberation Front (TPLF, formed in 1975)—had gained strength, despite renewed governmental efforts to defeat them. In 1990, Ethiopia lost Soviet support and ground; the EPLF held the Eritrean port of Massawa (Mitsiwa) and moved closer to seizing Asmera (Asmara), Eritrea's capital. Also fighting to topple Mengistu was the Ethiopian People's Revolutionary Democratic Front (EPRDF), formed in 1988 and allied with the TPLF. Aided by the Oromo Liberation Front (a smaller group formed in 1975 to seek autonomy for southern regions), the EPRDF and TPLF finally succeeded in deposing Mengistu (February–May 1991). The EPLF then took control of Eritrea, which later gained full independence (May 3, 1993), leaving Ethiopia a landlocked country. More than 250,000 persons had died in the 31-year-long war, aggravated by drought and famine.

Ethiopian-Italian Wars   See   ITALO-ETHIOPIAN WARS.

Ethiopian-Somali Border War (1963–88)   The birth of the Republic of Somalia, formed by the union of the former colonies of Italian Somaliland and British Somaliland in 1960, was accompanied by demands from the new nation for additional territories in French Somaliland (Djibouti), Kenya, and the vast region of the Haud, partly located in Ethiopia's Ogaden area. The Somali people, who are not indigenous to the areas they demanded in the Horn of Africa, had received permission under a British protectorate to graze their herds in the Haud; as early as 1963, Somalis and Ethiopians had fought each other in the border area; rebel Somalis would not accept Ethiopian control of the Ogaden. The discovery of oil in the Ogaden (1973), the fall of Ethiopia's imperial government, and a major but abortive revolt of Somalis in the Ogaden (1977) complicated the issue. In March 1978, Ethiopian troops, with aid from the Soviet Union and Cuba, drove the Somalis out of the Ogaden, only to have them return in three months, now calling themselves the Western Somali Liberation Front. Claiming an unattested victory, the Somalis were next troubled by Ethiopian bombing of small border towns. After 1978, sporadic guerrilla-style fighting occurred along the border, without major clashes, for many years. Ethiopia stated there would be no peace until Somalia renounced its claim to the Ogaden. In 1980, Somalia agreed to allow the United States the use of military bases in exchange for modern weapons and economic aid in 1981 and subsequent years. Somalia then was overwhelmed by about 1.3 million refugees from the Ogaden; the U.S. provided most of the food supplies to them. Two "western Somali" liberation groups continued waging war in the Ogaden, along with smaller clan-based guerrillas in other parts of the country. In 1988, the Somali National Movement (SNM), an antigovernment organization, caused a rebellion in northern Somalia, where the regional capital, Hargeysa (Hargeisa), and the port of Berbera came under siege. By November, government forces had curbed the rebellion. Meanwhile, Somali-Ethiopian negotiations over the Ogaden, which had begun in 1986, resulted in a peace agreement on April 3, 1988; Ethiopia withdrew from border territory it had held since 1983 and agreed not to support antigovernment organizations; Somalia also ended its support for rebel groups in Ethiopia. See also SOMALIAN CIVIL WAR OF 1988–90.

Etruscan-Roman Wars, Early (c. 509–308 B.C.)   About 800 B.C., migrants from Anatolia (Turkey) brought to Italy the high culture of the Bronze and Iron ages. Named *Tyrrhenoi* by the Greeks (whence, Tyrrhenian) and *Tusci* by the Latins (whence, Tuscany), they called themselves the Rasenna. We know them as the Etruscans. Their apparently peaceful commercial infiltration enabled them to set up a loose, never unified confederation of city-states and to control western Italy from Lake Como to the Tiber River, but it also initiated political and military conflict with aggressive Latin tribes, whose territories they entered about 625. They crossed the Tiber and took over a cluster of disconnected villages called Roma (founded, according to Roman scholars Livy [59–17] and Varro [116–27], about 753); their action established the Tarquin dynasty of the Roman city-state. Rome was drained, sewered, and platted as an Etruscan city; the original Forum was paved, and the Temple of Jupiter (burned in 83 B.C.) was built on the Capitoline Hill. A coup in 509 ousted the last Tarquin king and established the Roman republic. The Roman-Etruscan conflict became active while the Etruscans controlled more than one-third of Italy; wishing for dominance, they permitted the ousted Tarquinius Superbus (d. c. 503) to attempt to regain Rome. Three battles took place in which his sometime Etruscan ally, the king of Clusium (Chiusi), besieged and took the city for Clusium. Tarquinius then allied with the Sabines, some Latins, and the Greeks of Cumae to defeat the Clusian army, force it back to Rome, and force Clusium to withdraw in favor of the republics' rulers. Another defeat returned Tarquinius to Cumae, where he soon died. Rome then began to eliminate each city-state, one by one. Veii (Veio) resisted a cross-border raid (485), fought a 10-year war (c. 483–474) in which a Veiian attack on Rome almost succeeded, and won a 40-year truce. The Romans attacked from 438 to 426 (see ROMAN WAR WITH VEII, FIRST), allowed a second truce, and then laid siege to the city from 405 until its surrender in 396 (see ROMAN WAR WITH VEII, SECOND). Veii had help from only three Etruscan city-states, and, after invasions from the north led to the loss of Etruria's northern territories (see ROME, CELTIC SACK OF), they were slated for punishment. Veii's citizens were sold into slavery. Roman domination of Italy continued more swiftly as Etruria weakened; the cities of Sutrium and Nepi fell in 387, Caere and its port of Pyrgi in 384. To protect itself, Tarquinii began to fight from 358 to 351, won a truce, but involved itself in an alliance with Sutrium (they rebelled jointly but were subdued in

309). Perusia (Perugia) fell to the Romans in 309. In two centuries, Etruria had dwindled to a narrow area between the Apennine Mountains and the Cumian forest.

Etruscan-Roman Wars, Later (c. 302–264 B.C.) The truce of 308 (see ETRUSCAN-ROMAN WARS, EARLY) held for only six years. Local strife at Arretium (Arezzo) involving a struggle for power between the bourgeoisie and the powerful Cilnii family, Etruscan friends of the Roman rulers, led Rome to intervene in 302. Defeated in an ambush, the Romans foiled a second ambush near Rusellae (Roselle) and won with a cavalry charge. A two-year truce did not stop the hopeful Etruscan remnant, who acquired allies, including Gauls, only to lose near Volterra (298), suffer the loss of 25,000 men at Sentium (295), and lose again the rebellious towns of Rusellae, Perusia (Perugia), and Volsinii (Bolsena) in 294. A 40-year truce and heavy indemnities failed to prevent an Etruscan-Gallic offensive (283) and two consecutive defeats at Lake Vadimo. Even the coming of King Pyrrhus (319–272) of Epirus helped only briefly: when Pyrrhus decided to attack Rome with his Greek forces, his Etruscan allies in Vulci and Volsinii surrendered to the Romans, and Pyrrhus retreated to Tarentum (Taranto) on the southern Italian coast (see ROMAN WAR AGAINST PYRRHUS OF EPIRUS). Vulci lost its independence; Volsinii rebelled against the Romans in 264 and was thoroughly sacked, 2,000 bronze statues being stolen to pay for Rome's First PUNIC WAR. Etruria in central Italy was no longer an independent state; as a subject nation under close scrutiny as a result of Rome's new policy of founding colonies in Etruscan territories, it could only act as a thorn in Rome's side. It sabotaged Roman armament shipments during the Second PUNIC WAR and supported the Gracchi (Roman social reformers) in the SOCIAL WAR OF 91–88 B.C. But the bloody revenge taken by the victorious Roman general, Lucius Cornelius Sulla (138–78), against his opposition thoroughly devastated Etruria, whose two remaining "free" cities, Valathrii (now Volterra) and Perusia, fell, respectively, in 80 and 40. Etruria became a mere district (the seventh region) in Greater Rome, but its cultural influence outlasted both its own demise and that of Rome's power in the West (see ROME, FALL OF).

Eureka Stockade Miners' Rebellion (1854) The discovery of gold in Australia in 1851 caused not only immigration of a non-agricultural class of workers but also the enactment of severe laws against miners: expensive monthly licenses (regardless of mining success) and frequent inspections—both a form of economic and social control. Unfranchised, the miners used protests to show their unhappiness with the restrictions, one demonstration so tumultuous that troops were called up.

Leaders experienced in Welsh and English Chartism caused a mass movement for universal suffrage, but the Australian government acted only when miners burned licenses, and then it sent troops. In December 1854, miners in the Eureka goldfield organized themselves into military units, erected a stockade, and, though poorly armed, manned it against government troops. Some 400 troops assaulted the stockade, guarded by 150 miners; 30 persons were killed in the clash, which ended with a rout of the miners. Then the troops terrorized miners in their tents, killing a few and injuring many. But their efforts merely reinforced the demand for social change. See also LAMBING FLATS RIOT.

F

Falkland Islands/Islas Malvinas War   (1982) The dispute over what country has territorial rights to the Falkland Islands (Islas Malvinas in Spanish) in the South Atlantic dates back to the 17th century. In 1833, Britain reinforced its claim by occupying the islands and deporting Argentines living there. Argentina, however, continued to press its rights with the support of most Latin American nations. When negotiations about British yielding of sovereignty over the Falklands ended in inaction on February 27, 1982, Argentina threatened to use other means to settle the matter. On March 19, 1982, a group of Argentine scrap-metal salvagers raised their country's flag on South Georgia Island, a Falklands dependency. On April 2, 1982, Argentine forces invaded the Falkland Islands themselves and captured all key points, including the capital, Port Stanley. Eventually, the islands were occupied by almost 20,000 Argentine soldiers, mostly raw recruits. Extensive diplomatic efforts by the United States and the United Nations failed to defuse the crisis. Britain's Prime Minister Margaret Thatcher (1925–), with Parliament's approval, dispatched a large naval task force under the command of Rear Admiral John Woodward (1932–) to the area and declared a 200-mile war zone around the Falklands. South Georgia was retaken by British forces, which were well trained, well equipped, and highly motivated to mount an offensive. The Argentine air force and its bombs and missiles, especially the Exocet, inflicted severe damage on the British fleet, sinking two destroyers, two frigates, and several other warships and downing a number of aircraft. British submarines sank several enemy vessels. On May 21, 1982, Argentine troops began battling invading infantry under Major General Jeremy Moore (1928–) at Port San Carlos in the Falklands. After establishing a bridgehead, the British advanced inland, using World War II-style tactics, and, within a few hours, forced the surrender of the Argentines under General Mario Menéndez (1930–) at Stanley on June 14, 1982. Some 750 Argentines and 256 British had been killed. The British victory boosted the reputation of Thatcher's conservative government, while defeat brought the downfall of Argentina's President Leopoldo Fortunato Galtieri (1926–). The war did not end the dispute over the islands' sovereignty. Galtieri, who was acquitted (1985) on charges related to the ARGENTINE "DIRTY WAR", received (1986) 12 years in prison after being convicted of negligence and incompetence stemming from Argentina's humiliating defeat in the war.

Fallen Timbers, Battle of   (1794)   General Anthony Wayne (1745–96), who succeeded General Arthur St. Clair (1736?–1818) as commander of the U.S. Army in the Northwest Territory (see ST. CLAIR'S DEFEAT), was directed to destroy the troublesome Indian tribal confederation in the territory. With a 1,000-man army, which had been trained for nearly two years, Wayne advanced in the direction of Fort Miami, a British stronghold, on the Maumee River in present-day Ohio, where some 2,000 Indians had gathered to do battle with Wayne's army. Wayne's offers of peace were rejected. By mid-August 1794, Wayne, who had skillfully maneuvered his soldiers, was face-to-face with the Indians, who had taken cover behind a natural stockade of fallen timbers near present-day Toledo, Ohio. For several days he played a waiting game with the Indians, who expected an attack. On August 20, while many of the Indians were at Fort Miami for food supplies, Wayne attacked and, in less than two hours, had forced the Indians to retreat. The British failed to give promised aid to the warriors, and Wayne's men laid waste to Indian villages and cornfields. On August 3, 1795, Chief Little Turtle (1752–1812), representing the Indian confederation, signed the Treaty of Greenville, ceding to the United States most of Ohio and parts of Indiana, Illinois, and Michigan.

February (March) Revolution, Russian (1 9 1 7) The BOLSHEVIK REVOLUTION began in Petrograd (Leningrad, formerly and today St. Petersburg) on March 8, 1917 (February 23 by the Old Style calendar), when a spontaneous outbreak of strikes and riots occurred by factory workers protesting low wages, lack of food, war defeats, and corrupt government and by frustrated women and youngsters angered by long waits in breadlines. Strikes increased, and rioting spread to university students in a generalized demonstration for "Bread, Peace, and Freedom." Czar Nicholas II (1868–1918) ordered the strikers and rioters suppressed, but the only troops in Petrograd were still in training and would not fire on their countrymen. Soldiers in Moscow mutinied in support of the revolt on March 10, 1917, and all discipline was soon lost. Police seeking to restore order were slain. The Duma (national assembly) refused to obey the czar's order for its prorogation on March 11. The czar commanded that troops from the war front move to Petrograd, but they were never sent, as the revolution reached such a turmoil that military control would have been futile. An elected soviet (council) of workers and soldiers managed Petrograd's defense against the czar. To counter this radical threat and preserve the monarchy, a committee of the Duma reluctantly established on March 15 (March 2, O.S.) a provisional government, headed by Prince Lvov (1861–1925). Nicholas abdicated. See also KORNILOV'S REVOLT; OCTOBER REVOLUTION.

February Revolution, French. See FRENCH REVOLUTION OF 1848.

Fenian Raids (1866, 1870) The fiery Irish-American Fenian Brotherhood planned to liberate Ireland from British rule by involving the United States in a war with Great Britain; it hoped to do this by attacking Canada, a British dominion. On June 1, 1866, Fenian forces from Buffalo, N.Y., crossed the border and seized the Canadian town of Fort Erie. Canadian volunteers failed to repulse the Fenians, some 1,500 strong, until three days later, when they drove the invaders back across the Niagara River. A similar raid occurred the next week from Vermont into eastern Canada (Quebec), but it also failed. Though U.S. authorities took action against the Fenian raiders, Fenian troubles persisted and eventually led to other unsuccessful raids into Canada from Vermont and New Hampshire on May 25–27, 1870. By the next year the Fenian scare had ended because of public pressure and a crackdown on offenders.

Ferrarese War (1482–84) The refusal by the Ferrarese to comply with convention rights granted to the Venetians served as a pretext for the latter, allied with and incited by Pope Sixtus IV (1414–84), to attack the city of Ferrara. Genoa, Siena, Florence, Milan, and Naples supported Ferrara in the war. Papal troops, which lost battles to the Florentines in Castello and Rimini, withdrew after the pope was forced to conclude a five-year peace treaty. Not heeding the pope's order for a cease-fire, the Venetians advanced and routed the Ferrarese forces at Argenta. After a combined Italian army was formed, the tide turned against the Venetians, whose fleet on the Po River was scattered and whose land forces in Milanese and Ferrarese territory were defeated. By the end of 1483, Ferrara had regained most of its lost territory. In August 1484, Venice, seeing the Italian alliance against it falling apart, secretly concluded with Milan the Peace of Bagnolo, whereby, despite battle defeats, Venice retained convention rights over Ferrara and regained Rovigo and Polesine. This marked the furthest limit of Venetian expansion on the mainland.

Ferrarese War against the Papal States (1 5 1 2) During the French invasion of Italy (see HOLY LEAGUE, WAR OF THE), the duke of Ferrara, Alphonse I (1486–1534), who had been excommunicated by Pope Julius II (1443–1513) in 1509, in concert with the French, ordered attacks on papal, Spanish, and Venetian forces outside Ravenna, which was seized. During the war, the Swiss moved in successfully to evict the French from Milan, and the Holy League armies ensured the return of the Medici to power in Florence. The defeated Ferrarese managed to retain their ruling house of Este only because Pope Julius II died in 1513. They made peace with succeeding popes.

Fetterman Massacre (1866) As miners flocked to the West, the U.S. government assisted their efforts by building the Bozeman Trail to link the mining towns with the East. The trail, however, encroached on Sioux Indian hunting grounds, and Chief Red Cloud (1822–1909) warned that it would not be tolerated. Fort Phil Kearney was built to guard the trail in northern Wyoming, but the Sioux frequently attacked U.S. troops. When a work force from the fort was set upon, an 82-man force under Captain William Judd Fetterman (c. 1833–66) was sent to its rescue. Once outside the fort, Fetterman's party was lured into a trap by about 1,500 Sioux under Chief High Backbone (fl. 1860s) and massacred on December 21, 1866. Parts of the Bozeman Trail were closed afterward. See also SIOUX WAR OF 1865–68.

"Fifteen, The" See JACOBITE REBELLION OF 1715–16.

Fifteen Years' War See AUSTRO-TURKISH WAR OF 1591–1606.

Finnish War of Independence (1918–20) Although the Russian provisional government (see BOLSHEVIK REVOLUTION; FEBRUARY REVOLUTION) granted Finland, a Russian grand duchy, its own democratic government, the Finns declared their complete independence from Russia on December 6, 1917. Russia's new Soviet government (see OCTOBER REVOLUTION) recognized Finnish independence on January 4, 1918, but Finland's coalition government, headed by Pehr Svinhufud (1861–1944), was overthrown by Bolshevik-backed Finnish radicals on January 28, 1918, precipitating the start of civil war throughout the country. Finland's north was held by the "Whites," led by Baron Carl Gustaf Mannerheim (1867–1951), who opposed Bolshevism, and the south was controlled by the native Red Guards and their fellow communists (or Bolsheviks), who held the capital, Helsinki. After seizing Vaasa, Mannerheim led his forces south, taking Tampere, but was halted by the Red Guards in mid-April 1918. German forces under Count Rudiger von der Goltz (1865–1930) came to the aid of Mannerheim, seizing Helsinki and driving the Reds out of the country. At the Battle of Vyborg on April 29, 1918, the White Army, supported by Germans, forced the Reds to surrender en masse (12,000 captives). With this triumph, the Whites launched a brief reign of terror, killing thousands of suspected communists. A Finnish republic was set up on June 17, 1919. Conflicting claims to the region of western Karelia led to desultory fighting between the Finns and Russians from June 1919 to October 14, 1920, when the Treaty of Dorpat (Tartu) ended hostilities, reaffirmed Finland's independence, and awarded the Arctic port of Pechenga to the Finns. See also RUSSIAN CIVIL WAR OF 1918–21.

"Five Days" Revolt (1848) The killing of a Milanese citizen by soldiers triggered a violent protest against Austrian autocratic rule in Milan, which lasted for five days (March 18–23, 1848). Citizens took to the streets, massing household objects into 1,650 barricades throughout the city, and fought battles nearly everywhere against Austrian troops. The 14,000-man army of Austrian field marshal Joseph Radetzky (1766–1858) was forced to withdraw from Milan and waited as a coalition of Italian forces gathered in Lombardy (see ITALIAN REVOLUTION OF 1848–49). Milanese independence was short-lived, for Austrian rule was reimposed several months later.

Five Pecks of Rice (A.D. 190–215) While Chinese peasants were revolting in Shantung (Shandong) and Shansi (Shanxi) provinces (see "YELLOW TURBAN" REBELLION), unrest broke out farther south in central China, where a small Taoist cult had been flourishing since the early 100s. The cult had been founded by Chang Ling (Zhang Daoling) (34?–156?), a faith healer, whose patients gave him five pecks of rice annually either for their cures or for membership in his cult. In 190, Chang Ling's grandson, Chang Lu (fl. 3rd cent.), who was now leader of the Way of Five Pecks of Rice, established his own army and an independent theocratic state in what is now Szechwan province; he abolished private property, distributed grain to the inhabitants, constructed "inns of quality" for travelers, and promoted the Taoist religion. His "citizens" were encouraged to work on improving the roads to atone for their sins. Although the Han emperors sent imperial armies against Chang Lu and his so-called rebels, they did not succeed in subduing them and crushing the separate state. After 25 years of warfare, Chang Lu surrendered to the great Han general Ts'ao Ts'ao (Cao Cao) (155–220), who pardoned him and gave him a large piece of property and a high official title.

Flammock's Rebellion (1497) Thomas Flammock (d. 1497), a Cornish landowner of an old family, objected to the tax imposed by King Henry VII (1457–1509) to support military action punishing Scotland for aid to Perkin Warbeck (see WARBECK'S REBELLION). Objecting also that only northern barons were obliged to guard the Scots frontier, Flammock, with a townsman, Michael Joseph (d. 1497), agreed to lead Cornish protesters to London to set their grievances and demands before the king. A vast mob entered Taunton, killed its provost, marched to Wells, acquired a noble leader (Lord Audley), and continued to London. There, on June 22, 1497, at Deptford Strand, the English rebels were thoroughly defeated by the royal troops of Henry VII; Flammock and the other leaders were seized and executed.

Florentine-Milanese War of 1351 This war was the first of a series in which Florence sought to counter the threat of Milan's Visconti family. After Giovanni Visconti (1290?–1354) became ruler of Milan, he expanded Milanese territory by acquiring Bologna in 1350, allied himself with the Ghibellines in Tuscany, and ordered an invasion of Florentine territory. After two months of fighting, the Florentines managed to halt the Milanese advance at Scarperia and eventually forced the invaders to retreat to Bologna. Visconti prepared to renew his attack but died before it got underway. As a result of this war, the Florentine Guelphs (Guelfs) instituted a reign of terror against Ghibelline officeholders (the Guelphs and Ghibellines were opposing factions in Italian politics, the former sympathetic to the papacy and the latter sympathetic to the Holy Roman Emperor).

Florentine-Milanese War of 1397–1402 The Milanese under ruler Gian Galeazzo Visconti (1351–1402) waged an undeclared war in northern and central Italy, taking control of Verona, Padua, Pisa, Siena, Perugia, and other cities. After ravaging Tuscany, Visconti turned his attention to Florence, which, however, was saved from destruction when, on the eve of battle in September 1402, Visconti died of the plague. His conquests were divided among his sons and mercenaries, dispersing the Visconti family power and threat.

Florentine Revolt of 1343 The citizens of Florence, Italy, chafed under the oppressive taxation and cruelty of their elected lord (signore) Walter of Brienne, and by 1343 his policies had spawned three conspiracies to oust him. With outside help from Tuscany and Bologna, Walter of Brienne rounded up 300 important Florentine citizens whom he suspected of subversion and made plans to execute half of them. Joining forces, the conspirators led a revolt that prevented the executions. The lord was besieged in his palace until most of his foreign troops deserted him; he then granted the Florentine bishop authority to enact reforms; but the citizens, in a frenzy of uncontrollable rage, slaughtered most of the lord's supporters. The lord withdrew from the city, and soon a democratic and commercial republic was flourishing there.

Florentine War against the Great Company (1358–59)   The "Great Company" was one of many "bands of adventure" of roving German mercenaries hired out to a league of Italian princes fighting Milan. When the league could no longer pay, the company took to plundering and terrorizing the entire Italian peninsula. Florence refused to allow the plunderers into Tuscany, closing the mountain passes and marshaling the mountain people to defeat them at Scalella Pass on July 24, 1358. When the marquis of Montferrat, wishing to hire the Great Company, urged the Florentines to buy it off, he gathered an all-Italian army for a battle at the Tuscany border. The company circled the Florentine territory without entering, failed to confront the Italians, and finally left to fight for other princes elsewhere.

Florentine War with the Papal States (1485–86) Pope Innocent VIII (1432–92) supported the revolt of the Angevin barons against King Ferdinand I (1423–94) of Naples (see NEAPOLITAN REVOLT OF 1485–86). When Lorenzo de' Medici (1449–92), ruler of Florence, sent military assistance to Ferdinand, who, however, was not popular in Florence, papal forces were dispatched to Florence and Naples to break the alliance, as well as aid the barons. Florence successfully backed Ferdinand and drove out the papal soldiers. With a general peace in 1486, Lorenzo managed to regain control of the town of Sarzana, which had been lost to Genoa in 1478.

Florentine Wars against Pisa (1313–1406)   One aim of Florence during the 14th century was to gain access to the sea through the port of Pisa. Sporadic warfare occurred through the years without conclusion. In the war of 1362–64, Pisa defended its independence with the help of an English company under Sir John Hawkwood (d. 1394), and subsequently the city negotiated with French king Charles VI (1368–1422) for protection from the Florentines. In 1405, Florence induced France to hand over Pisa in return for supporting the French-backed antipope Benedict XIII (Pedro de Luna) (1328?–1423). When Pisa's citizens rebelled, Florence imposed a six-month land and naval siege. Pisa fell on October 9, 1406, giving Florence its long-sought seaport and facilitating the development of its maritime trade.

Fort Mims Massacre (1813)   A large force of young Creek Indians, the "Red Sticks," went on the warpath to avenge a recent ambush of them by American white settlers and to recover Indian lands taken by the whites (see CREEK WAR). On August 30, 1813, the Creek under Chief Red Eagle (William Weatherford) (1780?–1824) made a surprise raid on Fort Mims, a temporary fortification at the confluence of the Alabama and Tombigbee rivers in lower Alabama. Despite Red Eagle's calls for restraint, the Indians massacred some 500 whites, causing a concerted effort by U.S. militiamen to seek revenge and crush the Creek nation.

Fort William Henry, Massacre at (1757)   In 1755, British colonial forces under William Johnson (1715–74) built Fort William Henry at the southern end of Lake George, N.Y., a strategic point for both the British and French during the FRENCH AND INDIAN WAR because it opened the way north to Canada. On August 9, 1757, French general Louis Joseph de Montcalm (1712–59) attacked the British fort with a large force of soldiers and Indians. Greatly outnumbered, Colonel Monro (fl. 1757) surrendered; his men laid down their arms and marched out of the fort with the honors of war, having been promised safe conduct by Montcalm. But the Indians furiously set upon the defenseless prisoners, to Montcalm's horror. At the risk of his own life, he managed to restore order, but by that time many of Monro's men had been slain and the fort destroyed; Monro and other survivors were able to escape and reached safety at Fort Edward on the Hudson River.

"Forty-five, The" See JACOBITE REBELLION OF 1745–46.

France, Battle of (1940) For years the French had felt secure against attacks from Germany because of their heavily fortified, but incomplete, Maginot Line along the French-German border, but their sense of security was shaken when the powerful armies of Adolf Hitler (1889–1945), Germany's Führer (leader), suddenly invaded Denmark and Norway (April 9, 1940), then Luxembourg, Holland, and Belgium a month later (see WORLD WAR II), and seized French ports on the English Channel (see DUNKIRK, EVACUATION OF). In June 1940, a German offensive opened in France's Somme River area, where the Germans outflanked the Maginot Line. Meanwhile, other German armies swept through the northern coastal area into Brittany, and a third force broke through at Champagne and attacked the Maginot Line from the rear. On June 10, 1940, Italy declared war on France, and Italian troops advanced in Savoy and north of Nice in southern France. As the Germans steadily advanced westward, French forces disintegrated and withdrew. On June 14, 1940, Paris, France's capital, fell without a fight, and German troops marched in triumph down the city's Champs-Elysées. The French government fled to Tours and then Bordeaux, but on June 22, 1940, it accepted Hitler's terms for an armistice. The aged general Henri Philippe Pétain (1856–1951) became French premier, assisted by Pierre Laval (1883–1945), a Nazi collaborator; they set up a new French government at Vichy while German forces occupied most of the north and east. Although France had succumbed to

the Germans, thousands of French troops escaped to continue fighting along with the Allies, and thousands more joined the French Resistance to fight covertly on their native soil.

Franco-Algerian Wars of 1832–47 See ABD EL-KADER, WARS OF.

Franco-Austrian War of 1477–93 When Charles the Bold (1433–77) of Burgundy died (see BURGUNDIAN-SWISS WAR OF 1474–77), the expansionist French under King Louis XI (1423–83) immediately laid claim to Burgundy. Thwarted by the 1477 marriage of Mary of Burgundy (1457–82), Charles the Bold's daughter and heiress, to Austrian archduke Maximilian (1459–1519), Louis invaded the contested lands, only to suffer defeat by Mary's forces at Tournai (1477). A sporadic war ensued, aided by Maximilian's troubles with the Netherlanders (see AUSTRIAN NETHERLANDS CIVIL WAR OF 1477–93). Defeated in the minor Battle of Guinegate (1479), the French agreed to a truce, but they connived secretly with rebellious Flemish cities opposing Maximilian and promoted the humiliating Peace of Arras in 1482. Under it, to ensure the continuing amity of France toward the Flemish territories and their cooperation, Maximilian agreed that his infant daughter would marry the French dauphin and give immediately as her dowry the territories of Burgundy, Artois, and Franche-Comté. Thus Maximilian's son Philip (1478–1506) became a "Burgundian without a country" trying to rule, through Netherlander agents, a recalcitrant country advised by the French. His father had to bear the brunt, and he stopped the French war to fight the Netherlanders until 1486, when, as Holy Roman Emperor-elect, he occupied St. Omer in Flanders. Two abortive Austrian invasions followed (1486, 1487), peace was made with France (1489), and Maximilian now faced a new revolt in Flanders. When it was finally crushed in 1492, he renewed the war with France, his army defeating the French at Dournon in 1493. By the Peace of Senlis that same year, France ceded Artois and Franche-Comté to Austria. Maximilian recovered his daughter, whom the dauphin had jilted to gain Brittany and its duchess (see "MAD WAR"); he also gained a non-aggression agreement and a cooperative venture in which France controlled certain border forts militarily while Philip was in charge of civil administration. Burgundy, however, remained permanently French. See also FRANCO-BURGUNDIAN WARS.

Franco-Burgundian Wars (1464–65, 1467–77) Attempts by King Louis XI (1423–83) of France to strengthen his central authority encountered hostility and opposition from many powerful French nobles, including Charles the Bold (1433–77) of Burgundy, who helped form (1464) an alliance of the nobility—the League of Public Weal—to wage war against Louis, who was able to rally the lesser gentry and the bourgeoisie to his side. Louis's forces were defeated by the league at the Battle of Montlhéry (July 13, 1465); by the Treaty of Conflans (1465) the French king was forced to give back territory to rebel nobles; Charles received lands along the Somme River but later became angry when Louis encouraged the townspeople there to revolt. On the death of his father in 1467, Charles succeeded him as duke of Burgundy and began a long struggle against Louis to make Burgundy wholly independent of France. Meanwhile, through adroit diplomacy, Louis had managed to destroy the League of Public Weal; he tried to negotiate with Charles at Péronne (1468), was captured there by him when a revolt fomented by Louis's agents erupted at Liège, and was forced to make concessions in order to regain his freedom. Forcibly extending his rule to the Rhine, Charles plotted with other states (including England, with which he had an alliance) to destroy Louis and then partition France among them, but Louis foiled him by diplomatic maneuvers, making peace with or bribing Burgundy's allies. In 1473, Holy Roman Emperor Frederick III (1415–93) refused to crown Charles king of Burgundy (which would thus be raised to the status of a kingdom). French, Swiss, and German (Holy Roman Empire) forces attacked Charles's reorganized, well-disciplined army, which had freed the Burgundians from French control (see BURGUNDIAN-SWISS WAR OF 1474–77) and conquered much territory, including Lorraine in 1475. Charles's death in battle outside Nancy ended Burgundian defiance of Louis, who later gained complete sovereignty over Burgundy by the Peace of Arras in 1482. See also FRANCO-AUSTRIAN WAR OF 1477–93.

Franco-Chinese War of 1883–85   See SINO-FRENCH WAR OF 1883–85.

Franco-English Wars   See ANGLO-FRENCH WARS.

Franco-Flemish War of 1300–03   See ANGLO-FRENCH WAR OF 1300–03; SPURS, FIRST BATTLE OF THE.

Franco-German War of A.D. 978–80   Lothair (941–86), penultimate Carolingian king of France, decided unwisely in his capital, Paris, to militarily recover Lotharingia (Lorraine), lost to Germany in 925, from his liege, the Holy Roman Emperor Otto II (955–83). Otto, whose family had drastically reduced the Frankish Empire left by Charlemagne (742–814), liked his French kings weak. He reacted strongly to Lothair's invasion (978), capture of the city of Aachen, and near-capture of Otto himself; Otto's German forces invaded France. However, a reconciliation in 980 ended the war without serious strife, and Lothair repudiated all his claims. Nevertheless, in 983, Otto died and an infant German, Otto III (980–1002), was proclaimed Holy Roman Emperor; a civil war over the succession ensued. Lothair invaded Lotharingia again in 985 but died during the campaign, leaving his throne to the young Louis V (c. 967–87), aptly nicknamed "the Sluggard."

Franco-Prussian War (Franco-German War) (1870–71) After the Prussian victory in the SEVEN WEEKS' WAR, Otto von Bismarck (1815–98), Prussia's premier, began working to bring the independent southern German states into unity with the anti-French North German Confederation. When a Prussian effort was made to put a Hohenzollern prince, related to the Prussian royal house, on the Spanish throne in 1870, Emperor Napoleon III (1808–73) of France became alarmed by the possible threat of a Prussian-Spanish, two-front war against France. Bismarck, seeking to provoke war, published on July 14, 1870, the Ems telegram, a communication between the Prussian king and himself. He altered the telegram in such a way that both France and Prussia felt insulted about the failed talks, held the day before, between the countries about the Spanish throne. Relations were ruptured, and on July 19, 1870, France declared war (Napoleon had been told the French army was invincible and a "sure" victory would regain his declining prestige at home). French troops marched east under Achille Bazaine (1811–88) but lost and retreated to a vain stand at the Battle of Gravelotte on August 18, 1870. There, the French were blocked on their march toward Verdun by the first and second Prussian armies, totaling 190,000 men, led by Count Helmuth von Moltke (1800–1891). The Germans attacked and suffered heavy losses at first, but the French failed to counterattack and were defeated. Bazaine's forces retreated to the fortress at Metz. After the defeat of another French army at Sedan, France, on September 1, 1870 (Napoleon, sick in the midst of his troops, surrendered and was taken prisoner), Bazaine and his army of 170,000 were besieged at Metz for 54 days, finally surrendering (Bazaine was later convicted of treason and sentenced to 20 years' imprisonment). A French provisional government of national defense was set up in Paris, deposed Napoleon, and established the Third Republic. The Prussians besieged Paris from September 1870 to January 1871, when famine forced the city's surrender. French and German forces continued to battle each other in France's provinces until an armistice ended the war, but by March the FRENCH CIVIL WAR OF 1871 had begun. By the Treaty of Frankfurt on May 10, 1871, Germany received the regions of Alsace and Lorraine, and France had to pay a heavy indemnity of $1 billion and remain occupied until it was paid. King William I (1797–1888) of Prussia was pro-

claimed German emperor in 1871 (condescendingly, at Versailles). Peace among the major powers of Europe, with France no longer dominant, lasted until the outbreak of WORLD WAR I.

Franco-Spanish War of 1547–59 See HAPSBURG-VALOIS WAR OF 1547–49.

Franco-Spanish War of 1648–59 With the conclusion of the THIRTY YEARS' WAR, civil strife erupted in France (see FRONDE, WARS OF THE), and rebel leaders, including the imperious Louis II de Condé (1621–86), quickly allied themselves with the Spanish. In the 1650s, when Spain was preoccupied with England (see ANGLO-SPANISH WAR OF 1655–59) and England was fighting the Dutch (see DUTCH WAR, FIRST), French troops under Henri, vicomte de Turenne (1611–75), outmaneuvered superior Spanish forces under Condé, now a Spanish general, in northern France. On August 25, 1654, Turenne won the Battle of Arras but lost the Battle of Valenciennes on July 16, 1656. Following the Spanish defeat at the Battle of the Dunes and the capturing of nearby Dunkirk in northern France in June 1658, Spain's resistance was broken, and France had become the principal power in Europe. The Peace of the Pyrenees on November 7, 1659, established the Franco-Spanish border at the Pyrenees mountains; France acquired Roussillon, Artois, and some fortresses in the Spanish Netherlands (Belgium and Luxembourg). See also DUTCH WAR, SECOND; NORTHERN WAR, FIRST.

Franco-Spanish War of 1727 See ANGLO-SPANISH WAR OF 1727–29.

Franco-Spanish War of 1823 After warily watching nearly three years of factional struggles in Spain over the government, the international powers at the Congress of Verona (October 1822), alarmed by the capture of Spain's King Ferdinand VII (1784–1833) by armed revolutionaries opposed to absolutism, authorized France to intervene in the conflict (see SPANISH CIVIL WAR OF 1820–23) and restore Ferdinand to his throne, despite Britain's objection. On April 17, 1823, French forces led by Louis Antoine de Bourbon, duke of Angoulême (1775–1844), crossed the Pyrenees into Spain, welcomed by the Basques and Catalonians. The duke dispatched a force to besiege San Sebastián while he launched an attack on Madrid, Spain's capital, held by the revolutionaries. The rebel government withdrew to Seville, Madrid's military commander secretly capitulated and fled to France, and the leaderless Madrid garrison could not keep out the French, who seized the city and installed a Spanish-chosen regent pending Ferdinand's return. From there, the French moved south to besiege the revolutionaries under Colonel Rafael del Riego y Núñez (1785–1823) at Cádiz, where the Cortes (national legislature) had taken Ferdinand. Riego's forces suffered defeat at the Battle of Trocadero on August 31, 1823, and when Cádiz fell to the French on September 23, 1823, Ferdinand was handed over to them and restored to the throne. Renouncing his prior promise of amnesty for the revolutionaries, the king ordered ruthless measures of reprisal against them while French troops stood by helplessly.

Frankish-Alemannic War of A.D. 496 When the Ripuarian Franks' kingdom of Cologne (Köln) on the Rhine River was invaded by the Alemanni, a Germanic people, the Ripuarians requested help from the Salian Franks under King Clovis (c. 466–511). The Franks, led by Clovis, defeated the Alemanni at the decisive Battle of Tolbiac (Zulpich) southwest of Cologne in 496. During the battle, Clovis had reputedly prayed to his wife's god, pledging to convert to Roman Catholicism if he was victorious. Afterward he converted to Christianity, being baptized (supposedly with some 3,000 of his followers) by St. Remi (437?–533?), bishop of Rheims, in 496.

Frankish-Avarian War of A.D. 791–96 Charlemagne (742–814) and his son Pepin (d. 810) led Frankish armies against the Avars, a Mongolian people who had taken control of the central Danube River valley and who had acquired great wealth by plundering. In the first part of the war, the Franks were unsuccessful in tracking down and crushing the Avars, and Charlemagne returned home to strengthen his forces on the eastern frontier. In 796, a Frankish army under Pepin defeated the Avars, who were driven beyond the Tisza (or Theiss) River on the Hungarian plain. Frankish troops under Eric of Friuli found the Avars' hidden treasury and delivered 15 carts of stolen loot to Charlemagne. By 805, the Avars had submitted to Charlemagne's rule.

Frankish-Byzantine War of A.D. 803–10 The Franks under their king, Charlemagne (742–814), waged war against the Byzantines for control of Venetia and Dalmatia, two regions along the Adriatic Sea. Charlemagne's land and naval forces were generally successful. In 809, Byzantine emperor Nicephorus I (d. 811) became occupied in battle with the Bulgars (see BULGARIAN-BYZANTINE WAR OF A.D. 809–17) and began to seek terms with the Franks. In 810, Charlemagne made peace with Nicephorus, giving up most of his conquests (he kept Istria, a peninsula on the Adriatic) in return for Byzantine recognition of him as emperor of the West.

Frankish Civil War, First (A.D. 670–79) Two Frankish tribes, the Salians and the Ripuarians, dominated the land of the Germanic Franks, which was split into three kingdoms: Neustria (western Gaul, or France, north of the Loire), Austrasia (eastern Gaul north of the Loire and west of the Rhine), and Burgundy, after this region's conquest by the Ripuarians. Each kingdom had, by custom, a king and a mayor of the palace (prime minister), and all suggestions for changing this practice brought inter-Frankish strife. By the end of the fifth century, only the Austrasians had set up a hereditary kingship, under the Merovingian dynasty, after its founder Mérovée (fl. 448–58); the other kingdoms kept an elective practice. In 670, a Neustrian named Ebroin (d. 681), desirous of a single mayorship, was captured by Leodegar (Leger) (d. 679), a Burgundian. He escaped, captured Leodegar, had him killed, and ruled as the tyrannical mayor of the combined kingdoms of Neustria and Burgundy until his assassination in 681 ended the dominance of Neustria. **Second Frankish Civil War** (A.D. 687). Pepin II of Heristal (d. 714) acted as mayor of the Austrasian palace from 680 to 714. He successfully resisted the ambitions of Neustria without fighting until a new king, an infant Merovingian, was enthroned for Austrasia. Then, in opposition to Pepin, the mayor of Neustria's palace and its king mobilized the nobles of Neustria and Burgundy. During the Battle of Tertry, Pepin and his forces won, and Pepin united all three Frankish kingdoms under himself as mayor and the infant as king. In doing so, he advanced the new Carolingian dynasty (of mayors only until 751) founded by his father, Pepin of Landen (d. 639?), but named for the Heristal Pepin's illegitimate son Charles Martel (688?–741). **Third Frankish Civil War** (A.D. 714–19). After Pepin II of Heristal died, his kingdom was divided among three grandsons, for his sons had already died, with his widow acting as regent. His illegitimate son Charles Martel escaped from imprisonment by the regent, seized power as mayor of Austrasia, and stood ready to fight against his rivals and seize their territories. Between 716 and 718, his forces battled successfully against the Neustrians three times, finally thoroughly defeating them and their king and mayor at Vinchy in 718; Charles set up a puppet Neustrian king. Burgundy did not wait for defeat to submit to Charles's rule. Aquitaine, which had remained heretofore independent of the Frankish kingdoms, submitted in 719, when Moorish (Spanish Muslim) attacks on the region in 718 made it realize the need for Charles's help in the future (see FRANKISH-MOORISH WAR, FIRST). As mayor, Charles performed such royal functions as issuing decrees, presiding over royal courts, and leading the army. His son Pepin the Short (714?–68) was the first Carolingian to be both mayor and king. See also CHARLEMAGNE, CONQUESTS OF.

Frankish-Moorish War, First (A.D. 718–32) After conquering the Visigoths in Spain, the Moors (Spanish Muslims) attempted to raid north of the Pyrenees, invading Aquitaine and southern France in 718 and capturing the city of Narbonne in 719. Frankish forces under Eudes (Eudo) (665–735) defeated them at Toulouse in 721 and drove them back to Spain, but in 725–26 the Moors conquered all of Septimania (region in southern France adjoining Burgundy). Later a new Moorish offensive, led by Abd-ar-Rahman (d. 732), the Muslim governor of Spain, began that led to Eudes's defeat at Garonne, the burning of Bordeaux, and the laying waste to Aquitaine by the Moors as they marched north past Poitiers in west-central France (see TOURS, BATTLE OF). Eudes asked for help from Charles Martel (688?–741), mayor of the Frankish kingdom (see FRANKISH CIVIL WAR, THIRD), whose army defeated the Moors in 732, causing them to flee back to Spain and earning Charles his name Martel ("the Hammer"). **Second Frankish-Moorish War** (A.D. 734–59). Reduced to just staging raids, the Moors were easily controlled by Eudes and his Franks. Eudes's death in 735 caused a brief rebellion by his sons against Charles Martel, who came to the Bordeaux area to keep control, forcing the sons to pay homage. Moorish raids continued, including the brief occupation of Arles and an attack up the Rhone River valley. The Franks checked them at Valence in 737 and Lyon in 739. When Charles Martel died, his sons Carloman (d. 754) and Pepin the Short (714?–68) served jointly as mayors of the palace, administering the Frankish kingdom and thwarting Moorish invasions. When Carloman entered a monastery (747), Pepin became sole ruler and drove the Moors, who had captured Narbonne again, out of Septimania, which he annexed to his kingdom (France), and across the Pyrenees. Afterward the Moors gave up their northernly raids, partly because of Abbasid-Ummayyad strife, chiefly because the Christian kingdoms of Navarre and Asturias (both in northern Spain) acted as buffers between them and the Pyrenees.

Fredonian Rebellion (1826–27) In 1821, Spain opened Texas to American settlement, and the policy was continued by the newly independent government of Mexico the following year (see MEXICAN REVOLUTION OF 1821). An American, Hayden Edwards, secured a charter from Mexico and established a colony of about 200 families near Nacogdoches in eastern Texas. The land had already been claimed by some Mexican settlers, who, however, could not show clear title to it. An angry dispute arose, causing the Mexican government to revoke Edwards's charter and to order him out of Texas. He and some followers then seized Nacogdoches, proclaimed the independent republic of Fredonia, and adopted a constitution on December 21, 1826. Edwards's 200-man army, allied with some Cherokee Indians, was overwhelmed by a larger Mexican force in January 1827, and the Fredonian government was ended. See also TEXAN WAR OF INDEPENDENCE.

French and Indian War (1754–63) This was the last and most decisive of a long series of confrontations among the French, British, Indians, and colonists for control of the St. Lawrence River and Ohio River valleys. Virginia's lieutenant governor, Robert Dinwiddie (1693–1770), sent militiamen under George Washington (1732–99) to build a fort at the juncture of the Allegheny and Monongahela rivers in order to protect the region from French seizure. The French, who had already erected Fort Duquesne (Pittsburgh) on the site, attacked Washington, who had built Fort Necessity nearby, and forced him and his men to surrender (July 3, 1754); Washington was allowed to return home with the survivors in his command. The next year General Edward Braddock (1695–1755) led British redcoats and colonial forces to attack Fort Duquesne, but they were ambushed and routed by the French and their Indian allies near the fort on July 9, 1755. Colonial troops under William Johnson (1715–75), a British official in the Mohawk Valley, were more successful, defeating the French and Indians at the Battle of Lake George (September 8, 1755) during the Crown Point campaign. A British expedition against French-held Fort Niagara failed, however. France and Britain formally declared war in 1756 (see SEVEN YEARS' WAR), and Marquis Louis Joseph de Montcalm (1712–59) took charge of all French forces in Canada, while General John Campbell (1705–82), fourth earl of Loudoun, became commander of the British forces in America. Advancing from Fort Ticonderoga, French forces under Montcalm besieged, captured, and destroyed Fort William Henry, built and held by the British at the south end of Lake George (see FORT WILLIAM HENRY, MASSACRE AT). Greatly upset, the British made plans to drive the French from North America; Campbell was replaced by General James Abercrombie (1706–81), whose attempt to defeat the French at Fort Ticonderoga failed (July 8, 1758) and led to his replacement by Baron Jeffrey Amherst (1717–97). The French blew up and abandoned Fort Duquesne just before it was captured by a colonial-British force in late November 1758. Meanwhile, Amherst and General James Wolfe (1727–59) and their forces invested the French fortress of Louisbourg in Nova Scotia (see KING GEORGE'S WAR) and compelled its surrender after much fighting (July 27, 1758). Now Amherst, with an 11,000-man army, successfully stormed Fort Ticonderoga and Crown Point in June-July 1759. At the same time, British troops, aided by the Iroquois Indians, were driving the French from the Ohio and Illinois areas. The climax of the war was the battle fought on the Plains of Abraham near the city of Quebec, Canada, on September 13, 1759, when Montcalm and Wolfe faced each other. Both men were killed in combat; the British won and captured Quebec, which the French tried unsuccessfully to retake in 1760. British forces seized Montreal in September 1760, and Canada was now in British hands. In 1762, naval ships under Admiral George Rodney (1719–92) defeated the French in the West Indies, forcing the surrender of St. Lucia, Grenada, St. Vincent, and Martinique. But peace did not formally come until the end of the Seven Years' War in Europe, and in the Treaty of Paris (1763) France lost all its North American territories, except New Orleans and the islands of St. Pierre, Miquelon,

Guadeloupe, and Martinique. See also KING WIL-LIAM'S WAR; PONTIAC'S WAR; QUEEN ANNE'S WAR.

French-Canadian Rebellion of 1837   See PAP-INEAU'S REBELLION.

French Civil War of 1871   During the FRANCO-PRUSSIAN WAR, after the surrender and capture of France's Emperor Napoleon III (1808–73) at Sedan, the Third Republic was established at Paris, where the proud inhabitants withstood the German siege until forced to capitulate on January 28, 1871, because of starvation. By then, the Third Republic's National Assembly had relocated in Bordeaux and soon negotiated peace terms with the Germans. Humiliated by German troops in their city and the "dishonorable" peace agreed to by the largely monarchist assembly, the French leaders remaining in Paris set up an independent republican government, the Commune of Paris, and refused to obey the assembly, which sent government troops to occupy the city in March 1871, but were driven out. Faced with civil rebellion by the "radical" Communards, who squabbled among themselves and tried futile experiments in municipal government, the assembly, which had moved to Versailles, induced the victorious Prussians, who affected neutrality, to release French prisoners in order to form an army to besiege Paris. Entering the city, the government troops met desperate, fierce resistance by the Communards behind barricades during "Bloody Week" (May 21–28, 1871) and ruthlessly shot down thousands of them. The Communards, who were gradually pushed to the center of the city, murdered hostages they had taken, including the archbishop of Paris, and burned the Tuileries Palace, the city hall, the Palace of Justice, and other prominent buildings before being crushed. Summary executions of at least 17,000 prisoners were carried out by the victors, who imprisoned or exiled to penal colonies many others. Communes in other French cities, notably Marseilles, Toulouse, and Saint-Étienne, were also overthrown with merciless reprisals afterward in 1871. The radicals were left leaderless, the

citizenry demanded a stern republic, and the monarchists worked for restoration, even of an absolutist French regime.

French Indochina War of 1858–63   Under Emperor Napoleon III (1808–73), France wanted to contain Siamese (Thai) expansionism in Indochina (Vietnam, Cambodia, Laos), to gain a larger share of overseas markets there, and to end the Vietnamese persecution of French Christian missionaries. Continued Vietnamese hostility to westerners led to a joint French and Spanish expedition's bombardment and seizure of the port city of Tourane (Da Nang, Vietnam) in the late summer of 1858. Faced with problems from tropical disease and food shortages, the expedition decided not to move against the Vietnamese capital of Hue to the north, but instead sailed south to Saigon (Ho Chi Minh City) in Cochin China (southern Vietnam). Saigon was seized in 1859, and a 1,000-man Franco-Spanish garrison was left there while forces returned to Tourane to meet renewed threats. With its troops ravaged by cholera and engaged also in a war in China (see OPIUM WAR, SECOND), France tried unsuccessfully to negotiate a peace with Vietnamese king Tu Duc (1829–83). The Franco-Spanish garrison at Saigon withstood a nearly yearlong Vietnamese siege until a French force arrived to relieve it in February 1861. French troops, freed from duty in China, moved into the three eastern provinces of Cochin China. Faced with an insurrection in Tonkin (north Vietnam), Tu Duc sued for peace (1852); he ceded to the French the three eastern Cochin China provinces (Saigon, My Tho, Bien Hoa) and the Poulo Condore (Con Son) islands and agreed to open three ports to French trade, to allow religious freedom, and to pay a large indemnity. Under French military pressure, Tu Duc ratified the peace treaty in April 1853. That same year Cambodia's King Norodom (1834–1904) accepted a French protectorate over his country. In 1867, Siam gave up its claims in Cambodia to the French.

French Indochina War of 1873–74 By 1867, Vietnamese emperor Tu Duc (1829–83) had conceded all of Cochin China (southern Vietnam) to the French, who were looking for a trade route into southwestern China. French explorer François Garnier (1839–73) was sent with a small force to Hanoi to settle a dispute between local officials and a captured French trader-smuggler. Hanoi's refusal to capitulate to Garnier, who sided with the French trader, led to the storming and seizure of the Hanoi fortress; Garnier went on to seize other forts in the Red River delta area and extended his control over most major Vietnamese cities in the north. A joint Vietnamese-Chinese force, called the "Black Flag Pirates," opposed Garnier and killed him in a battle in late 1873. French ships were captured, and pro-French Christian towns were torched in Tonkin (north Vietnam), which the French decided was not worth trying to control and temporarily abandoned the effort, withdrawing from Hanoi and other cities. Tu Duc was impelled to recognize that the French hold over Cochin China was indisputable and the Christian missionaries and converts were free from persecution (his promise); the French gained use of the Red River as a trading lane.

French Indochina War of 1882–83 In 1881, China declared sovereignty over Annam or Vietnam, sending troops down the Red River to occupy its northern region, Tonkin. France, angered by continuing Vietnamese persecution of Christian missionaries, renewed its colonial expansionism in Indochina (Vietnam, Laos, and Cambodia), which China opposed. French captain Henri Laurent Rivière (1827–83) was sent with a small force to Tonkin's administrative center, Hanoi, to evict the Chinese and to subdue the rebel "Black Flag Pirates." He captured the Hanoi fortress, Nam Dinh's coast, and the Hon Gay coal mine. During a Vietnamese counterattack, Rivière was killed. French reinforcements were sent to the area, and France obtained a Vietnamese agreement on a treaty ceding Tonkin (1882). When China renounced the agreement, the French seized Haiphong and Hanoi and bombarded the Vietnamese capital of Hue (1883).

During the fighting, both sides negotiated and finally signed a treaty (August 25, 1883) that recognized French protectorates over northern Vietnam (Tonkin) and central Vietnam (Annam); southern Vietnam (Cochin China) was already under French control. Ten years later Siam relinquished to the French its claims to Laos, which was incorporated into a federation known as French Indochina. See also SINO-FRENCH WAR OF 1883–85.

French Indochina War of 1946–54 The French were not in a strong position to immediately reassert their authority in their former colony, French Indochina, after the Japanese invaders withdrew at the end of WORLD WAR II. In the north, the Vietminh, a political party led by Ho Chi Minh (1890?–1969), proclaimed the independent Democratic Republic of Vietnam. France agreed to recognize Vietnam as a free state within the French Union, but negotiations dragged on. In December 1946, Vietminh forces attacked French garrisons, and during the ensuing years guerrilla activity increased in the countryside. In 1949, a Vietnamese provisional government, headed by Emperor Bao Dai (1913–97), was established, which was recognized by France and, in 1950, by the United States. The communist-dominated Vietminh rejected any remnant of French authority and consequently attacked French outposts along Vietnam's border with China, from whom they received substantial military aid. In 1951, the Vietminh created a common front with communist groups in Laos and Cambodia (Kampuchea) and became more and more aggressive. They were led by General Vo Nguyen Giap (1912–), who launched an attack on March 13, 1954, against the strategic French stronghold at Dienbienphu in northwestern Vietnam. Giap's siege lasted 56 days; his Vietminh troops continually attacked with artillery and mortar fire until the French defenders, short of ammunition, surrendered on May 7, 1954. Meanwhile, an international conference in Geneva was working out an agreement whereby the fighting would cease and the French would withdraw. The Vietminh set up a government north of the 17th parallel, while the Vietnamese non-communists set up a government south of the demarcation line. The war was unpopular in France, most of whose citizens were relieved when it was over, despite the defeat and the loss of influence in Southeast Asia. In July 1954, Vietnam was divided into the Democratic Republic of Vietnam (North Vietnam) and the Republic of Vietnam (South Vietnam). See also VIETNAMESE CIVIL WAR OF 1955-65; VIETNAM WAR.

French-Iroquois Wars   See IROQUOIS-FRENCH WARS.

French Revolution (1789–92)   After the so-called Assembly of Notables refused to impose taxes required to avert bankruptcy, King Louis XVI (1754–93) of France was forced to summon the Estates General (legislative body) on May 5, 1789. Immediately the Third Estate, representing commoners, demanded that deputies vote jointly by head rather than separately by Estate, assuring a numerical advantage over the clergy and nobility. When Louis vacillated, the Third Estate proclaimed itself a National Assembly. Three days later, reformist deputies and their supporters gathered at a royal tennis court, swearing to secure a constitution. The king nominally recognized the Assembly but surrounded Versailles, the royal palace, with troops. On July 14, 1789, angry mobs stormed the despised Bastille prison in Paris—the symbol of absolutism. In response to ensuing peasant uprisings, the so-called Great Fear, nobles and clergy relinquished all privileges on August 4, 1789, and the Assembly soon issued the seminal Declaration of the Rights of Man and Citizen, followed by measures nationalizing church lands and outlawing monasticism. These decrees were combined in the constitution of 1791, institutionalizing separation of powers, individual liberty, and civil equality. But noble *émigrés* (royalists) fomented anti-revolutionary sentiment abroad, leading the Assembly, its support eroded by its anti-ecclesiastical stand, to declare war against Austria (see FRENCH REVOLUTIONARY WARS). "Spontaneous" mobs killed hundreds of royalist prisoners in

the SEPTEMBER MASSACRES of 1792. The Assembly established a new ruling body, the National Convention, which abolished the constitutional monarchy in favor of a republic on September 21, 1792. Louis was tried for treason and executed, setting off royalist insurrections, notably in Vendée, and a struggle for power among groups wishing to dominate the whole French government. In this period, called the Reign of Terror (1793–94), thousands were arrested, summarily tried, and executed as counterrevolutionaries. A new constitution in 1795 established a new government, the Directory, which was marked by corruption and bankruptcy and eventually overthrown by a coup d'état under Napoleon Bonaparte (1769–1821) on November 9, 1799. See also NAPOLEONIC WARS.

French Revolutionary Wars (1792–1802)   Pressured by the Girondists, a moderate republican faction, France's National Assembly declared war upon Emperor Francis II (1768–1835) of Austria, a signer of the Declaration of Pillnitz supporting restoration of France's *ancien régime* (see FRENCH REVOLUTION). Charles William Ferdinand (1735–1806), duke of Brunswick, led the Austrians and their Prussian allies across the Rhine, threatening to destroy Paris should the royal family be harmed. Resulting French resentment contributed to the abolition of the monarchy. In 1792, the French defeated the invaders at Valmy and then pressed an attack against the Austrian Netherlands, defeating the Austrians at Jemappes and subsequently overrunning what is now Belgium. The French offensive drove the Prussians across the Rhine; a French army conquered Savoy and Nice in November 1792. Meanwhile, alarmed by French boldness to propagate revolution abroad, Britain, Holland, Spain, Austria, Prussia, and Russia established the First Coalition against France (see COALITION, WAR OF THE FIRST). The allies at first won victories against the French on all fronts, but by 1793 French citizen armies, created through a system of universal conscription, were pushing the allies back across the Rhine. As the French conquered territory and took control, they created buffer republics between France and its foreign enemies.

Thus, Holland became the Batavian Republic in 1795, and Switzerland the Helvetic Republic in 1798. Sardinia, meanwhile, had been prosecuting its own war against France since 1792, when the French occupied Savoy and Nice. By early 1796, the Italians were easily keeping the starving, overextended French at bay. Then Napoleon Bonaparte (1769–1821) took command, and, in the first of his brilliant military campaigns, brought the Sardinians to their knees with an armistice at Cherasco within three weeks. After Napoleon's victories in Italy in 1796–97, many republics were established. Under the leadership of the Russian czar, a second coalition against France was formed by Russia, Britain, Austria, Portugal, Naples, and the Ottoman Empire (see COALITION, WAR OF THE SECOND). Initial allied successes were compromised by dissension, leading to disastrous defeat in Switzerland and Russian withdrawal from the war. In 1800, Napoleon, now First Consul, settled with the Ottoman Empire in the Convention of el-Aresh by evacuating Egypt (the French fleet had been destroyed by the British under Horatio Nelson [1758–1805] at the Battle of the Nile in 1798). Napoleon's victory at Marengo and Jean Victor Moreau's (1763–1813) victory at Hohenlinden broke Austrian resistance and forced Austria out of the war in February 1801. Britain, however, with naval superiority, continued to win victories on the high seas in the Mediterranean, the West Indies, and elsewhere. Malta, taken by Napoleon in 1798, was recaptured by the British in 1800. Nevertheless, the British, demoralized by new opposition from Denmark, accepted the Treaty of Amiens in 1802, restoring France's colonies in return for French evacuation of the Papal States and Sicily. See also NAPOLEONIC WARS; ORANGES, WAR OF THE; SWISS REVOLT OF 1798.

French Revolution of 1830 (July Revolution) An inept ruler, King Charles X (1757–1836) inspired resentment in the French middle class and its press, especially against ultra-royalist advisers; when he directed his reactionary favorite Jules de Polignac (1780–1847) to form a new ministry, the Chamber of Deputies hotly objected. Charles's angry dismissal of the chamber (1829) turned an attempt to curb a hated functionary into the total collapse of the regime. An 1830 French election revealed even greater opposition in the chamber, and Charles again dismissed it as he and Polignac published the "July Ordinances," which established strong press controls and reduced the electorate. As usual, the Parisians revolted and blockaded the streets on July 27, 1830; among those manning the barricades were army units and former members of the National Guard disbanded in 1827. Charles acted too late in annulling the new ordinances and dismissing Polignac (July 30, 1830); the minister was arrested and condemned to life imprisonment and later (1836) amnestied. Charles fled, then abdicated in favor of a grandson; the rebels, divided into republicans favoring the Marquis de Lafayette (1757–1834) and monarchists desiring the conservative Duke of Orleans, Louis-Philippe (1773–1850), argued among themselves until the dismissed bourgeois legislature declared the throne vacant and proclaimed Louis-Philippe king. His ineptness and rightist actions led his "July Monarchy" to the FRENCH REVOLUTION OF 1848 and the Second Republic.

French Revolution of 1848 (February Revolution) Like the FRENCH REVOLUTION OF 1830, a conservative minister was the focus of resentment in France in 1848, but this later revolt also included working-class members angry at the government's failure to relieve the depression of 1846–47. The offending minister was François Guizot (1787–1874); the unpopular monarch was King Louis-Philippe (1773–1850). France's opposition parties, forbidden direct campaigning for a forthcoming election, instead wittily held a "banquet campaign"; when their most important gathering, slated for February 22 in Paris, was forbidden by the king and Guizot, the Parisians gathered in force at the banquetting place, and street fighting erupted. At its worst on February 23, 1848, when some government troops opened fire while others either laid down their arms or joined the rebels, the revolution forced the dismissal of Guizot and, the next day, the abdication of Louis-Philippe. A provisional government, the Committee of Public Safety, guided by Alphonse de Lamartine (1790–1869), was established by the Chamber of Deputies; it declared the Second Republic and tried to meet all demands, setting up national workshops, declaring a right-to-work law, and calling for national elections. The revolution had been generally local; the French national response was predominately moderate. An executive committee, again including Lamartine, replaced the provisional government and attempted to meet the new public resentment (May 1848). It dissolved the national workshops, provoking an abortive workers' rebellion ("June Days," June 23–26, 1848). It also produced a very democratic constitution. In new elections, the French Assembly changed its balance again, monarchists outnumbering radicals five to two and moderates six to one. The revolution was now defunct, and the republic was soon to wither. Prince Louis Napoleon (1808–73), long a Bonaparte claimant and a conservative, was elected president in December 1848. The Second Republic lasted until 1852, when Louis Napoleon, by a masterly coup d'état, proclaimed himself Emperor Napoleon III of the Second Empire.

French-Vietnamese Wars   See FRENCH INDO-CHINA WARS.

French War of 1635–48   French cardinal Richelieu (1585–1642), chief minister of King Louis XIII (1501–43), had designs on obtaining the Rhineland for France during the THIRTY YEARS' WAR. Catholic France promised to give financial and military aid to Protestant German princes who accepted Catholicism in order to continue the war against the Holy Roman Empire or the Catholic Hapsburgs, whose power the French wanted to contain. In 1635, the Holy Roman Emperor made peace with Saxony and the Lutheran states. Spain, allied with the Hapsburgs, launched a military campaign against the Netherlands, and Richelieu, fearing increasing Hapsburg imperial power, strengthened his ties with Sweden's Chancellor Oxenstierna

(1583–1654), head of the Protestant forces, and allied himself with the Dutch, and then declared war on Spain on May 21, 1635. With French forces divided to fight in separate European regions according to Richelieu's strategy, Spanish and Bavarian armies invaded France in 1636 but were eventually driven back. French forces were successful in stopping an invading Spanish army in the south (1637) but were repulsed in Italy and the Netherlands (1638). In 1639, a Dutch naval fleet decimated a strong Spanish fleet at the Battle of the Downs. Unrest and uprisings in France, Spain, and Portugal hindered major French and Spanish campaigns during 1641–42. French troops led by Louis II de Condé (1621–86) won a resounding victory at Rocroi on May 19, 1643, nearly wiping out the whole Spanish army and almost eliminating Spain from the war. In Germany, Swedish forces steadily advanced southward while the French pushed northward across the Rhine. Imperial representatives began peace negotiations with Sweden at Osnabrück and with France at Münster and continued over several years while bloody battles occurred. A final attempt by combined Hapsburg-Spanish forces to invade France ended in failure at the Battle of Lens on August 2, 1648, when Condé won another victory. Emperor Ferdinand III (1608–57) decided to sign the Peace of Westphalia on October 24, 1648, concluding the conflict for a brief while (see FRANCO-SPANISH WAR OF 1648–59). See also BÉARNESE REVOLTS.

Fries Rebellion   ("Hot Water War") (1799)   In July 1798, the U.S. Congress passed a direct federal property tax to raise money in anticipation of war with France (see AMERICAN-FRENCH QUASI-WAR). Certain Pennsylvania German farmers in Bucks, Montgomery, and Northampton counties, led by "Captain" John Fries (1750–1818), a popular traveling auctioneer, rose up in armed resistance to federal tax assessors sent to survey houses and land in February 1799. Angry housewives in Bucks County threw boiling water on the assessors when they tried to measure the windows (they misunderstood this to mean they had to pay a levied window tax). The officials were driven out by the rebels under Fries, who later was apprehended in Bethlehem and tried twice for treason (the second time before U.S. Supreme Court Justice Samuel Chase [1741–1811]). Found guilty and sentenced to be hanged, Fries received a pardon from President John Adams (1735–1826), who had earlier sent federal troops that successfully put down the insurrectionists. See also WHISKEY REBELLION.

Fronde, Wars of the (1648–53) In 1648, the Parlement of Paris refused to approve the French Crown's revenue measures, presented during the regency of the minority of King Louis XIV (1638–1715). This opposition was an attempt to limit the growing authority of the Crown and to assert the ideas and grievances of an increasingly discontented nobility, especially their anger at the heavy tax loads imposed by the royal ministers. The initiating measure of the first phase of the opposition, the Fronde of the Parlement (1648–49), was a Crown plan requiring court magistrates to give up (that is, pay) four years' salary in order to gain reappointment. The Parlement, instead, sought for itself the right to discuss and modify royal decrees and approve new taxes; it listed other requested reforms. Involved in the THIRTY YEARS' WAR, France's government was forced to give in until the Peace of Westphalia (1648) released royal troops. Then Parlement members were arrested. Parisians rose up, blockaded streets, and secured their release. A royal blockade of Paris failed in 1649, and the French court signed the 1649 Peace of Rueil, granting both amnesty and concessions to the Parlement. But a second Fronde (opposing political party), that of the Princes, broke out when Prince Louis II de Condé (1621–86), who had aided the Crown, was arrested because he had rebelled at the absence of a political reward. In a series of provincial uprisings in 1650, his supporters failed to gain his release. The government then backed down, released him for a brief moment of triumph, indicted him, and forced his flight to Spain in 1651. Civil war ensued, but the defection of his military leader caused the defeat of Condé after a triumphal entry into Paris (1652). Condé fled to the Spanish Netherlands; with all Condé's supporters either self-exiled or repentant, the Crown returned to Paris in 1652, followed by its ministers the next year. Both Parlement and the nobility had lost effectiveness as a loyal opposition; the foundation was laid for the later absolutism of King Louis XIV.

G

Gabriel's Rebellion (1800) Gabriel (c. 1776–1800), also known as Gabriel Prosser, a deeply religious black slave, planned a major slave rebellion in Henrico County, Va., hoping to establish an independent black state in Virginia. After months of preparations, on the night of August 30, 1800, Gabriel's "army" of more than 1,000 slaves, armed with guns, swords, and clubs, began a march on Richmond, Va., from a meeting point some six miles from the city. Their march soon became impossible because of a violent rainstorm, which washed out bridges and flooded roads. The slaves were forced to disband, and before they could regroup, Governor James Monroe (1758–1831) of Virginia, who had learned of the plot, ordered out 600 state militiamen. Many slaves were arrested, including Gabriel and 34 of his loyal followers. All were tried, found guilty, and hanged in September 1800.

Gallic Wars (58–51 B.C.) These wars against the numerous tribes that inhabited Gaul (roughly the area of modern France) proved the military genius of the Roman general Julius Caesar (100–44), who, with Pompey the Great (106–48) and Crassus (115–53), formed an informal union, often called the First Triumvirate, which secured political dominance in Rome (60–51). His first campaign in 58 was against the Helvetii, a German-Celtic tribe that wanted to move to the southwest. Caesar and his legions pursued them, cut the tribe in two as it attempted to cross the Saone River, and defeated them for good at the Battle of Bibracte (Mount Beuvray) in July 58. He then helped a friendly tribe repulse a band of German invaders. The following year Caesar pacified the Belgae in the north, but during the winter they broke their alliance and attacked his garrisons. To retaliate, Caesar built a fleet and successfully attacked the leaders of the revolt, the Veneti (another Celtic people), in their stronghold in Armorica (Brittany). Thereafter the Romans controlled the Atlantic waters off Gaul. In 55, Caesar with his soldiers practically wiped out two Germanic tribes, the Usipetes and Tencteri, that had invaded Gaul from the east. To discourage future intrusions, he built a great bridge across the Rhine River (near modern Bonn, Germany), punished a few tribes sternly as he marched into Germany, and then withdrew, destroying the bridge as he left. Afterward he made a brief exploratory expedition to Britain (August 55), where he returned the next year with a large force that subdued the southern Britons. During the winter of 54–53, the tribes in Belgian Gaul again rebelled, destroyed one Roman legion in its winter quarters, and threatened to do the same to another when Caesar arrived and put down the revolt. The next year a more serious rebellion occurred under the leadership of Vercingetorix (d. 46), Gallic chieftain of the Arverni. Caesar led his legions across the Alps in the winter to put down this threat, while Vercingetorix and his disciplined army withdrew to their capital, Gergovia, a naturally fortified stronghold, burning villages and destroying food supplies and crops useful to the Romans as they went. The Romans laid siege to Gergovia but without success (April–May 52). Calling on his Gallic allies for help, Vercingetorix formed a 90,000-man army but failed to defeat Caesar at the Battle of the Vingeanne (a small tributary of the upper Saône). Taking the offensive, Caesar pursued the Arverni chieftain and invested him at the fortified hilltop town of Alesia (Alise-Sainte-Reine, near Dijon). The besieging Romans (about 60,000 men), who had erected walls of circumvallation and contravallation, were themselves besieged by a huge Gallic relief army (over 200,000 strong) coming to the aid of Vercingetorix; they repelled it while continuing their siege of Alesia. To save his people from starvation, Vercingetorix surrendered in October 52; he was later brought to Rome as a prisoner, exhibited there, and executed. In 51, Caesar moved about Gaul supressing all remaining resistance, and by the end of the year Roman authority was firmly established. Henceforth the Gauls were loyal supporters of Caesar and Rome itself. See also ROMAN CIVIL WAR, GREAT.

Gallipoli Campaign   See DARDANELLES CAMPAIGN.

Gascon Nobles' Revolt (1368) Edward the Black Prince (1330–76), ruler of Aquitaine, earned the wrath of the Aquitainians for his high living, his administrative oppression, and his imposition of high taxes to pay English war expenses. This led the highest lords of Gascony to appeal to King Charles V (1337–80) of France for relief in 1368. A clever man and a lawyer, Charles, called "the Wise," saw that the Treaty of Brétigny was legally invalid because no mutual renunciations of suzerainty had occurred; as overlord, he shrewdly summoned the Black Prince, his vassal, to Paris. The Black Prince refused, as expected, and Charles resumed the HUNDRED YEARS' WAR in 1369. The conquered territories rose in rebellion, and the French enjoyed a period of good fortune in war, despite some setbacks (see LIMOGES, MASSACRE AT).

Gaugamela (Arbela), Battle of (331 B.C.) In one of the truly decisive battles of history, the Macedonian forces of Alexander the Great (356–323) defeated the Persians under Darius III (d. 330) at Gaugamela near Arbela (Irbil) in present-day northern Iraq (see ALEXANDER THE GREAT, CONQUESTS OF). Alexander's battle-trained troops, who had marched from Egypt across the Tigris and Euphrates Rivers, consisted of 40,000 infantrymen and 7,000 cavalrymen, and Darius's forces, headquartered in Arbela, numbered 250,000, including 15 elepants. To avoid the elephants, which crazed the cavalry's horses, the Macedonians charged on the Persian left, opening a large gap in the center. Alexander charged into the gap, then wheeled behind the elephants to attack the Persian right flank and rear. Darius fled, and his troops followed, with Macedonians pursuing. An estimated 40,000 to 90,000 Persians were killed; Macedonian casualties were less than 500.

Gempei War (Taira-Minamoto War) (1180–85) When Yoritomo (1147–99), a son of the slain Minamoto clan leader, who had been exiled to Kwanto in eastern Japan at the time of his father's death (see HEIJI WAR), learned that the Taira clan leader, Kiyomori (1118–81), had ordered him to be executed, he raised the white standard of the Minamoto family and took to the field. At first the Taira military forces in Kwanto almost annihilated his troops, but his ranks grew steadily with men who were discontent with the harsh Taira rule. Within two years Yoritomo and his army drove the Taira out of Kwanto, and in 1183 they advanced upon and seized the capital at Kyoto. They then turned west where the Taira were still powerful and gradually reduced their numbers. The Taira were finally destroyed in April 1185, in the fierce naval Battle of Dan-no-ura, which is at the western end of the Inland Sea. Much of the Minamotos' success was due to the brilliant military leadership of Yoritomo's young half-brother, Yoshitsune (1159–89), of whom Yoritomo became increasingly suspicious. Yoshitsune fled to the north where he later committed hara-kiri (suicide by disembowelment). In 1191, Yoritomo, who by that time had gained military control of the whole empire, visited the emperor in Kyoto who appointed him Sei-i-tai-Shogun for life. He was the first to receive this title.

Genghis Khan, Conquests of (1190–1227) Temujin, the original name of Genghis (Jenghiz, Chingis) Khan (1167?–1227), began life as the son of an obscure Mongol tribal chief. Deprived of his father through poisoning by another Mongol group, the Tatars (Tartars), he lived as an outlaw from the age of nine, shepherding his mother and his siblings and developing the magnetic personality and organizing genius that enabled him to become the dominant leader of the Mongols in 1202 after more than 10 years of terrible but successful warfare against the Tatars and other tribes. In 1206, Genghis Khan was proclaimed supreme ruler (khakhan) of the Mongols, and by the time of his death he had conquered and become the ruler of central Asia and northern China (see MONGOL CONQUESTS). Though he could neither read nor write, his keen intellect and natural administrative talent enabled him to transform the usually independent and fractious nomad tribes into a disciplined military force organized by a decimal scheme until it reached 200,000 men; he devised inexorable blitzkrieg strategies for an armored, sword-and-lance-equipped heavy cavalry and a bow-and-javelin-aided light cavalry, teaching famous generals new tactics; he learned by listening and imitating, hiring engineers to conduct his sieges; he made use of a system of post houses on caravan routes and developed an efficient communication and intelligence network. Ruthless in war and vengeful, believing that those who resisted his demands for surrender should be slaughtered, Genghis Khan invented an effective kind of psychological warfare so powerful that he received surrenders before his armies made appearances. He began his conquests by warring against the Hsia Empire (see GENGHIS KHAN'S WARS WITH THE HSIA EMPIRE); he conquered the Chin Empire (see GENGHIS KHAN'S WAR WITH THE CHIN EMPIRE), had his Mongols invade Russia (see MONGOL INVASION OF RUSSIA, FIRST), India (see MONGOL INVASIONS OF INDIA), and Persia (see MONGOL-PERSIAN WAR, FIRST), and made plans to attack Europe (see MONGOL INVASION OF EUROPE). After each campaign, he repaired to his tent-capital at Karakorum in what is now Mongolia. His sons and grandson completed his work and divided the conquered domains among themselves. See also TAMERLANE, CONQUESTS OF.

Genghis Khan's First War with the Hsia Empire (1206–9) The Hsi Hsia (Xi Xia) Empire, located south of the Gobi Desert and west of the Chin Empire (Cathay), was the weakest in China. Ruled by Tanguts, Tibetan in race and Buddhist in religion, the Hsia kingdom was warlike, conducting border raids in a struggle with the Sung (Song) Empire over control of the Yangtze (Chang) River valley. It was also a thorn in the Mongols' southern flank; a war would allow Genghis (Jenghiz, Chingis) Khan (1167?–1227) to test the performance of his massed, disciplined Mongol raiders, and conquest would give the Mongols control of revenues from caravan routes connecting China to the West. The war involved no cities, for the Mongols had not yet learned the art of siege making; it was a war of attrition in which the Mongols ravaged the countryside so thoroughly that the Hsi Hsia sought peace terms and accepted Mongol suzerainty in 1209. The victorious Mongols were now free to move against the Chin Empire and to plan for further westward expansion (see GENGHIS KHAN'S WAR WITH THE CHIN EMPIRE). **Genghis Khan's Second War with the Hsia Empire** (1226–27). Genghis Khan had a personal reason for resuming his conquest of the Hsi Hsia Empire: it had not acted as a compliant vassal state should. To mobilize for the First MONGOL-PERSIAN WAR, the Mongol leader had demanded troops; the Tangut tributary ruler replied that if Genghis Khan had too few soldiers, he had no right to supreme power. Besieging the Hsia capital Ning-Hsia (Hsing-ch'ing) while involving the open country in annihilative warfare avenged the insult. After Genghis Khan's death in 1227, the capital fell, and the entire population was put to the sword. Tangut power, intact after the first war, was now completely destroyed.

Genghis Khan's Sack of Peking (1215) Early history gave Peking (Beijing) many names; the Chin called the city Yen-king and Yen-chu; Kublai

Khan (1216–94), the Mongolian emperor, was to call it Tai-Tu; the Turks named it Khanbaligh, from which Marco Polo (1254?–1324?), the Venetian traveler who arrived there in 1266, derived Cambulac and Kanbalu. However labeled, Peking in 1214 was a disheartened place: the Chin court had moved south after an earlier, unsuccessful Mongol encirclement; Chin engineers had joined Genghis (Jenghiz, Chingis) Khan (1167?–1227) and were now directing the Mongols in a second siege. Though low in morale, the Chinese were obstinate within their well-fortified city, and the siege was long and painful. A Mongol blockade weakened its defenders, and, with help from Chinese defectors, the walls were finally breached. The Mongols entered to loot palaces and public buildings. Peking's governor committed suicide, and many inhabitants were massacred. The city was only partially destroyed, but contemporary records indicate that it burned for a month. The Mongols established control, and then Genghis Khan took his armies west (see MONGOL-PERSIAN WAR, FIRST), leaving the city's Tangut bureaucracy in place.

Genghis Khan's War with the Chin Empire (1211–15)   The move by the Mongols under Genghis (Jenghiz, Chingis) Khan (1167?–1227) against Chin territories, known to the West as Cathay (China), had been carefully planned. Genghis Khan had earlier won over both the Turkish Önguts and the Chi-tan, benefiting from the Öngut location on Cathay's northern border and the Chi-tan desire for revenge against Peking (Beijing). All he needed was a reason to commence. In 1210, Peking ordered him to do homage to a new Chin ruler; Genghis Khan refused and mobilized his forces, ordering Öngut raids on the northern Chin border and conducting raids deep into the area south of the Great Wall of China in 1211. As he captured Chin engineers knowledgeable in siegecraft, he developed a more systematic plan; his armies now divided and made a three-pronged attack into Hopei and Liao-ning. When he began to threaten Peking, the Chin court moved 200 miles south to K'aifeng. By 1214, Genghis Khan's forces had begun to surround the Chin capital, and by 1215, the sack of Peking was over (see GENGHIS KHAN'S SACK OF PEKING). A call

for aid from Kara-Khitai (see MONGOL-PERSIAN WAR, FIRST) interrupted the Mongol action against the Chin until 1231 (see MONGOL CONQUEST OF THE CHIN EMPIRE).

Georgian Civil Wars of 1991–93   After the republic of Georgia, bordering the Black Sea in the west, declared its independence from Soviet rule in April 1991, pro-democracy civilians joined rebel national guardsmen to overthrow the increasingly dictatorial government of President Zviad Gamsakhurdia (d. 1993?). Serious and bloody fighting between paramilitary rebels and government troops finally forced Gamsakhurdia from office in January 1992. At the time, Georgia was embroiled in secessionist revolts by ethnic minorities in the Georgian territories of Abkhazia and Mingrelia (in the northwest along the Black Sea coast) and South Ossetia (in the north bordering North Ossetia in Russia). With aid from two military leaders, Eduard A. Shevardnadze (1928–), the former Soviet foreign minister, was elected Georgia's president in March 1992. Fighting erupted between Georgian troops and South Ossetians, predominantly Muslim, who wanted to unite with North Ossetia, eventually leading to a tripartite accord (June 1992) among Georgia, South Ossetia, and Russia, establishing a peacekeeping coalition force along the South Ossetia border. In October 1992, a rebel militia seized part of Abkhazia, where war escalated the following year. Abkhazian and Russian forces failed to capture the seaport of Sukhumi (Abkhazia's capital) in March and July; a cease-fire was then signed, with Georgian forces leaving the area. In late September 1993, Abkhazian forces overran Sukhumi and took control of the entire region; some 200,000 ethnic Georgians fled from Abkhazia after all Georgian troops abandoned it. United Nations-sponsored talks resulted in a peace agreement (December 1) to fix Abkhazia's autonomy within Georgia, and deployment of a UN-peacekeeping force. Gamsakhurdia, in exile in Chechnya, had failed to regain power in September 1993 when his private troops first occupied towns in western Georgia, advanced to Kutaisi, but were driven back by government forces with Russian support. He later reportedly killed himself. Georgia and Russia agreed to further economic and military cooperation in 1994. Shevardnadze escaped an assassination attempt, was reelected president in 1995, attempted to secure protection for ethnic Georgians wishing to return home in Abkhazia and South Ossetia, and escaped another bombing attack in 1998. See also ARMENIAN-AZERBAIJANI WAR OF 1988–94.

German Civil War of 1077–1106   Henry IV (1050–1106) became king of Germany in 1056; in the course of the regency during his minority, episcopal power had grown dominant. To regain control for himself after 1065, Henry attempted to pick bishops he could dominate. Pope Gregory VII (1020?–85) resisted both the lay investiture and Henry's demand that he (Henry) be crowned Holy Roman Emperor. A crisis occurred in 1076: Henry had a synod declare Gregory deposed; in return, Gregory deposed the rebellious synod clergy and excommunicated Henry, forbidding his exercise of kingship. Henry's nobles gave him an ultimatum: either gain Gregory's absolution by February 22, 1077 or lose their allegiance. On his way to the 1077 Diet at Augsburg, Germany, Pope Gregory rested at Canossa; there, barefoot in the snow, Henry appeared as a penitent, surrendered to Gregory's jurisdiction, and gained his absolution. The Diet nevertheless reversed Henry's election and chose an antiking. The papal party, the Welfs (Guelphs in Italian), gained support from Gregory in 1080; most German nobles backed Henry and formed the Waiblingen party (named for a castle of Henry's Hohenstaufen family; Ghibelline in Italian). In 1080, a Waiblingen council at Brixen (Bressanone) again deposed Gregory and set up an antipope, Guibert of Ravenna, called Clement III (1030?–1100). Henry's forces went to war against the Welfs, only to be defeated in Thuringia in 1080. The defeat, however, was a political victory: the antiking died and his successor was a nonentity who weakened Welf power. Most Germans felt God had voted for Henry, not Gregory; but when Gregory demanded the new antiking's fealty, Henry turned the civil war into a vain attack on Rome itself (1081–82). Henry's forces finally occupied Rome in 1084, replaced Gregory with Clement (who crowned Henry emperor), but were forced to retreat by Gregory's Norman allies led by Robert Guiscard (1015?–85), whose troops sacked Rome for three days in 1084. Gregory, now loathed by the Romans, was then escorted by Guiscard to Salerno, where he died in exile the next year. Later, Henry, who had returned to Germany in triumph, fought and defeated another rival in 1086–88, was compelled to lead another vain attack on Rome in 1090–92, and contended with putting down rebellions of his sons in Germany, supported by Gregory's successors, between 1093 and 1106. Henry IV's son Henry, later Henry V (1081–1125) as the German king and the Holy Roman Emperor, who wanted reconciliation with the pope, forced his father to abdicate after imprisoning him in 1105. Henry IV escaped, however, raised an army, defeated Henry V's forces near Visé in present-day eastern Belgium, but suddenly died in Liège in 1106. See also HOLY ROMAN EMPIRE–PAPACY WAR OF 1081–84.

German Civil War of 1197–1214   The death of Holy Roman Emperor Henry VI (1165–97) established a classic pattern for civil war: the emperor-elect, Frederick (1194–1250), was an infant; two nobles, Philip of Swabia (1176?–1218), Henry's brother, and Otto of Brunswick (1175?–1218) represented Waiblingen (Ghibelline; national) and Welf (Guelph; papal) contenders for the throne; in addition, a new pope, Innocent III (1160?–1216), maneuvered behind the scenes. Frederick, crowned king of Sicily, sat out most of the war. The adult contenders destroyed much of Germany in their warring: Philip, irregularly crowned in 1198, assisted by southern Germans and France, clashed with Otto, aided by northern Germans, the archbishop of Cologne, and the English, beginning in 1198. Pope Innocent pretended to be neutral until Otto insincerely agreed to donate Italian lands to the papacy in 1201. Cologne's archbishop then soon reversed himself and crowned Philip at Aachen in 1205. Philip's forces defeated Otto's in 1206, and Philip gained Innocent's recognition in exchange for concessions, only to be murdered in 1208. Otto inevitably regained prominence, sealing a charter ending the German monarchy's control of the

German church at Speyer in 1209. His forces then invaded Italy and compelled his coronation as Holy Roman Emperor Otto IV (1209), who afterward reneged on the Speyer agreement and invaded Sicily. Innocent now fomented rebellion in Germany and backed Frederick, who was crowned the German king as Frederick II in 1212. The war in Germany, now purely political, ended with the Battle of Bouvines (July 27, 1214), where the French under King Philip II (1165–1223) defeated the combined forces of Otto, King John I (1167–1216) of England, and the counts of Flanders. Frederick, recrowned in Aachen in 1215, reinstated the Speyer concessions and immediately took the Cross. Innocent had won, but the terrible cost to Germany continued in further civil strife and later conflicts with the papacy.

German Civil War of 1314–25   Germany's princes, lay and spiritual, gained additional territorial and administrative power (at the expense of royal imperial authority) during the reign of Holy Roman Emperor Henry VII (1275?–1313). Upon the death of Henry, a dispute arose over the election of his successor. The majority of the prince-electors, who were pro-Hapsburg, wanted the duke of Austria, Frederick III "the Handsome" (1286?–1330), and the minority supported Duke Louis IV (1287?–1347) of Bavaria (Wittelsbach dynastic family). Frederick and Louis were both elected king of Germany by their constituencies (1314); they began a long, bitter civil war to settle the claim and decide who would be Holy Roman Emperor, a title they both assumed. At the time the papacy was vacant, thus canceling the pope's rightful adjudication of contested elections (since 1201). In 1322, Louis's imperial troops won an important victory at Mühldorf; Frederick was captured there and put in prison (1322–25) and finally recognized his rival as emperor. Although the war ended in 1325, Pope John XXII (1249–1334) strongly opposed Louis, not acknowledging his right to govern. Louis defied him and stated he did not need papal confirmation to rule, just majority approval. In 1327–28, he led an expedition to Rome, which he captured; Nicholas V (d. 1333), Imperial antipope, was established there as a rival to Pope John XXII at Avignon; Louis was

crowned emperor at a "lay" coronation in 1328. Nicholas was excommunicated by John (1329); and realizing he had little support, Nicholas gave up his illegal claim to the papacy (1330).

German Civil War of 1400–1411   Between 1125 and 1806, the kings of the Romans (German kings in the Holy Roman Empire) were elected, not hereditary. This system prevented abuses by tyrants and ineffective rulers, but also had the potential of enabling the electors, both lay and clerical, to become rulers in their own right and of serving as a basis for civil strife. Wenceslaus (1361–1419), king of Germany from 1378 to 1400, was perceived in 1384 and 1387 as ineffective as Holy Roman emperor; he drank and was very lazy, increasingly so in the 1390s. In 1400, he was deposed, and Rupert of the Palatinate (1352–1410) was elected in his place. But Wenceslaus was popular. He constantly claimed his rights as Germany's king and influenced many people enough to be the subject of a potential war of restoration, happily avoided by Rupert's death. Wenceslaus named himself a candidate for the German throne. Unwilling to face the embarrassment of reelecting him, the electors named to the kingship his brother, Sigismund (1368–1437), king of Hungary, and Jobst (1351–1411), margrave of Moravia. Jobst was elected in 1410 but died in 1411. Wenceslaus again stood for election, but Sigismund, partner to a scheme to let Wenceslaus keep the title and receive a pension, was named German king and Holy Roman Emperor-elect in 1411. (See HUSSITE WARS.) Later, Sigismund, childless, his Luxembourg dynasty's tradition of providing Germany its kings at an end, and his treasury depleted, named a Hapsburg, Frederick of Hohenzollern (1371–1400), elector of Brandenburg, and his successor.

German Colonial Wars in Africa (1903–8) The Germans promoted white settlement as the key to their economic policy of making their African colonies self-sufficient. Often native tribes were dislodged by force from their traditional hunting and grazing areas. In 1903, the Hottentots (Khoikhoi tribe) revolted in German South-West

Africa (Namibia), and violence spread across the land. The Herero tribe rose in rebellion in South-West Africa in 1904, fiercely fighting the German oppressors and enslavers. Troops from Germany arrived to squash the African rebels and, with great difficulty and much bloodshed, did so by 1908. About 80 percent of the Herero people and 50 percent of the Hottentots were killed. Africans also revolted in German East Africa (Tanzania) (see MAJI MAJI UPRISING) and in Cameroon in West Africa, where German forces brutally suppressed them. Most Africans were reduced to virtual slavery in the mines and on the plantations. See also ARAB UPRISING IN GERMAN EAST AFRICA; WAHEHE WAR.

German Invasion of Poland See BLITZKRIEG.

German Revolution of 1848 Like so many of the European revolutions of 1848, the German one was ultimately a failure; however, unlike the others, its chief impetus was nationalism rather than liberalism. Feudalism was not dead in Germany, and although liberals tried to free the land and the individual, and some worker groups pressed for "socialism," the greater pressure concerned achieving a united Germany. After the fall of France's King Louis-Philippe (1773–1850) (see FRENCH REVOLUTION OF 1848), popular demonstrations for a national German parliament began and resulted in many German states, beginning with Baden, adopting liberal reforms; the Hanseatic states became democratic republics in March 1848. No violence occurred until the fall of the Austrian statesman Metternich (1773–1859) in the AUSTRIAN REVOLUTION OF 1848–49; the next month, April, saw Berlin, a center of excessive unemployment, erupt into bloody revolt, forcing the Prussian king to make concessions and to accept a degree of national unity he did not really want. The National Assembly convened on May 18, 1848, at Frankfurt and almost immediately split over whether Austria was to be included in the new German confederation. While labor agitation for a democratic republic was put down, the assembly developed a liberal rather than democratic constitution envisioning a constitutional monarchy and excluding Austria. By December 1848, most of the German radical impetus was dead; attitudes began to move to the right. King Frederick William IV (1795–1861) of Prussia rejected the crown offered by the Frankfurt constitution as too restrictive to his authority and offered instead his own conservative plan. Radical uprisings in southwest Germany were quelled by forces supporting princely authority. January and February 1849 led to another constitution, the cancellation of many 1848 liberal decrees, and Austria's return (with Russia's help) to a position so powerful as to humiliate Frederick William IV. As a result, the old German Confederacy Assembly, with Austria as head, reconvened in 1849 with little protest. The dramatic drive for a united Germany was stagnant. See also SEVEN WEEKS' WAR.

Ghanian Civil War of 1994–95 On February 3, 1994, longtime enmity between the Konkomba and Nanumba tribal ethnic groups erupted into fighting in the Northern Region of Ghana in West Africa. Konkombas, who originated in neighboring Togo, demanded similar traditional landowning rights held by the native Nanumbas. Ghanian troops were sent to restore order after at least 1,000 persons had been killed and more than 150,000 displaced as a result of the violent clashes; President Jerry John Rawlings (1947–) also imposed a state of emergency in seven districts and successfully sought a peace agreement between the warring factions that would settle the land dispute (signed in the capital of Accra on June 9, 1994). But in 1995, hostilities resumed in the north, notably around Tamale. About 100 persons died in fighting between Konkombas and Nanumbas, who had gained an alliance with the Dagomba and Gonja ethnic groups, before the government secured a peace settlement and allocated $1.2 million to aid some 200,000 persons displaced since the war began. See also TOGOLESE CIVIL WAR OF 1991–92.

Ghassanid-Lakhmid Wars (A.D. c. 500–583) Struggles between the Byzantine, or Eastern

Roman, Empire and Sassanid Persia for dominance in Arabia affected two pre-Islamic Arab dynasties: the Ghassanids, whose pro-Byzantine kingdom was located in parts of present-day Syria, Jordan, and Israel, and the Lakhmids, whose kingdom centered at al-Hirah in present-day south-central Iraq was allied with Persia. Almost incessant war was waged between these two Arab kingdoms, chiefly at the behest of the Byzantines or Persians. Under al-Mundhir III (503–54), the Lakhmids challenged Ghassan's power with some success, but suffered a momentous defeat in 528 at the hands of al-Harith ibn Jabalah (d. 569), who became the Ghassanid king the next year. Vigorous Lakhmid attacks on Byzantine Syria and Ghassan were unsuccessful in mid-century. In 583, orthodox Byzantine leaders, angry at Ghassanid Monophysitic heresy (believing Christ's human and divine natures as one rather than two), made Ghassan a vassal state and sent imperial troops to guard its borders. In 602, the Lakhmid dynasty ended with the death of its last ruler, a Nestorian Christian (a believer in Christ's dual nature with the corollary that Mary is not the Mother of God) opposed by Persia. Both kingdoms collapsed and disappeared during Arabia's conquest by Muslims in the seventh century. See BYZANTINE-MUSLIM WARS; MUSLIM CONQUEST OF PERSIA.

Gladiators' War   See SERVILE WAR, THIRD.

Glencoe Massacre (1692) Attempts by King William III (1650–1702) of England, Scotland, and Ireland to control the Highland Jacobites (see JACOBITE REBELLION OF 1689–90) took several forms: he constructed forts, gave money to clan chiefs to buy loyalty, and then required oaths of allegiance on pain of death. Former king James II (1633–1701), however, anticipating these oaths, required the chiefs to swear. One chief was late; another, MacIan MacDonald of Glencoe, refused. William, ordering the clan's extirpation, sent soldiers under MacIan's relative. The soldiers were received hospitably. Then one night government troops closed the approaches to the valley of Glencoe. The visiting soldiers, aided by rival Scottish clansmen, the Campbells, then slaughtered the sleeping MacDonalds and burned their houses. William's reputation in Scotland was ruined because the guards allowed a few MacDonalds to escape and tell the sad tale.

Glendower's Revolt (1402–9) The reign of English king Henry IV (1367–1413) was plagued by rebellions, the worst of which was probably that of the cunning and ruthless Owen Glendower (1359?–1416?). One of the most powerful of Welsh lords and an able leader, he quickly drove Henry's forces out of castles and towns in Wales because of a countrywide resentment against high taxes and poor administration. Proclaimed prince of Wales in 1400, Glendower gained the support of Edmund de Mortimer (1367–1409) in 1402 and the English Percys in 1403 (see PERCY'S REBELLION). After seizing the key castles of Aberystwyth and Harlech in 1404, he was recognized by King Charles VI (1368–1422) of France, with whom he made an alliance. However, Glendower's forces lost from 1405 through 1409 because the French failed to appear. Aberystwyth and Harlech were retaken by the English. Broken, Glendower fled into the mountains of Wales.

Glorious Revolution (1688) King James II (1633–1701) of England, Scotland, and Ireland was perhaps the most arrogant of the Stuart kings. Apparently lacking considerable political sense, he avenged MONMOUTH'S REBELLION bloodily, slaughtering the misguided rebels and then ordering the Bloody Assizes, a court that hanged some 300 rebels and scourged, fined, or transported to Barbados another 1,000. He openly declared his intention to convert England to Catholicism, established a standing army officered by Catholics, appointed Catholic officials, prorogued an insubordinate parliament, and arrested Anglican bishops who protested his Declarations of Indulgence. There was much alarm throughout Britain. The king seemed unconscious until it was too late that a conspiracy would bring his Protestant daughter Mary (1662–94) from Holland to replace him; then conciliatory efforts by James failed. Mary and her husband,

William of Orange (1650–1702), landed at Devonshire, England, with a Dutch army, gathered many supporters, and marched to meet James's royal forces at Salisbury. James fled, was caught in Kent, brought back to London, and finally allowed to leave for France on a dirty fishing smack. The Convention Parliament of 1689 ruled that the throne was "vacant" and offered it to William and Mary, who were heading a provisional government in England. They became the first rulers appointed by parliament. Except for the Jacobites (see JACOBITE REBELLION OF 1689–90), all of the British kingdom was delighted by this glorious (and bloodless) revolution. See also IRISH WAR OF 1689–91.

Golden Horde Dynastic War (1359–81) Jöchi (d. 1227), the eldest son of Genghis (Jenghiz, Chingis) Khan (1167?–1227), became ruler of a Mongol territory north and west of the Caspian Sea that became known historically as the Kipchak Khanate or, from the second ruler's opulence, the "Golden Horde." Jöchi's last Mongol successor died in 1359, and the territory became the locus of disputes and wars. Two non-Mongols tried ruling: Mamak (Mamai) (d. 1380) and Urus (d. 1380); but Tamerlane (Timur) (1336–1405) strove to procure the throne for his protégé Toktamish (Tuqtamish) (d. 1406), an ungrateful pensioner of Mamak, proclaiming him khan (ruler) in 1377. But Mamak still ruled and when he lost (1380) to Dmitri Donskoi (1350–89), prince of Moscovy, who led Russians refusing to pay Mongol levies in the first Russian victory over the Mongols, Toktamish attacked Mamak, losing twice. Mamak died, then Urus, and Toktamish became the legal ruler (1380–81); he renewed the Mongol yoke by warring in Russia in the destructive fashion of his forebears. Victorious, he forgot his allegiance to his mentor; Tamerlane made two wars within 10 years to temper his rebellious ambition (see TAMERLANE'S WARS AGAINST TOKTAMISH).

Golden Horde-Il-Khan Civil War (1261–62) The great Mongol assembly (kuriltai), convened by Arik-Böke (d. 1266), which precipitated the MONGOL CIVIL WAR OF 1260–64, caused a second conflict between his brother Hülegü (d. 1265), the Il-Khan (Mongol dynasty) ruler of Persia, and Berke (d. 1266), khan (ruler) of the Golden Horde (Kipchak Khanate in the Mongol Empire's western part), a result of Arik-Böke's attempt to interfere in the affairs of the White Horde (a Mongol khanate or realm north of the Aral Sea). Hülegü conducted a military campaign against an Arik-Böke protege, and Berke, a Muslim already angry at Hülegü (see MONGOL CONQUEST OF THE ABBASID CALIPHATE), signed a treaty with the Il-Khan's Mamluk Turk enemies. In 1262, Hülegü's forces marched north, defeated an army of Berke's by surprise, and then lost when ice on the Terek River gave way, drowning many of Hülegü's troops during an attempted crossing. Hülegü retreated and then ended the strife by making a politically advantageous marriage to a princess from Byzantium, a constant Muslim enemy. The khanates remained hostile until the end of the Il-Khan dynasty in 1335; TAMERLANE'S INVASION OF RUSSIA had its roots in this old Kipchak-Persian rivalry.

Gothic (Italian) War of A.D. 534–54 Italy was governed by a succession of weak Gothic rulers after the death of Theodoric the Great (454?–526), king of the Ostrogoths and conqueror of Italy. Hoping to reunite the Western Roman (Italian) and Eastern Roman (Byzantine) empires, Emperor Justinian I (483–565), who resided at Constantinople (Istanbul), directed his most capable general, Belisarius (505?–65), to head a campaign against the Goths in Italy. After invading and seizing Sicily, the imperial forces landed in southern Italy, marched north, and captured in 536 Naples and Rome, where they withstood a yearlong siege by the Goths (537–38). They then moved north but were hampered by lack of supplies and reinforcements and by attacks by the Goths. At Ravenna, Belisarius forced the Gothic king, Vitiges (fl. 536–39), to surrender in late 539; Vitiges was sent as a prisoner to Constantinople, to which Belisarius later returned in 541 at the emperor's request (Justinian feared that he might become Roman Emperor of the West). The war seemed to be over, for most Gothic strongholds had been taken. A new Gothic king, Totila (Baduila) (d. 552), nephew of Vitiges, ascended the throne and immediately began recapturing the cities and strongholds the imperial forces had won until he controlled most of Italy. Upon Justinian's urgent request, Belisarius came back to conduct five more campaigns against the Goths; his chief success was recapturing Rome, but he was unable to hold it. He was again recalled. Totila now extended his power over Sicily, Sardinia, and Corsica. In 552, Justinian renewed his efforts to regain Italy by sending Narses (478?–573), a Byzantine general, and a well-equipped naval fleet and army to the Adriatic. Crossing the Apennine Mountains and advancing on Rome, some 20,000 troops under Narses decisively routed about 15,000 Goths under Totila at the Battle of Taginae (near Gubbio, Italy) in July 552; many Goths, including Totila, were slain. With their leader dead, the Goths shortly capitulated to Narses's forces at Rome and other places in Italy, which now came under Justinian's rule for a brief period. Much of the country lay in ruin, and Justinian's treasury was drained from fighting the war. See also THEODORIC'S WAR WITH ODOACER; VANDAL-ROMAN WAR IN NORTH AFRICA.

Gothic-Roman Wars See ROMAN-GOTHIC WARS.

Gothic-Sarmatian War (A.D. 332–34) The Sarmatians, a Scythian-Germanic people, who had settled in Dacia (roughly Rumania), found themselves pressured by intruding Goths and other Germanic tribes; they asked for help from Roman emperor Constantine I "the Great" (280?–337), whose eldest son led a force north across the Danube River and joined the Sarmatians. Together they routed the Goths and their allies in 332–33, but the uncivil Sarmatians began to make raids into the Roman Empire. Constantine now urged the Goths to crush the Sarmatians, who received no Roman aid as Goths overwhelmed them. Ironically, the emperor allowed about 300,000 surviving Sarmatians to settle in the empire. For a while, the Goths remained quiet and good neighbors because of the Christianizing efforts of Bishop Ulfilas (311?–81) and the assignment of *foederati* status, under which they received subsidies in exchange for military services. See also ROMAN-GOTHIC WARS.

Gowrie Conspiracy (1600) Scotland's King James VI (1566–1625), later England's King James I, was invited to Gowrie House in Perth by the Ruthven barons, sons of the Gowrie executed after the RAID OF RUTHVEN; the barons sought to wrest away his royal power. What happened remains a mystery. Apparently promised a newfound treasure, James allowed himself to be escorted upstairs. Then he cried out for help, and his rescuers killed the Ruthven sons before an actual kidnapping plot could be ascertained. The only account of the event is James'; he reacted by stripping the Ruthvens of titles, lands, and dignities forever.

Gracchi, Revolt of the (133 B.C., 121 B.C.) Tiberius Gracchus (163–133 B.C.) and his brother Gaius Gracchus (153–121 B.C.), known as the Gracchi, both tried to carry out democratic reforms against the Roman governing aristocracy. In 133 B.C., elected tribune of the plebeians, Tiberius managed to pass an agrarian law alloting public land in Italy to free farmers at the expense of wealthy Roman landowners. Tiberius, who had used his power contrary to custom (which left provincial affairs to the Senate), was killed, along with about 300 of his supporters, during an election-day riot fomented by his political enemies. Ten years later, Gaius, also tribune of the plebeians, forced the enactment of new agrarian and social laws, challenging the Senate's financial and provincial controls and thus avenging his brother. Followers of Gaius, who failed to win a third term as tribune, opposed possible repeal of the Gracchian laws, armed themselves, and vainly fought senatorial troops in Rome in 121 B.C. Gaius fled and ordered a slave to kill him (which he did); some 250 followers died in battle and 3,000 others were executed by senatorial decree. See also SERVILE WAR, FIRST.

Granada, Siege of (1491–92) Most of the Moorish (Spanish Muslim) kingdom of Granada in southern Spain had fallen to invading Christian Castilian forces by 1491 (see SPANISH CHRISTIAN-MUSLIM WAR OF 1481–92). In the kingdom's capital, Granada, the inhabitants refused to recognize the suzerainty of King Ferdinand V (1452–1516) and Queen Isabella I (1451–1504) of Castile and Aragon. They called on Sultan Muhammad XI, better known as Boabdil (d. 1527), to break his truce agreement with Ferdinand and lead them in the defense of their homes; he did so. In April 1491, Castilians invested the city and constructed a western command post, Santa Fé, that effectively cut Granada's links with the outside world. Moorish sorties were repulsed by the superior Christian forces. Facing eventual starvation, Boabdil entered into peace negotiations and capitulated on January 2, 1492, the day after the Alhambra, the splendid palace-fortress of the Moorish monarchs of Granada, was taken over by the Castilians. On January 6, 1492, Ferdinand and Isabella entered the city; their rule over it was magnanimous, granting freedom of worship and local self-government. The Moors had the option of immigration to North Africa. Granada's fall concluded Muslim rule in Spain.

Grand Alliance, War of the (War of the League of Augsburg) (1688–97) The territorial aggressions of France's King Louis XIV (1638–1715) in Germany during the Third DUTCH WAR resulted in a defensive alliance of England, the United Provinces (independent Netherlands, especially Holland), and the Austrian Hapsburgs, called the League of Augsburg and, after 1689, the Grand Alliance. Louis had hoped for a brief, unimpeded war in Germany, but the GLORIOUS REVOLUTION toppled King James II (1633–1701) and brought England under King William III (1650–1702) into the fray to stop Louis's expansionism. To distract William, Louis created a diversion in Ireland in support of the deposed Stuart king (see IRISH WAR OF 1689–91), but William's victory there at the Battle of the Boyne upset his plans. Possessor of what was then Europe's finest navy, Louis attempted to cripple the Grand Alliance on the sea, his warships decisively defeating an Anglo-Dutch fleet at the Battle of Beachy Head in 1690 but later losing so disastrously in the 1692 Battle of LA HOGUE that his naval power was almost useless. Restricted to military land actions, Louis had to fight the alliance (now enlarged to include Savoy, Sweden, Spain, the Holy Roman Empire, Bavaria, Saxony, and the Palatinate) collectively and separately. In a brilliant double envelopment by French cavalry at the Battle of Fleurus in 1690, some 6,000 English, Spanish, and German troops were killed and 8,000 taken prisoner; this French victory, and the navy's at Beachy Head, made Louis seem invincible. A key city in the Spanish Netherlands, Namur, suffered two battles; the first in 1692 was a bloody French triumph. It was followed in two months by a slaughterous French victory at the Battle of STEENKERKE and in 1693 by a massacre of the alliance's forces at the Battle of NEERWINDEN. Louis was also victorious over Saxony in 1693, causing its withdrawal from the war the next year and a separate peace treaty in 1696. Although Louis continued the war, the death of his undefeated general, Marshal Luxembourg (1628–95), and a defeat at the second Battle of Namur in 1695 caused him to enter into secret peace negotiations with William. The war ended with the Treaty of Ryswick (Rijswijk) between September 20 and October 30, 1697, by which Louis recognized William's right to the English throne, the Dutch received trade concessions, and France and Grand Alliance members gave up most of their conquests since 1679. See also KING WILLIAM'S WAR; LOUIS XIV'S RHENISH INVASION; SPANISH SUCCESSION, WAR OF THE.

Great Indian Mutiny   See INDIAN MUTINY.

Great Java War   See JAVA WAR, GREAT.

Great Kaffir War   See KAFFIR WAR, EIGHTH.

Great Locomotive Chase   See ANDREWS'S RAID.

Great Northern War   See NORTHERN WAR, SECOND OR GREAT.

Great Peloponnesian War   See PELOPONNESIAN WAR, SECOND OR GREAT.

Greco-Persian Wars (500–448 B.C.)   3By 500 B.C., the sprawling Persian empire under King Darius I (559?–486) was the largest the ancient world had known. The IONIAN REVOLT, aided by Athens, caused Darius to seek revenge against Greece. His first attempt was negated by the wit and speed of Athenian forces at the Battle of MARATHON in 490. Darius considered a Persian invasion through Europe as his best option; in 480, a huge force under his son Xerxes I (519?–465) bridged and crossed the Hellespont (Dardanelles), conquered Thessaly, and won the Battle of Thermopylae (480), where Spartans and their allies, led by Leonidas (d. 480), made a heroic stand in the mountain pass (see PERSIAN INVASION OF GREECE). But the combined Greek city-states defeated the Persian fleet at Salamis in 480 and destroyed it at Cape Mycale in 479. Meanwhile, the Greek armies, against heavy odds, cleverly overthrew the Persian base at Plataea in southern Boeotia. With the threat of the Persian invasion over, the Ionian city-states, guided and helped by Athens, formed the Delian League in 478. Greek forces led by Cimon (507?–449), an Athenian general and the son of Miltiades (540?–489), then regained control of the city-states in Thrace and along the Aegean basin. In 466, Cimon's forces defeated the Persians in a great naval and land battle at Eurymedon River in Asia Minor. Later rebellions in Egypt were helped by the Athenians, now led by Pericles (495?–429), who blockaded Memphis, the capital, in 459. Confronted there by Persians, the Greeks lost two squadrons in battle by 456 and were bottled up, along with the rebels, on an island in the Nile; the Persians besieged them, finally crushing them in 454 after changing the course of the river. Cimon, a political rival whom Pericles had ostracized upon coming to power, was recalled and led the Athenians to victory over the Persians at Sala-mis, Cyprus, in 450; he recovered most of Cyprus before his death at the siege of Citium (Larnaca) the next year. The Peace of Callias concluded the war in 448, with Persia agreeing to stay out of the Aegean, and it lasted 40 years. See also PELOPONNESIAN WAR, FIRST.

Greco-Turkish War of 1897 (Thirty Days' War) Anger among the Greek populace over the Turkish maltreatment of Christians during the CRETAN UPRISING OF 1896 reinforced Greece's government's determination to annex Crete during the uprising and forced the Porte (Ottoman government) into war against Greece. The Greeks carried on two separate campaigns, one in Crete and the other in Thessaly. The Turks won consistently in both places, forcing the Greeks to withdraw from Crete and to accept an armistice in Thessaly on May 19, 1897. A peace settlement was reached four months later. The war proved disastrous for Greece, which was compelled to pay an indemnity and lost part of Thessaly. In addition, an international commission was set up to control Greek finances. The Ottoman Empire was to withdraw its troops from Crete and allow it to become an international protectorate under Prince George (1863–1913) of Greece. The Turkish troops left in 1898, and the 1913 Treaty of London, ending the First BALKAN WAR, enabled Crete, finally, to become part of Greece.

Greco-Turkish War of 1921–22   Turkish resistance to the allied occupation and dismemberment of the Ottoman Empire, led by Mustafa Kemal, later known as Kemal Ataturk (1881–1938), from Ankara, seat of his provisional nationalist government, had as one of its goals the expulsion of the Greek army from western Anatolia (Asiatic Turkey). Granted the Smyrna (Izmir) area by the 1920 Treaty of Sèvres, the Greeks wanted both Thrace and as much of Anatolia as they could control. Despite inadequate military equipment and very tenuous supply lines, Greek forces advanced on Eskişehir, were repulsed in two battles at Inonu (January and March 1921), but nonetheless moved doggedly on toward Ankara. At the Sakarya River, about 70 miles from Ankara, they were seriously defeated in a three-week battle (August 24–September 16, 1921) and forced to begin an agonizing, yearlong, 250-mile retreat toward Smyrna, which Kemal's forces besieged and captured on September 9–11, 1922. Thousands of Greek soldiers and civilians were seized and slain by the Turks. The Treaty of Lausanne, which superseded the Sèvres treaty, on July 24, 1923, ended the conflict and forced the Greeks to return eastern Thrace to the Turks, to remove all occupation troops, to return Turkish islands, and to exchange their Turkish minority population for the former Ottoman Empire's minority Greek inhabitants. See also TURKISH WAR OF INDEPENDENCE.

Greek Civil War of 1944–49   Toward the end of WORLD WAR II, Greek communists attempted to take over Greece, then occupied by British forces, but after six weeks of fighting (December 3, 1944–January 11, 1945) were suppressed. The British arranged a truce between the rival factions (moderate and left-wing) and helped set up a regency government under a Greek Orthodox archbishop. In May 1946, after the Greek people had voted to restore the monarchy and King George II (1890–1947), communist rebels, supported by Albania, Yugoslavia, and Bulgaria, began seizing control of parts of the country. Government officials, who got some support from the British, sought international aid, and U.S. president Harry S. Truman (1882–1972), under the Truman Doctrine, extended economic and military aid to Greece (and Turkey), and the United Nations called on Albania, Yugoslavia, and Bulgaria to cease their assistance to the rebels. By 1947, the communists had been driven into the northern border areas, and in late August 1949, their main stronghold was captured in the mountains of the Greco-Albanian frontier, despite help from the UN-condemned governments of Bulgaria and Rumania. A year earlier Yugoslav aid had been withdrawn and its frontier closed. The civil war ended on October 16, 1949.

Greek War of Independence   (1821–32) Western ideas, Ottoman Turkish oppression, and the rediscovery of Greek cultural heritage created the Greek desire for independence from Turkish rule. Before 1821, this desire found a double expression: Greek nationalistic societies, particularly the Philike Hetairia ("Society of Friends"), attracted the educated, and banditry and violence practiced by the klephts (Greek mountain brigands) drew the less educated. The war began in 1821 with the YPSILANTI REBELLIONS, followed by a declaration of Greek independence at Epidaurus, Greece, on January 13, 1822. Greek rebels under Demetrios Ypsilanti (1793–1832) acted in concert on land and sea, seizing control of garrisons and key ports in the Morea (Peloponnesus) and blockading Turkish ships bringing supplies. They captured Tripolitza (Tripolis), the chief Turkish fortress in the Morea, and Athens, considered the Ottoman sultan's personal property. During 1822–23, invading Turkish forces failed to take the key Greek fortress of Missolonghi at the entrance to the Gulf of Corinth and withdrew. Meanwhile, Janissaries (Turkish corps) fought on Crete and massacred Christians (see CRETAN REBELLION OF 1821–22); other Turks destroyed the whole island of Chios, making slaves of some 100,000 persons. But the Turks could not recapture the Morea. In 1822, the Greeks made the mistake of easing their fighting in order to set up a constitutional government. Dissension occurred among them and a civil war erupted. In 1825, when Ottoman sultan Mahmud II (1784–1839) asked for aid from the pasha of Egypt, Muhammad Ali (1769?–1849), the Greeks were very weak. The pasha's son, Ibrahim (1789–1848), led an Egyptian land and sea expedition to the Morea and soon regained full control of the peninsula. Invading Turks from the north besieged and captured Missolonghi in 1826, and Athens fell to the Turks the next year. European nations were aroused by the Greeks' struggle to throw off the barbarous Turks, and Britain and Russia signed a protocol agreeing to mediate between the Greeks and Turks, aiming for Greek autonomy. France joined Britain and Russia, and the trio demanded the withdrawal of the

Egyptians. When the Egyptians refused and the Porte (Ottoman government) rejected an armistice, the three allied European nations sent naval forces to Greece and destroyed much of the Turko-Egyptian fleet at the Battle of Navarino on October 20, 1827. The rest of Ibrahim's forces were expelled from Greece by the French. Then the RUSSO-TURKISH WAR OF 1828–29 further reduced Turkish power, and by the Treaty of Adrianople (1829) the Ottomans gave up the Danubian Principalities (Moldavia and Wallachia) and recognized Greek automony. Independent Greece was reluctantly accepted by the Porte in 1832 when the Treaty of London went into effect. See also JANISSARIES' REVOLT OF 1826.

Greek War of 323–322 B.C.   See LAMIAN WAR.

Grenada, Invasion of (1983) At dawn, on October 25, 1983, U.S. Marines, Army Rangers, Navy Seal commandos and elements of the 82nd Airborne Division invaded the small Caribbean island of Grenada, a member of the British Commonwealth. The announced mission of the American surprise attack, in which troops from a number of Caribbean nations took part, was to ensure the safety of some 1,000 Americans, whose presence on Grenada (most were medical students) was considered endangered by the new marxist military government that had seized power from and murdered Prime Minister Maurice Bishop (1944–83) six days earlier. The Organization of Eastern Caribbean States and Grenada's Governor-General Sir Paul Scoon (1935–   ) had requested U.S. help to combat the growing influence of Cuba and other communist countries on the island. The small Grenadian army, assisted by Cuban soldiers and workers who were constructing a large airport at Point Salines, put up fierce resistance for several days, but were eventually overwhelmed by the invasion force, which had grown from about 1,200 to over 7,000. Numerous rebels fled to the interior jungles and kept fighting; within a month the leaders of the military government were arrested, and Cubans, Russians, North Koreans, Liby-

ans, East Germans, Bulgarians, and suspected Grenadian communists had been rounded up and put in a detention camp. By mid-December 1983, all U.S. combat forces had left Grenada, and Scoon had appointed a nine-member advisory council to govern until elections could be held.

Guanajuato Massacre (1810) After the Mexican priest Miguel Hidalgo y Costilla (1753–1811) called for the end of Spanish rule in Mexico (see MEXICAN REVOLT OF 1810–11), he led his motley army of Indians and mestizos (persons of Spanish and Indian blood) into the town of Guanajuato in central Mexico. There Hidalgo's followers captured Spanish-government officials, Creoles (Spanish American natives of European descent), and others—all of whom had barricaded themselves in a warehouse—and massacred them; afterward the town was plundered.

Guatemalan Civil War of 1961–96   Rampant human rights abuses by the Guatemalan army and government, supported by powerful business and landholding interests, caused communist-led guerrillas (extreme leftists) to begin an active political war of terror in 1961. Also, promised social, agrarian, and economic reforms were blocked. In 1967–68, rightist groups were using the same terrorist tactics as the communists to attack the government, which slowly began to implement programs to improve the lives of the poor Indian peasants (Guatemala's population is more than 50 percent pure Indian; most of the remainder is of mixed Spanish and Indian descent, called Ladino). Communist guerrillas fatally shot two U.S. embassy military attachés in Guatemala City, the capital, on January 16, 1968, and they also killed the U.S. ambassador on August 18, 1968, when he resisted a kidnap attempt. By 1970, leftist dissidents, abetted by rightist dissidents, had created widespread fear and turmoil through violence and murder. Leftist terrorists kidnapped and killed the West German ambassador on April 5, 1970, when the government rejected their demands ($700,000 ransom and the release of 25 political prisoners). In mid-1978, General Romeo Lucas Garcia (1924–) became president and reportedly ordered the deaths of some 5,000 persons, including 76 opposing political leaders. His brutal, corrupt regime brought a cut-off of U.S. military aid. He was ousted in 1982 when dissident army officers seized power. In 1983 two military coup d'états occurred (August and October), and in 1984 a constituent assembly was elected to draft a new constitution. Civilian rule returned to Guatemala in 1986 with the election of President Marco Vinicio Cerezo Arévalo (1942–), followed five years later by President Jorge Serrano Elías (1945–). Serrano's attempt to suspend constitutional rights in 1993 led to his ouster by military, business, and political leaders. Later a temporary cease-fire with guerrillas restored some sense of democracy and led to a peace agreement (December 29, 1996) signed by four top leftist rebel leaders and government representatives. The war had left some 150,000 people dead, most of them Indian civilians, and some 50,000 missing; a difficult rebuilding of the country lay ahead.

Guatemalan Revolution of 1954 With the support of the army and several left-wing political parties, liberal colonel Jacobo Arbenz Guzmán (1913–71) was elected president of Guatemala in 1950. He later signed a communist-backed agrarian reform law (1952), expropriating the property of big private land-owners, including the United Fruit Company. In March 1954, the United States and several Latin American nations met at an inter-American conference and condemned the increasing communist movement in the Western Hemisphere. Soon a Polish ship landed communist-made arms in Guatemala, while the United States sent arms to Honduras and Nicaragua for their defense. On June 18, 1954, a 2,000-man anti-communist army under Lieutenant Colonel Carlos Castillo Armas (1914–57) invaded Guatemala from Honduras and quickly penetrated the country, encountering little resistance from Arbenz's army. The Guatemalan government sought help from the United Nations Security Council and from the So-

viets, and the Organization of American States began an investigation into the conflict. But before the international bodies made any decisions, Arbenz was ousted (June 28, 1954) and fled to Mexico; the capital, Guatemala City, was occupied by Castillo Armas, who became head of a ruling junta and later was elected president.

Guatemalan War (1885) A long period of conservative rule in Guatemala ended in 1871, when the liberals led by Miguel García Granados (1809–78) and Justo Rufino Barrios (1835?–85) captured the capital, Guatemala City, after a military campaign of 90 days and overthrew the government. Granados served as president for two years until he retired in 1873 and was succeeded by Barrios, the commander in chief of the army. Ruling like a dictator, Barrios decreased the power of the church and strengthened the Guatemalan economy by fostering the cultivation of coffee, a major commercial crop. In 1876, he attempted unsuccessfully to bring about a peaceful union of Central American states. On February 25, 1885, Barrios called for the establishment of a united Central American republic with himself as president and army commander. The proposed confederation gained the support of Honduras, which allied itself with Guatemala, but it was rejected by El Salvador, Nicaragua, and Costa Rica. Mexican president Porfirio Díaz (1830–1915) also opposed it and deployed troops along the Mexican-Guatemalan border. Hoping to establish the confederation by force, Barrios led his army into El Salvador, where he suffered defeat and was killed at the Battle of Chalchuapa on April 2, 1885. Another effort to unify Central America had failed.

"Güglers" War (1375–76) Lord Enguerrand VII de Coucy (1340–97), later count of Soissons, claimed (as the right of his mother) the Swiss territory of Aargau, which was held by his Hapsburg cousin, Duke Leopold III (1351–86) of Austria. During the second phase of the HUNDRED YEARS' WAR, de Coucy gained both permission and gold from the French king to assemble a 10,000-man army of French and English mercenaries, who were joined by knights at de Coucy's invitation. The army marched across France to Alsace, devastated areas while moving south to Basel, crossed the Jura Mountains, and entered the lower Aargau in November 1375; the mercenaries wore heavy cloaks with pointed hoods (called *Güglers* in Swiss-German, hence their nickname and the war's name). Leopold, comfortably ensconced at Breisach to the north, refused to fight; instead, he earned the undying hatred of the Swiss by ordering a systematic destruction of Aargau, leaving de Coucy's troops no villages, no people, no booty, and, most important, no food. The Güglers' army mistakenly divided into thirds to fight opposing citizen armies of the small Swiss Confederation, already experienced in resisting Austrian aggression. The Bernese, coming to the aid of the Swiss, overwhelmed the Güglers at Fraubrunnen (December 26, 1375), and the latter were forced in the spring of 1376 to battle their way westward across the Jura into France. See AUSTRO-SWISS WAR OF 1385–88.

Guinea-Bissauan War of Independence   (1962–74) In 1956, Amilcar Cabral (1921–73) founded the African Party for the Independence of Guinea and Cape Verde (PAIGC), which tried unsuccessfully through negotiations to gain independence for Portuguese Guinea (Guinea-Bissau) and the Cape Verde Islands, two Portuguese overseas provinces. The PAIGC prepared for an armed struggle by gaining the solid support of the Guinean villagers on the West African mainland. In late 1962, small guerrilla bands began attacking Portuguese army posts and police stations, and many areas were soon cleared of foreigners. Each band established a base in the forest from which it staged its operations. The Portuguese retaliated by bringing warplanes and more troops from Lisbon; guerrilla bases were subsequently bombed and raided. African tribalism and a widespread belief in witchcraft threatened the unity of the guerrillas until Cabral called a council of his commanders and explained that the liberation movement would fail unless its soldiers treated the people justly and forsook witchcraft; the PAIGC

was, Cabral said, "a dual revolution" against colonialism and old, outmoded beliefs. By 1973, the PAIGC had obtained control of two-thirds of Portuguese Guinea; it proclaimed independence and renamed the province the Republic of Guinea-Bissau. Portugal refused recognition, but a military coup in Lisbon (1974) installed a new national government that granted independence to Guinea-Bissau later that year; Luis de Almeida Cabral (b 1931–) became president, his brother Amilcar having been assassinated in early 1973. Under a separate agreement with Portugal, the Cape Verde Islands became an independent republic in 1975. See also ANGOLAN WAR OF INDEPENDENCE; MOZAMBICAN WAR OF INDEPENDENCE.

Gunpowder Plot (1605) The underground wars of Catholic countries to overthrow England (usually prompted by Spain) engendered a homemade English conspiracy: a plan to blow up Parliament and kill King James I (1566–1625) on November 5, 1605 (the day set for the king to open Parliament). This supposedly would start a great uprising of English Catholics that would lead to the establishment of a reformed government free of the severe penalties against Roman Catholicism. The conspirators, from the Catholic West Midlands, filled a cellar under the House of Lords with 36 barrels of gunpowder guarded by one Guy Fawkes (1570–1606). The plot was discovered through a mysterious letter sent to a lord, who was urged not to attend Parliament's opening so as to avoid "a terrible blow." Fawkes was arrested while entering the cellar and, under torture, revealed the names of fellow conspirators, who were seized. Fawkes was hanged, the others were executed or imprisoned, and most English, remembering Mary, Queen of Scots (1542–87) and the SPANISH ARMADA, sighed with relief. Harsher laws were laid down against English Catholics as a result of the plot.

Gun War, Basuto (1880–81) Though the Basuto chiefs of Sotho in southern Africa had requested British protection against the Boers (see BASUTO WAR), they were not prepared to surrender their own tribal authority. So when the British, alarmed at the spread of weaponry, ordered that the Basutos be disarmed, a rebellion ensued. Casualties were heavy, and by late 1881, an impasse had clearly been reached. Both sides agreed to accept the arbitration of Sir Hercules Robinson (1824–97), British high commissioner, who decreed that the Basutos must register and license their guns and pay compensation. But since government troops had been withdrawn, this face-saving gesture toward the Cape Colony was unenforceable.

Gupta Dynasty, Conquests of the   (A.D. 320–467) The last of India's political units established by the foreign invaders after the collapse of the Mauryan Empire (see MAURYAN EMPIRE, CONQUESTS OF THE) was ruled by a Kushan dynasty founded by Asiatic nomads about A.D. 40. It began to reveal weaknesses in the third century and was very weak when Chandragupta I (d. 335) inherited the kingdom of Magadha (c. 320) upon his marriage to a Licchavi princess. Although unrelated to his earlier namesake, he imitated him by first enlarging his kingdom westward, reaching Allahabad by the time of his death. His son Samudragupta (c. 330–80) extended the kingdom east to Assam and west to the borders of the Punjab, gaining homage from 12 kingdoms in the Deccan plateau area and battling the Shakas (Scythians) in their capital at Ujjain (in modern Madhya Pradesh state). His son Chandragupta II (fl. c. 380–414) caused the Gupta dynasty's holdings to be further enlarged by conquering the rest of the Shaka kingdom (modern Bombay state). From capitals at Pataliputra (Patna) and Ujjain, the Gupta dynasty now controlled all of northern India except the northwestern corner containing passes through which invaders always came. This shortcoming ultimately destroyed the kingdom, which because of its prosperity and high culture is considered by most historians as the embodiment of India's classical age. Successful invasions by White Huns weakened the kingdom so thoroughly that with the death of the last Gupta ruler (c. 467) only a Bengal

remnant of its power existed, and then only until 499. Both northern and southern India were reduced to their pre-Mauryan condition of small, constantly contentious states warring for dominance over trade routes and ports—in the north, the Indus and Ganges river valleys; in the south, the coastal regions below the Tropic of Cancer. See also CHALUKYA DYNASTY, WARS OF THE; CHALUKYAN WAR AGAINST HARSHA.

Gurkha War (1814–16) The Gurkhas, the ruling ethnic group in Nepal who were renowned for their military valor, made the British East India Company nervous by annexing villages and taking revenues in territories from Darjeeling to Simla in India. The company sent an ultimatum to Katmandu, Nepal's capital; the Gurkhas rejected it, and subsequently the British entered Nepal, setting up police forts. The Gurkhas retaliated with ambushes against the British troops. In order to conquer Nepal, the British next sent four divisions by four separate mountain routes and eventually forced the Gurkhas to surrender, with honor, in 1815. A brief truce followed, but disputes over treaty provisions caused renewed fighting. In 1816, the British under Sir David Ochterlony (1758–1825) won a decisive victory in the Katmandu Valley. Nepal lost control of some areas, including Sikkim and Simla; later Gurkha regiments in the British and Indian armies became militarily famous.

Guyanan Rebellion of 1969   Invading rebel bands from Brazil seized the towns of Lethem and Annai in southwestern Guyana near the border (January 2, 1969), but in a few days they were driven out by Guyanan army forces. Several policemen and some others lost their lives. The rebel invasion had been apparently sponsored by Americans who owned large cattle ranches in the region and hoped to establish a separate state there that they could control without interference from Guyana's repressive government under Prime Minister Linden Forbes Burnham (1923–85).

H

Haitian Civil War of 1806–20 In 1804, Jean-Jacques Dessalines (1758–1806) assumed the title Emperor Jacques I of Haiti (see HAITIAN-FRENCH WAR OF 1801–3). While attempting to crush a mulatto insurrection, he was murdered in 1806; a civil war for control of the island of Hispaniola soon erupted between Henry Christophe (1767–1820) in the north and Alexandre Pétion (1770–1818) in the south. In the island's eastern part, Santo Domingo (the Dominican Republic), some French forces remained and were confronted with an uprising by Spanish colonists there in 1808. With British aid, the insurgents defeated the French, drove the invading Haitians out of Santo Domingo, and declared their allegiance to Spain by the Pact of Bondilla in 1808. In the west, Christophe proclaimed himself king of all Haiti as Henri I in 1811, while continuing to battle Pétion and his mulatto rebels, and built a great palace, Sans Souci, and a fortress in the hills south of Cap-Haïtien. Pétion established a republic in southern Haiti and served as its elected president until his death in 1818. His successor, Jean Pierre Boyer (1776–1850), a mulatto, fought successfully against Christophe until the latter's suicide in 1820; he then brought all of Haiti under his control, assuming the presidency. See also HAITIAN RECONQUEST OF SANTO DOMINGO.

Haitian Civil War of 1991 Two coup attempts in 1991 against newly elected Haitian president Jean-Bertrand Aristide (1953–) dimmed the promise of democracy in Haiti. On January 6, 1991, Roger Lafontant (d. 1991), former leader of the infamous Tontons Macoutes militia, and his collaborators stormed the presidential palace and forced the resignation of provisional president Ertha Pascal Trouillot (1943–). Lafontant, who wanted to prevent Aristide from taking office, declared himself provisional president. Next morning, loyalist forces recaptured the palace, set Trouillot free (her travel was later restricted) and imprisoned Lafontant and his men. Meanwhile, thousands swarmed the streets, burning barricades and blocking access to the airport. Lafontant's headquarters was destroyed and many of his known and suspected supporters hacked to death. Also gutted were the archbishop's residence and the region's oldest cathedral. At least 75 people were killed and 150 injured. On January 27, rumors that Lafontant (subsequently sentenced to life imprisonment) had escaped from prison led to violent protests, including attacks on two police stations, and 17 deaths in Port-au-Prince, the capital. Aristide's bold and populist reforms rankled the neo-Duvalierists—those sympathetic to the recently ousted dictatorial regime of the Duvalier family—especially the powerful military whose members launched a coup d'état on September 29, 1991. Next day, Raoul Cédras (1949–) and his troops captured Aristide (later granted safe passage to Venezuela), established a three-man ruling junta and assumed control of the radio and television. The military violently suppressed all street protests and enforced strict curfews. Within weeks of the coup, about 500 people had been killed in armed confrontations. The United States and the European Community suspended economic aid to Haiti, while the Organization of American States (OAS) tried to isolate the ruling junta and demanded Aristide's return to power. Aristide urged the UN Security Council to help restore democracy. However, U.S. support for him was waning amid reports of alleged human rights violations during his tenure. Many countries, including the U.S., imposed a trade embargo but it was unevenly enforced. As economic hardships and worsening human rights abuses at home forced thousands of Haitians to seek refuge in neighboring countries, the OAS and the UN mediated several agreements to restore democracy to Haiti. Only the Governor's Island Accord in New York of July 3, 1993, negotiated directly between Aristide and Cédras for the former's return to power, had any hope of succeeding. However, its implementation was derailed by growing right-wing violence and repression in Haiti and different U.S. policies. Responding to pressure, the U.S. government agreed (under the UN Security Council's Resolution 940) to lead an international military team to end the crisis in Haiti. Finally Haitian military leaders stepped down, and on October 15, 1994, Aristide finally returned home to resume office.

Haitian-French War of 1801–3 As governor-general of the island of Hispaniola, François Dominique Toussaint Louverture (1743–1803) restored order and reorganized the government with a new constitution in 1801 (see TOUSSAINT LOUVERTURE, REVOLT OF). Planning to regain control of the island and to reinstitute slavery there, the French leader Napoleon Bonaparte (1769–1821) sent his brother-in-law Charles Victor Leclerc (1772–1802) with about 25,000 French troops to Hispaniola. When they landed at Cap-Français (Cap-Haïtien, Haiti) on February 5, 1802, they found the city set ablaze by retreating black troops under the leadership of Henry Christophe

(1767–1820). The French met savage resistance inland and were wasted by disease, especially yellow fever. In late March 1802, Leclerc's forces defeated some 1,200 blacks under Jean-Jacques Dessalines (1758–1806) at Crête-à-Pierrot; soon after, Dessalines, Christophe, and most of their followers defected to Leclerc. Offered amnesty, Toussaint laid down his arms but was treacherously seized and sent as a prisoner to France, where he died about a year later on April 7, 1803. For a while, Christophe and Dessalines served the French in attempting to put down the black and mulatto guerrillas who continued to fight, but they deserted upon learning that Napoleon intended to reestablish slavery on the island. The French troops, many sick with yellow fever, were unable to receive reinforcements from France because of a British blockade of French ports (see NAPOLEONIC WARS) and were forced to capitulate to the black leaders and evacuate Hispaniola in November 1803. In early 1804, Dessalines proclaimed Haiti an independent republic with himself as head. See also HAITIAN CIVIL WAR OF 1806–20.

Haitian Reconquest of Santo Domingo (1822) The restoration of the reactionary king Ferdinand VII (1784–1833) to the Spanish throne in 1814 led to discontent among the once loyal people of Santo Domingo (the Dominican Republic), a Spanish colony formerly ceded to France and conquerd by the Haitians (see TOUSSAINT LOUVERTURE, REVOLT OF). On November 30, 1821, Santo Domingo declared its independence from Spain, assumed the name Spanish Haiti, and sent an envoy to the South American liberator Simon Bolívar (1783–1830) seeking to unite with Greater Colombia (see COLOMBIAN WAR OF INDEPENDENCE). Before the message reached Bolívar, Jean-Pierre Boyer (1776–1850), president of Haiti, declared that Santo Domingo had submitted to the laws of Haiti, led his army into the colony and drove out the Spaniards, and brought the entire island of Hispaniola (Haiti and the Dominican Republic) under his control. See also HAITIAN CIVIL WAR OF 1806–20; SANTO DOMINGO, REVOLUTION IN.

Haitian Revolt of 1858–59 Haiti went through a long period of oppression and instability following the presidency of Jean-Pierre Boyer (1776–1850), whose corrupt and financially inept regime was overthrown in 1843. Four years later Faustin Élie Soulouque (1785–1867), a former black slave, became Haiti's president, and in 1849, he proclaimed himself emperor as Faustin I. An extremely repressive ruler, with a lavish court, he failed several times to conquer the neighboring Dominican Republic and finally was deposed in a bloody revolt (1858–59), mainly by mulattoes who had once backed him but whom he had turned against. Soulouque fled into exile, and one of his generals, Nicholas Fabre Geffrard (1806–79), who led the revolt, declared a republic, became president, and tried to institute needed reforms with little success. Counterrevolutionaries constantly disrupted his government, which was recognized by the United States in 1862. After Geffrard was ousted and exiled in 1867, disorder and repression returned to the country, which experienced a series of insurrections (1870, 1874, 1876, and 1888–89) before some law and order was restored; intense hostility between blacks and mulattoes still remained a problem. Likewise, in the Dominican Republic, a succession of strongmen ruled harshly during the last half of the 19th century, crushed frequent uprisings, and repelled Haitian invasions.

Haitian Revolt of 1915 In early 1915, Vilbrun Guillaume Sam (d. 1915) and his followers seized control of the government of Haiti, a country then in disarray because of revolutionaries. Sam held the presidency until a hostile Haitian mob assassinated him on July 28, 1915. With the country in anarchy, U.S. Marines who had recently landed at the Haitian capital of Port-au-Prince carried out the orders of U.S. president Woodrow Wilson (1856–1924), protecting foreigners and foreign property and supervising the election of a new president. Philippe Sudre Dartiguenave (1863–after 1922) became president and enforced a treaty under which Haiti was proclaimed (September 16, 1915) a political and economic protectorate of the United States, with customs turned over to American officials and a Haitian gendarmerie (police corps) under American control.

Haitian Revolt of 1918–19 In 1918, in a plebiscite under U.S. military supervision, a new constitution was adopted by the questionable, lopsided vote of 98,225 to 768 and went into effect in Haiti, which had been constituted in 1915 as a political and financial American protectorate for 10 years (see HAITIAN REVOLT OF 1915). No elections for office were held; Philippe Sudre Dartiguenave (1863–after 1922) remained in the Haitian presidency, while American officers ran the government. The country's gendarmerie (police corps) revived the *corvée* (labor draft) to put rural Haitians to work. In late 1918, in the area around Hinche, Haitians led by Charlemagne Péralte (d. 1919) and Benoît Batraville (d. 1919) revolted against the *corvée* and the U.S. presence in Haiti. The rebels, numbering between 20,000 and 40,000, were poorly armed but felt invincible because of their belief that Vodun (Voodoo) potions would protect them. Causing much terror, they finally attacked the Haitian capital of Port-au-Prince, where the gendarmerie, reinforced by U.S. Marines and air support, crushed them; Péralte and Batraville were shot to death. Peace was restored in Haiti under American occupation, which was later extended until 1934.

Halidon Hill, Battle of (1333) When the earls of Douglas and Moray forced the newly crowned Edward Balliol, king of Scotland, over the English border (see DUPPLIN MOOR, BATTLE OF), King Edward III (1312–77) of England sent troops, which met the Scots at Halidon Hill near Berwick-upon-Tweed in northeast England on July 19, 1333. Using the strategy successful at Bannockburn in 1314, the Scots charged down a hill toward the English, with a marsh between them. The Scots, however, unwisely entered the marsh, became enmired, and were slaughtered by English longbows. Ten-year-old King David II (1324–71) of Scotland was sent to France, and his regent ruled Scotland north of the

Forth. To the south, Edward Balliol, dependent on English forces, was "restored" to the second Scottish throne.

Hannibalic War   See PUNIC WAR, SECOND.

Hannibal's Destruction of Himera   (409 B.C.) Carthage never forgot its defeat at Himera on the north coast of Sicily during the CARTHAGINIAN-SYRACUSAN WAR. Hamilcar's death there in 480 was recalled by his grandson, an early Hannibal (d. 406). He gathered a large invasion force and again laid siege to Himera. This time, the opposition of Syracuse was deficient. Hannibal and the Carthaginians entered the city-state, took booty, and departed only after permanently reducing it to ruins.

Hannibal's Sacking of Acragas   (406 B.C.) Carthaginian forces returned to Sicily to begin a sequel to HANNIBAL'S DESTRUCTION OF HIMERA in 409, this time led not only by Hannibal (d. 406), Hamilcar's grandson, but also by his illustrious grandnephew Himilco (d. 397). Their actions involved laying siege to the south coastal settlement of Acragas (Agrigento). During this siege, the early Hannibal died, but Himilco gained renown by forcing the city to capitulate. His troops ravaged it severely. Further attacks on coastal cities followed during HIMILCO'S WAR.

Hapsburg-Bohemian War of 1274–78   Holy Roman Emperor Rudolf I of Hapsburg (1218–91) claimed Austrian territory as his imperial right, but he was opposed by Bohemia's King Ottokar II "the Great" (1230?–78), who had annexed Austria, Styria, and Carniola. In 1274, the Diet of Regensburg nullified Ottokar's acquisitions, and Rudolf, supported by some Bohemian nobles challenging their king, led forces against Ottokar. After adding Bavarian knights to his forces, Rudolf invested Vienna, which Ottokar had fortified. Ottokar's troops proved disloyal and deserted. The Bavarian knights seized the provision center of

Klosterneuberg near Vienna, and its ample supplies sustained Rudolf's forces during the siege. Cut off from Bohemian help, the Viennese surrendered and recognized Rudolf as their king. Ottokar, whose troops had been beaten several times, soon capitulated and relinquished all his acquired lands, except Bohemia and Moravia (1275). Embarrassed by his losses and by the recognition of Rudolf's suzerainty over Bohemia and Moravia, Ottokar assembled an army in Prague and, spurning Rudolf's attempt to negotiate, marched on Vienna. Rudolf's forces, reinforced by Alsatian and Swabian troops, engaged and defeated Ottokar's army at the Battle of Marchfeld on August 26, 1278; Ottokar was slain. Later, Bohemia, under Ottokar's successor, King Wenceslaus II (1271–1305), recovered its strength and status, and Rudolf cemented his conquests through strategic marriage contracts for his children.

Hapsburg Brothers' "War"   (1606–12) Matthias (1557–1619), Hapsburg governor of Austria, had been assigned by a Hapsburg family conference (1605) the powers of his psychotic brother, Holy Roman Emperor Rudolf II (1552–1612), over Hungary, chiefly to avoid war with the threatening Turks. Matthias reversed the Hapsburg policy of aiding the Counter-Reformation in Hungary by making concessions to its Protestants, thus weaning them away from dependence on the Turks. An ardent Roman Catholic, Rudolf attempted to interfere, and Matthias proclaimed himself head of the family in 1606. Rudolf remained emperor, but Matthias took control of Bohemia and Austria. Rudolf protested, for Matthias, who allied himself in 1608 with nobility from Hungary, Austria, and Moravia, failed to win the nobles of Bohemia, who backed Rudolf. A fraternal war was avoided by compromise until the paranoid Rudolf invited the archduke of Austria, his cousin and a Catholic bishop, to plunder from Austria to Prague, Bohemia. An army of the archduke's did just that in 1611. The Bohemian nobles changed sides; Matthias's allies then forced Rudolf to abdicate the Bohemian throne and retain only the title of emperor (1611), which Matthias acquired (with its powers) upon Rudolf's death the next year. See also THIRTY YEARS' WAR.

Hapsburg Dynastic War of 1439–57 The death in 1439 of Albert II (1397–1439), the first Hapsburg Holy Roman Emperor, created a relatively bloodless dynastic and family crisis for the House of Hapsburg. He had ruled Austria, Bohemia, and Hungary before becoming emperor, and his only heir was a posthumous son, Ladislas (1440–57). Albert's cousin, Frederick V (1415–93), duke of Inner Austria (Styria, Carinthia, and Carniola), became head of the Hapsburg family upon Albert's death. Coveting Ladislas's inheritance, he took control of the boy without legal designation as regent. But he was opposed by the Hungarian general John Hunyadi (1387–1456), the real power in Hungary, who wished to have possession of Ladislas to preserve his own authority. Hunyadi led Hungarian troops into Styria in 1446 and demanded Ladislas from Frederick, who turned him over to his arbitrator, a cardinal. Without Ladislas, Hunyadi was talked into a crusade against the Turks instead (see HUNGARIAN-TURKISH WAR OF 1444–56). Frederick soon faced insurrectionist Austrian nobles in 1451, who demanded Ladislas, but he successfully retained his illegal regency. Also in 1451 he settled Bohemian claims for the boy by naming George of Podebrad (1420–71) as Bohemian regent (and, thus, the ruler; later he became king of Bohemia). In 1452, he, now Holy Roman Emperor Frederick III, was surrounded in his capital at Wiener Neustadt, Austria, by 16,000 soldiers under Ulrich of Cilli (d. 1456), a cousin of Ladislas and power holder of Austria. Frederick surrendered Ladislas, who was taken to Vienna, where Ulrich fell from power in a coup in 1453 but retained and counseled Ladislas. Ladislas was crowned as Ladislas V in 1453 and asserted his majority in 1455, opposing both Hunyadi and Podebrad and ruling his Bohemian and Hungarian kingdoms briefly until his death, probably by poisoning, in 1457. For all his trouble, Frederick seems not to have benefited from his 13-year illegal regency.

Hapsburg-Valois War of 1547–59 After the death of King Francis I (1494–1547) of France, his son and successor, Henry II (1519–59), renewed the Valois (French dynasty) struggle against the Hapsburgs (house of Austria), particularly Holy Roman Emperor Charles V (1500–1558), who was also the king of Spain as Charles I (see ITALIAN WARS BETWEEN CHARLES V AND FRANCIS I). After the ANGLO-FRENCH WAR OF 1549–50, French forces invaded Tuscany but suffered defeat by an imperial army at the Battle of Marciano on August 2, 1553. French commander Blaise de Montluc (1501?–77) was boxed in at Siena, which had overthrown the Spanish for French rule, but was forced to surrender after a 15-month siege of the city by imperial forces under Cosimo de' Medici (1519–74), duke of Florence. Siena then reverted to Spanish control in 1555. French troops invaded southern Italy and established a stronghold in northern Naples, but they were forced to withdraw in 1557 (see ANGLO-FRENCH WAR OF 1557–60). The Treaty of Cateau-Cambrésis in 1559 ended the war; France relinquished all claims in Italy, except for the border region of Saluzzo; Savoy and Piedmont, save for Turin and a few towns, went to Emmanuel Philibert (1528–80), and the Two Sicilies and Milan went to King Philip II (1527–98) of Spain, leaving only Venice, Genoa, Lucca, and San Marino independent republics.

Harmar's Defeat (1790) General Josiah Harmar (1753–1813) was ordered by the governor of the Northwest Territory, Arthur St. Clair (1736?–1818), to lead a punitive expedition against the militant Indians along the Maumee River in present-day Ohio. On September 26, 1790, Harmar set out with about 1,100 militiamen, 320 of whom were regulars, the rest poorly trained and armed. A loose coalition of Indians under Chief Little Turtle (1752–1812) lured the troops deep into Indian territory and ambushed them. Harmar's counterattacks against the Indians near present-day Fort Wayne, Ind., proved disastrous, and he was forced to retreat. Harmar represented the clashes as victories in dispatches. Later Congress demanded an inquiry, which exonerated Harmar, who nevertheless resigned his commission. See also ST. CLAIR'S DEFEAT.

Harpers Ferry Raid   See BROWN'S RAID ON HARPERS FERRY.

Hawaiian Wars of 1782–1810   The Pacific archipelago now called Hawaii was divided into separate warring chiefdoms when Kamehameha I "the Great" (1758?–1819) and his cousin inherited (1782) the reign of the largest island (also called Hawaii). The two quarreled and waged a war in which Kamehameha's cousin was slain at the Battle of Mokuohai (1782). While battling rival chiefs at home, Kamehameha boldly set out to conquer the islands to the west (according to legend, he would unite the islands under his rule as a rebel, a killer of chiefs). In 1790, Maui fell to his invading warriors, who allegedly killed so many of the enemy near Wailuku that their corpses clogged a stream. A year later Kamehameha, who bought firearms from American and European traders, fought enemy chiefs from Oahu and Kauai, who reclaimed Maui and attacked Hawaii. He drove off the attackers, became sole ruler of Hawaii (1792), and three years later, in 1795, sent his war fleet (some 1,200 sailing canoes and 12,000 men) against the chiefs on Molokai, Lanai, and Oahu. Many Oahu defenders were trapped at the head of the Nuuanu Valley, where they were pushed or jumped in desperation to their deaths off Nuuanu Pali, a 1,200-foot cliff near present-day Honolulu. Only the islands of Kauai and Niihau remained outside Kamehameha's control. While attempting in 1800 to sail across the treacherous channel between Oahu and Kauai, his fleet was forced to turn back when a storm arose that capsized many canoes. In 1804, he was ready to try another crossing when an epidemic—probably cholera or plague—killed many of his warriors; he abandoned the plan and later began peaceful negotiations with Kauai's chief, who, in 1809, recognized Kamehameha as sovereign and, in return, was allowed to rule his island until his death. By 1810, all the Hawaiian islands were consolidated into Kamehameha's kingdom.

Heiji War (1159–60)   After Japanese emperor Shirakawa II (1127–92) abdicated in favor of his son (see HOGEN WAR), his supporters in the Taira and Minamoto families began to grow suspicious of each other. Jealousy and friction increased between the two families, and the Minamotos conspired to dispose of their rivals at the imperial court. The conspiracy was discovered, however, and fighting between the two clans broke out. The men on both sides were trained soldiers, and they fought stoutly and well. In 1190, the Tairas subdued their enemies, and their leader, Kiyomori (1118–81), assumed almost dictatorial power. The Minamoto leader, Yoshitomo (1123–60) and all his kinsmen at court were slain; only four young sons were spared. One of these, Yoritomo (1147–99), would 20 years later avenge his family's defeat (see GEMPEI WAR).

Henry of Bolingbroke's Revolt (1399)   In the later years of his reign, King Richard II (1367–1400) of England avenged himself against the Lancastrians, especially those who had controlled him early in his reign. When his uncle and former regent, John of Gaunt (1340–99) died, Richard seized his estates and refused to give the exiled Henry of Bolingbroke (1367–1413) the inheritance of his father's (John of Gaunt's) wealth. Bolingbroke invaded Yorkshire at Ravenspur in 1399, claiming he had come for his inheritance. Many flocked to his side, and when Richard returned from Ireland, Bolingbroke captured him, forced his abdication, imprisoned him at Pontefract Castle (where Richard was murdered or starved to death), and usurped the throne as Henry IV, the first Lancastrian king of England. See also HUNDRED YEARS' WAR.

Henry II's Campaigns in Wales (1157, 1165)   The chaotic reign of England's King Stephen (1097?–1154) gave the Welsh an opportunity to rise against the Norman marcher barons assigned to control them. Two Welsh leaders, Owain of Gwynnedd (d. 1170), prince of north Wales, and Rhys ap Gruffydd (1132?–97), leader of the south, won back lands taken earlier from them. Forces under England's King Henry II (1133–89) invaded Wales in 1157, and, although the English were defeated, managed to gain Owain's homage. English fortresses in Wales were rebuilt, but Owain incited a rebellion in 1165, causing Henry to invade again. Bad weather and short supplies ended the campaign indecisively, with the Welsh leaders generally driven back but retaining autonomy in their districts. Henry rebuilt new fortresses. See also ANGLO-FRENCH WAR OF 1159–89.

Henry VII's First Invasion of Brittany (1488) After becoming king of England (see ROSES, WARS OF THE), Henry VII (1457–1509) tried to safeguard the throne and its territories. He was aware that Brittany, a duchy in English hands, was in danger of falling to King Charles VIII (1470–98) of France. Popular feelings toward Brittany in England enabled Henry to obtain money to send three warships and a body of volunteers to the area; he also sent envoys to Paris and Brittany. The English force was, however, defeated by the French, and the Breton duke, Francis II (1435–88), promised to obey Charles, who wanted to marry his daughter, Anne of Brittany (1447–1514). England was compelled to renew a truce with France under the Treaty of Sablé. **Henry VII's Second Invasion of Brittany** (1489–92). Within two weeks of the treaty, Francis II was dead, and Charles claimed both Brittany and his daughter, Anne. Stalling for time, Henry supported a Breton regency; he offered to be mediator, promised troops to the Bretons, and made an alliance with Spain under which Catherine of Aragon (1485–1536) would marry his son Arthur (d. 1502). Then he sent troops. However, Anne of Brittany yielded to Charles, whom she agreed to marry, and Spain made a secret alliance with France (see "MAD WAR"). Henry then sailed to France (1490), laid siege to Boulogne (1491), accepted a peace offer of 745,000 gold crowns and a pension from the French at the Treaty of Etaples (1492), and abandoned the war. Brittany was now absorbed into France.

Himilco's War (405 B.C.) Carthaginian forces under Himilco (d. 396) proposed to duplicate the success of HANNIBAL'S SACKING OF ACRAGAS when they invaded the southern coast of Sicily, opposing the forces of Dionysius I (c. 430–367), tyrant of Syracuse. Syracuse lost the cities of Gela and Camarina (Santa Croceo). For the first time in its struggles against the Carthaginians, Syracuse was forced to enter into a treaty. It acceded to Carthaginian terms, allowing it control of half of Sicily, a sovereignty that lasted only until the DIONYSIUS WARS of less than a decade later.

Hittite Conquest of Anatolia (c. 1700–c. 1325 B.C.) The Hittites, an ancient Indo-European people, appeared in Anatolia (Turkey) about 2000 B.C. By 1340, they were one of the dominant powers in the Near East, but after 1190 they had ceased to be of major political and military importance, for their empire was the victim of migrating "Sea People" and the ever-expanding Assyrian Empire. By 710, they had entirely disappeared politically. Between about 1700 and 1325, however, the Hittites had two major periods of greatness. From a capital in central Anatolia, Hattusa (Bogazköy), an apparently eponymous King Hattusilis (fl. c. 1650–c. 1620) and his descendants led troops to so many victories that, by the time of the collapse of the Hittite Old Kingdom (d. 1500), the capital was situated on the northern fringe of the territory they controlled. Hattusilis ventured south to the plains of northern Syria near Antioch and southwest in Anatolia through Cilicia, acquiring as enemies the Hurrians of Mitanni and the Syrians of Aleppo. Cilicia came under Mitanni control, was lost, then reacquired, with help from Aleppo. Hattusilis was wounded enough in battle to return home to ail and die. Three incompetent sons of his ruled badly, but a grandson, Mursilis (c. 1620–1590), marched and conquered Aleppo, overcame Mitanni (c. 1595), and destroyed the Amorite capital at Babylon (c. 1590). He was murdered, and a period of weakness (the Middle Kingdom, c. 1500–c. 1400) saw the resurgent Mitanni establish the kingdom of Hanigabat in northern Syria (see HITTITE-HURRIAN WARS). Around 1400, a new king, Suppiluliumas (c. 1375–c. 1335), established the New Kingdom (c. 1400–c. 1190); he settled accounts with Mitanni about 1370 and went on to complete his eastward aggression by seizing the Mitanni city of Carchemish on the Euphrates (1340) and by setting up a buffer state between the Hittite and Assyrian Empires. Peace was brief. About 1325, allied Mitanni and Assyrian forces conquered the area; the Hittites again declined, fighting the Egyptians (see KADESH, BATTLE OF) and vainly opposing migrants into Anatolia and the powerful Assyrians (see ASSYRIAN-HURRIAN WARS). See also HURRIAN CONQUESTS.

Hittite-Hurrian Wars (c. 1620–c. 1325 B.C.) The Hurrian people were the chief rivals of the Hittites for control of Anatolia (Turkey) for about 300 years during the second millennium. About 1620, while the Hittites were fighting with the kingdom of Arzawa in the southwest, they left the Anatolian south and southeast unprotected, and the maturing Hurrian kingdom of Mitanni took control of these areas. The Hittite warriors pushed the Hurrians back for a brief time, only to face them in a struggle for the city of Aleppo (c. 1600), which ended in a Mitanni defeat about five years later. The Hittite leader was later murdered; nearly destroyed internally by succession problems, the Hittites lost possession of Cilicia to the Hurrians of Mitanni, who established the subkingdom of Kizzuwada (c. 1590). To cut the Hittites off from northern Syria, the Mitannis set up a southeastern kingdom called Hanigabat, prompting war over Syria with a rejuvenated Egypt about 1470 (see MEGIDDO, FIRST BATTLE OF). About 1400, the Hittite Empire (Old Kingdom, c. 1400–c. 1200) revived under a king named Suppiluliumas (c. 1375–c. 1335), who decided to end the Hurrian problem by invading Syria. He took a new invasion route by marching from the eastern Euphrates Valley. His action surprised the Mitannis, who resisted weakly and lost territory north of Damascus and all of what is now Lebanon (c. 1370) because their Egyptian allies offered no help. The remnants of the Mitanni kingdom then allied with Assyria, another rival of the Hittites. The forceful Hittites seized the

Mitanni city of Carchemish on the Euphrates (c. 1340), set up a buffer state between themselves and the Assyrians, using the former Mitanni provincial capital of Wassukani as their base, and lost the area about 1325 to the Mitanni-Assyrian alliance. The Hurrian subkingdom of Hanigabat was restored. The Assyrians, however, were swallowing up all of Anatolia, and both the Hittites and the Hurrians were soon to be of minor importance politically and martially. See also ASSYRIAN-HURRIAN WARS.

Hogen War (1156) For almost a century it had been the custom of Japanese emperors to abdicate in favor of a young son, to retire to a monastery, and from there to continue to rule and direct affairs at court. One such cloistered emperor was Toba (d. 1156), who in 1141 forced his son Sutoku (1119–64) to abdicate and replaced him with a second son, who died in 1155. Toba replaced him with a third son, Shirakawa II (1127–92). At Toba's death in 1156, Sutoku decided to leave the monastery and resume his place on the throne. The large imperial family was split asunder with some favoring Shirakawa and others favoring Sutoku. Both factions turned to the powerful Taira and Minamoto families for help. A brief but bitter armed struggle ensued in which Shirakawa and his followers were victorious. Sutoku was driven into exile, and his supporters were killed. Two years later Shirakawa abdicated in favor of his son and tried to continue the practice of actually ruling from a monastery, but it no longer worked, for the real power had passed into the hands of the military men who had triumphed in the war of insurrection. See also HEIJI WAR.

Holy League, War of the (1510–14) French support for Alfonso I (1486–1534) of Este against papal control led Pope Julius II (1443–1513) to form a Holy League of Italian states (including Venice, a recent papal enemy [see LEAGUE OF CAMBRAI, WAR OF THE], Swiss cantons, Spain and England) to evict France from Italy. By May 1512, the French had been driven out of Milan and other cities. After a

Swiss-Italian force won a resounding victory over the French at the Battle of Novara on June 6, 1513, the French withdrew from Italy and made separate peace agreements with the Swiss and their allies. When Pope Julius died, the Holy League soon came to an end. The Swiss, who had helped restore Massimiliano Sforza (1491–1530) as ruler of the Milanese duchy, had also taken advantage of the chaos caused by the war in Lombardy, northern Italy, and had seized Locarno, Lugano, and Ossola. In 1515, the new French king, Francis I (1494–1547), invaded Lombardy and routed the Swiss at the Battle of Marignano on September 13–14, 1515, thereby regaining Milan. In a peace treaty with the new pope, Leo X (1475–1521), Francis also gained Parma and Piacenza. The Venetians, now French allies, took Bergamo, Peschiera, and Brescia and besieged Verona in 1515–16. Peace and alliances were made by the French and Swiss, who retained most of the Alpine passes, with the French holding rights to enlist Swiss mercenaries.

Holy Roman Empire–Papacy War of 1081–84

Although he had lost an important battle in 1080 to the Papal (Guelph) Party (see GERMAN CIVIL WAR OF 1077–1106), the recently excommunicated and deposed German king, Henry IV (1050–1106), continued his long struggle with Pope Gregory VII (1020?–85) by invading Italy and establishing a long siege of Rome in 1081. The city held out against Henry's soldiers, but the Vatican area and St. Peter's fell in 1083. Bribes gained the surrender of the Romans in 1084, and Henry entered the city triumphantly. With Gregory taking refuge in the castle of St. Angelo, Henry installed the antipope Clement III (1030?–1100) in the Vatican and in return was crowned Holy Roman Emperor. But Norman aid requested in 1083 by Gregory arrived, led by Robert Guiscard (1015?–85), ruler of Apulia and Calabria. The Normans attacked Rome with so great a force that Henry's troops gave no resistance and fled to Germany. The city was brutally, if unintentionally, plundered; Gregory was rescued and, virtually a prisoner, was escorted by the Normans to Salerno, where he grew ill and died in 1085. At a very high

cost, the papacy had been vindicated; lay investiture ceased within a generation, and the authority of the Holy Roman Empire over ecclesiastics was greatly diminished.

Holy Roman Empire–Papacy War of 1228–41

The struggle for domination between the Holy Roman Empire and the papacy, begun with the GERMAN CIVIL WAR OF 1077–1106, continued for centuries, almost as a traditional conflict. Frederick II (1194–1250), made emperor during the GERMAN CIVIL WAR OF 1197–1214 and crowned in 1220 after being reared under papal auspices since 1198, was expected to be docile and obedient. Instead, he proved so obstinate a champion of the rights of lay rulers that he angered three popes. Pope Honorius III (d. 1227) had him take the Cross to regain Jerusalem, but conditions in Sicily, of which Frederick was king, demanded his attentions. His sending of troops failed to please Honorius, who had him marry the heiress to the kingdom of Jerusalem in 1225 and forced him to sail to the Holy Land in 1227 (see CRUSADE, SIXTH). Frederick's early return home because of illness caused his excommunication by Gregory IX (1143?–1241), a new pope who proved to be more formidable than his earlier namesake. And this Gregory was more devious: he forced Frederick to sail again to the Holy Land in 1228 and then fomented rebellions in Frederick's territories while the emperor recovered Jerusalem (1228–29), became its king, and returned home. The pope, however, excommunicated him again, for the disobedient Frederick stubbornly fought to regain Sicily, which the papacy had taken control of in his absence. The Peace of San Germano in 1230 allowed a period of ill-natured cooperation. Frederick, however, continued his efforts to unite Italy, facing Lombard opposition (in part, cultivated by Gregory) in 1231; taking time out to discipline his son, the king of Germany, in 1235; and to call a general Diet of the Empire at Piacenza in 1236 to force Italian cooperation. He then annexed church lands, prompting another excommunication and a renewal of the war. Victory alternated between the Holy Roman Empire and the papacy. In 1236 and

1237, Frederick's forces conquered the Veronese March, smashed Milan, and defeated the Lombard League's army at Cortenuova. In 1238, after unsuccessfully besieging Brescia, Frederick annexed papal territories. The pope, allied secretly with Genoa and Venice, excommunicated him again in 1239. An imperial siege of Milan failed, and Rome was attacked in 1240. Peace negotiations were underway until Gregory arbitrarily stopped them in 1241 and called for a General Council, whose delegates Frederick kept from assembling. Then the pope died, and both sides maneuvered until the start of the HOLY ROMAN EMPIRE–PAPACY WAR OF 1243–50.

Holy Roman Empire–Papacy War of 1243–50

The death of Pope Gregory IX (1143?–1241) provided a rancorous interlude between wars (see HOLY ROMAN EMPIRE–PAPACY WAR OF 1228–41). Both sides temporized. Holy Roman Emperor Frederick II (1194–1250) went to Sicily while the church elected a new pope, Celestine IV (d. 1241), who died of old age and sickness only 17 days after his election. Frederick's officials then subdued the remnant of the Papal States and planned a naval attack on Genoa and Venice, allies of Rome. Frederick himself vainly strove for the election of a lenient pontiff. The new pope, Innocent IV (d. 1254), proved wily and eventually outmaneuvered the emperor. Frederick had petitioned him for the lifting of his 1239 excommunication, and negotiations were proceeding when Innocent, who distrusted the emperor, reacted to the subduing of the Papal States by having his army besiege Viterbo, an independent Italian city, in 1243. Innocent next incited rebellion against Frederick in Lombardy, and in 1244, after entering Rome in full panoply, he forced a futile peace upon Frederick which would have destroyed his life's work had its stipulations been fulfilled. Frederick, instead, began to make demands contrary to the agreement, causing Innocent to flee, first to Genoa and then to Lyons. There, in 1245, an ecumenical council, successful despite Frederick's blocking of the Alpine passes to France, excommunicated Frederick again and deposed him on a triple charge: constant violation of the peace, sacrilege,

and suspicion of heresy. A new king of Germany was named in 1246. Papal-influenced rebellion developed in Sicily against the Holy Roman Empire; the Germans rose against the antiking. Meanwhile, Frederick's forces devastated Viterbo and attacked Piacenza in 1245, defeated a Guelph (papal) army bloodily at Parma in 1246, but were repulsed at Parma after a long siege in 1248. Frederick's losses in Italy were compounded by the loss of Tuscany (1249) and the capture of his son, the king of Sardinia. Later, in 1249, Frederick began to win again, overcoming another rebellion in Sicily and recapturing Parma. But his death in 1250 ended the war. An able man, Frederick died proclaiming that he was trying to reform the church by limiting it to its true (spiritual) sphere. A herald of the future, he prepared the way for the Reformation struggles to save the rights of lay rulers. See also CRUSADE, SEVENTH; MONGOL INVASION OF EUROPE.

Honduran Civil War of 1909–11

Manuel Bonilla (1849–1913), former president of Honduras, led his conservative supporters in revolt against liberal president Miguel R. Dávila (d. 1927), who had been placed in power by the Nicaraguan dictator-president José Santos Zelaya (1853–1919) after the HONDURAN-NICARAGUAN WAR OF 1907. The ensuing civil war was inconclusive, and on February 8, 1911, both sides agreed to an armistice and to the decision of the forthcoming elections. Bonilla was elected president on October 29, 1911. See NICARAGUAN CIVIL WAR OF 1909–12.

Honduran Guerrilla War of 1981–90

Many thousands of Salvadorans, Miskito Indians, and anti-Sandinista Nicaraguans took refuge in Honduras, which feared that the civil strife in the neighboring countries would spread across the border and help escalate leftist hostilities against the government (see NICARAGUAN CIVIL WAR OF 1982–90; SALVADORAN CIVIL WAR OF 1977–92). Cuban-trained marxist guerrillas attacked government targets and committed many acts of urban terrorism, such as shooting at the U.S. embassy in Tegucigalpa, the

Honduran capital, and seizing a Honduran airliner, to dramatize their cause. Police and military forces stepped up their effort to suppress the guerrilla rebels, whose growing insurgency caused the United States to increase its military aid to the government. Nicaraguan Democratic Force (FDN) rebels, based in Honduras, continued to make raids across the border into Nicaragua, heightening the tension between the two countries. In response, in 1986, Nicaraguan (Sandinista) forces crossed the border to crush FDN bases in Honduras. U.S. military helicopters ferried Honduran troops to battle the Nicaraguans at the border. In support of the anti-Sandinista rebels (*contras*), the U.S. dispatched (1988) about 3,200 combat troops to Honduras, where left-wing violence increased because of resentment over American military presence in the country. In 1990, hostilities largely ceased following the electoral defeat of the Sandinista regime in Nicaragua and the reduction of U.S. aid. Nonetheless, Honduran peasant organizations, seeking agrarian reforms, called for land seizures unless the government acted; landless peasants were attacked and killed (1991) while trying to farm unused countryside; officials promised to stop abuses.

Honduran-Nicaraguan War of 1907   José Santos Zelaya (1853–1919), who became president of Nicaragua after a successful liberal revolt in 1893, ruled the country as a virtual dictator and meddled in the affairs of other Central American countries, which he sought to unite by force under his leadership. In 1903, the Honduran conservative leader Manuel Bonilla (1849–1913) toppled the liberal government of Honduras, which Zelaya had supported, and became the country's president. Honduran rebels attempted in 1906 to overthrow Bonilla, receiving assistance from Zelaya. After Honduran government troops invaded Nicaragua in pursuit of rebels, Zelaya demanded reparations for war damages, but Honduras refused to give any. Nicaraguan forces then invaded Honduran territory and, on March 18, 1907, fought and won the Battle of Namasigue, which marked the first time machine guns were used in war in Central America. Teguci-

galpa, the Honduran capital, was occupied by Nicaraguans; Bonilla fled to the United States; and Zelaya named Miguel R. Davila (d. 1927) to head the new regime in Honduras. See also HONDURAN CIVIL WAR OF 1909–11.

Honduran-Salvadoran War of 1969   See SOCCER WAR.

"Hot Water War"   See FRIES REBELLION.

Huguenot Wars   See RELIGION, WARS OF.

Hukbalahap Rebellion (1946–54)   During the 1930s, a number of communist and socialist organizers were active in the rich agricultural areas of central Luzon in the Philippines, where landless peasants sought reforms. After the Philippines were occupied by the Japanese in 1942 (see WORLD WAR II IN THE PACIFIC), many Filipinos formed guerrilla bands called Hukbalahap (meaning "People's Anti-Japanese Army"), or Huks. Guided by their communist leaders, the Huks killed thousands of Japanese soldiers and Filipino collaborators. By 1945, they had gained control of most of the large estates in central Luzon and had set up a regional government that collected its own taxes and administered its own laws. After WORLD WAR II ended, elections were held in April 1946 for the new Philippine government that would come into being on July 4 that year when the Philippines gained its independence from the United States. The Huks took part in the elections, and one of their candidates won a seat in the Philippine Congress. However, he was summarily dismissed. The Huks then withdrew to their jungle hideouts in anger and began a rebellion against the central government. Many sympathizers joined their ranks, and government troops were unable to dislodge them. By 1950, the Huks felt strong enough to launch an attack on Manila, the Philippines' capital. As they were about to do so, their secret headquarters in the capital was raided, and all their political leaders in the city were arrested, so the attack was called off. About the same time the United States began sending large quantities of arms and other material to the Philippine government army, which made it more effective. With the election of Ramon Magsaysay (1907–57) to the presidency in 1953 and his subsequent reforms, popular support of the Huks waned. In 1954, the Huks' leader surrendered, and the long rebellion ended.

Hundred Days' War (1815)   Napoleon (1769–1821) escaped from Elba (see NAPOLEONIC WARS), landed near Cannes and was joined by Michel Ney (1769–1815) and a large French army. He marched to Paris, where he resumed power, driving King Louis XVIII (1755–1824) from the throne and beginning his rule of a "Hundred Days." Austria, Britain, Russia, and Prussia formed an alliance against Napoleon and planned to invade France. Taking the offensive, Napoleon, at the head of a 125,000-man army, marched north into Belgium, planning to crush the nearest allied armies. He seized Charleroi and won a victory over the Prussians under Gebhard von Blücher (1749–1819) at Ligny on June 16, 1815. That same day, French forces under Ney suffered defeat by the British under Sir Arthur Wellesley, Lord Wellington (1769–1852), at Quatre-Bas nearby but managed to prevent Wellington's forces from aiding Blücher's against Napoleon. At Waterloo on June 18, 1815, Napoleon attacked Wellington, whose forces, aided by Blücher's Prussians, routed the French. The allies then marched without opposition to Paris, forced Napoleon to abdicate, and shipped Napoleon as a prisoner of war to St. Helena in the South Atlantic, where he remained the rest of his life. See also NAPOLEON'S INVASION OF RUSSIA.

Hundred Years' War (1337–1457) King Edward III (1312–77) of England assumed the title "King of France" in 1337, continuing a dynastic controversy originating in the NORMAN CONQUEST of 1066. Attacking to punish the failure of King Philip VI (1293–1350) of France to return Guienne, Edward was also avenging French interference in his Scot-

tish campaign (see DUPPLIN MOOR, BATTLE OF), replying to his feudal lord's assertions of authority in English continental territories, and forwarding his plan to control Flanders. The war occurred in four phases, the first from 1337 to 1360. Before his army invaded France through Flanders, Edward won (1340) a great naval victory at Sluys (see SLUYS, BATTLE OF). A campaign from Cherbourg in 1346 engendered a battle at Crécy (CRÉCY, BATTLE OF), where English longbows trounced French crossbows decisively. Taking Calais in 1347, Edward, upon Philip's death in 1350, concluded a truce, broken in 1356 when Edward, the Black Prince (1330–76), the king's eldest son, captured French king John II (1319–64) at Poitiers (see POITIERS, BATTLE OF). Wartime pressures caused French peasant rebellions in the JACQUERIE of 1358 and civil war in Brittany (see BRETON SUCCESSION, WAR OF THE). A 1360 treaty in Bretigny regained Aquitaine and ended Edward's claim to the throne. Phase two began in 1369 in the French king's clever reaction to the GASCON NOBLES' REVOLT of 1368; he confiscated Aquitaine and began a methodical reconquest, using the new strategy of avoiding formal battles and advocating local rebellions (see LIMOGES, MASSACRE AT). When John of Gaunt (1340–99) succeeded the Black Prince in 1371, England lost even more rapidly. Under him, Poitiers, Poitou, and La Rochelle surrendered in 1372 and a devastating naval battle occurred. In 1373, a new Gaunt campaign failed miserably and Aquitaine and Brittany were lost (see PEASANTS' REVOLT, ENGLISH). An English raid from Normandy to Bordeaux resumed the war in 1412 (phase three); King Henry V (1387–1422) of England separately took Harfleur and gained an astounding victory at Agincourt (see AGINCOURT, BATTLE OF). Normandy was recovered by England in 1419, and the French government signed the 1420 Treaty of Troyes acknowledging control of northern France by Henry and the duke of Burgundy. Dauphinists lost at Cravant in 1423; the French at Verneuil in 1424; and the English focused on Orléans in 1428 (see ORLÉANS, SIEGE OF), laying an unchivalric siege until the charismatic Jeanne d'Arc, or Joan of Arc (1412–31), relieved the city in 1429 and proceeded to Rheims to see the dauphin crowned Charles VII (1403–61). No peace was signed. A reformed French government and army began phase four in 1449. Normandy soon fell to the French, and Charles conquered Guienne in 1451. The English captured Bordeaux (see BORDEAUX, FALL OF) in 1452 and tried to reconquer Guienne but found the new French cannon to be more effective than longbows. Defeated at Castillon in 1453, the English withdrew to Bordeaux, which the more powerful French recovered. No peace was signed, but the war was essentially over. It had achieved little for the English except to bankrupt the government, discredit the Lancastrian dynasty, and prepare for civil war with the Yorkists (see ROSES, WARS OF THE). The war's effect on France was more positive, for the country became unified and its movement out of feudalism was well underway. See also EDWARD THE BLACK PRINCE, RAIDS OF; "GÜGLERS'" WAR; PORTUGUESE-CASTILIAN WARS OF 1369–88.

Hungarian-Bohemian Wars   See BOHEMIAN-HUNGARIAN WARS.

Hungarian Civil War of 1301–8 With the death of Hungary's King Andrew III "the Venetian" (d. 1301), the Árpád dynasty came to an end. There ensued a war of succession among aspirants to the Hungarian crown of St. Stephen, involving principally Bohemia's Wenceslaus III (1289–1306), Bavaria's Duke Otto III (d. 1312), and Naples's Charles Robert of Anjou (1288–1342), who was supported by his uncle, Germany's King Albert I (1250?–1308), and Pope Boniface VIII (1235?–1303). Albert demanded that Bohemia's King Wenceslaus II (1271–1305), father of Wenceslaus III, renounce any claim and remove his son from the Hungarian throne (the Hungarian Diet had elected Wenceslaus III in 1301). Upon Wenceslaus II's refusal, Albert launched an invasion of Bohemia in 1304. Wenceslaus II's forces repulsed Albert and were preparing to invade Austria when their king died. In 1305, Wenceslaus III, now king of Bohemia but unable to assert his authority in

Hungary because of dissension, gave up his throne to Duke Otto. Disorder and chaos ensued until Charles Robert was at last chosen by the Diet to be Hungary's King Charles I in 1308 (he was crowned two years later).

Hungarian Civil War of 1439–40 King Albert II (1397–1439), ruler of Hungary and Bohemia, died in 1439, leaving his wife pregnant, and immediately a crisis occurred concerning his successor to the Hungarian throne. The nobility chose Poland's King Ladislas III (1424–44), who was backed by the successful general and noble John Hunyadi (1387–1456) (see HUNGARIAN-TURKISH WAR OF 1437–38). Other Hungarians supported the Hapsburg party candidate Ladislas (1440–57), the just-born infant son of Albert, who was placed under the inept guardianship of Frederick III (1415–93), the German king and later the Holy Roman Emperor. A civil war ensued that secured Ladislas III as the Hungarian king, Uladislas I; Hunyadi's aid was instrumental to the king. Later, when Ladislas III perished at the Battle of Varna in 1444 (see HUNGARIAN-TURKISH WAR OF 1444–56), the young four-year-old son was chosen Ladislas V "Posthumous" of Hungary, with Hunyadi as regent governor.

Hungarian Civil War of 1526–29 With Turkish assistance, John Zápolya (1487–1540) of Transylvania was elected king of Ottoman Hungary after the HUNGARIAN-TURKISH WAR OF 1521–26. But Austria's Archduke Ferdinand (1503–64), later Holy Roman Emperor, claimed the throne as the brother-in-law of the preceding Hungarian king, Louis II (1506–26), and the Hungarian Diet approved him in 1527. Ferdinand's troops invaded Hungary, attacking and seizing Raab, Gran (Esztergom), and Buda. At the Battle of Tokay (1527), Zápolya and his forces were defeated; he then sought help from Ottoman sultan Süleyman I "the Magnificent" (1496–1566), who returned to Hungary with an army, recaptured Buda, and restored Zápolya to the throne in 1529. Zápolya accompanied the sultan during his campaign against Vienna (see AUSTRO-TURKISH WAR OF 1529–33).

Hungarian Civil War of 1540–47   By the secret Treaty of Nagyvárad during the AUSTRO-TURKISH WAR OF 1537–47, Hungary was partitioned, with Austria's Archduke Ferdinand (1503–64) receiving Croatia, Slavonia, and western sections and John Zápolya (1487–1540) retaining the royal Hungarian title (king) and the rest of the country, including the capital, Buda (the throne and his lands were to go to Ferdinand on his death). However, upon Zápolya's death, his infant son was chosen king as John II Sigismund (1540–71). Ferdinand claimed the kingdom and besieged Buda, causing Zápolya's widow to seek support for her son's claim. Finding an Austrian presence in Hungary unacceptable, Ottoman sultan Süleyman I "the Magnificent" (1496–1566) invaded, seized Buda and other cities, and instituted Turkish administration throughout the country. Fighting lasted until 1547, when Persian troubles (see TURKO-PERSIAN WAR OF 1526–55) finally compelled the sultan to sign a five-year truce, which again divided Hungary. Ferdinand kept his original lands (Austrian Hungary) but was forced to pay an annual tribute. John II Sigismund received Transylvania and neighboring areas, along with the title "prince," and the Ottoman Empire got southern and central Hungary. Holy Roman Emperor Charles V (1500–1558), the pope, France, and Venice were all signatories, accepting for the first time Turkish influence and power as factors in European politics. See also AUSTRO-TURKISH WAR OF 1551–53.

Hungarian Civil War of 1921   Former Austro-Hungarian emperor Charles I (1887–1922), in exile in Switzerland since early 1919 (see KUN'S RED TERROR), suddenly returned to Hungary to regain his Hungarian throne, calling on Nicholas Horthy de Nagybánya (1868–1957), regent and head of state, to relinquish his powers in March 1921. But opposition to Charles was so violent both in and out of the country that he departed; the monarchists'

question whether he was still legally Hungary's king remained unsettled. That same year, in October, Charles arrived at Ödenburg (Sopron), Hungary, and marched on Budapest with troops to recover the throne. Government forces repulsed them with gunfire and arrested Charles, who was exiled to Madeira. The Hungarian Diet then nullified all Austrian (Hapsburg) claims to the throne.

Hungarian-Czechoslovakian War of 1919   See KUN'S RED TERROR.

Hungarian Pagan Uprising of 1046   At his death, King Stephen I (later Saint Stephen) (975?–1038) had not finished Christianizing many pagans in his domain. Many had resisted; and even his ruling Árpád dynasty was not completely converted (Stephen had exiled his reluctant relatives and was forced to choose as his successor a distant relative, Peter Orseolo [1011–46], son of the doge of Venice). Peter, however, became the victim of court intrigue (1041) and fled to Holy Roman Emperor Henry III (1017–56) for refuge. With Henry's troops, Peter regained his throne in 1044, but many of his subjects hated him as a foreigner, as Henry's vassal, and as a bringer of foreign advisers. Even church officials despised him. In 1046, two of the exiled Árpáds came with Russian troops from Kiev, entered pagan Hungary, and immediately gained the support of all pagan and opposition factions. The invaders and this fanatic mob (which massacred a welcoming delegation of bishops and Hungarian nobles) marched toward Peter's palace; he fled, was captured, imprisoned, blinded, and died of his wounds. One Árpád, Andrew I (d. 1060), converted in Russia, became the Hungarian king (1047), but used the renascent paganism to his own ends, keeping it under a veneer of Christianity as he continued Hungary's resistance to the Holy Roman Empire.

Hungarian Revolt of 1956   Liberal elements in Hungary deeply resented Soviet control in the country. On October 23, 1956, students, workers, and others began demonstrating and rioting in Budapest against the Hungarian communist government, demanding free elections, economic reforms, withdrawal of Soviet troops, and reinstatement of former premier Imre Nagy (1896–1958), who had been critical of Soviet influence in Hungary and had been expelled from the Communist Party in early 1956. Most Hungarian soldiers joined the demonstrators, leaving the government helpless. The next day, October 24, Soviet tanks moved in to quell the uprising; Nagy was recalled as premier; and revolutionary councils immediately sprang up throughout the country in support of freedom. The Hungarian communist government was toppled (October 25), and a pro-Western, democratic regime was set up as revolutionaries took over public buildings and industrial plants and freed the imprisoned anticommunist leader Cardinal Jozsef Mindszenty (1892–1975). Soviet forces withdrew from Budapest at the end of October 1956, and Nagy renounced the Warsaw Pact (Soviet defense alliance with Hungary and other Eastern bloc countries) and asked the United Nations for international neutrality status for Hungary. On November 4, 1956, quietly assembled Soviet forces—some 200,000 troops and 2,500 tanks and armored vehicles—swept into Budapest and other Hungarian centers. Nagy appealed to the UN for aid without success, and Hungary's freedom fighters put up a valiant but unsuccessful resistance. Nagy fled (later he was seized by Soviet police), and János Kádár (1912–89) replaced him as premier, establishing an all-communist government. Though they kept the border open for the flight of about 150,000 Hungarians to the West, the rebels were completely crushed by the Soviets, who later legalized their military presence through signed agreements with Kádár (1957), thus providing the basis for continued communist control.

Hungarian Revolution of 1848–49 In a fiery speech before the Hungarian Diet on March 3, 1848, nationalist leader Louis Kossuth (1802–94) denounced the Austrian (Hapsburg) governmental system under Emperor Ferdinand (1793–1875), who was also king of Hungary, and demanded a democratic constitution as a prerequisite for the continuation of the monarchy (see AUSTRIAN REVOLUTION OF 1848–49). Hungarian peasants, workers, radical students, and especially the Magyar gentry demonstrated in support of Kossuth and self-government. The Diet's March Laws (1848), setting up an independent government at Budapest, were reluctantly accepted by the emperor. But the revolutionary nationalistic movement brought disunity; Croatian nobleman Joseph Jellacic (1801–59), an Austrian general, refused to accept the Diet's authority and sought autonomy for Croatia. Serbs, Slovaks, Bohemians, and Rumanians also craved autonomous governments. Ferdinand withdrew his initial support for Premier Louis Batthyány (1806?–49), head of Hungary's government, and backed Jellacic, making him commander in chief of the imperial forces operating against the Hungarians. Kossuth's call for resistance found many thousands of persons harassing the invading Austrians under Prince Alfred Windischgrätz (1787–1862). The Hungarian government was moved to Debrecen as cities fell to the invaders throughout the country in a multipronged attack, which culminated in the surrender of Budapest and the arrest of Batthyány and other Hungarian leaders on January 5, 1849. Hungarian troops under Arthur von Görgey (1818–1916) took refuge in the mountains north of Budapest, which Polish commander Henryk Dembinski (1791–1864) and his Hungarian army attempted to set free but were defeated by Windischgrätz's forces at the Battle of Kápolna on February 26–27, 1849. Austrian premier Felix Schwarzenburg (1800–1852) requested and received outside help from the Russians to quell the rebels in the empire. In Transylvania, Joseph Bem (1794–1850) and a small army, allied with Kossuth, miraculously held off superior Austrian forces until Russian reinforcements crushed them in late July 1849. Meanwhile, in the spring of 1849, Görgey's troops were victorious and forced Windischgrätz to retreat from Hungary, which had been proclaimed an independent republic on April 13, 1849, with Kossuth as "governor-president." But invading Russians and Austrians, in June–July 1849, drove Görgey to southeastern Hungary, where the ever disputatious Hungarian government took refuge.

Austrian troops led by Baron Julius von Haynau (1786–1853) thoroughly defeated Görgey's Hungarians at the Battle of Temesvár (Timişoara) on August 9, 1849. Kossuth then gave up leadership of the government to Görgey and fled with other leaders to the Ottoman Empire; two days later Görgey surrendered to the Russians. Haynau headed the unexpected, brutal Austrian revenge against the Hungarians; Batthyány and many Hungarian officers were executed; hundreds of civilians were hung or imprisoned. Austria reorganized the country under a German-speaking bureaucracy.

Hungarian Revolution of 1918   Increasingly agitated by defeats and food shortages during WORLD WAR I, Hungarian leftists and nationalists sought independence from Austrian (Hapsburg) rule, to split away from the Austro-Hungarian Empire. The Hungarian Diet called its troops home, and a ruling liberal national council was established by Count Michael Károlyi (1875–1955) on October 25, 1918. In support of Károlyi, Hungarians rebelled publicly for an end to the war, dismissal of the Diet, universal suffrage, and the end of the dual monarchy (Austria-Hungary). Emperor Charles I (1887–1922) was compelled to make Károlyi premier in hope of restoring order (October 31, 1918), and a radical-socialist coalition came to power in Hungary. But ethnic nationalism threatened the state, with Slovaks, Serbs, and Rumanians considering withdrawal. To preserve national unity, Károlyi accepted the peace terms with France mandating the withdrawal of Hungarian troops from southeastern areas; Serb troops occupied the south, Rumanians moved into Transylvania, and Czech (Bohemian) soldiers were stationed in Slovakia. The Austro-Hungarian monarchy had collapsed, and the emperor had renounced all participation in state affairs. On November 16, 1918, the national council declared Hungary a republic. See also KUN'S RED TERROR.

Hungarian-Turkish War of 1437–38   The Ottoman Turkish advance into Europe and Hungarian territory was successfully checked by forces led by John Hunyadi (1387–1456), a Transylvanian nobleman. The city of Belgrade had been heavily fortified against the Turks, who moved along the Danube River to the south and besieged the Semendria (Smederevo) fortress. But Hunyadi and his men relieved the fortress spectacularly and evicted the Turks in 1437. As a result, King Albert II (1397–1439), king of Hungary and Bohemia, appointed Hunyadi military governor (*bán*) of Severin in Wallachia (part of Rumania), where he became even more deeply involved with the Turks (see HUNGARIAN-TURKISH WAR OF 1441–44). See also HUNGARIAN-VENETIAN WAR OF 1378–81.

Hungarian-Turkish War of 1441–44   In retaliation against Hungary's support for the "false Mustafa" and his claim to the Turkish sultanate, the legal Ottoman sultan, Murad II (1403?–51), mounted a campaign against Hungary in 1440. Responding to advancing Turkish troops, an army of mainly Slavs and Magyars was assembled under the leadership of John Hunyadi (1387–1456) and was victorious at the Battle of Semendria (Smederevo) in 1441 and at the Battle of Herrmannstadt in 1442. The Turks also lost later at Vassag and Nagyszeben (Sibin). Pope Eugenius IV (1383–1447) then urged King Ladislas III (1424–44), ruler of Hungary and Poland, to wage full war against the Ottoman Empire, promising to launch a supporting crusade. The king assembled a large army, moved south across the Danube, and drove the Turks from Semendria. In 1443, Hunyadi soundly defeated the Turks at Nish (in Serbia) and then captured Sofia. Joining the forces of Ladislas, Hunyadi's defeated Murad's army at the Battle of Snaim (Kustinitza) in 1443, thus destroying Ottoman power in the Balkan region. Fearful of possible future losses, Murad entered into peace negotiations at Szeged, Hungary, which culminated in a 10-year truce (July 12, 1444) with Hungary, which was granted control over Serbia and Wallachia.

Hungarian-Turkish War of 1444–56   Hungary capitalized on Ottoman weakness following the abdication of Sultan Murad II (1403?–51) at the end of the HUNGARIAN-TURKISH WAR OF 1441–44 by breaking the 19-day-old truce. In alliance with Venice, King Ladislas III (1424–44), ruler of Hungary and Poland, along with his brilliant general, John Hunyadi (1387–1456), and Cardinal Julian Cesarini (1398–1444), marched with troops to the Black Sea, where they decimated a Turkish fleet, seized Sunium, Pezech, and Kavanna, and then invested Varna. Recalled to the throne, Murad led a great army to Varna and won a spectacular battle there against a Hungarian army on November 10, 1444; Ladislas and Cesarini were killed fighting, and Hunyadi escaped. Afterward Murad retook control of Serbia and Bosnia. In 1448, Hunyadi led an army into Serbia but was defeated in a two-day battle at Kosovo when his Wallachian troops treacherously left him; though Hunyadi made good use of mercenaries armed with handguns, his troops were overwhelmed by the far larger Ottoman army led by Murad. After securing Constantinople in 1453 (see CONSTANTINOPLE, FALL OF), Murad's son and successor as sultan, Muhammad II (1430–81), initiated new pressure on the Hungarians and other Christians; some 50,000 Serbs were abducted by the Turks. Hunyadi, who had led a successful punitive expedition against the Ottomans in Serbia in 1449, again invaded the region in 1454 and eventually forced the Turks to fall back from Semendria (Smederevo) to Krusevac, where Hunyadi and Muhammad met without making peace. The city of Belgrade was besieged by Muhammad's soldiers for three weeks in July 1456, until Hunyadi's troops breached a line of blockading ships on the Danube, defeated the Ottomans, and took the city. Muhammad withdrew to Constantinople. On August 11, 1456, Hunyadi died from an epidemic in his camp, and his sad, leaderless troops were unable to follow up on the victory. See also HAPSBURG DYNASTIC WAR OF 1439–57; VENETIAN-TURKISH WAR OF 1443–53.

Hungarian-Turkish War of 1463–83   Hungary, Venice, and the pope formed an alliance in 1463 to counteract Ottoman Turkish conquests in Serbia; after Bosnia fell to the Turks (see BOSNIAN-TURKISH WAR OF 1459–63), King Matthias Corvinus (1440–90) of Hungary came to the aid of the Bosnians. Hungarian troops ousted Ottomans from many fortresses. In the spring of 1464, Turks under Sultan Muhammad II "the Conqueror" (1429–81) invested the Bosnian town of Jajce, but Hungarian forces managed to hold it and some of northern Bosnia; the rest of the territory fell to the Ottomans, who subjected it fully in 1483. In 1479, King Matthias, displeased by the peace between the Venetians and Turks (see VENETIAN-TURKISH WAR OF 1463–79), seized the Turkish-built stronghold of Szabács on the Save River. The war wound down to skirmishes, especially after the death of Muhammad in 1481. The region of Herzegovina, south of Bosnia, fell to the Ottomans in 1483.

Hungarian-Turkish War of 1492–94   Invading Ottoman Turks under Sultan Bayazid II (1447–1513) launched a surprise attack on Belgrade but were unable to take the city from the Hungarians. In 1492, the forces of Holy Roman Emperor Maximilian I (1459–1519) defeated the Turkish invaders at Villach in Carinthia (southern Austria). Later Bayazid's troops advanced into Transylvania, Croatia, Styria, and Carniola. Maximilian sought help from other European Christian rulers, but none was forthcoming. The above regions were disturbed by skirmishing rather than all-out war during this period.

Hungarian-Turkish War of 1521–26   Ottoman sultan Süleyman I "the Magnificent" (1496?–1566) demanded tribute from King Louis II (1506–26) of Hungary. Louis's refusal, with an insult to the Turkish ambassador, prompted Süleyman to march toward Hungary in 1521. Hungarian fortresses were destroyed, including those at Sabac and Belgrade, which was used as a Turkish base for further incursions to the north. Hungary was bolstered by an anti-Turkish alliance with Persia and the Holy Roman Empire, while France under King Francis I (1494–1547) supported the Ottoman Empire, despite Francis's mixed feelings about an alliance with the Ottoman "infidels." Having advanced along the Danube River, some 200,000 Turkish troops led by Sultan Süleyman arrived at the plain of Mohacs in present-day southern Hungary, where about 30,000 Hungarians under King Louis had confusedly gathered. There, on August 29, 1526, the two sides met in battle, during which the Hungarians suffered severe casualties (about 15,000 deaths) and fled in tatters; Louis drowned in the disorganized flight. The Turks, including the elite Janissaries (sultan's corps), had bad losses, too, but the sultan regrouped them, advanced to Buda, occupied the city without a fight, but soon withdrew from the country with 105,000 captives because of demands in eastern Anatolia (Turkey) (see TURKO-PERSIAN WAR OF 1526–55). See also AUSTRO-TURKISH WAR OF 1529–33; HUNGARIAN CIVIL WAR OF 1526–29.

Hungarian-Venetian War of 1171   Hungarians under King Stephen III (d. 1172) moved along the Dalmatian coast, capturing towns and cities held by the Venetians, who were waging war then against the Byzantine Empire (see VENETIAN-BYZANTINE WAR OF 1170–77). In response, Venice sent forces with Norman assistance that recaptured the Dalmatian seaports of Zara (Zadar) and Ragusa (Dubrovnik) in 1171. Two years later Byzantine emperor Manuel I Comnenus (1120?–80) forcibly helped place Bela III (d. 1196) on the Hungarian throne, and the latter attempted twice in wars (1181–88, 1190–91) to recover Dalmatian territory. The Hungarians were only partly successful, managing to retake Zara and other Venetian-held cities.

Hungarian-Venetian War of 1342–46   Charles Robert of Anjou (1288–1342), who became Hungary's King Charles I in 1308, lost control of Dalmatia to Venice, which had to go to war against Charles's eldest son and successor to the Hungarian throne, King Louis I "the Great" (1326–82), who wanted to reconquer Dalmatia. The Venetians, however, successfully engaged the invaders, defeating them at the Adriatic port city of Zara (Zadar, Yugoslavia) in 1346. The

murder of Louis's younger brother, Prince Andrew (d. 1345), at the court of Queen Joanna I (1326?–82) of Naples (she had supposedly conspired against Andrew, her former and first husband) had hindered and enraged Louis, who sought revenge and the solidification of Angevin rule over Naples by invading the Italian kingdom twice (1348, 1350); each time Joanna fled. With the pope's intervention, she made peace with Charles and returned to Naples in 1352.

Hungarian-Venetian War of 1357–58   Hungary's King Louis I "the Great" (1326–82), who established a brilliant civilized court at Buda, wished to restore his kingdom to the status of a great power, especially in the Balkans, where his forces temporarily halted the Ottoman Turks' advance by a victory in northern Bulgaria (1356). Turning his attention to Venetian-controlled Dalmatia, he mounted a military campaign in the area and succeeded in gaining possession of many towns; in February 1358, Venice ceded to Hungary most of its Dalmatian territory by the Treaty of Zara (Zadar).

Hungarian-Venetian War of 1378–81   The prolonged, bitter struggle by King Louis I "the Great" of Hungary to dominate all of Dalmatia on the Adriatic came to a successful conclusion during the War of CHIOGGIA (1378–81). In alliance with Genoa, longtime rival of Venice, Louis undertook a military operation to force the Venetians to relinquish control of the Dalmatian coast. Though the Genoese met defeat, the Hungarians, who had earlier asserted their authority in the east, the Balkan area, by winning campaigns against the Ottoman Turks (1366, 1377), succeeded in wresting control of virtually the entire Dalmatian territory; the Peace of Turin (August 18, 1381) confirmed Hungary's authority over the region. Louis, who had been crowned king of Poland (1370), became the most powerful ruler in eastern Europe, with his Hungarian kingdom as sovereign in surrounding dependencies in the Balkans, Galicia, and elsewhere.

Hungarian War with the Holy Roman Empire
(1477–85) Frederick III (1415–93), king of Germany and Holy Roman Emperor, also claimed the Hungarian throne, which was held by King Matthias Corvinus (1440–90); in 1458, a general diet in Buda and Pest had elected Matthias king despite protestations from Emperor Frederick III of the Austrian House of Hapsburg, who sought to keep his dynastic power intact while plagued by feudal claims from powerful nobles throughout his empire. Matthias overcame internal dissension, strengthened Hungarian defenses against the Turks, and improved the political and social conditions of his sovereignty. In 1477, the Hapsburg power and fortune increased with the marriage of Frederick's son, Maximilian (1459–1519), to the duchess and heiress of Burgundy, Mary (1457–82), daughter of Charles the Bold (1433–77); this seemed to confirm Frederick's imperial monogram: AEIOU (*Austriae est imperare orbi universo* [Austria's will to rule the world] or *Alles Erdreich ist Osterreich untertan* [all the earth is under Austria's rule]). But Matthias contested Frederick's authority, received help from the emperor's adversaries in Austria and Germany, and initiated military campaigns (1477, 1479, 1482), ravaging much of Austria. The Hapsburg capital of Vienna was besieged and captured (1485) by Matthias, who expelled Frederick and occupied the city until 1490. After Matthias's death, Maximilian retook Vienna and other Austrian lands held by the Hungarians, who had dominated much of central and southeastern Europe for five years. Maximilian, elected king of the Romans or German king in 1486, assumed most of the imperial power in 1490.

Hun Raids on the Roman Empire (A.D. c. 375–454) The Huns, a nomadic Asian people, swept down from the steppes north of the Black Sea to invade and pillage the Roman Empire for about 80 years before returning home. They fought the Goths in 375, defeating the Ostrogoths (East Goths) and driving the Arian Christian Visigoths (West Goths) increasingly westward as they pushed toward a Danubian base. Next the Huns subjected other barbarian groups and slowly developed the concept of

a king and tribal unifier. Attila (406?–53), their most famous leader, was dedicated to gaining the riches of a still wealthy Roman Empire (as early as 434 the Huns knew gold was available, for leaders at Constantinople [Istanbul] contracted to pay 700 pounds of gold annually to prevent their raids). Nonetheless, the Huns often attacked when this monetary blackmail was in arrears. In 441–42 and 447, they devastated the Balkan provinces, reaching as far south as Thermopylae and Constantinople itself, and collecting indemnities in exchange for peace. In the West, taking advantage of Frankish internal strife, Attila "the Hun" attacked Gaul (France), plundering Metz and cities in Belgium, then turning south toward Orléans. In 451, Attila's forces were stopped by an allied army of Gaulish Romans, Visigoths, and Alans under Flavius Aëtius (396?–454), a Roman general, at the Battle of Châlons-sur-Marne; forced to charge uphill, the Huns broke the Alan center, but the Visigothic right flank and the Gauls pushed them back to their camp. Attila withdrew across the Rhine River, never again offering a pitched battle. The Huns turned to Italy, sacking the town of Aquilea so ruthlessly that it never recovered, its refugees founding Venice to the southwest. In 452, Milan and Pavia suffered from Hun raids. To prevent the destruction of Rome, Pope Leo I "the Great" (390?–461) led a mission to Attila; whatever was said is unknown, but the Huns spared Rome and, laden with loot, went north over the Alps. In 453, Attila died on his wedding night. His sons soon were defeated by rebellious Gepidae (Germans) in 454; no details of the defeat exist, but it caused a Hun retreat homeward. See also ROMAN-GOTHIC WARS.

Huntly's Rebellion (1562) Although a hero at Solway Moss (see ANGLO-SCOTTISH WAR OF 1542–49), George Gordon, fourth earl of Huntly (1514–62), ran from the fight at Pinkie Cleugh and was captured by the English. Returning to Scotland in 1548, he secretly maneuvered for his own sake and England's, although both John Knox (1505–72) and Queen Mary (1542–87) were suspicious. Huntly openly tried to wed his son to Mary and may have been party to the son's attempt to abduct her in 1562. During the queen's trip to the north later that year to punish him, Huntly's Scottish rebels engaged her at Corrichie near Aberdeen and were overwhelmed. Huntly died of an apparent stroke, his son was executed, and the earldom was forfeited.

Hurrian Conquests (c. 1700–c. 1500 B.C.) Apparently migrating south from the Caucasus region, the Hurrians, a non-Semitic people, gradually settled in northern Mesopotamia and areas east of the Tigris, forming small feudal-like states about the beginning of the second millennium. By about 1700 they had gained sufficient numbers to unite and overthrow their Semitic rulers, taking control over first the area between Lake Van and the Zagros Mountains. The Hurrians established commercial centers and pushed ever westward and southward until they dominated eastern Anatolia (Turkey) and northern Syria by about 1500. A northern Mesopotamian area, Hurri, memorializes their name. In Anatolia and northern Syria, they are remembered as the rulers of the kingdom of Mitanni, which warred with Egypt over Syria about 1470 and suffered defeat at the hands of King Thutmose III (fl. c. 1500–1447) of Egypt (see MEGIDDO, FIRST BATTLE OF). Later an Egyptian-Mitanni alliance was formed, but was of little help when the Hittite and Assyrian empires began to grind Mitanni between them (see ASSYRIAN-HURRIAN WARS; HITTITE-HURRIAN WARS). After 1350, Mitanni shrank to the small kingdom of Hanigabat, which was conquered by the Assyrians about 1245; by 1000, the Hurrians had lost their separate ethnic identity in the Near East.

Hussite Civil War (1423–34) The Hussites, followers of John Huss (1369–1415) in Bohemia and Moravia, split into two groups, the radical Taborites and the moderate Utraquists, during the HUSSITE WARS. In 1423, fighting broke out between the two groups, and John Ziska (1360?–1424) led the Taborites to victory at the battles of Horid and Strachov. The following year Ziska put down further

dissension, defeating the Utraquists at Skalic and Malesov. Prokop the Great, who became leader of the Hussites after Ziska's death in 1424, was unable to prevent renewed war between the Taborites and Utraquists in 1433. He and other Taborite leaders were killed at the Battle of Lipany on May 30, 1434, when the Utraquists, joined by the Bohemian nobles, won victory. The Utraquists had accepted the Compactata, a religious compromise, and been taken back into the Catholic Church the year before.

Hussite Wars (1419–36) John Huss (1369–1415), Bohemian religious reformer, was convicted of heresy by the Roman Catholic Church and burned at the stake in 1415. His followers, the Hussites, suffered continual persecution and took up arms in 1419 against the Catholics and German king Sigismund (1368–1437), who had inherited the Bohemian crown and was implicated in the burning of Huss. The Hussites, who were divided into two factions, the radical Taborites and Utraquists, were led successfully in battle by John Ziska (1360?–1424) and withstood the anti-Hussite crusade declared by Pope Martin V (1368–1431) in 1420. They won victories at Sudoner in 1419, at Kuttenberg in 1421, and at Nebovid in 1422. When a civil war broke out between the Taborites and Utraquists in 1423, Ziska, a Taborite, managed to contain it and kept the Hussites together. After Ziska's death in 1424, Prokop the Great (1380?–1434) led the Hussites to victory against the Catholic crusaders and made raids into Germany, Hungary, and Silesia between 1426 and 1432. Internal warfare between the Taborites and Utraquists broke out in 1433 and resulted in the defeat of the Taborites at the Battle of Lipany in 1434. Many Hussites, now dominated by the Utraquists, accepted a Catholic compromise on doctrine (the Taborites refused to) and recognized Sigismund as king of Bohemia in 1436. See also HUSSITE CIVIL WAR.

Hydaspes (Jhelum) River, Battle of the (327 B.C.) As a military strategist, Alexander the Great (356–323) had no peer in ancient times; his masterpiece came in India at the Hydaspes River, now called the Jhelum. As at Granicus and Issus (see ALEXANDER THE GREAT, CONQUESTS OF; ISSUS, BATTLE OF), he had a river to cross, but at Hydaspes he had special problems: the river was in flood state, the hostile Indians possessed 200 horse-crazing elephants, and the Greek camp was in the open in full sight. Alexander began a war of nerves; his launching of boats and rafts, gathering of supplies, and cavalry exercises made the Indians complacent and lax. Leaving a large force in camp, Alexander took 11,000 men along the river, crossed over, defeated the Indian chariots, then charged right (see GAUGAMELA, BATTLE OF) while moving a second force left behind the elephants, destroyed the Indian infantry, and had his own infantry attack the elephants with axes. Although the Indians were defeated, their leader, Porus (d. 321?), rajah of Lahore, became Alexander's friend and later guided him down the Indus River (see ALEXANDER'S INVASION OF INDIA). The chief Greek casualty at the battle was the death of Bucephalus, Alexander's beloved warhorse, for whom the city Bucephala was built nearby as a monument in his honor.

Hyksos Invasion of Egypt (c. 1674–1567 B.C.) An ancient Semitic people, called the Hyksos by the Egyptians (from the phrase *heqakhase*, meaning "ruler of/from a foreign country"), overran Egypt during a period of dynastic weakness about 1700 B.C. and founded the concurrent 15th and 16th Egyptian dynasties. The Hyksos successfully besieged the city of Memphis about 1674, but ruled lower Egypt from a capital called Avaris on the Nile River delta. An Egyptian historian who wrote in Greek, Manetho (fl. c. 300 B.C.), wrote about the Hyksos using evidence now lost, labeled their advance an "invasion," but archaeological data suggest that they infiltrated the area without battles until they had sufficient strength in numbers to overthrow lower Egypt's capital and oust the legitimate ruler. Thereafter they were peaceful rulers, placing the legitimate rulers as vassal-puppets in upper Egypt and allying with the recently independent country of Nubia. Under Kamose (d. 1570), a 17th Dynasty king, the native rulers of Egypt began to recover power; in 1567, they were strong enough to regain Memphis and expel the Hyksos interlopers. Egyptian records from this period are scant, but they contain no mention of the Hyksos after 1567, and, as an ethnic group, they seem to have disappeared from history.

I

Iconoclastic War, First (A.D. 726–31) Byzantine emperor Leo III (680?–741) declared himself against the worship of icons (sacred images and figures), considered heretical and idolatrous. The clergy and the pope at Rome, Gregory II (669–731), opposed Leo and other iconoclasts (those who rejected image worship). In 727, a revolt broke out in Greece against inconoclasm, which led to a rebel fleet sailing to Constantinople with an antiemperor aboard. Leo's fleet destroyed it. The people of the exarchate of Ravenna, Italy, revolted, causing Leo to launch a fleet to capture the city. The fleet, partly destroyed in a storm, was repulsed at Ravenna in 731. Failing to restore Byzantine authority, Leo placed Calabria, Sicily, and Illyria (all under the pope's jurisdiction) under control of the Constantinople patriarch. **Second Iconoclastic War** (A.D. 741–43). Leo's successor, Emperor Constantine V (718–75), began persecuting the icon worshipers more severely than ever before. While he was away on a military campaign (see BYZANTINE-MUSLIM WAR OF A.D. 741–52), his brother-in-law, Artavasdos (fl. 740s), led an open military and religious revolt, supported by the icon worshipers, and won a battle against imperial forces. Afterward he proclaimed himself emperor in Constantinople and restored icon worship there. Artavasdos's forces were defeated twice, at Sardes and Modrina, in 743, and Constantine was able to retake the throne. Artavasdos was blinded for his contumacy.

Illyrian War, First (229–228 B.C.) The Greek rulers normally shunned the barbarian, warlike Illyrians, but the expansive Romans undertook to deal with Queen Teuta (fl. 230s–220s) of Illyria when Illyrian pirates robbed and murdered some Italian merchants in 230. Rome sent ambassadors, who were received haughtily by the militant queen and were ambushed and killed on their way home. The Roman senate ordered vengeance, interrupting Illyrian moves to besiege neighboring Greek city-states. At Corcyra (Kerkira, or Corfu), Greece, used by Roman ships, an Illyrian siege preceded the arrival of a Roman fleet and soldiers in 229. With little or no fighting, they relieved Illyria's siege, and the queen surrendered in 228, renouncing her land claims and promising indemnity payments. Having achieved their goal of ensuring the safety of the waters between Italy and Greece, the Romans allied with Macedonia to have it guard Illyria's flank. **Second Illyrian War** (219 B.C.). In 220, Demetrius of Pharos (d. 214), now the ruling leader of Illyria, broke the peace of 228 by invading territories under Roman protection and resuming the piracy that had precipitated the First Illyrian War. Because of the danger of war with Carthage, the Romans had to act quickly. Demetrius had built defenses in two cities, Dinale and Pharos. The former city fell to the Romans after a seven-day siege; the latter, squeezed between two large Roman armies, capitulated in one day. Demetrius fled, and the conditions established in 228 were resumed.

Inca Revolt (1535–36) Spanish expeditions under Francisco Pizarro (1475?–1541) and Diego de Almagro (1475?–1538) took control of the Inca Empire in Peru with relative ease in 1532–33. (The Inca Emperor Atahualpa [Atabalipa] [1500?–1533] was treacherously seized, imprisoned, and murdered for plotting against the Spanish.) The "conquerors" then crowned Manco Capac II (1500?–1544) as puppet emperor. Manco collaborated temporarily with the Spaniards, but in 1536, during the absence of Pizarro and Almagro, called for an Inca revolt. The natives rose up, massacred many Spaniards, and laid siege to the Spanish-held Inca capital of Cuzco (Cusco) for 10 months. Repelled, they simply gave up and returned to their homes and crops. Manco fled to the mountains, established an Inca government in exile, and continued to lead sporadic raids until his murder by traitorous followers in 1544. See also SPANISH CONQUEST OF PERU.

Indian Civil War of 1947–48 During 1947, efforts to effect an India independent of Great Britain but also unified throughout the subcontinent failed when the Muslim League and the Hindu Congress Party could not agree, despite British attempts to create a federal union. Riots between Muslims and Hindus (traditional rivals) in the "Great Calcutta Killing" of August 16–20, 1946, had spread east and west in the country; partition into India and Pakistan was announced for August 14, 1947. Partition was followed on August 16 by civil war between Hindus and Muslims in the Punjab; fighting spread throughout the country. At least 5,500,000 refugees moved each way between West Pakistan and western India; some 1,250,000 moved from East Pakistan into West Bengal; 400,000 Hindus fled from Sind in West Pakistan into India. Rioting was constant, and perhaps a million refugees died because India's first prime minister, Jawaharlal Nehru (1889–1964), would not permit British troops to intervene in the war. Dissatisfaction with the status of Kashmir in the partition brought on the INDO-PAKISTANI WAR OF 1947–48, exacerbating both ill-feeling and the refugee problem; thousands poured into Delhi, where additional riots occurred. When Hindu nationalist and spiritual leader Mahatma Gandhi (1869–1948) tried to achieve harmony, he was shot by a Brahmin assassin; his words had failed, but his murder restored order and unified the government of India.

Indian Mutiny (Sepoy Rebellion) (1857–58) On May 10, 1857, native soldiers, or *sepoys*, in the Bengal Army at Meerut in northern India mutinied against their British officers, following the spread of rumors that cartridges were being greased with animal fat, thus threatening religious taboo to both Muslims and Hindus. This mutiny immediately incited other Indians, who resented the British annexaton of Oudh (region in north-central India) and their threat to end the Mogul Empire; soon the revolt at Meerut spread throughout northern India as a full-scale Anglo-Indian war. The mutineers captured nearby Delhi, proclaiming the aged Mogul emperor as their leader, and, when revolt seemed imminent in Oudh, they seized Lucknow and Kanpur. The British quickly lost control over the Ganges heartland and portions of the Punjab and Deccan; rural Indian rebellions and guerrilla activity spread. Both sides committed atrocities; British vengeance became ferocious after the discovery of the massacre of more than 200 British women and children at Cawnpore in July 1857. Internal conflicts undermined the Indian rebels' efforts, and the British soon recaptured Delhi (September 20, 1857) and eventually retook the beleaguered Lucknow (March 16, 1858). The rebels were largely quelled by June 1858. Reforms were later instituted, including the transfer of India's governmental power from the British East India Company, fiercely hated by the natives, to the British Crown in London. But much bitterness remained, helping to fuel the growth of Indian nationalism.

Indian-Nepalese War of 1814–16 See GURKHA WAR.

Indian Stream "War" (1835) Living near the uncertain, remote border between Canada and New Hampshire, the 360 inhabitants of Indian Stream established a provisional, free republic with a constitution, bicameral legislature, and 40-man army (1832–35). Some inhabitants wanted to be Canadians; others wished to join New Hampshire, which (along with the U.S. government) rejected Indian Stream's independence. In 1835, pro-Canadians attacked and routed two sheriffs from New Hampshire, which finally (November) sent in 50 militiamen, who easily won the "war" without any casualties. Indian Stream later (1836) united with New Hampshire.

Indochina Wars See FRENCH INDOCHINA WARS.

Indonesian-Malaysian War of 1963–66 In 1963, Indonesia's dominating "Lifetime President" Achmed Sukarno (1901–70) refused to recognize the newly proclaimed democratic Federation of Malaysia (Malaya, Sabah, Sarawak, and Singapore, which broke away in 1965 and became an independent republic). His vitriolic rhetoric whipped up Indonesian enthusiasm for a war to "crush" Malaysia, which gained British military support to battle infiltrating Indonesian guerrillas in Sabah and Sarawak (both on Borneo) and elsewhere. Bands of Indonesian paratroopers landed at several locations on the Malay peninsula, and frogmen exploded bombs in Singapore's harbor. The war, although limited, was extremely costly monetarily for Indonesia, which was shaken by an attempt by communists to seize power on September 30, 1965. Immediately General Suharto (1921–) led the Indonesian army in squashing the attempted coup d'état and afterward carried on a bloody anticommunist purge throughout the country (an estimated 300,000 communists and leftists were killed) (see INDONESIAN MASSACRE OF 1965). Sukarno, who had increased the country's ties with communist China and had been backed by the Indonesian Communist Party (PKI), failed to regain full governmental control; his replacement of anticommunist officials with leftists brought on riots and protests in Djakarta, the capital, and other cities in Java (1966). Eventually he was compelled to surrender all executive authority to Suharto, who became acting president (1967) and then elected president (1968). The PKI was banned. Indonesia and Malaysia entered into peace negotiations at Bangkok, agreed to end hostilities (June 1, 1966), and signed a treaty at Djakarta (August 11, 1966).

Indonesian Massacre of 1965 Political and economic instability led a band of army conspirators, headquartered at Halim Air Base, to join with members of the Indonesian Communist Party (PKI) to attempt a coup d'état on September 30, 1965. They kidnapped and killed six generals, including the army chief of staff, and then announced they had control of the government. President Achmed Sukarno (1901–70) immediately named General T.N.J. Suharto (1921–) temporary army chief of staff, and a brutal anticommunist, anti-Chinese campaign was launched throughout Indonesia. Entire towns on Java and Bali were destroyed in reprisals against the PKI, and some 300,000 suspected communists were massacred. His power base significantly weakened, the left-leaning Sukarno was gradually forced to yield government control to Suharto. In 1990 former high-ranking U.S. officials admitted that they had supplied as many as 5,000 names of PKI leaders to Suharto in 1965—part of the U.S. campaign to ensure communists did not gain power in Indonesia, on the south flank of Vietnam, where the U.S. was fighting communist guerrillas in the VIETNAM WAR.

Indonesian War in East Timor (1975–) Three major rival factions contended for power in Portuguese Timor (East Timor), the eastern half of Timor island in the Malay Archipelago (the western half—formerly Dutch Timor—became part of Indonesia in 1950). The Revolutionary Front for the Independence of East Timor (FRETILIN) called for full independence; another Timorese faction favored a merger with Indonesia; and a rightist group wanted continued federation with Portugal. Civil war erupted in August 1975, and became so severe that the Portuguese governor and his staff left along with thousands of refugees. FRETILIN gained control of the government and renamed the area the People's Democratic Republic of East Timor; opposing parties contested this and called on Indonesia to intervene, which it readily did. Invading U.S.-armed Indonesian troops captured the coastal capital city of Dili on December 7, 1975, and later that month drove the FRETILIN fighters into the mountains, from which they continued their resistance. Despite a United Nations' vote of condemnation of the aggression and a Security Council resolution calling for the withdrawal of Indonesian troops, Indonesia formally annexed East Timor as a province on July 17, 1976 (Portugal had relinquished its sovereignty over the colony in 1975 before the Indonesian invasion). FRETILIN guerrillas, holed up in mountain strongholds and supported by the Soviets and Portuguese communists, continued sporadic warfare against Indonesian troops, while East Timor lay in ruins, its towns and farms in shambles, and its people suffering from rampant disease and famine (many as political prisoners in internment camps). Indonesia sealed East Timor from the outside world and used brutal tactics to crush pro-independence demonstrations, as well as the guerrillas. About 200 demonstrators were massacred at a cemetery in Dili in November 1991, causing human rights organizations to demand international intervention, by the United Nations or others. Talks began (1994) between Indonesian and Timorese leaders, who sought more autonomy, free speech, religious freedom (East Timor is 90% Roman Catholic, whereas Indonesia is almost 90% Muslim), and less government and military interference. Two East Timorese activists—Bishop Carlos Filipe Ximenes Belo (1948–) and José Ramos-Horta (1950–)—won the 1996 Nobel Peace Prize, which drew the world's attention to Indonesia's bloody presence in East Timor, where the continuing war, famine, and disease have killed about 250,000 inhabitants. Talks between Indonesia and Portugal led to an announcement (March 1999) by UN Secretary General Kofi Annan (1938–) that East Timor would vote in a UN-sponsored referendum on independence or autonomy within Indoesia (no date was set for the vote). To the north, across the Banda Sea from Timor, bloody sectarian fighting erupted between Muslims and Christians on the island of Ambon in March 1999.

Indonesian War of Independence (1 9 4 5 – 4 9) The Dutch East Indian islands of what is now Indonesia were occupied by the Japanese during WORLD WAR II from 1942 to 1945, when Indonesian nationalists proclaimed an independent republic in the area (August 17, 1945). The Netherlands did not recognize the new Indonesian government, and Dutch and British soldiers soon landed at Batavia (Djakarta, Java) with instructions to restore the status quo before 1942 (i.e., Dutch control), as well as to disarm and repatriate Japanese troops there. But fighting broke out between the Dutch and British occupiers and the Indonesian People's Army, especially in the Javanese cities of Bandung and Surabaja (1945). Dutch-Indonesian negotiations resulted in the Cheribon Agreement (1946), by which the Dutch recognized the creation of the United States of Indonesia under the Netherlands Crown. Differences of interpretation of the agreement finally led to disorder in Java and elsewhere; a large-scale Dutch "police action" began (July 20, 1947) to restore order in the region; repressive actions roused world public opinion against the Dutch (the British had left Indonesia in November 1946). Dutch forces proceeded with "mopping-up" operations in important sections and continued to blockade the "rebels" or republicans' territory. Meanwhile, extremist Muslims who wanted an Islamic state were carrying on guerrilla warfare against both the Dutch and the republicans, and communists in the People's Democratic Front staged an uprising at Madioen (Madiun), Java, against the Indonesian republican government (September 1948), which promptly and severely crushed it. The Dutch seized the rebels' capital, Jogjakarta, and the principal republican leaders in late 1948. But rebel villagers continued to engage in guerrilla warfare against the Dutch, who were increasingly condemned by the United Nations. Indonesian and Dutch representatives met at a round-table conference at The Hague (August 23–November 2, 1949); the Netherlands then transferred full sovereignty to the United States of Indonesia, whose government was headed by Achmed Sukarno (1901–70) as president and Muhammad Hatta (1902–80) as premier. Intermittent guerrilla warfare, especially in the eastern areas, continued in 1950, when the new nation was reconstituted as the Republic of Indonesia.

Indonesian Wars of 1957–62   (Dutch-Indonesian War of 1962)   Under the authoritarian rule of Achmed Sukarno (1901–70), Indonesia was disrupted by indigenous military revolts in 1957, when rebel army officers on Sumatra, Celebes, Borneo, and other islands repudiated the central government and set up their own regimes. Sukarno, whose reinforced army suppressed the rebels with dispatch, made the country a virtual dictatorship after dissolving the constituent assembly (1959); his leftist-leaning government accepted more and more communists. Continued Dutch rule of West New Guinea angered Indonesia, which claimed the territory as West Irian (Irian Jaya) and had asked the United Nations to help resolve the issue, without success. In December 1957, the Indonesian government ordered a 24-hour strike against Dutch-owned businesses in the country, forbade the Dutch airline to land at Indonesian airports, banned Dutch publications, expelled Dutch citizens, and expropriated Dutch holdings; this led to a mass exodus of some 40,000 Netherlanders from Indonesia. When Indonesian-Dutch diplomatic talks failed, the Dutch built up their defenses in West New Guinea and prepared the native people for self-determination, while the Indonesians obtained warships and planes from the Soviet Union. In 1962, Indonesian paratroopers landed in West New Guinea and, along with rebel guerrillas, fought against the Dutch, whose forces attacked enemy torpedo boats off the coast. The threat of a full-scale war led the United States and the UN to forsake their neutral positions and sponsor peace negotiations, which resulted in an Indonesian-Dutch agreement (August 15, 1962), whereby the Netherlands first transferred the administration of West New Guinea to the UN (1962), which, in turn, later transferred it to Indonesia (1963).

Indo-Pakistani War of 1947–48   The partition of the Indian subcontinent into India and a divided Pakistan (East and West) left undecided the status of Jammu and Kashmir, an independent kingdom bordering West Pakistan whose chiefly Muslim population was ruled by an autocratic Hindu. Coveted by both India and Pakistan, Kashmir was troubled by its ruler's wish to make it "the Switzerland of Asia" and by the desire of the Hindu-Muslim All-Jammu and Kashmir National Conference to democratize it first. These feelings and Pakistani demands combined in October 1947: Pathan Muslims in Poonch, or Punch, revolted against oppressive Kashmiri Hindu landowners. Pakistan sent troops on October 22, seizing Muzaffarabad and Uri, burning villages, slaughtering civilians, and advancing toward the Kashmiri capital at Srinagar. Ceding his state to India, the Kashmiri ruler requested and received Indian help (October 27, 1947). Sikh troops pushed the invaders toward Pakistan, which, poised to send troops until its British officers threatened to resign, transferred "volunteers" into the invaded area to hold it as Azad ("free") Kashmir. Hindu refugees poured into Delhi and Calcutta, increasing factional tension and rioting (see INDIAN CIVIL WAR OF 1947–48). The turmoil rose to such a pitch that the revered Hindu leader Mahatma Gandhi (1869–1948), who opposed the war and wished to create Muslim-Hindu harmony, was assassinated by a Hindu factionalist (January 30, 1948). His death, however, united India's Hindus and Muslims. Intervention by the United Nations resulted, after three weeks of fighting in April 1948, in a cease-fire and a de facto boundary at the battle line. Pakistan's involvement with Kashmir was not over, for disputes about water rights went unresolved until 1960, and Indian promises of a Kashmiri plebiscite were never fulfilled.

Indo-Pakistani War of 1965   Hostility between India and Pakistan increased after 1958, when General Muhammad Ayub Khan (1907–74) seized power in Pakistan and signed a friendship treaty with China, which placed in jeopardy Kashmir's boundary with Peking's territory. Negotiations failed and tensions increased, inciting a border clash between Indian and Pakistani troops in the Rann of Kutch (April 9–30, 1965). A cease-fire permitted the withdrawal of troops in early July that year, but the conflict erupted again in late August and early September, when both Indian and Pakistani forces crossed the cease-fire line established during the INDO-PAKISTANI WAR OF 1947–48. A full-scale war began on September 6, when India launched a three-pronged drive toward Lahore involving some 900,000 troops. Lahore was not attacked, but 450 Pakistani tanks were destroyed before a cease-fire was finally arranged by the United Nations on September 27. The cease-fire forestalled a threat of intervention by China and permitted both armies, now short of supplies, to pull back to the pre-August battle lines. Mediation efforts by Britain, the United States, and the Soviet Union led to a conference in Tashkent (1966), in which promises of cooperation, friendship, and a Kashmiri plebiscite (to decide whether to incorporate into India or not) were exchanged. India's representative, Prime Minister Lal Bahadur Shastri (1904–66), died within hours of the conference; and although his successor Indira Gandhi (1917–84) fulfilled most of India's promises, the PAKISTANI CIVIL WAR OF 1971 intervened and caused the INDO-PAKISTANI WAR OF 1971, further postponing the long-delayed Kashmiri plebiscite.

Indo-Pakistani War of 1971   The PAKISTANI CIVIL WAR OF 1971 forced more than 10 million refugees from East Pakistan (Bangladesh) into West Bengal, one of India's poorest districts. India appealed for international assistance, but received almost none. Backing its client state, Pakistan, the United States, through President Richard M. Nixon (1913–94), declared that the Pakistani civil war had evolved from an Indian attempt to destabilize Pakistan. Nixon cut off India's American credit. When Pakistani warplanes attacked Indian airfields in Kashmir (December 3, 1971), Indian forces began a 12-day war the following day, attacking areas in both West Pakistan and Bangladesh. The latter's sovereignty was recognized by India on December 6, 1971, 10 days before a combination of Indian air and ground forces caused the downfall of Dacca and the surrender of Pakistani forces in Bangladesh. India captured some 90,000 prisoners and established a cease-fire in both West Pakistan and Bangladesh (December 17, 1971). Pakistan emerged badly from the struggle, having lost not only the war but half its population. Its army and economy were on the verge of collapse, and its national morale was very low, despite America's encouragement and help, which delayed Washington's (U.S.) recognition of Bangladesh until April 4, 1972; Pakistan finally recognized the new republic in 1974.

Indus River, Battle of the (1221)   Motivated by his principle of leaving no potential attacker alive, Genghis (Jenghiz, Chingis) Khan (1167?–1227) led his Mongol forces in pursuit of Jalal-ad-Din (d. 1231), son of the defeated shah of Khwarizm (see MONGOL-PERSIAN WAR, FIRST), into the Hindu Kush (mountains), fought the Battle of BAMIAN, then followed him to the banks of the Indus River, India. The Mongols' 40,000 men faced 30,000 Muslims, who organized militarily with their backs to the river, their right flank safeguarded by its bend and their left protected by a mountain ridge. The Muslims charged, sending the right forward, followed by the center. Genghis Khan saw the weakness on their left, sent some troops (now able mountain cavalry) over the ridge to attack it, enveloped the Muslims, and caused heavy slaughter. The wily Jalal-ad-Din escaped again; the Mongols, however, in order to solidify their control of Khorasan, declined to continue in India and returned to Persia. See also MONGOL-PERSIAN WAR, SECOND.

Ionian Revolt (c. 500–493 B.C.)   The sixth-century Persian Empire controlled the Greek city-states of Ionia, a coastal region and adjacent islands in western Asia Minor (Turkey), by assigning tyrants as rulers. The Ionian port of Miletus revolted about

500 after receiving help from Athens and Eretria, but not Sparta. Other Ionian cities eagerly joined the rebels, who dethroned the tyrants. In 498, the Persian satrap (governor) was ousted from his capital, Sardis, in Lydia, and the city was burned by rebels, who then, foolishly, dispersed. Quickly retaking Sardis, the Persians repulsed the invading Greeks and recaptured the rebellious Ionian city states. In 494, they besieged Miletus; King Darius (558?–486) commanded a large Persian fleet that blockaded the city, defeated the Ionians at the Battle of Lade (a tiny island nearby), and captured and sacked Miletus, all of whose male inhabitants were then slain. See also GRECO-PERSIAN WARS.

Ipsus, Battle of (301 B.C.) In 306, Antigonus I (c. 382–301), having proclaimed himself king of Macedonia, had taken 30,000 soldiers into Asia Minor in an attempt to reunite the Alexandrian empire (see DIADOCHI, WARS OF THE). He was opposed by Cassander (358–297), also self-proclaimed as king, with his own 30,000 men, accompanied by Seleucus I (358?–280) and Lysimachus (c. 355–281). In this crucial fight among the Diadochi—the successors of Alexander the Great (356–323)—Antigonus and some 22,000 of his Macedonians were killed in battle, and the distribution of the spoils thereafter ruined the old empire. Seleucus received Syria and founded the Seleucid dynasty that lasted until 64 B.C. Cassander gained Macedonia (and thus all of Greece), and Ptolemy I (d. 283?), who had not participated, got a free hand in Egypt.

Iranian Revolution of 1979 Iran's Shah Muhammad Reza Pahlavi (1919–80) was opposed by liberals and intellectuals, who found him autocratic and dictatorial, and by conservatives, who considered him too Westernized and progressive. These two disparate groups joined together during 1978 under the leadership of an exiled conservative Muslim religious leader, the Ayatollah Ruhollah Khomeini (1901–89), whose rigidity was eventually to cause this unlikely union to fight within itself and finally to split. Riots disrupted the government, forcing the shah to flee to Egypt in January 1979, after naming a regency council to rule in his absence. In exile in France, Khomeini urged the overthrow of the weakened government. Strikes, demonstrations (some with more than a million marchers), the defection of the army into neutrality, and the return of Khomeini to Iran all combined to destroy the government in less than a month (February 1979). As leader, Khomeini declared Iran to be a religious (Islamic) rather than a secular republic, asserted that all laws were subject to review on Islamic (especially Shi'ite) principles, and established a revolutionary council to help him rule. Trials and executions of opponents and subversives ensued, and, despite marches by dissident women and ethnic revolts, especially by the Kurds, a referendum on March 30, 1979 indicated 99 percent of the people approved of Khomeini's views and methods. Mock trials and executions continued, disorders belying the referendum's results made necessary the establishment of the Army of the Guardians of the Islamic Revolution (May 6, 1979), and further executions by the revolutionary council carried on the reign of terror. Khomeini, meanwhile, had broken Iranian relations with the West and, more tragically, with the rest of the Islamic world. For the West, Khomeini's reactionary lawlessness reached its zenith on November 4, 1979, when staff members of the United States embassy at Tehran were seized by militants, who vowed to hold them hostage until the shah and his vast assets were returned to Iran. The shah's death, in Egypt in July 1980, failed to end the hostage crisis, which was finally resolved, mainly by Algerian mediation and a U.S.-Iranian financial and political agreement, on January 20, 1981. After 444 days in captivity, 52 Americans were released. Iranian rival revolutionary factions fought for power until the start of the IRAN-IRAQ WAR OF 1980–88.

Iran-Iraq War of 1980–88 (Persian Gulf War of 1980–88) The neighboring nations of Iran and Iraq have had a long-time dispute over control of the Shatt al-Arab, a 120-mile-long tidal river flowing past Iraq's chief port of Basra and the Iranian port of

Abadan to the Persian Gulf (the eastern bank of the river's lower course forms part of the Iraqi-Iranian border). After the IRANIAN REVOLUTION OF 1979, Iraq under President Saddam Hussein (1937–) became the target of the Iranian terrorist group Al Dawa ("the Call") and Iranian vitriolic propaganda, both directed by Iran's leader, the Ayatollah Ruhollah Khomeini (1901–89). Iranians tried to kill Iraq's deputy premier, created disturbances in the Iraqi capital of Baghdad, attacked Iraq's embassy in Rome, attempted to arouse Iraq's Shi'ite minority to rebel, and shelled Iraqi towns, causing civilian casualties. In response, on September 21–22, 1980, Iraqi warplanes and troops invaded Iran, hoping to quickly topple the Khomeini regime; Iranian gunboats in the Shatt al-Arab were bombed and sunk; airfields and oil refineries at Abadan and other places were damaged by invading Iraqis. Iranian forces retaliated against the enemy as Khomeini saw the war as an opportunity to rally his troublous people for a national cause; Iran called for total mobilization and fanatical military actions (martyrdom on the battlefield) against strongly equipped Iraq (using Soviet-made tanks, missiles, and heavy artillery and French-built fighter planes) and threatened to disrupt oil shipments through the Strait of Hormuz in the Persian Gulf. The United Nations and an Islamic conference of many nations failed to stop the war, which soon became one of the most costly and futile in Middle East history. Iraqi troops, ensconced in trenches, earthen parapets, and sandbagged bunkers, regularly turned back massive Iranian offensives (human waves of teenage Revolutionary Guards and others) along a 300-mile front stretching from the marshlands of Basra (closed to shipping) north to the Iraqi border towns of Mandali and Khanaqin. Neither side proved capable of occupying enemy territory or of mounting a decisive offensive; Iraq, with about 500,000 men under arms, was accused of using chemical weapons; Iran, with some 2 million under arms, and Iraq both sought to cut the other's economic lifeline (oil shipments). Their air attacks against tankers plying the gulf (especially around Iran's Kharg Island) dangerously escalated this war of attrition, and the United

States, holding Iran responsible for much terrorism against Americans in the Middle East, eventually tilted politically toward Iraq and pledged to keep the Persian Gulf open to international shipping to safeguard the main source of oil for Western Europe and Japan. In February 1986 Iranian troops gained territory on two fronts, but Iraq later recaptured the lost ground. An Iraqi warplane accidentally fired a missile at an American naval frigate, U.S.S. *Stark*, patrolling in the Persian Gulf, on May 17, 1987; Iraq apologized for the attack, which killed 37 American sailors. Another accident occurred on July 3, 1988, when an American warship in the Gulf (U.S.S. *Vincennes*) inadvertently shot down an Iranian commercial airliner, misidentifying it as an F-14 fighter jet, killing all 290 persons on the plane. After several Iranian military setbacks in 1988, Khomeini agreed to a UN resolution calling for cease-fire negotiations with Iraq, which had earlier sought to end the conflict. A cease-fire took effect on August 20, 1988, ending hostilities but leaving the status of the Shatt al-Arab waterway unresolved.

Irish Convict Revolt See   AUSTRALIAN IRISH CONVICT REVOLT.

Irish Raids in Britain (A.D. c. 395–405)   While suffering raids by the Saxons, Picts, and other invaders, Roman-occupied Britain was also beleaguered by hit-and-run raids from the west, where men of Ireland (then called Scots) ruled by Niall of the Nine Hostages (d. 405), high king of Ireland at the end of the fourth century, attacked from Strathclyde south to Wales, destroying coastal villages and carrying off thousands as slaves. Among the most famous of the captives was a Briton named Patricius, captured about 400 and forced to be a swineherd. He escaped and later returned to Ireland as St. Patrick (389?–461?). About 400, the ruler of Gwynedd, the northernmost kingdom in Wales, expelled the Scots; afterward the raids gradually slowed to a stop. Niall accidentally repaid his exactions: as great-great grandfather of St. Columba (521–97), Irish founder of the monastery of Iona

(563) and apostle of Celtic Christianity, Niall was indirectly responsible for the early Christianization of the British Isles. See also SAXON RAIDS.

Irish Rebellion, Great (1641–49) Despotic treatment, Protestant immigration to Ulster, and religious fanaticism combined with opportunity to incite an Irish rebellion when King Charles I (1600–1649) and England's Parliament were most at odds (see ENGLISH CIVIL WAR, FIRST). In Ireland, Catholics and the "Old" English tried to seize Dublin and, failing, took over Ulster and incited uprisings in Leinster in 1641. Parliament reacted with panic and ineptitude, refused to give Charles an army, promised Irish lands to volunteers, and sent Scottish troops in 1642. By then, almost all of Ireland was in rebel hands, and the Scots fared poorly. A provisional rebel government was established in Kilkenny in 1642, and James Butler (1610–88), the first duke of Ormonde and Charles's lieutenant, arranged a truce, which both the Irish and English parliaments rejected. The rebellion continued sporadically, despite interference by a papal nuncio (diplomatic envoy), with a rebel victory in 1645, rebel losses until 1647, a vain truce attempt in 1648, and a Protestant royalist defeat at the Battle of Rathmines in 1649. Only the coming of Cromwell ended the strife (see CROMWELL'S IRISH CAMPAIGN).

Irish Tithe War See TITHE WAR, IRISH.

Irish War of 1689–91 England's King James II (1633–1701) was one of the earliest Jacobites (see JACOBITE REBELLIONS). Ousted as king (see GLORIOUS REVOLUTION), he requested help from the Irish, still smarting from Cromwellian confiscations (see CROMWELL'S IRISH CAMPAIGN), and he received it. Landing in Ireland (1689) with troops and money from France's King Louis XIV (1638–1715), James was acknowledged as king by an Irish parliament at Dublin (it confiscated all Protestant lands), assembled an Irish-French army, and marched on Londonderry, whose Protestants had affirmed their allegiance to King William III (1650–1702) and Queen Mary II (1662–94). Londonderry was besieged for 15 weeks without victory. William landed in Ireland (1690) with an Anglo-Dutch army, which engaged and defeated James's forces at the Battle of the Boyne on July 11, 1690. James fled to France, but his supporters continued to resist the English advance and subjugation. The Battle of Aughrim on July 12, 1691 ended in defeat for the allied Irish and French, and Limerick, the Jacobite headquarters, finally surrendered after successfully resisting two sieges. The pacification of Limerick permitted free transport of Irish soldiers to France and freedom of religion (Catholic) in Ireland. But the Irish Protestants objected and passed in their parliament, predominantly Protestant, oppressive anti-Catholic legislation that caused sporadic fighting by Irish Catholics until 1696.

Iroquois-French Wars (1642–96) Ever since French explorer Samuel de Champlain (1567?–1635) had accompanied a Huron Indian war party and shot dead some Iroquois Indians in 1609, the Iroquois harbored an abiding hatred for the French. Soon after Champlain's death, they began to terrorize the French settlements along the St. Lawrence and Ottawa Rivers, making travel by foot or water hazardous. Missions started by French Jesuit priests were stormed and destroyed and their inhabitants cruelly tortured to death. The Huron were practically annihilated in the IROQUOIS-HURON WAR in 1650. Iroquois fighting posts were built at various strategic points, and their warriors were divided into forces that patrolled the forests and waterways relentlessly, winter and summer, day and night. Peace terms were negotiated periodically, but were soon broken by the bellicose Iroquois, who were armed by Dutch supporters at Fort Orange (Albany, N.Y.). The continuous conflict was also a war for control of the rich beaver fur trade, which the Iroquois tried to divert to Fort Orange by preventing the French and their Indian allies from taking their furs to Quebec, Canada. In 1660–61, Montreal was threatened, and 1661 saw the slaughter of a French band at Long Sault; but in 1666 newly arrived soldiers from France took the offensive and defeated the Mohawk, an Indian tribe of Iroquoian stock, in their homelands. The Indians sued for peace, which lasted uneasily for almost 20 years. But tensions rose again as the French moved westward, and antagonisms developed between the French and English. A new French governor, the marquis de Denonville (d. 1710), arrived in 1685, and he determined to teach the warring Seneca, another Indian tribe of Iroquoian stock, a lesson. He lead a large force into western New York and destroyed four Seneca villages in 1687. The Indians were furious about this and other treacherous acts by the French; they had their revenge two years later when they swooped down the St. Lawrence in large numbers, massacred the inhabitants of Lachine, and spread terror through the countryside as far as Montreal. They returned again there and elsewhere with surprise attacks against French forts, towns, and small settlements. When the comte de Frontenac (1620–98) returned as governor of New France (Canada) in 1689, he made war against the Iroquois a priority. The Indians were finally subdued in 1696, but during the 1700s they fought the French again as allies of the British (see FRENCH AND INDIAN WAR).

Iroquois-Huron War (1648–50) The Huron Indians, who inhabited present-day Ontario, Canada, and the Iroquois Indians, who occupied large areas to the south, were traditional enemies. In 1648, the Iroquois received firearms from the Dutch settlers and traders at Fort Orange (Albany, N.Y.) and then invaded Huron territory. Two French Jesuit missionaries, Jean de Brébeuf (1593–1649) and Gabriel Lalemant (1610–49), who had converted the Huron to Christianity, were captured and brutally tortured to death by the Iroquois, who nearly exterminated the Huron in the war. Those Huron who escaped fled in all directions, seeking refuge with neighboring tribes. But the Iroquois pursued them relentlessly, and in 1649, they furiously attacked the Tobacco Nation, the Tionontati Indians with whom the Huron had found safety, and slaughtered much of it. In 1650, the Iroquois invaded and almost wiped out the Neutral Nation, an Indian confederation that had taken in remnants of the Huron.

Isaurian War (A.D. 492–98) Zeno (Zenon) (426–91), emperor of the Eastern Roman (Byzantine) Empire, was a native of Isauria, a mountainous region in what is now south-central Turkey; he appointed many of his clansmen to positions of importance and power in the empire. Upon Zeno's death, the new emperor Anastasius I (430?–518) removed these officials and expelled Isaurian troops from Constantinople (Istanbul), the capital of the East. These actions brought on a revolt by the Isaurians, a wild and bellicose people, who invaded western Anatolia (Turkey). Anastasius declared war on them, and his army (mostly made up of Goths) routed the Isaurians at the Battle of Cotyaeum (Kutahya) and forced them back into Isauria in 493. Although greatly outnumbered, the Isaurians continued to fight the imperial troops and were often defeated. Eventually all their strongholds were destroyed; large numbers of them were resettled in Thrace; and their power to threaten the peace in Anatolia was broken for good.

Israeli-Arab Wars See ARAB-ISRAELI WARS.

Israeli Invasion of Lebanon See LEBANESE CIVIL WAR OF 1975–90.

Issus, Battle of (333 B.C.) The second great battle between King Darius III (d. 330) of Persia and Alexander the Great (356–323) took place at Issus in present-day Turkey (see ALEXANDER THE GREAT, CONQUESTS OF). Alexander's 35,000 troops were greatly outnumbered by the Persians, but the latter were poorly trained. From a hideout in the Syrian plains, Darius had marched his forces north along one side of a mountain range to cut Alexander off; on the other side, Alexander had moved his army south from Issus to reach the hideout and then had marched them north again. The armies met across the Issus River. To avoid Persian catapults, Alexander charged across the river, found a gap in the left of Darius's line, and sent in his heavy cavalry. The Persians broke, then fled, leaving Greek mercenaries isolated. They were slaughtered. Alexander's troops pursued the Persians, killing 110,000 of them (Macedonian losses were 302). Darius escaped, leaving the royal family behind to be captured by Alexander.

Italian Revolts of 1831–34 Stimulated by French ideas of independence and revolution and inspired by Italian patriot Giuseppe Mazzini (1805–72) and his work for a republican government in a united Italy, a number of Italian states, dominated by Austrian autocratic rule, attempted to seize power from oligarchic groups and legates and establish provisional governments. An assembly in Modena proclaimed the fall of Duke Francesco IV (1779–1846) in 1831, and soon Parma, Romagna, the Marches and Umbria set up provisional governments and together formed a united provincial government at Bologna, whose papal prolegate had earlier been forced to yield power to a commission. At the pope's request, Austria intervened and, using force, restored the duke of Modena and the duchess of Parma, suppressed the Romagna revolt, terminated the fledgling republican federation, and reestablished the status quo antebellum. See also ITALIAN REVOLUTION OF 1848–49.

Italian Revolution of 1848–49 (Italian War of Independence of 1848–49) The Risorgimento (movement for the liberation and unification of Italy), under the leadership of King Charles Albert (1798–1849) of Sardinia, demanded the expulsion of the Austrians from Italy (see ITALIAN REVOLTS OF 1831–34). Immediately following Milan's "FIVE DAYS" REVOLT, the kingdom of Sardinia (the island of Sardinia, Piedmont, Savoy, and other parts of Italy) declared war on Austria. Italian patriots in Venice revolted and proclaimed an independent republic under Daniele Manin (1804–57), who was made president. Support for the war came from Piedmont's Count Camillo Cavour (1810–61), Pope

Pius IX (1792–1878), and leaders in Modena, Parma, Tuscany, and Naples. Allied Italian forces under Charles Albert drew the smaller, 70,000-man Austrian army under Field Marshal Joseph Radetzky (1766–1858) into a "quadrilateral" fortress area: Mantua, Verona, Peschiera, and Legnago. Skillful offensive and defensive tactics by Radetzky and vacillation by Charles Albert brought success for the Austrians, who routed the Tuscan army and took the papal army hostage. This engendered alarm in the Italian allies, and the Neapolitan army was called home. Piedmontese forces, left to fight alone, suffered overwhelming defeat by Radetzky's forces at the Battle of Custoza near Verona on July 23–25, 1848. Radetzky then reoccupied Milan. Austria had regained all its Italian territory, save Venice. After Radetzky defeated the Piedmontese again, at the Battle of Novara on March 23, 1849, Charles Albert abdicated in favor of his son, Victor Emmanuel II (1820–78), who acquiesced to harsh peace terms. In the Kingdom of the Two Sicilies, King Ferdinand II (1810–59) ordered the bombardment of Messina and Palermo to crush the disorders. In Rome, where a revolutionary tribunal ruled, the pope's request to be reinstated was considered (Pius IX had fled from Rome to Gaeta because of rioting). Louis Napoleon (1808–73) sent a French expeditionary army to protect "Roman liberties." It advanced to the walls of Rome by the end of April 1849. The Roman force, which included 5,000 legionnaires ("the Red Shirts") under Giuseppe Garibaldi (1807–82), suspicious of the foreign soldiers, confronted the French and forced their withdrawal. To aid the French, the Austrian army was sent from the north, Neapolitans from the south, and Spanish landed on the Tiber River. After the Romans with Garibaldi's help drove back the Neapolitans, the Spanish withdrew, but increasing reinforcements for the French finally compelled Garibaldi's legionnaires to retreat, and Rome fell in June 1849 and papal rule was reestablished. At Venice, Manin's forces held out for four months (May–August 1849) against Radetzky's army, suffering terribly from bombardment, hunger, and cholera. Two weeks after Sardinia made peace with Austria, Manin surrendered. See ITALIAN WAR OF INDEPENDENCE OF 1859–61.

Italian Uprisings of 1914 While a new Italian government was being formed by Premier Antonio Salandra (1853–1931), a moderate conservative, radicals of all kinds were extremely vocal, resisting taxation, demanding wage increases, and opposing militarism. On June 7, 1914, popular uprisings ("Red Week") began in the Marches and Romagna, with rebellious landless laborers confronting strike breakers hired by local landowners. Incited by firebrands like Benito Mussolini (1883–1945), then editor of a socialist newspaper in Milan, the strikers and rebels staged an antidraft demonstration in Ancona, provoked gunfire from the police, and attempted reprisals. Bologna was taken over by dissidents who effected a general strike, sacked shops, and destroyed telegraph lines and railroad tracks. Ancona and other towns proclaimed themselves independent communes; Romagna declared itself a republic; Ferrara and Ravenna capitulated to the rebels. More than 100,000 soldiers had to be called into action before order was restored; but by early July 1914, Italy—despite its alliance with Germany and Austria—was so preoccupied with moves to declare neutrality that the problems of its restless laborers were temporarily shelved. See also WORLD WAR I.

Italian War between Charles V and Francis I, First (1521–25)   With the accession of Charles V (1500–1558) to the throne of the Holy Roman Empire began more than 40 years of Hapsburg-Valois struggles (Imperial versus French forces) for supremacy in Italy. After allying himself with the papacy against Francis I (1494–1547) of France in 1521, Charles moved to replace French rule in Milan with Francesco Maria Sforza (1491–1530), an ally. On April 27, 1522, French and Swiss troops were defeated by Imperial forces at the Battle of Bicocca near Milan; the French then withdrew from Lombardy. Although Italy was the main battleground, some fighting took place in the region of

Navarre in northern Spain; an invading French army lost to the Spaniards near Pamplona in 1521 and was driven out. In 1524, the French under Francis launched another invasion of Italy to regain lost territory. An Italian-Spanish-German army defeated the invaders at the Battle of Pavia on February 24, 1525, and Francis was captured and imprisoned in Madrid, where he signed a treaty giving up all claims to Italy and surrendering Burgundy, Artois, and Flanders to Charles. **Second Italian War between Charles V and Francis I** (1526–30). Alarmed by increasing Hapsburg power, Pope Clement VII (1478–1534) withdrew papal support for Charles and formed the League of Cognac with Francis (who had repudiated the Treaty of Madrid, saying he had signed it under duress), Sforza of Milan, and the rulers of Venice and Florence in 1526. Spanish and German mercenaries invaded Italy to oppose the league and sacked Rome in early May 1527. Their commander, Constable Bourbon (1490–1527), was killed, leaving them without strong leadership, and the mercenaries, starving and unpaid, committed many atrocities in the city. Pope Clement was briefly imprisoned. The French suffered several disastrous defeats and lost their main base in Italy, Genoa, which allied itself with the emperor. Despite a rallying effort led by Vicomte de Lautrec (d. 1528), French forces were anxious for peace, and in 1529 Francis and Charles signed the Treaty of Cambrai, the former again renouncing all French claims to Italy and the latter withdrawing his claim to Burgundy. Pope Clement, realizing his long-term interests lay with Spain, signed the Treaty of Barcelona in 1529 in return for Imperial help from Charles in overthrowing the rebellious Florentine republic, which had continued to wage war against the empire. Florence fought bravely but surrendered in 1530, and Alessandro de' Medici (1510–37) became duke. The independent Italian states, except for Milan and Genoa, submitted to Spanish control. Pope Clement crowned Charles king of Lombardy in 1530. **Third Italian War between Charles V and Francis I** (1535–38). On the death of Duke Sforza of Milan in 1535, Emperor Charles took possession of Milan (the

Treaty of Cambrai had determined this) and gave its governorship to his son Philip (1527–98), later King Philip II of Spain. A large French army invaded Italy to regain some control and seized Turin. Charles's Imperial troops advanced into Provence in southeastern France and prepared to fight Francis's forces at Avignon. However, both sides backed off, and the Truce of Nice was agreed to, keeping the status quo with the French in control of northwestern Italy. **Fourth Italian War between Charles V and Francis I (1542–44).** To the astonishment of many French, Francis concluded an alliance with Ottoman Sultan Süleyman I "the Magnificent" (1496?–1566). The city of Siena lent France its support for a final French invasion of Italy, thus breaking the truce. A joint French-Turkish naval force bombarded, besieged, and sacked the Imperial town of Nice in 1543. Charles invaded Picardy in northern France and made plans with the English, whose King Henry VIII (1491–1547) had allied himself with Charles in 1542, for a two-pronged invasion of France (see ANGLO-FRENCH WAR OF 1542–46). On April 14, 1544, a French army won an "inconclusive" victory at the Battle of Ceresole, south of Turin in Italy (cavalry played a major role backing up infantry). Because the English and Imperial advances into France were not well coordinated and slow, the French managed to ready their forces and check them. Francis and Charles agreed to the Peace of Crépy in 1544, which reaffirmed the old status quo; for the third time Francis gave up all claims to Naples. See also HAPSBURG-VALOIS WAR OF 1547–59.

Italian War of Charles VIII (1494–95)   Regent Lodovico Sforza (1451–1508), to ward off an attack from Naples because of his usurpation of the duchy of Milan (see NEAPOLITAN REVOLT OF 1485–86), invited French king Charles VIII (1470–98) to pursue his Angevin claim to Naples. French forces, led by Charles and accompanied by Swiss troops and strong artillery, crossed the Alps into Italy in 1494 and moved easily through Lombardy. In Florence, Pietro de' Medici (1471–1503) was overthrown and a constitutional republican government was insti-

tuted under the inspiration of Girolamo Savonarola (1452–98), who welcomed Charles as the fulfillment of a prophecy to reform Florentine society. Pope Alexander VI (1431?–1503) made concessions to ease Charles out of papal lands and then formed the League of Venice against him. Charles's conquest of Naples was shortened by disease and military failures, and he returned to France in 1495, after barely escaping defeat at the Battle of Fornovo (Taro). King Ferdinand II (1452–1516) of Aragon, whom Pope Alexander awarded the title "the Catholic" because of his interventions in Italy, was reinstated as ruler of Naples. Charles gained nothing by his warring venture, which, however, revealed Italian inability to unite against an external threat and foreshadowed later French campaigns that would end the independence of Italian states.

Italian War of Independence of 1848–49   See ITALIAN REVOLUTION OF 1848–49.

Italian War of Independence of 1859–61   Seeking to create a northern Italian kingdom, Napoleon III (1808–73) of France and Prime Minister Camillo Cavour (1810–61) of Piedmont (part of the Kingdom of Sardinia) formed an alliance to expel Austria from the area, thus provoking Austria to declare war and to invade Piedmont in April 1859. In June 1859, French-Piedmontese forces defeated the Austrians at Magenta and Solferino and occupied Milan. However, fearful of Italian power, Napoleon unexpectedly signed the Peace of Zurich, granting Lombardy to Piedmont and allowing Austria to retain Venetia (dominated by Venice) and thus perpetuating Italian disunity. Most Italians were enraged. On April 15, 1860, Cavour, after agreeing to the cession of Savoy and Nice to France, held a plebiscite, whereby Parma, Modena, Tuscany, and Romagna voted to join Piedmont (the Kingdom of Sardinia was to become the Kingdom of Italy). In the south, Giuseppe Garibaldi (1807–82) and his "Thousand Red Shirts" landed at Marsala, Sicily, having sailed from Genoa; marched inland, aiding the rebelling Sicilians against Francis II (1836–94), king of the Two Sicilies; defeated the Neapolitans at Calatafimi on May 15, 1860; and seized Palermo. Cavour, initially opposed to Garibaldi's tactics, now supported the revolt in the south and sought to annex the Two Sicilies to the northern Italian kingdom. Garibaldi, who mistrusted Cavour, crossed to the mainland, seized Naples, but was stopped by the Bourbon (French) army at the Liri River. Piedmontese forces invaded the Papal States, taking Umbria and the Marches and decisively defeating the papal army at Castelfidardo on September 18, 1860. Cavour moved into Naples, hoping to pressure Garibaldi to give up his territory. After plebiscites affirmed the Italian people's desire to join Piedmont, Garibaldi relinquished his conquests and retired to Caprera. An emergency government was formed, and its all-Italian parliament at Turin in February 1861 declared King Victor Emmanuel II (1820–78) of Sardinia the constitutional "King of Italy." Only Venetia (under Austrian rule) and Rome (occupied by the French) remained out of the Kingdom of Italy. After Cavour died, Garibaldi rallied volunteers to his banner and prepared to attack Rome, but the Italian government, fearing an international crisis, sent troops to intercept Garibaldi's force. At the Battle of Aspromonte on August 29, 1862, Garibaldi suffered defeat, was wounded, and captured (later he was pardoned). In 1866, Italy allied itself with Prussia against Austria (see SEVEN WEEKS' WAR). Victor Emmanuel refused an Austrian offer to let Venice join the kingdom in return for Italy's withdrawal from Prussia. Although Italy lost important battles on land (Custoza on June 24, 1866) and sea (Lissa on July 20, 1866), it received Venetia by the terms of the Treaty of Vienna that concluded the war. Garibaldi and his supporters again attempted to take Rome but were crushed by the French at Mentana on November 3, 1867. When France withdrew its soldiers from Rome because of the FRANCO-PRUSSIAN WAR in 1870, Italian forces invaded the city and took possession with little difficulty. After the Romans voted to join Italy, the Italian government's capital was transferred from Florence to Rome. See also ITALIAN REVOLUTION OF 1848–49.

Italian War of Louis XII (1499–1503) Louis XII (1462–1515) succeeded Charles VIII (1470–98) as king of France in 1498 and hoped through alliances with the Venetians and Swiss to pursue his claim to Milan inherited from his grandmother Valentina Visconti (1366–1408). Lodovico Sforza (1451–1508), duke of Milan, fled from the city to form an army and returned to find the French under Gian Giacomo Trivulzio (1441?–1518), an Italian condottiere (leader of mercenary soldiers) in service to the French, in possession of Milan. At the Battle of Novara, which ensued in 1500, Sforza's Swiss mercenaries refused to fight those hired by France, and the French won and Louis XII became duke of Milan. Sforza was taken to France as a prisoner. Louis, aided by Ferdinand II "the Catholic" (1452–1516) of Aragon, conquered Naples in 1501 (in the Treaty of Grenada of 1500, Louis and Ferdinand had agreed to divide the Kingdom of the Two Sicilies—Sicily and Naples—thereby discounting the illegitimate Aragonese line claim). A quarrel developed between the two, and, after the French suffered battle defeats by the Spanish at Cerignola and Garigliano, Louis recognized the Two Sicilies to be under the Spanish Crown. Genoa and Milan were at most times under French control until 1528 and 1535, respectively.

Italo-Ethiopian War of 1887–89 The Italians, helped by the British, who were trying to control Sudanese Muslim fanatics called Mahdists, secured a base on Ethiopia's Red Sea coastline at Massawa (Mitsiwa) in Eritrea in 1885; the Italians also purchased the port of Aseb in Eritrea from a local ruler. Desirous of exploiting more than the coastline area, they made a pact with the chieftain of Shewa (who later became Ethiopia's Emperor Menelik II [1844–1913] in 1889) and began, with British encouragement, to penetrate the Eritrean hinterland. Ethiopian forces of Emperor Yohannes (John) IV (1831–89) marched against the Italians, some 500 of whom were surrounded and nearly all killed at the Battle of Dogali on January 26, 1887. Italy sent an army of 20,000 men in response, garrisoning it in Eritrea, but little fighting took place; eventually dysentery and fever caused its recall. Yohannes became preoccupied fighting the invading Mahdists in northern Ethiopia and died at the Battle of Metemma (Gallabat) on March 12, 1889. With the support of the Italians, Menelik now took the throne and soon negotiated the Treaty of Uccialli with Italy (May 2, 1889). The Italians interpreted the treaty as giving them a protectorate over Ethiopia, which Menelik rejected as unjustified according to the text (1891). But Britain accepted the Italian protectorate over Ethiopia.

Italo-Ethiopian War of 1895–96 The wording of the Italian and Amharic versions of the Treaty of Uccialli differed (see ITALO-ETHIOPIAN WAR OF 1887–89): Italy claimed suzerainty over all of Ethiopia, but Ethiopia's Emperor Menelik II (1844–1913) said this was not so according to the text. In 1895, the Italians made further encroachments into Ethiopia and occupied the district of Tigre. Menelik's forces defeated about 2,400 Italians at Mekele and gained their surrender. In response, Italy sent reinforcements—some 20,000 soldiers—who met 80,000 Ethiopians at the Battle of Aduwa (Adowa or Adwa) on March 1, 1896. The Ethiopians won an overwhelming victory, killing about 6,500 of the enemy and taking some 2,500 prisoners. The defeated Italian general Oreste Baratieri (1841–1901) was forced to retire afterward, and the Italians were compelled to sue for peace and signed the Treaty of Addis Ababa on October 26, 1896. Italy recognized Ethiopia's independence and held only a coastal colony in Eritrea. A treaty in 1900 reduced the Italian holdings in Ethiopia to about 80 square miles, another humiliation.

Italo-Ethiopian War of 1935–36 As early as 1928, Benito Mussolini (1883–1945), dictator of Italy since 1922, had planned to avenge the Italian defeat in the ITALO-ETHIOPIAN WAR OF 1895–96. In a blatantly underhanded way, he sought to convince the world of Italy's right to Ethiopia, appealing to the League of Nations after altering the treaty documents of 1887, 1896, and 1900 and a great power

agreement of 1908. His ploy worked: the League of Nations suggested partition, but Ethiopia rejected the Hoare-Laval plan, which would have given Italy most of the country. In 1934, a bloody clash occurred between Italian and Ethiopian forces at Ualual, a disputed area on the Italian Somaliland border. Ethiopia's Emperor Haile Selassie I (1891–1975) pulled his troops back 20 miles from the Eritrean border, but nonetheless the Italians invaded Ethiopia without declaring war on October 3, 1935. Using aircraft and modern weapons, Italian forces slowly destroyed Ethiopia, which had little means to defend itself. The Ethiopian capital of Addis Ababa was captured on May 5, 1936; Haile Selassie fled and made a vain appeal for help to the League of Nations; Italy, however, had already called its king "emperor of Ethiopia," had annexed Ethiopia, and had united it with Eritrea and Italian Somaliland to form Italian East Africa. The Italians executed the archbishop of the Ethiopian Coptic Church, massacred monks, and decimated Addis Ababa. Although Italy had failed to conquer the entire country, it occupied it until 1941, when Ethiopia was liberated by British, Free French, and Ethiopian troops during WORLD WAR II. Haile Selassie regained his throne on May 5, 1941.

Italo-Turkish War of 1911–12 During the dismemberment of the Porte's (Ottoman government) African holdings in the late 1800s, France took over Tunisia as a protectorate, and Italy objected, always having desired to establish a colony in North Africa. To prepare for an annexation of the Turkish provinces of Tripolitana and Cyrenaica (Libya), Italy sent both immigrants and merchants to the areas between 1880 and 1910. Using the pretext that the Italians were being maltreated there, Italy's government issued a 24-hour ultimatum on September 28, 1911, threatening to invade. Declaring war the next day, Italy sent 50,000 troops and caught the Porte at Constantinople (Istanbul) both unprepared and sorely hampered. After bombarding Tripoli, Libya's capital, Italian forces seized control in October 1911. Egypt, declaring neutrality, refused to allow the passage of Ottoman troops, and thus only a few, mostly officers, landed to enlist native Arab aid, occupy some coastal areas, and help force a stalemate in the war by November, 1911. As a diversion, Italy began a naval campaign (1912), bombarding Beirut and Smyrna, occupying Rhodes, Kos, and other Dodecanese Islands, and, by bombarding forts protecting the Dardanelles, forcing the closing of the straits. The CUP-led Ottoman government fell; by the peace Treaty of Ouchy, near Lausanne, Switzerland, concluding the war on October 15, 1912, the Turks ceded Libya, Rhodes, and the Dodecanese Islands to Italy. See also BALKAN WARS; YOUNG TURKS' REBELLION.

J

Jacobite Rebellion of 1689–90   After Holland's stadholder William (1650–1702) of Orange was invited by the English Parliament to accept England's throne (1688), Tories loyal to King James II (1633–1701) and the Stuarts banded together, becoming known as Jacobites (Latin *Jacobus* equals "James"). In 1689, while James was in Ireland, the Jacobites in the highlands of Scotland pressed for James's restoration (see GLORIOUS REVOLUTION). William, already recognized as king by the majority of Scots, sent troops to suppress them, almost losing at Killiecrankie, until the Jacobite leader, viscount of Dundee, was killed. The Jacobites dispersed. At Dunkeld, the Jacobites lost again in a savage encounter and retreated to their hills and glens. Another Jacobite attempt at Cromdale ended in disaster in 1690, as did James's Irish campaign at the Battle of the Boyne on July 1 of that year. James died in exile in France in 1701 without trying again to retake the English throne. William built forts in Scotland and tried vainly to win Highland loyalty (see GLENCOE MASSACRE).

Jacobite Rebellion of 1715–16   ("The Fifteen") Losers the first time in their attempt to restore James II (1633–1701) to the English and Scottish thrones (see JACOBITE REBELLION OF 1689–90), the Jacobites opposed the Union of Scotland and England in 1707 and, by four votes, lost a repeal motion in 1713. After the death of Queen Anne (1665–1714),

James's second daughter, the Jacobites based new hope on James Edward (James Francis Edward Stuart) (1688–1766), James's son, who asked for a clan uprising in Scotland. The earl of Mar led the rebellion, proclaiming James Edward king (James III in England; James VIII in Scotland) in 1715 and denouncing the union. Seizing Perth, Mar's forces failed to go on to Stirling, allowing English troops to travel north. Mar's men dashed south and joined with English Jacobites, whose poor judgment permitted a royalist victory at Preston on November 14, 1715. Civil war developed in Scotland just as Dutch mercenaries fought an indecisive battle with Mar's forces at Sheriffmuir in mid-November 1715. In the meantime, English royalist troops increased in number. James Edward came to Scotland, but, overwhelmed by English forces in 1716, he and Mar escaped to France. The government in London acted swiftly, deporting and executing rebels, declaring peerages forfeit, disarming clans, and fortifying but never truly gaining the Scots' loyalties. See also JACOBITE REBELLION OF 1745–46.

Jacobite Rebellion of 1745–46   ("The Forty-five") Mostly stubborn Scots, the Jacobites plotted untried uprisings in 1719 and 1742 in support of the descendants of former king James II (1633–1701) (see JACOBITE REBELLION OF 1715–16). In 1745, Charles Edward Stuart (1720–88), son of James Edward (1688–1766), known as the "Old

Pretender" to the throne, came to Scotland with seven men. After his father was again proclaimed King James III, he gained support rapidly, went to Edinburgh, captured Perth, and then defeated two government regiments at Coltbridge. "Bonnie Prince Charlie" was an able leader: he chased two royalist regiments of English dragoons at the Battle of Prestonpans with a single charge on September 21, 1745, and then invaded Lancashire, taking Carlisle and Manchester. Moving on to Derby, he returned to Scotland for a spring offensive; his Scottish Highlanders defeated the English royalists at the Battle of Falkirk in early 1746 but were slaughtered by the English at Culloden Moor on April 16, 1746 (Charles barely escaped with his life). Despite a reward of 30,000 pounds, he wandered unhindered in the Highland until he returned to France, a perpetual exile.

Jacquerie (1358) Forgotten during the HUNDRED YEARS' WAR were the French peasants, who suffered from both the invading English soldiers and their own lords. Losing their homes to pillage, the peasants could work only if sentinels were posted; they spent their nights in caves, marshes, and forests. Soldiers demanded money and food on pain of death; lords demanded crops and animals to pay ransoms or recoup losses caused by the Black Death (plague). The Jacquerie, revolt of the French peasantry or collection of Jacques or Jacques Bonhomme (scornful nickname used by the nobles to refer to a peasant), began near Beauvais, north of Paris, in May 1358; peasants under Guillaume Cale (d. 1358) ravaged the countryside, burned castles, and murdered nobles—all in a vain attempt for justice. They joined the Parisian rebels under Étienne Marcel (d. 1358), who was trying to overthrow French king Charles V (1338–80). Marcel was murdered after the Parisians were crushed. Nobles, led by Charles II (1332–87) of Navarre and others, acted against the peasants, slaying many, capturing and executing their leaders, and massacring the dispersing peasant rebels for their insolence. See also PEASANTS' REVOLT, ENGLISH.

Jameson's Raid (1895–96) Cecil John Rhodes (1853–1902), British prime minister of the Cape Colony, plotted with Sir Leander Starr Jameson (1853–1917), British colonial administrator of Mashonaland, to overthrow the Boer government of the Transvaal under President S. J. Paul Kruger (1825–1904). Rhodes, who controlled extensive diamond mines, envisioned a federation of all South Africa under the British flag. On December 29, 1895, Jameson, disregarding Rhodes's request to delay any action, invaded the Transvaal with some 600 mounted men but suffered defeat at Krugersdorp on January 1, 1896, and surrendered the next day. The Boers handed him over to the British, at their request; Jameson was tried and convicted in London and served only several months in prison. Others in the raiding party were eventually released by the Boers in exchange for a large payment. See also BOER WAR, SECOND OR GREAT.

Jamestown Massacre (1622) The English colonists who had settled at Jamestown, Va., in 1607 maintained peaceful relations with the surrounding Algonkin-speaking Indian tribes, joined into a confederation under Chief Wahunsonacock (1550?–1618), known as Powhatan to the English. After Powhatan died, he was succeeded by his elderly brother, Opechoncanough (d. 1644), who outwardly remained friendly with the colonists for four years. On March 22, 1622, he led the Indians in a surprise attack on Jamestown and the environs, slaying some 350 men, women, and children. The so-called POWHATAN WAR had begun.

Janissaries' Revolt of 1621–22 Created as a non-Turkish elite force by Sultan Murad I (1319–89) and reformed as a salaried guard under direct control of Sultan Murad II (1403–51), the Janissaries proved to be neither as docile nor as loyal as expected. By 1600, the corps had become a powerful political force and was often the unwitting tool of the ambitious; the Janissaries' revolts or threats to revolt became a constant danger, especially in peacetime, when they received no salaries. In 1618, they had deposed the imbecile Sultan Mustafa I (1591–1639) and enthroned the adolescent Osman II (1604–22), who had dreams of martial glory. Raising a huge army to fight the Poles, whose Ukrainian Cossacks had skirmished with the Ottoman Empire's Crimean Tatars (Tartars), Osman led it to the Dniester River and vainly attacked Chozim in 1621. The disgruntled Turkish troops, having experienced heavy losses, refused to fight further. When Osman returned to Constantinople (Istanbul) claiming a momentous victory, his Janissaries (who had not been paid) upbraided him and threatened to revolt. Osman tried to overcome them by setting up a new militia that would pretend to march to Asia; instead, it would double back to exterminate the Janissaries. The secret leaked; the Janissaries revolted and stormed the palaces (1622). Osman promised to revoke his scheme, but they entered the royal seraglio, demanded the person of Mustafa I, killed the grand vizier and chief black eunuch, crowned Mustafa as sultan, and paraded Osman to their barracks, where they had him strangled—the first regicide in Ottoman history. His ear was sent to the Sultana Valide (queen mother), who had authorized Osman's execution in order to rule through Mustafa. Their reign was brief. In 1623, Murad IV (1609–40) was on the throne, but only because the military had demanded the change. See also TURKO-PERSIAN WAR OF 1623–38.

Janissaries' Revolt of 1703 The failure of the Porte (Ottoman Turkish government) to pay its troops, the Janissaries, in 1703 caused a six-week revolt that almost became a civil war. Ottoman sultan Mustafa II (1664–1704) hid in Adrianople, gathering a rival army and refusing to come to Constantinople (Istanbul), the Turkish capital, as demanded. The Janissaries, possessing the Prophet's sacred standard, came to him, achieved the defection of the rival army, and forced his abdication in favor of Ahmed III (1673–1736). But Ahmed, installed through violence, was himself to be the victim of the JANISSARIES' REVOLT OF 1730.

Janissaries' Revolt of 1730 Despite the success of Persia's Nadir Shah (1688–1747) in forcing Turkish squatters out of many Persian territories (see PERSIAN CIVIL WAR OF 1725–30), the Ottoman Empire's elite corps, the Janissaries, were not called into action; unemployed, they were also unpaid. When the Persian police action spilled over into Ottoman territory to spark the TURKO-PERSIAN WAR OF 1730–36, the Janissaries delayed involvement for two months by supporting a rebellion among 12,000 Albanian troops. In Constantinople (Istanbul) rebels strangled the Ottoman grand vizier, the chief admiral, and other senior officials; they also forced the abdication (but not the execution) of Sultan Ahmed III (1673–1736) and the enthronement of his nephew, Mahmud I (1696–1754). Even the change of sultan failed to end the revolt. A scheme developed by the new sultan and the Divan (Turkish privy council) succeeded as many Janissaries ceased to back the rebels, whose leader was invited to a meeting of the Divan, seized, and strangled in front of the sultan. Then, for three weeks, a general massacre of the rebels occurred in which 7,000 died, thus weakening their rebellious ardor. The massacres and consequent banishments reduced the military by some 50,000 men, but the war against the Persians was now ready to proceed.

Janissaries' Revolt of 1807–8 Difficulties with the undependable Janissaries led Ottoman sultan Selim III (1761–1808) to decree in 1805 the formation of a "New Order": regiments trained after the current French model. The European Janissaries objected with some violence, and the decree was withdrawn. However, in 1807, auxiliary troops (Yamaks) rebelled against the European-style uniforms, and the Janissaries joined them. Reformers among the sultan's counselors and ministers, blocked by a ruling of the grand mufti that such uniforms were contrary to Muslim law, were tried and executed. Selim was deposed; his relative Mustafa IV (1779–1808) acceded briefly until Selim's supporters stormed the palace, only to discover that Mustafa had ordered Selim strangled. The unruly Janissaries now dragged Mustafa from his throne, had him strangled with the usual bowstring, and proclaimed Mahmud II (1784–1839) sultan. The Janissaries' leader became the new grand vizier, who enthusiastically introduced Selim's New Order. But the Janissaries then proved they could be subtle as well as obstinate, for they feigned acceptance, detained the grand vizier, and murdered him, postponing their own annihilation for less than two decades.

Janissaries' Revolt of 1826 Ottoman sultan Mahmud II (1784–1839), nicknamed "the Reformer," wanted to eliminate the ungovernable Janissaries (elite corps), the throne's most powerful enemy within the Ottoman Empire. Convinced that modernization was necessary and aware that earlier attempts at military reform had met with violent resistance, he gained the support of the grand mufti and quietly concentrated on improving the artillery in his own personal army before decreeing a "New Order," with a difference: instead of dismissing the Janissaries, he would put 150 from each battalion into each division of his new corps, meanwhile explaining that he was reviving an old Ottoman order. The Janissaries, contumacious as usual, stormed the palace, where Mahmud's soldiers sprayed them with grapeshot. Retreating to their barracks, the Janissaries found themselves there the targets of the sultan's artillery, as well as the victims of Turkish mobs; 4,000 Janissaries died, and thousands of others were soon slain in the provinces. The term Janissary was proscribed, and their abettors, the Bektashi dervishes, were outlawed.

January Insurrection See POLISH REBELLION OF 1863–64.

Japanese Civil War of A.D. **672** In Japan this war of imperial succession was called Jinshinno-ran. When Emperor Tenchi (Tenji) (626–71) died, the aristocratic Nakatomi and Soga families, who had opposed his efforts to centralize the government, put Prince Otomo (fl. 672) on the throne instead of Prince Oama (673–86), the dead emperor's son. The latter was furious and set about raising an army. His warriors clashed with Otomo's forces outside his capital in Omi province (Shiga Prefecture) and beat them severely. Oama then ascended the throne as Emperor Temmu Tenno. He established a new capital at Asuka in Yamato province (Nara Prefecture), far away from the homes of the troublesome Nakatomi and Soga families.

Japanese Civil War of A.D. **764–65** After Empress Koken (718–70) gave up the Japanese throne (758) in favor of the young emperor Junnin (d. 766?), she donned the robes of a nun but continued to wield power with advice from an ambitious and attractive Buddhist priest named Dokyo (d. 772), who became presumably her lover. Junnin's favorite and leading minister Oshikatsu (Nakamaro) (d. 765), of the Fujiwara family, grew jealous of Dokyo when the latter acquired dominant influence in the government. And subsequently the power struggle between the two erupted into a civil war in 764; after some fierce fighting, Oshikatsu and most of his chief followers were defeated and killed. Koken reascended the throne as Empress Shotoku and arrested the emperor, who was banished to the distant island of Awaji; she soon made Dokyo her prime minister and later gave him the title *Ho-o* ("pope"). Upon the empress's death, Dokyo failed to ascend to the throne because of strong opposition from government officials, many of whom were Fujiwaras; his false prediction from an oracle that he should be emperor embittered many. Dokyo was banished from the capital, and the Japanese, leery of female rulers, did not allow another empress to reign until the 17th century.

Japanese Civil War of A.D. **936–41** The latter part of the 10th century was generally a peaceful time in Japan, during which art and literature flourished at the elegant and cultured court at Kyoto. However, intense civil strife did disturb the peace. Pirates had long been a menace in the Inland Sea, and in 936 the government sent Sumitomo (d. 941) of the Fujiwara family west to subdue them. He was successful in his mission, but once it was accomplished, he and his followers began plundering the western provinces themselves in defiance of imperial orders. Troops were dispatched against them; the chief of the local military family of Minamoto joined these forces in crushing the rebels. After Sumitomo's death in battle, anarchy subsided and peace returned to the area. Meanwhile, in the eastern region of Kanto, Masakado (d. 940) of the Taira family had been expanding his territory. In 939, he felt strong enough to declare himself emperor of Kanto. He set up his own government modeled after that at Kyoto. But his reign was short. Another chieftain of the Taira family turned against him, and in 940 Masakado was quashed. Although neither disturbance was long or had lasting significance, they did signal the rise of the Japanese military class upon which the court would increasingly depend for protection and strength.

Japanese Civil War of 1156 See HOGEN WAR.

Japanese Civil War of 1159–60 See HEIJI WAR.

Japanese Civil War of 1180–85 See GEMPEI WAR.

Japanese Civil War of 1221 See JOKYU WAR.

Japanese Civil War of 1331–33 The imperial court at Kyoto and the military headquarters, the Bakufu, at Kamakura both wanted to control Japan. The Hojo shogunate had wielded the actual power for decades, but even its supporters, the Minamotos, became distrustful and discontent. In 1331, the agents of the shogunate discovered that Emperor Daigo II (1287–1339) was planning to destroy Kamakura. The emperor tried to resist the troops sent against him, but he was taken prisoner in 1332 and exiled to the island of Oki. The following year he escaped, returned to the mainland, and raised his standard. Warriors from all over Japan flocked to his support. Many of the most powerful officers at the Bakufu deserted in his favor. Ashikaga Takauji (1305–58), a Minamoto general ordered to lead the

Bakufu army against the imperial army, turned himself and his troops over to the emperor. He and another former Bakufu general then burned Kamakura to the ground and ended the rule of the Hojo shogunate. Peace was short-lived, however, and strife swept the country again in a few years (see JAPANESE CIVIL WARS OF 1336–92).

Japanese Civil War of 1467–77 See ONIN WAR.

Japanese Civil War of 1863–68 See MEIJI RESTORATION.

Japanese Civil Wars of 1336–92   Ashikaga Takauji (1305–58), the general who had deserted his former colleagues and destroyed Kamakura for the emperor (see JAPANESE CIVIL WAR OF 1331–33), soon turned against Emperor Go-Daigo (1287–1339). In 1335, he sided with a rebellious movement in Kanto, set himself at the head of its army, and in 1336 captured the capital at Kyoto. Go-Daigo was imprisoned, but he escaped the following year and fled to the mountains in the Yamato district with the imperial regalia. Takauji placed a puppet upon the throne, who rewarded him by naming him shogun, a title that would remain in his family for the next 245 years. Go-Daigo denounced both the shogun and puppet emperor as rebels and set up a rival court in the south at Yoshino. The rivalry between the two courts soon engulfed the whole country. Feudal lords sided with one faction and then the other, and lawlessness and brigandage were rampant. This period of continual sporadic fighting in one province and then another has been called "The Age of the Turncoats." In 1367, the ablest of the Ashikaga shoguns, Yoshimitsu (1358–95), came to power and realized that the internal strife was impoverishing the country. He restored friendly relations with China and Korea, attempted to suppress piracy, and tried to reestablish order in the countryside. In 1392, he persuaded the ruler of the southern court to abdicate in favor of the northern emperor. The legal regalia were returned to the north, and the deposed ruler received a handsome pension and official recognition as a former emperor. Feuding and fighting continued in the provinces for some years, but generally Japan was at peace with itself and its neighbors.

Japanese Civil Wars of 1450–1550   Known in Japan as the "Epoch of the Warring Country," this was a period of continual civil wars, rebellions, banditry, feuds, and strife. Both the shogunate and the imperial court lost all semblance of authority, and central control of the empire disintegrated, except for the area immediately adjacent to the capital at Kyoto. The warrior class (samurai) became dominant and replaced the knights who once supported the shogun. They gave their allegiance to local leaders, some of whom became territorial lords known as daimyo. These daimyo ruled their domains as they pleased and paid no taxes nor gave any loyalty to the emperor. Instead they set up their own tax collectors, armies, and systems of governance. Many peasants left the land and joined the private armies in which, if they were capable, they could rise in rank. Of course, the daimyo, like the petty princes of Europe during the Middle Ages, made constant war on each other in efforts to extend their holdings and increase their power. Rival factions within a domain also fought for leadership. Great families or clans arose, only to fall (see ONIN WAR). Even monks in the Buddhist monasteries made war on each other (see MONKS, WAR OF THE). It was a time of political chaos and widespread turmoil similar to the dark and Middle Ages in Western Europe.

Japanese Civil Wars of 1560–84   Oda Nobunaga (1534–82) became the territorial daimyo (lord) of Owari in eastern Japan at age 16, and his powerful neighbor to the north thought it would be easy to overcome the young ruler and absorb his domain. In 1560, the head of the Imagawa family amassed his troops and invaded Owari, but he had underestimated Nobunaga. The invader's army was badly defeated and driven from Owari, and he himself was slain. Nobunaga then made an alliance with Tokugawa Iyeyasu (1542–1616), daimyo of Mikawa,

and with the daimyo of Kari. Once he felt secure in the east, Nobunaga turned westward in 1562 and in two years conquered the province of Mino. Then he invaded Ise to the south, and although he was unable to conquer it completely, his able general, Toyotomi Hideyoshi (1536–98), persuaded most of the provincial daimyos to join Nobunaga's standard. In 1567, Nobunaga was invited to Kyoto, Japan's capital, to restore order, for there were bloody feuds over the succession of the shogun. The following year he completed his task and became vice-shogun, usually a subordinate position but one that Nobunaga made powerful. Fearing the rise of a strong central authority, his former allies turned against him; only Iyeyasu and minor daimyos of Ise remained loyal. From 1570 to 1573, civil war raged between these rivals, and after Nobunaga was victorious, his fortunes improved. He subdued the Kwanto in the northeast and the area between it and five provinces around Kyoto. He also attacked the Buddhist monasteries in the Hiyesian hills above Kyoto because they had aided his enemies, and ruthlessly destroyed their settlements and slaughtered their soldier-monks. He then smashed, with less severity, the monasteries in the provinces under his control. In 1582, while preparing to go to the aid of Hideyoshi, who was fighting on the island of Shikoku, Nobunaga was assassinated by one of his vassals who promptly proclaimed himself shogun. Hideyoshi concluded an advantageous truce with his Shikoku opponent and rushed back to the capital with more than 30,000 men and avenged Nobunaga's death. The following year he was given the office of kwampaku (regent) of the empire. But Nobunaga's heirs and retainers resented the rise to power of this peasant-soldier and turned against him. Once more an alliance was split into two warring factions. By diplomacy and superior arms, Hideyoshi triumphed, and by 1584 he was recognized as the central authority of Japan. A treaty with Iyeyasu strengthened his position. By 1590, the entire country from north to south and west to east was unified as one nation, and Hideyoshi's concilatory behavior toward his former foes won their loyalty and support.

Japanese Conquest of Korea (1592–99)   After he had succeeded in unifying Japan (see JAPANESE CIVIL WARS OF 1560–84), Toyotomi Hideyoshi (1536–98) embarked on a grandiose plan to conquer Korea and then China. In May 1592, the first Japanese expeditionary force landed at Fusan (Pusan) in southern Korea and 18 days later reached Seoul. Within six weeks the Korean government collapsed; in desperation it appealed to China for help. Although the Japanese controlled the Korean peninsula, they did not control the 120 miles of ocean between the two countries. The Koreans had a far superior naval fleet consisting of turtle or tortoise boats that had iron-plated roofs studded with spikes to prevent the enemy from boarding. They were propelled by oars and were so designed that they could be rowed in both directions. The Japanese on the other hand, had only open transports that were slow and unwieldy. The turtle boats would pretend to flee and, after a Japanese ship set off in pursuit, they would reverse direction, ram the transport with their powerful beaks, and send it to the ocean bottom. These first ironclads in history prevented Hideyoshi's reinforcements from reaching Korea. The first Chinese troops that came to the aid of Korea were defeated, but in January 1593, a stronger army arrived, and it began driving the Japanese back south. In May of that year a preliminary truce was arranged, and the Japanese withdrew to the southern coast. Negotiations dragged on for years. When, in the spring 1597, Hideyoshi received a letter from the Chinese emperor ordering him to behave like a loyal vassal of China, he was so angry that he ordered the resumption of hostilities. Again thousands of Japanese soldiers landed in southern Korea and fought their way north. As earlier, they were initially successful but unable to win a decisive victory. Then in August 1598, Hideyoshi died, and the invasion came to a halt. Soon the Japanese troops returned home, leaving behind a desolated land, a starving population, and thousands of dead. Despite the armistice, many of their transports were attacked by turtle boats and sunk by those strange looking but deadly, effective vessels.

Japanese Earlier Nine Years' War   (1051–62)   The Abe family or clan ruled the section of Mutsu province that bordered the Kitakami River in northeastern Japan. It refused to pay taxes or contribute to the province's expenses. When the clan began to expand its domain, the governors of Mutsu and Dewa provinces joined forces and marched against them. Their army was defeated and compelled to retreat. When the imperial court learned of this, it ordered Minamoto Yoriyoshi (988–1075) and his son, Yoshiie (1039–1106), to go to Mutsu and crush the rebellious family. Yoritoki Abe (d. 1056) was pierced by an arrow in the first engagement, but his son, Sadato (1019–1062), took over the command and continued the war. He cut the Minamoto troops to pieces at Kawasaki in 1058, and only a few escaped in a snowstorm. Four years later the Minamotos returned with a fresh army and 10,000 additional men from the Kiyohara family in Dewa. The second Abe son soon surrendered and was exiled, but Sadato fought on despite two defeats. In the third battle at his base in Kuriyagawa, his fort was set on fire, and he was slain. His severed head was sent to the emperor in Kyoto.

Japanese Later Three Years' War   (1083–87)   The Kiyowara clan or family of Japan's northern province of Mutsu had many branches, which constantly quarreled with each other. The governor of Mutsu, Minamoto Yoshiie (1039–1106), tried to stop the fighting between the clan leaders, and when the violence continued, he determined that he would have to intervene with his own warriors. In 1086, he attacked the fort where Iyehira (fl. 1080s) and his Kiyowara rebels had withdrawn for the winter, but his siege was unsuccessful. Many of Yoshiie's men died from intense cold and hunger; the survivors had to retreat. He then assembled a new army, which was reinforced with troops brought by his younger brother and the Fujiwara family. Together they laid siege to the Kiyowara fortress at Kanazawa. After four months their enemy gave in, and the Kiyowara leaders were killed while trying to escape from their burning stockade. The dates of this war are misleading, for the name refers to the period of actual fighting and does not count periods of inactivity.

Japanese War of Succession See JAPANESE CIVIL WARS OF 1336–92.

Javanese-Chinese-Dutch War (1740–43) For centuries Chinese merchants had been trading with the ports of Java (Indonesian island). When the Dutch East India Company set up its headquarters at Batavia (Djakarta, Java), many Chinese settled there and were active in the commercial life. In time the Chinese population on Java greatly outnumbered the Europeans, and the Dutch became worried about the large number of unemployed Chinese and began to deport them to Ceylon (Sri Lanka) and the Cape of Good Hope (Cape Province, South Africa). In 1740, the Chinese rebelled in Batavia, where many were massacred by the well-armed Dutch in a panic. With the support of Javanese dissidents, the Chinese throughout Java began waging war; the sugar industry on the island came to a halt while the Javanese rulers debated which side to support. Mataram's King Pakubuwono II (d. 1743), who originally backed the Chinese and whose troops slaughtered a Dutch garrison in Kartosuro, soon switched sides when he realized the Dutch were far stronger than the Chinese. Peace finally came after Pakubuwono agreed to cede his northern coastal region to the Dutch. The Chinese, although seriously depleted in number, remained in their own communities in the port cities and towns of Java and, by the end of the century, became indispensable middlemen in the Javanese economy.

Javanese War of Succession, First (1704–7) During the 17th century the Dutch firmly established themselves in the coastal city of Batavia (Djakarta, Java, Indonesia) and frequently meddled in the affairs of rival kings and sultans in the East Indies (the Malay Archipelago). A runaway Balinese slave named Surapati (d. 1707) organized a force of natives against the Dutch in the early 1700s, and when the Dutch tried to capture him, he sought and received refuge from King Amangkurat III (fl. 1703–8) of Mataram, a kingdom in central Java. Surapati then moved to Java's northeastern part and set himself up as king. To punish Amangkurat for harboring Surapati, the Dutch supported a rival claimant to the Mataram throne, Pakubuwono I (d. 1719), who was Amangkurat's uncle. Together they defeated Amangkurat, who fled eastward to safety with Surapati; Pakubuwono was enthroned (1704). The Dutch, however, pursued Amangkurat and crushed him and Surapati, who was killed; in 1708, Amangkurat was forced into exile in Ceylon (Sri Lanka). **Second Javanese War of Succession** (1719–23). Upon the death of King Pakubuwono of Mataram, many native princes claimed the throne and initiated war. Again the Dutch on the island of Java intervened and supported whom they thought would be most pliable to their wishes. It took four years of bloodshed to capture all the rival claimants and send them into exile; the Dutch expanded their territorial control in Java. **Third Javanese War of Succession** (1749–57). Mataram had become a virtual vassal kingdom of the Dutch East India Company. King Pakubuwono III (fl. 1743–57), involved in a dynastic dispute, received Dutch military support against two royal challengers, who had joined in a war to dethrone him. In 1751, the Dutch suffered a serious defeat, and their commander was slain. One of the challengers eventually agreed to peace (the Gianti Agreement, 1755), by which Mataram was split in two: Pakubuwono's eastern part with its capital at Surakarta, and the western part centered at Jogjakarta. The other challenger resisted until 1757, when he made peace with the Dutch and consequently was given a portion of eastern Mataram.

Java War, Great (Dipo Negoro's War) (1815–30) Prince Dipo Negoro (c. 1785–1855), the eldest son of the third ruler of Jogjakarta, was passed over in the succession to the throne, which was taken by a Dutch-supported younger claimant in 1822 (see JAVANESE WAR OF SUCCESSION, THIRD). Dutch land reforms on Java had economically hurt many indigenous Muslim aristocrats, who rallied to Dipo Negoro's side when he invoked the name of Muhammad (570–632) and preached a jihad (Muslim holy war) against the infidel Dutch in an effort to overthrow their rule. The war was precipitated when the government built a road over land beside a sacred tomb; the Javanese common people and aristocracy believed the "just prince," Dipo Negoro, would cast out the infidels, right wrongs, and bring peace. Under Negoro's skillful military leadership, the Javanese carried on successful guerrilla warfare until 1828, when the Dutch won a major battle and then proceeded to establish a number of strongholds around the country and connected them with good roads on which "flying" columns could operate. This expensive system turned the tide. In 1829, two of Dipo Negoro's top aides surrendered, and the following year the prince agreed to negotiate peace. During a meeting, when he refused to give up his title and his claim to be a protector of Islam, the Dutch, despite their promise of safe conduct, arrested him and sent him into exile in Celebes. The Dutch, who had suffered about 15,000 soldier deaths in the war, regained power and gradually instituted fairer economic policies. See also ANGLO-DUTCH WAR IN JAVA; PADRI WAR.

Jenkins' Ear, War of (1739–43) Deteriorating relations between England and Spain in the 1730s led ineluctably to the War of the AUSTRIAN SUCCESSION. Predatory raids by both sides on trading ships, despite the 1713 Peace of Utrecht, caused the opposition to the prime ministry of Robert Walpole (1676–1745) to exploit the sensational 1738 claims of Captain Robert Jenkins (fl. 1730s) that he had lost both his ship *Rebecca* and his ear to Spanish coast guards in 1731. Walpole reluctantly declared war in October 1739. Admiral Edward Vernon (1684–1757) captured the Spanish fort of Porto Bello, Panama, in 1739; in 1740, defeat accompanied both Vernon and Georgia governor James E. Oglethorpe (1696–1785), respectively, at Cartagena, Colombia, and in a military attempt to capture St. Augustine, Florida. Oglethorpe's troops repulsed a Spanish attack on St. Simon's Island, Georgia, in the Battle of Bloody Marsh on June 9, 1742. In a second assault on St. Augustine, Oglethorpe again suffered defeat in 1743 and withdrew from Florida.

Jerusalem, Siege of (A.D. 70) During the JEWISH REVOLT OF A.D. 66–73, Roman forces led by Titus (40?–81) besieged the zealot-controlled city of Jerusalem, which was surrounded and guarded by a number of walls. They breached the vulnerable outer wall in the north and west and then attacked an inner wall, using huge assault towers. Titus stopped the assault when a false offer of surrender allowed Jerusalem's defenders to withdraw into the Upper City and the temple areas; he continued until the Romans had breached the walls surrounding the now-empty area. Afterward, with his troops checked, Titus had a huge siege wall built around the entire city to starve out its defenders. A few Jews surrendered, but most, faced with a choice of slavery or death, fought on more fiercely. The captured Jews, often 500 in a night, were crucified in the sight of the defenders. Titus now focused on taking the Antonia fortress, which safeguarded the temple, and used rams day and night until it fell. The zealots held out in the fortified temple until the Romans gained entrance by burning the gates; accidentally set ablaze, the temple was taken and looted of its treasure by the Romans. But the siege was not over, for the defenders held the Upper City. When peace negotiations failed, the Romans burned the Lower City, which was filled with rotting dead, and then attacked and breached the walls of the Upper City, finding it empty of all but the dead. Burning the rest of Jerusalem, the Romans took prisoners, who were executed, made slaves, or brought to Rome for Titus's triumphal procession. See also MASADA, SIEGE OF.

Jewish Revolt of 168–143 B.C. See MACCABEES, REVOLT OF THE.

Jewish Revolt of A.D. 66–73 Ultra-orthodox Jewish zealots, who were dedicated to the expulsion of all foreigners from the Jewish state of Palestine, antagonized the inept Roman provincial governor

Cestius Gallus (fl. 1st cent.) in his base in Syria and the money-grubbing Roman procurator of Judea (Judah) Gessius Florus (fl. 1st cent.), both of whom considered Jews beneath contempt. Because of a dispute in Caesarea, the capital of Judea, Florus demanded payment of a large fine by the temple at Jerusalem. Refused, he came to Jerusalem, met with a large Jewish delegation opposed to his looting, grew angry, and ended the meeting by ordering the slaying of some 3,600 Jerusalemites. A revolt against the Romans was promptly under way, spreading rapidly through Jewish Palestine. Zealots captured outlying fortresses, including Masada (66), which held out heroically through 73 (see MASADA, SIEGE OF). Gallus led forces to Jerusalem, the zealots' headquarters, but failed in an assault on the temple. In his withdrawal through Jerusalem's suburb of Bezetha, he lost 6,000 men, baggage, and a siege train to a Jewish army. Greatly annoyed, Roman emperor Nero (37–68) sent soldiers under Titus Flavius Vespasian (9–79) to quell the revolt. Beginning in Galilee, Vespasian beset Jotapata, a key Galilean fortress commanded by Joseph Ben Matthias (37–95?); after 47 days the fortress fell, and its commander became not only a prisoner of the Romans but also the official historian of the conflict, changing his name to Flavius Josephus and writing, in his *Jewish War*, the only eyewitness account of its violence. Vespasian, a restrained commander unwilling to do unnecessary harm, tried to parley for peace until forced to do battle at Tiberias, Gischala, and the fortress Gamala; his troops punished many rebel cities, advancing southward toward Jerusalem in 68. Jerusalem had been weakened by civil disturbance from the zealots' pogrom against Romans and their supportive Jews. Italy, too, was upset by civil strife following the murder of Nero; Vespasian was compelled to leave the battlefield for Rome and to secure the emperorship; he turned the army over to his son Titus (40?–81), who arrived at and besieged Jerusalem in the spring of 70 (see JERUSALEM, SIEGE OF).

Jewish Revolt of A.D. 115–17   Cyrenaica (eastern Libya), a Roman province since 67 B.C., contained both a large Greek and large Jewish population. The Jews had earlier felt their rights slighted by the Greeks; now regarding their Roman rulers as worse oppressors than the Greeks, they began a zealot-influenced revolt in the city of Cyrene (115). Their leader, named either Lukuas or Andreas (fl. 2nd cent.), was mocked by the Romans as "king of the Jews." At Cyrene, Greeks and Romans were slain or injured, and buildings burned; special forces sent by Roman emperor Trajan (53–117) cruelly crushed the Jews by 117. Meantime, the revolt spread to Jews in Egypt, Cyprus, Asia Minor, Judea, and Mesopotamia (116–17); in all places, bloody violence and destruction occurred until the Romans regained control. In Alexandria, Jews briefly triumphed in the suburbs; in Salamis, Cyprus, all non-Jews were slaughtered and the city was sacked, but in the end all Jews were expelled. Mopping-up operations outlasted Trajan's reign, and ruthless governors were sent to all places of revolt to keep the Roman *pax* (peace imposed by force of arms).

Jewish Revolt of A.D. 132–35   See BAR COCHEBA'S REVOLT.

Jokyu War   (1221)   A military government called the Bakufu was set up at Kamakura in Japan in 1192. It was directed by a shogun (hereditary commander in chief), but this person soon became a puppet ruler much like the emperor. The real power passed into the hands of the Hojo family whose leaders assumed the title of shikken (regent). In the early part of the twelfth century the Bakufu and the imperial court at Kyoto functioned quite independently of each other. Toba II (1180–1239), the emperor, had abdicated, as he realized he had very little influence in the country and thought he might have more if he manipulated important officials off the throne. In 1221, he gained the backing of the large Japanese monasteries, which had great military strength, and tried to break the power of the Bakufu. An uprising in Kyoto was quickly suppressed by the Hojo forces, however. The rebellion was crushed almost as soon as it started. Toba was banished. The most important consequences were that the Hojos installed two of their own as military governors in Kyoto, took command of the court and the imperial succession, and confiscated the estates of Toba's followers and distributed them among their own adherents. These actions strengthened the feudal system and the control of the military establishment in Japan.

Jordanian Civil War of 1970–71 After the SIX-DAY WAR (1967), nearly 400,000 Palestinians left the West Bank territory (lost to Israel) and joined the 700,000 resident in Jordan. From there and from parts of Lebanon and Syria, the Palestinians conducted terrorist attacks against Israel, which made retaliatory raids against them. The more militant of the Palestinian refugees, controlled by Yasir Arafat (1929–) of the Palestine Liberation Organization (PLO), asserted that Jordan's laws did not apply to them and claimed the West Bank as a future homeland. Jordan's King Hussein (1935–99), whose life was threatened by the Palestinians, saw his country becoming an armed camp and himself a contestant for authority. On September 6–9, 1970 ("Black September"), when Palestinian terrorists hijacked commercial jetliners and flew them to Amman, Jordan's capital, Hussein resolved to destroy the violent Palestinians in his land. He declared martial law on September 16, 1970, and for 10 days his troops surrounded refugee camps, disarmed guerrillas, and deported many militant leaders. Syrian support for the refugees faded by September 24, and the next day a cease-fire was arranged by Arab heads of state. Battles against guerrilla bands continued into 1971: Amman was freed of Palestinians in April, and July saw the destruction of Palestinian bases in north Jordan. The Palestinians moved to Lebanon and ultimately helped bring on the LEBANESE CIVIL WAR OF 1975–90.

Juchen Mongol Conquest of the Liao (1114–22) In what is now Manchuria, the Juchen Mongol tribes in the north acknowledged the suzerainty of the Liao dynasty in the south until 1114, when their chieftain severed relations with his Liao (Khitan) overlord (nomadic Khitan tribes had founded the dynasty about 947). The warrior Mongol tribesmen swept into southern Manchuria, conquering as they went. Seizing the opportunity to take revenge on their former vassals, the Khitans, the Chinese attacked them from the south while the Mongols moved on them from the north. Within two years, the Mongols possessed all of southern Manchuria, and they then proceeded to seize Liao territory in northern Shansi (Shanxi) and Chihli (Hopeh) in China. They set up their capital at Peking (Beijing) and established the Chin ("golden") dynasty. Remnants of the Liao fled westward and founded a new state in the Ili River valley, calling it Kara-Khitai. See also CHINESE WAR WITH THE KHITANS.

Juchen Mongol Invasion of the Sung Empire (1125–62)   The Juchen Mongols (Chinese Chin dynasty) turned against their former ally, the Chinese Sung, who had helped them drive the Liao (Khitans) from southern Manchuria and the Chinese provinces of Shansi (Shanxi) and Chihli (Hopeh) during the JUCHEN MONGOL CONQUEST OF THE LIAO. In 1125, they invaded Sung territory north of the Yellow River (Huang Ho), and, the next year, they crossed the river and laid siege to the Sung (Song) capital, K'ai-feng. In 1127, the capital fell, and the Sung emperor, Hui Tsung (Hui Zong) (1082–1135), and his family were taken prisoner and sent away. One of the emperor's sons, Kao Tsung (Gao Zong) (1107–87), escaped to Nanking in the south, where he established the Southern Sung dynasty and was proclaimed emperor. In 1129, the Mongols followed, crossed the Yangtze River, and captured Nanking (Nanjing), Kao Tsung's capital. Kao Tsung fled to Hangchow and ruled from there. Sung armies led by General Yo Fei (Yue Fei) (1103–41), supported by the Sung fleet on the Yangtze, defeated the Mongol forces and pushed them north of the river. For a decade the Sung drove the Chin back, retaking their cities as they progressed. A palace dispute among the Sung over continuing the war led to a decision to make peace with the Chin; Yo Fei, labeled a warmonger, was recalled and executed. In 1141, the Sung and Chin agreed to a treaty whereby the watershed that divides the Yangtze River valley from the Yellow River valley would be the boundary between them. The uneasy peace was broken in 1161, when Chin armies attempted unsuccessfully to invade the Southern Sung empire; the invaders were routed near Nanking by the apparent use of explosives for the first time in battle. Kao Tsung signed a new treaty with the Chin (1162). See also MONGOL CONQUEST OF THE CHIN EMPIRE; MONGOL CONQUEST OF THE SUNG EMPIRE.

Jugurthine War (Numidian War) (112–106 B.C.) Numidia was an ancient country in North Africa that was an ally of Rome. In 118, the Numidian kingdom was inherited by two royal sons and a nephew, Jugurtha (156?–104), who had one of his cousins assassinated, and the other fled to Rome to seek help. In 112, Jugurtha and his troops captured his cousin's capital and killed him and its defenders, many of whom were Romans. A Roman army was dispatched to Numidia in 111, but it was repulsed. Later Jugurtha went to Rome to justify his conduct and while there had a rival claimant to his throne killed. The war resumed, and again the Romans were defeated. In 109, Quintus Caecilius Metellus (d. 99), a Roman general, took command of the African army and began to lay waste Numidia. Jugurtha responded by resorting to guerrilla warfare. Two years later Gaius Marius (155?–86) became Roman general in Numidia and continued devastating the villages and forts, but Jugurtha and his loyal troops continued to fight. When Jugurtha's father-in-law treacherously turned him over to the Romans, Marius returned to Rome in triumph with Jugurtha as his prisoner.

Jülich Succession, War of the (1609–14) With the death of Duke John William (d. 1609) of Jülich, a struggle began for succession to his territories—the duchies of Jülich, Cleves, Mark, and Berg. The elector of Brandenburg and the count of Palatinate-Neuburg claimed title by descent from the female line, while the elector of Saxony claimed right of Imperial fief and the Holy Roman Emperor wished to grant the lands to Spain. Brandenburg and the Palatinate reached agreement to rule jointly as "the Possessor." Austrians under Leopold (1586–1633), brother of the emperor, captured and held the duchies (1609–10) until Dutch and German Protestant forces, supported by the French, invaded and evicted them; despite the assassination of France's King Henry IV (1553–1610) and his successor's support for Spain and Austria, allied Dutch-German troops besieged and captured Jülich's fortress on September 1, 1610. In 1613, the Possessors' ruling agreement collapsed; Neuburg now sought Catholic help. Battle lines were drawn between Catholics and Protestants, but no fighting occurred, and peace was reached by the Treaty of Xanten on November 12, 1614. Brandenburg received the duchies of Cleves and Mark (and Ravensberg), and Neuburg gained control of Jülich and Berg (and Ravenstein). To retain the support of the Catholic League, Neuburg sought to proselytize as a convert to Catholicism in its new lands. Elector John Sigismund (1572–1619) of Brandenburg, a Calvinist, ruled more tolerantly in his new acquisitions. See also THIRTY YEARS' WAR.

July Revolution, French See FRENCH REVOLUTION OF 1830.

July Revolution, Spanish See SPANISH REVOLUTION OF 1854.

Justinian's First Persian War (A.D. 524–32) Like other Roman or Byzantine emperors in the East before him, Justinian I (483–565) was plagued on his eastern frontiers by invading Persians. About 524, the Persians began intrusions into Mesopotamia, and Justinian was compelled to send troops to repulse them. In 527, he directed his best general, Belisarius (505?–65), to lead a campaign against them. Belisarius won a great victory at Dara in 530, defeating a combined Persian-Arab army of 40,000 in a brilliant defensive use of infantry and offensive deployment of cavalry. Though he repelled Persian invaders the next year, he was badly defeated by a superior army at Callinicum and withdrew with his weary army to Sura on the Euphrates, where he stood firm against repeated Persian attacks. After the death of Persia's King Kavadh I (d. 531), his son and successor Khosrau (Chosroes) I (d. 579) concluded an "eternal" peace with Emperor Justinian. But the eternity did not last long. Fearing growing Eastern Roman strength and intolerance of the Persians' religion, Khosrau declared war and invaded Syria. **Justinian's Second Persian War** (A.D. 539–62). Khosrau's forces penetrated to the heart of Syria, seizing Antioch, the third largest city in the Roman world at the time, and sacking it. The Persians won success in Mesopotamia, on the Black Sea, and in Lazica (Colchis or western Georgia). An armistice in 545 did not last long, although Justinian tried to keep the peace by paying the Persians a large subsidy each year. Fighting was intermittent until 561, when a 50-year peace between the Eastern Romans and Persians was signed. Lazica was returned to the Romans, and Persia was to continue receiving a subsidy in gold coins annually for Roman-held forts in the Caucasus. See also NIKA REVOLT; ROMAN-PERSIAN WAR OF A.D. 502–6; VANDAL-ROMAN WAR IN NORTH AFRICA.

Jutland, Battle of (Battle of the Skagerrak) (1916) Part of the British strategy against Germany in WORLD WAR I was to maintain a firm naval blockade; a fleet regularly patrolled the North Sea to keep all shipping away from German ports. Either deliberately or accidentally Germany tested Britain's strength when its High Seas Fleet under Admiral Reinhard Scheer (1863–1928) put to sea and sailed into the Skagerrak, an inlet of the North Sea between Jutland (Denmark) and Norway. About 60 miles off Jutland's coast on May 31, 1916, a German scouting fleet under Admiral Franz von Hipper (1863–1932) encountered British squadrons under Admiral David Beatty (1871–1936) and Admiral Hugh Evans-Thomas (1862–1928). Accurate German gunnery compelled the British, suffering severe losses, to turn back to join the entire British Grand Fleet under Admiral John R. Jellicoe (1859–1935), who carried on the naval battle against Scheer's High Seas Fleet, which Hipper had joined by then. British naval maneuvers to cut the Germans off from their home ports and to entrap and destroy the High Seas Fleet nearly succeeded that day. But because of darkness and fog and skillful naval tactics, the Germans managed to escape and lost only nine warships out of their total of 103. Although the British lost more ships (14 out of their 151) and more lives (more than twice as many as the enemy) in the battle, they maintained their supremacy in the North Sea. The German navy was demoralized and thereafter avoided battle during the course of the war.

Kadesh, Battle of (c. 1294 B.C.) The Hittites suffered a severe loss of territory and prestige in wars with the Hurrian kingdom of Mitanni and the emerging Assyrian Empire (see ASSYRIAN-HURRIAN WARS; HITTITE-HURRIAN WARS). The ruler of the Hittites, Muwatallis (fl. c. 1306–c. 1282), was determined to control Syria; Ramses II (fl. 1292–1225), fourth Egyptian king of the 19th Dynasty, was equally determined to restore his crumbling kingdom. With his army, Ramses retook control of Palestine and then marched north to the Hittite stronghold of Kadesh on the Orontes River, near modern Homs, Syria. There one of the greatest ancient battles and the first for which tactics and formations are known took place. Ramses had about 20,000 troops, including Numidian mercenaries; Muwatallis had some 16,000 Hittites; nonetheless, the latter had an advantage: 2,500 chariots, each holding three men. The Egyptians, all on foot, were surprised at first and surrounded by a Hittite assault and pincer movement; only the personal bravery of Ramses enabled his soldiers to hold out and escape defeat. The Hittites then stopped to loot their fallen foes, allowing the Egyptians to regroup and launch a counterattack. Kadesh was besieged unsuccessfully by Ramses, who eventually withdrew his troops but considered the battle a victory. It really was a draw, a label justified by a 1272 peace treaty, in which neither side gained or lost territory; instead, the treaty set up a dynastic marriage between the contestants and established a peace lasting the rest of Ramses's long reign.

Kaffir War, First (1779) South African Boer (Dutch) cattle farmers migrating to remote regions 400 miles northeast of Cape Town and the Bantu-speaking Xhosa tribe, also cattle farmers, competed for rich pasture land along the Great Fish River. Attempts to designate the river as a boundary were violated by both groups, and in 1779 a major conflict erupted when Kaffirs (as the Africans were known to the Boers), possibly to avenge the killing of a tribesman, raided European cattle and murdered some herdsmen. The Boers retaliated with commando raids, driving the Xhosa back across the river and capturing more than 5,000 head of cattle. The essential issues, however, remained unresolved for a century. **Second Kaffir War** (1793). Boer frontier people looked for help from the Dutch East India Company, which sent a man named Maynier (fl. 1793) to negotiate a settlement with the Xhosa. Lacking troops or police, he was unable to prevent continued mutual raiding, and in 1793 a serious drought provoked Boer farmers seeking pasture to cross into Kaffirland. A farmer named Lindeque (fl. 1793), defying orders, organized a cattle raid, to which the Xhosa responded by invading Boer territory. Maynier raised a commando force and expelled the intruders but irked the Boers by declining to demand cattle as compensation for their losses. **Third Kaffir War** (1799–1801). Burghers of Swellendam and the newly organized Graaf-Reinet declared independence in 1795 but were soon taken over by the British, who had allied with Holland

against France and thus inherited Boer-Kaffir disturbances. When conflicts over pasture and cattle once
again broke out, the Xhosa banded with the Boers'
Khoisan servants, who deserted with guns and
horses. The British caretaker government in Cape
Town succeeded in undermining the alliance
through concessions to the Khoisan but fell short of
its goal of expelling the Xhosa altogether. By 1802,
the war had cooled, and in 1803, the Cape reverted
to the Dutch in accordance with the Treaty of
Amiens between France and Britain. **Fourth Kaffir
War** (1811). Hostilities in Europe resumed, this
time with Holland allied with France against Britain, and in 1806 a strong British fleet took control
of the Cape. The almost continuous conflict between Boer and Xhosa, compounded by an influx of
African refugees fleeing from wars elsewhere, again
exploded into open warfare in 1811. The British,
blaming the unruly Boers for the conflicts, attempted to maintain inviolate borders. But, like the
Dutch, they lacked resources to force compliance
from either side, though a line of forts was set up
after the Xhosa were driven back across the Great
Fish River. **Fifth Kaffir War** (1818–19). The Xhosa,
more desperate with each succeeding war, succumbed to internal dissension. Though a quarrel
between two rival chiefs, Ndlambi (fl. 1810s) and
Gaika (fl. 1810s), ended in Gaika's defeat, the Cape
government persisted in recognizing his claims and
sent troops to quell Ndlambi's followers. Ndlambi
responded by attacking Grahamstown, pitting Boer
against Xhosa once again. When hostilities ended,
Lord Charles Somerset, the British governor, sought
to establish a neutral strip between the Great Fish
and Keiskama rivers—a policy doomed because it
declared off-limits land needed by both sides. British
settlers authorized to farm the neutral zone quickly
fled to outlying areas. **Sixth Kaffir War** (1834–35).
In their constant search for pasture, Boers penetrated farther into Kaffirland. The desire of British
settlers in Port Elizabeth to carry on trade with both
sides exacerbated tensions, and war erupted in 1834.
After expulsion of the Xhosa, Sir Benjamin D'Urban (1777–1849), the governor, opened former
Xhosa lands to settlement. But he could not prevent

Xhosa incursions and soon disannexed the new
province. Many Boers, disillusioned by British policy toward the Africans and lured by the promise of
open lands, began a northward migration known as
the Great Trek. **Seventh Kaffir War.** See AXE, WAR
OF THE. **Eighth Kaffir War** (1850–53). The Xhosa
naturally resented British annexation of their territory and curtailment of their chiefs' authority (see
AXE, WAR OF THE). Encouraged by the claim of a
Xhosa witch doctor that his charms could fend off
bullets, the Xhosa launched another war. Though a
number of setbacks to the British prolonged the
struggle, including loss of a ship carrying reinforcements, all the Xhosa chiefs were eventually forced
to surrender. The Xhosa actually participated in
their own downfall by ritual destruction of their own
cattle and crops, intended to call forth the aid of
their ancestral heroes. **Ninth Kaffir War**
(1877–78). After their disastrous defeat in 1853, the
Xhosa engaged in further superstitious destruction
of their own cattle and crops, reducing their own
numbers drastically. It took them a full generation
to rebuild their strength and resources, but in 1877
they made one last attempt to recover their lands.
This uprising was suppressed, resulting in the annexation of all of British Kaffiraria and reduction of
the Xhosa to a state of economic dependence. See
also BLOOD RIVER, BATTLE OF.

Kalka River, Battle of the (1223)   While
Genghis (Jenghiz, Chingis) Khan (1167?–1227)
was conforming Mongol control in Khwarizm (see
MONGOL-PERSIAN WAR, FIRST), a detached Mongol
army under the famed General Subedei (d. c. 1258)
marched west of the Caspian Sea toward the Sea of
Azov in southern Russia (see MONGOL INVASION OF
RUSSIA, FIRST). Russian princes and Cuman (Ku-
man) leaders hastily assembled an 80,000-man
army, including a remnant of Kipchaks, which was
poorly trained to withstand the blitzkrieg tactics of
the Mongols. Near the mouth of the Dnieper River
in 1223, the Russian-Cuman force met the smaller
Mongol army led by Subedei, who had his men
circle and attack repeatedly until his Mongol archers had nearly annihilated the enemy. The victori-

ous Mongols then marched northward but soon turned back and made a 3,000-mile trek to join the main Mongol armies under Genghis Khan in Persia. See also MONGOL INVASION OF EUROPE.

Kalmar, War of (Kalmar War) (1611–13) The attempt by King Charles IX (1550–1611) to control the old Finnmark region (the northernmost part of the Scandinavian peninsula), valuable to the Danish-Norwegian kings for fishing and fur trapping, and to limit Danish trade in the eastern Baltic, particularly the Gulf of Riga, provoked King Christian IV (1577–1648) of Denmark and Norway to send a naval fleet to protect trade in the Öresund (Danish Sound). After Charles refused to negotiate Swedish-Danish borders and differences, both he and Christian declared war. In a two-pronged attack, Danish forces moved through Västergötland, while Christian's troops besieged the Swedish port-city of Kalmar. Although Charles and his son Gustavus Adolphus (1594–1632) came to Kalmar's aid, the arrival of Danish reinforcements forced their retreat to nearby Visby, and Kalmar fell to the Danes in the summer of 1611. Angered by the defeat, Charles offered to settle the dispute with a duel, but Christian refused, attacked Visby, but retreated by sea to Copenhagen after a three-day battle. Charles died in late October 1611, and his son, now Gustavus II, carried on the war. The Norwegians pushed the Swedes out of Finnmark, and the Danes seized the port of Älvsborg in southeastern Sweden in May 1612. Fighting ended with the Peace of Knäred in early 1613; Finnmark came under Danish-Norwegian sovereignty, and Älvsborg was to be returned to Sweden in exchange for Swedish tribute. Kalmar, after which the war was named, returned to Swedish control.

Kalmar Civil War of 1520–23 (Swedish Civil War of 1520–23) In 1520, the Danish army under King Christian II (1481–1559), who was attempting to retain his position as the king of Sweden under the Kalmar Union (a union of the three crowns of Denmark, Sweden, and Norway), invaded and con-

quered Sweden; Christian's rival, Stan Sture the Younger (1493?–1520), Swedish regent, was mortally wounded in battle at Bogesund. With Sture's death, the Swedish government fell apart, and the Diet (legislative assembly) was forced to recognize Christian as king. Further resistance dissipated, and Christian was crowned king of Sweden in Stockholm on November 5, 1520, amid supposedly joyful demonstrations. Three days later he convened a spiritual court that provided a religious "rationale" for a country-wide massacre of all opponents (later called the Stockholm Massacre or Bloodbath because of the killing of opposing Swedish nobles in the marketplace in Stockholm). In reaction to this extreme cruelty, Gustavus Eriksson (1496–1560), a Swedish noble who had escaped from Danish imprisonment and whose father and brother-in-law had been beheaded, persuaded the peasants of Dalecarlia (Dalarna) in central Sweden to follow him in revolt against the Danes. Attracting soldiers as he conquered areas, Gustavus moved through Uppsala and successfully besieged Stockholm, having been proclaimed Sweden's liberator and administrator by a diet in August 1521. Christian was deposed as king and driven out of Denmark and Sweden, and Gustavus became king of Sweden as Gustavus I, thus ending the Kalmar Union. A year later, in 1524, Gustavus and Christian's Danish successor, Frederick I (1471?–1533), met to settle differences. The province of Blekinge in southwestern Sweden was returned to Denmark, and a congress of deputies was charged with the resolution of outstanding differences.

Kalmar War with Holstein (1409–35) Erik VII (Erik of Pomerania) (1382–1459), king of the Kalmar Union (a combination of the three crowns of Denmark, Sweden, and Norway), disputed the count of Holstein's possession of the duchy of Schleswig, and in 1409 he seized the duchy. In desperation, Holstein opened its ports to the Victualling Brothers (pirates), who forced Erik's withdrawal from Schleswig to Denmark. During 1416–18, Erik's defeats continued, losing territory, but in 1419 he recaptured Fehmarn Island in bloody encounters. When Erik attempted to weaken the commercial power of the Hanseatic League by his edict of 1422, which allowed only Danes to pursue trades and crafts, the league allied with Holstein (see KALMAR WAR WITH THE HANSEATIC LEAGUE). Fearing a Kalmar invasion of Pomerania, Erik left the battle arena; his army successfully held Flensburg, and his Danish navy defeated the league's ships in the Öresund (Danish Sound). When Erik imposed a toll on vessels sailing through the Öresund (1428), Holstein's and the league's forces immediately besieged Copenhagen to end the tax, but the city's inhabitants rallied to defend it successfully, led by Erik's queen. In 1431, Flensburg fell to the league and Holstein, and Erik made peace with both on their own terms, four years later. Schleswig was returned to Holstein; and Erik had achieved nothing during his more than 25 years of struggle.

Kalmar War with the Hanseatic League (1422–35)   In 1422, the Hanseatic League (mercantile league of cities in northern Germany and the Baltic area) declared war on Danish king Erik VII (1382–1459), ruler of the Kalmar Union (a combination of the three crowns of Denmark, Sweden, and Norway). The league feared loss of trade to Norway and exorbitant trade tariffs and hoped to break Erik's monopoly of tax levies on shipping traffic through the Öresund (Danish Sound). Erik conquered the city of Flensburg, a Baltic port, and took control of the Öresund's entrance. In 1428, the league's land and sea forces moved against Copenhagen but were repelled. A long sea battle at Stralsund on the Baltic left the Swedish fleet nearly totally destroyed. In 1431, Flensburg surrendered to the league, and in 1435, Erik, confronted with internal revolts, reluctantly made an unfavorable peace. Schleswig was surrendered to Holstein, an important ally of the Hanseatic League. See also KALMAR WAR WITH HOLSTEIN; SCANDINAVIAN REVOLT OF 1433–39.

Kampuchean Civil War of 1978–98   Premier Pol Pot (1925–98) of Kampuchea (Cambodia) directed the Khmer Rouge (communists) in drastically changing the country after 1976 (see CAMBODIAN CIVIL WAR OF 1970–75); his brutal regime took control of all lands and means of production and was guilty of monstrous violations of human rights. Border clashes with Vietnam led to Kampuchea cutting off diplomatic relations with its neighbor in late 1977. The Vietnamese, who stepped up their border attacks, encouraged Kampuchean rebels to overthrow the Pol Pot regime. In late 1978, about 200,000 Vietnamese troops invaded and occupied Kampuchea, whose capital, Phnom Penh, fell on January 9, 1979; Heng Samrin (1931–   ), a dissident Khmer Rouge, became president of a Vietnamese-supported government. Khmer Rouge loyalists, however, continued to fight in rural areas and jungles, attacking enemy supply lines and avoiding direct, large-scale battles. Pol Pot, who had fled to the northwest jungle, was recognized by the United States and China, both of which refused to accept Soviet-backed Vietnamese aggression. In 1982, three main anti-Vietnamese Khmer forces united in a coalition to oust the Vietnamese military occupiers of their country, while Prince Norodom Sihanouk (1922–   ), the country's former head of state, formed a coalition government-in-exile (which included Pol Pot's Khmer Rouge), recognized by the United Nations and available to replace the Vietnamese-aided regime. The Vietnamese launched strong attacks on the camps of Khmer "freedom fighters" along the Thai-Kampuchean border; in 1984, Vietnam showed increasing dependence on Soviet aid to combat the stiff guerrilla resistance. In 1987–88, Sihanouk met several times with Phnom Penh leaders without success. Urged by the Soviets, Vietnam began to withdraw some of its 140,000-man occupying army, with plans to be completely out by 1990. The Khmer Rouge (40,000 strong) tried to regain territory, while another rebel force, the noncommunist Khmer People's National Liberation Front (KPNLF), had internal strife. In 1989, the Phnom Penh regime renamed the country Cambodia, and Vietnam sped up its withdrawal of troops. A UN-brokered peace agreement was signed in Paris on

October 23, 1991, by the four Khmer factions—Sihanoukists, KPNLF, Khmer Rouge, and the Phnom Penh government—and ministers of 19 other countries that participated in peace talks. Disarming of some of the factions then began under the UN Transitional Authority in Cambodia (UNTAC), which also aided in the return of 375,000 refugees along the border of Thailand. In 1991, Sihanouk returned to Phnom Penh and became the elected president, replacing Heng Samrin. Khmer Rouge rebels, however, refused to cooperate and attacked UNTAC forces in 1992; the ruling party in Phnom Penh was torn by factionalism. Major clashes occurred in Batdambang province in the west, where Khmer Rouge rebels gave up their bases in Pailin and Phnom Malai without fighting in 1996; Pol Pot's Khmer Rouge began to disintegrate in its hidden jungle exile. Uncovered in 1995–96 were the mass graves of up to 2 million people who perished during the "killing fields" rule of Pol Pot in 1975–79. Tensions increased in the unstable coalition government between rival co-prime ministers, Hun Sen (1950–) and Prince Norodom Ranariddh (son of Sihanouk). These warlords tried to boost their strength by enlisting Khmer Rouge rebels as allies. Fighting broke out in Phnom Penh in July 1997; Hun Sen took power, overthrowing Ranariddh, who escaped; Sihanouk (ill with cancer) later left the country. Weakened by mass defections, Pol Pot's Khmer Rouge turned against their leader, replaced him with Ta Mok (Pol Pot's longtime comrade), and later in 1997, in a show trial in the jungle, sentenced Pol Pot to house arrest for life. In 1998, remnants of the Khmer Rouge became torn by factional infighting in Cambodia's northern jungles; they no longer posed a military or political threat to the government, and Pol Pot was killed or died of illness (April 15, 1998) in a jungle hideout before he could be brought to trial for genocide. The last main Khmer Rouge force surrendered to the government, laying down arms, in December 1998.

Kampuchean-Thai Border War   (1977–95) Thousands of refugees from Kampuchea (Cambodia) crossed the border into Thailand to escape starvation and death after the communist Khmer Rouge takeover of their country in 1975. Khmer troops attacked Thai border areas near Aranyaprathet. Thailand closed its border, put its army on alert, and later used air and artillery attacks to drive the enemy back. In 1979–80, Vietnamese occupation forces in Kampuchea made incursions into Thai territory, often seeking rebel guerrillas supposedly hidden in refugee camps (where many Laotians and Vietnamese refugees had also settled). Sporadic skirmishes continued along the border, while Thailand's military-dominated government fought insurgents inside the country, including Thai communists, rebellious Meo tribesmen, Thai Muslim separatists, opium warlords, and others. From 1985 to 1988, Vietnamese troops in Kampuchea periodically made raids to wipe out Khmer Rouge border camps in Thailand, which remained, along with China, major supporters of Khmer Rouge resistance (see KAMPUCHEAN CIVIL WAR OF 1978–98). By 1992, United Nations peacekeeping forces (over 16,000 strong) were implementing a possible political settlement and peace process in Cambodia (no longer called Kampuchea since 1989). UN forces assisted in the repatriation of about 375,000 refugees from the Thai border, and by August 1992 an estimated 100,000 had returned home to Cambodia. The border war had wound down considerably, but Khmer Rouge terrorism in 1993 caused many persons to flee to Thailand. In September 1995, Cambodia and Thailand, their strife quieted, set up a commission to govern their common border (excluding their rival claims in the Gulf of Thailand).

Kappel Wars (1529, 1531)   Catholic-Protestant tensions in Switzerland in the 16th century echoed those in Germany (see PEASANTS' WAR, GERMAN; SCHMALKALDIC WAR). The Swiss city and canton of Zürich was Protestant and strongly influenced by the Protestant religious reformer Huldreich Zwingli (1484–1531); it began to proselytize its Swiss neighbors and to embargo those cantons still loyal to Rome. Five Catholic cantons of the Swiss confederacy—Uri, Schwyz, Luzern, Unterwalden, and Zug—formed the Christian Union to restrict

Zürich's Protestant influence. In 1529, forces from Zürich skirmished with the union. An armistice signed at Kappel (on the border between Zürich and Zug) forced the Christian Union to break its tie with Austria, its ally, and to allow religious freedom within its member cantons. Convinced that a sixth canton, Thurgau, was being forcibly Protestantized, the union suddenly declared war on Zürich in 1531 and defeated its hastily assembled army at the Battle of Kappel on October 11, 1531; Zwingli was killed at the battle. The second Peace of Kappel (1531) recognized the rights and freedoms of Catholics within the union's cantons. See also VILLMERGEN WARS.

Karmathian Revolt of A.D. 899–906 The Karmathians (Karmatians, Carmathians, or Qarmatians), a large communistic Shi'ite sect living in lower Mesopotamia, revolted against orthodox rule of the caliphate. In 899, Caliph al-Mu'tadid (d 902) dispatched a Muslim army to subdue the rebels but was unsuccessful. Led by Abu Sa'id al-Djannabi (d. 913), the Karmathians overran much of Mesopotamia and Syria, seizing important Muslim cities, including Basra on the Shatt al-Arab near the Persian Gulf. Finally, they withdrew into Arabia, where they established an independent state on the shores of the Persian Gulf, near what is now the country of Bahrain. Remaining Karmathians in Syria were soon subjugated by the caliphate's forces. See also MECCA, SACK OF.

Kashmiri Insurgency of 1988– Another crisis in Kashmir, site of two wars between India and Pakistan (see INDO-PAKISTANI WAR OF 1947–48, INDO-PAKISTANI WAR OF 1965) since partition in 1947, began in 1988 when Kashmiri Muslims, feeling marginalized by the policies of the central government toward Kashmir, launched an armed struggle for autonomy. India responded by dispatching troops to the region in December 1989. This led to mass protests with the dissidents (there are 13 rebel groups, the Jammu Kashmir Liberation Front being the most prominent) stepping up their campaign of bombings, kidnappings, and strikes against civilians, especially Hindus. Most of the Hindus, who constitute a minority in Kashmir, fled to refugee camps in Jammu and Delhi. Meanwhile, the Indian security forces were accused of horrendous human rights violations—burnings, killings, abductions, rapes, and torture—against detainees, Kashmiri civilians, and medical personnel. An increasingly alienated Muslim civilian population supported the secessionist movement. India refused to part with Kashmir while Pakistan supported the plebiscite in the hope that it would mean union with Pakistan but not independence. The murder of a prominent Muslim cleric in Srinagar in May 1990 led to massive protests and the resignation of the Indian-appointed governor. The Indian troops fired at the crowds, wounding 300 and killing 47 people. The two countries exchanged gunfire in 1990 and in 1991 and, in May 1991, Indian forces killed 66 militants in one week. In February 1992, Pakistan shot Azad Kashmir dissidents. In October 1993, troops surrounded the famous Hazratbal mosque in Srinagar where the rebels were reportedly hiding. Twenty-nine people died in the standoff. The destruction of the Char-e-Sharif, a 15th-century shrine dedicated to Kashmir's patron saint, in May 1995 led to retaliatory violence across the state. Curfew was imposed and 35 secessionists killed. Pakistan reportedly intensified its efforts to arm and train the rebels. The international community called on India to reduce its military presence (estimated at 500,000 to 700,000) in the region and to initiate a dialogue with the dissident groups. India announced plans to strengthen the democratic process in the state and to jump-start the state's economy by introducing developmental programs. It hoped to isolate the militants and deal with the situation on a proactive basis. By the end of 1998, the struggle had claimed more than 20,000 lives, and no resolution appeared to be in sight.

Katyn Massacre (1940) Some 15,000 captive Polish soldiers and officers were deported to three Soviet prison camps in late 1939 after the outbreak of WORLD WAR II, when Germany invaded western

Poland and the Soviet Union, then a German ally, marched into eastern Poland and remained there until Germany (turned foe) drove the Soviets out in 1941. Two years later German Nazis discovered 4,143 bodies of Polish officers in eight mass graves in the Katyn Forest, south of Smolensk, in western Russia. The bodies of the 11,000 other Polish captives have never been found. The Germans and Soviets blamed one another for the Katyn Massacre, which fostered a Polish distrust of the Soviets during the four decades Poland spent as a client state of the Kremlin after the war. In 1987, a joint Soviet-Polish commission was established to investigate the massacre; most Poles and Western historians, based on wartime International Red Cross and Polish Red Cross reports, had concluded that the Soviet secret police, known as the NKVD (*Narodny Kommisariat Vnutrennikh Del*), had committed the massacre in April or May of 1940 (well before the Germans invaded the region, but possibly committed by Nazi request). In 1990 the Soviet government admitted culpability for the crime.

Kett's Rebellion (1549)   When England's landed nobles, lacking money, began to enclose common land for livestock grazing, the poor suffered, but the nobles were indifferent to them and their agricultural needs. In 1549, a tanner named Robert Kett (Ket) (d. 1549) led an orderly revolt of supposedly more than 15,000 persons, mainly peasants, protesting against the land enclosures in Norfolk County, England. They captured Norwich, the county town, tore down enclosing fences and hedges, and plundered rich landowners. English soldiers, aided by German mercenaries, suppressed the rebellion with much bloodshed. Kett was captured, tied in chains, and suspended from Norwich Castle to starve to death for his crime; his brother, a participating rebel, suffered the same fate, except from his parish steeple.

Khmer-Cham War of 1050-51   Unsettled conditions and constant anarchy in the kingdom of Champa (central Vietnam) and the southern part of the Khmer Empire (Cambodia) were finally ame-liorated in 1050, when Jaya Paramesvarman (d. 1060), the Cham king, and his son Yuvaraja Mahasenapati (d. c. 1092) suppressed a revolt in Panduranga. Yuvaraja's forces went on to victory over the Khmers, seizing Sambhupura, where they destroyed all the temples and donated stolen treasures and prisoners to the Mi-son temples. This military activity helped lead to the southern Khmers' rebellion (1051) under a leader variously identified as a Khmer vassal king or a Cham chieftain, who received Cham support and seized all of the empire's southern part. Khmer armies led by celebrated generals were sent against the rebels, but to no avail. Eventually the leading Khmer general decisively crushed them, and their leader then took refuge in Champa. The victorious Khmers donated their booty to an Isvaran temple at Rajatirtha. See also VIETNAMESE-CHAM WAR OF 1000–1044.

Khmer-Cham War of 1144–50   King Suryavarman II (d. c. 1150) of the Khmer Empire (roughly Cambodia and Laos) was angered by the peace between Dai Viet or Annam (northern Vietnam) and the kingdom of Champa (central Vietnam) and the latter's refusal to join his invasion of Dai Viet (see VIETNAMESE-KHMER WAR OF 1123–36). In 1144–45, his forces moved into Champa and seized the Cham capital of Vijaya (Binh Dinh), overthrowing King Jaya Indravarman III (d. 1145?); Suryavarman installed himself as ruler. In Panduranga, however, the Chams installed Rudravarman (d. 1147) and, after his death, his son Jaya Harivarman I (d. 1166/67) as their king. In response, Suryavarman sent his greatest general, Senapati Sankara (fl. 12th cent.), with Khmer and Vijayan troops to attack. Jaya Harivarman engaged this army at Chaklyang in the Phanrang Valley (in southern Vietnam) and totally destroyed it. A second large army was sent in 1148, and it too was destroyed at Kayev in the Virapura plain. Suryavarman now made his brother-in-law Harideva (d. 1149?) Champa's king and dispatched generals to lead Khmer troops for his protection. Jaya Harivarman and his forces then advanced north, captured Vijaya, and annihilated Khmer and Cham soldiers at Mahisa, killing Harideva and his chiefs. Jaya Harivarman was then crowned king at Vijaya. In 1150, Suryavarman sent a final force into Champa, and it, too, was destroyed. See also CHAM CIVIL WAR OF 1150–60.

Khmer-Cham War of 1167–90 Upon becoming ruler of the kingdom of Champa (central Vietnam), Jaya Indravarman IV (d. after 1177) launched an invasion of the neighboring Khmer Empire (roughly Cambodia and Laos), lured by its rich treasures. In 1171, the Chams, who had learned from a shipwrecked Chinese mandarin the advantages of using horses instead of elephants in battle, gained a victory against the Khmers. But King Jaya Indravarman later failed to obtain horses in China's Kwangtung and Hunan provinces for use in an invasion of Khmer. A Cham sea attack was successful in 1177. They sailed up the Tônlé Sap ("Great Lake" in central Cambodia) and the Siemréab River and captured the defenseless Khmer capital of Angkor (originally called Yasodharapura), the city's wooden structures were burned, and Angkor Wat (temple complex) was looted and soon fell into ruins, and the Khmer rebel, King Tribhuvanadityavarman (fl. 1166–77), was killed. Afterward the Khmers were inspired by King Jayavarman VII (c. 1120–c. 1215) to fight for their freedom and regained control of their land. Jayavarman was aided by Thai soldiers and Cham refugees living in Khmer in a retaliatory campaign against Champa. After a sea victory in 1181, he was able to rebuild the city of Angkor (Angkor Thom), north of the old capital. In 1190, he launched another invasion of Champa, ravaging its territory and its capital of Vijaya (Binh Dinh). Champa was conquered and split into two puppet vassal states.

Khmer-Cham War of 1191–1203 In 1191, the Chams rebelled against Khmer rule imposed the year before (see KHMER-CHAM WAR OF 1167–90), One of the two Khmer puppet rulers, Prince In (d. after 1203), was ousted and replaced by a Cham prince, who soon became King Jaya Indravarman V

(d. 1192?). He conquered the Khmer puppet ruling the other half of Champa, which was then reunited as a kingdom under his rule. The Chams defeated two invading Khmer armies. But, in 1203, the Khmer king, Jayavarman VII (c. 1120–c. 1215), supported by Cham rebels, achieved victory with an invasion and established on Champa's throne a puppet Cham prince, Ong Dhanapati-grama (d. after 1220), who was supported by Khmer troops. Champa became virtually a Khmer province for some 20 years.

Khmer-Thai Wars of c. 1352–1444 The Thai people of the kingdom of Ayutthaya (south-central Thailand), established by Rama Thibodi I (1312–69) about 1350, began invading the Khmer Empire (Cambodia) to the east. About 1352, King Rama Thibodi put his son Prince Ramesuen (d. 1395), governor of Lop Buri (province to the south), in charge of the invading forces. Ramesuen sent part of his forces ahead—a strategic mistake; the Khmer crown prince was able to stop the invasion by defeating the 5,000 advance troops. Upon hearing news of this, Rama Thibodi sent Prince Boromoraja I (d. 1388), governor of Sup'an, to rescue the stalled expedition. He achieved victory over the Khmers and annexed the Khorat and Chanthaburi districts (eastern Thailand). According to recent historical research, Thai invaders (Ayutthayans) occupied the Khmer capital of Angkor in 1369 and 1389; frequent Thai and Cham attacks threatened to destroy the hydraulic irrigation system that sustained the Khmer Empire, which was further weakened by intermittent Thai participation in Khmer royal politics, dynastic infighting, and the loss of soldiers as prisoners of war. Ayutthayan forces under Boromoraja II (d. 1448) besieged Angkor for seven months (1430–31), finally capturing the city through the treachery of two Buddhist monks and Khmer officials, who later, after the death of the Khmer king, Dharmasoka (d. c. 1444), secretly joined the Ayutthayans. Angkor was sacked by the Thais, who were driven out (1432) but returned later and destroyed it (1444). The Khmer court was moved to Phnom Penh, the new capital, and in the following years the empire contracted to a small kingdom centered around it.

Khorasan Rebellion of A.D. 806–9 Abbasid caliph Harun al-Rashid (766–809) traveled to the Persian province of Khorasan to investigate complaints against the governor, Ali ibn Isa b. Mahan (fl. early 800s), who ruled despotically. Al-Rashid, receiving many gifts and hearing nothing about wrongdoing, confirmed Mahan in his post and departed. Muslim rebels, led by Rafi b. Laith (fl. c. 805–10), then revolted against the governor, whose army suffered defeat in Transoxania in 806. The rebellion continued despite the governor's flight from the province and the caliph's pleas to stop and his promise of a new government sympathetic to the rebels' demands. Laith set up an independent Muslim province in Transoxania. Al-Rashid personally set out to squash Laith in 809 but died en route. His troops returned to Baghdad without confronting the rebels. See also MUSLIM CIVIL WAR OF A.D. 809–13.

Khurramites' Revolt (A.D. 816–38) The Khurramites, a communistic sect in Azerbaijan on the southwestern shore of the Caspian Sea, began attacking Muslim forces in Persia and Mesopotamia, proclaiming their mission to be the abolition of the religion of Islam. The forces of Caliph Allah al-Ma' mun (785–833) were unable to subdue the rebels, who received much Byzantine support (see BYZANTINE-MUSLIM WAR OF A.D. 830–41). When Abu Ishak al-Mu'tasim (d. 842) became caliph, he was determined to crush the Khurramites and the Byzantines. Muslim forces of the caliphate, led by al-Afshin (fl. 830s), governor of Media (near Azerbaijan), pursued the rebels constantly and finally defeated them in 838; the Khurramites' leader, Babak al-Khorrami (d. 838), was killed.

Kiel Mutiny (1918) Germany began to discuss a possible armistice with the Allies near the end of WORLD WAR I. At that time the German navy was in a mutinous state. When the German High Seas Fleet was ordered to sail to the North Sea for a major battle against the British, the German sailors in Kiel refused to go and took up arms, setting off by their mutiny (October 29–November 3, 1918) an open revolution throughout Germany; only the U-boat (submarine) crews remained loyal to the German emperor. Major revolts occurred in Hamburg, Bremen, and Lübeck (November 4–5) and spread to Munich (November 7–8); Bavaria declared itself a democratic and socialist republic. The emperor was forced to abdicate, and on November 11, 1918, the war ended.

King George's War (1744–48) The War of the AUSTRIAN SUCCESSION in North America was fought mainly by New Englanders against the French on the Nova Scotia peninsula. Governor William Shirley (1694–1771) of Massachusetts authorized Colonel William Pepperell (1696–1759), a wealthy Maine merchant, to lead a New England militia, supported by a squadron of the British Royal Navy, in an attack against the heavily fortified French stronghold at Louisbourg (Louisburg) on Cape Breton, Nova Scotia. While the navy bombarded the fortress and town, Pepperell and his men established a beachhead out of range of the French cannons. They employed unconventional commando tactics and attacked the fortress from the rear. After a 49-day siege (April–June 1745), both the town and fortress surrendered. In 1746, a French expedition to retake Louisbourg was wrecked in a storm off the coast of Nova Scotia. The French and their Indian allies raided towns in northern New England and New York, and the British and their Iroquois allies retaliated with raids in Canada (1746–48). All this warring effort was for naught, for by the Treaty of Aix-la-Chapelle in 1748 the status quo was restored, and Louisbourg was returned to France in exchange for Madras, India (see CARNATIC WARS).

King Philip's War (1675–76) Metacom or Metacomet (d. 1676), known as King Philip to the English colonists, was the son of Massasoit (d. 1661) and sachem (hereditary chief) of the Wampanoag

Indians. Humiliated by the Plymouth colonists' laws regulating Indians, he led his and neighboring tribes in southern New England in raids against English settlements. Beginning in June 1675, they burned, sacked, killed, and terrorized throughout the region. The white colonists responded by forming the New England Confederation and sending militia against the unorganized tribes. First the Narraganset Indians and their chief, Canonchet (d. 1676), were defeated, and then the Nipmuck and Wampanoag were subdued, following a successful campaign by colonists, who were assisted by friendly Mohegan Indians, in the Connecticut River valley (June 1676). King Philip was killed (August 12, 1676) by an Indian in the service of the colonists after his hideout at Mount Hope (Bristol, R.I.) was discovered, and 10 days after colonists had seized his wife and son (who were probably doomed to slavery, along with many other captive Wampanoag, Nipmuck, and Narraganset). Indian tribal power was virtually destroyed in southern New England, but Indian raids persisted in the northern parts until peace was concluded in April 1678. See also SWAMP FIGHT.

King William's War (1689–97) The European War of the GRAND ALLIANCE was extended to North America, where the British, allied with the Iroquois Indians, fought against the French and their Indian allies for control of the upper Hudson River valley, the St. Lawrence River valley, Acadia (now Nova Scotia and New Brunswick), and the Hudson Bay area. The British led by Sir William Phips (1651–95) seized Port Royal (Annapolis Royal, Nova Scotia) in 1690, and the French under Count Frontenac (1620–98) made successful raids on towns in New York and New England. The British failed to take Quebec, the main objective; the French were unable to take Boston, their main target, but recaptured Port Royal. The Treaty of Ryswick in 1697 ended the fighting until the outbreak of QUEEN ANNE'S WAR.

Kiowa War of 1874 The Kiowa Indians lived in the northern part of Texas in a forbidding-looking area known as the Starked Plains, through which tributaries of the Red River flowed, creating deep canyons. The Indians spent the winters in these canyons, where there was grass for their ponies and protection from blizzards. The U.S. Army was intent upon destroying this militant tribe, led by Chief Satanta (d. 1878), and six cavalry and infantry columns were sent against them from different directions. They attacked the major Kiowa village and took many prisoners. A scout then discovered their secret refuge in Palo Duro Canyon. Early the next morning the soldiers descended the steep walls of the canyon and charged the sleeping Kiowas, who were routed from their camp and pursued for five miles. The commander ordered that their ponies be rounded up and killed. This was the beginning of the end of a proud tribe that had long hated the white man, although they continued to fight (see RED RIVER INDIAN WAR).

Knights' War (1522–23) In Germany, the Lutheran Reformation caused a period of violent social change, usually purposing to cut the powers of the nobility and the church. In 1522, Franz von Sickingen (1481–1523) and Ulrich von Hutten (1488–1523), two Imperial (free) knights and advocates of the Reformation, initiated war in order to preserve the traditional status of the Imperial knights and to free and secularize noble and ecclesiastical lands. Their league of knights unsuccessfully laid siege to the Catholic city of Trier in 1522. In retaliation, the German princes of Hesse, Trier, and the Palatinate besieged Sickingen in his own castle at Landstuhl, forcing him to surrender on May 6, 1523; Sickingen died from battle wounds the next day. Von Hutten escaped to Zürich and the Swiss Protestant reformer Huldreich Zwingli (1484–1531) but died there after a few months. The German nobility were again victorious in the PEASANTS' WAR of 1524–25.

Korean-Chinese Wars See SINO-KOREAN WARS.

Korean War (1950–53) In order to disarm the Japanese occupiers, at the end of WORLD WAR II, the

Allies established the 38th parallel as a "temporary" dividing line between communist North Korea and democratic South Korea; efforts later by the United Nations to reunite the country failed. On June 25, 1950, North Korean troops suddenly and without warning invaded South Korea, and within two months they had pushed south almost to the tip of the Korean peninsula, where South Korean defenses were thrown up around Pusan (the Pusan Perimeter). Two days after the invasion, the UN called on its members to help South Korea, and 15 did so. The international force was under the command of U.S. general Douglas MacArthur (1880–1964), who planned and executed a successful amphibious landing behind enemy lines at the west-coast port of Inchon (September 15, 1950) and cut their supply lines. The North Koreans were driven northward and eventually back to the Yalu River (November 24, 1950), the boundary between China and North Korea. UN forces, using two columns, on each side of Korea's central mountain spine, planned to reunite Korea under southern control, but the plan was never realized because, on November 26, 1950, a large communist Chinese army invaded the north in support of the North Koreans and helped them drive the UN forces south after much bitter fighting. By January 1, 1951, the North Korean-Chinese army of about 485,000 men had forced MacArthur's 365,000 UN troops back to the 38th parallel. The South Korean capital of Seoul fell into enemy hands, but a counteroffensive by UN forces retook the city on March 14, 1951. Both sides began a "talking war" to reach an accord; negotiations dragged on while the fighting continued intermittently around the dividing line. MacArthur publicly advocated attacking and bombing Chinese bases in Manchuria, contrary to UN and American orders. On April 11, 1951, U.S. president Harry S. Truman (1884–1972) summarily dismissed MacArthur from command of UN and American forces in the Far East and appointed General Matthew B. Ridgway (1895–1993) in his place. Offensives and counteroffensives were launched by both sides, which suffered heavy casualties. Ridgway's truce negotiations, which hinged largely on the repatriation of prisoners, sick and wounded, broke down in October 1952; the UN forces had taken over 70,000 prisoners, and UN negotiators insisted that they be allowed to choose whether to return to the north or to stay in the south. The latter view ultimately prevailed, and three out of four prisoners remained in South Korea (21 American prisoners elected to stay with the communists). In April 1953, peace talks resumed and led to the signing of an armistice at Panmunjom on July 27, 1953; but no formal peace treaty has ever been concluded. U.S. officials have repeatedly refused North Korea's demand for the withdrawal of American troops from South Korea.

Kornilov's Revolt (1917) Conservative Russian generals, backed by Alexander F. Kerensky (1881–1970), who had replaced Prince Lvov (1861–1925) as premier in the provisional government, decided to form a military dictatorship to end the increasing anarchy and lack of army discipline after the FEBRUARY REVOLUTION. When Kerensky realized that General Lavr G. Kornilov (1870–1918), whom he had appointed army commander in chief, aspired to become sole dictator, he declared him a traitor and dismissed him. In response, Kornilov dispatched his Cossack troops to Petrograd (St. Petersburg), hoping to reform the soviet (revolutionary council) and the provisional government along more conservative lines. Kerensky withdrew his support for a rightist military takeover and sought help from the Soviets' central committee and leftist forces. Workers, armed by the Bolsheviks and urged to resist Kornilov's threat to their revolution, persuaded the Cossacks to defect, and the counterrevolution collapsed after five days (September 9–14, 1917). Kornilov was arrested and jailed; he escaped from Petrograd after the OCTOBER REVOLUTION. See also BOLSHEVIK REVOLUTION.

Kosciusko's Uprising See POLISH REBELLION OF 1794.

Kosovo Uprising of 1998 Sporadic fighting between ethnic Albanian guerrillas and Serbian police in the Serbian province of Kosovo in southern Yugoslavia escalated to a high-profile conflict in early March 1998 when Serbian police and paramilitary forces began blasting ethnic Albanian villages in the area surrounding the capital, Pristina, killing dozens of defenseless residents. Fearing the possibility of another full-scale Balkan war, the "Contact Group" (consisting of the United States, Britain, France, Germany, Italy, and Russia) set up to monitor adherence to the Dayton Accords of 1995, which ended the BOSNIAN CIVIL WAR OF 1992–95, imposed an arms embargo on Yugoslavia on May 9. Alone among Contact Group members, the U.S. favored harsher penalties against the Serbs; in the meantime it was discovered that the Russians had agreed to sell arms to Yugoslavia the previous December, in violation of the Dayton Accords. The province of Kosovo, 90 percent of whose 2 million inhabitants are ethnic Albanians, had been stripped in 1989 of its autonomous status within the republic of Serbia by then-president of Serbia, Slobodan Milosevic (1941–) in reaction to the province's demand for independence. In the following years a movement of peaceful civil resistance among the Kosovars (ethnic Albanians in Kosovo) led by moderate Ibrahim Rugova (1944–) had achieved a certain degree of success by boycotting Serbian administrative institutions. Rather than compromise by offering Kosovo the status of autonomous republic within the state of Yugoslavia—the status of Serbia and Montenegro—Milosevic, who subsequently became president of Yugoslavia, persisted in a policy of police rule in Kosovo. The police sweeps of March 1998, an action diplomats considered a foolish move, merely served to galvanize resistance among the vast Albanian majority. As Serbian forces continued to shell villages, the Kosovo Liberation Army (KLA), which began as a small band of poorly equipped men but quickly swelled with volunteers and arms supplied by Albania, gained control of 40 percent of the province. In early June, Milosevic stepped up his campaign of flushing Kosovars from their homes, causing thousands of refugees to flee for their lives to Albania. Meanwhile U.S. efforts to help settle the conflict failed, and Contact Group members continued to

disagree about sanctions. In August 1998, a Serbian offensive drove KLA rebels from their strongholds, and fighting centered on escape routes into Albania, where Kosovars maintained sanctuaries; both sides reviewed a blueprint for peace negotiations. Serbian terrorism against villagers brought UN condemnation. Clashes between Serbian security forces and rebels (as well as civilians) resulted in about 50 killings in December 1998, adding urgency to efforts by the Contact Group members to negotiate a permanent peace. The warring sides sent delegations to peace talks in Rambouillet, France, in February 1999. Serb forces continued attacks on Kosovo Albanians, while Belgrade fortified its border with Macedonia (the likely staging area for any NATO peacekeeping force). U.S. envoy Richard C. A. Holbrooke (1941–), architect of the Dayton Accords, unsuccessfully tried to persuade Milosevic to sign onto a U.S.-sponsored peace plan (March 10, 1999), and NATO began a strategic bombing campaign on March 24. More than 2,000 people have died and 300,000 have been displaced since the fighting began.

Kronshtadt Rebellion (1921)   Angered by the Bolshevik failure to distribute food to Russian cities and by the restriction of freedoms and the enactment of harsh labor regulations, the sailors at the Kronshtadt (Kronstadt) Naval Base supported striking urban workers by establishing a provisional revolutionary committee. The sailors, contributors to the success of the OCTOBER REVOLUTION of 1917, demanded an end to the Communist Party dictatorship, full power to the soviets (district councils), release of non-Bolshevik prisoners, and fuller political freedoms and rights. Leon Trotsky (1879–1940) and Mikhail N. Tukhachevsky (1893–1937) led soldiers across the ice from Petrograd (St. Petersburgh), crushed the rebellion, and shot or imprisoned the survivors. The unsuccessful rebellion nonetheless had forced the New Economic Policy of March 1921. See also RUSSIAN CIVIL WAR OF 1918–21.

Kun's Red Terror (1919) The new Hungarian republic (see HUNGARIAN REVOLUTION OF 1918) was soon menaced when Béla Kun (1885–c. 1939), a Bolshevik sent from Russia by Vladimir I. Lenin (1870–1924), established the Hungarian Communist Party on December 20, 1918. When Count Michael Károlyi (1875–1955), Hungary's president, resigned (March 21, 1919) in protest against the Allies' demands for more Hungarian territorial concessions, a coalition government of Communists and Social Democrats was formed under the leadership of Kun, who soon pushed out the latter and secured a Communist dictatorship. Appealing to Hungarian nationalism and promising to gain Russian aid (which never arrived), Kun and his followers formed a Red Army that shortly reconquered Slovakia from the Czechs. At home, nationalization of Hungary's landed estates, instead of division among the peasantry, lost Kun the support of the peasants, and the bourgeoisie withdrew its backing because of his increasing terror tactics against opposition. The Allies forced Kun to relinquish Slovakia, and Hungarian counterrevolutionaries attempted to overthrow Kun and the Communists. Earlier, to stop a possible Hungarian reconquest of Transylvania (under Rumanian control), a Rumanian army had invaded Hungary in April 1919 and had repelled Kun's attack on it. Kun's army refused to fight as Rumanian troops advanced on Budapest; Kun fled to Vienna on August 1, 1919; four days later the Rumanians occupied Budapest, which they pillaged before withdrawing on November 14, 1919. Admiral Nicholas Horthy de Nagybanya (1868–1957), who had led the counterrevolutionaries and their government, entered Budapest and was appointed regent and head of state in March 1920. He restored the monarchy, albeit separated from Austria, and thwarted two attempts (March and October 1921) by former Austrian emperor Charles I (1887–1922) to regain the Hungarian throne (see HUNGARIAN CIVIL WAR OF 1921).

Kurdish Guerrilla Wars of 1984– Wracked by internecine fighting and ever-shifting political loyalties, the Kurdish people (numbering today about 25 million and spread mostly across northern Iraq, eastern Turkey, and Iran) attempted for decades since the 1920s to gain autonomy, either within their respective countries or as an independent nation. But it is unlikely that the area, called Kurdistan (a geographical, not political, designation), will ever in fact be united: first, the western powers want to avoid further instability in Turkey and Iraq, which support of a sovereign Kurdish state would cause; second, creation of a solid national identity and political cohesion among the many Kurdish clans and factions has proven elusive. In 1984, for example, Turkish Kurd terrorists formed the Kurdistan Workers Party (PKK) and set about killing Kurds they considered loyal to the Turkish state; the Turkish government responded with counterinsurgency measures that resulted by 1996 in about 20,000 casualties and 2 million refugees. In addition to battling each other, the Kurds have been victims throughout the 20th century of systematic killing campaigns and political manipulation by Turkey, Iraq, and Iran. Recent massacres include the execution by Iraqi president Saddam Hussein (1937–   ) of some 8,000 males of the anti-Iraq Barzani clan and the notorious 1988 Al-Afan operation in which approximately 180,000 Kurds were either gassed in their villages or taken in busloads to southern Iraq where they evidently were shot en masse. In early 1991, Kurd guerrillas from Iraq's two main Kurd parties, the Kurdistan Democratic Party (KDP) and the Patriotic Union of Kurdistan (PUK), made important territorial gains, pushing Saddam's forces from their homeland in the oil-rich north. Over 1 million refugees from the fighting found safety in a security zone near the Turkish border set up by allied troops; a few months later when the troops left and Saddam predictably sent in his army, the Kurds once again pushed them back. In April 1992 elections were held for a national Kurdish assembly (a concession Saddam had granted for political show only). However, by May 1994 any hope of a long-term united effort among Kurds was shattered after the KDP and PUK resorted to violence in their competition for control. In April 1995 they set up a well-intentioned parliament in The Hague, but in September 1996 the KDP, now allied to Saddam, drove PUK rebels from

Irbil (Erbil), then took Sulaymaniyah (Sulaymania) and Dokan (Dukan), gaining only temporary control of Iraqi Kurdistan. In a counteroffensive in October 1996, PUK forces, supported by Iran, retook much of the territory, including Sulaymaniyah. By then, peace talks had begun through U.S. mediation and led to a cease-fire agreement by the KDP and PUK on October 23, 1996. Clashes between these rivals shattered the cease-fire about a year later. At the time (1997), Turkish forces, aided by the KDP and Barzani, crossed into northern Iraq to attack PKK rebels based there. The PKK suffered heavy losses, and the Turks ceded some land to the KDP. Turkey's capture of Abdullah Ocalan (1941–), fugitive Kurdish rebel leader of the PKK (who was taken out of hiding from the Greek embassy in Kenya and transported to Turkey for arrest), immediately ignited massive protests on February 16, 1999, as enraged Kurds seized embassies and consulates and held hostages in at least 21 European cities. Although Turkish officials claimed victory over Ocalan's rebel movement, they are under growing international pressure to grant the Kurds greater civil and political rights. See also PERSIAN GULF WAR OF 1990–91.

L

La Hogue (Hougue), Battle of (1692)   During the WAR OF THE GRAND ALLIANCE, France's King Louis XIV (1638–1715), possessor of Europe's finest navy, planned to defeat both the English and Dutch fleets. His expectations and a proposed invasion of England were destroyed (May 29–June 2, 1692) at La Hogue, an anchorage off Point Barfleur in northwest France. His admiral, comte de Tourville (1642–1701), victor at the 1690 Battle of Beachy Head, possessed only 44 ships against more than twice that number in the Alliance fleet. Reinforcements from Toulon failed to arrive; nevertheless, Tourville attacked. On the first day, French skill and seamanship gained the day. That night, he began to withdraw westward, sending 20 ships to St. Malo. Of the remainder, 15 were destroyed in the next four days' fighting, including Tourville's flagship. Tourville escaped, but the French naval supremacy was broken.

Lambing Flat Riots (1860–61)   The severe Australian laws that prompted the EUREKA STOCKADE MINERS' REBELLION were finally modified (1854); however, the Australian conservatives, whom the miners regarded as "the real aborigines," were never really defeated by liberal movements. Struggles over trade unionism revived (1855), and strikes occurred during periods of high unemployment, especially against the imported Chinese laborers. The settlement of Lambing Flat (Young) in New South Wales saw the worst of the riots against the Chinese, many of whom were attacked, robbed, beaten, or killed by white miners who wished to force them from the goldfields in the area. Some of the rioters were arrested; others fought gun battles with the police, who finally restored order in mid-1861. Alarmed by the protests, the effective passive resistance of the Chinese, and the spread of racism to include the Australian aborigines, the older Australian colonists who formed the legislative bodies merely restricted the Chinese to certain areas and, to discourage immigration by others, charged a residence tax.

Lamian War (Greek War) (323–322 B.C.)   This war postponed the struggle for power among the Diadochi (see DIADOCHI, WARS OF THE) because, as a general revolt in Greece, it demanded the attention of every Alexandrian successor. It had two causes: an Athenian revolt against Alexander's decree recalling exiles (see ALEXANDER THE GREAT, CONQUESTS OF) and disturbances caused by returning troops and exiles in the mercenary market of Taenarum. The war took its name from the besieging by Athenians of the Macedonian regent, Antipater (d. 319), at Lamia in Greece. Macedonian reinforcements broke the siege. The Athenians, whose Greek allies deserted them, lost at sea in 323 and on land in 322 at the Battle of Crannon in Macedonia. Athens surrendered unconditionally;

some of its leaders were executed (Demosthenes [385?–322], killed himself with poison). Athens also paid a huge indemnity, became an oligarchy, and had its port, Piraeus, occupied by Macedonian troops.

Laodicean War See SYRIAN-EGYPTIAN WARS, SECOND AND THIRD.

Laotian-Burmese Wars See BURMESE-LAOTIAN WARS.

Laotian Civil War of 1954–73 The Geneva Conference (1954) recognized Laos, part of French Indochina, as a neutral independent state; soon the Pathet Lao (an anti-French, pro-communist Laotian party) controlled the country's two northern provinces, gained support from infiltrating Vietminh troops from neighboring Vietnam, and attacked the Laotian government. In 1958, Laotian Premier, Prince Souvanna Phouma (1901–), allowed Pathet Lao leaders in the government, but in the elections he was ousted; a pro-Western, rightist government, supported militarily and economically by the United States, attempted to destroy the Communist-backed Pathet Lao. Much of the fighting between the Laotian army and Pathet Lao forces took place on the Plain of Jars in north-central Laos. In 1960, a military coup toppled the government in Vientiane, leading to the return of Souvanna Phouma, neutralist leader, as premier; but he fled into exile in Cambodia for awhile after a three-way struggle for governmental control erupted involving the Pathet Lao, rightists, and neutralists (1960). The Pathet Lao under Prince Souphanouvong (1909–95) agreed to a cease-fire (1961), and a coalition government was formed with representatives from the three factions (1962), each of which maintained its own army. In 1964, rightists briefly ousted Souvanna Phouma as premier until he agreed to expand rightist representation in the government; the Pathet Lao, backed by North Vietnamese forces, protested, severed its ties with the government, and overran the Plain of Jars. The battle lines in Laos fluctuated with the seasons in the next years, but gradually the communist Pathet Lao occupied the country's eastern, southern, and northern sections. Despite U.S. air support, Laotian government forces of Souvanna Phouma lost ground to communist counteroffensives (1970–72). The Pathet Lao and the government signed a cease-fire in 1973, and soon a coalition government of neutralists, rightists, and communists (Pathet Lao) was formed, with Souvanna Phouma as premier and Souphanouvong as president. After the communist takeover of South Vietnam and Cambodia in 1975, the Pathet Lao took effective control of Laos. See also FRENCH INDOCHINA WAR OF 1946–54; VIETNAM WAR.

Laotian Guerrilla War of 1977–90 In Laos, in 1975, the Pathet Lao leaders abolished the old monarchy and the coalition government and established a communist regime, the People's Democratic Republic; many Laotians fled to Thailand. In 1977, royalist Meo tribesmen in Laos began guerrilla warfare against the government, especially in Xieng Khouang province. The Meo and Hmong peoples (both persecuted minorities) gained support from China in their rebel attacks throughout the country, where the presence of some 45,000 Vietnamese troops (Laos and Vietnam were allied) was vehemently opposed by the rebels and Chinese. Laotians continued to escape to Thailand. In 1982, an anti-Pathet Lao "Royal Lao Democratic Government," backed by China, was set up in southern Laos with plans to ally with anti-Vietnamese forces in Cambodia. Rebel guerrilla groups continued to harass the Pathet Lao and Vietnamese forces. From 1984 to early 1988, Laos and Thailand intermittently fought over a disputed border area, where three villages were claimed by both countries. Rebel groups lacked sufficient strength to challenge the forces of the ruling Pathet Lao (the Lao People's Revolutionary Party), which accused Thailand of supporting right-wing Laotian guerrillas and harboring them along the border. In 1988, about half of the Vietnamese troops in Laos were withdrawn, and China (Vietnam's enemy) ceased to support anti-Pathet Lao resistance. Laotian business relations greatly improved with China, Thailand, Vietnam, and other countries. Discussions between Laos and Thailand over guerrilla attacks led first to a suspension in hostilities in 1990 and then to the withdrawal of Thai troops from the border area in 1991. Rebel groups had been checked by the Pathet Lao army, and the repatriation of some 60,000 Laotian refugees in Thai camps began.

Latin Empire–Byzantine Empire War, First (1204–22)   The Fourth Crusade (see CRUSADES) caused the momentary collapse of the Byzantine Empire. A Latin Empire known as Romania was proclaimed under the leadership of Baldwin II (1171–1205), but, because many of its territories were still to be conquered and its internal and external enemies were numerous, it always remained weak. In 1205, at Adrianople (Edirne), the Latins were routed by a Bulgarian-Cuman force. Baldwin was taken prisoner, and the Latins were forced to withdraw from Asia Minor. Henry of Flanders (1174?–1216) became the second Latin emperor in 1206 and, after an attempt to invade Asia Minor, was forced by the emperor of Nicaea to sign a two-year armistice. The Latins then made a secret alliance with the Seljuk Turks, who fought Nicaea from 1209. The Latins' defeat in 1211 was a great boost for the Nicaeans and aided minor Nicaean victories in 1212 and an armistice in 1214, when the Latins recognized and promised to respect Nicaea's boundaries. Henry died in 1216, further reducing Latin power and morale. In 1219, the southern Slavs recognized Nicaea as the heir to the Byzantine Empire and the center of Greek orthodoxy. The Latin Empire consisted only of Constantinople after 1222, when Nicaea wrested Seleucia from the Latins. **Second Latin Empire–Byzantine Empire War** (1224–37). Nicaea under John III (d. 1254) became the real savior of the Byzantine Empire by gaining control of once-independent Bulgaria. In 1224, with Bulgaria's Ivan II (d. 1241) as an ally, John gained territory in Asia Minor and the Aegean islands but failed to capture Constantinople. Ivan then went over to the Latin side. Nevertheless, by 1225, John had won almost the entire Latin territory in Asia Minor but had lost

Thrace to Epirus. Baldwin II (1217–73), then a minor, was named co-emperor of the Latin Empire in 1228, with Ivan as regent. But when Baldwin was joined in 1231 by John of Brienne (1170–1237), Ivan's regency was voided. Ivan declared war against the Latin side; his forces attacked Constantinople in 1235 and 1236 but were thwarted. John III, with Mongol assistance, then oppressed Ivan and reduced both Bulgaria and the Latin Empire to pawns. **Third Latin Empire–Byzantine Empire War** (1261–67). After 1250 the Latin Empire began to collapse entirely. Forces of Michael VIII Palaeologus (1225–82), who had usurped, in true Byzantine fashion, the throne of Nicaea, took Constantinople from the Latins in 1259 and restored the Byzantine Empire. The war continued against Charles I (1227–85) of Naples and Sicily, an outgrowth of costly actions against Epirus. In 1261, Michael was named emperor and began to consolidate the Byzantine Empire's power against its many enemies. A treaty with Genoa and victories in Peloponnesian territories and Latin islands also marked 1261. In 1262, Michael crushed a rejuvenated Bulgaria, and in 1263, after a defeat of the Genoese fleet, he made an alliance with Venice. A Byzantine victory over Epirus in early 1264 was marred by a serious defeat at Makry-Plagi later in the year. By 1267, however, through small skirmishes and naval victories and through careful diplomacy (including a brief reunion of the Roman and Orthodox churches), Michael's forces had made secure the restored Byzantine Empire, avoiding other major wars and bringing relative peace to the empire. See also BYZANTINE CIVIL WAR OF 1222–24; BYZANTINE CIVIL WAR OF 1259; BYZANTINE WAR OF 1207–11; CRUSADE, FOURTH; CRUSADE, SIXTH; CRUSADE, EIGHTH.

Latin War   (340–338 B.C.)   Rome was but one city on the Latium or Latin plains of central Italy for many decades, but it gradually rose to dominate the area. Many of the Latin cities were bound together in a loose confederation or league with Rome, but in 340, several of the larger cities challenged Rome's leadership and left the league. They were supported by other rebellious peoples, including the Campanians. At the Battle of Vesuvius (339), Publius Decius Mus (d. 339) sacrificed himself in a futile attack against the rebel Latin forces so that his colleague, Titus Manlius Imperiosus Torquatus (fl. mid-4th cent.), could withdraw safely with the rest of the Roman army. Soon thereafter Manlius led the Romans to victory at the Battle of Trifanum (338), and the defeated Latins were forced to accept an alliance with Rome. Unlike previous agreements in which all league members were considered equal, this time Rome was recognized as the leader, and the other cities were bound to it by offensive and defensive alliances. They also exchanged citizenship rights.

Latvian War of Independence (1919–20)   After Germany's defeat in WORLD WAR I, the Latvians (Letts) proclaimed an independent state with Karlis Ulmanis (1877–1940) as prime minister, but in early January 1919, Soviet (Bolshevik) forces invaded the country and seized its capital, Riga, where a Soviet government was set up. However, German-Latvian troops, with the approval of the Allies, forced the Soviets to withdraw in March 1919. Though the Treaty of Versailles required the Germans to leave the area, they attempted to take over Latvia and occupied Riga, but were expelled finally in late November 1919. Under Allied pressure, the Soviets, who had again tried to take over, were evicted from the country completely in January 1920, and concluded an armistice with the Latvians a month later. By the Treaty of Riga on August 11, 1920, the Soviet government recognized Latvia's independence (in 1940, during WORLD WAR II, Latvia, while occupied by Soviet troops, was constituted as one of the Soviet republics and did not regain its independence until 1991).

Lava Beds War   See MODUC WAR.

League of Augsburg, War of the   See GRAND ALLIANCE, WAR OF THE.

League of Cambrai, War of the (1508–10)   Angered when Venice took the region of Romagna to which the papacy had title, Pope Julius II (1443–1513) in 1508 united Venetian enemies—Holy Roman Emperor Maximilian I (1459–1519), King Louis XII (1462–1515) of France, and King Ferdinand II (1452–1516) of Aragon—into the League of Cambrai to divide up Venice's acquired mainland territories and bring papal lands under direct papal rule. The league's armies moved against Bologna, a main city in Romagna, after taking Perugia to the south, and made a massive attack on Venice, defeating the Venetians at the Battle of Agnadello in 1509. Venetian mainland possessions were dissolved, and Venice lost its claim to independence in church issues, as well as its claim to the cities in Romagna. The League of Cambrai, however, fell apart when Emperor Maximilian lost control of Padua and when the pope grew fearful of foreign control of Italy. Although Venice eventually regained its mainland cities, it never again achieved its former power. See also HOLY LEAGUE, WAR OF THE.

Lebanese Civil War of 1958   After being elected president of Lebanon in 1952, Camille Chamoun (1900–87) oversaw a predominantly Christian (Maronite) government that stressed closer ties to Europe and the United States. Lebanese Muslims, who made up about half of the country's population, favored instead stronger economic and political relationships with the surrounding Arab nations. On May 9–13, 1958, Muslim groups openly rebelled against Chamoun's regime, rioting and fighting in the streets of Tripoli and Beirut, Lebanon's capital. The newly formed United Arab Republic (a political union of Egypt and Syria) had allegedly instigated the violence against the pro-Western policies of President Chamoun, whose government seemed on the verge of collapse as rebels under several Muslim leaders and Druse (Druze) chieftain Kamal Jumblatt (1918–77) overcame army troops. Refusing to resign, Chamoun appealed to the United States for help; U.S. president Dwight D. Eisenhower (1890–1969) ordered American forces from the Sixth Fleet to land near Beirut to support the government, as well as to protect American lives and to guard against a possible Egyptian-Syrian invasion of Lebanon (July 15–20, 1958). About a month later the Lebanese government and army, assisted by more than 14,000 U.S. troops, had control of the situation. General Fuad Chehab (1902–73), a Maronite Christian, succeeded Chamoun as president on September 23, 1958; a new cabinet of four Christians, three Muslims, and one Druse was formed; the U.S. backed the new government and completely withdrew its troops from Lebanon by late October that year.

Lebanese Civil War of 1975–90 Lebanon's different Muslim groups, principally the Shi'ite, Sunni, and Druse (Druze) sects, which made up about half the population, were discontented with the 1943 National Pact, which established a dominant political role for the Christians (Phalange Party or Phalangists), especially the Maronites, in the central government. Palestinian Muslims also live in Lebanon, particularly in the south in refugee camps or in bases from which guerrillas of the Palestine Liberation Organization (PLO) carried out attacks on neighboring Israel. Lebanese Muslims tended to sympathize with the PLO. When a bus carrying many Palestinians was assaulted by Phalangists and the passengers slain (April 13, 1975), a long and bloody civil war was triggered. At first a leftist Muslim coalition fought rightist Christians; in early 1976, the PLO joined the Muslims after Christians raided a Palestinian refugee camp. Israel supplied arms to Christians. With the backing of the League of Arab States, Syria sent 30,000 troops to restore order in Lebanon and to implement a peace plan (1976). Elias Sarkis (1924–85), a Maronite Christian, was elected Lebanon's president and, with Syrian, Israeli, U.S., and Saudi support, attempted to establish authority. By 1977, Lebanon was divided into a northern section, controlled by Syrian forces, and a coastal section under Christian control, with enclaves in the south dominated by leftist Muslims and the PLO. Syrians and Christian militiamen were soon battling each other, and the for-

mer shelled the Christian part of Beirut, Lebanon's capital. In retaliation for a Palestinian guerrilla terrorist attack on Israel, Israeli troops invaded southern Lebanon (March 14, 1978) to wipe out PLO bases and occupied the area as far north as the Litani River. The Israelis complied with a United Nations' demand for their withdrawal from the area, which was then occupied by a UN peacekeeping force (1978). In 1980, Syria concentrated forces in central Lebanon's Bekaa (al-Biqa) Valley and later moved Soviet-made surface-to-air (SAM-6) missiles there. When the Phalangists (Christians) occupied the hills around Zahle near the strategic Beirut-Damascus highway, Syria launched a major offensive against them; Israeli jets intervened and attacked the Syrians and also bombed areas of Beirut in retaliation for PLO rocket attacks from Lebanon into northern Israel. A cease-fire went into effect on July 24, 1981, but it was temporary. To dispel the PLO, invading Israeli troops reached the outskirts of Beirut and forced the evacuation of PLO guerrillas in 1982. Lebanon's Phalangist president-elect Bashir Gemayel (1947–82), chosen to succeed the retiring Sarkis, was assassinated on September 14, 1982; his brother, Amin Gemayel (1942–), a more moderate Christian leader, became president—just days before 328 Palestinian civilians had been massacred by alleged Phalangists at Sabra and Shatila refugee camps in west Beirut (September 16–18, 1982). Afterward U.S. Marines and United Kingdom, French, and Italian troops arrived in Beirut as a peacekeeping force. A bomb blast killed more than 50 people at the U.S. embassy in Beirut on April 18, 1983. Israeli forces withdrew from Lebanon's Shuf Mountains, which the Druse under their leader Walid Jumblatt (1947–) occupied after heavy fighting against Christians and the Lebanese army. Without warning, 241 Americans and 58 French died in separate suicidal bomb attacks on U.S. and French military headquarters in Beirut (October 23, 1983). At Tripoli, PLO leader Yasir Arafat (1929–) and his loyalists were attacked and besieged by PLO dissidents, supported by Syria, for six weeks until they were forced to evacuate on a UN flag-flying Greek ship on December 20, 1983. U.S. warships off the coast bombarded Syrian and Druse positions. Faced with his country's disintegration into various mini-states, Gemayel sought national reconciliation talks to settle differences among political leaders—Phalangist, Maronite, Druse, Sunni, Shi'ite, and others—in order to stabilize the government. U.S. Marines left Beirut in February 1984, with Lebanon occupied in part by Syrian and Israeli troops and divided by bitter feuds and warring factions. A peacekeeping accord in 1986 soon fell apart, with ferocious battles between Druse and Shi'ite militias in Muslim west Beirut; Syrian forces invaded and quelled the turmoil in February 1987. Amin Gemayel's presidency expired in September 1988, and was followed by Christian leader General Michel Aoun's government. Christian east Beirut, controlled by Aoun (1935–), and Muslim west Beirut, where Prime Minister Selim al-Hoss (1930–) established a rival government, became a bloody battleground in 1989; feuding militias shelled each other mercilessly; western officials made vain appeals for a ceasefire. Finally, in October 1989, a tentative peace accord was approved, and a new Lebanese president was selected. In 1990, the Syrian-backed, Arab League–mediated peace plan, which addressed the concerns of both Christians and Muslims, began to be implemented in Beirut, where rival militias withdrew from the city, Lebanese Army troops took full control (for the first time since 1975), and the "green line," which split the city into Christian and Muslim sectors, was dismantled. But Lebanon, recognized by Syria as an independent state in 1991 (for the first time since 1943), failed to secure an Israeli pullout from the south. The 1975–90 civil war claimed over 144,000 lives, largely civilian; over 197,000 persons were wounded, and thousands of others were abducted by rival militias and never found. In the 1990s, Israeli forces periodically raided and bombarded Hizballah (Hezbollah), the Iranian-backed Shi'ite Muslim militia that had been fighting the Israelis in south Lebanon since 1982. PLO guerrillas there continued rocket attacks on northern Israel. In 1998, Israel accepted a UN resolution for troop withdrawal from south Lebanon, where the village of Arnoun was seized by Israeli troops in February 1999; Israel denied expansion of its so-called security zone, objecting to guerrilla attacks from Arnoun on its outpost at the former Crusader castle of Beaufort. See also PALESTINIAN GUERRILLA RAIDS.

Lechfeld, Battle of (A.D. 955) After their devastating raid into France and northern Italy in 954 (see MAGYAR RAIDS IN FRANCE), the Magyars marched across the Carnic Alps to the Drava and Danube valleys; they were optimistic about victory in Germany, where King Otto I (912–73) was involved in quelling civil strife. After a brief stay in their homeland (Hungary), some 50,000 Magyars invaded Bavaria and besieged the city of Augsburg, whose courageous German bishop, awaiting help from Otto, led a charge that confused the enemy (August 955). On the next day, Otto arrived with a 10,000-man army, causing the Magyars to lift their siege and battle Otto. At first the more numerous Magyars seemed to be winning, seizing the German camp and routing a third of Otto's army. With the support of reinforcements led by Conrad "the Red" (d. 955), duke of Lorraine and former rival of Otto, the Germans rallied, and their mail-clad cavalry proved superior to the lightly covered cavalry of the Magyars, who broke apart, fled, and suffered heavy casualties (Conrad, unfortunately, was slain at the time of victory). Pursued by Otto's army, the Magyars hastened eastward, never to return to Germany and too weak militarily to conquer Austria in the 960s and 970s. The Magyar menace had ended for good.

Leisler's Rebellion (1689–91) When the Protestants William (1650–1702) and Mary (1662–94) ascended the English throne in the GLORIOUS REVOLUTION (1688), there were a number of uprisings in the American colonies against royal officials suspected of being Catholics. In New York City, discontented artisans and small traders seized the fort on Manhattan and proclaimed their leader, Jacob Leisler (1640?–91), a German immigrant merchant, commander in chief. Supported by farmers, city workers, and the militia, Leisler acknowledged the sovereignty of William and Mary and ruled southern New York in their name. Leaders in Albany, N.Y., did not recognize Leisler until 1690, when they needed his militia to protect them from a feared Indian attack. In March 1691, Major Richard Ingoldesby (fl. early 1690s) arrived from England with troops and demanded that the fort be surrendered to him, which Leisler refused to do—an act that was subsequently construed as treason. When the new English governor arrived, Leisler was seized (March 30, 1691) after surrendering the fort and tried as a traitor. Convicted, he was hanged in New York City on May 16, 1691.

Lelantine War (c. 670 B.C.)   Rivalry over trade and colonial trading posts caused Greece's biggest military conflict since the TROJAN WAR. The cities of Chalcis and Eretria fought land battles on the Lelantine Plain, a natural boundary between them in the district of Boeotia. On its side, Chalcis had Corinth, Samos, and the Thessalian League; Eretria had Aegina, Miletus, and possibly Megara. Fought on land and sea during the early seventh-century period of intense colonization, the war's final battle took place on the plain that gives the war its name. Thessalian cavalry defeated the Eretrians, who nonetheless later became the more prominent and prosperous city-state.

Lepidus, Revolt of (78–77 B.C.)   Marcus Aemilius Lepidus (d. c. 77) was the consul of Rome in 78 who championed the cause of the poor and dispossessed and attempted to alleviate their lot. When his efforts failed, the people of Etruria in west-central Italy revolted, and Lepidus supported them. He raised an army in northern Italy and marched on Rome but was defeated by the forces of Quintus Lutatius Catulus (d. 60) and Pompey the Great (106–48). Lepidus and his followers escaped to the island of Sardinia, where he died shortly afterward. His followers in northern Italy were crushed by Pompey's soldiers.

Liberian Civil War of 1989–97   An eight-year struggle for leadership of the West African republic of Liberia began on December 24, 1989, when U.S.-educated rebel leader Charles Taylor (1948–) invaded Liberia from neighboring Côte d'Ivoire (Ivory Coast). Taylor's forces, called the National Patriotic Front of Liberia (NPFL), sought to take power from brutal dictator Samuel K. Doe (1951?–90), whose military regime had ruled the country since seizing power in a 1980 coup against President William R. Tolbert, Jr. (1913–80). By September 1990 Taylor controlled most of Liberia but had not been able to take the capital, Monrovia, where President Doe held out in the executive palace. The warring factions, largely divided along ethnic lines, were complicated by a split that year between Taylor and Prince Yormie (Yeduo) Johnson (1959–), head of the Gio tribe. The three-way fighting now was between Johnson's small Gio group, Taylor's more numerous Mano tribe (with many Gio who had stayed loyal to him), and Doe's forces (consisting mainly of the Krahn and Mandingo tribes). A peacekeeping force organized by five West African nations from the Economic Community of West African States (ECOWAS), ostensibly sent to stabilize the situation, was spurned by Taylor, who mistrusted the force's neutrality. (Early in the war President Doe had sought help from the United States without success.) In September 1990 Prince Johnson's small band caught, tortured, and killed Doe, and Johnson declared himself president; at the same time, the head of Doe's presidential guard, General David Nimblay, assumed leadership of Doe's supporters, now called the United Liberation Movement of Liberia for Democracy (ULIMO). Johnson and Nimblay then agreed to support an interim government chosen by ECOWAS. ECOWAS forces joined Johnson's rebels to fight against Taylor (bearing out Taylor's suspicions), although their relationship was not friendly. Now a stalemate set in, with all three factions still vying for control. Following a peace agreement in August 1995, Taylor, Johnson, and General Alhaji G. V. Kromah formed a ruling council with three other warlords (relatively powerless), each of whom occupied his own floor in the executive palace and ran various ministries. A January 1996 peace plan brokered by several African states was ineffectual, and in April 1996 ferocious fighting again erupted in Monrovia among rebels and government troops and West African peacekeeping forces. Taylor then made a tenuous alliance with the republic of Nigeria, and on July 19, 1997, with Nigerian help, free elections were held in Liberia. Taylor won a landslide victory, and hostilities ended. During the war, at least 150,000 civilians suffered death during routine looting and killing rampages carried out by various militias, or by starvation caused by agricultural and industrial ruin. See SIERRA LEONEAN CIVIL WAR OF 1991– .

Libyan-Egyptian War of 1977   Hostilities between Libya and Egypt increased greatly in April–May 1977, when demonstrators in both countries attacked each other's consulates. Colonel Muammar al-Qaddafi (1943–), Libya's head of state, accused Egypt of provoking a war so that it could seize the Libyan oil fields, a charge Egypt denied. In June 1977, al-Qaddafi ordered the 225,000 Egyptians working and living in Libya to leave the country by July 1 or face arrest. An exchange of gunfire by troops along the Libyan-Egyptian border on July 21, 1977, immediately caused a four-day war, in which both sides used tanks and airplanes in several battles along the desert border. A number of Libyan aircraft were destroyed on the ground during an Egyptian strafing attack. After Algeria's president intervened as a peacemaker, both sides agreed to a cease-fire on July 24, 1977; both countries had suffered heavy losses of men and materiel.

Liegnitz, Battle of   See WAHLSTADT, BATTLE OF.

Limoges, Massacre at   (1370) The resumption of the HUNDRED YEARS' WAR in 1369 saw the English, again claiming the French throne, encounter a new French military strategy: encouragement of revolts in English territories; raids, ambushes, night attacks and general harassment; and the avoidance of formal battles. Reacting, John of Gaunt (1340–99), anxious to appear the equal of his now invalid

brother, Edward the Black Prince (1330–76), led merciless English raids against the French. When the city of Limoges rebelled, the English, led by John and Edward (who was suffering from a mortal disease at the time), mined the walls, stormed the city, and slaughtered more than 3,000 inhabitants. Other French cities revolted, and the English began to lose; naval defeat in 1372 and the loss of Aquitaine and Brittany in 1373 forced a 1374 truce.

Lithuanian War of Independence   (1918–20) Russian-ruled Lithuania declared itself an independent state (February 16, 1918) following the overthrow of the Russian czar (see BOLSHEVIK REVOLUTION; OCTOBER REVOLUTION). Immediately Soviet (Bolshevik) forces invaded, but the Germans, recognizing the new state, soon drove them out. After Germany's surrender (November 11, 1918) in WORLD WAR I and the forced withdrawal of German troops from Lithuania, the Soviets again invaded the country and seized its capital, Vilna (Vilnius), in early January 1919. The Poles intervened in support of the Lithuanians and drove the Soviets out of Vilna, helping to precipitate the RUSSO-POLISH WAR OF 1919–20. In December 1919, the Lithuanian-Polish border was defined by the Allied powers, which gave Vilna to Lithuania. Fighting continued until the Soviets and Lithuanians signed the Treaty of Moscow on July 12, 1920; Lithuania's independence was recognized. However, Polish raiders led by General Lucian Zeligowski (1865–1947) captured Vilna by surprise (October 9, 1920), established a provisional government there, and held a plebiscite (January 8, 1922) that showed a majority of Vilna's citizens wanting union with Poland. All relations between Poland and Lithuania were severed because of this, and by the end of 1922 Lithuania had been recognized as a democratic republic. See also MEMEL, INSURRECTION AT.

Livonian War   (1558–83)   Seeking access to the Baltic Sea and laying claim to Livonia (Estonia and almost all of Latvia), Czar Ivan IV "the Terrible" (1530–84) of Russia launched an invasion of the region, which was ruled by the Livonian Knights. After losing control of Narva, Dorpat (Tartu), and other places, the languishing knights dissolved their order (1561), placing ownership of parts of Livonia under the protection of Poland, Lithuania, Sweden, and Denmark. At first the Russians were victorious in war against their four adversaries and committed unspeakable outrages against the Livonians, but when Ivan became embroiled with problems at home (see BOYARS' REVOLT OF 1564), the tide began to turn, especially after Lithuania formed a political union with Poland in 1569. Through diplomatic maneuvering, Ivan diverted Denmark from its Livonian interest, the island of Oesel. When Stephen Báthory (1533–86) came to the Polish throne, he continued the war vigorously after 1576 and achieved numerous victories, recapturing many cities, including Polotsk (1579), and besieging Pskov. In 1582, Russia made peace with Poland through the mediation of a Jesuit envoy sent by the pope and gave up its claims to Livonia. The next year Ivan made peace with the Swedes, ceding to them the Russian-held towns on the Gulf of Finland. See also NOVGOROD, SACK OF.

Lombard League, Wars of the (1167–83) In the 11th and 12th centuries, the Holy Roman emperors and the popes were involved in prolonged power struggles concerning spiritual and temporal matters, particularly the right of investiture of abbots and bishops. Holy Roman Emperor Frederick I Barbarossa (c. 1125–90) conducted six military expeditions into Italy (1154–86) in an effort to control the papacy; he also hoped to gain predominance over the Lombard cities of northern Italy. At first Frederick's forces were successful in subjecting cities; Pope Alexander III (c. 1105–81) was forced by the emperor to take refuge in France (1162), while three opposing Imperial antipopes were enthroned successively from 1159 to 1178. Frederick's fourth expedition to Italy (1167–68) resulted in the formation of the Lombard League, whose member cities included Milan, Mantua, Venice, Padua, Lodi, and Brescia, to resist the invading German army, which captured Rome but was forced to leave Italy when malaria broke out among the troops. Alexander, who had excommunicated the emperor (1165), allied himself with the league, which built the fortress city of Alessandria to defend the northern mountain passes. Frederick's fifth expedition (1174–77) suffered a disastrous defeat at the Battle of Legnano (May 29, 1176), where the superior Lombard forces (pikemen and cavalry) crushed the German knights on horseback; Frederick fled from Italy in disguise afterward; the victory foreshadowed the sequent importance of infantry over cavalry. The Peace of Venice (1177) was concluded between Frederick and the papacy; a six-year truce between the emperor and the Lombard League was converted into the Peace of Constance (1183), by which the Lombard cities gained virtual autonomy but remained Frederick's fealty. Lombard and Tuscan disputes led to Frederick's sixth expedition (1184–86), which succeeded in establishing firm imperial political control in Milan and parts of central Italy. The league, which had split into rival factions after 1183, was revived in 1226 to meet the threat of Holy Roman Emperor Frederick II (1194–1250), who reasserted the Imperial claim to Lombardy. At the Battle of Cortenuova (1237), his Imperial troops crushed the Guelph (Guelf) army of Milan and the Second Lombard League. See also HOLY ROMAN EMPIRE–PAPACY WAR OF 1228–41.

Long March (1934–35) After holding off Kuomintang (Chinese Nationalist) troops in the mountainous regions of Kiangsi (Jiangxi) in southern China for a year (see CHINESE CIVIL WAR OF 1930–34), the Chinese Communist army of about 200,000 men was driven from its positions and started, in October 1934, an orderly retreat through Hunan, Kweichow (Guizhou), and Szechwan (Sichuan) provinces into, eventually, northern Shensi (Shaanxi). During the remarkable, year-long, 6,000-mile trek, the Communists crossed 18 mountain ranges, five of which were snow-covered, 24 rivers, a vast swamp of mud, and two enemy lines; they also fought Kuomintang and hostile provincial armies along the way; about 50,000 men of the original 200,000 survived, along with some 50,000 others who had joined the march. Chu Teh (Zhu De) (1886–1976) and Mao Tse-tung (Mao Zedong) (1893–1976) led the largest force, the Eighth Route Army, which marched the longest distance and later joined up with other Communist (Red) armies in Shensi.

"Long War" See AUSTRO-TURKISH WAR OF 1591–1606.

Lopéz War See PARAGUAYAN WAR.

Lord Dunmore's War (1774)   John Murray (1732–1809), fourth earl of Dunmore, was transferred from the colonial governorship of New York to Virginia in 1771. Shawnee, Ottawa, and other Indians attacked white hunters and settlers in the western territories, causing Lord Dunmore to launch a two-pronged campaign to reduce the "redmen." One force of some 1,500 Virginians, led by Colonel Andrew Lewis (1720–81), moved west down the Kanawha River, while a second force, led by Lord Dunmore from Fort Dunmore (Pitt) near present-day Pittsburgh, Pa., proceeded down the Ohio River. On October 10, 1774, the Shawnee under Chief Cornstalk (1720?–77) attacked Lewis at Point Pleasant at the mouth of the Kanawha in present-day West Virginia; they suffered defeat in a hard, bloody, daylong battle and then fled. Later they concluded a peace treaty with Lord Dunmore at Camp Charlotte on the Pickaway Plains of Ohio and ceded their Kentucky claims to the Virginians. See also CRESAP'S WAR.

Louis XIV's Rhenish Invasion (1688–89)   The city of Cologne (Köln) was a satellite for France's King Louis XIV (1638–1715), useful for keeping the lower Rhine open for France, already in control of Strasbourg and other areas after 1681. Louis became mortified when his candidate for archbishop of Cologne, whom he could influence, was rejected by the pope. Taking advantage of the Holy Roman Emperor's activities in the Balkans against the Turks, Louis declared war against the Holy Roman Empire, citing the archepiscopal selection, Orleans's unsettled claims in the Palatinate, and the presence of fortifications at Philippsburg as causes for his actions. His planned war was expected to be short, but his Rhenish invasion triggered the Pan-European WAR OF THE GRAND ALLIANCE. Finding little resistance, French forces captured the Palatinate, Trier, Mainz, and Cologne, then violently and destructively invaded Franconia and Swabia in a deliberate campaign of terror. The emperor and German princes made a truce with the Turks, rushed home, and declared war on France. Franconia was freed, Frankfurt was garrisoned, and Heidelberg was advanced upon by the allies; the French retreated, burning Mannheim, Worms, Speyer, and other cities as they went. Meanwhile, the Grand Alliance began its military actions, managing to regain Mainz and Bonn in Germany in 1689, thus liberating the lower Rhine. But the French recovered Heidelberg even as Louis initiated peace efforts; accidental fire destroyed the entire city. The fighting in Germany ended in 1689, but settlement, deferred until the 1697 Treaty of Ryswick (Rijswijk), forced Louis to give up territories gained in 1688, but allowed him to retain Alsace and Strasbourg.

"Lovers' War"   See RELIGION, SEVENTH WAR OF.

Lovewell's "War" (1725)   After the Massachusetts colonial government placed a £100 bounty on Indian scalps in late 1724 (see ABNAKI WAR, THIRD), John Lovewell (1691–1725), an enterprising farmer, led an 87-man expedition up the Merrimack River near Lake Winnipesaukee, surprised 10 sleeping Indians, and returned home with their scalps (February 1725). In the spring a 34-man party under Lovewell journeyed north into southern Maine, where they were suddenly attacked by some 80 Indians near present-day Fryeburg on Sunday, May 9, 1725 (evidently the party's chaplain had just slain and scalped an Indian that day!). The Indians killed Lovewell and 16 others, whose surviving cohorts escaped death when the Indians withdrew because their medicine man had been shot.

Lübeck's War of 1531–36   The northern German port city of Lübeck, a leader of the mercantile Hanseatic League, sought to preserve its trading supremacy and power in the Baltic area, mainly by overruling the Swedes, Danes, and Dutch. Using the pretext that repayment of a war debt incurred by a Swedish count (the brother-in-law of Sweden's King Gustavus I [1496–1560]) was less than Lübeck's claim, Jürgen Wullenwever (1488?–1537), Lübeck's burgomaster (mayor), ordered a Swedish ship to be confiscated as restitution; in response, Gustavus embargoed all of Lübeck's ships in Swedish ports. Lübeck and other Hanseatic allies, encouraged and helped by Danish rebels, declared war on both Sweden and Denmark and captured the cities of Malmö and Copenhagen. But Lübeck and its allies couldn't sustain their gains; an expedient temporary Danish-Swedish alliance succeeded in driving out the invaders and finally gaining victory over Lübeck, which made peace (Treaty of Hamburg, 1536) and never again monopolized trade in the Baltic. The 1536 treaty did, however, retain some toll exemptions for Lübeck's ships; the war debt was declared paid. Forced to leave Lübeck, Wullenwever was captured, imprisoned, tortured, and executed (1537). See also COUNT'S WAR; KALMAR CIVIL WAR OF 1520–23.

Lübeck's War of 1563–70   See DANISH-SWEDISH WAR OF 1563–70.

Lubomirski's Rebellion   (1665–67) Polish nobleman and soldier George Lubomirski (1616–67), who took part in the RUSSO-POLISH WAR OF 1658–67, attempted with the support of fellow nobles to prevent a royal election. In 1664, the Polish parliament (Sejm) convicted him of treason and sentenced him to exile. Lubomirski was joined by many supporters, who disturbed the parliament for nearly two years before withdrawing to form their own confederation. His forces engaged the royal army and won a victory at Lake Goplo on July 13, 1667. As a result, Poland's King John II Casimir (1609–72) lost power and was forced to abdicate in 1668. Lubomirski eventually withdrew into Austrian Silesia. By weakening Poland at a critical phase in its war with Russia, he forced Polish acceptance of the Treaty of Andrusovo, by which Poland permanently lost most of its eastern lands to Russia.

Luccan-Florentine War   (1320–23) By April 1320, the ambitious Ghibelline leader Castruccio Castracani (1281–1328), ruler of Lucca in central Italy, had openly declared war on the Guelphs (Guelfs) of Florence (the Ghibellines and Guelphs were rival political factions whose loyalties were to the emperor and the pope, respectively). Luccan forces ravaged Florentine territory but were finally checked by fresh Florentine troops. Castruccio then allied himself with Pistoia, another city in central Italy, and Luccan forces pillaged to within 10 miles of Florence in mid-June 1323. Florence desperately negotiated and raised a new army. Aided by Milanese troops, the Luccans decisively defeated the Florentines at the Battle of Altopascio in 1325. Castruccio ordered the plundering of Florentine lands to pay war debts and again threatened to take Florence, which sought help from other Guelph supporters. Castruccio, who was now in control of almost all of Tuscany, came into conflict with the papacy, finally stopped hostilities, and later suddenly died, leaving his "empire" in disarray and allowing Florence soon to retake most of its lost holdings.

Lusitanian War   (147–139 B.C.) A group of fierce Celtic tribes called the Lusitani, who lived in present-day central Portugal and western Spain, fought the Romans during the CELTIBERIAN WARS. In 150, the Roman proconsul ordered the slaughter of thousands of Lusitanians with whom he had made a treaty. A survivor of the massacre, Viriathus (d. 139), who was a shepherd, rallied his people to further resistance and formed a guerrilla army that repeatedly crushed the Romans. One army was trapped by Viriathus, but instead of destroying it, he made peace and allowed it to leave. Lusitanian resistance collapsed soon after Viriathus was assassinated by a traitor bribed by the Romans. See also NUMANTIAN WAR.

Ly Bon's Rebellion (A.D. 541–47) The people of Nam Viet or Annam (northern Vietnam) rose in rebellion (541) under the leadership of Ly Bon (d. 547), a Vietnamese of Chinese descent, against their oppressive Chinese governor (see CHINESE CONQUEST OF NAM VIET). Ly Bon's forces expelled the Chinese and then repulsed an attack (543) from the kingdom of Champa to the south. Ly Bon, who declared himself king, could not retain hold and was defeated and killed by the Chinese in 547.

M

Maccabees, Revolt of the (168–143 B.C.) The Maccabees were a devout Jewish family famous for their dedication to religious and political freedom. When Antiochus IV Epiphanes (d. 163), Seleucid king of Syria, desecrated the temple in Jerusalem and tried to force the Jews to adopt pagan rites, the Jewish priest Mattathias (d. 166) resisted and killed a Syrian soldier. He then fled to the mountains with his sons, and a long period of guerrilla warfare followed between Jews and Syrians. On the death of Mattathias, his son Judas Maccabeus (d. 161) became leader of the rebellious Jews and defeated two Syrian armies sent against him. In 165, Judas retook Jerusalem and rededicated the temple (Hanukkah, or Chanukah, the Jewish Festival of Lights, commemorates this event). Judas was killed while fighting a third Syrian army, and his brother Jonathan (d. 143) became the Jewish leader. Jonathan was a clever diplomat who concluded treaties of friendship with Rome and Syria, but he was deceived by a Syrian general who proffered peace but instead took him prisoner and slew him and his captured troops. The last brother, Simon (d. 135), built forts and strongholds throughout Judea (southern Palestine); the Syrian king recognized him as high priest, governor, and leader of the Jews. Thereafter Judea enjoyed a period of independence and peace, but after Simon's death the area was disrupted by internal strife and frequent invasions by the Seleucid Syrians and bordering Arab tribes. See also SELEUCID WAR WITH EGYPT.

Macdonald Rebellion (1411) The 1406 capture of Scottish king James I (1394–1437) and his 18-year imprisonment in England permitted Scottish barons to gain extraordinary power. In Scotland's northwest, the Macdonald clan called themselves "Kings of the Isles" and acted like autonomous monarchs. In a dispute over control of the earldom of Ross with the nephew of James's regent, forces under Donald Macdonald, with assistance from the Macleans, marched in 1411 to attack Aberdeen. Under the Maclean leader, Red Hector of the Battles, the Macdonald army engaged the regent's forces in the indecisive but savage Battle of Red Harlaw. Red Hector was slain, the Macdonald army withdrew, and a long peace ensued. See also DUBH'S REBELLION; OG'S REBELLION.

Macedonian Insurrection of 1902–3 To strengthen its claim to Macedonia against its rivals Serbia and Greece, Bulgaria established (1899) a Macedonian Commission. Run from the Bulgarian capital of Sofia, the commission's object was to make Macedonia autonomous but controlled, with the permission of the Ottoman Empire (Turkey), by a Bulgarian inspector. Part of the Bulgarian plan was to force a diplomatic maneuver through covert terrorist activity; and to this end, Bulgarian revolutionary bands called *komitadji* were sent on raids into Macedonia. They helped precipitate insurrection within the country in 1902–3. The *komitadji* murder of a Rumanian professor opposed to the arguments of the commission and their capture of a female American missionary forced Austria and Russia to suggest reforms in the *vilayets* (administrative divisions) of Salonika, Monastir (Bitola), and Kossovo (1903). Accepted by the Ottomans, these reforms were never implemented. Further internal strife led inexorably to the FIRST BALKAN WAR and the division of Macedonia among the three rival claimants.

Macedonian War, First (215–205 B.C.) Macedonia, located in what is now northern Greece, was a warlike nation in the ancient world. King Philip V (238–179) of Macedon was ambitious and wanted to extend his empire. While Rome was preoccupied with fighting Carthage (see PUNIC WAR, SECOND), he made war against Roman forces in the east; the fighting dragged on for a decade with no decisive results. Philip then turned his attention southward to the Greek city-states and began to extend Macedonia's influence there. Hitherto Rome had remained neutral in the quarrels of the Greek states, but it now hoped to expand Roman influence there, precipitating a new war. **Second Macedonian War** (200–196 B.C.). Roman legions resoundingly defeated Philip V's phalanxes at the Battle of Cynoscephalae in 197, forcing the Macedonians to withdraw entirely from Greece. Philip was forced to pay a large indemnity to Rome, which proclaimed itself the liberator of the Greek states and assumed a benevolent protectorate over them. Philip's son, Perseus (212?–166), succeeded him on the throne in 179 and began to make alliances with various Greek states. Rome was displeased at this interference, and another war broke out. **Third Macedonian War** (172–167 B.C.). At Pydna in southeastern Macedonia, the Roman army was victorious; Perseus was taken to Rome in chains; and Macedonia was divided into four republics. But this experiment in representative government failed, for the republics bickered among themselves, and confusion and discontent were rampant. In 152, a pretender to the throne attempted to reestablish the Macedon monarchy, setting off a fourth war. **Fourth Macedonian War** (151–146 B.C.). Once again the Macedonian forces were crushed by superior Roman armies. This time the country of Macedonia was annexed to Rome and became the first province in the soon-to-expand Roman empire. See also PUNIC WAR, THIRD.

Mackenzie's Rebellion (1837) Canadian journalist William Lyon Mackenzie (1795–1861), strongly advocating a republican form of government for Upper Canada (Ontario), called for the overthrow of the British-dominated ruling clique, the Family Compact. About 800 followers of Mackenzie tried but failed to establish a provisional government at Toronto and were forced to flee to Navy Island on the Niagara River. There Mackenzie proclaimed a government. After Canadians loyal to the Upper Canada government crossed the river and burned the U.S. steamer *Caroline*, which had been carrying supplies to Mackenzie's rebels, Mackenzie abandoned Navy Island and fled to the United States, where he was imprisoned for 11 months for violating the neutrality laws. Later, under a proclaimed general amnesty, he returned to Canada in 1849. See also PAPINEAU'S REBELLION.

Madagascar Revolt of 1947–48 In 1946, the island of Madagascar became a French overseas territory, prompting the establishment of its first formal political party, called the Mouvement Démocratique de la Rénovation Malagache (MDRM), whose objective was independence for Madagascar. In less than a year, Malagasy nationalist tribesmen rose in revolt in the island's eastern part; after receiving reinforcements, resident French soldiers were able to quell it, but not before much bloodshed had occurred (more than 11,000 persons were killed in the fighting). The MDRM was outlawed, and the revolt continued as a guerrilla war through 1948. Ten years later France allowed Madagascar's natives to decide their own fate; they voted to become autonomous within the French Community, and the Malagasy Republic was proclaimed on October 14, 1958 (it became fully independent in 1960). The country was renamed Madagascar in 1975.

Madagascar Wars with France (1883–85, 1895) In 1882, the French claimed a protectorate over the northwestern part of Madagascar, but the Hovas, the chief Malagasy people, refused to recognize it. By a 1868 treaty the French had accepted Hova control over the entire island, but they disregarded it in favor of 1840 treaties with local chieftains, which gave the French some islands off the northwest coast. Upon the Hova government's rejection of French demands, French warships bombarded the coastal towns of Majunga and Tamatave, which was captured and occupied by French troops in June 1883. The French formed a native army that helped them secure a treaty in 1885 after two years of desultory warfare; the French protectorate was recognized, along with the French settlement at Diégo-Suarez on the island's northern tip, and a French resident was allowed at the native capital of Tananarive. Later the Hova government increasingly opposed the French. In 1895, a French expeditionary force of 15,000 men landed on Madagascar at Majunga and, after delays because of sickness and transportation problems, moved inland toward Tananarive. After being bombarded, the capital promptly surrendered on September 30, 1895; the native queen became a mere figurehead under French rule. Widespread revolt broke out against the French when they declared Madagascar a French colony in 1896. Order was finally restored under French governor-general Joseph S. Gallieni (1849–1916), who deposed the native queen, ended the Hova supremacy, and treated all the Malagasy tribes on an equal basis.

"Mad Mullah," Holy Wars of the (1899–1920) Somali chieftain Muhammad ibn Abd Allah Hasan (1864–1920), a leader of a militant puritanical Muslim Sufi brotherhood called the Salihiyah, rabidly opposed the foreign "infidel Christian" colonials, believing their influence would destroy the purity of Islam in Somaliland (Somalia), and consequently he declared a jihad (holy war) to expel the British and other aliens from the area. Between 1900 and 1904, his Muslim dervish followers defeated combined British, Italian, and Ethiopian forces four times; in 1905, he agreed to settle with his followers in Italian Somaliland, where he set up a theocratic state. By 1908, he was again militant and initiated another jihad. Called the "Mad Mullah" by the British, he had about 10,000 followers who terrorized the entire area, killing almost a third of the male population. Left control of the interior by the British (1910), he nonetheless attacked coastal Somaliland. In 1913, Salihiyah forces annihilated the British-led Somali Camel Constabulary at Dul Madoba; during WORLD WAR I, with Turkish and German support, they harassed the British from a stronghold at Taleh. Bombed out of Taleh in 1920, the Mad Mullah fled to Ethiopia, where he died. The Salihiyah dissolved, but in some Somali areas the Mad Mullah continued to be regarded as a hero of wars of national liberation.

Madura Revolt of 1334–35 In India, the Delhi sultanate's control proved precarious because the organization of its distant territories was chiefly feudal and revolts in small Hindu kingdoms were frequent. The establishment of provincial governors seemed to solve the rebellion problem until 1334, when the Delhi-appointed governor of Madura or Madurai, a Tughluk Turk (related to the new Tughluk dynasty in Delhi), declared an independent sultanate with a capital at Gulbarga. Originally established as a province in 1311 (see DELHI SULTANATE RAIDS IN SOUTH INDIA), Madura was, in theory, an administrative center under Delhi's direct control. To assert its authority, Delhi sent troops; but violent rebellions in Lahore and Delhi itself caused the troops to return north (1335) before they could punish the offending Madura governor, whose desire for autonomy proved infectious. See also BAHMANI-DELHI SULTANATE WAR; VIJAYANAGAR CONQUEST OF MADURA.

"Mad War" ("Guerre Folle") (1488–91) Insurgents supporting claims of Duke Louis (1462–1515) of Orléans to the regency during the minority of King Charles VIII (1470–98) of France, including Duke Francis II (1435–88) of Brittany, were crushed at Saint-Aubin-du-Cormier in 1488 by royal forces of the king's sister, Anne of France (1460–1522). The Treaty of Sablé stipulated evacuation of foreign troops from Brittany; moreover, Anne of Brittany (1477–1514), Francis's heir, could not marry without royal consent. After her father's death, Anne married King Maximilian (1459–1519) of Austria by proxy. Charles, threatened by Austrian encirclement, petitioned Anne to repudiate this union in favor of one with himself, triggering a dispute in which King Ferdinand II (1452–1516) of Aragon and King Henry VII (1457–1509) backed Maximilian. After a royal show of force at Rennes, France, Anne agreed by the Treaty of Laval to marry Charles in exchange for an affirmation of Breton autonomy.

Magyar Raids in France (A.D. 907–54) THE MAGYAR RAIDS IN THE HOLY ROMAN EMPIRE spilled over into France in 907, when the Magyar warriors crossed the Rhine River to harass Alsace and eastern France, especially Burgundy. Using bases in Germany, they attacked Burgundy from 917 to 919, threatening the heart of the kingdom. King Charles III "the Simple" (879–929) of France tried to obtain help from his barons to fight the Magyar menace, but failed; rivalries among the various duchies and barons may be directly blamed for the inadequacy of the French Carolingian defense. Rivalries explain an unopposed Magyar advance in 926, endangering Rheims, and later a devastation of Burgundy in 937, despite opposing French troops led by the ill-fated King Rudolf (Raoul) of Burgundy (d. 936). The invaders continued ravaging France and northern Italy; Aquitaine was raided in 951, as were the outskirts of Cambrai, Laon, and Rheims in 954. The great Magyar raid of 954 swept from northeastern France south through Burgundy into Italy via the Great St. Bernard Pass. See also LECHFELD, BATTLE OF.

Magyar Raids in the Holy Roman Empire (A.D. c. 894–955) According to Hungarian history, seven tribes of the Finno-Ugric-speaking Magyars chose

as their unifying leader Árpád (c. 840–907) and moved westward from their northern Caucasus home about 889. About 894 or 896, they invaded Frankish Pannonia (eastern Austria, western Hungary, and part of Yugoslavia), gaining full control of it about 900. From this base, the Magyars raided in all directions, overcoming Moravia in 906, defeating a Bavarian army at Ennsburg, and taking over the Hungarian Great Plain. They conducted some 33 raids between 898 and 955, going north to Bremen, south to Otranto, west to Orléans, and east to Constantinople (Istanbul). Many of their raids were in the Holy Roman Empire, particularly in Saxony and Thuringia in 908, in Bavaria in 909 and 910 (resulting in defeat and victory, respectively), and in Alsace in 917. During the 919–36 reign of Germany's King Henry I "the Fowler" (876?–936), the Magyars were relatively quiet, especially after 924, when Henry's seizure of an important Magyar leader brought a nine-year truce. Henry fortified his towns in Saxony and reorganized his army. Breaking the truce in 933, he was victorious against the Magyars at Riade, taking their camp and forcing them to flee. Conditions changed after 936, however, when Holy Roman Emperor Otto I (912–73) faced civil war upon his accession to the throne. Still Magyar raids into Thuringia and Saxony were beaten back, as were incursions into Bavaria in 948–49, after which Saxon troops marched into Hungary itself. The Magyars instead staged raids in France from 951 to 954, made an incursion into Germany in 954, and lost disastrously at the BATTLE OF LECHFELD in 955.

Mahabat Khan's Insurrection (1626–27) India's Mogul throne of Emperor Jahangir (1569–1627) had been saved by his general, Mahabat Khan (d. 1634) (see SHAH JAHAN'S REVOLT); Nur Jahan (d. 1645), the empress, was angered by Mahabat's success however. She was fearful of his growing power and popularity, disturbed that he still backed Khurram (Shah Jahan [1592–1666]) as heir to the throne, and angry that he failed to support her rival claimant. She inveigled the emperor into making Mahabat the governor of distant Bengal, supposedly as a reward for his service; then she drummed up false charges against him and persuaded Jahangir to order his return to Lahore for trial. Mahabat disobeyed the order, led his army to the court in the Punjab, and seized Jahangir after being refused an audience. Nur Jahan and her rival claimant escaped, but failed to free the emperor, who, by tricking Mahabat, escaped and fled to Kashmir. Mahabat hastened to Khurram in the Deccan area, where he was persuaded to submit to the emperor. But Jahangir died, and no punishment was given to Mahabat. The rival claimant to the throne stole the imperial treasury at Lahore, only to be caught and blinded; the empress, outwitted, graciously agreed to retire on a pension. The throne was Mahabat's; to safeguard it, however, he adopted the Ottoman custom of executing all possible contenders; in this case, a brother, two nephews, and two cousins died. He mounted the throne as emperor Shah Jahan on January 24, 1628. See also MOGUL CIVIL WAR OF 1657–59.

Mahdist War   See SUDANESE WAR OF 1881–85.

Mahmud of Ghazna, Conquests of (c. 1000–30) A conqueror of northwestern India and, after 998, third Turkish ruler of Ghazna (Ghazni, Afghanistan), a kingdom then consisting of present-day Afghanistan and the northeast section of Iran, Mahmud of Ghazna (971–1030) was the first invader of India whose motives stemmed, in part, from Islamic principles. Although his 17 or more invasions between about 1000 and 1026 involved the destruction of Hindu temples and shrines as heretical, his chief motive seems to have been an accumulation of plunder to make Ghazna into a second Baghdad (Islam's most splendid city about 800). When Mahmud died, his kingdom included Kashmir, the Punjab, and most of modern Iran, which he first raided in 977. Three of his raids on India are especially noteworthy. In 1001, his 15,000-man light cavalry had such superior skill and training as to defeat an Indian army of almost triple its size near Peshawar; the Indian leader was killed. A revived Punjabi force almost defeated the Ghaznavids in

1108, again near Peshawar; some 30,000 Indians charged and caused a Ghaznavid retreat, but a panic among the Indians' elephants allowed the enemy's regrouping and victory and annexation of the Punjab. Mahmud's greed was shown in an invasion (1024) of the southern coastal province of Kathiawar; there he captured Somnath and completely sacked its rich Hindu temple, taking its ornamental gates before returning home. His rule of the conquered territories was harsh; he did not, however, force conversions to Islam; he even used Hindu troops without fear of mutiny for his robbery and desecration of Hindu houses of worship.

Maillotin Uprising (1382) THE HUNDRED YEARS' WAR had devastated France financially, and the French people—who bore most of the taxation the conflict made necessary—showed their displeasure in several abortive uprisings, especially in 1380 and 1382. Among the most violent was the Maillotin Uprising in Paris, named for the lead maillots (mauls) carried by the insurrectionists. Beginning as a riot over yet another tax, it became a large-scale uprising in which Jews and tax-collectors were hunted down to be beaten and killed, houses were pillaged, and the prisons of the Chatelet were stormed and opened. France's King Charles VI (1368–1422) was only 14 in 1382, but he, his Council of Twelve, and other officials attempted to negotiate with the rebels. The uprisings, however, did not end until its leaders were arrested; most were put to death. The hated tax was abolished, but a secondary effect occurred: court interest in the support of the Parisian municipal government ceased for 150 years, to be revived only because King Francis (1494–1547) showed some concern. See also JACQUERIE.

Maji Maji Uprising (1905–7) The native peoples of German East Africa (Tanzania) resented being forced to work for and pay taxes to their new masters from Europe. Native unrest increased when the German government started an ill-advised cotton-growing experiment at the expense of growing food crops. An African religious cult developed whose members believed that if they received special water, called maji, they would be immune to gunfire. Reinforced by this belief, the Africans revolted against the Germans. The uprising spread rapidly through the territory because the Germans were unprepared at first. In two years the rebellious Africans were fiercely crushed through harsh military actions and scorched-earth tactics. An estimated 200,000 natives reportedly perished by hanging, shooting, starvation, and disease. See also GERMAN COLONIAL WARS IN AFRICA.

Malacca, Siege of (1640–41)   Since the beginning of the 17th century the Portuguese and Dutch had been struggling for supremacy in the East Indies (see PORTUGUESE-DUTCH WARS IN THE EAST INDIES). The former had captured the strategic site of Malacca (Melaka) on the Malay peninsula's west coast in 1511 and made it the center of its trading activities in the area. The Achinese (Achenese or Atjehnese) people of northern Sumatra, who had frequently warred against the Portuguese without success in attempts to expel them, briefly joined the Dutch, and together they laid siege (August 1640) to Malacca's fortress, which had walls 32 feet high and 24 feet thick. Earlier in June that year the Dutch had blockaded the Malaccan port with the help of Johore's fleet. The fortress's defenders (about 250 Portuguese and 2,000 Asians) received no aid from Goa, India, or other Portuguese outposts and eventually capitulated in January 1641; some 7,000 lost their lives fighting or from disease and starvation. With control of this important port, the Dutch were assured an almost complete monopoly of the highly valued spice trade.

Malay Jungle Wars of 1948–60   (Malayan Emergency)   In 1948, communist terrorists, many of whom were Chinese, began disrupting village life in the jungles of the newly established Federation of Malaya (under the rule of a British high commissioner). They carried on hit-and-run guerrilla warfare against army outposts, police stations, and other government places; a state of emergency was declared, and British and indigenous Malay forces fought back. In 1949, an intense campaign was mounted against the guerrillas, hundreds of whom were slain or captured. One effect of the jungle warfare was to bring leaders of the various ethnic and religious communities closer together with more mutual understanding. The government-implemented Briggs plan (1950) resettled so-called "squatter" Chinese farmers, who were easy prey for raiding guerrillas, in protected Malay areas. In 1951, the terrorists increased their activities, destroyed rubber trees, intimidated plantation workers, and assassinated the British high commissioner. Sir Gerald Templer (1898–1979), the new high commissioner (1952), headed the government forces, began a concerted antirebel campaign, and encouraged cooperation among the diverse Malay peoples. Rigid food control in suspected rebel areas forced many terrorists to surrender or starve. By 1954, the communist high command in Malaya had moved to Sumatra. After the Malay Federation became an independent state in the British Commonwealth (1957), the war petered out; increasing numbers of terrorists surrendered (a government amnesty was offered to them in 1955, and many accepted it). Still, a hard core of several hundred communist guerrillas continued to operate in the thick jungles along the Malay-Thai border until 1960, when they were defeated.

Malian Civil War of 1990–96   Longstanding hostility between the Tuareg (Touareg), nomadic Berber Muslim people, and Mali's dictatorial president Moussa Traoré (1936–) erupted into bloody conflict between Tuareg separatists and government troops in the Menaka area in late June 1990. Although a military coup overthrew Traoré in 1991 and civilian Alpha Oumar Konaré (1946–) was elected president in 1992, various Tuareg liberation groups continued to clash with troops in the northern region of Mali, a large, landlocked West African country lying partly in the Sahara Desert. Despite peace accords signed in 1991 and 1992, fighting continued along the Mali-Mauritanian frontier and in the Bamba and Gao areas (the Niger Bend). Later, the powerful Tuareg coalition force, the Unified Movements and Fronts of Azawad (MFUA), signed two agreements with the government (1993 and 1994) that allowed the incorporation of some 7,000 Tuareg rebels into the regular army and other government bodies. In October 1995, Mali began the repatriation of some 120,000 Tuareg refugees living in camps in neighboring Mauritania, Algeria, Burkina Faso, and Niger. The Popular Front for the Liberation of Azawad and other Tuareg rebel groups agreed to disarm and demobilize, thus officially ending the war (March 27 1996) and again permitting free movement across Mali's northern region. See also NIGERIEN CIVIL WAR OF 1990–95.

Mamluk-Ottoman War of 1485–91   Relations between the Ottoman Empire and the Mamluk (Mameluke) rulers of Egypt and Syria became fearful in the 1470s, when military campaigns during the TURKOMAN-OTTOMAN WARS OF 1400–1473 reached as far as the Syrian Euphrates. The Mamluks then supported Djem (1459–95) in his power struggle with his older brother, Bayazid II (1447–1513), during the OTTOMAN CIVIL WAR OF 1481–82, and Bayazid was pressed by his military leaders to seek revenge against the Mamluks. In 1485, when a conflict arose over a Turkoman territory ruled by the Mamluk-backed Duldakir dynasty in Cappadocia (part of Turkey), the result was an intermittent war. The Mamluks interfered in Cappadocia by stirring up eastern Turkoman nomads and asserting authority over Lesser Armenia; five of six annual Ottoman campaigns were not decisive against the Mamluks, who won a small victory in 1488. The peace meetings of 1491 gained the Mamluks territorial concessions, along with an inimical suspension of fighting until the MAMLUK-OTTOMAN WAR OF 1516–17.

Mamluk-Ottoman War of 1516–17   When Ottoman military campaigns of Sultan Selim I (1467–1520) in the TURKO-PERSIAN WAR OF 1514–16 threatened Mamluk (Mameluke) Syria, the aged Mamluk sultan of Egypt, Kansu al-Gauri (d. 1516), led forces north to invade the Ottoman Empire from Aleppo. Using artillery, Selim's army thoroughly defeated the Mamluks at the Battle of Marj-Dabik (Dolbek) on August 24, 1516; Kansu died of a stroke in the battle near Aleppo, which immediately surrendered. The Mamluks retreated to Egypt, giving up Syria. Selim's campaign then gathered speed; he seized Damascus, Beirut, Gaza, and Jerusalem; installed Ottoman governors in these places; made Lebanon's princes his nominal vassals; and offered peace to the new Egyptian sultan, Tuman Bey (d. 1517), on condition that he accept Ottoman suzerainty. This was rejected. After sending the caliph (Islam's chief leader) to Cairo to read Friday prayers in the Ottoman sultan's name as a sign of a coup, Selim and his army advanced on the city, defeated Tuman's Mamluks at the Battle of Reydaniyya on January 22, 1517, and soon after conquered Cairo and Egypt. Tuman, who had escaped, tried guerrilla warfare but was captured and hanged. The grand sherif (magistrate) of Mecca sent Selim the keys to Arabia's holy places as a sign of his surrender, and the caliph brought the sacred cloak and standard of the prophet Muhammad (570–632) to Constantinople (Istanbul) to signify that the Ottomans had become the protectors of Muslim pilgrims and of all Islam in general. Selim took no reprisals against the Mamluks and made many of them officials in his administration. According to legend, the caliph conferred his title and power on Selim.

Manchu Conquest of China (1618–50)   The Manchus were descendants of the Juchen Mongol tribes of northern Manchuria (see JUCHEN MONGOL CONQUEST OF THE LIAO; JUCHEN MONGOL INVASION OF THE SUNG EMPIRE). Under the capable leadership of Nurhachi (T'ien Ming) (1559–1626), a chieftain of a Manchurian tribe, the Manchus united the neighboring tribes and began to expand their domain. In 1618, Nurhachi declared war against China under the Ming dynasty, issuing a list of seven grievances. His well-trained troops gained control of all Chinese territory north of the Great Wall within a few years and even breached the wall in poorly defended places. In 1644, when China was torn by internal strife (see CHINESE CIVIL WAR OF 1621–44) and the Chinese imperial capital of Peking (Beijing) was occupied by a rebel general, the Ming general Wu San-kuei (Wu Sangui) (1612–78), who was guarding the northern Chinese frontier, appealed to the Manchus for assistance against the rebel usurper. Help was gladly given, and together their forces descended on Peking and defeated the rebel army. The usurper fled to the west but was eventually captured and killed. The Manchus now controlled the capital and proclaimed their own prince emperor of China and Manchuria. Several Ming princes had escaped to the south, and for six years they and their forces struggled to halt the advance of the Manchu armies. The cities of Nanking (Nanjing), Hangchow (Hangzhou), and Canton (Kuang-chou, Guangzhou) fell to the invaders, and by 1650 the Manchu conquest of mainland China was complete. The Manchus established the Ch'ing (Qing) dynasty, which would rule China until 1911 (see CHINESE REVOLUTION OF 1911–12). See also CHINESE WAR WITH KOXINGA.

Manchu Conquest of Korea (1627)   Korea had recognized the suzerainty of the Ming dynasty in China for decades and had given military aid to the Mings against the invading Manchus from the north of Manchuria. In 1627, however, the Manchu armies swooped down the Korean peninsula. The Koreans were no match for these tough, well-trained fighters, although they resisted boldly. The invaders soon conquered the country, and the Korean king was forced to switch his allegiance to the Manchu (Ch'ing) dynasty whose capital was at Mukden (Shen-yang). The Manchus did not make their Korean subjects wear pigtails as symbols of subservience as they did the Chinese, and the tribute they requested was more an exchange of presents than an observance of vassalage. In general, the Manchus left the Koreans alone after the invasion.

Mandingo-French War, First (1885–86)   French colonial forces waged war against the black Mand-

ingo (Malinke) tribes, led by Chief Almamy Samory (d. 1900), in the interior of the Ivory Coast in West Africa. The Mandingos were eventually defeated in battle (1886); Samory escaped being captured; and French rule was established. **Second Mandingo-French War** (1894–95). The French proclaimed a protectorate over the entire Ivory Coast but were unable to occupy the hinterland because of resistance by the Mandingos under Samory. French military campaigns failed. **Third Mandingo-French War** (1898). The French initiated a new military campaign against the Mandingos and finally defeated them, breaking their hold on the Ivory Coast's interior region. Samory, captured (September 29, 1898), was exiled to Gabon.

Maniaces, Revolt of (1043)   George Maniaces (d. 1043), Byzantine general who helped suppress the BULGARIAN REVOLT OF 1040–41, was afterward imprisoned on a charge of treason. Byzantine emperor Michael V Calaphates (d. after 1042) released him and gave him the rule of the Italian provinces. While campaigning against Muslim invaders there in 1043, Maniaces was again accused of treason. Ordered to return to Constantinople by Emperor Constantine IX Monomachus (c. 1000–55), who had helped depose Michael, Maniaces refused, was proclaimed emperor by his troops, and defeated Imperial forces in battle. While leading a march on Constantinople, he was killed by an arrow in an accident, and the revolt fell apart.

Manipuri-Burmese Wars   See BURMESE-MANIPURI WARS.

Mantuan Succession, War of the (1628–31)   By treaties in 1615 and 1617, the House of Savoy gave its duchy of Montferrat to the Gonzaga family of Mantua (northern Italian city) pending the Holy Roman Emperor's disposition. The sole Gonzaga heir was a daughter, who received Montferrat while Mantua passed to the French duke of Nevers, whose son married the Montferrat heiress to secure both Italian states. But Savoy then sought to renew its

Montferrat claim, and a distant Gonzaga relative claimed Mantua. At the same time, Emperor Ferdinand II (1578–1637) sent his army over the Alps to seize both Mantua and Milan; the former city was sacked in 1630. Savoy now agreed to divide Montferrat, but France's King Louis XIII (1601–43) marched his army to the aid of the duke of Nevers and, consequently, saved Mantua from total destruction by Imperial forces. The ensuing war was concluded when Cardinal Richelieu (1585–1642), leading French troops, successfully supported the duke of Nevers's claim to both Mantua and Montferrat. See also THIRTY YEARS' WAR.

Maori War, First See BAY OF ISLANDS WAR; WAIRAU MASSACRE.

Maori War, Second See TARANAKI WARS.

Maratha-Mogul War of 1647–65 During the reigns of the Mogul (Muslim) emperors in India, mistreatment and humiliation of the Hindus by the Moguls was commonplace. The desire to protect and preserve Hinduism was thus one motive behind the actions of the Yavada prince Shivaji Bhonsle (1627–80), who assumed at age 20 the administration of his family's lands and began (1647) to create an empire free from Mogul tyranny. From a Hindu homeland in the Western Ghats near Poona, he attacked the declining Muslim state of Bijapur and built hilltop forts; by 1653, his forces controlled territory from Goa north to the Bhima River and were moving eastward across the Deccan region. Calling his new state Maharashtra to memorialize both the Marathas (Hindu warrior people) and the Rashtrakutas, Shivaji began raiding other Mogul territories. The raids caused concern at Delhi, the Mogul capital, but not enough to send troops. Free from opposition, Shivaji formed a navy in the Arabian Sea to discourage European intervention; then, in 1664, his forces attacked Surat on the Gulf of Cambay, site of a large English factors' compound. Mogul emperor Aurangzeb (1618–1707) sent his ablest general, Jai Singh (fl. 1600s), to Bijapur, where he won over the Muslim sultan's assistance and defeated Shivaji in a drive against the Maratha fort of Purandhar (1665). A treaty forced Shivaji to surrender 23 of his 25 forts and to send his son as a "representative" (hostage) to Agra (seat of the Mogul court before Delhi). Later Shivaji went himself, but his discovery that he was considered an inferior under house arrest made him devise a cunning escape. Within three years, he had prepared himself to resume his interrupted assault upon the Moguls (see MARATHA-MOGUL WAR OF 1670–80). See also AURANGZEB, WARS OF.

Maratha-Mogul War of 1670–80 The kingdom of Maharashtra under Shivaji Bhonsle (1627–80) resumed its war against the Moguls (see MARATHA-MOGUL WAR OF 1647–65) by recapturing lands and forts ceded in the 1665 Treaty of Purandhar. Shivaji's troops sacked Surat a second time (1670) and later invaded Khandesh and Berar. Mogul reinforcements were rushed to Jai Singh (fl. 1600s), heading the war against the Marathas, and helped check the rebels; an enlarged Mogul army with a new general, Bahadur Khan (fl. 1600s), was briefly effective in 1672. But Shivaji easily seized parts of Bijapur, whose sultan had died (1672); because other Mogul wars tied up troops, Shivaji managed to take over former Mogul areas and crowned himself *chatrapati* ("lord of the universe") in 1674. Aware that the Moguls had attempted to use Bijapur as a base for attacking Maharashtra, he invaded the Carnatic region, allied himself with Golconda, conquered Jinji, and forced Bijapur to cede territories in return for help against Moguls anxious to suppress the autonomous but weak Muslim state (1676–80). By this time, Shivaji's holdings extended from the Narmada (Narbada) River south to Goa and eastward to Nagpur in the middle of India. Shivaji's sudden death from illness stopped the war briefly (see MARATHA-MOGUL WAR OF 1681–1705). See also RAJPUT REBELLION AGAINST AURANGZEB.

Maratha-Mogul War of 1681–1705 The death of Shivaji Bhonsle (1627–80) brought to the Maratha throne his son Sambhagi (1657–89), whose experience as a Mogul hostage had made him briefly defect to the Muslim side (see MARATHA-MOGUL WAR OF 1670–80). It also brought a new element into the conflict: the defection of Crown Prince Akbar (d. 1704), son of Mogul emperor Aurangzeb (1618–1707), to the Hindu side during the RAJPUT REBELLION AGAINST AURANGZEB. Because Akbar was trying to cajole Sambhagi into joining him and the Rajputs (Hindus) against Agra, Aurangzeb and the court came to the Deccan (1681), living in a vast tent city 30 miles in circumference for the next 24 years while Aurangzeb acted as his own commander in chief. At first, Aurangzeb was successful, but not against the Marathas, who raided from their forts. Instead, he seized the dying sultanate of Bijapur (1686) and the Shi'ite sultanate of Golconda (1687). He accidentally captured Sambhagi and other leaders and executed them barbarously after severe torture (1689). The war went on under Sambhagi's brother Raja Ram (d. 1700) until his death, and then under Raja Ram's widow, who conducted civil war from new Maratha capitals at Jinji and Satara. The now elderly Aurangzeb moved his huge entourage from one Maratha hill fort to another, only to have the abandoned forts recaptured by the enemy. In 1705, too old and ill to continue and perhaps conscious that the Deccan area was to be the grave of his reputation as well as his body, Aurangzeb went north to Ahmadnagar, where he died in 1707. See also MARATHA WARS.

Maratha War, First (1775–82) The collapse of the kingdom of Maharashtra in India in the early 1700s forced the development of the Maratha Confederacy, a union of five clans and their territories, with a capital at Poona near Bombay. The peshwa (prime minister) at Poona was, in theory, the confederacy's leader; however, constant rivalry among the clans, especially for his office, weakened the confederacy's united stand against territorial aggressions by the British East India Company. A 1775 contention for the prime minister's position caused the company to support a former peshwa ousted in 1774 and to sign a treaty promising troops in return for gold, jewelry, and lands. Attacking Poona, the contender failed when his troops were overwhelmed (1775). The British then intervened, defeating the Maratha forces in 1779, forcing the confederacy to withdraw from both this war and the FIRST MYSORE WAR. The peace of Sabai in 1782, through which the company gained only an island near Bombay, kept the confederacy neutral for 20 years and allowed the company to fight for other territories, especially Mysore (Karnataka). **Second Maratha War** (1803–5). The conquest of Mysore by the British in 1799 (see MYSORE WAR, FOURTH) left the Maratha Confederacy as the only impediment to the British East India Company's total control of central and southern India. Continued rivalry for the position of peshwa proved fortunate for the British. A young peshwa, Baji Rao (1775–1851), was opposed by the Sindhia clan; the British, in the 1802 Treaty of Bassein, had promised him protection. The Sindhai seized Poona and set up a puppet peshwa; the Holkar clan, a British ally, then recaptured Poona and drove out the puppet. With little military activity, the company placed a British resident in Poona, who became the real ruler of the confederacy. He achieved order in central India by bringing in Pindari, Maratha soldiers turned mercenaries and looters; the company's later efforts to replace the Pindari with regular soldiers and establish a bureaucracy constituted one cause of a third war. **Third Maratha War** (1817–18). The British East India Company attempted to keep Baji Rao a puppet ruler while the British resident remained the true ruler of the Maratha Confederacy, but Baji Rao stubbornly tried to revive Maratha pretensions to power and so angered the other clans. When a British force chasing Pindari robber bands crossed Maratha territory, three of the five Maratha clans rose against Baji Rao. Rather than protect him, the British used full military power against Poona, secured its defeat, then pensioned off and exiled the beleaguered peshwa. Later annexing Maratha territory to its Bombay area holdings, the British East India Company fully established British supremacy in India.

Marathon, Battle of (490 B.C.) Persia, attempting to punish Athens for supporting the IONIAN REVOLT, launched a fleet to invade Greece, but it was wrecked by a storm in 492. In 490, a second

Persian fleet with probably about 50,000 soldiers sailed across the Aegean, attacked and sacked Eretria, and then sailed south to the Plain of Marathon, to a spot designated by the Athenian Alcmeonid (pro-Persian) faction, which hoped to be restored to power by the Persians. Under Miltiades (540?–489), the Athenian citizen-army camped stolidly near the plain, refusing battle until the disgusted Persians sent their fleet and formidable cavalry to attack Athens from the west. Miltiades' forces then immediately and boldly attacked and beat the Persian infantrymen and, to forestall the Persian fleet, force-marched back to Athens, whose citizens had learned of the victory by the messenger-runner Pheidippedes (fl. 490). The Persian fleet wisely declined to land. Afterward the Alcmeonid faction reprehended Miltiades for an unauthorized and unsuccessful attack on Paros, a Greek island that had aided the Persians; he died of a leg wound from an accident before being disgraced. See also GRECO-PERSIAN WARS.

Marches, Rebellion of the (1322) The relationship of King Edward II (1284–1327) of England with his barons, especially with regard to executive appointments, was stormy. One favorite, Piers Gaveston, had been executed in 1312. Hugh le Despenser (1262–1326), Edward's chamberlain, was next. By marrying a Clare, he had gained control of Glamorgan on the Welsh border, and the Marcher lords were displeased. The earl of Lancaster united opposition against Despenser and maneuvered his exile, angering Edward, whose royal troops attacked the Marcher lords at Boroughbridge in 1322. Using the novel tactic of dismounted men-at-arms and archers against cavalry, Edward's troops defeated the rebels. The king had Lancaster and several associates executed and recalled Despenser to his side.

"March on Rome" (1922) In the summer of 1922, Italy seemed on the verge of a civil war among its political parties; its government especially couldn't cope with the Fascists, who seized power in Bologna, Milan, and other cities. Benito Mussolini (1883–1945), head of the National Fascist Party, demanded the resignation of Italy's premier, Luigi Facta (1861–1930), a liberal though weak leader, and the formation of a Fascist government, threatening dire consequences if his demands were not met. The "March on Rome" (October 28, 1922) by his Fascists compelled Facta to declare (belatedly) a state of siege and to decree martial law. King Victor Emmanuel III (1869–1947), Italy's constitutional head of state, refused to sign the decree, however, and dismissed Facta. Arriving in Rome from Milan in the comfort of a railroad sleeping car on October 30, 1922, Mussolini found only some 25,000 of his black shirts (Fascists) occupying the capital; but by the next day thousands more of his followers came on special trains, surrounded the royal palace, and cheered the victory of Mussolini, whom the king permitted to form a government to reestablish order. See also D'ANNUNZIO'S WAR.

March Revolution See FEBRUARY REVOLUTION, RUSSIAN.

Marne, First Battle of the (1914) In August 1914, German armies invaded Belgium and northeastern France (see WORLD WAR I) and advanced to the Marne River within 15 miles of Paris, where the German drive became snarled and stopped. The retreating French decided to stage a desperate counterattack; one army attacked the Germans' right flank on September 6, 1914, and when it turned to fight, a gap opened in the German line. Both French and British troops advanced into this opening and attacked the other German flank. They were reinforced by some 6,000 additional troops who had been driven from Paris in taxi cabs. As the German armies were pushed farther and farther apart, they began to retreat. When they reached the northern bank of the Aisne River, they halted and dug trenches, beginning the type of warfare (trench warfare) that would characterize much of the fighting for the next four years (see WORLD WAR I ON THE WESTERN FRONT). This six-day battle at the Marne (September 5–10, 1914) squashed the Germans' expectations for a quick and easy victory over the French. **Second Battle of the Marne** (1918). In late May 1918, German forces began a powerful offensive against French positions, which were thrown off balance, and fought their way to the Marne, less than 40 miles from Paris. They wanted to capture Rheims and divide the Allied armies on the Western Front, but encountered stiff resistance. At Château-Thierry American troops fought with great determination and repeatedly repulsed German attacks. The final German offensive came on July 15 and troops succeeded in crossing the Marne, but after two days it ground to a halt. One German division was trapped and surrendered. On July 18, the French, British, and American troops under Marshal Ferdinand Foch (1851–1929), the supreme Allied commander, began counterattacking against the faltering Germans along a long front. By mid-August 1918 the Germans were in full retreat, and a month later they had been driven back to the "Hindenburg Line," a strongly fortified position just outside the prewar German border. The Germans were soon to sue for peace to end World War I.

Maroons' Rebellion of 1795 On the West Indian island of Jamaica, freed or escaped black slaves called maroons (a name from the French *marron* and Spanish *cimarrón*, meaning "untamed"), who lived in the thick woods and mountains, frequently harried the British colonials until 1739, when a treaty granted them autonomy and territory. In 1795, when two maroons were severely whipped by the British for stealing swine, the maroons rose in rebellion, causing much bloodshed until the British brought in bloodhounds to chase them. Overpowered, the maroons who refused to make peace were shipped to Halifax, Nova Scotia, and later (1800) to Sierra Leone in West Africa. The remaining maroons were no longer a threat to the British colonists in Jamaica.

Marsic War See SOCIAL WAR OF 91–88 B.C.

Maryland's Religious War (1644–46) The Great ENGLISH CIVIL WAR (1642–46) had its repercussions in colonial Maryland, where fighting occurred between Puritans (English Protestants) and Roman Catholics. Upon returning to the colony from consultations in England, Maryland's proprietary governor, Leonard Calvert (1606–47), a royalist, was forced to flee to Virginia in 1644 to escape Puritan rebels. In 1645, Richard Ingle (fl. 1642–53), a Protestant seaman and tobacco trader, led raids in Maryland and seized the colony's predominantly Catholic capital, St. Mary's. With aid from Governor William Berkeley (1606–77) of Virginia, Calvert recaptured the Maryland colony in 1646. After Calvert's death, as a concession to the Protestants, a Virginia Puritan, William Stone (1603?–60), was made proprietary governor of Maryland, whose council was reorganized to include an equal number of Protestants and Catholics. The Toleration Act of 1649 was an attempt to end religious conflicts by granting religious tolerance to all who believed in Jesus Christ.

Masada, Siege of (A.D. 72–73) After the successful ROMAN SIEGE OF JERUSALEM in 70, some of the Roman forces marched to crush Jewish rebels hidden in fortresses in the desert. The fortress at Herodium fell quickly, and the one at Machaerus succumbed only after its leader was accidentally captured in 71. Masada, however, proved almost impregnable; a mountaintop fortress some 1,400 feet above the level of the nearby Dead Sea, it was the site of two ornate palaces and complex fortifications erected by Herod the Great (73–4 B.C.), king of Judea. Since Herod's death, Romans had held Masada, but Jewish zealots seized it in 66, when the JEWISH REVOLT OF A.D. 66–73 began. Less than 1,000 men, women, and children defended the fortress against almost 15,000 besiegers—the Roman Legion X Fretensis—who were thwarted for nearly two years. The Romans dug a siege wall, established eight camps, and built a huge ramp for a siege tower and battering ram; their only damage to Masada was a single breach in its stone wall. Quickly repaired by the Jews with wood and earth, the weakness in the wall still left Masada vulnerable. The Romans set fire to the wooden wall and gained entrance to the fortress, but found alive only two women and five children, all hidden in a cave. Choosing death over slavery, the Jewish zealot-defenders had burned their food stores and committed suicide en masse. Modern Israelis and others visit Masada annually as a shrine memorializing Jewish heroism.

Masaniello's Insurrection (1647)   When the oppressive Neapolitan nobles levied a new tax on fruit to raise money for the tribute to Spain (Naples was then an appanage of the Spanish Crown), a young fisherman, Masaniello (1620–47), originally named Tommaso Aniello, was chosen to lead an insurrection of the lower classes in protest. On July 7, 1647, Masaniello's rebels burned the customs house and rampaged through Naples, forcing the Spanish viceroy to flee. Many nobles were killed before Masaniello and the viceroy reached an agreement pardoning the rebels, granting citizens' rights, and abrogating the onerous tax. Seemingly gone mad because of his success, Masaniello urged his followers to slaughter more nobles but was himself murdered on July 16, 1647, either by agents hired by the nobles or the viceroy or by some of his own disillusioned men. When the viceroy ignored his agreement, renewed violence flared up in the city and surrounding provinces against the lords and the Spaniards. A Spanish fleet arrived at Naples and bombarded it; Spanish troops attempted to take the city but were driven out by enraged Neapolitan rebels. Naples temporarily supported a French Anjou descendant to the throne who led opposition to Spain, but his arbitrary ways infuriated many. The gates of the city were opened to Spanish forces in 1648. The Anjou duke was imprisoned in Spain, and Spanish rule reimposed. Rebel leaders were caught and executed.

Mascates, War of the (Peddlers' War) (1710–11)   The inhabitants of Olinda and Recife, two neighboring towns in Pernambucco in eastern Brazil, clashed over authority in the district. Olinda, the district's administrative capital, contained wealthy, aristocratic plantation owners, who resented the immigrant ship workers and traders at Recife and labeled them *mascates*, meaning "peddlers." When the Portuguese royal government made Recife a wholly separate town with its own government in 1710 (at the request of its people), civil war ensued between Recife and Olinda that lasted until 1711, when a new district governor mediated peace and promised amnesty to both sides. While Olinda declined in importance, Recife prospered and eventually became the capital of Pernambucco in 1827.

Matabele-British War (1893)   While the main body of Matabele (Ndebele) warriors were in the north fighting to conquer the Mashonas, another Bantu people, armed columns of the British South Africa Company invaded Matabeleland in present-day western Zimbabwe in the fall of 1893. The king of the Matabeles, Lobengula (1870–94), was furious at this encroachment and made plans for war against the invaders. On the plains of the Shangani River, the Matabeles attacked the British, whose Maxim guns overpowered and killed many of the enemy. En route toward the Matabele capital of Bulawayo, the British withstood a surprise attack; again the warriors' spears were no match for the Maxim guns. The British occupied the capital (November 4, 1893) and took control of Matabeleland afterward. Lobengula fled north and died on the march on January 23, 1894. His people, whose livelihood was based on farming and livestock, were deprived of much land and frequently were conscripted to work in the British gold mines.

Mau Mau Uprising (1952–56)   The Mau Mau was a secret black terrorist organization or movement that sought to eliminate white European settlers from British East Africa (Kenya) and to restore control of the area to the native Africans. It grew rapidly among the Kikuyu, Meru, and other black tribes located in the "white highlands" and around the capital city of Nairobi. Mau Maus murdered whites and burned their homes and fields; they forced many reluctant black Africans to join them, beating or killing outright those who refused. The British responded to the Mau Mau terrorist uprising with force; declaring a state of emergency (October 20, 1952), the government dispatched thousands of troops and arrested Kikuyu and other tribal nationalist leaders, including Jomo Kenyatta (c. 1894–1978), suspected head of the Mau Mau, who was imprisoned (1953–61) and later became Kenya's first prime minister. As the Mau Mau movement spread, violence increased, and both sides committed terrible atrocities. British troops herded suspects into concentration camps; tribal villages were placed under strict security guard. Many tribesmen fled to the forests in the Aberdare and Mount Kenya areas, but the British army pursued them and routed them from their hiding places. After the capture and execution of Mau Mau leader Dedan Kimathi (d. 1956), the rebellion subsided as the British regained control, but at a high price (some £60 million were spent and about 50,000 troops were committed to fight the Mau Mau). Much property had been destroyed, and nearly 11,000 terrorists had been killed. The uprising succeeded, however, in calling attention to genuine African grievances, such as the need for land reform and more self-government.

Mauryan Empire, Conquests of the (c. 325–232 B.C.) Until the invasions of Turkish Muslims in the north after A.D. 1175 (see MUHAMMAD OF GHUR, CONQUESTS OF), the history of India is best described in terms of a group of small, sometimes petty, states continually at odds with each other. Two factors prevented the subcontinent (India) from developing a political unity: constant invasions from central and southwestern Asia and the divisive tenets of Hinduism. Despite these factors, one Gangetic kingdom, Magadha, lasted, in various guises, from 500 B.C. until the fifth century A.D. and provided a foundation for two worthy attempts at coordination. In 600 B.C., Magadha had been one of at least 16 competitive political units; within a hundred years the contestants had been reduced to four and then to Magadha alone, with a capital at

Pataliputra (Patna), as controller of the Ganges trade routes. Magadha's second form, that of the Mauryan Empire, began about 325 B.C., when Chandragupta Maurya (fl. c. 325–c. 290) seized the Magadhan throne, took land east of the Indus River south to the Narmada (Narbada) River, and—in an effort to close the mountain passes in northwestern India over which invaders came—defeated in 303 the forces of Seleucus Nicator (358?–280), the Macedonian general. Chandragupta's son Bindusara (fl. 298–273) extended the Mauryan Empire's southern boundary deep into the Deccan plateau (central India) and into what later became Mysore (Karnataka) state. His grandson Asoka (fl. 269–232) completed the empire by bloodily conquering the east coast kingdom of Kalinga to the Godavari River (271), giving the empire control of all the subcontinent except the southern tip. Under Asoka, the empire was at peace, with a centralized government; however, Asoka's policy of nonviolence reduced the army, encouraged internal conflicts, and made India prey to Bactrian, Scythian, and Parthian invasions. By 150 B.C., Indo-Hellenic forces had reached Pataliputra. The empire was defunct. Indo-Greek and other foreign rulers were enthroned through the third century A.D. Magadha, however, survived to be revitalized in the fourth century by the Gupta dynasty.

Mayan Revolt   See SPANISH CONQUEST OF YUCATAN.

Mecca, Sack of (A.D. 930)   During the first decades of the 900s, the Karmathians (Carmathians), a heretical Muslim sect living in northeastern Arabia, invaded Mesopotamia several times and harassed the caliphs in Baghdad. In 930, Abu Tahir al-Djannabi (d. 943), son of Abu Sa'id al-Djannabi (d. 913), leader of the KARMATHIAN REVOLT OF A.D. 899–906, led a sensational raid on Mecca. Islam's holiest city, located in western Arabia. The Karmathians plundered the city and carried off the most sacred Islamic object, the Black Stone, from the Kaaba (Caaba), the Muslim shrine at Mecca. Ten years later they returned the stone under pressure from the Fatimids, a Muslim dynasty in North Africa.

Mecca-Medina War (A.D. 624–30) Muhammad (570–632), the Prophet of Islam, denounced the pagan Arab religion of the native Qurayshite tribe of Mecca. To escape being murdered, he fled from Mecca to Medina in 622 (the Hegira) and sought revenge. In March 624, Muhammad, with 300 followers, intercepted a caravan of 1,000 Meccans traveling from Syria with Ummayyad leader Abu Sufyan (563–651) of Mecca (the Ummayyads at first rejected Muhammad's teachings but later accepted them). Muhammad's force seized the caravan, violating its pagan sanctity, forcing the Meccans to take Muhammad seriously. In 625, the Qurayshites won a tenuous victory over Muhammad's followers at the hill of Uhud (Ohod) near Mecca. Abu Sufyan, fearing Muhammad's growing religious support, led a 10,000-man force to Medina in 627, hoping to crush Muhammad, but was repulsed by Muhammad's 3,000-man army. The Treaty of al-Hudaybiyah was arranged, which allowed Muhammad to make a pilgrimage to Mecca in 629. However, some Meccans broke the treaty by attacking Muhammad's followers in November 629. In January 630, Muhammad countered by leading an attack on Mecca, where he met no resistance and destroyed more than 350 pagan idols. Thereafter he won a large following among the Meccans, who allowed him to establish Mecca as the holy city of Islam. See also MUSLIM REVOLT OF A.D. 656.

Median-Lydian War of 590–585 B.C. The collapse of the Assyrian Empire (see NINEVEH, FALL OF) and the subsequent division of Assyrian territories by Babylonia and Media caused the downfall of the kingdom of Lydia. Long the dominant power in western Anatolia (Asian Turkey), Lydia suffered two severe jolts in six decades and finally collapsed in 546 B.C. The first involved Lydia's King Alyattes (c. 619–560) and Media's King Cyaxares (d. 585), the latter attempted to take over the ancient Ana-

tolian territory of Urartu (Armenia). The Median effort brought them to the eastern boundary of Lydia at the Halys (Kizil Irmak) River about 590: battles that lasted five years successfully kept the Medians on the river's eastern bank. Details are not recorded, but it is known that the ruler of Babylonia and the Syenneses of Cilicia successfully mediated. Since neither Lydia nor Media had gained an advantage and both were worn out, the Halys became the official boundary between the two kingdoms. According to Greek historian Herodotus (484?–425?), Alyattes's daughter became the bride of Cyaxares's son, and peace lasted until the second jolt, the PERSIAN-LYDIAN WAR OF 547–46 B.C., destroyed Lydian power.

Median-Persian Revolt of 550–549 B.C. A new Persian empire was established when Cyrus II "the Great" (600?–529), ruler of the Median (Persian) kingdom of Anshan, turned against his grandfather, Astyages (fl. 584–549), king of the Medes and overlord of the Persians from about 584 to 550. Son of a Persian father (Cambyses I [fl. 600–559]) and a Median princess, Cyrus founded the Achaemenid dynasty and eventually revived the Persian Empire; the dynasty held power until its defeat by Alexander the Great (356–323) about 330. Cyrus's original goal was not to resuscitate Persia but to reform it. He led rebellious Medians unwilling to tolerate the continued harshness of Astyages, who was so unpopular that he caused dissension within his personal army. After a series of indecisive battles in 550, Cyrus took advantage of an army mutiny, captured Astyages, and spared his life, an act of clemency that led to the PERSIAN-LYDIAN WAR OF 547–546 B.C.

Megiddo, First Battle of (c. 1469 B.C.) Southward expansion of the kingdom of Mitanni (see HURRIAN CONQUESTS) caused Egyptian influence in Syria and Palestine to decline; King Thutmose III (fl. c. 1500–1447) of Egypt was determined to restore Egyptian power to its former preeminence. In the 1470s, he began a successful military campaign in the Near East, regaining control of Palestine and entering northern Syria. But, according to the partial records still extant, he faced an opposing Syrian-Palestinian coalition of some 330 rebellious princes led by the Mitanni king of Kadesh. About 1469, near the northern Palestinian fortress-city of Megiddo, gateway to Mesopotamia, the princes' army engaged the Egyptian force, which divided into three groups, began a surprise attack at dawn, and forced the enemy troops to flee to safety within the city. Pausing to loot the enemies' camp, the Egyptians under Thutmose then laid a successful seven-month siege of Megiddo. Important because it established an Egyptian empire in southwestern Asia, Thutmose's campaign gained the subservience of all members of the coalition except its Mitanni leader and prompted Babylonia, Assyria, and the Hittites to pay tribute. Thutmose went on to ravage southeastern Mitanni, especially the area around Carchemish, but he was unable to subdue the kingdom, which, under a later Egyptian ruler, became briefly an Egyptian ally. **Second Battle of Megiddo** (609 B.C.). The scene of several main battles in pre-Christian times and prophesied to be the location of the great Battle of Armageddon (occurring between the forces of good and evil at the end of the world), Megiddo became involved in the collapse of the Assyrian Empire after the fall and destruction of NINEVEH in 612. As an Assyrian ally, Egypt under King Necho II (fl. c. 609–593) wished to help the Assyrians recapture their newly established capital at Harran (Haran), now in Urfa province in Turkey. Necho informed the kingdom of Judah that he wished to cross its territory; Judah refused permission and sent a small force to stop Necho's large Egyptian army already under way. Judah's soldiers were defeated at Megiddo, and King Josiah (fl. c. 638–609) of Judah was killed in the battle by an arrow. Pushing north, Necho and his army made a vain effort to be of use at Harran, and then returned to Palestine and managed to keep out the Babylonians. See also CARCHEMISH, BATTLE OF.

Meiji Restoration (1863–68)   Since the early 17th century, Japan had been governed by a Tokugawa shogun, a hereditary position giving its owner command of the military and leadership of the administration. His capital was at Yedo or Edo (Tokyo), while the emperor, who was mainly a figurehead, had his capital at Kyoto. The coming of foreign traders to Japan in the mid-19th century altered the relationship of the two nominal rulers and their vassals. The daimyos (lords) of the western provinces of Choshu, Satsuma, Hizen, and Tosa had originally tried to expel the foreigners (see SHIMONOSEKI "WAR"), but they changed their minds and, being against the shogun, advised representatives of the foreign powers to deal directly with the imperial court. In November 1865, a fleet of British, French, and Dutch warships sailed into the port of Hyogo (Kobe) near Osaka where the shogun and his ministers were meeting. They did not want to risk a bombardment and promised to persuade the emperor to approve the trade treaties, which he reluctantly did. The following year Choshu rebelled, and the shogun convinced the emperor to initiate a campaign against it, but when the shogun died in September, the military operation was halted. Early in 1867, the emperor died and was succeeded by his 14-year-old son. That fall the western daimyos presented a letter to the shogun urging him to resign and pointing out that the division of political authority was endangering the existence of the country. The shogun did resign in November, expecting to be appointed to a prominent position in the new government. But this did not happen. In January 1868, the ban against Choshu was lifted. Clansmen of the four western provinces immediately descended upon Kyoto and seized military control of the city from Tokugawa troops. The former shogun withdrew to Yedo and prepared for war, but he soon realized he had no chance against the forces assembled under the new imperial standard. He surrendered his city and lands and retired to private life. His followers in the north continued to resist until mid-1869, but by then the new authority of the Meiji emperor had been firmly established. This drastic change in government was achieved with minimal bloodshed and destruction. See also SATSUMA REVOLT.

Melilla, War of   See RIF WAR OF 1919–26.

Memel, Insurrection at (1923)   The predominantly German city of Memel (Klaipeda) in western Lithuania on the Baltic had been under inter-Allied control since the end of WORLD WAR I (1918). Although Lithuania asked that the Allied powers grant it control of the city and the district (Memel-land), the Allies instead established a French garrison in the city for administrative purposes. On January 11, 1923, an insurrection broke out, engineered by the Lithuanians, whose troops occupied Memel and forced the French to leave. Within several days, Lithuania had possession of the entire district. The Allied powers protested, investigated the situation, and decided to make Memel (city and district) an autonomous region within Lithuania, which officially accepted the decision by signing the Memel Statute on May 8, 1924. See also LITHU-ANIAN WAR OF INDEPENDENCE.

Messenian War, First (c. 736–716 B.C.)   Dorians (northern Greeks) invaded the Peloponnesus between 1100 and 950 B.C., conquered the eastern portion of the peninsula, and settled in the valley of Lacedaemon, making Sparta their capital. The remaining native stock was reduced to serfdom and called Helots. Attracted by the fertility of the western areas, the Spartans subdued first the Laconians and then (c. 736) began a 20-year war against the Messenians, another native group in the Peloponnesus. Resistance centered around Mount Ithome, key to the rich Stenyclarus plain. Led by their legendary king Theopompus, the Spartans were victorious about 716. They demanded half of all Messenian produce and caused Messenians to suffer other indignities. **Second Messenian War** (c. 650–630 B.C.). Formerly sharers in Mycenaean culture, the Messenians resented their repression and revolted (c. 650). Under their semilegendary leader Aristomenes (fl. 7th cent.), they waged a long and costly war, one that nearly bankrupted their adversaries, the Spartans. Defeated at Mount Eira about 630, they made the Spartans realize the necessity of having a trained citizen army. Under the legendary Lycurgus (fl. 7th cent.), Sparta's entire social system changed to conform to a Cretan model: all males would be trained to a perfection of physical fitness and to a practiced skill at arms. Sparta was the first civilization devoted primarily to war. The Messenians were reduced to Helots. **Third Messenian War** (c. 464–455 B.C.). A very severe earthquake at Sparta (464) afforded the Helots of Laconia a chance to rebel, but their masters, the Spartans, led by the semi-legendary king Archidamus (fl. 476–427) suppressed them. The Messenians then entrenched themselves at Mount Ithome in 463 and successfully resisted clumsy Spartan attempts to besiege them. Appealing to allies for help, the Spartans received 40,000 hoplites (heavily armored foot soldiers) from Athens but soon dismissed them, supposedly because many were antagonistic to the Spartans, thus helping ignite the FIRST PELOPONNE-SIAN WAR. By 457, Messenian resistance began to weaken, and, in 455, Mount Ithome fell. The surviving Messenians were freed but exiled from the Peloponnesus; many of them joined Athens in the ongoing larger war against Sparta and managed to refound their "country" after the Battle of Leuctra (see THEBAN-SPARTAN WAR OF 379–371 B.C.).

Messiah War   See SIOUX WAR OF 1890–91.

Messinan Rebellion of 1674–79   Disputes often arose between the Spanish viceroy (governor) of Messina, Sicily, and the Messinans over the constitutionally defined duties of the viceroy; in 1674, fighting and rioting between the Merli (aristocrats) and Malvezzi (democrats) led to his eviction. King Louis XIV (1638–1715) of France was offered control of the city, and a Sicilian-French alliance, if he supplied help. After being declared king of Sicily, Louis sent a powerful naval fleet to take Messina in 1676 (see DUTCH WAR, THIRD). After three years of naval battles with Spanish and allied Dutch warships, the French were victorious in the war but faced financial problems at home. Louis and the French fleet fled from Messina, leaving its citizens terrified of Spanish reprisals. Messinans involved in the rebellion were rounded up and executed or exiled; Spain revoked Messina's rights, and the city, which lost more than half its population, never regained its former brilliance.

Mexican Civil War of 1871–77 In 1871 President Benito Juárez (1806–72) of Mexico declared his candidacy for a fourth term of office; Sebastián Lerdo de Tejada (1825–89) and Porfirio Díaz (1830–1915) also declared their candidacies. When the incumbent was reelected and Lerdo was appointed chief of the supreme court, Díaz led a revolt, which was crushed, and then fled into the mountains, where the Indians protected him from federal troops. When Juárez died in 1872, he was succeeded by Lerdo as president; an amnesty was declared that allowed the return of Díaz. Upon the reelection of Lerdo in 1876, Díaz again revolted. His forces defeated, they crossed the border into the United States to reorganize and rearm. His army then recrossed into Mexico, while Díaz sailed to Havana, Cuba, and then to Veracruz and proceeded to Oaxaca to head another army. Two rebel armies under Díaz and General Manuel Gonzalez (1833–93) defeated the government forces near Tlaxcala on November 16, 1876. Lerdo fled into exile as Díaz entered the capital, Mexico City; Díaz was elected president in 1877.

Mexican Civil War of 1911 Francisco I. Madero (1873–1913), a U.S.-educated lawyer and liberal, called for the ouster of Mexican dictator Porfirio Díaz (1830–1915) and opposed him in the 1910 presidential election. Díaz had Madero arrested and, after the balloting, proclaimed himself the victor. On November 20, 1910, Madero and his supporters launched an armed revolt. Although the Porfirian army contained most of the outbreaks in 1911, Pascual Orozco (fl. 1910s) maintained resistance in Chihuahua state, and in May 1911, rebel forces under him and Francisco "Pancho" Villa (1877–1923) captured Ciudad Juárez. Thus encouraged, revolutionaries throughout Mexico took up arms. With his own support crumbling, Díaz was forced to accept the Treaty of Ciudad Juárez stipulating his prompt resignation, and Madero was elected president in October. But Madero could not control the forces he had unleashed, and the events of 1911 ushered in two decades of bloodshed (see MEXICAN REVOLT OF 1914–15).

Mexican Civil War of 1920 Venustiano Carranza (1859–1920) tried to dictate who would succeed him as president of Mexico (see MEXICAN REVOLT OF 1914 15); he chose a little-known diplomat named Ignacio Bonillas (fl. 1915–20). Álvaro Obregón (1880–1928), who had helped put Carranza in office and served as his minister of war, felt the office should be his. Obregón's former comrade-in-arms, Adolfo de la Huerta (1881–1955), then governor of the state of Sonora, and General Plutarco Elías Calles (1877–1945), chief of the Sonoran armed forces, called for Carranza's resignation. When Carranza sent federal troops into Sonora to break a labor strike, Huerta declared Sonora an independent republic. Obregón and Calles marched south, collecting arms and volunteer troops as they went. Finding no soldiers willing to oppose Obregón and his rebel army, Carranza fled from the capital, Mexico City, toward Veracruz aboard a train loaded with gold he had taken from the national treasury. En route, he learned that the governor of the state of Veracruz had joined the rebels; he then fled on horseback into the mountains, where he was betrayed and murdered. Obregón entered Mexico City unopposed; Huerta became provisional president and, after a special election, was succeeded by Obregón later in 1920.

Mexican-French War of 1838 See PASTRY WAR.

Mexican-French War of 1861–67 After the War of the REFORM, financially troubled Mexico under President Benito Juárez (1806–72) declared in 1861 a two-year moratorium on payment of foreign debts. Britain, France, and Spain sent a joint expeditionary force to collect their due from Mexico; the forces landed at Veracruz and moved to Orizaba. After conferring with the Mexicans, the British and Spanish withdrew, convinced that Juárez would compensate them, but the French seized the opportunity to interfere in Mexican politics (Napoleon III [1808–73] hoped to set up an empire in Mexico). French troops under General Charles Ferdinand Latrille de Lorencez (1814–92) moved toward Mexico City but were defeated by Mexicans under Ignacio Zaragoza (1829–62) at Puebla. Napoleon sent reinforcements and placed the French army in Mexico under the command of General Élie-Frédéric Forey (1804–72), who marched on Puebla, now defended by forces under Jésus González Ortega (1824–81); after two months the Mexicans surrendered there in May 1863. Forey's troops entered the undefended capital, Mexico City, on June 7, 1863, while Juárez fled northward and established his headquarters near the Texas border. French forces under General François Achille Bazaine (1811–88) marched west from the capital, occupying cities almost without resistance. In 1864, Napoleon placed the Austrian archduke Ferdinand Maximilian (1832–67) on the Mexican throne as a puppet emperor, promising him military support through 1867 in return for the collection of French debts. Though many Mexican conservatives supported Maximilian, the liberals opposed him and made guerrilla raids against his troops. When the AMERICAN CIVIL WAR ended in 1865, American troops led by General Philip Sheridan (1831–88) advanced to the Rio Grande, the U.S.-Mexican border, and the U.S. government protested the French presence in Mexico. Napoleon deserted Maximilian and withdrew the French troops in 1867. Moving south, Mexican liberal forces under Mariano Escobedo (1827–1902) besieged Maximilian and his loyal Mexican followers at Queretaro for 71 days, until Maximilian was betrayed into capitulation. Court-martialed and found guilty, Maximilian was shot to death on June 19, 1867. Juárez reassumed his post as Mexican president.

Mexican Insurrections of 1926–29   Mexico's election of 1924 brought to the presidency Plutarco

Elías Calles (1877–1945), who implemented the previously unenforced anticlerical provisions of the 1917 constitution. In early 1926, officials of the Mexican Roman Catholic Church issued a condemnation of the provisions. Calles responded by closing Catholic schools, convents, and seminaries, by forcing the registration of priests, and by accusing the Catholic hierarchy of treason. In mid-1926, Catholic laypersons retaliated by stopping all but their essential purchases, and soon the Catholic clergy ceased performing clerical functions. Terrorists called the *cristeros*, whose cry was *Viva Cristo Rey* ("Long Live Christ the King"), took up arms against the anticlerical government and caused widespread destruction and murder in a dozen Mexican states. Although the Catholic hierarchy disavowed any connection with the *cristeros*, the government ordered the nationalization of church property, the deportation of several bishops, priests, and nuns, and the execution of a number of Catholics. Government forces crushed most of the *cristeros* by early 1928. Although Álvaro Obregón (1880–1928) was elected Mexican president on July 1, 1928 (he was assassinated later that month and was succeeded by Emilio Portes Gil [1891–1978], who was appointed provisional president), the undisputed political power in Mexico still lay with Calles. In March 1929, another insurrection erupted under the leadership of politically and religiously discontented generals, whose followers ravaged the country for about two months before the government restored order. Calles influenced the election to the presidency of Pascual Ortiz Rubio (1877–1963) in 1929; a half-hearted military insurrection against Ortiz failed, and Ortiz assumed office as Calles's puppet and continued his anticlerical policies.

Mexican Revolt of 1810–11   On September 16, 1810, Miguel Hidalgo y Costilla (1753–1811), parish priest in Dolores, called for the end of Spanish rule in Mexico, issuing the *Grito de Dolores* ("Cry of Dolores"), a document for racial equality and redistribution of land. Tens of thousands of Indians and mestizos flocked to Hidalgo's banner, taking over several Mexican towns (see GUANAJUATO MASSA-

CRE), and began a march on Mexico City. Frightened by the rebels, royalist forces marched against them and crushed Hidalgo's motley army at the Battle of Calderón Bridge, near Guadalajara, on January 18, 1811. Hidalgo fled but was caught and shot to death. He and his "Cry" ignited the Mexicans in a struggle for independence.

Mexican Revolt of 1914–15   By a successful coup d'état, Victoriano Huerta (1854–1916) gained the presidency of Mexico on February 18, 1913, overthrowing Francisco I. Madero (1873–1913), but Huerta was opposed by the separate forces of Emiliano Zapata (1880–1919) in the south, of Venustiano Carranza (1859–1920) in the northeast, of Francisco "Pancho" Villa (1877–1923) in the north, and of Álvaro Obregón (1880–1928) in the northwest. These four opposing forces increased their military activities until they controlled about three-quarters of Mexico by the spring of 1914, confining Huerta and his followers to the areas around Mexico City, the capital, and Veracruz. U.S. president Woodrow Wilson (1856–1924) refused to recognize Huerta's government, whose hostile acts resulted in American forces seizing and occupying Veracruz (April 21, 1914). When Villa's forces seized Zacatecas and Obregón's took Guadalajara and Queretaro, Huerta resigned as president. The rival leaders, Villa and Obregón, raced for the capital; Obregón arrived first and proclaimed his friend Carranza "First Chief" of Mexico. The leaders later met at Aguascalientes to organize a government in late 1914, but now Mexico was torn by anarchy; Villa and Zapata occupied Mexico City, while Carranza and Obregón took control of Veracruz. Although Villa and Zapata had more troops and held about two-thirds of the country, Carranza was recognized by the United States and eight other nations in the Western Hemisphere as de facto president of Mexico. Carranza controlled the northeastern border area with the United States, from which he could purchase arms; he also had the expert military assistance of Obregón and the shrewdness to promise the people social reform. In early 1915, Obregón and his troops occupied the capital, forcing Villa to flee to the surrounding countryside. Villa and his forces were pursued to the town of Celaya, where Obregón employed military tactics developed in WORLD WAR I. His troops dug trenches and strung barbed wire around Celaya, and in a three-day battle in April 1915, they won a decisive victory over Villa, who retreated northward. Villa's men pulled up railroad tracks to prevent pursuit by their foes. Both Villa and Zapata continued guerrilla warfare against Carranza, who later became president officially. Obregón was appointed minister of war. See also MEXICAN CIVIL WAR OF 1911; MEXICAN CIVIL WAR OF 1920; VILLA'S RAIDS.

Mexican Revolt of 1996   While trying to conclude an accord with the Zapatistas (see CHIAPAS REBELLION OF 1994), the Mexican government under President Ernesto Zedillo (1951–   ) confronted another armed guerrilla group, the Popular Revolutionary Army (EPR), based in the village of Aguas Blancas in the southwestern Mexican state of Guerrero. The EPR, entirely separate from the Zapatistas, called the Zedillo regime corrupt, illegitimate, and antidemocratic. In August 1996, EPR rebels launched coordinated attacks against government targets in six Mexican states, inciting a large military offensive by Zedillo against them. The guerrillas were forced to retreat into mountain areas and hamlets, where they undertook a propaganda and harassment campaign against the government in 1997. EPR leaders, bolstered by some leftist politicians, called for a newly written constitution for Mexico.

Mexican Revolution of 1821   After the liberals took power in Spain in 1820, forcing King Ferdinand VII (1784–1833) to reinstate the liberal constitution of 1812, conservative groups in Mexico concluded that the best recourse for maintaining the status quo was independence for Mexico. In an effort to subvert the colonial government, Agustín de Iturbide (1783–1824) persuaded the viceroy, Juan Ruiz de Apodaca (1767–1835), to give him command of the Spanish armies in order to crush the Mexican rebel guerrillas of Vicente Guerrero (1782–1831). Iturbide then marched with 2,500 soldiers in pursuit of Guerrero, who won some minor battles but was persuaded to join forces with Iturbide. On February 24, 1821, these two leaders issued the Plan of Iguala, calling for an independent Mexican monarchy (preferably a constitutional one under Ferdinand), Roman Catholicism as the country's sole religion, and racial equality for all Mexicans. The plan attracted rebels like Nicolás Bravo (1787?–1854) and Guadalupe Victoria (1789–1843) and conservatives like Anastasio Bustamante (1780–1853), who led 6,000 troops to fight for the cause. Most of the royal army deserted as the Mexican army under Iturbide (Guerrero had accepted his leadership) swept through the country. The new Spanish viceroy, Juan O'Donoju (1755–1821), soon met with Iturbide and signed the Treaty of Córdoba of 1821 that established Mexico's independence. Proclaimed Mexican emperor as Agustín I by his soldiers, Iturbide placed the crown upon his own head on May 19, 1822 (a Mexican national congress had reluctantly accepted the proclamation, fearing Iturbide as a dictator).

Mexican Revolution of 1823   Emperor Agustín I (1783–1824) of Mexico attempted to rule with a national congress wary of his imperial powers. His extravagance led to a need for more money. Because a small Spanish garrison remained on the island of San Juan de Ulloa off Veracruz and blocked the emperor's collection of duties, Agustín resorted to confiscation as a means to raise revenues, but he soon lost the support of the soldiers, many of whom had not been paid for months. Sent by the emperor to capture San Juan de Ulloa, General Antonio López de Santa Anna (1794–1876) took command of the Mexican army and issued a call for the establishment of a Mexican republic. He was joined by General Guadalupe Victoria (1789–1843), and together they set forth the Plan de Casa Mata in February 1823, calling for the end of the empire and the creation of a republic with a new constitution and a new congress. The army favored the plan, and

Augustín was forced to abdicate in March 1823 and to go into exile in Europe. A republic was established with Guadalupe Victoria as president.

Mexican War   (1846–47)   Relations between the United States and Mexico turned hostile when Mexico refused to accept the U.S. annexation of Texas in 1845. Mexico also rejected the U.S. claim that the Rio Grande was the southern border of Texas, stating that the border was farther north, at the Nueces River. In 1845, U.S. president James Polk (1795–1849) sent John Slidell (1793–1871) to Mexico to negotiate the boundary question and to purchase California and New Mexico; Mexico refused to negotiate. On April 25, 1846, Mexican troops crossed the Rio Grande and attacked U.S. troops under General Zachary Taylor (1784–1850), who had been ordered into the disputed Texan area. The U.S. Congress, at Polk's request, declared war on Mexico on May 13, 1846. A U.S. army under Taylor crossed the Rio Grande, defeated Mexican forces, and captured Monterrey on May 24, 1846. Later, on February 22–23, 1847, Taylor's army won the Battle of Buena Vista against a Mexican army led by General Antonio López de Santa Anna (1794–1876). Meanwhile, U.S. troops under Colonel Stephen W. Kearny (1794–1848) seized Santa Fe, and proceeded to California, where American settlers under Captain John C. Frémont (1813–90) had already declared their independence from Mexico. U.S. forces under General Winfield Scott (1786–1866) landed at Veracruz, took the city, advanced inland to defeat the Mexicans at Cerro Gordo, Contreras, and Chapultepec, and captured Mexico City on September 14, 1847. The Mexican leaders capitulated. By the Treaty of Guadalupe Hidalgo, signed on February 2, 1848, Mexico ceded to the United States most of what are now the states of New Mexico, Arizona, Utah, and California; the U.S. government assumed the claims of its citizens against Mexico. See also BEAR FLAG REVOLT.

Miguelite Wars   (War of the Two Brothers) (1828–34)   Portuguese monarchal absolutists led by Dom Miguel (1802–66) opposed the establishment of a Cortes (representative national assembly). After accepting the parliamentary charter that his brother Emperor Pedro I (1798–1834) of Brazil had promulgated (see PORTUGUESE CIVIL WAR OF 1826–27), Dom Miguel was appointed regent during the minority of Queen Maria II (1819–53), also called Maria de Glória, whom he had married by proxy. But Dom Miguel violated his oath to Pedro, replacing moderate governors and military officials with autocrats, and the Cortes was replaced by a docile body that proclaimed Miguel king of Portugal in May 1828. Queen Maria II, Pedro's little daughter, who was en route from Brazil to Portugal, was diverted to England, where she took refuge. Constitutionalists at Oporto and other places supported Pedro and Maria but were decisively defeated by the "Miguelites" near Coimbra on June 24, 1828. Dom Miguel was crowned king on July 11, 1828, and his absolutists began to wage a bloody war of reprisal. All Portugal fell to them save the Azores, an island group in the Atlantic west of Portugal, where a regency on behalf of Queen Maria II was established in 1829. Pedro abdicated his Brazilian throne in favor of his son and traveled to Europe to finance an army for the conquest of Portugal. In April 1831, he landed in the Azores, assembled an expedition with British support, and then sailed to Oporto in February 1832. Oporto was taken and subsequently withstood a yearlong siege by the Miguelites, who finally retook the city; French general Louis Auguste Victor de Bourmont (1773–1846) helped Miguel at Oporto. But soon afterward, Miguelite naval forces suffered defeat by a "liberation" fleet commanded by Sir Charles James Napier ("Carlo Ponza") (1782–1853) off Cape St. Vincent on July 5, 1833. Lisbon fell to the constitutionalists on July 24, 1833. Miguel's sheltering of Don Carlos (1788–1855), absolutist Spanish pretender to the throne of Spain, at his base near Coimbra resulted in a Spanish invasion to capture Don Carlos and helped prompt the formation of the Quadruple Alliance of Britain, France, Spain, and Portugal to preserve constitutionalism and to counter the absolutist Holy Alliance of Austria, Russia, and Prussia. With Spanish aid, the constitutionalists captured Viseu, Coimbra, and Tomar and defeated the Miguelites at the Battle of Santarém on May 16, 1834. In return for a general political amnesty, Dom Miguel surrendered 10 days later at Évora-Monte, gave up his claim to the throne, and retired to Germany. Pedro reinstated the 1826 constitution, and Queen Maria II was crowned after being declared of age (1834). See also CARLIST WAR, FIRST.

Milanese Civil War of 1447–50 After Filippo Maria Visconti (1402–47), duke of Milan, died with no male heirs, his territorial acquisitions were divided, and after about 200 years of autocratic rule in Milan, a republic was restored. However, Visconti's son-in-law, Francesco Sforza (1401–66), seized much of Milan, took Piacenza, and in 1448 declared war on Venice (see VENETIAN-MILANESE WAR OF 1448–54). After his victory at the Battle of Caravaggio, Sforza changed sides, allying himself with Venice against Milan, which then refused him entrance in response to his deception. Sforza laid siege to Milan, and in 1450 he was granted entrance and declared duke.

Milanese-Florentine Wars See FLORENTINE-MILANESE WARS.

Milanese Revolt of 1848 See "FIVE DAYS" REVOLT.

Milanese-Venetian Wars See VENETIAN-MILANESE WARS.

Minangkabau War See PADRI WAR.

Minisink Massacre (1779) During the AMERICAN REVOLUTION all the Iroquois tribes, except the Oneida, sided with the British and terrorized the western frontier settlements of the Americans. Joseph Brant (1742–1807), a wily and very capable Mohawk chief, directed many of the Iroquois raids (see CHERRY VALLEY MASSACRE). On the night of July 19, 1779, Brant and 60 Indians, accompanied by 27 British Tories disguised as Indians, swept down on the village of Minisink in central New York. Rousing the sleeping residents with their wild war cries, the raiders burned houses, barns, a mill, and a small stockade to the ground, drove off livestock, laid waste orchards and farms, and killed or took captive many of the defenseless people, whose possessions were seized as booty. Some residents fled to the nearby mountains. The local militia took off in pursuit of the Indians but was ambushed by Brant; most of the militiamen were slain in the bloody confrontation.

Mithridatic War, First (88–84 B.C.) Mithridates VI "the Great" (c. 132–63) became king of Pontus, a region in central Asia Minor, at a young age, and when he grew to adulthood, he began to unite the peoples in the surrounding areas into his empire. Conflict wit3h the Roman presence in Asia was inevitable. In 88, Mithridates seized almost every city in Asia Minor and ordered that thousands of Romans be massacred. Allies in Greece confronted a Roman army led by Lucius Cornelius Sulla (138–78), who defeated the Greeks in 85, while another Roman army under Gaius Flavius Fimbria (d. 84) drove Mithridates and his troops back to Pontus. Mithridates was forced to relinquish most of his conquered territory and to pay a large indemnity. **Second Mithridatic War** (83–81 B.C.). War began when an ambitious Roman general named Lucius Licinius Murena (fl. 83–82) led an invasion of Mithridates's land in the Kizil Irmak River area. He was defeated. In 75, Mithridates joined forces with Quintus Sertorius (d. 72), a Roman general in Spain, thus precipitating another war. **Third Mithridatic War** (75–65 B.C.). Sertorius's murder ended the threat from the west on Rome, and Lucius Licinius Lucullus (110?–56), a Roman general, was sent to deal with Mithridates in the east. Although the Romans were victorious in many battles, including Cyzicus, Cabira (Sivas), Tigranocerta, and Artaxata, and succeeded in driving Mithridates from Pontus, Lucullus's worn-out army threatened to mutiny and did not win the war. When Pompey the Great (106–48) assumed command (67), he succeeded in ending the conflict, utterly defeating Mithridates at the Battle of Lycus in

66. Mithridates fled to the Crimea, where, shamed by his failure, he ordered a slave to kill him. Mithridates's son-in-law and ally, King Tigranes (140?–55) of Armenia, was defeated and captured; he handed over to the Romans all of his conquests in 65. See also ROMAN-ARMENIAN WAR OF 72–66 B.C.

Mitre's Rebellion (1874) In 1868, Bartolomé Mitre (1821–1906) lost the Argentine presidency to Domingo Faustino Sarmiento (1811–88), who had the backing of the military and whose administration carried on educational reform and economic development. Mitre remained a strong political figure in Buenos Aires, whose financial superiority over other Argentine provinces dominated national life. In 1874, Mitre, leader of a liberal faction, failed to regain the presidency in the election; claiming his defeat was fraudulent, he led a rebellion, but federal troops under Sarmiento defeated the rebels at Buenos Aires (November 6, 1874) and forced Mitre to capitulate. The victorious presidential candidate Nicolás Avellaneda (1836–85), a minister in Sarmiento's government, then took office and governed until 1880, when he was succeeded by General Julio Argentino Roca (1843–1914), who had gained national fame in a successful war (1878–79) against the Indians of Patagonia, who had been pushed south of the Río Negro, thus opening up the pampas to colonization. See also ARGENTINE CIVIL WAR OF 1861.

Modoc War (Lava Beds War) (1872–73) In 1870, a band of Modoc Indians, led by Chief Kintpuash, known to the whites as Captain Jack (1837?–73), left the Klamath Indian Reservation in southern Oregon to reclaim Modoc ancestral lands near Lost River in northern California. Attempts to return the Indians to the reservation failed. About 80 Modoc warriors and their families retreated to the lava beds, a natural fortress of caves and ravines, near Tulelake, Calif. In November 1872, U.S. cavalry began a series of sieges against the Modoc, who successfully held their ground. At a peace conference in April 1873, Captain Jack shot General

Edward R. S. Canby (1817–73) to death, causing the U.S. troops to intensify their efforts to crush the Modocs. In late May 1873, Captain Jack with a much reduced force was forced out of the lava beds, pursued, and captured. He was hanged at Fort Klamath on October 3, 1873. Some of the Modocs were returned to the reservation in Oregon, and some were sent to Oklahoma.

Mogul-Afghan War of 1565–81   Unlike Hinduism, Islam had no tradition of primogeniture, and succession wars after the death of a ruler were commonplace. India's Muslims solved the problem in two ways: by dividing a kingdom among the heirs or by adopting the Ottoman practice of the strongest slaughtering all rivals. Akbar (1542–1605), Mogul emperor of Hindustan (the Ganges plain in north India), chose the first way; Emperor Aurangzeb (1618–1707) the second (see AURANGZEB, CONQUESTS OF). But the first method did not always ensure peace. Akbar's half brother, Mirza Hakim (d. 1585), had been allowed to retain control of Kabul, but nonetheless he became a stone in Akbar's slipper. In 1565, Uzbek nobles rose against Kabul, and Mirza Hakim fled to India and requested Akbar's help. While Akbar marched toward Lahore, disloyal Moguls persuaded Mirza Hakim to rebel. The appearance of the imperial Mogul army frightened him enough to force flight to Kabul. Akbar made a generous peace, and put down other rebellions among relatives and tributaries with ferocity (see MOGUL WAR AGAINST GUJARAT, SECOND). Even these examples of Akbar's stern justice did not keep Mirza Hakim peaceful, and Akbar had to advance against him in 1581. He was now less generous; a governor responsible to Delhi was installed in the person of Akbar's half sister. Though virtually powerless, Mirza Hakim reigned until his death, at which time Kabul was annexed to the Mogul Empire.

Mogul Civil War of 1600–05   The reign of Akbar (1542–1605), Mogul emperor of Hindustan (the Ganges plain in north India), ended with a low-key quarrel between Akbar and his oldest son, Salim, who later reigned as Jahangir (1569–1627). Salim held court in Allahabad as if he were an independent prince, thus angering Akbar, who was openly and obsessively hostile to him. Salim roamed about India with a large army (1600–02), referring to himself as emperor and disobeying his father's orders. In 1602, he marched toward Agra with 30,000 troops, but Akbar dissuaded him before any fighting occurred. But Salim laid plans to use his troops to assassinate his hated rival, his father's chief adviser. Warned, the adviser nonetheless faced his enemy, was seized, and beheaded; when his head was brought to Salim, Salim ordered it thrown in an outhouse. Akbar did not retaliate, for he thought Salim was a pitiable alcoholic; a reconciliation took place (1603) during which Salim surrendered 350 elephants as a symbol of disarmament, and Akbar placed the royal turban on Salim's head as crown prince. But soon Salim was placed under house arrest and forbidden alcohol and opium. The court, appalled, openly favored his son Khusrau (d. 1622), whose followers fought against Salim's during an elephant joust (1605). At Akbar's order, the fight was stopped by Salim's 13-year-old son Khurram (1592–1666), later Shah Jahan, who was also to rebel against his father and to be an accomplice in Khusrau's murder (1622). Ill on his deathbed, Akbar reasserted that Salim was his chosen successor.

Mogul Civil War of 1607   Civil wars marked the opening and close of the reign of India's Mogul emperor Jahan-gir (1569–1627); indeed, internal strife on various levels marked all of Jahangir's tenure from 1605 to 1627, during which the empire created by Akbar (1542–1605) gained little in territory and began to lose its sense of community. Jahangir himself had been a rebellious son (see MOGUL CIVIL WAR OF 1600–1605), and he was anxious to avoid the disorder and bloodiness of internal conflict. His strategies failed. He restrained his eldest son Khusrau (d. 1622) in the court, for Khusrau had wrangled with him before his enthronement. A reconciliation in 1605 only briefly resolved their conflict, for Khusrau fled the court in 1607, gathered a mob of followers, and laid siege to Lahore in the hope of gaining a territory of his own to govern. An imperial army quickly defeated the rebels; Khusrau was captured, returned to Lahore in chains, and degraded in many ways. His titles, perquisites, and status as crown prince were transferred to his brother Khurram (1592–1666), later known as Shah Jahan. To prevent further rebellions, Jahangir punished the rebels sadistically, beheading and impaling hundreds, and earned the permanent enmity of the Sikhs by executing their leaders and keeping Khusrau in golden chains for a year. Not unexpectedly, upon release, he advocated the assassination of his father; he was partially blinded as punishment and remained a prisoner of the court until 1622, when he was ordered strangled by Khurram, who was then involved in his own revolt against Jahangir (see SHAH JAHAN'S REVOLT). See also SHAH JAHAN, CONQUESTS OF.

Mogul Civil War of 1657–59   A Mogul military commander at age 16, Aurangzeb (1618–1707) won almost every war his father, Shah Jahan (1592–1666), had ordered undertaken (see AURANGZEB, WARS OF), while his eldest brother and Shah Jahan's favorite, Dara Shikoh (1615–59), was ensconced in the court in an effort to keep him from rebelling (rebellion by princes against their emperor-fathers was a habitual Mogul practice). Dara ventured out to lead an army only once, and then unsuccessfully. Fearful of his younger brother, Dara and his faction had actually undercut Aurangzeb in wars against Golconda and Bijapur (1656–57), substituting huge indemnities for conquest and annexation. Dara was given the reins of government and ended all communication with his brothers, thus provoking a war of succession. Shuja (d. c. 1658) and Murad (d. 1661), two of Dara's brothers, had themselves proclaimed emperor separately, mobilized armies, and planned to move against Agra, the Mogul capital. Shuja was defeated (February 24, 1658) and chased to Bengal. Murad and Aurangzeb allied and defeated an imperial force at Dharmat (April 25, 1658) and Dara at Samugarh, near Agra (June 8, 1658). Dara fled, was defeated and captured

at Deodari, and executed on false charges. Aurangzeb, free of Murad (in prison and executed later) and Shuja (ambushed and killed in Bengal), now deposed Shah Jahan, imprisoned him in the Agra fortress, refused to visit him, and had himself proclaimed emperor (June 26, 1658). By early 1659, he was securely enthroned; his father remained a prisoner, within sight of the Taj Mahal, until his death.

Mogul Civil War of 1707–8   Although Mogul emperor Aurangzeb (1618–1707) had proposed a partitioning of the empire to avoid a war of succession, his death found three of his sons contending for power. Princes Azam (d. 1707) and Kambakhsh (d. 1708), both in the Deccan region of India, were angered when their elder brother Muazzam (1643–1712), who was governor of Kabul (now in Afghanistan), assumed the Mogul throne in 1707 as Bahadur Shah I. Azam was defeated and killed in a battle with Bahadur, and later his brother Kambaksh died from wounds received in a skirmish (1708). Now free to attempt the revival of imperial fortunes, Bahadur pacified the Rajputs by releasing Ajit Singh (1678–c. 1720), a Crown prisoner since the RAJPUT REBELLION AGAINST AURANGZEB (1679), to be ruler of Marwar (Jodhpur); Bahadur subverted the Marathas by freeing Shahu (d. 1749), their ruler, who immediately began a civil war against those who had directed Maratha military actions since the 1689 execution of his father Sambhagi (1657–89) (see MARATHA-MOGUL WAR OF 1681–1705). Only the Sikhs stoutly resisted Bahadur's authority. Readily the emperor initiated a campaign (1710) and went to Lahore (now in Pakistan) to lead the fight against the Sikhs; the war was inconclusive, though the Moguls drove the rebels into the mountains. Bahadur's death in 1712 brought on the MOGUL CIVIL WAR OF 1712–20. See also MOGUL-SIKH WARS.

Mogul Civil War of 1712–20   The death of Bahadur Shah I (1643–1712), the Mogul emperor, touched off a succession struggle that accelerated the decline of the Mogul Empire in India. Bahadur had four sons, and the strongest was the eldest, who assumed the throne as Jahandar Shah (d. 1713) and proved to be the most incompetent of all the Mogul emperors. His claim to the throne was disputed by a relative, Farrukh-Siyar (d. 1719), who, with the help of the powerful Sayyid brothers (Husayn Ali [d. 1720] and Abdullah [d. 1721?]), staged a successful coup in 1713 and had Jahandar Shah strangled to death. Long a puppet of the Sayyid brothers, Farrukh-Siyar was enthroned, backed the Sayyids in defeating the rebellious Rajput leader Ajit Singh (1678–c. 1720) and the Sikh leader Banda Singh Bahadur (1670–1716), but turned against his masters (1719), who then deposed, blinded, and finally murdered him. Unable to be emperors because of dynastic constraints, the Sayyids crowned successively two sickly boy emperors (February–November 1719) before enthroning a grandson of Bahadur Shah I, Muhammad Shah (1702–48). By 1720, the growing power of the Marathas, warrior Hindus, had extended into Hindustan (the Ganges plain in north India). Bahadur was involved in a conspiracy against Husayn Ali, who was poisoned; Abdullah was defeated and seized by the emperor at the Battle of Hasanpur, near Delhi; this terminated Sayyid control. The Mogul Empire, however, continued to weaken until, in 1764, the Emperor Shah Alam II (1728–1806) became a pensioner of the British East India Company. See also AFGHAN REBELLIONS OF 1709–26; BENGALESE-MOGUL WAR OF 1742; PERSIAN INVASION OF MOGUL INDIA.

Mogul Conquest of Rajasthan (1561–95) The long absence of Mogul emperor Humayun (1508–56) from India (see MOGUL WARS AGAINST THE SUR DYNASTY, EARLY) had enabled the Hindu princes of central and western India to become autonomous. Strengthened by loose alliances, these kingdoms together formed Rajasthan or Rajputana and threatened the economic stability of the Mogul Empire. Humayun's son and successor, Akbar (1542–1605), began a double approach to the problem in 1561, part military and part diplomatic. His forces conquered the central kingdom of Malwa, situated north of the Deccan region, in 1561; then, in 1562, he married a princess of Amber (Jaipur) and

gained a friendship with its ruler that lasted throughout his reign. This double solution gained him, between 1562 and 1564, control of Jodhpur, Bhatha (Rewa), and a large territory in the Punjab and western Rajasthan. From 1567 to 1570, he gradually gained authority over all of Rajasthan by seizing its huge fortresses; Chitor, supposedly impregnable, occupied his forces from 1567 to 1568 and cost some 30,000 lives; Ranthambhor required a long siege during 1568–69. The next year Akbar called a conference of Rajput rulers; four kingdoms promptly acknowledged his sovereignty; four others joined shortly later. Only the western Mewar kingdom held out from an island in a man-made lake at Udaipur. Despite military and diplomatic efforts, Mewar remained independent for the rest of Akbar's rule. Major fighting was over, but Akbar continued to enlarge the Mogul Empire by annexing Kashmir (1586), taking Sind (1590), annexing Orissa to Bengal (1592–94), and conquering Baluchistan (1595). Only western Mewar, Assam, and the Deccan remained outside Mogul control at the time of his death in 1605.

Mogul-Maratha Wars   See MARATHA-MOGUL WARS.

Mogul-Persian War of 1622–23   Shah Abbas I "the Great" (1557–1628?) of Persia coveted the strategic fortress-city of Kandahar, held by the Moguls. His soldiers tried to capture it in 1605–6, but the Mogul emperor Jahan-gir (1569–1627) sent an imperial force that compelled the Persians to retreat. In 1622, Abbas led an army against Kandahar and, after a 45-day siege, captured it. Jahangir again planned to send forces to recover the city and its supposedly impregnable fortress. However, because he was too preoccupied with his gardens, wine, poetry, and women to fight himself, Jahangir ordered his son Khurram (1592–1666), later called Shah Jahan, to lead an army from the Deccan into present-day Afghanistan. Khurram delayed, was judged by the imperial court to be in revolt, and finally took up arms, but against his father. His revolt (see SHAH JAHAN'S REVOLT) prevented Mogul retaliation: the imperial army that finally reached Kandahar in 1623 was too weak to recover the city.

Mogul-Persian War of 1638   Exactly one century before the PERSIAN INVASION OF MOGUL INDIA, the forces of Mogul emperor Shah Jahan (1592–1666) recaptured the city of Kandahar, lost in the MOGUL-PERSIAN WAR OF 1622–23. Shah Jahan now hoped to repossess his ancestral Timurid homeland of Samarkand; Kandahar was to be a step along the way. Shah Jahan offered a huge bribe to the Persian governor of Kandahar, who accepted it, and thus gained the city's surrender without having to establish a formal siege. He then spent large sums on the fortification of Kandahar and its dependencies. During the MOGUL-PERSIAN WAR OF 1649–53, he delayed the imperial Mogul force, which arrived to find that the city had once again fallen into Persian hands. Kandahar was never recovered again by Mogul armies.

Mogul-Persian War of 1649–53   Shah Jahan (1592–1666), the Mogul emperor in India, was not able to be complacent concerning the aggressive Persians, who captured the Afghan city of Bamian (1639) and seemed likely to try to reconquer Kandahar to the south. The Moguls strongly fortified Kandahar, and when no Persian attack came, Shah Jahan's son Murad (d. 1661) was sent to invade Uzbek-controlled Badakhshan in 1646. His army was unsuccessful. In response, the Persians began to mobilize for an attack on Kandahar; Shah Jahan postponed sending troops until 1649, by which time the city had fallen to an alliance of Persians and Uzbek Turks. The Mogul army, led by Shah Jahan's son Aurangzeb (1618–1707), attacked Kandahar without success in 1650; the army was too small and had too little ordnance to mount a winning siege. Aurangzeb withdrew and in 1652 brought a powerful army; after two months of fighting, superior Persian forces caused a second withdrawal. Disgraced, Aurangzeb deferred to his oldest brother,

Dara Shikoh (1615–59), whose army also failed to retake the fortress-city after a five-month siege in 1653. Mogul forces never again attempted to recover Kandahar. See also AURANGZEB, WARS OF.

Mogul-Sikh War of 1675–1708   The Sikhs were a religious community combining Muslim and Hindu elements, located in northern India. Appreciated by the liberal Mogul (Muslim) emperor Akbar (1542–1605), the Sikhs were disliked by the orthodox, especially so because they supported the liberals in Mogul succession disputes. In 1606, the fifth Sikh guru (spiritual teacher), Arjun (1563–1606), was arrested and tortured to death by order of Mogul emperor Jahangir (1569–1627) for allegedly supporting the rebellion of Khusrau (d. 1622) (see MOGUL CIVIL WAR OF 1607). The seventh guru, Har Rai (1630–61), supported the Muslim prince and scholar Dara Shikoh (1615–59) against Mogul emperor Aurangzeb (1618–1707) and had to send his son as hostage to the Mogul court. After each incident, the Sikhs became more militant. The ninth guru, Tegh Bahadur (1621?–75), reacted to Aurangzeb's Islamic fanaticism by leading a revolt in the Punjab. Captured by imperial troops, Tegh Bahadur was brought to Delhi, the Mogul capital, where he was beheaded for refusing to convert to Islam. His execution had two results: Tegh Bahadur's son and the 10th and last guru, Gobind Rai Singh (1666–1708), organized the Sikh army of the Khalsa ("pure") and waged sporadic defensive war in the Punjab against vastly superior Mogul forces until his assassination in 1708. See also MOGUL CIVIL WAR OF 1707–8.

Mogul-Sikh War of 1709–16   In an effort to reestablish Mogul control over several rivals, Bahadur Shah I (1643–1712), India's Mogul emperor, at first gained the help of the Sikhs under Guru Gobind Rai Singh (1666–1708) against the Marathas. But when Gobind died in 1708, the Sikhs under Banda Singh Bahadur (1670–1716) became opponents of Mogul garrisons in the Punjab, seized the fort at Sirhind (1710), and became virtual rulers of the Punjab.

Only the city of Lahore remained in Mogul hands, and Banda continued to raid from the hills. Bahadur Shah's death allowed Banda to recover Sadhaura and Longarh. His raiding increased when a succession war (see MOGUL CIVIL WAR OF 1712–20) reduced Mogul opposition. After the successor to Bahadur Shah, Farrukh Siyar (d. 1719), defeated and captured Banda in 1711, the Sikhs' leader was dragged to Delhi to be humiliated by being paraded in chains and was eventually tortured to death with red-hot irons in June 1716.

Mogul War against Gujarat, First (1 5 3 5 – 3 6) The death of Babur (1483–1530), first Mogul emperor of India, elevated to the throne his son Humayun (1508–56), whose reign nearly cost the Moguls their young empire in India (see BABUR, CONQUESTS OF). In 1530, Mogul India had been merely a military occupation by the invaders; territorial consolidation was left to the somewhat feckless Humayun, whose real interests were wine, opium, poetry, and astrology. He began badly, failing to subdue militarily the Hindu principality of Kalinjar in Bundelkhand, to the south of Delhi (1530). Then Humayun picked a long-term quarrel with the Sur (Afghan) dynasty's Sher Khan (1486–1545), governor of vassal Bihar, by failing to take his fortress at Chunar (see MOGUL WARS AGAINST THE SUR DYNASTY, EARLY). His next move was to the south and west, invading Malwa and Gujarat (1535). At first this campaign went well: he seized the forts of Mandu and Champaner; he drove Sultan Bahadur (d. 1536?) of Gujarat down India's west coast to seek refuge among the Portuguese. But Humayun's angry vassal Sher Khan had declared his independence and invaded Bengal (1536); Humayun returned to Delhi without leaving behind occupation forces. Bahadur came home freely, and once again took control of his territories, continuing his opposition to Delhi's authority. **Second Mogul War against Gujarat** (1572–73). Following his conquest of most of Rajasthan from 1561 through 1570, Akbar (1542–1605), emperor of Hindustan (the Ganges plain in north India), made the logical move of pushing westward toward the kingdom of Gujarat,

which had opposed Muslim authority since the time of the Delhi sultanate (see MOGUL CONQUEST OF RAJASTHAN). Gujarat was protected by a system of fortresses and fortified cities, and each had to be conquered by siege. In November 1572, Ahmadabad was easily captured; a month later Akbar seized the fortress at Cambay and defeated a hostile kinsman at Sarnal. He then returned to the court city of Fatehpur Sikri, specially created for Akbar to replace Agra and Delhi. The hostile kinsman crushed at Sarnal had not given up; thinking summer monsoon rains would keep Akbar away, he lay siege to Ahmadabad (1573). Akbar, however, was undaunted; his troops slogged more than 500 miles in 11 days despite the bad weather, defeated 20,000 rebel Indians, and captured his rival kinsman, who was imprisoned. The Portuguese, who had supported Gujarat (whose island of Diu they occupied), made peace with Akbar, who returned to his new capital briefly before pursuing his war against the Sur dynasty. See also PORTUGUESE CAMPAIGNS AGAINST DIU.

Mogul Wars against the Sur Dynasty, Early (1535–36) By failing to seize the Bihari fortress of Chunar in 1532, India's Mogul emperor Humayun (1508–56) earned the undying rivalry of the Sur (Afghan) governor of Bihar, Sher Khan (1486–1545), who had accompanied Babur (1483–1530) from Kabul to victory in India (see BABUR, CONQUESTS OF). Humayun's absence from Delhi in 1535 to fight the MOGUL WAR AGAINST GUJARAT prompted Sher Khan to assert independence and invade Bengal. His action forced Humayun to abandon Gujarat, push his forces east despite a monsoon, and reach Bengal in 1537. However, as in the Gujarat war, he was called away, this time to a revolt in Delhi by younger brothers. Sher Khan had managed to place his troops between Humayun and Delhi; the emperor's forces, reduced by monsoon weather, were massacred at Chausa in 1539. Humayun escaped to Agra, pardoned his brothers, and confirmed one of them, Kamran (d. 1557), as ruler of Kabul and Kandahar before fleeing west, only to suffer defeat again at Kannauj in 1540.

He escaped to Lahore while Sher Khan established himself as emperor. The new emperor pursued the first, who fled to Sind, then east to Rajasthan, then back to Sind (where his successor, Akbar [1542–1605], was born). He next fled to Kandahar, where his brother refused to receive him, and finally withdrew into Persia (Iran), where he tried to bribe its shah with the Koh-i-nur diamond in exchange for an army. By 1547, Humayun was on his way back, but he had to spend seven years fighting Kamran before he could reenter India (1554) to fight the armies of the Surs. Involved in a three-way war of succession, the superior Sur forces were nonetheless defeated by the inferior Mogul-Persian army in the Punjab and finally were crushed entirely at Rohtas (Rohtak) in 1555. Humayun went directly to Delhi and Agra, reclaimed his throne, and held it for one year before a drunken fall down stone steps killed him.

Mogul Wars against the Sur Dynasty, Later (1556–57, 1575–76) The third and greatest Mogul emperor of India, Akbar (1542–1605), inherited, at age 13, all the problems his father, Humayun (1508–56), had left unresolved, chiefly the continuing disruptive rivalry of the Sur dynasty, as well as the hostility of the Hindu Rajput rulers (see MOGUL CONQUEST OF RAJASTHAN). He also had minor problems of his own: an aggrandizing half-brother (see MOGUL-AFGHAN WAR OF 1565–81), the hostility of Gujarat (see MOGUL WAR AGAINST GUJARAT, SECOND), and trouble with his oldest son (see MOGUL CIVIL WAR OF 1600–05). Fighting with the Surs continued because Humayun's 1555 victory at Rohtas (Rohtak) had merely crippled the rival claimants to the Sur throne. Sikander Sur (d. 1558) was disturbing precarious Mogul authority in the Punjab when Akbar became emperor, and Akbar, with his regent, went immediately west, only to discover that Hemu (d. 1556), Hindu prime minister of Sur-ruled Bihar and Bengal, had seized Delhi and Agra, establishing himself as the Rajah Vikramaditya. The imperial Mogul army dashed east and, at the second Battle of Panipat, was losing its left and right wings to a Hindu charge involving some 1,500 elephants when

Hemu was struck in the eye with an arrow; his army fled; Hemu was captured and beheaded. Relieving Delhi and Agra and consigning them to a military commander's rule, Akbar returned west to defeat Sikander Sur at Sirhind (1557). The remaining Sur pretender to the throne fled to Orissa; Akbar, noting his weakness, left him alone until the 1574 conquest of Bihar caused the Orissa Sur to invade Bengal. Akbar won a battle at Tukra (1575) and occupied Bengal. The Sur ruler tried again (1576) to seize Bengal, but his defeat and death at Rajmahal ended an opposition the Timurid rulers had faced since 1536. See also BABUR, CONQUESTS OF.

Mohi (Sajo River), Battle of (1241) During the Mongol advance into Hungary (see MONGOL INVASION OF EUROPE), King Bela IV (1206–70) of Hungary left his main army at Pest (Budapest), where he expected the Mongols to strike in force, and took 100,000 men to the plain of Mohi on the Sajo River in Tokaj (Tokay). He engaged the Mongols under Batu (d. 1256) with a small detachment at a bridge and kept most of his men in camp. Meanwhile, Mongol forces led by General Sübedei (d. c. 1258) had hidden on the east side of the Sajo, crossed over at night, and attacked on April 11, 1241, Europe's most formidable army from the rear; other Mongol detachments immediately attacked its wings. The Hungarians were completely surprised, and when the main Mongol force made a frontal attack, between 40,000 and 70,000 were slain. Fully demoralized, Bela fled, with the Mongols in pursuit until they decided to rest and enjoy the spoils of war; they would have renewed the conquest of Europe in the winter of 1242 had not the death of their supreme ruler (khakan), Ögedai (d. 1241), demanded the return of the Mongol armies to Karakorum for the election of a new ruler.

Moldovan Civil War of 1991–92 Lying in the fertile, hilly plains between the Prut and Dniester (Dnestr) rivers, the small former Soviet republic of Moldova (Moldavia) became embroiled in a bloody inter-ethnic conflict after proclaiming its independence in September 1991. Fighting erupted between Moldovans (ethnic Rumanians, but culturally distinct) and Slav separatists (ethnic Russians and Ukrainians), who feared Moldova would join with neighboring Rumania in the west and sought self-rule in the region east of the Dniester River (Trans-Dniester). The 14th division of the Russian army, stationed in Moldova, provided arms and sometimes troops to the Slav insurgents, who defeated the Moldovan forces in several battles, notably that for Tighina (Bendery), in June 1992. An agreement signed by Russia's President Boris Yeltsin (1931–) and Moldova's President Mircea I. Snegur (1940–) in July 1992 led to a cease-fire and a joint peacekeeping force in the Trans-Dniester region, where the residents established (1993) the autonomous "Dniester Republic" and later (1995) held legislative elections and approved a separatist constitution. Moldova, which adopted a new constitution in 1994, secured the eventual withdrawal of Russian troops from its territory and signed a peace memorandum with the breakaway Dniester Republic on May 8, 1997.

Mongol-Burmese War of 1277–87   Kublai Khan (1216–94), founder of the Mongol (Yüan) dynasty in China (see MONGOL CONQUEST OF THE SUNG EMPIRE), attempted to exact tribute from the Burmese king of Pagan, Narathihapate (d. 1287), who refused to accept Mongol vassalage and, in 1273, executed Kublai's envoy sent to demand payment. In 1277, Narathihapate's soldiers, mounted on elephants, advanced into China's Yunnan region after making successful raids along the border. At the Battle of Ngasaunggyan (1277), Mongol archers on horseback dismounted when their horses became frightened by the elephants, regrouped on foot, dispersed the elephants, remounted, and made a victorious charge against the Burmese, who outnumbered them about three to one. Later, after stopping another Burmese border raid, the Mongols invaded and crushed the Burmese near Bhamo (1283). Kublai's grandson Yesin Timur (1267–1307) led invaders down the Irrawaddy Valley, captured the city of Pagan (from which Narathihapate had fled south to Bassein), and set up a puppet government. Deciding to recognize Mongol suzerainty, Narathihapate was murdered by his son soon after (1287).

Mongol-Burmese War of 1299–1300   When the Shans, a Mongoloid Thai group in northeast Burma overthrew the Mongol puppet government at Pagan on the Irrawaddy River (see MONGOL-BURMESE WAR OF 1277–87), a small Mongol army was dispatched to reestablish control of the area. At the fortified, three-walled town of Myinsaing, Shan forces checked the Mongols, of whom about 500 were killed in battle. The Shan leaders, fearful of possible Mongol reinforcements, offered the Mongol commander a large bribe; he accepted it and withdrew with his army to Yünnan province in southwestern China. Later, the Mongol commander was executed by Yünnan's governor for his actions; the Mongols, however, decided not to invade again.

Mongol-Chinese War of 1356–68   The seeds of rebellion that caused the collapse of the Yüan dynasty established by Kublai Khan (1216–94) were unwittingly planted by Kublai himself. Unlike his grandfather, Genghis (Jenghiz, Chingis) Khan (1167?–1227), who had a renowned Chinese adviser, Kublai distrusted the Chinese and appointed mostly Muslim advisers, thereby offending the mandarins (high Chinese officials). He offended the intellectuals by disbanding the Confucian system of civil service examinations, and he angered all Chinese by denying the privilege of learning Mongol and by treating them as second-class citizens. Minor rebellions occurred early, but one so alert and magnetic as Kublai Khan quelled them easily. As the quality of the Yüan emperors declined, as the Mongols increasingly distanced themselves from the Chinese, and as the court became more frationalized and more dissolute, the Mongols lost all authority. In the 1350s, rebellions in the Yangtze (Chang) River valley grew uncontrollable. Warlords set themselves up as independent rulers, and one—the first Ming emperor, Chu Yüan-chang (Hung-wu) (1328–98)—established his dynasty, with its capital at Nanking (Nanjing). Taking Peking (Beijing) (1368), and driving the Mongols first to Shang-tu and then to Outer Mongolia, where for a century they vainly considered themselves the legitimate rulers of China.

Mongol Civil War of 1260–64   The death of the great Mangu Khan (1207?–59) threw the Mongol Empire into disunity. His brother Kublai (1216–94), representing the modern, sinicized Mongol, found himself confronted by the old Mongols, led by his younger brother Arik-Böke (d. 1255). Both of them summoned separate great Mongol meetings (kuriltais); Kublai first at Shang-tu (May 1260), then Arik-Böke about two weeks later at Karakorum. Both were elected supreme ruler (khakhan). Their actions unleashed forces neither side could control, and the Mongol hostilities lasted for the rest of the century. Arik-Böke had alienated his brother Hülegü (d. 1265), a supporter of Kublai, and had set him against Berke (d. 1266), leader of the Golden Horde, thus precipitating the GOLDEN HORDE–ILKHAN CIVIL WAR. In 1260, Kublai sent an army toward Karakorum; Arik-Böke then retreated westward. Their armies clashed and withdrew without a decisive victory (1261), and Arik-Böke tried vainly to recapture the capital, Karakorum. He finally capitulated after losing in battle to Kublai in 1264. Arik-Böke was allowed to go free, an inconsequential political figure until his death two years later.

Mongol Conquest of the Abbasid Caliphate   (1255–60)   Mangu Khan (1207?–59), the Mongols' supreme ruler (khakhan) from 1251 until his death, planned to eradicate the Muslim Assassins, a secret order of hashish-eating terrorists and murderers, and to reach the borders of Egypt by conquering the Abbasid caliphate (dominion). His brother Hülegü (d. 1265), founder of the Il-Khan dynasty bordering the caliphate, was put in charge of the conquest; he therefore marched his forces from the Oxus (Amu Darya) River almost to the Nile. Persia wanted to have Mongol control reestablished, particularly against the Muslim ambitions. Effecting Hülegü's

careful, thorough plan, officered by his general Ked-Buka (d. 1260), the Mongols departed from Samarkand in 1256, obliterated the Assassins in their Elburz Mountains' caves and castles (1256), beseiged Baghdad, the caliph's capital, from three sides (1257), secured its defeat (1258), and then looted and burned it. Then Hülegü murdered the caliph by rolling him in a carpet and allowing horses to kick and trample him to death. With 400,000 Mongols, he took control of the remainder of Mesopotamia (Iraq) in 1258, attacked Syria the next year, and conquered Aleppo, Damascus, Gaza, and Sidon in 1260. Egypt was threatened, but the death of Mangu Khan forced Hülegü to return home, leaving Ked-Buka in charge with 10,000 soldiers. Afterward the Egyptians attacked them and killed Ked-Buka and won (the second Mongol defeat of the thirteenth century). Psychologically uplifted by this victory, Egypt became a strong Muslim power and was able to retake Syria, thus destroying Mangu Khan's original expectation.

Mongol Conquest of the Chin Empire   (1231–34)   The second supreme ruler (khakhan) of the Mongols was Ögedei (d. 1241), son of Genghis (Jenghiz, Chingis) Khan (1167?–1227), who decided to fight the Chin (northern Chinese dynasty) in the east and then begin a MONGOL INVASION OF EUROPE. Since the Chin still held territories in Honan (Henan) province and were furthermore exceedingly rich, Ögedei, his brother Tolui (d. 1232), and General Sübedei (d. c. 1258) led forces to the Chin holdings. A double military strategy governed: Ögedei and Sübedei would advance from the north and west to form a left wing; Tolui would advance from the south (right wing). With some 30,000 men, Tolui met no opposition until reaching the mountains; there, although harried by the Chin warriors, the Mongols outwitted them until the Chin withdrew to K'ai-feng, the Chin capital, where the other Mongols waited. Tolui died, and Sübedei commanded the siege of the capital, whose many inhabitants looked over their 40-mile circuit of defensive walls to see a second set of walls being erected for siege machines, liquid fire balls, and gunpowder-aided projectiles. Starvation and plague helped the besiegers under Sübedei, who attacked, aided now by Sung (Song) soldiers. The Chin emperor fled, sacrificed his wives, and hanged himself. K'ai-feng was entered; Ögedei's Chinese adviser saved both valuable artifacts and buildings, gained mercy for scholars and peasants, and prevented wholesale looting and slaughter. Ögedei next declared war on the Sung Empire (see MONGOL CONQUEST OF THE SUNG EMPIRE). See also GENGHIS KHAN'S WAR WITH THE CHIN EMPIRE; JUCHEN MONGOL INVASION OF THE SUNG EMPIRE.

Mongol Conquest of the Sung Empire (1234–79) The Mongol war against the Sung or Song (Chinese dynasty) lasted through the reigns of five great khans (rulers) not only because the Sung proved to be the most formidable foe encountered by the Mongols but also because the demands of other wars and civil strife from 1234 to 1264 (see MONGOL CIVIL WAR OF 1260–61; MONGOL CONQUEST OF THE ABBASID CALIPHATE; MONGOL INVASION OF EUROPE) diverted men, money, and attention from its vigorous pursuit. Speeded up in the 1260s, after the accession of Kublai Khan (1216–94) as the Mongols' supreme ruler (khakhan), the conquest of the Sung had begun as a war of sieges led by the famous General Sübedei (d. c. 1258). Even Kublai Khan was personally involved in the early period: in 1252, after he established his Honan capital Shang-tu (the poet Coleridge's Xanadu), he led 100,000 soldiers through Tibet into Yunnan, turned back a flank of the Sung, then marched his men through what is modern Laos to attack the Sung southern flank. By 1254, he had marched north to encounter his first Sung forces using elephants, which he fought with flaming arrows. His losses were heavy, however, and by 1254 he commanded only 20,000 soldiers. Nonetheless, the Mongols under Kublai Khan's brother, Mangu Khan (1207?–59), won a series of brilliant campaigns between 1257 and 1259. The sudden death of Mangu Khan from dysentery halted the war and subsequently allowed the Sung to revive. In 1260, Kublai Khan was elected khakhan and did not turn

his full attention to subjugating the Sung until 1268. The Mongols led by Bayan (1237–95), Sübedei's grandson, won many battles, seizing many large Sung cities, including the never-before ravaged Sung capital of Hangchow (Hangzhou) in 1276, but the war dragged on in the outlying provinces. A loyal Sung force protected the boy emperor in a fleet in the Bay of Canton, where a Mongol fleet destroyed the Sung ships in a battle in 1279 (the emperor drowned). The Mongols had won, and their wish expressed in 1260 to unite China was fulfilled when Kublai Khan, placating the Chinese gentry by assuring property rights, established the Yüan dynasty. As khakhan, Kublai Khan gave little attention to the other areas of the huge Mongol Empire, and so each of the subsidiary khanates became almost independent kingdoms after the Sung capitulation. See also VIETNAMESE-MONGOL WAR OF 1257–88.

Mongol Conquests (1206–1405) Eurasian history relates many accounts of the victories of migrating pastoral nomads—the Huns, Magyars, Turks, and others—but none so fascinates and impresses the reader as that of the explosive Mongols. From a group of loosely knit tribes with a penchant for isolated raids, the Mongols, and other peoples attracted to their prowess, were transformed into a united and disciplined military machine that, by the end of the 13th century, controlled territories stretching from the Sea of Japan to the Mediterranean and from the Siberian steppes to the Arabian Sea. The uniting and disciplining force was Genghis (Jenghiz, Chingis) Khan (1167?–1227), originally named Temujin, whose organizing genius and charisma enabled him to become the Mongols' supreme ruler (khakhan) in 1206 (see GENGHIS KHAN, CONQUESTS OF). He molded the usually unruly tribes into a victorious army, conquering Central Asia and northern China by the time of his death. His descendants, assigned subordinate control in Mongol territories, completed his work, extending Mongol rule by 1300 over Persia (see MONGOL-PERSIAN WAR, SECOND), southern Russia (see MONGOL INVASION OF RUSSIA, SECOND), and most of China (see

MONGOL CONQUEST OF THE SUNG EMPIRE). The Mongols also stormed Europe (1237–42) but did not remain to govern it (see MONGOL INVASION OF EUROPE). A grandson, Kublai Khan (1216–94), founded China's Yüan dynasty in 1260 and made attempts to control Japan, Indochina, and northern India. But disunity among the Mongol leaders in the 14th century led to a weakening of control, the loss of Il-Khan Persia, the collapse of the Yüan dynasty, civil war in the Kipchak (Russian) territories (see GOLDEN HORDE DYNASTIC WAR), and a last blazing of Mongol intrepidity in the conquests of Tamerlane (see TAMERLANE'S INVASION OF RUSSIA), who was a Turk reared in the Mongol traditions. The Mongol tribes finally declined to warring among themselves. For almost 200 years, the incandescence of Mongol militance had amazed Asia and frightened Europe. See also TAMERLANE, CONQUESTS OF.

Mongol Invasion of Europe (1237–42)   Long proposed, the Mongol assault on Europe was carefully planned at a great assembly (kuriltai) in 1235, and by 1236, some 150,000 troops were marching west. A leisurely conquest of Russian principalities (1237–40) marked their entry into Europe and gained these territories for the Golden Horde (see MONGOL INVASION OF RUSSIA, SECOND). The winter of 1240 found the Mongols in Poland, where the brilliant strategies of General Sübedei (d. c. 1258) enabled them to attack Lublin, sack Sandomierz, rout the Poles at Boleshlav and Chmielnik, burn Cracow, and defeat 40,000 Poles, Germans, and Teutonic Knights at WAHLSTADT near Liegnitz (Legnica) in 1241. Liegnitz resisted entry and was leveled by the Mongols. Still energized, the Mongol army swiftly turned southward to Hungary over the Carpathian Mountains, entering from Galicia, marching from Moldavia into Transylvania and German Saxony, and reaching the Danube River. The Hungarians, frightened and weakened by battles with the Kipchaks, who were blamed for the coming of the Mongols, had little room to maneuver in the four-way pincer action initiated by the Mongols. King Bela IV (1206–70) of Hungary mistakenly thought the main Mongol force would come from the north (near Pest, now Budapest) and sent some troops along the Sajo River. The Battle of MOHI in 1241 crippled Hungary and allowed the Mongols to burn Pest (Christmas Day, 1241), make a westward raid into Austria, and then rest and rearm for the summer of 1242. There would have been a resumption of the campaign had not the death of the Mongols' supreme ruler (khakhan) Ögedei (d. 1241) summoned everyone back to Asia.

Mongol Invasion of Japan, First (1274)   In power in Korea, the Mongols were curious about Japan and issued their standard summons to surrender; Japan refused. Kublai Khan (1216–94) sent a Mongol-Korean fleet, which seized two offshore islands and then made a landing at Hakata (Fukuoka) in northern Kyushu. Japanese weapons proved to be inferior to those of the Mongols, and a Mongol bridgehead was almost fully established when a big storm wrecked part of the invaders' fleet. This and the gathering of more Japanese warriors compelled the Mongols to retreat back to Korea. Convinced that another invasion was due, the Hojo rulers of Japan erected fortifications. **Second Mongol Invasion of Japan** (1281). Angered because the Japanese had killed Mongol envoys and rejected Mongol suzerainty, Kublai Khan launched a large Mongol-Korean armada (4,500 junks with supposedly 150,000 men) from north China and Korea. The invaders again seized the offshore islands and again landed on northern Kyushu; they met a double-edged resistance: fortifications kept the Mongols from advancing inland, and a Japanese fleet made successful raids against the larger Mongol fleet. The fighting on land lasted two months; then a severe storm destroyed most of the armada. With their supplies running low, the Mongols were soon defeated; only a few thousand of them escaped death and managed to return to Korea. The Japanese, convinced of their islands' sacredness, gave credit to divine winds (kamikaze) sent by the gods for their reprieve. Kublai Khan forbore a third invasion attempt, and problems in his empire after his death in 1294 saved Japan thereafter from the Mongols.

Mongol Invasion of Russia, First (1221–23) A
pursuit of the renegade shah of Khwarizm after the
Mongol destruction of Bukhara, a city in central
Uzbek, brought the Mongols to Russia for the first
time. Two Mongol generals tracked the shah to the
Caspian area and found him dead in 1221. Their
armies then raided through Azerbaijan into Georgia, conquered the city of Tiflis (Tbilisi) in 1221,
ruined the town of Maragha, annihilated the population of Hamadan, and then (1222) entered the
steppes north of the Caucasus region. The Mongols
next confronted an alliance of Alans, Cherkess, and
Kipchak Turks (the last known as Polovtsians and
Cumans; perpetual enemies, they later figured in the
MONGOL INVASION OF EUROPE). The Kipchaks were
routed and fled west; the others, along with Russian
princes, were defeated at the Battle of the KALKA
RIVER in 1223. The Mongols then captured the
Genoese port of Sudak on the Crimean peninsula,
advanced up the Volga River to chastise the Muslim
Bulgars and Kangli Turks, and later returned to
Emperor Genghis (Jenghiz, Chingis) Khan
(1167?–1227) in Persia. This territory, to be assigned to Genghis Khan's eldest son, Jöchi (d. 1227),
became the Kipchak Khanate (the "Golden
Horde") after a battle at Kiev in 1240. **Second
Mongol Invasion of Russia** (1236–40). The earlier
Mongol invasion had not given the Golden Horde
control; its second khan (ruler), Batu (d. 1256)—he
of the golden tents that gave the khanate its nick-
name—had to fight to gain the Russian land he was
to rule. In 1236, Mongol divisions gathered in Great
Bulgaria near the Volga, destroyed that state and its
capital, and proceeded to march into Europe; forces
under Mangu (1207?–59), his friend Batu Khan, and
General Sübedei (d. c. 1258) paused to establish
Mongol suzerainty. In 1236, Mangu fought the
Bashkirs and Kipchaks in the area then called
"Great Hungary," driving the latter before him into
Hungary itself by 1241. Batu Khan remained after
the Mongols crossed the Volga into a politically
divided, weak Russia and annihilated the cities of
Riazan and Kolomna in 1237; he then moved into
central Russia, conquered the princedom of
Vladimir (Suzdal) in 1238, attacked Tozhok, and

advanced toward Novgorod but became bogged
down in a muddy spring thaw and turned back; he
rested for all of 1239 until fresh Mongol troops and
horses overcame heavy losses. In 1240, Batu Khan's
forces attacked the middle Dnieper area, cultural
center of old Kievan Russia, devastated many cities,
destroyed Kiev for killing Mongol envoys, established complete control there, and afterward joined
other Mongol soldiers as they marched toward Poland.

Mongol Invasions of India (1221–1398) Unlike
those in Persia, China, and Europe, the Mongol
raids into India lacked detailed plans for total conquest. The earliest raid was an accidental result of
the FIRST MONGOL-PERSIAN WAR; the son of
Khwarizm's shah, Jalal-ad-Din (d. 1231), had escaped Mongol clutches, mobilized Khorasan, fled to
Afghanistan and further mobilized, then moved to
the Hindu Kush (mountains). The Mongols under
Genghis (Jenghiz, Chingis) Khan (1167?–1227) followed Jalal-ad-Din, fought the slaughterous 1221
Battle of BAMIAN, and then quickly pursued Jalal-
ad-Din into India to fight the strategically remarkable Battle of the INDUS RIVER the same year. The
Mongols also conducted raids into India in 1241,
1292, and from 1299 to 1308, chiefly in the vicinity
of Lahore in the Punjab. The city of Delhi was
threatened by them in 1329; the biggest campaign
in India, however, occurred nearly 70 years later in
1398 during the Mongol invasion under Tamerlane
(Timur) (1336–1405), which resulted in Delhi's
destruction (see TAMERLANE'S INVASION OF INDIA).

Mongol Invasions of Korea (1231–41) The murder of a Mongol envoy in 1231 caused Ögedei (d.
1241), son of Genghis (Jenghiz, Chingis) Khan
(1167?–1227) and the second supreme ruler (khakhan) of the Mongol Empire, to order an invasion
led by General Sübedei (d. c. 1258). Korea had
suffered incursions as early as 1218 as a result of
Genghis Khan's continuing struggles with Chin vassal states, but relations generally had been amicable.
Sübedei's Mongol invasion secured the submission

of the larger Korean cities, and Mongol governors were put in charge. However, a rebellion in 1232 caused the frightened puppet king of Korea to flee his country. Ordered to appear at Karakorum, the capital of the Mongols, the king refused, and in 1235 Ögedei dispatched a punitive expedition to Korea. The slow-paced Mongol expedition took six years to regain control; the king submitted, sent hostages, and was reinstalled as puppet ruler.

Mongol-Persian War, First (1218–21) The Mongol war initiated by Genghis (Jenghiz, Chingis) Khan (1167?–1227) against Persia, then made up of Khwarizm, Transoxiana, and Khorasan, was the bloodiest conflict ever fought by the Mongols. Unexpected, it was the sad result of Genghis Khan's attempt to prepare a peaceful future for his territories. Genghis Khan had interrupted his fighting with the Chin Empire (see GENGHIS KHAN'S WAR WITH THE CHIN EMPIRE) to come to the aid of Muslim Turks opposed in Kara-Khitai ("Black Cathay") by an usurper, the former king of the Naimans, defeated earlier in the century. Liberated by two divisions of Mongols, Kara-Khitai lay to the east of Khwarizm, and Genghis Khan sent a peaceful Mongol trade mission to its oppressive and ambitious shah. Afraid of spies, some men of Khwarizm seized the caravan and executed the mission's members. Genghis Khan demanded reparation; receiving none, he declared war (1218) on Persia. Pillaging and sacking all cities that refused to surrender, the 200,000-man Mongol army saved only engineers and artisans (whom they recruited) as it smashed Utrar and Khojend in 1219. Once subjugated, the conquered Persian cities were allowed to rebuild and to resume trade. The Khwarizmian shah fled, and the Mongols pursued him; his flight resulted in the destruction of BUKHARA (1220), the sacking of the capital, Samarkand (1220), and the surrender of Herat and Merv (1220). The war continued with the 1221 pursuit of the shah's heir into Afghanistan, the destruction of BAMIAN, the MONGOL INVASION OF INDIA, the Battle of the INDUS RIVER and the destruction of suddenly rebellious Herat and Merv. By 1221, Genghis Khan's empire stretched from Peking to the Aral Sea, and in 1222 he rested during the FIRST MONGOL INVASION OF RUSSIA before renewing his war with the Hsia (see GENGHIS KHAN'S SECOND WAR WITH THE HSIA EMPIRE).

Second Mongol-Persian War (1230–43). The escape of Jalal-ad-Din (d. 1231), son of the defeated shah of Khwarizm, from the Battle of the Indus River led him to a cordial reception in Delhi; he married the sultan's daughter, gained his father-in-law's help, and recrossed the Indus (1225) after inflicting punishment on Lahore and the Punjab. Occupying dominions formerly controlled by a brother in western Mesopotamia (Iraq), Jalal-ad-Din's forces captured Tabriz (1225) and Tiflis (Tbilisi) in Georgia, took Armenia (1227), and defeated a small Mongol army. In 1230 a large Mongol force was sent by Khakhan Ögedei (d. 1241) to crush him; the force surrounded him at Diyarbakr in 1231, only to have him escape to his death in Kurdistan that year. Pushed westward by expansionist zeal, the Mongols continued warfare from a center near Azerbaijan, systematically conquering Syria, Syrian Mesopotamia, and Anatolia (Turkey). They attacked Christian kingdoms like Georgia and Armenia (1235–36) to keep lines of communications open for a war in Europe set for 1236–37. The Mongols' westward march shattered Georgian unity, gutted Armenia's capital (1239), and, despite the eventual MONGOL INVASION OF EUROPE, buffeted Muslim Rum (Byzantine Empire) in 1241, reducing it to vassalage by 1243. The major fighting ceased when the chief Mongol leader Khakhan Ögedei died in 1241; other leaders then returned to Karakorum, the Mongol capital, for the election of his replacement. However, continued warfare against Rum briefly gave the Mongol Empire a Mediterranean outlet.

Mongol Revolts of 1755–60   Numerous strong Mongol tribes, including the Dzungars, in Chinese or Eastern Turkistan and western Mongolia, were constant rebels on China's northwestern frontier. Chinese emperor Ch'ien Lung (Qianlong) (1711–99) dispatched armies under his able but ruthless general Chao-hui (Zhaohui) (1708–64) to subjugate these peoples and take control of the region. After some difficulty in 1757, Chao-hui defeated the Dzungars and other Mongols who had refused to pay annual tribute to the Chinese government and had killed officials sent to collect payments. Meanwhile, Muslims in southern Chinese Turkistan had revolted, and Chao-hui and his forces moved south to suppress these rebels, who finally submitted to Chinese rule after long, fierce battling. Chinese Turkistan and western Mongolia, including Dzungaria, became the Sinkiang-Uigur Autonomous Region under China's suzerainty. See also MUSLIM REBELLION IN CHINA.

Monks, War of the (1465) Although most Japanese were Buddhists by the 15th century, there were several Buddhist sects that vied with each other for power, land, and influence. Since the ninth century the Tendai had exerted authority from their monasteries on the Hiyesian, a large hill northeast of Kyoto, Japan's capital, while the Shin had established themselves within the capital. Both sects had warrior monks, and both had competed with each other for decades, but they had been kept in hand by the shoguns. However, when the shoguns, like the emperors, were reduced to mere figureheads, the antagonism between the sects broke into open conflict. The monks of Hiyesian marched into Kyoto and put the Hongwanji Temple, which was the headquarters of the Shin, to the torch and burned it to the ground. In the countryside the different sects also fought each other and destroyed property. These religious wars were one more manifestation of the general anarchy that prevailed in Japan during the fifteenth century. See also JAPANESE CIVIL WARS OF 1450-1550; ONIN WAR.

Monmouth's Rebellion (1685) The reign of King Charles II (1630-85) of England, Scotland, and Ireland, like his father's, contained impassioned struggles between the Crown and Parliament (see ENGLISH CIVIL WAR, FIRST OR GREAT). Religion, not money, was the chief concern, focusing on the Catholicism of James (1633-1701), duke of York, later crowned King James II (VII in Scotland) in 1685.

Political parties had emerged for the first time: the Tories supported James and Catholicism; the Whigs opposed both. Three Whig-controlled parliaments, attempting to exclude James, had been dissolved, and Charles had ruled without a parliament. The first earl of Shaftesbury, Anthony Ashley Cooper (1621-83), had proposed Charles's acknowledged but illegitimate son James Scot (1649-85), duke of Monmouth, as heir (see COVENANTERS' REBELLION OF 1679). After receiving some acclaim, Monmouth had been forced to flee to Holland by those fearing another civil war. After Charles II's death, he landed at Dorsetshire, England, where he proclaimed himself king and raised an army of 4,000 men. At the Battle of Sedgemoor, his army was routed by James's troops; Monmouth was captured and beheaded. Planned coordination with the COVENANTERS' REBELLION OF 1685 had failed.

Mons Graupius (Grampians), Battle of (A.D. 84) The Roman Empire's disastrous defeat in Germany in A.D. 9 (see TEUTOBURG FOREST, BATTLE OF THE) was later countervailed in the British Isles in 84, when the Romans were victorious over a horde of Picts in Highland Caledonia (Scotland). Led by Gnaeus Julius Agricola (40-93), Roman legions from 77 to 83 had conquered Wales and then advanced in 84 almost to modern Aberdeen. The historian Tacitus (56?-120?), in his *Life of Agricola*, reports that 11,000 Roman cavalry and infantrymen, the latter including loyal Britons, met and fought 30,000 Picts or Caledonians under Galgacus (Calgacus) (fl. 84) at Mons Graupius, an unidentified site in the Grampian Mountains. The battle was fierce; reportedly 10,000 Picts died; the Roman loss was 360. The victory kept the Picts from ever again seriously bothering the Romans, but they remained warlike north of the Roman territories—so much so that Emperor Hadrian (76-138) ordered the building of a wall from the Tyne River to the Solway Firth in 122. See also ROMAN CONQUEST OF BRITAIN.

Montenegrin-Turkish Wars   See TURKO-MONTENEGRIN WARS.

Montevideo, Siege of (1843–51) In the 1830s, two major political parties, the conservative Blancos and the liberal Colorados, evolved in Uruguay; the Blancos were mainly backed by ranchers, merchants, and the clergy, and their geographic strength was in the interior; the Colorados were strong in the port city of Montevideo and the coastlands. In 1835, Manuel Oribe (1796?–1857), a Blanco, was elected Uruguayan president and later became involved in factional strife with José Fructuoso Rivera (1790?–1854), a Colorado, who had been the country's former president. Rivera led a revolt that deposed Oribe in 1838 and took over the presidency, while Oribe fled to Buenos Aires and allied himself with Juan Manuel de Rosas (1793–1877), dictator of Argentina, who had meddled in Uruguayan affairs during the 1830s in the hope of taking control of the country, whose independent status he rejected (see ARGENTINE-BRAZILIAN WAR OF 1825–28). Britain and France sought to preserve Uruguay's independence and to protect their commercial interests in the area. Later, Rosas armed Oribe to begin a civil war (1842) against Rivera at Montevideo, which was besieged by Oribe's forces for eight years (1843–51); the Italian patriot Giuseppe Garibaldi (1807–82), in exile in Uruguay, was one of the defenders of Montevideo. British and French naval forces arrived in the area, occupied parts of Uruguay and Martín García Island at the mouth of the Uruguay River, and blockaded the Río de la Plata (1845–49). An Argentine provincial governor, Justo José de Urquiza (1800–1870), allied with the Colorados and led a revolt against Rosas. Oribe, who was forced to abandon the siege of Montevideo, signed a treaty (1851) allowing the Colorado government to stay in power. Fearful of Argentine annexation of Uruguay, Brazil supported Urquiza against Rosas, and the Uruguayan Blancos and Colorados joined temporarily in a successful coalition to defeat the Argentine dictator. At the Battle of Monte Caseros on February 3, 1852, Urquiza and some 20,000 insurgents, including Argentines, Uruguayans, and Brazilians, decisively defeated Argentine government troops under Rosas, who fled to England, thus ending his tyrannical rule and his threat to Uruguayan independence. See also ARGENTINE CIVIL WAR OF 1859.

Moorish-Christian Wars in Spain See SPANISH CHRISTIAN-MUSLIM WARS.

Moorish-Frankish Wars See FRANKISH-MOORISH WARS.

Moors' Conquest of Spain See MUSLIM CONQUEST OF SPAIN.

Morant Bay Rebellion (1865) In 1865, impoverished peasants on the British island of Jamaica petitioned Queen Victoria (1819–1901) for permission to use government-held lands for planting, but were denied. Discontent centered in the Jamaican parishes of St. Ann and St. Thomas, where a mob of natives stormed and set fire to the courthouse in Morant Bay while the parish council was in session; the chief magistrate and 18 other white persons were killed. Declaring martial law, Jamaica's Governor Edward John Eyre (1815–1901) ruthlessly suppressed the rebellion, one of whose leaders, George William Gordon (d. 1865), a member of the Merchants and Free Persons of Color, was tried, convicted, and executed. Eyre, who had exaggerated the extent of the threat of the native rebels to the white planters, induced the Jamaican assembly to vote itself out of existence. In 1866, he was recalled to England, and the British Parliament established Jamaica as a crown colony under a new royal governor.

Morgan's Raids on Panama (1668–71) Welsh-born British buccaneer Henry Morgan (1635?–88) was important as a Crown-paid harasser of ships on the Spanish Main (South America's coastal areas between Panama and the Orinoco River). In 1668, he directed a fleet of 36 ships and some 2,000 buccaneers to the Isthmus of Panama, where he and his fellows stormed the supposedly impregnable Spanish fort-city of Porto Bello, defeated a large

Spanish force, and sacked the city. They then hacked their way across the isthmus and dallied as pirates in the eastern Pacific for awhile. In early 1671, Morgan's men defeated a large Spanish force near Panama City, which they looted and burned. Morgan then deserted his followers, returned to his ship, and made off with most of the booty. Because the latter raid had occurred after an Anglo-Spanish peace treaty, Morgan was escorted back to England to face charges of piracy. But Anglo-Spanish relations had deteriorated drastically by the time of his arrival, and he was knighted (1673) and made deputy governor of Jamaica (1674), where he spent the rest of his life.

Moriscos, Revolt of the (1568–71) Because the Moriscos (Spanish Muslims forcibly baptized as Christians) continued to speak, write, and dress like Muslims, they suffered persecution by the Spanish Christians (King Philip II [1527–98] of Spain forbade the Moriscos' language and traditions in 1566). Harsh subjugation of the Moriscos in Andalusia, a large region in southern Spain, led to a revolt in Alpujarra on December 25, 1568. In retaliation for heavy damage to Granada by the Moriscos, Spanish royal troops slaughtered many Morisco rebels at Alfajarali Pass in 1569. Don Juan (John of Austria) (1547–78) was ordered to terminate the revolt, and by 1571 his forces had successfully suppressed the Moriscos in Andalusia. The Moriscos, relocated and scattered throughout Spain, continued their particular Muslim ways until 1605–9, when they were expelled from Spain by royal order and settled mainly in North Africa.

Mormon War See UTAH WAR.

Moroccan War of 1907–12 At the start of the 20th century, major European powers vied for political and commercial influence in Morocco, which France and Spain agreed by a secret treaty (1904) to partition eventually between them. At the Algeciras Conference (1906), the powers reaffirmed Morocco's territorial integrity and trade opportunities for all and entrusted the French and Spanish with policing the country. In 1907, Moroccans rioting against foreign workers in Casablanca were violently crushed by French troops, who killed several thousand persons and occupied the city. Native opposition to foreign encroachment persisted. In 1908, Morocco's Sultan Abd al-Aziz IV (1880–1943), who was accused of neglecting the Muslim culture, was deposed by his brother, who was declared sultan at Fez in 1909 but could not maintain order and had to secure help from the French and Spanish. Rif tribesmen attacked Spanish workers in Melilla on Morocco's coast (see RIF WARS); Spanish troops suffered defeat (1909). A Rif attack on Fez brought on a French advance and occupation of the city. Germany was upset by French military movements, felt its interests were threatened in Morocco, and seemed to threaten war with France upon the arrival of the German gunboat *Panther* at Morocco's Atlantic port of Agadir (1911). Germany and France averted war through negotiations, resulting in the former recognizing French authority in Morocco in return for the latter's cession of some French territory in the Congo, Africa, to Germany. Morocco's sultan signed the Treaty of Fez (March 30, 1912), agreeing to a French protectorate over his country; subsequently, France and Spain split Morocco into four zones, with the French ruling most of the area.

Moro Wars (1901–13) The Moros are Muslim tribespeople who inhabit central and western Mindanao, the second largest island in the Philippines. They have lived there for centuries, quite apart from the rest of the Filipino people, most of whom are Christians. The Spanish, who ruled the islands until 1898, when they were driven out by Americans (see SPANISH-AMERICAN WAR), let them follow their age-old way of life and did not try to convert them, but the Americans felt differently. They wanted them to become assimilated, but the Moros resisted with sporadic outbreaks beginning in 1901. In 1903, they attacked American troops stationed near Lake Lanos in the interior of Mindanao. On the nearby island of Jolo in 1906, some 600 rebellious Moros who had taken refuge inside the crater of a large volcano (Mt. Dajo) were slaughtered by U.S. troops under General Leonard Wood (1860–1927). This raised a cry of indignation from the public. Fighting ceased after June 1913, and the Moros continued to practice their religion and traditions in peace.

Mountain Meadows Massacre (1857) Relations between the Mormons (Latter-day Saints) and the U.S. government were tense and suspicious when a band of 140 emigrants from Arkansas passed through southern Utah in September 1857 on their way to California. They camped in a valley called Mountain Meadows and were attacked by Paiute Indians. They drew their wagons into a circle, dug trenches, and defended themselves for several days. Then a group of white men approached and offered to escort them to safety if they would disarm. As soon as they had handed over their guns, they were murdered on the spot; only 17 infants were spared. The Mormons later admitted that they had directed the Indian attack and were responsible for the wanton killings, but it was not until 1874 that John Doyle Lee (1812–77), a fanatical Mormon who apparently led the killers, was arrested. Convicted of murder, Lee was executed at Mountain Meadows in 1877.

Mozambican Civil and Guerrilla Wars of 1976–92 The Front for the Liberation of Mozambique (FRE-LIMO), which had spearheaded the successful armed independence movement against Portuguese rule (see MOZAMBICAN WAR OF INDEPENDENCE), installed a marxist government and became the only legal political party in Mozambique. By 1976, most of the whites with technical skills had fled. There were shortages of food and imported goods, and these ills were exacerbated by the government's policies of nationalizing all industry, banks, transportation, and privately owned urban land, of increasing taxes, and of pushing for the collectivization of agriculture. Discontent was rampant, as were corruption and lawlessness. The government dealt harshly with rebellious activities;

"people's tribunes" sent many persons to reeducation camps, and the prisons were packed to capacity. Mozambican black guerrillas made raids into neighboring white-ruled Rhodesia (Zimbabwe), clashing with Rhodesian troops and causing the border between the countries to be closed in 1976. Clashes continued and the border remained closed until early 1980, when Rhodesia gained its independence. FRELIMO's marxist regime tried to curb increasing attacks against it by several anticommunist factions, including the Mozambican National Resistance (MNR), which sabotaged rail and communications lines and oil pipelines throughout the country. FRELIMO troops battled South African forces trying to destroy bases in Mozambique from which the rebel African National Congress (ANC) launched raids into South Africa. President Samora Moisès Machel (1933–) of Mozambique took personal control of the armed forces (1983) and stepped up actions against the rebel groups. In a 1984 agreement, Mozambique vowed to expel ANC rebels, and South Africa promised to stop supporting the right-wing MNR (also called Renamo). But covert South African aid for MNR guerrillas continued. Aided by Zimbabwe and Zambia, President Joaquim Chissanó (1939–), who replaced Machel in 1986, and his ruling FRELIMO regime waged a mainly defensive war against wandering, anti-government guerrilla bands, who engaged in wanton destruction, torture, and killing in rural villages throughout the country, which came to be known as "Mozambleak" in 1988–89 because of the thousands of deaths from war, starvation, and disease. About 2 million rural Mozambicans were driven from their lands, helping to further bankrupt the economy. In 1989, the MNR leader Afonso Dhlakama (1954–) began to talk with Roman Catholic clergy to devise a peace plan, although random rebel attacks and terrorism persisted. President Chissanó met with guerrilla leaders through mediation of Zimbabwe's President Robert Mugabe (1924–) and active church leaders. In 1990, the FRELIMO party abandoned the marxist system, agreed to many MNR demands, and adopted a new constitution that granted civil liberties and a free market economy and provided for multiparty elections and three branches of government. MNR rebels continued to sabotage power lines, railways, and government installations until negotiations between warring parties ended in a ceasefire agreement (October 4, 1992) signed by Chissanó and Dhlakama. Severe drought helped to deplete both sides. United Nations peacekeepers coordinated the disarming of guerrillas and organized multiparty elections, which took place in October 1994 with Chissanó winning the presidency. The return of 1.7 million Mozambican refugees officially ended in mid-1995.

Mozambican War of Independence (1962–74) In 1962, several small nationalist groups seeking independence for Portuguese East Africa (Mozambique) gathered in Dar-es-Salaam, the capital of Tanzania, and formed a coalition called the Front for the Liberation of Mozambique (FRELIMO) under the leadership of Eduardo Mondlane (d. 1969). FRELIMO began training several hundred volunteers in guerrilla warfare tactics in Algeria, while black rebels carried on sporadic fighting against their Portuguese rulers in East Africa. In 1964, FRELIMO was ready to take to the field, and its troops soon overran the two northern provinces of Portuguese East Africa. The Portuguese were forced to send more troops and materiel to hold the south (this was an expensive drain on the national treasury). In 1969, Mondlane was murdered in Dares-Salaam by Portuguese agents, and a year later Samora Moises Machel (1933–   ), a marxist, assumed command of FRELIMO. He opened new fronts against the Portuguese (who maintained more than 40,000 soldiers in the country), and by the time of the 1974 military coup in Lisbon (a leftist regime was installed) his forces (no more than 10,000 strong) controlled the middle and northern provinces. The Portuguese attempted to negotiate a settlement with the rebels whereby Portugal would retain some rights, but FRELIMO refused. In 1974, a cease-fire was signed when Portugal agreed to grant Mozambique full independence. White rebels tried to sabotage the process of independence by seizing control of the government (1975), but they

were suppressed by FRELIMO and Portuguese troops. Machel was elected the first president of independent Mozambique in 1975. See also ANGOLAN WAR OF INDEPENDENCE; GUINEA-BISSAUAN WAR OF INDEPENDENCE.

Muhammad of Ghur, Conquests of (1175–1206) The greatest Ghurid leader, Mu'izz-ud-Din Muhammad ibn Sam (d. 1206), better known as Muhammad of Ghur, was one of the founders of Muslim rule in India. With his brother, who took the Ghurid throne, he came into power in 1162 and learned his military skill in successful wars for Ghurid control of Khorasan (he was enthroned himself in 1202). In 1173, he and his forces seized Ghazna (see AFGHAN WAR BETWEEN GHUR AND GHAZNA), and afterward he involved himself in 12 military campaigns in India from 1175 until his death. In 1179, he destroyed the Ghaznavid garrison in Peshawar. Subduing Sind in 1182, capturing the Ghaznavid principality of Sialkor (Kashmir) in 1185, taking Lahore in 1186, and conquering the Punjab in 1187, he completed the Ghurid conquest of the Ghaznavid empire in India; the Ghaznavids were driven east into the Bihar and Bengal regions, to be conquered later by the Ghurids about 1200. Only one of Muhammad's campaigns ended in defeat— that of 1191, when the Rajput rulers, including the western Chalukyas, overcame him at Taraori near Thanesar on the Sarsuti River. However, in 1192, he returned to the same spot to defeat them. The next year he conquered Delhi and continued to enlarge his empire in India by seizing Kannauj and sacking Benares (Varanasi) in 1194, taking the fortress of Gwalior in 1195, overcoming Bihar in 1197, and leading the first Ghurid campaign against Bengal in 1198 (destroying Indian Buddhism by accident). His rule was overbearing, because the Muslims were a minority and the Hindus were regarded, after extensive plundering, as only a colonial people. But the Indian people did not rebel, perhaps because of Muslim émigrés and their rumors of Mongol fighting in Persia (Iran). Assassinated in Lahore in 1206, Muhammad was ably succeeded by his slave lieutenant Qutb-ud-Din Aybak (d. 1210), who founded the "slave dynasty" (1206–90) and the Delhi sultanate, the forerunner of the later Mogul Empire. See also DELHI SULTANATE WARS WITH GHAZNA AND GHUR.

Munich Putsch See "BEER HALL PUTSCH."

Muqanna, Revolt of (A.D. 775–78) Muslim Shi'ites rejected the ruling Abbasid caliphate's basis for power, which derived from Abbas (d. 653), uncle of the prophet Muhammad (570–632); instead, they derived the caliphate from Ali (600?–661), husband of the Prophet's daughter Fatima (606–32). Shi'ite-dominated Khorassan in Persia rose in rebellion, despite the attempt of the Abbasid caliph, Muhammad al-Mahdi (742–86), to preserve himself by persecuting the opposition. The unorthodox responded by following al-Muqanna or Mokanna ("the Veiled Prophet") (d. 779), whose real name was Hashim ibn Hakim. Imbued with Shi'ite, Zoroastrian, and Manichaean beliefs, Muqanna spent about three years battling in the field before retiring to his fortress of Sanam. Defeated in 778, he committed suicide (779) and left the struggle over Muslim religious authority, still current today, in the hands of others.

Murrel's Uprising (1835) John A. Murrel (1794–1844), a wealthy plantation owner in Tennessee, led an outlaw band that engaged in stealing horses and slaves in several southern states. He planned a bizarre, large-scale slave uprising, hoping to establish an underworld empire in the South (on July 4, 1835, southern slaves were to rebel in Nashville, Memphis, Natchez, New Orleans, and other cities, and Murrel and his "army" were to take control). Authorities got word of Murrel's plans, and he was arrested. The uprising, already set to start, foundered without his leadership, though there were outbreaks in a few cities that had to be contained by force. Some 30 blacks and 15 whites were caught in Mississippi and Tennessee, found guilty of conspiracy, and hanged. Murrel himself was sent to prison for 10 years and died soon after his release.

Muslim-Byzantine Wars See BYZANTINE-MUSLIM WARS.

Muslim Civil War of A.D. 657–61 The Muslim governor of Syria, Mu'awiyah (602?–80), believed that Ali ibn Abi Talib (600?–661), the fourth caliph, was involved in the murder of his cousin, Uthman ibn Affan (d. 656), the third caliph (see MUSLIM REVOLT OF A.D. 656). To put down a revolt by Mu'awiyah, Ali invaded Syria and fought a prolonged battle at Siffin in 657. After three months of indecisive fighting, a truce was established, and negotiations were begun to determine who was the true caliph. Mu'awiyah proclaimed himself caliph in Jerusalem in 660. Ali was murdered the next year by a member of a Muslim sect that developed out of his own camp during the negotiations—the Kharijites, who believed that piety, not birthright, should be the criterion for ascension to the caliphate. Ali's oldest son, al-Hassan (628–73), yielded the caliphate under pressure from Mu'awiyah in 661. Mu'awiyah became the first Ummayyad caliph and proclaimed Damascus the new Muslim capital that same year. Two Islam sects were thus created: the Shi'ites, who believe in the divine right of the sons of Ali, and the Sunnis, who refuse to recognize Ali and support the Ummayyad clan.

Muslim Civil War of A.D. 680–92 The death of the Ummayyad caliph Mu'awiyad (602?–80) led to new fighting by Muslim claimants to the caliphate. Mu'awiyah's son, Yazid I (645?–83), became caliph but was widely opposed in Syria and Mesopotamia. The Kufans, a Muslim group, chose Husayn ibn Ali (629–80), the second son of Ali ibn Abi Talib (600?–661), as caliph (see MUSLIM CIVIL WAR OF A.D. 657–61). Husayn advanced from Mecca to fight Yazid, whose supporters attacked and killed him after the Kufans had deserted him at Kerbela in 680. The Meccans and Medinans, led by Abdallah ibn Zubayr (d. 692), successfully defended Mecca against Yazid's army in 682. As a result, after Yazid died in 683, Zubayr was recognized as the caliph of Arabia, Mesopotamia, and Egypt. However,

Zubayr's supporters were defeated by the forces of another caliphate claimant, Marwan ibn al-Hakam (623–85), at the Battle of Marj Rahit near Damascus in 684. Despite al-Hakam holding the caliphate, tribal warfare between Muslims intensified in the Arab empire and a split developed between northern and southern Muslims. After al-Hakam's death, his son Abd al-Malik (646–705) became caliph and attempted to unify the various Arab tribes. His Syrian forces besieged Mecca and killed Zubayr, who had been ruling as a rival caliph.

Muslim Civil War of A.D. 743–47   The Muslim empire, ruled by three weak caliphs between 743 and 744, was torn by rebellion among various dissident groups until Marwan II (d. 750) became caliph. Marwan, the last Ummayyad caliph, used force to defeat rebels in Syria, Mesopotamia, Arabia, and Persia. However, a strong rebel group in the Persian province of Khorasan, the Abbasids, joined the Shi'ites, who opposed the ruling Ummayyads, and raised a great rebellion in 747 (see ABBASID REVO-LUTION OF A.D. 747–50).

Muslim Civil War of A.D. 809–13   In 802, Abbasid caliph Harun al-Rashid (766–809) declared that his two sons should rule the Muslim empire jointly after his death. As outlined in the Meccan Document, al-Rashid proclaimed son Muhammed al-Amin (785–813) his successor as caliph, and son Abd Allah al-Ma'mun (785–833) ruler of Khorasan and the eastern half of the empire, but under his brother's imperial rule. Upon al-Rashid's death, al-Ma'mun revolted, backed by some of the Khorasanian guard under the Persian general Tahir ibn Husain (d. 822). Tahir's forces routed al-Amin's troops in Khorasan, marched to Mesopotamia, seized most of the caliph's provinces, and took Baghdad in 811 after a two-year siege. In 812, al-Amin surrendered but was killed the following year during an attempted escape. Al-Ma'mun was now recognized as the caliph, but the brothers' war had weakened the central authority of the caliphate, allowing Syria, Mesopotamia, and Egypt to grow beyond the

caliph's control for a decade. See also KHORASAN REBELLION OF A.D. 806–09; SHI'ITE REBELLION OF A.D. 814–19.

Muslim Civil War of A.D. 861–70   The inclusion of Turks into high offices of the caliphate caused major disruptions in the Muslim empire. Powerful Turkish military leaders manipulated the government, installing four separate caliphs between 861 and 870. The caliphs were murdered or dethroned when they displeased the Turks. Because of the lack of a strong, stable central authority, provincial governments were wracked by various religious and military revolts in Persia, Transoxania (region of Turkistan), Mesopotamia, Arabia, and Egypt. In 869, black slaves began a rebellion in southern Mesopotamia that lasted for nearly 15 years (see Zanj Rebellion). It is unclear why the Turks discontinued their radical, murderous rule within the caliphate, but after draining the Muslim treasuries to maintain the army and the court and receiving little income from the provinces, the Turkish leaders ended their rule, allowing al-Mo'tamid (d. 892) to govern unharassed as caliph from 870 until his death.

Muslim Civil War of A.D. 936–44   The strength of the caliphate was never regained after its dissolution during the reign of the Turkish guards in the MUSLIM CIVIL WAR OF A.D. 861–70. By 936, the caliphate consisted of little more than the province of Baghdad. The Abbasid caliph, Ahmad ar-Radi (d. 940), appointed an adventurer, Muhammad ibn-Ra'iq (d. 942), commander of the caliphate's army and gave him financial power over the realm (the Abbasid dynasty ruled only over spiritual matters afterward). Ibn-Ra'iq gained control of Syria, defeating the Hamdanids there and repulsing an invasion by the Ikhshidites of Egypt. After the death of Ibn-Ra'iq, the Hamdanids captured the cities of Aleppo and Hims and occupied northern Syria. In 944, the war ended with an insecure truce.

Muslim Civil War of A.D. 945–48   The Hamdanids, led by Sayf al-Dawla (d. 967), fought against the invading Ikhshidites of Egypt for control of Syria. Aleppo in northwestern Syria was held by the Hamdanids, who won victories over the Ikhshidites at first but became involved in checking incursions by the Byzantines in the north and had to give up central and southern Syria to the Ikhshidites by 948. Al-Dawla used skillful military strategy to ward off the Byzantines and hold onto northern Syria. See also BYZANTINE-MUSLIM WAR OF A.D. 960–76.

Muslim Civil War of A.D. 976–77   Southern and central Syria were controlled by the Fatimids after this Muslim sect, which claimed descent from Fatima (606?–32), daughter of the prophet Muhammad (570–632), had invaded and defeated the Ikhshidites at Ramleh in 969 (see MUSLIM CIVIL WAR OF A.D. 945–48). The Hamdanids in northern Syria allied themselves with the Karmathians (who had been thwarted in their invasions of Egypt by the Fatimids in 971 and in 974) and drove the Fatimids out of Syria in 976. With new forces, the Fatimids returned the next year and routed the Hamdanids and Karmathians at the Battle of Ramleh. The southern half of Syria was now under Fatimid rule. See also BYZANTINE-MUSLIM WAR OF A.D. 960–76.

Muslim Civil War of 1102–8   While the crusaders occupied the city of Edessa (see CRUSADE, FIRST), Syria and northern Mesopotamia were continually wracked by internal warring between the strong Seljuk Turks, at that time holding most of the cities in central and southern Syria, and rival Muslim groups, holding mainly the rural land. Seljuk leader Kilij Arslan I (d. 1108) seized control of the chief city in northern Mesopotamia, Mosul, in 1102. Opposed by another Seljuk leader, Ridwan (d. 1117), Kilij led his Turkish forces against Ridwan's at the Battle of Khabur River in 1108. Kilij was defeated and killed. Afterward Ridwan and his successors attempted, without much success, to subjugate other Muslim and Turkish groups. See also BYZANTINE-SELJUK TURK WAR OF 1064–81; BYZANTINE-SELJUK TURK WAR OF 1110–17.

Muslim Conquest of Persia (A.D.   634–51)   Sweeping out of Arabia, Muslim warriors and marauders, followers of the Islamic prophet Muhammad (570–632), attacked the Byzantine and Sassanid Persian empires (see BYZANTINE-MUSLIM WAR OF A.D. 633–42). They relentlessly pursued and successfully fought Byzantine armies in the eastern Byzantine provinces of Syria and Palestine, capturing important cities and subjugating the native peoples (634–44). The Muslims' eastward advance was temporarily set back in Mesopotamia (Iraq), at the Battle of the Bridge (634) on the Euphrates, where the Sassanid Persians routed and drove them back to the city of Hira. The pursuing Persians were stopped at the Battle of Buwayb (635), south of Kufah (in Iraq). A new Muslim army (about 30,000 strong), sent by the imperial Muslim caliph Omar (581?–644), entered Mesopotamia and was victorious over a 50,000-man Persian army at the Battle of al-Qadisiyah (637). Later that year the Sassanid winter capital at Ctesiphon on the Tigris (south of Baghdad) was captured and sacked by the Arabs, who again won at the Battle of Jalula (December 637), some 50 miles to the north. Central Persia (Iran) came under the control of the invaders, who continued to battle and finally won the decisive victory at Nahavand (641), where the Muslims, supposedly outnumbered five to one, feigned defeat on the battlefield, withdrew with the Persians in pursuit, surprised them between two narrow mountain passes, and slew about 100,000 of them. (By then invading Arabs had also nearly conquered Egypt after taking the cities of Pelusium and Heliopolis in 640.) In Persia, opposition to the Arabs steadily fell apart until the last Sassanid king, Yazdegard III (d. 651), who had taken refuge in Merv, was murdered; Muslim supremacy in the country had been achieved.

Muslim Conquest of Spain (A.D. 711–18)   At Ceuta, in northwestern Africa, Muslim Arabs urged their viceroy (governor) Musa ibn-Nusayr (660?–714?) to launch an invasion of Visigoth-controlled Spain to regain lost Arab territory. In 711,

Musa dispatched an army of Arabs and Berbers, led by Tarik ibn-Ziyad (d. c. 720), which crossed the Strait of Gibraltar and decisively defeated the Visigoths under their last king, Roderick (d. 711), at Laguna de Janda, near the Guadalete River (Río Barbate) on July 19, 711; while attempting to escape, Roderick was either slain or drowned. The Visigoths, who had sown seeds of disunity in Roderick's army, now joined Tarik, whose forces moved to the north, pillaging the country and seizing Córdoba and the Visigothic capital, Toledo. Musa himself arrived with 18,000 Arabs at Algeciras in June 712, moved inland, and seized Medina-Sidonia, Seville, and Merida (June 30, 713). He was joined by Tarik, who had gained the support of Spanish Jews, and continued his successful march. A separate campaign under Tarik was victorious in the northwest, at León and Astorga. In 713, Musa returned home to Damascus, Syria, and left his son Abd-al-Aziz (d. 716) as the first emir (Muslim commander) of southern Spain. Abd-al-Aziz made peace with the Visigothic lord at Murcia, granting him some independence in return for tribute and cooperation. About 714, Saragossa (Zarogoza) fell to the Muslims; Barcelona fell about 717 and was opened to Arab shipping from the eastern Mediterranean. By 718, the Spanish Christians and Visigoths had been pushed into the mountains of the north and west, and the Muslims or Moors of Spain had advanced as far north as the Pyrenees Mountains. See also FRANKISH-MOORISH WARS.

Muslim Dynastic War of 1196–1200 To forestall a succession struggle after his death, Saladin (1137?–93), sultan of Egypt and Syria, founder of the Ayyubid dynasty, divided most of his Muslim empire among his male relatives. He failed, however, to designate a successor to the sultanate of Cairo. In 1196, a struggle for power in Cairo began between Saladin's sons—one the ruler of Syria, the other of Egypt—and grew to include their uncle al-Malik al-Adil (d. 1218), who fought on both sides until his own forces gained supremacy in battle in Egypt in January 1200. Ruling as the sultan, al-Adil took complete control of Saladin's empire, reuniting

Syria and Egypt under his leadership. Constant family friction, however, weakened the Ayyubid line, which eventually ceased to exist when its last sultan was murdered by rebellious Mamluks (Mamelukes) in 1250.

Muslim Rebellion in China (1863–77) Muslim tribes in Eastern or Chinese Turkistan, west of Tibet, rebelled against their Manchu (Ch'ing) overlords in 1863. They were led by Yakub Beg (1820–77), who established an independent government at Kashgar. The Russian government, which controlled the adjacent territory, feared the revolt would spread to their lands and with this pretext sent Russian troops to occupy the northern areas of Turkistan around Kuldja on the Ili River in 1871. The following year the Russians concluded a commercial treaty with Beg, thereby recognizing his sovereignty. But the Manchus did not take rebellions lightly and ordered General Tso Tsungt'ang (1812–85) to restore order in Turkistan. The general and his army advanced very slowly over the rough terrain and by 1876 reached Kashgar. There Beg's forces were beaten in battle, and by 1877, the defeated Muslims again acknowledged China's authority over them. The Russians were reluctant to leave the territory they had occupied, but in 1881 agreed to a treaty in which most of the land reverted to China and Russia received 9 million rubles to pay for the cost of the occupation. See also MONGOL REVOLTS OF 1755–60.

Muslim Revolt of A.D. 656 After the murder of the third caliph, Uthman ibn Affan (d. 656), Ali ibn Abi Talib (600?–661), the cousin and son-in-law of the prophet Muhammad (570–632), became the fourth caliph and immediately faced a revolt by two followers of the Prophet, Talha (d. 656) and Al-Zubair (d. 656). The two Muslims, supported by the Prophet's widow A'ishah (614–78), raised a 30,000-man army and met Ali's forces near Basra in Mesopotamia (Iraq) on December 4, 656. "The Battle of the Camel," as the clash came to be called because A'ishsh sat on a camel amidst the soldiers, ended when both Talha and Al-Zubair were slain. A'ishah was captured and exiled. Turmoil about Ali's ascension to the caliphate continued, finally resulting in the MUSLIM CIVIL WAR OF A.D. 657–61. See also MECCA-MEDINA WAR.

Muslim Revolt of A.D. 699–701   Al-Hajjaj ibn Yusef (d. 714), Muslim governor of the eastern provinces of the caliphate, dispatched his famous Peacock Army (so called because of its colorful military dress) into what is now southeast Afghanistan to restore the Arab position after a smaller Muslim army had been stopped by the Afghans. The Peacock Army, led by Kindah tribesman Ibn al-Ash'ath (d. 704), suppressed the Afghan rebels and was ordered to remain in the area indefinitely. Ibn al-Ash'ath defied the order, as well as al-Hajjaj's demands for individual tribal homage, and, with part of the army, marched back to Mesopotamia, gathering support for his revolt along the way. In January 701, troops of al-Hajjaj encountered Ibn al-Ash'ath's force at Tustar and were defeated. Ibn al-Ash'ath then captured Basra and marched against al-Hajjaj at Kufa, near which the former won the Battle of Dayr al-Jamajim. Al-Hajjaj gathered Syrian reinforcements, consigned by the caliph Abd al-Malik (646–705), attempted unsuccessfully to negotiate a truce with Ibn al-Ash'ath, and decisively defeated Ibn's rebel army at the Battle of Maskin on the Dujail River in 701.

Mysore War, First (1767–69)   Established in 1600 to break the Dutch monopoly in India, the British East India Company enjoyed relatively easy prosperity until the mid-1700s, when the breakup of the cooperative Mogul empire and competition from the French caused it to seize Indian states for self-protection. Acquiring control of Bengal by 1765, the company had two formidable competitors for supremacy, Mysore (Karnataka) and the Maratha Confederacy (see MARATHA WAR, FIRST). Mysore, a Hindu state taken over in 1762 by its Muslim commander in chief, Haidar (Hyder) Ali Khan (1722–82), would have been a useful ally

against the Marathas, but the British East India Company alienated Haidar Ali in 1767 and continued to do so until Mysore's virtual extinction (1799). Mysore was attacked by the company's forces in 1767, which were victorious until Indian allies (Hyderabad and the Marathas) withdrew in 1768. Thereafter, Haidar began to win steadily, once threatening the company's government headquarters at Madras, until 1769, when peace was virtually dictated by Mysore. **Second Mysore War** (1780–84). Creditors forced the nawab (ruler) of Arcot to attempt to repay his debts by attacking Mysore; the British supported him. Allying himself with the Maratha Confederacy, Haidar Ali retaliated fiercely. His army appeared outside the walls of Fort St. George (1780), almost costing the company the Carnatic (Goa) region. British soldiers came to relieve Madras from attacks by the Marathas (1780), and the Marathas withdrew to make a separate peace. Haidar Ali died in 1782, and promised French military aid arrived too late to help his son, Tippoo (Tipu) Sahib (1749–99), so that Mysore was defeated. The 1784 Treaty of Mangalore restored conditions to the pre-1780 status. **Third Mysore War** (1790–92). Tippoo, young and ambitious but neither as bright nor as judicious as his father, was still angry at the British East India Company, which, under Lord Charles Cornwallis (1738–1805), wanted to annex Mysore. The company needed only a pretext to attack. Cornwallis excluded Tippoo's name from a 1790 list of the company's "friends," and Tippoo attacked in response. Refused alliances with the Marathas and Hyderabad, Tippoo's forces were still strong enough to withstand three British campaigns led personally by Cornwallis. The last campaign, a 1792 move against Mysore's capital at Seringapatam, cost Mysore half its territory. **Fourth Mysore War** (1799). Tippoo, understandably, regarded the British with hostility and showed his ire by receiving envoys from Napoleonic France and planting a "Freedom Tree" in the garden of his palace. A new British governor-general, Richard Wellesley (1761–1842), dedicated to both excising French power in India and annexing Mysore, attacked Seringapatam with help from Hyderabad in 1799. Tippoo was killed during the battle, and the lands left over after the Third Mysore War were divided: one half went to the British India Company and the northern territories to Hyderabad. The small remaining land was returned to the Hindu family cast out by Haidar Ali in 1762 before the First Mysore War.

N

Namibian War of Independence (1966–90) In 1966 a United Nations resolution terminated South Africa's mandate over the former German colony of South West Africa, also known as Namibia. The white-minority government of South Africa, however, refused to give up its administration and domination of the territory. Black nationalist Africans promptly established a guerrilla liberation front, the South West Africa People's Organization (SWAPO), and began to harass the whites. SWAPO was weak and ineffective at first; however, when the Portuguese were driven out of neighboring Angola (see ANGOLAN WAR OF INDEPENDENCE), the guerrillas were offered aid and bases there, as well as training by Cuban soldiers. The guerrilla war for independence escalated sharply. South African government troops began raiding guerrilla bases in Angola, while SWAPO forces hit back in Namibia. In 1976, the UN condemned South Africa for "illegal occupation" of the territory, and the following year the UN General Assembly recognized SWAPO as the sole legitimate representative of Namibia. In 1978, the UN called an international conference to resolve the conflict; South Africa's Prime Minister John Vorster (1915–83) agreed to free elections to be supervised by the UN to determine the fate of Namibia; he then reneged. In 1979, Vorster, now president, again rejected a UN proposal to settle the dispute. Two years later a peace conference in Geneva also failed to win concessions from the South African government; control of Walvis Bay, Na-

mibia's only deep-water port, was a major point of contention. The United States supported South Africa's refusal to withdraw from Namibia unless Cuban troops pulled out of Angola; a commission was set up to monitor a cease-fire agreement in 1984. A new, multiracial government was installed in Namibia by South Africa in 1985, but SWAPO's armed struggle continued because of lack of progress toward implementing UN Resolution 435 on independence for Namibia and the withdrawal of Cuban troops from Angola. In December 1988, a U.S.-mediated peace agreement linked to UN Resolution 435 was signed by South Africa, Cuba, and Angola, setting a timetable for Namibian independence; at the same time Cuba and Angola agreed to a phased withdrawal of Cuban troops from Angola. However, during Namibia's transition period, SWAPO forces based in southern Angola swarmed into Namibia on April 1, 1989, in violation of the peace agreement. Waiting for the guerrillas were Namibian security police, who killed several hundred of them and stopped the SWAPO incursions. Afterward, thousands of Namibian refugees and exiled SWAPO members, including Samuel S. Nujoma (1929–   ), longtime political leader, returned peacefully to Namibia. A Constituent Assembly was then elected to frame a constitution; Nujoma took office as president when South Africa relinquished its control and gave Namibia full independence on March 21, 1990. SWAPO gained a major electoral victory in 1994, and Nujoma remained president.

Naning War (1831–32) In the 17th and 18th centuries, many Minangkabau immigrants from Sumatra settled in the Malay state of Naning, near Malacca (Melaka), and paid an annual tribute to the Dutch East India Company, which dominated the area. The company, through mismanagement, became seriously in debt and was taken over by the Dutch government in 1799, at a time when the British and Dutch were intense rivals in the area (see ANGLO-DUTCH WAR IN JAVA). The Anglo-Dutch treaty of 1824 gave Malacca and the other "Straits Settlements" (Singapore and Pinang) to the British, who claimed they had inherited the rights to the tributes previously paid to the Dutch by the native peoples. Naning's ruler refused to hand over annually one-10th of his state's crops, demanded by the British in 1829. A British expedition was sent against Naning in 1831, but was defeated. Another expedition was mounted the next year and was victorious after three months of grueling fighting. This embarrassing and expensive war slowed British acquisition of trading and extraterritorial rights in the Malay peninsula for the next 40 years. See also PADRI WAR.

Nanking, Sack of ("Rape of Nanking") (1937–38) On December 13, 1937, at the beginning of the SINO-JAPANESE WAR OF 1937–45, the Japanese Imperial Army captured China's capital, Nanking (Nanjing), a port city of over 1 million people. An orgy of violence followed within a few days, lasting through January 1938. Japanese soldiers burned much of the city to the ground, raped more than 20,000 women, and killed at least 30,000 captive Chinese soldiers. They used prisoners for bayonet practice; they mutilated and beheaded people, and roasted them alive; they forced Chinese fathers to rape their daughters, and sons their mothers. The mindless Japanese depravity also included hanging persons by their tongues from hooks, burying others up to their necks and driving over them with tanks, and drowning still others in frozen lakes. Members of the international community in Nanking courageously established a "safety zone" to shelter Chinese refugees. One foreigner, John Rabe (d. 1950), a German Nazi businessman living there since 1908, attempted in vain to influence Adolf Hitler (1899–1945) to stop the savagery as more than 200,000 civilians were murdered. For 50 years afterward, Japan officially downplayed or denied the atrocities.

Napoleonic Wars (1803–15)   The FRENCH REVOLUTIONARY WARS gradually evolved into a prosecution of Napoleon's (1769–1821) personal ambitions. His incorporation of Piedmont and continued intervention in Italy, Germany, Switzerland, and the Netherlands aroused the distrust of the British, who defied the precarious Treaty of Amiens (1802) by retaining Malta and in 1803 declared war. Napoleon assembled a large army but could not deter Britain from systematically seizing French colonial possessions. His plans for a naval invasion of England were frustrated by weather, tides, and British blockades, and on October 21, 1805, the British fleet under Lord Horatio Nelson (1758–1805) dealt his doomed fleet a stunning defeat at the Battle of Trafalgar. Meanwhile, Napoleon, now emperor, annexed Genoa and crowned himself king of Italy, prompting formation in 1805 of the Third Coalition against him by Britain, Austria, Russia, and Sweden (see COALITION, WAR OF THE THIRD). By the Treaties of Tilsit in 1807, France made peace with Russia, whose troops helped the French defeat Sweden in 1808. Failing to subdue Britain, Napoleon instituted the Continental System, a costly and ultimately unsuccessful trade boycott. By 1809, Napoleon had redrawn the map of Europe, having placed relatives on the thrones of Spain and Naples and brought most of the continent into subjugation. Austria, seeing Napoleon preoccupied in Spain, attempted to regain autonomy. Napoleon soon entered Vienna but was held off both in Tirol and north of the Danube, where he was forced to backtrack at Essling-Aspern in May 1809. Heartened by this hint of weakness, the British launched an abortive expedition to the Netherlands, and small revolts sprang up across Europe. But Napoleon recrossed the Danube and defeated the Austrians at the Battle of Wagram in July 1809. The Peace of Schönbrunn, imposed by Napoleon on Austria in October 1809, relieved Austria of its Illyrian provinces. Napoleon turned his attention to Spain and Portugal (see PENINSULAR WAR) and was ultimately forced back into France. France's relations with Russia worsened, especially after Russia made peace with Britain in June 1812. Napoleon's INVASION OF RUSSIA was disastrous and a serious blow to his power. His Prussian allies, smelling weakness, formed a coalition with Russia, Sweden, and Austria to wage a "War of Liberation." After his defeat at the "Battle of the Nations" in Leipzig on October 16–19, 1813, Napoleon rejected a peace offer stipulating the Rhine and the Alps as France's boundaries and stubbornly held his ground. But in March 1814, Paris was captured by the allies, whereupon Napoleon abdicated and accepted exile in Elba. Louis XVIII (1755–1824) ascended the French throne. Remarkably, Napoleon was able to rally his followers and return triumphantly to Paris in March 1815. Louis fled, inaugurating the "Hundred Days" of Napoleon's attempt to rebuild his empire (see HUNDRED DAYS' WAR). But the alarmed allies rose against him, and in June 1815, after a brave showing at Ligny, he capitulated at Waterloo to the British under Sir Arthur Wellesley, Lord Wellington (1769–1852), reinforced by the Prussians under Gebhard von Blücher (1749–1819). Napoleon was permanently banished to the remote island of St. Helena, ending some 23 years of almost constant warfare. See also RUSSO-SWEDISH WAR OF 1808–9; TYROLEAN REBELLION OF 1809–10.

Napoleon's Invasion of Russia (1812)   Russian renunciation of the Continental System (Napoleon's scheme of economic warfare against Britain during the NAPOLEONIC WARS had been ruinous to Russia's economy), compounded by differences over French influence in Poland, Sweden, and the Balkans, caused Napoleon to invade Russia with his Grand Army of nearly 500,000 soldiers in June 1812. Outnumbered, the Russians retreated, destroying crops in their wake and stretching French supply lines thinner and thinner. After winning bitter battles at Smolensk (August 17) and

Borodino (September 7), Napoleon's troops entered Moscow (September 14), only to find themselves holding a city burned and gutted by its fleeing inhabitants. The Russians under Mikhail I. Kutuzov (1745–1813) repulsed Napoleon's further advances, and the czar refused to negotiate a truce. Nothing remained but retreat for the French, who were now seriously suffering from lack of food, severe cold, disease, and fatigue. The retreating French were decimated even more by Kutuzov's pursuing forces and incessant Cossack attacks, especially while crossing the Berezina River on November 26–28, 1812. Napoleon left his war-weary, tattered troops in December to return to Paris to put down a rumored plot against him and to raise a new army. Only about 30,000 French soldiers survived the invasion and the retreat. See also HUNDRED DAYS' WAR.

Navaho War of 1860–65   See APACHE AND NAVAHO WAR OF 1860–65.

Neapolitan Revolt of 1485–86   The harsh taxation policies of King Ferdinand I (1423–94) of Naples resulted in a revolt by the Angevin barons, who attempted to replace the king with either René II (1451–1508) of Lorraine or with Ferdinand's second son. The barons were suppressed through a series of arrests, trials, and executions in 1486. Later Ferdinand allied himself with Lorenzo de' Medici (1449–92) of Florence, leading Lodovico Sforza (1451–1508) of Milan, fearful of Ferdinand's intentions, to call on King Charles VIII (1470–98) of France to intervene in Italian affairs. See also ITALIAN WAR OF CHARLES VIII.

Neapolitan Revolt of 1820–21   Soldiers under Muratist officers, followers of the former French king of Naples Joachim Murat (1767–1815), who had tried to carry out democratic reforms, rebelled at the town of Nola on July 1–2, 1820, against the reactionary government of Ferdinand I (1751–1825), king of the Two Sicilies (Naples and Sicily). When the regular army refused to oppose the rebels, the frightened king granted a constitution to Naples. In October 1820, the new Neapolitan parliament cancelled its ruling agreement with the Sicilian junta that opposed the constitution and dispatched forces under Pietro Colletta (1775–1831) to suppress the Sicilian government. When another revolt occurred at Palermo, Sicily, the Holy Alliance of European powers met and called for troops to intervene and restore order—that is, despotism. Ferdinand, sent to the then Austrian city of Ljubljana (now the capital of Slovenia) to stop imperial intervention, betrayed his orders by requesting aid, and in March 1821, Austrian forces approached the Neapolitan border, the rebel army fled, and Ferdinand reestablished himself on the throne and repudiated the constitution. An imperial occupation force remained until 1827, carrying out a tyrannical repression in Naples.

Neerwinden, Battle of (1693)   During the fourth summer of the WAR OF THE GRAND ALLIANCE, King William III (1650–1702) of England, commander of the Alliance armies, took up a strong position near the village of Neerwinden in eastern Belgium on July 29, 1693. His formidable center was aided by flanks fronted by small streams; it was attacked so strongly by the undefeated French that reserves were called from the flanks. The French then charged both weakened flanks simultaneously, buckled the Alliance line, and forced many Alliance troops into the streams to drown. The charges cost the French over 8,000 men; in contrast, the Alliance forces had lost about 18,000 in their third major defeat of the war. See also STEENKERKE, BATTLE OF.

Netherlands War of Independence   See EIGHTY YEARS' WAR.

Neuchâtel, Insurrection at (1856–57)   At the end of the NAPOLEONIC WARS, the Congress of Vienna (1814–15) accorded Neuchâtel an unstable dual status as a canton in the reorganized Swiss Confederation and as the personal property of the king of Prussia. The dissatisfied Swiss, caught up in the spirit of the revolutions of 1848, revolted and made the canton a republic (1848), angering the major powers, which in the London Protocol (1852) acknowledged the rights of Prussia's King Frederick William IV (1795–1861) but advised him not to take power unless they concurred. Nonetheless, Frederick William encouraged Neuchâtel's royalist aristocrats to attempt a coup d'état there in 1856; it failed, and 530 of the aristocrats were arrested. Neuchâtel refused to release them, and Prussia prepared for war. The Swiss armed too, but action was delayed while diplomatic endeavors were made by French emperor Napoleon III (1808–73). When France announced support for Neuchâtel and Britain backed France, Frederick William accepted a face-saving suggestion: he would retain for life the title prince of Neuchâtel, but would renounce his sovereignty over it. Neuchâtel returned to its former state as a republic and a canton, the aristocrats were released, and both armies were demobilized, much to the relief of Europe.

Neville's Cross, Battle of (1346)   When the English longbowmen of King Edward III (1312–77) defeated the French at Crécy in 1346 and the French asked the Scots for a diversionary campaign, Scottish forces of King David II (1324–71) invaded Yorkshire. Encountering an English army much stronger than theirs, the Scots were defeated at Neville's Cross on October 17, 1346, and David was taken prisoner. During David's 11-year "dalliance" at the elegant English court, Robert Stewart, later Robert II (1316–90), ruled in David's stead. He recaptured Berwick, taken after Halidon Hill (see HALIDON HILL, BATTLE OF); and yielded power when the thoroughly Anglicized and heavily ransomed David returned as Scottish king in 1357.

New Caledonian Uprising of 1984–85   In the French overseas territory of New Caledonia in the South Pacific, ethnic Kanaks (Melanesians) under the leadership of Jean-Marie Tjibaou (1937–89) established the Front de Libération Nationale

Kanake et Socialiste (FLNKS), a militant independence movement, in 1984. In November, violent clashes began occurring between Kanaks and European settlers (mainly French), called *caldoches*, who generally opposed independence from France. In January 1985, while fighting went on between police and Kanak rebels (FLNKS leader Eloi Machoro was slain in an exchange of gunfire), many demonstrators denounced an independence proposal and rioted in Nouméa, the capital. A state of emergency was imposed, lasting for six months, and a transitional regime was instituted, allowing different groups to express their concerns about New Caledonia's progress toward independence in association with France. In 1988, Kanak separatists attacked a police station on the island of Ouvéa (Uvéa) and held 27 hostages, causing French security forces to retaliate in a bloody massacre of 19 Kanaks. Pro- and anti-independence groups agreed to the Matignon Accord (1988), which provided for a framework of new provincial administrative centers, a major development program, and a referendum on the territory's political future in 1998 (when New Caledonians voted overwhelmingly for continuing ties to France but having more autonomy).

Nez Perce War (Chief Joseph's Uprising) (1877) When gold was discovered along the Salmon River in present-day western Idaho, U.S. forces moved in to dislodge the peaceful, highly civilized Nez Perce Indians, who had been ceded the area by the U.S. government. The Indians led by Chief Joseph (1840?–1904) resisted stoutly, routed the soldiers in White Bird Canyon (June 17, 1877), and advanced eastward into Idaho and Montana. U.S. troops under General Oliver O. Howard (1830–1909) failed to defeat the elusive, well-disciplined Nez Perce. But Chief Joseph soon realized that his warriors could never prevail against the white man and sought to lead his people north into Canada. In one of the most masterly retreats in military history, he guided about 1,000 Nez Perce over some 1,500 miles of harsh mountainous and plains terrain, evading two pursuing armies under Howard and General Nelson A. Miles (1839–1925). While resting in

northern Montana, about 40 miles from the Canadian border, Joseph and his depleted tribe were overtaken by the soldiers, who fought them for four days. On October 5, 1877, Joseph surrendered to Miles, giving an eloquent speech that ended: "Hear me, my chiefs; I am tired; my heart is sick and sad. From where the sun now stands, I will fight no more forever." In 1878, he and his band were sent to a reservation in present-day Oklahoma, where many died of illness. Joseph and the remnants of his tribe were later allowed to move to Washington state—to a reservation where he devoted the rest of his life to the peaceful betterment of his people.

Nicaraguan Civil War of 1909–12 In 1909, a conservative revolt broke out in Nicaragua against the liberal dictator-president José Santos Zelaya (1853–1919), whose bellicose actions and interference in other Central American nations were opposed by the United States; two U.S. citizens aiding the rebels were captured and executed, causing an angry protest by U.S. secretary of state Philander C. Knox (1853–1921). When Zelaya was forced to resign on December 16, 1909, Nicaragua was in a state of near anarchy, and a power struggle between conservative and liberal factions ensued. In May 1911, the conservative Adolfo Díaz (1874–1964) became provisional president and promptly requested U.S. aid. A treaty was reached between the United States and Nicaragua, whereby New York banks made loans to furnish working capital for Nicaragua, and an American customs collectorship was instituted to retire domestic and foreign debts. When the U.S. Senate rejected the treaty, President William Howard Taft (1857–1930) enacted the plan by executive agreement, but the loans were restricted. With the call "Down with Yankee Imperialists," Nicaraguan liberals rose in rebellion in July 1912. At the request of Díaz, about 2,500 U.S. Marines were soon landed in Nicaragua to protect the conservative government, and in two months the rebellion was quelled. Under U.S. military supervision, elections were held in 1912, with Díaz being elected president of Nicaragua; a legation guard of about 100 U.S. Marines remained in the country for 13 years. See also HONDURAN CIVIL WAR OF 1909–11.

Nicaraguan Civil War of 1925–33   In 1925, a coalition government was formed in Nicaragua upon the election of President Carlos Solórzano (fl. 1920s), a conservative, and Vice President Juan Bautista Sacasa (1874–1946), a liberal; shortly the U.S. Marines left the country after 13 years of occupation (see NICARAGUAN CIVIL WAR OF 1909–12). On October 25, 1925, General Emiliano Chamorro Vargas (1871–1966) and Adolfo Díaz (1874–1964) seized power by a coup d'état, driving Sacasa and other liberals out of the government; after Solórzano's resignation, Chamorro became president in January 1926, but he was not recognized by the United States, which sent gun-boats and troops to Nicaragua after a liberal revolt broke out under General Augusto César Sandino (1893–1934), whose supporters seized U.S. property. A truce was arranged; Chamorro resigned and left the country in October 1926; and the Nicaraguan congress elected the conservative Díaz president. However, Sacasa returned from exile in Mexico and, with Mexican aid, established a rival liberal government on Nicaragua's east coast. A civil war erupted between liberal rebels under General José María Moncada (1868–1945) and the government under Díaz, who requested and received military assistance from the United States. In 1927, U.S. warships arrived and landed some 2,000 Marines and materiel. Angry at American interference in Nicaraguan affairs, Sandino joined the war, engaging in guerrilla actions against the gringos (white foreigners). U.S. president Calvin Coolidge (1872–1933) sent his personal representative, Henry L. Stimson (1867–1950), to settle the conflict, and Stimson induced the rival leaders, Díaz and Moncada, to disarm and to allow U.S. supervision of forthcoming elections. The liberal Moncada was elected president of Nicaragua on November 4, 1928, but Sandino refused to accept this and continued his guerrilla attacks on Marine detachments. In response, U.S. warplanes bombed the guerrillas' mountain strongholds; fleeing to Mexico, Sandino vowed not to lay down his arms until the removal of the Marines from Nicaragua. In 1932, Sacasa was elected president and attempted to reach an accord with Sandino, who capitulated after the Marines withdrew in early 1933. In Managua in 1934, Sandino was assassinated by national guardsmen angry over the amnesty given to him by the government.

Nicaraguan Civil War of 1978–79   Since 1937, the Somoza family had dominated Nicaragua politically and economically, amassing a huge fortune from its business enterprises and agricultural holdings. Opposition to Nicaraguan president Anastasio Somoza Debayle (1925–80) came chiefly and increasingly from the leftist Sandinista National Liberation Front, named in honor of Augusto César Sandino (1893–1934), a Nicaraguan freedom fighter assassinated allegedly on orders by Somoza Debayle's father, Anastasio Somoza García (1896–1956), head of the national guard and later president of Nicaragua. In 1977 the U.S. State Department cited the Somoza regime for human rights violations, and Nicaragua's Roman Catholic hierarchy accused the government of torturing and executing civilians in its anti-Sandinista campaign. The murder of Pedro Joaquin Chamorro (1924–78), opponent of the Somoza regime and publisher of the newspaper *La Prensa*, brought on rioting by thousands of Nicaraguans, who blamed Somoza for Chamorro's death. Antigovernment activity increased, and Somoza's resignation was called for. In August 1978, Sandinista guerrillas invaded the national palace and held more than 1,500 persons hostage, including the deputies in the lower assembly, until they won release of 59 political prisoners and safe conduct out of the country. Invading Sandinistas from Costa Rica ignited a successful revolution on May 29, 1979 and, after about seven weeks of fighting against Somoza's national guardsmen, forced Somoza to flee into exile in the United States on July 17, 1979. The Sandinistas, who broadcast over the government radio that a cease-fire was in place, installed a five-member junta to rule and immediately set about reforming the country's institutions and economy.

Nicaraguan Civil War of 1982–90   Former Nicaraguan national guardsmen, called Somocistas because of their loyalty to the late president Anastasio Somoza Debayle (1925–80), opposed the leftist Sandinista National Liberation Front government that took control of Nicaragua in 1979; many of them went into exile in neighboring Honduras and Costa Rica and began preparations to overthrow the Sandinistas. These anti-Sandinistas were aided by Nicaragua's Miskito Indians, who fled to Honduras when the Sandinista government attempted to resettle them away from the Coco River (the Nicaraguan-Honduran border). In January 1982, Sandinista troops crossed the border into Honduras, raided several Indian settlements, and shot more than 100 Miskitos; this act alienated many Sandinista symphathizers inside and outside Nicaragua. Some Miskitos joined the Somocistas, and others became allied with another antigovernment guerrilla group, the Democratic Revolutionary Alliance (ARDE), operating in the south of Nicaragua; the latter group accused the Sandinistas of establishing a "Soviet-style Stalinist regime" and of betraying the people. These two rebel groups operated separately. In 1983 and 1984, antigovernment insurgents, the *contras*, based in Honduras and supported by the United States, made incursions into Nicaragua and inflicted costly damage by blowing up bridges and oil tanks. The Sandinista regime became limited in its apparent ability to aid leftist revolutionaries in Central America, being tied up fighting the rebels within the country. In 1985 and 1986, the Sandinista army intensified the war against the largest contra group, the Nicaraguan Democratic Force (FDN), which operated from Honduran territory (see HONDURAN GUERRILLA WAR OF 1981–90). But the guerrilla groups, helped by the U.S. embargo on trade to Nicaragua, put up strong resistance, despite losing ground and internal strife (especially among the ARDE rebels). At the time, U.S. military aid to the *contras* was forbidden by law; the diversion of money (from secret arms sales to Iran) to them caused a major scandal for U.S. president Ronald W. Reagan (1911–). A peace plan, effected by Costa Rica's President Oscar Arias Sanchez (1942–), called for cessation of outside aid for the rebels and negotiations between warring parties; Central American leaders signed a treaty based on the Arias plan in August 1987. The Sandinista National Liberation Front and President Daniel Ortega Saavedra (1945–), head of Nicaragua's ruling junta since 1979, were finally ousted in February 1990, when free elections were held; a 14-party anti-Sandinista coalition, led by Violeta Barrios de Chamorro (1929–), won legislative and presidential control. The new government signed a peace accord with the rebels, who then began demobilizing and registering with UN peacekeepers in May–June 1990. About 27,500 *contra* rebels eventually and voluntarily surrendered their weapons. The war had cost some 30,000 lives and helped push Nicaragua close to economic ruin. See also SALVADORAN CIVIL WAR OF 1977–92.

Nicopolis, Crusade of   (1396) Conquests by the Ottoman Turks in the Balkans and their sieges of Constantinople (Istanbul) in the 14th century so frightened Europe that Pope Boniface IX (c. 1355–1404) proclaimed a crusade against them. Almost 100,000 men responded to his call, gathering in Buda under Sigismund of Hungary (1368–1437) and marching down the Danube to seize two Ottoman fortresses and pillage areas they should have freed, until they reached and besieged Ottoman-controlled Nicopolis (Nikopol, Bulgaria). Ironically, the crusaders had neither a battle plan nor a unified chain of command. Restless as they confronted an Ottoman army under Sultan Bayazid I (1347–1403), a force that had besieged Constantinople since 1391, hotheaded French knights under John "the Fearless" (1371–1419) disregarded the sage advice of the experienced Sigismund and recklessly (and successfully) charged the first Ottoman line, unaware of the standard Ottoman tactic of sacrificing its vanguard. But they next faced a second Turkish line, which surrounded them and Sigismund's relieving main army of 16,000, weakened by unexpected Wallachian and Transylvanian soldiers' desertions. Thousands of crusaders died—in battle, in flight, or by drowning in the Danube. More than

10,000 of them were taken prisoner (including many of their noble leaders, who were ransomed later) and executed by the Turks. Sigismund and other nobles escaped by ship. Bayazid continued to conquer in Thessaly and the Morea (Peloponnesus) until the coming of Tamerlane (Timur) (1336–1405) into Asia Minor momentarily halted the Ottoman conquest of the Balkans (see ANGORA, BATTLE OF; TAMERLANE, CONQUESTS OF).

Nien Rebellion (1853–68)   In the early 1850s, the Chinese living in the Yellow River (Huang Ho) valley suffered famine because of repeated flooding of the river; many of them joined outlaw bands, called *nien*, which had been plundering the provinces of Anhwei, Honan, and Shantung during the first half of the century. While the Manchu (Ch'ing, Qing) government was preoccupied with the TAIPING REBELLION in the south, the Nien bands formed armies, notably under the leadership of Chang Lohsing (d. 1863), and fortified their villages and took advantage of the mobility of their strong cavalry to harass and evade imperial troops seeking to crush them. They soon controlled a large area in north China that was virtually independent of the rest of the country. However, their movement lacked strong direction after Chang Lo-hsing was killed, and the Nien were unable to coordinate their actions with the Taiping rebels in the south. Imperial forces led successively by Generals Seng-ko-linch'in (d. 1865), Tseng Kuo-fan (1811–72), and Li Huang-chang (1823–1901) surrounded the Nien fortresses, starved them into submission, and sacked their strongholds. By 1868, the rebels were defeated, and the emperor's forces were again in command of their area.

Nieuwpoort (the Dunes), Battle of (1600)   Outside Ostend among the sand dunes of Nieuwpoort, or Nieuport (in northwest Belgium), Maurice of Nassau (1567–1625) brought to its zenith his long guidance of the United Provinces's resistance to Spain. His 11,000 infantrymen met an equivalent army led by Albert the Pious (1559–1621), arch-

duke of Austria, on July 2, 1600. The Dutch were less formally arranged than the Spanish, who were gathered in four great squares, despite the terrain. The greater mobility of the Netherlanders under Maurice and their constant, heavy musket fire wore down the Spanish, whose line broke toward the end of the day. The Spanish under Albert suffered heavy casualties in this, the only major land battle of the EIGHTY YEARS' WAR, but they were left with sufficient strength to take Ostend the following year.

Nigerian-Biafran War (1967–70)   When Nigeria gained independence from Britain in 1960, three large and culturally different peoples—the Hausa, Yoruba, and Ibo—made up much of the population. The Ibo, who came from the eastern region, tended to be better educated and thus held most of the civil service and administrative posts. The Hausa, in the north, began to resent the Ibo "outsiders" and rioted against them (1966), killing thousands and destroying their property. The Ibo withdrew to their eastern homeland. The Nigerian government's decision to break up the region into three states promptly sparked the often-threatened Ibo secession; Ibo leaders, headed by Lieutenant Colonel Chukwuemeka Odumegwu Ojukwu (1933–), the military governor in the east, proclaimed their eastern region the independent Republic of Biafra on May 30, 1967. The Organization of African Unity (OAU) tried but failed to mediate the differences. Nigerian federal troops invaded Biafra, met stiff resistance, and eventually captured Enugu, the Biafran capital (October 4, 1967). Peace talks were futile in the spring of 1968, and the Nigerian government, which had set up an economic blockade of Biafra, renewed its offensive, having received military aid from Britain, the Soviet Union, and Italy. The Biafrans, who had secured arms from France, fought doggedly but unsuccessfully to hold on to Port Harcourt, Aba, and Owerri. In 1969, they retook Owerri, and crossed the Niger River, but were driven back by an enlarged, better-equipped Nigerian army of nearly 200,000. With its people starving and its economy ruined, Biafra surrendered on January 12, 1970; Ojukwu had fled by air into exile in the Ivory

Coast the day before. The slow process of the reintegration of the Ibo people into Nigeria's national life now began; nearly 2 million had died (chiefly from starvation) in the war.

Nigerian-Sierra Leonean War of 1997–98   See SIERRA LEONEAN CIVIL WAR OF 1991– .

Nigerien Civil War of 1990–95   Independent-minded among Nigeriens or Nigerois (inhabitants of Niger), the ethnic Tuareg (Touareg) people in the northern desert regions frequently opposed the central government at Niamey, the capital. In May 1990, army troops retaliated against attacking Tuareg separatists in Tchin Tabaraden, killing hundreds of nomadic Tuaregs and arresting many others. But rebel attacks on security forces and tourists persisted in the northern regions, and in August 1992 army reprisals resulted in the arrest of members of the Tuareg Liberation Front of Air and Azawad (FLAA), one of the various Tuareg groups. The government declared a state of emergency in the north, sought to aid thousands of refugees, and succeeded in prolonging a FLAA-declared truce through much of 1993. Meanwhile, Niger was torn by strikes, student protests, and mutinous soldiers because of a desperate economy. In 1994, the main Tuareg coalition, the Coordination of Armed Resistance (CRA), agreed to limited autonomy in a region to be set aside for some 750,000 Tuaregs. The CRA also signed a peace pact with the government on October 9, 1994, in Ouagadougou, Burkina Faso. Other Tuareg representatives agreed to peace on April 24, 1995, leading to the National Assembly granting full amnesty to former separatists and releasing all captive Tuaregs. The only Tuareg rebel group not signing the 1995 peace accord—the Democratic Renewal Front—acknowledged it in 1997. See also MALIAN CIVIL WAR OF 1990–96.

Nika Revolt   (A.D. 532)   Justinian I (483–565), Eastern Roman (or Byzantine) emperor, attempted to stop the corruption and despotic behavior of many of his imperial administrators, but his efforts were only partially successful. In 532, some of the populace of Constantinople (Istanbul), capital city of the empire, rebelled against the high taxes and government extortion; their cry was "Nika," meaning victory. An angry mob surrounded the imperial palace where Justinian, his wife, Theodora (508?–48), and their court were residing. Soon the mob gained control of the city, much of which was destroyed by fire. Justinian considered fleeing to a safer place, but Theodora would not leave (she was determined to show firmness like a veritable empress). Generals Belisarius (505?–65) and Narses (478?–573) called out the imperial bodyguard and other forces, led them into the city, and soon restored order with much cruelty. Some 30,000 rebels, who had proclaimed Hypatius (d. 532) emperor, were slain; Hypatius was seized and executed. Afterward Justinian removed some of the offending officials as a concession to the people. This revolt was the only internal one of his long reign.

Nineveh, Fall of   (612 B.C.)   The fourth and most splendid capital city of the Assyrian Empire, Nineveh (the Hebrew form of the Assyrian name *Ninua*), located on the Tigris River opposite modern Mosul, Iraq, was theoretically impregnable, surrounded by walls seven and a half miles long and up to 148 feet thick. Nonetheless, a coalition force of Medes, Babylonians, and some Scythians and Persians captured and destroyed the city, thus apparently fulfilling the prophecy in the Old Testament of Nahum and Zephaniah. No military records are extant to describe what happened in detail, but a Median chronicle notes that the Tigris was in flood and that battering rams were mounted on rafts, suggesting that entry to the city was made through a weakness in its long riverside walls. Otherwise, the fall, destruction, and abandonment of Nineveh remain, for the most part, an historical mystery, which extensive archeological work has not solved. The city was still empty about 200 years later, when the Greek historian Xenophon (434?–355?) reported visiting it. See also ASSYRIAN WARS OF c. 746–609 B.C.

Nine Years' War, Earlier   See JAPANESE EARLIER NINE YEARS' WAR.

Nore Mutiny (1797)   Impressed by the successful SPITHEAD MUTINY a month earlier, British sailors at the Nore, a famous anchorage in the Thames estuary near Sheerness, England, mutinied under the leadership of Richard Parker (d. 1797) and blockaded the mouth of the Thames River. Instead of humbly petitioning the Admiralty and the Commons and stating their grievances, they made angry demands, including a call for a bigger share of prize money. Equally angry, the British government rejected their stipulations. National feelings rose against them, and Parliament passed a law forbidding all communication with them. Within three weeks (June 1797), most of the mutineers had drifted back to their tasks. Parker was arrested, convicted, and hanged from the yardarm of his ship; other leaders were executed, too. The rest were shown clemency, but gained no immediate relief.

Norman-Byzantine War, First (1081–85)   Although the Norman adventurer Robert Guiscard (1015?–85) had been invested by the pope in 1059 with Apulia, Calabria, and Sicily, these lands had still to be conquered. With the aid of his brother, Roger I (1031?–1101), Guiscard wrested Sicily from the Muslims, between 1061 and 1091. Gaining control of the southern Italian areas brought Guiscard into conflict with the Byzantine Empire. He, along with his eldest son Bohemund I (1056?–1111), sailed east in 1081 to attack the Balkans, conquering Corfu and capturing Dyrrachium. Guiscard now coveted the imperial crown for himself and captured Byzantine emperor Alexius I Comnenus (1048–1118) in 1082. But conditions in Italy required Guiscard's presence during 1083–84, and when he returned to attack Cephalonia (Kefallinia) in 1085, to the gratitude of the Byzantines, he died of plague. **Second Norman-Byzantine War** (1098–1108). Guiscard's son Bohemond continued his father's strategies, but his plan to control the empire was disguised while he helped lead the FIRST CRUSADE to save the Holy Sepulcher. Made prince of Antioch in 1099 after breaking a 1097 oath to Emperor Alexius I by attacking a year earlier, Bohemond, for security, became a vassal of Geoffrey of Bouillon (1053?–1100), Latin ruler of Jerusalem. Bohemond, however, was held by the Muslims from 1100 to 1103. Upon release, he returned to Europe, married the daughter of Philip I (1052–1108) of France, and mounted a private crusade against Alexius I. Defeated in 1108, he was forced to renew his vassalage.

Norman Conquest (1066)   Edward the Confessor died without issue on January 5, 1066; this led to a three-way rivalry for the throne of England. One adversary was Harold Hadrada (d. 1066), Norway's king. Another was Harold Godwinson (1022?–66), scion of England's most powerful baron. The third, William (1027?–87), duke of Normandy, a cousin once removed, proved to be the most significant. Other actions before Edward's death had complicated the struggle. Edward had constantly wrestled for power with Godwin (d. 1053), earl of Wessex, whose exile had failed to deter him. Looking to Normandy for succor (and perhaps under duress) in 1051, Edward had orally promised William the throne. In 1064–65, Harold Godwinson, visiting Normandy, vowed support over sacred relics to William. But on his deathbed, Edward assigned the throne to Harold. When the English magnates concurred, Harold had three rivals: his power-hungry brother Tostig (d. 1066), Hadrada, and William. Tostig, defeated and exiled, joined Hadrada and accompanied him in an invasion designed to establish a king and powerful baron. Harold met the Norwegians at Stamford Bridge on September 25, 1066; Hadrada and Tostig were both slain. Then Harold rushed south to meet William and his forces, who had invaded on September 27 between Pevensey and Hastings. On October 13, 1066, Harold reached Hastings, erected defensive earthworks, and repelled William's first charge. During the second charge, Harold was killed and his leaderless army surrendered. William's Christmas Day coronation set in motion processes that profoundly changed the course and nature of English culture.

Normandy, Invasion of (1944) June 6, 1944, was D-day for the Allies in WORLD WAR II. General Dwight D. Eisenhower (1890–1969), supreme Allied commander in Western Europe, directed the daring invasion of the European mainland that day. Thousands of troop ships, amphibious craft, and warships transported British, French, American, Canadian, and other Allied troops across the stormy English Channel to Normandy in northwestern France. Before the invasion, the Allied air forces and navies had been pounding the strong German fortifications along the French coast, but even so the Allies found the enemy entrenched and well equipped to resist them. U.S. forces encountered stiff resistance on Utah and Omaha beaches, while to the east British troops, later reinforced by Canadians, fought resolutely for the stubbornly German-defended port of Caen. The hedgerow terrain of Normandy was fairly easy to defend, and the Germans made the most of it. Nonetheless, by the end of July 1944, after seven weeks of intense fighting, the Allied bridgeheads were firmly established. The invasion had succeeded, and the Allied armies were united along the coast. In early August 1944, the U.S. Third Army broke through the German lines in the west and rushed into Brittany, south to the Loire River, and then east toward Paris. A German attempt to split the American forces failed, and instead a British force driving from the south trapped the German Seventh Army and wiped it out. See also WORLD WAR II ON THE WESTERN FRONT.

Norman-French War (1077–82) King Philip I (1052–1108) of France, alarmed by the NORMAN CONQUEST of England, made it his policy to prevent the union of Normandy and England under one ruler. He persuaded and encouraged the young Robert Curthose (c. 1054–1134), William the Conqueror's oldest son, to rebel against his father. Robert, however, was easily defeated. He and his father became reconciled until further disagree-

ments caused him to be exiled. Nonetheless, in 1087, he became Robert II, duke of Normandy, when his father died. Philip, a decade after his maneuvering, had gained his wish.

Norse Raids See VIKING RAIDS.

North African Campaign (1940–43) The principal objective of the Axis powers in North Africa during WORLD WAR II was to seize the Suez Canal and hence control of the Mediterranean, while the Allies sought to retain control of these strategically important areas. Much of the fighting took place along the shores of Libya and Egypt; tanks, aircraft, and land mines were employed extensively. In September 1940, an Italian army penetrated Egyptian territory, but the British drove it back, and by February 1941, the Italians were overwhelmed. The German Afrika Korps, which was especially trained for desert warfare by its commander, General Erwin Rommel (1891–1944), known as the "Desert Fox," took over the fighting in March 1941, and forced the British out of Libya and back into Egypt. The British Eighth Army counterattacked in November that year and drove the Germans westward. In May 1942, the Germans under Rommel took the offensive again, routed the British in a great tank battle at the Knightsbridge crossing during the Battle of Gazala-Bir Hakim (May 28–June 13, 1942), and pushed them about 250 miles into Egypt. There the British established a strong battle line stretching from El Alamein on the coast to the Qattara Depression, an impassable badlands. Though they tried repeatedly, the Afrika Korps could not break this defensive line. On October 23, 1942, the British Eighth Army under General Bernard L. Montgomery (1887–1976) launched an attack after heavy artillery and air bombardments of German positions. The British broke through the German lines and forced Rommel to begin one of the longest retreats in history, westward to Tunisia. The Battle of El Alamein prevented Rommel from capturing Cairo and the Suez Canal and ranks as one of the most decisive of the war; it greatly boosted Allied morale. On May 12, 1943, the Axis forces in North Africa capitulated after being defeated by the British and Americans in Tunisia.

Northern Expedition (1926 28)   After the death of Sun Yat-sen (Sun Wen, Sun Yixian) (1866–1925), the Kuomintang or Chinese Nationalist Party that he had founded in southern China was split into pro-communist and rightist factions, while in the north rival military commanders vied for power. Following Sun's admonitions to reunite the country, the Kuomintang forces under General Chiang Kai-shek (1886–1975) set out northward from their capital at Canton (Guangzhou) in July 1926. By August they had gained control of Hunan province and by October the cities of Wuchang, Hankow, Hanyang, and Nanchang. In the spring of 1927, they exerted authority over all the provinces south of the Yangtze (Chang) River and Honan (Henan) province in the north. One reason for the Kuomintang success was that their soldiers had been trained not to prey on civilians, and for the first time in China's history, troops were warmly welcomed by the people. Effective propaganda played a part too. But a rift widened in the Kuomintang during the summer. To solve the conflict Chiang Kai-shek resigned his command and the party dismissed its Russian advisers, expelled the communists and radicals, and reorganized itself. In the spring of 1928, Chiang was recalled to lead the army, and the northward push resumed. The northern armies were defeated in the field, and a sympathetic northern general captured Peking, China's capital, in June 1928, while the opposing general fled to Manchuria. This victory reunited China, and the capital was moved from Peking (Beijing) south to Nanking (Nanjing). The first phase of Sun's plan for national reconstruction—military unification—was completed, and the second phase—political tutelage—began. See also CHINESE CIVIL WAR OF 1930–34.

Northern Ireland Civil War of 1969–98   Underlying a persistent conflict in Northern Ireland (Ulster) are three factors: a centuries-old antago-

nism between the British and the Irish, long seen as strife between Protestants (British) and Roman Catholics (Irish); pressures to force Ulster (about 60 percent Protestant) into political union with Eire or Ireland (about 95 percent Roman Catholic); and the presence in Ulster of a Roman Catholic minority held back by economic and political power. This explosive mixture began to ignite in 1968, when Catholics staged civil rights protests and the resulting violence led to the importation of British troops. Militant groups like the Irish Republican Army (IRA), its radical offshoot, the Provisional Wing (Provos) of the IRA, and the Protestant Ulster Defense Association intensified hostilities through demonstrations, street fights, bombings, and assassinations in 1969. The animosity was so fierce that the British government suspended the Northern Irish Stormont (parliament) in 1972 and ruled directly. When a 1973 plebiscite indicated that an overwhelming Ulster majority rejected union with Eire, a new parliamentary election was held, and a coalition government was formed by Catholic groups and others. But Protestant militants like the Reverend Ian Paisley (1926–) vowed to destroy the coalition, elected hard-liners to the Westminster (British) parliament, and forced, through a general strike, the collapse of the new Stormont government (1974). Violence continued, and the Irish showed their resentment of the "invading" British forces by killings in both Ulster and Britain. In 1983, a Northern Ireland bill in Westminster attempted a third home rule government; Protestants held the majority, and the Roman Catholic members boycotted the sessions. A new plan for union with Eire was developed in 1984. But the tradition of strife was so firmly a part of Northern Ireland's culture that its approval by a majority did not stop civil antagonism. Outbreaks of violence continued between paramilitary groups during the 1990s. The IRA declared a ceasefire in September 1994 in response to the Downing Street Declaration of late 1993, in which the British and Irish governments (Britain and Ireland) agreed to begin peace talks that were to include unarmed, nonviolent groups only; Protestant paramilitary groups joined the ceasefire in October. A further step toward stability was taken in February 1995 with the Framework document, which addressed crucial political issues, including Ireland's claims on Ulster and the right of Ulster's people to determine their own future. These concessions, it was thought, would reduce the influence of the terrorists, whose premise that a political solution was impossible now seemed proven untrue. But the cease-fire was broken in February 1996 with a bomb set off in London by the IRA, which objected to certain procedural steps in negotiations then being held as a prelude to formal talks. The worst street fighting since 1968 followed in July 1996 in the town of Portadown, when Protestant Orangemen insisted on conducting a march with a politically provocative theme through a Catholic neighborhood. Determined to be part of the peace talks, the IRA reinstated the ceasefire in July 1997, and Sinn Fein (the IRA's political wing), under the leadership of Gerry Adams (1948–   ), was admitted to the talks in September 1997. Despite revenge killings by splinter groups on both sides in early 1998, the legitimate opposition parties, including Sinn Fein, continued to attend the peace talks. On April 10, 1998, representatives of eight political parties agreed to a landmark document, under which Protestants and Catholics in Northern Ireland would govern jointly in a 108-seat National Assembly, which would work with the Irish Republic in a newly formed North-South legislative council. This power-sharing peace accord was endorsed by the majority of voters in referendums in the Irish Republic and Northern Ireland on May 22, 1998. In 30 years of fighting, more than 3,000 men, women, and children were killed by one side or the other. Afterward, hard-liners opposed to the peace attempted to undo it through church bombings and other violent acts, notably a car bomb in Omagh that killed 28 people and wounded over 330 (August 15, 1998). Strong public revulsion against the so-called Real IRA, which claimed responsibility for the Omagh attack, forced it and other Irish republican groups to suspend violent campaigns. Northern Ireland's major Protestant and Catholic parties clashed over different interpretations of the peace

agreement in December 1998, while the outlawed IRA was refusing to disarm.

Northern War, First (1655–60) Swedish king Charles X (1622–60) wished to extend Sweden's possessions in the Baltic area (see POLISH-SWEDISH WAR FOR LIVONIA, SECOND), and when Polish king John II Casimir (1609–72), pressing his father's claim to the Swedish throne, refused to recognize Charles as "Protector of Poland," Charles declared war. Invading Swedish armies seized Warsaw after a three-day battle and conquered Poland (see RUSSO-POLISH WAR OF 1654–56; RUSSO-SWEDISH WAR OF 1656–58). To the northeast, Swedish forces took control of Lithuania. Frederick William (1620–88) of Brandenburg, who had allied himself with Sweden and had become sovereign over Prussia, made peace with Poland. With the Polish front secure, Charles moved to seize Holstein, Schleswig, and most of Jutland from Denmark, which had allied itself with Poland. In a daring attack across the ice from Jutland, he took Fünen (Fyn) Island and threatened Copenhagen, the capital of Denmark. Charles, dissatisfied with the terms of a Danish-Swedish peace, the Treaty of Roeskilde, laid siege to Copenhagen and sought to control the Öresund (Danish Sound). A Dutch fleet helped the Danes repel the Swedish fleet blockading Copenhagen. Driven from Holstein and Schleswig by Poles and from Bornholm and Trondheim by Danes and Norwegians, Sweden sought peace. Negotiations broke down, but after Danish troops won the Battle of Nyborg and captured Sweden's best troops in November 1659, Sweden's regency government, which had succeeded Charles (who had died of a fever while planning an invasion of Norway), signed the Treaty of Oliva in 1660. The treaty confirmed Swedish control of Livonia, Danish control of Bornholm and Trondheim, and Brandenburg's title to East Prussia. **Second or Great Northern War** (1700–1721). On becoming Sweden's king in 1697, Charles XII (1682–1718) faced three threats to Swedish supremacy in the Baltic: Danish king Frederick IV (1671–1730) wished to incorporate Holstein-Gottorp into Denmark; Polish king Augustus II

(1670–1733), elector of Saxony, hoping to retake Livonia, besieged Riga, Livonia's chief city; and Russian czar Peter I "the Great" (1672–1725), desiring Ingermanland, besieged Narva. First, Charles invaded Denmark and took Copenhagen, forcing the Danes to seek peace. Second, he lifted the Russian siege of Narva. Third, he relieved Riga, his forces invading Livonia, occupying Courland and Lithuania before advancing on and seizing Warsaw and Cracow in Poland. Charles's army won a resounding victory against Augustus's much larger army at the Battle of Pultusk on April 13, 1703. The Polish Diet (assembly) elected Charles's candidate, Stanislaus I Leszczyński (1677–1766), king in 1704. In 1706, Charles moved on to subdue Lithuania and pursued Augustus in Saxony, forcing him to cede his royal claim to Stanislaus. In September 1707, Charles left Saxony with 80,000 soldiers and marched through eastern Poland and Lithuania into Russia. Winter weather, lack of supplies, and Russian resistance prevented him from reaching Moscow, and a detour into the Ukraine to join forces with Ivan Mazeppa (1640?–1709), who was leading a Cossack uprising against Peter, proved disastrous in 1708–9. With greatly reduced forces, Charles suffered a terrible defeat by the Russians at the Battle of Poltava (Pultowa) on June 28, 1709, and afterward, accompanied by only 1,800 men, fled to Turkish Moldavia. In the north, Augustus returned to Poland and ousted Stanislaus; Peter moved on Ingermanland, Livonia, and Finland; and Prussia took Pomerania. Sweden now faced an enemy coalition of Poland, Russia, Prussia, Saxony, Hanover, and Denmark, which had reentered the war in 1709. Swedish troops repelled the Danes in Skane (extreme southern Sweden) and defeated a Danish-Saxon army in Pomerania. However, a combined Russian, Danish, and Saxon army in Holstein forced the Swedes to surrender, and the Swedish fleet fell to Russia. Ensuing peace negotiations halted when Charles, who had managed to get the Turks to briefly enter the war against Russia (see RUSSO-TURKISH WAR OF 1710–11), appeared in the German city of Stralsund on the Baltic, issuing orders to recommence hostilities. But the allies besieged Stralsund and, in December 1715, it fell. Charles fled to Sweden, raised another army to invade Norway (then ruled by Denmark), but was shot dead in the trenches while his army was preparing to besiege Fredrikshald (Halden) in December 1718. After his death, Sweden's army returned home, and conditions of peace were determined. By the treaties of Stockholm (1719–20), Sweden awarded the duchies of Bremen and Verden to Hanover for a large indemnity and gave the city of Stettin (Szczecin) and parts of west Pomerania to Prussia. Denmark gave up its conquests, except for Schleswig, for a payment. By the Treaty of Nystad (1721), Livonia, Ingermanland, part of Karelia, and many Baltic islands were ceded by Sweden to Russia, which gave up Finland. Russia had become a dominant power in Europe.

Northumberland's Rebellion (1408)   Henry Percy (1342–1408), first earl of Northumberland, never forgave King Henry IV (1367–1413) for Shrewsbury (see PERCY'S REBELLION). Though Northumberland surrendered to the English king, he was pardoned by his peers and, by 1405, was involved in a new conspiracy to dethrone Henry and crown Edmund Mortimer (1376–1409). Alerted to the plot, Henry had Northumberland's fellow conspirators, the earl of Nottingham and Richard Le Scrope, the archbishop of York, beheaded. Northumberland fled to Scotland. Leading Scottish troops in 1408, he was trapped and killed by a force led by the sheriff of Yorkshire at Bramham Moor.

Northwest Rebellion   See RIEL'S SECOND REBELLION.

Norway, Invasion of (1940)   Although Norway had proclaimed itself neutral at the beginning of WORLD WAR II, the Germans disregarded this on April 9, 1940, when their warships entered all the major harbors on the Norwegian coast and seized control of them. The Luftwaffe (German air force) bombed Norwegian airfields and radio stations while troop ships landed soldiers, who occupied the cities. The swiftness of the German invasion was aided by Nazi sympathizers, who were Norwegian traitors called Quislings, named after the leader of Norway's Nazi Party, Vidkun Quisling (1887–1945). Most Norwegians, however, resisted the Germans. British submarines and other naval vessels sank Nazi troop ships and warships in Norway's harbors; a landing force drove the Germans from the northern port of Narvik for several months. An Anglo-French expeditionary force arrived to help and engaged the Germans in fierce fighting around Oslo, Norway's capital, and other strategic centers. The Germans responded with blitzkrieg tactics—swift, sudden attacks by tanks, artillery, and aircraft. Norway's King Haakon VII (1871–1957) and his cabinet escaped to London after it became clear that the Germans had successfully occupied their country. Many Norwegian ships and trawlers also escaped to England, where they aided the Allied cause, as did many Norwegians who joined the Resistance movement.

Norwegian Invasion of Scotland (1263)   Scotland's kings dreamed of gaining the Hebrides, or Western Islands, from Norway, but only King Alexander III (1241–86) succeeded. King Haakon IV (1204–63) of Norway had sent a great fleet of 100 ships toward Largs, Scotland, in the summer of 1263. Alexander craftily negotiated until the fall, when expected storms battered and destroyed too many Norse ships for a sea battle and left the Norse troops too confused to fight effectively. After losing the Battle of Largs in the Clyde River, Haakon fled toward Norway but died at Kirkwall in the Orkney Islands. His successor, Magnus IV (1238–80), sold Alexander the islands' sovereignty in the 1266 Treaty of Perth and had his sons marry Alexander's daughters.

November Insurrection   See POLISH REBELLION OF 1830–31.

November Revolution   See OCTOBER REVOLUTION, RUSSIAN.

Novgorod, Muscovite Conquest of (1471–79) Grand Prince Ivan III "the Great" (1440–1505) of Moscow carried on the work of his father, Basil II (1415–62), to enlarge and strengthen the Muscovite (Russsan) state (see RUSSIAN CIVIL WAR OF 1425–53). To the northeast lay Novgorod, a great trading center with extensive territorial possessions in northern Russia, which had vied with Moscow for supremacy during the past centuries. Novgorod's Roman Catholic Lithuanian allegiance was an anathema to Moscow's Orthodox Christians. In 1471, when Novgorod allied itself strongly with Poland, Ivan declared war and advanced his troops against the Novgorodians, winning victories on the Shelon River and the Shilenga River (1475). Without promised Polish military aid, Novgorod decided to surrender, granting Ivan more than 15,000 rubles as indemnity and the right to nominate his own archbishop for the city. It also had to pledge against any Lithuanian alliance. Protesting Ivan's title of "lord" of Novgorod, rebels disrupted the city in 1477, causing Ivan, with help from Pskov and Tver (Kalinin), two cities that had supplied troops earlier for his victories, to march toward Novgorod. Refusing to negotiate, Ivan forced the city to capitulate when its rebellious leader resigned in January 1478. He then confiscated Novgorod's monastery estates and abducted some boyars (aristocrats). Novgorod made another attempt, with Polish aid, to restore its independence in 1479, but Ivan's forces quashed the revolt, taking many Novgorodians captive.

Novgorod, Sack of (1570)   A convicted Russian criminal, seeking a commutation of his sentence, which Russia's Czar Ivan IV "the Terrible" (1530–84) granted to those who exposed disloyalty, planted a forged letter supposedly written by the metropolitan (archbishop) of Novgorod requesting an alliance with Lithuania (a joint kingdom with Poland since the Union of Lublin on July 1, 1569). In December 1569, Ivan set out to observe the destruction of the city of Novgorod, which he had decreed. En route Ivan's forces destroyed towns, including Tver (Kalinin), and massacred the inhabitants before arriving in Novgorod on January 2, 1570. Churches and monasteries were looted and burned, and about 60,000 Novgorodians were methodically murdered (500 to 1,000 were slain a day). Finally Ivan pardoned the surviving citizens, many of whom ironically soon succumbed to the plague. The metropolitan and other Novgorodian leaders, whom Ivan had executed, were brought back with him to Moscow and displayed in a gory public spectacle. See also LIVONIAN WAR.

Numantian War (137–133 B.C.) During the CELTIBERIAN WARS a Roman army captured the fortified Celtiberian hill town of Numantia located near modern Soria, Spain, on the upper Duero River. The Numantians, who had previously repelled many Roman assaults, vehemently opposed Roman rule. In 137, they forced the surrender of a 20,000-man Roman consular army led by Gaius Hostilius Mancinus (fl. mid-2nd cent.), who promised peace. The Roman Senate did not acknowledge the defeat, however. In 134, the consul Scipio Aemilianus (185?–129) took charge of the demoralized Roman troops in Spain and laid siege to Numantia. After eight months, the 4,000 starving defenders surrendered to Scipio Aemilianus, whose army of 60,000 men had blockaded Numantia by setting up continuous ramparts around it. The town-fort was completely razed, and its inhabitants were slain or enslaved. See also LUSITANIAN WAR.

Numidian War See JUGURTHINE WAR.

Octavian's War against Antony (33–30 B.C.) As the leading members of Rome's Second Triumvirate, it was inevitable that Octavian (63 B.C.–A.D. 14), later Emperor Augustus, and Mark Antony (83?–30) would become rivals for the dominant position. When Octavian refused to support his Parthian campaigns (see ROMAN-PARTHIAN WAR OF 55–36 B.C.), Antony turned to Queen Cleopatra (69–30) of Egypt for help. She was anxious to revive the Egyptian Empire and thought Antony would be of assistance. The two became lovers, and in 32, Antony divorced his Roman wife, Octavian's sister, and married Cleopatra. Meanwhile, a propaganda war was being waged on both sides throughout Italy and the Roman territories. The divorce and later the discovery of Antony's purported will, in which he left everything to Cleopatra and her children, enraged most Romans. Octavian utilized this emotion to have all peoples in Italy and the western provinces swear allegiance to him. Antony's titles were abrogated, and the Roman Senate declared war on Cleopatra. Antony and Cleopatra assembled an army and fleet that sailed to Greece for the winter of 32–31 (see ROMAN CIVIL WAR OF 43–31 B.C.). In the spring, Octavian and his general, Marcus Vipsanius Agrippa (63–12), crossed the Adriatic with a force about equal to Antony's and engaged the enemy at Actium, a promontory in Greece on the Ionian Sea, on September 2, 31. Agrippa blockaded Antony's navy, while Octavian cut the supply routes of the army. Realizing he was losing the battle, Antony ordered the army to retreat and the fleet to run the blockade. Only a few ships made their way through, including the one carrying Antony and Cleopatra. The remaining ships and most of the army promptly surrendered. In 30, Octavian and his men invaded Egypt but were initially repulsed by Antony's forces as they advanced on Alexandria. Supposedly misinformed that Cleopatra had killed herself, Antony committed suicide in grief. Unable to influence Octavian and facing humiliation as a displayed captive in Rome, Cleopatra committed suicide, probably by means of a poisonous asp. Octavian was hailed as savior of the ancient world.

Octavian's War against Pompey (40–36 B.C.) Sextus Pompeius Magnus, called Pompey the Younger (75–35), the youngest son of Pompey the Great (106–48), fled to Egypt and then Spain after his father's defeat and death in the Great ROMAN CIVIL WAR and continued to fight Julius Caesar (100–44) and his successors. With his forces, he seized Sicily, and his pirate fleet prevented grain from being transported to Rome. Then Pompey wrested Sardinia from Octavian (63 B.C.–A.D. 14), later Roman emperor Augustus, in 40. The next year Octavian, Mark Antony (83?–30), and Pompey concluded the Treaty of Misenium, by which Pompey was given the governorship of Sicily and Sardinia and compensated for his father's property in return for conveying grain to Rome. But the treaty did not hold, and Octavian's forces regained possession of Sardinia, thus precipitating the war again in 38. Pompey's warships and a storm destroyed Octavian's fleet when it tried to capture Sicily. Two years later, with 120 warships under the command of Marcus Vipsanius Agrippa (63–12), Octavian's best general, Pompey's fleet was defeated in a battle off the northeast coast of Sicily near Naulochus (Mylae or Milazzo). Pompey escaped to Asia Minor but, in 35, was captured by Antony, an ally of Octavian at the time, and killed. Thereafter Rome's grain supply was secure. See also OCTAVIAN'S WAR AGAINST ANTONY.

October (November) Revolution, Russian (1917) After an abortive attempt by the Bolsheviks (radical marxist party) to seize power from the provisional government in Petrograd (Leningrad, St. Petersburg) in July 1917, Bolshevik leader Vladimir I. Lenin (1870–1924) fled to Finland, and Russian socialist Alexander F. Kerensky (1881–1970) succeeded the liberal Prince Lvov (1861–1925) as premier (see BOLSHEVIK REVOLUTION; FEBRUARY REVOLUTION). A reactionary coup failed (see KORNILOV'S REVOLT) but weakened Kerensky's power; support for the Bolsheviks increased as the Russians, exhausted and suffering severe privations from fighting WORLD WAR I, grew suspicious of military and governmental leaders. In early November 1917 (late October by the Old Style calendar), soviets, or revolutionary councils, throughout Russia voted to form a Soviet government that would end the war and establish citizen-run industries and farms. The Bolshevik leader Leon Trotsky (1879–1940) took over the military revolutionary committee at Petrograd, where the troops voted to obey only the committee's orders. Kerensky demanded rescission of the vote and sent soldiers on November 6, 1917 (October 24, O.S.), to shut down the Bolshevik press in Petrograd. The Bolsheviks, along with sympathetic troops and the workers' Red Guards, marched upon and peacefully took over the government buildings and public utilities. While Kerensky gathered his forces to oust the Bolsheviks, his ministers at the Winter Palace surrendered in the face of Bolshevik armed might. Then Kerensky's troops marched to Gatchina near Petrograd, and there the pro-Kerensky committee of public defense ordered the military-school trainees to arrest the military revolutionary committee and to attack Bolshevik or Soviet-held areas. The Bolsheviks withstood this assault and took charge of the military schools. Trotsky moved to Gatchina, where his troops defeated government forces in two days; Kerensky then fled abroad. Lenin became president of a Council of People's Commissars, the name of the new government, in which Trotsky and Joseph Stalin (1879–1953) were chief commissars. The Bolsheviks soon took Moscow after bloody street fighting, and within a month they controlled the country. In January 1918, Lenin dissolved the freely elected socialist-dominated national assembly, thereby ending Russia's first attempt at democracy. See also RUSSIAN CIVIL WAR OF 1918–21.

"October Revolution, Second" See RUSSIAN REBELLION OF 1993.

"October War" See ARAB-ISRAELI WAR OF 1973.

Offa's Wars (A.D. 771–96) Offa (fl. 757–96), who became king of Mercia after a brief, successful civil war (757) against the murderers of his cousin King Aethelbald (fl. 716–57), asserted control directly and indirectly over much of Anglo-Saxon England south of present-day Yorkshire; by 774, he was labeled "king of the English." The wars he fought were chiefly disciplinary: the reduction to vassalage in 771 of the small kingdom of Hastings between Kent and Sussex and the quashing of Kentish revolts in 775, 795, and 796 (one with the help of his son-in-law, the king of Wessex). Wessex, before the reign of Offa's son-in-law, had to be disciplined at the Battle of Bensington (779). A more violent defeat and punishment affected an insubordinate subking of East Anglia—he was beheaded (794). In the west, Offa's forces had many skirmishes with the Welsh; he had an earthen wall, called Offa's Dyke, built, less as a fortification than as a boundary between England and Wales. A civilizing monarch, Offa codified laws and established a new coinage. See also AETHELBALD'S WARS.

Ogaden War　See ETHIOPIAN-SOMALI BORDER WAR.

Og's Rebellion (1480)　Despite the failure of the MACDONALD REBELLION in 1411, the Macdonald clan was a source of constant headache to the Scottish Crown. An agreement between the Crown and the "Lord of the Isles" turned his bastard son Angus Og (d. 1490) against both his father and the central government, splitting the western Highlands into two feuding groups. At the 1480 Battle of Bloody Bay, Angus Og, with help from the Macleod and MacKenzie clans, fought what is recorded as an unusually violent and bloodthirsty fight, capturing and imprisoning his own father and two Maclean lieutenants. Thereafter, Angus Og kept the Highlands in turmoil until his assassination in 1490. See also DUBH'S REBELLION.

Old Zürich War (1436–50)　This war illustrates the tension between the burgeoning modern and declining feudal ages. The imperial (free) city of Zürich had acquired various feudal domains and expected to do so when the Toggenburg district near Lake Constance was freed by the 1436 death of its last count. Its competitor was Schwyz, another Swiss imperial city. Schwyz acted first, establishing communes in the Toggenburg and barring the road to Zürich; a 1437 conference of its canton officials agreed with the action. Their decision cut off some of Zürich's markets, and Zürich turned to the conservative Imperial Diet for relief in 1440. Frederick III (1415–43), a hidebound Hapsburg, duke of Austria and king of Germany, agreed to help Züurich (1442), forcing Schwyz and its ally Glarus to declare war on both Zürich and Austria. Zürich's forces retreated when its burgermeister (mayor) w3as killed; the Diet issued a conciliatory order, and Zürich broke with Austria, which rejected the Diet's order. The Swiss Confederacy aided Schwyz, laying

siege to Zürich with 20,000 troops. Frederick asked for help from France, whose King Charles VII (1403–61), seeking to regain Basel, sent 40,000 men. The troops beat a retreat in battle in 1444, and a peace was arranged at Ensisheim (which Zürich would not sign). A new Peace of Constance (1446) broke the Austrian-Zürich alliance officially, regained some territory for Zürich, and gave Schwyz most of the Toggenburg. More important, a 1450 court of arbitration ordered Austria out of the Aargau—that is, out of Switzerland—and replaced it with the House of Savoy.

Onin War (1467–77)　During the Middle Ages in Japan, powerful families or clans ruled large estates farmed by peasant serfs. When Yoshimasa (1435–90), the Ashikaga shogun, decided to retire, a dispute arose over succession and provoked a war between two rival military families serving the shogun in western Japan. Fighting centered chiefly in or near the capital city of Kyoto, which was soon left in ashes. Though Yamana Mochitoyo (1404–73) and his son-in-law Hosokawa Katsumoto (1430?–73), the leaders of the two warring groups, died during the Onin War (so called from the name of this period in Japanese history), hostilities dragged on and ended in a stalemate in 1477. Meanwhile, the war involved more than a dozen great families, notably the Shiba and Hatakeyama, and plunged the provinces into a struggle for the redistribution of feudal power. With the breakdown of authority from the imperial court and the shoguns, families turned against each other in an effort to increase their holdings. The countryside was laid waste by the destructive armed rivalry of warlords; thousands were killed and terrorized; and estates were decimated and their rulers bankrupted. See also JAPANESE CIVIL WARS OF 1450–1550.

Opium War, First (1839–42)　China tried unsuccessfully to restrict foreign trade and residence in its territory and forbade the importation of opium; British merchants ignored Chinese regulations and continued to import the forbidden drug. On March

30, 1839, a Chinese imperial commissioner ordered the opium in British warehouses and ships in Canton (Guangzhou) to be seized and destroyed. In retaliation, Britain sent warships and troops to attack China's coastal cities, including Hangchow (Hangzhou), Hong Kong, and Canton. British blockades were set up; an amphibious force moved up the Pearl (Zhu, Chu) River, stormed the forts around Canton, and captured the city in May 1841. The coastal cities of Amoy (Xiamen) and Ningpo (Ningbo, Ninghsien) fell soon after, but the British operation bogged down because the soldiers suffered from lack of supplies, poor food, disease, and typhoon-weather conditions. In the spring of 1842, a new energetic English commander arrived and began concerted military activities on the Yangtze (Chang) River; Shanghai and then Chinkiang (Zhenjiang) were taken. The Chinese were no match for the British with their modern weapons and navy, and when the British reached Nanking (Nanjing) in August 1842, the Chinese sued for peace. The Treaty of Nanking was a harsh one in which the Chinese were forced to pay a $20 million indemnity, cede Hong Kong to the British Crown, and open the ports of Canton, Amoy, Foochow (Fuzhou, Minhow), Ningpo, and Shanghai to British trade. **Second Opium War** (*Arrow* War) (1856–60). By 1856, the British wanted more concessions from the Chinese and teamed up with the French to send an expedition against China. After Chinese officials seized the *Arrow*, a Chinese-owned ship registered in Hong Kong flying the British flag and engaged in the illegal opium trade, an Anglo-French force attacked and occupied Canton in late 1857. They then sailed north to capture briefly the Taku forts near Tientsin (Tianjin). Peace was made with the Treaties of Tientsin between China and Britain, France, Russia, and the United States; China agreed to open more ports to trade, allow foreign legations at Peking (Beijing), and legalize opium importation. When foreign diplomats were refused entrance at Peking and invading British forces were slaughtered by the Chinese near Tientsin (1859), an Anglo-French

expedition seized the Taku forts, moved upriver and took Tientsin, and defeated a Chinese army outside Peking (1860). The Chinese emperor fled, and his intimidated commissioners concluded four new treaties, which opened more ports to foreign trade, gave British, French, Russian, and American diplomats the right to live in Peking, and established the principle of extraterritoriality whereby the foreigners had extensive rights in their spheres of influence on China's coast. Peking's Summer Palace was burned in retaliation for the earlier Chinese seizure and torture of peace envoys led by Sir Harry Smith Parkes (1828–85); some in the party were killed. See also BOXER UPRISING.

Oporto, Revolution at (1820) Portugal was ruled by a regency established by the British after they had defeated the French in the PENINSULAR WAR, an important phase of the NAPOLEONIC WARS. The Portuguese king, John VI (1769–1826), remained in Brazil, where he had fled during the war and had set up court. Fearing the rise of Portuguese Jacobinism (extreme radicalism in politics), William Carr Beresford (1768–1854), British marshal in charge of the Portuguese army, went to Brazil to persuade John to return because he believed the king could prevent a Portuguese revolution. While Beresford was away, liberal unrest increased and was stimulated by the outbreak of the SPANISH CIVIL WAR OF 1820–23. On August 24, 1820, members of the Jacobin Club at Oporto (Porto), Portugal, along with high-ranking army officers who sought Beresford's ouster, staged a coup; two colonels with their troops declared the establishment of a national junta, and with a volley of shots the "revolution" was accomplished. In Lisbon, the capital, a revolt occurred on September 15, 1820, with a junta evicting the ruling regency and calling a meeting of the Cortes (legislature). The resident British military were evicted, and Beresford returned to England. In 1821, John returned to Portugal to rule as a constitutional monarch. See also BRAZILIAN WAR OF INDEPENDENCE; PORTUGUESE CIVIL WAR OF 1823–24.

Oranges, War of the (1801)   Napoleon Bonaparte (1769–1821), French dictatorial leader, demanded that Portugal cede to France much of its national territory and close its ports to British trade (see FRENCH REVOLUTIONARY WARS). Spain reluctantly agreed to join with France in an invasion of Portugal when Napoleon's demands were rejected. French forces invaded in April 1801, and were joined by Spanish troops under Manuel Godoy (1767–1851). After defeating the Portuguese near Olivenza on the Spanish border, Godoy sent a triumphant message, along with oranges picked from nearby Elvas, to the Spanish queen, saying he would march to Lisbon (the war thus received its name from that gift of fruit). Portugal then readily signed the Peace of Badajoz on June 6, 1801, pledging to shut its ports to the British, to grant trade privileges to France, to cede Olivenza to Spain and part of Brazil (Portuguese Guiana) to France, and to pay war reparations. Napoleon, however, disavowed the terms, which Spain prepared to defend in the face of Napoleon's threats to destroy it, as well as Portugal. But he did not fulfill them because of British challenges to France elsewhere. See also NAPOLEONIC WARS.

Orléans, Siege of (1429)   The 1420 Treaty of Troyes (see HUNDRED YEARS' WAR) made King Henry V (1387–1422) of England heir to the French throne, despite denunciations by the dauphin, later Charles VII (1403–61), and his large following at Bourges. Henry's death in 1422 caused the regent for King Henry VI (1421–71) to attack the south of France, winning several victories. He mounted an English siege at Orléans, the dauphin's key city, in 1428—an unchivalric action, for its duke was a prisoner. French resistance continued for months, until Jeanne d'Arc or Joan of Arc (1412–31), a deeply religious peasant girl, led the French to victory. Joan's army drove the English from the Loire River valley, raising French morale. The English were forced out of Troyes, Châlons, and Rheims, where Charles was crowned. Though executed as a heretic in 1431, Joan had fatally weakened the English.

Osaka Castle, Siege of (1614–15)   After the Battle of SEKIGAHARA, the infant Hideyori (1598–1615), Japan's nominal ruler, and his mother went to live in the great castle that his father, Toyotomi Hideyoshi (1536–98), had built in Osaka, Japan, in 1583. The chief of the board of regents, Tokugawa Iyeyasu (1542–1616), remained friendly with Hideyori even though the child's family had been implicated in the 1600 conspiracy against him led by Ishida Mitsunari (1563–1600). Hideyori was encouraged to spend some of his great wealth to rebuild the temple of Hokoji, which had been destroyed by an earthquake in Kyoto. When the temple was ready to be dedicated, Iyeyasu objected to an inscription on the bell and prohibited the ceremony. Furious, Hideyori returned to his castle and invited discontented daimyo (lords) to join him there to plot Iyeyasu's overthrow. Before they could take any overt action, Iyeyasu and his large army laid siege to the castle in December 1614. Although doggedly holding off the besiegers, Hideyori's forces could not break out of the well-fortified castle. In January 1615, a truce was agreed upon, which stipulated, among other things, that the outer ramparts of the castle be torn down and the wide moats be filled with earth. When this was done, Iyeyasu found a pretext to renew the siege in May 1615. With its defenses considerably weakened, the castle was successfully stormed and burned by Iyeyasu's army; Hideyori committed *seppuku* (suicide by ripping out the bowels), and his family and followers were slain or exiled. Iyeyasu was the undisputed ruler of Japan, and his Tokugawa heirs would govern the country until 1867 (see MEIJI RESTORATION). See also SHIMABARA REVOLT.

Oswald's Wars (A.D. 633–41)   The death of Deiran king Edwin (585–632) enabled the Bernician nobility under Oswald (605?–41), son of Bernician king Aethelfrith (fl. 593–616), to regain dominance in the united Northumbrian kingdoms of Bernicia and Deira (see AETHELFRITH'S WARS). Oswald, exiled from Northumbria after 616, sought the help of another Anglo-Saxon ruler, Penda (577?–655), king of Mercia. Their enemy was Cadwallon (Cadwallader) (d. 634), ruler of the northern Welsh kingdom of Gwynedd. Styling himself "king of the Britons," Cadwallon had slain Edwin in the 632 Battle of Heathfield, carried Edwin's severed head to York, and then ravaged both Deira and Bernicia "like a furious tyrant," in the words of the English historian Bede (673–735). Oswald and Penda defeated and killed Cadwallon near Heavenfield in 634 after a year of fighting. Most of Oswald's reign was spent securing his Northumbrian borders and extending his authority southward; a dynastic marriage made him overlord of Wessex. He desired a peaceful kingdom, established a monastery at Lindisfarne (Holy Island) to introduce Celtic Christianity into Northumbria, but his move toward Wessex turned his ally Penda into a competitor, for they fought at Maserfeld (Oswestry?) in 641, and Oswald was slain. Mercia then became the dominant Anglo-Saxon kingdom for the next 150 years. Oswald was canonized as a saint. See also AETHEL-BALD'S WARS.

Ottoman-Byzantine Wars   See BYZANTINE-OT-TOMAN TURK WARS

Ottoman Civil War of 1403–13   The death of Ottoman sultan Bayazid I (1347–1403) after his defeat and capture at the Battle of ANGORA shattered the young Ottoman Empire. Four of his six sons fought among themselves for the sultanate, each from separate strongholds. Muhammad (1389–1421) seized Karaman, Süleyman (d. 1411) controlled the empire's European holdings, and Isa (d. 1405) and Mustafa (d. 1413) seized territories in Anatolia (Turkey). At first, Süleyman seemed to have supreme power; he allied himself with the Byzantines in 1405, then defeated and strangled Isa. His brother, Mustafa, next (1406) tried to defeat him and the Byzantine co-emperor in Thrace; however, Mustafa's Serbian and Bulgarian allies deserted him, and Süleyman and his forces occupied the Ottoman European capital at Adrianople (Edirne). His power was short-lived: Mustafa led Turks and Wallachians against him, coaxed his Janissaries

(elite soldiers in the sultan's army) into defection, then captured him and ordered his strangulation (1411). Mustafa's forces attempted to besiege Constantinople (Istanbul), but they lost their fleet and the struggle. Still dominant, Mustafa raised a large army (1412) by falsely accusing the Byzantine emperor of soliciting Timurid aid; he punished the Serbians for their desertion in 1406 and conquered Salonica, blinding its ruler, the son of Süleyman. But Muhammad, Bayazid's youngest son, appeared as Süleyman's avenger, backed by powerful Turkish notables. Allying with the Byzantines, he helped raise another of Mustafa's sieges of Constantinople, won back the Janissaries, and fought Mustafa three times before defeating him and ordering his strangulation (1413). No longer opposed within the family, Muhammad I began the difficult task of reuniting the Ottoman Empire.

Ottoman Civil War of 1481–82   Sultan Muhammad II "the Conqueror" (1429–81) strengthened the Ottoman Empire by developing a principle of indivisibility of rule. He alone had power, an absolutism protected by the peculiarly Ottoman custom of permitting a reigning sultan to execute his brothers. Muhammad's sons, however, proved less heartless, to their mutual misfortune. His son Bayazid (1447–1513), governor of Amasya when Muhammad died, arrived at Constantinople (Istanbul) first to find the Janissaries had revolted, killed the grand vizier as a supporter of his younger brother, and harassed Christians and Jews. Promises of amnesty and increased pay won him the Janissaries' support, and he was made Sultan Bayazid II in 1481. His younger brother, Djem (1459–95), governor of Karaman, went to the old Ottoman capital of Bursa to avoid the Janissaries, was proclaimed sultan, and reigned there 18 days. He proposed an amicable solution: Bayazid could rule Europe. The indivisibility doctrine, reinforced by religious arguments and Bayazid's ambition, caused Djem to battle Bayazid at Yenishehr in 1481; in defeat, Djem fled to Cairo. In 1482, Djem returned with Mamluk assistance, tried vainly to rouse Karaman, was defeated, and then fled to Rhodes. There the Knights Hospitalers

(Order of St. John) under Pierre d'Aubusson (1423–1503), who had successfully defended Rhodes against Muhammad's fleet in 1480, kept Djem captive (for an annual fee) until his death, perhaps at Bayazid's order; during those 13 years Bayazid refrained from European wars because of the threat of Djem's release to resume the civil war. Relieved at his brother's demise, Bayazid felt free to war against Venice (see VENETIAN-TURKISH WAR OF 1499–1503)).

Ottoman Civil War of 1509–13 Enthroned during a period of revolt and fraternal rivalry (see OTTOMAN CIVIL WAR OF 1481–82), Sultan Bayazid (1447–1513) was doomed to exit under similar circumstances: his sons, his Turkoman inhabitants, and the Janissaries (his elite soldiers) all rebelled against him. Even his death was a reflection: the poisoning of his brother, Djem (1459–95), perhaps at his order, mirrored Bayazid's own poisoning in 1513, perhaps by order of his son, Selim I (1467–1520). Bayazid had chosen his son, Ahmed (d. 1513), to be his successor, but Selim, governor of Trebizond, wanted greater power. When Bayazid showed his readiness to abdicate in Ahmed's favor, Selim and his men marched to Adrianople (Edirne), demanding that Selim be given a European province to govern (with Bayazid as sultan); he soon seized the city, only to be defeated and forced to flee back to Trebizond (1509–10). Meanwhile, the influence of Ismail I (1486–1524), the Safavid shah of Persia, caused Shi'ite Turkoman nomads to rebel in 1511 and capture Bursa, 150 miles from Adrianople. Bayazid, whose grand vizier was absent to suppress the rebellion, was then surprised by Ahmed, anxious for his promised inheritance; Bayazid prevented a revolt of the Janissaries against Ahmed by refusing to abdicate. Afterward Ahmed and his brother Kortud (d. 1513) tried to gain power in Anatolia (Turkey). In 1512, Ahmed's forces, with Persian aid, were defeated by an army under Selim, who then rushed to Adrianople, received the Janissaries' assistance, and forced Bayazid's abdication. Within a month, Bayazid was dead, as was Kortud. Ahmed was defeated and stran-

gled to death in 1513. All of Selim's nephews were similarly slain. To complete his removal of all possible opposition, Selim, nicknamed "the Grim" because of his cruelty, had eliminated four out of five of his sons and ordered the massacre of 40,000 Anatolian Shi'ites. Unjustly, he died of old age. See also PERSIAN CIVIL WAR OF 1500–1503; TURKO-PERSIAN WAR OF 1514–16.

Ottoman Civil War of 1559 Viewed strictly as a militarist, Sultan Süleyman I (1496–1566) deserves the sobriquet "the Magnificent" bestowed on him by historians. But his personal life deserves less praise, for, like many Ottoman sultans, he allowed the harem to either influence or dictate policy. Süleyman's attitude toward his favorite wife, Roxelana (d. 1559), was uxorious. She persuaded him to believe the falsehood that his eldest son Mustafa (d. 1553) was plotting to usurp the throne, and Süleyman had him beheaded in 1553. Upon Roxelana's death, her and Süleyman's sons Selim (1524?–74) and Bayazid (d. 1561) became rivals. Bayazid raised an army to oppose Selim, whom Süleyman favored, but was defeated at the Battle of Konya in 1559 and afterward fled to Persia. In 1561, the Persian shah delivered Bayazid to executioners sent by Selim with the approval of Süleyman, who paid the shah handsomely for his help.

Ottoman-Druse War of 1585 Descended from the original followers of al Hakim (d. 1021), considered an incarnation of God in 1017 while he functioned as the sixth caliph of Egypt's Fatamid dynasty, the Druse (Druze), still a small Islamic sect today, became politically important in what is now Lebanon in the 11th century, especially as opponents of the then dominant Shi'ite sect. After the Ottoman conquest of the Mamluks (see MAMLUK-OTTOMAN WAR OF 1516–17) and the Ottoman establishment of controls in Lebanon, Sultan Selim I (1467–1520) recognized the importance of placating the Druse by naming Fakhr ad-Din (d. 1544) of the house of Ma'n the emir ("native ruler") of the Druse in the Ottoman Empire, for Selim regarded himself as the punisher of the unorthodox, particularly the militant Shi'ites. However, in one of Lebanon's many attempts to achieve some autonomy, an insurrection began in 1585, led by Yusuf Sayfa (fl. 1580s), Shi'ite ruler of Tripoli, and grew into a war involving many Muslim religiopolitical groups. Fakhr's son, Korkmaz (Qurqomaz) (1544–85), a Druse leader, had to be executed by the Ottomans, who regained control in the area. He was succeeded first by an uncle and then by the first emir's grandson, Fakhr ad-Din II (1572–1635), who became leader of the Druses in 1590 and made them the dominant force in Lebanese politics.

Ottoman-Druse War of 1611–13 After 1590, Fakhr ad-Din II (1572–1635), emir (independent ruler) of the Druse (Druze) from 1607, had consolidated and extended his influence until the Druse controlled the dominant religiopolitical party (the Kaysis) in what is now Lebanon. Aware of the Ottoman preoccupation with war in Europe and Asia (see AUSTRO-TURKISH WAR OF 1591–1606. TURKO-PERSIAN WAR OF 1603–12), Fakhr sought security and trade by allying himself with Tuscany in Italy (that is, the Holy Roman Empire) in 1608. Alarmed by this development and regarding it as making possible a crusader state in the Fertile Crescent, Ottoman sultan Ahmed (1589–1617) ordered the pasha (governor) of Damascus to begin a punitive expedition against Fakhr and the Druse. As holder of territories from Nazareth in the south to Mount Carmel in the north, and leader of his own 40,000-man army, Fakhr was hard to control under the best of conditions, and the Ottoman police action failed at first. But a successful offensive by the pasha in 1613 forced Fakhr into exile in Tuscany, to the pleasure of Ahmed. However, in 1618, the new Ottoman sultan, Osman II (1604–22), a teenager, welcomed Fakhr back to expand his territories in all directions, with the blessings of the Porte (Ottoman government), unaware that Fakhr remained secretly allied with Tuscany.

Ottoman-Druse War of 1631–35 The territorial ambitions of the Druse (Druze) ruler Fakhr ad-Din II (1572–1635) continued to offend his local Lebanese enemies, whom he put down in 1625 despite assistance from the pasha (governor) of Damascus. He continued his opposition to the Porte (Ottoman government) with secret aid from the grand duke of Tuscany in Italy and bribed Ottoman officials at Constantinople (Istanbul) to prevent military actions. But Ottoman sultan Murad IV (1609–40), planning yet another campaign in the TURKO-PERSIAN WAR OF 1623–38, doubted the allegiance of the Druse (who might support the Persians in Syria and Mesopotamia) and ordered a land and sea expedition against Fakhr in 1633. While the Ottoman navy blockaded the Lebanese coast, a Turkish (Syrian-Egyptian) 80,000-man army encountered and defeated 25,000 Druse, Maronites, and mercenaries, led by Fakhr, who escaped capture to the mountains. One of his sons was captured and executed. In late 1634, Fakhr himself was seized, transported to Constantinople, and there beheaded (1635) along with two of his other sons. The Ma'n dynasty (Fakhr's) died out in 1697, but Druse belligerence has lasted to the present day.

Ottoman-Mamluk Wars See MAMLUK-OTTOMAN WARS.

P

Pacific, War of the (1879–84) Peru, Bolivia, and Chile all wanted control of the Atacama Desert region; Peru claimed Tacna, Arica, and Tarapacá; Bolivia claimed Antofagasta; and the boundary there between Bolivia and Chile was uncertain. In the 1860s, the nitrates found in the desert became valuable, and consequently Chilean companies moved into the area. In 1866, Chile and Bolivia established their boundary at the 24th parallel; Chile promptly began to mine its area and to expand northward. Peru and Bolivia secretly allied in 1873 to defend their territories in the Atacama. Property of the Chilean nitrate companies was seized by Peru in 1875 and by Bolivia in 1878. Chilean president Aníbal Pinto (1825–84) sent 200 troops to occupy the port of Antofagasta in February 1879, and on April 5, 1879, Chile declared war on Bolivia and Peru. The first stage of the war was fought largely at sea, where Chilean warships took the offensive and blockaded coastal ports. The Peruvian ironclad *Huáscar*, commanded by Admiral Miguel Grau (1838–79), harassed the Chilean navy until it was destroyed in a battle off Antofagasta on October 8, 1879; Grau and many of his crew were killed. The war's second phase occurred on land, with Chilean forces confronting and rolling back combined Bolivian-Peruvian armies in the Tarapacá region in late 1879. After occupying Antofagasta and Tarapacá, Chile sent an expedition north to Arica and Tacna and seized these towns by June 1880. The Bolivians were clearly defeated, but the Peruvians

continued to fight to regain Tarapacá. Peace negotiations began. A Chilean force of almost 25,000 men landed at Pisco, Peru, routed the Peruvians as it moved north, and captured the Peruvian capital of Lima on December 17, 1879. Resistance completely broke down in Peru, which was nearly on the verge of national collapse. By the Treaty of Ancón (October 20, 1883), Peru ceded Tarapacá province to Chile, which was allowed to keep Tacna and Arica for 10 years, after which a plebescite would determine their ownership. The Treaty of Valparaiso between Chile and Bolivia (April 4, 1884) provided for Chilean control of Antofagasta (city and province, including the Atacama), but the terms were not officially recognized until 1904.

Padri War (Minangkabau War) (1821–37) Since at least the 16th century a civilized Muslim people had inhabited the Minangkabau country of central-western Sumatra. In the early 1800s, three Muslim pilgrims, returning home from Mecca and passing through the northern Sumatran port of Pedir, as all pilgrims did, were fired with zeal for reforming their Minangkabau Islamic society along puritanical lines. They soon attracted many followers who became known as the "white people," or Padris, because of the white robes and turbans they wore. The Pedri-advocated reforms were forced upon many people, who were severely punished if they did not conform. The local chiefs, who inherited their lands and titles through the female line (a practice forbidden by Islamic law), became alarmed by the reformers, whom they feared would set up a form of religious government. Resorting to armed conflict to maintain their authority, the chiefs failed to defeat the Padris and then sought help from the Dutch in Java. Seeing the Muslim reformers as a threat, the Dutch intervened, although their doing so antagonized some feudal nobles, who joined the Padris. The Padris' headquarters was in the well-fortified city of Bondjol, which withstood a 15-year siege by the Dutch. Even after the Padris surrendered in 1837, some die-hards continued to wage guerrilla warfare in the mountains. See also NANING WAR; JAVA WAR, GREAT.

Pahang Civil War (1857–63)   Upon the death of Sultan Bendahara Tun Ali (d. 1857), his two sons claimed his throne, which governed the Malay state of Pahang, whose eastern coast borders the South China Sea. The oldest son, Tun Mutahir (d. 1863), was supported by Johore (Johor), a Malay sultanate to the south, and by the British, who were then opposing Siamese (Thai) domination of Malaya. Wan Ahmad (fl. 1860s), the other son, was helped by the Trengganu (Terengganu), a sultanate to the north, and by the Siamese. Both sides, whose outside supporters had ulterior motives, engaged chiefly in raids and ambushes, with occasional battles near fortifications. Siamese vessels sent to assist Wan Ahmad in 1862 were routed by a British warship. The war ceased soon after Tun Mutahir's death in 1863, and Wan Ahmad was recognized as the new sultan.

Pakistani Civil War of 1971   Relations between East and West Pakistan became strained during the late 1960s because the eastern portion, which provided three-fourths of Pakistan's foreign trade, received few of the economic benefits. In 1966, a general strike and strong demands for increased autonomy for the east were followed by riots in 1968 and 1969, when a new Pakistani president, General Agha Muhammad Yahya Khan (1907–74), was in-

stalled. He ordered a 1970 vote—the first since 1947—for a national assembly. Assigned 163 seats, East Pakistan filled almost all of them with representatives from the Awami League, a movement for full eastern autonomy, led by Sheik Mujibur Rahman (1920–). Yahya Khan's responses —two postponements of the opening of the assembly and cancellation of the election results—brought on a general strike in East Pakistan and the withholding of taxes. Yahya Khan then declared martial law and moved 60,000 first-rate troops to East Pakistan, where negotiations failed to resolve the crisis. Rahman was arrested; and the troops, assigned to keep order, fired on student dormitories and crowded bazaars in Dacca (March 25, 1971). East Pakistan's independence as the nation of Bangladesh was declared the next day. West Pakistani forces, however, were so militarily efficient that hundreds of thousands of "rebels" were killed and some 10 million eastern refugees poured into India's West Bengal area. Attacked in Kashmir on December 3, 1971, India carried on a two-front war (see INDO-PAKISTANI WAR OF 1971), and by mid-December had secured the surrender of the West Pakistani troops in Bangladesh. Yahya Khan resigned in favor of his prime minister, Zulfikar Ali Bhutto (1928–); Rahman was released to rule Bangladesh as its prime minister. Tensions between Pakistan and Bangladesh were eased diplomatically in 1972, and an exchange of prisoners was arranged in 1973. Pakistan however, did not recognize the sovereignty of Bangladesh until 1974.

Pakistani (Sindh) Civil War of the 1990s   Conflict arose in Pakistan's Sindh (Sind) province between the indigenous Sindhi peoples and the Mohajirs (Muhajireen), Urdu-speaking immigrants from India who settled mainly in the urban areas of Sindh after the partition between Pakistan and India in 1947. The native-settler relationship, initially warm and welcoming, became strained during the mid-1960s following the implementation of the one-unit scheme (the joining of all four provinces as one unit for representation purposes in the central government) and the centralization of the bureaucracy in the

Punjab province. The consequent marginalization of the other three provinces (of which Sindh was the largest) led to feelings of alienation and frustration among their residents. For instance, 8 million acres of Sindhi lands were given to the military and other settlers without any compensation. Also, Sindh was deprived of its share of Indus River water and its rich natural resources were exploited. Sindhi medium schools in the city of Karachi were closed down. The Sindhis viewed the domination of non-Sindhis in Sindh's affairs as an affront to their hegemony, and thus was born the Jeeve Sindh movement and the Sindh National Alliance (SNA). Anti-Mohajir sentiments festered and were exploited by politicians on both sides. The two communities, never culturally homogeneous, drifted apart. The Mohajirs, treated as outsiders in a place they called home, organized the Mohajir Qaumi Movement (MQM) in March 1984, and in 1994 they launched a full-fledged struggle for a separate province. Since then, Sindh's urban areas have been turned into virtual battlefields by the warring factions—with riots, arson, looting, dacoities, and cold-blooded massacres exacerbated by police brutalities. The militancy of their leaders compounded by the easy availability of arms (via Afghanistan) and the lack of a political forum to redress their grievances, created an explosive situation in Sindh. The military crackdown, which began on May 27, 1992, temporarily suppressed the insurgency but brought to light the MQM's torture and coercive practices. Eventually, it split into the Altaf Hussain and the Haqiqi factions. The action was not drastic as many other parties and influential families in Sindh were also involved in clandestine criminal activities. Likewise, interpersonal rifts surfaced between the Sindhi nationalist leaders. Hostilities escalated in March 1994 when the government announced a new administrative district in Karachi and used force to curb the growing violence in the city. The army withdrew in November 1994 and both factions of the MQM unleashed a new wave of terror in the city using car bombs, rocket attacks, weekly strikes, and secret killings of non-Urdu speakers and MQM's media and civilian

critics. During the next few days, factional, ethnic, sectarian (between Shias and Sunnis), and gang violence claimed several hundred lives in Karachi, bringing the annual toll to over 750. The paramilitary, brought in to restore normality, began meddling in civilian affairs. The death toll between December 1, 1994, and March 15, 1995, was 542 human lives; by mid-1995, 800 had died, and 2,000 had lost their lives by year's end. The sectarian violence subsided in May 1995, but the MQM stepped up its campaign of terror, creating near civil war atmosphere in Karachi, where no one was safe and law enforcement officials perpetrated horrific crimes on those in their custody. By mid-1995, over 5,000 lives had been lost in the conflict, and 500 more were slain in 1996, and 270 more in the first few months of 1997, when the MQM-Muslim League governing coalition in Sindh released many militants from prison, thus unleashing another cycle of violence. In 1998, Karachi continued to be plagued by daily random attacks and a political resolution did not appear imminent.

Palan Wars (A.D. c. 800–1025)   The failure of Harsha Vardhana (c. 590– c. 647) to reconstitute the former Gupta Empire (see CHALUKYAN WAR AGAINST HARSHA) left north India in a chaotic state. As a result, many small Indian kingdoms attempted to expand themselves. The most persistent was the Bengal kingdom under the Pala dynasty, established about A.D. 750. During the next three centuries, the Palas made three attempts to push westward; each time more aggressive kingdoms defeated them. Their ruler Dharmapala (fl. 770–810) had extended Palan influence as far west as Kannauj, Harsha's former capital, encountering the resistance of the burgeoning Rashtrakutas. His successor, Devapala (fl. 810–50), claimed ancient rights to the Deccan region and advanced militarily along the Narmada (Narbada) River, only to be overwhelmed by Rashtrakutan forces. A large, loosely federated Rajput alliance resented Palan activity along the eastern Ganges River, and its forces marched victoriously into Bengal in 916. Palan aggression quieted until the reign of Mahipala I (fl. 988–1038); his extension of Palan influence west to Benares (Varanasi) and south along India's east coast caused the Cholas to begin a military campaign in the north in 1021. The Cholas entered Bengal in 1025, defeated the Palas under Mahipala, and caused the Pala dynasty to decline until invasions by the forces of Muhammad of Ghur at the end of the century brought about its collapse (see MUHAMMAD OF GHUR, CONQUESTS OF).

Palestinian Guerrilla Raids (c. 1960–93) Palestinian guerrilla groups, such as the Syrian-backed Al Saiqa, the marxist-oriented Popular Front for the Liberation of Palestine (PFLP), and Al Fatah, headed by Yasir Arafat (1929–), engaged in guerrilla raids against Israel, their enemy, as a means of keeping it on the defensive. Under the theoretical leadership of Arafat, who founded the Palestine Liberation Organization (PLO) in 1964 and became its leader in 1968, the raids were orchestrated before and between major Arab-Israeli wars. The guerrillas bombed Israeli schools, buses, and marketplaces; conducted random assassinations; and fired rockets at civilian centers. Before 1967, these terrorist raids came chiefly from Syria; after the SIX-DAY WAR (1967) the guerrillas were based in Jordan until they were forced into Lebanon during the JORDANIAN CIVIL WAR OF 1970–71. Arafat's Palestinians were forced out of Lebanon in 1983 (see LEBANESE CIVIL WAR OF 1975–90). Palestinian raids eventually became more infrequent, being replaced by imitative raids from Shi'ite groups. Two of the Palestinian attacks received worldwide condemnation: their "Black September" (September 6–9, 1970) hijacking of commercial jetliners (which forced 435 passengers to become hostages in Amman) and the 1972 raid at the Munich Olympic Games, during which 11 Israeli athletes were killed. In late 1987, Palestinians in Gaza rioted against Israeli police, resulting in further violence in other Israeli-occupied territories. The PLO consequently proclaimed an independent state in 1988, nominally recognized Israel, and gained minor diplomatic contact with the U.S. In uprisings termed "intifadeh," Palestinians opposed Israeli troops in the West Bank and Gaza in 1989 and 1990; scores of Palestinians were injured or killed. Negotiations between the PLO and Israel led to historic agreements in September 1993: Israel accepted the PLO as the Palestinians' representative, the PLO granted Israel's right to exist, and the Palestinians gained limited self-rule in the West Bank and Gaza (officially signed in 1994 and augmented in 1995). Palestinian anger and despair over paralysis in the peace process, brought on by the election in May 1996 of Israel's hard-line prime minister Benjamin Netanyahu (1949–), helped lead to furious confrontations between armed Israelis and Palestinians in late September 1996, after the opening of the ancient Hasmonean tunnel, dug by Israelis in Arab East Jerusalem (proposed capital of a future Palestinian state). The U.S. tried to find diplomatic ways to restart the peace process, and in early 1997 Israel agreed to a partial withdrawal from the West Bank city of Hebron. Extremists on both sides continued to clash on the roads and in Jerusalem, various Jewish settlements, and some religious sites. Israeli-Palestinian coexistence remained tenuous despite new Israeli-Palestinian peace talks and accords at Wye River, Md., mediated by the U.S. (mid-October 1998); Israel agreed to concede territory in return for strengthened security. See also ARAB-ISRAELI WAR OF 1973.

Panama, U.S. Invasion of (1989) By late 1988, the flamboyant strongman, General Manuel Antonio Noriega (1938–) virtually ruled Panama as head of the National Defense Forces. Increasing social turmoil and suppression of opposition (including Noriega's nullification of presidential election results in May 1989) caused the United States to intensify its diplomatic and economic pressures against Noriega, who had been indicted in the U.S. for drug trafficking. There were futile efforts by the Organization of American States (OAS) and various nations to mediate U.S.-Panamanian differences. After a military coup attempt against Noriega failed on October 3, 1989, Panama's government curtailed civil rights and issued emergency "war" measures; the assembly made Noriega "maximum leader" on December 15. U.S. president George

H.W. Bush (1924–) launched "Operation Just Cause"—American armed forces' invasion of Panama—in the early morning of December 20, with the intention of capturing Noriega after routing resistance and installing a stable, democratic government. About 14,000 U.S. troops invaded to join 12,700 troops already stationed in Panama to guard the Panama Canal. The capital, Panama City, suffered heavy damage in fighting between National Defense Forces (along with paramilitary troops) and American forces. Looting was widespread without an effective police force. Noriega, who took refuge in the Vatican diplomatic mission, eventually surrendered on January 3, 1990, and was taken to Miami, where later (1992) he was convicted and imprisoned on drug-running charges. Supported by the U.S., Guillermo Endara Galimany (1936–) who probably would have won the 1989 election nullified by Noriega, became president.

Panamanian Revolution of 1903   By the Hay-Herrán Treaty (January 22, 1903), Colombia was to lease land across the isthmus of Panama to the United States for the construction of a canal (Panama at that time was a part of Colombia). Colombian president José Manuel Marroquín (1827–1908), whose war-torn country was nearly bankrupt (see THOUSAND DAYS, WAR OF A), favored the treaty, but the Colombian congress rejected it on August 12, 1903. Philippe Jean Bunau-Varilla (1860–1940), who had been involved in the unsuccessful attempt by the French to build a canal and held canal-building rights, was supported by the U.S. government in his endeavor to raise funds to construct a Panama canal; he helped organize a revolt in Panama against Colombia. On November 3–4, 1903, at Colón, Panama, a small group of railroad workers, firemen, and soldiers rose up in revolt and proclaimed the independence of Panama. Offshore the U.S. cruiser *Nashville* deterred the landing of Colombian troops under General Rafael Reyes (1850?–1918) sent to put down the rebels. With unusual haste, U.S. president Theodore Roosevelt (1858–1919) recognized Panamanian independence on November 6, 1903, and soon after

received Bunau-Varilla, minister from the newly formed republic of Panama. On November 18, 1903, the United States and Panama signed the Hay-Bunau-Varilla Treaty, by which the former acquired a 10-mile-wide strip of land across the isthmus (the Panama Canal Zone) for a payment of $10 million, plus $250,000 annually for a lease, to Panama.

Panay Incident (1937)   The American gunboat U.S.S. *Panay*, which patrolled the Yangtze River near Nanking (Nanjing), China, was used as a bomb shelter for foreign embassy staff during the Japanese bombing of the area (see SINO-JAPANESE WAR OF 1937–45). On December 12, 1937, Japanese warplanes suddenly and without provocation dive-bombed repeatedly the *Panay* and a British gunboat, both of which were moored in the river; the American vessel was sunk, and the British one severely damaged. The U.S. public was outraged by this attack, which caused two deaths and 48 casualties. Claiming its pilots had not seen the U.S. flags painted on the *Panay*'s decks and sides, Japan apologized and paid the indemnity demanded by the United States. See also NANKING, SACK OF.

Papacy–Holy Roman Empire Wars   See HOLY RO-MAN EMPIRE–PAPACY WARS.

Papineau's Rebellion (1837)   French-Canadian political leader Louis Joseph Papineau (1786–1871) protested publicly against the British government's "unfair" treatment of French-Canadians in Lower Canada (Quebec). His speeches called for the breakup of the British-dominated governing clique, the Château Clique, and incited riots and fighting in Montreal. A series of armed clashes between Papineau's French-Canadian rebels and the better-trained and -equipped Canadian government militia, aided by British soldiers, took place at St. Denis, St. Charles, and St. Eustache in the Montreal area (November 1837). The rebels were easily defeated, and order was restored. Papineau escaped to the United States, then to France (1839), and later returned to Canada (1845) after receiving a general amnesty. See also MACKENZIE'S REBELLION.

Papua New Guinean Civil War of 1988–98
Decade-long, bloody strife on Papua New Guinea's island of Bougainville, in the southwest Pacific Ocean, killed almost 20,000 people, rendered 40,000 people homeless, and virtually destroyed the country's economy. It began as a fight over compensation between Bougainville Copper Limited (BCL), an Australian-owned mining company, and the hundreds of indigenous landowners it displaced in Panguna. The company destroyed over 220 hectares of forests, dumped toxic pollutants in the rivers, left 1,400 natives without fishing rights, and imported workers from elsewhere in Papua New Guinea, which upset the Bougainvillians who are racially and ethnically distinct from other Papua New Guineans. The landowners protested and tried for years to negotiate a fair settlement with BCL and the government. Finally, late in 1988, they were forced to close the copper mine. In March 1989, the government sent in the police and the military (financed, trained, and equipped by Australia), in what became the brutal and prolonged Operation Tampara. They isolated Bougainville through an air and sea blockade imposed in May 1990, hoping to force the natives into a settlement by denying them basic humanitarian aid and trying to turn them against the secessionist Bougainville Revolutionary Army (BRA), which had proclaimed independence. Two New Zealand-brokered agreements—the Endeavour Accord and the Burnham Declaration—were short-lived, as was the Honiara Agreement of September 1994. Early in 1997, Papua New Guinea's government hired mercenaries (the Sandline affair) to root out the BRA. Instead, the resulting controversy forced the resignation of Prime Minister Julius Chan (1939–). In July 1997, New Zealand again hosted peace talks. On April 30, 1998—amidst much jubilation—the two opposing parties signed a permanent ceasefire; the government would withdraw its troops and assure freedom of movement on the island, which would be patrolled by a multinational peacekeeping force.

Paraguayan Civil War of 1947   General Higinio Morínigo (1897–1983), named president of Paraguay in 1940, suspended the constitution and ruled as a military dictator. Under his regime, Paraguay suffered frequent disturbances, including labor and general strikes and student riots. The military, which received 45 percent of the national income, remained loyal to Morínigo and crushed his opposition. In July 1946, he permitted the resumption of political activity, banned since 1940, and formed a two-party cabinet. The next year the Febreristas resigned from the cabinet and, under their party's leader, Rafael Franco (1896–1973), a former Paraguayan president, tried to seize control of the government with the help of other liberals. They were defeated in a civil war from March to August 1947. Morínigo remained in office until ousted by a military coup on June 6, 1948. Paraguay had five presidents in the next 15 months.

Paraguayan Revolt of 1954   Federico Chávez (d. 1978), president of Paraguay since 1949, managed to be reelected in 1953, despite the weakness of his government and political dissension. On May 5, 1954, General Alfredo Stroessner (1912–), commander in chief of the armed forces, led a revolt with the support of the army and liberals, toppling the government and deposing Chávez. Running unopposed for president, Stroessner was "elected" in 1954 and established an authoritarian government that put down all opposition and imprisoned or exiled many political adversaries. This dictator withstood several unsuccessful revolts against him, managed to stabilize Paraguay's currency, and embarked on large public works projects.

Paraguayan Revolt of 1989   The harsh regime of General Alfredo Stroessner (1912–), who had ruled Paraguay since 1954 (see PARAGUAYAN REVOLT OF 1954) and been criticized for violations of human rights, was toppled in a revolt led by General Andrés Rodríguez (1923–), Stroessner's second-in-command, on February 3, 1989. Military forces loyal to Rodríguez violently seized control of the government in Asunción, the capital, where an estimated 300 people, both civilian and military, were killed. Stroessner was placed under house arrest and allowed to go into exile abroad; Rodríguez, an alleged cocaine trafficker, became president, vowing to restore democracy and respect human rights. In 1993, he was succeeded by Juan Carlos Wasmosy (1939–), Paraguay's first ever democratically elected civilian president, who faced a struggle to control the military and its authoritarian influence.

Paraguayan Uprisings of 1959–60   Many Paraguayans opposed to the harsh regime of General Alfredo Stroessner (1912–), president of Paraguay since 1954, had fled across the border into Argentina, where they established a base from which to stage attacks on their homeland in the hope of toppling the government. In September 1959, Stroessner ordered the country's southern border closed; on December 12, 1959, about 1,000 rebels, based in Argentina, crossed over and penetrated several miles until they were repulsed. Paraguay's government declared a state of siege. Border incidents continued to strain relations between Paraguay and Argentina. Six times in 1960 rebels attempted to invade Paraguay; quickly stopped by Stroessner's forces, they helped foment guerrilla activities in the south. The rebels and guerrillas were eventually subdued by the army.

Paraguayan War   (López War or War of the Triple Alliance) (1864–70)   Francisco Solano López (1827–70), president-dictator of Paraguay, dreamed of ruling a great Platine state in South America, with Paraguay as its center. Brazilian military intervention in Uruguayan political affairs in support of the Colorados (1864) caused López, who backed the Blancos, rivals of the Colorados, to demand the withdrawal of Brazilian imperial troops. When Brazil paid no heed, Paraguayan forces invaded and occupied the Brazilian state of Mato Grosso in late 1864, and López declared war on Brazil. Denied permission to cross Argentine territory so that his

soldiers could invade southern Brazil, López declared war on Argentina on March 18, 1865. Brazil, Argentina, and Uruguay formed the Triple Alliance against Paraguay (May 1, 1865) and organized allied armies under the command of Argentine general Bartolomé Mitre (1821–1906). Brazilian naval forces won a major battle on the Paraná River south of Corrientes in mid-1865, forcing the Paraguayans to retreat and afterward fight a defensive war from their own soil. López led his army to victory against the invading allies at the Battle of Curupayti (September 22, 1866) after suffering several defeats. Slowly allied forces pushed up the Paraguay River in 1867, capturing the strategic river fortress of Humaitá as López withdrew his men north to Angostura and Ypacaraí. After these two towns fell to the allies in late 1867, Paraguay's capital of Asunción was seized and sacked by the Brazilians, whose commander, Luís Alves de Lima e Silva, duke of Caxias (1803–80), replaced Mitre as head of the allied forces. Fleeing with partisan troops, López carried on a guerrilla war in northern and eastern Paraguay until he was killed on March 1, 1870, while fighting Brazilians in Concepción province. Paraguay's provisional government and the allies concluded a peace treaty (June 20, 1870), by which Argentina and Brazil received 55,000 square miles of Paraguayan territory. The war devastated Paraguay, whose former population of about 525,000 was reduced to some 221,000, of whom only 29,000 were adult males; it was the bloodiest conflict in Latin American history.

Paraguayan War of Independence   (1810–11)   In 1776, Paraguay had been combined with Argentina, Bolivia, and the Banda Oriental (Uruguay) into the viceroyalty of the Río de la Plata. After Napoleon (1769–1821) deposed King Ferdinand VII (1764–1833) of Spain (see NAPOLEONIC WARS; PENINSULAR WAR), the Argentines at Buenos Aires formed a ruling junta of the United Provinces of the Río de la Plata and invited outlying provinces to give their allegiance to this central authority. In 1811, one year after the Paraguayans had stated their autonomy, a force under Manuel Belgrano

(1770–1820) was sent from Buenos Aires to Asunción to force Paraguayan compliance, but Belgrano was defeated and withdrew. Paraguayans then ousted the Spanish royal governor, declared Paraguay's independence from Spain, and established a revolutionary junta at Asunción. In 1814, absolute governing power was given to the first consul, José Gaspar Rodríguez de Francia (1766–1840), who was declared "perpetual dictator" two years later. See also ARGENTINE WAR OF INDEPENDENCE.

Parthian-Roman Wars   See ROMAN-PARTHIAN WARS.

Parthian-Syrian Wars   See SYRIAN-PARTHIAN WARS.

Pastry War (1838)   During the early years of the Mexican republic, foreigners often found their property destroyed during civil strife. Unable to secure compensation from Mexico, they looked to their own governments for help. A French pastry cook, claiming his shop had been ruined by looting Mexican soldiers, appealed to France's King Louis-Philippe (1773–1850); France demanded 600,000 pesos for damages to its nationals and sent a fleet, which bombarded and seized the Mexican fortress of San Juan de Ulúa, near the port of Veracruz. Mexico declared war in 1838. General Antonio López de Santa Anna (1795?–1876) came out of retirement and, without authority, led the Mexican forces against the French at Veracruz, which the French occupied briefly. Soon the Mexican government of President Anastasio Bustamante (1780–1853) promised to pay the 600,000 pesos, and the French forces withdrew. In a skirmish at Veracruz, Santa Anna was wounded in a leg, which had to be amputated.

Paulician War of A.D. 867–72   The Paulicians, a dualist Christian sect that developed in Armenia in the mid-600s, established a Paulician state at Tephrike (Divrigu, Turkey) in the Byzantine Empire. Persecuted as heretics by the Byzantines, the Paulicians, nonetheless, survived and spread their teachings; they sided with the Muslims against the Byzantines (see BYZANTINE-MUSLIM WAR OF A.D. 851–63). In 867, Byzantine emperor Basil I (813?–86) began a military campaign to end the power of the Paulician state, and by 872, Byzantine troops had overrun Tephrike, killed the Paulician leader Chrysocheir (d. 872) and many others, and forced the remaining Paulicians to flee to Armenia and Syria.

Pearl Harbor (1941)   At 7:55 A.M. on Sunday, December 7, 1941, a swarm of Japanese aircraft swooped out of the sky and attacked the U.S. naval and air bases at Pearl Harbor on Oahu Island, Hawaii. This attack was a complete surprise, although tensions between the United States and Japan had been building up for some time (see WORLD WAR II). No one was prepared to do battle early on a Sunday morning in Hawaii, and for two hours the Japanese planes, aided by submarines and midget submarines, wreaked havoc on the U.S. fleet. Of the eight battleships present, three were sunk, another capsized, and the remainder were badly damaged; three cruisers, three destroyers, and five other vessels were sunk or seriously damaged; and 247 planes, 175 of which were destroyed on the ground, were lost. Only 29 of the 360 Japanese planes were shot down before the rest returned to their distant aircraft carriers. About 4,500 persons were killed or wounded, including the deaths of 2,330 American military personnel. The next day the U.S. Congress declared war against Japan; U.S. president Franklin D. Roosevelt (1882–1945) declared that December 7, 1941 was a "day that shall live in infamy." See also WORLD WAR II IN THE PACIFIC.

Peasant and Cossack Revolts   See CHMIELNICKI'S REVOLT; PUGACHEV'S REVOLT; RAZIN'S REVOLT.

Peasants' Revolt, English (Tyler's Revolt) (1381)   Plague and economic turmoil in England during the HUNDRED YEARS' WAR caused the peasants to suffer miserably. Attempts to control wages angered English journeymen, and rises in wages upset villeins (village peasant-serfs), who received no wages. The poll taxes ordered by John of Gaunt (1340–99) for war purposes angered everyone, especially in 1381: a shilling (a week's pay for a free peasant) from every adult. A village in Essex threw out an over-zealous tax collector in 1381, igniting a revolt that spread to Kent, where Wat Tyler (d. 1381) was chosen as leader. Soon all of England was affected by the peasants' revolt. Essex men under Jack Straw (fl. 1381) and Kent peasants under Tyler marched to London, burned Gaunt's palace, met with the young king Richard II (1367–1400), and were granted pardons and promised relief. A mob of London riffraff seized the Tower of London, killed the archbishop of Canterbury and others, and turned government opinion against all the rebels. A second meeting with Richard produced new demands, the murder of Tyler, the dispersal of the rebels, and the king's breaking of his earlier promises. Nationally, the revolt was quelled somewhat less violently than that of the JACQUERIE in France in 1358; however, the revolt slowed the decay of English feudalism.

Peasants' Revolt, Hungarian See DOZSA'S REBELLION.

Peasants' Revolt, Rumanian (1907) Proclaimed a kingdom in 1881, Rumania was, in theory, a representative democracy; in actuality, city dwellers had most of the power, and poorer rural dwellers were kept by complex rules from exercising their franchise. Rumania's economy improved, but only the powerful became wealthy; rural dwellers, especially landless farmers, grew steadily poorer. In March–April 1907, peasants united in revolt, burning the houses of rich landowners and destroying their crops until the army crushed the rebels with vigor. Reforms introduced into the Rumanian legislature passed, but they were administered in such a way before WORLD WAR I as to benefit only the large landholders.

Peasants' Revolt, Transylvanian (1784) Many indigenous Vlach (Wallachian) peasants, led by Rumanian patriot Nicolae Hora or Horea (1730–85), wishing to escape abusive Magyar nobles and their oppression, rose in violent revolt in November–December 1784 in Transylvania, part of Hungary under Austrian bureaucratic rule at the time. During the insurgency, the armed peasants raided and destroyed villages and homes, while massacring an estimated 4,000 Magyar nobles and other Hungarians (including government commissioners). Imperial troops finally ruthlessly crushed the insurgents; Hora was captured and executed on February 28, 1785.

Peasants' War, German (1524–25) Uprisings, mostly abortive and usually unsuccessful, were the rule in pre-Reformation Germany, especially "peasant clog" (*Bundschuh*) uprisings by poor rural inhabitants eager to gain freedoms and privileges as the Swiss had (see AUSTRO-SWISS WAR OF 1499). This conflict was politically, socially, and economically centered against the grave inequalities of German feudalism; it was also inspired by some of the Protestant ideas of Martin Luther (1483–1546), Huldreich Zwingli (1484–1531), and John Calvin (1509–64), although these ideas were extremely attenuated and simplified. In 1524, peasants organized armies in Swabia and Franconia and made pillaging raids in the southern German countryside. As local landholders and even some towns gave the rebels support and the war spread into Hesse, Thuringia, Saxony, and the Tyrol, the German nobility became determined to put the peasants down. Even Luther, angered by the rebels' penchant for disorder, repudiated them in 1525. In that year, the combined forces of the Lutheran prince of Hesse and the Catholic duke of Saxony cooperated in battling the insurgents at Frankenhausen in Thuringia. The battle there ended in defeat for the peasants, whose insurgency lost impetus when Thomas Müntzer (1489?–1525) was captured and beheaded. The German peasants, of whom some 100,000 were slain in the war, were crushed, but the Austrian poor fought on into 1526, gaining little before being suppressed, too. See also KNIGHTS' WAR.

Peasants' War, Swedish See DACKE'S WAR.

Peddlers' War See MASCATES, WAR OF THE.

Peloponnesian War, First (460–445 B.C.) The Delian League (see GRECO-PERSIAN WARS) gradually turned into an Athenian maritime empire and aroused the enmity of both Sparta and Corinth, Greek city-state rivals of Athens. Beset by a revolt of its Helots (see MESSENIAN WAR, THIRD), Sparta alienated Athens by rejecting its proffered aid; Athens then allied with Spartan enemies (462). Megara quarreled with Corinth and requested and received Athenian aid, setting off war in 460. At first victorious, Athens progressively established a land empire in Greece after defeating the Corintian fleet (460) and a Corintian army sent to raid Megara (459). Aegina, Corinth's ally, was besieged and captured by Athens in 457. Sparta created a diversion by sending an expedition to Boeotia to bolster its ally Thebes; it won the Battle of Tanagra (457) against the Athenians near Thebes, but recalled its forces. The Athenians then defeated the Thebans at Oenophyta (457) and took control of Boeotia. Under the leadership of Pericles (495?–429), Athens seized a long coastal strip of Achaea in 455, receiving the vassalage of Sparta's Helots, ordered to colonize the Corinthian Gulf. In 451, a five-year truce began. After Boeotia revolted against Athens, the tide turned in favor of Sparta and its allies; Megara, Phocis, and Euboea revolted (see SACRED WAR, SECOND). A Spartan army marched toward Athens but was checked in time by Pericles's forces. Euboea was recovered by Athens. but its land empire was gone. A peace was negotiated in 445, allowing Athens its maritime empire and Sparta its land empire; they called for 30 years' amicability, but only 14 had elapsed before contentious colonies and allies of Sparta and Athens caused renewed fighting. **Second or Great Peloponnesian War** (431–404 B.C.). Begun with an Athenian victory over The-

bans at Plataea, an ally of Athens, the early part of the war followed Pericles's policy of avoiding set battles, and a Spartan siege of Athens failed (see ARCHIDAMIAN WAR). But the plague killed Pericles and one-quarter of Athens' population; and Cleon (d. 422), the new Athenian leader, altered the war policy, which had been to raid and blockade and had successfully closed the Gulf of Corinth in 429. Under Cleon, Athens now put down a revolt in Lesbos (428), vainly attempted to capture Boeotia (427), and seized all but one base in the Corinthian Gulf. Then the Athenians spectacularly established a base in Spartan territory at Sphacteria in 425. Their victory over Megara and its port Nisaea in 424 seemed to prove the new war policy correct. But a campaign in Boeotia failed at Delium, morale fell, and an Athenian peace party led by Nicias (d. 413) opposed Cleon; Athenian policy became decided politically, and the results were often disastrous. Spartans under General Brasidas (d. 422) defeated the Athenians at Amphipolis in 424. A one-year truce was followed by a futile Athenian attempt to retake Amphipolis (see BRASIDAS'S INVASION). After the deaths of Cleon and Brasidas, Nicias, the new Athenian leader, concluded a misguided peace (421): Athens was to retain Pylos (harbor in Messenia) and Sparta Amphipolis. The mercurial Athenian statesman Alcibiades (c. 450–404) forced a break with Sparta, making Athenian alliances with Argos, Mantinea, and Tegea (former Spartan allies). The peace that was to last 50 years ended. Alcibiades apparently persuaded Nicias and his council to back a flamboyant plan to conquer Syracuse, Sicily. The Athenian sea and land forces departed in 415 for Syracuse, but Alcibiades, called back to face charges of religious sacrilege, defected to Sparta, which he persuaded to send troops to help the Syracusans. The Athenians led by Nicias lost a Syracusan siege and became the besieged in 414; their great general Lamachus (d. 414) died in battle, and their fleet was destroyed by a Spartan-Corinthian-Syracusan navy in 413. All Athenian survivors became slaves; Athens lost over 40,000 men, 240 ships, and their leaders Nicias and Demosthenes (d. 413), both of whom were captured and executed.

Under Alcibiades' guidance, Sparta planted a garrison on Attic soil at Declea, threatening Athens, whose treasury suffered, for its silver mines at Laurium became unreachable. The Persian satrap of Sardis made a treaty with Sparta and urged Athens' colonies in Asia Minor to revolt (Sparta had agreed to Persian sovereignty over them and thus had gotten Persian money to support its navy). Miraculously, Athens rebuilt its fleet and recovered some rebellious states (412), and Alcibiades secretly negotiated to rejoin Athens and was recalled after promising to help crush the Athenian oligarchs (411). Appointed commander of the fleet, Alcibiades led the Athenians in victory over the Spartan fleet at Cynossema and Abydos in 410. At the Battle of Cyzicus (410) Spartan-Persian sea and land forces were decisively beaten, and Sparta requested to make peace, with the status quo, but Cleophon (d. 405), the new Athenian ruler and a demagogue, refused. Byzantium again came under Athenian control when Alcibiades seized it in 408; he returned to Athens in triumph but soon lost influence when his squadron (he had left it at Ephesus) was defeated by a Spartan-Persian fleet under Lysander (d. 395) off Notium in 406. The Athenian fleet was then blockaded at Mytelene, but a totally new fleet was raised (wondrously since Athens was nearly bankrupt) and defeated the Spartans at the Battle of Arginusae in 406. A Spartan offer to make peace was again rejected by Cleophon. In 405, the Athenian fleet of almost 200 ships, moored for the night, was surprised by Lysander's naval force and utterly destroyed at the Battle of AEGOSPOTAMI near the Hellespont (Dardanellas); the Athenian crews were captured and slain. Lysander sailed to Piraeus and Athens and besieged both, forcing the starving Athenians to capitulate after a six months' siege. Cleophon was tried and executed. Thus, after the destruction of its fortifications, reduction of its fleet to 12 ships, transformation into an oligarchy, and designation as a subject ally to Sparta, ancient Athens was never again a political power.

Peninsular War (1808–14)   Even before Austria's attempt to regain autonomy during the NAPO-

LEONIC WARS, Napoleon (1769–1821) encountered trouble on the Iberian peninsula—trouble that would end only with his reign. When Britain's ally Portugal rejected the Continental System (a trade boycott initiated by Napoleon against Britain), Napoleon secured permission to invade Portugal via Spain. Ensuing Spanish discontent led King Charles IV (1748–1819) of Spain to abdicate in 1808 in favor of his son King Ferdinand VII (1784–1833), who was received enthusiastically by the people. Napoleon, however, forced Ferdinand to return the crown to his father, who then resigned his rights to the French emperor, whereupon Napoleon crowned his own brother, Joseph Bonaparte (1768–1844), sparking a national uprising backed by Britain. The French, after setbacks at Bailén and Vimeiro in 1808, surrendered Lisbon. Then Napoleon himself took command of the French forces and nearly defeated the British, who narrowly escaped at Coruña in early 1809. That year, with France preoccupied in Austria, the British under Sir Arthur Wellesley, Lord Wellington (1769–1852), returned to drive the French from Portugal and invade Spain, overcoming the French at Talavera on July 28, 1809. But Napoleon's reinforcements restored French ascendancy. In 1811 Wellington's forces began their inexorable recovery of Portugal's frontier fortresses. They proceeded to Salamanca and Madrid, evicting the French from southern Spain by 1812. Wellington failed to take Burgos but in 1813 routed the French at Vitoria and pursued them back into France, where he laid siege to Bayonne and Bordeaux, his actions merging with the general allied liberation effort. The Peninsular War brutalized Spain and detonated revolutions throughout Latin America.

Penruddock's Revolt (1655)   The dismissal by Oliver Cromwell (1599–1658), "Lord Protector" of England, Scotland, and Ireland, of an uncooperative parliament in early 1655 made him a military despot. Royalist uprisings resulted, for many wished the return of the Crown. In Wiltshire, England, John Penruddock (1619–55), royalist son of a knight's family, had already suffered financially because of his politics. With 200 followers, he occupied the town of Salisbury and seized judges trying royalists for treason. Penruddock spared them and then marched into Devon, only to be captured by a Cromwellian regiment. Tried before the judges he had captured in Salisbury, he was found guilty and was decapitated. Cromwell, however, revealed some generosity: Penruddock's children were granted some of his sequestered estate. See also ENGLISH CIVIL WAR, FIRST OR GREAT.

Pequot War (1637) The warlike Pequot Indians, who lived in the forests of southern New England between Narragansett Bay and the Connecticut River, were involved in warfare with rival Indians in the area. When English colonists began to settle in the Connecticut River valley, the Pequot were displeased by this encroachment on their homeland, and confrontations were frequent. In 1636, John Oldham (1600?–1636), an English trader, was killed on Block Island, presumably by a Pequot, and a punitive English expedition from Massachusetts raided and ruined several Pequot villages in retaliation in 1637 (the English were also angry because of Pequot interference with their trading with the Dutch). A colonial force and friendly Indians, led by Captain John Mason (1600?–1674), successfully stormed the main Pequot stronghold at Mystic, Conn., and killed more than 500 Indian defenders. Much of the Pequot tribe was wiped out; those captured were sold as slaves in the West Indies or to the colonists. In 1655, the colonists granted the remnant of the tribe a reservation on the Mystic River, where some of their descendants still live.

Perak War (1875–76) British influence in Perak, a state in northwestern Malaysia, began in 1818 when trading agreements were first made with local chiefs. The Pangkor Treaty of 1874 allowed Britain to send its first resident, James W.W. Birch (d. 1875), to take charge of governmental administrative affairs. Soon after his arrival later in 1874, Birch changed many old-fashioned and inefficient procedures and policies, especially those concerning revenue collection and slavery. The sultan of Upper Perak and other Malay chiefs met secretly in July 1875, and decided to get rid of Birch, whose ways of modernization they opposed, and to end all foreign influences. While in Upper Perak on tax business, Birch was murdered by one of the chiefs and his warriors. British troops were promptly sent into Perak and quickly stamped out all resistance. By mid-1876, the dissident chiefs were arrested, and later tried and punished; the sultan was deposed. The Malayans had failed to halt the increasing British political and economic influence; subsequent British residents, however, did not try to make changes on their own but instead operated jointly with the native Malay rulers.

Percy's Rebellion (1403) King Henry IV (1367–1413) of England was a usurper, but he nonetheless carelessly offended his barons. The Percy family, led by the earl of Northumberland, had supported Henry's usurpation until 1402, when Northumberland's son, Sir Henry "Hotspur" Percy (1366–1403), captured the Scottish leader, the earl of Douglas, at the Battle of Homildon Hill (the English had repulsed the Scottish invaders there). Afterward King Henry IV improperly and illegally demanded Douglas and the right to ransom. Angered, the Percys then supported Edmund Mortimer (1376–1409), who had a right to the English throne, marched troops to join promised Welsh support from Owen Glendower (1359?–1416?), but were intercepted by the royal forces of King Henry IV and Prince Hal, later Henry V (1387–1422). At the Battle of Shrewsbury on July 21, 1403, the Percys were defeated before Glendower could aid them; Hotspur was slain, and his troops surrendered (see NORTHUMBERLAND'S REBELLION).

Perónist Revolts of 1956–57 After the overthrow of Juan Domingo Perón (1895–1974), dictator of Argentina (see ARGENTINE REVOLT OF 1955), first General Eduardo Lonardi (1896–1956) and then General Pedro Pablo Eugenio Aramburu (1903–70) became head of a provisional government backed by military leaders. Aramburu, who ousted Lonardi in a bloodless coup on November 13, 1955, was determined not to allow Perón or any of his followers to regain political power. The Perónista Party was declared illegal, but subversive activities and violence were widespread. From exile in Paraguay, Perón ordered his sympathizers to harass the government through riots, sabotage, and terrorism. On June 14, 1956, Perónist rebels rose in revolt in the provinces of Santa Fe, La Pampa, and Buenos Aires. Declaring martial law, the government sent in troops to restore order. Many on both sides were killed and wounded before the revolt was suppressed; more than 2,000 civilians and military men were arrested, 38 of whom were executed. Later in 1956 other Perónist plots were uncovered and squashed. A neo-Perónist Popular Union party urged voters to cast blank ballots in the forthcoming elections for a constituent assembly. Violent clashes between proponents for and against the restoration of a constitutional government became frequent. When the elections were over in 1957, the single largest block of votes was blank, but those who did vote elected pro-reform candidates who held about 60 percent of the assembly seats. The assembly voted to restore the 1853 constitution, but little else was accomplished. The government was hindered by strikes by telephone and telegraph employees and by general strikes by antigovernment workers, most of whom were Perónists. These disputes caused much damage, large production losses, and general political and economic chaos.

Persian-Afghan War of 1726–38   By the end of the AFGHAN REBELLIONS OF 1709–26, the Afghans had control of about half of Persia and had forced the abdication of the Safavid (Persian) shah Hussein (1675?–1726) in favor of the Ghilzai Afghan Ashraf (d. 1730). The uncrowned Safavid shah, Tahmasp II (d. 1739), relied on the advice of his general Nadir Khan, later called Nadir Shah (1688–1747), who engaged in war against the rebellious Afghans. Developing a disciplined army by degrees, Nadir conquered areas near Afghan-held Herat, wisely avoiding open battles until his troops

were ready. Capturing Mazandrin from the Ghilzai Afghans in 1728, he closed routes to Tehran. His troops, ready in 1729, advanced on Herat, defeated the Abdali Afghans in four battles, and made them his chief ally against their rivals, the Ghilzai. The false shah, Ashraf, and his troops were defeated by Nadir's forces at Mihmandust in 1729, thanks mainly to the Abdalis, who helped defeat Ashraf again at Murchalkur near Isfahan in 1729. Ashraf then fled to Shiraz; Nadir captured Isfahan, had Tahmasp crowned shah, received the voluntary surrender of the Ghilzai in Kirman, rested his troops, and then marched toward Shiraz. After suffering another defeat at the Battle of Zarghan (1730), Ashraf fled toward the Afghan city of Kandahar, only to be murdered by its ruler, a cousin. Rebellion at Herat occupied Nadir through 1731 and 1732. Tahmasp was deposed by Nadir in 1732 and succeeded by Tahmasp's infant son, whom Nadir later (1736) deposed to become shah. Meanwhile, Nadir moved more than 100,000 Abdalis and related Afshars to Meshed to safeguard Khorasan, pursued his war with the Ottoman Empire (see TURKO-PERSIAN WAR OF 1730–36), and stabilized Persia. In 1737, he moved against Kandahar, at that time the best fortified city in the world, with 80,000 soldiers, mostly Abdali cavalry. From a newly built city, Nadirabad, he directed the long siege of Kandahar, which fell by deceit in 1738. Non-Ghilzais were moved into Nadirabad. Kandahar was partly razed with great difficulty; its walls, often 30 feet thick, stand as ruins today. The Ghilzais were exchanged for Khorasan Abdalis, and Nadir rested two months before beginning his PERSIAN INVASION OF MOGUL INDIA. See also PERSIAN CIVIL WAR OF 1725–30.

Persian-Afghan War of 1798   The Persian shah, Fath Ali (1766–1834), was induced by the British to pressure Afghan king Zaman (d. 1801?) not to march on British India. Zaman, one of 22 powerful Barakzai brothers (a ruling dynasty in Afghanistan), had planned an armed attack on Delhi and Kashmir. His forces invaded Indian territory, but while Zaman was there, Fath Ali encouraged Zaman's older brother, Muhammad (fl. 1798–1816), to seize the Afghan throne. Aided by Persians, Muhammad seized the city of Kandahar and then the Afghan capital of Kabul. Zaman returned from India and was captured, blinded, and imprisoned. Muhammad was the new king.

Persian-Afghan War of 1816   Persian troops of Fath Ali Shah (1766–1834) marched to Ghorian, a Persian fortress on the frontier, in preparation for an invasion of Afghanistan to take Herat, a city claimed by the Persians. The Persian invaders were bought off by Herat's Afghan governor, who promised a large payment of coins stamped with the name of Fath Ali. The vizier (high Muslim official) at the court of King Muhammad (fl. 1798–1816) of Afghanistan ordered the governor to be seized and deported. Immediately Persian troops approached Herat on orders from Fath Ali, who was angered by the vizier's seizure of the governor. To halt the Persian advance, Muhammad blinded the vizier (demanded by Fath Ali), whose relatives avenged him by seizing the throne from Muhammad.

Persian-Afghan War of 1836–38   Under Russian influence, Muhammad Shah (1810–48), king of Persia, prepared to invade Afghanistan, marshaling his troops in Khorasan before marching into Afghan territory toward the city of Herat. The Persians began a siege of Herat on November 23, 1837, but the Afghans, aided by the British who opposed the Russians for control of the area, held them for 10 months and forced the Persians to withdraw on September 28, 1838. Afghan ruler Dost Muhammad (1793–1863) now sought to launch a second Islamic holy war against Peshawar, an eastern border district occupied by the Sikhs, a Hindu sect (his first war there failed because of internal Afghan dissension), but the British opposed him. Dost Muhammad then accepted Russians in his court (see AFGHAN WAR, FIRST).

Persian-Afghan War of 1855–57   The 1855 Treaty of Peshawar officially established peace and friendship between the British and Afghans, ending 12 years of hostility. That same year the Persians invaded Afghanistan to capture Herat (see PERSIAN-AFGHAN WAR OF 1836–38), and the Afghans called for and received British aid to fight the invaders (see ANGLO-PERSIAN WAR OF 1856–57). In 1857, the Persians withdrew, leaving Dost Muhammad (1793–1863) to unite Afghanistan, then under many independent local rulers, under his kingship.

Persian Civil War of 522–521 B.C.   Struggles for power within the Achaemenid dynasty of Persia were frequent. King Cambyses II (d. 522), son and successor of Cyrus II "the Great" (600?–529), secretly murdered his brother, Smerdis (d. c. 525), in order to rule Persia alone. He then led a Persian invasion of Egypt, defeating the Egyptians under King Psamtik III (d. c. 523) at Pelusium (525) and capturing Heliopolis and Memphis. While commanding an unsuccessful campaign up the Nile against Nubia and Ethiopia, Cambyses learned that Gaumata (d. 521), a Magian priest from Media, had impersonated Smerdis (whose murder had remained a secret) and usurped the Persian throne during a rebellion (522). Rushing home to regain control, Cambyses perished from an infection from a sword wound or by his own hand. The "false Smerdis" reigned for seven months before he was overthrown and slain by Cambyses's distant cousin, Darius I (558?–486), later called "the Great," whose troops had to overcome foes in almost every province of the Persian Empire. As a member of the Achaemenid royal family, Darius was declared the rightful successor of Cambyses. See also PERSIAN REVOLTS OF 521–519 B.C.

Persian Civil War of 1500–1503   Revenge sought by the Turkoman tribes for their 1473 defeat and forced migration into western Persia (see TURKOMAN-OTTOMAN WARS OF 1400–1473) was delayed while Uzun Hasan (1420–78), a Turkoman leader, established a short-lived dynasty in Azerbaijan, only to have it collapse and become Safavid-ruled in 1501. The revenge occurred as the TURKO-PERSIAN WAR OF 1514–16; its prelude was civil war in Persia.

The Turkoman "white sheep" (Al Koyunlu) dynasty, mildly heterodox because of its dervish-influenced ideas, offended its more heterodox population by reforming Timurid and Mongol laws according to orthodox (Sunni) canons. It especially offended the Sufi-Shi'ite sheikh Heydar of Ardebil, who died at the hands of a Sunni in 1488. His son, Ismail (1486–1524), avenged him by taking over his father's "redhead" (Kizilbash) organization, using dynastic infighting within the white sheep (nine rulers from 1478 until 1501) to his advantage, and warring as necessary to establish the Safavid dynasty. By 1501, the charismatic Ismail had seized the city of Tabriz and declared himself shah. He defeated the last white sheep ruler at Shurur in 1501, quickly conquered most of modern Iran and Iraq, captured Hamadan in 1503, and—making Shi'ism the official religion—converted most of the orthodox Sunni. He later became the religious and political leader of all Turkoman groups in Anatolia (Turkey), with his influence spreading as far west as southern Rumania.

Persian Civil War of 1725–30   Afghan invasions of Persia in the early 1700s (see AFGHAN REBELLIONS OF 1709–26) helped initiate the decline of Safavid (Persian) power and the rise of a Khorasani (Turkoman) general named Nadir Khan, later known as Nadir Shah (1688–1747). Persia's incompetent Shah Hussein (1675?–1726) was murdered by an Afghan and former Safavid vassal, and the resulting confusion and civil strife enabled the Ottoman Turks to occupy territories from Georgia to Hamadan. In 1726, Nadir Khan, then governor of Khorasan, became the leading military strategist for Tahmasp II (d. 1739), uncrowned shah of Persia, and headed an ever-enlarging, ever-victorious army until, by 1730, he had forced the Ottomans out of Hamadan, Kirmanshah, and Tabriz. His aggressions widened to become the TURKO-PERSIAN WAR OF 1730–36 and the PERSIAN-AFGHAN WAR OF 1726–38, during which Nadir Khan became so powerful as to depose Tahmasp (1732) in favor of an infant son, who himself was deposed (1736) when Nadir Khan became Nadir Shah and replaced the Sa-

favid dynasty with the Afshar until his assassination in 1747.

Persian Civil War of 1747–60   The death of Persia's great leader Nadir Shah (1688–1747) ended his 11-year Afshar dynasty and momentarily destroyed the Persian Empire, for Nadir's military commanders were dividing it among themselves. In 1747, six contenders for power were involved; by 1760, central and southern Persia were a unit ruled by the powerless infant shah Ismail III (fl. c. 1755–80), grandson of the last Safavid shah, through his strong regent, Karim Khan (1705?–79), founder of the Zand dynasty. Karim Khan had defeated three of the contenders by 1757 to establish Ismail on the throne, had tolerated if not supported an Afshar state in Khorasan ruled by Shah Rokh (1748–95), the blind grandson of Nadir, and had contained the rebellious Kajar family, founders of the next Persian dynasty (see PERSIAN CIVIL WAR OF 1779–94), in Mazanderan. After 1760 and until his death, Karim Khan, who never took the title of shah (king), attempted to reinvigorate Persia, erecting fine buildings, relieving some taxation, and developing trade.

Persian Civil War of 1779–94   Following the death of Persian leader Karim Khan (1705?–79) of the Zand dynasty, a power struggle ensued first among his Zand successors, who fought over their legacy until 1789, when their last important clansman, the gallant Lutf Ali (d. 1794), became dominant. His principal enemy was a member of the rival Kajar family so dexterously controlled and contained by Karim Khan during and after the PERSIAN CIVIL WAR OF 1747–60. The Kajar, Agha Muhammad Khan (1742–97), was a cruel, avaricious fighter who hunted down Loft Ali until he defeated and captured him at the city of Kerman. Agha had him killed; then he had Kerman's citizenry massacred, mutilated, or blinded for their support of the last Zand leader. Crowned "king of kings" (shahanshah) in 1796, Agha attacked rebellious Khorasan and tortured its blind ruler to death. His quest for power destroyed Persia's prosperity and economy, but despite rebellions and adversaries, his family, the Kajars, remained in control of Persia until the coming of the Pahlavi dynasty (see PERSIAN REVOLUTION OF 1921). Justice repaid Agha's extreme cruelty—he was assassinated in 1797.

Persian Conquests of 559–509 B.C. King Darius I "the Great" (558?–486) followed his consolidation of authority within Persia (see PERSIAN REVOLTS OF 521–519 B.C.) by military campaigns designed to protect and enlarge his empire's borders. First he strengthened his frontiers; then, according to the Greek historian Herodotus (484?–425?), he began a punishment of the vicious and destructive Scythians, first by warring victoriously east of the Caspian Sea. These actions added territory as far east as the Indus Valley. In 513, Darius turned his attention westward, subduing the Scythians in eastern Thrace and the eastern Getae territory—a major offensive that took Persia into Europe for the first time. Crossing the Bosporus (and eventually the Danube River) over a bridge of boats, his armies pushed the Scythians and Getae people into what is now modern Rumania. Then the Persian invaders experienced trouble; their enemies had practiced a scorched-earth policy, which caused the Persians a severe supply problem. Darius abandoned the campaign, ordering his satraps (governors) to complete the subjugation of Thrace and Greek cities in Asia Minor, to force the submission (but not the surrender) of Macedonia, and to capture the Aegean islands of Lemnos and Imbros (Imroz Adasi) by 509. Persia was now in a position to move against mainland Greece, a campaign delayed until 500 (see GRECO-PERSIAN WARS).

Persian-Greek Wars   See GRECO-PERSIAN WARS.

Persian Gulf War of 1980–88   See IRAN-IRAQ WAR OF 1980–88.

Persian Gulf War of 1990–91   (Iraqi Invasion of Kuwait)   In July 1990 President Saddam Hussein (1937–) of Iraq accused the small, neighboring state of Kuwait, on the north end of the Persian Gulf, of grossly overproducing oil in violation of OPEC quotas and of surreptitiously stealing oil from Rumaila, a border territory claimed by both Iraq and Kuwait. Hussein also had grievances over oil pricing and Kuwaiti loans to Iraq. On August 2, 1990, a large Iraqi army invaded and overran Kuwait, after briefly encountering strong resistance from outnumbered Kuwaiti troops. Hussein announced a new military government for Iraqi-occupied Kuwait (now declared its 19th province), deployed about 120,000 troops along Kuwait's border with Saudi Arabia, and warned other countries not to come to Kuwait's assistance. The Arab League condemned the Iraqi invasion and demanded an immediate withdrawal, as did the United States, Japan, and the 12-member European Community, all of which feared Iraq might turn next to invading other vulnerable Persian Gulf nations, notably oil-rich Saudi Arabia. On August 6, the United Nations Security Council ordered a worldwide economic embargo on trade with Iraq and then authorized military action to enforce the embargo. The U.S. and the European Community also suspended arms sales to Iraq and froze its assets abroad. In response, Hussein seized foreign assets in Iraq owned by nations participating in the embargo. U.S. president George H.W. Bush (1924–) deployed air, land, and sea forces—the Rapid Deployment Force (RDF)—to Saudi Arabia and the Persian Gulf region. On November 29, 1990, the U.N. Security Council voted 12 to 2 to give Iraq until January 15, 1991, to pull its troops out of Kuwait, after which the U.S. and its allies could use military force. After Hussein ruled out unconditional withdrawal and threatened to use chemical weapons if attacked, the U.S. Congress gave Bush authority to wage war. On January 17, 1991, allied coalition forces (U.S., British, French, Egyptian, Saudi Arabian, and others) under U.S. Army general H. Norman Schwarzkopf (1934–) launched a massive offensive, called Operation Desert Storm, against Iraq to liberate Kuwait. During the next month, allied warplanes bombed and strafed Iraqi forces hidden in the desert and in cities, destroyed chemical stockpiles and artillery and aircraft, and established complete air supremacy. Iraq attacked Israel with Scud missiles, set fire to some Kuwaiti oil facilities, and sabotaged Kuwait's main supertanker loading pier, dumping millions of gallons of oil into the Persian Gulf. On February 24, a massive allied ground assault, including about 450,000 U.S. troops, called Operation Desert Sabre, began against an estimated 1 million Iraqi military personnel, including some 350,000 occupying Kuwait, who were deceived into believing the allied main attack would be directed against Kuwait City, the capital. Instead, the real allied assault was a two-pronged outflanking maneuver. Forty-one Iraqi divisions were effectively destroyed and enormous amounts of armored equipment were captured. After the Republican Guard divisions (Hussein's elite military forces) near Basra were defeated by U.S. and British units on February 27, the Iraqis in Kuwait collapsed and fled northward, suffering heavy casualties and forcing Hussein to accept a cease-fire on February 28. Hussein's forces, using mostly older Soviet-made weapons, had been overpowered by the allied electronic warfare systems, modern helicopters, battle tanks, and Patriot and cruise missiles. An estimated 85,000 Iraqi soldiers died in the war—a stark contrast to allied deaths of less than 240 personnel. Iraq agreed to discard all poison gas and germ weapons and to allow U.N. inspectors to check sites; trade and military sanctions remained in effect, pending Iraqi compliance. The allies imposed "no-fly" zones in southern and northern Iraq to protect Shiite Muslim and Kurdish rebels respectively. See also IRAN-IRAQ WAR OF 1980–88, KURDISH GUERRILLA WARS OF 1984– .

Persian Invasion of Greece (480–479 B.C.) After the Persian defeat at MARATHON, King Darius I (558?–486) began preparations to invade and conquer Greece, assembling a vast army and fleet. But he died before the start, and his son and successor Xerxes I (519?–465) led the invasion in 480. The Persians attacked from Macedonia, seizing Thessaly and moving south. To defend the Greek isthmus, a large army under King Leonidas (d. 480) of Sparta went to Thermopylae while a mostly Athenian naval fleet engaged the Persian ships in the Aegean. A Persian attack from the rear trapped Leonidas's troops in a narrow pass and, despite brave resistance, Thermopylae fell. Superior Greek naval activity at the Battle of Salamis in September 480 destroyed much of the Persian fleet. Xerxes fled back to Asia Minor with about half of his force, leaving Mardonius (d. 479) in charge with the remainder. Mardonius's attack on Boeotia in 479 was thwarted at Plataea, where a beleaguered Greek force, through ingenious maneuvers by its leader Pausanias (d. 471), captured and sacked the Persian camp after killing Mardonius. A Greek fleet destroyed the Persian navy at Cape Mycale near Samos, ending all danger of a Persian invasion through Europe. See also GRECO-PERSIAN WARS.

Persian Invasion of Mogul India (1738–39) Because the Mogul emperor had aided the Afghans in the PERSIAN-AFGHAN WAR OF 1726–38, Nadir Shah (1688–1747) of Persia decided to invade the Mogul Empire (India), then in a state of decline. With 50,000 men, he forced Kabul to surrender in September 1738, and marched toward the Punjab. Victorious against the Moguls at the Khyber Pass, the Persians then seized Peshawar and Lahore, raiding the countryside as they advanced on Delhi, the Mogul capital. At Karnal, almost 300,000 Indians and 2,000 elephants assembled to halt the invaders. Nadir skirted their encampment, set up an ambush close to a nearby village, lured part of the Indian force (the right flank) from the camp, and severely routed it. The Indian center fought bravely but unavailingly against musket fire, and the Indian left failed to move at all during a battle lasting four hours (February 24, 1739). Following the Indian surrender, Nadir entered Delhi. A rumor that he had been murdered caused his soldiers to riot; Nadir was almost assassinated when rebellious Indians resisted the Persians. Nadir then ordered massacres, and supposedly 20,000 Indians died; his troops looted and burned throughout Delhi. Exacting a toll from every citizen, he amassed an indemnity of 700 million rupees, and after advising the Mogul emperor (whom he left on the throne) on the art of government, he started back to Persia. Annexing all Indian territory west of the Indus River and taking the Indian treasury, the crown jewels, the Koh-i-nor diamond, and the Peacock Throne (royal chair), Nadir led a baggage train miles in length on his journey home.

Persian-Lydian War of 547–546 B.C. Cyrus II "the Great" (600?–529), ruler of the former Median vassal state of Anshan, became its overlord or king after the MEDIAN-PERSIAN REVOLT OF 550–549 B.C. He entered the Median capital at Ecbatana without serious fighting and removed its treasury to the Anshan capital at Susa. Lydia's King Croesus (d. 547) laid plans for the rescue and restoration of his brother-in-law Astyages (fl. 584–549), the last king of Media, held captive by Cyrus. Cyrus, whom the Babylonians began to label "king of Persia," neutralized them by assuring that they had nothing to fear, then occupied Cilicia (region in southern Turkey) to block all land routes for aid to Lydia (in northwest Turkey). After vainly asking help from Babylonia and Egypt, Croesus attacked Cyrus across the Halys (Kizil Irmak) River in 547, fought an indecisive battle, and then (considering the fighting season at an end) returned to his capital at Sardis. Unconventionally, Cyrus continued toward Sardis; his forces defeated Croesus's army and laid siege to Sardis, which fell after two weeks (546); Croesus was captured and spared. Cyrus then marched west to conquer the Greek cities of the Aeolic and Ionian areas, which had been Lydian vassals. Only the city of Miletus, with some Spartan help, resisted and thus suffered serious punishment.

Persian-Mogul Wars See MOGUL-PERSIAN WARS.

Persian Revolts of 521–519 B.C. The ascendance of Darius I (558?–486) to the Persian throne during the PERSIAN CIVIL WAR OF 522–521 B.C. was followed by two years of struggle to ensure his power, which he had to impose in some quarters with much force. Darius began by dashing to Media to kill a son

of Cyrus II "the Great" (600?–529), who had usurped that throne; this done, he then, either personally or through representatives, put down revolts in Susiana, Babylonia, Sagartia, and Margiana, where independent governments had been established. In Persia itself (Iran) and in Babylonia (during a second revolt there), Darius crushed imposters claiming to be descended from Cyrus or Cyaxares (d. 585). He was also forced to send troops to Armenia and Parthia, so that by 519, when another (the third) revolt was quashed in Susiana, he had, according to an inscription in the village of Behistun (Bisitun, Iran), defeated nine rebel leaders in 19 battles. Free to move against rebellious satraps (Persian provincial governors)—military actions of 518 and 517—Darius began to invade territories and earned, like Cyrus, the epithet "the Great." See also PERSIAN CONQUESTS OF 519–509 B.C.

Persian Revolution of 1906–9 In the early 1900s, Persia (Iran) was in dire straits: its weak shah was ill, its finances were imperiled by a fall in the value of silver and its default on a loan from Russia, and the commercial rivalry of Britain and Russia had victimized it. Yielding to popular pressures for a constitution, the shah signed in late 1906 the Fundamental Law, a modern document based on Western models that established a constitutional monarchy. He died soon after and was succeeded as shah by his son Muhammad Ali (1872–1925), who attempted to overthrow the new constitutional assembly (majlis). He formed a Persian Cossack brigade with the help of the Russians and, using bombs as persuasion, prorogued the assembly. The shah's reactionary prime minister was murdered, a new assembly developed an absolutist constitution (1907) without abrogating the 1906 document, the new liberal prime minister and others upholding the first instrument were arrested (December 1907), the assembly was dispersed by the Cossacks (June 1908), and a third assembly abolished the 1906 document as contrary to Muslim law. Muhammad Ali then tried to rule absolutely, but the Persians at Tabriz rose in rebellion against him in 1908; those in Rasht and Isfahan followed in 1909. At Tabriz, Russian forces aided the shah's besieging army in brutally crushing the rebels in March 1909. Rebellious Bakhtiari tribesmen and troops from Rasht attacked and captured Tehran, Persia's capital, in July 1909, and forced the abdication of Muhammad Ali in favor of his 12-year-old son, Ahmed Mirza (1898–1930), who, under a regency, took the throne as the last Kajar ruler.

Persian Revolution of 1921

Persia (Iran) in 1921 was on the verge of collapse. Its ruler, Ahmed Shah (1898–1930), the last of the Kajar dynasty, was both weak and corrupt; its finances were confused and dominated by Great Britain and Russia, whose interests were strictly commercial and strategic. To end this chaos, Reza Khan Pahlavi (1877–1944), an army officer, led some 3,000 Cossacks to Tehran, Persia's capital, to stage a successful coup d'état on February 21, 1921, overthrowing the shah and establishing a new government. Reza Khan made himself minister of war and commander in chief and used his power, including the right to tax, to gain control of the entire country. Despite the autocratic nature of his regime, he introduced many reforms, remodeled the army, got Russia to withdraw its troops (1921), became prime minister (1923), negotiated with Britain to remove troops stationed in Persia since WORLD WAR I, and, manipulating a submissive national assembly (majlis), had the absent shah (in Europe) formally deposed (1925) after being invested with dictatorial powers the same year. He then changed his name to Reza Shah Pahlavi to found the Pahlavi dynasty in late 1925.

Persian-Roman Wars   See ROMAN-PERSIAN WARS.

Persian-Russian Wars   See RUSSO-PERSIAN WARS.

Persian-Turkish Wars   See TURKO-PERSIAN WARS.

Persian Wars   See GRECO-PERSIAN WARS.

Perusian Revolt   See ROMAN CIVIL WAR OF 43–31 B.C.

Peruvian-Bolivian Confederation, War of the

(1836–39)   In 1835, a confederation of Peru and Bolivia was established after Bolivian dictator Andrés Santa Cruz (1792–1865) invaded Peru to end a Peruvian army revolt; the union was welcomed by the Peruvians. Fearing a change in the balance of power, Chile and Argentina opposed it; the former held grievances against Peru due to commercial competition and unpaid debts from the PERUVIAN WAR OF INDEPENDENCE. Chilean statesman Diego Portáles (1793–1837) agitated for war, which was declared by Chile on November 11, 1836; Portáles's assassination by mutinous soldiers seven months later helped popularize the Chilean war effort. An initial expedition to Peru in 1837 resulted in a standoff; Santa Cruz offered to make peace by the Treaty of Paucarpata, but Chile rejected it. In 1838, a Chilean army under General Manuel Bulnes (1799–1866) captured Lima, Peru's capital, which was later that year recaptured by Santa Cruz's forces. The two opposing armies again met at the Battle of Yungay on January 20, 1839, and the confederation's troops were decisively beaten. Santa Cruz fled to Ecuador, and the confederation was broken up. See also PERUVIAN-BOLIVIAN WAR OF 1841.

Peruvian-Bolivian War of 1841

Peruvian President Agustín Gamarra (1758–1841) sought to annex Bolivia to Peru and launched an invasion of the neighboring country in 1841. The Bolivians under President José Ballivián (1804–52) defeated the invaders at the Battle of Ingavi on November 18, 1841: Gamarra was killed in action. In June 1842, a peace treaty was signed, ending the efforts to unite Peru and Bolivia. See also PERUVIAN-BOLIVIAN CONFEDERATION, WAR OF THE; PERUVIAN CIVIL WAR OF 1842–45.

Peruvian Civil War of 1842–45

Following the death of President Agustín Gamarra (1785–1841) at Ingavi in the PERUVIAN-BOLIVIAN WAR OF 1841,

Peru became torn by civil war in 1842. In early 1843, Manuel Ignacio Vivanco (fl. 1840s), calling himself "The Regenerator," seized power and ruled the country as a dictator with the support of the army; he ignored the 1839 constitution, failed to convene the Peruvian congress, and punished disloyalty with the firing squad. Beginning in 1844, opposition to Vivanco centered in southern Peru, where Ramón Castilla (1797?–1867) and others led armies in support of the former constitution. Constitutionalist troops seized control of Peru's capital, Lima, while Vivanco was absent. At the Battle of Carmen Alto on July 22, 1844, constitutionalist armies under the direction of Castilla won against Vivanco's forces, compelling Vivanco to flee into exile. Factional strife continued until Castilla was elected president in 1845 and brought some order to Peru.

Peruvian-Ecuadoran Border War of 1995   See ECUADORAN-PERUVIAN BORDER WAR OF 1995

Peruvian Guerrilla War of 1980–   In the mid-1980s, a guerrilla group known as Sendero Luminoso ("Shining Path"), whose ideology was a blend of Maoist communism and ancient Inca tribalism, began to terrorize areas in Peru, attacking and destroying private and government property and murdering community leaders and others. At first their terrorist activities centered around Ayacucho, but they soon spread to Lima, the capital, and its port of Callao. Senderistas apparently attacked a prison in Ayacucho and helped about 250 prisoners escape (1982); they also bombed electricity pylons, railways, and public buildings. In early 1983, eight Peruvian journalists investigating the terrorism near Ayacucho were killed by villagers, who reportedly believed they were Senderistas and perhaps responsible for the assassinations of local politicians in the region the year before. The Senderista guerrillas later massacred 66 villagers, including women and children. In Lima, in 1983, explosions destroyed a chemical plant and cut off the city's electricity supply; afterward a burning hammer and sickle appeared on a hill in the nearby countryside, signifying

the blasts were caused by Sendero Luminoso. For the rest of the 1980s, the Senderistas increased their violent attacks on political, economic, and civilian targets, notably in Lima and Callao, and attempted to destabilize the center-left government of President Alan García Perez (1949–   ), in office from 1985 to 1990. In 1988 Senderista guerrillas backed a general strike that paralyzed Peru, and later they supported the Movimiento Revolucionario Tupac Amaru (MRTA), another guerrilla movement, trying to topple the new government of President Alberto Fujimori (1938–   ), who took office in mid-1990. Fujimori, who escaped an assassination attempt (1992), declared "war" on the guerrilla groups and captured some of their leaders, notably Abimael Guzmán (1935–   ), defiant head of the Sendero Luminoso. Terrorist violence, with car bombings and killings, continued while Fujimori sought to stabilize the country politically and economically, with some success. Senderistas mainly terrorized in the upper Huallaga Valley and around Lima. On December 17, 1996, in Lima, 14 MRTA guerrillas invaded the Japanese ambassador's residence during a reception and took more than 600 hostages (including foreign dignitaries), most of whom were later released. The guerrillas, who demanded the release of hundreds of MRTA comrades in prison, were killed when Peruvian commandos attacked them about four months later, on April 22, 1997, and freed the remaining 72 hostages. Guerrilla sabotage and terrorism remained a national dilemma in 1998 and 1999.

Peruvian Revolt of 1780–82   José Gabriel Condorcanqui (1742?–81), who had assumed the name of his great ancestor, Tupac Amaru, the last Inca chieftain, led the Indians of the Peruvian highlands in revolt against the Spanish government, which was charged with cruelty in connection with forced labor practices. In November 1780, about 75,000 poorly armed Indians, supported at first by some creoles (natives of Spanish descent), rose up and soon took control of much of what is now southern Peru, Bolivia, and northern Argentina. Tupac Amaru, who proclaimed himself liberator of his

people, led two unsuccessful attacks on Cuzco (Cusco), but he and his family were captured in March 1781, brought to Cuzco, and executed there (after watching the killing of his wife and sons, Tupac Amaru was tortured and beheaded). The revolt, however, continued, led by Tupac Amaru's half-brothers. La Paz was twice besieged by the Indians before Spanish officials were able finally to quell the revolt in 1782, using some 60,000 troops throughout the region to do so. The Indians were issued a general pardon to appease them.

Peruvian Revolt of 1948   The Alianza Popular Revolucionaria Americana (APRA), or Partido Aprista, a reformist Peruvian political party founded and led by Víctor Raul Haya de la Torre (1895–1979), helped José Luis Bustamante y Rivero (1894–1989) be elected president of Peru in 1945. The Apristas, who had won numerous seats in both houses of the legislature and accepted three posts in the cabinet, were determined to push through social and economic reforms but encountered strong conservative political opposition in the government. In 1947, the murder of a conservative newspaper editor was blamed on Apristas; during the controversy the Aprista cabinet members resigned, non-Aprista senators refused to attend sessions of the senate, all legislation was consequently blocked, and the government was paralyzed. The Aprista-conservative struggle culminated in a revolt by dissident Apristas in the port city of Callao in October 1948; a number of sailors and civilians seized some warships; and the country seemed on the verge of civil war. On October 27–29, 1948, the conservative Peruvian army chief of staff, General Manuel Odría (1897–1974), led an anti-APRA military revolt that overthrew Bustamante and his government; a military junta headed by Odría took power. The APRA and communist parties were outlawed; numerous Apristas were jailed or exiled; and Haya de la Torre took asylum in the Colombian embassy in Lima. On July 2, 1950, Odría was legally elected Peru's president.

Peruvian War of Independence   (1820–25)   José de San Martín (1778–1850), South American revo-

lutionary leader of Spanish descent, believed that until Peru, long a bulwark of Spanish royal authority, was liberated there would be no freedom in South America. After defeating the Spanish in Chile (see CHILEAN WAR OF INDEPENDENCE), San Martín transported about 4,000 troops by sea, escorted by the Chilean fleet commanded by Lord Thomas Cochrane (1775–1860), from Valparaiso, Chile, to Pisco, Peru, in 1820. San Martín's army camped at Huacho and attracted many Peruvian recruits. When the Spanish viceroy left Lima, Peru's capital, for the interior, the city's inhabitants invited San Martín to enter in July 1821. San Martín immediately declared the independence of Peru, which at the time included present-day Bolivia, known as Upper Peru then. Needing military assistance, San Martín appealed to Simón Bolívar (1783–1830), leader of the South American revolutionaries in the north, for help. On July 26–27, 1822, the two leaders met and joined their forces at Guayaquil; San Martín turned over control to Bolívar and retired from further revolutionary activities. Bolívar and Antonio José de Sucre (1785–1830) arrived in Peru in 1823 and, leading a 9,000-man army, defeated Spanish royalists under José Canterac (c. 1775–1835) at the Battle of Junín on August 6, 1824. Sucre led about 6,000 soldiers to victory against 9,300 royalists under José de La Serna (1770–1832) at the Battle of Ayacucho on December 9, 1824; La Serna's whole army was captured, forcing the Spanish leaders to capitulate and agree to withdraw all royal troops from Peru. Revolutionaries in Upper Peru, who had been waging an unsuccessful war of liberation there, were now aided by the soldiers of Bolívar and Sucre and were able to defeat the 4,000-man Spanish force in 1824. Bolívar would have united Peru and Upper Peru into one nation, but Sucre had already agreed with leaders of Upper Peru to create a separate state there. By naming the new state the republic of Bolívar or Bolivia, Sucre assuaged Bolívar and was made the first president of Bolivia. See also ARGENTINE WAR OF INDEPENDENCE; COLOMBIAN WAR OF INDEPENDENCE; VENEZUELAN WAR OF INDEPENDENCE.

Peterloo Massacre (Manchester Massacre) (1819) Early 19th-century England contained a privileged class fearful of revolution after the NAPOLEONIC WARS and lower classes hungry for parliamentary and economic reforms. A clash was inevitable, and it came on August 16, 1819, at Manchester's St. Peter's Field, at a peaceful rally, the last of a series of 1819 gatherings to protest economic depression, high food costs, and government inaction. About 60,000 persons attended; the large number and their concerns frightened the civil authorities, who had assembled the 15th Hussars, the Cheshire Volunteers, and an untrained civic guard to keep order. No disorder developed except that caused by the authorities, who ordered the rally disbanded immediately after speeches began. The speakers were to be arrested, but the amateur guard made a general attack on the crowd. A cavalry charge cleared the field in 10 minutes, but resulted in 11 deaths and more than 400 wounded persons. An inquiry cleared the authorities, but public indignation earned the bloody outrage its ironic name, a bitter pun on Waterloo (see HUNDRED DAYS' WAR).

Philippine Guerrilla Wars of 1969–   Hostility toward the central government by ideological and religious factions disturbed the Philippines after 1946, when it gained independence from the United States. At first, the opposition focused on central Luzon, where Hukbalahap (Huk) militants, communist in ideology, were brought under control in 1954 (see HUKBALAHAP REBELLION). But, in 1969, during the presidency of Ferdinand Edralin Marcos (1917–89), the Huks renewed hostilities, which were echoed by nationalistic Moro (Muslim) rebellions in Mindanao. Typhoon floods in Luzon caused Marcos to declare martial law throughout the island nation in 1972 and, because military action by his Philippine government exacerbated the guerrilla resistance, he tried a carrot-and-stick approach, offering amnesty to those who surrendered weapons. In the communist New People's Army (NPA; military arm of the outlawed PKP, Partido Kommunista ng Pilipinas), many Filipinos complied; but the Moros, with aid from Malay rebels

and Libya, refused and spread their rebellion to the Philippine Sulu Archipelago. The Moro attacks reached a peak in 1974, when the Sulu city of Jolo was devastated and government security forces there grew to 35,000 men. Afterward guerrilla activity became endemic but sporadic and, combined with Marcos's assumption of virtual dictatorial power in 1973, led to riots and demonstrations in Manila, the Philippine capital, against the government in 1980, 1982, 1984, and 1985. In 1981, the National Assembly was recalled and given token power, with the lifting of more than eight years of martial law. But unremitting, internecine communist and Moro campaigns against Marcos continued. Helped by a military rebellion in 1986, Corazon C. Aquino (1933–) toppled Marcos, became president, and attempted to negotiate peace with the NPA and the Moro National Liberation Front (MNLF), the Muslim group fighting for a separate state in Mindanao and the southern Philippines. But these guerrilla groups continued their bloody attacks to destabilize the Aquino government, which struggled to cope with dissident military officers and attempted coups. Two related military movements—Reform the Armed Forces Movement (RAM) and the Young Officers' Union (YOU)—became a greater threat than the NPA, which gradually declined in strength because of government military pressure and the worldwide decline of communism in the 1990s. Many NPA guerrillas, nonetheless, carried out assassinations of officials, U.S. servicemen, and others. In 1992, Fidel V. Ramos (1928–) succeeded Aquino, who had survived seven coup attempts during her presidency. Torn by internal strife, the NPA's strength fell to about 13,000 rebels (half what it had in 1987). In 1994, Ramos declared a general amnesty for all rebels and dissident police and soldiers accused of subversive crimes. His peace talks led to a signed treaty with the MNLF's leader, Nur Misuari, who was made governor of the newly formed Autonomous Region in Muslim Mindanao (ARMM) in 1996. But the Moro Islamic Liberation Front (MILF), a radical offshoot of the MNLF, refused to accept the treaty, ambushed army troops, and raided towns in Mindanao and elsewhere. MILF's leader, Hashim Salamat, rejected Ramos's attempts to negotiate and engaged in bombings and kidnappings, along with insurgency, in 1997–98.

Philippine Insurrection of 1896–98   Opposed to the corrupt Spanish colonial government in the Philippines, many Filipinos joined the Katipunan, a secret revolutionary society, founded by Andres Bonifacio (1863–97) in Manila. When the Spaniards found out about the Katipunan, Bonifacio promptly called for an armed revolution to gain independence for the Philippines (August 26, 1889). Spanish troops won battles against the rebels, who were forced to retreat to northern Luzon, but Filipino resistance stiffened after the arrest and public execution of José Rizal (1861–96), a patriotic writer who had inspired the movement for independence. Bonifacio and Emilio Aguinaldo (1869–1964), the Filipino mayor of Cavite on Luzon, became rivals for power while carrying on the fight against the Spanish; in 1897, Aguinaldo had his foe shot for alleged treason. Cavite province became the center of much of the fighting and, by the latter part of 1897, was mostly under Spanish control. On December 15, 1897, both sides agreed to the Pact of Biak-na-bato, which ended the insurrection temporarily; Aguinaldo and other rebel leaders went into exile in Hong Kong, accepting 400,000 pesos and Spanish promises to introduce governmental reforms in the Philippines. After the outbreak of the SPANISH-AMERICAN WAR in 1898 and the U.S. fleet's victory over Spanish warships in Manila Bay, Aguinaldo returned to the Philippines on May 19, 1898, and, with American support, organized a Filipino army that helped U.S. troops defeat the Spanish, who had reneged on their promised reforms. For a payment of $20 million, Spain sold the Philippines to the United States. See also PHILIPPINE INSURRECTION OF 1899–1902.

Philippine Insurrection of 1899–1902   Though the Philippines under the leadership of Emilio Aguinaldo (1869–1964) had declared independence

from Spain on June 12, 1898, Spain ceded the islands to the United States for $20 million by the Treaty of Paris (see SPANISH-AMERICAN WAR). Refusing to accept the treaty, Aguinaldo and fellow Filipinos set up the Philippine Republic under the Malolos Constitution (January 20, 1899); Aguinaldo was named president. Hostilities against American rule began on February 4, 1899, when Filipinos and U.S. troops fired on each other near Manila. Initially the Filipinos were forced to retreat, but under General Antonio Luna (1866–99) they retaliated with an attack on Manila on February 22–24, 1899. American forces led by General Arthur MacArthur (1845–1912) pushed them back and eventually captured their capital at Malolos (March 31, 1899); Aguinaldo had to flee. He later disbanded his army and instituted guerrilla warfare; U.S. forces carried the war against the rebels into southern Luzon, the Visayan Islands, Mindanao, and Sulu. On March 23, 1901, Aguinaldo was captured through a stratagem by U.S. general Frederick Funston (1865–1917) and Filipino scouts in U.S. service. The insurrectionary leader was compelled to swear allegiance to the United States and issued a proclamation calling for peace. The guerrilla war continued for another year until most of the Filipino generals had surrendered; it ended on May 6, 1902. A civil government under American control was established in the Philippines, with William Howard Taft (1857–1930) as the first civil governor.

Phocas's Mutiny (A.D. 602)   Phocas (d. 610), a centurion in the Byzantine army camped on the Danube (see BYZANTINE-AVARIAN WAR OF A.D. 595–602), led a mutiny by Byzantine troops in the winter of 602. Angered by pay cuts and the severe cold, the troops replaced their leader Priscus with Phocas, who then marched them back to Constantinople and murdered Byzantine emperor Maurice (c. 539–602) and his five sons. Phocas became the new emperor.

Piedmontese Revolt of 1821   Influenced by the FRENCH REVOLUTION, liberal nobles and the Car-

bonari (secret society that advocated political freedom) rebelled in Piedmont against the reactionary
rule of King Victor Emmanuel I (1759–1824) of
Sardinia, who had refused to accept a constitution
(the region of Piedmont in northwest Italy was
then a part of the Kingdom of Sardinia). The
rebels, supported by Charles Albert (1798–1849)
of Savoy, successor-designate to the throne,
forced Victor Emmanuel to abdicate in favor of
his brother Charles Felix (1765–1831). The revolt was crushed on March 10, 1821, and, in
Charles Felix's absence, Charles Albert became
regent and proclaimed the Spanish constitution.
However, Charles Felix opposed the constitution's adoption, and on April 8, 1821, combined
Austro-Sardinian royal forces defeated the Piedmontese forces at the Battle of Novara. Piedmont
was again firmly under Sardinian rule; Charles
Felix purged the army, executed three leading
conspirators, and jailed others. Liberal resentment was engendered by Charles Albert's later
reconciliation with Charles Felix.

"Pig War" (1906–9)   In an attempt to reduce its
economic dependence on the Austro-Hungarian
Empire, Serbia began (1904) to import French
rather than Austrian munitions and established
(1905) a customs union with Bulgaria, making
tariff-laden Austrian goods unsalable in Serbia.
Long used to setting economic policy, Austria responded in 1906 by closing its borders to Serbian
pork. Serbia refused to bow to Vienna, gained
French investment to build new packing plants for
international trade, began to order materials from
the Austrian rival Germany, and pressured the Aus-
trian-administered provinces of Bosnia and Herzegovina for a trade outlet on the Adriatic Sea.
Russia supported Serbia's actions, and war between
Austria-Hungary and Russia was averted only because of a German ultimatum (1909) demanding
the cessation of Russian aid to Serbia. Serbia and
Austria developed a new commercial treaty (1909),
but Serbia covertly stirred up trouble among the
southern Slavs in newly Austrian-annexed Bosnia

and Herzegovina, actions that contributed to the
start of WORLD WAR I. See also BALKAN WARS.

Poitiers, Battle of (A.D. 732)   See TOURS, BAT-
TLE OF.

Poitiers, Battle of (1356)   In an attempt to stop
the raids by Edward the Black Prince (1330–76),
King John II (1319–64) of France had his superior
force adopt the English tactic of dismounted men-
at-arms. But his Frenchmen were weary, and crossbows were no match for longbows. John's charge
failed, and the Black Prince counterattacked the
arrow-riddled French to win a complete victory on
September 19, 1356. King John and his son were
captured and sent to England under 3 million
crowns' ransom. Afterward King Edward III
(1312–77) of England returned to the HUNDRED
YEARS' WAR, attacking Rheims and concluding the
Treaty of Brétigny in 1360, in which he gained
Aquitaine and was made heir to the French throne
upon John's death. See also EDWARD THE BLACK
PRINCE, RAIDS OF.

Polish-Bohemian War of 1305–12   Bohemia's
strength and prestige were much restored through
the efforts of King Wenceslaus II (1271–1305) after
he assumed full control in 1290 (see HAPSBURG-BO-
HEMIAN WAR OF 1274–78). Financed by profits from
rich silver mines, he waged a victorious campaign
in Little Poland and gained the Polish Crown in
1300. After he died, his son and successor, King
Wenceslaus III (1289–1306), had difficulty asserting his authority and, while marching to claim his
inherited Polish throne, was assassinated at the
Moravian city of Olomouc in 1306. Duke Ladislas
"Lokietek" (1260–1333) of Kujavia, a notable Polish fighter, aspired to unite the separate principalities of Poland. With the approval of church leaders,
he led a successful campaign, taking control of Little
Poland in 1305 and Great Poland in 1312 and
uniting the two. In 1320, he was crowned King
Ladislas I of Poland. The 1306 death of Wenceslaus
III ended the Premyslide dynasty. Several aspirants

sought the Bohemian throne, and in 1310 it was given to Count John of Luxembourg (1296–1346), son-in-law of Wenceslaus II. See also HUNGARIAN CIVIL WAR OF 1301–8.

Polish-Bohemian War of 1438–39   In 1438, King Albert II (1397–1439) of Germany (of the Austrian House of Hapsburg) succeeded his father-in-law, Sigismund (1368–1437), as Holy Roman Emperor, taking the thrones of Hungary and Bohemia. An opposing faction, however, wanted the crown to go to Ladislas III (1424–44), king of Poland since 1434, who would later (after 1440) also be king of Hungary as Uladislas I. War erupted between the forces of Ladislas and Albert, who also participated in a disastrous campaign against the Turks and died in Hungary in 1439. After Ladislas became Hungarian king, he contended with strong opposition from Slovakian Hussites under John Jiskra z Brandysa (d. 1470); in 1440, they took control of Slovakia in Bohemia. Following the death of Ladislas in battle against the Turks, his skillful Hungarian general John Hunyadi (1387–1456) declared himself overseer of Slovakia. Jiskra z Brandysa resisted Hunyadi, defeating him in battles several times (most notably at Lucenec in 1451). Finally a truce was arranged that allowed Jiskra z Brandysa to control most of Slovakia. See also BOHEMIAN CIVIL WAR OF 1448–51; HUNGARIAN-TURKISH WAR OF 1441–44; HUSSITE WARS.

Polish Civil War of 1382–84   Following the death of Poland's King Louis (1326–82), his vacant throne was fought over by two nobles who desired to be king. Several provinces were ravaged by the contenders' forces. Finally Louis's youngest daughter, Hedwig (c. 1373–99), was selected for the throne with the proviso that she marry a prince chosen by the Polish people. Because Hedwig was underage, her mother accepted the throne for her but appointed one of the feuding nobles regent during her minority. Angry Poles rejected the regency, and Hedwig was crowned in Cracow in 1384 and two years later married the grand duke of Lithuania. Poland and Lithuania were thus united.

Polish Civil War of 1573–74   Poland's King Sigismund II Augustus (1520–72) died without heirs, leaving the choice of a successor to the citizenry. Opposition to the Union of Lublin, whereby Poland was united with Lithuania, was widespread, and chaos in the country was avoided with the convening of a Warsaw assembly in April 1573, to select a new king from among five foreign candidates. Earlier, the Compact of Warsaw on January 28, 1573, had settled religious disagreements, giving all non-Catholics religious freedom, and it helped pave the way for the election of Henry of Valois (1551–89), duke of Anjou, as Polish king. The reformed constitution and the Henrician Articles of 1573 so constricted Henry's actions that when, 13 months later, his brother, France's King Charles IX (1550–74), died, Henry fled from Poland to assume the French throne as Henry III (see RELIGION, FIFTH WAR OF). In the midst of renewed disputes, the Polish nobles elected Prince Stephen Bathory (1533–86) of Transylvania as king, supporting him with military force.

Polish Civil War of 1768–73   In 1768, an organization of Polish Catholic nobles, called the Confederation of Bar, was formed in Poland to oppose Russian influence and demands for religious and political equality for Protestants and Orthodox. Actively supported by France, the nobles and their forces sought to rid Poland of interference by Catherine II "the Great" (1729–96) of Russia and to force Poland's King Stanislaus II Augustus (1732–98) to abdicate because he had granted, at Catherine's insistence, rights to non-Roman Catholics. The Turks, who wanted to stop Russian expansionism, aided the Confederation of Bar. In June 1770, Russian troops invaded Poland to suppress the ongoing civil war between the government and the confederation, which declared Stanislaus deposed. When Austrian troops threatened to move against the Russians, Catherine, whose professional armies had overwhelmed the smaller Polish volunteer armies on the battlefield, sought aid from King Frederick II "the Great" (1712–86) of Prussia, who feared involvement in a general European war but wanted Polish territory. In February 1772, Russia and Prussia agreed to a treaty by which the First Partition of Poland was arranged; Austria received its share of Polish territory in August that year. Poland lost almost 30 percent of its lands in the partition, which the Polish parliament was forced to accept in 1773. See also CATHERINE THE GREAT'S FIRST WAR WITH THE TURKS.

Polish Rebellion of 1606–7 (Zebrzydowski's Insurrection) King Sigismund III (1566–1632) of Poland incurred his people's resentment through pursuing his claim to the Swedish throne, his flagrant anti-Catholicism, his pro-Austrian policies, and his attempts to revamp the Polish constitution in order to increase royal power at the expense of parliament. Seething discontent erupted in open rebellion in 1606, when Polish nobles under Mikolaj Zebrzydowski (fl. 1605–7), governor of Cracow, rose up in protest against Sigismund's order for a permanent army under royal authority. Zebrzydowski and his dissidents drew up a series of demands, which the king rejected. The rebels created havoc until Sigismund brought troops home from duty in Sweden to defeat them in battle in July 1607. In 1609, Poland's parliament declared amnesty for the rebels and guaranteed the constitution, thus establishing parliamentary power over the king and the preeminence of the Polish Catholic nobility.

Polish Rebellion of 1715–17   After Augustus II (1670–1733) regained the Polish throne (see NORTHERN WAR, SECOND OR GREAT), the Saxon troops he billeted in Poland incensed the inhabitants by their thievery and destruction. In response, Poles rebelled with full support of the nobility, bringing on clashes between the king's soldiers and the rebels. Augustus could not control the situation in which hundreds of citizens were murdered. When his army suffered heavy losses, he requested aid from the Russian czar. With that threat, the Polish nobles agreed to enter into negotiations, and peace was reached between the king and them in 1717. The Saxons were to depart from Poland and the size of the Polish army was reduced to just 18,000 men.

Polish Rebellion of 1794 (Kosciusko's Uprising) After Prussia and Russia took over most of Poland in the Second Partition of Poland in 1793, exiled Polish patriots under Thaddeus Kosciusko (1746–1817) gathered at Leipzig, Germany, to plan a rebellion. In March 1794, Kosciusko went to Cracow, where he received the support of dissident Polish officers, declared a national uprising, and assumed dictatorial powers. Leading troops en route to Russian-held Warsaw, he defeated a superior Russian army. This victory inspired the Poles, who joined the cause in great numbers to fight and recover three-fourths of Poland's lost territory. Warsaw and Vilna were taken from foreign hands in bloody street fighting, but the Poles were defeated by large Prussian-Russian armies at Kulm (Chelmno) and elsewhere. Cracow fell to the Russians, causing the citizens of Warsaw to grow alarmed by possible traitors. Suspected informers were slain until Kosciusko restored order. Afterward Warsaw withstood a monthlong siege by a Prussian-Russian force, which unexpectedly withdrew in early September 1794, to quell Polish uprisings in Prussian-controlled territory. By then, Kosciusko had control of most of Great Poland, but Lithuania had fallen to Russia. Advancing Russian troops overwhelmed a Polish army while proceeding toward Warsaw. When Kosciusko suffered defeat and was captured at Maciejowice on October 10, 1794, the rebellion collapsed. Warsaw soon fell amid the slaughter of civilians by enemy troops in surrounding towns. In 1795, the Third Partition of Poland was arranged, giving Russia control of Lithuania and the Ukraine, Prussia control of Warsaw and all northern Poland, and Austria Cracow and the southern region; Poland as a country ceased to exist.

Polish Rebellion of 1830–31 (November Insurrection)   By various indignities and the withholding of rights, the Russian administration ruling Poland after the Third Partition (see POLISH REBELLION OF 1794) angered its Polish subjects, instilling in them a desire to rebel for independence. Polish soldiers in their secret society called the National Association against Russia conspired to overthrow their Russian overlords, receiving inspiration from the FRENCH REVOLUTION OF 1830. Confident of French aid, Polish members of the Warsaw training school, who feared their replacement by Russians, openly rebelled on November 29, 1830, attacking Russian cavalry companies and assaulting the Russian grand duke's residence in Warsaw. Polish army regiments, citizens, and prisoners joined the insurrection, causing increasingly brutal anarchy. Grand Duke Constantine (1827–92), brother of Czar Nicholas I (1796–1855) of Russia, fled, and General Joseph Chlopicki (1771–1854) was set up as dictator of Poland by his countrymen. Czar Nicholas refused to recognize this and sought to crush the Poles, who announced the end of the Russian succession to its throne on January 25, 1831. Despite Polish success against Russian forces in several battles, the Russians advanced until they were brought to a standstill at the Battle of Grochow on February 25, 1831. The Russians then rested for the rest of the winter, and the Poles became divided by internal political dissensions. On May 26, 1831, Russian forces won the Battle of Ostroleka, moved westward and seized Warsaw on September 8, 1831. The rebellion collapsed with its leaders fleeing from Poland. Russia, which had quelled sympathetic uprisings in the Ukraine and elsewhere, incorporated Poland totally into the Russian state and attempted to destroy all vestiges of Polish nationality. This repressive Russification of Poland served ironically to increase Polish nationalism. See also CRACOW INSURRECTION.

Polish Rebellion of 1863–64 (January Insurrection)   Despite efforts by Czar Alexander II (1818–81) to gain the support of the Poles by liberal reforms in education, religion, and administration, the czar's Polish administrator, by his authoritarian manner, provoked both the moderate gentry and more radical youth to demonstrate for independence in 1861. The following year the czar appointed his brother Constantine (1827–92) viceroy of Warsaw and granted local voting rights. But the Poles were not satisfied and attempted to assassinate Constantine. When the harsh administrator tried to draft young rebels, mostly students, into the Russian army, many of them fled to the forests and formed a revolutionary assembly to overthrow the government. Open rebellion erupted on January 22, 1863, spreading rapidly throughout the country and into Lithuania. Bands of poorly equipped and inexperienced youths conducted guerrilla warfare against Russian soldiers for almost two years. Attempts by Britain, France, and Austria to end the fighting failed and instead produced a strong nationalist reaction in Russia. The Polish rebels set up a clandestine government in Warsaw and Lithuania but, lacking sufficient military aid promised by France's Emperor Napoleon III (1808–73), who disliked Prussian support of Russia, were suppressed by May 1864. The Russians killed or exiled the participants and confiscated their property. Poland lost all vestiges of self-government and was reorganized as a Russian province; the Russian language became obligatory in Poland's schools.

Polish-Russian Wars   See RUSSO-POLISH WARS.

Polish Succession, War of the (1733–38)   When Poland's King Augustus II (1670–1733) died, Stanislaus I Leszczynski (1677–1766), now father-in-law of France's King Louis XV (1710–74), sought again to take the Polish throne (see NORTHERN WAR, SECOND OR GREAT), receiving diplomatic and military support from France, Spain, and Sardinia. Most Polish nobles wanted him king, but others, notably Lithuanians, gained support from Russia and Austria for their candidate, Augustus III (1696–1763), elector of Saxony and son of Augustus II. A Russian army marched to Warsaw and forced a rump parliament there to declare Augustus III king in 1733, forcing Stanislaus to flee to Danzig. Russian and Saxon troops besieged Stanislaus and his supporters, including a French relief force, from January to June 1734, when Stanislaus fled from Danzig just before its surrender. The war was then primarily fought on two fronts. In the Rhineland it was inconclusive except for the French siege and capture of Philippsburg after occupying Lorraine in 1734. In Italy the Austrians won at the Battle of Parma on June 29, 1734, the French at the Battle of Luzzara on September 29, 1734, and the Austrians again at the Battle of Bitonto on May 25, 1735, the final major engagement of the war. Meanwhile, Poland was in the throes of civil strife between rival factions backing Stanislaus and Augustus. A preliminary peace in 1735 was finally settled by the Treaty of Vienna on November 18, 1738, by which Stanislaus renounced the Polish throne and was made the duke of Lorraine (which was to devolve to the French Crown on his death), and Augustus III (whose coronation had taken place in Cracow in 1734) was recognized as the Polish king. See also SPANISH-PORTUGUESE WAR OF 1735–37.

Polish-Swedish War for Livonia, First (1600–1611) The struggle between Poland and Sweden for Livonia (Estonia and parts of Latvia) broke into open warfare when Swedish troops invaded and overran most of Livonia in 1600. Polish forces successfully defended the city of Riga, launched a counteroffensive, won battles at Dorpat (Tartu), Reval (Tallinn), and elsewhere, but were unable to gain control of the area. A 15,000-man Swedish army led by newly crowned king Charles IX (1550–1611) invaded Livonia in 1604, marched toward Riga, but was routed by a 4,000-man Polish force under Jan Karol Chodkiewicz (1560–1621) at the Battle of Kirchholm. After Charles's death, an armistice halted hostilities in 1611. **Second Polish-Swedish War for Livonia** (1617–29). When the armistice fell apart, the war resumed, with Swedish forces led by Gustavus II seizing several Baltic ports in Livonia in 1617. An armistice stopped the fighting until 1620, when Gustavus led an invading 16,000-man army that besieged and captured Riga in September

1621. The Swedes soon occupied all of Livonia and Courland (southwestern Latvia). They then invaded and took all of northern Prussia, threatening Poland's outlet to the Baltic Sea in 1626. Gustavus, who had returned home for the winter, brought reinforcements with him in the spring of 1627 and successfully drove the Polish troops southward to Poland's border by 1628. A war of attrition developed, with several standoffs between Swedish and Polish cavalry. Gustavus, whose forces had control of the Baltic coast, concluded the war by the Truce of Altmark in 1629; Poland lost Livonia, and Sweden gained the use of all Prussian ports, except Danzig (Gdansk), Konigsberg (Kaliningrad), and Puck (a fortified port on the Vistula). See also THIRTY YEARS' WAR.

Polish-Turkish War of 1444–56   See HUNGARIAN-TURKISH WAR OF 1444–56.

Polish-Turkish War of 1484–1504   During the reign of King Casimir IV (1427–92) of Poland, clashes between Poles and Turks increased in Moldavia, a region that Poland had incorporated. In an attempt to cut off Poland from the Black Sea, Turkish naval forces seized Kiliya and Akkerman (Belgorod-Dnestrovsky) at the mouths of the Danube and Dniester rivers, respectively. To combat this threat to Polish commerce, Casimir formed a league against the Ottoman Empire, forcibly evicted the Turks from Moldavia, and advanced with 20,000 troops to Kolomyya on the Pruth River in 1485. There Ottoman sultan Bayazid II (1447–1513) entered into peace negotiations. A decision on the disposition of captured fortresses by both sides could not be reached, but a truce was declared, which lasted until Casimir's death. In 1496, King John I Albert (1459–1501), Casimir's son and successor, initiated a campaign to help Stephen "the Great" (1433?–1504) of Moldavia fight the Turks (Stephen's forces had heroically routed the Turks at Racova in 1475 to keep Moldavian autonomy). But, suspecting that John I Albert wanted to depose him, Stephen and his troops resisted the invading Poles, defeating them at Suceava in 1497. Ottoman troops also entered the region, fought some skirmishes, but withdrew during the unusually cold winter of 1498. A truce was reached in 1500, ending hostilities between Poles and Turks, and yet the Moldavians held out until Stephen's death (1504) and then were compelled to pay tribute to the Ottoman sultan to maintain their autonomy.

Polish-Turkish War of 1614–21　　Poland encouraged rebellions in Turkish-controlled Moldavia and Wallachia, causing the Turks, allied with the Tatars (Tartars), to make bloody raids in the Polish Ukraine in retaliation. General Stanislas Zolkiewski (d. 1620) advanced with 10,000 Polish troops into Moldavia and, joined by some Cossacks and Moldavians, defeated a superior Turkish-Tatar army at the Battle of Jassy (Iasi) on September 20, 1620. In response, Ottoman sultan Osman II (1604–22) moved an army from Constantinople (Istanbul) into the area, compelling Zolkiewski to retreat in the face of much larger numbers. But Zolkiewski and his troops were annihilated in battle in Moldavia in late 1620. The war continued, nonetheless, and another Polish army of 75,000 men, led by Stanislas Lubomirski (1583–1641), fought the sultan's army to a standstill at the Battle of Chocim (Khotin) on the Dniester River in 1621. A truce was signed soon after, but both sides continued to make raids. See also RUSSO-POLISH WAR OF 1609–18; THIRTY YEARS' WAR.

Polish-Turkish War of 1671–77　　Cossacks, allied with Turks and Tatars (Tartars), refused to accept Polish authority in the western Ukraine (Polish Ukraine) after the RUSSO-POLISH WAR OF 1658–67; they made bloody raids in the region. Poles under John Sobieski (1624–96) dispersed the belligerent Cossacks but were forced to retreat when some 250,000 Turks under Ottoman sultan Muhammad IV (1641–91) invaded the province of Podolia and captured the fortress of Kamieniec in 1672. Poland's King Michael (1638–73) reluctantly accepted the Treaty of Buczacz (1672), by which Podolia was ceded to the Turks and the Polish Ukraine became independent under Turkish protection. The treaty was not ratified by the Polish parliament, and the Poles united under Sobieski to renew the war. At the Battle of Chocim (Khotin) on November 11, 1673, Sobieski's soldiers routed the Turks, who then withdrew from Poland. The day before the battle Michael had died; Sobieski marched in triumph to Warsaw where he was chosen the new king—John III. In 1675, an invading army of more than 150,000 Turks and Tatars seized Podolia but were eventually defeated at the Battle of Lvov. Beset by internal strife and court intrigues, John was unable to raise a large army but, with less than 20,000 troops, repulsed another invading army, 200,000 strong, at the Battle of Zorawno in October 1676. The Turks were greatly impressed by John's courage and returned much of Polish Ukraine to the Poles but retained Podolia by the Treaty of Zorawno on October 16, 1676. See also RUSSO-TURKISH WAR OF 1678–81.

Polish-Turkish War of 1683–99　　See AUSTRO-TURKISH WAR OF 1683–99.

Polish Wars with the Teutonic Knights　　See TEUTONIC KNIGHTS' CONQUEST OF PRUSSIA; TEUTONIC KNIGHTS' WAR WITH POLAND OF 1309–43; TEUTONIC KNIGHTS' WAR WITH POLAND AND LITHUANIA OF 1410–11; THIRTEEN YEARS' WAR.

Pontiac's War (Pontiac's Rebellion or Conspiracy) (1763–66)　　Pontiac (1720–69), chief of the Ottawa Indians, was furious when the broad lands in the Ohio River valley were given to the British by the 1763 Treaty of Paris (see FRENCH AND INDIAN WAR). Under his leadership, the tribes west of the Appalachian Mountains formed a confederacy to protect their hunting grounds and drive out white settlers. In May 1763, Pontiac led a surprise attack against Fort Detroit, which stood firm when reinforcements arrived; he then laid siege to it until November. During this period, the British attacked Pontiac's camp but were severely defeated at the

Battle of Bloody Run on July 31, 1763. Detroit never fell to the Indians, however. Meanwhile, other tribes stormed British forts and outposts from northern New York to Virginia and destroyed nearly all except Forts Niagara and Pitt (formerly named Duquesne). A relief force led by Colonel Henry Bouquet (1719–65), advancing to Fort Pitt, routed a group of Indian tribes at the Battle of Bushy Run on August 6, 1763; the fort was then relieved. In the spring of 1764 the British sent two armies into the wilderness and gradually subdued the Indians. Pontiac did not sue for peace until 1766, when he signed a treaty and was pardoned by the British.

Portuguese Campaigns against Diu (1509–47) To fulfill its objective of monopolizing the East Indian spice trade, Portugal had to wrest control of the Arabian Sea from Egyptian Muslims. In addition to establishing forts and equipping trading posts in India (see PORTUGUESE CONQUESTS IN INDIA AND THE EAST INDIES), the Portuguese began a military offensive against the Muslims by attacking and sinking an Egyptian fleet off the island of Diu, a possession of India's Muslim state of Gujarat, in 1509. In 1531, the Portuguese began a concerted effort to conquer Diu, which had control through conquest of port cities on India's west coast, like Goa. Diu's defenders were both Egyptians and Gujarati soldiers, but they succumbed in 1533 to allow Portuguese control for more than four centuries. A siege of Diu by Gujarati forces in 1538 failed, and Diu, along with Goa and Daman (conquered in 1538), became a triumvirate of fortified Portuguese trade centers dominating the eastern end of the Arabian Sea. Portuguese control was not yet absolute; another Gujarati siege of Diu in 1546–47 was so successful that the Portuguese viceroy in Goa had to send relief forces to hold the line. Diu, Daman, and Goa remained in Portuguese hands until 1961, when they were seized by India.

Portuguese-Castilian War of 1140 After leading the Portuguese to victory over the Moors (Muslims) at the Battle of Ourique (its site is uncertain, prob-ably not present-day Ourique in southern Portugal), Count Alfonso Henriques (1112–85) proclaimed his independence from his cousin, King Alfonso VII (d. 1157) of Castile and León, and was crowned the first king of Portugal (all in 1139). He then pursued his mother's rightful claim to lands in southern Galicia (northwest Spain). In response, the Spanish king raised an army and invaded Portuguese territory in 1140. Alfonso Henriques met with Alfonso VII, and they decided to settle the dispute by a tourney at Val-de-Vez. The Portuguese knights were victorious in the mock combat; the lands became Portuguese; and Alfonso Henriques was reluctantly accepted as Portugal's king. Alfonso VII formally recognized his crown in the Peace of Zamora in 1143.

Portuguese-Castilian Wars of 1369–88 During the HUNDRED YEARS' WAR, King Pedro I "the Cruel" (1320–67) of Portugal was involved in a dispute with Count Henry of Trastamara (1333–79) over the Castilian throne. On Pedro's murder, his son Ferdinand I "the Handsome" (1345–83) became Portuguese king, and several Castilian towns offered their allegiance to him, which he accepted. In 1369, Count Henry took the throne of Castile (and León) as King Henry II and promptly launched an invasion of Portugal. Ferdinand was forced to accept the Peace of Alcoutin (1371), by which he gave up claim to Castile and promised to marry Henry's daughter. Instead, he desired Leonor Teles (d. 1386), a Portuguese noblewoman who was already married (later he secured an annulment of her marriage and made her his queen). In 1372, Henry again invaded Portugal, besieged its capital of Lisbon, and forced Ferdinand to surrender various castles and break his alliance with John of Gaunt (1340–99), English duke of Lancaster, who claimed the Castilian throne through his marriage to the elder daughter of Pedro I. After Henry died, Ferdinand resumed his alliance with England, whose forces joined the Portuguese in an invasion of Castile in 1381. But the war was a disaster for Ferdinand, who made peace (August 1382) and reluctantly married his daughter and heiress, Beatrice, to Castile's King John I (1358–90).

When Ferdinand died as an unpopular sovereign, Portuguese citizens, opposing Castile's title to Portugal, chose Pedro I's illegitimate son, John (1357–1433), grand master of Aviz, as "defender of the realm." Queen Leonor, who had assumed the regency, was driven out of Lisbon and fled to Santarem, where invading Castilians under John I came to her aid in 1384 (she was soon sent to a convent). Because of the plague and weak support from rebellious Portuguese, the Castilian siege of Lisbon failed, and John and his troops returned to Spain. On April 6, 1385, the Portuguese Cortes (legislature) at Coimbra declared John of Aviz the new king, and immediately he laid siege to areas resistant to his rule. This brought the return of John of Castile with his army and allied French soldiers. At the Battle of Aljubarrota, near Lisbon, on August 14, 1385, the outnumbered Portuguese, aided by English archers, defeated the Castilian-French army, which then withdrew from the country; Portugal's independence was decisively secured. In 1386, Portugal and England signed the Treaty of Windsor, establishing a permanent alliance between the countries. John of Gaunt pressed his claim to the Castilian throne and, with Portuguese aid, invaded Castile without success in 1387. He made peace at Bayonne, France, in 1388, relinquishing claim to Castile in return for a financial settlement. The Portuguese-Castilian truce of 1387 was extended until an official peace was concluded in 1411.

Portuguese Civil War of 1449   In 1446, Alfonso V (1432–81) became king of Portugal and married the daughter of his uncle, the former regent Pedro (d. 1449), duke of Coimbra. Alfonso's brother, whom he appointed duke of Braganza, sought to influence the king against Pedro, who, aware of his disfavor, withdrew to Coimbra. Accusations against Pedro continued, convincing Alfonso to demand his arms. When Pedro refused to relinquish them, the duke of Braganza forced a confrontation, but his troops were routed by Pedro's supporters at Penella. Alfonso then assembled 30,000 soldiers on the Alfarrobeira River on May 21, 1449, and in the ensuing battle with Pedro's forces, Pedro and his men were slain, ending the war.

Portuguese Civil War of 1481–83   After assuming the Portuguese crown in 1481, King John II (1455–95) sought to curtail the expanding power of the nobility, who were guilty of financial and governmental abuses. The Cortes (legislature) he convened at Évora in 1481 instituted restrictions and a loyalty oath requirement for the nobles. Displeasure with these regulations was manifested in conspiracies and revolts by the nobles, which were quashed by the king with bloodshed and executions. John personally killed two rebel cousins in the palace itself. Despite these ruthless dealings with the aristocracy, John's policies were fully supported by the Portuguese middle class and peasants.

Portuguese Civil War of 1823–24   During the drafting of Portugal's democratic constitution in 1823, Portuguese royalists staged two unsuccessful insurrections in an attempt to restore an absolute monarchy: the first from Vila Real and the second from Vila Franca de Xira. The latter was supported by Dom Miguel (1802–66), the third son of Portugal's King John VI (1769–1826). On April 30, 1824, Dom Miguel and his absolutist followers moved against the government at Lisbon, where the soldiers in the garrison there acknowledged him as king; Dom Miguel was joined by his mother, the Portuguese queen. Lisbon's police chief and others were arrested for allegedly plotting against the royal family, and King John was left alone in Bemposta Palace when his moderate advisers fled in fear. Miguel installed his own followers as military officers. The Portuguese citizenry, angered by this headstrong treatment of their sovereign, John, withdrew support for Dom Miguel, who was forced to seek forgiveness from his father. Assisted by the diplomatic corps, John was able to reimpose his rule, and the arrested Dom Miguel was exiled to Vienna. The king authorized a constitution reestablishing the Cortes (national legislature). In 1825, he accepted Brazilian independence, with succession rights to both Brazil and Portugal vested in his son Pedro I (1798–1834), emperor of Brazil (see BRAZILIAN WAR OF INDEPENDENCE). See also OPORTO, REVOLUTION AT.

Portuguese Civil War of 1826–27   When King John VI (1769–1826) of Portugal died, his son, Emperor Pedro I (1798–1834) of Brazil, was recognized as the new Portuguese king, Pedro IV (see PORTUGUESE CIVIL WAR OF 1823–24). To the satisfaction of the liberals, he issued a constitutional charter for Portugal (based on the British parliamentary system) but remained in Brazil, abdicating the Portuguese throne to his infant daughter Maria da Gloria (1819–53) provided she was betrothed to his younger brother, Dom Miguel (1802–66), who was to accept the constitutional government. Civil war broke out between the absolutist supporters of Miguel, the so-called "Miguelites," who took control of Lisbon, and the constitutionalists, who were aided by General John Carlos de Oliveira e Daun Saldanha (1791–1876) at Oporto. A 5,000-man British force landed at Lisbon in January 1827, and assisted the constitutionalists in putting down Miguel's followers. The British left when Miguel agreed to Pedro's charter (earlier, his marriage to Maria had taken place by proxy, but it was never consummated), and Miguel was appointed regent. See also MIGUELITE WARS.

Portuguese Conquest of Ceuta   (1415)   The fortified port city of Ceuta on the Strait of Gibraltar in northwest Africa had been left undefended by the Moors (Muslims) while their sultan (ruler) put down a revolt in the Maghreb (part of Morocco, Algeria, and Tunisia). To gain favor with the pope and the Castilian (Spanish) king as a Christian crusader, King John I (1357–1433) of Portugal and his sons, including Prince Henry (1394–1460), later renowned as "the Navigator," who he wished to give experience in battle, sailed with a naval fleet from Lisbon on July 25, 1415, to attack Ceuta. The fleet anchored at Tarifa and then moved on Ceuta, which

withstood the first assault. The city's inhabitants had put candles in their windows to appear as if they numbered many more than they did. Moorish mountain people descended to protect Ceuta, but on the second attack the Portuguese captured it (August 24, 1415). This marked the start of Portuguese expansion on the African mainland. A small force left at Ceuta withstood repeated assaults over the next three years, most notably by the Moors from Granada.

Portuguese Conquests in India and the East Indies   (1500–1545)   In 1498, Portuguese explorers under Vasco da Gama (1469?–1524) landed at Calicut (Kozhikode) on the Malabar Coast of India. After three months, they sailed for home, loaded with spices and convinced that India offered Portugal an opportunity to obtain Christian converts, acquire rich spices, and defeat the trade monopoly of the eastern Mediterranean Muslims, whom the Portuguese hated for their encroachment upon Christendom. The 1498 visit led to a plan for a most unusual Portuguese empire: a string of forts and trading posts from the East Indies to the Arabian Sea, protected by a heavily armed fleet. No Portuguese colonies were to be established, and none was organized until 1557, when Macao on China's coast was acquired. However, to show the friendly rajahs (Hindu princes) and hostile sultans (Muslim rulers) the superiority of Christian traders, expeditions until 1505 arrogantly fired cannons from their spice-laden ships on departure for home. Portuguese viceroys came, beginning in 1505 with Francisco de Almeida (c. 1450–1510) and, from 1509 to 1515, Alfonso de Albuquerque (1453–1515); the latter developed the final Portuguese empire-building plan. Forts were set up at Calicut, Cochin, and Cannanore in India, on Socotra (island off Southern Yemen's coast), and on the East African coast. An Egyptian fleet was destroyed by the Portuguese off Diu (Indian island) in 1509 (see PORTUGUESE CAMPAIGNS AGAINST DIU). After two military campaigns, the Portuguese seized Goa on the Malabar Coast from the Shiite shah of Bijapur and the ruler of Vijayanagar; in 1511, Albuquerque began to conquer the East Indian spice-growing areas by seizing Malacca (Melaka, Malaysia). Achin and Pasei fell in 1516, Ternate and Tidor in 1521 and Macassar in 1545. By then, four wars had been fought with Calicut (1505, 1509, 1510, and 1525–26), a cruel but victorious war had been fought for Chaud (1520), Bombay was under Portuguese control (1534), Diu had been conquered (1533), and Daman had been overcome (1538). Violently hostile to Muslims of any country and friendly and open to intermarriage with Hindus, the Portuguese had, in less than half a century, become controllers of the spice monopoly and possessors of one of the greatest trade empires of all times. See also VIJAYANAGAR WARS OF 1509–65.

Portuguese-Dutch Wars in the East Indies

(1601–41) Early in the 17th century, the Dutch began to assume superiority in the East Indies (the Malay Archipelago together with Indochina and India) and to replace the Portuguese, who had dominated the area for more than 100 years. In 1601, the Dutch made an alliance with the ruler of Ceylon (Sri Lanka), and together they drove the Portuguese out of that island. A strong Portuguese naval force suffered defeat by the Dutch off the Banda Islands (in east Indonesia) in 1602. To the north the Portuguese-held island of Amboina (Ambon) was seized by the Dutch (1605), who later (1608) forced the Portuguese to agree to a 12-year armistice. In 1619, the Dutch captured and razed the Javanese settlement of Jakarta (Djakarta) and built the walled town of Batavia nearby, which became the headquarters of the Dutch East India Company. From there Dutch ships sailed against the hated Portuguese, as well as the British and indigenous rulers in the area. Gradually, the Dutch gained control of the rich spice trade with Amboina, Banda, Ternate, Ceylon and Java and set up outposts or factories in these and other East Indian islands. They pursued their warring as far as Portuguese India. Ceylon's chief port and spice center, Point de Galle (Galle), under Portuguese rule since 1507, was invaded and captured by the Dutch in 1640. That year the Portuguese-held port city of Malacca

(Melaka) on the southern Malay peninsula was also besieged (see MALACCA, SIEGE OF). When the city fell in 1641, the Dutch became the new European masters in the East Indies, for the Portuguese commercial empire there had been ruined. See also AMBOINA MASSACRE.

Portuguese-Mogul War of 1631–32

Hooghly or Hugli, located in the Ganges-Brahmaputra delta, was founded by the Portuguese in 1537 and soon became Portugal's foremost port on the Bay of Bengal in eastern India. Its success was also its downfall. There the Portuguese controlled a monopoly on salt, managed most of Bengal's mercantile trade for a high fee, and placed a duty on tobacco, which they refused to share with the Moguls. This arrogance was compounded by the Portuguese practice of seizing both Muslim and Hindu children to sell as slaves. After vainly ordering these actions stopped, Shāh Jāhan (1592–1666), the Mogul emperor, prepared militarily to destroy Hooghly, its fort particularly (1631). On June 24, 1632, some 150,000 imperial Mogul troops began a three-month siege of Hooghly, which was defended by 300 Portuguese soldiers and a native Christian force of 700. Hundreds of inhabitants were drowned in an attempted escape by boats; about 1,000 Mogul soldiers died before Hooghly fell; and 400 surviving defenders were taken as prisoners to Agra, the Mogul capital, and executed later (1635) for refusing to convert to Islam. The port never regained its earlier prosperity.

Portuguese-Moroccan War of 1458–71

European fear of the Muslim Ottoman Turks following the fall of CONSTANTINOPLE (1453) was reflected in the agreement by Portugal's King Alfonso V "the African" (1432–81) and Castile's King Henry IV (1425–74) to launch a crusade against the Muslims; Henry was to subjugate the Moors in Granada, Spain, while Alfonso was to conquer the Muslims in present-day Morocco in northwest Africa. In 1458, Alfonso sailed with a 25,000-man army across the Strait of Gibraltar, hoping to destroy Tangier, a Muslim stronghold, but was persuaded to march inland to besiege the city of Alcázarquivir (Ksar el-Kebir). The city fell to the Portuguese invaders. In 1464, Alfonso finally launched his assault on Tangier, the chief port of the Muslims in Morocco, but it was a disaster, with the king himself barely escaping with his life. For several years he feared to risk another military campaign. In 1468, the Portuguese captured and destroyed the Muslim town of Anfa (Casablanca) on the Atlantic. Three years later, leading some 30,000 troops, Alfonso marched on Tangier, massacring Muslims en route. The terrified citizens of Tangier abandoned their city, which the Portuguese then took over. See also SPANISH CHRISTIAN-MUSLIM WAR OF 1481–92.

Portuguese-Moroccan War of 1578   King Sebastian (1554–78) of Portugal, educated by the Jesuits, dreamed of a great crusade against the infidels (Muslims) in present-day Morocco. Despite the contrary advice of Pope Gregory XIII (1502–85) and King Philip II (1527–98) of Spain, Sebastian led an expedition of some 25,000 soldiers, mainly mercenaries, to the region in June 1578, in support of a pretender to the throne of Fez, Morocco. They marched overland to Alcázarquivir (Ksar el-Kebir), where a superior force of Muslims under the king of Fez awaited their enemy, short of provisions and debilitated by the heat. There, in the "Battle of the Three Kings" on August 4, 1578, the Portuguese and their mercenary troops under the headstrong command of Sebastian, who was accompanied by the Moroccan pretender, suffered a disastrous defeat by the Muslims. The king of Fez, Sebastian, and the pretender-king all died on the battlefield; about 8,000 of Sebastian's men died, 15,000 were captured and the rest managed to escape. The captive nobles were ransomed by the Muslims for a hefty sum, nearly bankrupting Portugal, where rumors persisted that Sebastian had not been killed and grew into a movement known as Sebastianism (a messianic belief that he would return to help the Portuguese overthrow Spanish domination). See also SPANISH-PORTUGUESE WAR OF 1580–89.

Portuguese-Omani Wars in East Africa (1652–1730) From the island of Mombasa, off present-day Kenya, the Portuguese had dominated the gold and slave trade on the eastern coast of Africa for many years. In 1652, the natives of Mombasa asked the sultan of Oman on the Arabian peninsula for help to drive out the Portuguese; he sent a fleet that raided the Portuguese-held island of Zanzibar to the south of Mombasa. This was the start of a long struggle between the Omanis (Arab Muslims) and the Portuguese (white Christians) for control of the East African coast, its natural resources, and the profitable African slave trade. In 1687, a former king of Pate (island off Kenya) appealed to the Portuguese for help in regaining his kingdom from the Omanis. When the Portuguese fleet arrived at Pate, it found a stronger Omani fleet waiting and was forced to retreat to Mombasa in the south. In 1696, an Omani fleet sailed into the chief port of Mombasa and laid siege to Fort Jesus; the siege lasted three years before the Portuguese admitted defeat; by then they had lost all their coastal trading posts north of Cape Delgado. In 1727, the Arab garrison at Fort Jesus mutinied, and the king of Pate solicited Portuguese aid in expelling the Omanis; at the time Oman was beset with civil disorders and could not send help. The Portuguese recaptured Mombasa and Pate with little fighting and reestablished a slave trading station on Zanzibar. Dissension soon arose between the native peoples and the Portuguese, whose garrisons were besieged and eventually starved into surrendering. By 1730, the Portuguese had been expelled from Zanzibar, Mombasa, and Pate and had fled to their colonies of Goa in western India or Portuguese East Africa (Mozambique).

Portuguese Revolution of 1640 (December 1st Revolution) The Portuguese, weary of oppressive Spanish rule, turned to John (1605–56), duke of Braganza, for deliverance and rioted in Lisbon, Braga, and Évora. Spain, alarmed at John's popularity and afraid of a conspiracy, ordered all Portuguese nobles and troops to assemble in Madrid. However, with the ousting of the Spanish governor in Portugal on December 1, 1640, the nobles offered the Portuguese crown to John, who accepted and became King John V on December 15, 1640.

Portuguese-Spanish Wars   See SPANISH-PORTU-GUESE WARS.

Portuguese War against Ternate (1 5 5 0 – 8 8) During the 16th century, Portugal was a leading maritime power with far-flung outposts around the world. Some of these were in the Molucca Islands of the East Indies where Portugal held a monopoly on the lucrative spice trade. Ternate was a Molucca island where cloves were grown, and, with the consent of its ruling Muslim sultan, Hairun (d. 1570), the Portuguese erected a fortress there (1522) and made the island a major spice-collecting center. The rapacity of the Portuguese sailors and administrators soon turned the sultan against them, and war ensued. In 1565, the Christian communities were almost overwhelmed but were saved by the arrival of a fleet from Goa, India. Peace was restored, but within several years tensions rose again where it was discovered that the Portuguese were keeping more of the spice trade profits than their agreement with Ternate stipulated. To avoid bloodshed, the sultan swore on the Koran and the Portuguese viceroy swore on the Bible to maintain peace, but the next day while Hairun was visiting the fortress, he was murdered. His son and successor Baabullah (fl. 1570s) swore vengeance and laid siege to the fortress, which was captured after four years in 1574 and the Portuguese garrison was massacred. Five years later the English buccaneer Francis Drake (1540?–96) visited Ternate, was well received by the sultan, and sailed away with five tons of cloves. In 1581, the Portuguese once again were driven out. The previous year the throne of Portugal had been united with that of Spain, and together the two powers later retook Ternate. However, the defeat of the SPANISH ARMADA off the shores of England in 1588 ended Spain's control of the seas, and the Portuguese and Spanish were again expelled from Ternate.

"Potato War"   See BAVARIAN SUCCESSION, WAR OF THE.

Pottawatomie Massacre (1856)   The fighting in Kansas territory between pro- and antislavery settlers and others in the mid-1850s (see WAKARUSA WAR) foreshadowed the U.S. CIVIL WAR that was to come in 1861. On May 21, 1856, a group of proslavery "border ruffians," armed thugs from Missouri, raided the town of Lawrence, Kans., burning and destroying buildings owned by free-soilers (those opposed to slavery in the western territories). A fanatical American abolitionist named John Brown (1800–1859), who had come to Osawatomie, Kans., to join his sons in 1855 and to help the antislavery forces there, was enraged by the "sack of Lawrence" and decided to take revenge. On the night of May 24–25, 1856, he and six of his followers, including four of his sons, dragged five men from their cabins in a proslavery settlement at Pottawatomie Creek, Franklin County, Kansas, and, one by one and in cold blood, hacked them to death. This "massacre" helped greatly to fuel the sporadic guerrilla border war in "bleeding Kansas." Federal troops finally had to intervene to stop the bloodshed and lawlessness. By the time Kansas entered the Union as a free (nonslave) state in 1861 more than 200 persons had been killed in clashes. See also BROWN'S RAID ON HARPERS FERRY.

Powhatan War (1622–44)   English survivors of the JAMESTOWN MASSACRE invited the Indian leaders of the Powhatan Confederacy (some 30 Algonquian-speaking tribes that had been united by former Chief Powhatan [1550?–1618] in eastern Virginia) to a supposed peace conference, at which they attacked the Indians. Chief Opechoncanough (d. 1644) and others managed to escape and began warring against the white colonists, who were determined to break the confederacy and carried out three expeditions annually for that purpose for about 14 years. A lull in hostilities was broken by a sudden Indian attack in 1641; then a lull occurred again, and a final Indian raid in 1644, in which some 500 whites were killed. The English, now aided by friendly Christianized Indians, launched a campaign that crushed the Powhatan Confederacy (Opechoncanough was caught and shot dead). The colonists made peace with the individual tribes and designated lands to each.

Praguerie (1440)   This was a five-months' revolt by French nobles and princes against King Charles VII (1403–61) of France, following similar contemporary struggles in Bohemia and Prague, whence comes the revolt's name of Praguerie. The HUNDRED YEARS' WAR had diminished the authority of the French monarchy and given power to the nobility, at times almost to the point of complete autonomy. When Charles asserted his power by forbidding the raising and maintenance of private armies (and, thus, outlawed private wars), some nobles and princes, including Charles's own son, the dauphin, later King Louis XI (1423–83), and the captains of mercenary armies began a revolt in Poitou in February 1440. Outgeneraled by the royal army there, the rebels moved into Bourbon territories under the leadership of the duke of Bourbon, only to suffer defeat again. The Peace of Cusset ended the fighting, and the rebels and their leaders, including Jean II (d. 1476), duke of Alençon, who had fought with Joan of Arc (1412–31) at Orléans in 1429, were treated leniently. The rivalry between the monarchy and the nobility, however, was not over until Louis's forces were able to destroy the power of the great nobles, led by Charles the Bold of Burgundy (1433–77), in 1477. See also ANGLO-FRENCH WAR OF 1475; BURGUNDIAN-SWISS WAR; HUSSITE WARS; ROSES, WARS OF THE.

Public Weal, War of the   See FRANCO-BURGUNDIAN WARS.

Pueblo Uprising (1680)   In the late 1500s, the Spanish began to send Catholic missionaries to the community villages of what is now New Mexico that were inhabited by various Indian tribes the Spanish called Pueblo. The Indians were soon colonized, but as the decades passed, they became resentful of their Spanish conquerors, who destroyed their sacred objects. In 1680, a medicine man and chief, Popé (d. c. 1690), united the Hopi, Zuni, and other Pueblo tribes under his leadership, and they rebelled against the Spaniards in August of that year. They killed some 400 Spanish colonists and missionaries, burned the missions, and drove the Spanish from their capital at Santa Fe. Almost all marks of Spanish culture were destroyed by the Pueblo, whose unity fell apart soon after Popé's death. In 1692, the Spanish reconquered the area and razed a number of Pueblo villages.

Pugachev's Revolt (1773–74)   In 1773, Emelyan Ivanovich Pugachev (1726–75) suddenly appeared on the steppes (vast Russian plains) east of the Volga, claiming to be the deposed Czar Peter III (1728–62), who had actually been murdered in the RUSSIAN REVOLUTION OF 1762 when his wife Catherine II "the Great" (1729–96) had seized the throne. Pugachev's imperial claims, fervent "Old Believer" preachings, and promises to abolish serfdom once in power allowed him to assemble an "army" of oppressed Cossacks, peasants, and lowclass workers as he traveled about. In 1774, Pugachev's army besieged but failed to take Orenburg on the Ural River. Imperial armies sent by Catherine were at first unable to defeat the rebels, who sacked Kazan and seized Saratov. Finally, while peasants and others throughout Russia awaited the coming of Pugachev as a savior, his ill-equipped, untrained men were overwhelmed by Catherine's forces, led most notably by Count Aleksandr Suvorov (1729–1800), and were thoroughly defeated at Tzaritsyn (Volgograd) in September 1774. Pugachev was seized but escaped. Betrayed and recaptured, he was brought to Moscow and executed in 1775. Imperial reforms entrenched more firmly the institution of serfdom in Russia.

Punic War, First (264–241 B.C.)   As Rome was expanding its territory on the Italian peninsula, Carthage, a Phoenician city in North Africa, was extending its control over the western Mediterranean and its shores, including the island of Sicily. When Carthage threatened to seize Messana (Messina) and close the straits between Sicily and the

Italian coast, Rome felt it had to protect its colonies, and war broke out. Most of the fighting took place in Sicily. Rome soon realized that it needed a strong navy to contest Carthage's control of the seas and proceeded to build and man several fleets, an expensive venture. Despite numerous losses in Sicily, North Africa, and at sea, the Romans did manage to gain control of the Mediterranean, and the Carthaginians in Sicily, lacking reinforcements and supplies from Carthage, were forced to surrender in 241, following the decisive defeat of the Carthaginian fleet at the Battle of the Aegates (Egadi) Islands. Under the peace terms, Sicily became a Roman province, and Carthage had to pay an enormous indemnity. Despite defeat, the Carthaginian general Hamilcar Barca (270?–228) thirsted for revenge and began to establish colonies in Spain. After his death, his son, Hannibal (247–183), took over the work in Spain and, by 218, had raised a large army there. Hannibal and his forces (with about 80 elephants) marched rapidly through southern France and across the Alps and invaded northern Italy, precipitating a new war.

Second Punic War (Hannibalic War) (218–202 B.C.). The Romans were not prepared for Carthage's large, well-equipped army, which was augmented by Gauls. Hannibal defeated one Roman force after another at the battles of Ticinus River (218), Trebia River (218), and Lake Trasimere (217), and at the Battle of Cannae on August 2, 216, he almost annihilated the Roman army (about 60,000 Romans were slain). Hannibal had expected the conquered Italians to rebel against Rome and join him, but few of them did. A new Roman general adopted the policy of refusing open battle with the Carthaginians and instead eluded them and forced them to exhaust their supplies and men in futile chases. In 204, Scipio Africanus (237–183) led a Roman expeditionary force to North Africa, and Hannibal rushed there to defend Carthage. However, the Romans decisively crushed his army at the Battle of Zama in 202. Rome took Spain as a province, the Carthaginian fleet was forced to surrender, another large indemnity was imposed, and Rome assumed control of Carthage's foreign policies. More than 50 years later Carthage had revived much of its maritime prosperity and, without Rome's consent, defended itself against an attack by the Numidians, Rome's allies. Rome used this as a pretext for war.

Third Punic War (149–146 B.C.). King Masinissa (238?–149) of Numidia had supposedly provoked war against the Carthaginians, who occupied and refused to leave Numidia. Invading Roman forces were held off for three years until 146, when an army under Scipio Aemilianus (185?–129) successfully assaulted and completely destroyed Carthage. Nine-tenths of the city's inhabitants perished in battle or by starvation or disease; survivors were sold as slaves. Rome took over control of North Africa, the Carthaginian estates became Roman, and other Punic cities usurped the trade that had once been dominated by Carthage. See also CELTIBERIAN WARS.

Quadruple Alliance, War of the (1718–20) The ardent wish of King Philip V (1683–1746) of Spain, grandson of France's King Louis XIV (1638–1715), to gain the French Crown was secretly encouraged by his premier, Cardinal Giulio Alberoni (1664–1752). At the same time, Philip's ambitious second wife, Elizabeth Farnese (1692–1766) of Parma, wanted her children to inherit the familial holdings in Italy. However, any alliance between Spain and France was opposed by Britain and Holland, as well as by Holy Roman Emperor Charles VI (1685–1740) (see SPANISH SUCCESSION, WAR OF THE). On August 2, 1718, the Quadruple Alliance was formed by Britain, Holland, France, and the Holy Roman Emperor to uphold the terms of the 1713 Peace of Utrecht, which Philip had violated by militarily occupying Sardinia and Sicily. When Spain refused to withdraw its troops from Sicily, a British fleet landed Austrian forces there in early August 1718; a Spanish naval force was destroyed by British warships under Admiral George Byng (1663–1733) off Cape Passaro, Sicily, on August 11, 1718. The Austrian forces seized Messina, Sicily, from the Spaniards. In 1719, a Spanish expedition attempted unsuccessfully to bring men and supplies to the Jacobites in Scotland; it was dispersed by a violent storm off the Scottish coast (see JACOBITE REBELLION OF 1745–46). French troops invaded the Basque region of northern Spain and ravaged it and Catalonia before stormy weather and sickness forced their return home in late November 1719.

The Spanish ports of Vigo and Pontevedra on the Atlantic were attacked and captured by British marines. Seeing the war as a disaster for Spain and as the result of Alberoni's foreign policy, King Philip banished him from the country (December 1719) and soon after signed the Treaty of The Hague (February 17, 1720), by which Spain evacuated Sicily and Sardinia. Savoy received Sardinia and ceded Sicily to Austria, and afterward Savoy's dukes titled themselves kings of Sardinia. Philip relinquished his Italian claims in return for an Austrian pledge that the duchies of Parma, Piacenza, and Tuscany would be inherited by his and Elizabeth Farnese's eldest son, Charles (1716–88). The Holy Roman Emperor recognized the Spanish Bourbons and yielded his claims to Spain. See also ANGLO-SPANISH WAR OF 1727–29; AUSTRIAN SUCCESSION, WAR OF THE.

Quantrill's Raids (1861–65)   Bloodthirsty adventurer William Clarke Quantrill (1837–65), a former schoolteacher whose sympathies were with the South during the U.S. CIVIL WAR, organized and led a pro-Confederate guerrilla band of killers, including Cole Younger (1844–1916), William Anderson (d. 1864), and Frank James (1843–1915), whose younger brother Jesse (1847–82) joined the group in 1864 (see ANDERSON'S RAID). In Kansas and Missouri, Quantrill's men defeated Union detachments with regularity, raided and pillaged communities under the guise of fighting for the Confederacy (stealing money, jewelry, and other valuable property was their real intent), and killed indiscriminately. Quantrill's most notorious actions occurred at Olathe, Kansas, which was burned and looted on September 6, 1862; at the antislavery stronghold of Lawrence, Kansas, where Quantrill and some 450 cohorts shot to death about 180 men, women, and children and burned most of the buildings on August 21, 1863; and at Baxter Springs, Kansas, where a Union force (nearly 100 strong) was defeated on October 6, 1863, and afterward all of the captives (including noncombatants) were shot to death. Later Quantrill's band split apart because of rivalry for leadership. With about 20 loyal followers, Quantrill moved to Kentucky but was tracked down by Union soldiers, surprised, shot in the back while trying to escape and caught. He died in pain from the wound in a Louisville prison on June 6, 1865.

Queen Anne's War (1702–13)   The North American phase of the War of the SPANISH SUCCESSION involved fighting between the British and French for control of the continent. The war began with a British raid on St. Augustine in Spanish Florida in 1702. The French and their Indian allies attacked English settlements throughout New England (see ABNAKI WAR, SECOND); their massacre of the Puritan colony at Deerfield, Mass., in 1704 intensified the hostilities. In 1710, a British expedition under Francis Nicholson (1655–1728) captured Port Royal (Annapolis Royal), a key French stronghold, in Acadia (what is now Nova Scotia and New Brunswick), but the French rebuffed subsequent expeditions against Quebec and Montreal. Under the Treaty of Utrecht in 1713, the French retained New France, including Cape Breton and Prince Edward Island, but lost Newfoundland, Hudson Bay, and Acadia. See also JENKINS' EAR, WAR OF; KING GEORGE'S WAR.

R

Rajput Rebellion against Aurangzeb (1679–1709)
An ultraorthodox Muslim, India's Mogul emperor
Aurangzeb (1618–1707), who assumed the title
Alamgir ("Conqueror of the World"), was determined to exalt Islam by abasing both Hindus and
their rulers. In 1678, he seized the infant Rajput
(Hindu) heir to the throne of Marwar (Jodhpur),
Ajit Singh (1678–c. 1720), and precipitated the
militant opposition of both Marwar and Mewar in
1679. Aurangzeb moved the imperial court to
Ajmer in the supportive Hindu state of Amber
(Jaipur), recaptured Ajit Singh (who had been
briefly rescued by Rajput soldiers), defeated and
annexed Marwar (1679), reimposed the hated poll
tax (*jizya*) lifted by former emperor Akbar
(1542–1605) in 1562 because it was paid only by
Hindus, and ordered the destruction of more than
250 Hindu shrines in all three Rajput states. The
war with Mewar continued on a major level until
1681, when two events occurred: Aurangzeb's
crown prince Akbar (d. 1704) rebelled, and later
Mewar made peace. Citing as reasons Aurangzeb's
rebellion against his father (see MOGUL CIVIL WAR
OF 1657–59) and the court's cruel oppression of the
Hindus, Prince Akbar left Ajmer, taking his army
with him. Although his forces outnumbered
Aurangzeb's, the latter's intrigues made the Rajput
princes desert Akbar, who fled to the Deccan region
vainly seeking help and afterward went into exile in
Persia, where he died. Mewar made peace, ceding
territory in lieu of *jizya* payments. Though his vic-
tory made Rajput loyalty dubious, Aurangzeb
moved the court to the Deccan, never again to see
Delhi or Hindustan (the Ganges plain in north
India) (see MARATHA-MOGUL WAR OF 1681–1705).
Minor Rajput clashes continued until 1707, and
Ajit Singh, hauled about the Deccan as a royal
prisoner, was set free in 1709 after the MOGUL CIVIL
WAR OF 1707–8. See also AURANGZEB, WARS OF.

Rashtrakutan-Cholan War of A.D. c. 940–72
The first of the CHALUKYAN-RASHTRAKUTAN WARS
in India gave the Rashtrakutas, former vassals of the
Chalukyas, an opportunity to enlarge their territories by annexing Malwa, a kingdom north of the
Narmada (Narbada) River, and to prepare under
their king, Krishna III (fl. 939–68), to take over
former Pallavan territory not already under Cholan
control. But the Cholas under Parantaka I (fl.
907–53) had already begun to annex these lands to
their kingdom. In 940, they took Nellore from the
Rashtrakutas. Later Krishna and his successor, Indra
IV (ceased to rule in 973), however, defeated the
Cholas, who suffered major territorial losses, including the Vengi and Tamil plains (948–67) and the
battered Cholan–then Pallavan–then Cholan capital at Kanchipuram, captured by the Rashtrakutas
in 972. The victory briefly gave the Rashtrakutas
control over the south, but the Rashtrakuta dynasty
underwent a swift decline during the second
Chalukyan-Rashtrakutan War, which ended in 975

with the founding of the second western Chalukya dynasty and led to the CHALUKYAN-CHOLAN WARS.

Razin's Revolt (1665–71)   After the RUSSO-POLISH WAR OF 1658–67, Stenka Razin (d. 1671), whose brother had been killed in a campaign against the Cossacks in 1665, became leader of a band of landless Cossacks, setting up an outpost on the upper Don River near the Volga. For three years he made raids throughout the lower Volga and Caspian Sea areas. A fleet with goods for the Russian czar was seized and Muslim settlements were sacked by the Don Cossacks, who routed a Persian fleet sent by the shah to crush them (1669). Forces of Astrakhan's governor captured Razin, who swore his allegiance to the governor and was allowed to return to the Don with his men and loot. In 1670, Razin's followers, numbering 7,000 Cossacks, attacked and captured Tzaritsyn (Volgograd), murdered many nobles, incited thousands of peasants to join them, advanced up the Volga, and took Saratov and Simbirsk (Ulyanovsk). Russian government troops marched against Razin's undisciplined army of 20,000, defeating them near Simbirsk in October 1670. Fleeing back to the Don, Razin was captured by landowning Cossack betrayers, transported to Moscow, and executed there. The czarist troops destroyed the rebels' villages and successfully besieged Astrakhan (December 1671), which had become a major rebel stronghold.

Rebecca Raids (1842–44)   Members of a secret society in rural Carmarthenshire, Wales, protested against many wrongs: British governmental resistance to the industrial and political reforms of Chartism, agrarian distress, increases in land taxes, and "reforms" of the Poor Laws (1834) that worsened the lot of the poor. But they directed wrath chiefly at the tollgates and tollhouses on the public roads of Wales. New gates and increases in toll charges were the last straw. The conspirators took their motto from Genesis: "And they blessed Rebekah and said to her, '. . . may your descendants possess the gate of those who hate them!'"; they called each leader "Rebecca" and each follower "her daughter." Dressed in feminine apparel, the male raiders made surprise night attacks on tollgates and houses with axes and torches, ultimately destroying 120. The startled tollkeepers were not generally disturbed. In 1843, soldiers and police attempted to quell the raids, which stopped after turnpike trust laws were amended and the number of tollgates was reduced (1844).

"Red Eyebrow" Rebellion (A.D. c. 17)   Wang Mang (33 B.C.–A.D. 23), a nephew of the dowager empress of the Han dynasty in China, served as chief minister for about 10 years before disposing of an infant emperor and assuming the throne himself. He introduced sweeping reforms such as abolishing slavery and imposing an income tax. These made the powerful Chinese landlords angry and hostile and also aroused the animosity of the peasants. In 17, heavy rains and neglect of the dikes caused the Yellow River (Huang Ho) to flood severely, and thousands were driven from their homes. A peasant revolt, led by an energetic woman called Mother Lu, broke out in Shantung (Shandong) and spread through the central plains of China. The rebels were inspired by religious fervor and painted their eyebrows red to make them look like demons. Wang Mang was not able to withstand the combination of opposition from both the powerful high class and the lowly peasants. He was killed, ending his short-lived Hsin ("New") dynasty; the Han dynasty was restored.

Red River Indian War (1874–75)   In the late 1860s, many American Indians—Cheyenne, Arapaho, Comanche, Kataka, and Kiowa—were put on reservations in Oklahoma and Texas, but many of them loathed the confinement and slipped away to raid white settlements. U.S. cavalry and infantry, headed by General William T. Sherman (1820–91), moved against the Indians in the fall of 1874 and fought 14 pitched battles, mainly in the Red River valley in northern Texas. American forces destroyed the winter camps of several Indian tribes in Palo

Duro Canyon (see KIOWA WAR OF 1874) and proceeded to harry all the Indians in Texas through the following winter; they never gave them time to repair their tepees and belongings, to hunt, to prepare dried meat, or to rest. One battle involved the destruction of the camp of a Cheyenne chief who was deceived into believing that the attacking force was much larger and stronger than it actually was. Slowly the Indians capitulated and returned to the reservations; their leaders were sent to Florida as prisoners. Some Cheyenne fled to Kansas but were chased and brutally slaughtered. The Comanche avoided most of the war by staying far out on the Starked Plains, but they also eventually surrendered when they realized they could never defeat the armed whites. By the end of 1875, there were no free Indians roaming America's southern plains, and most of the buffalo were gone as well.

Red River Rebellion See RIEL'S FIRST REBELLION.

Reform, War of the (1857–60) The reforms embodied in the Mexican constitution of 1857 were supported by the liberals and opposed by the conservatives. Mexico's liberal president, Ignacio Comonfort (1812–63), was forced into exile by conservative general Félix Zuloaga (1814–76), who took control of the capital, Mexico City, and assumed presidential powers in early 1858, until he was replaced by Miguel Miramón (1832–67), a conservative. A rump congress met in Querétaro and proclaimed Benito Juárez (1806–72), a liberal, president in 1858. In Mexico City, the conservatives controlled the regular army and were supported by the church and the wealthy. The government of the liberals, who had a poorly equipped militia, was forced to flee from Querétaro to Guadalajara, from there to the Pacific coast and then to Panama. Finally, it made its capital the Mexican port of Veracruz on May 4, 1858. The United States recognized the Mexican government there in 1859 and gave arms to the liberals. The liberal army under Santos Degollado (d. 1861) fought in the west but lost every major battle, including notable defeats at

Tacubaya (April 11, 1859) and Celaya (November 1859). Miramón and his forces attempted to drive Juárez out of Veracruz in early 1859, but many of his men sickened and died in the lowland. Degollado marched on Mexico City but suffered defeat at Chapultepec in April 1859. Desperately needing money, Juárez's government confiscated church property and thus was able to better arm and equip its armies. Jesus Gonzalez Ortega (1824–81) led liberal troops to victory near Guadalajara and afterward at Calderón (1860). Ortega's decisive defeat of Miramón's forces at the Battle of Calpulalpam on December 20, 1860, opened the way to Mexico City, which Juárez entered on January 1, 1861; he then assumed full control of the country and put into effect the reforms in the constitution. See also MEXICAN-FRENCH WAR OF 1861–67.

Regulators' Revolt (War of the Regulation) (1771) The frontier farmers in the western counties of North Carolina had many grievances against the eastern aristocrats who controlled the colonial government, and in 1768, they formed an association to protest unequal taxation and corrupt justices. The next year a group of frontier farmers and settlers, calling themselves the "Regulators," won control of the provincial assembly, but the British colonial governor, William Tryon (1729–88), dissolved the assembly before it could take any actions. Peaceful at first, the Regulators became increasingly violent. After a lawyer convicted of extortion was allowed to go free, they wrecked the courthouse and beat up the lawyer. In 1771, the government passed the Bloody Act, which stated that rioters were guilty of treason. Tensions continued to mount, and in May of that year Tryon sent 1,200 militiamen into the area. They confronted about 2,000 poorly armed Regulators on May 16, 1771, at the Battle of Alamance Creek and completely routed them. Six Regulator leaders were hanged, and the rest were forced to swear allegiance to the eastern Tidewater government.

Religion, First War of (1562–63) Incensed by the Edict of January (1562), extending toleration to

French Protestants or Huguenots, supporters of the Catholic duke François of Guise (1519–63) massacred a Protestant congregation at VASSY. The Huguenots, led by Louis I of Condé (1530–69) and Count Gaspard of Coligny (1519–72), retaliated by seizing Orleans, triggering widespread skirmishes. Antoine of Bourbon (1518–62), Condé's brother, was killed when Catholics attacked Rouen, a Protestant stronghold. At the bloody but indecisive Battle of Dreux, the opposing commanders, Condé and Duke Anne of Montmorency (1493?–1567), were both captured. In March 1563, despite the recent assassination of Guise, the two prisoners negotiated the Peace of Amboise stipulating limited toleration. Both sides joined to evict English troops who had seized Le Havre in support of the Huguenots. **Second War of Religion** (1567–68). Fearing an international Catholic conspiracy, Condé and Coligny led an unsuccessful attempt to capture the royal family at Meaux. Other Protestant contingents were more effective, however, and by late 1567, threatened Paris. In the Battle of St. Denis, Condé managed to sustain his position against numerical odds and Montmorency met his death. The ensuing Peace of Longjumeau extended additional concessions to the Huguenots. **Third War of Religion** (1568–70). An unsuccessful plot to seize Condé and Coligny, compounded by royal repression of Calvinism, dissolved the tenuous peace. After much skirmishing, royalists under Gaspard de Tavannes (1509–73) surprised and defeated the Huguenots at Jarnac in March 1569, killing Condé. Seven months later, Catholic forces swelled by Swiss sympathizers again vanquished the Huguenots and their German reinforcements at Moncontour. But Coligny was able to regain the initiative, leading to the Peace of St. Germain, a compromise that once again extended many religious freedoms to the Protestants. **Fourth War of Religion** (1572–73). The infamous MASSACRE OF ST. BARTHOLOMEW'S DAY, which saw the slaughter of some 3,000 Protestants, including Coligny, who had gathered in Paris to celebrate the wedding of Henry of Navarre (1553–1610) and Marguerite of Valois (1553–1615), triggered renewed warfare. The *politiques*, a moderate Catholic faction, surfaced during this period, pressing for conciliation with the Protestants in the name of national unity. Though little actual fighting took place, aside from an unsuccessful royalist siege of La Rochelle, the Protestants were able to gain ascendancy in southwestern France. **Fifth War of Religion** (1575–76). Fighting once again erupted, and although Catholic troops under Duke Henry of Guise (1550–88) scored a victory at the Battle of Dormans in October 1575, the Protestants managed on the whole to retain the upper hand. French king Henry III (1551–89), impressed by the *politiques'* support of the Huguenots, agreed to the Peace of Monsieur, once again renewing ineffectual promises of religious freedom. Guise, rejecting the treaty, organized a Holy League and gained backing from King Philip II (1527–98) of Spain for an attempt to seize the throne. **Sixth War of Religion** (1576–77). Henry III tried to coerce the Holy League into supporting a renewed attack on the Protestants. Though the Catholic nobility dissolved the league to avoid submitting to royal authority, Henry's troops subdued the Protestants, who had lost the support of the *politiques*. Concessions stipulated in the Peace of Bergerac were never carried out by the vacillating Henry III. **Seventh War of Religion** (1580). The so-called "Lovers' War," an inconsequential action, had less to do with the friction between Catholics and Huguenots than with the romantic escapades of the beautiful and promiscuous "Queen Margot," wife of the equally lascivious Henry of Navarre. **Eighth War of Religion** (1585–89). Growing concern over the Protestant Henry of Navarre's position as heir to the throne of the childless Henry III injected the issue of succession into the ongoing Catholic-Huguenot disputes. Henry of Guise, determined to avert this outcome, reorganized the Holy League to do battle with resentful Protestants in the so-called "War of the Three Henrys." Henry of Navarre overcame a numerically superior royalist army at Coutras in 1587, but subsequent Catholic victories at Vimory and Auneau led to Henry's capitulation to Guise at Paris in 1588. But in the ensuing web of intrigue, Guise and his brother, Cardinal Louis of Guise (1555–88), were assassinated. Henry III, fleeing the rage of the league, was himself assassinated in 1589. Henry of Navarre ascended the throne as Henry IV, supported by Protestants and Catholic *politiques*, though not by the league. **Ninth War of Religion** (1589–98). The Holy League, led by Duke Charles of Mayenne (1554–1611), induced Spain to join the fight against Henry IV. Though Henry won important victories at Arques in 1589 and Ivry in 1590, civil war raged throughout France, and Paris was in a state of siege. After three years of inconclusive maneuvering, Henry reembraced Catholicism in 1593, thereby bringing most of France under his banner and averting an invasion planned by Spain and the league. The following year he triumphantly entered Paris. The remainder of the war focused on evicting the Spanish, who were attempting to enforce the claims of a Spanish pretender to the French throne. In 1598, the Peace of Vervins, by which Spain recognized Henry as king, and the Edict of Nantes, extending substantial toleration to the Huguenots, brought the wars of religion to a close.

Revolutionary War, U.S.   See AMERICAN REVOLUTION.

Revolution of 1688   See GLORIOUS REVOLUTION.

Revolutions of 1848   See AUSTRIAN REVOLUTION OF 1848–49; FRENCH REVOLUTION OF 1848; GERMAN REVOLUTION OF 1848; HUNGARIAN REVOLUTION OF 1848–49; ITALIAN REVOLUTION OF 1848–49.

Rhodes, Siege of (305–304 B.C.)   In his continuing struggle with Ptolemy I (d. 283?) (see DIADOCHI, WARS OF THE), Antigonus I (c. 382–301) erred in ordering the siege of Rhodes (the island and city). In losing Cyprus in 307, Ptolemy had no source of seamen; Rhodes's supplying of ship timbers to Egypt was therefore unimportant. But Antigonus ordered his son Demetrius I (337?–283) to punish Rhodes for failing to support him in his war with Egypt. In 305, Demetrius arrived with 200 warships, 170 transports, 40,000 troops, and 30,000 workmen; he attacked Rhodes's harbor with warships behind a floating boom, which the Rhodians destroyed. He then erected his armored tower Helepolis ("Taker of Cities") against the walls; the Rhodians built two inner walls and burned the Helepolis. Demetrius tried silent surprise; it failed. He tried blockade, but the Rhodian cruisers destroyed his supply ships, and Ptolemy sent Rhodes provisions and mercenaries. After one year of besieging, Demetrius received orders to quit. The Rhodians gained the right to be neutral in Antigonus's Egyptian war, gave Demetrius the ironic nickname Poliorcetes ("Besieger"), and built the Colossus of Rhodes to express their joy of victory.

Rhodesian Civil War of 1971–80   In late 1971, the rival African factions working for black-majority rule in white-controlled Rhodesia (Zimbabwe) formed a coalition, the Front for the Liberation of Zimbabwe, which became a joint guerrilla effort to overthrow the government. The black guerrillas operated from bases in Zambia and from FRELIMO-controlled areas in Mozambique and made periodic raids in Rhodesia. With the collapse of the Portuguese empire in Africa in 1974–76 (see ANGOLAN WAR OF INDEPENDENCE; MOZAMBICAN WAR OF INDEPENDENCE), Rhodesia's Prime Minister Ian Douglas Smith (1919–   ) saw his country surrounded on three sides by unfriendly African nations and declared a state of emergency to combat the rebel guerrillas. Mozambique closed its 800-mile-long border with Rhodesia, but Rhodesian government troops frequently violated it in "hot pursuit" of guerrillas. In 1976, Rhodesian soldiers destroyed a United Nations refugee camp, declaring it was hiding guerrillas. Black antigovernment rebels also operated from three fronts in Zambia. As the violence increased on both sides, the United States and Great Britain tried to negotiate a peaceful settlement; white Rhodesians, however, were unwilling to relinquish political and economic power, and the black Africans were divided by tribal, ideological, and political differences. In 1978, guerrillas attacked one of Rhodesia's main cities, Umtali, with mortar fire; in retaliation, the Rhodesian army bombed bases some 125 miles within Mozambique. Finally, in 1978, an agreement was reached on a constitution to transfer power to the black majority. The country's name was changed to Zimbabwe Rhodesia, and in the general election (April 24, 1979) Bishop Abel Muzorewa (1925–) became the country's first black prime minister when his party won more than 67 percent of the vote. However, the two powerful black nationalist factions led by Joshua Nkomo (1917–) and Robert Mugabe (1924–) denounced the agreement and the results and continued fighting. In the fall of 1979, Britain called a peace conference in London to which all African leaders were invited. Eventually a new agreement was hammered out that was acceptable to everyone. The UN economic sanctions imposed on Rhodesia since 1966 were lifted in late 1979. In elections in 1980, Mugabe was chosen prime minister, receiving almost 63 percent of the popular vote. Britain handed the reins of government to him; the new republic's name was officially shortened to Zimbabwe.

Riel's First Rebellion (Red River Rebellion) (1869–70) When the Hudson Bay Company transferred land it owned in what is now southern Manitoba to the Canadian government in 1869, French-Canadians of Indian ancestry, called métis, feared they would lose their traditional rights to the Red River settlements in the area. Louis Riel (1844–85), of French and métis parentage, led an armed revolt and seized Fort Garry (Winnipeg) in November 1869. There the métis set up a provisional government with Riel as president. Fighting occurred between Riel's followers and the English settlers in the region. British regulars under Colonel Garnet J. Wolseley (1833–1913) were dispatched to suppress the rebels, who gave up Fort Garry without a fight on August 24, 1870. Riel fled the country. The disputed area became part of the province of Manitoba in 1870, and many of the rights Riel demanded, such as separate French schools for the métis, were guaranteed. **Riel's Second Rebellion (Northwest Rebellion) (1885).** Métis and Indians moved westward to settle in what is now Saskatchewan, where they fought to retain title to their lands. Upon the appeal of the métis, Riel returned to lead them in open revolt, which he urged the Indians to join, and set up a provisional government. The Royal Canadian Mounted Police, which had been organized in 1873, and the Canadian army joined forces to squelch the rebels; they surrounded Riel's headquarters at Batoche and decisively defeated him on May 12, 1885. Riel was captured, tried, and hanged for treason, which provoked an outburst of protest among the French-Canadians in Quebec and a bitter controversy over sectarian schools in Manitoba and Quebec.

Rif War of 1893 Muslim Berbers called the Rif (Riff), who inhabited the er-Rif region in northern Morocco, menaced the Spanish possessions there along the Mediterranean coast. When Morocco's sultan failed to check the Rif, Spain fortified its Melilla enclave, which was soon besieged by Rif tribesmen. The attack plus the killing of Melilla's military commander caused a severe public outcry in Spain, and in November 1893, a 25,000-man force was sent to Melilla and eventually drove the Rif back. By the Treaty of Fez (1894) the sultan agreed to pay Spain a war indemnity of 20 million pesetas and to punish the Rif. In addition, Spain could proceed with its fortification of Melilla, where a buffer zone was established between it and Morocco.

Rif War of 1919–26 (Abd el-Krim's Revolt) In 1919, the Spanish possessions in northern Morocco were being attacked in two sectors: in the east by the Rif (Riff), Muslim Berber tribes, under chieftain Abd el-Krim (1882–1963), and in the west by Moroccans under the brigand Ahmed ibn-Muhammad Raisuli (1875–1925). The Spanish high commissioner of Morocco, Dámaso Berenguer (1873–1953), achieved success against Raisuli, but General Fernández Silvestre (d. 1921) met disaster at the hands of Abd el-Krim. Silvestre and some 12,000 Spanish troops (out of a total of 20,000) were slain by the Rif at the Battle of Anual on July 21, 1921. This forced Spain's withdrawal from the eastern sector, where Abd el-Krim set up the "Republic of the Rif," with himself as president, and prepared to drive out the French and control all of Morocco. With a well-equipped force of 20,000 Rif, he moved south and captured many French blockhouses on the way to Fez in 1925. The French and Spanish, putting aside their rivalry in Morocco, formed an alliance to counter Abd el-Krim. Spain's dictator Miguel Primo de Rivera (1870–1930) personally led a large Spanish-French expeditionary force, which landed at Alhucemas Bay on Morocco's Mediterranean coast in September 1925, and began advancing on Abd el-Krim's headquarters, Targuist. From the south, a 160,000-man French army led by Marshal Philippe Pétain (1856–1951) moved rapidly northward, squeezing the fiercely fighting Rif troops into the area north of Taza (1925). Faced with defeat by superior forces, Abd el-Krim surrendered on May 26, 1926; he was exiled to the island of Réunion. At a Paris conference (June 16–July 10, 1926), France and Spain restored the borders of their Moroccan zones, which had been set by a 1912 treaty.

Río de la Plata, Wars of the   See ARGENTINE WAR OF INDEPENDENCE; PARAGUAYAN WAR OF INDEPENDENCE; URUGUAYAN REVOLT OF 1811–16.

Rogue River Wars (1855–56)   In the mid-19th century the governor of the Washington Territory and the U.S. Army clashed over Indian policy; the governor, supported by white settlers, wanted to remove the Indians to obtain their lands; the army opposed such land grabs. In Oregon's mountainous Rogue River area, the commander of Fort Lane had often interposed his men between the Indians and the settlers, for the latter had begun to attack Indian villages. In October 1855, he moved Indian women and children into the fort for their own safety; then some violent settlers raided the Indian village, killing 27 braves. In reprisal, the Indians slew 27 set-tlers; the surviving whites made random attacks on Indian camps during the winter. On May 27, 1856, when Fort Lane had arranged for the surrender of the Indians at Big Meadow, the Indians instead attacked the soldiers. Warned of this, the army commander dug in his troops, who used rifles and a howitzer to fight off successive waves of attackers until reinforcements arrived (May 28); the Indians fled, but surrendered within a month, to be herded into reservations on the Pacific coast.

Rohan's Revolts   See BÉARNESE REVOLTS.

Rohilla War (1774)   The Rohillas, an Afghan people pushed eastward by Persia's King Nadir Shah (1688–1747), settled in the district of Rohilkhand (Uttar Pradesh) in north-central India in 1740. Threatened by the Marathas in 1771, they requested help from the nawab (viceroy) of Oudh, who provided mercenaries. The Rohillas failed to pay for the assistance and, instead, began to advance against Oudh, which was itself subject to Maratha attacks. The British governor-general of Bengal, Warren Hastings (1732–1818), who wanted Oudh as a buffer state between the Marathas and eastern India, agreed to lend the nawab a brigade of the East India Company's soldiers. In 1773, Oudh and British brigades forced the Marathas to retire. The British mercenaries were next used by the nawab to defeat the Rohillas at Miranput Katra in February 1774; Rohilkhand was then annexed to Oudh. Hastings had gained a buffer state; Oudh had enlarged its territory; but the British Parliament in London was not pleased; Hastings was impeached for abuse of power, tried, and acquitted. See also MARATHA WARS.

Roman-Alemannic War of A.D. 271   The Alemanni, a Germanic people, advanced westward to occupy an area called by the Romans the Agri Decumates, now the West German state of Baden-Württemberg. About 270, they began an invasion of northern Italy. Roman emperor Aurelian (212?–75) hurriedly marched an army northward to

Milan and confronted them at Placentia (Piacenza), where he was severely defeated. Moving south toward Rome, the Alemanni were followed by Aurelian, who rallied and reorganized his soldiers and overtook the barbarian invaders at Fano in central Italy. There he won a victory, and the Alemanni withdrew northward. Aurelian's forces pursued them and won a second battle at Pavia, where the invaders were nearly wiped out. The remnants of the Alemanni fled over the Alps homeward. To safeguard Rome, the Agri Decumates area was abandoned in the late 270s; new forts were built by the Romans on the south bank of the Danube River; and the city of Rome was walled.

Roman-Armenian War of 93–92 B.C.   The Parthian empire of King Mithridates II "the Great" (124?–87) dominated the Armenian kingdom of Tigranes I "the Great" (140?–56), who had been the former's hostage until he supposedly bought his freedom by ceding 70 valleys. Tigranes began to enlarge his kingdom by annexing surrounding areas in eastern Asia Minor; he allied himself with King Mithridates VI "the Great" (c. 132–63) of Pontus, whose daughter he married (see MITHRIDATIC WARS). In 93, Tigranes invaded the Roman client state of Cappadocia, in east-central Asia Minor; Lucius Cornelius Sulla (138–78), Roman general and praetor of the Asiatic region, and Orobaze (d. 91?), Parthian envoy for Mithridates II, met along the Euphrates (the river was accepted by both as a common border), where they made an alliance against Tigranes. But before Parthian help could arrive, Roman forces succeeded in driving out the Armenian invaders of Cappadocia. When Orobaze returned home, he was convicted of committing a lèse majesté (taking a seat below Sulla's at their Euphrates meeting) and was thus beheaded.

Roman-Armenian War of 72–66 B.C.   King Mithridates VI "the Great" (c. 132–63) of Pontus, defeated by the Romans under Lucius Licinius Lucullus (110?–56) in the THIRD MITHRIDATIC WAR, sought refuge with his son-in-law, King Tigranes I

"the Great" (140?–56) of Armenia, who refused to surrender him to the Romans. Lucullus then invaded Armenia and captured its rich capital city, Tigranocerta, after a battle there in the autumn of 69. The following year he attempted to subjugate the rest of the country but was unprepared for the rough mountainous terrain and inhospitable climate. Mithridates quickly trained a new Armenian army in Roman methods, but Tigranes's soldiers were defeated at Artaxata in 68. Lucullus forced his way north, and his exhausted troops had nearly reached the new Armenian capital when they refused to go any farther and compelled Lucullus to retreat to the Euphrates Valley. Mithridates returned to Pontus to confront the Romans again; Lucullus followed but was recalled to Rome in 66. Pompey the Great (106–48) took the Roman command in the east and, aided by a disloyal son of Tigranes, subdued the Armenian king (66), who was forced to pay a large indemnity and ruled thereafter as a client king of Rome.

Roman-Armenian War of A.D. 113–17   See ROMAN EASTERN WAR OF A.D. 113–17.

Roman-Armenian War of A.D. 162–65   See ROMAN EASTERN WAR OF A.D. 162–65.

Roman Civil War, Great (49–44 B.C.)   Julius Caesar (100–44) was a Roman military hero for conquering Gaul (see GALLIC WARS) and championing the rights of the people; the Roman Senate feared him and his legions. His rival, Pompeius Magnus, or Pompey the Great (106–48), backed the senatorial party, which in early January 49, ordered Caesar to give up his province of Gaul. Caesar refused and crossed the Rubicon River into Italy, an act that set off the long-expected civil war with Pompey. As Caesar advanced under arms toward Rome, gaining strength along the way, Pompey and his army and most of the Senate went to Greece to gather new forces. While they were there, Caesar hastened to Spain and defeated the legions of Pompey there. On Caesar's return to Rome, he reestablished order and then set out for Greece, where he crushed Pompey's army at the Battle of Pharsalus on August 9, 48, using brilliant tactics. Pompey fled to Egypt, where he was murdered as he stepped ashore. Caesar followed, and in Alexandria, Egypt, he found King Ptolemy XII (95?–51) and his sister-wife, Cleopatra (69–30), competing for power. Caesar supported Cleopatra and left her firmly placed on the throne when he departed overland through Syria to put down King Pharnaces II (fl. 63–47) in Pontus (see CAESAR'S WAR IN PONTUS). He returned to Rome for the winter of 47–46 to quell a mutiny in the army and, in the spring, set off for North Africa, where the senatorial party had raised new forces, including Numidians under King Juba I (c. 85–46). These were decisively routed by Caesar's legions at the Battle of Thapsus in 46. Meanwhile, the sons of Pompey were assembling an army in Spain, Caesar and his soldiers confronted it on March 17, 45, and in the Battle of Munda, probably near Montilla, Spain, defeated the final efforts of Pompey and the Senate to oppose him militarily. He then returned to Rome and assumed the office of dictator, a temporary one. Whether or not he intended to make himself king will never be known with certainty, but many of his enemies and even patriotic friends believed he did. A conspiracy was formed against Caesar, and on March 15, 44, he was stabbed to death in the Senate building by a group including former Pompeians and some disgruntled associates, among whom was Marcus Junius Brutus (85?–42). Civil strife erupted again (see ROMAN CIVIL WAR OF 43–31 B.C.).

Roman Civil War of 84–82 B.C.   While Roman general Lucius Cornelius Sulla (138–78) was in Asia Minor fighting King Mithridates VI "the Great" (c. 132–63) of Pontus in the FIRST MITHRIDATIC WAR, his enemies in Rome gained control of the government and sent Gaius Flavius Fimbria (d. 84) to replace him as commander in the east. Sulla won Fimbria and his army over to his side and, in 83, returned to Italy seeking revenge. He encountered resistance from some of the Italian tribes and Roman forces, which he either defeated or converted. In a last effort, his enemies attempted to seize Rome, but Sulla met them with his legions at the Colline Gate and annihilated them in a bloody battle in November 82. The Roman Senate passed laws making Sulla dictator and legalizing all his past actions.

Roman Civil War of 43–31 B.C.   This was a confusing period marked by intrigues, suspicion, propaganda on all sides, revenge, and betrayal. After the death of Julius Caesar (100–44) (see ROMAN CIVIL WAR, GREAT), his grandnephew and heir, Octavian (63 B.C.–A.D. 14), later called Augustus, rose to the forefront as a leader along with Mark Antony (83–30) and Marcus Lepidus (d. 13). The Roman Senate designated the three as the Second Triumvirate with power to rule jointly for five years; this was renewed in 37. Before undertaking to crush the army raised by Caesar's assassins, Marcus Junius Brutus (85?–42) and Gaius Cassius Longinus (d. 42), they made Rome secure by executing all the leaders of the senatorial party and confiscating their property. They then embarked for Macedonia, where their legions defeated their enemies at the battles of Philippi in October 42; both Cassius and Brutus committed suicide after their defeats there. The victors then divided the empire among themselves, but inevitably dissension arose. Antony's wife and brother stirred up a revolt (41) against Octavian, which was put down at Perusia (Perugia). Octavian also faced opposition from the pirate fleet commanded by Pompey the Younger (75–35), which threatened Rome's grain supply. Twice Octavian was defeated, but at the third encounter, in 36, at Naulochus, off Sicily, he was successful thanks to Octavian's able general Marcus Vipsanius Agrippa (63–12). Lepidus was suspected of being in league with Pompey and was dismissed from the triumvirate. Meanwhile, Antony was attempting to conclude the war in Parthia (see ROMAN-PARTHIAN WAR OF 55–36 B.C.). When Octavian refused to send him troops, he turned to Cleopatra (69–30), with whom he had established a liaison, for help. His campaign in Parthia was a disaster, and he returned to Egypt. Octavian was consolidating his position in Rome, and he used Antony's relationship with

Cleopatra to rouse popular opinion against him. When Antony divorced his Roman wife (Octavian's sister) in 32, married Cleopatra, and willed his possessions to her and their children, hatred of him swept through Italy. The Senate declared war on Cleopatra, and both sides prepared a fleet and army. They met at the Battle of Actium near Préveza on the Ionian Sea (September 2, 31). While Agrippa's warships blockaded Antony's fleet, Octavian's army cut off his land supply routes. Seeing a hopeless situation, Antony made a desperate and successful breakout with Cleopatra through the blockade; their army and navy, however, promptly surrendered. Octavian was now master of the Roman world, and a period of civil peace ensued. See also OCTAVIAN'S WAR AGAINST ANTONY.

Roman Civil War of A.D. 68–69   The cruel, despotic rule of Emperor Nero (37–68) caused much discontent in the Roman Empire. Roman legate (governor) of Gaul Gaius Julius Vindex (d. 68) led a revolt that was joined by Servius Sulpicius Galba (3–69), legate in Spain, who was declared emperor by his troops (on the advice of Vindex). However, Lucius Verginius Rufus (15–69), legate of Upper Germany, crushed the revolt by Vindex (who committed suicide afterward) and, refusing to be saluted as emperor by his own troops, supported instead Galba, who was acclaimed by the Roman Senate after being recognized by the Praetorian Guard (the emperor's bodyguard); Nero, condemned by the Senate, killed himself. Nonetheless, Aulus Vitellius (15–69), legate of Lower Germany, whose legions had declared him emperor, marched toward Italy to seize power, while Galba was slain by the fickle Praetorians, who had switched their support to Marcus Salvius Otho (32–69), legate of Lusitania (Portugal) and a leader in Galba's struggle against Nero. Otho gained senatorial recognition as emperor and, three months later, marched with troops from Rome to confront rival Vitellius, whose forces were victorious at the First Battle of Bedriacum (April 16, 69) near Cremona in northern Italy; Otho subsequently killed himself. Vitellius entered Rome and was acclaimed emperor by the Senate. Meanwhile,

Vespasian (9–79), a competent commander in Judea, was proclaimed emperor with the backing of the Roman legates of Syria and Egypt and sent a large army, led by Antonius Primus (fl. 60s), from the Danube area to Italy. At the Second Battle of Bedriacum (November? 69), Antonius was victorious over the main army of Vitellius, who was murdered in Rome when the victors arrived (December 20, 69) to successfully take control. A day later the Senate acknowledged Vespasian as emperor.

Roman Civil War of A.D. 193–97   The powerful but fickle Praetorian Guards murdered Roman emperor Publius Helvius Pertinax (126–93), whose strict economic measures they disliked, and afterward sold the imperial crown to the highest bidder, one Marcus Didius Julianus (133–93). But promptly three rivals claimed the emperorship with the full support of their legions: Clodius Septimus Albinus (d. 197) in Britain, Lucius Septimius Severus (146–211) in Pannonia, and Pescennius Niger (d. 194) in Syria. Marching to Rome, Severus usurped power; the Roman Senate had just executed Didius Julianus because of its antipathy to his purchase of the throne. Severus reformed the Praetorians with new legionnaires and deceitfully gained the support of rival Albinus by accepting him as his successor. Advancing east into the empire, Severus and his troops were victorious over Niger at the battles of Cyzicus (193), Nicaea (193), and Issus (194); Niger was caught fleeing and slain. Byzantium (Istanbul), occupied by Niger's loyal troops, withstood a long siege by Severus, who finally seized and sacked the city (196). Friction developed between Severus and Albinus, who declared himself emperor and, leading the legions of Britain, moved into Gaul to engage the Pannonian legions led by Severus, who had interrupted his campaign in Mesopotamia (see ROMAN-PARTHIAN WAR OF A.D. 195–202) to return to the west. Albinus was defeated and killed at Lugdunum (Lyons), which was nearly destroyed by Severus afterward (197). Severus then returned to his Mesopotamian campaign; the military dominated Rome's government, to the chagrin of the Senate, during Severus's reign as emperor.

Roman Civil "War" of A.D.235–68   The large Roman Empire endured a period of almost incessant anarchy and civil strife (235–68), during which numerous rivals were fighting among themselves for the title "Augustus" (emperor) and for power in various provinces (see ROMAN CIVIL WAR OF A.D. 238). Corruption, constant intrigues, taxes, government confiscations, and a 15-year plague (251–65) also helped to weaken the empire, whose frontiers began to disintegrate from pressures from invading Germanic tribes (see ROMAN-GOTHIC WARS). During the reign (253–68) of Emperor Publius Licinius Egnatius Gallienus (d. 268), who ruled jointly with his father Valerian (d. 261?) until 260, insurgents and pretenders continually competed throughout the empire, especially in Gaul (France), Illyria or Illyricum (Yugoslavia and Albania), and provinces in the east. So many imperious contenders either established independent domains or sought the throne that Gallienus's reign has been called the "Age of Thirty Tyrants" by some, although the English historian Edward Gibbon (1737–94) counted only 19 "tyrants." Roman infantry had lost its supremacy on the battlefield to the cavalry, and Gallienus, who remained in control through defensive maneuvers, transferred the command of his armies from senators to expert equestrian officers. While attempting to crush a revolt at Milan, he was murdered by his own soldiers in 268. See also AURELIAN'S WAR AGAINST TETRICUS; AURELIAN'S WAR AGAINST ZENOBIA.

Roman Civil War of A.D. 238   Roman emperor Gaius Julius Verus Maximinus "Thrax" (173–238), a strong Thracian who spent most of his reign leading legions against invading barbarians in Germany, gained no recognition from the Roman Senate, which gave the imperial dignity in 238 to Clodius Pupienus Maximus (d. 238) and Decimus Caelius Balbinus (d. 238), who then became co-emperors. However, insurgent Roman troops in northern Africa elected the elderly Gordianus I (158–238) as emperor. His son Gordianus II (192–238) ruled with him but was slain in battle near Carthage by Numidian supporters of Maximinus; soon afterward Gordianus I killed himself in grief, and his grandson Gordianus III (224?–44) was declared emperor. Meanwhile, the Senate had deposed Maximinus, who marched south into northeastern Italy and besieged Aquileia, capital of the region; a stalemate resulted and he was killed by his own troops. Pupienus Maximus and Balbinus were murdered by Praetorian Guards, who preferred Gordianus III and helped him secure the throne.

Roman Civil War of A.D. 284–85   After the death of his father, Marcus Aurelius Carus (223?–83), during the ROMAN-PERSIAN WAR OF A.D. 282–83, his surviving son, Carinus (d. 285), was proclaimed Roman emperor of the West. Meanwhile, the soldiers in the east had selected Diocletian (245–313), a commander under Carus, as Roman emperor of the East. Carinus wanted to be emperor of both the west and east, so he led an army eastward to confront Diocletian; he won several encounters in Moesia (Bulgaria). At the Battle of Margus (Morava), his western army seemed to be winning, when Carinus was apparently murdered by one of his officers. Diocletian was victorious and became sole emperor of a reunited Roman Empire. See also ROMAN-GOTHIC WARS.

Roman Civil War of A.D. 306–7   After Roman emperor Diocletian (245–313) abdicated in 305 because of ill health, the Roman Empire became wracked by civil war; previously Diocletian had appointed Galerius (d. 311) "Caesar" (emperor) of the East and Constantius I (250?–306) "Caesar" of the West. At Constantius's death, his army chose his son Constantine I (280?–337) to succeed him, but Galerius supported Severus (d. 307) as emperor. Then Maxentius (d. 312) put forth his claim. Galerius and Severus joined forces against him, but Maxentius's father, Maximian (d. 310), came out of retirement to help him. Their armies met Severus's outside of Rome; Severus's men deserted him, and he gave himself up to Maximian, who ordered him killed. In 307, Maxentius proclaimed himself Roman emperor. By 310, there were five self-proclaimed emperors ruling different parts of the Roman Empire, and intrigues and conspiracies were prevalent.

Roman Civil War of A.D. **311–12**   Emperor Constantine I "the Great" (280?–337) invaded northern Italy with a 40,000-man army, winning victories at Susa, Turin, and Milan against superior forces under generals of rival emperor Maxentius (d. 312). After two more successes, at Brescia and Verona, Constantine marched south toward Rome, gathering reinforcements as he went. Maxentius and his 75,000-man army confronted him at the Milvian (Mulvian) Bridge over the Tiber River outside Rome in 312. Constantine's smaller army (about 50,000 strong) won a decisive victory there; while fleeing, Maxentius drowned in the river. The battle is memorable because, before it began, Constantine is said to have seen a flaming cross in the sky; he adopted the cross as a symbol for his fight and vowed to become a Christian if he was victorious. The following year, 313, he and the Roman emperor of the East, Licinius (270?–325), met in Milan and signed an edict permitting toleration of Christianity and the restoration of confiscated church property.

Roman Civil War of A.D. **313**   Licinius (270?–325), Roman emperor in the East, was opposed by Maximinus, called originally Daia (d. 313), a contender for his title, who planned to take control of the entire eastern part of the Roman Empire. In 313, the latter crossed the Bosporus with an army, unsuccessfully attacked Licinius's forces in Thrace, and then fell back into Asia Minor. Leading some 30,000 loyal soldiers, Licinius marched against Maximinus's forces in western Asia Minor, where at the Battle of Tzurulum he won a decisive victory. Maximinus retreated into Asia Minor, where he soon died. Licinius promptly annexed all his territory and was now the unchallenged ruler of the Eastern Roman Empire.

Roman Civil War of A.D. **314–24**   Hostilities erupted between Licinius (270?–325) and Constan-

tine I "the Great" (280?–337), Roman emperors in the east and west, respectively, when the former attempted to foment a revolt against the latter. With 20,000 soldiers, Constantine marched into the eastern empire and fought an indecisive battle in southeastern Pannonia in 314; Licinius and his men withdrew, pursued by Constantine. After losing the Battle of Mardia, Licinius agreed to recognize all of Constantine's European territory except Thrace; Constantine agreed to forgo his rights as senior emperor. Tensions mounted and quarrels arose over the treatment of Christians. In 323, Constantine's forces pursued a horde of Goths into Thrace in violation of the agreement, and the war resumed in earnest. Constantine took the offensive and defeated Licinius's army at Adrianople (Edirne) on July 3, 323; his son Flavius Julius Crispus (d. 326) led his 200-ship fleet to victory over Licinius's 350-ship fleet at the Hellespont (Dardanelles) that same month and year. Licinius fled into Asia Minor, put together a large army, and fought a long, bloody battle at Chrysopolis (Scutari) in September 323, finally being routed thoroughly by Constantine. Licinius again fled but later surrendered and was executed for stirring up fresh intrigues. See also ROMAN-GOTHIC WARS.

Roman Civil War of A.D. **350–51**   After the death of Roman emperor Constantine I "the Great" (280?–337), the empire was divided among his three sons: Constantine II (317?–40) received Gaul (France), Spain, and Britain; Constantius II (317–61) got Asia Minor, Egypt, and Syria; and Constans (323?–50) Italy, Africa, and Illyricum (Balkan Peninsula). Constantine II soon became angry at the high-handed behavior of his younger brother, Constans, and invaded Italy in 340. He was slain in an ambush, and Constans assumed control of the western portion of the empire. He was, however, not liked by the army, and in 350 a military conspiracy succeeded in killing him; the army selected a barbarian officer named Magnentius (d. 353) to succeed him. Constantius marched westward to avenge Constans; Magnentius invaded Illyricum, where at first his army did well until it met

Constantius's armored cavalry at the Battle of Mursa (Osijek, Yugoslavia) in 351; Magnentius lost, but both sides suffered heavy casualties. Magnentius fled to northern Italy, while Constantius regained control of Africa, Spain, and southern Italy. When he began to pursue Magnentius in the north, the latter withdrew to Gaul, where he committed suicide when the populace and his soldiers rose up against him. Constantius thus became the sole Roman emperor.

Roman Civil War of A.D. 360–61   In the mid-350s, hostile Persians invaded the Christian kingdom of Armenia; Roman emperor Constantius II (317–61) led an army to the east to crush the Persians, but suffered defeat. He commanded his Christianized cousin Julian (331–63), who had successfully repulsed the Franks and Alemanni in Gaul (France) and was popular with his soldiers, to come to his aid. Julian was ready to go, but his army mutinied and refused to leave Gaul. The soldiers proclaimed Julian their emperor, and he accepted. When Constantius heard this news, he decided to return to the west to put down this rebellion, precipitating a civil war. For his part, Julian determined to confront his uncle. Both forces began to march toward Constantinople (Istanbul) from opposite directions. Julian marched swiftly with his army through southern Germany to Pannonia (parts of Austria, Hungary, and Yugoslavia), where he captured Constantius's legate at Sirmium (Sremska Mitrovica) without a fight. He then continued on toward Constantinople and learned that Constantius, en route to challenge him, had fallen ill and died in Asia Minor. Meanwhile, Julian publicly repudiated Christianity and converted to paganism, thus becoming known as "Julian the Apostate." Julian, whom Constantius had named as his successor, continued the war against the Persians as the new emperor (see ROMAN-PERSIAN WAR OF A.D. 337–63). See also VISIGOTHIC RAIDS ON THE ROMAN EMPIRE, EARLY.

Roman Civil War of A.D. 387–88   In 375, three "Augusti" (emperors) ruled the Roman Empire: Gratian (359–83) in the west; his half-brother Valentinian II (372–92) in Italy, Illyricum (Balkans), and Africa; and their uncle Valens (328?–78) in the east. In 378, the latter was killed in a battle with the Visigoths at Adrianople (Edirne) (see ROMAN-GOTHIC WAR, FIFTH). Gratian appointed Theodosius I "the Great" (346?–95) Valens's successor. Gratian himself was an indifferent ruler, and there was much discontent, especially in Britain, where the army elected its commander, Magnus Clemens Maximus (d. 388), Augustus in 383. Gratian, with his army, marched against him in Gaul (France), but was deserted by his soldiers, captured, and murdered. Valentinian and Theodosius reluctantly acknowledged Maximus as emperor of Gaul, Spain, and Britain. In 387, when Maximus invaded Italy to usurp power there, Valentinian fled to Theodosius for help. The latter assembled large land and naval forces and set out on a campaign against Maximus in Illyricum, where he defeated Maximus in two engagements, one in a courageous and sudden river crossing (388). Maximus withdrew to Italy, pursued by Theodosius, whose navy controlled the Adriatic Sea. At Aquileia (near Venice) Maximus was besieged; his soldiers betrayed him, delivering him to Theodosius, who ordered his execution and restored Valentinian as emperor. Although the fourth century was marked by repeated attempts by individuals to gain military control, the Roman Empire was still regarded as a united entity. This was to change in the following century. See also HUN RAIDS ON THE ROMAN EMPIRE; VISIGOTHIC RAIDS ON THE ROMAN EMPIRE, LATER.

Roman Civil War of A.D. 394   Arbogast (d. 394), a powerful pagan Frankish general in the Roman army, who had pacified the barbarians in Gaul and along the Rhenish frontier of the Roman Empire (388–89), turned against Roman emperor Valentinian II (372–92) of the West, whose murder he evidently instigated. He then proclaimed his pagan protégé Eugenius (d. 394), a former rhetoric teacher, as emperor. Refusing to recognize these two pagan usurpers, Roman emperor Theodosius I "the Great" (346?–95) of the East (since 379) and West (since 392) marched with a large army to avenge Valentinian's death, traveling from Constantinople (Istanbul) to northeastern Italy, where he confronted Eugenius, Arbogast, and their forces at the Frigidus (Vipacco) River, near Aquileia. The first day of battle (September 5, 394) ended in near defeat for Theodosius, who was saved only by darkness; that night he prayed (being a baptized Christian) and reorganized his troops, who attacked and won the next day, thanks mainly to the brilliant generalship of Theodosius's commander Flavius Stilicho (359?–408) (see STILICHO'S WARS WITH THE VISIGOTHS); Eugenius was killed and Arbogast committed suicide; their pagan revolution had failed; the empire was reunited. At the death of Theodosius, the Roman Empire's eastern portion was left to his son Arcadius (377?–408) and the western portion to his younger son Flavius Honorius (384–423), both of whom were ill-prepared to cope with the invading barbarians on the frontiers and elsewhere.

Roman Conquest of Britain (A.D. 43–61) Although the Roman general Julius Caesar (100–44) had successfully invaded Britain during his GALLIC WARS, the conquest of the island did not begin until Claudius I (10 B.C.–A.D. 54), the Roman emperor, sent a four-legion army under Aulus Plautius (fl. before mid-1st cent.) to subjugate the intransigent tribal kingdoms. After landing on the coast at Rutupiae (Richborough, Kent) in 43, the Roman invaders surprised and defeated belligerent Catuvellauni and Trinovantes tribesmen, who retreated toward Londinium (London) but suffered another defeat near Durobrivae (Rochester). Claudius soon arrived to take command of the campaign personally; the Catuvellauni leader Caratacus (fl. 30–60), whose brother Togodumnus (d. 43) had died fighting the Romans, fled westward, rallying various tribes (the Silures and Ordovices of Wales) to his cause. The Romans dispatched separate expeditions that crushed opposition; some tribes readily submitted to Roman rule. By 47, southeastern Brit-

ain, including the three principal centers of Romanized life on the island—Londinium, Camulodunum (Colchester), and Verulamium (St. Albans)—was securely in Roman hands; in the west, the frontier was set along the road known as the Fosse Way, which Roman legions crossed to invade the territory of the Brigantes. Caratacus, whose forces were defeated in north Wales, fled to Brigante queen Cartimandua (fl. 30–70) for help, but in 51 she turned him over to the Romans, who had backed her position of power in a number of anti-Roman revolts among her subjects (later, in 57, they helped her put down a revolt led by her husband and coruler). After a serious but unsuccessful outbreak of resistance (see BOUDICCA'S REBELLION), the British frontier was securely added to the Roman Empire in 61, during the reign of Emperor Nero (37–68). See also MONS GRAUPIUS, BATTLE OF.

Roman Eastern Frontier Wars of 20 B.C.–A.D. 19 Roman emperor Augustus (Octavian) (63 B.C.–A.D. 14) stationed legions in the empire's distant provinces in the east, where he faced considerable hostility, especially from Armenia (a rebellious Roman tributary) and independent Parthia. In 20 B.C., his stepson Tiberius (42 B.C.–A.D. 37) campaigned in Armenia and recovered from the Parthian king, with whom he made a peace treaty, legion standards captured in 53 B.C. during the ROMAN-PARTHIAN WAR OF 55–36 B.C. Thus Roman honor was vindicated, and great acclaim was bestowed on Tiberius, who became emperor on the death of Augustus. The Parthians soon disputed Roman control of Armenia, and Augustus sent generals to the east to campaign repeatedly (17–13, 1–4) but with limited success. Judea was made a Roman province in A.D. 6, and Syria was occupied by legions. A two-year campaign (18–19) in Parthia finally succeeded in restoring Roman control over Armenia, which continued to be a troublesome client state. See also ROMAN-ARMENIAN WARS; ROMAN EASTERN WARS.

Roman Eastern War of A.D. 113–17 Roman emperor Trajan (53–117) was an unusually fair and well-qualified administrator as well as a capable general. In 113, he set out with an army for the east after the Armenian king had been ousted and a Parthian placed on the throne without Rome's consent. He invaded Armenia in 114; encountering little resistance, he overthrew the king and made the country an imperial province. Trajan then advanced into Mesopotamia, again met little opposition, and established there the new province of Assyria. The next year, however, while the Roman forces were far south in Babylon, the new provinces rebelled, and Parthians invaded both Armenia and Assyria. Trajan hastened north with his army to regain his territory; he soon recovered Mesopotamia and checked the Parthian advance in Armenia. A Parthian nobleman loyal to the Romans was named king of Parthia. In 117, Trajan planned another campaign in Mesopotamia to support his appointed king but became ill and died at Selinus (Selindi, Turkey).

Roman Eastern War of A.D.162–65   At the beginning of the reign of Roman emperor Marcus Aurelius (121–80), Vologesus III (fl. 147–91), king of Parthia, launched an invasion of Armenia, defeated the Roman army stationed there, continued on into Mesopotamia, overran the Roman garrisons, and devastated the countryside. Marcus Aurelius sent his adoptive brother, Lucius Aurelius Verus (130–69) to command Roman forces in the east and to restore order. Armenia was retaken in 163. During the following two years the fighting continued in Mesopotamia, where Roman troops led by Avidius Cassius (d. 175) captured Seleucia and Ctesiphon, the Parthian capital. The Parthians sued for peace. A virulent pestilence sweeping through the east and Europe killed thousands, including the Roman soldiers returning from the war, and thus the conquerors were unable to permanently subdue the Parthians.

Roman-Etruscan Wars   See ETRUSCAN-ROMAN WARS.

Roman Gothic War, First (A.D. 249–52)   The Goths were a fierce Germanic people who began to threaten the frontiers of the Roman Empire in the third century (later they split into two divisions: the Ostrogoths [East Goths] and Visigoths [West Goths], with their names reflecting the regions in which they settled in Europe). In 249, a Gothic horde crossed the Danube River and proceeded south into Lower Moesia (Bulgaria). A Roman army under Emperor Decius (201–51) attacked and defeated them, but the Goths soon continued on into northern Greece. The next year Decius pursued them, was ambushed, and defeated in turn. Decius recouped his losses and with fresh troops set out after the Goths again in 251. The ensuing battle seemed to go in his favor at first, but his luck turned. The Goths managed to surround his army and cut it to pieces; both Decius and his son were slain. The new Roman emperor, Gallus (205?–53?), who had fought under Decius, concluded an inglorious peace, allowing the Goths to keep their plunder, to withdraw peacefully across the Danube, and to receive an annual Roman tribute if they did not invade the empire again. **Second Roman-Gothic War** (A.D. 253–68). This consisted of a series of Gothic raids into Roman territory in the Balkans and Asia Minor. In 253, the Goths attacked the Aegean coastal regions and some years later crossed the Hellespont (Dardanelles) and raided the cities on the Ionian coast. Loaded with booty, they turned inland, raiding as they went. Eventually the Goths reached the Black Sea and were able to sail back to their homelands in the north. In 267, they set sail southward and again attacked the coast of Greece; many cities as far south as Sparta were assailed; Athens was captured and looted. Roman emperor Gallienus (d. 268) led an army into Moesia to cut off the Goths' retreat by land. The opposing forces met at Naissus (Nish), where thousands of Goths were slaughtered on the battlefield; the survivors fled to armed encampments. Gallienus had to return to Italy to cope with problems there and thus did not pursue the Goths. **Third Roman-Gothic War** (A.D. 270). Gallienus's successor, Claudius II "Gothicus" (214–70), took over command of the Roman imperial army;

his campaign against the Goths was marked with victories that won him the surname Gothicus. He forced captives to resettle or to join the Roman army. Claudius was succeeded by Aurelian (212?–75) in 270, who finished the task of subduing the Goths. He gave them Dacia (Rumania) to settle in, and for the next century relative peace reigned between the Romans and Goths beyond the Danube and Rhine Rivers. **Fourth Roman-Gothic War** (A.D. 367–69). This was caused in part by the westward movement of the Huns, nomadic people from Mongolia, who drove the tribes of eastern Europe west and south. The Visigoths, led by their chief Athanaric (d. 381), pushed southward from Dacia, invading Thrace repeatedly and forcing the Roman emperor of the East, Valens (328?–78), to send armies against them. In 369, the Romans won a great victory, and Athanaric had to accept peace terms stipulating that the Visigoths would remain north of the Danube. The peace, however, was short-lived. The Huns had overrun the Ostrogoths in the Ukraine and were putting much pressure on all the Germanic tribes, some of which asked Valens for permission to settle in Thrace. This was granted, but corrupt Roman officials exploited the new settlers, who took up arms. **Fifth Roman Gothic War** (A.D. 377–83). The Roman generals of Emperor Valens were unable to restrain the roaming, plundering Visigoths, despite reinforcements, so, in 378, Valens came to lead the army himself. Although outnumbered, he attacked the Goths and their allies at Adrianople (Edirne) with disastrous results (see VISIGOTHIC RAIDS ON THE ROMAN EMPIRE, EARLY). Valens was killed, as were two-thirds of his men; the defeat at Adrianople left the eastern Roman provinces practically defenseless. The next emperor, Theodosius I "the Great" (346?–95), continued the war against the Visigoths in the Balkans, but it was inconclusive and costly. Resorting to diplomacy, he negotiated an unprecedented peace, in which the barbarians were permitted to settle in designated places and to retain their own government and national identity in return for serving as military allies to the Romans. See also VISIGOTHIC RAIDS ON THE ROMAN EMPIRE, LATER.

Roman Northern Frontier Wars of 24 B.C.–A.D. 16

To establish a secure Roman border protecting Italy and Gaul (France), Emperor Augustus (Octavian) (63 B.C.–A.D. 14) moved legions northward and eastward from the Rhine border fixed by Julius Caesar (100–44) in 51 B.C. Augustus founded Aosta in northern Italy (24) and took control of Illyria (roughly Yugoslavia) and Moesia (northern Bulgaria). When invading German tribesmen were victorious in 16, Augustus personally went to Gaul to direct operations; his stepsons Tiberius (42 B.C.–A.D. 37) and Drusus (38–9) headed at the same time triumphant punitive expeditions in Rhaetia (Bavaria), Noricum (Austria), and Pannonia (western Hungary), all of which were annexed to the Roman Empire. In Gaul, legions under Drusus turned back a German invasion (12), marched into Germany, and won at the Lippe River against much superior forces (11); Drusus, victorious, paraded his army back and forth between the Rhine and Elbe rivers to show Roman power. After Drusus died from injuries received falling from a horse, Tiberius carried on his beloved brother's campaigning in Germany until 7, when conquest and subjugation stopped. In A.D. 4, he returned to Germany to quell tribal revolts, leading expeditions (naval and land) to the Elbe; he left the Roman consul Varus (d. A.D. 9) in command there and went to Pannonia and Illyria to suppress uprisings successfully (6–9). The disastrous Roman defeat in the Battle of the TEUTOBURG FOREST, in 9, stopped further Romanization of Germany. Nevertheless, a number of punitive campaigns led first by Tiberius and then by Germanicus Caesar (15 B.C.–A.D. 19), son of Drusus, inflicted severe damages on the Germans in revenge for the Teutoburg catastrophe (11–16). See also ROMAN-GOTHIC WARS.

Roman-Parthian War of 55–36 B.C.

In the ancient world, Parthia was a country situated in what is now northern Iran. Its relations with Rome had been cordial until 65. There was no cause for war 10 years later when Crassus (115–53) set off from Rome with a large army; Crassus desired the glory and bounty of a victorious campaign; he was disappointed. In 54, he crossed the Euphrates River and began to invade Parthia, but his soldiers were not experienced in desert warfare. They were surrounded in heavy dust by Parthian horsemen and archers who decimated the Roman legions. Crassus was slain while trying to escape from Carrhae. Seventeen years later Mark Antony (83?–30) resumed the war, attempting to invade Parthia over the Armenian mountains, but the Armenian king refused to help, and Parthian horsemen raided Mark Antony's supply train and destroyed his siege guns. His attempt to seize the fortress of Praspa failed, and the Romans were forced to retreat with severe losses.

Roman-Parthian War of A.D. 56–63   Vologesus I (fl. 51–77) became king of the Parthians in 51, and when the Roman puppet king of Armenia was killed, he attempted to place his brother, Tiridates (d. 73?), on the Armenian throne. This displeased Roman emperor Nero (37–68), who directed his general in Asia Minor, Corbulo (d. 67), to set up another puppet king. In 57, Corbulo and his forces invaded Armenia and drove Tiridates from the throne. Vologesus was occupied with threatening domestic problems in Parthia at that time and could not spare soldiers to oppose Corbulo. In 61, however, Vologesus invaded Armenia, forced the Roman legions from the country, and reestablished Tiridates as king. Corbulo negotiated a settlement whereby Tiridates remained king but acknowledged Nero as overlord.

Roman-Parthian War of A.D. 195–202   While rival emperors were struggling for control in Rome, King Vologesus IV (fl. 191–209) of Parthia invaded Armenia and besieged the city of Nisibis (Nisibin or Nusaybin). After becoming emperor, Lucius Septimius Severus (146–211) led a Roman army eastward across the Euphrates River and occupied the Parthian city of Seleucia. The army proceeded against Ctesiphon, which also fell after fierce fighting. When the Romans turned north, Vologesus and his soldiers lifted the siege of Nisibis and then retreated to the mountains. However, the Parthian

fortress of Hatra stood firm against the Romans in 197 and again in 199. Severus captured Nisibis and made it the capital of a Parthian province in the Roman Empire. Despite the failure at Harta, Severus's campaign against the Parthians was successful.

Roman-Persian War of A.D. 230–33   About 226–27, an upstart king of Persia, Ardashir (Ataxerxes) I (d. 241), revolted against his Parthian overlord, overthrew him, conquered the Parthian Empire, and founded the Sassanid dynasty. He then claimed all of Asia Minor for the new Persian Empire. In 230 and 231, he invaded Roman Mesopotamia and defied Rome by minting his own gold coins. The young and militarily inexperienced Roman emperor, Marcus Aurelius Alexander Severus (208?–35), tried unsuccessfully to negotiate peace and was forced to take to the battlefield to put down this threat in his eastern provinces. In 232, three Roman armies attempted to invade Persia from different directions. The army under Alexander Severus's command was badly defeated, and the two others were only partially successful. Ardashir's Persian losses were so severe, however, that he was unable to follow up his "victory." Alexander Severus returned to Rome and celebrated a triumph. There was no formal peace, but the Roman frontier was reestablished.

Roman-Persian War of A.D. 241–44   Shapur I (d. 272), Sassanid king of Persia and son of Ardashir I (d. 241), continued his father's policy of enlarging the Persian Empire at the expense of Rome. His cavalry and foot soldiers invaded and seized most of Syria and threatened the city of Antioch. Roman emperor Marcus Antonius Gordianus III (224?–44) and his father-in-law and most able general, Gaius Furius Sabinus Aquila Timesithesus (d. 243), arrived in Syria with a Roman army in 242, defeated Shapur's Persians at the Battle of Resaena in 243, and drove Shapur out of the country. However, the death of Timesithesus and the murder of Gordianus, some say by his successor, Philip "the Arabian"

(204?–49), prevented the Romans from exploiting their success. Emperor Philip made peace with Shapur, and the former Roman-Persian boundary was reestablished.

Roman-Persian War of A.D. 257–61   Taking advantage of Rome's internal disintegration, King Shapur I (d. 272) of Persia conquered Armenia and placed a Persian puppet on its throne. His forces made raids into Mesopotamia and Syria and seized the city of Antioch in 258. Roman emperor Valerian (d. 261?) set out for Asia Minor with an army and drove the Persians from Antioch, but was unable to defeat Shapur and his troops at the Battle of Edessa (Urfa) in 260. The Roman army was encircled, and Valerian desperately entered into peace negotiations with Shapur, during which the Roman emperor was taken prisoner. This threw the Romans into disarray, and they surrendered. Valerian was brought to Persia, where he later died in captivity. Shapur's forces quickly overran Syria, retook Antioch, and raided other eastern Roman territories. While returning home laden with plunder, the Persians were defeated in battle by a prince of Palmyra, and this ended Shapur's aggressive practices in Asia Minor and Syria.

Roman-Persian War of A.D. 282–83   In 282, the new Roman emperor, Marcus Aurelius Carus (223?–83), accompanied by his younger son Marcus Aurelius Numerianus (d. 284), led a military campaign against the Persians under King Bahram I (d. 276). The Roman forces succeeded in retaking upper Mesopotamia from the Persians and captured their capital, Ctesiphon. Weakened by disorders in their eastern territory, the Persians negotiated a peace with Carus, who had marched east of the Tigris River with the intention, possibly, of undermining the Sassanid Persian Empire. In 283, Carus died mysteriously near the Tigris, allegedly struck by lightning; it was rumored, however, that he was murdered by his Praetorian prefect, Arius Aper (d. 285). The Roman army now returned westward through Asia Minor; Numerianus, now joint Ro-

man emperor with his brother Carinus (d. 285), was found dead after the army had reached the Bosporus. Aper, accused of his murder, was personally slain by Diocletian (245–313), who had fought as a commander under Carus. The army proclaimed Diocletian emperor (see ROMAN CIVIL WAR OF 284–85).

Roman-Persian War of A.D. 295–97   For many years the Roman Empire had been beset with rebellions within its far-flung provinces and by invasions by outside barbarians. Narses (d. c. 302), Sassanid king of Persia, took advantage of the disorders elsewhere and seized the Roman protectorate of Armenia. The Roman "Caesar" for the east, Galerius (d. 311), and a relatively small army marched against the Persians, won some minor victories in Mesopotamia, but were decisively routed at the Battle of Carrhea (Harran) in 296. The following year, with a reinforced army, Galerius marched again to confront the Persians, and this time he was victorious, nearly annihilating a much superior army in a surprise attack somewhere along the upper Tigris River. There Galerius captured much booty and many Persians, including Narses's harem and family. Narses was compelled to accept Rome's peace terms. By the Peace of Nisibis (Nisibin or Nusaybin), in 297, the Persians returned upper Mesopotamia to the Romans, ceded five provinces northeast of the Tigris to them, and recognized the Roman puppet, Tiridates III (238?–314), as king of Armenia. Narses's family and concubines were given back to him.

Roman-Persian War of A.D. 337–63   Upon the death of Roman emperor Constantine I "the Great" (228?–337), his second son Constantius II (317–61) became ruler of the eastern part of the Roman Empire. He was engaged in constant but indecisive war with Shapur II "the Great" (309–379), the Persian king who was trying to repossess Armenia and northern Mesopotamia. After Constantius returned to Italy, Shapur and his soldiers invaded Mesopotamia again in 359. Constantius returned to the east but died in Tarsus in Cilicia before reestablishing his authority. His successor, Roman emperor Julian (331–63), continued the war against Shapur, at first successfully, but he was unable to seize Ctesiphon and, as previous Roman generals, was plagued with problems of desert warfare. While retreating from Ctesiphon, Julian was killed in a skirmish. Shapur was then free to develop the prosperity of his Persian empire without Roman interference. See also ROMAN CIVIL WAR OF A.D. 360–61.

Roman-Persian War of A.D. 421–22   Soon after he secured the Sassanid Persian throne and the support of the nobles, King Bahram V (d. 439), called Gor ("the wild ass"), reversed the policy of his father, Yazdegerd I (d. 420), and revived the violent persecution of Christians, which angered the Romans and brought on war by them against the Persians. In some minor battles in Mesopotamia, Bahram's forces suffered defeat, and the king agreed to peace terms in which Christianity was tolerated throughout the Persian Empire. In turn, the Romans agreed to tolerate Zoroastrianism, the religion of Persia.

Roman-Persian War of A.D. 441   The Sassanid king of Persia, Yazdegerd II (d. 457), son and successor of Bahram V (d. 439), began to persecute the Jews and Christians in his empire (see ROMAN-PERSIAN WAR OF A.D. 421–22). This provoked a brief war with Rome, which sent forces against the Persians after failing to reverse Yazdegerd's policy peacefully. Roman troops were successful in minor engagements, and the king made peace, permitting the Jews and Christians to worship in their own ways without interference.

Roman-Persian War of A.D. 502–6   The Sassanid king of Persia, Kavadh I (d. 531), asked the eastern Roman emperor, Anastasius I (430?–518), for financial aid in paying a tribute to the Ephthalites ("White Huns"), who had helped Kavadh regain his throne from which he had been deposed by his brother. When Anastasius refused the request and began to interfere in affairs in Per-

sian Armenia, Kavadh invaded Roman Armenia with an army in 502 and captured the major city there, Theodosiopolis (Erzurum). He triumphed again the next year in Roman Mesopotamia, seizing Amida (Diyarbakir) after a three-month siege. Repulsed at Edessa (Urfa), the Persians were gradually beaten by the eastern Romans (Byzantines), who recaptured Amida and then made peace. The Roman-Persian border was restored to what it was before the war. See also GHASSANID-LAKHMID WARS; JUSTINIAN'S FIRST PERSIAN WAR.

Roman-Persian War of A.D. 524–32   See JUSTINIAN'S FIRST PERSIAN WAR.

Roman-Persian War of A.D. 539–62   See JUSTINIAN'S SECOND PERSIAN WAR.

Roman-Persian War of A.D. 572–91   Khosrau (Chosroes) I (d. 579), Sassanid king of Persia, broke the peace treaty made with Eastern Roman emperor Justinian I (483–565) in 561 when he invaded Roman Armenia and seized the fortress of Dara on the Euphrates River (see JUSTINIAN'S SECOND PERSIAN WAR). His forces also conquered parts of the Caucasus (region between the Black and Caspian Seas) but were less successful in Mesopotamia. In 579, the Romans (Byzantines) and Persians began peace negotiations, which ceased, however, upon Khosrau's death. His son and successor, Ormizd (Hormizd) IV (d. 590), refused to give up any of his father's conquests, and the war resumed. The Sassanid Persian Empire was also disrupted by widespread internal rebellion and by Arabic invaders, who overran most of Khorasan. The able Persian general Bahram Chobin (d. 591?) was successful against the Arabs and regained much lost territory. Turning against the Romans, he suffered severe defeats at Nisibis (Nusaybin or Nisibin) and the Araxes (Aras) River in 589. Nevertheless, Bahram was powerful enough to head a conspiracy against Ormizd that led to the latter's deposition and assassination. Bahram proclaimed himself king in 590, while the rightful heir, Khosrau II (d. 628), Ormizd's son, fled to Syria and sought help from Eastern Roman emperor Maurice (c. 539–602). Maurice consented, and his army accompanied Khosrau back to Persia, en route defeating Bahram's forces at the Battle of the Zab (590). In Media (northwest Iran) Bahram's army was crushed (591); Bahram escaped but soon was killed or died; Khosrau was restored to the throne, and peace was concluded with the Romans. Former frontiers were reestablished on both sides, and Roman subsidies paid to Persia for Caucasus forts ceased.

Roman War against Pyrrhus of Epirus (281–272 B.C.) Tarentum (Taranto), a Spartan (Greek) colony on the southern Italian coast, resented Roman expansion in its area, declared war on Rome, and asked King Pyrrhus (319–272) of Epirus in Greece, an able general, for assistance, which he readily gave. For the first time, Romans met a Greek army in battle at Heraclea in 280 and were badly defeated. The following year the Greeks under Pyrrhus again beat the Romans in southern Italy, this time at Asculum (Ascoli), but suffered such heavy losses on the battlefield that Pyrrhus declared, "One more such victory and I am lost." From this is derived the expression a "Pyrrhic victory." See also CARTHAGINIAN WAR AGAINST PYRRHUS OF EPIRUS.

Roman War with the Quadi and Sarmatians (A.D. 374–75) Just as Rome had problems with invading barbarians (see ROMAN-GOTHIC WARS), so did the earlier migrants. The Quadi, a Germanic people, had been pushed ever westward by the Huns until they were settled, by 359, east of the Danube River in Dacia (roughly Rumania). They remained peaceful until Roman emperor Valentinian I (321–75) extended Roman fortifications on the south bank of the river into Quadi territory. The Quadi king, Gabinus (d. 374), led a force to complain of this violation of Quadi rights, but the Roman commander of the fort murdered him for his presumption. The resulting rebellion brought the Quadi with their allies, the Sarmatians, across the Danube; they devastated Moesia (Bulgaria) and Pannonia (parts of Austria, Hungary, and Yugoslavia) and routed feuding Roman legionaries. Roman forces under Theodosius (346?–95), the future emperor, checked the Sarmatians, forcing them into a separate peace (374), while Valentinian marched with an army from Gaul (France) into Quadi territory (375), devastating it before returning to winter quarters. Convinced that further resistance was useless, the Quadi sent envoys to Valentinian; when they excused their rebellion as the effect of Roman aggression, Valentinian became so angry that he suffered a fatal stroke. The Quadi remained peaceful until 405, when they joined the Visigoths in invading Italy (see STILICHO'S WARS WITH THE VISIGOTHS). See also GOTHIC-SARMATIAN WAR; ROMAN-GOTHIC WARS.

Roman War with the Cimbri and Teutones (104–101 B.C.) For many years the Cimbri and Teutones, Germanic tribes who originally inhabited Jutland (Denmark and part of north Germany), had been making their way south into Roman Gaul (roughly France). They defeated several Roman armies before advancing west toward Spain. In 104, these barbaric tribes turned toward northern Italy and planned to invade it in three large groups. Meanwhile, the capable Roman general Gaius Marius (155?–86) had been recruiting and training new troops to meet the invaders; he built a strong fortified camp at the junction of the Rhône and Isére rivers, where his forces repelled attacks by Teutones and Cimbri in 102. Moving down the Rhône, a large Teutonic horde planned to march over the Maritime Alps into Italy, but it was ambushed and routed by Marius's army at the Battle of Aquae Sextae (Aix-en-Provence) in 102. A horde of Cimbri, which had moved through Switzerland to the east and then through the Brenner Pass, crushed a Roman force in the Adige River valley in northern Italy and marched south into the Po River valley. Rushing back to Italy, Marius and his men joined other Roman troops and thoroughly defeated this Cimbri horde at the Battle of Vercellae in 101; supposedly 140,000 barbarians were slain, and more than 50,000 taken captive there. A third horde of barbarians turned away and did not bother Rome again.

Roman War with the Vandals (A.D. 468) By 468, the Vandals, a Germanic people, under the leadership of their king Genseric (Gaiseric) (390–477), had assumed authority over Roman Africa, Sicily, and other islands in the eastern Mediterranean, where their ships controlled the seas (see VANDAL RAIDS ON THE ROMAN EMPIRE). Leo I "the Great" (400?–474), eastern Roman emperor, sent a naval expedition against them under the command of his brother-in-law, Basiliscus (d. 478). Through carelessness (or treachery, according to some historians), Basiliscus maneuvered his fleet so ineptly and postponed attacking the Vandals so long that Genseric's fire ships were able to wreak havoc on the Roman forces near Cape Bon (Ras Addar, Tunisia). The expedition ended in disaster; Basiliscus fled back to Constantinople (Istanbul); and the Vandals remained masters of the Mediterranean. See also VANDAL-ROMAN WAR IN NORTH AFRICA.

Roman War with Veii, First (438–426 B.C.) The powerful Etruscan city of Veii (Veio), situated about 12 miles north of Rome on the right bank of the Tiber River, had an important outpost downriver a short distance above Rome. The Romans sought to take possession of this post, called Fidenae, and attacked it about 438. In the course of one battle King Tolumnius (d. c. 430) of Veii was killed by a Roman general. Veii called on other cities in the Etruscan League to come to its aid, but few responded. After a protracted siege, the Romans took Fidenae in 426 and added it to their own territory. **Second Roman War with Veii** (405–396 B.C.). A Roman army attempted unsuccessfully to besiege Veii, whose citizens had foreseen this and had strongly fortified their cliff-top city. Then the Roman dictator Marcus Furius Camillus (d. c. 365) initiated a siege that lasted nine years; his Roman soldiers gained control of the level land north of Veii and reputedly crawled through drainage tunnels into the heart of the city, which they captured and

mercilessly sacked. Veii was destroyed; its inhabitants and their territory were absorbed by Rome; its fall signaled the end of Etruscan dominance in central Italy and the ascendancy of Rome. See also ETRUSCAN-ROMAN WARS; ROME, CELTIC SACK OF.

Rome, Celtic Sack of (390 B.C.)   Celts (or Gauls) crossed the Alps into northern Italy, took the city of Melpum (Milan) in 396, and continued south into central Etruria, besieging the Etruscan city of Clusium (Chiusi) about 391. According to the Roman historian Livy (59 B.C.–A.D. 17), calls for aid from Clusium brought a peace delegation from Rome, which tried in vain to persuade the Celts to return north. The invaders, led by chieftain Brennus (fl. later 4th cent.), defeated an opposing Roman army at the Allia (July 390) and then stormed Rome, all of which was captured except the citadel and the Temple of Jupiter on the Capitoline Hill. Many of the chiefly wooden buildings were burned to the ground, and looting and murder were rampant. After several months, the Celts, unable to conquer the hill and learning that their territories in the Po Valley were threatened by the Illyrian Venetii tribe, accepted a large payment of tribute offered by the Roman leader Marcus Furius Camillus (d. c. 365) and departed from Rome. According to legend, when the gold tribute was being weighed, a Roman tribune complained about the inaccurate scale weights; immediately Brennus placed his sword on the scale, exclaiming, "Vae victis!" (woe to the vanquished!). See also ETRUSCAN-ROMAN WARS, EARLY.

Rome, Fall of (A.D. 476) During the two decades following the sack of Rome by the Vandals in 455 (see VANDAL RAIDS ON THE ROMAN EMPIRE), Italy was ruled by a succession of barbarian generals, and the Roman emperor of the west was little more than a puppet or figurehead. In 476, the Germanic mercenary soldiers who comprised the majority of the Roman army revolted and proclaimed their chief, Odoacer (Odovacar) (434?–93), king. At the Battle of Pavia on August 23, 476, Odoacer defeated the

Roman general Orestes (d. 476), sent against him; Orestes was captured and executed; Odoacer then seized Ravenna, which had become the capital of the Western Roman Empire, and deposed Emperor Romulus Augustulus (d. after 476), Orestes's son, who was allowed to retire to a villa in Campania. Afterward Odoacer ruled Italy but did not call himself emperor and did not consider his territory part of the Roman Empire in the East. The date, 476, is significant, for it marks the total and final breakdown of the centuries-old political system in western Europe and the dawn of the so-called Dark Ages. Further weakening of the Roman Empire occurred in A.D. 486, when Clovis (A.D. c. 466–511), king of the Salian Franks, defeated Syagrius (A.D. 430?–86), the Gallo-Roman governor, at Soissons. Clovis then expanded his power north of the Loire, annexing Roman dominions in Gaul (France). See also THEODORIC'S WAR WITH ODOACER.

Rome, Muslim Sack of (A.D. 846) In the early 800s, Spanish Muslim pirates dominated the Mediterranean Sea, capturing Palermo, Sicily, in 831 and establishing small Muslim states on Italy's southern coast at Taranto and Bari (840). From these bases, they terrorized the Adriatic and Tyrrhenian Seas, often coming inland to raid. Repulsed at Naples in 846, they came north to the Tiber River, overcoming a fort built at its mouth by Pope Gregory IV (d. 844). They landed on the south bank of the Tiber and marched toward Rome. As the Muslims advanced, they looted and burned Roman suburbs. The Vatican hill area, then outside Rome's defensive walls, suffered extensively, with the old St. Peter's basilica being desecrated. After the raiders escaped with their booty, Pope Leo IV (800?–855) had walls built around the Vatican area. Known for years as the "leonine walls," they safeguarded the "Leonine City," a nickname still in use today.

Rome, Visigothic Sack of (A.D. 410) In 408, the Visigoths' demands upon Rome for tribute and Pannonia (Roman province south and west of the Danube) were rejected by the government in Ra-

venna; Alaric (370?–410), the Visigothic king, blockaded Rome, gained a sizable ransom, and then withdrew to Tuscany to fight Roman armies. When Roman officials at Ravenna refused to meet Alaric's new demands, the Visigoths seized Rome's port city of Ostia in 409; Alaric forced the Roman Senate to elect a puppet emperor, who named him commander in chief. Alaric then besieged Ravenna but withdrew when 4,000 relief soldiers arrived from Constantinople, the capital of the Eastern Roman Empire (Ravenna was the capital of the West). A truce followed; the puppet emperor was deposed, but an attack on Alaric's camp by the Romans broke the truce (410). Determined to sack Rome and then take the Visigoths to North Africa, Alaric invaded northern Italy from Illyricum (Roman colony along the Adriatic's east coast) and besieged Rome. The city suffered starvation; the Roman Senate agreed to more tribute for Alaric, but Ravenna overruled its vote. Three weeks later, the city's Salarian Gate was opened by treachery; Visigoths and Roman slaves then destroyed Rome, sparing only the churches. Many died, while others were held for ransom or enslaved. Loaded with loot, the Visigoths marched south (see VISIGOTHIC RAIDS ON THE ROMAN EMPIRE, LATER). See also ROME, FALL OF.

Roses, Wars of the (1455–85) A power struggle for the throne of England, this war involved only two houses in the English royal line. Other social classes were indifferent or neutral, except when armies crossed their fields. The struggle began as an opposition to the Beaufort (Lancastrian) family's desire to end the HUNDRED YEARS' WAR after Orléans (see ORLEANS, SIEGE AT). The Beauforts controlled the young king Henry VI (1421–71), and the loss of Bordeaux (see BORDEAUX, FALL OF) turned the English to the Yorkists, led by Richard (1411–60), duke of York, recognized in 1450 as heir to the then childless king. Protector when Henry became insane, Richard was ousted from power and rebelled. Victorious in 1455 at St. Albans, he again became Protector. Henry's queen, Margaret of Anjou (1430?–82), gathered troops, and the Yorkists, declared traitors, fled, to return to victory at

Northumbria in 1460. The king was captured and Richard declared his heir. Margaret sponsored another Lancastrian army that won victory over the Yorkists at Wakefield in late 1460. Richard was killed, but his son was named heir; the earl of Warwick, the "kingmaker," now led the Yorkists. Margaret's forces won at a second St. Albans' battle, but the Lancastrians lost at Mortimer's Cross and Towton in 1461, compelling Margaret to flee to Scotland to raise resistance. In London, Richard's son was proclaimed King Edward IV (1442–83), giving power to Warwick until 1467, when Edward dismissed Warwick's appointees (see WARWICK'S REBELLION). Warwick was forced to flee to France, where he allied himself with the French king and became reconciled with Margaret. With an army, Warwick and Margaret returned to London in 1470, deposed Edward, and restored Henry to the throne. Edward fled to Burgundy, returning to England with aid in 1471 and defeating the Lancastrians at Barnet, where Warwick died, and at Tewkesbury, where Henry's late-born son succumbed and Margaret and Henry were captured. Henry then died mysteriously. Relative peace lasted until 1483. Then Edward's son became King Edward V (1470–83) briefly, only to have his uncle, later Richard III (1452–85), usurp the throne (see BUCKINGHAM'S REVOLT). This action gained the enmity of Henry Tudor, a Lancastrian claimant, who became Henry VII (1457–1509) when Richard died at Bosworth Field in 1485 (see BOSWORTH FIELD, BATTLE OF). Marrying Edward IV's daughter, Henry united the warring houses, thus ending both the war and feudalism in an England whose nobles were too weak to overthrow the Tudor line (see SIMNEL'S REBELLION).

Ruandan Civil War of 1959–61   After WORLD WAR II, Ruanda (Rwanda), a former German colony in east-central Africa, became part of the Belgian-administered United Nations trust territory of Ruanda-Urundi. Historically the very tall Tutsi (Watusi or Tusi) people had dominated the area, although they made up only 15 percent of the population. In November 1959, the suppressed Hutu (Bahutu) people, the majority of the population, long held in feudal bondage, rose in revolt against the ruling Tutsi, who were supported by the Twa (Pygmies); Belgium had just granted self-government, and the Hutu felt they did not have a voice in Ruanda's affairs proportionate to their numbers. Bloody tribal warfare ensued in which the Hutu were eventually victorious. The people were allowed to choose their form of government. In 1961, in a UN-supervised referendum, more than 80 percent of the Ruandans voted to abolish the monarchy and depose the Tutsi mwami (king); a republic was proclaimed, causing more than 150,000 Tutsi to flee to neighboring countries (see BURUNDIAN CIVIL WAR OF 1972). In 1963, armed Tutsi émigrés invaded Hutu-controlled Rwanda, which had become an independent nation the year before and then changed the spelling of its name. Hutu forces repelled the invaders, massacred many Tutsi in reprisal, and checked another invasion in 1964.

Ruandan Civil War of 1990–94   See RWANDAN CIVIL WAR OF 1990–94.

Rumanian Rebellion of 1989 (Rumanian Revolution of 1989)   On Christmas Day 1989, the communist dictator Nicolae Ceausescu (1918–89) and his wife, Elena (1919–89) were executed in secret by members of the nascent National Salvation Front (NSF), thus bringing 24 years of gross misrule to an abrupt and dramatic end. Ceausescu rose to leadership of Rumania's Communist Party in 1965 and became president in 1974. Initially he was praised in the West for his anti-Soviet stances, including his denunciation of the 1968 SOVIET INVASION OF CZECHOSLOVAKIA. But increasing frustration among ordinary Rumanians with Ceausescu's bizarre megalomania, his steady destruction of Rumania's economy, his refusal to allow dissenting views of any kind, and his cruel social policies—including plans for mass relocation of peasants and denying medical care to the elderly—came to a head in mid-December 1989, when Ceausescu's elite security forces (the Securitate) arrested Laslo Tokes (1953–   ), an outspoken ethnic Hungarian pastor working in the western city of Timisoara. Mayhem ensued as Securitate forces gunned down hundreds of angry citizens who took to the streets in defense of Tokes. Rebellion quickly spread to Bucharest, the capital, where hundreds more were killed by Ceausescu's men. Meanwhile the army, which turned against the regime in support of the people, engaged in fierce fighting with the Securitate in cities across Rumania. In the midst of the chaos, the Ceausescus fled and were captured, tried, and sentenced to death by the NSF. This hastily formed group, comprised of 60 self-appointed members including former communists who had fallen out with the regime, assumed power, named a 37-member transitional government, and promised to hold free elections in the spring. To broaden its appeal the NSF admitted dozens of representatives from new political parties, local militias and citizens' committees. Interim president Ion Iliescu (1930–   ) and Prime Minister Petre Roman (1946–   ), both reform communists, now faced the formidable challenge of building a new Rumania. In the meantime it fell to the army to maintain stability in the traumatized nation. May 1990 elections confirmed Iliescu as president, but dissatisfied opposition members and Ceausescu-like ranting on the part of Iliescu, combined with high unemployment, currency devaluation, and ethnic tensions, promised a rough transitional period.

Rum Rebellion   See AUSTRALIAN RUM REBELLION.

Russian-Bulgarian War of A.D. 969–72   After the death of their czar, Symeon (d. 927), the Bulgars were without strong leadership and confused about Symeon's attempts to make Bulgaria a cultural rival of the Byzantine Empire. In 969, Kievan Russians under Prince Sviatoslav (d. 972) moved southward to seize the city of Philippopolis (Plovdiv) and other Bulgarian territory. To halt the Russian advance and expansionism, the Byzantines of Emperor John

Tzimisces (925–76) decided to crush the Russians (see BYZANTINE-RUSSIAN WAR OF A.D. 970–72).

Russian Civil War of 1425–53   At the age of 10, Basil II (1415–62) succeeded his father Basil I (1371–1425) as the grand prince of Moscow, but his uncle Yuri (d. c. 1434) sought control of the principality through the help of the Tatars (Tartars). The boyars (Russian aristocrats) supported Basil's rule until 1432, when Yuri gained their favor because of a marriage contract dispute with Basil. A simmering civil war broke wide open, and Yuri and his supporters managed to hold Moscow briefly before death terminated his claim to the throne. Yuri's son carried on the fight until 1435, when he was defeated, captured, and blinded. When Basil refused to help the Tatars and drove their leader (khan) from Muscovy (ancient Russia) to Kazan on the Volga River, he ignited the rage of the Tatars, who attacked and harassed Moscow for a century afterward. In 1443 and 1451, the Muscovites repulsed the invading Tatars at their city walls; for a time the Tatar leader captured and held Basil for ransom and also expropriated boyar estates. Another son of Yuri's, Dimitri Shemiaka (d. 1453), prince of Galicia, along with other princes, seized control of Muscovy in 1446, and imprisoned and blinded Basil, but was compelled to restore Basil to the throne in 1447. Shemiaka's animosity ultimately led to an invasion by Basil's young son Ivan (1440–1505) into Galicia, where Shemiaka was defeated and fled to Novgorod; Galicia was rejoined to Muscovy. In 1453, Shemiaka died of poisoning at his Novgorod refuge. Muscovy had now become a strong, politically unified Russian state under Basil and was later to grow more powerful and larger and more consolidated under Ivan, his successor as Ivan III "the Great" (see NOVGOROD, MUSCOVITE CONQUEST OF).

Russian Civil War of 1604–13   See "TIME OF TROUBLES," RUSSIAN.

Russian Civil War of 1918–21   Several months after the popularly elected Russian assembly was disbanded as a counterrevolutionary body (see OC-

TOBER REVOLUTION), civil war broke out in 1918 between the ruling Bolsheviks (or communists) and the anti-Bolshevik "Whites." It was triggered by a clash between Czech troops in transit through Siberia and the Bolsheviks, whose punishment of the Czechs provoked the Czechs to raid Siberian villages. Taking advantage of the situation, the Whites began battling the newly formed Bolshevik Red Army, successfully taking almost all of Siberia. During the struggle, Czar Nicholas II (1868–1918) and his family were murdered at Yekaterinburg (Sverdlovsk) in July 1918. A month later, British, French, Japanese, and American troops, in support of the Whites, landed at Vladivostok on the Pacific Ocean's Sea of Japan, and British and Americans disembarked at Archangel (Arkangelsk) on the White Sea and helped a new provisional government to establish itself there. Through these foreign efforts, Bolshevik rule was eliminated east of the Ural Mountains. However, the Red Army under Leon Trotsky (1879–1940), communist military affairs commissar, waged fierce battles and ultimately defeated three White armies from the Caucasus, Baltic, and Siberia areas. The Czechs withdrew, but the Allied foreign powers continued to furnish troops and supplies to fight the communists. Terrorism and assassinations increased on both sides, and communist distrust of non-Bolsheviks was hardened. After peace negotiations failed, a White army advanced toward Moscow, reaching Orel, about 200 miles to the south, and another White force came within 10 miles of Petrograd (Leningrad, St. Petersburg), but the Red Army turned them back and won victory at Novorossiysk on the Black Sea. After the western Siberian city of Omsk, headquarters of the anticommunist forces of Admiral Aleksandr V. Kolchak (1874–1920), fell to the Reds in November 1919, and the withdrawal of foreign forces from the war, the Whites were gradually crushed as they fought in hostile territory. The bloody civil war, in which the KRONSHTADT REBELLION occurred, ended with the Soviets (Bolsheviks or communists) firmly in control of the government and the country (including Siberia) by 1921. See also FINNISH WAR OF INDEPENDENCE; RUSSO-POLISH WAR OF 1919–20.

Russian Conquests in Central Asia (1865–81) The Central Asian Turkoman and Tatar (Tartar) nomads on the steppes (vast plains) south of Siberia came under Russian control in the 19th century. Fortresses erected by Czars Alexander I (1777–1825) and Nicholas I (1796–1855) were instrumental in subjugating the Kirghiz tribe up to the Syr Darya River. South of the Aral Sea, the emirate of Bukhara and the khanates of Khiva and Kokand were attacked by Muslim extremists, bringing on the conquest of the territories by Russian military governors. Russian troops occupied the main cities of Tashkent (1865) and Samarkand (1868), and a Russian governor-general was installed in the newly formed Turkistan province (1867) between the Aral Sea and Lake Issyk-Kul. Two years after suffering defeat in battle, Bukhara's emir (Muslim ruler) accepted Russian control in 1868 in return for retaining his throne. Khiva's khan (ruler) agreed to the same in 1873, and a Trans-Caspian province was created between the Caspian Sea and the Amu Darya River. When Kokand's khan refused to submit to Russian rule, his khanate was overrun and made a part of Russia in 1876. By 1881, Russian Turkistan was formed—a large central Asian region stretching from the Caspian Sea eastward to the Chinese border and from the Irtysh watershed southward to the Afghan frontier.

Russian Dynastic War of A.D. 972–80   On his death, Prince Sviatoslav (d. 972) left the Russian state to his three sons: Oleg (d. 977?), Yaropolk (d. 979?), and Vladimir (956–1015). The three brothers went to war for the throne, and in 977 Yaropolk's forces from Kiev defeated Oleg's from Drevlian territory; Oleg was slain in flight. From Novgorod, Vladimir went to Scandinavia to seek aid, and in 978 he returned with Norse mercenaries, seized Polotsk, and regained control of Novgorod after evicting Yaropolk's administrators. Advancing toward Kiev, Vladimir's men captured Yaropolk, who gave up the city without a battle and was executed on Vladimir's orders. By 980, Vladimir was the sole ruler of the Russian state. See VLADIMIR, CONQUESTS OF.

Russian Dynastic War of 1015–25   When Russia's Grand Prince Vladimir (956–1015) died, he left his empire divided among his many heirs. His ambitious nephew Sviatopolk "the Damned" (d. 1021) sought to gain sole control of it; he murdered his young brothers Boris and Gleb (in 1015) and took over Kiev. However, a third brother, Yaroslav (d. 1054), who had inherited Novgorod, marched with forces against Sviatopolk at Kiev. Routed in battle, Sviatopolk fled to Poland and the court of his father-in-law Boleslav I (d. 1054). In 1019, Sviatopolk, Boleslav, and a large army invaded and drove the Russians back to Kiev (see RUSSO-POLISH WAR OF 1019–25). Sviatopolk regained his Kievan crown, and Yaroslav withdrew to Novgorod. But Sviatopolk turned against his Polish supporters, who received aid from Yaroslav to defeat Sviatopolk, who was killed in flight. Russia was now ruled by Yaroslav, the grand prince of Kiev and Novgorod. A later successful military campaign by another heir resulted in a brief, temporary division of the realm between him and Yaroslav, but upon the former's death all Russian lands reverted to Yaroslav.

Russian Rebellion of 1993   ("Second October Revolution") Russia's most serious internal crisis since the dissolution of the Soviet Union in 1991 came to a head in two days of bloody street fighting in early October 1993 when communist members of the Supreme Soviet (parliament) tried to bring down the government of President Boris Yeltsin (1931–) by force. Exasperated by numerous hardline legislators' continual blockage of his efforts to liberalize the economy and other aspects of Russian life, Yeltsin had drafted a new constitution in June 1993 which would not only give the presidency much stronger powers but also dissolve both the Congress of People's Deputies (supreme legislature) and the Supreme Soviet and replace them with a bicameral legislature. Although the Constitutional Committee of the Congress of People's Deputies participated in the drafting process, the Supreme Soviet, dominated by conservatives and communists, instantly rejected the draft. After two months of increasing intransigence on both sides, Yeltsin

unilaterally dissolved the two legislative bodies on September 21 and announced elections for a new two-chamber parliament for December. The Congress's speaker, Ruslan Imranovich Khasbulatov (1942–), and Yeltsin's vice president, Alexander Vladimirovich Rutskoi (Rutskoy) (1947–), along with 150 supporters, promptly occupied the parliament building (the "White House"); the Supreme Soviet then dismissed Yeltsin and declared Rutskoi president, naming new key ministers as well. Efforts of the Russian Orthodox Church to effect a compromise failed. Western governments and former Soviet states supported Yeltsin, who decided not to use force unless the opposition did so first. On Sunday, October 3, thousands of pro-communist demonstrators, many from the provinces, appeared on Moscow's streets, easily breaking through police barriers at the White House and mayor's offices but failing in a bloody struggle to take the Ostankino TV studio, an important strategic site. On Sunday night Yeltsin ordered the army—whose loyalties he had not been entirely certain of—to mobilize, and at 7:30 on Monday morning tanks began firing on the White House. During sporadic cease-fires defenders inside the burning building were allowed to leave; Khasbulatov and Rutskoi surrendered late in the afternoon and were taken to Lefortovo Prison. Perhaps 200 persons had died in the fighting, and over 150 were arrested. Yeltsin had triumphed, but formidable barriers remained: strong communist opposition in regional and federal councils; the growing popularity of fanatical nationalist Vladimir Volfovich Zhirinovsky (1946–); a populace angry at continued economic hardship and skeptical about the value of democracy; and an army expecting to be repaid for having saved Yeltsin's presidency. Approved in the December elections, a new constitution expanded Yeltsin's powers and created a bicameral parliament consisting of the State Duma (lower chamber) and the Federal Council (upper chamber). Communists made strong gains in parliamentary elections nonetheless.

Russian Revolution of 1762   Czar Peter III (1728–62) of Russia aroused the hostility of many because of his policies, notably his pressure on the Orthodox Church to adopt Lutheran practices. His ambitious and admired German-born wife, Catherine (1729–96), conspired to seize power with the help of Russia's imperial guards, led by her lover Grigori Orlov (1734–83). The unwillingness of Peter's troops to join his Danish campaign (Peter hoped to help his native Holstein take over Schleswig) provided a fortuitous climate for a coup d'état by Catherine, and while Peter was away at Oranienbaum, near St. Petersburg (Leningrad), Catherine, Orlov, and the imperial guards traveled to St. Petersburg, where the senate and the church welcomed them on July 9 (June 28 by the Old Style calendar), 1762. Immediately Catherine was crowned empress (czarina) at Kazan Cathedral and announced Peter's dethronement so quickly that supporters of their son Paul (1754–1801), whom Catherine disliked intensely, could not act in opposition. That very night Catherine marched with her troops to Oranienbaum, where she completed the bloodless coup by formally obtaining Peter's abdication on July 10. A week later, while held in custody, Peter was killed in a brawl arranged by Grigori's brother, Aleksei Orlov (1737–1809), a fellow conspirator. See also SEVEN YEARS' WAR.

Russian Revolution of 1905   The presence of many dissatisfied groups in Russia—peasants, workers, nobles, and border ethnic populations—produced an unstable regime, which was further exacerbated by Russia's defeat in the RUSSO-JAPANESE WAR OF 1904-5. On January 22, 1905 ("Bloody Sunday") workers led by Father Georgi Gapon (1870?–1906) marched on the Winter Palace, the royal residence, in St. Petersburg (Leningrad), to present a petition of grievances to Czar Nicholas II (1868–1918), who was not at the palace at the time. Government troops opened fire on the procession, killing about 70 and wounding almost 300 workers. This outrage set off strikes throughout the country. Russia's interior minister proposed a new moderate constitution, which only galvanized leftist opposition and culminated in a spontaneous general strike throughout Russia on October 20–30, 1905. Two

power centers emerged: a Soviet (council) of Workers' Deputies with Leon Trotsky (1879–1940) as vice chairman and the Constitutional Democratic (Kadet) party. Demanding "land for the people," peasants seized or destroyed landowners' property, and workers during a rail strike in Moscow demanded civil rights reform, as well as a general pardon. The czar yielded to his adviser, Count Sergei Witte (1849–1915), who issued the October Manifesto (October 30, 1905) granting civil liberties, a constitution, and an elected Duma (national assembly). The revolution's goals had seemingly been achieved, but the czar remained autocratic and supported reactionary terrorism (see BLACK HUNDREDS, RAIDS OF THE). When nearly 200 members of the St. Petersburg soviet were arrested and imprisoned on December 16, 1905, workers rebelled in protest a week later in Moscow. Street fighting in the two Russian cities was crushed by loyal government troops.

Russian Revolution of 1917   See BOLSHEVIK REVOLUTION; FEBRUARY (MARCH) REVOLUTION, RUSSIAN; KORNILOV'S REVOLT; OCTOBER (NOVEMBER) REVOLUTION, RUSSIAN.

Russian-Tatar War of 1571–72   Hoping to attack Moscow while Czar Ivan IV "the Terrible" (1530–84) was involved with the RUSSO-TURKISH WAR OF 1568–69, the leader (khan) of the Crimean (Krim) Tatars (Tartars) set out with a group of cavalry, moving northward ravaging the countryside. The Tatars raided into Muscovy (ancient Russia) to reach the walls of Moscow in 1571; they then captured and set fire to the city, except for the Kremlin, and supposedly carried off about 100,000 captives before being driven off. Russians returning from the Turkish war (the Turks had retained control of the Crimean khanate) helped repulse another assault on Moscow in 1572. After suffering defeat at the Battle of Molodi, about 25 miles from Moscow, that same year, the Tatars withdrew to their territory.

Russo-Afghan War of 1885 After occupying the city of Merv (Mary) in 1884, Russian forces crossed the disputed Afghan border and drove Afghan troops out of the Penjdeh district in 1885. The British, already alarmed because Russia had halted negotiations by the Anglo-Russian boundary commission to establish peaceably the Afghan-Russian border, began military preparations to protect the city of Herat, which was considered vital to India's protection. In a temporary settlement, Russia agreed to proceed no farther until the border was fixed, but Russian troops, in violation of their orders, waged a fierce battle at Ak-Teppe on March 30, 1885, severely defeating the Afghans. War seemed likely between Britain and Russia, but British prime minister William Gladstone (1809–98) resisted militaristic sentiment at home and managed, through negotiations, to reach an agreement on September 10, 1885, whereby Russia was granted the Penjdeh district, with Afghanistan securing the Zulfkar Pass. The rest of the border was fixed in 1887.

Russo-Chechen Civil War of 1994–96 See CHECHEN REVOLT OF 1994–96.

Russo-Finnish War of 1918–20 See FINNISH WAR OF INDEPENDENCE.

Russo-Finnish War of 1939–40 (Winter War) When hostilities broke out in Europe in 1939 (see WORLD WAR II), Soviet Russia demanded of Finland the lease of a naval base on the Hanko Peninsula, the demilitarization of its Mannerheim Line (fortified line of defense against the Soviets, across the Karelian Isthmus), and the cession of several islands in the Gulf of Finland. Finland refused, and when negotiations fell apart in November 1939, Soviet armies totaling an estimated 1 million men invaded the small neighboring country. For more than three months (November 30, 1939–March 12, 1940), some 300,000 Finnish troops (of whom about 80 percent were mobilized reservists) held the "Russian bear" at bay, skillfully using the severe Finnish winter (deep snow and subzero temperature) to their

advantage. At the village of Suomussalmi in eastern Finland, the Finns won a brilliant monthlong battle in which their artillery and infantry nearly annihilated two Soviet divisions (December 11, 1939–January 8, 1940). Although they were joined by sympathetic volunteers from Sweden, Norway, and the Allies, Finnish forces were unable to halt the incessant Russian assaults on the Mannerheim Line in February 1940; aided by tremendous artillery bombardments and aerial attacks, the Russians, who suffered heavy losses, breached the line and pressed on toward Viipuri (Vyborg). War-weary and without needed foreign aid, the Finns sued for peace and accepted the Soviet terms on March 12, 1940, ceding the Karelian Isthmus and Viipuri as demanded. In June 1941, they joined the Germans in their invasion of the Soviet Union (see WORLD WAR II ON THE RUSSIAN FRONT).

Russo-Japanese War of 1904–5 In 1903, the Japanese government proposed to the Russian government that each should recognize the other's special interests and economic privileges in Manchuria and Korea. Unbeknownst to the Russians, Japan had been building up its navy and army. The Russians negotiated in a desultory way, and in anger the Japanese ambassador broke off the talks on February 6, 1904 and returned home. Three days later a Japanese fleet sank two Russian warships at Chemulpo (Inchon), Korea, and torpedoed the main Russian force in Port Arthur (Lushun), on China's Liaotung peninsula. The rest of the Russian fleet was icebound in the port of Vladivostok. Once it had achieved superiority of the seas, Japan was able to send thousands of troops into Korea and Manchuria. Korea was overrun speedily, and by May 1 the Japanese had advanced into Manchuria. By September the Russians had been driven northward to Mukden (Shen-yang), and Port Arthur was surrounded. Two bloody but indecisive battles in the fall forced the Russians farther north. On January 2, 1905, Port Arthur surrendered after a grueling Japanese siege. Meanwhile the Russians had dispatched from the west a large naval force. In Manchuria, the Japanese took the offensive again in early 1905, won the

Battle of Mukden (February 21–March 10), and drove the Russians 70 miles farther north. In May 1905, the Russian fleet arrived from the west and made for Vladivostok, but on the way it encountered the Japanese navy in a strait off the Japanese islands of Tsushima. The Battle of Tsushima raged for two days (May 27–28, 1905), during which the Russian fleet was utterly destroyed, while the Japanese lost only three torpedo boats. U.S. president Theodore Roosevelt (1858–1919) offered to mediate a peace, and on August 10, 1905, representatives of the warring powers met in Portsmouth, New Hampshire, where a peace treaty was signed on September 5, 1905. Russia ceded the part of the island of Sakhalin below the 50th parallel to Japan, recognized Japanese "political, military, and economic interests" in Korea, transferred to Japan the territory it had leased from China in Liaotung, agreed to pay the Japanese costs of maintaining Russian prisoners, and granted fishing rights off the coast of Siberia. Most of all, however, Japan's stunning and unexpected victory gained it recognition as a world power. See also SAMIL INDEPENDENCE MOVEMENT; SINO-JAPANESE WAR OF 1894–95.

Russo-Persian War of 1722–23　Despite Russia's exhaustion after the Second or Great NORTHERN WAR, Czar Peter I "the Great" (1672–1725), apprehensive over the Turkish push toward the Caspian Sea, launched a war against Persia weakened by the AFGHAN REBELLIONS OF 1709–26. Without much opposition, Russian forces seized the Persian cities of Derbent in 1722 and Baku and Resht in 1723. The Turks, threatened by Russian penetration, responded by seizing Tiflis (Tbilisi), the capital of Georgia, in northwestern Persia. By the Treaty of St. Petersburg on September 12, 1723, Russia gained control of the coastal areas between Derbent and Resht on the Caspian Sea, and the Persian shah received the loan of czarist troops for domestic peacekeeping. But the Ottoman Empire, backed by Britain, disputed Russia's Caspian Sea acquisitions. A direct Russo-Turkish war was avoided by the Treaty of Constantinople (1724), by which the Ottomans received western Persia (occupying Tabriz,

Kermanshah, and Hamadan in 1724–25) and the Russians northern Persia (holding three Caspian regions and captured territories).

Russo-Persian War of 1804–13　When Russia annexed Georgia (1800) and Karabakh, Caucasian regions under the suzerainty of Persia, rebel factions resisted and asked for Persian aid. Invading Russians besieged the city of Erivan (Yerevan) in 1804 but were compelled to withdraw with the arrival of reinforcements under Shah Fath Ali (1762?–1835) and Crown Prince Abbas (1783–1833). Inconclusive warfare persisted until 1812, when the Russians surprised and annihilated a superior Persian force under Abbas Mirza at the Battle of Aslanduz. Despite Russia's deep involvement with NAPOLEON'S INVASION OF RUSSIA, the shah signed the Treaty of Gulistan (1813), ceding Georgia, Karabakh, and other Caucasian areas to Russia. See also TURKO-PERSIAN WAR OF 1821–23.

Russo-Persian War of 1825–28　Ambiguities in the 1813 Treaty of Gulistan (see RUSSO-PERSIAN WAR OF 1804–13) and Russian haste in incorporating its new territorial acquisitions provoked Persia to reject the treaty and attempt to retake Georgia in 1825. But it lost the Battle of Ganja on September 26, 1826, when its cavalry was terrified by Russian artillery and fled. Advancing afterward into Persia, Russian troops under Ivan Paskevich (1782–1856) took Erivan (Yerevan) and Tabriz in 1827. When Persian troops dispersed with the coming of winter that year, the Russians marched upon and seized Tehran, where the entire Persian artillery arsenal was captured. This terminated the war, and the Treaty of Turkomanchi set the Aras River as the Russian-Persian border, granted Russia the sole right to station warships in the Caspian Sea, imposed an indemnity to be paid by Persia, and gave territorial and commercial rights to Russia.

Russo-Persian War of 1911　After the PERSIAN REVOLUTION OF 1906–9, Russia sent troops to the northern Persian city of Kazvin to protect its interests there and refused to remove them, in violation of the Anglo-Russian agreement of 1907. William Morgan Shuster (1877–1960), an American serving as Persia's treasurer-general to help put in order its finances, clashed with Russia, which evidently backed an unsuccessful military attempt by the former shah, Muhammad Ali (1872–1925), to regain power in mid-1911. The Russians issued two ultimatums for the Persians to remove Shuster, but the national assembly (majlis) rejected both (November 1911). In northern Persia, Russians committed atrocities at Tabriz, took over Azerbaijan, and then advanced on Tehran. Persia's regency government during the minority of Ahmed Shah (1898–1930), with the cabinet, enacted a coup on December 24, 1911, suddenly closing down the assembly, forming a ruling directory, and accepting Russia's demand for the dismissal of Shuster.

Russo-Polish War of 1019–25   Russian ruler of Kiev, Sviatopolk (d. 1021), after being routed in battle by his brother, the grand prince of Novgorod, Yaroslav (d. 1054), fled to safety at the court of his father-in-law, Boleslav I (d. 1025), duke of Poland. There Sviatopolk urged Poles to regain territories lost to the Novgorodians and to restore his rule in Kiev. Boleslav led a large Polish army into Russia, where he won a lengthy battle at the Bug River against Yaroslav and his troops in 1020. Boleslav then occupied Kiev and restored Sviatopolk's rule as Yaroslav withdrew to Novgorod. But Sviatopolk began to chafe under the Polish presence in his city and made plans to massacre the foreign troops. The plan was revealed, and angry Poles retaliated by plundering the city and then departed, pursued by Kievan forces under Sviatopolk. At the Bug River, Sviatopolk was defeated and retreated afterward to Kiev, which fell to the attacking Poles within a short time. Boleslav returned to Poland a victor, and at his death he controlled an area from the Elbe to the Bug and from the Baltic to the Danube, and called himself king.

Russo-Polish War of 1499–1503   When Alexander I (d. 1506), king of the newly formed Polish-Lithuanian state, failed to comply with his marriage contract, his father-in-law Ivan III "the Great" (1440–1505), grand duke of Moscow, initiated war against him. Ivan's forces pillaged Polish lands and won a major battle against Lithuanian soldiers on July 14, 1500. But the Russians were unable to capture Lithuanian-held Smolensk. The war subsided until the Lithuanians, aided by the Livonian Knights, defeated the Russians at Siritza but were unsuccessful during a siege of Pskov in 1502. A peace was arranged the next year, giving Russia all its conquered territory and making Ivan sovereign of Russia.

Russo-Polish War of 1506–8   Desultory skirmishing between the forces of Sigismund I (1467–1548), duke of Lithuania and king of Poland (after 1506), and those of Basil III (1479–1533), grand duke of Moscow, finally broke into open warfare when some foreign princes supporting Basil were ordered by him to lay waste Lithuania. Sigismund made preparations for a large-scale military campaign. Fighting, but no significant battles, had occurred when a truce was signed in 1508. The Russians kept all their conquered lands, but their relations with the Poles and Lithuanians remained hostile.

Russo-Polish War of 1512–21   When Grand Duke Basil III (1479–1533) of Moscow learned of a secret Polish treaty with the Crimean Tatars (Tartars), who were to attack the Muscovy–White Russian border area, he resumed open warfare with the Polish-Lithuanian state. Basil's Russian forces made two unsuccessful sieges of the Lithuanian-held city of Smolensk in December 1512. Seizing other territory, they eventually took the city in June 1514. At Orsha, however, the Russians suffered a severe defeat (some 30,000 casualties) by the Lithuanians. Although the Muscovites (Russians) managed to keep control of Smolensk, their weakness prompted Sigismund I (1467–1548), duke of Lithuania and king of Poland, to instigate an unsuccessful attack by the Tatars against the Russians at Tula, south of Moscow, in 1517. Afterward peace negotiations began, with the war continuing as border fighting. Nothing was concluded until the Crimean Tatars renewed their attacks in 1521; then Moscow obtained an armistice allowing Smolensk to be under Russian control.

Russo-Polish War of 1534–37   When Moscow's Grand Duke Basil III (1479–1533) died, he left his wife to run his Russian kingdom until his son Ivan, later Ivan IV "the Terrible" (1530–84), was of age to assume control. In the atmosphere of heightened court intrigues between the boyars (Russian aristocrats) and royal supporters, she suspected even relatives of duplicity and moved to imprison some of them. Basil's brother, while fleeing to Poland for help from King Sigismund I (1467–1548), was intercepted and jailed for treason. Forming a powerful army, Sigismund fought an inconclusive war against the Russians, who were able to quell insurrectionists backed by the Poles and Lithuanians. Smolensk was retained by the Russians. The war was terminated by a truce in 1537.

Russo-Polish War of 1609–18   Capitalizing on instability during Russia's "TIME OF TROUBLES" and hoping to seize the throne of Moscow for himself, King Sigismund III (1566–1632) of Poland invaded Russia with an army and besieged the city of Smolensk in 1609. He called on all Poles in Russia to help him. The Russian leader Basil IV Shuiski (d. 1612) marched with 30,000 men to relieve Smolensk, but a small Polish force under Stanislas Zolkiewski (d. 1620) ambushed and defeated them at the Battle of Klushino in September 1610. Basil fled to Moscow but was deposed as ruler because of the defeat. Polish forces seized Moscow on October 8, 1610 (Smolensk surrendered about six months later), and the throne was offered to Sigismund's son Ladislas (1595–1648) under terms of a previously signed Smolensk Treaty. Sigismund balked, wanting the throne himself, and sent Poles and Germans into the Kremlin to establish his government. In 1611, Moscow's citizens, along with Russians in the provinces, rebelled against the invaders, who burned much of Moscow to subdue the rebels but were besieged in the Kremlin by attacking provincial forces. Muscovites were able to stop a Polish army attempting to relieve their beleaguered colleagues in the Kremlin, which soon fell to the Russians. In 1613, Michael Romanov (1596–1645) was elected the new Russian czar. Exhausted Polish troops retreated to the border region, where sporadic fighting continued. In 1617, Ladislas and his men failed in an attack on Moscow. A 15-year armistice was signed on December 1, 1618, ending the war and leaving the Poles in control of Smolensk. See also RUSSO-SWEDISH WAR OF 1613–17.

Russo-Polish War of 1632–34   (War of Smolensk)   Conscious of the approaching expiration of the armistice with Poland (see RUSSO-POLISH WAR OF 1609–18), Czar Michael Romanov (1596–1645) made military plans to recover the Polish-controlled city of Smolensk. Upon the death of Poland's King Sigismund III (1566–1632), the czar, claiming the armistice applied only during both signatories' reigns, dispatched Russian troops to the walls of Smolensk in September 1632. For nearly a year the Poles, greatly outnumbered, held off the besiegers until food shortages caused concern. King Ladislas IV (1595–1648) led a Polish army to help Smolensk and overwhelmed the Russians in battle. The withdrawing Russian army was pursued, besieged for six months, and forced to capitulate in February 1634. The Treaty of Polianovka in 1634 gave Poland possession of Smolensk and the surrounding province and much of the northeastern Baltic coastal region. In addition, Ladislas renounced his claims to the Russian throne and recognized Michael Romanov as czar. See also THIRTY YEARS' WAR.

Russo-Polish War of 1654–56   In retaliation for his defeat by the Poles in the Ukraine (see CHMIELNICKI'S REVOLT), Bogdan Chmielnicki

(1593?–1657) and his Cossacks allied with the Russians and moved against the Poles at Kiev and Smolensk in 1654. At the same time, Czar Alexis (1629–76) and more than 100,000 men overwhelmed smaller Polish armies and occupied much of Lithuania; in 1655, Alexis declared himself grand duke of Lithuania. While Poland was preoccupied by Swedish attacks on its territories during the FIRST NORTHERN WAR, Russo-Cossack forces recovered much of the Ukraine and made raids into Poland. Poland's King John II Casimir (1609–72) fled to Silesia, leaving his country in the hands of the Russians and Swedes. From there, he negotiated an alliance with Holy Roman Emperor Leopold I (1640–1705) and signed a truce with the czar, who pulled his forces back to the Ukraine, freeing Russian forces to challenge Swedish Livonia (see RUSSO-SWEDISH WAR OF 1656–58). The war ended with the Treaty of Nimieza in 1656, in which Russia and Poland made an anti-Swedish pact, which lasted until the RUSSO-POLISH WAR OF 1658–67.

Russo-Polish War of 1658–67

The Poles under King John II Casimir (1609–72) renewed their fighting against the Russians in Lithuania when the three-year pact with Russia terminated (see RUSSO-POLISH WAR OF 1654–56). After suffering defeats at Vilna and Kaunas, Polish armies drove the Russians out of Lithuania and invaded the areas of Vitebsk and Polotsk in 1660. In the Ukraine, a well-equipped Russian army was routed by a smaller Polish force, aided by Tatars (Tartars), led by George Lubomirski (1616–67), at the Battle of Lubar (1660), and a large Cossack army was also crushed by Lubomirski shortly after. The war then dwindled down to border fighting until the Polish victory at the Battle of Lublin promised favorable peace negotiations in 1664. However, LUBOMIRSKI'S REBELLION disrupted the Polish government, allowing Moscow to dictate the peace terms. By the Treaty of Andrusovo, in 1667, Poland ceded Smolensk and Kiev (for two years, but Poland never regained Kiev) to Russia, and the Ukraine was divided between the two countries along the Dnieper River. The Cossacks were to be under joint control. See also POLISH-TURKISH WAR OF 1671–77.

Russo-Polish War of 1919–20

As German troops withdrew from Poland according to the 1918 armistice's terms (see WORLD WAR I), Soviet (Bolshevik) troops advanced westward over Polish-held territory to the Bug River by February 1919. In response, Polish forces under General Józef Pilsudski (1867–1935) pushed the Soviets back to the Berezina River and into the Ukraine. The Allies' supreme council approved a temporary eastern Polish border within Russia, but on January 28, 1920, Soviet leaders sought one along the actual war front, farther west. Pilsudski hoped to restore Poland's border of 1772 and seize the Ukraine. Allied with anti-Soviet Ukrainians under Simon Petlyura (1879–1926), Pilsudski's forces marched upon and captured Kiev (April 25–May 7, 1920). A strong Soviet counterattack drove the Poles out of Kiev and Vilna (Vilnius), where troops under Mikhail Tukhachevski (1893–1937) put the Poles to flight. By mid-August 1920, Soviet armies had moved to the outskirts of Warsaw, where the Poles, now with aid from the French under General Maxime Weygand (1867–1965), fought and routed the invaders in a fierce 10-day battle. Polish armies went on the offensive and defeated Tukhachevski's troops in battles near the Niemen River in September 1920. An armistice was agreed to on October 12, 1920, with a preliminary Treaty of Riga, which became definitive on March 18, 1921. Poland's territorial claims in the east were accepted by the Soviets. See also LITHUANIAN WAR OF INDEPENDENCE; RUSSIAN CIVIL WAR OF 1918–21.

Russo-Swedish War of 1240–42

Sweden, Denmark, and Lithuania hoped to take advantage of the confusion following the second MONGOL INVASION OF RUSSIA to gain territory and extend Christianity. Supported by Pope Gregory IX (1147?–1241), the Swedish soldier-statesman Birger (d. 1266) led an army of Swedes, Danes, and Livonian Knights into Russia to challenge the city of Novgorod's territorial claims on the Neva River and Gulf of Finland. In 1240, Novgorod's Prince Alexander (1220?–63), a supporter of Orthodox Christianity, and his forces engaged the enemy near present-day Leningrad on the Neva River and won an illustrious victory. After constructing forts to preserve his triumph in the area, he returned home to Novgorod to receive the surname Nevski ("of the Neva") in honor of his victory. But after his departure, the enemy seized Pskov. Urged on by the pope, the Livonian Knights exacted tribute, built a fort at Koporié on the Neva, and ravaged the Estonian area. Alexander then led an army to drive the knights out of Koporié and Pskov, and on April 5, 1242, decisively defeated them at the famous "Battle of the Ice" on an icy channel leading to Lake Peipus. Afterward Alexander returned to Novgorod, where peace was concluded.

Russo-Swedish War of 1590–95   Russian czar Fëdor I (1557–98) wanted to secure Swedish-controlled northern Estonia, including Revel (Tallinn), its principal city. A Russian army advanced westward toward Narva, near which it defeated a Swedish force of some 20,000 men in early 1590. While besieging Swedish-defended Narva, the Russians also pillaged Estonia. Both sides entered into peace negotiations, signing a one-year armistice that granted Russia control of several towns but put off settlement of Estonia itself. Sweden's King John III (1537–92), chafing under the armistice, strengthened his forces in the region with the intention of regaining the ceded towns from Russia. He died as negotiations over Narva and northern Estonia broke down and fighting resumed. By 1595, Sweden had control of Estonia's Baltic coast and had conquered much of Livonia (Estonia and parts of Latvia). See also NORTHERN WARS.

Russo-Swedish War of 1613–17   After the end of Russia's "TIME OF TROUBLES", the Muscovites advanced against the city of Novgorod, occupied by the Swedes, who had attempted to gain control of the Russian throne. The Swedes' chance had been lost with the election of Czar Michael Romanov (1596–1645). Sweden's King Gustavus II (1594–1632) led an army against Moscow after stopping the expedition against Novgorod. However, when the strong frontier fortress of Pskov successfully checked the Swedes during a six-month siege in 1614, Gustavus decided to withdraw and made little effort to seize Russian territory afterward. Peace negotiations began and resulted in the Treaty of Stolbovo on January 26, 1617. Sweden ceded Novgorod to Moscow and gained possession of all territories on the Gulf of Finland. Russia gave up claim to Estonia and Livonia.

Russo-Swedish War of 1656–58   While the First NORTHERN WAR raged, Czar Alexis (1629–76) of Russia saw a chance to regain lost lands under Swedish control, made peace with Poland (see RUSSO-POLISH WAR OF 1654–56), and initiated an offensive into Livonia and Estonia. Alexis's forces seized several towns and fortresses as they drove toward Riga, which was besieged in July–August 1656. The Swedes finally made a sortie, killing and capturing thousands of Russians; Alexis fled, pursued. Strengthening its defenses in the Baltic area and repelling another Russian offensive in 1658, Sweden secured its territories there and forced Alexis to conclude a truce that same year.

Russo-Swedish War of 1741–43   Sweden's ascendant Hattar Party (the "Hats") advocated a war with Russia to regain lost Swedish territory. Under French influence, Sweden, ill-prepared and with only a 20,000-man army, initiated hostilities (1741), but Russia, which had just concluded the RUSSO-TURKISH WAR OF 1736–39, took the offensive, winning the Battle of Wilmanstrand in Finland on September 3, 1741. At St. Petersburg (Leningrad), a bloodless coup occurred that brought Elizabeth Petrovna (1709–62) to the Russian throne. She sought peace with Sweden but found Swedish terms totally unacceptable. Russian troops again invaded Finland, overwhelmed the main Swedish army, and forced the surrender of 17,000 Swedes at Helsingfors

(Helsinki) on August 20, 1742. Though fighting ceased, peace discussions lasted for nearly a year, ending with the Treaty of Åbo (August 7, 1743). Russia retained the southern part of its Finnish territory to the Kymmene River, which became the border. In exchange for the mitigating peace terms, Sweden's King Frederick I (1676–1751), being childless, had agreed to Elizabeth's election of Holstein's Duke Adolphus Frederick (1710–71) to inherit the Swedish crown. See also AUSTRIAN SUCCESSION, WAR OF THE.

Russo-Swedish War of 1788–90   During CATHERINE THE GREAT'S SECOND WAR WITH THE TURKS, Sweden's King Gustavus III (1746–92), without the Diet's approval, launched an invasion of Russian Finland in June 1788 (he hoped to countervail possible Russian or Prussian advances on Swedish territory). His military campaign was ineffective in 1788 and 1789. Swedish officers refused to fight this illegal war, resulting in a disastrous defeat at the Finnish town of Fredrikshamm (Hamina), and formed a conspiracy (Anjala League) to negotiate peace with Czarina Catherine II "the Great" (1729–96) of Russia. At sea, Sweden suffered several defeats, with the loss of many warships. After the winter of 1790, Gustavus returned to the front and waged a successful Finnish campaign, marching toward St. Petersburg (Leningrad). His land forces were checked at Vyborg and his fleet blockaded until the Swedes won the great naval Battle of Svensksund (July 2–9, 1790); a third of the Russian fleet of 151 ships was sunk or captured. Denmark, which had joined Russia, invaded Västergötland in southwestern Sweden and besieged the city of Göteborg. England and Prussia soon mediated a Danish truce, and on August 15, 1790, Russia and Sweden signed the Treaty of Wereloe, which restored the prewar status quo.

Russo-Swedish War of 1808–9   During the NAPOLEONIC WARS, France and Russia made peace (1807) and called on Sweden to drop out of the anti-French alliance with Britain. When Sweden's King Gustavus IV (1778–1837) refused, Czar Alexander I (1777–1825) launched a Russian invasion of Swedish Finland in February 1808. After seizing the fortress of Sveaborg, Russian troops moved successfully through Finland, forcing the Swedes to evacuate by the end of 1808. Gustavus's despotic policies led to a coup d'état that overthrew him (March 13, 1809) and forced his exile. In the summer of 1809, Russia, refusing to discuss peace with Sweden's unstable government, expanded the fighting, seized the Åland Islands, and won two battles in northern Sweden. Finally, the new Swedish king, Charles XIII (1748–1818), made peace with the czar; by the Treaty of Fredrikshamm (September 17, 1809), Sweden ceded Finland and the Åland Islands to Russia; Finland became a grand duchy under the czar.

Russo-Turkish War of 1568–69   Ottoman grand vizier Muhammad Sokollu (1505–79) under Sultan Selim II (1524?–74), seeking to check Russian expansion, wanted to construct a canal linking the Don and Volga rivers to enable ships to pass between the Black and Caspian seas, thereby gaining Turkish access to Persia and opening a route to Central Asia. In 1568, he sent troops to Azov with the intention of seizing Astrakhan from Russia. Troops moved up the Don River to begin canal construction. With a third completed, technical problems forced a halt, and vessels had to be portaged to the Volga River, from which Astrakhan was invested in 1569. When the siege failed, the Turkish troops withdrew and were lost returning home in a storm on the Black Sea. The sultan ordered Sokollu to abandon the canal project.

Russo-Turkish War of 1678–81   Ottoman sultan Muhammad IV (1641–91) disliked the terms of the Treaty of Zorawno that ended the POLISH-TURKISH WAR OF 1671–77 and sent Turkish forces under Grand Vizier Kara Mustafa (d. 1683) to drive the Russians and Poles out of the Ukraine. Though seizing and destroying towns, the Turks suffered severe casualties and lost many artillery pieces, finally withdrawing. On January 8, 1681, the Treaty of Radzin was signed, by which the Ottoman Empire gave up its claims to the Ukraine.

Russo-Turkish War of 1695–1700   Russia's Czar Peter I "the Great" (1672–1725), urged by his Swiss-Scotch friend François Lefort (1656–99), an officer in the Russian service, ordered an assault on the Turkish-held city-fortress of Azov at the Don River delta. The first siege in 1695, personally led by Peter, failed with the Russians suffering heavy casualties; they had been unable to blockade Azov because Russia had no navy. Peter built a fleet, which blockaded the city in 1696 and captured it in July of that year. Over 30,000 Russians lost their lives in the effort to secure it. Peter then planned a great expedition to end forever the Ottoman threat and traveled throughout Europe seeking allies and learning about western technical and scientific knowledge. While the Hapsburgs made a separate peace to end the AUSTRO-TURKISH WAR OF 1683–99, Peter abandoned his Turkish cause to join Poland against Sweden at the start of the Second or Great NORTHERN WAR. In 1700, Russia signed a truce with the Ottoman Empire, reluctantly giving up its Black Sea fleet but retaining Azov.

Russo-Turkish War of 1710–11   After his army was decimated in Russia during the Second or Great NORTHERN WAR, Sweden's King Charles XII (1682–1718) fled with a handful of troops into Turkish Moldavia. In October 1710, Czar Peter I "the Great" (1672–1725) ordered the Ottoman sultan to evict Charles, but the sultan, responding to the appeals of Charles, initiated war against Peter. With the Turks pressing at the Russian border, confident Peter marched with 60,000 soldiers to invade Moldavia in 1711. A superior Ottoman army drove the Russians back to Pruth River, where Peter, who had received no expected aid from Slavs, Moldavians, and Wallachians (with all of whom he had secret alliances) and whose troops were suffering from lack of supplies, entered into peace negotiations. By the Treaty of the Pruth on July 21, 1711,

Russia returned Azov to the Turks (see RUSSO-TURKISH WAR OF 1695–1700) and destroyed border fortresses; Charles was granted free passage to Sweden but stayed in Turkish territory for three more years trying vainly to get the Ottomans to launch a major campaign against Russia.

Russo-Turkish War of 1722–24   See RUSSO-PERSIAN WAR OF 1722–23.

Russo-Turkish War of 1736–39   (Austro-Turkish War of 1737–39)   Discovering that France was seeking military aid from the Ottoman Empire during the War of the POLISH SUCCESSION, Russia declared war on the empire in 1736, sending armies into the Turkish areas north of the Black Sea. Allied with the Tatars (Tartars), the Turks inflicted heavy losses on the invaders, who were compelled to withdraw into the Russian Ukraine. Tatar raids into that region were very destructive and impelled Russia's ally, Austria, to declare war on the Turks in January 1737. Austrian troops invaded Bosnia, Wallachia, and southern Serbia but, meeting stiff resistance, fell back. In the Turkish Ukraine, Russian and Turkish armies fought for possession of Azov, Ochakov, and other cities, capturing, losing, and recapturing them. Though a peace agreement was reached through French mediation, the war continued as the Turks advanced along the Danube toward Belgrade in 1738. Austrian forces failed to check the Turks in the Balkan area, but in Moldavia an invading Russian army under Count Burkhard C. von Münnich (1683–1767) decisively defeated a large Turkish army, captured Chocim (Khotin) and Jassy (Iasi), Moldavia's capital, and made plans to march on Constantinople (Istanbul), the Ottoman capital. At Belgrade, the Austrians signed a treaty on September 18, 1739, after the city had fallen to the Turks; they ceded Belgrade, northern Serbia, and parts of Bosnia and Wallachia. The Turks now marched on Münnich's forces, but Russia, fighting now alone, decided to make peace. By the Treaty of Nissa on October 3, 1739, Russia relinquished all of its conquests except Azov, whose fortifications it agreed to destroy, and also agreed to a ban on Russian naval vessels in the Sea of Azov and the Black Sea.

Russo-Turkish War of 1768–74 See CATHERINE THE GREAT'S FIRST WAR WITH THE TURKS.

Russo-Turkish War of 1787–92 See CATHERINE THE GREAT'S SECOND WAR WITH THE TURKS.

Russo-Turkish War of 1806–12 In 1806, Ottoman sultan Selim III (1761–1808) dismissed the Russian-backed governors of Moldavia and Wallachia for inciting revolts in the two principalities. The French ambassador to the Porte (Ottoman government) urged the sultan to declare war on Russia (see NAPOLEONIC WARS). War was declared by the Porte in 1806. A British naval fleet sailed to Constantinople (Istanbul) and ordered the Porte to evict the French ambassador and make peace with Russia (1807), but the sultan refused, and Constantinople's citizens rallied and fired 1,000 guns at the fleet, which withdrew severely damaged. In June 1807, Russian warships defeated the Turks at the Battle of Lemnos. Napoleon (1769–1821) mediated an armistice (August 1807) between the Turks and Russians, who withdrew their troops from Moldavia and Wallachia; the Turks retired to Adrianople. Skirmishing continued, however, between the two sides until the Treaty of Bucharest on May 28, 1812—the result of British mediation this time. Moldavia and Wallachia remained under Ottoman control, but the Turkish-Russian border was set along the Pruth River, with Bessarabia going to Russia.

Russo-Turkish War of 1828–29 On April 26, 1828, Russia declared war on the Ottoman Empire, coming to the aid of Greece in the GREEK WAR OF INDEPENDENCE and seeing a chance for territorial expansion. Russian forces successfully besieged Braila in Wallachia and crossed the Danube to secure Turkish fortresses at Ruschuk (Ruse) and Widdin (Vidin), while another Russian army captured Varna after a three-month siege in 1828. In the Caucasus, invading Russians seized Kars and won a victory at Akhaltsikhe before being halted by Kurdish resistance. In 1829, the Turks lost Silistra, and the Russians under General Hans Diebitsch-Zabalkansky (1785–1831) won battles at Tcherkovna (June 11) over Grand Vizier Mustafa Reshid Pasha (1802–58) and at Sliven (August 12). Eight days later Diebitsch-Zabalkansky and his army, greatly depleted and suffering from plague, marched into Adrianople (Edirne). Meanwhile, another Russian force won at Erivan (Yerevan) before learning that Diebitsch-Zabalkansky had expeditiously signed the Treaty of Adrianople on September 16, 1829, granting the Danubian Principalities (Moldavia and Wallachia) semiautonomy, Russia control of the mouth of the Danube, all peaceful states access to the Turkish straits, and Greece its independence. The Ottoman Empire was assessed high war reparations and confirmed Orthodox rights in its territories (see CATHERINE THE GREAT'S FIRST WAR WITH THE TURKS). See also CRIMEAN WAR.

Russo-Turkish War of 1877–78 Despite Russian aid to Serbian rebels (see SERBO-TURKISH WAR OF 1876–77), the Ottoman Empire maintained its control of Serbia and repression of Orthodox Christians there. When the Turks refused to institute reforms, Russia, acceding to its powerful pan-Slav movement, declared war on the empire on April 24, 1877. Rumania (a union of Moldavia and Wallachia in 1862) joined Russia in the war. Invading Russian forces in the Balkans captured the Shipka Pass and Plevna, which fell after a heroic five-month stand by the Turks in 1877. Moves and countermoves to dislodge both sides from strategic fortresses and areas were generally futile. In the Caucasus, however, the Russians attacked and took the Turkish fortress of Kars on November 18, 1877, and then besieged Erzurum. By January 30, 1878, a strong Russian army under Mikhail D. Skobelev (1843–82), who had captured Plevna, Plovdiv, and Adrianople (Edirne), was just outside the Ottoman capital, Constantinople (Istanbul). Both sides began negotiating truce terms at Adrianople, leading to a formal treaty signed at San Stefano on March 3, 1878. Rumania and Serbia were granted independence, and an enlarged Bulgaria became autonomous under Russian authority.

Ruthven, Raid of (1582)   Scottish Protestant barons, fearful that young King James VI (1566–1625), later England's King James I, would be turned Catholic by his court counselors, plotted with the English to assume power. Led by the earls of Angus and Gowrie (family name: Ruthven), the barons seized James at Ruthven Castle, near Perth, in 1582. Taking over the government and receiving the blessing of the General Assembly of the Kirk of Scotland, they imprisoned James at Falkland Castle. He escaped, fled to St. Andrews, and proclaimed himself king in fact as well as name. Gowrie was executed in 1584, and James punished the Kirk by naming himself head of church and state. See also GOWRIE CONSPIRACY.

Rwandan Civil War of 1990–94   In one of history's most horrendous genocides, more than 850,000 Rwandans were brutally killed from April to July 1994 in Rwanda (formerly Ruanda) in east-central Africa—victims of an internal power struggle that ironically ended a four-year civil war between Rwanda's two main ethnic groups, the Tutsi (Watusi or Tusi) and Hutu (Bahutu). The roots of Rwanda's tribal strife have been attributed to Belgium's earlier colonial policies, which initially favored the wealthier and better-educated Tutsi. The resentful Hutu majority took power in the RUANDAN CIVIL WAR OF 1959–61, after which Ruanda became the independent nation of Rwanda on July 1, 1962. Many Tutsi fled to neighboring Uganda, where they remained for the next three decades. In 1990, a rebel group, the Rwandan Patriotic Front (RPF), infiltrated Rwanda from Uganda with the intention of regaining control of the country. The Hutu-led Rwandan government, mired in debt, unable to adequately feed the population, and threatened by the RPF, ceded some power to the Tutsi under the Arusah Accords of August 1993. However, President Juvénal Habyarimana (1937?–94), who had grabbed power in a 1973 coup, stalled the process, and the agreement was not fully put into effect. But with tensions rising, some Cabinet posts were granted to the Tutsi, and the following April Habyarimana attended a conference in Tanzania to address the Hutu-Tutsi problem. On his return to the capital, Kigali, his plane exploded, killing Habyarimana as well as the Hutu president of Burundi, Cyprien Ntaryamira (see BURUNDIAN CIVIL WAR OF 1993–). The suspicious explosion was immediately blamed on the RPF, but was in fact the work of the hard-line Hutu palace guard, who were bitterly opposed to any rapprochement with the Tutsi. Events set off a 14-week killing spree, during which both the Hutu army and militant Hutu death squads mercilessly butchered hundreds of thousands of civilians, mostly Tutsi but also many Hutu political moderates. Acting prime minister Agathe Uwilingiyimana (d. 1994), a Tutsi, was murdered, along with 10 UN peacekeepers who tried to save her, within hours of the plane crash. The Tutsi rebels did not engage in mass slaughter of the Hutus; nonetheless, more than 3 million Hutus, fearing Tutsi reprisals, fled Rwanda for neighboring Congo (Zaire), Tanzania, Burundi, and Uganda, setting up huge refugee camps where monumental food distribution problems and rampant disease strained the resources of world relief organizations. Despite the decimation of the Tutsi, the RPF defeated the Hutu army, and the Arusha Accords were finally fully implemented in July 1994, with rebel leader Major General Paul Kagame (1957?–) as vice president and defense minister and moderate Hutus as president and prime minister.

S

Sacred War, First (c. 590 B.C.) The Sacred Wars, so-called because they concerned the shrine of Apollo at Delphi, became political as well as religious conflicts. The first involved the Amphictyonic League, "dwellers around" Thermopylae and later Delphi, formed to administer the temporal affairs of the religious shrines and to conduct the Pythian Games. Their target was Crisa, a Phocian city and overlord of Delphi, the port for the shrine; the cause was Crisa's sacrilegious demand that pilgrims to Delphi pay tolls. Besieged on its landward side by the league and blockaded by the fleet of Cleisthenes (Clisthenes) (fl. early 6th cent.), tyrant of Sicyon, the city fell and was destroyed. The war gave the league full control of the shrine, advanced the celebrity of Cleisthenes, and initially introduced into Phocis the influence of Thessalian city-states, chiefly Thebes. **Second Sacred War** (c. 449–448 B.C.). As a military action, this conflict was fairly unimportant; its significance lay in Sparta's entry into the concerns of the Amphictyonic League. Phocians had taken control of the city of Delphi, claiming its administration as their right; the league protested that control of both the city and the shrine was theirs. Spartan troops expelled the Phocians, apparently without a fight, but Athenian troops under Pericles (c. 495–429) reinstated the Phocians. Athens then signed a treaty with Sparta. The league, to which Athens belonged, was offended by this unilateral political action. Thebes rebelled and Athens failed to put it down, and Phocis, no longer

allied to Athens, remained in control of Delphi. A shaky peace lasted almost a century. **Third Sacred War** (355–346 B.C.). From a small beginning, this war threatened to involve all of Greece. Thebans and other Thessalonians in the Amphictyonic League charged their ancient enemy Phocis with cultivating lands sacred to Apollo. Phocis was fined, as was (belatedly) Sparta for its seizure in 382 of the Cadmea at Thebes (see THEBAN-SPARTAN WAR OF 379-371 B.C.). Under Philomelus (d. 354), Phocis refused to pay; it armed, captured the Delphic shrine and its treasury in 355, and gained secret Spartan help. Locria vainly tried to force the Phocians out, Athens and Sparta made peace, but the Thebans declared war in 355, defeating Philomelus at Neon in 354 and causing a Phocian retreat in 353. Anxious to gain power in Greece, Philip (382–336) of Macedon aided Thebes, forcing Athens and Sparta to support Phocis. Philip helped Thebes conquer Phocis from 351 to 347, seeking peace with Athens at the same time. The Peace of Philocrates in 346 gave Philip mastery of northern and central Greece, including Thermopylae and Delphi; the Amphictyonic League, remembering the original cause of the war, punished Phocis severely. **Fourth Sacred War** (Amphissean War) (339–338 B.C.). This war began like the third: cultivation of sacred lands, punishment by fine, refusal to pay, and a declaration of war by the Amphictyonic League in 339. But the Amphisseans drove the Delphians back, and the league again received help from the expansionist

Philip of Macedon. He first seized Elatea in northern Boeotia, frightening Athens, whose Demosthenes (384?–322) persuaded Athens's long-standing enemy Thebes to enter an alliance. In a winter campaign in 339, the Greeks won, but Philip defeated them at Chaeronea in 338. In the Peace of Demades that followed, Thebes suffered occupation, but Athens retained its fleet. Greek liberty was lost, however; in 337 a Panhellenic league under Macedonian hegemony had replaced all earlier alliances.

Saint Albans Raid (1864)   The Canadians' fear of attack from the United States was an impetus that helped form a federal union of all British North America (Canada) in 1867. During the U.S. CIVIL WAR, some 25 Confederate agents based in Canada crossed the border into Union territory and attacked the town of Saint Albans, Vt. (October 19, 1864). After killing a man and stealing about $200,000 from three banks, they fled back to Canada; a U.S. posse pursued them across the border and caught several, but had to hand them over to Canadian officials. Soon about half of the Confederate raiders were arrested, but when they were released unpunished by a Canadian court, talk of war with Canada and Britain was heard in the United States. The stolen money was returned; five of the raiders were rearrested and held for breaking Canadian neutrality; the war scare grew, however, prompting the stationing of 2,000 Canadian militiamen along the border in early 1865.

St. Bartholomew's Day, Massacre of (1 5 7 2) Catherine de Médicis (1519–89) opposed the influence of Count Gaspard of Coligny (1519–72), Huguenot (French Protestant) leader, on her son King Charles IX (1550–74) of France. After Catherine's plan to assassinate Coligny failed on August 22, 1572, she persuaded Charles to order the deaths of Huguenot leaders, many of whom were gathered in Paris to celebrate the wedding of Henry of Navarre, later King Henry IV (1553–1610), and Marguerite of Valois (1553–1615). At a set time on St.

Bartholomew's Day, August 24, 1572, Parisian mobs rose up and killed the Huguenot leaders, including Coligny, throughout the city. Despite a royal order to cease, the killing spread to the provinces and lasted through September 1572. Some 3,000 Protestants were slain in Paris alone; an estimated 50,000 were killed in France during the general massacre, which resulted in renewed civil war between Catholics and Protestants (see RELIGION, FOURTH WAR OF).

St. Clair's Defeat (1791)   When Josiah Harmar (1753–1813) failed to subdue the Indians in the Northwest Territory (see HARMAR'S DEFEAT), Arthur St. Clair (1736–1818), the territory's governor and commander of the federal army, set out with a 2,100-man force on October 3, 1791, moving northward from Fort Washington (Cincinnati). While camped near the upper Wabash River, St. Clair's force, which had been reduced to about 1,400 because of desertions, was surprised and attacked by Indians under Chief Little Turtle (1752–1812) on November 4, 1791. After a bloody three-hour battle, St. Clair retreated, having lost more than half of his men. The defeat was a great humiliation that led to an investigation by Congress. St. Clair was eventually exonerated, and blame was placed on the inexperience of the soldiers. See also FALLEN TIMBERS, BATTLE OF.

St. George's Day Revolt   See ESTONIAN REVOLT OF 1343–45.

Sajo River, Battle of   See MOHI, BATTLE OF.

Sakdal Uprising (1935)   Sakdal, meaning "accuse" in Tagalog, one of the major languages in the Philippines, signified the discontent and anger of the poor, landless peasants who worked on the large plantations in central Luzon, Philippines, in the early 1930s. Many of these peasants joined the Sakdal movement, founded and headed by Benigno Ramos (fl. 1930–35), who called for lower taxes for the poor, land reform, and the Philippines' immediate independence from the United States. The movement gradually evolved into a political party, which drew many votes in the 1934 Philippine fall elections. On the night of May 2, 1935, throngs of Sakdals, many of whom were armed, took control of government buildings in 14 towns in Luzon. The next day government troops were called out and quickly suppressed the rebellious peasants, about 100 of whom were slain in the violence. Ramos escaped to Japan, and the Sakdal party was declared illegal and disbanded.

Saladin's Holy War (1187–89) After gathering a large army of Muslims of various groups in the Middle East, Saladin (1137?–93), sultan of Egypt and chief warrior of Islam, launched a Holy War against the Christian Crusaders to take control of the Latin Kingdom of Jerusalem (the plundering of a Muslim caravan by Christians under Reginald of Châtillon (d. 1187] had violated a truce). At the Battle of Hattin in 1187, Saladin's Muslims, called Saracens by the Christians, defeated the Crusaders under Reginald and Guy of Lusignan (1129–94), both of whom were taken prisoner (Reginald, castigated for truce breaking, was beheaded by Saladin when he refused to become a Muslim; Guy was released when he ceded the port of Ascalon). Saladin then successfully besieged Jerusalem, entering the city on October 2, 1187. His siege of Acre in June 1189 was thwarted by the arrival of reinforcements under King Richard I Lion-Heart (1157–99) of England (see CRUSADE, THIRD). See also CRUSADER-TURKISH WARS.

Salvadoran Civil War of 1977–92 In 1977, a conservative civilian-military government came to power in El Salvador, which saw increasingly violent clashes between opposing leftist and rightist factions. With the country being torn apart by kidnappings, assassinations, arbitrary arrests, and torture, a military coup overthrew the government (October 15, 1979), and the new ruling junta called on both the right and left to lay down their arms,

but to no avail. On March 24, 1980, El Salvador's Archbishop Oscar Arnulfo Romero (1918–80), an outspoken champion of human rights and the poor, was assassinated by a right-wing terrorist as he officiated at a mass in San Salvador, the capital; at the prelate's funeral, panic swept through the large crowd after explosions and gunfire by snipers, and 31 persons were killed and some 200 were injured. Later that year (December 4, 1980) four missing U.S. churchwomen were found slain in El Salvador, causing a temporary cutoff of U.S. economic and military aid to the government. While wiping out rebels, government forces errantly massacred some 750 men, women, and children in El Mozote and surrounding hamlets in December 1981. Leftist guerrilla rebels, supported by Cuba and Nicaragua, operated mainly in the countryside, raiding towns, police stations, and military posts to obtain arms and gaining control of about a third of the country. Right-wing death squads, formed to eliminate suspected leftists, were blamed for killing thousands of civilians, including Jesuit priests, nuns, labor organizers, peasant leaders, alleged communists, and democratic reformers. A succession of U.S.-supported centrist and rightist governments failed to defeat the rebels of the marxist-led Farabundo Martí National Liberation Front (FMLN), which rejected (1987) both a Central American peace plan and a unilateral cease-fire by the government. By early 1989, the FMLN guerrillas were militarily deadlocked with the Salvadoran armed forces and had gained almost no political power. During elections in March 1989, the FMLN mounted a bold offensive, attacking about 20 towns; the rightist Nationalist Republican Alliance (ARENA) won control under Alfredo Cristiani (1947–). But charges of widespread corruption continued; defiant FMLN rebels launched another bold offensive in San Salvador in November 1989. President Cristiani then engaged in UN-mediated negotiations for 21 months until a peace accord was reached on January 16, 1992, followed by a permanent cease-fire on February 1. Afterward, FMLN forces gradually disbanded, government forces were cut in half, and political and economic reforms were instituted. The war had cost about 80,000 lives, uprooted about 1 million people, and destroyed the country's productive infrastructure. See also NICARAGUAN CIVIL WAR OF 1982–90.

Salvadoran-Honduran War of 1969   See SOCCER WAR.

Salvadoran Revolt of 1948   General and President Maximiliano Hernández Martínez (1882–1966) ruled El Salvador dictatorially from 1931 to 1944, when he resigned following a general strike (May 1944) in protest against his ruthless suppression of a military revolt the month before. The country's military-ruled government put Salvador Castañeda Castro (c. 1888–1965) in the presidency and expunged some liberties during the next three years, but Castañeda also introduced a number of education and labor reforms and promoted the union of El Salvador and neighboring Guatemala. Nonetheless, he was ousted by an army revolt of young officers (December 12–14, 1948), who demanded economic and social reforms to raise the standard of living. Major Oscar Osorio (1910–69), a member of the junta that had seized power, headed the government until his election as president in 1950; he legalized labor unions, improved housing, and encouraged industrial and agricultural development.

Samarkand, Mongol Destruction of   See BUKHARA, MONGOL DESTRUCTION OF.

Samil Independence Movement (March First Movement) (1919–20)   In 1910 the Japanese annexed Korea against its will, and at the end of WORLD WAR I the Koreans tried unsuccessfully to persuade the Paris Conference to consider them an oppressed people with a right to self-determination. On March 1, 1919, 33 Korean cultural and religious leaders came together to sign a "Proclamation of Independence," which they read that day before a huge gathering in the Korean capital city of Seoul.

The independence movement spread like wildfire to other cities and towns. During the following year more than 1,500 demonstrations, which were attended by about 2 million persons, were held throughout the country. Although the demonstrations were peaceful, the Japanese police and military reacted with harsh severity against the anti-Japanese demonstrators; nearly 23,000 were killed or wounded in clashes. Of about 47,000 who were arrested, some 5,000 were sent to prison. After the demonstrations were suppressed, the Japanese government reformed its governance of Korea and gave the Koreans a small measure of self-government. Today March 1 is celebrated in both North and South Korea as a national holiday in honor of the demonstrators' patriotism. See also SINO-JAPANESE WAR OF 1894–95.

Samnite War, First (343–341 B.C.)   The warlike Samnite tribes occupied what is today the Abruzzi region of Italy, mostly in the southern Apennine Mountains, and as these peoples were expanding their territory in the fourth century B.C., it was inevitable they would clash with Rome. The first confrontation came in 343, when Capua, a town in the Latin League, requested Rome's help against the Samnites. Rome responded with troops, who won a minor victory at Mount Gaurus in 342, but mutinies and heavy losses made Roman aid generally ineffectual. A peace treaty (341) gave several towns in Campania to the Samnites, which caused great resentment among Rome's Latin allies (see LATIN WAR). Most of Campania came under the protection of Rome. **Second Samnite War** (327–304 B.C.). In 327, the Samnites supported a faction in a struggle for control of Naples. Rome laid siege to the city, which was garrisoned by Samnites who were persuaded to leave, and Naples became an ally of Rome. This led to renewed war. The Samnites were better fighters in mountainous terrain, and they trapped a Roman army in a narrow Apennine pass called Caudine Forks and forced it to surrender in 321; the Romans were made to march out under the yoke, an ignominy they never forgot. Rome then reorganized its forces and adopted military maneuvers more suitable for mountain warfare. The fighting resumed in 317, and the next year the Samnites won another victory at Lautulae. But the Romans recovered rapidly, won an important battle at Ciuna (315), and regained lost territory, driving the Samnites from Campania and putting them on the defensive. Rome also established colonies around the edges of Samnium (the country of the Samnites) that acted as fortresses and bases for attack, and it built the Via Appia (Appian Way), a paved road, from Rome to Capua that ensured communications even in the rainy season. The Samnites induced the Etruscan cities in the north to revolt against Rome, but the Etruscans were defeated at the Battle of Lake Vadimo (310) and forced to make peace (308). The Samnites then encouraged tribes in the central Apennines to withdraw from the Roman alliances, but these tribes also were subdued. After losing the Battle of Bovianum (305), the Samnites and their remaining allies agreed to a peace treaty in 304. **Third Samnite War** (298–290 B.C.). Fighting erupted when the Samnites joined the Gauls, Etruscans, and Sabines in opposing Roman expansion to the north, and together they made raids on Roman outposts. A combined army of Etruscans, Gauls, and Samnites met a Roman army at Sentinum (Sassoferrato) near the Adriatic Sea and was badly defeated in 295. Afterward the tribes made peace, except for the Samnites, whose countryside was systematically ravaged by the Romans and who suffered defeat at the Battle of Aquilonia (293). Eventually the Samnites were forced to sue for peace in 290. Recognized for their valor, they were allowed to become allies, not subjects, of Rome. Italy was now dominated by the Romans.

Samoan Civil War of 1880–81   Desultory tribal warfare had long occurred on Samoa, an archipelago in the south-central Pacific, where the United States, Germany, and Britain all signed treaties that gave them commercial and other rights (1878–79). In 1880, the three foreign powers agreed to recognize Malietoa Talavou (d. 1880) as Samoa's king, whose death later that year brought on a civil war between contentious groups seeking power. About eight months later, Malietoa Lau-

pepa (d. 1898) secured the throne with the foreign powers' recognition.

Samoan Civil War of 1887–89   Natives of Samoa, an island chain in the South Pacific, resented the collection of large taxes by a German trading company, which threatened that those who did not pay would have to mortgage their land. German warships landed soldiers in support of a local chief, Tamasese (fl. 1880s), who was proclaimed *tafaifa* ("king of all Samoa") in 1887; the old king, Malietoa Laupepa (d. 1898), was exiled. Samoans under Mataafa (d. after 1899), a powerful chief, rebelled against Tamasese in September 1888. The German consul at Apia (on the Samoan island of Upolu) led Tamasese's warriors against the insurgents, but was forced to retreat to Mulinu'u Point, where a German gunboat afforded protection. British and U.S. officials protested when the gunboat shelled rebel villages. Mataafa's forces plundered German plantations and wiped out an invading contingent of Germans. The German consul, furious, declared a state of martial law; his request for two marine companies was denied because they might cause U.S. intervention. In 1889, Malietoa was restored as king under an agreement by the United States, Britain, and Germany, all of which gained administrative rights in Samoa.

Samoan Civil War of 1893–94   In the spring of 1893, Mataafa (d. after 1899), a leading Samoan chief, rejected a warrant to come to Apia, the capital of Samoa, and instead waged war against his traditional enemy, Malietoa Laupepa (d. 1898), the Samoan king. The Malietoan forces, however, proved to be stronger, and Mataafa was driven onto the small Samoan island of Manono. German and British warships arrived to quell the fighting, and Mataafa was finally induced to surrender and, with some of his supporters, was taken by a German ship to the Marshall Islands.

Samoan Civil War of 1898–99   On the death of Samoa's King Malietoa Laupepa (d. 1898), his longtime rival Mataafa (d. after 1899) returned from exile aboard a German warship and was shortly elected the Samoan king as virtually a German puppet. The U.S. and British consuls strongly opposed him, backing instead the dead king's son. Fighting erupted between Samoans; in January 1899, the capital city of Apia was thrown into chaos with foes fighting in the streets, looting, and burning buildings. At first Mataafa and his Samoan and German supporters gained the upper hand until U.S. and British warships shelled Apia (March 15, 1899). Anglo-American troops took control of coastal roads, but were unable to defeat the enemy in the interior. All fighting ceased with the arrival of a tripartite (U.S.-British-German) commission on May 13, 1899. Both sides agreed to give up their firearms, for which they were fairly compensated, and the monarchy was abolished. By the tripartite treaty (1899), Germany received the western Samoan islands, of which Savaii and Upolu (the site of Apia) are the most important; the United States obtained the eastern islands (American Samoa, with its capital at Pago Pago on Tutuila); and Britain withdrew from the area for recognition of rights on Tonga and the Solomons.

Sand Creek Massacre (Chivington Massacre) (1864) On November 28, 1864, a band of American cavalry and artillery that had been marching across the plains in the cold for five days learned from its mixed-race guide that an Indian camp lay ahead. Their commander, Colonel John M. Chivington (1821–94), demanded to be taken to it. As day was breaking, the cavalry dashed into the Cheyenne and Arapaho camp on Sand Creek, a tributary of the Arkansas River in southeastern Colorado. The Cheyenne chief, Black Kettle (d. 1868), raised an American and white flag above his tepee to show friendship, while a white trader with the Indians tried to dissuade the troops from violence. But in the confusion a melee broke out, and both sides started shooting at each other. The Indians were driven up the sandy creek, fighting as they went, but their bows and arrows were no match for the firearms of the soldiers, who shot women and children as well as warriors during their hot pursuit. After it was over, only two Indian women and five children remained alive, and they were taken away as captives. Seven soldiers were killed and more than 400 Indians. The troops confiscated the goods in the Indian camp and continued on their way. An army commission later investigated the incident and Chivington's responsibility for it, but no firm decision was ever reached in the controversy of who was to blame. See also CHEYENNE AND ARAPAHO WAR OF 1864–68.

Sandino's Revolt See NICARAGUAN CIVIL WAR OF 1925–33.

Santo Domingo, Revolt in See HAITIAN CIVIL WAR OF 1806–20.

Santo Domingo, Revolution in (1844) Haitian rule over Santo Domingo (the Dominican Republic) was harsh and oppressive (see HAITIAN RECONQUEST OF SANTO DOMINGO). In the 1830s, Juan Pablo Duarte (1813–76) organized and led a secret revolutionary society, "La Trinitaria," to fight the Haitians. A rebellion broke out in Haiti against the corrupt rule of President Jean Pierre Boyer (1776–1850), who was forced to flee in 1843. Taking advantage of the unstable situation, Duarte and some 100 fellow conspirators seized the fortress of Puerta del Conde and the city of Santo Domingo on February 27, 1844; the Haitians were expelled; and the independence of the Dominican Republic was proclaimed. See also HAITIAN CIVIL WAR OF 1806–20.

Sanusi Revolt of 1915–17 The Sanusiyah brotherhood, founded by Muhammad ibn Ali as-Sanusi in 1837, adopted Muslim Sufi mystical and puritanical tenets and established itself firmly in Cyrenaica (eastern Libya), where its politically motivated, militant followers called the Sanusis (Senussis) fought unsuccessfully against French expansionism in the Sahara (1902–13) and Italian colonization and pacification of Libya (1911–34). During

WORLD WAR I, under the influence of Ottoman Turkish propaganda, the Sanusis attacked British forces in the Libyan Desert of Egypt. At first, in November 1915, they were successful, necessitating British reinforcements to check them. A British offensive in February–March 1916, drove them, still hostile and unsubdued, into the Suva Oasis. In 1917, the British took over the oasis and drove out the surviving Sanusis, who returned to Libya to antagonize the Italians and eventually gain control there after WORLD WAR II. The Sanusi leader and grandson of as-Sanusi, Idris I (1890–1983), became the first king of independent Libya in 1951 and reigned until he was deposed in a military coup led by Colonel Muammar al-Qaddafi (1942–) in 1969.

Sardinian Revolt of 1821   See PIEDMONTESE REVOLT OF 1821.

Satsuma Revolt (1877) Since the 12th century the samurai were the hereditary warrior class in Japan, and their grievances against the shogun led to the downfall of the Tokugawa shogunate (see MEIJI RESTORATION) in 1867 and the unification of the country under the emperor. The powerful daimyos (lords) voluntarily handed over their domains to the Crown, the first step in abolishing the feudal system that had existed for centuries. By 1871, the samurai were the only remaining vestige of feudalism. They were granted pensions equal to one-half their former hereditary salaries and were given permission to set aside their two swords and to engage in trade, business, agriculture, or industry. In 1873, the samurai were offered the option of exchanging their pensions for lump payments, and in 1876 the commutation of pensions was made mandatory. At the same time a decree was issued forbidding the wearing of swords except by men in the newly organized army. This final insult to their pride caused many groups of samurai to revolt. Most were easily suppressed, but in Satsuma, in the south, 40,000 warriors trained in the use of modern and traditional weapons rebelled under the leadership of

Saigo Takamori (1827–77), one of the original reformers. The revolt broke out on January 29, 1877, and continued for the next eight months. The emperor sent 65,000 men into the field against the samurai, and in the end this army, made up of peasants and civilians, prevailed over the former military elite. Some historians contend that if Saigo had not wasted time and men besieging the castle of Kumamoto, the result might have been different. As it was, Saigo was killed during the final battle outside Kagoshima (September 24, 1877), and his devoted adherents committed suicide.

Saxon Raids of A.D. c. 205–369 Archaeological evidence suggests that Germanic raids in Roman-occupied Britain began early in the third century; the Romans labeled the raiders as "Saxons" and, by 250, had begun to erect nine defensive seashore forts from Kent west to modern Portsmouth in Hampshire, with a "count of the Saxon shore" in command of them at Rutupiae (Richborough). By 300, forts had been built as far west as Cardiff; London had a defensive river wall; and York had been fortified. The raids, hit-and-run affairs, involved pillage, slaying, rapine, and arson; they were directed either from the Amsterdam shore to Britain's Wash area, from the Boulogne area to Kent, or from the Cherbourg area toward the Isle of Wight. Coupled with attacks from Picts from present-day Scotland and from Scots (Irishmen) from the west, the frequent raids reached a climax in 367, when both the count of the Saxon shore and the duke of the northern army were killed in battle by the Saxons, who had been helped by the withdrawal of Roman troops to fight barbarians endangering Rome. Rural settlements were abandoned as residents sought refuge in walled towns in Britain; commerce and agriculture suffered severely until order was restored by Roman general (emperor after 379) Theodosius (346?–95) and upheld during the early reign of his son, Roman emperor Honorius (384–423).

Saxon Raids of A.D. c. 407–550   Saxons resumed their invasions of Britain in large numbers when Roman troops withdrew from the region to protect Rome or to assist troop-elected "emperors." They raided far inland; the fighting was without set battles until 429, when Verulamium (St. Albans) was attacked by Saxon and Pict pirates. Britain became chaotic because of invading Picts, Scots, and Saxons; its appeal to Rome for aid was rejected (446). Nonroyal tyrants took command of territories, among them Vortigern (d. c. 461), a Briton who hired barbarians to fight the Picts and offered them land in Kent as reward. The hired barbarians, "Jutes" (actually Jutes, Angles, Saxons, Frisians, and some Franks), rebelled, demanded more territory, and sent for relatives, who helped them win at Aylesford (c. 455) and Crayford (c. 457) and, by 475, establish the kingdom of Kent. Vortigern's death was followed by a westward trek of Britons and the immigration of many thousands to Armorica ("Little Britain," not Brittany). A union of Britons (c. 470) brought a lull in hostilities, for most Britons remained in the west while the Saxon kingdoms of Sussex (477) and Wessex (495) were established. A Briton war chieftain, unnamed by the historian Gildas (516?–70?) and called Artorius (Arthur) by the historian Nennius (fl. c. 796), profoundly defeated the Saxons in 516 or 518 at Badon Hill (Mount Badon, perhaps Liddington Badbury) by using cavalry, unknown to the Saxons. A line along the old Roman road called Fosse Way separated the Britons in the west from the Saxons in the east until about 550.

Saxon Raids of A.D. c. 550–77

By the end of the fifth century, the Germanic invaders who settled in Britain had begun to set up separate kingdoms (Kent, c. 475; Sussex, c. 477; Wessex, c. 495; East Anglia, c. 500; Essex, c. 505; Northumbria [Bernicia, 559, and Deira, c. 560], c. 605; Mercia, c. 606—a group called the "Heptarchy" by historians). Three types of conflict occurred in Britain after about 550: pillage raids, settlements battles, and expansionist wars between the kingdoms of the Anglo-Saxon Heptarchy. Until 552, the Britons stayed mainly in the west, occupying the Welsh kingdom of Strathclyde (Scotland), Rheged, Manan Gododdin, Elmet, Cumbria; the Welsh kingdoms of Gwynedd, Dyged, and Gwent; and Dumnonia (Somerset, Devon, and Cornwall). Most fighting involving the Britons took place in the southwest and Wessex areas. The Britons attempted an offensive across the Fosse Way at Searoburh (Old Sarum) in 552, but they lost. In reprisal, the Saxons crossed the Fosse Way in 556 and 571, winning at Beranburh (Barbury) and Bedeanford (Bedford?). In 577, in the decisive and last important battle of the Anglo-Saxon invasions at Deorham (Dyrham, near Bath), the Britons of Dumnonia were slaughtered in great numbers. Dumnonia was not occupied, however. Celtic Britain was weakly alive, and although continental Saxons continued to raid sporadically in British Saxon areas, the wars of the Saxon invaders became chiefly internecine, involving the Britons only occasionally. See also AETHELFRITH'S WARS.

Scandinavian Revolt of 1433–39

Danish king Erik VII (Erik of Pomerania) (1382–1459), ruler of the Kalmar Union (the combined kingships of Denmark, Sweden, and Norway), imposed on Sweden an oppressive system of Danish bailiffs and levied heavy troop and monetary requirements to fight the KALMAR WAR WITH THE HANSEATIC LEAGUE. In June 1433, Swedish peasants and miners under Engelbrekt Engelbrektsson (d. 1436), a miner, rebelled against the Danish governor, attacking castles and evicting bailiffs. The provinces of Upland, Vermland, and Södermanland joined the revolt, and the Swedish council invited Norway and some Hanseatic towns to join, too. While Engelbrektsson was being declared Sweden's administrator in 1435, Erik was negotiating with Swedish nobles to reestablish the Danish-Swedish union and gain control of his throne. The Swedish post of administrator was abolished, but after Erik allowed his troops to ravage Swedish coastal areas on his return to Denmark, the Swedish council retaliated by again choosing an administrator, Karl Knutsson (1408?–70), to rule. Erik, refusing Danish and Swedish demands for constitutional forms of government in a new union, was deposed in Denmark and Sweden in 1439 (Norway deposed him in 1442). His nephew, Christopher of

Bavaria (1418–48), succeeded him as ruler of the Kalmar Union.

Scandinavian Seven Years' War See DANISH-SWEDISH WAR OF 1563–70.

Scandinavian War of 1026–30 Both Swedish and Danish influence in Norway diminished with the ascent of Olaf II (Olaf Haraldson) (995?–1030) to the Norwegian throne. When Denmark's King Canute II "the Great" (994?–1035) sought restoration of Denmark's Norwegian rights, King Olaf allied himself with King Anund (d. 1051) of Sweden. The Danes defeated the Swedes at the naval battle of Strangebjerg in 1026. While Canute was away, Olaf and Anund invaded Denmark, but in 1028, after Canute had returned, Swedish-Norwegian naval forces were crushed by the Danes at Helgeaa. Anund returned home. The Danes drove Olaf from Norway to Sweden, where he raised an army to reconquer Norway. He was defeated and killed at the Battle of Stiklestad in 1030.

Scandinavian War of 1448–71 After King Christopher III (1418–48), Danish ruler of Sweden, Norway, and Denmark, died, Sweden and Norway united in 1449 under the rule of Swedish noble Karl Knutsson (1408?–70), who became King Charles VIII. However, strong support for the new Danish king, Christian I (1426–81), induced him to form a united Scandinavian kingdom. Charles, disliked and betrayed by the clergy, was forced to flee in February 1457, and Christian was crowned "king of Scandinavia." In time, Christian lost popularity because of personal and monetary disputes with the church and onerous tax and police policies. The Swedish bishop of Linkoping nullified obligations of allegiance to the king and took up arms against him. Finally, the royal forces were pushed back to Stockholm, the Danes gave up, and the rebels recalled Charles to the throne in 1464. Christian, from Copenhagen, sought to restore good relations with Uppsala's archbishop, who helped marshal opposition to Charles. Defeated in battle in 1465,

Charles was forced again to flee and give up the throne. The archbishop ruled independently until his opponents' plotting caused him to solicit troops from Christian in 1466. The opposition renounced Danish rule and again sought Charles's return. Although opposing nobles joined pro-Danish clergy seeking his ouster, Charles was ultimately victorious on the battlefield, and the Danes entered into peace negotiations. After Charles's death in 1470, the post of administrator fell to Sten Sture (1440?–1503), whose decisive defeat of Christian at the Battle of Brunkeberg, near Stockholm, in October 1471, ended Danish intervention in Sweden.

Schleswig-Holstein War See DANISH-PRUSSIAN WAR OF 1864.

Schmalkaldic War (1546–47) In 1531, nine German states formed the Schmalkaldic League as a defensive alliance of Protestants within the Holy Roman Empire; it hoped to counter any antagonistic moves by Catholic Holy Roman Emperor Charles V (1500–1558). Charles, however, was not at first concerned with the Lutheran Protestant Reformation and seemed not to understand what was taking place and therefore ignored it. But, in 1544, fearing the league would ally itself with his enemy King Francis I (1494–1547) of France, he gave it de facto recognition. Then he decided (1546) to destroy its power, declaring war from Regensburg ostensibly because the Protestants had declined his invitation to the frequently delayed Council of Trent (its first session, 1545–47). Charles's war declaration was made when neither of his formidable foreign armies was near him, and the league's forces could have overcome either. But the league dallied. The opposing armies finally arrived at Muhlberg in April 1547; the league's forces were still not unified at the time, and some league members now went over to Charles's side. Charles's forces, led by the duke of Alva (Alba) (1508–82), routed the league's Saxon army and captured its leader, John Frederick (1503–54), elector of Saxony. The league's Hessian leader, Philip (1504–67), landgrave of Hesse, was also taken prisoner at Muhlberg, and both he and John Frederick were paraded at the Diet of Augsburg, which attempted to settle (1548) the religious differences in the Holy Roman Empire. See also HAPSBURG-VALOIS WAR OF 1547–59; ITALIAN WARS BETWEEN CHARLES V AND FRANCIS I.

Scottish-English Wars   See   ANGLO-SCOTTISH WARS.

Scottish Invasion of Ireland (1315–18)   Edward Bruce (d. 1318), brother and heir of Robert (1274–1329), possessed some hereditary claim to the earldom of Ulster and invaded Ireland in 1315. With 6,000 men, Edward routed the forces of the earl near Connor and, gaining the allegiance of Irish inhabitants in Connaght and West Meath, was crowned king in 1316. His power increased as many Anglo-Irish came to his support. In 1317, he and Scottish king Robert campaigned as far south as Limerick, losing support as they inflicted heavy damage. They established no strongholds, however, and their forces were pushed back to Ulster by Anglo-Irish forces under Roger de Mortimer (1287?–1330), English lord lieutenant. Robert then returned to Scotland. King Edward emerged from Ulster in 1318 to face Mortimer and died at Faughard near Dunkirk. See also SCOTTISH WAR OF 1314–28.

Scottish Uprising against Mary of Guise (1559–60) Despite the Catholic opposition of Mary of Guise (1515–60), widow of James V (1512–42) and regent of Scotland, Protestantism gained favor in Scotland. Nobles drew up the "First Covenant," a plan for a reformed national church, but neither the Scottish clergy nor parliament would meet their requests. In 1559, the fiery John Knox (1505–72) preached so eloquently that mobs attacked and pillaged churches. Mary asked for help from France. The Protestants received help from Queen Elizabeth I (1533–1603), who sent an English fleet and an army, which besieged French forces at Leith for six months. Mary died in 1560, and the Catholic resis-

tance diminished. The 1560 Treaty of Edinburgh withdrew foreign forces and established the Kirk of Scotland under Knox.

Scottish Uprising against Mary, Queen of Scots (1567–68)   The mysterious murder of Lord Darnley (1545–67), husband of Mary, Queen of Scots (1542–87), earned the queen the hatred of Protestants and Catholics alike and cost her the Crown. Her sudden marriage to James Hepburn (1536?–78), fourth earl of Bothwell, three months later did additional damage. Protestant lords, led by the earl of Moray, raised forces on the pretext of saving her from Bothwell, believed to be Darnley's murderer. When Bothwell and his men encountered Moray's soldiers at Carberry Hill on June 15, 1567, his men ran; Mary was taken prisoner and Bothwell escaped to Scandinavia. Abdicating in favor of her infant son, James VI (1566–1625), Mary soon escaped from imprisonment at Lochleven Castle and gathered a force of 6,000 men but was defeated by Moray's forces at Langside in 1568. Mary immediately fled to England, where she was held prisoner by Queen Elizabeth I (1533–1603) for the rest of her life.

Scottish War of 1295–96   In 1284 Scottish nobles recognized Princess Margaret, Maid of Norway (1283–90), infant granddaughter of Scotland's King Alexander III (1241–86), as heir apparent to the throne. Also, England's King Edward I (1239–1307) negotiated with Norway's King Erik II (d. 1299) and succeeded in forming the marriage treaty of Edward I's eldest son, Prince Edward of Caernarvon (King Edward II [1284–1327] of England), to Princess Margaret, Erik II's daughter. In July 1290 this marriage was approved by a Scottish assembly in the Treaty of Brigham, which stressed that Scotland would remain independent. But the unexpected death of Margaret (Alexander III's last successor), while voyaging from Norway to Scotland, brought at least 13 legitimate claims to the Scottish throne, chief among them being the noble contenders Robert Bruce (1274–1329) and John Balliol (1249–1315). King Edward I was invited to conciliate and, in 1291, chose Balliol, who was crowned Scottish king at Scone in 1292. Imposing vassalage and other demands on Scotland, Edward caused Balliol to rebel. Scotland signed an alliance with France in 1295, mobilized troops, and prepared to invade northern England in 1296. Edward made a counterthrust, receiving homage from many, including Bruce. Then Edward's forces sacked Berwick, defeated and imprisoned Balliol, and took Edinburgh, Stirling, Perth, Elgin, and other castles. After receiving Scottish homage, Edward stole the Stone of Scone and departed, leaving Scotland kingless as a "forfeited fief" annexed to England and under the charge of three commissioners and many garrisons. See also BANNOCKBURN, ENGLISH DEFEAT AT; BRUCE'S REVOLT; SCOTTISH WAR OF 1314–28; WALLACE'S REVOLT.

Scottish War of 1314–28   Scottish forces under Robert the Bruce (1274–1329) raided frequently across the border into England in 1314 (see BANNOCKBURN, ENGLISH DEFEAT AT). England suffered continued raids by the Scots under the leadership of James "Black" Douglas (1286?–1330) from 1315 to 1318, while Robert campaigned in Ireland with his brother (see SCOTTISH INVASION OF IRELAND). The English stronghold at Berwick was recaptured in 1318, and in 1319 Robert sent a diversionary force under Douglas into Yorkshire, where, at Myton, so many monks and clergy were involved in a skirmish that the Scots referred to their victory as "the chapter of Myton." Until 1322, Robert avoided any major battle with the English. Then, when King Edward II (1284–1327) attempted another invasion of Scotland, Robert's forces met the English at the Battle of Byland, winning a victory by a surprise attack, and forcing Edward to flee from the battlefield and retreat into Yorkshire. Though a truce was established in 1323, border incursions occurred until 1328, when the Peace of Northampton gave Scotland its legal independence. See also BRUCE'S REVOLT; SCOTTISH WAR OF 1295–96; WALLACE'S REVOLT.

Sekigahara, Battle of (1600)   Before he died, Toyotomi Hideyoshi (1536–98) appointed his loyal ally and the most powerful daimyo (lord) in Japan, Tokugawa Iyeyasu (1542–1616), chief of a board of regents, which was to rule the country on behalf of Toyotomi's infant son, Hideyori (1598–1615). A board of five ministers had been appointed in 1585 to administer the government, and its head, Ishida Mitsunari (1563–1600), soon began to conspire against Tokugawa. When he learned of the matter, Tokugawa, who was a shrewd statesman, persuaded many of Ishida's followers not to support him and further enlarged his own body of confederates. The opposing sides met in battle at Sekigahara in Mino province on October 16, 1600. By that time the Japanese had acquired firearms from the Europeans, and they fought with guns as well as swords. Ishida's motley 100,000-man force, torn by internal dissension, was no match for Tokugawa's well-trained, cohesive 80,000-man army, which was completely victorious by the end of the day and killed more than 30,000 of the enemy; Ishida was captured and executed. This was one of the most decisive conflicts in Japanese history, for it set the stage for the beginning of the Tokugawa shogunate, which would rule Japan for the next 250 years. See also OSAKA CASTLE, SIEGE OF.

Selangor Civil War (1867–73)   The Malay chiefs of Selangor, a state in southwest Malaya, quarreled politically and economically (especially over the collection of duties on Selangor's valuable tin exports), and they split into two opposing factions in the 1860s. The dissident chiefs of the upper Klang (Kelang) River area carried on intermittent warfare against those of the lower river and Selangor's sultan. About 1870, the area's Chinese immigrant tin miners, who belonged to two Chinese secret societies, took sides in the war; the Ghee Hin society joined the upper river group, while the Hai San joined the lower river group. Much of the fighting now took place in the tin miners' jungle camps. British intervention on behalf of the lower river chiefs, who had been aided by an army from nearby Pahang, turned the tide and led to the dissidents' defeat in late 1873. The next year Selangor became a British protectorate.

Seleucid War with Egypt (171–168 B.C.) King Antiochus IV Epiphanes (d. 163) of Seleucid Syria controlled lands—Coele Syria (Bekaa Valley, Lebanon), Phoenicia, and Palestine—which the Egyptians claimed and prepared to invade. Antiochus, however, led an invasion of Egypt beforehand and was victorious in battle. Pelusium, Egypt's main frontier fortress, was captured, and the Egyptian kingdom, except for its capital of Alexandria, came under the rule of Antiochus, who then returned home to quell disturbances. Ptolemy VI Philometor (186?–145) and his brother Ptolemy VIII Euergetes (184?–116), Egyptian rulers, requested help from Rome. In 168, Antiochus again invaded Egypt, invested Alexandria, but withdrew on the threat of Roman intervention; Egypt was restored to the Ptolemies. While returning home, Antiochus stormed and captured the Jewish stronghold of Jerusalem, sought to extirpate Judaism, and thus brought on a revolt (see MACCABEES, REVOLT OF THE). See also SYRIAN-EGYPTIAN WARS.

Seljuk Turk-Byzantine Wars See BYZANTINE-SELJUK TURK WARS.

Seminole War, First (1817–18) The Spanish colony in Florida was a refuge for runaway black slaves who found new homes among the Seminole Indians. However, U.S. troops frequently pursued the slaves across the border, causing resentment among the Seminoles, who retaliated by ambushing and scalping a force of Americans. The U.S. Army sent an expedition to recapture the slaves and to destroy the Spanish fort on the Apalachicola River, and war broke out in earnest. In 1817, U.S. general Andrew Jackson (1767–1845) assumed command and, without specific authorization, marched south with a small force and seized the Spanish forts at St. Marks and Pensacola. He also captured several Seminole chiefs and two British Indian traders, Alexander Arbuthnot and Robert Ambrister, all of whom he ordered to be executed (1818). This created a furor of protest from the British and most members of the U.S. president's cabinet, but no action was taken. In contrast, Jackson was hailed as a hero in the American West. In 1819, John Quincy Adams (1767–1848), U.S. president, negotiated a treaty whereby Spain ceded all its territory east of the Mississippi River to the United States for $5 million. **Second Seminole War** (1835–42). Hostilities broke out when Chief Osceola (1800?–1839) and most of his Seminole tribe refused to acknowledge a treaty of removal that had been signed by some Indian chiefs and the U.S. government. Rather than leave their homeland in Florida and move west of the Mississippi, the Seminoles retreated into Florida's Everglades and fought there in the swamps for seven years, pitting some 1,500 warriors against more than 40,000 U.S. troops. In 1837, with 8,000 soldiers at his command, General Thomas S. Jesup (1788–1860) won several battles, but none was decisive. Osceola was then promised safe conduct to a peace conference, but was treacherously seized and sent to a jail in North Carolina, where he later died. Jesup's trickery outraged the public. In 1838, General Zachary Taylor (1784–1850), who had earlier defeated some Seminoles at Lake Okeechobee (December 25, 1837), took over command from Jesup, but was unable to bring the war to a conclusion, though organized Seminole resistance had collapsed. At his own request in 1840, Taylor was relieved of command in Florida, where finally some 3,800 Seminoles agreed to emigrate west to live on a reservation in what is now Oklahoma. About 400 remained holed up in the Everglades. This Indian war, the most expensive fought by U.S. troops, cost more than $40 million and the lives of 1,500 soldiers, plus many Indian lives and homes. **Third Seminole War** (1855–58). After Florida became a U.S. state in 1845, the remaining Seminoles held tenaciously to their ancestral lands and resisted encroachment by the whites. Ten years later, a concerted effort was made to hunt down and remove several hundred of the Indians from their homes in the Everglades. Fights were minor. The U.S. government eventually paid the most recalcitrant of the

Seminoles to move West. Nonetheless, a small band stayed in the swampy lands and did not make peace until 1934. The Seminole Wars were the only Indian wars the U.S. did not win.

Senegalese Border War of 1989–91   Bloody ethnic violence between Senegalese and Mauritanians in the Senegal River valley (the border region between Senegal and Mauritania) erupted in mid-April 1989, following the killing of two Senegalese peasants apparently by Mauritanian border guards, in a simmering dispute over animal grazing rights. Fighting soon forced the white (*bidan*) Moors, who controlled trade in the region, to flee north; their rivals, the Poular-speaking blacks (Tukulors and Fulani), fled to safety on the south side of the river valley and made retaliatory raids into Mauritanian territory. Much looting and bloodshed by both sides occurred, while at least 250,000 persons fled their homes into forced exile elsewhere. Attempts by the Organization of African Unity (OAU) to mediate failed in 1990. Senegal's President Abdou Diouf (1935–   ) managed to work out a prudent agreement, which was signed by the two countries on July 18, 1991. The border was later reopened, and refugees and exiles began to return to their homes in the valley. That same year (1991), President Diouf arranged a cease-fire agreement with separatist rebels in Casamance, a rainy region in southwestern Senegal, bounded by Gambia (north) and Guinea-Bissau (south); guerrillas of the Mouvement des Forces Democratiques de Casamance received total amnesty, having battled the government for two years.

Sepoy Rebellion   See INDIAN MUTINY.

September Massacres (1792)   After King Louis XVI (1754–93) of France had been stripped of his functions and the royal family imprisoned (see FRENCH REVOLUTION), many French people believed that royalist sympathizers in prisons planned to rise up and join a counterrevolutionary plot. Radicals demanded the deaths of all such conspirators. On September 2, 1792, an armed group of Parisians attacked and killed prisoners being transferred from one jail to another in the city. "Spontaneous" mobs then seized suspects from prisons in Paris, Versailles, Lyons, Orléans, Rheims, and elsewhere and, after hasty trials, summarily executed them. Some 1,200 prisoners died in five days, and their deaths became a political issue among the various factions vying to rule the French government.

Serbian Uprising, First (1804–13)   The Ottoman Empire had tried for a long time to crush the rise of nationalism in its Serbian subjects, who were virtual bondslaves of their Turkish-controlled lands. The Serbs also loathed the tyrannical rule of the Janissaries (elite Turkish corps) in the pashalik (province) of Belgrade. Under the leadership of Karageorge (1762–1817), son of a Serbian peasant, they revolted against the Turks, driving out the Janissaries in December 1806. Karageorge, whose request for Serbian autonomy had been rejected by the Porte (Ottoman government) in 1805, formed an alliance with Russia, which was also fighting the empire (see RUSSO-TURKISH WAR OF 1806–12). After the Turks lost battles to Serbo-Russian forces at Varvarin and Loznica in 1810, Serbia was liberated, but NAPOLEON'S INVASION OF RUSSIA (1812) compelled the Russians to conclude a treaty with the Ottomans at Bucharest. Free to concentrate solely on Serbia, the Turks invaded in full force, defeated the Serbs in 1813, and regained control; Karageorge fled to Austria. **Second Serbian Uprising** (1815–17). A peasant revolutionary, Milosh Obrenovich (1780–1860), who was a rival of Karageorge, led the Serbs in a new and successful revolt against the Turks (1815), who granted considerable autonomy to Serbia afterward. In 1817, Karageorge returned home and was murdered on orders by Milosh (this initiated the long blood feud between the rival Karageorgevich and Obrenovich families). Named prince of Serbia (1817) by the Serbian national assembly, Milosh later (1827) obtained Turkish recognition of his title as hereditary. By 1830, Serbia, under Turkish suzerainty and Russian protection, was an internationally acknowledged autonomous principality.

Serbo-Bulgarian War of 1885–86   The Balkan peace established by the Conference of Berlin in 1878 (see RUSSO-TURKISH WAR OF 1877–78; SERBO-TURKISH WAR OF 1876–78) was broken when Bulgaria, under Prince Alexander Joseph of Battenberg (1857–93), invaded Eastern Rumelia (southern Bulgaria) and took control in 1885. Serbia, unhappy with its limited territorial boundaries, demanded that Bulgaria give it some Bulgarian lands. When an international conference failed to reach an agreement about Bulgaria's expansion and Serbia's demands, Serbia declared war, sending troops into Bulgaria. Alexander's forces, however, responded by driving them back into Serbia and advancing toward Belgrade. As protector of Serbia, Austria became alarmed, especially when the Serbs were decisively defeated at the Battle of Slivnitza on November 17–19, 1885. A Bulgarian takeover of Serbia was stopped only by Austrian intervention. Alexander accepted an armistice, and later, by the Treaty of Bucharest in 1886, the old Serbo-Bulgarian border was reestablished, and Alexander's annexation of eastern Rumelia was confirmed.

Serbo-Turkish War of 1876–78   Christian inhabitants of Herzegovina and Bosnia rebelled in 1875 against their Muslim Turkish rulers and appealed for help from Serbia, then an autonomous state within the Ottoman Empire. This and rampant Serbian nationalism and Russian promises of support for the rebels caused Serbia to declare war on the empire on June 30, 1876; Montenegro did the same a day later. The Montenegrins were immediately victorious, defeating the Turks in Herzegovina and remaining there throughout the war. The Serbians fared less well, for the promised Russian support did not arrive. Turks invaded Serbia and won a ferocious battle at Aleksinac on August 9, 1876, causing Serbia to appeal to the great powers for mediation. A second Serbian defeat at Aleksinac on September 1, 1876, brought a brief armistice, which

Serbia broke three weeks later. Russia ordered the Turks to stop fighting but to no avail. The war continued until the Turks were virtual masters of Serbia when another armistice forced a separate peace (1877) between the Porte (Ottoman government) and Serbia under the auspices of the great powers. However, conflict between the Russians and Turks resulted in war (see RUSSO-TURKISH WAR OF 1877–78). Britain's displeasure with the Treaty of San Stefano, ending the wars in 1878, led to the Conference of Berlin, whose treaty, in addition to giving Serbia, Montenegro, and Rumania independence, gave Austria-Hungary Bosnia and Herzegovina, humiliated Russia as a naval power, and, in failing to consult the Balkan countries, laid the foundation for future conflicts, especially WORLD WAR I. See also TURKO-MONTENEGRIN WARS.

Sertorian War (80–72 B.C.)   Quintus Sertorius (d. 72) was an able general who was appointed governor of Lusitania (Portugal and western Spain) in 83. He was forced to flee to North Africa in 81, when Lucius Cornelius Sulla (138–72) became Roman dictator and took vengeance upon all former enemies, among them Sertorius (see ROMAN CIVIL WAR OF 84–82 B.C.). A year later the Lusitanians revolted against Rome and asked Sertorius to return to lead them, which he did. Rome's legal governor in Lusitania was defeated by Sertorius at the Battle of the Baetis (Guadalquivir) River in 80. Sulla sent an army under Quintus Metellus Pius (d. c. 64) to squash the revolt, but it was overcome by Sertorius's forces. By 77, Sertorius controlled most of what is now Spain and Portugal. A new Roman army under Pompey the Great (106–48) marched from Italy over the Pyrenees to join forces with Metellus, but Sertorius out-generaled them in a series of campaigns (76–73). After the arrival of reinforcements, the Romans gradually began to win the upper hand. Sertorius initiated strict discipline and severe punishments for infractions in his army, which roused dissension among his troops. Marcus Perperna (d. 72), his chief officer, stirred up more disaffection, helped murder Sertorius, and assumed command of the army. He was shortly thereafter defeated by Pompey, taken captive, and killed.

Servile War, First (Slave War in Sicily, First) (135–132 B.C.) Most of the grain that fed Rome was grown on large agricultural estates in Sicily, and the estates' owners were dependent upon cheap slave labor captured by Rome's victorious armies. These captives were brutally treated, and it was inevitable that they would revolt against their overlords. Some 70,000 of them, led by a Syrian named Eunus (d. c. 132), rose against their owners in 135, and for more than three years they managed to tie down Roman armies in Sicily before they were suppressed. **Second Servile War** (Slave War in Sicily, Second) (104–99 B.C.). The slaves in Sicily again revolted in protest against their harsh treatment. Led by Salvius, Tryphon, and Athenion (presumably they all died in the war), the slaves gained control of most of the open countryside and laid siege to the cities, which were almost subdued by starvation. The first Roman army sent against them was defeated, but the second succeeded in putting down the revolt. **Third Servile War** (Gladiators' War or Spartacus, Revolt of) (73–71 B.C.). This took place in southern Italy and was the largest of the slave revolts. The Thracian slave-gladiator Spartacus (d. 71) and some 70 of his friends escaped from the gladiator training school at Capua and took refuge on Mount Vesuvius. They recruited other gladiators and runaway slaves and other discontents, defeated two Roman armies sent against them, and rapidly overran Italy south of the Apennine Mountains. In 72, Spartacus's army of 40,000 men split in two, with his German and Gallic recruits following another leader, and the rest following Spartacus. The former were routed in Apulia in 72, but Spartacus marched north, planning to flee to Thrace in Greece. His men refused to leave Italy and turned south, plundering as they went. Spartacus retired to southern Italy again, where a Roman army under Marcus Licinius Crassus (115?–53) confronted him at Brundisium (Brindisi) in 71. There Spartacus was killed in battle, and his followers were overwhelmed. After surrendering, about 6,000 of them were crucified, and those who escaped were soon hunted down and killed by Pompey the Great (106–48) and his army.

Seven Oaks Massacre (1816) The Scotch philanthropist Thomas Douglas (1771–1820), fifth earl of Selkirk, who owned a controlling interest in the Hudson Bay Company, decided to establish a colony of Scotch settlers in the fertile Red River basin near present-day Winnipeg, Manitoba. His first settlers arrived in 1812, much to the consternation of the North West Company, the Hudson Bay Company's principal rival, whose fur traders used the region for transporting their goods. The settlers were persuaded to leave in 1815, but a new group arrived and restored the Red River colony the following year. North West Company traders then stirred up their halfbreed Indian allies against the colonists, whose outlying posts and crops were destroyed in June 1816. At a place called Seven Oaks, about 25 colonists confronted their harassers (some 60 strong) to end the destruction; a fight broke out, and 21 colonists were killed. The Red River colony fell into the hands of the North West Company. In response, Douglas hired a group of Swiss mercenaries to capture the chief North West post at Fort William, which they did. The ringleaders of the Seven Oaks Massacre were arrested, and in 1817 colonists were brought back to the Red River. This time they survived and prospered.

Seven Reductions, War of the (1752–56) For a long time Spain and Portugal fought over Banda Oriental (southern Uruguay) along the Río de la Plata, most of which came under Spanish control by 1724. A Spanish-Portuguese agreement (1750) proposed that seven Jesuit-established and -operated *reducciones* or reductions (mission-settlements for the Christianization, protection, and agricultural training of the native Guaraní Indians, whom the Spaniards often tried to exploit as laborers) along what is now the Uruguay River be swapped for Portuguese-founded and -controlled Colonia, an important coastal trading town on the Río de la

Plata. Both the Jesuits and the British, trading partners with the Jesuits and Portuguese, opposed the plan, but only the Jesuits acted, instigating the Guaraní to rebel against their forced immigration to Brazil and thus beginning four years of action by both Portuguese and Spanish troops to subdue them. Four "rebel" Jesuits were ordered to Lisbon for arraignment; by 1759, Portugal's chief minister Sebastião José de Carvalho e Mello (marquês de Pombal) (1699–1782) had dismissed all Jesuits from governmental, educational, and colonial administrations. Spain acquired Colonia in 1777.

Seven Weeks' War (Austro-Prussian War) (1866) To overcome Austrian dominance of the German Confederation and to unite the German states under Prussian hegemony, Otto von Bismarck (1815–98), Prussia's premier, ignored the objections of his king, William I (1797–1888), and provoked war by occupying the duchy of Holstein, administered by Austria under the terms of the treaty after the DANISH-PRUSSIAN WAR OF 1864. This occupation quickly pitted Austria and its allies, Württemberg, Saxony, Hanover, Baden, and other smaller German states, against Prussia and its ally, Italy. Prussian troops overran Saxony, Hanover, Electoral Hesse, and Bohemia, crushing the Austrians at the Battle of Sadowa (Königgrätz) in eastern Bohemia on July 3, 1866. In Italy, Austria was victorious on land at Custozza, where 80,000 Austrians met 120,000 Italians led poorly by Victor Emmanuel II (1820–78), king of Sardinia, and at sea near Lissa (Vis), where the battle involved armored ships for the first time in Europe. Preliminary peace talks began, with Emperor Napoleon III (1808–73) as mediator, which led to the Treaty of Prague on August 23, 1866, ending the war of seven weeks' duration. By the treaty, Austria was excluded from German affairs, Prussia gained control of Schleswig-Holstein, Hanover, Hesse, Nassau, and Frankfurt, and the old German Confederation was replaced by a Prussian-dominated North German Confederation—a prelude to the 1871 declaration of the German (Prussian) Empire after the Franco-Prussian War. Despite Austria's victories in Italy, it was persuaded

by Napoleon to relinquish control of Venetia to the Italians (the Treaty of Vienna). Austria then reorganized its remaining territories as the Austro-Hungarian Empire (1867).

Seven Years' War (1756–63)   Colonial rivalry between Great Britain and France and the continuing struggle for supremacy between Austria and Prussia, begun in the War of the AUSTRIAN SUCCESSION, eventually led to a worldwide conflict fought in Europe between Prussia, Britain, and Hanover on one side and France, Austria, Russia, Saxony, Sweden, and, for a while, Spain on the other; in India and North America between France and Britain (see FRENCH AND INDIAN WAR); and in India between the same latter two enemies. The war, containing more than 30 battles in Europe and overseas, was the last great conflict involving all the great powers of Europe before the FRENCH REVOLUTIONARY WARS. Prussian and Austrian armies did so much of the fighting that the label "Austro-Prussian War of 1756–63" is often encountered. Prussia invaded Saxony in 1756 to begin the war; the Holy Roman Empire (Austria) declared war in 1757 on Prussia's King Frederick II "the Great" (1712–86), whose forces next invaded Bohemia but suffered defeat by the Austrians under Marshal Leopold von Daun (1705–66) at Kolin on June 18, 1757, thus forcing Frederick to raise the Prussian siege of Prague and withdraw from Bohemia. In Saxony, the Prussians under Frederick defeated a French-Austrian force at Rossbach on November 5, 1757; in Silesia, an Austrian army at Leuthen on December 6, 1757; and in Brandenburg, Russian invaders at the bloody Battle of Zorndorf on August 25, 1758. British and Hanoverian armies were victorious against the French at Krefeld on June 23, 1758, and at Minden on August 1, 1759; the latter was the last major French threat to Hanover and to Prussia during the war. Prussia's fortunes, however, declined in 1759 at Maxen, where 12,000 Prussians surrendered to the Austrians, and in a crushing defeat at Kunersdorf, where a 90,000-man Austro-Russian army completely overwhelmed 50,000 Prussians led by Frederick, who was seriously demoralized afterward and considered abdication. The Prussian decline continued into 1760, for the Russians captured Berlin, Frederick's capital. A brief change in fortune occurred with Frederick's costly victory against Daun's troops at the Battle of Torgau on November 3, 1760. But Prussia was in trouble: a 1761 British election threw Prussia's supporters out of office and thus British subsidies to Prussia ended. A change in Russian rulers, however, counterbalanced this; Peter III (1728–62) briefly became czar and supported Prussia; upon Peter's assassination, Russia dropped out of the war. In 1762, Sweden made a separate peace with Prussia, and shortly after the Austrians under Daun lost to Frederick's soldiers at Burkersdorf in Silesia. In the Carnatic area, in southern India, British forces gained control after defeating French troops at Wandiwash in 1760 and seizing Pondicherry in 1761. The British also warred successfully against Spain in Europe, Cuba, and the Philippines in 1762. Nevertheless, for most of the warring countries, peace was being sought because the prolonged conflict had exhausted their resources. By the Treaty of Paris on February 10, 1763, France renounced to Britain its claims in North America and India, and by the Treaty of Hubertusburg, six days later, peace with a return to the status quo was established among Austria, Saxony, and Prussia, which retained Silesia. See also CARNATIC WARS; MYSORE WARS; SPANISH-PORTUGUESE WAR OF 1762.

Shah Jahan, Conquests of (1613–21) For many years the chief military commander of India's Mogul emperor Jahāngīr (1569–1627) was Crown Prince Khurram (1592–1666), his son, who later proclaimed himself Shah Jahan as emperor. Jahāngīr himself fought no wars after his enthronement in 1605; content to be pleasure-loving and idle, he gradually gave way to two undermining influences: a double addiction to alcohol and opium and the power of his Persian wife, Nur Jahan (d. 1645), and her family, who did the actual ruling of the empire while Jahāngīr sat on the throne. The territory of the empire did not grow during Jahāngīr's royalty, but Khurram extended its authority. In 1613, he led

an army against Mewar, which even Akbar (1542–1605) had not been able to conquer (see MOGUL CONQUEST OF RAJASTHAN), and the double force of his army and personality accomplished an accommodation under which the rana (Indian prince) of Mewar became a friendly tributary of the empire, giving up not territory but his son to the court. Mewar's neighbor, Kangra, was attacked and defeated in 1620, accepting tributary status after that date. The troublesome Deccan region also submitted to the imperial authority at Delhi after Khurram's successful campaigns of 1616–17, only later to rebel and suffer subjugation, but not annexation, in 1620–21. Khurram's last military success turned Nur Jahan against him, for she realized that his power and personality would allow her no control after his enthronement. She began to favor a son-in-law and influenced Jahāngīr so effectively that Khurram was forced into rebellion against his father (see SHAH JAHAN'S REVOLT). See also MOGUL CIVIL WAR OF 1607.

Shah Jahan's Revolt (1622–26) In 1622, Persia's Shah Abbas I "the Great" (1557–1628?) began a second and successful attempt to seize Kandahar from the Mogul Empire (his first, in 1605, had failed), and Mogul emperor Jahangir (1569–1627) ordered his son, Crown Prince Khurram (1592–1666), better known later as Shah Jahan, to lead an army from the Deccan region to Afghanistan against Abbas (see MOGUL-PERSIAN WAR OF 1622–23). Aware of the destructive intrigues of the empress, Nur Jahan (d. 1645), against him (see SHAH JAHAN, CONQUESTS OF) and unwilling to leave a power base close to Delhi to allow him control of the throne should his ailing father die, Khurram did not march; instead, he sent messages explaining the necessity to wait out the rainy season. Nur Jahan saw his delay as incipient rebellion, convinced the emperor of this, and engineered a severe reprimand. In 1623, Khurram marched, but toward Agra, not Kandahar; his forces tried unsuccessfully to capture the former court city of Fatehpur Sikri and retreated into the Deccan. An imperial Mogul force under the generalship of Mahabat

Khan (d. 1634), who himself was a rebel against the empress in 1627, pursued Khurram, drove him into Bengal, and then followed him back into the Deccan. Khurram had acquired some followers but no territory. Exhausted and overwhelmed in 1625–26, he yielded completely to his father's demands and was forgiven and made governor of Balaghat in the Deccan. See also MAHABAT KHAN'S INSURRECTION.

Shays's Rebellion (1786–87) Faced with low prices and high taxes in the economic depression following the AMERICAN REVOLUTION, farmers in western Massachusetts demanded relief in the form of paper money, a moratorium in debts, and an end to debt imprisonment. When the state legislature adjourned without granting relief, Daniel Shays (1747?–1825) led an armed rebellion in August 1786, aiming to prevent farm foreclosures in the civil courts. When the farmers threatened to take the federal arsenal at Springfield, Mass., in early 1787, Governor James Bowdoin (1726–90) called out the state militia under General Benjamin Lincoln (1733–1810). The rebels were routed at Petersham and forced to disperse in February 1787. Shays fled to Vermont and later received a pardon. The rebellion gave urgency to revising the Articles of Confederation and to ratification of a new federal constitution.

Shi'ite Rebellion of A.D. 814–19 Shi'ite extremists revolted against the attempt by Abbasid caliph Allah al-Ma'mun (785–833) to end the division in the Islamic world between the Shi'ites (believers in the divine right of Ali ibn Abi Talib [600?–661] and his descendants) and the Sunnites (believers in the divinity of the three caliphs before Ali, the fourth caliph). Rebel Shi'ites, the Alids, occupied the holy cities of Mecca and Medina, seized southern Mesopotamia, and threatened the Muslim capital of Baghdad. Al-Ma'mun's loyal general, Harthma b. Ayan, led the imperial forces to victory against the Alid rebels, whose leader Abu 'l-Saraya (d. 818) was seized and beheaded. To pacify the Alids, al-Ma'mun declared a Shi'ite, Ali ar-Rida (d. 818), his successor. However, Sunnites in Baghdad were an-

gered, proclaimed al-Ma'mun deposed, and elected his uncle, Ibrahim (779–839), an Abbasid related to the third caliph, as the new caliph. Ar-Rida mysteriously died of poisoning, and al-Ma'mun, who had been residing at Merv, returned to Baghdad with many supporters in August 819, and took control of the caliphate, subduing the Alids. See also MUSLIM CIVIL WAR OF A.D. 657–61.

Shimabara Revolt (1637–38) Catholicism had been introduced into Japan by a Portuguese priest in 1549; he was followed by numerous other Christian missionaries, who converted large numbers of Japanese to their faith. The Tokugawa shoguns (military rulers) frequently expelled missionaries and forbade the Japanese to practice Christianity. In 1623, the new shogun reissued all the old anti-Christian decrees, and foreign and Japanese Christians were ruthlessly persecuted, especially on the southern island of Kyushu, where the people had come into contact with the Portuguese and Spanish. Catholicism had taken root very early on the Shimabara peninsula, east of Nagasaki on Kyushu, and on the nearby Amakusa Islands; many Christian converts had been executed in this area. At the end of 1637, thousands of militant Christians rose in open revolt against the oppressive religious, agrarian, and taxation practices of the Tokugawa regime. About 37,000 rebels—men, women and children—withdrew to the abandoned castle of Hara on Shimabara's coast in early 1638, and for three months they withstood a besieging Tokugawa army of some 100,000 troops. A Dutch warship, called in by the Japanese government, bombarded the rebel stronghold. Finally, starving and lacking musket ammunition, the defenders could no longer hold the ramparts: the castle was stormed and captured, and most of those within who were still alive were quickly put to the sword; only 105 were taken. The collapse of the revolt spelled the end of Christianity as an organized religion in Japan.

Shimonoseki "War" (1863–64) The daimyo (lord) of the Choshu clan, whose territory stretched along the northern shores of the strategic Straits of Shimonoseki in Japan, supported the party that advocated expelling all foreigners from the country. On June 26, 1863, two of his ships attacked an American steamer anchored at the entrance to the strait, and in July shore batteries and warships fired upon French and Dutch vessels. In retaliation, an American naval ship sank two Choshu ships, and a French warship burned a small village and destroyed a shore battery. Undismayed, the Choshu batteries continued to fire upon any foreign ship that came within range. In March of the following year the British consul at Yedo or Edo (Tokyo) persuaded his foreign colleagues that force would have to be used to open the straits to foreign ships and to make Japan observe trade treaties it had signed with European powers. They decided to act in concert, and on September 5, 1864, a fleet of 17 ships from France, Great Britain, the Netherlands, and the United States steamed into the Straits of Shimonoseki and for three days systematically destroyed all the batteries on the Choshu coast. The allied commanders then negotiated a treaty that assured free passage and nonfortification of the straits, the right to trade at Shimonoseki, and the payment of a large indemnity. Thereafter the Japanese did not try to get rid of foreigners but rather began to imitate them and learn their superior mechanical and technological skills. See also MEIJI RESTORATION.

Siamese-Burmese War of 1548   Siam or Ayutthaya (Thailand) watched apprehensively the military maneuvers of Burma's King Tabinshwehti (1512–50) of Toungoo (see BURMESE CIVIL WAR OF 1535–46). The encroachment of his troops on Siamese soil was an excuse for a retaliatory attack on Tavoy in southern Burma, thus unleashing an attempt by Tabinshwehti to conquer Siam. Burmese forces, supported by Portuguese mercenaries, marched east through Three Pagodas Pass to Kanchanaburi and to Ayutthaya, the Siamese capital, which was besieged for four months (1548). Dressed as men, Siamese queen Suriyodaya (d. 1548) and her daughter perished fighting; the Siamese king's son Rameshvara (d. 1564) and son-in-law were both

captured, but later freed in return for a safe retreat by the Burmese forces, who had run out of war supplies and failed to take the capital. Depressed by defeat and unable to command his unruly kingdom, Tabinshwehti turned to drinking; in 1550, a Mon revolt erupted in Pegu (Lower Burma), where a Mon prince assassinated Tabinshwehti and proclaimed himself king. Tabinshwehti's brother-in-law, Bayinnaung (1515–81), suppressed the revolt and ascended the throne.

Siamese-Burmese War of 1563–69   Burma's King Bayinnaung (1515–81) wanted to keep the Ayutthayans or Siamese from allying with the Shan states in Upper Burma (he eventually destroyed the power of the Shans and enlarged Burma to approximately its present size). Using as a pretext for an invasion of Siam (Thailand) the refusal of the Siamese king, Mahachakrabarti (d. 1569), to send him a sacred white elephant, Bayinnaung advanced southward, with his troops using cannons atop wooden towers, overran the Sukhotai area (1563), and seized the Siamese capital city of Ayutthaya (1564). Faced with his subjects' opposition to war, Mahachakrabarti negotiated a peace and turned over resistance leaders, including a son, to the Burmese. Mahachakrabarti's son Mahindra (d. 1569) took control of Siam, but when he failed to reconquer the northern provinces from Burma, his father regained control (1568). The Burmese now received the support of Mahachakrabarti's son-in-law, Maha Dhammaraja (d. 1590), "Lord of the White Elephant," whose daughter was consequently held hostage by the grandfather. Bayinnaung responded by sending a huge army into Siam, where it besieged the city of Ayutthaya for ten months. Fierce Siamese resistance was finally overcome on August 30, 1569, when a treasonous monk helped the Burmese enter the city, shortly after Mahachakrabarti's death. Mahindra died as a captive, and Bayinnaung installed Maha Dhammaraja on the throne as his vassal. Thousands of Siamese were deported to Burma as slaves. See also BURMESE-LAOTIAN WAR OF 1564–65.

Siamese-Burmese War of 1584–92   Burma dominated Siam (Thailand) for 15 years after the SIAMESE-BURMESE WAR OF 1563–69. In 1584, Phra Naret (c. 1555–1605), governor of Siam's northern province of Phitsanulok and son of vassal king Maha Dhammaraja (d. 1590), renounced his allegiance to Burma's King Nanda Bayin (d. 1599), son and successor of Bayinnaung (1515–81). A two-pronged Burmese invasion of Siam was launched through Three Pagodas Pass and Chiengmai (northwest Thailand); the invaders were defeated and turned back. In late 1586, three Burmese armies invaded Siam from different directions and advanced to the Siamese capital of Ayutthaya. They invested and attacked the city from January to May 1587, finally being forced to withdraw because of lack of supplies, disease, and Phra Naret's strategies and refusal to capitulate. In 1590, another Burmese invasion failed; Phra Naret assumed the Siamese throne as King Naresuan upon his father's death. Nanda Bayin launched an invasion in 1592 in a final attempt to crush Naresuan and his independence movement; at the Battle of Nong Sa Rai, a large Burmese army led by Crown Prince Minkyizwa (d. 1592) engaged Naresuan and his forces; in a hand-to-hand combat between the two leaders, who rode elephants, the crown prince was slain. The demoralized Burmese then retreated; Siam had finally been liberated from Burmese rule. See also SIAMESE-CAMBODIAN WAR OF 1587.

Siamese-Burmese War of 1593–1600   After the death of Burma's heir apparent at Nong Sa Rai and the withdrawal of Burmese forces from Siam (see SIAMESE-BURMESE WAR OF 1584–92), Siamese king Naresuan advanced into Burma's peninsular area, seizing Tavoy and Tenasserim provinces in 1593. His troops marched north to attack successfully Moulmein and Martaban in 1594. Meanwhile, Naresuan launched an offensive into Cambodia to the east; after savage fighting, the Cambodian capital of Lovek (just north of Phnom Penh) fell, and Naresuan established suzerainty over the country (1594). When Laotian soldiers overran Chiengmai (northwest Thailand) in 1595, Chiengmai's ruler secured the aid of Naresuan in driving out the invaders; afterward the Siamese king took control and made Chiengmai's ruler his vassal. By 1596, Burma's King Nanda Bayin (d. 1599) had been compelled to retreat to Pegu, the Burmese capital, and safeguard it from Siamese attack. Later, when the BURMESE CIVIL WAR OF 1599 erupted, Naresuan mounted another offensive against Pegu, seizing and occupying the city until the Burmese rebels, who had ousted and killed Nanda Bayin, regrouped and defeated the Siamese. See also SIAMESE-CAMBODIAN WAR OF 1593–94.

Siamese-Burmese War of 1607–18   Burma fell into disunity after the destruction of Pegu (see BURMESE CIVIL WAR OF 1599), until Anaukpetlun (d. 1628), ruler of Ava in Upper Burma, sought to reunite the country by capturing the towns of Prome (Pye) in 1607, Toungoo in 1610, and Syriam in 1613 (see BURMESE-PORTUGUESE WAR OF 1613). Anaukpetlun's Burmese forces invaded the Siamese-held areas of Tavoy and Tenasserim in southeastern Lower Burma (1613–14); Tavoy was seized and held for a period; Siamese and Portuguese forces checked the invaders in Tenasserim; and Siam's western borders were restored. At the same time (1614) Burmese invaded the kingdom of Chiengmai (northwest Thailand), seeking to replace Siamese or Ayutthayan suzerainty there with Burmese, and successfully besieged the city of Lampang. Skirmishing continued until 1618, when Burma and Siam signed a treaty that granted the former control of Chiengmai and the latter Tavoy.

Siamese-Burmese War of 1660–62   Seeing an opportunity to regain control of the Burmese-dominated region of Chiengmai (northwest Thailand), King Narai (1632–88) of Ayutthaya or Siam (Thailand) marched his troops into the area, captured several towns, but was repulsed (1660) and forced to withdraw (1661). But Burmese dynastic unrest lured him to try again. After reshuffling his military command, Narai sent 100,000 troops to conquer the area, particularly Lampang, Lamphun, and Chiengmai (the city); in 1662, his men seized and pillaged Chiengmai and routed a Burmese relief force. Narai stationed strong forces along the Burmese border, which brought on a Burmese attack that was repulsed; Narai then marched into Burma, seizing Martaban and Rangoon. When supplies ran out, he was compelled to return home, giving up the territory to the Burmese. See also BURMESE-CHINESE WAR OF 1658–61; THAI WAR OF 1660–62.

Siamese-Burmese War of 1764–69   Burmese king Hsinbyushin (d. 1776), of the Konbaung dynasty, pursued a policy of expansionism at the expense of neighboring countries (see BURMESE-MANIPURI WAR OF 1764). In 1764, his forces marched eastward into Siam (Thailand), seizing the Chiengmai area before invading Laotian territory. The successful campaign then moved south to the Siamese capital city of Ayutthaya, which was besieged and captured in April 1767, thanks mainly to the skillful Burmese general Maha Nawraha, who died shortly before victory. The city was sacked; many of its rich, artistic treasures were destroyed or taken; afterward the Burmese capital was moved south to Thon Buri and then Bangkok. Thousands of captives were carried off as slaves to Burma. Siamese general Phya Taksin (1734–83), whose forces had been defeated at Ayutthaya, had escaped and recruited a new army, which marched on the capital and was victorious in 1768. Taksin, having assumed the Siamese throne (1767), confronted and defeated two rivals for the crown in 1769, subsequently unifying the country again. See also BURMESE-CHINESE WAR OF 1765–69; SIAMESE-VIETNAMESE WAR OF 1769–73.

Siamese-Burmese War of 1775–76   Phya Taksin (1734–82), who had secured the Siamese throne during the SIAMESE-BURMESE WAR OF 1764–69, made an unsuccessful military attempt in 1769 to regain control of Chiengmai (northwest Thailand), which had been seized by the Burmese. Six years later (1775) his invading troops were triumphant; an effort by Burma's King Hsinbyushin (d. 1776) to retake Chiengmai failed the following year.

Siamese-Burmese War of 1785–92   Burma's King Bodawpaya (d. 1819), of the Konbaung dynasty, who had assumed power in 1782 after defeating several rivals, invaded the neighboring coastal kingdom of Arakan to the west in 1784. Arakan was conquered and became a Burmese province; its king was captured; and over 20,000 Arakanese captives were brought to Burma as slaves. Emboldened by his success, Bodawpaya led an army eastward to invade Siam (Thailand), where his troops were generally routed because of his inept leadership. The war continued intermittently, and eventually the Burmese seized control of the coastal regions of Tavoy and Tenasserim (southeast Lower Burma).

Siamese-Cambodian War of 1587   Cambodia's King Sattha (d. 1596) supported Siamese prince Phra Naret (c. 1555–1605) and his declaration of independence from Burma (see SIAMESE-BURMESE WAR OF 1584–92). Troops led by Sattha's brother were provided for Phra Naret's attack on the Burmese in Chiengmai (northwest Thailand) in April 1586. Phra Naret, however, in response to a slight by the brother, had Laotian captives impaled. Upset by Phra Naret's actions, Sattha broke his ties with the Siamese prince and launched an invasion of southern Siam (1587), seizing Prachim (Prachin Buri). Cambodia's requests for aid from Portugal and Manila proved futile. Instead of pursuing the retreating Burmese (they had failed to capture Ayutthaya, the Siamese capital), Phra Naret forced the Cambodians to retreat, retook Prachim, and invaded Cambodia, where he captured Battambang and Pursat (Pouthisat) and advanced as far as the capital, Lovek, before lack of supplies necessitated his withdrawal. He vowed to punish Sattha for breaking the alliance.

Siamese-Cambodian War of 1593–94   Having freed Siam (Thailand) of Burmese control (see SIAMESE-BURMESE WAR OF 1584–92), Siam's King Naresuan (Phra Naret) (c. 1555–1605) sought revenge on Cambodia's King Sattha (d. 1596) (see SIAMESE-CAMBODIAN WAR OF 1587). In May 1593, a Siamese invasion force of some 100,000 men moved eastward into Cambodia, taking the towns of Battambang and Pursat (Pouthisat). At the head of this force, Naresuan pushed on to Lovek, the Cambodian capital, where two other Siamese armies joined forces with him after having captured Siĕmréab, Bassac (Champassak, Laos) and other towns in the north. Despite his failure to obtain Spanish aid in Manila, Sattha refused to capitulate; he imprisoned a Siamese diplomat and began counterattacks against Lovek's besiegers. In July 1594, Lovek fell after a bloody assault. Sattha escaped and took refuge in Luang Prabang (Louangphrabang), where he died in 1596. His brother, Prince Srisuphanma (d. 1618), was imprisoned in Ayutthaya, and Cambodia was put under the rule of a Siamese military governor.

Siamese-Cambodian War of 1603 After arriving in Cambodia in 1596 to help King Sattha (d. 1596), who had already been deposed, Spanish forces killed a usurper to the Cambodian throne and installed a son of Sattha's in 1597. But many Cambodians resented the power wielded by the foreigners, and in mid-1599, the Spanish soldiers at Phnom Penh were attacked and massacred. Afterward three weak, corrupt princes held the throne until the queen mother asked Siam's King Naresuan (c. 1555–1605) to enthrone Prince Srisuphanma (d. 1618), Sattha's brother. In 1603, Srisuphanma returned to Cambodia with a 6,000-man Siamese army; soon overcoming the resistance, he became king as a vassal of Naresuan. See also SIAMESE-CAMBODIAN WAR OF 1593–94.

Siamese-Cambodian War of 1622 After the death of Cambodia's vassal king, Srey Sauryopor (d. 1618), formerly called Prince Srisuphanma, his son and successor Chettha II (d. 1625) proclaimed Cambodia independent from Siamese domination. King Songtham the Just (Intharaja II) (d. 1628) of Ayutthaya or Siam (Thailand) dispatched expeditions by land and by sea to restore Siamese control (1622). The fleet saw no action and soon sailed back to Siam. After deceitful guides led the Siamese army astray and off the good roadways, Cambodian forces dared to attack; the Siamese sustained severe losses in men, horses, and elephants and retreated. After this defeat, Songtham tried in vain to obtain English and Dutch help for another invasion.

Siamese-Cambodian War of 1714–17 In a civil war of succession in 1714, the new Cambodian king, Prea Srey Thomea (fl. 1710s), was overthrown by his uncle, Keo Fa (d. c. 1720), who had been the former king and had help from a Vietnamese army and some Laotian troops in regaining the throne. The ousted king promptly fled to Siam (Thailand), where he requested aid from King Bhumindaraja or Phra Chao Thai Sa (1681–1733), who wanted to offset increasing Vietnamese power in Cambodia. But attempts to restore Prea Srey Thomea as rightful king failed in 1715 and 1716. In 1717, Bhumindaraja sent two large expeditionary forces into Cambodia, the larger via Siĕmréab in the north, the other with naval support along the Gulf of Siam. At the Battle of Banteay Meas, the southern force was crushed by a combined Cambodian and Vietnamese force because the Siamese fleet panicked under attack, took to sea, and was ruined in a storm. The northern Siamese force, however, was victorious, advancing to the Cambodian capital of Udong (north of Phnom Penh). There, in return for his surrender and allegiance to Siam, Keo Fa was allowed to keep his throne; Prea Srey Thomea's cause was given up.

Siamese-Cambodian War of 1831–34 (Siamese-Vietnamese War of 1831–34) After Ang Chan II (1791–1835) regained the Cambodian throne (see CAMBODIAN REBELLION OF 1811–12), Siamese forces moved into Cambodia's northern areas and then southward, defeating the Cambodians at the Battle of Kompong Chang and forcing Ang Chan to flee to Vietnam (1832). The Siamese advanced to

Chau-doc and Vinh-long in southern Vietnam before being confronted by Vietnamese troops and forced to pull back. A general uprising broke out in Cambodia and eastern Laos (under Siamese control) while a 15,000-man Vietnamese army marched against the Siamese (1833) and assisted Ang Chan in returning to Udong, the Cambodian capital (north of Phnom Penh). With the withdrawal of the Siamese, almost total Vietnamese control was exercised over Cambodia. See also SIAMESE-VIETNAMESE WAR OF 1841–45.

Siamese Civil War of 1610–12 (Yamada's Guards' Revolt) In the early 1600s, Japanese fleeing from the repressive Tokugawa shogunate of Japan were welcomed in the Thai kingdom of Ayutthaya or Siam (Thailand), where they established themselves under their compatriot Yamada Nagamasa (d. 1632) as the privileged palace guard at the capital city, Ayutthaya. When Songtham the Just (Intharaja II) (d. 1628) became the Siamese king in 1619, the Japanese guards revolted in support of another aspirant to the throne. Simultaneously a Laotian army invaded from the north, ostensibly to back the guards, and moved into Lop Buri, just north of the Ayutthayan capital. Songtham evicted the Laotians and, after quelling the guards' revolt, allowed the Japanese to maintain their military position in return for ceding their citadel at Phetchabun. See also THAI WARS.

Siamese Civil War of 1630–36 In 1630, the throne of the Thai kingdom of Ayutthaya or Siam (Thailand) was usurped by Phra Chao Prasatthong (d. 1656), a high nobleman and official, after he poisoned former King Songtham the Just (Intharaja II) (d. 1628) and ousted his two sons. A bloody conflict ensued, with numerous factions opposing Prasatthong, who poisoned rival Yamada Nagamasa (d. 1632), leader of the Japanese palace guard in Ayutthaya. Upon the refusal of Japan's Tokugawa shogun to acknowledge his rule, Prasatthong attempted to slaughter the guards, most of whom managed to flee successfully by sea. Some 3,000 persons, including members of the legitimate royal family, were seized and put to death—all in order to ensure Prasatthong's rule. Prasatthong's forces were sent south to crush a rebellion against him in the province of Pattani, on the Malay peninsula (1634–36). They failed completely, and Pattani became virtually autonomous.

Siamese Civil War of 1733 On the death of King Bhumindaraja or Phra Chao Thai Sa (1681–1733) of Siam (Thailand), a fierce struggle for the throne erupted between his second son, Prince Aphai (d. 1733), and the dead king's younger brother, Boromokot (d. 1758), who had the imperial rank of *uparat* (roughly heir apparent); earlier Bhumindaraja had tried to change the royal succession from his brother to Aphai. At first the prince's forces seemed superior, but as Boromokot's troops pushed toward the Thai grand palace, Aphai's troops deserted him, allowing Boromokot to become king and take control of the capital, Ayutthaya. The fleeing Aphai and a brother of his were soon captured in a swamp and killed; Boromokot ruthlessly slaughtered all of his major enemies. After suppressing an attack on the palace by 300 rebel Chinese (1733), the king reigned in peace until his death.

Siamese-Laotian War of 1826–29 Laotian king Chao Anou (1767–1835) wanted to end Siamese hegemony over his city-state of Vien Chang (Vientiane) and thus strengthened his ties with Vietnamese emperor Minh Mang (1792–1841). In 1826, upon hearing a rumor (actually baseless) that a British fleet planned to attack Bangkok, the capital of Siam (Thailand), he mounted a three-pronged invasion, with armies from Vien Chang, Roi Et, and Ubon, marching quickly toward Bangkok on the pretext that he was coming to defend Siam against the British. Soon discovering that Chao Anou sought to liberate his country, the Siamese rallied and drove the Laotian invaders, who had come within a three-day march of Bangkok, back to Korat (Nakhon Ratchasima) and Ubon. In 1827, the bloody seven-day Battle of Nong-Bua-Lamphu was waged, forcing the Laotians to retreat north across the Mekong River. The pursuing Siamese captured and laid waste Vien Chang; Chao Anou took refuge in the jungle while many of his people were carried off as slaves to Siam. In 1828, Chao Anou persuaded the Vietnamese emperor to give him troops to retake his land; most of the soldiers, however, deserted while en route to Vien Chang, where Chao Anou met defeat and fled north to Tran Ninh (Xieng Khouang), whose ruler handed him over to the Siamese to stop an invasion. Brought to Bangkok in a cage, Chao Anou was tortured to death. See also SIAMESE-CAMBODIAN WAR OF 1831–34.

Siamese-Vietnamese War of 1769–73   Cambodia had long been under Siamese suzerainty, but its eastern provinces had been falling under Vietnamese control. In 1769, Cambodia's King Ang Non (d. 1779) was deposed by his brother, who received help from Vietnam and afterward refused to pay tribute to Siam (Thailand). Siamese armies of King Phya Taksin (1734–82) marched east and occupied the Cambodian areas of Siĕmréab and Battambang. In 1770, when the Vietnamese attacked the Siamese towns of Trat and Chanthaburi, Taksin launched a land and sea invasion of Cambodia, seizing Banteay Meas, Phnom Penh, and other places. As the Siamese advanced on the capital at Banteay Pech, the Vietnamese-backed puppet ruler fled, and his brother Ang Non was restored on the throne as a vassal of Siam. But Vietnam again intervened: one force occupied Rach Gia on the Gulf of Siam; another sailed up the Mekong River to Phnom Penh, won a battle there, and restored the puppet on the throne. By 1773, however, the Vietnamese had suffered defeat, and Ang Non once again held the throne in 1775. He checked a Vietnamese attack on him the next year.

Siamese-Vietnamese War of 1831–34   See SIA-MESE-CAMBODIAN WAR OF 1831–34.

Siamese-Vietnamese War of 1841–45   After the failure of Siam (Thailand) to regain hegemony over Cambodia (see SIAMESE-CAMBODIAN WAR OF 1831–34), a Vietnamese-installed queen reigned on the Cambodian throne as her country increasingly came under the yoke of Vietnam. Vietnamese oppression caused a general uprising in 1841, with Cambodians slaughtering their Vietnamese overlords and others, soliciting help from Siam, and requesting Cambodian prince Ang Duong (1796–1860) to return from exile in Bangkok and become king. Siamese king Rama III (d. 1851) sent an army that installed Ang Duong on the Cambodian throne (1841). Vietnam, which had more than 50 garrisons throughout Cambodia, waged a savage four-year war against rural insurgents and Siamese troops, sustaining defeat in general but refusing to withdraw from the country. Finally, in 1845, both sides agreed to a compromise peace, which placed Cambodia under joint Siamese and Vietnamese protection but with a Siamese predominance. In 1848, Ang Duong was formally crowned Cambodia's king.

Siamese Wars   See THAI WARS.

Siberia, Conquest of   (1581–98)   The Cossack Yermak Timofeyevich (d. 1584), leader of a gang of thieves who plundered the Russian countryside, was pursued for murder by government troops, fled up the Volga River, and was hired by the Stroganov merchants to protect their western Siberian holdings menaced by Tatars (Tartars). With about 850 Cossacks, Yermak set out on September 1, 1581, advancing up rivers, across the Ural Mountains, and to the Tatar khanate of Sibir by the spring of 1582. The Cossacks, using guns and cannons, triumphed over the numerically superior Tatars, armed with bows and arrows, and seized their capital, Kashlyk (Sibir), in western Siberia. Czar Ivan IV "the Terrible" (1530–84), at first opposed to involvement in Siberia, was excited by Yermak's success; he gave Yermak a pardon and welcomed his Cossack envoys in Moscow. Troops sent by the czar aided Yermak, but the Tatar leader (khan) sent forces from the south that attacked and annihilated Yermak and a band of Cossacks in August 1584. According to legend, Yermak drowned in the Irtysh River while swimming across in flight, weighted down by a coat of armor, a gift from the czar. In 1586, Russian forces secured control of the Sibir khanate, but the Tatars persisted in raiding into Russian territory and were not completely subdued in the khanate—that is, Siberia—until 1598.

Sicilian-Byzantine War of 1147–58   The ambition of Norman king Roger II (1095–1154) of Sicily rendered him the scourge of the 12th-century Mediterranean world. By making Sicily dominant over the former Norman states of Apulia, Calabria, and Capua, he upset the papacy's balance-of-power politics, thwarted the Italian ambitions of the Holy Roman Emperor, and threatened the western holdings of the Byzantine Empire. All became his enemies, but Sicily warred chiefly against Manuel I Comnenus (1120?–80), the Byzantine emperor. Roger craftily backed favorable factions in papal politics and aided rebels in the Holy Roman Empire to prevent an Empire-Byzantine alliance. During 1147–48, he invaded Corfu and Neapolis, laid waste Euboea, and plundered Thebes. Luck played a role, too: the death of King Conrad III (1093–1152) of Germany thwarted a planned Empire-Byzantine campaign against Sicily. Instead, the papacy and the Holy Roman Empire allied (1153), and Emperor Frederick I Barbarossa (c. 1125–90) threatened to invade Sicily. Roger's death halted the invasion, but his policy was continued by his son William I (d. 1166), who offered peace to Manuel, was refused, and then deprived the Byzantines of a war fleet by making peace with Venice. With papal help, Manuel invaded Italy, seized Capua (1155), but suffered total defeat at Brindisi (1156). The pope was compelled to make a separate peace (1157) and invested William as ruler of Sicily, Apulia, Capua, Naples, Amalfi, Salerno, and the Marsi. In that year William's troops ravaged the coasts of the Greek empire, forcing a peace (1158) upon Manuel and a Sicilian alliance with the papacy against Frederick, who still wanted land and power in Italy. See also LOMBARD LEAGUE, WARS OF THE; NORMAN-BYZANTINE WARS.

Sicilian-Byzantine War of 1170–71   The expansionist policies of the Norman rulers of Sicily persisted under its last Norman king, William II (1154–89). Sicily's special enemy continued to be Byzantine emperor Manuel I Comnenus (1120?–80). In this war, William played an ancillary role, aiding the Venetians, who in 1170 were driven completely out of the Aegean, but were determined to reverse this. William also allied with Genoa to keep its war fleet from Byzantine control. His secondary role was dictated by an offer from Manuel for a dynastic marriage to his daughter; but when Manuel withdrew the offer (1172) and turned instead to the prince of the Holy Roman Empire, William aided the Venetians, who had been victorious over the Byzantines at Ragusa (Dubrovnik) and Chios in 1171, by supporting an abortive action at Ancona in 1173. The war thereafter dwindled to a draw and ceased in 1177. William, however, was not satisfied; allying with the Holy Roman Empire and gaining England as a distant ally by marrying Joan (1165–99), daughter of King Henry II (1133–89), he began in 1177 preparations for a major military campaign for the future (see SICILIAN-BYZANTINE WAR OF 1185).

Sicilian-Byzantine War of 1185   After the death of Byzantine emperor Manuel I Comnenus (1120?–80), who was Norman Sicily's traditional enemy, a succession dispute broke out in the Byzantine Empire, ending in the dethronement and murder of Alexius II Comnenus (1168?–83) by his uncle, Andronicus I Comnenus (1110?–85). Always anxious to expand his territory, Sicily's King William II (1154–89) sent some 80,000 troops across the Balkans, capturing Durazzo (Durrës, Albania) and Salonika, then marching to the outskirts of Constantinople (Istanbul), the Byzantine capital. Immediately peace negotiations began, but the Sicilians broke faith by attacking during them, so greatly angering the Byzantines that they defeated the huge Norman army, which retreated westward, only to lose at Salonika. Although William planned another campaign, it was postponed; after William's death, his Sicilian throne passed through his aunt to her husband, the future Holy Roman Emperor Henry VI (1165–97), who was too involved in securing his inheritances in Sicily and Italy to be concerned with Constantinople. See also SICILIAN VESPERS, WAR OF THE.

Sicilian Vespers, War of the (1282–1302) Responding to the Sicilian rebels' request for help against the ruling Angevin French (see SICILIAN VESPERS REBELLION AND MASSACRE), King Pedro III (1239–85) of Aragon led an expedition to Sicily in 1282 and was proclaimed king of Sicily by the rebels. Charles I (1226–85), Angevin French king of Naples and Sicily, who was then in Calabria in southern Italy planning an expedition against Constantinople (he hoped to set up an Angevin empire in the East), rushed to Sicily, where his forces became engaged in battle against Sicilian-Aragonese forces. The Sicilian-Aragonese admiral Roger de Loria (1245?–1304) won important naval victories against the Angevins off Messina in 1283 and Naples in 1284. His fleet also defeated the French fleet of King Philip III (1245–85), who had entered the war in full support of Charles (see ARAGONESE-FRENCH WAR OF 1284–85). The war lasted for 20 years, with the Angevin kings of Naples battling the Aragonese kings of Sicily for possession of Sicily. By the Treaty of Anagni in 1295, King James II (1260?–1327) of Aragon, son of Pedro III, relinquished control of Sicily and in recompense was made king of Sardinia and Corsica by the pope (the papacy backed the Angevin claim to Sicily). However, the Sicilians rebelled and crowned James's brother, Frederick II (1272–1337), who continued the war against the Angevins until securing the Peace of Caltabellotta in 1302. The pope and the Angevin king of Naples recognized Frederick as king of Sicily.

Sicilian Vespers Rebellion and Massacre (1282) Sicilians chafed under the oppressive Angevin French rule of Charles I (1226–85), king of Naples and Sicily (the Two Sicilies). When some Sicilians attending vespers at a church near Palermo, Sicily, on Easter Monday, March 30, 1282, assaulted and killed several insulting French soldiers, a rebellion broke out in Palermo that spread throughout Sicily. During the night of March 30–31, 1282, Sicilians massacred about 2,000 French inhabitants of Sicily and then turned to the Aragonese and their king, Pedro III (1239–85), Charles's rival for the Sicilian throne, for help (see SICILIAN VESPERS, WAR OF THE).

Sierra Leonean Civil War of 1991– Linked to the National Patriotic Front of Liberia (NPFL), a rebel movement known as the Revolutionary United Front (RUF) sought to overthrow the republican government of Sierra Leone in West Africa, launching attacks from bases in neighboring Liberia in 1991 (see LIBERIAN CIVIL WAR OF 1989–97). An interstate border war ensued as well between Liberian rebels under Charles Taylor (1948–) and Sierra Leonean troops. Territory seized by RUF guerrillas near Pujehun in southern Sierra Leone was later (1994) recaptured by government troops. The guerrillas continued their attacks, killing over 50 civilians at Telu, razing villages near Bo, and bringing retaliatory attacks on them near Kenema (August 1994). Thousands of Sierra Leoneans fled to safety in neighboring Guinea. In 1995, President Valentine E.M. Strasser (1966–), whose troops had overthrown Sierra Leone's government in a violent coup (1992), vainly sought a peace agreement with the RUF. Strasser was later ousted in a bloodless military coup, and that same year (1996) Ahmed Tejan Kabbah (1932–) won the presidency in democratic elections, returning Sierra Leone to civilian rule. Kabbah negotiated and signed a short-lived peace settlement with the RUF (November 1996); at least 10,000 persons had been killed and over a million others left homeless in five years of civil war. Kabbah was ousted in May 1997, when mutinous troops attacked and fought peacekeeping Nigerian troops stationed in Freetown, Sierra Leone's capital, to defend the government against rebel militias. A military junta led by Major Johnny Paul Koroma took control of the country, which was plunged into violence and anarchy. Nigeria sent naval ships and troops to try to restore Kabbah, who had fled the country. The Economic Community of West African States (ECOWAS) applied sanctions in an effort to force Sierra Leone to restore democracy. In February 1998, Nigerian forces bombarded and seized Freetown, sending the ruling junta leaders in flight to Liberia. Kabbah returned a month later when a coalition of West African peacekeepers (largely Nigerian troops) had calmed much of the country. Resistance came from the interior Kono district, where RUF rebels began killing and pillaging in April 1998; thousands of persons fled to Guinea to escape the rebels, who killed more than 3,000 persons in an attack on Freetown (February 1999) as they attempted to free a rebel leader. Nigeria said its troops would remain in Sierra Leone for now (March 1999).

Sikh Golden Temple, Siege of the (1984) The majority of the inhabitants of India's Punjab state are Sikhs, a monotheistic sect combining Hindu and Islamic elements. While the Sikhs' Akali Dal party pressed the Indian government for greater political and religious autonomy for Punjab, Sikh extremists carried out a campaign of terrorism and murder throughout the region. Sikh civil disobedience in the city of Amritsar, Punjab, turned violent, causing the Indian army (some 12,000 strong) to be sent there in early June 1984; the Sikhs' holiest shrine, the Golden Temple (Harmandir) in Amritsar, was reportedly a hideout for militants and terrorists. On June 6, 1984, the army stormed and seized the Golden Temple complex, whose defenders fired on troops with machine guns and antitank rockets; more than 500 Sikhs and 55 troops were killed and about 1,500 Sikhs were captured. Immediately afterward the army raided other Sikh places of worship in Punjab; active rebel resistance ceased. The Akali Dal party protested the army action.

Sikh War, First (1845–46) After 1818, the sole rival to British control in India was the young Sikh kingdom of the Punjab, with a huge army of Khalsas ("the pure": soldier-saints) numbering 100,000. Considered too powerful to assail, the Punjab under Ranjit Singh (1781–1839) was left alone by the British, who, however, were upset in 1838 that Ranjit Singh neither sent troops nor permitted their passage to the British in Afghanistan (see AFGHAN WAR, FIRST). Weakness in the Punjab after Ranjit Singh's death caused the British to provoke hostilities. They first conquered Sind on the Punjab border in 1843, then moved troops toward that border in 1844, and in the next year seized Lahore within three months. An 1846 treaty cost the Punjab Kashmir and all fertile lands between the Beas and Sutlej Rivers. **Second Sikh War** (1848–49). A spirit of national independence among the Sikhs and the British desire to control all of India combined to provoke another war, which began as a national Sikh revolt. The British troops fared badly in 1848 and lost again at Chilianwala in early 1849, but within two months they had won all of the Punjab—the granary region of the British Empire and, later, the heartland of Pakistan. The British ruled as benevolent despots, bearing "the white man's burden"; the Sikhs, to avoid worse treatment from the Muslims, chose to stay loyal to the empire.

Silesian War, First (1740–42) In 1740, King Frederick II "the Great" (1712–86) of Prussia, heir to Brandenburg territories and privileges, made a very shaky dynastic claim to Silesia, then a part of Bohemian Crown lands. His claim was immediately opposed by Maria Theresa (1717–80), Hapsburg queen of Hungary and Bohemia. Attempting to negotiate the claim, Frederick offered Maria Theresa a military alliance in exchange for Silesia (a region now divided between the Czech Republic and Poland) and the Brandenburg vote to elect her husband Holy Roman emperor; his offer refused, he led 40,000 troops into Silesia in 1740 and, with his army outnumbering the Austrians 10 to one, gained full control within seven weeks. Maria responded by sending 20,000 soldiers in 1741; Frederick's superior infantry defeated them at Mollwitz in the only major battle of the war. Although the larger Austrian cavalry at first routed Frederick's and pushed him into flight, Prussian infantry resisted five heavy charges to win what is often regarded as the opening battle of the pan-European War of the AUSTRIAN SUCCESSION. During this larger war, Austria made a separate peace with Prussia at Breslau in 1742, with England as mediator; Frederick gained almost all of Silesia. **Second Silesian War** (1744–45). Made aware of a secret coalition involving Austria, England, Holland, Sardinia, and Saxony, an alliance to deprive him of both Silesia and his inheritance, Frederick invaded Bohemia in 1744 with 80,000 troops. He was successful in capturing Prague in early September 1744, but his luck turned around, and an effective Austrian army forced him to withdraw 100 miles northeast into Silesia, where his troops won three historically important battles in 1745 at Hohenfriedeberg, Hennersdorf, and Kesseldorf to profoundly influence the War of the Austrian Succession. By the Treaty of Dresden in 1745, Frederick's Silesian acquisitions during the First Silesian War were confirmed, but the greater war was continued. **Third Silesian War.** See SEVEN YEARS' WAR.

Simnel's Rebellion (1486–87)   Among King Henry VII's (1457–1509) enemies, his queen, Elizabeth of York (1465–1503), daughter of Edward IV (1442–83), was often ferociously anti-Lancastrian (see ROSES, WARS OF THE). With her sister and John de la Pole (1464–87), she had Lambert Simnel (c. 1475–1525) trained to impersonate Edward, earl of Warwick, a Yorkist imprisoned in the Tower of London. Introduced to Yorkist Ireland in 1486, Simnel gathered strong support and was crowned king. Simnel returned to England in 1487 with several thousand mercenaries led by Pole and paid by Burgundy. Royal troops killed Pole and captured Simnel. Henry pardoned him. Legend states that Simnel became a scullion in the royal kitchens.

Sinai War   See ARAB ISRAELI WAR OF 1956.

Sino-Burmese Wars   See   BURMESE-CHINESE WARS.

Sino-French War of 1883–85   Since the early 1860s, the French had slowly expanded their sphere of influence in Cochin China (southern Vietnam), Annam (central Vietnam), and Cambodia, all of which were nominally part of the Chinese Empire. In 1882, the king of Annam called upon the Chinese for help in stopping French encroachments on his kingdom. The following April French forces seized Hanoi, the chief city of Tonkin (northern Vietnam), which was under Annamese control; some months later Annam's king was forced to sign a treaty making his kingdom a French protectorate. Chinese troops were sent to Tonkin to assist the native armies against the invading French. Meanwhile, French naval forces moved against the Chinese port of Foochow (Minhow) and destroyed enemy naval ships and land fortifications in 1884. Chinese forts on Formosa (Taiwan) held out against French attacks until 1885, when they surrendered. In Tonkin, the French suffered a severe defeat after initial success and then withdrew from the area. However, neither side wanted to continue this undeclared war, and a peace was negotiated in the Treaty of Tientsin (Tianjin), which was signed on June 9, 1885. China recognized the French agreement with Annam and evacuated its troops from Tonkin; France returned Formosa and the nearby Pescadores Islands, which it had occupied, to China. See also FRENCH INDOCHINA WAR OF 1882–83.

Sino-Indian Border Dispute (1959–62)   Since gaining independence in 1947, India had claimed that its borders with China were those established by the British, but the Chinese took the position that borders drawn by an imperialistic power are illegal and should be renegotiated. The disputed areas were in the Aksai-Chin plateau, which India insisted was part of Ladakh, in eastern Kashmir, and along the McMahon Line in the Northwest Frontier Agency locale. In the late 1950s, the Chinese constructed a road across the Aksai-Chin plateau to western Tibet. The Indians were unaware of this until they sent troops to the area in 1959 and found the Chinese military already entrenched there. Inevitably incidents of serious fighting between the two sides occurred. Efforts to negotiate a settlement failed. In 1962, the Indian government ordered its troops to cross the line controlled by the Chinese. China protested, and when the Indians refused to return to their side of the line, the Chinese army attacked. The Indians withdrew after being badly beaten. China then proclaimed a cease-fire and withdrew several miles behind the line established on November 7, 1959.

Sino-Indian War of A.D. 648–49   Friendly diplomatic relations between the Chinese court and the Indian kingdom of Kanauj were established in 641. In 647, Emperor T'ai Tsung (Taizong) (600–649) of China dispatched a delegation to call on the Indian king. When it arrived, the delegation discovered that the former king was dead and that a usurper, Arjuna (fl. mid-600s), had gained the throne. The new ruler appropriated the gifts and tried to kill all the Chinese officials. The ambassador and one colleague managed to escape and made their way to Nepal, where they raised a sizable army reinforced with Chinese cavalry. Ambassador Wang Hsuan Tze (fl. mid-600s) led this army into Kanauj, besieged and then stormed the capital, took the usurper prisoner, and marched him back to the Chinese capital of Ch'ang-an (Sian, Xi'an) in chains.

Sino-Japanese War of 1894–95   In June 1894, a revolt by the Tonghak Society broke out in southern Korea against the government and the monarchy, which promptly appealed to both China and Japan (rivals for predominance in Korea) for help in squashing it. Chinese and Japanese troops were sent to Korea but would not withdraw when the revolt was quelled. In July 1894, the Japanese attacked the palace at Seoul, seized the royal family, and instituted a new government, which immediately repudiated all Korean treaties with China and asked the Japanese to remove Chinese troops from the country. After several clashes on land and sea, Japan and China declared war on each other on August 1, 1894. The Chinese were defeated at Pyongyang and soon were driven from the Korean peninsula. The

opposing navies met at the Battle of the Yalu River (near its mouth), where the Japanese severely damaged the Chinese fleet while suffering some damage themselves (September 17, 1894). The Japanese followed up this victory by capturing Port Arthur (Lü-shun) at the tip of the Liaotung (Liaodong) peninsula (northeastern China) on November 21, 1894, and by winning the naval and land Battle of Weihaiwei in Shantung (Shandong) on February 12, 1895. Defeated at every turn, China sued for peace in March 1895. The terms of the Treaty of Shimonoseki were harsh—China was forced to cede Formosa (Taiwan) and the Pescadores Islands to Japan, recognize the independence of Korea, open four more ports to Japanese merchants, and pay a huge indemnity—but they would have been harsher if Russia, France, and Germany had not intervened and prevented the cession of territory on China's mainland.

Sino-Japanese War of 1937–45   For years the Japanese had been replacing the Russians and Chinese as the dominant foreign influence in Manchuria (northeast China) and had set up a puppet state there called Manchoukuo. The Japanese had also extended their influence into the Chinese provinces north of the Great Wall, and Generalissimo Chiang Kai-shek (1887–1975) feared to oppose them, for he knew they had superior weapons and equipment. In July 1937, Chinese and Japanese troops exchanged shots at the Marco Polo Bridge north of Peking (Beijing). Both sides tried to negotiate a settlement, but the affair could not be localized. Other clashes occurred, and soon an undeclared war was raging. The Japanese moved swiftly. Bombers from Manchoukuo pounded the northern Chinese cities. Japan's fleet bombarded Shanghai, which the Chinese defended valiantly. When this city's fate appeared certain, the Chinese dismantled their factories there and moved their machinery, piece by piece, far into the interior. Nanking, China's capital, fell in December 1937 (see PANAY INCIDENT), and Hankow (Hankou) became the new capital. The Japanese razed much of Nanking (Nanjing), raping thousands of women and killing upwards of 200,000 Chinese civilians (see NANKING, SACK OF). The following year Canton (Guangzhou) and Hankow were captured, and the capital moved again to Chungking (Chongqing) in the mountains above the Yangtze (Chang) River gorges. By the end of 1938, the Japanese occupied all the coastal ports and controlled the railroad lines and major cities of China. Then a stalemate developed that lasted until 1941, when the Japanese expanded their "Co-prosperity Sphere" into Southeast Asia and when the United States entered the war (see WORLD WAR II IN THE PACIFIC). When the Burma Road and other supply routes were closed by the Japanese, the Allies, mostly Americans, flew supplies and war materiel to Chungking from India "over the hump" of the Himalayan Mountains (see WORLD WAR II IN CHINA). With a newly trained air force, the Chinese, assisted by U.S. planes, began bombing Japanese strongholds. In the north Chinese communist guerrillas had been harassing the Japanese throughout the occupation by ambushing convoys, attacking small garrisons, and blowing up bridges and rail links. The Japanese were never able to occupy the Chinese countryside nor could they induce many Chinese to participate in puppet governments. After Russia entered the war on August 8, 1945, its armies swept into Japanese-held Manchuria and liberated it, and by the time Japan formally surrendered on September 2, 1945, many of the coastal areas of China had been retaken. Japan had failed in its grand design to dominate the Far East, while the Chinese had failed to resolve their fundamental political differences (see CHINESE CIVIL WAR OF 1945–49). See also BURMA CAMPAIGN; WORLD WAR II.

Sino-Korean War of A.D. 610–14   In the 600s, the Korean peninsula was divided into three kingdoms, the two northernmost of which, Kokuryo and Paekche, had had close relations with China and had once been tributaries. Chinese emperor Yang Ti (Yang Di) (569–618) of the Sui dynasty was determined to reestablish this relationship and sent a message to the Korean king of Kokuryo demanding that he recognize China as his overlord. The king

refused, and Yang Ti retaliated by ordering his chief general to conquer the kingdom. Two Chinese invasions were driven back, but the third, led by the emperor himself, was more successful. Yang Ti had just about completed his conquest when he learned that a rebellion had broken out at Loyang, his capital, and he rushed back to raise the siege there. Yang Ti was forced to flee to southern China, where he was later killed.

Sino-Korean War of A.D. 645–47   Chinese emperor T'ai Tsung (Taizong) (600–649) of the T'ang dynasty wanted to expand his empire into the Korean peninsula. In 645 he led a large army into the northern Korean kingdom of Kokuryo, where he won several battles and seized a number of cities, but he was unable to crush the main Korean army before winter set in and compelled him to return home. Two years later T'ai Tsung attempted again to subjugate Kokuryo and again was forced to withdraw.

Sino-Korean War of A.D. 660–68   On the Korean peninsula, war broke out when the northern kingdoms of Kokuryo and Paekche combined forces to invade their longtime rival in the south, the kingdom of Silla. The Sillans appealed to the Chinese emperor Kao Tsung (Gao Zong) (628–83) for help, which was readily sent because of the emperor's desire to conquer the peninsula. A Chinese army marched through Manchuria into Kokuryo, and a naval force attacked along Paekche's coast. In 662 and 663, Japan intervened on behalf of Paekche, but its land and sea forces were defeated; the Chinese navy destroyed the Japanese fleet. Paekche was conquered and made part of Silla, which accepted Chinese suzerainty. The Kokuryos stubbornly resisted conquest by the Chinese and Sillans until their capital was captured in 668. Silla was enlarged to include the area south of the Taedong River, and most of Kokuryo was annexed by China.

Sino-Tibetan War of A.D. 641   In 634, the Tibetan king Srong-brtsan-sgam-po (c. 608–50) sent an emissary to the Chinese emperor T'ai Tsung

(597–649), who received him with great courtesy. Four years later T'ai Tsung reciprocated by sending a group of high officials to visit Srong-brtsan-sgam-po, who mistook this act of friendship to mean that the Chinese feared him or wanted his help. He arrogantly demanded a Chinese imperial princess for a wife, and his request was refused. In 641, Srong-brtsan-sgam-po invaded China at the head of a large army. His forces were no match for the well-trained Chinese frontier soldiers, who defeated his troops and drove the Tibetans back to their mountains. Once he defeated Srong-brtsan-sgam-po, T'ai Tsung magnanimously gave his former foe an imperial princess.

Sino-Tibetan War of A.D. 763–821   The Tibetans took advantage of internal difficulties within the Chinese Empire to continually invade its western provinces. In one early raid they succeeded in reaching the capital at Ch'ang-an (Sian, Xi'an), which they seized and sacked. They spread terror all along the frontier with wanton destruction, burning, and killing. Chinese armies sometimes defeated them, but the Tibetans then retreated to their mountain fortresses and waited to strike again. In 798, the Chinese T'ang emperor concluded an alliance with a Muslim chieftain in the west and gained the support of Nanchao (a Thai kingdom) against the Tibetans. With the help of these powerful allies, the Tibetans were eventually decisively defeated and in 821 were forced to agree to a treaty of peace with China.

Sino-Tibetan War of 1750–51   For centuries the Chinese emperors had supported the Dalai Lamas, the spiritual leaders of Tibet, as a wise way to prevent the rise of a military power on their western frontier. By the early part of the 18th century they had established two representatives, called *ambans*, at Tibet's capital of Lhasa. In 1750, the ambans arranged the murder of the Tibetan regent, and the people were so angry they in turn murdered all the Chinese living in Lhasa. Emperor Chien Lung (Qian-Long) (1711–99) dispatched a Chinese army to the mountainous Tibetan kingdom to restore order. They found the going hard but did manage to crush the resistance. Chinese authority was reestablished by giving the ambans control over the Dalai Lama's political actions and a say in identifying his successor. The Chinese also gave greater support to the Panchen Lama of Tashilumop, the second-highest religious figure in Tibet, to act as a check against the Dalai Lama.

Sino-Vietnamese War of 1979   Although communist China had backed North Vietnam in its struggle against South Vietnam and the United States (see VIETNAM WAR), the Chinese and Vietnamese were traditional enemies; tensions between the two increased when Vietnam strengthened its ties with the Soviet Union, invaded Laos and Cambodia (Kampuchea) in late 1978, and expelled Chinese living in Vietnam. On February 17, 1979, some 120,000 well-equipped Chinese troops crossed the border into northern Vietnam in several places and seized control of several towns; they penetrated 25 miles into Vietnamese territory, encountering stiff resistance. Divisions from Vietnamese occupying forces in Cambodia arrived to reinforce the resistance, which was unable, however, to prevent the Chinese capture of Lang Son, a vital center in Vietnam's northern provinces, on March 3, 1979. About the same time, a separate Chinese force reached the coastal town of Quang Yen, some 100 miles from Hanoi, after several days of fierce fighting against Vietnamese units. Meanwhile, Vietnamese counteroffensives across the border into China's Yünnan province were repulsed. Declaring its punitive military operation against Vietnam a success, China began withdrawing its forces about March 6, 1979, and within two weeks they were all back on Chinese territory. Subsequently, there were many exchanges of fire along the Chinese-Vietnamese border and numerous talks to reach an accord, but no treaty or settlement was concluded.

Sioux War of 1862–64   Poor hunting grounds remained for the Sioux Indians after they ceded lands east of the Red and Big Sioux Rivers in Minnesota and Iowa; they became increasingly hostile to white settlers and traders, many of whom encroached on Indian territory and were unscrupulous in their dealings. Suddenly, in August 1862, a band of Sioux warriors under Chief Little Crow (1803?–63) ambushed and destroyed an army detachment from Fort Ridgely on the upper Minnesota River and then besieged the fort itself; whites were massacred at New Ulm, Minn., when the Sioux attacked the settlement on August 24, 1862. Minnesota's Governor Henry H. Sibley (1811–91) raised a volunteer militia force at Fort Snelling and set out to punish the Sioux, who had created panic by their barn burnings, slaughter of men, women, and children, and destruction of crops. At Wood Lake in what is now North Dakota, Sibley decisively defeated Little Crow (September 23, 1862), who escaped westward but returned the next year and was shot dead by a Minnesota farmer. Earlier, 307 captive Indians were sentenced to death; most had their sentences commuted, but 38 were hanged on December 26, 1862, in the largest mass execution in U.S. history. Meanwhile, a large military operation was begun by Sibley in cooperation with General Alfred Sully (1821–79). Sibley and his men were victorious against Sioux bands in North Dakota (July 1863), and Sully was, too, in a simultaneous but separate campaign. The latter led another expedition that marched into the Badlands and crushed a large Sioux force at Killdeer Mountain (July 28, 1864); it then swept westward to the Yellowstone River, killing those of the Sioux who decided to stand and fight, before returning to the newly established Fort Rice near present-day Bismarck, N. Dak.

Sioux War of 1865–68 As more and more wagon trains crossed the Great Plains and miners moved into present-day Colorado and Montana, the Oglala or Dakota Sioux Indians became increasingly belligerent toward the white trespassers on their hunting grounds. They constantly harassed U.S. Army units sent to build forts to protect the Bozeman Trail, a shortcut from Fort Laramie in Wyoming to the gold mines in Montana. In 1866, the Sioux ambushed and slaughtered 83 soldiers ordered to rescue a besieged working party (see FETTERMAN MASSACRE). The Sioux were expert horsemen and sharpshooters, and their tactics were to attack unexpectedly and then disappear. There were so many incidents of Indian raids and depredations (see WAGON BOX FIGHT) that the citizenry became aroused, and in 1867 the U.S. Congress established an Indian Peace Commission to stop the fighting. The following year Chief Red Cloud (1822–1909) agreed to a peace treaty, the terms of which stipulated that the U.S. Army abandon the forts on the Bozeman Trail and the trail itself. In turn, the Sioux would relinquish some of their territory and move to a reservation by 1876. All this was done, and the Sioux were relatively peaceful for several years.

Sioux War of 1876–77 By 1876, gold had been discovered in the Black Hills (southwestern South Dakota), a region the Sioux Indians considered sacred and the U.S. government had promised to respect. Although it tried, the U.S. Army could not keep white prospectors out of the area; the Sioux's legitimate grievances against the whites increased. Many roving Indian bands refused to go by the government deadline of February 1, 1876, to the reservations set aside for them. A military expedition was sent out against them. One column under General George Crook (1829–90) destroyed the village of Sioux chief Crazy Horse (1849?–77), but shortly afterward it was defeated by the Indians. Crook retired briefly to obtain reinforcements and then moved north again. Meanwhile, another column under General Alfred Howe Terry (1827–90) was advancing westward from Dakota; it included the Seventh Cavalry led by Colonel George Armstrong Custer (1839–76). When a large Indian band was reported on the Rosebud River (southeastern Montana), the cavalry were sent ahead as scouts, but Custer disregarded his orders and pursued the Indians south to the Little Bighorn River. There, not waiting for reinforcements and unaware or heedless of the numerical superiority of the Indians (about 2,500 Sioux and Cheyenne warriors under Chiefs Sitting Bull [1834–90], Gall [1840?–94], and

Crazy Horse), Custer decided to attack immediately and vaingloriously. He divided his command into three units, sending two units farther upstream to encircle and attack the Indians and led the third unit of 266 soldiers in a direct charge on the morning of June 25, 1876. The Indians surrounded Custer on a hill and killed him and every one of his men (later called "Custer's Last Stand"). The two other units failed to relieve Custer; they were attacked and forced to retreat but were saved from annihilation by the arrival of Terry and his troops. Terry and Crook continued their campaign against the Indians, especially the Sioux, with vigor. Crazy Horse was defeated and surrendered in 1877; he was presumably killed while trying to escape. Sitting Bull and Gall and other warriors fled to Canada, and most of the other Sioux were either slain or captured and forced to settle on reservations. In 1881, both Sitting Bull and Gall returned, surrendered, and were pardoned.

Sioux War of 1890–91 (Messiah War) Life was not easy for the Sioux and other Indians settled on reservations in the Dakotas and Montana. Crops failed, there was much disease and poverty, and pressure to sell land to the whites mounted year by year in the 1880s. To help make life bearable, many of the Sioux turned to a new mystical religion that predicted that an Indian messiah would come in the spring of 1891 and would unite all the Indians in an earthly paradise. Believers practiced a ghost dance that produced trances, visions, and mass frenzy. Indian agents for the U.S. government grew alarmed at these practices. When the military was called in to stop the dances, the Sioux rebelled in anger. At Grand River, Chief Sitting Bull (1834–90) was shot dead by Indian police for resisting arrest. Two weeks later, on December 29, 1890, the U.S. Seventh Cavalry fought and defeated the Sioux on the Black Hills reservation at Wounded Knee Creek (South Dakota); more than 200 Indian men, women, and children were massacred; the cavalry had gotten its revenge for its defeat at Little Bighorn (see SIOUX WAR OF 1876–77). After a few more skirmishes, the Sioux surrendered on January 16, 1891. This was the

last major Indian conflict, and like all the others it ended in defeat for the Indians.

Six-Day War (1967) Egypt's President Gamal Abdel Nasser (1918–70) demanded (and obtained) the removal of the United Nations emergency force (UNEF) from Egyptian territory in May 1967. Shortly afterward, he ordered a shipping blockade of the Strait of Tiran, effectively closing the Israeli port of Elat on the Gulf of Aqaba. At this time Syrian, Egyptian, and Israeli forces had mobilized along their respective borders, where guerrilla raids had taken place frequently since the end of the ARAB-ISRAELI WAR OF 1956. Suddenly, on June 5, 1967, Israeli warplanes attacked and bombed two dozen Arab airfields, destroying more than 400 Egyptian, Syrian, and Jordanian planes on the ground. Israeli land forces invaded the Sinai peninsula, Jerusalem's Old City, Jordan's West Bank, the Gaza Strip, and the Golan Heights and occupied these areas when the war ended with a United Nations–sponsored cease-fire on June 10, 1967. See also ARAB-ISRAELI WAR OF 1973; JORDANIAN CIVIL WAR OF 1970–71.

Skagerrak, Battle of the See JUTLAND, BATTLE OF.

Slave Rebellions, U.S See GABRIEL'S REBELLION; MURREL'S UPRISING; TURNER'S REBELLION; VESEY'S REBELLION.

Slave Wars in Sicily See SERVILE WARS, FIRST AND SECOND.

Slovakian Uprising of 1944–45. During WORLD WAR II (1939–45), Monsignor Josef Tiso (1887–1947) headed the German puppet state of Slovakia, which had separated from Czechoslovakia with support from Germany's Nazi dictator Adolf Hitler (1889–1945) in 1939. Tiso's authoritarian regime was opposed by many Slovaks, causing Hitler to send troops in mid-1944 to maintain control and also defend Slovakia from invading airborne Soviet and Allied guerrillas. Beginning in Banská Bystrica in central Slovakia on August 29, 1944, more than 80,000 armed Slovaks openly resisted the German army, secured control of the mountainous heartland, and freed Allied airmen who had been shot down and captured. The Soviet army overturned Tiso's regime in April 1945, and Tiso was later tried for treason and hanged in Bratislava on April 18, 1947.

Slovenian War of Independence (1991)   After the communist dictator Josip Tito died in 1980, longstanding ethnic, religious, and economic tensions within Yugoslavia became more apparent. Although the country comprised six republics and two self-governing provinces, Serbia (the largest republic) dominated the federal government and army. Resentment of Serbia grew when Slobodan Milosevic (1941–), who eventually became president of the republic, began stirring up Serbian nationalism in 1987. The prosperous republics of Slovenia and Croatia, no longer willing to subsidize less-developed Serbia or to accept a centralized federal government under its control, declared their independence from Yugoslavia on June 25, 1991. After Slovenia took control of its border crossings, its defense forces blockaded federal army bases in the republic and captured about 2,300 federal soldiers. Meanwhile, the federal army moved tanks in and bombed the airport in Ljubljana, the Slovenian capital, and some border posts. Fighting continued until mid-July 1991 by which time several dozen people had been killed. The war ended when the federal army withdrew its tanks and troops to concentrate on the neighboring secessionist republic of Croatia (where, in contrast to ethnically homogeneous Slovenia, there was a significant Serb minority). In February 1992 the European Community recognized Slovenia as a state, and in May 1992 the country joined the United Nations. See CROATIAN WAR FOR INDEPENDENCE; BOSNIAN CIVIL WAR OF 1992–95.

Sluys, Battle of (1340)   The 1337 Flanders campaign of King Edward III (1312–77) of England was only moderately successful in the HUNDRED YEARS' WAR. Edward returned to England for more men and ships to try again. The French assembled a fleet of 150 ships, holding 40,000 men, to prevent Edward's return. However, Edward's strategy, emphasizing longbowmen and the maneuvering of ships to put the sun in the eyes of the French, gave the English an advantage and eventually won victory. In the daylong fight, which the French chronicler Jean Froissart (1333?–1401?) called "bloody and murderous," most of the French ships were sunk or captured. The English gained a yearlong truce and command of the English Channel.

Smolensk, War of   See RUSSO-POLISH WAR OF 1632–34.

Soccer War (Guerra de Fútbol) (1969)   In the 1950s and 1960s, some 300,000 landless peasants and unemployed workers from El Salvador migrated to areas in western Honduras and there succeeded in cultivating the land and making a better life for themselves. In 1969, the Honduran government enforced an agrarian reform law that gave the Salvadoran "squatters'" fields to native Hondurans. Salvadorans were often evicted just as they were about to harvest their crops; about 17,000 of them were deported and returned to El Salvador with reports of persecution. Ill feelings in both countries increased. When Honduras was defeated by El Salvador in a three-game soccer series, rioting broke out in the former country against the Salvadoran migrants and precipitated a brief war (July 14–18, 1969). Salvadoran planes dropped bombs on Honduran airports, and invading troops occupied Honduran territory. Although bombing the enemy in retaliation, Honduras maintained a defensive position and was relieved when the Organization of American States (OAS) arranged an armistice and persuaded the Salvadoran troops to withdraw. More than 2,000 persons perished in the fighting, and much land was laid waste. Despite the establishment of a demilitarized zone along the border of the two nations, sporadic fighting occurred for several years.

Social War of 357–355 B.C. (War of the Allies) Athens, accused of meddlesome practices as head of the Delian League (see PELOPONNESIAN WAR, FIRST), resumed such practices when Thebes caused Euboea to revolt in 357. Necessary to Athens's Hellespontine grain routes, Euboea was punished and Athens's control of other allied city-states was tightened. Chios rebelled, as did Rhodes, Byzantium, and, later, others—all desiring to be Athens's social and political equals. Athens put Samos under siege in 356, and the Athenian fleet sailed to Byzantium to lose at Embata that same year. In 355, Persia sent an ultimatum concerning a general remaining after Embata and causing troubles in Persian satrapies. Athens gave in to another "King's Peace" (see CORINTHIAN WAR), allowing its allies independence and losing harbors in the north in return for continued trade in the Aegean. Athens's acquiescence made impossible restraint of the rampant imperialism of Macedonia (see SACRED WAR, THIRD).

Social War of 219–217 B.C. (War of the Allies) This war tested the mettle of Philip V (238–179), newly crowned king (221) of a weakened Macedonia. The most important member of the Hellenic League, Macedonia was to be asked to arbitrate problems among its membership, for Achaeans operating in Messenia appealed (220) to the 18-year-old king for action against Aetolia, which permitted private citizens to practice piracy. The league's ruling against Aetolia made it prepare for war. Philip, reluctant because of possible Roman interference, delayed a response (see ILLYRIAN WAR, SECOND). But when Aetolia attacked Macedonia in 219, Philip acted swiftly—invading the Peloponnesus; punishing Elis, Aetolia's ally; overcoming almost treasonous intrigue by some officials; attacking Aetolia, especially its federal center at Thermon in 218; plundering Laconia to immobilize Sparta; waging violent war in Aetolia's Aegean outpost, Phthiotic Thebes, in 217; and overseeing the Peace of Naupactus in 217. Philip became the beloved of most of Greece. Nothing was gained or lost in the war, but peace delayed further Roman activity for five years.

Social War of 91–88 B.C. (War of the Allies or Marsic War) In 91, Marcus Livius Druses (d. 91), tribune of the people, introduced a bill in the Roman Senate that would have extended Roman citizenship to all Italians, but he was assassinated before any action was taken. In disgust, the peoples in the mountainous areas of southern and central Italy, especially the Marsians (Marsi), revolted and established an independent federation called Italia. Their soldiers had often fought with and for the Romans, and their army was as well trained and capable as the Roman army. The Romans were unable to put down the revolt, and the *Socii* (Latin for allies) of Italia were unable to overpower Rome, so a stalemate developed. Then, in 90, the Roman consul Lucius Julius Caesar (d. 87) suggested a law (the Julian Law) that was passed—citizenship would be granted to those allies who had not joined the revolt and had remained loyal (mostly Umbrians, Etruscans, and Latins) and to those who laid down their arms immediately. Resolute rebels defeated Roman forces under Lucius Porcius Cato (d. 89) at Fucine Lake in 89; Cato was slain, but his cohort Gnaeus Pompeius Strabo (d. 87) won a conclusive victory at Asculum in 89, ending the war in the north. That same year the citizenship law was extended to all who registered within 60 days, whether they had revolted or not. Meanwhile, Romans led by Lucius Cornelius Sulla (138–78) won success in the south, including the capture of Pompeii from the rebels. By 88, almost all of the Italians had accepted the Roman offer of citizenship and Roman sovereignty.

Somalian Civil War of 1988–90   After the army overthrew the civilian government of Somalia in 1969, the country was wrenched constantly by strife and famine. Bitter cross-clan feuding fed by the inept and brutal one-party rule of Muhammad Siad Barre (Siyad Barrah) came to a head in the spring of 1988 when the Somali National Movement (SNM) began taking over towns and military installations in the north. Thousands were killed, and hundreds of thousands of refugees fled to neighoring Ethiopia. Somalia's capital, Mogadishu, remained in the hands of the socialist government. In March 1989 soldiers of the Ogadeni clan mutinied in Kismayo (Chisimaio), and fighting continued until government troops gained the upper hand in July. In the meantime the SNM made major gains. The fighting forced United Nations staff and other aid workers to abandon the country in May, and the assassination of the Roman Catholic bishop of Mogadishu on July 9, 1989, led to more violence. Under pressure from the rebels and civilian street fighting President Barre, who had nationalized most of the economy in the 1970s, promised to hold multiparty elections. But united rebel groups thwarted elections and eventually launched a successful coup against Barre in late December 1990; Barre fled the country a month later. See also SOMALIAN CIVIL WAR OF 1991– .

Somalian Civil War of 1991–   Following three years of civil upheaval that ended briefly in 1990 when free elections were promised (see SOMALIAN CIVIL WAR OF 1988–90), a new power struggle between rival clans started once again in Somalia. Factions marked by complex relationships and changing loyalties were divided primarily between General Muhammad Farrah Aidid (Aydid), a member of the Hawiye clan and head of the Somali National Alliance (SNA), and Ali Mahdi Muhammad, also of the Hawiye clan (but a different subclan) and head of the Somali Salvation Alliance (SSA). President Muhammad Siad Barre (Siyad Barrah), who had imposed a dictatorship after President Abdi Rashid Ali Shirmarke was assassinated in October 1969, clung tenaciously to power but was finally ousted in January 1991 by the rebels. Ali Mahdi assumed the presidency but was challenged in September by Aidid, who was chairman of the ruling United Somali Congress (USC). Fighting broke out in Somalia's capital, Mogadishu; no one group was powerful enough to form a government. Meanwhile, in May, under the leadership of Muhammad Ibrahim Egal, the northeastern part of the country had seceded; the new entity, Somaliland, achieved relative stability, but antisecessionists resisted in the region's capital, Hargeysa (Hargeisa),

and Somaliland was not recognized internationally as a separate sovereign nation. Virtual destruction of Somalia's economy and agricultural activity combined with severe drought left 2 million Somalis facing starvation. In an effort to avoid the results of a full-scale famine, in August 1992 the United Nations shipped tons of food to Somalia. However, distribution was hindered by various stalling tactics or prevented altogether by a number of Muslim warlords. In December 1992 the first of some 28,000 UN troops arrived in order to transport food and quell the chaos. In June and July 1993 UN peacekeepers and Somali citizens were killed in Mogadishu when the UN, encouraged by the United States, broadened its mandate to include capturing or killing Aidid. Heated dissension among member countries over the purpose of the UN's mission further confused the situation, and in March 1994 most U.S. and European Union forces left Somalia. The same month, Aidid and Mahdi met in Kenya to form a joint government, but fighting again broke out in Mogadishu in May and December. The remaining 19,000 UN troops left Somalia in March 1995. A stalemate persisted between Aidid and Mahdi, both of whom continued to occupy Mogadishu. The Somali Salvation Democratic Front (SSDF) controlled the northeast, and three lesser groups controlled other areas. Aidid was weakened when his powerful right-hand man Osman Hassan Ali switched his allegiance to Mahdi. Aidid died on August 1, 1996, from a battle wound, and was succeeded by his son, Hussein Aidid (Aydid). Split between political factions based on clans and subclans, Somalia remained disunited, with a non-functioning government, in 1997–98 and into 1999; a split within the SSDF had led to the formation of a self-declared independent state (Puntland) in the northeast in mid-1998.

Sonderbund, War of the (1847) Protestant Swiss liberals, seeking a revised constitution, stronger central government, freedom of worship, and secular education (expulsion of the Jesuits), tried to impose their views upon the whole Swiss confederation, encountering stiff resistance from Catholic

Swiss in the early 1840s. To protect Catholic interests and prevent more federalization, seven Catholic Swiss cantons (Lucern, Uri, Schwyz, Unterwalden, Fribourg, Zug, and Valais) formed a defensive alliance called the *Sonderbund* ("Separatist League") in 1845. When a reformist majority in the Swiss Diet voted through a measure ordering the dissolution of the Sonderbund (1847), the seven Catholic cantons refused, took up arms, and appealed for outside help (in vain). In a brief and almost bloodless civil war (November 4–24, 1847), federal troops under General Guillaume Henri Dufour (1787–1875) defeated the forces of the Sonderbund, which was far outnumbered on the battlefield. The Sonderbund was dissolved, and its former members were compelled to pay the cost of the war. The victors adopted a new constitution (1848) that established a strong Swiss federal government, while preserving the local cantonal governments.

South African Rebellion of 1990   South Africa's apartheid system (separation of blacks and whites), officially approved by the white-dominated government in 1948, resulted in more racial tension and violence in subsequent decades. In the 1980s, the government began to force blacks to move into self-governing, black territories, or "homelands," and to renounce their citizenship, igniting strong criticism from other nations and thus compelling the government to make reforms to end apartheid. In February 1990, South Africa's President Frederik W. de Klerk (1936–) lifted the ban on the principal anti-apartheid party, the African National Congress (ANC), and freed black ANC political leader Nelson R. Mandela (1918–), imprisoned since 1962. In March 1990, savage fighting broke out between Mandela's ANC supporters and the rival Zulu-based Inkatha party, led by Mangosuthu G. Buthelezi (1928–), after thousands of Zulus were forced out of their homes in ANC-loyal areas of the southeastern province of Natal. There Zulu Inkatha members, armed with guns, knives, and sticks, battled for control of the villages in the rugged Edendale Valley, where South African troops helped police stop the bloodshed and restore order. Fac-

tional fights broke out in other areas that police struggled to halt. From July to September 1990, the bloodiest clashes in modern South African history occurred when Inkatha launched raids in the Transvaal townships, where an estimated 800 persons were slain and ANC supporters boldly defended themselves. Police with machine guns stifled the hostilities, but afterward sporadic fighting between rival factions took place until 1994. The government ended some apartheid laws (1991), dissolved the black "homelands" (1993), and held the country's first one-person one-vote election (1994), in which the ANC won a clear majority, with Mandela becoming president.

South African War   See BOER WAR, SECOND OR GREAT.

Southampton Insurrection   See TURNER'S REBELLION.

Soviet Invasion of Afghanistan   See AFGHAN CIVIL WAR OF 1979– .

Soviet Invasion of Czechoslovakia   See CZECHOSLOVAKIA, SOVIET INVASION OF.

Spanish-Algerine War of 1775   Spain's King Charles III (1716–88) tried hard to establish calm in Muslim-troubled northern Africa; he made peace with Morocco in 1767 only to have it broken in 1774 when the sultan ordered all Christians out of his land and laid siege to Melilla. The Spanish turned back the attack and blamed (unjustly) the British for causing the problem. Charles then decided to crush Morocco for all time by sending 18,000 troops against the dey (governor) of Algiers, an ally of the Moroccan sultan. Under the Irish general Alexander O'Reilly (1722–94), Jacobite reformer of the Spanish army, the Spanish advanced threateningly toward the city of Algiers. Instead of gaining victory, they were decisively defeated, losing several thousand men and drawing increased Muslim opposition.

Spanish-American War (1898) The mistreatment of the Cubans by the Spanish authorities was widely publicized, frequently sensationally, by the press in the United States (see CUBAN WAR OF INDEPENDENCE). On February 15, 1898, the battleship U.S.S. *Maine* was mysteriously blown up and sunk while moored in Havana harbor in Cuba; 260 of its crewmen were killed. Though the exact cause of the disaster was never found out, Spain was blamed, and American intervention on behalf of the Cubans increased despite Spain's agreeing to an armistice on April 9, 1898. The United States declared war on Spain on April 25, 1898. Fighting took place in the Atlantic and the Pacific, where the U.S. Asian fleet under Commodore George Dewey (1837–1917) sailed into Manila Bay, the Philippines, and completely destroyed a larger Spanish fleet on May 1, 1898. Two months later about 11,000 American troops under General Wesley Merritt (1834–1910) arrived at Manila Bay and, aided by Filipino rebels under Emilio Aguinaldo (1869–1964), captured the city of Manila on August 13, 1898. In the Atlantic, meanwhile, a Spanish fleet under Admiral Pascual Cervera y Topete (1839–1909) sailed to Santiago de Cuba harbor, where the U.S. Atlantic fleet commanded by Admiral William T. Sampson (1840–1902) blockaded it (May–July 1898). A U.S. expedition of about 17,000 troops under General William R. Shafter (1835–1906) landed at Daiquirí, Cuba, and began to move on nearby Santiago. At the Battle of San Juan Hill and El Caney, on July 1, 1898, the Americans under Shafter, including the First Volunteer Cavalry (the "Rough Riders") under Colonel Leonard Wood (1860–1927) and Lieutenant Colonel Theodore Roosevelt (1858–1919), who led the Rough Riders in a successful attack up nearby Kettle Hill that day, won a hard-fought victory, gained a commanding position overlooking Santiago, and repelled Spanish attempts to dislodge them. Cervera attempted to break through the American

blockade, but his Spanish fleet suffered utter defeat at the naval Battle of Santiago Bay on July 3, 1898. Two weeks later the Spaniards at Santiago capitulated, and on July 25, 1898, an American force under General Nelson A. Miles (1839–1925) landed on Puerto Rico and had almost defeated the Spanish there when an armistice was signed (August 12, 1898). By the Treaty of Paris on December 10, 1898, Spain gave up sovereignty over Cuba and ceded Puerto Rico, Guam, and the Philippines to the United States, which made a payment of $20 million for the latter territory. See also PHILIPPINE INSURRECTION OF 1896–98.

Spanish Armada, Defeat of the (1588) In order to avenge himself for England's interference in the Netherlands, to overthrow Queen Elizabeth I (1533–1603), and to gain the English throne as the son of a Lancastrian, King Philip II (1527–98) of Spain developed an elaborate plan to conquer England. He planned to have a Spanish armada (fleet) of 500 warships to meet the duke of Parma's armies in Flanders for a grand invasion. Only 130 ships and some 28,000 soldiers sailed from Lisbon in May 1588, under the duke of Medina-Sidonia; held up by storms, they failed to join with Parma's forces. Instead, the ships entered the English Channel, fought a several-days' running battle with a Dover-based English squadron equipped with superior guns, and hastened to the French Channel port of Calais, where a large English fleet under Lord Charles Howard (1536–1624) of Effingham used fireships to scatter them on the night of August 7–8, 1588. During the next day, off Gravelines, the English attacked and almost destroyed the disorganized Spanish Armada. A shift of winds enabled surviving Spanish ships to escape northward around Scotland to Ireland and then home to Spain; only 76 ships returned. Not one English warship was lost in the conflict. See also ANGLO-SPANISH WAR OF 1587–1604.

Spanish-Chilean War of 1865–66 See SPANISH-PERUVIAN WAR OF 1864–66.

Spanish Christian-Muslim War of A.D. 912–28

Muslim Arabs, Berbers, and Muwallads (Spanish converts to Islam) contended for control of al-Andalus or southern Spain. The Muslim Ummayyad emir (commander) Abd-ar-Rahman III (891–961) failed to restore calm by granting amnesty to rebels and attempted to subdue Toledo, the controlling center of Muslim or Moorish Spain. His 40,000-man army was victorious in battle against the Arab rebel Ibn Hafsun (d. 917) and his army of dissenters and tribesmen. Most of southern and eastern Spain came under Abd-ar-Rahman's rule, though Arab rebels continued to wage war against him for some time. In Galicia (northwest Spain), especially in the kingdom of León, Spanish Christians under King Ordoño II (d. 923) attacked and defeated the Moors, managing to keep the invaders at bay. In 921, however, Ordoño lost against the Moors at Val-de-Junquera, where he was aiding the Christian king of Navarre. The sons of Ibn Hafsun continued to fight both Abd-ar-Rahman and the Spanish kings until their surrender in 928. A year later Abd-ar-Rahman became the first caliph (Muslim spiritual and civil head) of Córdoba. Frontier fighting between the Christians and Muslims became frequent and resulted in much bloodshed. See also MUSLIM CONQUEST OF SPAIN.

Spanish Christian-Muslim War of A.D. 977–97

Caliph Hisham II (d. 1013?) was a weak Muslim Ummayyad ruler of Córdoba, Spain, whose power was usurped by Muhammad ibn-abi-Amir (939–1002), helped by his father-in-law General Kalib (d. 981). However, Kalib began to fear ibn-abi-Amir's power and thus allied himself with the Christian kings of León, Navarre, and Castile. Having previously built up his Muslim (Moorish) army, ibn-abi-Amir invaded Galicia (northwest Spain) in 977 and defeated Kalib, who died in battle. He then turned against King Ramiro III (962–82) of León, defeating him at the Battle of Zamora (981) and at Simancas, where earlier the Spanish Christians under King Ramiro II (923?–50) had severely defeated the Muslims and Caliph Abd-ar-Rahman III (891–961) in 939. Because of his triumphs, ibn-abi-Amir assumed the honorific title al-Mansur bi-Allah ("victorious through Allah") and ruled Muslim Spain as regent in the reign of Hisham II. In 982, civil war erupted in León, where Vermudo II (d. 999) usurped the kingdom with the help of troops from al-Mansur and the Christian king of Navarre. In 985, Barcelona was captured by al-Mansur, who torched the city. When Vermudo evicted Córdoban mercenaries from León in 987, al-Mansur and his forces invaded and plundered the entire León kingdom in 988. In 989, in Castile, he instigated a rebellion, which he used as an excuse to invade and triumph over the Christians at Medinaceli; he exacted tribute in return for peace. Al-Mansur's Moors rampaged through Galicia, where they stole the cathedral bells from the church at the holy city of Santiago de Compostela. By 997, the Moors had conquered most of the Iberian peninsula (Spain and Portugal).

Spanish Christian-Muslim War of 1001–31

With a Muslim army, Muhammad ibn-abi-Amir al-Mansur (939–1002) marched up the Duero River to subjugate Christian rebels in Castile, Spain. He encountered a large Christian force near Calatanazar (1001) and was compelled to withdraw. Upon his death in 1002, al-Mansur was succeeded by his older son, Abdulmalik-al-Muzaffar (d. 1004?), as Muslim regent of Córdoda in the reign of Ummayyad Caliph Hisham II (d. 1013?). Despite growing internal dissension among the Muslim leaders, Abdulmalik-al-Muzaffar was victorious in several battles with the Christians. His early death, however, brought on open civil war, and his younger brother Sanjul (d. 1009) seized power, coercing Hisham to declare him his heir. This caused a rebellion at Córdoba and the abdication of Hisham in favor of Muhammad II Mahdi (d. 1010), who was opposed by Berber mercenaries and their candidate for caliph, Sulayman al-Mustain (d. 1016). Sanjul was murdered in 1009. With help from Count Sancho Garces (d. 1021) of Castile, the Berbers overthrew the usurping caliph Muhammad II in November 1009, and the combined Christian-Muslim forces then looted Córdoba and installed Sulayman as caliph.

Because the Muslim central authority was weakened, a number of independent emirates and kingdoms were established throughout Spain. Muhammad II allied himself with Barcelona's Count Ramón Borrell I (d. 1018) and his brother, and a joint Muslim-Christian army invaded Córdoba, conquered the Berbers, and burned the city in June 1010 (Córdoba was seat of the government of Muslim Spain). After the joint army left, Muhammad II was assassinated, and Hisham II managed to regain the caliphate, albeit briefly, for in May 1013, he was again forced to abdicate, and in the ensuing chaos the caliphate changed hands regularly as the Ummayyad and Hammudid Muslim dynasties vied for power. In 1031, the caliphate at Córdoba collapsed entirely with the forced resignation of the reigning caliph, Hisham III (d. 1031). The last vestige of unity in Moorish Spain was thereby eliminated.

Spanish Christian-Muslim War of 1172–1212

After fighting unruly nobles and establishing his authority as king of Castile, Alfonso VIII (1155–1214) undertook a campaign against the Muslim Almohad invaders (see ALMOHAD CONQUEST OF MUSLIM SPAIN) and succeeded in taking the kingdom of Cuenca from them in 1177. The Christian Castilians continued triumphantly until 1195, when Alfonso was resoundingly defeated at the Battle of Alarcos, near Ciudad Real, by Almohad caliph Abu-Yusef Ya'qub al-Mansur (d. 1199). Afterward, Castile was invaded by troops from León and Navarre, as well as by Moors (Spanish Muslims), but Alfonso's forces managed to repel the intruders. With the assistance of Pope Innocent III (1161–1216) and Spanish clergy, Alfonso now made preparations for a coordinated assault on the Almohads and other Muslims. His army won victories. In 1212, Alfonso had his greatest victory at the Battle of Las Navas de Tolosa, which gave him and his Castilians firm control of central Spain. Almohad power, which had peaked in 1195, soon declined both in Spain and North Africa.

Spanish Christian-Muslim War of 1230–48

King Ferdinand III (1199–1252) of Castile and León, a Christian zealot nicknamed "the Saint," initiated a vigorous military crusade to destroy Moorish (Spanish Muslim) rule in southern Spain. His forces invaded the Guadalquivir River valley to attack Moorish strongholds, winning a series of battles and capturing Córdoba (1236), Jaén (1246), and Seville (1248), the capital of the Moorish region called al-Andalus (Andalusia). For the first time in Muslim Spain, the Christian conquerors evicted defeated Moorish inhabitants from their homes, an action that resulted in eventual economic ruination in the area. The kingdom of Murcia came under Castilian occupation, and only the Moorish kingdom of Granada remained intact but as a vassal state of Castile. Thus Ferdinand had, in effect, completed the Christian reconquest of Spain from the Moors. Periodic fighting with the Moors in Granada continued until about the early 1400s.

Spanish Christian-Muslim War of 1481–92

In southern Spain, peace between the Moors (Spanish Muslims) and Christians was broken when King Muley Abdul-Hassan (d. 1485) of Granada suddenly raided and captured the Zahara fortress near Ronda on December 26, 1481, enslaving the Christians. In response, in a similar surprise attack, the marquis of Cádiz seized the Moorish town of Alhama, close to Granada, on February 28, 1482. Abul-Hassan then invested Alhama, but news of the approach of a Christian force led by King Ferdinand V (1452–1516) of Castile and Aragon caused him to abandon the siege; Ferdinand entered the city on May 14, 1482. Ferdinand's Queen Isabella I (1451–1504) helped him prepare for a siege of Moorish-held Loja, launching a fleet to prevent Moorish reinforcements from the sea. But Ferdinand was defeated at the Battle of Loja on July 1, 1482. Abdul-Hassan's son, Boabdil (d. 1527), besieged Lucena in April 1483, but he was seized by the Christians while in flight; he acknowledged Ferdinand's suzerainty over the kingdom of Granada to gain his release, but Abdul-Hassan rejected it. The Christians continued to invest Granada on land while a Spanish fleet cut off provisions from North Africa. Isabella personally participated in the war against the Moors, seeing it as a holy mission. Christian Castilian forces advanced and took Ronda (May 1485) and Loja (May 1486). When Málaga fell to the Christians in August 1487, the Moors were forced to withdraw to the fortresses of Baza and Almería, both of which fell in 1489 after extended sieges. The Castilians had control of southeastern Spain by 1490, and the Moors under Boabdil were surrounded at the city of Granada. Reneging on his earlier agreement, Boabdil refused to give up sovereignty over Granada. With the Christian conquest of the city (January 2, 1492), the centuries-long Muslim rule of Spain ended (see GRANADA, SIEGE OF).

Spanish Civil War of 1820–23   The inept rule of Spain King Ferdinand VII (1784–1833), who refused to accept the liberal constitution of 1812, provoked widespread unrest, particularly in the army. The king sought to reconquer the Spanish colonies in South America that had recently successfully revolted and consequently had deprived Spain of a major source of revenue (see ARGENTINE WAR OF INDEPENDENCE; CHILEAN WAR OF INDEPENDENCE; COLOMBIAN WAR OF INDEPENDENCE; VENEZUELAN WAR OF INDEPENDENCE). At Cádiz, Spain, in January 1820, troops who had assembled for an expedition to America were angry over infrequent pay, bad food, and poor quarters and mutinied under the leadership of Colonel Rafael del Riego y Núñez (1785–1823). Pledging fealty to the 1812 constitution, they seized their commander, moved into nearby San Fernando, and then prepared to march on Madrid, the capital. Despite the rebels' relative weakness, Ferdinand accepted the constitution on March 9, 1820, ushering in a period of popular rule. But in this liberal atmosphere, political conspiracies of both the right and left proliferated. Liberal revolutionaries stormed the king's palace and virtually made Ferdinand a prisoner for the next three years. A mutiny occurred in the Madrid garrison, and civil war erupted in the regions of Castile, Toledo, and Andalusia. The Holy Alliance (Russia,

Austria, and Prussia) refused Ferdinand's request for help, but the Quadruple Alliance (Britain, France, Holland, and Austria) at the Congress of Verona (October 1822) gave France a mandate to intervene and restore the Spanish monarchy (see FRANCO-SPANISH WAR OF 1823). French troops invaded Spain, captured Madrid, and drove the revolutionaries south to Cádiz and Seville. On August 31, 1823, rebel forces were routed in battle near Cádiz, and soon after, the French freed Ferdinand, who had been taken from Madrid as a captive, and placed him on the throne. Unexpectedly, he took ruthless revenge on his opponents, revoked the 1812 constitution, and restored absolutism (despotism) to Spain.

Spanish Civil War of 1840–43   After the FIRST CARLIST WAR, Maria Cristina (1806–78), regent during the minority of her daughter, Queen Isabella II (1830–1904), sought to abolish the constitution of 1837 and to limit the independence of Spain's cities. Urban uprisings occurred, forcing her to accept the more liberal constitution of 1812, but the uprisings continued when the central government imposed its choice of officials at the local level. General Baldomero Espartero (1792–1879), a hero of the Carlist War, gained much popularity by refusing to heed Maria Cristina's order to quell the rebels; he was made ministerial president. Moderate reforms were then enacted that so constrained Maria Cristina's power that she, along with Isabella, left the country (October 1840) to reside in France, where she fomented insurrections against Espartero, who was now the dictatorial head of government. Cristina-instigated insurrections were put down at Pamplona in October 1841, and at Barcelona in December 1842. Maria Cristina's agents aided Colonel Juan Prim y Prats (1814–70) to stir up rebellion in the south in 1843. Espartero's regime was toppled when General Ramón María Narváez (1800–1868) led opposing troops from Valencia to Madrid, the capital, which was seized. Espartero fled to England but later returned (1848). In November 1843, Isabella, though only 13, was declared of age and made head of government; Cristina was recalled; and

Narváez became president of the ministry. See also SPANISH REVOLUTION OF 1854.

Spanish Civil War of 1936–39   Constant strife between political extremists on the right and left, aggravated by economic suffering during the Great Depression, doomed Spain's centrist republic established in 1931. When the leftist "Popular Front" won the 1936 elections and continued secular reforms, the rightist Falange (Fascist) Party, headed by General Francisco Franco (1892–1975), conspired to stage a military coup against the government. A revolt by army officers at Melilla in Spanish Morocco on July 17, 1936, immediately set off revolts in garrisons at Cádiz, Seville, Bourgos, Saragossa, Huesca, and other places in Spain. These rebel troops and insurgent "nationalists" overwhelmed Loyalist government forces to take control of Spain's south and west; with the capture of Badajoz on August 15, 1936, they united their conquests. In the north, insurgents moved on Irun and San Sebastián. In the south, rebels threatened the capital, Madrid, which the Loyalists fortified with international brigades (volunteer forces from Britain, France, and the United States, as well as anti-Fascist Italians and Germans); Madrid withstood a 28-month siege before capitulating. On October 1, 1936, Franco was named "Chief of the Spanish State" by the insurgents, and he proceeded to impose a centralized, autocratic rule. Britain and France initiated a policy of nonintervention in the war, but other powers, especially Germany, Italy, and the Soviet Union, violated it by sending aid to the particular side they supported. With Italian aid, the insurgents captured Málaga in February 1937, and with German aerial bombing, they were able to occupy Guernica and Durango in April 1937. Loyalists quelled an anarchist uprising in Barcelona with much bloodshed in May 1937; a new Loyalist government had to be formed as a result. After an 80-day siege, Bilbao fell to the insurgents on June 18, 1937. In the western Mediterranean, attacks on British ships by mysterious submarines led to the international Nyon Conference (September 1937), at which nine powers (Italy and Germany absent) adopted a system of naval patrol zones to stop "piracy" in the war. A strong Loyalist counteroffensive captured Teruel, which, however, was retaken by the insurgents' counteroffensive two months later in mid-February 1938. After the Soviets halted their aid to the Loyalists in 1938, the republican cause became hopeless, and the insurgents, who now held much of Spain, prepared a major offensive to capture Barcelona, seat of the Loyalist government since late October 1937. Franco's troops, assisted by Italians, routed Loyalist forces to seize Barcelona on January 26, 1939, precipitating the collapse of Loyalist resistance throughout Spain. At Madrid, the Loyalist Defense Council drew up honorable surrender terms, forcibly crushed communist opposition to them, and surrendered unconditionally (Franco's demand) on March 28, 1939. Despite pleas by Britain and France for moderation, special Fascist tribunals tried, convicted, and executed many Loyalists. Franco's regime was recognized by the United States on April 1, 1939. See also ASTURIAN UPRISING OF 1934; CATALAN REVOLT OF 1934.

Spanish Civil Wars in Peru   (1537–48)   When Spanish leader Diego de Almagro (1475?–1538) claimed the city of Cuzco (Cusco) in Peru in 1537, he was opposed by fellow Spanish leader Francisco Pizarro (1475?–1541), who initiated war against him. Almagro's forces were defeated, and Almagro was executed; his son began to conspire against Pizarro and, accompanied by supporters, attacked and murdered Pizarro at his palace on June 26, 1541. To put down the uprising caused by Almagro's son, Cristóbal Vaca de Castro (d. 1571?) was sent to assume the governorship of Peru. In 1542, Castro restored order and executed Almagro's son. Two years later Blasco Núñez Vela (d. 1546) arrived to be the first Spanish viceroy in Peru and to enforce the so-called New Laws, humanitarian laws, restricting the privileges of the conquistadors and protecting the rights of the Indians. Núñez's rule antagonized many, especially Gonzalo Pizarro (1506?–48), Francisco's younger brother, who led a successful popular revolt and defeated Núñez's loyal forces at the Battle of Anaquito in 1546. Núñez was caught and executed, and Gonzalo secured the governorship of Peru for himself (see XAQUIXAGUANA, BATTLE OF).

Spanish Conquest of Chile (1540–61) An early, unsuccessful Spanish attempt to conquer what is now Chile by Diego de Almagro (1475?–1538) was followed by an expedition under Pedro de Valdivia (1500?–1553), who set out with 150 Spaniards and some 1,000 Indian allies from Peru in January 1540. The expedition faced difficult travel over the Atacama Desert, successfully fought a succession of battles with the hostile Araucanian Indians, and founded the town of Santiago, Chile, on February 12, 1541. Six months later the Araucanians attacked and virtually destroyed the place; for two years the survivors held out on a small island until help arrived from Peru in 1543. In 1547, Valdivia returned to Peru to seek further help in his conquest; reinforced, he pushed farther south, establishing Concepción in 1550 and Valdivia in 1552. The next year the Araucanians under Lautaro (1535?–57) opposed the Spaniards and captured and killed Valdivia in battle. The Indians then seized Concepción in 1554 but were defeated in 1557 after an unsuccessful attack on Santiago. In 1561, Spanish forces crossed the Andes and founded the towns of Mendoza and San Juan, both of which belonged to Chile for more than 200 years. The region was under Spanish control, with the Indians pacified (the Araucanians remained bellicose until the 1800s).

Spanish Conquest of Mexico (1519–21) Hernán Cortés (Cortez) (1485–1547) led a Spanish expedition of 600 men from Hispaniola (island now occupied by Haiti and the Dominican Republic) to Mexico in 1519. After landing at a site near present-day Veracruz, he burned his ships to prevent his men, whom he welded into a small, disciplined army, from returning home. The Spaniards then invaded the interior of Mexico, defeating the Tlaxcalan warriors and making allies of other Indians. In November 1519, Cortés and his soldiers reached Tenochtitlán (now Mexico City), the capital of the Aztec Empire, and were permitted to enter by the Aztec emperor, Montezuma (Moctezuma) II (1480?–1520), who believed the invaders were descendants of the god, Quetzolcoatl. Cortés seized Montezuma and held him as a hostage for ransom (gold and other riches). Forced to return to the Mexican coast to deal with a Spanish agent, Pánfilo de Narváez (c. 1470–1528), sent to replace him, Cortés left Pedro de Alvarado (c. 1485–1541) in command at Tenochtitlán in mid-1520. Alvarado's harshness and slaying of many Aztecs caused an Aztec uprising, and, when Cortés returned to the city, he and his soldiers were attacked and forced to flee (Montezuma was killed in the battle) on June 30, 1520. Cortés made preparations to reconquer Tenochtitlán, assembling a Spanish-Indian force and disciplining it. His assault the next year was successful; the city fell on August 13, 1521, and the last Aztec emperor, Cuauhtémoc (c. 1495–1525), was captured. Cortés was master of Mexico with the collapse of the Aztec Empire, whose chieftains made promises of allegiance to him. See also SPANISH CONQUEST OF YUCATÁN.

Spanish Conquest of Peru (1531–33) A Spanish force of 180 men, 37 horses, and two cannons, led by Francisco Pizarro (1475?–1541), sailed south from Darien (Panama) and landed at Tumbes on the Peruvian coast in 1531. With his small army, Pizarro advanced inland and ascended the Andes to Caljamarca. where Atahualpa (Atabalipa) (1500?–1533), emperor of the Inca Indians, awaited with some 30,000 followers. Professing friendship, Pizarro lured Atahualpa, accompanied by some 3,500 men, mostly unarmed, into the great square at Caljamarca. There, after the emperor disdainfully flung the Bible to the ground (Pizarro had exhorted him to accept Christianity), the Spaniards opened fire and cut down the Incas from all sides. Pizarro himself grabbed Atahualpa, who was held for an enormous ransom, not released, and executed (he was charged with conspiracy and heresy—refusing to become a Christian). Pizarro, who had been joined by Spanish forces under Diego de Almagro

(1475?–1538), moved against the Incas at Cuzco (Cusco), the capital city, rich with gold medallions and ornaments, which fell without bloodshed in November 1533. The Spanish had gained control of the Inca Empire. See INCA REVOLT; SPANISH CIVIL WARS IN PERU.

Spanish Conquest of Puerto Rico (1508–11) In 1508, Juan Ponce de León (1460?–1521) led a Spanish exploring expedition to Boriquen (Puerto Rico), where the Spaniards at first were well treated by the Arawak Indian inhabitants. Relations with the Indians quickly deteriorated when they were forced to mine gold for the Spanish. Minor uprisings occurred until 1511, when the cacique (Indian chief), Agueybana II (d. 1511), planned an island-wide revolt. Informed about the plan, Ponce de León gathered 120 Spaniards, advanced through the forests, and attacked Agueybana and his men while asleep, killing hundreds of Indians. Agueybana and others escaped and, several days later, attacked the Spanish but were defeated, with the cacique dying in battle. The remaining Indians fell back; some made peace with Ponce de León; others fled to neighboring islands to join with their former enemies, the Caribs, in later struggles against the Spaniards.

Spanish Conquest of Yucatán (1527–46) Francisco de Montejo (1484?–1550?) joined his friend Hernán Cortés (Cortez) (1485–1547) in the SPANISH CONQUEST OF MEXICO and was assigned the task of conquering the Yucatán Peninsula. Montejo's campaign from the east in 1527–28 met strong resistance from the Maya (tribe of Central American Indians) who inhabited the region. The Spaniards withdrew. Between 1531 and 1535, Montejo directed a second campaign, this time from the west, but again was beaten back by the hostile Maya. Disheartened, he entrusted the task to his son and namesake, Francisco, who, at the cost of many lives, cruelly suppressed the Indians in the area and established Mérida, Campeche, and other settlements (a fierce Mayan revolt in 1546 was quickly and brutally quelled to end Indian defiance in Yucatán, but some

Maya managed to hold out in the jungles of Guatemala and were not subdued until 1697).

Spanish Conquests in North Africa (1505–11) During the reign of Spain's King Ferdinand II or V (1452–1516), his inquisitor general Cardinal Francisco Jiménez de Cisneros (1437–1517), organized and helped finance from his archiepiscopal revenues Spanish military campaigns against the infidel Muslims in North Africa. An able statesman and general, Jiménez personally led the 1509 amphibious operation on the port city of Oran, Algeria, capturing it in one day and installing Christian forces there before returning to Spain. The next year, 1510, the Mediterranean port of Bougie (Bejaia), Algeria, fell to the Spaniards, who soon captured Algiers, Tunis, and Tripoli (conquered in a separate campaign in 1510). By 1511, the Muslim rulers of these cities had been forced to pay tribute to Spain, and then Jiménez made preparations for a new African expedition but abandoned it when the pope asked his help against French dissidents.

Spanish-English Wars   See   ANGLO-SPANISH WARS.

Spanish-French Wars   See   FRANCO-SPANISH WARS.

Spanish-Moroccan War of 1859–60   Attacks by Muslim Arabs on the Spanish possessions of Ceuta and Melilla in Morocco resulted in a declaration of war (October 22, 1859) by Spain, whose premier, Leopoldo O'Donnell (1809–67), used damage claims by Spanish citizens as a pretext for war after Morocco's sultan failed to offer adequate compensation. O'Donnell took personal charge of the war, forming a 40,000-man army and blockading Moroccan seaports, but designing poor battle plans. The Spanish troops landed at a disadvantageous location, became bogged down on bad roads, and were stricken with cholera; besides, the Muslims were tough adversaries. Spanish honor was saved by a victory by General Juan Prim y Prats (1814–70) on January 1, 1860, and by the capture of Tetuán a month later. Under pressure from the British, peace was arranged on April 26, 1860; Spain, which had suffered many casualties, received an indemnity, and its Ceuta enclave was enlarged.

Spanish-Peruvian War of 1864–66 (Spanish-Chilean War of 1865–66) Spain, angered by attacks on Spanish Basque immigrants working on Peruvian plantations (see TALAMBO INCIDENT), sent a naval force to the Pacific in 1864, ostensibly to protect Spanish rights but actually in an effort to regain control of its former colony, Peru. On April 14, 1864, the Spanish force seized the rich guano-producing Chincha Islands, 12 miles off the Peruvian coast; on January 27, 1865, Spain and Peru concluded a treaty whereby the former virtually recognized Peruvian sovereignty and the latter acceded to Spanish demands to pay a 3 million-peso indemnity for losses to Spanish subjects at Talambo and for the return of the Chincha Islands. These provisions aroused Peruvian resentment, allowing General Mariano Ignacio Prado (1826–1901) to take control of Peru's government and to declare war on Spain on January 14, 1866. Fearing a return of Spanish power in South America, Chile under President José Joaquín Pérez (1800–1890) joined with Peru, which also made defensive alliances with Bolivia and Ecuador, and declared war on Spain. South American Pacific ports were closed to the Spanish fleet, and in retaliation Spanish warships bombarded the Chilean port of Valparaiso (March 31, 1866) and the Peruvian port of Callao (May 2, 1866). A week after the Callao bombardment, Spain ceased hostilities; later a truce was arranged in 1871 through mediation of the United States. Spain and Peru signed a treaty in 1879 that officially recognized the latter's independence.

Spanish-Portuguese War of 1580–89 King Philip II (1527–98) of Spain, in response to Portuguese disputes about succession following the deaths of King Sebastian (1554–78) and Henry "the Cardinal King" (1512–80), pressed his hereditary claim to the throne (Sebastian was his nephew) through negotiations while simultaneously preparing an invasion of Portugal. Henry's illegitimate nephew, Antonio (1531–95), was proclaimed the Portuguese king. Philip's troops then moved into Évora, seat of the Portuguese court. Under the command of Fernando Álvarez de Toledo, duke of Alva (Alba) (1507–82), Spanish soldiers defeated a Portuguese army of peasants and townspeople at the Battle of Alcántara near the Tagus River on August 25, 1580. Antonio fled to Oporto, Portugal, where he was defeated and escaped to France in May 1581. When Philip sent his Spanish fleet to the Azores, Antonio's only remaining Portuguese stronghold, Catherine de Médicis sent French reinforcements to the Portuguese but they were dispersed by the Spanish, thus dashing Antonio's hopes for recovering Portugal's throne. Later, in 1589, the year after the English defeat of the SPANISH ARMADA, Queen Elizabeth I (1533–1603) of England militarily supported Antonio's return to Portugal. An invasion of the country failed; English forces returned home, and Antonio returned to Paris, where he died in 1595. Portugal, whose throne was now firmly held by Philip, remained a dependency of Spain until 1640. See also PORTUGUESE-MOROCCAN WAR OF 1578.

Spanish-Portuguese War of 1641–44 To strengthen his position against Spanish efforts to regain control of Portugal, the new Portuguese king, John IV (1605–56), made alliances with England and the Netherlands and signed a treaty in 1641 with France promising to wage war on Spain. Fighting between Spanish and Portuguese began with minor military encounters at the forts of Elvas and Badajoz; both sides then hastily made preparations for large-scale campaigns. Portugal sought to weaken Spain by separating the region of Andalusia from it, and Spain in turn backed a conspiracy in Lisbon to overthrow King John. Portuguese troops won success at Olivenca and at the defense of Beira in 1642. General Mathias d'Albuquerque (d. 1646?) led a Portuguese invasion of Spain in May 1644, and won an important victory at the Battle of Montijo later that month. In 1644, general European peace negotiations commenced (see THIRTY YEARS' WAR), but Spain refused to join them until France dropped demands for recognition of Portuguese independence. The opening of negotiations produced an unofficial, albeit temporary, cessation of hostilities. See also SPANISH-PORTUGUESE WAR OF 1657–68.

Spanish-Portuguese War of 1657–68   After the death of Portuguese king John IV (1605–56), Portugal feared Spain would renew its attempts to regain control (see SPANISH-PORTUGUESE WAR OF 1641–44). Consequently, Portugal sought alliances with France, England, and Sweden and prepared for an expected Spanish invasion. The attack came first on Olivenca, where Spanish troops evicted the Portuguese. A planned Portuguese offensive at Badajoz was scuttled with the approach of Spanish reinforcements, and it was not until January 1659 that the Portuguese scored a victory at Elvas. In May 1662, Spanish forces under Don Juan (John of Austria) (1547–78) defeated Portuguese troops under Frederick Herman Schomberg (duke of Schomberg) (1615–90), German soldier of fortune in Portuguese service, provoking panic in Lisbon. Don Juan took Évora but suffered defeat at the Battle of Ameixal on June 8, 1663. Schomberg won victories at Valencia de Alcántara, Villaviciosa, and Montes Claras and successfully invaded Andalusia (1665). Through the mediation of England's King Charles II (1630–85), Spain finally recognized Portugal's independence and its ruling House of Braganza by the Treaty of Lisbon in 1668; all conquered territory was returned.

Spanish-Portuguese War of 1735–37   Spain under King Philip V (1683–1746) became involved in the War of the POLISH SUCCESSION, supporting the claim of Stanislas Leszczynski (1677–1766) to the Polish throne and allying itself with France against Austria. Spanish troops invaded Lombardy and Italy with the French, while another Spanish force took control of Naples and Sicily in 1734. In South America, the Spaniards initiated war (1735) against their longtime rivals, the Portuguese, by seizing their chief stronghold, Colonia, on the Río de la Plata in Banda Oriental (Uruguay). Not until the British induced the Spanish to return Colonia, founded in 1680 by Portuguese soldiers, did fighting stop (1737).

Spanish-Portuguese War of 1762   Spain under King Charles III (1716–88) was neutral at first in the SEVEN YEARS' WAR but, when a British victory over the French appeared likely to upset Spanish power in Europe and overseas (especially its colonial trade in America), it concluded a commercial, political, and military alliance—the Bourbon Family Compact (1761)—with France against Britain. In 1762, the Spanish, now much involved fighting the British (who had declared war on Spain early that year and would seize and occupy Cuba and the Philippines until 1763), invaded Portugal, whose powerful chief minister Sebastião José de Carvalho e Mello (marquês de Pombal) (1699–1782) called upon the British for help. The town of Braganza and the fortress of Almeida fell to the Spaniards, who received aid from the French; Count William of Schaumburg-Lippe (1724–77) reformed and led the Portuguese army, gained valuable help from British troops under John Burgoyne (1722–92), John Campbell (1705–82), and others, and repulsed the invaders of Portugal by the end of 1762. By the Treaty of Paris (1763), Britain obtained the territory of Florida from Spain, now sharing in the French defeat in the larger general war.

Spanish Revolution of 1854   (July Revolution) General Leopoldo O'Donnell (1809–67) and Antonio Cánovas del Castillo (1828–97) headed a conspiracy to overthrow the corrupt Spanish government of Maria Cristina (1806–78), the unpopular and secretive queen mother. In late June 1854, rival government forces fought to a draw on the outskirts of Madrid. Meanwhile, Cánovas stirred up Madrilenian public support for a rebellion by publishing his *Manifesto de Manzanares*, promising, among other government reforms, the restoration of the national militia, which gained countrywide liberal backing. In July 1854, revolts broke out in Barcelona, Valladolid, and Madrid, which became a capital city of chaos for 10 days. The premier resigned, and finally the throne agreed to establish a "Junta of Public Safety" and promised liberal reforms. Queen Isabella II (1830–1904) recalled the retired Baldomero Espartero (1792–1879) to restore order, which he did by the end of July. He became premier, with O'Donnell his war minister, to the chagrin of Maria Cristina, who, after much dissension, left Spain and went into exile on August 28, 1854. See also CARLIST WAR, FIRST; SPANISH CIVIL WAR OF 1840–43.

Spanish Revolution of 1868   The increasingly autocratic rule of Spain's Queen Isabella II (1830–1904), whose personal life was a public scandal, caused some of her ministers to foment a military rebellion to oust her in July 1868. But it failed, and the leading rebel generals were banished to the Canary Islands. Isabella was in France to sign an alliance with Emperor Napoleon III (1808–73) when Admiral Juan Bautista Topete y Carballo (1821–85) issued a revolutionary proclamation at Cádiz, Spain, on September 18, 1868. Quickly uprisings occurred in Madrid and other cities; the queen returned, and exiled liberal generals reentered the country, including Juan Prim y Prats (1814–70), who had led an abortive uprising in 1866. At the Battle of Alcolea, near Córdoba, rebel forces led by General Francisco Serrano (1810–85) decisively defeated the Spanish royal army under General Manuel Pavía y Lacy (1814–96) on September 28, 1868. Isabella fled to France the next day and was declared deposed. While Spain boiled in disorder, a provisional government was established that did away with reactionary laws, abolished the Jesuits and other religious orders, and ensured universal suffrage and freedom of the press. Serrano and Prim, the government leaders, summoned a constituent assembly (Cortes) that promulgated a new constitution after voting to have a monarchical government. See also CARLIST WAR, SECOND; FRANCO-PRUSSIAN WAR.

Spanish Saharan War (1976–91)   In 1976, after Spain ceded the northern two-thirds of its overseas province of Spanish Sahara to Morocco and the southern third to Mauritania, Moroccan troops led some 350,000 people in the forced "Green March" to settle in the territory, which Morocco claimed. Mauritanian troops also entered the area in 1976, but a Saharan guerrilla group called the Popular Front for the Liberation of Saguia el Hamra and Río de Oro (Polisario Front), supported by Algeria and Libya, began a struggle to gain the territory's independence as the Saharan Arab Democratic Republic (SADR), attacking both Moroccans and Mauritanians. In 1980, Mauritania signed a treaty with the Polisario Front, giving up sovereignty over its area to the Polisarios. Morocco's King Hassan II (1929–), however, annexed that area and sent troops to occupy it. In 1981, SADR's government-in-exile was recognized by more than 40 nations, including a majority of African countries, and Polisario guerrillas attacked the Moroccan forces, attempting to crush them in the deserts of what is now called Western Sahara. To prevent Polisario attacks, the Moroccan military constructed a defensive wall system from southern Morocco through Western Sahara down to Cape Bojador (Bujdur). The Organization of African Unity (OAU) pressed for a referendum on self-determination in the territory, while the United Nations advanced a similar proposal, which Morocco accepted in 1988. Meanwhile, Polisario forces made occasional attacks on the defensive wall, and the OAU vainly attempted to mediate between Morocco and the SADR, which claimed sovereignty over Western Sahara. In 1991, the war was suspended after an agreement between Morocco and the Polisario to hold a UN-supervised referendum. But both sides raised objections, mainly about the proposed voting lists to be used and procedures. As a result, the referendum was postponed year after year. In 1997, the new UN secretary-general, Kofi Atta Annan (1938–), named James Baker (1930–), former U.S. secretary of state, his special envoy to try to settle the dispute. Talks between Morocco and the Polisario, mediated by Baker, led to acceptance of terms for a referendum for self-determination in Western Sahara in 1998. But necessary preparation for the repatriation of refugees and other Saharans residing outside the territory who are eligible voters caused postponement of the referendum until December 1999, provided the parties fully cooperate.

Spanish Succession, War of the (1701–14) Fearful of a Spanish-French union, England, Holland, and Austria formed an anti-French alliance when Spain's King Charles II (1661–1700), a Hapsburg, chose a Bourbon as his successor, and thus France's King Louis XIV (1638–1715) claimed the Spanish throne. In Europe, the war, which was fought in North America as QUEEN ANNE'S WAR, took place in Italy, Germany, Spain, and the Spanish Netherlands (see GRAND ALLIANCE, WAR OF THE). French forces battled in Italy from 1701 until 1706, when they were driven out. Battles in Germany showed the great skill of England's duke of Marlborough (1650–1722), for he blunted and then stopped a 1703 French drive toward Vienna in battles at Donauwörth (1704) and BLENHEIM (1704). England, under the leadership of Queen Anne (1665–1714), vigorously pursued the war, capturing Gibraltar in 1704 and helping take Barcelona, Spain, where Austria's Archduke Charles (1685–1740) established himself as King Charles III of Spain. Most of the war's decisive fighting occurred in the Spanish Netherlands. In 1706, some 50,000 French troops, advancing east between Namur and Liège, encountered an equivalent English-Dutch-German force under Marlborough near Ramillies. In battle there, Marlborough feinted on the French left flank, then turned to the other flank while 25,000 of his cavalrymen charged the French, wheeled right, and covered the entire French rear. Allied infantry attacked the French frontally. The French were defeated disastrously, losing about three times as many men as the allies. The allied victory forced the surrender of Brussels, Antwerp, and surrounding Belgian areas. However, in 1707, allied defeats were unsettling, with French reoccupation of Brussels and Ghent. About 100,000 French troops then marched up the Scheldt River toward Oudenarde (Audenaarde), where they were surprised by an 80,000-man army under Marlborough on July 11, 1708 (Marlborough had hastened so swiftly from Brussels to meet the French that he had had no time to properly deploy). By day's end, the allied forces had enveloped the French right and forced a French retreat from the battlefield back toward Ghent; some 7,000 French surrendered and 6,000 were killed or wounded; allied losses totaled 3,000. The allies also won at Lille (1708), Tournai (1709), and Malplaquet (1709), where both sides suffered heavy losses. When Barcelona's King Charles III became Holy Roman Emperor Charles VI in 1711, England, now fearful of a Spanish-Austrian union, began peace talks with the French, called Marlborough home (his leadership might have prevented a 1712 allied defeat at Denain), and joined an armistice under the Peace of Utrecht in 1713. The Holy Roman Empire fought on until consenting to the treaties of Rastatt and Baden the next year. Louis XIV agreed that the crowns of France and Spain would remain separate; France recognized Protestant succession in England; the Empire was promised the Spanish Netherlands but did not accept Bourbon rule in Spain. From this active and costly war (and, later, from the War of the AUSTRIAN SUCCESSION), Europe began to learn that dynastic or national rights are inferior to careful maintenance of the balance of power. See also CAMISARDS' REBELLION; GLORIOUS REVOLUTION; QUADRUPLE ALLIANCE, WAR OF THE.

Spartacus, Revolt of See SERVILE WAR, THIRD.

Spartan-Achaean War of 228–226 B.C. The end of the Wars of the DIADOCHI left Greece divided, and Greek city-states fought among themselves for dominance. The chief contestants toward the end of the third century B.C. were Macedonia and Sparta; a third was the Achaean League (a confederation of Greek cities in Achaea), a former Macedonian ally, whose leader, Aratus of Sicyon (d. 213), was determined to bring the whole of the Peloponnesus into the league. In opposition, Sparta's King

Cleomenes III (c. 260–219) provoked the league by entering a disputed territory (229), winning over Aetolian cities and a wedge of territory around Manitea, in a section of Arcadia not under the league's control. In 228, Aratus captured part of the area, and Cleomenes began to march. The league declared war. Only skirmishes occurred at first. In 227, Aratus was reelected the league's general and, after a defeat at Lyceum, recaptured Mantinea. Made tyrant of Sparta after a revolt in 226, Cleomenes resumed war, recovered Mantinea, invaded Achaea, and crushed the league's army at Hecatobaeum. The league almost accepted him as its head but, bereft of allies, decided to opt for peace. Beginning in 225, the league began to fall apart, as Macedonia and Sparta (and, later, Rome) became the sole competitors for control of Greece.

Spartan-Achaean War of 193–192 B.C.

The Second MACEDONIAN WAR weakened Sparta and gave impetus to the revival and growth of the Achaean League. In a treaty (195), victorious Rome had assigned authority over Spartan seaports to the league as a reward for military assistance, but it had not granted possession. Philopoemen (253?–183), the league's general, wanted control of Sparta itself; revolts (193) in the Spartan seaports, incited by Nabis (207–192), tyrant of Sparta, offered an opportunity. The revolts had regained the cities for Sparta, and Nabis laid siege to Gytheum (193), which held an Achaean garrison. Philopoemen secured the help of Titus Quinctius Flaminius (230?–174), a famed Roman general. Advancing to Gytheum before the Roman armies arrived, Philopoemen opened a campaign that was completed successfully by the Romans while the league's armies pursued Nabis's forces toward Mount Barbosthenes (192). The Spartan forces were almost annihilated. Philopoemen went on to blockade Sparta and ravage Laconia. But the stronger Flaminius stopped fighting, restored the *status quo ante*, and disappointed Philopoemen's hopes for Sparta's annexation. The Spartan loss led to Nabis's assassination (192) and to Sparta's brief membership in the Achaean League.

Spartan-Achaean War of 189–188 B.C.

Because of Greek internecine struggles, the Roman Senate attempted to follow a philhellenic policy while still holding Macedonia in check. The Achaean League, still ambitious to control the entire Peloponnesus, annexed Messene and Elis and crushed a revolt in Sparta (191). However, the league's general, Philopoemen (253–183), had acted without permission of the Roman consul in quelling the Spartan revolt; he did so again when Sparta stormed Las near Gytheum (189). Philopoemen threatened war unless the Spartans guilty of the attack were surrendered; the Spartans instead killed 30 pro-Achaean citizens, voted secession from the Achaean League, and surrendered to Roman protection. Philopoemen declared war, and the league's forces invaded Laconia (188), captured between 80 and 350 of the Spartan secessionist faction, and executed them after a show trial. Sparta's city walls were dismantled; all mercenaries, anti-Achaeans, and enfranchised helots were exiled; all laws became Achaean; and a new treaty was forced upon Sparta. Philopoemen's harshness brought about Roman intervention, and restriction of the league's new power, and also forced the eventual return of the league to an alliance with Macedonia.

Spirit Lake Massacre (1857)

In revenge for the killing of several Sioux Indians by a white trader, a band of Sioux under Chief Inkpaduta (fl. 1850s) raided a newly built white settlement near Spirit Lake in northwestern Iowa on March 8–12, 1857. The Indians murdered 32 men, women, and children and carried off four women, two of whom were subsequently killed; of the two surviving female captives, one was set free voluntarily and the other was ransomed. A detail from Ft. Ridgely in Minnesota later pursued the Sioux under Inkpaduta but failed to catch them.

Spithead Mutiny (1797)

British sailors in their home port at Spithead on the English Channel engaged in monotonous and uneventful blockade work against the French (see FRENCH REVOLUTION-

ARY WARS). Demanding better treatment, Royal Navy crews mutinied on April 15, 1797, sending their officers ashore and operating both their ships and their base by committee. In an orderly manner, they presented petitions to the Admiralty and the Commons, citing harsh discipline, poor food, and low wages (unraised since the reign of King Charles II [1630–85]) as their grievances. Impressed by their decorum, British authorities found their requests reasonable and granted them, ending the mutiny within three weeks. See also NORE MUTINY.

Spurs, First Battle of the (1302)   As part of a 1207 Flemish trade alliance, English king Edward I "Longshanks" (1239–1307) sent troops to the land annexed in 1301 by King Philip IV "the Fair" (1268–1314) of France. Annexation and control being quite different conditions, Philip's army, sent to subdue Flanders, was often opposed by the English army, usually without important consequence (see ANGLO-FRENCH WAR OF 1300–1303). But in 1302, an army from the fortified Flemish city of Bruges, with English help, met a French army near Courtrai on July 11, 1302. The French were totally defeated. When the battle ended, a huge pile of golden spurs taken from slaughtered French knights became a symbol of victory and gave the conflict its name. **Second Battle of the Spurs** (1513). King Henry VIII (1491–1547) of England inherited longstanding enmity with France with his crown. Tempted by a desire to prove his mettle and be a European power to be reckoned with, he joined the Holy League of Pope Julius II (1443–1513) against France (see HOLY LEAGUE, WAR OF THE). Henry drilled his army near Bayonne while Spain fought in Navarre; he lost a naval battle and made vain attempts to retake Guienne (see HUNDRED YEARS' WAR). When the league made peace, Henry, unfulfilled, seized two French cities and fought the Battle of the Spurs (so-called because of the rapid departure of the defeated French) at Guinegate in northern France on August 16, 1513. Henry then made peace, married his young sister to the aging French king Louis XII (1462–1515), and returned home in satisfying triumph.

Sri Lankan Civil War of 1983–   Sri Lanka's post-independence history has been marked by ethnic tensions, leading to violent episodes (see CEYLONESE REBELLION OF 1971) between the Buddhist Sinhalese majority and the Hindu Tamil minority (18 percent of the population), which was discriminated against and felt increasingly marginalized by the policies of successive governments. The bloodiest and defining chapter, however, began in July 1983 when members of the Liberation Tigers of Tamil Eelam (LTTE), a group fighting for an autonomous state in northeast Sri Lanka, ambushed and killed 13 Sinhalese soldiers (apparently not without provocation) in the Jaffna district. On July 23, after their public burial in Sri Lanka's capital of Colombo, a frenzied mob went on a rampage (with the collusion of the police, army, and government supporters) looting and burning Tamil homes, businesses, and factories. The next day, 20 Tamils on a bus were brutally executed. Between July 25–27, prisoners in Welikaldi killed 52 Tamil inmates in their cells. Curfew was imposed in Colombo on July 26 and extended nationwide as the violence spilled into Kandy and Gampola. Already, 384 people had died and over 50,000 Tamils were rendered homeless. On July 28, Sri Lanka's President J. R. Jayewardene (1906–96) outlawed the Tamil United Liberation Front (TULF), the largest opposition party. The curfew was lifted on July 29 but reimposed after more clashes in Colombo. On August 5, 1983, the parliament banned (150-0) all political parties supporting separatism and also any public discussion anywhere of Tamil independence. Despite the extension of a state of emergency and curfews in several districts, violence erupted in the east on August 27–28 during a rally protesting the July killings. The government alleged that the violence had been instigated by the four leftist political parties to undermine it. Tamil businesses sustained $90 million in losses, over 100,000 Tamils were displaced, and the economy was severely crippled by the loss of nearly 30,000 jobs. The government appealed for international aid in rebuilding. Over the next few years, the violence intensified and became more organized. Meanwhile, India—which had secretly sheltered and armed the Tamil militants—had been asked to mediate in the conflict. However, the Indo–Sri Lanka Peace Accord, formalized four years and 6,000 lives later, was anything but that. Signed by President Jayewardene and India's Prime Minister Rajiv Gandhi (1944–91) on July 29, 1987, it granted local rule to two Tamil-dominated northeastern provinces, provided the rebels surrendered their arms to the 7,000-strong Indian Peace-Keeping Forces (IPKF) dispatched specifically to ensure compliance with the accord. Envisaged as a buffer, the IPKF's presence instead proved inflammatory. The Sinhalese rebels in the south wanted the accord annulled and stepped up their aggression. The IPKF's strong-arm tactics against Tamil rebels and civilians alike drew them into the conflict in the northeast. As the violence escalated, killing about 6,000 civilians, some 1,200 Indian soldiers, and 800 Tamil Tigers, so did the clamor for the immediate withdrawal of the IPKF, which did not happen until March 1990. Ranasinghe Premadasa's new government pledged to end discrimination against minorities. In 1991, Rajiv Gandhi was assassinated by a Tamil suicide bomber at a rally in southern India. Premadasa met the same fate in Colombo in May 1993. During the intervening years, the clashes continued. Chandrika Kumaratunga (1945–), elected president in 1994, tried to jumpstart the peace talks. Her focus was on a cease-fire (broken in 1995) and on rebuilding the war-torn northeast. But after the rebels attacked Kandy's holy Temple of the Tooth, the LTTE was banned and peace talks suspended. In 1998, its 50th year of independence, Sri Lanka was still reeling from the human (75,000 dead) and economic impact of this unresolved conflict, and a lasting peace appeared to be elusive.

Standard, Battle of the (1138) Through his marriage, King David I (1084–1153) of Scotland had become the earl of Huntingdon, thus controlling English lands in Northumbria and Durham. He wanted to add them to Scotland but did not try to annex them until he was offered Huntingdon, Northumbria, and Cumberland in exchange for supporting Matilda (1102–67) in her struggle with King

Stephen (1086–1154) over the English throne (see ENGLISH DYNASTIC WAR OF 1138–54). In April 1138, David led his forces into northern England and at Northallerton encountered an army of English barons surrounding a "standard" (pole with a banner) mounted on a wagon (whence the battle's name). The English standard displayed three local Yorkshire saints and the Sacred Host. Blessed by the archbishop of York, the English attacked and defeated the Scots, who heard false rumors of David's death and fled. Stephen allowed the lands to remain in Scottish hands during his reign.

Steenkerke, Battle of (1692) The French campaign in the Spanish Netherlands during the WAR OF THE GRAND ALLIANCE opened with a bloody, 36-day siege of Namur in southern Belgium. King William III (1650–1702) of England, victorious in the IRISH WAR OF 1689–91, took both supreme command and the offensive on the Alliance side, attempting to surprise the French camp at Steenkerke (Hainaut, Belgium). William's vanguard inflicted heavy casualties on the French, who reorganized to fight eight English regiments before falling back; they were relieved by fresh troops. The weary English infantry, involved in both gunfire and hand-to-hand combat, fell back before midday (August 3, 1692). The whole Alliance army then retreated, having lost over 8,000 men, among them two generals. See also NEERWINDEN, BATTLE OF.

Stilicho's Wars with the Visigoths (A.D. 390–408) The Visigoths broke a peace established in 381 by Eastern Roman emperor Theodosius I (346?–95), by allying with Huns to devastate Thrace in 390 (see VISIGOTHIC RAIDS ON THE ROMAN EMPIRE, EARLY). This action brought confrontation with the Roman general Flavius Stilicho (359?–408), a former Vandal who understood barbarian strategies. By 392, the Romans had suppressed Visigothic raiding. With the death of Theodosius and the elevation of Alaric (370?–410) as the Visigoths' king, raiding resumed in the southern and western Balkans. Greece suffered the destruction of the Temple of Demeter (396); of the northern cities, only Thebes held out. Stilicho, whose troops failed to win in Thessaly, was briefly transferred to Italy. He returned to Greece in 397 and blockaded the Visigoths in Arcadia, but his strategy was undercut because he was again sent to Italy to punish the African Moors' refusal to ship grain to Rome. Some Visigoths then devastated Epirus until Alaric, placated by bribes, made peace in 397; he was made *magister militum* of Illyricum (Croatia) and gained Epirus, an unfortunate reward, for he could now harass the Western Roman Empire. With a Gothic leader, Radagaisus (d. 405), Alaric formed a Danubian confederation, including Vandals and Alans. By 401, northern Italy, especially Milan, was under attack. Stilicho's forces drove the confederation armies westward and then defeated them in a bloody battle at Pollentia (Polenza) in northern Italy in 402, capturing Alaric's wife and family and forcing Alaric back to Illyricum. Within a year, he was back besieging Verona. Stilicho's forces could have massacred the Visigoths; however, Stilicho, who desired Rome's eastern throne, developed a treaty (403) aiming at an invasion of this younger empire. It failed because Radagaisus went instead to Italy, losing to Stilicho at Fiesole in 405. Alaric took over the Goths' base in Noricum (southern Austria), demanded a huge payment for Gothic service to Rome, and received it in 407. A mutiny among Stilicho's troops brought an allegation of treason, a trial, and Stilicho's execution in 408. Freed of effective opposition, Alaric began to threaten Rome itself (see ROME, VISIGOTHIC SACK OF).

Stockholm Massacre   See KALMAR CIVIL WAR OF 1520–23.

Streltsy, Revolt of the (1698) The streltsy (from *strelets*, meaning "musketeer") were an elite Russian military corps, part of whose duty was serving as the czar's bodyguard, which gradually acquired a formidable political power. They backed the Miloslavsky family's championing of Czar Ivan V (1666–96) and

his sister-regent Sophia Alekseyevna (1657–1704) over their half-brother Peter I (1672–1725). Peter became sole czar upon Ivan's death, and the streltsy, angry because Peter's reforms of the corps required greater activity and superior efficiency, fumed until Peter went on a European tour (1697–98). Then they began to fulminate against him and demonstrate in favor of Sophia's return to power. In Moscow in the summer of 1698, some 2,200 marched in arms to elevate Sophia but were quickly suppressed by Peter's mercenaries (Peter had returned from Vienna upon hearing news of the plot). His punishment of the conspirators was extreme: more than 1,000 were killed by torture or impalement; a reign of terror spread to other anti-Petrists; Sophia was forced to become a nun, imprisoned and under guard for the rest of her life; and the streltsy were disbanded.

Suburb (Arrabal), Revolt of the (A.D. 818) In 805, conspirators attempted unsuccessfully to overthrow al-Hakam I (d. 822), the Muslim Ummayyad emir (ruler) of Córdoba, Spain. Repressive acts and more taxes by al-Hakam increasingly angered Córdoban dissidents, ultimately leading to a violent revolt by the inhabitants of a suburb (*arrabal* in Spanish) of Córdoba in March 818. The emir's palace was stormed, but the palace guards slaughtered the attackers and went on to kill (by crucifixion) 300 of the suburb's notables. The suburb was sacked and entirely destroyed, and its approximately 60,000 inhabitants were expelled from Spain; some settled in Fez, Morocco; others became pirates, sailed to Alexandria, Egypt, and took control there until they were driven to Crete in 827. In Toledo, Spain, revolts by Spanish Christians and Jews were also savagely crushed by al-Hakam in 814 and by his successor as emir, Abd-ar-Rahman II (788–852), in 837.

Sudanese Civil War of 1956–   After Sudan in eastern Africa became independent in 1956, southern rebels, largely black Christians and animists, began fighting for autonomy from the national government at Khartoum, the capital, in the Muslim, Arabized north. The southern Sudanese resented the government's attempt to impose Islam and the Arab language and to monopolize Sudan's resources and wealth. Several military coups wracked the parliamentary government before General Gaafar Muhammad Nimeiry (1930–) led a successful military takeover in 1969. He withstood various efforts to overthrow him and declared an Islamic republic in 1983. Meanwhile, Arab militias practiced slaving raids in the south, which retaliated against government targets. After Nimeiry was overthrown in a popular uprising in 1985, the Sudan People's Liberation Army (SPLA), dominated by Dinka tribesmen, demanded repeal of a set of harsh Islamic laws (Shari'a), which called for floggings and amputations for criminal offenses even by non-Muslims. The SPLA, which controlled much of the rural south, also insisted upon the establishment of provincial parliaments. SPLA forces overran villages in 1988, bringing northern military reprisals. An estimated 3 million people fled from the south to escape fighting and starvation caused by crop failure through drought (1988). The continuing war severely hampered international relief efforts. A peace pact, signed on November 16, 1988, between the SPLA and government rulers fell apart. During a 1991–92 offensive by the Khartoum government, every major town in the south was seized, but victory eluded the north. Again, in 1994, a government offensive—aerial bombing and ground campaigns—failed to wipe out the rebels around Juba, Wau, and Kapoeta in the south. About 400,000 people sought refuge in camps across Sudan's borders with Zaire (Congo), Uganda, Kenya, and Ethiopia. By 1998, the country remained paralyzed by the war, which (along with famine and disease) had killed an estimated 1.5 million Sudanese. Local militias, encouraged by the government, have taken slaves as their compensation, although the Sudanese regime denies condoning slavery. The rebel SPLA, accused of forcibly inducting military-age boys, has not, however, taken Arab prisoners for slaves. In October 1998, the war seemed to intensify, as the government declared national mobilization and closed schools and universities.

Sudanese War of 1881–85 Muhammad Ahmad (1843?–85), a devout Muslim, withdrew to Aba Island on the White Nile River in Sudan, where his piety attracted many followers, including members of the militant dervish sect. He soon declared himself the Mahdi, "the expected guide," and began a holy war against the Egyptians, who were controlled by the British from Cairo. The government sent soldiers to capture him, but they were attacked by the Mahdi's followers and forced to retreat. On August 12, 1881, the dervishes were again victorious at the Battle of Aba. The Mahdi and his forces moved westward to Qadir Mountain in Kordofan, Sudan. Twice expeditions were sent against him, and twice they were ambushed and annihilated. Meanwhile thousands of Muslims flocked to the Mahdi's side, and Egyptian soldiers shied away from fighting fellow Muslims led by a man rumored to have great supernatural powers. In mid-1882, the Mahdi's forces took the offensive against government garrisons throughout Kordofan. One by one the garrisons fell, but when poorly armed fanatical Mahdists tried to storm the city of El Obeid, they were cut down by overpowering rifle fire. The Mahdists then besieged the city to starve it into submission; they destroyed an expedition coming to its relief; and on January 17, 1883, the city surrendered. A new army under the command of a British officer was organized and dispatched to recapture El Obeid; constantly harassed en route, it was finally routed. The British government advised the Egyptians to abandon the Sudan to the Mahdists and sent General Charles George "Chinese" Gordon (1833–85) to oversee the evacuation of Khartoum. Gordon decided to defend the city instead. For almost a year, the Mahdi's forces besieged Khartoum defended by Gordon and a small garrison, which awaited the arrival of a relief force. On January 26, 1885, the Mahdists overran the city's fortifications and killed the defenders, including Gordon. Two days later the relief force arrived but was ordered to withdraw. Though the Mahdi died five months later, his successor, the khalifa ("the adviser") Abdullah (1846?–99), led the dervishes to victory and liberated Sudan from foreign rule.

Sudanese War of 1896–99   Britain decided to reconquer the Sudan, which was controlled by the Mahdists under the khalifa Abdullah (1846?–99) and which was of increasing colonial interest to the Italians and French in Africa. An Anglo-Egyptian army led by General Horatio Herbert Kitchener (1850–1916) advanced south from Egypt up the Nile River into the Sudan. Accompanied by a river gunboat flotilla, Kitchener constructed a railway as he moved and encountered stiff resistance from the Mahdists. The Anglo-Egyptian force captured Dongola (September 21, 1896) and Abu Hamed (August 7, 1897) and was victorious against the Mahdists at the Battle of the Atbara River (April 8, 1898). A 40,000-man army of dervishes and Mahdists, under the command of the khalifa, savagely attacked Kitchener's army of about 26,000 men at Omdurman on the Nile, just north of Khartoum, on September 2, 1898. The attack was repelled with machine guns, and the khalifa suffered heavy casualties. Kitchener counterattacked, and his cavalry—the 21st Lancers, among whom was Winston Churchill (1874–1965)—bravely drove the dervishes from the field. The khalifa and his remaining forces took flight and were pursued into Kordofan, where they managed to hold their ground for more than a year. On November 24, 1899, the Mahdist forces were completely destroyed, and the khalifa was slain in battle. The condominium government of the Anglo-Egyptian Sudan was then established.

Suez War   See ARAB-ISRAELI WAR OF 1956.

Sukhothai Revolt   See THAI WAR OF 1371–78.

Surinamese Guerrilla War of 1986–92   The National Military Council, led by Lieutenant Colonel Désiré Bouterse (1946–), controlled the government of Suriname (formerly Dutch Guiana) between 1982 and 1988, a period when opposition leaders were murdered, natives were restrained, and human rights abuses regularly occurred. In Suriname's eastern region in 1986, increased rebel resistance under Ronnie Brunswijk, a former bodyguard of Bouterse, resulted in a declared state of emergency in December, thus compelling Bouterse to hold general elections that brought a democratic civilian government to power in January 1988. But Bouterse remained head of the army and, in 1989, refused to accept the conditions of a peace signed by Brunswijk and Suriname's representative in Kourou in neighboring French Guiana. Many of Suriname's native Indians also opposed the settlement, fearing that the army's withdrawal from the ethnic Bush Negroes' regions in the east (agreed to by the government) would threaten their security. In 1990, the army retook control of Moengo and Langatabbetje, on the Suriname–French Guiana border; in 1991, Bouterse and Brunswijk agreed to a cease-fire. The two principal guerrilla factions—the Surinamese Liberation Army or Jungle Commando (led by Brunswijk) and the Tucayana Amazonas (led by Thomas Sabajo)—finally stopped fighting in May 1992. They and other rebels signed a peace treaty with the government, which granted a general amnesty and integration of rebels into the civilian police. At Moengo on August 24, 1992, Brunswijk was the first to lay down his arms before mediators from the Organization of American States (OAS).

Swamp Fight   (1675) When the Narraganset Indians decided to join the Wampanoag in their war against the English colonists (see KING PHILIP'S WAR), they were concentrated in a fort on high ground in the middle of a swamp outside present-day Kingston, R.I. The white colonists' army of about 1,000 men from Massachusetts and Connecticut was commanded by Governor Josiah Winslow (1629–80) of Plymouth. On December 19, 1675, he led the Massachusetts contingent in an assault against the front gate of the Indian fort, but was repulsed by a wall of fire. Meanwhile, Captain Benjamin Church (1639–1718) had led the Connecticut and Plymouth soldiers around to the back, where they successfully forced open the rear gate. They set fire to the wigwams inside, and the Indians took flight across the icy swamp, fighting as they ran. Almost 1,000 Narraganset were said to have died; their chief, Canonchet (d. 1676), managed to escape but was killed the next year.

Swedish Civil War of 1520–23 See KALMAR CIVIL WAR OF 1520–23.

Swedish Civil War of 1562–68 After King Erik XIV (1533–77) succeeded to the Swedish throne, his half-brother John (1537–92), duke of Finland, sought to oust him and acquired a power base in Poland through marriage to the sister of Polish king Sigismund I Augustus (1520–72). Erik's forces seized John's capital, Åbo (Turku in southwestern Finland), and John was taken and imprisoned for treason. Erik, mentally deranged at times, then ordered the murders of members of the illustrious Sture family (Swedish nobles) for collusion with John. Set free after relinquishing his duchy, John fomented revolt among the nobility; civil war erupted after John seized Stockholm's fortress during Erik's wedding celebration in 1568. Stockholm was successfully besieged by John's troops, and Erik was persuaded to abdicate in favor of John in exchange for his personal safety (Erik was imprisoned in 1569 and probably died of poisoning in prison in 1577). John was proclaimed King John III in Stockholm and soon ended the long, ongoing DANISH-SWEDISH WAR OF 1563–70.

Swedish-Danish Wars See DANISH-SWEDISH WARS.

Swedish-Russian Wars See RUSSO-SWEDISH WARS.

Swedish War of 1630–35 At the height of the Holy Roman Empire's success following the Danish phase (see DANISH WAR OF 1625–29) of the THIRTY YEARS' WAR, well-trained Swedish troops led by Lutheran king Gustavus II (1594–1632), fearing the challenge of encroaching imperial power and desiring to prevent Protestantism's extinguishment, landed in Germany in June 1630, and began securing Pomerania. Johan, count of Tilly (1559–1632), replaced Count Albrecht von Wallenstein (1583–1634) as Imperial army chief when Emperor Ferdinand II (1578–1637), hoping to achieve German unity, ordered Wallenstein's dismissal to please powerful German princes who hated him. Tilly's forces besieged, captured, and sacked the Lutheran free city of Magdeburg (1630–31). The electors of Saxony and Brandenburg, followed by numerous German Protestant princes, immediately allied themselves with Sweden's Gustavus, who had gained financial support from France by the Treaty of Bärwalde. Near Leipzig at the Battle of Breitenfeld on September 17, 1631, Swedish-Saxon forces defeated Tilly's army and afterward advanced into the Rhineland, securing most of northwest Germany and threatening the empire by the end of the year. Gustavus's army moved south, engaged, and annihilated most of Tilly's army at the Battle of Lechs (April 15–16, 1632); Tilly himself was fatally wounded. Augsburg, Munich, and southern Bavaria fell to the Swedish king, who continued his drive toward Vienna. At Lutzen, imperial forces under Wallenstein, who had been recalled in desperation by Ferdinand, suffered defeat by the Swedes, who were, however, disheartened by Gustavus's death on the battlefield. Wallenstein's increasing ambition, conspiring to be king of Bohemia, proved a threat to Ferdinand, and he was murdered in 1634. After losing the Battle of Nördlingen in 1634, the Swedes withdrew from southern Germany, and when Ferdinand agreed to abrogate the anti-Protestant Edict of Restitution, the empire achieved peace with Saxony in 1635. Most German princes then acquiesced. Sweden, spent by the war, appealed for French help (see FRENCH WAR OF 1635–48).

Swedish War with Lübeck See LÜBECK'S WAR OF 1531–36.

Swiss-Austrian Wars   See AUSTRO-SWISS WARS.

Swiss-Burgundian Wars   See BURGUNDIAN-SWISS WARS.

Swiss Civil War of 1436–50   See OLD ZURICH WAR.

Swiss-Hapsburg Wars   See AUSTRO-SWISS WARS.

Swiss-Milanese War of 1478   As the number of mercenaries and traders passing through the St. Gotthard Pass on the Swiss-Italian border increased, clarification of the ill-defined border became necessary. The Val Levantina renounced its allegiance to Milan in 1475 and, supported by some armed Swiss, unsuccessfully besieged the nearby city of Bellinzona on the Swiss-Italian border near the St. Gotthard Pass. Later, on December 28, 1478, the disciplined Swiss infantrymen won a victory at the Battle of Giornico, defeating a larger Milanese force. Although most Swiss cantons refused to support further military efforts against the Milanese, the Swiss canton of Uri took Bellinzona in 1500.

Swiss Revolt of 1798   The Swiss region of Vaud under the leadership of Frédéric César de La Harpe (1754–1838) revolted against its hated Bernese rulers. At the suggestion of Napoleon Bonaparte (1769–1821), French revolutionary troops invaded Switzerland, ostensibly to help the Vaudois but actually to assist the change of Vaud to the "Lemanic Republic" (January 1798), which shortly became the canton of Leman and, after 1803, the canton of Vaud. Within several months, France had control of all Switzerland, renamed now the "Helvetic Republic." Bern declared war on France; two separate Bernese forces fought the French on March 5, 1798, winning one battle and losing another; Bern then surrendered. Most other Swiss cantons rose in revolt against the French and were successful at Rothenturm, Morgarten, and Lake Zug in May 1798. Afterward, in response to a French call for a peace convention, most Swiss laid down their arms and submitted to a constitution framed by the French for their own purposes. The canton of Unterwalden continued to fight but lost to superior French forces in July that year. Peace the next month on French terms destroyed the Swiss Confederation until 1815; the Swiss were required to aid the French in the NAPOLEONIC WARS and to permit an army of occupation. Only the half-canton of Nidwalden held out, but it finally capitulated after 1,000 men, 102 women, and 25 children were massacred at Stanz in September 1798. See also FRENCH REVOLUTIONARY WARS.

Swiss-Swabian War   See AUSTRO-SWISS WAR OF 1499.

Swiss War against Savoy   (1403–16)   In 1403, the two Swiss cantons of Uri and Unterwalden occupied the upper Ticino River valley, on the Swiss-Italian border, in an attempt to expand southward. In 1410, they called on the other members of the Swiss league of cantons for support and occupied also the Val d'Ossola at the southern end of the Simplon Pass. The Swiss lost this valley to the duchy of Savoy in 1414 but were able to regain it by the end of 1416. Most of the Alpine passes into northern Italy were now controlled by the Swiss.

Swiss War of Independence   See AUSTRO-SWISS WAR OF 1385–88.

Syrian-Egyptian War, First (Seleucid War) (274–271 B.C.)   After the death of Alexander the Great (356–323 B.C.), his Macedonian generals divided up his vast empire, and they and their descendants fought almost continually for dominance in Asia Minor for the next century (see DIADOCHI, WARS OF THE). The Ptolemies controlled Egypt, and the Seleucid dynasty reigned in Syria. In 274, the Syrians under King Antiochus I Soter (324–261) invaded the land of Palestine (parts of modern Israel, Jordan, and Egypt), which Ptolemy II

Philadelphus (309–246) claimed for Egypt. Antiochus was successful at first on land, but after three years Egypt's warships controlled the coastal ports on the Mediterranean. **Second Syrian-Egyptian War** (260–255 B.C.). This conflict went better than the first for the Syrians, who were now ruled by King Antiochus II Theos (286–247). His forces regained control of the cities lost by his father, Antiochus I, along the eastern Mediterranean. He eventually agreed to a peace in which he gave up his wife, Laodice (fl. 3rd cent.), and married Ptolemy II's daughter, Berenice (d. 246). The marriage was not a happy one, and after several years Antiochus left his second wife and their infant son and returned to Laodice. She, however, supposedly poisoned him, proclaimed her son, King Seleucus II (d. 226), and ordered her followers at Antioch to kill Berenice and her son. Their murders in 246 enraged Berenice's brother King Ptolemy II Euergetes (282?–221) and brought on warfare. **Third Syrian-Egyptian War** (Laodicean War or War of Berenice) (246–241 B.C.). Ptolemy II's Egyptian land forces invaded Seleucid Syrian territory and made their way to Babylonia, while his naval forces recaptured the territory lost in the previous war. Much of southern Asia Minor and Syria, as well as some Aegean ports, fell under Ptolemy II's control; these conquests marked the height of the Ptolemies' Egyptian empire. In 223, Antiochus III "the Great" (242–187) ascended the Syrian throne and set about rebuilding the Seleucid Empire. **Fourth Syrian-Egyptian War** (219–217 B.C.). Syrian forces under Antiochus III invaded Palestine and pushed south almost to the Red Sea. King Ptolemy IV Philopator (244?–203) raised an Egyptian army to counter this threat. In 217, the opposing forces met at Raphia (Rafa), where the Egyptians were victorious and soon recovered Palestine as Antiochus's forces retreated. **Fifth Syrian-Egyptian War** (202–198 B.C.). Antiochus III and his Seleucid Syrians attempted again to seize Palestine and were successful. They routed the Egyptians for good at the Battle of Panium in 198. Palestine and other Ptolemaic possessions in Syria and southeast Asia Minor, except for Cyprus, came under the control of the

Seleucids. To ensure the peace agreement, Antiochus gave his daughter, Cleopatra I (fl. 193–176), to King Ptolemy V Epiphanes (210?–181), in marriage. See also DAMASCENE WAR; MACEDONIAN WARS; SELEUCID WAR WITH EGYPT.

Syrian-Parthian War of 141–139 B.C. The king of Parthia, Mithridates I (fl. 171–138), called also Arsaces VI, and his forces had seized several Greek cities in Asia Minor and had made them vassals. The Greeks were oppressed by their Parthian overlord and begged the Seleucid king of Syria, Demetrius II Nicator (d. c. 125), to liberate them. In 141, Demetrius reluctantly consented and led an army into Parthia. At first he was victorious in several engagements, but in 139 his forces were decisively defeated and he was taken prisoner. For 10 years he was held captive by the Parthians but was allowed to maintain a royal household. Meanwhile, Antiochus VII Euergetes or Sidetes (158?–129), Demetrius's brother, had gained the throne of Syria; his forces expelled the Parthians from Syrian territory (Mesopotamia) and invaded Media, part of the Parthian kingdom (see SYRIAN-PARTHIAN WAR OF 130–127 B.C.). In 129, Demetrius was released by the Parthians, who perhaps hoped to foment civil war in Syria; however, Antiochus was killed during a surprise raid by the Parthians, and Demetrius regained the throne.

Syrian–Parthian War of 130–127 B.C. Antiochus VII Euergetes or Sidetes (158?–129) marched with a Syrian force into Parthia, regained control of lost territory, and supposedly forced Parthia's King Phraates (d. 128) to set free his brother, Demetrius II Nicator (d. c. 125), held captive for 10 years. Antiochus continued on into Media but was slain by Phraates's forces at the Battle of Ecbatana (Hamadan, Iran), Media's capital. Antiochus's allies, the Scythians, then invaded Parthia to reinforce the Syrian troops, causing Phraates to regroup his soldiers to meet the new attackers. The Parthian king led an army against them but was defeated and killed. Nevertheless, the Seleucid Syrians had been prevented from retaking Parthian lands they once controlled.

Syrian-Roman War of 192–189 B.C.   The Aetolians of central Greece wanted to supplant Macedonia as the dominant state in Greece after the Macedonian defeat at Cynoscephalae in 197 (see MACEDONIAN WAR, SECOND). In 192, they attacked Rome's allies in Greece and asked King Antiochus III "the Great" (242–187) of Syria to intervene on their behalf. He gladly did so and sailed across the Aegean with some 10,000 soldiers. His army, however, was defeated by the Romans at Thermopylae in 191, and the king was forced to flee back to Asia. The navies of Rhodes and Pergamum (Bergama) joined the Romans and twice won victories over Antiochus's fleets. The Romans were able to invade Asia Minor under the command of Publicus Cornelius Scipio Africanus (237–183) and his brother Lucius Cornelius Scipio (fl. 2nd cent.). The opposing armies met at the Battle of Magnesia near Smyrna in December 190. At first the Syrians under Antiochus III seemed to be winning, but they pursued one flank of the Roman cavalry too far, and another flank of Romans surrounded the Syrian foot soldiers and cut them to pieces. This was a disastrous battle for Syria, which lost its coastal territories, surrendered all but 10 of its warships, gave up its elephants (which had been an asset in battle), and were forced to pay a huge indemnity. Thereafter Syria was reduced to a landlocked nation.

Syrian War with Pergamum (224–221 B.C.) Pergamum (Bergama) was one of the Greek cities in northern Asia Minor founded by Alexander the Great (356–323), the Macedonian conqueror. About 230, its king, Attalus I Soter (269–197), scored a great victory over the Galatians, inhabitants of Galatia in central Asia Minor; this encouraged him to seek to expand his territory in other directions, causing him to come in conflict with the new young Seleucid king of Syria, Antiochus III "the Great" (242–187). While Antiochus and his forces were in the south fighting in Palestine, Attalus invaded northern Syria with an army and annexed much territory. Antiochus's cousin, Achaeus (d. 214), realized the threat by Attalus and went to meet it with force. Fighting ensued in several areas, and by 221 Pergamum's invading forces had been driven back to their original borders. Antiochus regained control of most of central Asia Minor.

T

Taiping Rebellion (1850–64)   In 1850, the Manchu (Ch'ing) rulers of China ordered the imperial troops to break up a religious society whose beliefs were partially based on Protestant doctrine. The Chinese emperor's army was soundly defeated, and the society, founded and led by a scholar, Hung Hsiu-ch'uan (Hong Xiuquan) (1814–64), was quickly transformed into a rebellion against the Manchus. The malcontents of southern China flocked to join the movement, which at first was poorly supplied. In 1852, they captured an arsenal at Yochow (Yüe-yang), and, once fully armed, they swept down the Yangtze (Chang) Valley and seized Nanking (Nanjing), where Hung Hsiu-ch'an proclaimed his new dynasty, the Taiping or "Great Peace." His followers wrought great destruction throughout southern China, and the provincial and imperial forces were unable to stop them. In 1860, the foreign powers, which had wrested major concessions for themselves from the Chinese in the First and Second OPIUM WARS, decided it was in their own best interests to come to the aid of the Manchus. An American naval officer organized a small imperial army along western lines, and its successes earned it the name "Ever Victorious Army." In 1862, the British officer, Charles George Gordon (1833–85), took command and under his leadership many walled towns and cities were retaken. Two Chinese armies raised and led by volunteers also aided in suppressing the rebels. In July 1864, Nanking was taken by storm, and a year later the last pockets of resistance were overwhelmed. Much of the once prosperous areas of China lay in ruin and desolation, and millions had died during the course of the rebellion that shook the Ch'ing dynasty profoundly. See also NIEN REBELLION.

Taira-Minamoto War   See GEMPEI WAR.

Tajikistan Civil War of 1992–   In landlocked Tajikistan in central Asia, armed Muslim rebels began battling the neocommunist-dominated government in 1992 (pro-democracy groups continued to vie for power). Seeking to make the country an Islamic state, the Tajik rebels at first centered their fighting in the south, notably around Kulyab and Kurgan Tyube. The factional warfare threatened to move to Dushanbe, the capital. By 1996, operating also from northern Afghanistan (on Tajikistan's southern frontier), the rebels began regularly clashing with some 25,000 Russian troops stationed there. Russia had placed the troops in Tajikistan to support its president, Imomali Rakhmanov (1952–), who had won office in 1994. The town of Kulyab, Rakhmanov's political stronghold, became a major military resupply base for Afghan forces opposed to the Taliban, the fundamentalist Islamic group that took control of Afghanistan in 1997 (see AFGHAN CIVIL WAR OF 1979–). After extensive negotiations under United Nations auspices, Rakhmanov signed a cease-fire agreement with his leading opponent, Sayed Abdullah Nuri, in Moscow on December 23, 1996. Though both sides agreed to complete peace talks, clashes continued between Islamic rebels and the hard-line government. About 100,000 people had died in Tajikistan since the war began.

Talambo Incident (1862) Peruvian laborers assaulted a group of Basque immigrants on the hacienda (plantation) of Talambo, Peru. The government of Spain dispatched a royal viceroy to Peru to demand compensation, but the Peruvian government resented the obvious Spanish contempt for Peru's independence and refused to receive the Spaniard. After negotiations failed, a Spanish squadron seized Peru's valuable guano-producing Chincha Islands in 1864. The Peruvian president agreed to Spain's demands, paying 3 million pesos for the return of the islands (1865); this infuriated most Peruvians and soon led to his ouster by General Mariano Ignacio Prado (1826–1901). See also SPANISH-PERUVIAN WAR OF 1864–66.

Tamerlane, Conquests of (1360–1405) Tamerlane, the English name for Timur Leng ("Timur the Lame") (1336–1405), is often regarded as a reincarnation of Genghis (Jenghiz, Chingis) Khan (1167?–1227), but he was a Turk of the Barlas clan, not a Mongol; a conservative Muslim, he was, not like Genghis, tolerant of other religions; and, though intellectually vigorous and illiterate like Genghis, he was too impatient to be concerned with civil administration. Raised as a Turkish chief's son in the traditions of the recently defunct (1335) Il-Khan empire, Tamerlane inherited Mongol approaches to military strategy and the manipulation of adversaries, making the Turks into an experienced, disciplined force for brutal conquest. He is well known for the Mongol-like barbarity of his wars, begun while he was still in his mid-20s. Then vizier (high Muslim official) to the White Horde (Chagatai Khanate), he directed its conquest of Transoxania (presently Uzbekistan) and Turkistan (region in Central Asia extending from the Caspian

Sea to the Gobi Desert). By 1369, Tamerlane had become supreme leader of the Turkish tribes, and under his command the Muslims regained their military superiority, bloodily finishing his wars in Transoxania. He took control of the White Horde khanate in 1375, conquered three-quarters of their land by 1380, and then ruthlessly subdued Persia to the Euphrates River by 1387. These conquests were interrupted by TAMERLANE'S FIRST WAR AGAINST TOKTAMISH, whom he had installed as khan (leader) during the GOLDEN HORDE DYNASTIC WAR. In 1392, Tamerlane's forces crossed the Euphrates to establish control of Georgia and Azerbaijan and the southern Russian states (the Crimean Tatars felt his strength during TAMERLANE'S SECOND WAR AGAINST TOKTAMISH). Afterward he returned to Samarkand, the capital of the Timurid Empire, but, as was his habit, stayed there only briefly to plan and begin his invasion of India, during which he ravaged Delhi (see TAMERLANE'S INVASION OF INDIA). Returning to Samarkand with Indian treasures, he next ravaged Georgia again after defeating Lithuania's Duke Witold (Vytautus) (1350–1430) (see TAMERLANE'S DEFEAT OF WITOLD). Like the Mongols (see MONGOL-PERSIAN WAR, SECOND), his forces advanced toward the Mediterranean, seizing Baghdad, Damascus, and Aleppo from the Mamluk Turks by 1400. In the Ottoman Empire, Tamerlane defeated Bayazid I (1347, 1403), Ottoman sultan and conqueror of Asia Minor, at the 1402 Battle of ANGORA. Now 66, Tamerlane returned to Samarkand, planned with careful detail an invasion of China, but died en route in 1405. His dynasty (the Timurids) lasted for a century, dedicating more to the advancement of scholarship, science, and art than to military activities. See also GENGHIS KHAN, CONQUESTS OF.

Tamerlane's Defeat of Witold (1399) The Golden Horde's (Kipchak Khanate's) domination over western and southern Russia was not restored after TAMERLANE'S INVASION OF RUSSIA. Witold (Vytautus) (1350–1430), the grand duke of Lithuania, briefly battled with Tamerlane (Timur) (1336–1405) for control in that area. Allied with his cousin the king of Poland, Witold had captured the cities of Kiev and Smolensk, almost reaching Moscow; moreover, he had sheltered Toktamish (Tuqtamish) (d. 1406), Tamerlane's main adversary in the area, when he fled the 1395 Battle of the Terek River (see TAMERLANE'S SECOND WAR AGAINST TOKTAMISH). The Golden Horde's vassal khan (leader) had asked for Toktamish's extradition; Witold refused it and planned a crusade against the khanate. Leading an army of Lithuanians, Poles, and 500 Teutonic Knights, Witold advanced into Kipchak territory. Tamerlane marched his army from Samarkand and attacked Witold's coalition from the rear at the Battle of the Vorskla River in 1399; Tamerlane's tactics confused the enemy, resulting in the slaying of two-thirds of Witold's troops. Witold took flight and was pursued by Tamerlane's destructive Tatars (Tartars) to the Dnieper River; he escaped capture while the Tatars regained Kievan tribute and continued their scorched-earth campaign into Poland. The campaign not only restored Golden Horde authority but it also freed Russia from its chief European medieval foes, the Teutonic Knights. Witold benefited, too; he helped destroy the Teutonic Knights' domination at the Battle of Tannenberg in 1410 (see TEUTONIC KNIGHTS' WAR WITH POLAND AND LITHUANIA OF 1410–11).

Tamerlane's First War against Toktamish (1385–86) As he had done to his rival Mamak (Mamai) (d. 1380), the Mongol leader Toktamish (Tuqtamish) (d. 1406) quickly forgot his obligations and gratitude to his mentor Tamerlane (Timur) (1336–1405) (see GOLDEN HORDE DYNASTIC WAR). In his actions to aid the enthronement of Toktamish, Tamerlane had taken over the former Golden Horde territory of Urganj; Toktamish vowed to take it back. Learning that Tamerlane was in the Caucasus, Toktamish decided to conquer his capital, Samarkand, furtively. His successful military activity in 1385 caused war to erupt in Khwarizm and Transoxania, for Tamerlane learned of his protégé's intentions and raced back to Samarkand, arriving earlier than Toktamish and immediately attacking him. Because Tamerlane's army was regarded as the

vanguard of a larger force, the invader withdrew, pursued by Tamerlane in 1386 after he had punished in horrible Mongol fashion Urganj, city and state, and the Jats of the White Horde, who had aided Toktamish. Then Tamerlane planned to meet Toktamish face to face in the Kipchak Khanate, departing from Samarkand in 1391 to discipline Toktamish and to invade Russia. **Tamerlane's Second War against Toktamish** (1391–95). Crossing the empty steppe north of the Caspian to reach the Great Bulgar state, Tamerlane learned that Toktamish and his army marched on the western side of the Ural River. He decided to attack, although his movement would require extensive marching for his undersupplied army across desert areas. When his army approached Toktamish's rear guard in 1391, the ungrateful protégé tried to stop it with gifts and fawning diplomacy, but Tamerlane, knowing the pain of betrayal, advanced and attacked. The three-day Battle of the Steppes (Kandurcha) at first saw Tamerlane's left side nearly destroyed until his reserve troops, placed at the rear of the center, circled and broke Toktamish's rear (in addition, a rumor from Tamerlane's camp that Toktamish had died demoralized the latter's men and helped in their defeat). Toktamish escaped, made an alliance with the Mamluk sultan of Egypt, and regrouped, harrying Tamerlane's frontier in 1394. Meanwhile Tamerlane invaded (see TAMERLANE'S INVASION OF RUSSIA), with his forces attacking and partially sacking Toktamish's Golden Horde capital at Sarai and supporting a puppet khan (leader) there. In 1395, Tamerlane again attacked Toktamish at the Battle of the Terek River, drove him from the battlefield, and afterward relentlessly followed him westward to the Ukraine. Toktamish, living the life of a fugitive, attempted a reconciliation with Tamerlane but with little success; the Golden Horde never regained its former glory before its eventual collapse to the Crimeans in 1502.

Tamerlane's Invasion of India (1398–99) Like Genghis (Jenghiz, Chingis) Khan (1167?–1227), Tamerlane (Timur) (1336–1405), the Turkish-Mongol leader, seldom made war without a public motive. Ostensibly, he was now reacting against the city of Delhi's over-kindness to non-Muslims; actually, he was taking advantage of dynastic controversy over its sultanate and Muslim-Hindu battles throughout India. Also, in accord with Mongol tradition, his invading troops entered India through Afghanistan, built a boat bridge to cross the Indus River, and plundered the Punjab during a leisurely march to the east. Tamerlane's goal was Delhi and its riches. The city was not besieged. His troops won a battle outside it (December 17, 1398) and took many prisoners; Tamerlane entered in triumph, was enthroned after one day, and collected ransom money. But conditions soon deteriorated: his soldiers looted and raped with abandon; Indian prisoners were taken and executed—as were those from the Battle of Delhi—to an estimated total of 50,000 to 80,000. Delhi was then burned. After 10 days, the conquerors left unhurriedly, hauling wagonloads of treasure with captured artisans to build Samarkand's now ruined cathedral mosque. Pillaging en route, they laid waste to Lahore, recrossed the Indus, and returned home. Delhi, a devastation ground, now contended with plague and famine (its historians note that nothing moved for two months) However, the tradition of Tamerlane, who had gained wealth and eliminated an enemy in his planned campaign against China, lived on in northern India; his great-grandson Babur (1483–1530) founded the great Mogul dynasty in 1526.

Tamerlane's Invasion of Russia (1391–95) After his first battle (1391) with his foe Toktamish (Tuqtamish) (d. 1406) in the second punitive war (see TAMERLANE'S SECOND WAR AGAINST TOKTAMISH), Tamerlane (Timur) (1336–1405) seized the city of Sarai, the capital of the Golden Horde (Kipchak Khanate), partially sacking it. Ever restless, Tamerlane led his 100,000-man army into Russia, conquering the city of Yelets, but stopping about 200 miles from Moscow. Instead of advancing, until 1395, Tamerlane's forces deviated toward Persia, massacring the non-Muslim population of Tenais (Azov), ravaging the lands of the Circassians and Alans, and destroying the Caspian Sea port of As-

trakhan. At the Battle of the Terek River (1395) Toktamish was defeated permanently, and Tamerlane completed the destruction of Sarai and fought the resisting Georgians on his way south. In northern Persia, his army entered the Elburz Mountains and, revealing an unusual capacity for mountain warfare, defeated two supposedly impregnable fortress-cities. Now the master of northern, mountainous Persia and the Caucasus region (as well as his earlier territories), Tamerlane and his forces, after about eight months of rest, returned to Samarkand, his capital, to prepare, with one interruption, for his invasion of India (see TAMERLANE'S INVASION OF INDIA).

Taranaki War, First (1860–61) In New Zealand, in 1859, a Maori subchief of the Taranaki area on North Island sold Waitara River land to Europeans without the consent of his tribe, which subsequently resisted confiscation. In early 1860, the British, forgetful of the veto provision of the Treaty of Waitangi (see WAIRAU MASSACRE), attacked Maori pas (fortresses), but without success at first. The British finally seized the Te Arei Pa or fortress in 1861, gained a truce, and allowed the Maoris to keep possession of a European-owned Tataramaika tribal block of land. Despite the 1861 truce, this series of skirmishes between the Maoris and British continued sporadically until 1872, resulting in a major loss of Maori territory, the disruption of Maori society, and the loss of 54 percent of the Maori population (more than 50,000 persons) The 12-year period, often referred to collectively as the Second Maori War, continued in 1863 and again in 1864 with the second and third Taranaki wars. **Second Taranaki War** (Waikato War) (1863–64). War with the Maori resumed in April 1863, after Sir George Grey (1812–98), governor-general of New Zealand, built a military attack road into the Waikato River area, a section on North Island coveted by the European settlers. Government forces drove the Maoris from the Tataramaika block, laid sieges at Maori fortresses, and used gunboats and forest-ranger units against the Maoris, who were now applying guerrilla tactics. British victories at Meremere and Rangiriri

(1863) and at Orakau Pa (1864) led to a cessation of military actions in the Waikato area, but fighting continued on North Island through 1872. **Third Taranaki War** (1864–72). In the period, the famous Maori Hau Hau—a religiomilitary cult of warriors who considered themselves immune to bullets—wreaked havoc on the British forces. The government had desired peace after its victory at Orakau Pa in the Second Taranaki War, but the British East India Company's desire for additional lands caused the battles to continue. By now the provisions of the 1840 Treaty of Waitangi had been forgotten by all concerned. The British won at Weroroa Pa in 1865, but each succeeding colonialist drive was halted through 1868, when a second religiomilitary cult, the Ringatu, also hampered British success. Until 1872, the war became a conflict without clear victories or defeats; however, when both sides stopped fighting because of total exhaustion, the Maori society was so thoroughly disrupted that only King Country in New Zealand remained closed to Europeans. Not until the 20th century did the Maoris show any progress toward recovery from the war. See also BAY OF ISLANDS WAR.

Tatar (Tartar) Conquests and Invasions   See MONGOL CONQUESTS AND INVASIONS.

Tay Son Rebellion   See VIETNAMESE CIVIL WAR OF 1772–1802.

Ten Thousand, March of the (401–400 B.C.) Some 10,000 Greek mercenaries in hostile Persian territory (see CUNAXA, BATTLE OF) began a march to the nearest friendly haven, the Greek colony of Trapezus on the Black Sea, about 1,000 miles away. Trailed by Persian troops, the Greeks encountered great difficulties, for they had to live off the land, fight barbaric hill people, and endure winter blizzards. But their adventures were many: strange foods, unusual customs, bizarre natives. After five months of marching and fighting, about 6,000 survivors reached Trapezus and continued by boat to Chalcedon on the Bosporus, facing Byzantium.

Xenophon (c. 430–c. 355), one of the leaders of the heroic retreat, later wrote about it in his *Anabasis*, a celebrated Greek military history.

Ten Years' War (1868–78) In Cuba, in the 1860s, many of the native people opposed their Spanish rulers, who upheld slavery, increased taxes, and excluded them from governmental posts. After Queen Isabella II (1830–1904) of Spain was deposed in the SPANISH REVOLUTION OF 1868, Cuban patriots led by Carlos Manuel de Céspedes (1819–74) proclaimed a revolution at Yara on October 10, 1868, issuing *el grito de Yara*, a demand for Cuba's independence; they embarked on 10 years of guerrilla warfare that cost the deaths of about 200,000 Cubans and Spaniards and settled little of lasting importance. In 1869, the rebels established a revolutionary republic in eastern Cuba, where much of the fighting and killing took place; Spanish forces held Havana in the west and controlled most of the wealthy sugar-growing plantations in that part of Cuba. No major battles occurred in the war; there were, however, numerous raids and reprisals carried out by both sides. Among the main revolutionist leaders were Antonio Maceo (1848–96) and his brother José (1846–96), Máximo Gómez y Báez (1836–1905), Calixto García Íñiguez (1836?–98), and Tomás Estrada Palma (1835–1908); the Spanish forces were under the command of General Valeriano Weyler y Nicolau (1838–1930), whose cruelty against the Cubans was protested by the United States. Although the United States refused to intervene in the war, its sympathy and unofficial support for the Cuban rebels increased after the Spanish seized the steamer *Virginius* (October 31, 1873), a rebel-owned ship carrying arms to Cuba and deceitfully flying the U.S. flag; after its seizure, many of its crewmen, including some Americans, were executed by their Spanish captors, almost causing war between the United Sates and Spain. The fighting dragged on until the Spanish general Arsenio Martínez de Campos (1831–1900), sent to Cuba in 1877, arranged the Treaty of Zanjón, which was concluded on February 10, 1878, and promised reforms. Spain, however, did not live up to its promises, though it abolished slavery in 1886, and the Cuban discontent continued to grow. See also CUBAN WAR OF INDEPENDENCE.

Teutoburg Forest, Battle of the (A.D. 9)   Roman forces controlled Germany west of the Rhine and were pushing eastward toward the Elbe when Publius Quintilius Varus (d. A.D. 9), Roman general and consul, was sent (A.D. 6) to govern the part of Germany already Romanized and to lead three legions and auxiliary troops. Arrogant and tactless, Varus angered Arminius (Hermann) (18 B.C.?–A.D. 19), a German officer in the Roman army, a Roman citizen, and chief of the German Cherusci tribe. Arminius, planning a rebellion, deceitfully persuaded Varus to lead his legions and auxiliaries in the late summer of 9 into the Teutoburger Wald (Teutoburg or Teutoberg Forest), with Arminius as head of a rear guard. There in the forest (supposedly near modern Detmold, West Germany) supply wagons mired and troops broke formation; German guerrillas attacked, the German recruits deserted, and the rear guard fell upon the unsuspecting Romans under Varus, who tried vainly to march west to safety. On the second day of fighting, his cavalry was annihilated; by the end of the third day, some 20,000 infantrymen had been slain. Varus, humiliated, committed suicide. This Roman defeat forced Emperor Augustus (Octavian) (63 B.C.–A.D. 14) to set the Rhine not the Elbe, as the eastern and northernmost limit of the empire's German domains. See ROMAN NORTHERN FRONTIER WARS OF 24 B.C.–A.D. 16.

Teutonic Knights' Conquest of Prussia   (1233–83)   In 1226, the Polish duke of Masovia (Mazovia) invited the crusading Teutonic Knights (German military and religious order) to settle in Poland subject to his authority; he hoped to strengthen Polish Christianity and Poland's position vis-à-vis its neighbors. In 1233, the Teutonic Knights, who had moved north and established a stronghold at Thorn (Torún) on the Vistula River in northwestern Poland, began the conquest and Christianization of the heathen Prussians to the east. The knights' grand master, Hermann von Salza (d. 1239), placed his conquered lands under papal suzerainty, aspiring to establish an independent German church state. The Poles attempted unsuccessfully to assert their claim to suzerainty over the knights, who proceeded to conquer Prussia in a successful 50-year military campaign. In 1242, the duke of Pomerania (Polish region on the Baltic), sensing danger in the growing eastern German state of the Teutonic Knights, began war by encouraging a Prussian insurrection, but failed to evict the knights during a 10-year campaign (the duke of Masovia failed to grasp the Teutonic threat and, at first, supported the knights against Pomerania). Between 1261 and 1283, the knights exterminated large numbers of native Prussians, advancing to the Neman (Niemen) River and firmly establishing control of Prussia.

Teutonic Knights' War with Poland and Lithuania of 1410–11   When the grand duke of Lithuania supported a 1409 revolt in Samogitia (Lithuanian territory occupied by the Teutonic Knights since 1398), he earned the enmity of the knights, who had established control of Prussia, Pomerelia (eastern Pomerania), and lands in Germany and the eastern Baltic region. The knights also wanted to break the newly formed union between Lithuania and Poland, both of which mobilized their forces to meet the invading knights. At the Battle of Tannenberg (between the villages of Tannenberg and Grünfelde in East Prussia, now northeastern Poland) on July 15, 1410, Polish-Lithuanian troops under King Ladislas II (1350–1434) of Poland decisively defeated the Teutonic Knights, whose grand master and majority of commanders were slain during the 10-hour battle. Large areas of Pomerania and Prussia surrendered to advancing Polish-Lithuanian forces, who were, however, unable to capture the knights' stronghold at Marienburg (Malbork) and eventually withdrew, allowing the knights to regain all lost territory. Nevertheless, the eastward expansion of the oppressive Teutonic Knights had been halted for good, and by the first Treaty of Thorn (Torún) on February 1, 1411, the knights gave Samogitia and the Dobrzyń land to Lithuania until Ladislas's death, However, in 1422, after three interim military confrontations, the knights relinquished all claims to Samogitia. See also THIRTEEN YEARS' WAR.

Teutonic Knights' War with Poland of 1309–43
When the German province of Brandenburg threatened to take Pomerelia (eastern Pomerania) from Poland, the Poles asked the Teutonic Knights to defend the region (see TEUTONIC KNIGHTS' CONQUEST OF PRUSSIA). The knights repulsed the Germans and then seized Pomerelia, including the city of Danzig (Gdańsk), in 1309 (they massacred many Polish soldiers and citizens of Danzig). The knights' grand master made his residence at Marienburg (Malbork) castle near Danzig. King Ladislas I (1260–1333) of Poland, hoping to regain Pomerelia, Poland's only access to the sea, entered into negotiations with the pope, who had influence with the knights, and allied himself with Lithuania, an enemy of the knights. While Ladislas was diverted by a Bohemian threat to the south, the Teutonic Knights invaded Poland in 1331 and 1332. On September 27, 1331, at the Battle of Plowce, the knights suffered defeat at the hands of the Poles but afterward continued plundering northwestern Poland and taking territory. After Casimir III "the Great" (1309–70) succeeded to the Polish throne, he managed to stop the war by the Treaty of Kalisz in 1343; Poland regained lost territory in exchange for leaving Pomerelia under the knights's control.

Teutonic Knights' War with Poland of 1454–66
See THIRTEEN YEARS' WAR.

Texan War of Independence (Texan Revolution) (1836) About 30,000 Americans had settled in Mexican-held Texas by 1836. Mexico then attempted to stop American immigration and to establish a more centralized control over Texas. The Texans rebelled and declared their independence on March 2, 1836. About 5,000 Mexican troops under General Antonio López de Santa Anna (1794–1876) marched into Texas to crush the re-

bels. For 12 days 182 Texans held off the Mexican army at the Alamo in San Antonio before being overwhelmed and slaughtered. Soon afterward a Texan force of 400 men surrendered near Goliad and more than 300 of them were massacred. Responding to the battle cry "Remember the Alamo! Remember Goliad!" a small Texan army, commanded by General Samuel Houston (1793–1863), defeated Santa Anna's Mexicans at the Battle of San Jacinto on April 21, 1836. Santa Anna, taken prisoner, was forced to sign a treaty recognizing Texan independence. Though later repudiating the treaty, Mexico made no further effort to reestablish control of Texas, which became an independent republic with a desire for annexation by the United States.

Thai War of 1371–78 In 1371, King Boromoraja I (d. 1388) of Ayutthaya (Thai kingdom in present-day south-central Thailand) led a military expedition north to reestablish control over the Thai kingdom of Sukhothai, which was declining under Thammaraja II (d. 1409) and was in revolt. To discourage possible Chinese involvement in the conflict, Boromoraja sent gifts to the Chinese emperor in Nanking (Nanjing). In 1372, Boromoraja's forces seized the towns of Muang Nakhon, Phangkha, and Sengcharao; the next year they moved on Chakangrao, where Boromoraja had the chieftain Sai Keo (d. 1373) killed and drove out the other chieftain, Kham Heng (fl. 1370s), with his army. The Ayutthayans ceased hostilities for about two years until Boromoraja returned to rebellious Sukhothai, taking control of the city of Phitsanulok, capturing its chieftain Khun Sam Keo (d. c. 1376), and enslaving many city residents. In 1376, Boromoraja attacked Chakangrao, defended by Kham Heng and his forces, which were not allied with the Thai kingdom of Chiengmai to the north (Chiengmai's king hoped to ensure his realm's safety by maintaining Sukhothai as an independent buffer state between Chiengmai and Ayutthaya). The allied army attempted to ambush Ayutthayan forces, but failed; its soldiers were slaughtered in battle near Kamphaeng Phet. The Sukhothai chieftain Thao Phadong (fl. 1370s) escaped but was again defeated in battle, and many Sukhothai state officials were captured. In 1378, Boromoraja besieged Kamphaeng Phet once again. This time, however, Thammaraja agreed to peace terms: his surrender and cession of western areas, including Kamphaeng Phet, to Ayutthaya. Thammaraja was allowed to rule Sukhothai under Ayutthayan suzerainty, from a capital at Phitsanulok. See also KHMER-THAI WARS OF c. 1352–1444.

Thai War of 1387–90   In 1387, 14-year-old Sen Muang Ma (1373–1411) ascended the throne of Chiengmai, a Thai kingdom in the jungled mountainous areas of present-day northern Thailand. His uncle, Prince Phrohm (fl. 14th cent.), began plotting to seize the Crown and, when he was unsuccessful, called on King Boromoraja I (d. 1388) of the Thai kingdom of Ayutthaya (south-central Thailand) for help. Boromoraja sent an army, hoping secretly to gain control of Chiengmai. The opposing forces met at the Battle of Sen Sanuk, near the city of Chiengmai. Sen Muang Ma's forces were victorious, and the Ayutthayans withdrew from the country. Sen Muang Ma and his uncle resolved their differences; the latter joined the royal retinue and gave his nephew, as a token of friendship, a holy Buddha statue he had stolen from Kamphaeng Phet's ruler, who protested the theft and the occupation of his city by Prince Phrohm's forces. In response, Boromoraja led troops on a march to help Kamphaeng Phet, which he captured; afterward he died en route home in 1388. Two years later Sen Muang Ma led troops ostensibly to help the Thai kingdom of Sukhothai (central Thailand) regain independence from Ayutthayan domination. But Sukhothai's King Thammaraja II (d. 1409), learning about the possible takeover of his kingdom by Chiengmai, confronted and defeated Sen Muang Ma, who was forced to flee on the backs of two servants in order to avoid capture.

Thai War of 1411   Following the death of King Sen Muang Ma (1373–1411) of Chiengmai (Thai kingdom in what is now northern Thailand), a succession dispute arose between his sons, Prince Sam Fang Ken (d. 1442) and Prince Yi Kumkam (fl. 1411–20). The latter prince requested help from King Intharaja I (d. 1424) of Ayutthaya (Thai kingdom in central Thailand), who sent an army under vassal king Thammaraja III (d. 1419) of Sukhothai to place Yi Kumkam on the throne of Chiengmai. To besiege and shoot into the town of Phayao, Thammaraja's Ayutthayan troops erected a 72-foot-high earthen hill fort nearby and fought a battle in which both sides allegedly used cannons. Phayao's defenders, who melted down brass tiles to make a cannon, repulsed the attackers and destroyed their fort. A short time later the Ayutthayans laid siege to the capital city of Chiengmai, which fiercely resisted all attempts to take it, until finally Sam Fang Ken suggested that the succession dispute be settled by a single contest between two champion warriors—one Chiengmai, the other Ayutthayan; Yi Kumkam agreed to renounce his claim to the throne if his warrior (the Ayutthayan) lost. After several hours of combat on foot between the rival champions, the Chiengmai candidate was declared the winner when his opponent was wounded in the big toe. Consequently, the Ayutthayans withdrew from Chiengmai, marched north, and captured the town of Chiengrai, where they carried off many captives to be slaves in Ayutthaya (indemnification for the cost of the war).

Thai War of 1442–48   King Sam Fang Ken (d. 1442) of Chiengmai (Thai kingdom in modern northern Thailand) was forced to abdicate by his sixth son, Prince Chao Lok (1411–87), who assumed the throne as King Sri Sutham Tilok. Immediately a dynastic dispute arose when Sam Fang Ken's 10th son, Prince Chao Joi (d. c. 1446), refused to support his brother-king, brought his father to the town of Muang Fang, and began a war to take power. When Sri Sutham Tilok seized Muang Fang, Chao Joi abandoned his father and fled to Thoen, where he successfully urged the town's governor to seek help from the Thai kingdom of Ayutthaya to the south. Ayutthaya's King Boromoraja II (d. 1448), seeking to extend his influence, was glad to march with troops to aid Chao Joi. However, before the arrival of Boromoraja at Thoen, the forces of Sri Sutham Tilok attacked and killed Chao Joi and the governor. While on the march, Boromoraja took captives until his advance was blocked by Chiengmai forces, which employed Laotian spies to infiltrate the Ayutthayan army and stampede its elephants by cutting off their tails. In the midst of the ensuing chaos, Chiengmai soldiers attacked and defeated the Ayutthayans. Boromoraja, becoming ill, returned home. In 1448, he again led a campaign against Chiengmai, but died before it could be completed.

Thai War of 1451–56   The enlarged Thai kingdom of Ayutthaya (central Thailand) was militarily strengthened under King Boromo Trailokanat (d. 1488), who desired ascendancy over the smaller Thai kingdom of Chiengmai to the north. In 1451, an insurrection broke out in the former Sukhothai kingdom against Ayutthayan rule; the Sawankhalok town leader and others asked Chiengmai's King Sri Sutham Tilok (1411–87) for help in an attempt to regain their independence. As a result, Chiengmai forces invaded Sukhothai but were compelled to withdraw. An Ayutthayan offensive led to the occupation of Chiengmai (1452). Later, Luang Prabang's Laotian king, Sai Tia Kaphat (d. 1479?), intervened in the war, forcing the Ayutthayans to retreat and the Chiengmais to defend themselves. A Chiengmai army later invaded Ayutthayan territory and briefly held Kamphaeng Phet; hostilities halted temporarily afterward.

Thai War of 1461–64   The neighboring, rival Thai kingdoms of Ayutthaya and Chiengmai again fell into hostilities after the conspiratorial town ruler of Sawankhalok (under the Ayutthayan yoke) left and became head of the Chiengmai town of Phayao. In 1461, Chiengmai forces of King Sri Sutham Tilok (1411–87) invaded Ayutthayan lands, moving south to take Sukhothai and besiege Phitsanulok. But a Chinese attack from Yunnan province on Chiengmai forced Sri Sutham Tilok to

withdraw his forces from Ayutthaya. In 1463, King Boromo Trailokanat (d. 1488) transferred his Ayutthayan capital to Phitsanulok in order to gain a more centralized and tighter military control. His forces repulsed another Chiengmai invasion and assault on Sukhothai, driving the invaders well back into their own land; at the Battle of Doi Ba (1463), fought in the moonlight and with the use of elephants, the Chiengmais drove Ayutthayan troops into a swamp and forced them to retreat. Peace was restored in 1464.

Thai War of 1474–75   Diplomatic encounters between the rival Thai kingdoms of Ayutthaya and Chiengmai to settle their differences only resulted in bloodshed for six years and eventually, in 1474, an Ayutthayan invasion and seizure of Chiengmai territory. King Sri Sutham Tilok (1411–87), whose Chiengmai forces suffered setbacks, sued for peace in 1475. Though no formal peace was made, hostilities ceased for about 10 years until envoys from Ayutthaya were murdered by Sri Sutham Tilok. An Ayutthayan invasion of Chiengmai was inconclusive (1486) and the fighting ended with Sri Sutham Tilok's death.

Thai War of 1492   War erupted again between the Thai kingdoms of Ayutthaya and Chiengmai—this time over a Chiengmai-owned crystal statue of Buddha stolen by the Ayutthayan king's son when he was in Chiengmai as a Buddhist priest. When his demand for the statue's return was not heeded, Chiengmai's King Phra Yot (fl. 1487–95) promptly attacked Ayutthaya and forced King Rama Thibodi II (1472–1529) to give back the statue taken by his son.

Thai War of c. 1500–1529   The larger Thai kingdom of Ayutthaya (also called Siam) was a menace to the smaller Thai kingdom of Chiengmai, which maintained an aggressive stance to keep from falling under its enemy's control. In 1507, Chiengmai's King Ratana (fl. early 1500s) began an offensive into Ayutthayan territory, but his forces were repulsed in a hard-fought battle near Sukhothai. The next year Ayutthaya took the initiative with an invasion of Chiengmai; after taking Phrae, the invaders lost a bloody battle nearby and were forced to withdraw. An Ayutthayan invasion in 1510 fared no better. Skirmishing persisted for five years until Chiengmai forces attacked Sukhothai and Kamphaeng Phet to the south. Ayutthaya's King Rama Thibodi II (1472–1529) and two of his sons mounted a strong offensive, evicting enemy troops from their soil and pushing them into Chiengmai as far as the Wang River, near Lampang; there Rama Thibodi was victorious in battle, then looted Lampang, and carried away a valuable Buddha statue. The Ayutthayans had received crucial Portuguese support (guns and a training corps) in this campaign. By the time of Rama Thibodi's death, Chiengmai forces had been ousted from Sukhothai and other Ayutthayan towns. See also SIAMESE-BURMESE WARS.

Thai War of 1660–62   A Chinese Manchu (Ch'ing) army attacked the Burmese capital of Ava (1659) in pursuit of a Ming pretender to China's peacock throne, Yung Li (d. 1662) (see BURMESE-CHINESE WAR OF 1658–61.) Fearing Ava's fall, Burma's king, who took refuge in Chiengmai (Thai city), requested help from King Narai (1632–88) of Ayutthaya (Siam). The Mons, who were in revolt in Lower Burma, also sought help from Narai. When the Chinese stopped their attack and withdrew, Chiengmai's officials tried to cancel the Burmese request for aid, but Ayutthayan forces were already on the march (Narai hoped to take control of the Burmese-dominated Chiengmai area). On their second attempt, Ayutthayan troops captured and plundered Chiengmai (1662) and afterward undertook a campaign deep into Lower Burma. In 1664, Chiengmai rebelled, evicted the Ayutthayans or Siamese, and restored Burmese rule; the region remained under Burmese control until 1727. See also SIAMESE-BURMESE WAR OF 1660–62.

Theban-Spartan War of 379–371 B.C.   In theory, the 386 King's Peace (see CORINTHIAN WAR) allowed the Greek city-states autonomy; in practice,

Sparta, anxious to please Persia, dominated tyrannically. Its chief opponent was Thebes, which Sparta purposely irritated by giving other Boeotian cities autonomy, by seizing the Cadmea, the citadel of Thebes, in 382, by causing a rebellion and then putting it down, and—to block Athenian and Chalcidian aid to Thebes—by capturing Olynthus in 379. The Thebans recaptured the Cadmea in 379, defeated two Spartan relief forces, and allied defensively with Athens in 378. From this date, Sparta's power declined rapidly. A second constitution-based Athenian League began, and Persia withdrew support for Sparta, which attempted several maneuvers: invasions of Boeotia (377 and 376), a treaty with Athens and the league (374), a Pan-Hellenic peace conference, which offended Boeotia (371), and a final vain military endeavor, ending in defeat at the Battle of Leuctra (371). Rebellions dissolved Sparta's Peloponnesian League; the strengthened Athenian and Boeotian leagues formed an Arcadian League with federal police powers, and Thebes became the dominant Greek city-state.

Theodoric's War with Odoacer (A.D. 489–93) The Ostrogoths (East Goths), a Germanic people, under their king Theodoric the Great (454?–526) had been making vexatious raids into the provinces of the Eastern Roman Empire. To get rid of the Ostrogoths, Roman emperor Zeno (Zenon) (426–91) of the East appointed Theodoric patrician (noble ruler) of Italy and commissioned him to lead his army into Italy to oust Odoacer (Odovacar) (434?–93), who had deposed the last Roman emperor of the West (see ROME, FALL OF) and become ruler of Italy. Leading more than 150,000 Ostrogoths, Theodoric marched across the Julian Alps and confronted Odoacer and his army in northern Italy, where the latter was defeated at the battles of Sontius (Isonzo) and Verona in 489; Odoacer then fled to his nearly impregnable capital of Ravenna, where he received reinforcements from the south and made a successful sortie against Theodoric's besiegers in 490. The Ostrogoths fell back to Pavia, were pursued by Odoacer's troops (half of them became preoccupied in battling an invading

Visigothic-Burgundian force), and won the Battle of the Adda River on August 11, 490. Odoacer again retreated to Ravenna, followed by Theodoric, whose forces besieged this city near the Adriatic Sea for three and a half years. Finally an Ostrogothic naval blockade forced Odoacer to make peace (February 27, 493); he agreed to a treaty by which he and Theodoric would rule Italy jointly. Shortly afterward, while attending a banquet with his sons and chiefs, Odoacer and the others were treacherously seized and murdered on the spot by Theodoric's men. Theodoric was proclaimed the sole ruler of Italy and enjoyed a long reign, although never officially recognized by the Roman emperor of the East.

Thirteen Years' War (1454–66) King Casimir IV (1427–92) of Poland longed to recover Baltic territory lost to the Teutonic Knights (German military and religious order) during previous wars (see TEUTONIC KNIGHTS' WAR WITH POLAND OF 1309–43; TEUTONIC KNIGHTS' WAR WITH POLAND AND LITHUANIA OF 1410–11.) The autocratic rule of the knights led to a Prussian revolt in 1454, which Poland supported. Casimir then declared war on the knights, who won an initial victory at Chojnice. But protracted war drained the knights' financial resources; in 1457, when mercenary soldiers could no longer be paid, the knights surrendered their capital-stronghold, Marienburg (Malbork), to the Poles. By 1462, the knights had been pushed back to East Prussia; they suffered a decisive defeat at the Battle of Puck (a fortress on the Vistula River south of Tczew) on September 17, 1462. Continuing Polish success led to the second Treaty of Thorn (Torún) on October 14, 1466; Poland was given Pomerelia and West Prussia, and the knights retained East Prussia, with a new capital at Königsberg (Kaliningrad), but their grand master became a vassal of the Polish king in that territory. The knights, formerly strictly a German order, were forced to accept Poles as members.

Thirty Days' War   See GRECO-TURKISH WAR OF 1897.

Thirty Years' War (1618–48) The underlying causes of this devastating, general European war were conflicts of religion: Protestantism versus Roman Catholic reform, pluralistic tolerance versus arbitrary imposition of faith, Lutheranism and Calvinism, and the Protestant Union and the Catholic League. It was also a conflict of politics: centralization of authority with the decline of feudalism versus the rise of independent German principalities. The Hapsburg (Austrian) dynasty sought to control as much as possible of Europe, helped by most German Catholic princes, while German Protestant princes and foreign powers (France, Sweden, Denmark, the Netherlands, and England) attempted to check the Hapsburg power. Spain periodically sided with the Catholic Hapsburgs and participated in the war. A revolt in Bohemia ignited the conflict (see BOHEMIAN-PALATINE WAR) when citizens elected the Protestant elector Palatine over the Catholic Hapsburg emperor, Ferdinand II (1578–1637), to the throne of Bohemia. Troops of the Catholic League were victorious, and Catholicism under the Hapsburgs was reimposed in Bohemia. Duke Maximilian (1573–1651) of Bavaria, with Spanish military aid, and Ferdinand's support, became the elector of the Palatinate. The inability of anti-Hapsburg countries to unite in aid to the Protestant states forced Denmark to wage alone the DANISH WAR OF 1625–29, thereby moving the battle theater from central to northern Europe. The Danes under King Christian IV (1577–1648) were badly defeated at the Battle of Lutter in August 1626 and at the Battle of Wolgast in September 1628; thus Denmark made peace with the Holy Roman Empire (Austria), agreeing not to interfere in German affairs by signing the Treaty of Lübeck in 1629. That same year, three months before the treaty, the Imperial high point of the war occurred when Emperor Ferdinand imposed the Edict of Restitution, divesting Protestants of all church lands acquired or taken since the Peace of Augsburg of 1555. Fearing the increasing Hapsburg threat and wishing to protect Protestantism from dissolution, Sweden's King Gustavus II (1594–1632) invaded Pomerania at the start of the SWEDISH WAR OF 1630–35 and, allied with Saxony,

Brandenburg, and most small German principalities, advanced to the Rhine River and then to the east, threatening Vienna itself in 1632. After Gustavus's death at the Battle of Lützen on November 16, 1632, when the Swedes defeated the Holy Roman Empire's forces led by Count Albrecht von Wallenstein (1583–1634), the German princes made peace upon the emperor's abrogation of the Edict of Restitution. Fighting alone and exhausted, Sweden appealed to France, whose forces thereafter entered the war (see FRENCH WAR OF 1635–48) Under the French leadership of Cardinal Richelieu (1585–1642), the conflict became a Hapsburg-Bourbon political struggle. The French defeated the Spanish to reach Alsace in 1639, while their Dutch allies disrupted Spanish supply lines at sea in the New World (America). France continued to push into southern Germany as Sweden pressured the Holy Roman Empire from the north. Many battles were fought, including Rheinfelden (a French-German army was victorious over Imperial forces in 1638), Breitenfeld (Swedes again won against imperial troops in 1642 after success there in 1631), Rocroi (French forces nearly annihilated the entire Spanish army in 1643), and Jankau (Swedish victory against Austrians and Bavarian allies in 1645). Complex peace negotiations took years while the fighting continued. The war's destruction was heightened by the pillaging and foraging necessitated to sustain many poorly paid mercenary troops and their dependents, who stripped the land bare, leaving much desolation throughout Germany The Peace of Westphalia concluded the war on October 24, 1648. German principalities gained autonomy under titular Imperial control; Sweden obtained territory on the Baltic and an indemnity; France received Alsace and most of Lorraine and a border at the Rhine; Switzerland and the United Provinces (northern states of the Netherlands) gained their independence; and the Holy Roman Empire granted equality to Catholic and Protestant states. Both Calvinism and Lutheranism were accepted. See also BÉARNESE REVOLTS; DANISH-SWEDISH WAR OF 1643–45; EIGHTY YEARS' WAR; FRANCO-SPANISH WAR OF 1648–59; FRONDE, WARS OF THE; MANTUAN SUCCESSION, WAR OF THE; TRANSYLVANIAN-HAPSBURG WAR OF 1645.

Thousand Days, War of a (1899–1903)   During the Colombian presidencies of Rafael Núñez (1825–94) and his successor Miguel Antonio Caro (1843–1909), both of whom were conservatives, the republic of Colombia was frequently disrupted by bitter political struggles between liberals and conservatives. Caro's successor, President Manuel Sanclemente (1820?–1902), was elected by the conservatives in 1898. Wrangling within the victorious conservative party, however, provided an opportunity for liberals to rise in revolt against the government in 1899. Vice President Jose Manuel Marroquín (1827–1908), a conservative, ousted Sanclemente from office in a successful coup d'état on July 31, 1900, and assumed the presidency. Violent, bloody clashes took place between armed liberals and conservatives, and Colombia fell into economic ruin as the civil war raged for three years. Marroquín's federal troops finally put down the liberal rebels and restored order; an estimated 100,000 Colombians lost their lives in the fighting, which ended in June 1903. Later that year Panama, a part of Colombia, declared its independence and, with the help of the United States, successfully broke away (see PANAMANIAN REVOLUTION OF 1903). In 1904, General Rafael Reyes (1850?–1921) was elected Colombian president and began to rebuild his humiliated, war-ravaged country.

Three Feudatories, Revolt of the (1 6 7 4 – 8 1) Three former Ming generals, including Wu Sankuei (Wu Sangui) (1612–78), had helped the Manchus take control of China and establish the Ch'ing dynasty in place of the Ming dynasty (see MANCHU CONQUEST OF CHINA). As a reward, the generals became governors of three feudatories (vassal states) in southern China, but later the Chinese Manchu emperor, K'ang-hsi (Kangxi) (1654–1722), felt threatened by the growing power of the three governors of Yünnan (ruled by Wu), of Kwangtung (Guangdong) and of Fukien (Fujian).

In 1673, the governor of Kwangtung gave up command of his army and retired; K'ang-hsi promptly abolished his feudatory. Wu refused the emperor's order to pay homage and to relinquish his rights, and he renounced his allegiance to the Manchus and declared his independence, taking control of Yunnan, Szechwan (Sichuan), Kweichow (Guizhou), Hunan (Henan), and Kwangsi (Guangxi Zhuangzu) provinces. The heirs to the Kwangtung and Fukien feudatories soon joined Wu in his rebellion. The emperor directed the imperial armies to squash the rebels in Kwangtung and Fukien first and this was done in several years after much bloodshed. Wu, who declared himself emperor and his dynasty the Chou, was driven back with his forces into Yunnan and Szechwan, where he continued to fight until his death from dysentery in 1678; his grandson carried on the revolt until it was crushed entirely three years later.

"Three Henrys, War of the"   See RELIGION, EIGHTH WAR OF.

"Three Sanchos, War of the" (1068) During the CASTILIAN CIVIL WAR OF 1065–71, King Sancho II (c. 1038–72) of Castile attempted to expand his territory at the expense of his neighbors. He launched a campaign against his cousin, King Sancho IV (1054–76) of Navarre, who summoned a cousin, King Sancho I (1043–94) of Aragon, to help him. Sancho II's Castilian troops were routed in battle in 1068, after some success at first, thanks largely to the leadership of Spanish soldier Rodrigo Díaz de Vivar (1040?–99), who won his sobriquet "el Cid Campeador" (lord champion) at the time (by killing the Navarrese champion in single combat). See also ALMORAVID CONQUEST OF MUSLIM SPAIN.

Three Years' War, Later   See JAPANESE LATER THREE YEARS' WAR.

Tiananmen Square Massacre (1989) Protests by students in China began with the death (April 15) of disgraced Communist Party chairman Hu Yaobang (Hu Yao-pang) (1915–89), a liberal reformer ousted in 1987 for not halting student demonstrations for democracy and human rights. In Beijing, university students eulogized Hu as a symbol of "modernization" and made peaceful daily marches of protest to Tiananmen Square, where they openly danced and debated over politics and corruption. Fearing their communist legitimacy threatened by the pro-democracy movement, the government leaders under Deng Xiaoping (Teng Hsiao-ping) (1904–97) ordered military forces to disperse the crowds and regain control. Supported by tanks and other armored vehicles, helmeted soldiers moved into Tiananmen Square and other Beijing neighborhoods late Saturday night June 3, 1989, and in the early morning hours the next day began throwing tear-gas shells and chasing students and others from the square. Some protesters held fast behind barricades, fighting with rocks and Molotov cocktails. Troops began firing their AK-47 assault rifles at the mobs, while tanks fired their cannons indiscriminately down thoroughfares. Within hours on June 4, the square was virtually emptied of all protesters, and hundreds of wounded were hustled away among smoldering vehicles and debris. The Chinese government proclaimed a great victory over "counter-revolutionary insurgents," and later issued harsh martial laws ordering the arrest of pro-democracy leaders and dissidents, similar to the practices in the CHINESE "CULTURAL REVOLUTION." An estimated 5,000 citizens were killed that day in Beijing. Chinese leaders since have largely silenced democracy and human-rights advocates, many of whom have been jailed or exiled.

Tientsin Massacre (1870) Many Chinese scholars and followers of China's many religions resented the white Christian missionaries who had flocked to China in the mid-19th century, and to stir up the common people they frequently circulated rumors that the foreigners were sorcerers. The French Sisters of Charity at their orphanage in the city of Tientsin (Tianjin) used to give small cash rewards to people who brought in homeless or unwanted children, which gave rise to the rumor that children were being abused, kidnapped, and used for witchcraft. On June 21, 1870, an angry Chinese crowd led by a local magistrate stood outside the orphanage; the French consul ordered his guards to fire on the mob to disperse it. Enraged by this, the Chinese stormed and sacked the orphanage, killing in the process 18 foreigners, including the consul and 10 nuns. A storm of protest issued from both Paris and Rome, and Western naval ships sailed to Tientsin. France demanded severe punishment for those responsible; 16 Chinese were executed, and China officially apologized to France.

Tiepolo's Rebellion (1310) The great council that governed Venice became an extreme oligarchy, membership in which was strictly through heredity. Shut out of governmental decisions, Venetians staged a popular rebellion (1300) that failed, with its leaders being hanged. Ten years later, Bajamonte Tiepolo (d. 1328) conspired with the patrician Querini family to take over the government. When the plot was leaked out, the conspirators were compelled to rebel before they were ready, seizing the piazza (public square) on June 15, 1310. Forces of the Venetian doge (chief magistrate), Pietro Gradenigo (1249–1311), soon suppressed the rebels in street fighting. The Querini leader was captured and executed, but Tiepolo managed to escape. Afterward a secret tribunal, the council of 10, was established ostensibly to "protect" the Venetian republic by uncovering conspiracies and tracking down rebels; in 1335, it became a permanent body, which gradually took over many governmental functions, notably financial and military affairs.

"Time of Troubles," Russian (1604–13) After the death of Czar Fëdor I (1557–98), his brother-in-law and chief adviser Boris Godunov (1551?–1605) engineered his own election as czar. But, in 1604, some boyars (Russian aristocrats) and important Poles who opposed Godunov put forth a czar pretender, "false Dimitri" (d. 1606), as Fëdor's legal successor (actually, Dimitri [1581–91], Fëdor's

younger brother, had been murdered in exile). On Godunov's sudden death in 1605, Poles and Cossacks enthroned the false Dimitri, who held power for about a year until he was murdered by hostile boyars. A Russian boyar, Basil IV Shuiski (d. 1612), seized the throne but was violently opposed by Poles and Cossacks. A second false Dimitri (d. 1610) appeared in 1608 and camped outside Moscow at Tushino (he later was known as "the thief of Tushino"). The forces of Basil suffered two defeats in battle against Cossacks and Poles, allowing the second false Dimitri to seize power (see RUSSO-POLISH WAR OF 1609–18). In 1610, Basil was ousted and the second false Dimitri was killed, and the Russian throne was contested for the next three years; a third and fourth false Dimitri claimed it, but the former was slain in 1611 and the latter was executed in 1613. The boyars offered the crown to the Polish king's son Ladislas (1595–1648), and lesser landowners offered it to the Swedish king's brother. In February 1613, however, the zemstvo (Russian representative assembly) elected Michael Romanov (1596–1645) the new czar. See also RUSSO-SWEDISH WAR OF 1613–17.

Timoleon's War (344–339 B.C.) The tyranny of Dionysius II (d. 344) was so harsh that Syracusan citizens appealed to their mother-city of Corinth for relief. Corinth sent Timoleon (d. 337), a statesman and general, remembered as "the scourge of tyrants," to fight against Dionysius and the supporting tyrant of Leontine (Lentini). Timoleon's antagonists were exiled and a new regime, a moderate oligarchy, was established. But Timoleon had inherited the struggle against the power of Carthage. In 341, he defeated a large Carthaginian force, regaining Acragas, Gela, and Camarina—cities lost in HANNIBAL'S SACKING OF ACRAGAS and HIMILCO'S WAR. A peace of almost 30 years was declared, to be disturbed by AGATHOCLES' WAR AGAINST CARTHAGE.

Tinchebrai, Battle of (1106) Robert Curthose (1054?–1134), duke of Normandy, had rebelled against his father (see WILLIAM I'S INVASION OF NORMANDY) and battled against his brother (see WILLIAM II'S WAR WITH ROBERT CURTHOSE). Upon his return from crusading in 1100, he attempted unsuccessfully the next year to seize the English throne from his younger brother, King Henry I (1068–1135). Later, Robert's misgovernment in Normandy caused Henry to lead an invasion and defeat his brother's followers at Tinchebrai, France, on September 28, 1106; Robert was captured and imprisoned at Cardiff, Wales, for the rest of his life. Tinchebrai is almost as important as the Battle of Hastings (see NORMAN CONQUEST), for it enabled the Anglo-Norman kingdom to reunite peacefully for the first time in three decades. See also ANGLO-FRENCH WAR OF 1109–13.

Tithe War, Irish (1831) Irish Catholics forced by law to pay tithes to the Church of Ireland (Anglican) banded together in the Catholic Association, founded in 1823 by Daniel O'Connell (1775–1847), to resist the unfair tax. Their success sorely impoverished Anglican clergymen. However, their passive resistance turned violent in 1831. At Newtownforbes, Ireland, 12 who opposed the impounding of cattle were shot dead; at Carrickshook, Irish peasants armed with farm tools killed 18 police; at Castlepollard, police shot 10; and at Gortroche, a clergyman ordered firing on officials, causing eight deaths and 13 injured persons. The government intervened, found the task of collecting to be onerous, and withdrew. Once again reasonably peaceful resistance continued in what has been called the "Tithe War" until partial relief was obtained in 1836.

Togolese Civil War of 1991–92 The disclosure (April 1991) of killings allegedly by security forces set off huge, violent demonstrations against the military-controlled government of President Gnassingbe Eyadema (1937–) of Togo (formerly French Togoland), on the south coast of West Africa. Under much public pressure for democratization, Eyadema then legalized opposition political parties and was forced (due to a general strike) to convene a national conference, attended by both military and civilian representatives (July–August 1991). Soldiers failed to halt the conference, which declared itself sovereign; civilians formed a governing council, with free, multiparty elections set for 1992 (later postponed). At the conference, militant troops invaded but withdrew through a show of civilian strength. Eyadema remained nominally president, and his loyal troops later (October 1992) occupied the National Assembly building in Lomé, the capital, holding civilian legislators hostage until they agreed to unfreeze the assets of Eyadema's party, the Rally of the Togolese People. Pro-Eyadema forces later attacked and killed opposition leaders, pro-democracy demonstrators, and dissident soldiers and others (1993–94), securing President Eyadema's hold on Togo's government.

Tours (Poitiers), Battle of (A.D. 732) During the FIRST FRANKISH-MOORISH WAR, the Moors (Spanish Muslims) invaded under their leader Abd-ar-Rahman (d. 732) far into the Frankish kingdoms (France). Eudes (Eudo) (665–735), ruler of Aquitaine, was unable to stop them and requested help from Charles (688?–741), the Frankish mayor of the palace (see FRANKISH CIVIL WAR, THIRD), who was moving with an army near Orléans. Marching south to Tours and Poitiers, Charles confronted Abd-ar-Rahman's forces somewhere between these two towns in early October 732. The Frankish infantry was arranged in a solid square, and when the wild, blitzkrieg cavalry charges of the Moors occurred, the infantry attacked both horses and men with swords and axes, a tactic used earlier to defeat the Moors at Toulouse in 721. Moorish charges continued from two to seven days, according to Muslim and Christian historical records, respectively. When Abd-ar-Rahman was slain in battle, the Moors fled southward, not pursued by the Franks. Muslim expansion in Europe was decisively halted by Charles, who gained the title of honor Martel, meaning "the Hammer," for his great victory.

Toussaint Louverture, Revolt of (1793–1803) The FRENCH REVOLUTION had repercussions in the French colony of Saint-Domingue (Haiti), where black slaves, desiring equal rights and liberty, rose in rebellion against their white masters in 1791. Afterward, François Dominique Toussaint (1743–1803), a self-educated black ex-slave, organized and led a black army, joining the invading Spanish forces in their war against the French in 1793 (see FRENCH REVOLUTIONARY WARS); Toussaint won success because of his swift military campaigns, adopted the name Louverture ("the opening"), and was joined by other black leaders, such as Jean-Jacques Dessalines (1758–1806) and Henry Christophe (1767–1820). In 1794, after learning that France had recently freed all slaves, Toussaint went over to the French side and later helped the French general Étienne Laveaux (fl. late 18th cent.) expel the Spanish from Santo Domingo (the Dominican Republic) in 1795 and oust the British, who had occupied the coastal areas of Saint-Domingue, three years later. By 1797, Toussaint, who had tried to ease tensions between blacks and whites, had become the virtual ruler of the island of Hispaniola (Haiti and the Dominican Republic). His only challenger was André Rigaud (1761–1811), a mulatto leader of a semi-independent state in the southern part of the island. In the summer of 1799, Toussaint's forces under Dessalines attacked the mulatto stronghold of Jacmel and, after a six-month siege, forced Alexandre Pétion (1770–1818), Rigaud's second in command, to surrender; Toussaint then defeated Rigaud himself at the Battle of Aquin, forced Rigaud and his 700 mulatto troops to leave the island, and within a year took control of the entire island, assuming the title governor-general (1801). See also HAITIAN-FRENCH WAR OF 1801–3.

Town War, German (1386–89) In the latter half of the 14th century, Germany was in chaos. The Holy Roman Empire was breaking up, and landholding nobles set themselves up as individual entities, with private armies and a system of secret courts (the "Veme," imported from Westphalia). Wenceslaus (1361–1419), king of Germany and Bohemia and the Holy Roman Emperor, found it difficult to control these private powers, whose strengths lay in ancient feudal privileges. Wars between and among nobles, Imperial (free) towns and cities, and even church units were frequent. Nobles and church units fought to stop annexations by towns, which attracted many rural workers because of their increasing wealth. The oligarchical towns fought to end excessive and illegal tolls on their commerce in raw materials and goods. Conditions were almost hopeless under weak King Wenceslaus, an alcoholic, who attempted to rule from Bohemia. A rebel noble, Duke Leopold of Austria (fl. c. 1380–1410), was exceptionally oppressive, and the large Swabian town league, allied with the Swiss Confederation, fought and defeated his forces at Sempach in 1386, thus setting off a general war between towns and nobles (1386–89). The towns fared badly, especially in southern Germany, for they were islands of autonomy in a sea of feudal (noble) territory. An unsatisfactory peace was arranged in 1389 by Wenceslaus, who sided with the nobles; it quieted the strife but did not stop it completely, for its echo is found in the OLD ZURICH WAR.

Transvaal Civil War of 1862–64 After the Boers (Dutch) made their Great Trek north to escape British authority in southern Africa, they settled in four areas of the Transvaal, each with a small capital. These district governments in the Transvaal continually quarreled with each other over boundaries, religion, and politics. In 1856, the South African Republic was organized in the southwest Transvaal, and Marthinus Pretorius (1819–1901) was elected its president. His attempt to unify the entire Transvaal was met with resistance; dissenting factions continued their separate governments. Also elected president of the adjoining Orange Free State to the south (1859), Pretorius tried unsuccessfully to unite the two republics while continuing to reconcile the factions in the Transvaal. Civil war broke out among the Boers; Pretorius resigned from the Free State presidency (1863) and spent his energies mediating the disputes between the warring parties. Early in

1864, he was able to negotiate an end to the strife; by this time the four districts had joined the South African Republic, and Pretorius was elected its president a second time (1864). See also BOER WAR, FIRST.

Transvaal Revolt   See BOER WAR, FIRST.

Transylvanian-Hapsburg War of 1645   During the THIRTY YEARS' WAR, Protestant Transylvania had successfully kept the Catholic Hapsburgs from effectively enforcing the Counter-Reformation in Hungary (Transylvania was formerly its eastern part). Under the leadership of George I Rákóczy (1591–1648), Transylvania had gained international stature as a champion of Protestantism and had attracted the attention of the Swedes, who had marched victoriously through Silesia to Moravia, taking the city of Leipzig in 1642. The Swedes and Transylvanians allied in 1644, declaring a war on the Hapsburgs, which began in 1645 with a renewed Swedish invasion of Bohemia, the Swedish defeat of an Austrian army and Bavarian cavalry at Jankau (March 6, 1645), and advances into Upper Austria. Rákóczy's forces marched north, endangering Vienna itself. On August 3, 1645, the combined Swedish and Transylvanian forces, aided by French and Hessian troops, drubbed the Imperial (Austrian-Bavarian) army at the Battle of Allerheim (or Nördlingen) in Bavaria, during which the courageous imperial commander, Baron Franz von Mercy (1590?–1645), was killed. The Peace of Linz on December 16, 1645, won religious freedom for Hungary and gained Transylvania more territory.

Transylvanian-Turkish War of 1657–62   The Ottoman Empire's vassal states in Europe often required police actions to keep them under control. Transylvania, subject to Turkish suzerainty, had independently and vainly battled against Poland in 1657 and caused the Porte (Ottoman government) to turn against its prince, George II Rákóczy (1621–60). A new prince was chosen, but Rákóczy took power again in 1658 and repulsed Turkish besiegers at Lippa, Transylvania's capital. Five months later, a double assault by Wallachians and Turks led by the grand vizier sacked Karlsburg and captured three other fortresses. Rákóczy was deposed and fled to his estates in Austrian Hungary. In 1659, with Hungarian recruits, he returned to Transylvania and was again proclaimed prince. In response, Turkish forces under the pasha (governor) of Buda invaded and attacked from Temesvar to Torda and Hermannstadt, victorious all the way. Rákóczy turned to Austrian Hungary for help, making land concessions, but the Austrians delayed, and an Ottoman army made a tour of destruction (1660) from northeastern Hungary, entered Transylvania, and defeated Rákóczy at Fenes, where he was mortally wounded. In 1661, the rebellious Transylvanians elected yet another prince, who, with only 10,000 troops and momentarily weakened by the retirement of Austrian forces in the face of four Turkish armies ravaging Transylvania, was trapped near Segesvar (Schäsburg), defeated, and murdered (1662). The Ottomans restored order in Transylvania, installed their own prince, and ironically expanded their victory into a defeat by initiating the AUSTRO-TURKISH WAR OF 1663–64.

Trinidadian Rebellion of 1970   Deteriorating social and economic conditions on the two-island nation of Trinidad and Tobago gave rise to much popular unrest, especially between the blacks (about 43 percent of the population) and the East Indians (about 40 percent). After a series of demonstrations led by black power leaders, who demanded government action to solve problems, including unemployment, the governor-general in the capital of Port-of-Spain declared a state of emergency, banned further protests, imposed a dusk-to-dawn curfew, censored the press, and arrested several black leaders. Widespread rioting and violence erupted throughout the islands; simultaneously several hundred army troops mutinied in support of black-power rioters, seized an arsenal, and held hostages. The islands' government asked for and received arms and ammunition from the United States, and U.S. and British naval vessels steamed to the area "to stand by." By April 25, 1970, about five days after the start of the riots and army mutiny, loyal government forces had suppressed the rebels. Further harsh measures were imposed to limit personal freedom and political activity. A state of emergency lasted until July 1972, at which time political prisoners were released; a month later imprisoned soldiers who had participated in the mutiny were freed.

Trinidadian Rebellion of 1990   In late July 1990, some 120 members of the militant Jamaat al-Muslimeen (meaning Group of Muslims in Arabic), founded (1984) and led by Iman Yasin Abu Bakr (1950?–), attempted to overthrow the government of Trinidad and Tobago, a two-island republic in the Caribbean off the northeast coast of Venezuela. This small black Muslim group, believed to have 250 to 300 members and involved in a land dispute with the government, had denounced many economic policies; Bakr, a former police officer, recognized only the "law of Allah," not "man's law," and sought a "new beginning in Trinidad." In the capital of Port-of-Spain, Bakr's rebels stormed and blew up the police station and seized the state TV station and parliament building with 42 hostages, including Prime Minister Arthur N. R. Robinson (1926–) and some cabinet ministers and legislators. At least 30 persons died in the fighting and looting during the rebellion, which drew little popular support and ended five days later on August 1, 1990. The rebels surrendered and released their hostages. Held captive for murder, treason, and other crimes were 114 Jamaat members, who were eventually released in July 1992 after a high-court judge upheld the validity of amnesty granted to them during the rebellion in order to secure the release of the hostages without bloodshed.

Triple Alliance, War of the   See PARAGUAYAN WAR.

Tripolitan War   (1800–1805) For many years the Muslim pirates of the Barbary States (Tripoli, Tunis, Algiers, and Morocco) had been exacting tribute and enslaving captured sailors from the ships of Christian nations plying the waters of the Mediterranean off North Africa. In 1800, the pasha of Tripoli demanded increased tribute from the United States and went so far as to declare war against it. U.S. president Thomas Jefferson (1743–1826) reluctantly decided the time had come to resist the pirates and sent a squadron of warships to the North African coast. Tripoli was blockaded for a while rather successfully, but a raid against the city failed. In 1803, Edward Preble (1761–1807) commanded another squadron to the Mediterranean; he sent the frigate *Philadelphia* to resume the blockade of Tripoli. During a storm the frigate was driven aground in the harbor and captured, and its crew was taken prisoner. The captors refloated the *Philadelphia* and began converting it for use in their own navy. One dark night in February 1804, U.S. lieutenant Stephen Decatur (1779–1820) and a small band boarded the frigate in Tripoli's harbor and set it on fire; this was the most daring exploit of the war. The U.S. blockade was vigorously pursued, and in 1805 the Tripolitans agreed to a peace treaty. The United States no longer paid annual tribute to Tripoli, although other Christian nations still did; the Americans continued to pay tribute to the other Barbary States until 1815 (see ALGERINE WAR). Not until France captured Algiers in 1830 did the menace of pirates cease in the Mediterranean.

Trojan War   (c. 1200 B.C.) The probability is high that the story of the Trojan War, mythologized in Homer's *Iliad*, is based on historical fact. Ancient records contain names found in the Homeric narrative, and Achaen Greek aggressions in the 13th century B.C. leading to their primacy in the eastern Mediterranean, the ancient city of Troy included, left archaeological evidence. As Homer relates it, the war began when Paris, son of Troy's King Priam, kidnapped Helen, wife of Menelaus, with the help of the goddess Venus. Menelaus called upon other Greek leaders to help him, and they and their soldiers were gathered under the direction of Menelaus's brother, Agamemnon, king of Mycenae. In order to gain favorable winds for the ships at Aulis loaded with Greek heroes, Agamemnon sacrificed his daughter, Iphigenia. The Greeks sailed across the Aegean Sea and ravaged the area of Troy (in northwestern Asia Minor) for nine years, but Hector, son of Troy's king, held out until the 10th year when the Greeks tried a *ruse de guerre* (war stratagem): An enormous wooden horse secretly filled with Greek soldiers was offered by them as a divine gift to the Trojans. The Greeks then ostensibly sailed for home. But when the horse was pulled inside Troy's walls, the Greeks returned, and those concealed inside the horse opened the city's gates to their fellows. Troy was overthrown.

Trung Sisters' Rebellion (A.D. 39–43) In what is now northern Vietnam, Trung Trac (d. 43) and her sister Trung Nhi (d. 43) became the leaders of an aristocratic independence movement after the former's husband was murdered by a Chinese official for conspiring with other lords to overthrow their Chinese Han rulers, whose bureaucratic control threatened indigenous Vietnamese feudal ways (see CHINESE CONQUEST OF NAM VIET). The fervid Trung sisters led a rebellion, seizing control within a year (39–40) of about 65 strongholds and forcing the Chinese commander to flee. Declaring themselves queens of a large independent state (modern north Vietnam), the sisters received no peasant support, and their untrained troops were soon overwhelmed by invading Chinese under General Ma Yuan (14–49). After suffering a defeat near present-day Hanoi, the Trungs withdrew to Hat Mon (Son Tay) and were decisively defeated there. Feeling disgraced, they drowned themselves at the confluence of the Red and Day Rivers; China took control of the region.

Tuareg Rebellions See MALIAN CIVIL WAR OF 1990–96, NIGERIEN CIVIL WAR OF 1990–95.

Tukulor-French Wars (1854–64) From the fourth through the 14th centuries, the Tukulor people dominated West Africa's Senegal River valley as the state of Tekrur; converted to Islam in the 11th century, they extended their influence northward to include Morocco and founded the Moravid dynasty. The Mali Empire conquered Tekrur in the 14th century; the Tukulors remained a subject people until the mid-1800s, when a charismatic leader, al-Hajji Omar (c. 1795–1864), founded the Tijaniyya Brotherhood and tried to revive Tekrur's past glory by beginning a jihad (holy war) against its neighbors. Omar failed to consider the attitude of the French, who had colonized coastal Senegal; under its governor Louis Faidherbe (1818–89), the French were contemplating inland expansion. So long as Omar focused his raids to the east of the upper Senegal, France was merely wary; when Tukulor attention turned west (1854), French troops began to skirmish with Omar's warriors and later (1856) checked their attacks on garrisons. The Tukulors now turned to non-French areas and seized the large Bambara kingdom of Segu (1861); with minor cost to France, they had power as far east as Timbuktu in central Mali. But the Tukulors were exploitative conquerors, and the French were usually bystanders as uprisings created disorder, caused the death of Omar, and so distressed his sons (who waged destructive dynastic wars of succession for many years) that the French were able, by 1890, to take control of Segu and Senegal without serious fighting.

Tupac Amaru's Revolt See PERUVIAN REVOLT OF 1780–82.

Tupamaros' Reign of Terror (1967–73) The Tupamaros, a leftist guerrilla organization, opposed the government of Uruguay and engaged in terrorist activities with raids, bombings, bank robberies, kidnappings, and assassinations. They attacked police stations, armories, and military bases to obtain arms and ammunition, and they abducted prominent people, both Uruguayans and foreigners, to gain large ransoms or the release of comrades who had been arrested. In 1971, more than 100 jailed Tupamaros made a daring escape through a 40-foot tunnel, and 38 women broke out of a maximum security prison. Up to this time, the police had been responsible for fighting and capturing the Tupamaros, but now the Uruguayan armed forces were put in charge. The terrorism against the government continued, and in April 1972, "a state of internal war" was declared, with Uruguay placed under martial law to help the police and military marshal the resources of the country against the guerrillas. On February 12, 1973, President Juan María Bordaberry (1928–) agreed to military control of his administration; he abolished congress and replaced it with a council of state four months later. The army used severe repressive measures, reportedly including mass arrests and torture, to crush the Tupamaros, some of whom fled to Argentina and there carried on their antigovernment campaign after 1973. All marxist parties were permanently outlawed in Uruguay on January 1, 1975, and by that time the military had such strong control over all aspects of life that subversion was almost impossible.

Turkish War of Independence (1919–23) After WORLD WAR I ended, the victorious allied European powers occupied the Ottoman Empire with the intention of dismembering it. The Young Turk (CUP) government fled into exile. The last Ottoman sultan, Muhammad VI Vahideddin (1861–1926), was convinced that resistance to the Allies was futile, but the Young Turk Mustafa Kemal, later called Kemal Atatürk (1881–1938), refused to capitulate, and the emergence of modern Turkey is a monument to his perseverance, immortalized in his name after 1934: Kemal ("the perfect") Atatürk ("Father of the Turks"). In 1919, he gained an official post in Anatolia (Asian Turkey), from which he led a national resistance movement against both the sultan's armies and Greek occupying forces. Kemal also became, in 1919, leader of the Association of the Rights of Anatolia and Rumelia at a congress at Erzurum; his group forced Constantinople (Istanbul), seat of the government, to yield in 1920 and pass a "National Pact" asserting Turkish territory to be the boundaries extant on November 11, 1918, Armistice Day ending World War I. In response, the Allies occupied Constantinople, arrested deputies, and began military opposi-

tion to the Kemalists, or nationalists. Civil war erupted, and Kemal, through a provisional parliament at Ankara, declared the sultan to be under foreign control and appealed for all Muslims to fight foreign aggrandizement. A new Fundamental Law in 1921 gave sovereignty to the Turkish people and named the nation Turkey. The civil war now flared up. The Greeks were defeated at the Battle of the Sakarya River in 1921 (see GRECO-TURKISH WAR OF 1921–22) and retreated painfully until they surrendered in September 1922, at Smyrna (Izmir). The Kemalists received international recognition in 1921 and 1922: a treaty with Russia, Italian withdrawal of troops, French abandonment of Cilicia in Turkey, the return of Constantinople and Thrace to Turkish control. In 1922, the Kemalist parliament began the abolishment of the sultanate, and the Lausanne Conference in Switzerland (November 1922–July 1923) established modern Turkey's borders, arranged the exchange of Greek and Turkish minorities, and made the straits of the Dardanelles and Bosporus international. Turkey was proclaimed a republic on October 29, 1923, with Kemal Atatürk as its first president. See also YOUNG TURKS' REBELLION.

Turko-Austrian Wars   See AUSTRO-TURKISH WARS.

Turko-Egyptian War, First (1832–33) Promised control of Syria and Crete as a reward for his son's military aid during the GREEK WAR OF INDEPENDENCE, Muhammad Ali (1769?–1849), pasha of Egypt, swore to avenge the Ottoman sultan's breach of promise in not granting him Syria (Crete was given to him). He laid plans with his French-officered army to invade Syria and, manufacturing as a pretext a personal quarrel with the pasha of Acre, sent his son Ibrahim (1789–1848) with a large army to attack in 1832. Egyptian success that year was total: Gaza and Jerusalem fell early, military siege and blockade overwhelmed Acre, and the new and inexperienced troops of Sultan Mahmud II (1784–1839) lost battles at Aleppo and Damascus. Ibrahim advanced into Anatolia (Turkey) itself, seizing Konya and moving toward Bursa, some 50 miles from Constantinople (Istanbul) The Porte (Ottoman government) asked for and received aid from Russia, which sent a fleet and 18,000 troops to Constantinople in 1833. Ibrahim quickly abandoned his plan to attack the city. Alarmed by the Russian move, the French and British negotiated (1833) a peace with Ibrahim, whose father was confirmed as pasha of Egypt and Crete; Egypt also took control of Syria and Adana. The French and British guaranteed to prevent further Egyptian intrusions in return for Russian withdrawal. But in the separate 1833 Peace of Hunkiar Iskelessi, the Turks allied offensively and defensively with Russia; secretly, Russian warships were granted the right, in time of war, to close the Dardanelles straits to all foreign ships. Muhammad Ali treated the peace as a mere truce. **Second Turko-Egyptian War** (1839–41). When Egypt declared independence by ending its tribute payments to the Ottomans in 1838, Sultan Mahmud II prepared an army to invade Syria. In 1839, when he was ready, he declared war, sent a war fleet into the Mediterranean, and invaded. Both land and sea expeditions ended in disaster. Many soldiers, bribed by Egyptian gold, deserted; the remainder were soundly defeated; the commander of the naval fleet was traitorous, for he sailed to Alexandria and surrendered to the Egyptians. With France supporting Egypt, the other Western powers were fearful lest Russian intervention occur, but Russia was unusually conciliatory and gave up its right to exclusive passage in the Dardanelles. Together, France, Britain, and Russia persuaded the Porte to make the pashalik (province of a pasha) of Egypt hereditary if the Ottoman fleet were returned (1840). Muhammad Ali foolishly refused, and the Western powers solved the problems with force. The British bombarded and destroyed forts at Beirut and Acre, landed troops, and, supported by an Arab revolt against Muhammad Ali's harsh rule, defeated the Egyptian armies of occupation in Syria. When Alexandria was threatened with bombardment, Muhammad Ali returned the Ottoman fleet, resumed his annual tribute to the Porte, agreed to reduce the size of his armies, and completely withdrew from Syria.

Turko-Greek Wars See GRECO-TURKISH WARS.

Turko-Hungarian Wars See HUNGARIAN-TURKISH WARS.

Turkoman-Ottoman Wars of 1400–1473 Territorial annexations by the Ottoman Turks before 1400 focused on the Balkans (see NICOPOLIS, CRUSADE OF), but under Ottoman sultan Bayazid I (1347–1403) annexations to the east began. The sudden arrival of Tamerlane (Timur) (1336–1405) and his victory at ANGORA (Ankara) in 1402 complicated the annexations, for he had established Timurid principalities. Two other problems faced the Ottoman sultans: gaining the adherence of non-Ottoman Turkish notables conscious of their political power and overcoming the resistance of Turkoman nomads whose religious beliefs made them oppose a centralized and orthodox administration. Little progress was made before 1421, in part because of the OTTOMAN CIVIL WAR OF 1403–13. But Sultan Murad II (1403–51) began his reign in 1421 and, by the time of his death, had forcibly made all Timurid principalities his vassals, with the exception of Karaman and Jandar, which retained some autonomy. The notables, who had put him on the throne, were hamstrung when he began to rely on non-Turkish groups and to create his own salaried army—the Janissary corps—from Christian slaves turned Muslim and loyal only to him. By 1444, after a revolt in ever-restless Karaman, the Ottomans had gained possessions in Anatolia (Turkey) extending almost to Azerbaijan. But the Turkoman nomad problem was still unsolved. Individually weak, the Turkoman tribes achieved a kind of unity from their allegiance to heterodox religious societies, which also functioned as political parties. Dominant was the "redhead" (Kizilbash) group, highly influenced by mystic dervishes; it was led by Uzun Hasan (1420–78), who was also leader of the Tatar (Tartar) "white sheep" (Ak Koyunlu) dynasty and province.

A second tribal federation, the "black sheep" (Kara Koyunlu), ruled what is now northern Iraq and Azerbaijan, moving into eastern Anatolia until 1466, when Hasan's forces defeated them and seized Baghdad. Hasan became so important as an opponent of the Ottomans that during the VENETIAN-TURKISH WAR OF 1463–79 he was persuaded by the papacy to have the white sheep and Karaman fight Constantinople (Istanbul) from the east. Ottoman sultan Muhammad II "the Conqueror" (1429–81) captured Karaman and forced Hasan eastward until the defeat of the white sheep at Bashkent (1473) pushed the nomads into Persia (Iran) and angered the Syrian Mamluks. The Porte (Ottoman government) now had only a shaky hold on eastern Anatolia, a hold complicated by the replacement (1501) of the white sheep dynasty by the Shiite Safavid dynasty in Azerbaijan and Persia, a coup that led to the TURKO-PERSIAN WAR OF 1514–16.

Turko-Montenegrin War, First (1852–53) Montenegro was a small Balkan tributary state that the Ottoman Turks were never able to subdue completely, for fighting the Turks was a perpetual occupation of the Montenegrins. Its movement toward independence began when its prince-bishop, Danilo II (1822–60), separated the offices of prince and bishop in 1851 and made the throne hereditary. These actions exceeded Danilo's authority since he was a vassal of the Porte (Ottoman government), which sent troops in 1852 to Montenegro. The Montenegrins forced the Turks to retreat after several victories. The war had interested Austria, whose emperor moved troops to the border of Bosnia and Herzegovina and ordered the Turkish commander Omar Pasha (1806–71) to withdraw from Montenegro, which the Turks did in 1853 after Russian pressure was added. No formal treaty was concluded. **Second Turko-Montenegrin War** (1861–62). Disorder and rebellion after the death of Danilo II caused the Ottomans to dispatch a large expedition under Omar Pasha to Montenegro. Turkish forces invested Cetinje, Montenegro's historic capital, failed to subdue it fully but overran the small country. The Convention of Scutari (Shkoder) left

affairs in *status quo ante*, except that Montenegro agreed not to build forts on its borders or to import arms. Montenegro did not receive its independence until 1878, when the Congress of Berlin permitted it to become autonomous. See also CRIMEAN WAR.

Turko-Persian War of 1473   See VENETIAN-TURKISH WAR OF 1463–79.

Turko-Persian War of 1514–16   After his bloody accession to the Turkish throne, Sultan Selim I (1467–1520) began to prepare for war against Shiite Persia, for he, a fanatic Sunni Muslim, believed he should punish the unorthodox Shi'ite Muslims and the Persians who had supported his brother Ahmed (d. 1513) in the OTTOMAN CIVIL WAR OF 1509–13. In 1514, he began the long march from Adrianople, his main base, to Azerbaijan, his troops suffering many periods of hunger, for the retreating Persians practiced a scorched-earth policy. Selim left the Persian city of Tabriz unharmed at first and went on to defeat the Persians, who lacked both artillery and sufficient infantry, at the Battle of Chaldiran on August 23, 1515. Returning to Tabriz, now partially populated, he captured it within two weeks, plundering the city and massacring its inhabitants, except for 1,000 craftsmen, sent to Constantinople (Istanbul). The Turkish army then fell back to Amasya and Angora (Ankara) to disperse. Selim soon launched a second campaign, during which the Turks captured the great fortress of Kamakh and established control over Kurdistan, formerly Safavid-ruled. The Turkish reduction and vassalage of Albistan, where the Duldakir dynasty was removed, angered the Syrian Mamluks (Mamelukes) and prompted the MAMLUK-OTTOMAN WAR OF 1516–17, which made further Turkish military action in Persia impossible. Shah Ismail I (1486–1524) of Persia, however, did not make use of this advantage to attack the Ottomans; the Turko-Persian war had merely stopped for a decade.

Turko-Persian War of 1526–55   After the end of the TURKO-PERSIAN WAR OF 1514–16, Safavid Persian attempts were made to foment rebellion in various Ottoman provinces. Busy in Europe (see HUNGARIAN-TURKISH WAR OF 1521–26), Ottoman Sultan Süleyman I "the Magnificent" (1496–1566) avoided major campaigns against Persia; instead, he tried to suppress Safavid propagandists and supporters in eastern Anatolia (Turkey); he also persuaded the Turkish Uzbeks in Transoxania to attack Persia from the east. Despite these efforts, war broke out in 1526 because of a Turkoman revolt in Cilicia; it continued in the Ottoman quelling of an uprising (1526–28) in Karaman involving Mamluk (Mameluke) troops led by the rebel Kalendar-Oghlu (d. 1528) and in the Ottoman invasion of Kurdistan because of its leader's defection to Persia. After the submission of Baghdad to the Porte (Ottoman government) in 1532, Süleyman, planning to invade Mesopotamia (Iraq), first seized Tabriz (1534) and Van, set up a new Ottoman province at Erzurum, and—after making an unprecedented winter march—entered Baghdad to establish control over Mesopotamia. Tabriz, recaptured by the Persians in early 1535, was seized again (and sacked) later that year by Süleyman on his return to Constantinople (Istanbul), the Ottoman Empire's capital. Border fighting persisted between the Turks and Persians, who refused to engage in set battles but retook Tabriz and Van, both of which were again recaptured by Süleyman in 1548. Safavid attacks on and seizure of Erzurum in 1552 renewed the war, with an Ottoman army led by Süleyman retaking Erzurum and then marching into western Persia, which was ravaged (1553–54). Declaring a truce in late 1554, Süleyman made peace at Amasya in 1555, abandoning all claims to Tabriz, Erivan (Yerevan), and Nakhjivan, but retaining control of Mesopotamia, Erzurum, western Armenia, and most of Kurdistan. He had realized that an all-out war, with its attendant high expenses, might overcome and control Persia, but conditions in the Porte and abroad would not permit one. See also AUSTRO-TURKISH WAR OF 1529–33; VENETIAN-TURKISH WAR OF 1537–40.

Turko-Persian War of 1578–90 After the death of Shah Tahmasp I (1514–76) of Persia, a civil war over the Persian succession seemed to be developing, leading the Ottoman Turks to believe the Persians could at last be conquered. In 1578, a large Ottoman offensive began with a surprise invasion from Crimea. Two Persian armies were overwhelmed in rapid succession, Georgia was conquered and Ottomanized, and Daghestan in Persia was invaded. This early Ottoman momentum did not last as the Persians began to resist more effectively; moreover, much effort and time was spent on securing Georgia, taking the great fortress at Kars in 1579, capturing and refortifying Erivan (Yerevan) in Armenia in 1583, and constructing defenses near Tiflis (Tbilisi) in 1584. Another Ottoman army, under great odds, completed the conquest of Daghestan and seized Shirwan in 1583. Azerbaijan was the goal of Ottoman actions from 1585 to 1588, but Persian counteroffensives relieved Tabriz from Turkish hands and momentarily overcame Tiflis and Erivan. Internal problems in Persia and Uzbek attacks on the Persians in the east reduced the size of the Persian forces fighting the Ottomans, who won successes at Ganna and Karabagh in 1588. The Persians were then forced to enter into peace talks. The Ottoman reconquest of Tabriz in 1590 and its dependent Azerbaijan territories led to a final peace settlement, with the Persian cession of Georgia, Azerbaijan, Shirvan, and other provinces. The war actually settled little; it had only reestablished the eastern border set earlier by Sultan Süleyman I "the Magnificent" (1496–1566).

Turko-Persian War of 1603–12 Persia wanted the lands ceded to the Turks at the end of the TURKO-PERSIAN WAR OF 1578–90, but fighting the Uzbeks prevented a new offensive until 1603. Shah Abbas I "the Great" (1557–1628) of Persia had sent ambassadors (1599) to Europe to promote an anti-Ottoman alliance. Unsuccessful in this diplomacy, he dispatched Caucasian and Azerbaijan troops to Anatolia (Turkey), causing the Turks to fight on three fronts: in Hungary (see AUSTRO-TURKISH WAR OF 1591–1606), Anatolia, and within the Ottoman Empire itself, beset by riots over the tax burden imposed by the wars. The Persians retook Tabriz after a lengthy siege in 1603 and then recaptured Erivan (Yerevan), Shirvan, and Kars in 1604. Angered by the Persian reconquests, Ottoman sultan Ahmed I (1589–1617) led a large army against a smaller Persian force under Abbas near Lake Urmia in 1606 but suffered defeat with heavy losses. Afterward Abbas took control of Baghdad, Mosul, and Diarbekh. This war, plus incidents in Egypt, Lebanon, the eastern Mediterranean, and the Cossack-bedeviled Black Sea area, caused Ahmed to be somewhat deferential at the Treaty of Zsitva-Török by which the Turks made peace with Austria in 1606. Returning Ottoman armies from Europe did no good. By 1608, Abbas had recovered all the areas lost in 1590 and had virtually destroyed Ottoman rule in the Caucasus. In a position to be victor, Abbas dictated the terms of a 1612 peace treaty, all of which favored Persia.

Turko-Persian War of 1616–18 Disputes arose over the terms of the treaty ending the TURKO-PERSIAN WAR OF 1603–12, thus causing a renewal of fighting in 1616. A strong Ottoman army besieged Erivan (Yerevan) in 1616, was repulsed, and forced to withdraw because of severe winter weather and pursuing Persian troops. In 1618, the Turks again invaded, moving on Tabriz, but Persian forces ambushed and destroyed part of the Turkish army, which later was thoroughly routed near Tabriz. Immediately peace negotiations began, resulting in a treaty that merely reiterated the terms of the 1612 agreement. The Ottoman eastern border had returned to its status before the TURKO-PERSIAN WAR OF 1526–55.

Turko-Persian War of 1623–38 This conflict began as a result of a struggle for power within the Ottoman cadre of Baghdad, where the pasha (governor) and the military vied for control. The struggle became crucial in 1621, when a Janissary officer formed a faction and for two years became more powerful than the pasha. The officer, after he and the Janissaries (elite Ottoman soldiers) were masters of Baghdad, futilely applied to the Porte (Ottoman

government) for recognition as the new pasha. He next turned to Shah Abbas I "the Great" (1557–1628) of Persia for aid, gaining a small Persian relief force just as the Porte agreed to recognize him. Renouncing Abbas, he found himself attacked by the Persians and was killed in 1623. To recover Baghdad and other areas in Persian hands, the Ottomans tried three campaigns: 1625–26, a failure because of lack of artillery and a Turkish army mutiny; 1629–30, literally a washout because of bad weather; and 1630, a Turkish success in the Battle of Mihriban and the sacking of Hamadan but a rebuff before Baghdad. A fourth campaign was postponed by Ottoman sultan Murad IV (1609–40) while his forces defeated what he considered to be potential traitors in the OTTOMAN-DRUSE WAR OF 1631–35. In 1635, Murad led an invading army, recapturing Erivan (Yerevan) but stalling at Tabriz. A fifth campaign, delayed until 1638 despite the Persian recapture of Erivan in 1636, advanced straight to Baghdad. There the Turks, led personally by Murad, struggled for seven months to take the city because the Persians intended to fight to the last man. After Baghdad's capture (1638), peace was made, allowing the Turks to keep the city while the Persians retained Erivan. The border of Mesopotamia with Persia became the eastern boundary of the Ottoman Empire. See also JANISSARIES' REVOLT OF 1621–22.

Turko-Persian War of 1730–36 Police actions by Nadir Khan, later called Nadir Shah (1688–1747), to rid Persian territories of Turkish occupiers (see PERSIAN CIVIL WAR OF 1725–30) spilled over into the Ottoman Empire to incite a formal Turko-Persian conflict, delayed at first by the JANISSARIES' REVOLT OF 1730. Despite Nadir Khan's preoccupation with a punitive campaign against the Afghans (see PERSIAN-AFGHAN WAR OF 1726–38), he was able to meet a weakened Ottoman army with consistent success. He won back control of Armenia and Georgia, recovered Ardebil, and developed his own navy in the Persian Gulf, severely reducing Ottoman authority in that area. His single failure was a 1733 siege of Baghdad, recovered later, however. In 1736, he was compelled to become the Persian shah (king) because his Safavid protégé, despite Nadir Khan's victories, had offered the Porte (Ottoman government) a conciliatory peace. The Treaty of Constantinople in 1736 restored Persia's western boundaries to those before the rule of Ottoman sultan Süleyman I "the Magnificent" (1496–1566) and freed Nadir Shah, as the first and only Afshar shah, to resume his fight against the Afghans.

Turko-Persian War of 1743–47   Attempts to ratify the treaty ending the TURKO-PERSIAN WAR OF 1730–36 were impeded by Persia's insistence that a small Shiite sect, the Ja'fari, be declared orthodox and by Ottoman haughtiness in torturing the ambassadors of Nadir Shah (1688–1747). In 1743, Nadir Shah declared war on the Turks and, after demanding the surrender of Baghdad, began a long march to Constantinople (Istanbul). But when he learned that the Ottoman *ulema* (Muslim legal council) had made respectable a holy war against Persia, he turned east after having captured Kirkuk, seizing Arbil and besieging Mosul as a threat to Baghdad. A challenge from Mongol China made Nadir Shah try a diplomatic ploy, a ruse to allow him to subdue revolts (1743–44) throughout Persia over high war taxes. Persian attacks on the Ottomans resumed in early 1744 as Nadir Shah marched west from Hamadan, besieging Kars and then dashing back to Daghestan to quell a revolt. He returned to meet and rout a huge Turkish army at the Battle of Kars in August 1745. The Turks fled west, raiding their own country as they went and prompting fighting among the various Turks. The war disintegrated. Nadir Shah, who was growing insane, punished his subjects by extorting monies and blinding or executing ineffective officials; the result, from early 1745 through June 1746, was further Persian revolt. In 1746, peace was secured; although Persia's boundaries were unchanged and Baghdad remained Ottoman, Nadir Shah had wisely dropped his demand for Ja'fari recognition. The Porte (Ottoman government) was pleased and dispatched an ambassador with a retinue of 1,000, but Nadir Shah had

been assassinated by an angry citizen before the group arrived. See also PERSIAN CIVIL WAR OF 1747–60.

Turko-Persian War of 1821–23   After severe losses in Georgia during the RUSSO-PERSIAN WAR OF 1804–13, Crown Prince Abbas Mirza (1783–1833) of Persia vowed to modernize his armies. He sent Persians to England to learn Western military techniques and invited British officers to train his troops, especially newly introduced infantry. Turkish defense of rebellious tribes from Azerbaijan led to Abbas Mirza's attack into eastern Anatolia (Turkey) in 1821. Fighting occurred in the Lake Van area and culminated in Persian success at the Battle of Erzurum (1821), where Abbas Mirza's army routed a superior Turkish force. Peace did not come until the Treaty of Erzurum two years later; both sides recognized the previous borders, with no territorial changes. See also RUSSO-PERSIAN WAR OF 1825–28.

Turko-Polish Wars   See POLISH-TURKISH WARS.

Turko-Russian Wars   See RUSSO-TURKISH WARS.

Turner's Rebellion (Southampton Insurrection) (1831)   Nat Turner, a literate and pious black slave, came to believe he was divinely chosen to lead his people out of bondage in Southampton County, Va. On August 21–23, 1831, he and about 75 followers went on a bloody rampage in the county, slaughtered 55 white persons (including Turner's master, Joseph Travis [d. 1831], and his family), and terrorized the Tidewater area. Soldiers from Fort Monroe and sailors from the navy were sent in to quell the rebellion. The blacks were dispersed; some were killed or captured. Turner escaped to the woods but was caught after a six-week manhunt and hanged along with 20 of his followers. The violence of the revolt caused the southern states to take sterner measures against slaves and to tighten their fugitive slave laws.

Tuscarora War (1711–13)   Iroquoian-speaking Tuscarora Indians who lived in the eastern part of present-day North Carolina became very hostile toward the English settlers after seizure of Tuscarora lands, encroachment on their hunting grounds, kidnapping of their children by white slave traders, and other depredations by the whites. Led by Chief Hancock, Tuscaroras suddenly attacked and massacred about 200 English colonists on the Chowan and Roanoke Rivers on September 22, 1711. The English retaliated with two punitive expeditions: the first was led by Colonel John Barnwell, consisted of some 50 whites and over 350 Indian allies, and ended in a flimsy truce (January–April 1712); the second expedition, commanded by Colonel James Moore leading about 35 whites and 1,000 allied Indians, resulted in the Tuscaroras' surrender after a three-day battle near Snow Hill, N.C. (March 1713). Under a ruthless peace treaty, surviving Tuscaroras trekked northward to eventually be incorporated into the Iroquois Confederacy (made up of the Mohawk, Oneida, Onondaga, Cayuga, and Seneca tribes) as the sixth tribal nation. Tuscarora resistance having been destroyed, North Carolina furthered colonization in the west.

Tutsi-Hutu Wars   See BURUNDIAN CIVIL WAR OF 1972; RUANDAN CIVIL WAR OF 1959–61; RWANDAN CIVIL WAR OF 1990–94.

26th of July Movement (1953)   This was the guerrilla movement and rallying cry of Fidel Castro (1926–   ) as he sought to gain the support of the Cuban people for the overthrow of Cuba's dictator Fulgencio Batista y Zaldívar (1901–73). July 26, 1953, commemorates the day on which Castro and about 200 young Cuban rebels attacked the Moncada army barracks at Santiago, Cuba. The effort was a futile one, and most of the attackers were killed. Fidel and his brother Raul (1931–   ) managed to escape. Months later they gave themselves up to stop Batista's brutal police from persecuting innocent people in Santiago who were accused of being part of the anti-government campaign. Castro

was sentenced to 15 years in prison on Cuba's Isle of Pines but was pardoned after serving only 11 months. He went to Mexico and then returned to continue the fight against Batista (see CUBAN REVOLUTION OF 1956–59). Castro's disastrous but daring 1953 attack and his long speech of self-defense at his trial made him a hero among the Cuban masses, especially among the young people.

Two Brothers, War of the   See MIGUELITE WARS.

Tyler's Revolt   See PEASANTS' REVOLT, ENGLISH.

Tyre, Siege of (333–332 B.C.)   Until the siege of AORNOS, the genius of Alexander the Great (356–323) as a besieger had never been tested more severely than it was at Tyre (see ALEXANDER THE GREAT, CONQUESTS OF). Considering itself invincible because it had fallen only once since the vain 13-year (585–573) Babylonian assault by Nebuchadnezzar II (c. 630–562), ancient Tyre was built on an island just off the mainland of Phoenicia. Trying to reach it from the landward side, Alexander ordered a mole (causeway) constructed; the clever Tyrians almost stopped the work by shooting the laborers and sending fireships to destroy the siege towers. To bolster morale after six months, Alexander reminded his men that the fall of Tyre meant the fall of the Persian fleet. Luckily, the Cypriot fleet surrendered, and then Alexander, with 220 ships, attacked from the sea, tying ships in pairs to hold rams and to allow siege towers to come to Tyre's walls. Some 8,000 Tyrians died in the successful nine-month siege; Tyrian captives were sold as slaves.

Tyrolean Rebellion of 1809–10   The Alpine region of Tyrol (Tirol) in western Austria was the scene of a peasant rebellion led by Andreas Hofer (1767–1810), a Catholic innkeeper loyal to Austria's House of Hapsburg, who desired to free his homeland (Tyrol) from Bavarian rule (Napoleon had placed it under Bavaria in 1805). Hofer's armed peasants, aided by Austrians, won minor battles against Bavarian and Italo-French forces occupying

Tyrol, where Hofer became commander in chief after decisively defeating the Bavarian army near Innsbruck in August 1809. However, by the Peace of Schönbrunn in October 1809, Austria ceded Tyrol to the victorious French (see NAPOLEONIC WARS), and Hofer's resistance failed against Italo-French occupying forces in Tyrol. Forced into hiding, Hofer was betrayed, seized by the French, and taken to Mantua, where he was shot on February 20, 1810, on Napoleon's orders.

Tyrone's Rebellion (1595–1603) The Irish, always contentious among themselves or against foreign rulers, resented both taxes used to maintain English troops and, propagandized by the papacy, the ecclesiastical policy of Queen Elizabeth I (1533–1603) of England. In 1595, Hugh O'Neill, second earl of Tyrone (1540?–1616), united dissenting groups, appealed to Spain for assistance, and in small encounters defeated some of Elizabeth's best commanders. Elizabeth spent 2 million pounds on the problem and, in 1598, after Spanish assistance had energized Tyrone's followers, sent the earl of Essex with 16,000 men to crush Tyrone. Suffering many reverses, Essex finally concluded a forbidden truce with Tyrone and subsequently was angrily recalled. The Spanish landed, but the English, by keeping them from uniting with Tyrone's men, forced their surrender. By 1603, Tyrone had yielded to the English and gone into self-exile.

U

Ugandan Civil War of 1978–79 In the fall of 1978, Ugandan troops, under orders from dictatorial president-for-life Idi Amin (1925–), invaded northern Tanzania and, after blowing up the only bridge over the Kagera River, occupied about 700 square miles of foreign territory, called the Kagera Salient. In response, President Julius K. Nyerere (1922–) of Tanzania sent an army, reinforced by Ugandan exiles who had fled their homeland to escape Amin's tyrannical rule, across the border into Uganda (October 1978). Soon the invaders were advancing through southern Uganda after winning some skirmishes. They surrounded the Ugandan capital of Kampala, but were halted briefly by a Libyan force that had come to Amin's aid. On April 11, 1979, Tanzanian troops and Ugandan exiles and nationalists entered Kampala, whose residents welcomed them as liberators. Eluding capture, Amin fled to Libya and left behind an impoverished Uganda and a brutalized people. During the eight years of his rule, he had expelled all Asians, killed thousands of tribespeople and Christians, spent excessively to build up his army, and nationalized all land without compensating the owners.

Ugandan Guerrilla and Civil Wars of 1986– Uganda in east-central Africa was in social and economic chaos following the tyrannical rule of Idi Amin (1925–) (see UGANDAN CIVIL WAR OF 1978-79). The corrupt regime of President Milton Obote (1925–), who assumed control in 1980, was toppled in a military coup (1985); the National Resistance Army (NRA), the main rebel force operating in Uganda, soon attacked the government forces of the new president, Tito Okello (1914–), who fled the capital, Kampala (January 1986). NRA commander Yoweri Kaguta Museveni (1944–) became president and sought national reconciliation among the warring rival groups (tribal and political). But the country remained in turmoil, especially in the north, where rebels loyal to Obote and Okello fought the government. In 1988, Museveni called on all insurgent organizations, including the Uganda Freedom Movement, the Federal Democratic Movement (FEDEMO), the Uganda People's Democratic Army, and the Uganda Federal Army, to lay down their arms, without success. Nonetheless, Museveni strengthened his grip on the government and managed to check rebel resistance with help from the NRA, which mounted successful offensives in the Soroti and Kumi districts in 1990. Clashes between Rwandan troops and Ugandan guerrilla forces on the border strained relations between the neighboring countries, resulting in their signing a security agreement in 1992 (see RWANDAN CIVIL WAR OF 1990-94). Tensions in Uganda eased when the constitution was amended (1993) to allow for the reestablishment of tribal rulers in four old southern kingdoms. But Museveni, backed by the Constituent Assembly, successfully opposed the reintroduction of multiparty democracy, while carrying on a program of economic reform with generous aid from other countries. In 1995, rebel offensives were suspended in the central and southeast regions, but a new Sudan-based guerrilla group, called the Lord's Resistance Army, began raiding villages in the Acholi district (north). Uganda's relations grew more strained with neighboring Sudan; both countries had aided various rebels' attacks on each other's government in the past. In 1997, Museveni received U.S. arms and military training for his actions with Sudan and the Congo (Zaire). Bold raids by the Lord's Ressistance Army prompted the government to confine all the Acholi people in protected villages in 1998. See ZAIRIAN CIVIL WAR OF 1996–97; SUDANESE CIVIL WAR OF 1956– .

Ugandan Religious Wars (1885–92)   By 1879, British Anglican, French Roman Catholic, and Arab Islamic missionaries had reached the equatorial African area known as Uganda. The native king, Mwanga (fl. 1880s), became increasingly fearful of the outsiders' influence over his people and decided to eradicate them. In 1885, he seized the chief Anglican missionaries and killed a bishop who approached the region from the east—the direction from which legend said the conquerors of Uganda would come. Persecution of Christians increased; converts were slaughtered in cold blood or burned at the stake. Mwanga's plan to put all the Christians and Muslims on an island in Lake Victoria and let them starve to death did not succeed; the king was forced to flee for his life, and his brother Kikewa (fl. 1880s) then took the throne. Hoping to achieve peace, Kikewa divided the main posts among the three religious groups. The Muslims, however, murdered many Christian native chiefs, whose followers fled but later rallied and defeated the Muslims in battle in October 1889. The next month the Muslims triumphed in another battle but were decisively defeated in February 1890. Thereupon the Catholics and Protestants began to quarrel. After the French Catholic factions attacked and were defeated by the British Protestants at Kampala in the spring of 1892, they took refuge on the Sese Islands in Lake Victoria, from which they preyed on the Protestants. Later in the year a British officer led an attack on the islands and routed the Catholics, who fled and settled in the southern part of Uganda. The Muslims resided in another area, while the Protestants gained control of the main parts of Uganda, which became a British protectorate in 1894.

United Irishmen's Revolt (1798)   Irish Catholic nationalists, known as the Society of United Irishmen and inspired by Theobald Wolfe Tone (1763–98), James Napper Tandy (1740–1803), and other leaders, openly revolted against British Protestant rule in order to secure independence for Ireland. British troops under the command of Gerard Lake (1744–1808) overpowered and beat the Irish rebels, many of whom were arrested. Angry, armed mobs of Irishmen rose up and seized control of County Wexford until they were forced to surrender at the Battle of Vinegar Hill, June 21, 1798. A French expeditionary force, organized and led by Tone, who intended to aid the fighting Irishmen, was intercepted and defeated by a British squadron off Lough Swilly, County Donegal. Tone, who was captured and court-martialed, committed suicide before he was to be hanged for treason. The revolt collapsed, and in 1801 Great Britain was united with Ireland as the United Kingdom.

Uruguayan Civil War of 1842–51   See MONTEVIDEO, SIEGE OF.

Uruguayan Revolt of 1811–16   The Banda Oriental (Uruguay) had long been an area of dispute between Spain and Portugal. In 1776, it was made part of the Spanish viceroyalty of Río de la Plata, which included present-day Argentina, Paraguay, and Bolivia. After Napoleon (1769–1821) deposed King Ferdinand VII (1784–1833) of Spain in 1808 (see NAPOLEONIC WARS; PENINSULAR WAR), Argentina took the lead in establishing control over the Banda Oriental, which was invited to join with it in the United Provinces of the Río de la Plata. When the Spanish viceroy, Francisco Javier de Elio

(1767–1822), was forced out of Buenos Aires (see ARGENTINE WAR OF INDEPENDENCE), he took refuge in Montevideo, where Uruguayans under José Gervasio Artigas (1764–1850) sought to remove him by force. Elio requested aid from Ferdinand's sister, Carlota Joaquina (1775–1830), wife of the Brazilian regent John (1769–1826). In 1811, a Portuguese force invaded the Banda Oriental to protect Elio from the revolutionaries in Montevideo and Buenos Aires who were seeking independence. Artigas led the revolutionaries to victory, took control of the Banda Oriental, and decided that it must remain separate from Argentina. In 1814, Argentine troops attacked Montevideo but were repulsed in 1815, leaving the Banda Oriental independent of Spain and Argentina. In the following year Brazilian forces invaded, drove out Artigas, and occupied the area, which was made part of Brazil in 1821 and remained so until after the ARGENTINE-BRAZILIAN WAR OF 1825–28, when it established its independence as the nation of Uruguay.

Uruguayan Revolution of 1933   In 1931, Gabriel Terra (1873–1942) of the liberal Colorado party was elected president of Uruguay, whose economy was being hurt by the Great Depression. He came into conflict with the national council of administration, which checked the executive power, and faced opposition from conservative Blancos and radical Colorados who desired more socialization of the economy. On March 30, 1933, Terra dissolved both the national council and the congress by sending soldiers in to eject their members; he abolished the constitution and assumed dictatorial powers. A new constitution, promulgated in 1934, concentrated authority in the presidency and provided proportional representation among the political parties in the cabinet and senate; reelected president, Terra ruled dictatorially and suppressed a small revolt against him the following year (1935). For a time freedom of speech was restricted and opposition newspapers were forbidden. However, under Terra's administration, Uruguay's economy improved and socialization occurred. In 1938, Terra stepped down and, in a relatively fair election, was succeeded as president by his brother-in-law, General Alfredo Baldomir (1884–1948), who then restored democratic government.

Uruguayan War of Independence   See ARGENTINE-BRAZILIAN WAR OF 1825–28; URUGUAYAN REVOLT OF 1811–16.

U.S. War of Independence   See AMERICAN REVOLUTION.

Utah War (Mormon War) (1857–58)   Utah, which was settled by the Mormons (Latter-day Saints) in the mid-1840s, was declared a U.S. territory in 1850, and Brigham Young (1801–77), the Mormon leader, was appointed governor. Federal officials complained of Young's dictatorial ways and the power of the church, while others were shocked at the Mormons' practice of polygamy. The Mormons, for their part, did not want non-Mormons in their territory and resented the flow of emigrants across and into their lands. Matters worsened, and in 1857 the U.S. president sent Colonel Albert S. Johnston (1803–62) and a force of 2,500 troops to Utah to install a new non-Mormon governor to enforce federal authority. The Danites, a Mormon militia, slowed Johnston's progress across the plains by stampeding horses, destroying wagon trains, and burning grass, while Young called settlers from throughout the territory to come to Salt Lake City to defend the capital. Before a serious confrontation took place, a federal mediator was able to arrange a compromise. The new governor was recognized and allowed to enter Salt Lake City, while the troops camped outside and soon returned East. Although the "rebels" were pardoned by the president, friction between the Mormons and the government continued for another four decades. It was only after the Mormon Church abolished polygamy that Utah was admitted into the Union in 1896. See also MOUNTAIN MEADOWS MASSACRE.

Vandal Raids on the Roman Empire (A.D. 406–533)   The Vandals, an ancient Germanic tribe from Jutland (Denmark) who had settled east of modern Berlin, Germany, in the fifth century B.C., entered the Danube River basin in the early third century, apparently with Roman imperial permission. Pushed out, they invaded Gaul (France) in 406, but were driven into Spain in 409. Despite imperial permission to remain, the Vandals nonetheless fought minor encounters with Roman forces and Visigoths, another Germanic people. In 428, Genseric (Gaiseric) (390–477), an Aryan Christian, became the Vandals' king. Pressed by the Visigoths, he led his people to North Africa in 429, overwhelmed Roman troops there, and by 435 controlled most of Roman Africa. The Vandals captured Carthage (439), making it their capital and using it as a base for raids on Sicily and southern Italy. Roman recognition of an independent Vandal nation (442) stopped the raids briefly. Upon the murder of Valentinian III (419–55), Roman emperor of the West, his widow appealed to Genseric for help against the usurping emperor Petronius Maximus (d. 455). Genseric sailed with a fleet to the mouth of the Tiber River and marched upon Rome in June 455. In flight, Maximus was slain by the Vandals, who occupied and sacked the city for a fortnight. Then, with Valentinian's widow as a hostage, they returned to Carthage. The Romans vowed to exterminate them at Carthage, but failed miserably during the ROMAN WAR WITH THE VAN-DALS in 468. By 476, the Eastern Roman emperor made peace with Genseric, who had made many pirate attacks and had gained control of North Africa, Sicily, Sardinia, Corsica, and the Balearic Islands. Genseric's death (477) ended the Vandal raids on Italy, but raids went on elsewhere until a defeat by a Roman-Byzantine army led by General Belisarius (505?–65) caused the Vandals to lose Carthage in 533 (see VANDAL-ROMAN WAR IN NORTH AFRICA). The Vandals soon disappeared from history. See also VISIGOTHIC RAIDS ON THE ROMAN EMPIRE, LATER.

Vandal-Roman War in North Africa   (A.D. 533–34)   Since the mid-400s, the Vandals, a Germanic people, had controlled North Africa (see VANDAL RAIDS ON THE ROMAN EMPIRE). They were harsh masters of the Romanized population there and intolerant of any religion except their own. In 533, the Eastern Roman emperor, Justinian I (483–565), sent an expedition to North Africa commanded by his capable general Belisarius (505?–65). The Vandals' king, Gelimer (Geilamir) (fl. 530–34), a staunch anti-Roman, had earlier usurped the throne from his pro-Roman cousin in 530; Justinian used this as an excuse to interfere. Belisarius's army defeated Gelimar's forces in battle near Carthage, the Vandal capital, and then captured the city. Three months later, in December 533, Gelimar's army was utterly destroyed on the battlefield; Gelimar fled to

Numidia (roughly Algeria), was pursued and captured (March 534), and taken to Constantinople (Istanbul); he later settled in Galatia in central Asia Minor. This defeat spelled the end of the Vandals as a distinct people. See also GOTHIC (ITALIAN) WAR OF A.D. 534–54.

Vassy, Massacre at (1562)   In France, the bitter hostility between Protestants (Huguenots) and Catholics was exacerbated by the unsuccessful conspiracy of Amboise (1560), by which the Protestants tried to end persecutions suffered at the hands of King Francis II (1544–60), who was dominated by the noble Guise family, champions of Catholicism. After failing to abduct the king from the royal castle of Amboise and arrest the Guise leaders, Huguenot conspirators were rounded up and ruthlessly hanged. The death of Francis, however, deprived the Guises of power. Hoping to avert civil war, Catherine de Médicis (1519–89), the ruling queen mother, granted the Protestants limited toleration in prescribed areas in the Edict of January (1562). Duke François of Guise (1519–63), claiming Huguenot violations of the law, ordered the partisans to fire upon Protestant worshipers at Vassy on March 1, 1562. This outrage, in which many innocents were killed, promptly ignited the FIRST WAR OF RELIGION.

Vellore Mutiny (1806)   The British East India Company's indifference to the religious and caste customs of its Indian (sepoy) troops led to the bloody and useless mutiny at Vellore, India, in May 1806. To replace the Indians' turban, the British had introduced a headdress resembling a hat; to ensure decorum, they had prohibited the troops from wearing ornaments and caste marks during parades. The 1,500 sepoys at Vellore split into two groups, one attacking and killing many of the 4,000 Europeans barracked there; the other firing at officers' houses, killing them as they entered their doorways. From the nearby town of Arcot came troops of British dragoons (mounted infantrymen), who blew down the gates of Vellore's fort held by the sepoys and cut down some 400 mutineers (about 130 British soldiers died in the fight). The governor-general of Madras was replaced (1807) for his carelessness.

Vendée, Wars of the (1793–1832)   Five uprisings against changes proposed by the government at Paris began in the rural, conservative Vendée, a department (administrative district) in western France. To the devoutly Roman Catholic and economically backward inhabitants of the Vendée, the anticlerical decrees of the Parisian revolutionaries were infuriating after the FRENCH REVOLUTION. In 1793, the conscription laws were introduced, setting off the first and most important uprising in the Vendée. A force of 50,000 Vendéans, joined by prominent royalist nobles and later called the "Grand Army," occupied local towns (February 1793) and, aided by unrelated counterrevolutionary uprisings in Lyons, Marseilles, and Normandy, seriously threatened the French Revolutionary government, which was already suffering from the FRENCH REVOLUTIONARY WARS. By June 1793, the Grand Army had seized the town of Saumur; it then crossed the Loire River and, bogging down in a vain siege of Nantes, failed to win Brittany, Normandy, and Maine toward a projected march on Paris itself. Relatively victorious otherwise until October 1793, the rebels, now 65,000 in number, were seriously defeated by government forces at Cholet, but a rebel remnant fought on, to be savagely trounced at Le Mans and Savenay in December 1793. Severe government reprisals provoked new but unsuccessful rebel resistance until an amnesty (December 1794) and a decree of freedom from conscription and of religious liberty (Treaty of La Jaunaie, 1795) stopped the fighting. A second uprising, a small effort, took place in June 1795, when exiled French nobles backed by Great Britain returned to Brittany, France, but were defeated the next month; the capture and execution of the nobles' leaders in 1796 ended the fight for good. Order was then swiftly restored by the French Revolutionary government at Paris. Later three mainly royalist rather than religious uprisings, also known as wars of the Vendée, occurred in 1799, 1815, and 1832 in the

Vendée. The rule of Emperor Napoleon Bonaparte (1769–1821) was opposed in 1815 and that of King Louis-Philippe (1773–1850) in 1832. See also FRENCH REVOLUTION OF 1830; NAPOLEONIC WARS.

Venetian-Byzantine War of 1170–77   The Byzantine inhabitants of Constantinople (Istanbul) resented the increasing presence of Venetian merchants and the privileges accorded them following the first two CRUSADES. Genoa, Pisa, and other trading rivals of Venice urged Byzantine emperor Manuel I Comnenus (1120?–80) to act; in 1171, in a single day, all Venetians in the Byzantine Empire were arrested and their goods briefly confiscated. The emperor seized Venetian outposts in the Aegean; other Venetian holdings in the Adriatic fell to Hungary (see HUNGARIAN-VENETIAN WAR OF 1171). The doge of Venice issued the first government bonds to finance an expedition to retake the Dalmatian coastal cities of Zara (Zadar) and Ragusa (Dubrovnik) and the Aegean Greek seaport of Negropont (Chalcis). With Norman aid, Venetians seized Ragusa and sacked the Byzantine-held Aegean islands of Chios and Lesbos (1171). In 1173, when Venetians lost at Ancona, the dreaded plague was brought back to Venice, and in the resulting chaos the doge was killed, Venice's government reorganized, and a deliberative assembly (the forerunner of the Great Council) was established. By 1177, all fighting had ceased and drawn-out negotiations had begun, lasting until 1183, when Andronicus I Comnenus (1118–85), newly crowned Byzantine emperor, resumed trade and political relations with Venice, to which he pledged compensation for losses.

Venetian Conquest of Friuli (1411–20) Threatened by the Hungarians under King Sigismund (1368–1437), the dukes of Friuli (historic region of northeastern Italy on the Adriatic, now partly in Slovenia) requested military aid from Venice in 1411. A successful Venetian campaign against the Hungarians led to Friuli being solidly in Venetian hands by 1420. Venice had pushed its borders northward to the Carnic Alps and eastward to the Julian Alps.

Venetian-Genoese War of 1255–70   Attempts by Venice and Genoa, commercial rivals in the eastern Mediterranean, to eliminate each other and to procure exclusive trading rights at Constantinople and in the Crusaders' Latin colonies led to war in 1255. Off the coast of Palestine, the Venetians won three naval battles against the Genoese, enabling them to expel the Genoese from Acre. A number of minor, undefined battles were fought among the Aegean islands and off the coast of Greece. The most decisive battle was at Trapani near Sicily in 1264, when a Venetian fleet destroyed a Genoese naval force and killed more than 1,000 Genoese seamen. When Venice secured additional trading rights from the emperor at Constantinople, a truce was signed by Venice and Genoa in 1270.

Venetian-Genoese War of 1291–99   Genoa's spice trade routes in the Black Sea and eastern Mediterranean were challenged by Venice, which allied itself with Pisa. The Genoese defeated a combined fleet from Venice and Pisa in the Gulf of Alexandretta in 1294, then sacked the Venetian port of Canea (Khania) on Crete and destroyed the Venetians' spice fleet there. At Constantinople, Genoese citizens attacked and killed many Venetians. In retaliation, the Venetian navy under Rogerio Morosini (fl. 1290s) sacked Galata, a Genoese trading port near Constantinople. Minor attacks and counterattacks continued fitfully until the Genoese under Lamba Doria (fl. 1290s) won a resounding naval victory off the Dalmatian coast near Curzola in 1299. More than 900 Venetians were killed or captured. A mutual nonaggression pact was signed by Venice and Genoa in 1299.

Venetian-Genoese War of 1350–55   When the Genoese seized a number of Venetian ships near Caffa (Feodosiya), a flourishing Genoese trading colony on the Crimean peninsula, war broke out again between Venice and Genoa. Soon afterward the Genoese captured the important Venetian colony at Negroponte (Évvoia or Euboea) in Greece. Quickly the Venetians made alliances with the eastern emperor at Constantinople and the king of Aragon. An indecisive battle was fought at the Bosporus. A Venetian victory off Sardinia in 1352 enabled Venice to blockade Genoa, which then concluded an alliance with Milan and went on the offensive. A Genoese victory at the Battle of Sapienza in 1354 forced Venice to make peace; both cities promised not to encroach on the other's territory and trade routes. See also CHIOGGIA, WAR OF.

Venetian-Genoese War of 1378–81   See CHIOGGIA, WAR OF.

Venetian-Milanese War of 1404–6   The conquests of Milanese ruler Gian Galeazzo Visconti (1351–1402) were lost, with many northern and central Italian cities reverting to local lords (see FLORENTINE-MILANESE WAR OF 1397–1402). Venetians took control of the Milanese possessions of Vicenza, Verona, Padua, and Bassano. In 1406, they ended the Carrara family line by strangling Lord Francesco II Novello da Carrara (d. 1406), who had retained the lordships of Padua and Verona under an agreement. Venice now dominated most of northeastern Italy.

Venetian-Milanese War of 1426   Filippo Maria Visconti (1402–47), duke of Milan, hoped to retake Verona and Vicenza, both lost after his father's death, and to rule all of northern Italy. In 1426, Venice, prompted by commercial advantage and the threat of Visconti's ambition, allied itself with Florence against Milan. Soon Siena, Ferrara, Savoy, and Mantua joined the Venetian-Florentine alliance and formed a large army under Francesco Carmagnola (1390–1432). When Carmagnola's forces entered Brescia, a prearranged revolt erupted, helping the imposition of a siege. Milanese defender Francesco Sforza (1401–66) surrendered, but reinforcements on both sides extended the fighting for eight months until November 1426, when the last

Milanese city stronghold fell with the help of a new weapon—artillery. With the intervention of Pope Martin V (1368–1431), a peace treaty was negotiated in Venice on December 30, 1426. Venice gained Brescia and the environs; Florence retook its lost territory; Savoy ruled the territory it acquired from Milan; and Milan was enjoined from interfering in any state between it and Rome.

Venetian-Milanese War of 1427–28   Almost immediately after the Peace of Venice was signed (see VENETIAN-MILANESE WAR OF 1426), Filippo Maria Visconti (1402–47), duke of Milan, attempted to ambush and kill Venice's General Francesco Carmagnola (1390–1432) at Chiari. Visconti rearmed his Po River fleet and renewed warfare. After fighting an inconclusive battle at Goltolengo, Carmagnola went to Cremona and, finding the city occupied by Visconti's forces, launched a full-scale attack outside it on Casa-al-Secco. Carmagnola's men piled up the bodies of dead soldiers to bridge Cremona's moat, gaining entrance and soon victory. Afterward Carmagnola ambushed and defeated Milanese forces in a swamp near Brescia. Florence, exhausted by the war and threatened by increasing Venetian power, sued for peace at Ferrara in April 1428. Venice was awarded Brescia and part of Cremona.

Venetian-Milanese War of 1429–33   After Florence broke the Peace of Ferrara in 1429 (see VENETIAN-MILANESE WAR OF 1427–28) by attacking Lucca and defeating a Genoese fleet on the Riviera, war broke out again between Venice and Milan. Francesco Carmagnola (1390–1432) led Venetian forces into battle in Cremona, where they were defeated on June 6, 1431 by the Milanese under Francesco Sforza (1401–66) at Soncino on the Po River. In addition, the Milanese fleet was victorious at a general naval battle at Bina. Carmagnola's battle failures led to his trial for treason in Venice. Found guilty, he was beheaded on April 5, 1432. The war ceased when the duke of Milan agreed to peace in 1433. Venice retained control of Brescia and Bergamo.

Venetian-Milanese War of 1448–54   When the duke of Milan, Filippo Maria Visconti (1402–47), died without a clear heir, the Venetians moved into the duchy of Milan to take advantage of Milanese unrest. Francesco Sforza (1401–66), chosen to lead the Milanese army, took the offensive in 1448, gaining much Venetian territory, destroying Venice's fleet, and winning the Battle of Caravaggio. All the while, however, he was secretly negotiating with the Venetians, and eventually he renounced his Milan connection to wage war for Venice. Sforza's forces blockaded Milan, which capitulated and whose citizens made Sforza the new duke. In 1452, Sforza allied himself with Florence, Genoa, and Mantua against Venice. The desultory warfare between Venice and Milan ended with the Peace of Lodi in 1454.

Venetian-Turkish War of 1416   In response to advances by the Ottoman Turks in the Aegean Sea area, the Venetian fleet under Pietro Loredan (d. 1439) defeated and destroyed the Turkish fleet in a naval battle off Gallipoli in June 1416. Venice consequently secured control of the Dalmatian islands and coast and also acquired new outposts in Greece and Euboea (Negroponte). Sultan Muhammad I (1389?–1421) was forced to seek peace, sending the first Turkish ambassador to a Christian power.

Venetian-Turkish War of 1425–30   Ottoman sultan Murad II (1403–51) launched Turkish warships that destroyed Venetian outposts along the Albanian coast and at Epirus in western Greece. In 1430, the Turks took Thessalonica (Salonica), a city on the Aegean Sea, where 1,400 Venetians were garrisoned. The city's inhabitants were massacred or sold into slavery, and its churches were converted into mosques. Entangled in war elsewhere, Venice was forced to make peace in 1430 (see VENETIAN-MILANESE WAR OF 1429–33).

Venetian-Turkish War of 1443–53   Venice contributed warships to the defense of Constantinople (Istanbul) against the Ottoman Turks of Sultan Muhammad II (1429–81). After the city's fall in 1453 (see CONSTANTINOPLE, FALL OF), the Turks moved on to conquer Greece and Albania, thus isolating Venetian outposts. The Venetians were driven out of Rumelia in the southern Balkan peninsula and Anatolia (Asian part of Turkey).

Venetian-Turkish War of 1463–79   Ottoman sultan Muhammad II "the Conquerer" (1429–81) strengthened the Turkish fleet, which captured the Greek port of Mytilene on the Aegean Sea and made raids along the Dalmatian coast. In 1470, Turkish sea and land forces took Negropont (Chalcis), a port on Euboea. The Venetians secured the aid of the Persians, who invaded Anatolia (Asian Turkey) but were defeated by Turks under Muhammad at the Battle of Erzinjan (Erzincan), on the upper Euphrates, in 1473. The Persians were forced to withdraw, depriving Venice of a formidable ally and leaving Muhammad virtually in control of Anatolia. The Turks now overran Albania and raided to the very outskirts of Venice. By the Treaty of Constantinople in 1479, the Venetians ceded all of the regions conquered by the Turks, including Scutari (part of Constantinople), whose Venetian garrison had heroically repulsed numerous Turkish assaults in 1478–79, Negroponte, the island of Lemnos, and other Venetian outposts in the Aegean. Venice also paid a 100,000-ducat indemnity and agreed to pay annual tributes to the Ottomans in return for trading rights. See also TURKOMAN-OTTOMAN WARS OF 1400–1473.

Venetian-Turkish War of 1499–1503   The Ottoman Turks continued their depredations against the Venetians, who received some help from the kings of France, Aragon, and Portugal but none from Rome and other rivals. The Turkish fleet, with improved naval discipline, won the Battle of Lepanto on July 28, 1499, soundly defeating the Venetian fleet, whose commander, Antonio Grimani (1436–1523), was captured and later returned in chains. Turkish victories in Pylos, Modon, and Coron and Turkish raids across the Julian Alps into Italy as far as Vicenza finally forced Venice to make peace in November 1503. The Turks took control of parts of Morea (Peloponnesus) and some islands but lost Cephalonia, largest of the Ionian islands.

Venetian-Turkish War of 1537–40   A presumed Venetian insult caused Ottoman sultan Süleyman I "the Magnificent" (1496?–1566) to wage war against Venice. Turkish forces harried Apulia in southern Italy in 1537. Süleyman prepared a large Turkish land and naval force to besiege the Venetian island of Corfu but abandoned his plans with the arrival of a strong Imperial-Venetian fleet commanded by Andrea Doria (1468?–1560). Turkish naval forces under Khair ed-Din Barbarossa II (1466?–1546), making sweeps of the Aegean and Adriatic seas, captured many Venetian-held islands and outposts and raided Crete in 1538. On September 27, 1538, Barbarossa's fleet won a victory against an Imperial-Venetian fleet under Doria at the Battle of Preveza. By 1540, Venice had ceded to the Turks its Aegean islands and mainland outposts in Morea (Peloponnesus), including Nauplia and Monemvasia.

Venetian-Turkish War of 1570–73   When the Venetians refused to cede Cyprus to the Ottoman Turks, Sultan Selim II (1524?–74) ordered an invasion of the island by Turkish land and naval forces. In the summer of 1570, about 5,000 soldiers at Nicosia fought off a besieging 50,000-man Turkish army but succumbed; the Turks then massacred the entire Venetian garrison and much of the population. Afterward the Turks besieged and blockaded Venetian-held Famagusta on Cyprus for nearly a year. After the defending Venetian force was cut in half to about 2,500 men, the Venetian governor at Famagusta accepted the peace terms offered by the Turks, who then mercilessly massacred the defenders in early August 1571. A fleet of the Holy League, consisting mainly of 200 Venetian, Spanish, and papal ships, under Don Juan (1547–78) of Austria,

tracked down and annihilated a Turkish fleet at the Bloody Battle of Lepanto, Greece, on October 7, 1571. Spain hesitated in following up the victory, and in 1572 a Turkish naval force checked the Venetians, forcing them to separate from the league and to sign a treaty on March 7, 1573. Venice ceded Cyprus and possessions in Albania and Epirus and paid a large indemnity to the Turks.

Venetian-Turkish War of 1645–69   See CANDIAN WAR.

Venetian-Turkish War of 1685–99   The Venetians under Francesco Morosini (1618–94) seized parts of Dalmatia and Morea (Peloponnesus) from the Ottoman Turks between 1685 and 1687. In September 1687, Athens was captured by Morosini, but the Venetians were later forced to abandon the city despite their control of most of Peloponnesus. The Aegean island of Chios was seized by the Venetians in 1591 but later returned to the Turks, who held it until the FIRST BALKAN WAR in 1912. The Treaty of Karlowitz in January 1699 ended the war, and Venice obtained the Peloponnesus and much of Dalmatia. See also AUSTRO-TURKISH WAR OF 1683–99.

Venetian-Turkish War of 1714–18   In retaliation for Venetian incitement of an uprising in Montenegro in 1714 (Venetians had invaded Bosnia and seized Turkish Mediterranean-based ships, too), the Ottoman Empire declared war on Venice and sent land and sea forces to capture Venetian islands and fortresses in the Aegean area. The Turks besieged and conquered the entire Peloponnesus after a year and, with naval help from Egypt and the Barbary States, drove the Venetians from the Aegean and Crete, where they had held on to small strongholds after the CANDIAN WAR. A Turkish assault on Corfu was repulsed by the Venetians, who received some help from Spain, Portugal, and several Italian states. By 1716, Austria was fighting alongside Venice (see AUSTRO-TURKISH WAR OF 1714–18). Through British and Dutch mediation, peace was established by the Treaty of Passarowitz on July 21, 1718. Venice gave up the Peloponnesus but acquired some Albanian and Dalmatian outposts.

Venezuelan Civil War of 1858–64   In March 1858, the autocratic Monagas brothers, who had ruled Venezuela since 1848 (see VENEZUELAN REVOLT OF 1848–49), were overthrown in a revolution engineered by Conservatives and Liberals, who were both vying for power. Promptly civil strife erupted among ambitious *caudillos* (military leaders) in the provinces, and Venezuela became embroiled in the so-called Federalist Wars mainly pitting Conservatives against Liberals, with the former wanting a centralized government and the latter federalism and democracy. Fighting was fierce, and the government was in different hands several times until José Antonio Páez (1790–1873), a former Venezuelan president, was recalled from exile to form a Conservative ministry (1861). But turmoil persisted as the Liberals fought against the repressive policies of Páez, who governed as a harsh dictator until his supporters were defeated in 1863; he again went into exile. By 1864, the Liberals, led by Generals Juan Falcón (1820–70) and Antonio Guzmán Blanco (1829–99), had gained control and promulgated a federalist constitution.

Venezuelan Civil War of 1868–70   A decentralized Venezuela under the leadership of President Juan Falcón (1820–70), a Liberal, led to increasing political disorder and fighting among strong provincial *caudillos* (military leaders). José Tadeo Monagas (1784–1868) headed a Conservative revolution that toppled Falcón in 1868; Monagas briefly regained power but died shortly after; and civil war broke out with much bloodshed. A counterrevolution led by the energetic Liberal caudillo Antonio Guzmán Blanco (1829–99) succeeded in overthrowing the Conservatives in 1870, and Guzmán Blanco, who had been vice president in the Falcón government, assumed power and later (1873) was elected constitutional president. Ruling as a be-

nevolent despot, he improved the country's economy and school system, proclaimed religious freedom, and suppressed the Roman Catholic Church. In 1888–89, a revolution led by his opponents destroyed his authority, and Guzmán Blanco, who was abroad at the time, was compelled to take up residence in Paris for the rest of his life.

Venezuelan Revolt of 1848–49   José Antonio Páez (1790–1873), leader of the Conservatives, dominated Venezuela either as the country's president or power broker from 1830 to 1848, a period of political stability and economic progress. His friend General José Tadeo Monagas (1784–1868), who was elected Venezuelan president as a Conservative in 1846, broke with Páez when he appointed Liberals as ministers. The Conservative congress was angered, and Páez led supporters in revolt against Monagas, whose forces were victorious; Páez went into exile. Between 1848 and 1858, Venezuela was under the dictatorial presidential rule of either Monagas or his brother, José Gregorio Monagas (1795–1858), who alternated in the country's highest office and tried to lengthen the presidential term from four to six years (see VENEZUELAN CIVIL WAR OF 1858–64).

Venezuelan Revolt of 1945   President Isaias Medina Angarita (1897–1953) of Venezuela relaxed governmental control sufficiently to allow the establishment of opposition political parties, including the Acción Democrática (Democratic Action), a socialist and leftist party that appealed to the middle class, workers, students, and young army officers. As the election of 1945 approached, the Acción Democrática became frustrated because under the constitution the next president would be chosen by the Venezuelan Congress rather than by popular election. The likely government choices were unacceptable to the party, and on October 18, 1945, some of the party's young officers led a revolt, ousted and jailed Medina, and placed a seven-man junta in control with Rómulo Betancourt (1908–81) as provisional president. The new government put forth the constitution of 1947, providing for new social legislation, and held the first free presidential election in Venezuelan history later that year.

Venezuelan Revolt of 1958   Venezuela's government under President Marcos Pérez Jiménez (1914–) was denounced for corruption, police oppression, and extravagant spending for the construction of public works and tourist hotels. Public dissatisfaction led to overt revolutionary actions by several air force units on January 1, 1958, when planes bombed the capital city of Caracas and caused much destruction and loss of life. By the next day Pérez Jiménez's forces had regained control. However, there was much unrest in the armed forces, and a week later a mutiny occurred in the navy. Pérez Jiménez frantically reorganized his cabinet several times in an effort to obtain strong leadership. On January 21, 1958, a general strike erupted in Caracas that brought life there to a halt; two days later all the armed forces joined the popular protest. Realizing he could not govern without the support of the military, Pérez Jiménez flew to Miami, Fla., taking a multimillion-dollar fortune with him. Five military officers set themselves up as a junta to head a provisional government until new elections could be held.

Venezuelan Uprisings of 1992   The radical Bolívarist Revolutionary Movement (MRB) accused high-level military leaders of corruption, especially profiteering through drug traffickers, and helped foment mid-level military unrest against Venezuela's government under President Carlos Andrés Peréz (1922–). In February 1992, rebellious officers briefly seized the paratroopers' base in Maracay near Caracas, the capital, before being overpowered by government forces. Another rebel faction then took control of Maracaibo before also being crushed, and 133 officers were arrested on insurrection charges. Afterward, an investigation began concerning armed forces' corruption, and some political and economic reforms occurred. Dis-

gruntled air force units, allied with civilian leftists, later failed in another military coup against President Pérez on November 27, 1992; aircraft attacked Peréz's office in Caracas, where heavy fighting occurred for half a day. Arrested were 240 soldiers and civilians. However, corruption charges leveled against Pérez led to his removal from the presidency in May 1993 and to his conviction for mismanagement of a multimillion-dollar government fund in May 1996.

Venezuelan War of Independence   (1811–21) After the Napoleonic invasion of Spain (see PENINSULAR WAR), the Spanish captain-general at Caracas was deposed, and a junta assumed authority in Venezuela. Simón Bolívar (1783–1830) was sent to England to secure aid for a war of liberation from Spanish rule. Soon Francisco de Miranda (1750–1816), a Venezuelan who had fought in the FRENCH REVOLUTIONARY WARS, returned to lead the struggle. On July 5, 1811, Venezuelan independence was proclaimed, but Miranda's forces were soon defeated, and the country was returned to royal rule (Miranda was arrested and imprisoned in Spain, where he later died). In 1813, Bolívar led the Venezuelans to victory against the Spanish under Domingo de Monteverde (1772–1823) and captured Caracas, gaining the title "Liberator." Though Bolívar won other battles, the Spanish defeated him at La Puerta, regained control of Venezuela, and forced him to flee to New Granada (Colombia); there and in Jamaica and Haiti he remained nearly two years in exile (see COLOMBIAN WAR OF INDEPENDENCE). In 1816, Bolívar returned to Venezuela and, aided by patriots under José Antonio Páez (1790–1873) and volunteer soldiers from Europe, established a headquarters at Angostura (Ciudad Bolívar). He was absorbed mainly in fighting in New Granada, liberating it from Spanish rule in 1819. Turning his attention to Venezuela, Bolívar signed an armistice with the royalists and then broke it to rout the Spaniards at the Battle of Carabobo on June 24, 1821. Venezuelans were liberated at last. See also CHILEAN WAR OF INDEPENDENCE; PERUVIAN WAR OF INDEPENDENCE.

Venizelists' Uprising See CRETAN UPRISING OF 1935.

Vercingetorix, Rebellion of See GALLIC WARS.

Verdun, Battle of (1916) Verdun, the major French fortress on the Meuse River, became the object of a German offensive in February 1916, during WORLD WAR I. After a heavy artillery bombardment, German troops advanced and captured several of the smaller forts surrounding Verdun. French forces counterattacked and stopped the German drive. The battle raged on for months. Areas were taken and retaken by both sides; there were strong attacks and counterattacks. "They shall not pass" became the cry of French resistance, and indeed Verdun did stand resolute against relentless German shelling. By August 1916, the Germans realized they could not capture the fortress and ceased their attacks. About a million Frenchmen lost their lives in this struggle, which was one of the most destructive of the war.

Vesey's Rebellion (1822) Denmark Vesey (c. 1767–1822), a talented, black freedman who worked as a carpenter, planned and organized a major slave rebellion in and around Charleston, S.C. (he hoped to relieve the blacks of their wretched conditions, take control of Charleston, and, if necessary, flee to the West Indies). Vesey and some colleagues collected many weapons, armed several thousand slaves in the area, and set the date for the rebellion for a Sunday in July 1822. When news of it leaked out (black betrayers informed the white authorities), Vesey moved the date up to Sunday, June 16, but the authorities quickly made preparations to defend Charleston and began arresting black suspects, including Vesey. In the ensuing trials of 136 black slaves, 67 were convicted on minor conspiracy charges, 32 were condemned to exile, and 37 (including Vesey) were hanged for active participation in the attempted rebellion. Four white men, convicted of plotting with the slaves, were fined and sent to prison.

Vienna, Siege of (1683) The Ottoman Turks secretly supported rebellious Hungarians and others in Hapsburg (Austrian) Hungary after the AUSTRO-TURKISH WAR OF 1663–64. Planning to overcome Austria and Holy Roman Emperor Leopold I (1640–1705), Ottoman sultan Muhammad IV (1641–92) assembled a large army at Belgrade for an invasion in 1683. After marching up the Danube River and being joined by a Transylvanian force, the Turks, now about 150,000 strong, reached Vienna, Austria's capital, in mid-July 1683, and immediately besieged the city, which was defended by a garrison of only 15,000 men (Leopold and his court had fled to Passau). For nearly two months the defenders, who made frequent sorties, checked the Ottomans, who, at times, breached the city's walls but were driven back. Some 30,000 Polish troops led by King John III Sobieski (1624–96) of Poland, responding to an appeal by the pope, marched to Vienna, were joined by about 45,000 Austrians and Germans, relieved the city, and defeated the Turks in battle on September 12, 1683. Afterward King John sent the captured standard of the Prophet to the pope. See also AUSTRO-TURKISH WAR OF 1683–99.

Vietnamese-Cambodian War of 1738–50 Cambodia was increasingly upset by its loss of power and territory to neighboring Annam or Vietnam, which had invaded and annexed Cambodian border provinces in the Mekong River delta area in the early 1700s. Vietnamese infiltration and colonization of Cambodian coastal regions, particularly Ha-tien (which had been taken by the Vietnamese during the SIAMESE-CAMBODIAN WAR OF 1714–17), led to a Cambodian military effort to reconquer lost lands. In a protracted conflict, Cambodian forces were repelled, and Vietnamese troops retaliated by marching into Cambodian territory and seizing additional tracts. By 1750, the Vietnamese had control of the region known as Cochin China (part of southern Vietnam), which included the rich rice-growing Mekong delta plain.

Vietnamese–Cham War of 1000–1044 South of the independent and expansionist state of Dai Viet or Annam (northern Vietnam) lay the kingdom of Champa, a primarily naval and maritime power with little agricultural development and interior settlement. Northern Champa became occupied by Vietnamese settlers and rice farmers, who were protected by their government. In retaliation, the Chams made forays into the Red River delta area and were successful until Vietnamese forces of ruler Le Dai Hanh (d. 1005) occupied and pillaged the Cham capital and exacted tribute. Soon the Cham region of Amaravati (Quang Nam) was ceded to the Vietnamese, and Vijaya (Binh Dinh) became the Cham capital. War continued intermittently between the two states. In 1044, the Vietnamese ruler Ly Thai-Tong (999–1054) led a naval attack on Champa, now torn by civil unrest. Vijaya was captured, along with some 5,000 Chams, 30 elephants, and the royal harem; Champa's king was killed.

Vietnamese-Cham War of 1068–74   Allied with the Khmers, the Chams saw an opportunity to recapture their capital of Vijaya (Binh Dinh), which had been seized by the Vietnamese or Annamese in 1044 (see VIETNAMESE-CHAM WAR OF 1000–1044). They launched an invasion into the three southern border provinces of Dai Viet or Annam (northern Vietnam). Ly Thanh-Tong (1022–72), the Vietnamese ruler, retaliated in 1068 by attacking the kingdom of Champa (central Vietnam), burning Vijaya, and capturing Rudravarman III (d. 1074), the Cham king. In 1074, Champa's three border provinces were ceded to Dai Viet as ransom for the captive king, who died soon after. See also CHINESE-ANNAMESE WAR OF 1057–61.

Vietnamese-Cham War of 1103   Upon hearing from a Vietnamese or Annamese refugee that he could easily recover the three northern provinces lost to Dai Viet or Annam (northern Vietnam), King Jaya Indravarman (d. 1113?) of Champa (central Vietnam) promptly halted his customary tribute payments to Dai Viet and began an attack on the three provinces. At first his forces were victorious, but they were able to hold the provinces only a few

months before they were defeated and driven out by the Vietnamese.

Vietnamese-Cham War of 1312–26   Tran Ahn-tong (d. c. 1314), the ruler of Dai Viet or Annam (northern Vietnam), sent troops to quell revolts in the southern provinces, which had formerly belonged to the kingdom of Champa (central Vietnam) but had been ceded to Dai Viet. In 1312, his forces invaded Champa, defeated the Chams, captured their king, Jaya Simhavarman IV (Che Chi) (1284–1313), and annexed the kingdom to Dai Viet. The Cham king's brother was named the provincial administrator as a feudal prince. Combined Vietnamese and Cham forces repulsed a Thai invasion in 1313. When Tran Ahn-tong abdicated, the prince led a Cham rebellion against the Vietnamese (1314–18), but was eventually defeated. Other minor rebellions were also suppressed. Dai Viet's new ruler appointed General Che A-nan (fl. 14th cent.) to rule Champa in 1318. Che A-nan, however, sought and secured Mongol help to gain Champa's independence; his forces were finally victorious over the Vietnamese in 1326, thus ending Champa's forced vassalage to Dai Viet. Che A-nan became king, and the two war-weary states were at peace for many years.

Vietnamese-Cham War of 1446–71   Having encroached on the territory of the kingdom of Champa since the 11th century, the Vietnamese or Annamese to the north invaded once again in 1446 and seized the Cham capital of Vijaya (Binh Dinh). The Chams, who refused help from the Chinese, were able to recapture their capital, but civil wars weakened their kingdom during the next decades, bringing five different rulers to Champa's throne. In 1471, Le-Thanh-Ton (1441–97), the Vietnamese ruler, initiated a bloody campaign against the Chams. Vijaya was seized and looted, about 40,000 Chams were slain, and more than 30,000 were captured, including 50 members of the royal family. Champa's king was killed, and most of the kingdom was incorporated into Dai Viet or Annam (Vietnam); only a small Cham kingdom remained in the south as a buffer between the Vietnamese and Khmers. In another 150 years Champa was totally swallowed up by Dai Viet.

Vietnamese-Chinese War of 1405–7   After Ho Qui Ly (d. 1407?) had usurped the throne of Dai Viet or Annam (northern Vietnam), the deposed Tran royal family appealed to China's Ming emperor, Yung Lo (Yonglo) (1360–1424), for help (see VIETNAMESE CIVIL WAR OF 1400–1407). A Chinese naval expedition under the emperor's Muslim eunuch Chen Ho (1371–1433) was sent and attacked Dai Viet's southern coast between 1405 and 1407, freeing Champa (central Vietnam) from Vietnamese control. In 1407, about 200,000 Chinese soldiers in two large armies invaded Dai Viet; Ho Qui Ly confidently moved opposing troops along the Red River, but his men's morale was undermined by conspirators seeking to restore the Tran dynasty. Vietnamese forces were thus easily defeated; the usurper and his son Ho Han Thuong (d. 1407?) were captured and taken to China. Instead of restoring the royal family, Yung Lo annexed the state of Annam (meaning "Pacified South") to the Chinese Empire; after nearly 500 years, the area was again under Chinese domination (see CHINESE-ANNAMESE WAR OF A.D. 907–39). A Chinese governor-general was appointed Annam's head of state, and Chinese officials reorganized the administrative branch of government.

Vietnamese-Chinese War of 1418–28   The people of Dai Viet or Annam (northern Vietnam) prized their independence and resented being ruled by the Chinese (see VIETNAMESE-CHINESE WAR OF 1405–7). Le Loi (1384–1433), a rich Vietnamese landowner who had begun a resistance movement in 1416, organized a guerrilla force in the Lam Son area, with the help of writer-poet Nguyen Trai (1380–1442). The anti-Chinese guerrillas first attacked outposts and supply lines of the occupying Chinese Ming armies, never engaging the enemy directly, hoping to wear it down. After losing three battles, Le Loi's troops withdrew to the Chi Linh

Mountains near Lam Son. In 1419, they obtained help from the Laotians, who decided later to aid the Chinese instead. With his troops again retreating, Le Loi sought and secured a two-year armistice in 1422. The power of the Chinese began to decline after the death of their Ming emperor, Yung Lo (Yonglo) (1360–1424). In 1426, using attack elephants, the guerrilla rebels seized Nghe An province south of the Red River delta and then advanced north against the Chinese, who controlled only the city of Hanoi by 1427. The Chinese offered to withdraw if a Tran dynasty descendant was placed on the Vietnamese throne. Le Loi agreed, installing Tran Cao (d. 1428?). However, when Le Loi intercepted a Chinese general's message requesting reinforcements, he resumed the war. Victorious over a 100,000-man Chinese force, most of whose generals were captured or killed, Le Loi took Hanoi after a prolonged siege (1427–28), forcing the surrender of the Chinese; he furnished junks to carry the Chinese troops back to China. After ordering Tran Cao killed, he became the first Le dynasty ruler and concluded a peace with the Ming dynasty.

Vietnamese Civil War of 1400–1407   Dai Viet or Annam (northern Vietnam) conquered the kingdom of Champa (central Vietnam) and then moved the Vietnamese capital southward from Hanoi to Thanh Hoa in 1398. Meanwhile, the debilitating effect of constant fighting with the Chams, together with a succession of weak and corrupt Tran rulers who were unable to suppress rebellious mountain tribes, had allowed an able but disgruntled Vietnamese general, Ho Qui Ly (d. 1407?), to have Tran Nghe Tong (d. 1394), the royal ruler, strangled to death. Ho Qui Ly became regent. Later he skillfully engineered the overthrow of Tran Thuan Tong (fl. 1388–1400) and made the three-year-old crown prince ruler. In 1400, however, he seized the Tran throne and founded the Ho dynasty with himself as sovereign. In only a year Ho Qui Ly abdicated in favor of his son Ho Han Thuong (d. 1407?) but retained a position of power and influence. Ho forces battled against Tran followers, who wanted to restore the deposed royal family and gained support from the Chams. The Chinese responded to a Tran call for help and sent a large naval expedition southward (see VIETNAMESE-CHINESE WAR OF 1405–7).

Vietnamese Civil War of 1772–1802 (Tay Son Rebellion) After the 16th century the imperial Later Le dynasty (1428–1787) had only nominal control of Vietnam; actual power was shared between two rival families, the Trinh in the north and the Nguyen, with their capital at Hue, in the south. Nguyen power was challenged by three brothers—Nguyen Hue (1753?–92), Nguyen Nhac (1752?–93), and Nguyen Lu (1752?–92)—who wanted political and social reforms and began a rebellion in their home village of Tay Son (1772). After the Tay Son brothers defeated Nguyen troops at nearby Qui Nhon (1773), their rebellion quickly spread. Hoping to benefit from the turmoil in the south, the Trinhs sent an army that seized Hue and helped the Tay Sons capture Saigon (Ho Chi Minh City). But the Tay Sons turned against the Trinhs and drove them from Hue in 1775. Two years later, at Saigon, they virtually destroyed the Nguyen family; 15-year-old Prince Nguyen Anh (1762–1820) took flight, joined by French missionary Pierre Pigneau de Behaine (1741–99); the Tay Son brothers now had control of southern and central Vietnam. In 1782–83, Saigon was occupied by Nguyen Anh's supporters until they were forced out; Nguyen Anh took refuge in Siam (Thailand), where he gained help in his struggle against the Tay Sons; Pigneau failed to obtain aid from France for Nguyen Anh, but privately recruited many Frenchmen. In 1786, the Tay Sons' forces seized the city of Hanoi in north Vietnam, now in a state of anarchy; the Later Le dynasty and the Trinh family were overthrown. Vietnam was reunited by the Tay Son brothers, each of whom ruled part of the country. In the north, Nguyen Hue proclaimed himself Emperor Quang Trung and, in 1788–89, led Vietnamese peasant forces to victory over an invading Chinese army. Meanwhile, Nguyen Anh with Siamese troops landed in the Mekong delta area and captured Saigon in September 1788. Bolstered by French help the next year, he gradually recovered

Nguyen territory and won successive victories against the Tay Sons, whose naval fleet was destroyed in 1792. After the deaths of the three brothers, their sons carried on the war, but were unsuccessful; Nguyen Anh captured Hue in 1801 and Hanoi in 1802. He promptly declared himself emperor of Vietnam, taking the title Gia Long and reviving the Nguyen dynasty; China officially recognized him in 1804.

Vietnamese Civil War of 1955–65 With American military advisory assistance, Premier Ngo Dinh Diem (1901–63) of South Vietnam (proclaimed as an independent republic after the FRENCH INDO-CHINA WAR OF 1946–54) gained control of the army, which he used to fight three rebellious, well-equipped religious groups (the Binh Xuyen, Hoa Hao, and Caodaist sects). In 1955, Binh Xuyen rebels in Saigon (Ho Chi Minh City), South Vietnam's capital, battled government troops until being driven out of the city; the rebels' continued harassment forced Diem to attack them at Can Tho and Vinh Long and in the Seven Mountains. When Diem refused to hold general elections in 1956 as promised, North Vietnam directed Viet Cong rebels (communist South Vietnamese insurgents) to begin a campaign of guerrilla warfare and terrorism to overthrow South Vietnam's regime. Diem suppressed a military revolt against him (1960), but his U.S.-trained army proved generally ineffective against the tactics of the Viet Cong, who established the National Front for the Liberation of South Vietnam. U.S. military aid increased in an effort to wipe out the Viet Cong; South Vietnam's "strategic hamlet program" was started in 1962 to resettle peasants in defended towns against the Viet Cong. Diem's government's harassment of opposing Buddhist priests led to riots and self-immolations. On November 1–2, 1963, a military coup toppled the South Vietnamese government; Diem was killed; and a military-controlled provisional regime was established. A period of political instability ensued, with South Vietnam trying to strengthen its anticommunist military effort. By 1965, the Armed Forces Council, headed by Generals Nguyen Cao

Ky (1930–) and Nguyen Van Thieu (1923–), was running the country. See also VIETNAM WAR.

Vietnamese-French Wars   See FRENCH INDO-CHINA WARS.

Vietnamese-Khmer War of 1123–36   Finding Dai Viet or Annam (northern Vietnam) weakened by a series of ineffectual rulers and involved in hostilities with China, King Suryavarman II (d. c. 1150) of the Khmer Empire (roughly Cambodia and Laos) decided to expand northward into Dai Viet, and to that end he coerced the kingdom of Champa (central Vietnam) to help him against the Vietnamese. In 1128, Suryavarman led about 20,000 soldiers on a march north along the "old ambassadors' route" from Savannakhet (in south-central Laos) to Nghe An (in northern Vietnam), but his forces were routed in battle. The next fall he sent more than 700 ships to lay waste Dai Viet's coastal areas, and continued skirmishing on land. In 1132, combined Khmer and Cham forces invaded Nghe An but were evicted. In 1136, Champa's King Jaya Indravarman III (d. 1145?) made peace with Dai Viet and refused to join Suryavarman in a new expedition against the Vietnamese; later the Khmer king took over substantial parts of Champa (see KHMER-CHAM WAR OF 1144–49). Further attacks were led by Suryavarman on Dai Viet in 1138 and 1150, but they were also inconclusive.

Vietnamese-Mongol War of 1257–88   While conquering China (see MONGOL CONQUEST OF THE SUNG EMPIRE), Kublai Khan (1216–94), the great Mongol leader, sought to gain control of the East Indian spice routes that passed along the coast of Dai Viet or Annam (northern Vietnam); he sent a Mongol army south into Dai Viet and Champa (central Vietnam). The Mongols traveled down the Red River and ransacked Hanoi in 1257, encountering little opposition at first. From 1260 on, Kublai Khan tried obstinately to obtain Dai Viet's and Champa's acknowledgment of his suzerainty. The conflict resulted in the formation of a Vietnamese-Cham alliance against the estimated 500,000 Mongol invaders, who pushed Vietnamese general Tran Hung Dao (d. 1300) and his forces south to Tranh Hoa. From mountain hideouts, the Chams carried on strong guerrilla warfare. Slowly Tran Hung Dao forced the Mongols back into China, counterattacking with success on both land and sea. In 1287, they again invaded (about 300,000 strong) and seized Hanoi, but met stiff resistance as they moved farther southward. Employing an old ruse (see CHINESE-ANNAMESE WAR OF A.D. 907–39), Tran Hung Dao lured the Mongol war fleet, in 1288, up the Bach Dang River, where the ships were torn apart by iron spikes, which had been driven into the river bottom so as to be concealed at high tide. Some 400 Mongol vessels were captured, along with thousands of troops. The remaining Mongol forces retreated but suffered defeat at Noi Bang pass. By then, both sides wanted to end this costly and troublesome war; the rulers of Dai Viet and Champa recognized Kublai Khan's suzerainty; and the Mongols ceased invading the areas. See also MONGOL CONQUESTS.

Vietnamese-Siamese Wars   See SIAMESE-VIETNAMESE WARS.

Vietnamese Uprisings of 1930–31   (Yen Bai Uprising) The failure of the Vietnamese to gain political concessions from the French colonial government led to the formation of clandestine revolutionary organizations, such as the Viet Nam Quoc Dan Dang (VNQDD) or Vietnamese Nationalist Party, founded in 1927. Many Vietnamese military officers and intellectuals joined the VNQDD, whose leader was Nguyen Thai Hoc (1904–30), a teacher, in hopes of achieving a democratic government free of the French. Engaging in terrorist activities, the VNQDD planned a general military uprising; on the night of February 9–10, 1930, native troops at the garrison of Yen Bai in Tonkin (north Vietnam) mutinied and killed their French officers. The French, alerted beforehand, brutally crushed the uprising a day later before other indigenous garrisons followed suit. Nguyen Thai Hoc and

12 cohorts were arrested and beheaded. Many followers of the VNQDD, which was virtually destroyed, joined the Indochina Communist Party, formed in 1930 by Nguyen That Thanh (later known as Ho Chi Minh) (1890–1969), which fomented serious peasant uprisings in Tonkin and Annam (central Vietnam). With much rigor, French forces overwhelmed the rebels and reestablished control; hundreds of Vietnamese were slain and thousands imprisoned. Nonetheless, disturbances continued against French rule and became increasingly more vehement. See also FRENCH INDOCHINA WAR OF 1946–54.

Vietnam War (1956–75) The country of Vietnam had been divided at the 17th parallel into the Republic of Vietnam (South Vietnam) and the Democratic Republic of Vietnam (North Vietnam) after the FRENCH INDOCHINA WAR OF 1946–54. In 1956, a civil war broke out between the communist government of the north, supported by the Vietminh, and the nominally democratic, U.S.-backed government of the south. At first the fighting was mainly bloody guerrilla warfare carried out by Vietminh soldiers—the so-called Viet Cong—who had returned to their homes in the south and there fought against the Army of the Republic of Vietnam (ARVN). The United States provided military advisers to the ARVN and, in 1961, authorized them to fight with the South Vietnamese units they were training. On August 2, 1964, North Vietnamese patrol boats reportedly attacked two U.S. destroyers in the Gulf of Tonkin; U.S. president Lyndon B. Johnson (1908–73) was given congressional authorization to repel any armed attack, and U.S. warplanes began bombing raids over North Vietnam. American troops were sent to South Vietnam to participate as allies of the South Vietnamese. North Vietnamese army units marched continuously down the Ho Chi Minh Trail in Cambodia to fight alongside the Viet Cong. In an attempt to clear the countryside, U.S. forces and the ARVN initiated the tactics called "search and destroy," "free fire zones," and "pacification." They also regularly bombed military and civilian targets in the north and supply dumps in Cambodia. At the end of January 1968, the communist-formed National Liberation Front (NLF) and the Viet Cong launched their great Tet Offensive against 36 provincial cities and wreaked wide destruction in South Vietnam before they withdrew with heavy losses. Their fighting ability, however, amazed the world. Meanwhile, protests and demonstrations occurred frequently in the United States against this undeclared war. At that time, 1968–69, about 500,000 American troops were in Vietnam. In July 1968, the U.S. announced a new policy of "Vietnamization," in which the South Vietnamese themselves would gradually do all the fighting. In May the next year, American army units began to leave, but air support units remained. In 1972, the communist forces of the NLF crossed the demilitarized zone (DMZ) around the 17th parallel and seized a northern South Vietnamese province. The U.S. retaliated by mining the harbors of Haiphong and other North Vietnamese ports. When the peace talks between the U.S. and North Vietnam, which had been going on sporadically since 1968, broke down entirely in December 1972, U.S. president Richard M. Nixon (1913–94) ordered 11 days of intensive "Christmas bombing" of North Vietnamese cities. Later talks resumed and led to a cease-fire agreement among the U.S., Viet Cong, and North and South Vietnam on January 27, 1973. But the fighting continued as before, with both sides accusing the other of violations. In 1974, the ARVN began withdrawing troops from distant outposts, and the NLF seized several provincial capitals. The long-expected communist offensive started in January 1975; NLF forces gained control of Vietnam's central highlands. When the South Vietnamese government decided to evacuate its northern cities of Quang Tri and Hue, its collapse and defeat were in sight. Southern coastal cities were abandoned, civilians and army troops took flight, and the remaining U.S. forces escaped from the country by sea and air. On April 30, 1975, South Vietnam surrendered unconditionally to the communists, who occupied its capital Saigon (Ho Chi Minh City) without a fight. North and

South Vietnam were formally reunited as the Socialist Republic of Vietnam on July 2, 1976.

Vijayanagar Conquest of Madura (1378) During the 1320s, two Telugu-speaking brothers were captured by Muslims, taken to Delhi, converted to Islam, and eventually made administrators in Kampili, in south India. In 1336, defeated in a military action against the Hoysalas, they reverted to Hinduism, gained the support of local Hindu landholders, and established an ideological state—Hindu against Muslim, Tamils governed by Telugu speakers—which prospered despite these oppositions. The first brother, Harihara I, reigned from 1336 to 1357; his brother Bukka I (reigned 1354–77) and Bukka's son Harichara II (reigned 1377–1404) took advantage of Hindu opposition to Muslims in other kingdoms to enlarge their Hindu kingdom of Vijayanagar ("city [and empire] of victory") so that it stretched, south of the Kistna or Krishna River, from coast to coast. Vijayanagar's perpetual enemy was the Bahmani sultanate, with which it fought during much of the 14th century (see VIJAYANAGAR WARS WITH BAHMANI) and during most of the 16th century (see VIJAYANAGAR WARS OF 1509–65). Almost stopped by the Bahmanis in 1377, the Hindu kingdom took advantage of the Bahmani sultan's assassination in 1378, seizing Goa and other west coast ports and relieving Madura or Madurai, the former Pandyan capital, from the Muslim oppression it had known since 1335 (see MADURA REVOLT OF 1334–35). All of south India became Hindu, not again to become Muslim until the fall of Vijayanagar in 1565.

Vijayanagar Wars of 1509–65 Founded in 1336 as a response to Mogul incursions in south India, the Hindu kingdom of Vijayanagar was almost perpetually at war (see VIJAYANAGAR WARS WITH BAHMANI). By the 16th century, its militarism had two purposes: to fight the Muslims and to preserve its business activities (its capital city, also called Vijayanagar, was one of the great trading centers of the world until 1565). Its status was precarious. The kingdom achieved its greatest power under Krishna Deva Raya (fl. 1509–29), despite internal opposi-

tion and invasions from northeastern Hindu kingdoms. A 1513–16 war with Orissa (Hindu state) gained it territory and a dynastic marriage. To give the kingdom authority on both coasts of India, Krishna engaged in "realpolitik," working with friendly Portuguese to take control of the Bahmani successor state of Bijapur. He began a tradition of Vijayanagar interference in Muslim affairs that ultimately destroyed the Hindu kingdom, for the other Bahmani successor states eventually united to oppose Vijayanagar. Krishna's successors, puppets controlled by the kingdom's chief minister, Rama Raya (d. 1565), faced invasions from the Muslim allies and at first kept power by manipulating their internal rivalries. An alliance (1560) between Golconda and Ahmadnagar against Vijayanagar and Bijapur attracted the other successor states; Rama Raya was disastrously defeated and killed at the Battle of Talikota in 1565. The city of Vijayanagar was sacked and destroyed; it never recovered. The diminished kingdom, however, continued in a chaotic fashion until 1652, when Mogul annexation of the entire Carnatic region gave Delhi almost total control of south India and forced the exile of the last Vijayanagar ruler.

Vijayanagar Wars with Bahmani (1350–1410) Vijayanagar, an independent Hindu kingdom created in 1336, and Bahmani, founded as an independent Muslim kingdom in 1346, automatically became enemies in India for as long as Bahmani existed. Although Bahmani's first years were spent chiefly in consolidating its control of the western Deccan region south almost to the Kistna or Krishna River, its second ruler, Muhammad Shah I (fl. 1358–75), continued a conflict with Vijayanagar that was to outlast the Muslim sultanate: 10 wars were fought between 1350 and 1410 over possession of the very rich land lying between the Kistna (Vijayanagar's northern border) and the Tungabhadra River (Bahmani's southern border), an area fought over long before either kingdom was established. Even though Muhammad Shah made use of then-novel artillery in two wars, he accomplished little. Bahmani won in 1365 and again in 1367, perpetrating a general massacre, but failed during 1377 and 1398 attacks upon its enemy's capital city. Succession wars in Bahmani undoubtedly contributed to the ineffectiveness of many Bahmani campaigns through 1398. Under Bahmani's ruler Taj-ud-Din Firuz (fl. 1397–1422), a brief peace was made in 1410; he had successfully attacked the capital of Vijayanagar, murdered its king's sons, collected a tribute payment, and married the king's daughter. But the disputed territory remained uncontrolled. Unremarkable as wars, these conflicts are unique because, while north India was demoralized by Hindu-Muslim campaigns, those in the south went on without interference of any kind from the Delhi sultanate, which suffered in 1398 the additional woe of TAMERLANE'S INVASION OF INDIA and the costly and bloody sack of Delhi by Turks and Mongols.

Viking Conquest of Man (1079) The last great Viking raid occurred in 1079 at Skyhill on the Isle of Man in the Irish Sea. Although Man had suffered raids since the early 800s and was under the control of Dublin Northmen in 1079, "Skyhill" made the island a dependency of Norway. Led by the Icelandic-born Godred Corvan, the Vikings had tried twice before to defeat the Manxmen, but not until the Viking victory at Skyhill did the Isle of Man come under Viking rule, which lasted until 1266, when the island was purchased by Scottish nobles. See also VIKING RAIDS.

Viking Defeat at Brunanburh (A.D. 937) To counteract Anglo-Saxon reclamation of the northeastern Danelaw (see VIKING RAIDS IN ENGLAND, LATER), Olaf Guthfrithsson (d. 941), leader of the Dublin Vikings, joined Scots warriors and the Strathclyde Britons to force Aethelstan (d. 939), king of England, out of power. The combined forces invaded England, recaptured York (taken by Aethelstan in 927), proceeded toward the Midlands, and met the English warriors at Brunanburh. In two days of fighting, five invading kings and seven Irish earls died. The English victors missed Guthfrithsson, who escaped to retake York in 939. Aethelstan's victory, which firmly established his hegemony in England, is celebrated poetically in an Icelandic saga and the *Anglo-Saxon Chronicle*.

Viking Raids (A.D. c. 800–c. 1016) For more than two centuries, pillaging raids disrupted life in Europe, especially for those dwelling near sea coasts or along navigable rivers. Without warning, a fleet of ships would appear anywhere from the Shetland Islands to Pisa, Italy, disgorging a few hundred Norwegian or Danish or Swedish warriors armed with axes and swords. The invaders would then overwhelm a church or monastery and its surrounding village; engage in robbery, destruction, and murder; and escape before outside help could arrive. The attacks were fierce, swift, and frequent; rich monasteries like Iona had only a few years to recover before being raided again. Once the Vikings had discovered the advantages of wintering at the mouths of great rivers like the Thames or Seine and then mounting large offensives, even cities were not safe: Paris, Aachen, Seville, Cologne, and many others suffered sieges and sackings, often repeatedly. Nothing seemed capable of stopping the raids—the walling of settlements, the erection of protective castles, nor the payment of protective tribute. Even the mailed cavalry of Charlemagne (742–814) was powerless against the marauders. Only the Vikings could stop themselves by changing their goals from destruction and pillage to colonizing and commerce, and this transformation had a profound effect upon European history. See also subsequent eight articles.

Viking Raids against Alfred (A.D. 871–96) A victory over the Danish Vikings at Ashdown gave determination to the Saxons during 871, the "Year of Battles." Two Viking armies, the East Anglian force and a fresh Danish army, overran eastern Britain and settled at Reading. Moving toward Wessex, they were opposed by the forces of Ethelred I (d. 871) and Alfred (849–99) and driven back. At Reading, the Wessex leaders attacked the Viking camp, but were repulsed after heavy losses. Inconclusive skirmishes followed, and Alfred, now king, attacked near Wilton. The Danes, feigning retreat to draw an attack, were victorious, and Alfred paid a large Danegeld to achieve an armistice, which the Danes broke, conquering Mercia in 872 and thereafter raiding southwest Britain. They made a surprise attack on Chippenham, Alfred's headquarters, in 878, overwhelming the West Saxons and causing Alfred to flee and order a general mobilization. At Ethandun (now Edington), later that year, Alfred fought a decisive battle. His forces pushed the Danes from the field and pursued and successfully besieged them at Chippenham. In 885, Alfred repelled an invasion of Kent, regained London, and became ruler of all Saxon England; he forced the Peace of Wedmore, gaining Danish promises to respect the boundary between Wessex and the Danelaw area. Fruitless attacks by European Danes followed from 892 through 896, but England was generally at peace. See VIKING RAIDS IN ENGLAND, LATER.

Viking Raids in England, Early (A.D. 793–870) The first recorded raid in England was the Norwegian Viking devastation of Lindisfarne's monastery. A smash-grab-and-kill assault, it was a prelude to similar attacks on Wearmouth, Jarrow, and Iona. Busily establishing bases on Scots islands (see VIKING RAIDS IN THE NORTH SEA), the Norwegians allowed relative peace until 835, when Danish Vikings raided the Thames island of Sheppey. Four important battles—all involving Danish Vikings—then followed. In 837, at Hingston Down, Cornwall, rebelling Britons aided by Vikings forced the West Saxons into the struggle for the first time. The Cornish were defeated, and King Egbert (775?–839) annexed the territory. Vikings, overwintered on Thanet Island in the Thames, attacked Aclea in 851 and were defeated by King Alfred's father Ethelwulf (d. 858). Wessex became the premier kingdom in the Anglo-Saxon heptarchy. In 866, Northumbria was the locus of a battle with a new kind of Viking: settlers in East Anglia in 865, with a land force, including cavalry. They entered York during a Northumbrian civil war, defeated and killed both kings, and ended Saxon power in north-

ern Britain. Four years later, at Hoxne (Suffolk), King Edmund (841?–70) of East Anglia was defeated, then beheaded for refusing to abjure Christianity. More than one-third of England was now Danish.

Viking Raids in England, Later (A.D. 899–1016) Successors of King Alfred (849–99) tried after 899 to gradually recover the Danelaw area. After a defeat in East Anglia in 902, Edward the Elder (870?–924) defeated Northumbrian Danes at Tettenhall in 910. In 918, his forces stormed Tempsford, killing its ruler and ending all resistance in East Anglia. York was recaptured in 927 and involved again in a Viking attack in 937 (see VIKING DEFEAT AT BRUNANBURH). In 980, heavy attacks by the Vikings resumed, especially near London. The Viking raider bands had changed, becoming more professional and larger in number, and England, under the weak King Ethelred II (965?–1016), could not withstand them. Ethelred tried paying tributes in increasing amounts, but the monies merely financed subsequent attacks. In 991, Norwegians won the Battle of Maldon, immortalized in Anglo-Saxon verse, and Ethelred fled to Normandy after paying 21,000 pounds in tribute. In 994, the Danes vainly attacked London, and in 1002 attacked again, gaining 24,000 pounds in tribute. Ethelred took revenge by murdering all native-born Danes in England. In 1011, Canterbury was raided and its archbishop murdered. Canute the Great (994?–1035), king of the Danes, invaded England in 1015. Ethelred died, however, in 1016, and his heir, Edmund Ironside (989?–1016), gained both the crown and the ongoing war. In 1016, he fought Canute and lost at Pen and Assundun (Ashingdon). Canute regained the Danelaw and Mercia, but a month later, Edmund died, and England became Danish until 1042.

Viking Raids in France, Early (A.D. 799–886) Viking raiders first attacked the Frankish Empire in 799; the raids continued until 810, when Frisia suffered. Charlemagne (742–814) then built up defenses on the empire's northern seaboard, so that a

Norse fleet at the Seine's mouth was effectively repulsed in 820. Danish Vikings first appeared in Frisia and Dorestad in 834, and the Frankish Empire, weakened after Charlemagne's death, could not withstand them. In 836, Antwerp and Noirmoutier were burned. Thereafter occurred other major raids and sackings: Rouen in 841, Quentovic in 842. Norse warriors in 67 ships entered the Loire in 842, stormed Nantes, took slaves, and settled down to stay near Noirmoutier. In 845, Reginherus, or Ragnar (fl. 9th cent.), entered the Seine with 120 Danish Viking ships. Charles the Bald (823–77) stationed Frankish troops on each side of the river. Reginherus's forces attacked and won; they hanged 111 Franks to honor Woden (the chief Norse god) and forced the first of 13 Danegeld payments. Reginherus's son attacked Paris in 857 and left only four churches standing. The Franks learned two new defenses: fortification of cities and the use of Danegeld to bribe the Vikings to fight their battles. In 861, 5,000 pounds of silver moved the Danes to oust the Norse from Noirmoutier. A fortified Paris, besieged in 885–86, held out for 11 months against 700 ships and 40,000 Vikings. Finally Charles the Fat (839–88) paid 700 pounds of silver to the Viking leader Siegfried Finric (fl. ninth cent.) to have the Vikings attack Frankish rebels in Burgundy.

Viking Raids in France, Later (A.D. 896–911) Among the Vikings leaving England in 896 empty-handed (see VIKING RAIDS AGAINST ALFRED) were Danes under Gonge-Hrolf, better known as Rollo (860?–931?). Son of the second earl of Orkney, and thus a Norwegian, Rollo did not return home but conducted raids on France between the Seine and Loire rivers. After 900, his forces settled there and became colonists. They did not cease raiding, for in 910 Rollo led unsuccessful attacks on Paris and Chartres. In 911, King Charles the Simple (879–929) belied his nickname by meeting with Rollo in St. Clair-sur-Epte, the eastern boundary of the Viking territory, and coming to peace terms. Rollo and his followers were deeded their settlement area in exchange for swearing allegiance to Charles. Vowing to protect their territory from other Vikings,

the poachers became gamekeepers. Baptized Robert in 912, Rollo became the first duke of Normandy, from which the next great Viking raid began in 1066. See also NORMAN CONQUEST; VIKING CONQUEST OF MAN.

Viking Raids in Ireland (A.D. 795–1014) The first recorded Viking attacks on Irish coastal settlements occurred in 795, perpetrated by Norwegians from the Orkney and Shetland islands. Raids increased in number, especially during the 830s, when the Vikings under the semilegendary Turgeis (d. 845) raided Armagh and Ulster, Connacht, and Meith and, in 837, sailed up the Liffey River. The Vikings then became residents, but only in coastal areas, building longphorts (fortified ship havens) and introducing the pastoral Irish to town life. Dublin, founded in 841, became a small Norse kingdom in 853. Other longphorts were established after raids at Waterford, Wexford, Wicklow, and Limerick. From them, the Vikings attacked Strathclyde, Mercia, and Northumbria. In 1014, Irish forces under King Brian Boru (926–1014) defeated the Danish Vikings at Clontarf near Dublin; Brian was killed during the battle. Though the Irish had wrested Dublin from them, the Vikings stayed on until Dublin was taken by the English in 1170.

Viking Raids in Russia (A.D. c. 825–907) Swedish Vikings, who were both warriors and traders and who called themselves the Rus or Ros, conducted raids in the early ninth century along the eastern Baltic. About 860–62, either by raids or because of Slavic invitations, their semilegendary leader Rurik (d. 879) took over Novgorod and founded a trading center near Lake Ladoga (Oneya). Using rivers for both raiding and trading, the Rus spread southward. Under Rurik's successor Oleg (d.c. 912), the Vikings seized Kiev in 882, uniting the northern and southern Rus. In 907, Oleg led a large fleet down the Dnieper River to the Black Sea, invaded Constantinople (Istanbul) without serious fighting, and emerged the holder of a treaty highly favorable to Rus traders. Called Varangians by the Byzantines, many of the Rus became members of the Byzantine emperor's Varangian guard.

Viking Raids in the North Sea (A.D. c. 800–994) Norwegian Vikings probably raided the Scots islands—the Shetlands and Hebrides—around 800, or perhaps a little earlier. The islands were used as Viking bases for attacks on ecclesiastical settlements until 825, and for raids on Ireland and Strathclyde in the years following (see VIKING RAIDS IN IRELAND). A Norwegian earldom was established in the 870s in the Orkney Islands, and raids on the Scots mainland enabled that base to rule Caithness and Moray as late as 1057. In 994, a Norse attack by King Olaf Tryggvason (963?–1000) produced the forcible conversion of the Orcadian Vikings to Christianity. The Orcadian Vikings were early settlers; later they acted as warriors in the expeditions of other Vikings in Ireland and England.

Villa's Raids (1916–17) Francisco "Pancho" Villa (1877–1923) is famed in Mexico as a revolutionary and in the United States as a violent bandit. The 1911 overthrow of Mexico's hated dictatorial president Porfirio Díaz (1830–1915) set off a struggle for power that Villa, who had American support, was winning until 1915, when the troops of Álvaro Obregón (1880–1928) defeated him and elevated as acting chief of Mexico Villa's enemy Venustiano Carranza (1859–1920). The United States recognized Carranza and repudiated Villa, who responded by attacking Americans in Mexico. Villa's men raided across the border into Columbus, N. Mex. (March 9, 1916), killing about a dozen Americans before being driven off. U.S. president Woodrow Wilson (1856–1924) ordered General John J. Pershing (1860–1948) to lead a punitive expedition into Mexico in pursuit of Villa, whose forces skirmished several times with the invaders. This American invasion, which was labeled a failure after 11 months (Pershing withdrew in February 1917) because Villa, whose raids continued, could not be captured, so angered his countrymen that Villa was regarded as a national hero, despite the fact that he

led rebels in northern Mexico until 1920, the year of Carranza's death. See also MEXICAN CIVIL WAR OF 1911; MEXICAN REVOLT OF 1914–15.

Villmergen War, First (1656) Uprisings and the threat of them in post-Reformation Switzerland were usually economic in origin; the Swiss peasants resented the demands of town officials for taxes for defense purposes, the necessity to use the often debased currency issued by each canton, and the generally inferior treatment. These grievances caused the abortive Swiss peasants' uprisings of 1653; they underlay the Villmergen Wars, but with the differences that the peasants were Catholics and the townspeople were Protestant. In 1656, five Catholic cantons went to war against the rich Protestant cantons of Zürich and Bern, whose forces were defeated at the Battle of Villmergen. Afterward the Third Land Peace of Baden (1656) asserted the right of each canton to enforce religious unity in its own territory. **Second Villmergen War** (1712). The Land Peace was broken when the abbot of St. Gall helped build a main road that disadvantaged the Protestants of the Toggenburg. Efforts at conciliation failed after forces from Zürich and Bern occupied Toggenburg, Aargau, Thurgau, and Rheintal. The Protestant Bernese defeated the Catholics at the second Battle of Villmergen, after which the Peace of Aargau (1712) repealed the second Peace of Kappel (see KAPPEL WARS) and set forth religious toleration by both Catholics and Protestants in the common lordships. The power base shifted back to the Protestant cantons.

Visigothic-Frankish War of A.D. 506–7 Clovis (c. 466–511), Roman Catholic king of the Salian Franks, waged war against Alaric II (d. 507), Arian king of the Visigoths (Arianism denied that Christ is of one substance with God). Frankish troops under Clovis decisively defeated the Visigoths at the Battle of Vouillé near Poitiers in 507; Alaric was slain by Clovis in the battle. The Franks penetrated as far south as the Visigothic capital of Toulouse. The Visigoths were compelled to withdraw over the

Pyrenees, retaining only the region of Septimania north of the mountains. Catholicism had triumphed over Arianism in western Europe because of Clovis, who would soon become Frankish ruler of most of Gaul and western Germany.

Visigothic Raids on the Roman Empire, Early (A.D. 332–90) The Visigoths, the most durable and compelling of Rome's Germanic invaders, first appeared in Roman chronicles in 332, when they were severely beaten as they invaded modern Danubian Yugoslavia and Bulgaria. The defeat made their king, Ermanaric (d. c. 376), turn their attention north, where they harried the Roman Empire; many became Arian Christians. Civil war in the empire prompted them to make raids in Byzantium (the Eastern Roman Empire), when, in 364–65, Procopius (d. 366) led a rebellion against the Roman emperor of the East, Valens (328?–78), and with Visigothic help, gained control of the Balkans. A Syrian army successfully quelled Procopius in 366; Gothic help was punished by Valens's crossing of the Danube River in 367–69, a military campaign that forced a second Visigothic leader, Athanaric (d. 381), into the Transylvanian area. The aftermath was civil war between Athanaric's followers and Arian Visigoths. Athanaric lost power to Fritigern (d. after 382), successor to Ermanaric and an Arian Christian. A confederation of Goths then rebelled against Valens, whom they killed in 378 during the Battle of Adrianople (Edirne), in which two-thirds of the Romans fell (see ROMAN-GOTHIC WAR, FIFTH). When Theodosius I "the Great" (346–95) became emperor of the East in 379, he warred against all Gothic groups, forcing the Ostrogoths (East Goths) west and allowing the Visigoths, who had devastated Macedonia and Thessaly, to settle in northern Thrace (382) in exchange for a supply of mercenary soldiers. But Theodosius's plan for peace did not last long, for in 390 the Visigoths, now led by Alaric (370?–410), faced Flavius Stilicho (359?–408), a Roman general, who became their chief antagonist for the next 18 years (see STILICHO'S WARS WITH THE VISIGOTHS). See also ROMAN-GOTHIC WARS.

Visigothic Raids on the Roman Empire, Later (A.D. 410–76) The Visigothic leader Alaric (370?–410) pursued his plan to take control of North Africa after sacking Rome (see ROME, VISIGOTHIC SACK OF). His Visigoths marched to Reggio di Calabria, set sail in ships, but were driven back by a storm (410). Alaric suddenly died; his replacement was his brother-in-law, Ataulphus (d. 415), who used one war prize from Rome, the emperor's sister Galla Placidia (c. 388–450), as a bargaining chip for a brief alliance with Rome employing Visigoths to quell uprisings in Gaul (France) and Spain in 412. But the Visigoths under Ataulphus soon resumed fighting against the Romans; Ataulphus attacked Marseilles and captured Narbonne (413), married Galla Placidia (414), and immediately faced a new Roman offensive that forced the Visigoths into Spain. Ataulphus's murder in 415 led to a new treaty, under which Galla Placidia was returned and the Visigoths were pledged, for food subsidies, to attack the Vandals and Alans in Spain. Their success as mercenaries gained the Visigoths lands from the Loire River to Bordeaux and *foederati* status in 418. Nevertheless, they again broke the peace by assisting the Vandals in a battle in 422. Later they became an independent nation and a Roman ally against the African Vandals between 426 and 437 (see VANDAL RAIDS ON THE ROMAN EMPIRE). The Visigoths supported the Romans against rebels in Spain (453), then helped establish Marcus Maecilius Avitus (d. 456) as emperor of the West, and fought the Suevians, a Germanic people, in Spain. By 458, however, the Suevians controlled the Roman Senate and had defeated the Visigoths at Arles (463), forcing them to lose independence and to return to foederati status. The Barbarian-Roman government employed the Visigoths until an Eastern Roman army began to fight the Visigoths under their king Euric (d. c. 484). An able strategist, Euric seized most of Gaul and Spain, capturing the cities of Arles and Bourges (470) and gaining acknowledgment in a peace pact (475) as an independent ruler west of the Rhone River. After Odoacer (Odovacar) (434?–93), a Germanic king, became the barbarian master of Italy in 476 and officially ended the

Roman Empire, Euric became master of Spain in 478. There the Visigothic kingdom lasted through 12 kings until the MUSLIM CONQUEST OF SPAIN.

Vladimir, Conquests of (A.D. 981–85) Installed as ruler (grand prince) at Kiev after the RUSSIAN DYNASTIC WAR OF A.D. 972–80, Vladimir I (956–1015) set out to conquer territory in the Dnieper River area. The Pechenegs (Patzinakes), a nomadic Turkish people, repeatedly attacked his forces, who constructed fortified towns along the steppe border. Vladimir took control of Galicia (southeastern Poland and the western Ukraine) in 981, subdued the heathen tribes in present-day White Russia in 983, and conquered the Bulgarian state in the south. His campaigns brought the entire area from Poland to the Volga River under Kievan Russian domination by 985. A pagan at first, Vladimir allied himself with the Byzantines for probably economic and political advantages and received Byzantine baptism to become the first Christian ruler of Russia (988?).

Wagon Box Fight (1867) A detail of men from Fort Phil Kearney in northern Wyoming was sent with Captain James Powell (fl. 1860s) to cut firewood on Big Piney Creek in order to build up the fort's supply for the coming winter. The captain knew that Red Cloud (1822–1909) and his Sioux warriors were on the warpath (see *SIOUX WAR OF 1865–68*), so he removed the wheels from his wagons and turned them on edge to make a miniature fort around his encampment. On August 2, 1867, about 1,500 Indians led by Red Cloud and Crazy Horse (1849?–77) swooped down a hill and attacked the detail outside the camp, stampeding the mules and horses; in the confusion the axemen and guards managed to flee to either Fort Phil Kearney or Powell's wagon-box fort. Armed with new breech-loading rifles, Powell and 32 others fired repeatedly on the attacking Indians, whose many charges were stopped by a blistering rain of bullets. The fight lasted throughout the day until a relief force from Fort Kearney arrived. The superior firepower of Powell's men had taken the lives of an estimated 1,000 Indians; of the 33 marksmen, two were killed and two wounded.

Wahehe War (1891–93) Carl Peters (1856–1918), German imperial high commissioner of the district of Kilimanjaro in German East Africa (Tanzania), decided to maintain the traditional Arab administration of local justice and governance (see *ARAB UPRISING IN GERMAN EAST AFRICA*). However, many of the petty Arab officials were corrupt and unscrupulous and felt no loyalty to Germany; they took advantage of their power to exploit the black African tribes. One martial tribe, the Wahehe, who lived along the Rufiji River, rebelled against the Arabs in protest. For two years they fought the Arabs until German and mercenary troops arrived and helped defeat them. Peters became known afterward as *mkono-wa-damu* or "the man with blood-stained hands." In 1897 he was relieved as commissioner because of his cruel treatment of the Africans.

Wahlstadt (Liegnitz), Battle of (1241) The Mongol victory at Wahlstadt near Liegnitz (Legnica, Poland) epitomized the great difference between Mongol efficiency and the laxness of European armies in the 1200s (see *MONGOL INVASION OF EUROPE*). The Mongols were disciplined, practiced warriors unified under a single system of command, dedicated to following a meticulously prepared plan, itself developed from carefully considered intelligence reports. The Europeans had a conscripted, unpracticed infantry and heavy cavalry made up of knights trained only in jousting; unused to cooperative fighting, they were not unified, lacking an overall battlefield strategy. At Wahlstadt on April 9, 1241, the Europeans included their chief leader, Henry of Silesia (d. 1241), with 20,000 hurriedly mobilized soldiers, troops from Moldavia under its heir, a contingent of Teutonic Knights, and others—all (about 40,000 men total) divided into four units. Noting this division, the Mongols used their strategy of "suicide" (mangudai): a small vanguard advancing and then retreating to tempt the enemy forces to follow between the hidden wings of the Mongols' main force. Without considering the others or the consequent European strategy, Henry led his own forces into the trap, only to be completely routed, as were the others by separate Mongol detachments. Though Henry escaped, he was pursued, caught, and beheaded. His rashness on the battlefield, however, had caused the flower of Polish chivalry to perish. Shown Henry's head, Liegnitz's citizens refused to surrender, causing the Mongols to assault and burn the city. Mongol losses were heavy, but within a month the invaders were battling in Hungary.

Waikato War   See TARANAKI WAR, SECOND.

Wairau Massacre (Wairau Affray) (1843) When New Zealand first began to be settled in 1840, William Hobson (d. 1842), lieutenant-governor of the New Zealand colony and consul to the Maori chiefs, wished to avoid the outrages caused by the British East India Company. He wisely developed the 1840 Treaty of Waitangi under which Maori chiefs ceded sovereignty in return for British protection; the chiefs were guaranteed possession of their lands, which they agreed to sell only to the Crown. An important provision was the right of senior chiefs to veto any proposed sale. The New Zealand Company, however, proceeded less morally, entering into sales agreements with subchiefs and illegally acquiring other tracts. The Maori became alarmed and resisted attempts to seize their lands. Their hesitation, however, led to the Wairau Massacre on June 17, 1843. Fifty Europeans, associated with the company, reported that Maori chiefs had refused to allow surveying of "purchased" areas; they wanted the chiefs arrested. Coming upon 90 Maoris and two chiefs (who refused to be arrested), the

Europeans conceded the chiefs' request that the government investigate the matter, but shots were suddenly fired; one of the chiefs' wives and 22 Europeans were killed. Later the company was found to be in error, and the Maoris were not punished, but the air of hostility contributed to the BAY OF ISLANDS WAR, also called the First Maori War.

Wakarusa War (1855) The Kansas-Nebraska Act of 1854 allowed the settlers in the Kansas-Nebraska territories to determine whether they wanted slavery or not by popular sovereignty (the vote of the people themselves). Pro- and antislavery groups in Kansas set up separate constitutions and rival governments at Lecompton and Topeka respectively (1855). The murder of an antislavery man in November 1855 brought on the so-called Wakarusa War, a series of clashes between pro and antislavery forces along the Wakarusa River near Lawrence, Kans. (November 26-December 7, 1855). A few casualties occurred, and armed proslavery Missourians, called "border ruffians," made plans to attack Lawrence, Kans., which was defended by Free-Soilers (opponents of the extension of slavery in the western territories). The attack and the "war" itself were aborted by the intervention of the territorial governor. In 1856, border ruffians did raid Lawrence, causing a retaliatory attack by abolitionists on settlers at Pottawatomie Creek (see POTTAWATOMIE MASSACRE). Hostilities between free and slave interests erupted into civil war, referred to as "bleeding Kansas," which lasted until federal troops intervened and restored order in 1860. See also CIVIL WAR, U.S.

Walker's Invasion of Mexico (1853–54) William Walker (1824–60), an American adventurer living in California, was involved in a scheme to establish American settlements in Mexico. He organized a filibustering expedition and, on the pretext of protecting Mexicans from the Apache Indians rampaging in northwestern Mexico, sailed from San Francisco on October 15, 1853. With his armed force, Walker landed at La Paz in Baja or

Lower California, which he proclaimed an independent republic with himself as president (November 3, 1853). He then announced the annexation of the Mexican state of Sonora (January 18, 1854). The Mexicans frequently attacked the American invaders, who were forced to flee from Mexico because of lack of provisions and ammunition. In May 1854, Walker surrendered to U.S. authorities at the border near San Diego. Soon tried for violating neutrality laws, he was acquitted and, about a year later, resumed his filibustering activities in Nicaragua.

Walker's Invasion of Nicaragua (1855–57) The American soldier of fortune William Walker (1824–60), with 58 followers, went to Nicaragua in June 1855, on the invitation of Don Francisco Castellón (d. 1855), leader of a liberal revolt against the country's conservative government. Joining the Nicaraguan rebels, Walker's armed force, called the American Phalanx, captured a U.S. steamer on Lake Nicaragua and afterward the city of Granada, a conservative stronghold on the lake. After Castellón died, Walker assumed control of the campaign against the conservatives, who were shortly crushed; in July 1856, he had himself elected president of Nicaragua and was briefly recognized by the U.S. government. This American filibusterer antagonized the Central American states and his former friend Cornelius Vanderbilt (1794–1877), an American magnate who desired control of the transit route across Nicaragua. In the fall of 1856, Costa Ricans under Juan Rafael Mora (1814–60) invaded Nicaragua and seized San Juan del Sur, Rivas, and the transit road; Guatemala's president, Rafael Carrera (1814–65), sent troops that seized Masaya and laid siege to Granada with the help of El Salvadorans and Nicaraguan conservatives. American recruits sympathetic to Walker were prevented from joining him. With his forces reduced by cholera, Walker evacuated Granada and moved toward Rivas, where he was besieged for weeks by the Costa Ricans. To avoid capture, he surrendered to U.S. commander Charles Henry Davis (1815–86) aboard the warship *St. Mary's* on May 1, 1857. Returning to Nicaragua later that year, Walker was arrested and deported. In 1860, again seeking power in Central America, he landed in Honduras, where he was arrested, condemned by court-martial, and shot.

Wallace's Revolt (1297–1305) Because King Edward I (1239–1307) of England used calculated terror as an instrument of his Scottish policy, a brawl involving William Wallace (1272?–1305) and English soldiers and his assassination of an English sheriff developed into a fast-spreading movement of national resistance. In 1297, Wallace's rebels defeated an invading English army at Stirling Bridge through ineptness of its commander, who ordered his large and overconfident force to cross a narrow bridge near the Abbey of Cambuskenneth, only to be wiped out by Wallace's smaller army. Edward invaded, defeated Wallace at Falkirk in 1298 by using longbowmen against massed pikemen for the first time, forcing Wallace to engage in guerrilla warfare. Edward then left Scotland to oppose his tax-angry barons, but returned in 1303 to defeat Wallace at Stirling. Wallace escaped, but the price on his head ensured betrayal; in 1305, he was tried, brutally hanged, drawn, and quartered. See also BRUCE'S REVOLT; SCOTTISH WAR OF 1295–96.

Warbeck's Rebellion (1495–99) Despite the failure of LAMBERT SIMNEL'S REBELLION in 1487, forces opposing the earlier English usurper King Henry IV (1367–1413) tried another impersonation plot. The new impostor was a Flemish-born silk worker named Perkin Warbeck (1474?–99), trained to pose as Richard, duke of York, a prince supposedly murdered by King Richard III (1452–85). Warbeck's backers were the Holy Roman Emperor, the ever-scheming duchess of Burgundy, the earl of Warwick, and the Scottish King James IV (1473–1513). Warbeck's invasion of England in 1495 failed. He then went to Scotland, convinced James of his authenticity, and married James's cousin. A Scottish-led invasion in 1496 also failed, partly because of a rift between James and Warbeck. Warbeck left Scotland and invaded Cornwall in 1497, but failed again at Exeter, where his 6,000-man rebel army backed down before the troops of King Henry VII

(1457–1509). He fled but was captured at Beaulieu in Hampshire in 1499. On a false promise of a pardon, Warbeck admitted the whole plot but was hanged after twice attempting to escape from the Tower of London.

War of a Thousand Days See THOUSAND DAYS, WAR OF A.

War of Berenice See SYRIAN-EGYPTIAN WARS, SECOND AND THIRD.

War of Chioggia See CHIOGGIA, WAR OF.

War of Demetrius See DEMETRIUS, WAR OF.

War of Devolution See DEVOLUTION, WAR OF.

War of 1812 (Second War of American Independence) (1812–14) When Britain was fighting France in the NAPOLEONIC WARS, neither side respected the rights of neutral merchant ships, and many U.S. vessels were seized. The British went further and impressed American sailors into their navy. They also stirred up the Indians in the Old Northwest Territory to attack American outposts and settlements. War Hawks in the West and South united under the slogan "Free trade and sailors' rights," and Congress narrowly voted to declare war on Britain. In 1812, an American three-pronged attack on Montreal failed miserably and Detroit fell, but on the high seas the young American navy scored five victories. In 1813, Detroit was retaken, Captain Oliver H. Perry (1785–1819) defeated a British fleet on Lake Erie, and General William H. Harrison (1773–1841) broke up Tecumseh's (1768?–1813) Indian confederacy at the Battle of the Thames, but American ships were bottled up in harbors by a British blockade. The British took the offensive in 1814 but were stopped for good at Plattsburgh. To the south the British navy commanded Chesapeake Bay and a land force captured Washington and burned the Capitol and White House. However, it was repulsed at Fort McHenry, Baltimore. In December 1814, another British naval and land force approached New Orleans, but was decisively defeated by Americans under General Andrew Jackson (1767–1845) on January 8, 1815, two weeks after the war had concluded with the Treaty of Ghent. The United States was now recognized as an independent entity. See also AMERICAN REVOLUTION.

War of 1812, Franco-Russian See NAPOLEON'S INVASION OF RUSSIA.

War of Jenkins' Ear See JENKINS' EAR, WAR OF.

War of the Austrian Succession See AUSTRIAN SUCCESSION, WAR OF THE.

War of the Axe See AXE, WAR OF THE.

War of the Bavarian Succession See BAVARIAN SUCCESSION, WAR OF THE.

War of the Emboabas See EMBOABAS, WAR OF THE.

War of the First Coalition against France See COALITION, WAR OF THE FIRST.

War of the League of Augsburg See GRAND ALLIANCE, WAR OF THE.

War of the Mascates See MASCATES, WAR OF THE.

War of the Oranges See ORANGES, WAR OF THE.

War of the Pacific See PACIFIC, WAR OF THE.

War of the Polish Succession See POLISH SUC-CESSION, WAR OF THE.

War of the Public Weal See FRANCO-BURGUN-DIAN WARS.

War of the Ramadan See ARAB-ISRAELI WAR OF 1973.

War of the Reform See REFORM, WAR OF THE.

War of the Second Coalition against France See COALITION, WAR OF THE SECOND.

War of the Spanish Succession See SPANISH SUCCESSION, WAR OF THE.

War of the Third Coalition against France See COALITION, WAR OF THE THIRD.

"War of the Three Henrys" See RELIGION, EIGHTH WAR OF.

"War of the Three Sanchos" See "THREE SAN-CHOS, WAR OF THE."

Wars of American Independence See AMERICAN REVOLUTION; WAR OF 1812.

Wars of Religion See RELIGION, WARS OF.

Wars of the Allies See SOCIAL WARS.

Wars of the Diadochi See DIADOCHI, WARS OF THE.

Wars of the Roses See ROSES, WARS OF THE.

Warwick's Rebellion (1469–71) The earl of Warwick, Richard Neville (1428–71), known as the "king maker," advised and controlled King Edward IV (1442–83) of England effectively and happily until 1465. Then, after Warwick had negotiated delicately in France about a queen for Edward, he discovered Edward's secret marriage to the nonroyal Elizabeth Woodville (1437?–92). Silently angry, Warwick was rebuffed again as a self-ruled Edward replaced Warwick's appointees with Woodvilles. He bristled when Edward unwisely allied with Burgundy, France's enemy, in 1467 and openly revolted in 1469, capturing Edward at Edgecote. Hopeful of reappointment, he released him. However, Edward's accusation of treason in 1470 made Warwick flee to France, where he became reconciled with his former enemy, Queen Margaret (1430?–82), consort of English king Henry VI (1421–71), imprisoned in the Tower of London. With French aid, Warwick and Margaret gathered forces, invaded England in 1470, and freed Henry for restoration to the throne. Edward fled to Burgundy, returning in 1471 to kill Warwick at the Battle of Barnet and, after Henry's son died, to recapture the royal family at Tewkesbury. Henry, recaptured, died in the Tower. Edward now possessed full power, and the war between the houses of York and Lancaster seemed to be over (see ROSES, WARS OF THE).

Waterloo, Battle of See HUNDRED DAYS' WAR.

Wat Tyler's Revolt See PEASANTS' REVOLT, ENG-LISH.

Western Saharan War See SPANISH SAHARAN WAR.

Whiskey Rebellion (1794) In 1791, the U.S. Congress authorized an excise tax on whiskey to help pay the national debt incurred during the AMERICAN REVOLUTION. Objections to the tax were voiced, but the most violent resistance occurred in western Pennsylvania in 1794, when federal revenue officers were attacked and buildings burned. In October 1794, President George Washington (1732–99), urged on by Secretary of the Treasury Alexander Hamilton (1755–1804), who had proposed the excise to raise money and assert the power of the national government, sent 13,000 state militiamen, led personally by Hamilton, to put down the rebellion (mostly by farmers). No battle was fought, and the rebels dispersed in November. Troops occupied the region. Of 20 rebels taken prisoner, two were convicted of treason but were later pardoned by the president. The determination and ability of the U.S government to enforce its laws had been shown for the first time. See also FRIES REBELLION.

White Lotus Rebellion (1796–1804) The White Lotus had been a secret Buddhist society in China since the mid-14th century. After the alien Manchus invaded China and became its rulers under the Ch'ing (Qing) dynasty (1644–1911), the White Lotus became dedicated to the overthrow of the Manchus and to the restoration of the former Ming dynasty (1368–1644). By 1796, thousands of disgruntled Chinese, suffering from food shortages and government indifference, had joined the society in the mountains of central China, drawn by the desire to get rid of the hated Manchus and by the promise of the return of Buddha (563?–483? B.C.) and good fortune. Bands of guerrillas attacked government troops, but their efforts were not well coordinated. On the other hand, a court favorite of the Chinese emperor embezzled the money that was intended to finance the war against the White Lotus rebels, and the army was riddled with corruption and incompetence. The White Lotus controlled such a large area that the government finally locked the peasants up in large stockades so that the rebels could not live off the land. The peasants were trained as local militia and given arms, which they then used against the White Lotus guerrillas and eventually broke their stranglehold on the land, notably the impoverished provinces of Shensi (Shaanxi), Szechwan (Sichuan), and Hupei (Hubei). With the peasants against them, the guerrillas were suppressed.

Whitman Massacre (1847) Dr. Marcus Whitman (1802–47) established a mission, Waiilatpu, near present-day Walla Walla, Wash., in 1836. Blaming the white missionaries for an outbreak of measles that killed many members of their tribe, the unfriendly Cayuse Indians, whose sick members Whitman tried unsuccessfully to treat, attacked the mission on November 29, 1847, massacring Whitman, his wife, and 12 others and kidnapping 53 women and children (whom they held captive until ransomed). The Cayuse reportedly fulfilled an Indian custom that permits the survivors of deceased relatives to take revenge on a medicine man. Settlers in this part of the Oregon Territory declared war on the Cayuse (see CAYUSE WAR).

William I's Invasion of Normandy (1076) William I "the Conqueror" (1027?–87) learned that subduing England (see NORMAN CONQUEST) and controlling Normandy in northwestern France demanded much of him. He had been forced to wrest the French region of Maine from the ambitious counts of Anjou in 1073, and his valiant but feckless eldest son Robert Curthose (1054?–1134), whom he had put in charge of Normandy, continually harassed him. Robert Curthose, gull of King Philip I (1052–1108), who wanted to enlarge France and bedevil William, his vassal, had become convinced that he should be duke of Normandy, not merely its caretaker. He led a rebellion; William and his forces invaded and subdued him, becoming reconciled with him in 1076. But the amity ceased, and Robert was briefly exiled. His ambition, however—even after he became duke of Normandy (1087)—made him struggle with his brothers when they became kings of England. See also TINCHEBRAI, BATTLE OF; WILLIAM II'S WAR WITH ROBERT CURTHOSE.

William I's Invasion of Scotland (1072) When the Normans conquered England (see NORMAN CONQUEST), the northern border of England was not fixed; King Malcolm III Canmore (d. 1093) of Scotland saw this as an advantage. Harboring Edgar the Atheling (1060?–1125), an English prince and claimant to England's throne, marrying Edgar's sister Margaret (d. 1093), and wishing to enlarge Scotland made Malcolm decide to invade Northumbria and Cumberland (1070–71). Norman political problems took William I "the Conqueror" (1027–87) away during the winter of 1071–72, but he returned to march with his forces through Northumbria and Lothian, confronting Malcolm at Abernethy. Malcolm did not offer battle to the first feudal lord seen in Scotland, but acknowledged William's suzerainty (1072) and paid homage. Edgar the Atheling sought refuge in Flanders. See ANGLO-SCOTTISH WAR OF 1079–80.

William II's Invasion of Scotland (1091–93)   Despite the homage offered William I "the Conqueror" (1027?–87) in 1072 (see WILLIAM I'S INVASION OF SCOTLAND), King Malcolm III (d. 1093) of Scotland persisted in attempting to enlarge Scotland. His forces invaded England in 1091, and King William II (1056?–1100) and his English troops pushed them back, gained homage, and went on to conquer Cumberland in 1092, establishing England's northern boundary at the Solway Firth (Hadrian's Wall). Malcolm, nonetheless, tried to invade again and died in a defeat at the FIRST BATTLE OF ALNWICK, Northumbria, in 1093. Internal strife followed, and William found some security in placing Malcolm's son on the Scottish throne in 1097.

William II's War with Robert Curthose (1089–96)   When William I "the Conqueror" (1027?–87) died, his Anglo-Norman kingdom was divided among his heirs according to feudal testamentary customs. His eldest son, Robert Curthose (1054?–1134), received Normandy, France, but Robert's hold on the duchy was feeble, as his father had predicted. Normandy's administrative problems, influenced by France's King Philip I (1052–1108), caused Robert's brother King William II (1056?–1100) of England to invade to secure control of the family holdings in France (1089, 1091, 1094). William's forces had limited success until Robert, determined to go on the FIRST CRUSADE, pawned the duchy to William to raise money (1096), thus enabling William to rule both England and Normandy. See also TINCHEBRAI, BATTLE OF; WILLIAM I'S INVASION OF NORMANDY.

Winnebago-Illinois War of 1671   The Winnebago Indians were a peaceful tribe that inhabited present-day eastern Wisconsin from Green Bay to Winnebago Lake in the seventeenth century. The Illinois Indians originally lived on the eastern shores of the Mississippi River, but they were pushed westward by the aggressive Iroquois. In 1671, the Illinois invaded Winnebago territory, and a series of raids and fights took place between the two tribes. The Winnebago were no match for the more warlike Illinois, and they gave way. The conflict reduced their number by more than 50 percent, and only about 3,000 Winnebagos survived.

Winter War   See RUSSO-FINNISH WAR OF 1939–40.

World War I (1914–18)   Although the assassination in Serbia of the heir to the Austro-Hungarian throne was the event that sparked the beginning of the so-called "Great War," international tensions and competition had been mounting for many years (see BALKAN WARS). On July 28, 1914, the Austro-Hungarian Empire declared war on Serbia. Russia began mobilizing troops along the German border, and Germany declared war on Russia and its ally, France. Immediately German armies went into action against France, planning to conquer it in a few months and then to turn the powerful German military machine against Russia. When German troops disregarded the neutrality of Luxembourg and Belgium by invading these countries to sweep through France from the northeast, Great Britain joined France to repel the invaders. The Central Powers of Austria-Hungary and Germany, later joined by the Ottoman Empire (Turkey) and Bulgaria, were aligned against the Allies of France, Great Britain, Serbia, Russia, and Belgium, which were later joined by Italy, Rumania, Portugal, Montenegro, Japan, Australia, the United States, and 20 other countries. Within a month German divisions reached the outskirts of Paris, but the retreating French rallied and counterattacked (see MARNE, FIRST BATTLE OF THE), driving the Germans back to the north. For the next four years the opposing armies faced each other, sometimes only a few hundred feet apart, in a long line extending from the North Sea to Switzerland (see WORLD WAR I ON THE WESTERN FRONT). Bloody battles were fought at Ypres, Artois, on the Somme, in the Meuse Valley and the Argonne Forest, and elsewhere (see MARNE, SECOND BATTLE OF THE; VERDUN, BATTLE OF) with staggering losses on both sides, but basically the line remained stationary until the fall of 1918. Austro-Hungarian troops had to face the Russians on their eastern border (see WORLD WAR I ON THE EASTERN FRONT) and Italians in the south (see WORLD WAR I ON THE ITALIAN FRONT), while they subdued Serbia and Montenegro (see WORLD WAR I IN THE BALKANS). When its navy could no longer operate from the North Sea (see JUTLAND, BATTLE OF), Germany resorted to unrestricted submarine warfare. This so angered the Americans that they declared war on Germany on April 6, 1917; although it was some time before they could send large numbers of men and materiel, their entry into the conflict gave the Allies a great moral boost. Despite a defeat at Gallipoli (see DARDANELLES CAMPAIGN), Britain remained master of the seas by protecting the Suez Canal (see WORLD WAR I IN EGYPT), and this enabled it to seize German colonies in Africa, to supply its armies in the Middle East (see WORLD WAR I IN MESOPOTAMIA; WORLD WAR I IN PALESTINE), and to transport troops from its Commonwealth countries. When Russia dropped out of the war in 1917 (see BOLSHEVIK REVOLUTION), the Germans were able to transfer troops from the eastern front to help the Austro-Hungarians and the Turks, whose empires were crumbling, but even fresh troops could not break the stalemate on the western front. As the French, British, and Americans slowly, doggedly drove the Germans back to the "Hindenburg Line," Bulgaria fell, the Ottoman Empire sued for peace, and Austria-Hungary collapsed. The war-weary Germans revolted, and their kaiser and generals were forced to sign an armistice on November 11, 1918. The ensuing Treaty of Versailles and other treaties changed the geographical face of Europe and the Middle East and brought about numerous political, economic, and social changes. The war had seen the introduction of tanks, airplanes, and poison gas and had caused enormous suffering and destruction wherever it was fought. More than 10 million persons had died, and many more were injured. See also RUSSO-POLISH WAR OF 1919–20; TURKISH WAR OF INDEPENDENCE; ZEEBRUGGE RAID.

World War I in Egypt (1914–17) As soon as the Ottoman Empire (Turkey) announced that it was entering World War I against the Allies, Great Britain declared Egypt a British protectorate and deposed the pro-German ruler. Egypt's Suez Canal was an essential lifeline and had to be protected at all costs; both the Turks and the Germans were anxious to gain control of the canal. In February 1915, three Turkish forces approached the canal by different routes, but the British had already fortified the western bank; the Turks were driven away with heavy losses. A year later the British began to fortify the eastern bank of the canal along an 80-mile stretch and to secure the Sinai Desert. As they slowly made their way north toward El Arish on the border with Palestine, they laid railroad tracks and a water pipeline. In July 1916, they were attacked by a sizable Turkish force, but again the Turks were severely beaten, and many prisoners were taken. By December that year, the British were within 20 miles of their destination, which was garrisoned by Turkish troops, who withdrew without a fight. Two Turkish contingents still remained in Egypt, but they were dispatched by surprise attacks by the British Camel Corps. By 1917, the last Turkish forces were gone from Egypt, and the Suez Canal was no longer in danger.

World War I in Mesopotamia (1914–18) Shortly after the Ottoman Empire (Turkey) entered World War I in November 1914, on the side of the Central Powers, the British sent a small force from India to the head of the Persian Gulf to establish a British sphere of influence in Mesopotamia to protect India and Egypt. The troops were ordered to move northward up the gulf to seize Baghdad eventually. At first the British forces were successful against the Turkish forces, but when the Anglo-French armies failed on the Gallipoli peninsula (see DARDANELLES CAMPAIGN), Turkish divisions were rushed to Mesopotamia. The British were driven back to Kut-el-Amara, which was surrounded and besieged. Several relief expeditions were dispatched, but they were unable to break through the Turkish lines. After a 143-day siege, the British surrendered in April 1916. The following year Allied reinforcements and gunboats were sent to the Persian Gulf, and the British quickly established themselves on both sides of the Tigris River as they proceeded north. After heavy fighting, Kut-el-Amara was captured, and the retreating Turks were pursued up the river to Baghdad. To prevent any counterattacks, the British continued their pursuit of the fleeing Turks and so gained control of most of Mesopotamia, including the Baghdad-Samara Railroad. Although all this action did not have great strategic significance for the war as a whole, it did boost the sagging morale of the Allies and dealt the Ottoman Empire a blow from which it never recovered.

World War I in Palestine (1917–18)   Once the British had driven the Turks from Egypt (see WORLD WAR I IN EGYPT), they continued to pursue their enemy north into Palestine. Their first two efforts to capture the stronghold of Gaza failed, but the third under the command of Edmund H. H. Allenby (1861–1936) succeeded. Earlier he had captured Beersheba to the east, and after the victory at Gaza his men proceeded northward, meeting little resistance until they reached Lydda, a junction point on the railroad between Jaffa and Jerusalem. After fierce fighting they dislodged the Turks and effectively cut their forces in two. The British next took Jaffa on the coast and then turned east toward Jerusalem, which was strongly fortified. Allenby devised a plan to surround the city and take all the outposts. This involved much hard fighting in diffi-

cult terrain and bad weather. After reinforcements arrived, an assault was made on the Holy City on December 8, 1917, and the next day the Turks surrendered. However, they regrouped and attempted to retake Jerusalem two weeks later, but to no avail. Gradually the British drove them from the hills and into what was then called Syria. Palestine became a British protectorate after centuries of Turkish rule.

World War I in the Balkans (1915–18)   The Balkan peninsula in southeastern Europe had long been seething with nationalistic rivalries and competing territorial desires (see BALKAN WARS). Although the Austro-Hungarian Empire declared war on the Balkan state of Serbia on July 28, 1914 (see WORLD WAR I), it was not until after combined Austro-Hungarian and German forces had driven the Russians from Galacia (see WORLD WAR I ON THE EASTERN FRONT) that the Austrians turned their attention to Serbia and invaded it from the north. In October 1915, Bulgaria joined the Central Powers (Germany, Austria-Hungary, and the Ottoman Empire) and promptly launched an invasion of Serbia from the south; Bulgarian troops were crushed by superior numbers and firepower. The Austrians then moved against Serbia's neighbor, Montenegro, and captured its capital in January 1916. Bulgarian and Austrian armies next invaded Albania from the north and east, but failed to drive an Italian force from the southern region. Rumania wavered for two years, debating which side was most apt to win the war; in August 1916, it decided to join the Allies and declared war on the Central Powers. Rumanian troops invaded Transylvania in Hungary with initial success, but were soon pushed back by two German armies. Soon Rumania itself was overrun by Bulgarians and Germans. In Greece, the Allies seized control of the telegraph and postal systems, the Greek navy, and large stores of munitions from the army and blockaded the coast. A French and British expeditionary force in Salonica, in northern Greece, made sure that Greece maintained its neutrality in the war, but it made no move against the Bulgarians in Macedonia until September 1918.

Reinforced by exiled Serbian soldiers and Greek troops, the Allies attacked on three fronts and, within two weeks, captured the major Bulgarian strong points. Bulgaria soon sued for peace and agreed to an unconditional surrender. The Allies continued their advance northward as they liberated both Serbia and Montenegro. Rumanian forces reentered the Balkan war arena and helped drive the Austro-Hungarian and German soldiers from its borders and southern Russia. The pro-German rulers of the Balkan states (present-day Albania, Greece, Rumania, Bulgaria, Yugoslavia, Macedonia, and the European part of Turkey) were deposed, and the fate of the states was decided at the forthcoming peace conference. See also HUNGARIAN REVOLUTION OF 1918; SERBO-BULGARIAN WAR OF 1885–86.

World War I on the Eastern Front (1914–17) When Austria-Hungary declared war on Serbia on July 28, 1914 (see WORLD WAR I), Russia began to mobilize its armies despite Germany's protests; on August 1, 1914, the two countries were at war. Russian troops invaded East Prussia but were badly defeated at the Battle of Tannenberg (August 29–30, 1914), where many prisoners and materiel were seized by the Germans, and at the Battle of Masurian Lakes (September 9–14, 1914). The Russians were more successful in Galacia (southeast Poland and western Ukraine) against the Austro-Hungarian forces, from whom they wrested key passes in the Carpathian Mountains and captured the capital city, Lemberg (Lvov), and the fortress city of Przemysl in early 1915. During the previous fall German armies had twice invaded Russian Poland and had twice failed to capture Warsaw, although they did control western Poland. By the winter of 1915, the opposing forces were facing each other from trenches along a 900-mile front. In May that year combined Austro-Hungarian and German armies struck in Galacia; their heavy artillery routed the Russians from their mountain strongholds; Lemberg and Przemysl were retaken. Then the Germans launched a major offensive, called "Hindenburg's Drive" after the brilliant strategist General Paul von Hindenburg (1847–1934), to drive the Russians out of Poland. By encircling maneuvers, they threatened to trap the Russians, who hastily retreated, leaving Warsaw, Brest-Litovsk, Vilna, and part of Lithuania to the enemy. A year later, in June 1916, the Russians began an offensive against Austria-Hungary in the area of the Styr and Sereth (Siretul) rivers and succeeded in advancing 20 to 50 miles along a 250-mile front; they were halted only when their supplies gave out. Meanwhile, discontent over the corrupt government of the czar was increasing in Russia; in March 1917, the czar's regime was toppled (see BOLSHEVIK REVOLUTION; FEBRUARY REVOLUTION). The new Russian government quickly made peace with Germany, and the war on the Eastern Front ended.

World War I on the Italian Front (1915–18) Italy remained neutral until May 23, 1915, when it decided to join the Allies and fight its traditional enemy, Austro-Hungary (see WORLD WAR I). The Italian army took the offensive in the Isonzo River valley, but the Austrians had already fortified the peaks in that mountainous area, and the Italians were unable to make any tangible headway, although they made assault after assault. They did manage to cross the river in the Caporetto area in the fall of 1915 and in 1916 captured Gorizia. The following year the Italians pushed forward again in several places, and the Germans, fearing their Austrian allies might withdraw, sent reinforcements. This turned the tide. After a heavy bombardment, the demoralized Italian troops began to retreat from Caporetto, and the retreat soon became a rout that stopped only when the army reached the Piave River. The other large-scale action on the Italian front occurred in the Trentino alpine area to the west where the Austrians launched an offensive in 1916 against ill-prepared Italian outposts. The Austrians swept across the border, and it seemed possible that they might seize Venice and cut off the armies on the Isonzo. However, an Italian force holding a commanding position on Monte Ciove held firm against overwhelming odds and stopped the Austrian advance. This offensive weakened Austria's eastern front and permitted the Russians to invade its territory in the Styr and Sereth (Siretul) Rivers region (see WORLD WAR I ON THE EASTERN FRONT). In November 1918, the Austrians surrendered to an Italian general whose troops had beaten them at Vittoria Veneto, and under the peace terms Italy regained Trieste and other territory the Austrians had seized in previous wars.

World War I on the Western Front (1914–18) At the beginning of World War I, the rapid and powerful German advance through Belgium and northeastern France was stopped by the French and British in September 1914 (see MARNE, FIRST BATTLE OF THE), and the German armies were forced back beyond the Aisne River. In the north the Allies contended with the Germans for control of Ypres in southwestern Belgium and the English Channel ports, while in the southeast the Germans were driven back to the mountains. By December 1914, both sides had dug into a series of fortified trenches almost 600 miles long and stretching from Ostend (Oostende, Belgium) to Douai, Saint-Quentin, Rheims, Verdun, Saint-Mihiel, and Lunéville (northeastern French towns) and then south to the Swiss border. This battle line remained almost stationary for the next four years, although there were frequent bombardments and waves of soldiers sent out of the trenches ("over the top") against the enemy, the gains in territory were insignificant, but the losses in lives were very high. Life in the trenches was miserable for all; many novels and memoirs have described the horror, mud, cold, and filth of that trench warfare. In 1916, the Germans launched a major offensive against the strongest Allied fortress (see VERDUN, BATTLE OF); there the French held fast. Another German offensive (see MARNE, SECOND BATTLE OF THE) was repulsed by the Allies in July 1918, and was followed by a massive counterattack in which the Allies under Marshal Ferdinand Foch (1851–1929) drove the Germans out of most of France and Belgium; a counteroffensive by American troops pushed the Germans from the Argonne Forest and Saint-Mihiel. The Western Front moved eastward as the war drew to a close.

World War II (1939–45)   The principal Axis power—Germany—felt cheated by the harsh terms of the Treaty of Versailles (see WORLD WAR I) and was eager to regain or expand its territories. Germany had become fascistic, and was ruled by a military dictatorship—under Adolf Hitler (1889–1945), it began to disregard treaties and commit acts of aggression. It remilitarized the Rhineland in 1935, annexed Austria and subsequently Czechoslovakia's Sudetenland in 1938, occupied Czechoslovakia in 1939, and annexed Memel in 1939 (see MEMEL, INSURRECTION AT). Also fascistic, Italy under Benito Mussolini (1883–1945) conquered Ethiopia (see ITALO-ETHIOPIAN WAR OF 1935-36) and seized Albania in 1939. Japan invaded Manchuria in 1931 and began an undeclared war against China (see SINO-JAPANESE WAR OF 1937–45). Most of the world wanted peace and watched these warlike acts with apprehension. When Hitler's troops invaded Poland (see BLITZKRIEG), Great Britain and France had to honor their agreement to protect the Poles, although it was too late to save them. At first Russia sided with the Axis powers and seized the Baltic states and Finland (see RUSSO-FINNISH WAR OF 1939–40), but in 1941 Hitler turned on his former ally and invaded Russian territory (see WORLD WAR II ON THE RUSSIAN FRONT). After conquering Poland (September 1939), Hitler turned his energies westward; Britain and France had declared war on Germany on September 3, 1939. Hitler's mechanized, powerful armies swept through Denmark and invaded Norway (see NORWAY, INVASION OF). A month later, May of 1940, German Nazi troops marched on Holland, Belgium, and Luxembourg, broke through France's defensive Maginot line (see FRANCE, BATTLE OF), and seized ports on the English Channel while dislodging a British expeditionary force (see DUNKIRK, EVACUATION OF). After occupying northern France and setting up the puppet Vichy government in the south, the Germans used their Luftwaffe (air force) to attempt to bomb Great Britain into submission, but without success (see BRITAIN, BATTLE OF). By the end of 1939, the war had expanded into the Balkan peninsula (see WORLD WAR II IN THE BALKANS) and to North

Africa, where the Italians invaded Egypt. Although the United States remained neutral, it did set up a Lend-Lease agreement with Britain, whereby food and supplies were shipped across the Atlantic in armed convoys to protect them from German U-boats or submarines (see ATLANTIC, BATTLE OF THE). The year 1941 was grim for Britain as it faced the Axis powers alone until Russia was invaded by the Germans and the U.S. naval base at PEARL HARBOR was attacked by the Japanese. In early 1942, Japan rapidly expanded its "Great East Asia Co-prosperity Sphere," but the Americans recovered quickly from their initial defeat and began to demolish the Japanese naval strength (see WORLD WAR II IN THE PACIFIC). Germany's Afrika Korps was beaten at El Alamein in northern Egypt (see NORTH AFRICAN CAMPAIGN), and the lifeline of the Suez Canal was preserved. The British, joined by Free French and American forces, which landed in Algeria and French Morocco, drove the Axis troops out of Africa by May 1943. The supposed German victory in Russia turned into defeat at Stalingrad (Volgograd) in early 1943, and the Allies invaded Sicily and Italy from their North African bases (see WORLD WAR II ON THE ITALIAN FRONT). The leaders of the Allies (chiefly Britain, France, Canada, Australia, Russia, Belgium, the Netherlands, China, and the United States) met at a number of conferences to decide future strategy and objectives and to sign the United Nations declaration. In the East, the Japanese fought doggedly against Chinese, American, British, and Australian forces in Burma (see BURMA CAMPAIGN) and the Pacific islands, but only in China were they successful (see WORLD WAR II IN CHINA). German-occupied Europe was severely bombed by the Allies before they landed troops to liberate the area (see NORMANDY, INVASION OF; WORLD WAR II ON THE WESTERN FRONT). By the end of 1944, an Allied victory was assured and, with some grievous setbacks (see BULGE, BATTLE OF THE), the Russians, Americans, and British advanced steadily on Berlin, Germany's capital, from the east and the west. Their forces met at Torgau in Saxony (now part of East Germany) on April 25, 1945, and a few days later Hitler and his mistress-turned-wife

presumably killed themselves in a bunker in Berlin. Germany surrendered unconditionally on May 7, 1945. After U.S. atomic bombs devastated two of its large cities, Hiroshima and Nagasaki, Japan surrendered on August 14, 1945. The United States and the Soviet Union emerged as superpowers after this most terrible of wars, in which millions of soldiers, sailors, airmen, marines, and civilians died in air raids, U-boat sinkings, rocket attacks, concentration camps, death marches, and bloody battles, and from disease, starvation, torture, and forced labor.

World War II in China　(1941–45) China, which had been at war with Japan for many years (see SINO-JAPANESE WAR OF 1937–45), entered World War II on the side of the Allies in late 1941. Most of the Chinese coast was in the hands of the Japanese, and the Chinese armies in the interior were supplied by materiel trucked in over the Burma Road. When the road was sealed off in 1942 (see BURMA CAMPAIGN), supplies were flown into China over the Himalayan "hump" by expert British and American fliers. The U.S. 14th Air Force set up bases in southeastern China, from which it effectively carried out bombing raids on Japanese shipping: U.S. General Joseph "Vinegar Joe" Stilwell (1883–1946) served as chief of staff of American forces for Chiang Kai-shek (1887–1975), supreme Allied commander of air and land forces in the Chinese war theater. In the spring of 1944, the Japanese mounted a new large offensive. First they occupied Honan (Henan) province, whose armies had fled, and then moved south along the rail line from Hankow (Hankou) to Canton (Guangzhou). The Japanese forces traveled by night to try to avoid the "Flying Tigers," P-40 fighter planes flown by the U.S. Volunteer Group in China, which unremittingly bombed and strafed their lines of march. Each time a Chinese force opposed the Japanese, it was overcome. By November 1944, the Japanese had fulfilled their objective of controlling the railroad from Indochina north to Peking (Beijing) and had taken eight Chinese provinces. In the north, however, they did not fare so well, for the Chinese Communist Eighth Route Army and peasant militia used guerrilla tactics to harass their garrisons and strongholds. Later, when the war ended, the Chinese communists would demand the surrender of the Japanese and take over their arms. Despite large amounts of British and American aid, the corrupt and strife-ridden Chinese Nationalist government at Chungking (Chongqing) never took an initiative against the Japanese, preferring instead to reserve its best troops for possible use against the communists.

World War II in the Balkans (1939–41) Benito Mussolini (1883–1945), Italy's dictator, dreamed of a glorious Italian empire obtained with the help of his Fascist ally in Germany, Adolf Hitler (1889–1945). In April 1939, Italian troops invaded and soon conquered Albania, and from there they invaded Greece in October 1940. The Greeks, however, were far better soldiers than the Italians, who were soon chased back to Albania. In August 1940, Russia demanded two provinces from Rumania, and Hungary demanded control of Transylvania; both demands were met reluctantly by the pro-German dictators of Rumania and Transylvania. To make sure of his allies on the Balkan peninsula, Hitler sent German troops into Hungary and Rumania in January 1941 and into Bulgaria shortly afterward. Yugoslavia's leaders signed a pact making them Nazi puppets, but its army objected and resolved to fight. On April 6, 1941, the Luftwaffe (German air force), accompanied by troops, attacked both Yugoslavia and Greece, neither of which could counter the superior German arms and forces. Yugoslavia was overrun in 11 days; its capital, Belgrade, was bombed mercilessly in "Operation Punishment"; and the remnants of the Yugoslavian army fled to the mountains, from which they waged damaging guerrilla warfare against the Nazis during the next three years. A British expeditionary force had been sent to aid the Greeks, but the most it could do was fight delaying actions. Greek forces surrendered in Albania on April 20, 1941, and in Greece proper four days later. The British were evacuated to Crete, but the Germans pursued them, and the Luftwaffe pounded this island into submission after a ten-day

aerial and naval battle. Turkey signed a friendship treaty with Germany and granted the Germans passage through the Dardanelles. The loss of the Balkans was a severe blow to Britain as it struggled alone against the Nazi war machine.

World War II in the Middle East (1941) Britain sought to prevent the Middle East from falling into the hands of the Axis powers in World War II. In Iraq, whose government had become pro-German, the British landed forces at Basra and Habbaniyah, their air base west of Baghdad. The Iraqis flooded the land between the Tigris and Euphrates rivers to thwart the British advance on Baghdad. After three weeks of scattered fighting, Iraqi resistance collapsed, and the British secured Baghdad. About a week later, on June 8, 1941, Free French forces, supported by British Commonwealth troops, invaded Syria and Lebanon from Palestine and Trans-Jordan; British forces from Iraq invaded Syria soon afterward. At the Lebanese city of Sidon, Vichy French forces resisted the invaders until British bombardments drove them out. Westward-moving Allied armies captured the Syrian cities of Aleppo and Latakia. The Germans made air strikes against the Allies without much success. An armistice was signed at Acre (Akko, Israel) on July 14, 1941; the Free French and British occupied Syria and Lebanon for the remainder of the war. In Iran, German technicians helped operate the oil fields, which the British wanted to control. In late summer of 1941, the Allies carried out an invasion of Iran with remarkable speed; Soviet troops moved down both sides of the Caspian Sea and seized major ports, while Soviet planes bombed Tehran; British forces invaded from Iraq and seized oil fields; the minuscule Iranian naval force was sunk. The Allied campaign ended successfully about four days after it began; Britain had gained its objectives with little loss of life and materiel.

World War II in the Pacific (1941–45) Hours after their surprise attack on PEARL HARBOR, Japanese bombers destroyed most of the U.S. planes on the ground at a field outside Manila in the Philippines; three days later they sank three British battleships in the Gulf of Siam. With little to stop them, the Japanese then seized Wake and Guam islands and the British base at Hong Kong and invaded the Philippines in full force. Bataan and Corregidor in the Philippines held out for almost five months before they fell. In February 1942, after the surrender of Thailand, the Japanese moved down the Malay Peninsula and seized the British port of Singapore, where they took 70,000 troops captive. Java, Borneo, Bali, Sumatra, Timor, and Burma fell in turn until the Japanese occupied all East Asia. Port Moresby on New Guinea was their next target; from there they planned to attack Australia. But the indecisive Battle of the Coral Sea (May 7–8, 1942) between the Japanese and American fleets prevented this from happening. Then the tide turned in the Battle of Midway (June 4, 1942), which was fought almost entirely by planes that tried to sink each other's warships; the Japanese suffered heavy losses. Afterward the Americans took the offensive; they won Guadalcanal after a bloody six-month fight in the jungles there (August 7, 1942–February 9, 1943) and Papua in New Guinea. In 1943, the Japanese were cleared out of the Aleutian Islands off Alaska. The Solomon, Gilbert (Kiribati), and Marshall islands were seized next by the Allies in large-scale amphibious operations supported by air and naval bombardments. Saipan, Tinian, and Guam in the Marianas were taken in August 1944. The Americans were now within flying distance of Japan, which they bombed repeatedly. On October 20, 1944, American forces landed on Leyte in the Philippines, and U.S. general Douglas MacArthur (1880–1964), supreme Allied commander in the Southwest Pacific, announced "I have returned." One of the greatest naval engagements of all times was fought in the Gulf of Leyte on October 23–26, 1944; the Japanese were defeated, but the fighting on land continued for four months before the Philippines were completely liberated. Iwo Jima was captured by U.S. Marines in March 1945, and Okinawa was invaded the next month; there the Japanese resisted for over two months. In July 1945, the

Allies sent Japan an ultimatum with terms that had been determined at the Potsdam Conference, but the Japanese ignored it. The agonizing American decision was then made to use the newly developed atomic bomb. On August 6, 1945, one such bomb was dropped on the Japanese city of Hiroshima, 90 percent of which was leveled, with about 130,000 persons killed or injured. A second bomb fell on Nagasaki on August 9, 1945, ruining a third of this Japanese city and killing or wounding about 75,000 persons. Five days later Japan's Emperor Hirohito (1901–89) overruled his military advisers and accepted the peace terms of Potsdam.

World War II on the Italian Front (1 9 4 3 – 4 5)
After defeating the Axis forces in the NORTH AFRICAN CAMPAIGN, the Allies turned their attention to Italy. On July 10, 1943, thousands of American and British soldiers landed under the cover of darkness on the shores of southern Sicily. They took the Germans and Italians garrisoned there by complete surprise and, within hours, gained control of 150 miles of the coast. After one battle at the Gela beachhead, Allied troops swept across the island, captured Palermo, and by August 17, 1943, secured all of Sicily. Meanwhile, the Italian dictator, Benito Mussolini (1883–1945), had been deposed, and his successor had sued for peace, which was granted on September 3, 1943, the same day the British landed on the toe of the Italian peninsula. Six days later U.S. forces made a large amphibious landing at Salerno, expecting little resistance. But Adolf Hitler (1889–1945), Germany's dictator, had sent German troops to occupy strategic places in Italy, and they fought the Allied invaders ruthlessly. Slowly the Allies moved up the peninsula, seized Naples, and by December 1943, reached Cassino Pass, south of Rome, which the Germans had fortified. Some of the toughest fighting of the war occurred in this mountainous terrain. In an effort to outflank the Germans, another Allied force was sent ashore at the Anzio beachhead, but German reinforcements arrived, and the Allies had to struggle to maintain their foothold. Finally, in May 1944, they overcame the Germans at Anzio and Cassino Pass

and advanced northward again. Rome was liberated on June 4, 1944, and Florence two months later. The Allies, however, were stopped at the German Gothic Line stretching across the Alps in northern Italy. A stalemate developed during which time Italian partisans harassed the Germans wherever they were stationed. In April 1945, Allied forces crossed the Po River and partisan forces seized Milan, Genoa, and Venice. Mussolini was captured by partisans as he tried to flee the country and was summarily shot to death with his mistress. On April 29, 1945, the Germans in Italy surrendered; shortly after the partisans handed over their arms and dissolved their resistance movement.

World War II on the Russian Front (1941–45)
Although the Soviet Union had entered World War II as an Axis power and had defeated Finland (see RUSSO-FINNISH WAR OF 1939–40) and absorbed the Baltic states, its Soviet leaders realized that Adolf Hitler (1889–1945), the German Führer (leader), was not to be trusted. There was worldwide surprise when three German armies, supported by Rumanian, Hungarian, Italian, Finnish, Slovak, and Spanish troops, invaded Russia on June 22, 1941. Even more surprise was shown at the valiant resistance displayed by Soviet soldiers and civilians. Hitler had expected to overrun Russia in four to six weeks, but he had underrated his opponents, the vast distances to be covered in Russia, and the scarcity of good roads and railroads there. At first the Germans were successful as they swept eastward in their tanks and armored vehicles against the retreating Russians. The city of Leningrad (St. Petersburg) was surrounded and besieged for two harrowing years; Kiev fell and half a million Soviet soldiers were killed or taken prisoner; the rich agricultural and industrial region of the Ukraine fell into German hands; Nazi troops were within sight of Moscow. But then winter set in, and the war bogged down. In the spring of 1942, the Germans resumed their offensive, intending to conquer the Caucasus region and its oil fields, but they were stopped at Stalingrad (Volgograd). The city was bombed to rubble, but the Russians fought stubbornly from house to house, factory to factory. In mid-November 1942, the Russian military high command assembled its remaining troops, which began to advance upon Stalingrad from the north and south. The two Russian forces met behind the German lines, trapping the enemy's army in the smoldering city. All efforts to break out failed, and on February 2, 1943, the Germans surrendered. The victory at Stalingrad was the turning point of the war; thereafter the Russians took the offensive and drove the retreating Nazis, who slaughtered and destroyed as they withdrew, from their country. By 1944, Russian troops had control of the Baltic states, eastern Poland, the Ukraine, Rumania, Bulgaria, and Finland. Early in 1945, they conquered East Prussia, Czechoslovakia, and eastern Germany, and in April that year they took Berlin, Germany's capital. As Napoleon I (1769–1821) had done before him, Hitler had underestimated the will of the Russian people and the severity of the Russian winters (see NAPOLEON'S INVASION OF RUSSIA).

World War II on the Western Front (1944–45)
Although British and American bombers had struck the principal industrial centers of Germany during 1942 and 1943 in World War II, it was not until the successful Allied landing on France's Normandy beaches in June 1944 (see NORMANDY, INVASION OF) that a Western Front was established on European soil. The mechanized U.S. Third Army moved southward into the Loire River valley and then proceeded east toward German-occupied Paris, which was liberated on August 25, 1944. A month later the American forces had advanced eastward to the Moselle River, had captured the fortress city of Liège, and were at the German border near Aachen, while the British had recaptured Brussels and Antwerp in Belgium and another Allied force had landed in southern France and was making its way north. But lack of supplies, especially fuel, slowed the Allied advance to a standstill until the continental harbors and ports could be reopened. An attempt to seize the Rhine bridge at Arnhem in the Netherlands failed in September 1944. Three months later the Germans launched a surprise

offensive against the weak American line at the Ardennes Forest (see BULGE, BATTLE OF THE), hoping to divide and conquer the Allied forces, but this last strike failed. In February 1945, the Allies again went on the offensive, cleared the retreating Germans from the west banks of the Rhine River, crossed the river at Remagen and later other places, and trapped some 300,000 German troops in the Ruhr Valley. Thereafter the Western Front moved rapidly eastward toward Berlin.

Wyatt's Rebellion (1554)   Many English were stunned in January 1554 to learn that Queen Mary (1516–58) was betrothed to Philip II (1527–98) of Spain. Unwilling to let England become a dependency of Spain and cognizant of Spanish interference in religious policy, several English nobles planned to rebel, depose Mary, and elevate Elizabeth (1533–1603) to the throne. France helped in the plan and promised troops, but leaked the plot, scheduled for March 1554. Mary swiftly imprisoned several of the major conspirators, forcing Sir Thomas Wyatt (1521?–54), the leader and son of the poet and diplomat Sir Thomas Wyatt (1503?–42), to act in February. His few fellows, without French aid, marched to London from Kent and, after fierce fighting in the city, surrendered. Wyatt, after exonerating Elizabeth, was tried and promptly hanged for high treason, as were several leading rebels.

Wyoming Valley Massacre (1778)   The British increased their attacks on frontier settlements during the AMERICAN REVOLUTION in 1778. Colonel John Butler (1726–96) led a force of 1,000 Tory rangers and Iroquois Indian allies in a sweep through the Wyoming Valley of Pennsylvania, where they met resistance from the 5,000 inhabitants. On July 3, 1778, Butler's men stormed the American-held garrison there, and it soon fell. About 360 men, women, and children, who had taken refuge in the fort, were slaughtered; others fled to the forests and soon died of hunger or exposure. General George Washington (1732–99), commander in chief of the American army, was so outraged at this "surpassing horror of the Revolution" that he sent an American force into the area, and it defeated the Tory rangers soundly in 1779. See also CHERRY VALLEY MASSACRE.

X

Xaquixaguana, Battle of (1548) The king of Spain sent Pedro de la Gasca (1485?–1567?), a lawyer and priest, as his representative to reestablish royal authority and to end the civil wars in Peru (see SPANISH CIVIL WARS IN PERU). Gonzalo Pizarro (1506?–48), who had established himself as governor at Lima, Peru, led the anti-royal forces against Gasca, to whose side came both Spanish and Indians disgusted with the brutality of Pizarro's rule. The forces of Pizarro and Gasca met at Xaquixaguana (Jaquijahuana) on April 5 or 9, 1548. Forty-five of Pizarro's men were slain, and the others surrendered (Gasca lost only one man). Pizarro was captured and promptly executed. Spanish royal authority was partially restored in Peru.

Xenophon's Retreat of the Ten Thousand   See TEN THOUSAND, MARCH OF THE.

Y

Yakima Wars (1855–58) The Yakima (Yakama) Indians lived along the Columbia and Yakima Rivers in Washington Territory, on land desirable for white settlement and mining. With great difficulty, U.S. officials negotiated a treaty with the Yakima and 13 other Indian tribes, all of whom ceded their lands and agreed to be placed on a single, large reservation. Some of the tribes decided to resist their removal and joined together under the leadership of Yakima chief Kamaiakan (fl. 1850s), whose forces successfully repulsed U.S. troops for about three years. Other Indians in the territory rose up in rebellion, following the lead of the Yakima, and many skirmishes, raids, and battles took place. Finally at the Battle of Four Lakes, near Spokane, Wash., the Indians were decisively defeated (September 1858) and afterward placed on reservations, although a few tribes remained outside them. Kamaiakan fled to Canada, but 24 other chiefs were captured and hanged or shot. The Yakima tribe was put on a reservation south of the present city of Yakima.

Yamada's Guards' Revolt See SIAMESE CIVIL WAR OF 1610–12.

Yamasee War (1715–16) The Yamasee Indians lived in northern Florida and southern Georgia until 1687, when they rebelled against Spanish rule and fled northward into the southeastern part of present-day South Carolina, where they became friendly with the English colonists. When fur traders and settlers encroached on their land, the Yamasee turned hostile and killed some 90 white traders and their families on April 15, 1715. The colonists rose in wrath against them but were unable to crush the Yamasee, who received aid from surrounding Indian tribes. Indian camps along the Savannah River were overrun and burned, while British trading posts and plantations were attacked and looted. With reinforcements from neighboring colonies, the British finally defeated the Yamasee, who then fled south to Florida and made friends with the Spanish as foes of the British. The British later attacked and destroyed their village near St. Augustine, Fla., in 1727, and the Yamasee tribe was wiped out in war with the Creek Indians in 1733.

"Yellow Turban" Rebellion (A.D. 184–c. 204) In east China in the 100s, many of the followers of the mystical religion of Taoism, founded by Lao-tse (Lao-Tzu) (c. 604–531 B.C.), had turned to magic and faith healing. One Taoist sect, the Taiping, was led by Chang Chüeh (Zhang Jiao; d. 184) and his two brothers, whose thousands of followers wore yellow headdresses to express their bond with the "earth" (Chinese philosophy envisioned five main powers changing the world: water, fire, metal, wood, and earth). In 184, the Yellow River (Huang Ho) flooded and drove the peasants from their farms;

epidemics and much discontent followed, and the Taiping "Yellow Turban" communities seemed to offer comfort and religious peace in which to live. Chang Chüeh led an open revolt against the Han emperor, associated with the red "fire" power, and his rapacious eunuchs, who had killed many scholars opposed to them. Chang Chüeh was slain, but the rebellion spread from the east coast to the north and west of China. By 188, almost 400,000 persons were in armed revolt and were battling large imperial armies that had superior weapons. The Yellow Turban rebels were eventually cruelly suppressed, but they weakened the Han dynasty and hastened its downfall in 221. See also FIVE PECKS OF RICE.

Yemenite Civil War of 1962–70 In September 1960, the crown prince of Yemen succeeded his just deceased father as imam (Islamic king); his reign, however, was cut short when rebellious army officers bombarded the royal palace, overthrew the monarchy, and proclaimed a "free Yemen republic" (September 27–30, 1962). The imam fled to the desert mountains, where he announced his intention to regain the throne and rallied many Arab tribesmen to join his royalist supporters. Egypt soon recognized the rebel government and sent troops and materiel in support, while Saudi Arabia and Jordan backed the imam. Clashes occurred along the Yemen-Saudi Arabia border, and mediation efforts by the United Nations and various countries failed to stop the bloody conflict. In 1963, in what is now South Yemen (Aden), a war for independence began, pitting the National Liberation Front (NLF) and the Egyptian-backed Front for the Liberation of Occupied South Yemen (FLOSY) against the British and local dynastic chieftains (the British had dominated the area since the 1950s). By 1967, the left wing NLF was the strongest faction and took control of the area, forcing the British to withdraw; on November 29, 1967, Southern Yemen became independent. Meanwhile, to the north, Egypt's President Gamal Abdel Nasser (1918–70) agreed to withdraw his troops if Saudi Arabia's King Ibn al Saud Faisal (1906?–75) would stop all military aid to the royalists (1967). On November 5, 1967, Yemen's republican government was overthrown in a military coup, and conservative leaders took charge. For a while it seemed that the new leaders would negotiate a peace, but an unsuccessful royalist offensive destroyed the initiative. The republicans, now aided by the Soviets, Syrians, and South Yemenites, repulsed numerous attacks by the royalists, to whom the Saudi government renewed its aid to counter foreign help to their enemy (1968). The Saudis later persuaded the royalists to seek a reconciliation with the republicans. In May 1970, an agreement was reached between the two warring parties; the royalists were granted positions in the government of Yemen, known also as the Yemen Arab Republic, which was then recognized by France, Britain, Iran, and Saudi Arabia.

Yemenite Civil War of 1986 A gunfight between President Ali Nasser Muhammad (1938–) and opposition leaders in a Politburo meeting on January 13, 1986, set in motion a brief but full-scale civil war in South Yemen, an Arabian marxist country with close ties to the Soviet Union and located at the tip of the Arabian Peninsula at the mouth of the Red Sea. During the following week an estimated 10,000 people were killed; many bodies were left rotting for days in the capital city of Aden, where the fiercest fighting took place. Muhammad, who had been in power since 1980, angered his more zealously pro-Soviet colleagues, among them former president Abdul Fattah Ismail (1939–86), because of his attempts to develop economic relationships with the country's non-marxist Arab neighbors. Somewhat surprisingly, the Soviet Union, to which South Yemen was important strategically, did not openly support Ismail and stated from the outset of the violence that it was not involved in the revolt; observers surmised that the Soviets were not displeased with Muhammad's economic successes. Nonetheless Muhammad's side was overpowered, he was formally disavowed by the Soviets, and he fled to exile in Ethiopia, another marxist state. On January 24 Haidar Abu Bakr al-Attas (1940?–), who had been prime minister in Muhammad's government, was appointed interim president and then, following parliamentary elections in October 1986, was elected president for a five-year term in November.

Yemenite Civil War of 1994 Following several weeks of skirmishes, full-scale hostilities broke out in Yemen on May 5, 1994, between President Ali Abdullah Saleh (1942–), representing conservative northern interests, and Vice President Ali Saleh al-Beidh (1938–), representing the formerly marxist south. The conflict was largely considered a personal power play between the two Arab political leaders, not a manifestation of opposition between ordinary Yemenites, who had welcomed the unification four years earlier of North Yemen, which had remained strongly Muslim after centuries of Ottoman Turkish domination, and South Yemen, which had forged ties with the Soviet Union after its independence from Great Britain in 1967. The viability of the resulting Republic of Yemen, despite the satisfaction of the majority of Yemenites, was eroded by the rivalry of Saleh and al-Beidh; from the beginning they refused to amalgamate the northern and southern armies or economies, and in 1993, after Saleh appointed his own men to 21 of the 31 Cabinet posts and would not accept socialist-sponsored legislation, al-Beidh left San'a (Sanaa), the capital in the north, for good, thus rendering the government nonfunctional. The conflict in Yemen highlighted the divisions among the Arab states; Saudi Arabia's King Fadh especially had been infuriated by Saleh's support of Iraq in the recent PERSIAN GULF WAR OF 1990–91. On June 1, 1994, the United Nations, led by the Saudis, issued a condemnation of the northerners and demanded a cease-fire. Although the northerners verbally accepted the cease-fire, they continued to attack Aden, the major city in the south (and former capital of South Yemen). On July 7, a little over two weeks after the south declared itself an independent state, Aden surrendered. The Republic of Yemen remained intact, but the north, edging out southern socialists and imposing greater Islamic influence over the nation, was clearly in charge.

Yemenite War of 1979 The pro-Western Yemen Arab Republic (North Yemen) blamed the neighboring Soviet-backed People's Democratic Republic of Yemen (South Yemen) for the murder on June 24, 1978, of its president; two days later South Yemen's president, a moderate marxist who had been working on a proposed merger of the two Yemens, was overthrown and executed by ultraleftists in a military coup. Mutual hostilities increased until February 24, 1979, when troops on both sides of the border fired on each other. North Yemenite forces were led by radical army officers across the border and attacked a number of villages in South Yemen; with Soviet, Cuban, and East German support, South Yemenite troops invaded the north. Alarmed by this invasion of its ally, Saudi Arabia called an emergency meeting of the League of Arab States and, along with the United States, rushed arms to North Yemen. A U.S. naval task force was sent to the Arabian Sea. Several cease-fires were arranged and then violated; finally a truce went into effect on March 19, 1979. Both sides withdrew their armies from the border, where a multinational Arab League patrol was stationed to enforce the truce. Leaders of North and South Yemen reached a reconciliation and planned to unite under one government; this was not readily achieved.

Yen Bai Uprising See VIETNAMESE UPRISINGS OF 1930–31.

Yom Kippur War See ARAB-ISRAELI WAR OF 1973.

Young Turks' Rebellion (1908–9) Although the Ottoman Empire had developed an almost absolutist constitution in 1876, Sultan Abdul-Hamid II (1842–1918) had suppressed it. His actions forced its supporters, mostly young, Westernized Ottomans (hence, Young Turks) to seek exile in Europe, where, as the Committee of Union and Progress (CUP), they propagandized for a reformed Ottoman Empire. In 1908, Young Turk officers of the Third Army Corps in Macedonia raised the standard of freedom at Salonika, demanding that the constitution be reinstated and that parliament, prorogued in 1877, be recalled. The rebellion, supported by the CUP in Paris, spread quickly; a threat to invade Constantinople (Istanbul) forced Abdul-Hamid to state, insincerely, that the Young Turks' demands would be met (July 24, 1908). Having achieved its basic aims, the CUP had no idea about running the Ottoman government, and administrative errors followed the peaceful military coup. The CUP allowed the old bureaucracy to function; it permitted the deceptive sultan to open the reestablished parliament in 1909. Abdul-Hamid promised to become a constitutional monarch while he secretly worked to cripple the CUP. His intrigues caused the very reactionary Muhammadan Union to become outspoken, and the union's pressure influenced the troops of the First Army Corps to storm the Chamber of Deputies demanding restoration of the Sacred Law and abolition of the constitution (April 1909). Feigning regret, the sultan acceded to the rebels' demands. The CUP government fell, and the new government, lacking the CUP, saw no error in the sultan's order for the annihilation of Armenians in Adana and Cilicia (see ARMENIAN MASSACRES OF 1909), the proclamation of martial law, the arrest of the 1908 rebels, or the reduction of the Constantinople garrison. In response, Salonika sent troops as an army of liberation under Mustafa Kemal, later known as Kemal Atatürk (1881–1938). It entered Constantinople, deposed the sultan with the approval of Muslim religious leaders, and named his brother Muhammad V Reshid (1844–1918) as ruler in a CUP-run administration faced with many complex national and international problems.

Ypsilanti Rebellions (1821) Two of the early military actions in the GREEK WAR OF INDEPENDENCE involved the Ypsilanti family, prominent Phanariots (Greeks of Constantinople) who were exiled to Russia because of differences with the Porte (Ottoman government). Alexander Ypsilanti (1792–1828) became a general in the Russian army and, in 1820, leader of the Philike Hetairia nationalists for Greek independence, entitling him to the honorific "prince." As leader, he assumed that all Balkan states would support a Greek rebellion and dreamed of a pan-Balkan uprising against the Ottoman Empire. In March 1821, leading a Sacred Battalion, he invaded Moldavia, seized its capital at Jassy (Iasi, Rumania), and entered Bucharest. Although the Phanariot governor of Moldavia backed him and Greeks in Wallachia rallied to his cause, the Russian czar, under pressure from Austria's foreign minister Metternich (1773–1859), repudiated him instead of giving support, and the Greek ecumenical patriarch excommunicated him. More important, Rumania did not aid Alexander because of impatience with oppressive Greek Phanariot officials and involvement in its own drive for independence. Rumania did not rebel in favor of the Greeks, especially so since Alexander's group had kidnapped and killed a Rumanian leader. Alexander's forces were sorely defeated by the Ottomans at the Battle of Dragasani, 90 miles west of Bucharest, on June 9, 1821. Alexander escaped into Austria, where the emperor had him arrested and imprisoned until 1827. His brother Demetrios Ypsilanti (1793–1832), who had also served in the Russian army and helped Alexander at Jassy, fled from Moldavia to Morea (Peloponnesus), where he gathered Greek rebels to begin the war of independence there.

Z

Zairian Civil War of 1996–97 An eight-month-long campaign under rebel leader Laurent Kabila (1940–) overthrew in 1997 Africa's longest-ruling dictator, President Mobutu Sese Seko (formerly Joseph D. Mobutu) (1930–97), whose plundering of Zaire's abundant natural resources had left the country's economy in ruins after 30 years. Kabila, headquartered around Lake Tanganyika in eastern Zaire, had been sporadically and ineffectively fighting Mobutu since the latter seized power in 1965. Kabila's opportunity to definitively oust Mobutu came in the fall of 1996, when tensions escalated between indigenous Tutsi (Watusi or Tusi), along with other ethnic groups, and Hutu (Bahutu) militia based in refugee camps bordering Rwanda in eastern Zaire. These sprawling camps resulted from the exodus from Rwanda of Hutu civilians after the 1994 genocide of Tutsi by Hutu troops (see RWANDAN CIVIL WAR OF 1990–94). International relief agencies maintained the camps, which extremist Hutu used as bases from which to conduct raids into Rwanda, whose government (formerly in Hutu hands) was now led by former Tutsi rebel leader Paul Kagame (1957?–) in a coalition with moderate Hutu leaders. After Hutu extremists convinced Zairian authorities to expel all Tutsi from the country, Kagame, supported by Uganda's President Yoweri Kaguta Museveni (1944–), gave Kabila command of some 2,000 Zairian Tutsi recruits, who had recently been trained in Rwanda and who had already driven the Hutu militia from the camps and seized much of eastern Zaire. Kabila now had enough troops to mount a credible attack against Mobutu; by February 1997 he controlled a corridor of land stretching from Watsa in the north to Kalémié in the south along the eastern border. With more support from Uganda, Burundi, and Angola, Kabila's troops marched across Zaire, arriving near the capital, Kinshasa, in May 1997. Six months before, Mobutu had flown to Kinshasa from the French Riviera, where he had one of his many lavish homes; at the time suffering from prostate cancer, he stayed but a few ineffectual days before flying back to France. Later Mobutu returned to Kinshasa and was persuaded by his generals and South Africa's President Nelson Mandela (1918–) to relinquish power; he then fled to his hometown, Gbadolite, about 700 miles to the north. A day later the rebel forces entered the capital without any fighting. Kabila's peaceful entry and transition to power were engineered beforehand through negotiations among Mandela, Mobutu, Kabila, and U.S. representative to the United Nations Bill Richardson (1947–). Mobutu went into exile and later (September 7) died in Rabat, Morocco. Kabila renamed the country the Democratic Republic of the Congo, what it was called before becoming the Republic of Zaire in 1971; Kabila also allowed only one political party—his Alliance of Democratic Forces for the Liberation of the Congo—despite pleas from other African leaders and the U.S. to include opposition members in his government. See UGANDAN GUERRILLA AND CIVIL WARS OF 1986– .

Zanj Rebellion (A.D. 869–83) Several thousand black slaves known as the Zanj (Zenj), taking advantage of the weak caliphate during the MUSLIM CIVIL WAR OF A.D. 861–70, began a rebellion in southern Mesopotamia to secure their freedom. Taken captive in East Africa, the Zanj mainly worked for Arab landowners in the salt marshes east of Basra; they were poorly treated, considered inferior infidels, and attracted many discontents (blacks and peasants) to their side. The rebels built their own capital in the salt marshes (870), sacked Basra (871), and took control of much territory. Muslim armies sent by the Abbasid caliph al-Mo'tamid (d. 892) battled the Zanj for almost 15 years. In 883, the rebels, who had thoroughly disrupted commerce and run amuck in the area, were defeated by an army led by the caliph's brother, al-Muwaffiq (fl. early 880s).

Zanzibar Rebellion of 1964 In 1963, Britain granted independence to the island of Zanzibar (together with nearby Pemba Island), whose governmental power was in the hands of two Arab-dominated political parties and whose head of state was an Arab sultan. On January 12, 1964, the government was overthrown in a violent leftist rebellion by black African nationalists, some of whom had been trained in communist China. A people's republic was declared; the Arab parties were banned; thousands of Arabs were arrested and imprisoned, and their property was confiscated; and the sultan was sent into exile. The new government, directed by the Afro-Shirazi party (whose supporters were black Africans), initiated land reforms and measures to abolish class privileges. To stabilize and strengthen its economy, Zanzibar merged (1964) with Tanganyika to form the United Republic of Tanzania under the leadership of President Julius Nyerere (1922–   ).

Zebrzydowski's Insurrection See POLISH REBELLION OF 1606–7.

Zeebrugge Raid (1918) After German forces invaded Belgium in 1914 at the start of WORLD WAR I, the Germans converted the Belgian port of Zeebrugge into a U-boat (submarine) base for preying upon Allied shipping in the North Sea and Atlantic Ocean. On the night of April 22–23, 1918, a daring British naval force under the command of Sir Roger J. B. Keyes (1872–1945) raided the port, sank three old cruisers filled with cement in the harbor channel, and knocked out some of the submarine operations, although three U-boats did manage to make their way out the next day. At the same time a British raid on the Belgian port of Ostend (Oostende) was unsuccessful. On May 9–10, 1918, however, a similar raid by Keyes and his men closed Ostend's harbor, whose entrance was blocked with a sunken cruiser.

Zulu Civil War of 1817–19 The Zulus were originally a small tribe that had migrated to the eastern plateau of present-day South Africa; they became a strong tribal nation largely due to the efforts of an ambitious chieftain named Shaka (c. 1787–1828). A rebellious young man, Shaka was estranged from his father, who was a Zulu chief, and became a warrior with the Mtetwa people. Dingiswayo (d. 1817), the Mtetwa paramount chieftain, helped Shaka become recognized as head of the Zulus after Shaka's father died in 1816. The two chieftains were close friends, and their warriors fought together against common enemies, such as the Ndwandwe headed by Zwide (d. 1819). After Dingiswayo was murdered by Zwide, the Mtetwa people placed themselves under Shaka and took on the Zulu name. Shaka revolutionized traditional ways of fighting by introducing the *assegai*, a light javelin, as a weapon and by organizing warriors into disciplined units that fought in close formation behind large cowhide shields. In the Battle of Gqokoli Hill in 1819, his troops and tactics prevailed over the superior numbers of the Ndwandwe people, who were routed; Zwide was killed. Most of the Ndwandwe abandoned their lands and migrated northward, leaving Shaka master of Zululand. Now began the Mfecane ("The crushing"), a series of tribal wars that devastated the region in the early 1820s, during which Shaka created a military Zulu empire and extended his rule, especially in the area of present-day Natal. Zulu warriors defeated local tribesmen and massacred many.

Zulu Civil War of 1856   Umpanda (d. 1872), the Zulu king, was a weak ruler, but he had two ambitious sons, Cetewayo (1836?–84) and Mbulazi (d. 1856), who were eager to succeed their father. Rivalry and competition between the sons led to civil war in Zululand in present-day South Africa. An army led by Cetewayo marched against another led by Mbulazi, and at the Battle of Tugela River in December 1856, the former won decisively. Mbulazi and all his followers who survived the battle were captured and executed. Cetewayo became ruler, even though his father lived for another 16 years.

Zulu Civil War of 1883–84   After Cetewayo (1836?–84), the Zulu king, was defeated by the British in the ZULU WAR of 1879, he went into hiding but was eventually captured and imprisoned. He behaved with such dignity as a prisoner that the British permitted him to return to Zululand in early 1883. There he discovered that a man named Zibelu (d. 1884?) had risen to power during his absence and had won the loyalty of many Zulus. Immediately civil war erupted between Cetewayo's faction and Zibelu's. After about a year of fighting, Cetewayo was killed, and his son, Dinizulu (d. after 1889), assumed the Zulu throne. As the war dragged on, Dinizulu sought the aid of the white man in ex-change for territory in northern Natal. This turned the tide, and Dinizulu's forces, with the white man's help, were victorious. However, Dinizulu soon quarreled with the white Europeans and resisted their encroachments. In 1889, he was placed under arrest and exiled to St. Helena, an island in the South Atlantic.

Zulu War   (1879) Upon annexation of the Transvaal state from the Boers (Dutch) in 1877, the British inherited the long-time Boer border dispute with the Zulus, a Bantu-speaking people in southern Africa (see BLOOD RIVER, BATTLE OF). When King Cetewayo (1836?–84) ignored British demands for de facto control, the British under General Frederic A. Thesiger (1827–1905), Baron Chelmsford, invaded Zululand. The Zulus, armed with spears, fought fiercely, defeating the British at Isandhlwana on January 22, 1879, and putting up strong resistance in other confrontations, notably at Eshowe and Kambula. British reinforcements arrived in April–May, 1879, and shortly after, with the killing of Louis J. J. Bonaparte (1856–79), son of former French emperor Napoleon III (1808–73) and a volunteer for the British, during a Zulu ambush while on a reconnaissance mission, the war became an international issue. On July 4, 1879, British troops under General Garnet J. Wolseley (1833–1913) won a decisive victory at Ulandi, effectively ending Zulu power. Cetewayo escaped but was caught in August and made peace. To terminate continued Zulu uprisings, however, the British officially annexed Zululand in 1887. See also BOER WAR, FIRST.

GEOGRAPHICAL INDEX

Listed Chronologically

Cambodia and Kampuchea

Sweden

Northern War, Second or Great (1700–1721)
Russo-Swedish War of 1741–43
Seven Years' War (1756–63)
Russo-Swedish War of 1788–90
Napoleonic Wars (1803–15)
Coalition, War of the Third (1805–7)
Russo-Swedish War of 1808–9

Switzerland—*see also* Holy Roman Empire
Burgundian-Swiss War of 1339
"Güglers' War" (1375–76)
Austro-Swiss War of 1385–88
Appenzell War (1403–11)
Swiss War against Savoy (1403–16)
Old Zürich War (1436–50)
Austro-Swiss War of 1460
Burgundian-Swiss War of 1474–77
Franco-Burgundian Wars (1464–65, 1467–77)
Swiss-Milanese War of 1478
Austro-Swiss War of 1499
Holy League, War of the (1510–14)
Kappel Wars (1529, 1531)
Villmergen War, First (1656)
Villmergen War, Second (1712)
French Revolutionary Wars (1792–1802)
Swiss Revolt of 1798
Napoleonic Wars (1803–15)
Sonderbund, War of the (1847)
Neuchâtel, Insurrection at (1856–57)

Syria—*see also* Assyria, Persia, Roman and
    Ottoman Empires
Diadochi, Wars of the (323–281 B.C.)
Corupedion, Battle of (281 B.C.)
Damascene War (280–279 B.C.)
Syrian-Egyptian War, First (274–271 B.C.)
Syrian-Egyptian War, Second (260–255 B.C.)
Syrian-Egyptian War, Third (246–241 B.C.)
Syrian War with Pergamum (224–221 B.C.)
Syrian-Egyptian War, Fourth (219–217 B.C.)
Bactrian-Syrian War (208–206 B.C.)
Syrian-Egyptian War, Fifth (202–198 B.C.)
Syrian-Roman War of 192–189 B.C.
Seleucid War with Egypt (171–168 B.C.)
Maccabees, Revolt of the (168–143 B.C.)
Syrian-Parthian War of 141–139 B.C.

Syrian-Parthian War of 130–127 B.C.
Aurelian's War against Zenobia (A.D. 271–73)
Ghassanid-Lakhmid Wars (A.D. c. 500–583)
Muslim Civil War of A.D. 657–61
Muslim Civil War of A.D. 680–92
Muslim Civil War of A.D. 743–47
Muslim Civil War of A.D. 809–13
Muslim Civil War of A.D. 861–70
Karmathian Revolt of A.D. 900–906
Muslim Civil War of A.D. 936–44
Muslim Civil War of A.D. 945–48
Muslim Civil War of A.D. 976–77
Crusades, the (late 11th through 13th cent.)
Crusader-Turkish Wars of 1100–1146
Muslim Civil War of 1102–8
Muslim Dynastic War of 1196–1200
Mongol-Persian War, Second (1230–43)
Mongol Conquest of the Abbasid
    Caliphate (1255–60)
Crusader-Turkish Wars of 1272–91
Mamluk-Ottoman War of 1485–91
Mamluk-Ottoman War of 1516–17
Druse Rebellion of 1925–27
World War II in the Middle East (1941)
Arab-Israeli War of 1948–49
Six-Day War (1967)
Jordanian Civil War of 1970–71
Arab-Israeli War of 1973
Lebanese Civil War of 1975–90

Thailand (Siam)
Khmer-Thai Wars of c. 1352–1444
Thai War of 1371–78
Thai War of 1387–90
Thai War of 1411
Thai War of 1442–48
Thai War of 1451–56
Thai War of 1461–64
Thai War of 1474–75
Thai War of 1492
Thai War of c. 1500–1529
Siamese-Burmese War of 1548
Burmese-Laotian War of 1558
Siamese-Burmese War of 1563–69
Burmese-Laotian War of 1564–65

INDEX

<hr>

Entries are filed letter by letter.